Microsoft®

Microsoft® Office Outlook® 2007 Inside Out

Jim Boyce
Beth Sheresh
Doug Sheresh

PUBLISHED BY
Microsoft Press
A Division of Microsoft Corporation
One Microsoft Way
Redmond, Washington 98052-6399

Library of Congress Control Number: 2006939800

Printed and bound in the United States of America.

2 3 4 5 6 7 8 9 QWT 2 1 0 9 8 7

Distributed in Canada by H.B. Fenn and Company Ltd.

A CIP catalogue record for this book is available from the British Library.

Microsoft Press books are available through booksellers and distributors worldwide. For further information about international editions, contact your local Microsoft Corporation office or contact Microsoft Press International directly at fax (425) 936-7329. Visit our Web site at www.microsoft.com/mspress. Send comments to mspinput@microsoft.com.

Acquisitions Editor: Juliana Aldous Atkinson
Developmental Editor: Sandra Haynes
Project Editor: Valerie Woolley
Editorial Production Services: Studioserv

Body Part No. X13-24144

For Cassie, a very special little girl

Contents at a Glance

Part 5: Customizing Outlook

Part 6: Managing and Securing Outlook

Part 7: Collaboration

Part 8: Working with Office Server and SharePoint Services

Part 9: Using Outlook with Exchange Server

Part 10: Mobility

Table of Contents

Part 3: Working with Contacts

Part 4: Managing Your Time and Tasks

Part 7: Collaboration

Part 8: Working with Office Server and SharePoint Services

Part 9: Using Outlook with Exchange Server

Part 10: Mobility

Acknowledgments

From Jim Boyce

I've authored and contributed to more than 50 books, and each project has been much the same in terms of compressed schedules and tight deadlines. This book was no different in that respect, but what made it very enjoyable and possible to accomplish was the phenomenal dedication to the project shown by everyone involved.

I offer sincere thanks to Sandra Haynes, Valerie Woolley, and Kathleen Atkins, who helped launch the project and kept it and the people involved all moving forward as a team. My sincere thanks also go to Juliana Aldous Atkinson for the opportunity to do the project and for her help in getting the project rolling. Carole McClendon, my agent at Waterside Productions, gets a well-deserved thanks, as well.

Thanks also go to Peter Harrison, Aline Phelps, and Mike Toot, who had the difficult task of not only verifying the accuracy of a wide range of information but also trying to do that with a moving target during the beta process. Vince Averello gets a nod for tech editing the programming chapters on the CD. I thank Jennifer Harris and Nancy Sixsmith, who served as copyeditors and did a great job tightening up and clarifying the manuscript. Thanks also to Shawn Peck, proofreader, for checking everyone's work and catching those errors that always seem to sneak by somehow.

My appreciation to the personnel at Waypoint Press for their outstanding project management, editorial, and production work.

Many thanks go to the other authors who contributed to this book: Beth Sheresh and Doug Sheresh, Rob Tidrow, Bill Zumwalde, and Sharyn Graham for the 2007 edition; Blair Rampling, Rob Tidrow, Deanna Maio, Tyler and Rima Regas, Dan Newland, John Durant, Matthew Nunn, and KC Lemson for their contributions to the previous edition. All of them poured heart and soul into their contributions. I offer an extra bit of thanks to Rob, Doug, Beth, Bill, and Sharyn for making time in their schedules to take on some extra material yet again and help us make our deadlines.

I also express sincere thanks to Westley Annis, who took the rough script code I developed for the CustomContactPrint and CustomMessagePrint scripts and performed a major overhaul of the code to make the scripts functional and presentable.

I offer my appreciation and admiration to the Microsoft Outlook development team for their efforts in making a great program even better!

Last but not least, I extend my deepest love and appreciation to my wife, Julie, for her tolerance of my obsessive work habits and understanding of my myriad other annoying character traits and bad habits.

From Beth Sheresh and Doug Sheresh

We want to offer our sincere gratitude to Jim Boyce for bringing us in on another interesting, if demanding, writing project, and especially for finessing multiple roles as author, editor, project manager, and technical advisor. Our thanks also to Carole McClendon at Waterside Productions for helping us navigate the contractual dimensions of this project.

We owe thanks to Brynna Owens for her ongoing technical assistance, Internet-based research, and encouragement in this and other writing projects. Our appreciation also goes to Jo Harms for once again supporting our technology endeavors and maintaining our e-mail server.

We thank Brian Boston for helping us with technical research, testing, and troubleshooting of Outlook features in Windows XP and Vista. We also want to offer our appreciation to Honora Wade and Alice Goodman for their elucidations of real-world applications of Microsoft Live Meeting.

On a personal note, we especially want to thank Sunrise and Jessica Fletcher (the Inn at Lucky Mud), Don and Kitty Speranza (the Inn at Crippen Creek), Kathleen Morgain (Twin Gables B&B), and Rob and Diane Stockhouse (Stockhouse Farms) for keeping us supplied with homemade goodies and fresh organic produce.

We'd Like to Hear from You!

Out goal at Microsoft Press is to create books that help you find the information you need to get the most out of your software.

The INSIDE OUT series was created with you in mind. As part of an effort to ensure that we're creating the best, most useful books we can, we talked to our customers and asked them to tell us what they need from a Microsoft Press series. Help us continue to help you. Let us know what you like about this book and what we can do to make it better. When you write, please include the title and author of this book in your e-mail, as well as your name and contact information. We look forward to hearing from you.

How to Reach Us

E-mail: nsideout@microsoft.com

Mail: Inside Out Series Editor
Microsoft Press
One Microsoft Way
Redmond, WA 98052

Introduction

Fifteen years ago, the average computer user spent most of his or her time using productivity applications such as Microsoft® Word or Microsoft Excel®. In the ensuing years, users have become more sophisticated, network implementations have become the rule rather than the exception, and collaboration has become a key facet of a successful business strategy. Perhaps the most significant change of all has been the explosive growth of the Internet. All these factors have led to a subtle but significant shift in the way people work. Today, most users of the 2007 Microsoft Office system spend a majority of their time in Microsoft Office Outlook® 2007. That change alone signifies a shift toward information management as an increasingly important everyday task. Getting a handle on daily information management can be critical to your productivity, success, and sanity.

Office Outlook 2007 is an extremely versatile program. Most of the other applications in the Microsoft Office system suite have a fairly specific purpose. Outlook 2007, however, serves as personal information manager (PIM), calendar, e-mail application, task manager, and much more. With so much power and flexibility at your fingertips, you need to have a good understanding of the Outlook 2007 features. Understanding the ins and outs will not only help you get the most from this program but will also have a positive impact on your workday.

Who This Book Is For

Understanding all of the Outlook 2007 features and putting them to work is the focus of *Microsoft Office Outlook 2007 Inside Out*. Most Outlook 2007 books act mainly as how-to guides for users who want to learn about the software. This approach leaves out workgroup managers and administrators when it comes to deployment, collaboration, server-side issues, and administration. *Microsoft Office Outlook 2007 Inside Out* offers a comprehensive look at the features most people will use in Outlook 2007 and serves as an excellent reference for users who need to understand how to accomplish what they need to do. In addition, this book goes a step or two further, providing useful information to advanced users and IT professionals who need to understand the bigger picture. Whether you want to learn Outlook 2007 for your own use, need to support Outlook 2007 on a peer-to-peer network, or are in charge of supporting Outlook 2007 under Microsoft Exchange Server, you'll find the information and answers you need between the covers of *Microsoft Office Outlook 2007 Inside Out*.

This book makes some assumptions about the reader. You should be familiar with your client operating system, whether it's Microsoft Windows® XP or Windows Vista™. You should be comfortable working with a computer and have a good understanding of how to work with menus, dialog boxes, and other aspects of the user interface. In short, *Microsoft Office Outlook 2007 Inside Out* assumes that you're an experienced computer user who might or might not have an understanding of Outlook 2007 and what it can do. The purpose of this book is to give you a comprehensive look at what Outlook 2007 can do, how to put Outlook 2007 to work, and how to manage Outlook 2007 at the user, workgroup, and server levels.

How This Book Is Organized

Microsoft Office Outlook 2007 Inside Out offers a structured, logical approach to all aspects of using and managing Outlook 2007. Each of the 10 parts of this book focuses on a specific aspect of Outlook 2007 use or management.

Part 1—Working with Outlook

Part 1 starts with the basics. Chapter 1 takes a look at the features that are new in Outlook 2007. Chapter 2 takes a look at the Outlook 2007 architecture and startup options. In Chapter 3, you'll learn how to perform advanced setup and configuration tasks such as setting up e-mail accounts, using profiles, making Outlook 2007 work with other e-mail services, configuring receipt and delivery options, and using add-ins that extend the Outlook 2007 functionality. Chapter 4 gets you up to speed using Outlook 2007 to send and receive messages, manage your workday, locate information on the Internet, and perform other common tasks. Chapter 5 rounds out Part 1 with a detailed look at how you can use categories to organize your data in Outlook 2007.

Part 2—E-Mail and Other Messaging

Part 2 delves deeper into the Outlook 2007 e-mail and fax messaging components and features. In Chapter 6, you'll learn how to manage address books and distribution lists. Chapter 7 explains how to set up Internet e-mail accounts. Chapter 8 will help you start to manage the e-mail features in Outlook 2007. Chapter 9 will make you comfortable with the range of features Outlook 2007 provides for creating messages both simple and complex. In Chapter 10, you'll learn how to find and organize your messages. Chapter 11 explains how to apply filters and rules to process messages automatically. Chapter 12 will help you exclude junk and spam e-mail senders. Look to Chapter 13 to learn how to generate automatic responses to incoming messages.

Because security is an increasingly important topic, Chapter 14 will help you secure your system and your data, send messages securely, and prevent others from impersonating you to send messages. Chapter 15 offers a comprehensive look at how the Outlook 2007 remote mail features can be indispensable for managing your mail online and offline. Chapter 16 explains how to use the new Really Simple Syndication (RSS) features to subscribe to and read RSS feeds in Outlook 2007. Chapter 17 rounds out the section with an explanation of Lightweight Directory Access Features (LDAP) features in Outlook 2007.

Part 3—Working with Contacts

Part 3 explores the Outlook 2007 features for managing your contacts. Chapter 18 starts with a look at how to manage contact information, including addresses, phone numbers, e-mail addresses, fax numbers, and a wealth of other information. You'll also learn how to sort, filter, and categorize your contacts, as well as share contact data with others. Chapter 19 looks at a Microsoft add-on product for Outlook 2007 called Business Contact Manager, which you can use to track business contacts, sales leads, products, and other business-related items.

Part 4—Managing Your Time and Tasks

Part 4 covers scheduling, one of the most widely used features in Outlook 2007. Chapter 20 provides an in-depth look at the Outlook 2007 appointment-scheduling capabilities. You'll learn how scheduling works, and you'll learn how to schedule appointments, create recurring appointments, use color effectively to manage your schedule, allow others to access your schedule, and publish your schedule to the Web. Chapter 21 takes a look at scheduling meetings and resources using Outlook 2007 and explains the subtle differences between scheduling appointments and scheduling meetings. Chapter 22 examines all aspects of managing tasks with Outlook 2007. You can use the Outlook 2007 Tasks folder to keep track of your own tasks as well as assign tasks to others. Integrating your tasks in Outlook 2007 can help you ensure that your tasks get done on time and are allocated to the appropriate person to complete them.

Chapter 23 offers a look at journaling, an important feature in Outlook 2007 that allows you to keep track of time spent on projects and documents and to track contacts and other items of interest. Chapter 24 takes a look at notes, a useful feature in Outlook 2007 that will help you get rid of those little slips of paper cluttering your desk and the sticky notes taking over your monitor. You'll learn how to create notes, assign categories to them, change their color, move them to other applications, put them on your desktop, and much more.

Part 5—Customizing Outlook

Customizing an application or the user interface for your operating system isn't just a matter of picking and choosing your personal preferences. Your ability to customize the way an application functions or appears can have a profound impact on its usefulness to you and to others. In short, the ability to customize an application allows you to make that application do what you want it to do in the way that makes the most sense to you. Chapter 25 starts the coverage of customization with a look at templates and how they can simplify the creation of e-mail messages, appointments, events, and other Outlook 2007 objects. You'll learn not only how to create and edit templates, but also how to share those templates with others.

Chapter 26 provides the detailed information you need to customize the Navigation Pane, the toolbar that appears by default to the left of the Outlook 2007 window and gives you quick access to the Outlook 2007 components. Chapter 26 also helps you customize the other aspects of the Outlook 2007 interface, including toolbars, Outlook

Today view, and folders. Chapter 27 explains how to create custom views and print styles for organizing and displaying your Outlook 2007 data. Chapter 28 takes a look at creating and using custom forms for a variety of tasks. Chapter 29 gives you a look at a host of ways you can automate tasks in Outlook 2007.

Part 6—Managing and Securing Outlook

Part 6 begins the transition to more advanced topics of interest to users, administrators, and IT professionals. In Chapter 30, you'll learn how Outlook 2007 uses folders to store your data and how to manage those folders. Chapter 30 also offers in-depth coverage of how to organize and archive your important data. In Chapter 31, you'll learn how to archive, back up, and restore your Outlook 2007 data. The chapter not only covers the importance of a sound backup and recovery strategy but will also help you develop and implement your own strategy that takes into account the unique requirements of Outlook 2007 and Exchange Server.

In Chapter 32, you'll learn how to move data in an out of Outlook 2007 using the program's import and export features. Chapter 33 will help you get a handle on all of your Outlook 2007 data, with a discussion of the new Instant Search feature and other features in Outlook 2007 for finding and organizing data. Chapter 34 includes an analysis of the importance of virus protection and how to guard against virus infections and outbreaks. You'll read about both client-side and server-side solutions. Because up-to-date virus definitions are the key to successful prevention, Chapter 34 takes a close look at developing a virus definition update strategy. You'll also find a detailed discussion of how to configure attachment blocking at the server as well as in Outlook 2007 itself.

Part 7—Collaboration

Chapter 35 will help you simplify your life by teaching you how to delegate many of your responsibilities–including managing your schedule–to an assistant. Chapter 36 will help you coordinate your schedule with others by teaching you to share your calendar. Chapter 37 explains how to integrate Outlook 2007 with other Microsoft Office system applications, such as performing a mail merge in Microsoft Office Word 2007 based on contacts stored in Outlook 2007.

Chapter 38 moves into the realm of Microsoft Office Project 2007, showing you how to integrate Office Project 2007 and Outlook 2007. Chapter 39 explores online collaboration through services such as Microsoft Office Live Meeting and other online collaboration services and tools.

Part 8—Working with Office Server and SharePoint Services

Although this part of the book contains only one chapter, you'll find Chapter 40 very helpful in understanding how Outlook 2007 integrates with Microsoft Windows SharePoint® Services. You'll learn how to work with shared contacts, set up and use alerts, work with shared documents, link a team calendar to Outlook 2007, and more.

Part 9—Using Outlook with Exchange Server

Outlook 2007 can be an effective information management tool all by itself, whether you use it on a stand-alone computer or on a network in collaboration with other users. Where Outlook 2007 really shines, however, is in its integration with and as a client for Microsoft Exchange Server. Part 9 steps up to a more advanced level to explain a broad range of Outlook 2007/Exchange Server integration topics. Chapter 41 turns the focus to the client, explaining how to configure Outlook 2007 as an Exchange Server client. Chapter 42 explores the wealth of features in Outlook 2007 specifically geared toward messaging with Exchange Server, such as the ability to recall sent messages before they are read, prioritize messages, and much more. This chapter also contains a detailed look at voting, an interesting feature in Outlook 2007. You can use Outlook 2007 as a tool to solicit input from others on any issue or topic, receiving and tallying their votes quite easily. Chapter 43 helps you continue working when you're away from the office or when your server is offline, covering how to use remote features to access and manage your Outlook 2007 data.

Part 10—Mobility

Life isn't just about working in the confines of your office, and Part 10 takes that into account. For example, Chapter 44 explains how to connect to Exchange Server using a Web browser such as Microsoft Internet Explorer® and Outlook Web Access (OWA). Chapter 45 completes this part of the book with a look at the mobility-related features in Outlook 2007–which you can use with Exchange Server 2003 and Exchange Server 2007–to take your Outlook 2007 data on the road.

Companion CD

The Microsoft Office suite offers an impressive ability to customize and integrate applications, and Outlook 2007 is no exception. Whether you need to create a few custom forms or develop full-blown interactive applications with Outlook 2007 and other Microsoft Office system applications, the first three articles provide the solutions you need. In Article 1, you'll expand on the topics covered in Chapter 28 and begin to delve into Outlook 2007 programming with a look at programming forms using Microsoft Visual Basic® Scripting Edition (VBScript). Article 2 continues the coverage of programming and development with a look at using Microsoft Visual Basic for Applications (VBA) to develop Outlook 2007 applications. Article 3 completes the discussion with a detailed look at integrating Outlook 2007 and other applications through VBA. Articles 4 and 5 cover a selection of features surrounding Microsoft Outlook Express and Windows Mail, including how to use these programs to work with Internet newsgroups and how to move data in and out of Outlook 2007 and Outlook Express/Windows Mail.

See the section "Conventions and Features Used in This Book" (page xli) for a list of some of the features you will find used throughout this book.

About the CD

The companion CD included with this book contains many tools and resources to help you get the most out of your Inside Out book.

What's on the CD?

Your Inside Out CD includes the following:

- **eBook** A complete, electronic version of *Microsoft Office Outlook 2007 Inside Out*.
- **Additional eBooks** In this section you'll find the following resources:
  - *Microsoft Computer Dictionary*, Fifth Edition
  - *First Look 2007 Microsoft Office System* (Katherine Murray, 2006)
  - Sample chapter and poster from *Look Both Ways: Help Protect Your Family on the Internet* (Linda Criddle, 2007)
  - Windows Vista Product Guide
- **Extending Office** Here you'll find links to Microsoft and other third-party tools that will help you get the most out of your software experience.
- **Resources** In this section, you'll find links to white papers, user assistance articles, product support information, insider blogs, tools, and much more.

System Requirements

The following are the minimum system requirements necessary to run the CD:

- Microsoft Windows Vista, Windows XP with Service Pack (SP) 2, Windows Server 2003 with SP1, or newer operating system.
- 500 megahertz (MHz) processor or higher
- 2 gigabytes (GB) storage space (a portion of this disk space will be freed after installation if the original download package is removed from the hard drive)
- 256 megabytes (MB) RAM
- CD-ROM or DVD-ROM drive
- 1.5 gigabytes (GB) available space
- Microsoft Windows or Windows Vista-compatible sound card and speakers
- Microsoft Mouse or compatible pointing device
- Microsoft Internet Explorer 6 or newer
- 1024x768 or higher resolution monitor

> **Note**
>
> An Internet connection is necessary to access the hyperlinks on the companion CD. Connect time charges may apply.

Support Information

Every effort has been made to ensure the accuracy of the contents of the book and of this CD. As corrections or changes are collected, they will be added to a Microsoft Knowledge Base article. Microsoft Press provides support for books and companion CDs at the following Web site: *www.microsoft.com/learning/support/books/*.

If you have comments, questions, or ideas regarding the book or this CD, or questions that are not answered by visiting the site above, please send them via e-mail to *mspinput@microsoft.com*.

You can also click the Feedback or CD Support links on the Welcome page. Please note that Microsoft software product support is not offered through the above addresses.

If your question is about the software, and not about the content of this book, please visit the Microsoft Help and Support page or the Microsoft Knowledge Base at *support.microsoft.com*.

In the United States, Microsoft software product support issues not covered by the Microsoft Knowledge Base are addressed by Microsoft Product Support Services. Location-specific software support options are available from *http://support.microsoft.com/gp/selfoverview/*.

Microsoft Press provides corrections for books through the World Wide Web at *www.microsoft.com/mspress/support/*. To connect directly to the Microsoft Press Knowledge Base and enter a query regarding a question or issue that you may have, go to *www.microsoft.com/mspress/support/search.htm*.

> **Note**
>
> This companion CD relies on scripting for some interface enhancements. If scripting is disabled or unavailable in your browser, follow these steps to run the CD:
>
> 1. From My Computer, double-click the drive that contains this companion CD.
> 2. Open the Webfiles folder.
> 3. Double-click Welcome.htm to open the CD in your default browser.

Conventions and Features Used in This Book

This book uses special text and design conventions to make it easer for you to find the information you need.

Text Conventions

Convention	Feature
Abbreviated menu commands	For your convenience, this book uses abbreviated menu commands. For example, "Choose Tools, Forms, Design A Form" means that you should click the Tools menu, point to Forms, and select the Design A Form command.
Boldface type	**Boldface type** is used to indicate text that you enter or type.
Initial Capital Letters	The first letters of the names of menus, dialog boxes, dialog box elements, and commands are capitalized. Example: The Save As dialog box.
Italicized type	Italicized type is used to indicate new terms.
Plus sign (+) in text	Keyboard shortcuts are indicated by a plus sign (+) separating two key names. For example, **Shift+F9** means that you press the Shift and F9 keys at the same time.

Design Conventions

> **Note**
>
> Notes offer additional information related to the task being discussed.

Cross-references point you to other locations in the book that offer additional information on the topic being discussed.

> **CAUTION!**
>
> Cautions identify potential problems that you should look out for when you're completing a task, or problems that you must address before you can complete a task.

INSIDE OUT **This statement illustrates an example of an "Inside Out" problem statement**

These are the book's signature tips. In these tips, you'll get the straight scoop on what's going on with the software—inside information on why a feature works the way it does. You'll also find handy workarounds to different software problems.

TROUBLESHOOTING

This statement illustrates an example of a "Troubleshooting" problem statement

Look for these sidebars to find solutions to common problems you might encounter. Troubleshooting sidebars appear next to related information in the chapters. You can also use the Troubleshooting Topics index at the back of the book to look up problems by topic.

Sidebar

The sidebars sprinkled throughout these chapters provide ancillary information on the topic being discussed. Go to sidebars to learn more about the technology or a feature.

PART 1

Working with Outlook 2007

CHAPTER 1

What's New in Outlook 2007

Microsoft® Office Outlook® 2007 sports a lot of new features that improve usability and add functionality. What's more, many of the familiar features in earlier versions have been revamped or fine-tuned in Office Outlook 2007. All of these changes come together to make Outlook 2007 an outstanding tool for communication, time and information management, and collaboration.

If you are an experienced Microsoft Outlook user, one of your first questions is no doubt, "What's new in Outlook 2007, and how do I find all of these new features?" That's what this chapter is all about. While we don't cover every little change or nuance of the new Outlook 2007 interface or new and improved features here, we offer a broad overview of the new features in Outlook 2007 to help you get up to speed quickly. Let's start with the most obvious–the user interface.

A New Interface

Certainly the most obvious difference in all of the 2007 Microsoft Office system applications is their new interfaces. Like the other Microsoft Office system applications, Outlook 2007 sports a new interface. In some ways, however, the differences in Outlook 2007 are not as pronounced as they are in some of the other applications, such as Microsoft Office Word 2007. Outlook 2007 blends some new interface components with improvements to its existing components to achieve a new look and feel. Fortunately, you should be able to become comfortable with this new look and feel in a short time. Once you've made that transition, you'll come to really appreciate the new interface.

Let's take a look at the biggest difference from earlier versions–the Ribbon.

The Ribbon

Unlike some of the other Microsoft Office system applications, the main Outlook 2007 window uses a familiar menu bar and toolbar combination to give you access to commands, options, and tools in Outlook 2007. These other applications, such as

Office Word 2007, use a new feature called the Ribbon to give you quick access to commonly used features. Outlook 2007 does make use of the Ribbon, however, as you can see in Figure 1-1. The new message form is one of the many forms in Outlook 2007 that sports a Ribbon rather than the more familiar menu bar/toolbar combination.

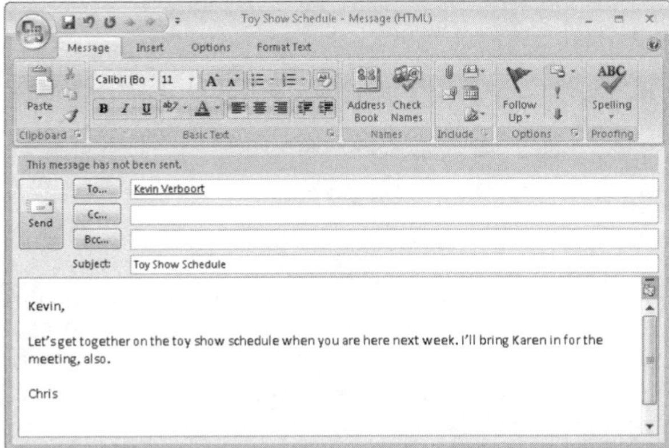

Figure 1-1. The Ribbon makes commands and features easily discoverable.

The Ribbon is something of a paradigm shift. Rather than provide a linear menu list of commands, the Ribbon divides features onto individual *tabs*, each of which comprises tools with related functions. For example, all of the tools that relate to inserting items into a new message are located together on the Insert tab of the new message form.

Each Ribbon tab is divided into *groups*, and each group organizes the features for a specific function. On the Message tab of the new message form, for example, the Basic Text group organizes the tools you use to format text in the message.

Is the new Ribbon design good or bad? After you spend the time to become familiar with it, you'll probably come to the conclusion that the Ribbon is an improvement over the "old" interface. The Ribbon helps expose some useful and powerful features that many people never used because they weren't aware they existed or they didn't take the time to dig through the menus to find them.

The Navigation Pane

The Navigation Pane was first introduced in Microsoft Outlook 2002 as part of Microsoft Office XP and took the place of the Outlook Bar. The Navigation Pane gives you quick access to all of your Outlook 2007 folders (Inbox, Calendar, and so on) and adapts depending on which folder you are using. For example, when you open the Calendar folder, the objects offered in the Navigation Pane change to reflect features available in the calendar, such as views.

The Outlook 2007 Navigation Pane looks at first blush to be much like the Navigation Pane in Outlook 2002 and Outlook 2003. The main difference in Outlook 2007 is the capability to show the Navigation Pane in a collapsed state, as shown in Figure 1-2.

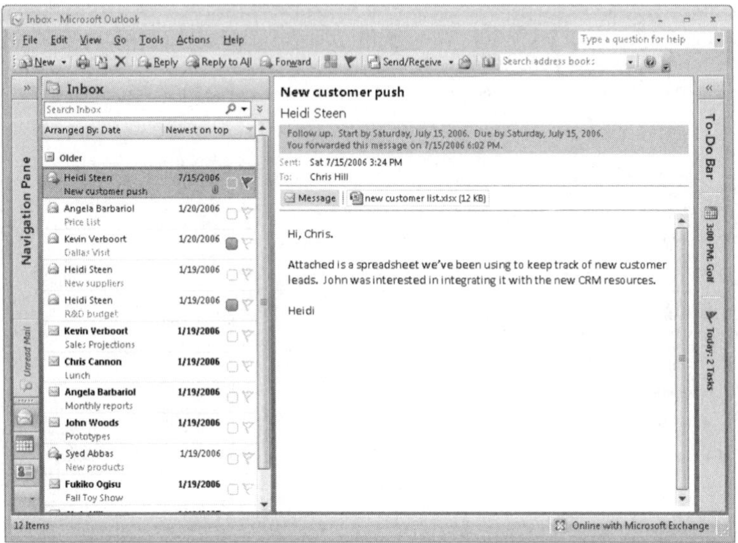

Figure 1-2. You can collapse, or autominimize, the Navigation Pane.

Essentially, the Navigation Pane, when collapsed, acts a little like the Microsoft Windows® taskbar in autohide mode. The Navigation Pane sits at the left edge of the Outlook 2007 window as a narrow vertical toolbar. You can click items in the Navigation Pane to expand them for use. For example, click the Navigation Pane section to display the Favorite Folders and folder list or views for the current folder. After you click a folder in the list to select it, the pane is hidden again. Using the Navigation Pane in collapsed mode makes more space available for displaying the contents of a folder (such as your monthly calendar) while still keeping the Navigation Pane's features readily available.

The To-Do Bar

The To-Do Bar, shown in Figure 1-3, is another new feature in Outlook 2007 that brings together information from different Outlook 2007 sources and makes it readily available. It combines the Date Navigator, appointments for the day, and current tasks in one pane.

As with the Navigation Pane, you can configure the To-Do Bar to automatically hide after you use it. In this mode, the To-Do Bar sits at the right edge of the Outlook 2007 window as a vertical toolbar. When you click the To-Do Bar, it expands to display its contents. You can then click a date to view its appointments in the Calendar window, work with tasks, and so on. When you click again in the main Outlook 2007 window, the To-Do Bar collapses back to a vertical toolbar.

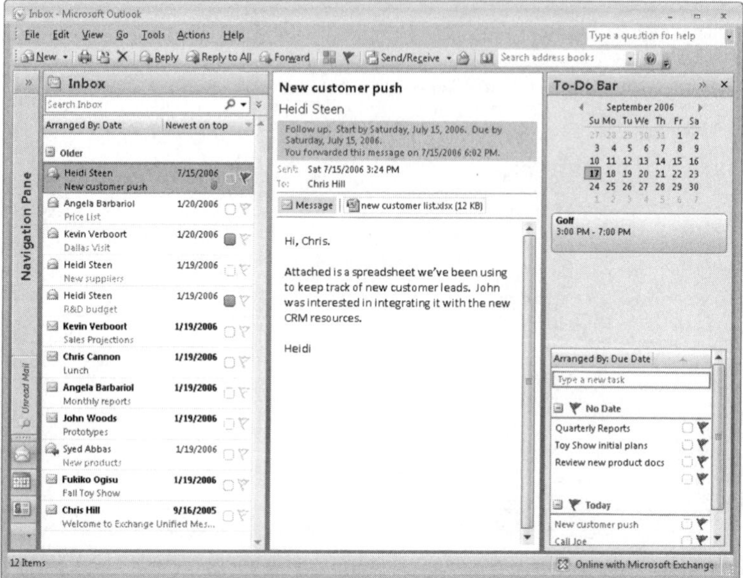

Figure 1-3. The To-Do Bar combines tasks, appointments, and the Date Navigator in one location.

Other Interface Changes

The Outlook 2007 interface is significantly changed in other ways in addition to the Ribbon, Navigation Pane, and To-Do Bar. For example, the Calendar window has been given a visual and functional overhaul. See the sections titled "Calendar Changes" and "E-Mail Changes" later in this chapter for details. Additional interface features are explored in other chapters where appropriate.

Instant Search

Outlook 2007 introduces its own Instant Search feature. For example, in the Inbox folder, you can click in the Search box and type a word or phrase, and Outlook 2007 quickly (but not quite instantly) displays the results of the search. You can work with the results of the search before the search is complete, so when you find the item you need, you can simply double-click it to open it–you don't have to wait for the search to complete.

Search is also improved in other ways in Outlook 2007. You can click the arrow next to the Search box to open the Query Builder, as shown in the upper-left corner of Figure 1-4, where you can specify additional search parameters to locate items. The contents of the Query Builder change according to the folder in which you are working. For example, the search criteria in the Inbox pane are different from the criteria in the Calendar pane.

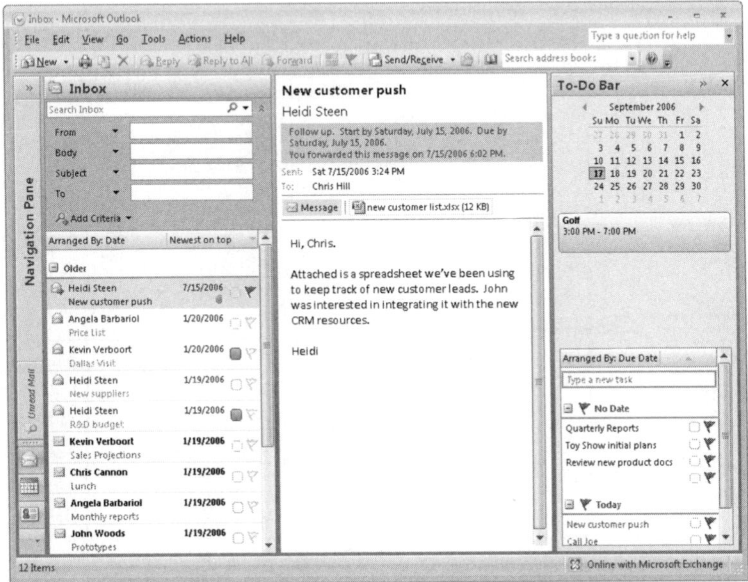

Figure 1-4. Use the Query Builder to perform advanced searches.

To learn more about these and the other added search features in Outlook 2007, see Chapter 33, "Finding and Organizing Outlook Data."

Calendar Changes

The Calendar folder has received some new interface changes and added features in Outlook 2007. For example, the calendar's appearance has been improved with additional color and visual elements. On the functional side, the calendar includes a Daily Task List pane at the bottom of the window, as shown in Figure 1-5. The Daily Task List shows the tasks that are due on the current date, such as tasks with that day as a due date or e-mail messages with a follow-up date of that day.

You can use the Daily Task List to open tasks and the other items it displays (such as messages), add new tasks, mark tasks as complete, assign tasks, print tasks, and perform other actions on the items. Tasks that you do not complete roll over to the next day, so they are not forgotten.

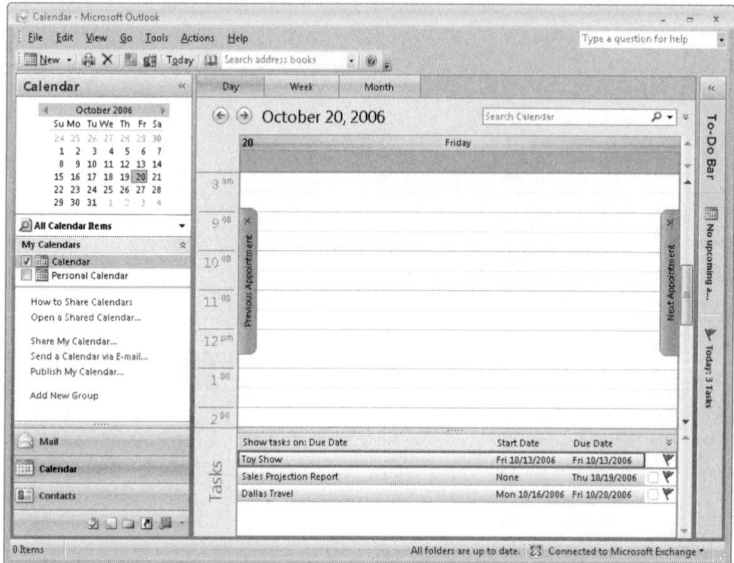

Figure 1-5. Use the Daily Task List in the Calendar folder to view your current tasks.

> **Note**
>
> The appearance of the Week view is another change in the Calendar folder. No longer a two-column day-planner view, the Week view is more like the Work Week view in earlier versions.

Scheduling also sees improvement in Outlook 2007. When Outlook 2007 is used in concert with Microsoft Exchange Server 2007 for scheduling meetings, attendee schedules are automatically reviewed and a time is then proposed for the meeting. Naturally, you can select a different time if needed. Figure 1-6 shows the Scheduling Assistant, which helps you choose a meeting time that works for the majority of attendees.

In addition, when you make a change to a meeting time, location, or agenda, the attendees receive an informational update rather than a request to accept the meeting changes.

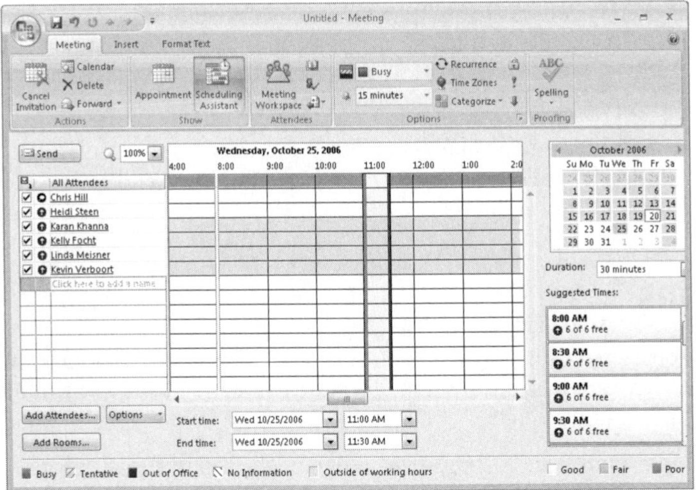

Figure 1-6. Use the Scheduling Assistant to easily schedule meetings.

Another useful improvement for scheduling is calendar overlay. In earlier versions of Microsoft Outlook, you could open another Calendar folder in a new window to view the appointments in that calendar. As in Outlook 2003, Outlook 2007 also lets you view calendars side by side. Even better, Outlook 2007 lets you overlay calendars, as shown in Figure 1-7. For example, if you keep personal appointments separate from business appointments, you can overlay the two calendars for a complete, overall, view.

Figure 1-7. Use calendar overlay to view multiple calendars in a combined view.

Calendar overlay extends to Microsoft Office SharePoint® sites. You can view calendars stored on a SharePoint site and even overlay them with your own calendar, all right within Outlook 2007. For example, you could overlay your team calendar over your personal calendar to identify scheduling conflicts.

There are many additional changes and improvements in the Outlook 2007 calendar and scheduling features. See Part 4, "Managing Your Time and Tasks," to learn more about scheduling and using the calendar.

E-Mail Changes

Many people spend a majority of their time working in the mail folders in Outlook 2007. So Microsoft has improved mail features in Outlook 2007 in a number of ways, both visual and functional.

For example, Outlook 2007 now can automatically set up e-mail accounts for you based on a small amount of information you provide, such as your e-mail address and name. Outlook 2007 will attempt to determine the appropriate mail server and other settings based on that information, simplifying account setup. If Outlook 2007 is unable to set up the account, you can specify settings manually.

Here's a list of the most notable mail-related feature improvements in Outlook 2007:

- **Attachment Previewing** You can preview certain types of documents right in the Reading Pane without having to open the attachment or the message containing it. You simply click the item to preview it in the Reading Pane. Outlook 2007 supports previewing of Outlook 2007 items, images and text files, and documents created by Microsoft Office Word, Office PowerPoint®, Office Excel®, and Office Visio®. This feature is extensible, enabling third-party developers to build preview capability for other attachment types.
- **Out Of Office Assistant** In earlier versions, Microsoft Outlook displayed a notification dialog box when you started Outlook with the Out Of Office Assistant turned on. In Outlook 2007, the notice appears on the status bar. A more important change to the Out Of Office Assistant is that you can now schedule the Out Of Office Assistant ahead of time, turning it on at the specified time. So a week or so before you will be out of the office, you can set it and forget it. The Out Of Office Assistant will turn on at the specified time all by itself and turn off at the set time, as well. In addition, you can specify different Out Of Office messages for recipients in your organization and those outside it. These last two features require Exchange Server 2007.
- **Unified Messaging** When Outlook 2007 is used with Exchange Server 2007, you can have your voice messages and faxes delivered to your Inbox along with your e-mail.

- **International Domain Names** Outlook 2007 supports internationalized domain names in e-mail messages, enabling people to specify addresses in their own languages in addition to English.
- **E-Mail Postmarks** Outlook 2007 stamps each message with a uniquely generated electronic postmark. This postmark serves two purposes. First, it helps reduce spamming by imposing a small processing load on the computer. This load is negligible when sending an average number of e-mail messages, but it imposes an unacceptable load on spammers trying to send messages to a large number of recipients. In addition, Outlook 2007 recognizes the postmark on messages that it receives, helping it to determine whether a message is not junk mail.
- **Junk Filter And Phishing Protection** Another improvement in Outlook 2007 is its enhanced junk filtering. Outlook 2007 also adds a phishing filter to help guard against phishing attacks in which official-looking but false messages attempt to direct you to malicious sites or obtain personal information such as credit card or banking information.
- **Managed Folders** This feature works in conjunction with Exchange Server 2007 to provide a means for archiving messages to meet legal requirements, such as Sarbanes-Oxley and HIPAA, and corporate policy requirements. Managed folders look and function like other message folders (such as the Inbox folder). However, the policies assigned to managed folders determine retention and other policy-based behavior. In addition, the user cannot move, rename, or delete managed folders. These restrictions ensure that the users cannot bypass retention policies.

Microsoft has introduced a handful of additional changes to improve e-mail features in Outlook 2007. These additional features are covered in Part 2, "E-Mail and Other Messaging."

Color Categories

You are no doubt familiar with categories in Outlook 2007. Categories in Outlook 2007 are like tags that you associate with Outlook 2007 items (such as messages, appointments, and tasks). In earlier versions of Microsoft Outlook, categories were defined using text only. You could choose from existing categories as well as create your own categories. You can organize Outlook 2007 items based on category–for example, grouping items in a folder based on their category assignments.

Outlook 2007 introduces color categories to make categories more visible and more useful, as shown in Figure 1-8. By associating a color with a category, you make it easier to quickly identify items that have a specific assigned category. This is particularly true when you are using a list view that is not grouped by category. For example, you might assign the Blue category to all e-mail messages from a certain sender. You can then identify at a glance when looking at the Inbox the messages from that sender.

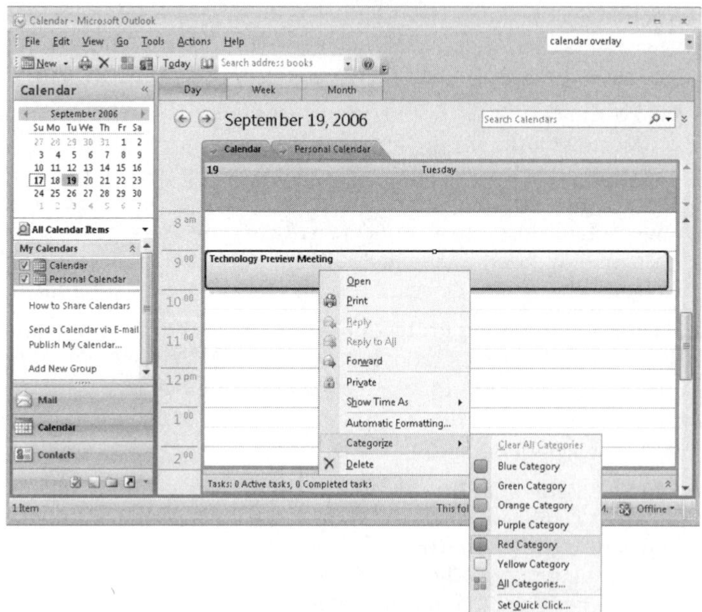

Figure 1-8. Outlook 2007 adds color to categories to make them more useful.

Although Outlook 2007 shifts the category paradigm to a color-based model, you can still rely on your old text categories. The primary difference is that you can now also associate a color with those categories. For example, in earlier versions of Microsoft Outlook, you could create a category named Toy Show. Now, with Outlook 2007, you can also associate a color with that category, making its items easily identifiable.

> **Note**
>
> You can also assign a shortcut key to each category, enabling you to assign that category to items by simply pressing the shortcut key sequence.

Collaboration and Sharing Improvements

Outlook 2007 adds several new features and improves on existing features to make collaboration and sharing even easier. SharePoint integration is a key new feature.

Integration with Office SharePoint Server

Outlook 2007 integrates with Microsoft Office SharePoint Server 2007 sites to enable you to interact with information stored on a SharePoint site. For example, you can connect shared calendars, document libraries, discussion lists, contacts, and tasks from a SharePoint site to Outlook 2007. SharePoint items show up in a folder named SharePoint Lists, which appears in the Navigation Pane along with your Outlook 2007 folders. You can then work with the items from the SharePoint site as if you were working on Outlook 2007 items. Changes that you make are updated on the SharePoint site.

> **Note**
>
> Outlook 2007 also integrates with Microsoft Windows SharePoint Services versions 2 and 3.

The following list summarizes many of the key tasks that you can perform in Outlook 2007 with SharePoint items:

- **Connect a SharePoint library to Outlook 2007.** Connecting a SharePoint library to Outlook 2007 makes the library and its items available within Outlook 2007. You connect the library to Outlook 2007 from the SharePoint site.
- **Download a file from a SharePoint library to Outlook 2007.** You can download just a list of available files or the files themselves, or you can have Outlook 2007 download files in the background. The SharePoint site administrator can control how and whether files are downloaded to client systems.
- **Open a file from a SharePoint library using Outlook 2007.** You can navigate to a SharePoint library in the Navigation Pane, locate the file you want, and simply double-click the file to open it.
- **Edit a file from a SharePoint library using Outlook 2007.** You can modify a document from a SharePoint library offline from Outlook 2007 and save the changes to the library (assuming that you have sufficient permissions in the library).
- **Remove a SharePoint file from Outlook 2007.** You can remove one or more files from a SharePoint library list in Outlook 2007 without actually removing the documents from the SharePoint library. The document remains on the server but is removed from your cached list. This feature simplifies browsing libraries that contain a large number of items.
- **Remove a SharePoint library from Outlook 2007.** If you don't need to see a particular library anymore, you can easily remove it from Outlook 2007. Removing the library does not affect it on the server, but only removes it from the Navigation Pane in Outlook 2007.
- **Add a file to a SharePoint library by sending an e-mail message.** If the SharePoint document library is configured to accept documents by e-mail, you can add a document to a library simply by sending an e-mail message, with the document attached, to the library.

Shared Calendars

Outlook 2007 adds some great new features to make it possible to share your schedule with others and to view their schedules as well. For example, you can create a *calendar snapshot* that you can send in an e-mail message to others. The recipient can open the calendar in Outlook 2007 or in a Web browser.

Outlook 2007 also supports Internet Calendars, which are calendars stored on an Internet service and available for download and synchronization in Outlook 2007. You can create a calendar in Outlook 2007 and publish it to an Internet service or use other applications to create the calendar. If you subscribe to a calendar-sharing service, Outlook 2007 can query the service on a periodic basis to upload and download calendar changes. Microsoft offers Internet Calendar sharing through the Microsoft Office Online Web site.

> **Note**
>
> In addition to these calendar-sharing features, you can still save your calendar to a Web page, enabling you to publish your calendar to any Web server.

Shared Business Cards

You are probably familiar with contacts in Outlook 2003. In Outlook 2007, you can create electronic business cards complete with photos, logos, text, and other content. Outlook 2007 stores these business cards in the Contacts folder. You can share these business cards with others through e-mail and receive their cards as well.

And More...

The features briefly explored in this chapter are just the main new features introduced in Outlook 2007. As you become familiar with Outlook 2007, you'll find lots of additional features that increase ease of use, make Outlook 2007 more reliable, simplify collaboration with others, and in general, make it easier to use Outlook 2007 to manage your contacts, schedule, e-mail, and other information. You'll find coverage of all of these new features throughout the rest of *Microsoft Office Outlook 2007 Inside Out*.

CHAPTER 2

Outlook Overview and Startup

This chapter provides an overview of the architecture in Microsoft® Office Outlook® 2007 to help you learn not only how Office Outlook 2007 works but also how it stores data. Having that knowledge, particularly if you're charged with administering or supporting Outlook 2007 for other users, will help you use the application more effectively and address issues related to data storage and security, archiving, working offline, and moving data between installations.

This chapter also explains the different options you have for connecting to e-mail servers through Outlook 2007 and the protocols—Post Office Protocol 3 (POP3) and Internet Message Access Protocol (IMAP), for example—that support those connections. In addition to learning about client support and the various platforms on which you can use Outlook 2007, you'll also learn about the options that are available for starting and using the program.

If you're anxious to get started using Outlook 2007, you could skip this chapter and move straight to Chapter 3, "Advanced Setup Tasks," to learn how to configure your e-mail accounts and begin working with Outlook 2007. However, this chapter provides the foundation on which many subsequent chapters are based, and reading it will help you gain a deeper understanding of what Outlook 2007 can do so that you can use it effectively and efficiently.

Overview of Outlook

Outlook 2007 was once primarily a tool for managing personal information such as contacts and e-mail, scheduling, and tasks. Today, Outlook 2007 provides all of these features but adds the benefits of enhanced collaboration. This collaboration comes in the form of group scheduling, data sharing, shared calendars, Microsoft Office InfoPath® forms integration, and Microsoft Office SharePoint® integration. While the capability to manage your e-mail, contacts, calendar, and tasks is still important, the ability to collaborate with your coworkers and business partners can be even more important.

Outlook 2007 provides a broad range of capabilities to help you manage your entire workday. In fact, a growing number of Microsoft Office system users work in Outlook more than 60 percent of the time. An understanding of the Outlook 2007 capabilities and features is important not only for using the Microsoft Office system effectively but also for managing your time and projects. The following sections will help you learn to use the features in Outlook 2007 to simplify your workday and enhance your productivity.

Messaging

One of the key features Outlook 2007 offers is messaging. You can use Outlook 2007 as a client to send and receive e-mail through a variety of services. Outlook 2007 offers integrated support for the e-mail services covered in the sections that follow.

> **Note**
>
> A *client application* is one that uses a service provided by another computer, typically a server.

Exchange Server

Outlook 2007 integrates tightly with Microsoft Exchange Server, which means that you can take advantage of workgroup scheduling, collaboration, instant messaging, and other features offered through Exchange Server that aren't available with other clients. For example, you can use any POP3 e-mail client, such as Microsoft Outlook 2007 Express or Microsoft Windows® Mail (the Windows Vista™ incarnation of Outlook Express), to connect to a computer running Exchange Server (assuming that the Exchange Server administrator has configured the server to allow POP), but you're limited to e-mail only. Advanced workgroup and other special features—being able to recall a message before it is read, use public folders, view group schedules, and use managed folders for archiving and retention, for example—require Outlook 2007.

Internet E-Mail

Outlook 2007 provides full support for Internet e-mail servers, which means that you can use Outlook 2007 to send and receive e-mail through mail servers that support Internet-based standards, such as POP3 and IMAP. What's more, you can integrate Internet mail accounts with other accounts, such as an Exchange Server account, in order to send and receive messages through multiple servers. For example, you might maintain an account on Exchange Server for interoffice correspondence and use a local Internet service provider (ISP) or other Internet-based e-mail service for messages outside your network. Or perhaps you want to monitor your personal e-mail along with your work-related e-mail. In that situation, you would simply add your personal e-mail account to your Outlook 2007 profile and work with both simultaneously. You can then use rules and custom folders to help separate your messages.

For more information about messaging protocols such as POP3 and IMAP, see the section "Understanding Messaging Protocols" later in this chapter.

HTTP-Based E-Mail

Outlook 2007 supports Hypertext Transfer Protocol (HTTP)–based e-mail services, such as Microsoft Hotmail®. HTTP is the protocol used to request and transmit Web pages. This means that you can use Outlook 2007 to send and receive e-mail through Hotmail and other HTTP-based mail servers that would otherwise require you to use a Web browser to access your e-mail, as shown in Figure 2-1. In addition, you can download your messages to your local Inbox and process them offline, rather than remaining connected to your ISP while you process messages. Another advantage is that you can keep your messages as long as you want—most HTTP-based messaging services, including Hotmail, purge read messages after a given period of time. Plus, HTTP support in Outlook 2007 lets you keep all your e-mail in a single application. Currently, Outlook 2007 directly supports Hotmail. Check with your e-mail service to determine whether your mail server is Outlook 2007–compatible.

> **Note**
>
> You can use Outlook 2007 with your Hotmail account only if you have a paid Hotmail account, such as MSN® Hotmail Plus or MSN Premium. You can't use Outlook 2007 to access a free Hotmail account.

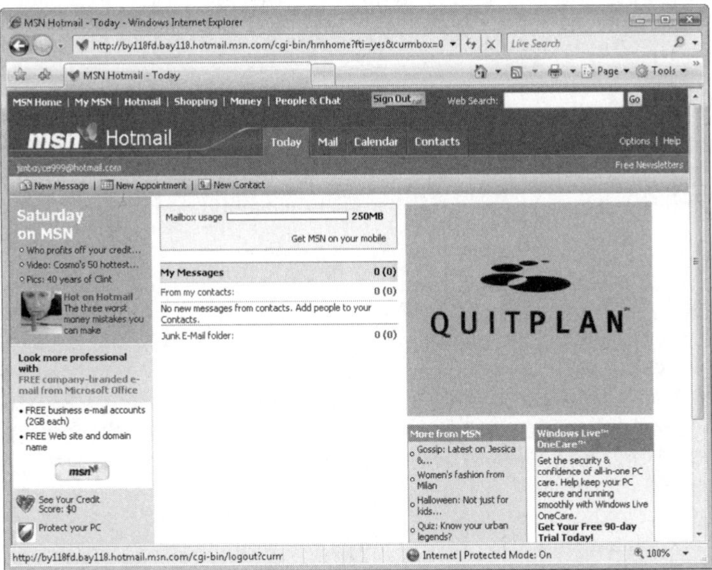

Figure 2-1. HTTP-based mail servers such as Hotmail have traditionally required access through a Web browser.

Fax Send and Receive

Outlook 2007 includes a Fax Mail Transport provider, which allows you to send faxes from Outlook 2007 using a fax modem. In addition, third-party developers can provide Messaging Application Programming Interface (MAPI) integration with their fax applications, allowing you to use Outlook 2007 as the front end for those applications to send and receive faxes. Both Microsoft Windows XP and Windows Vista include built-in fax services that support sending and receiving faxes. Both of these fax services can print incoming faxes and deliver a copy to a file folder, but neither will deliver faxes to your Outlook mailbox.

If you need to be able to deliver incoming faxes to your mailbox, you must use a third-party, MAPI-capable fax application. Or, if you use Exchange Server, you can choose a server-side fax application to provide fax support and delivery.

Extensible E-Mail Support

The Outlook 2007 design allows developers to support third-party e-mail services in Outlook 2007. Whatever your e-mail server type, Outlook 2007 provides a comprehensive set of tools for composing, receiving, and replying to messages. Outlook 2007 provides support for rich-text and HTML formatting, which allows you to create and receive messages that contain much more than just text, as shown in Figure 2-2. For example, you can send a Web page as a mail message or integrate sound, video, and graphics in mail messages. Outlook 2007 support for multiple address books, multiple e-mail accounts, and even multiple e-mail services makes it an excellent messaging client, even if you forgo the application's many other features and capabilities.

Scheduling

Scheduling is another important feature in Outlook 2007. You can use Outlook 2007 to track both personal and work-related meetings and appointments, as shown in Figure 2-3, whether you are at home or in the office–a useful feature even on a stand-alone computer.

Where the Outlook 2007 scheduling capabilities really shine, however, is in group scheduling. When you use Outlook 2007 to set up meetings and appointments with others, you can view the schedules of your invitees, which makes it easy to find a time when everyone can attend. You can schedule both one-time and recurring appointments. All appointments and meetings can include a reminder with a lead time that you specify, and Outlook 2007 will notify you of the event at the specified time. You can process multiple reminders at one time, a useful feature if you've been out of the office for a while.

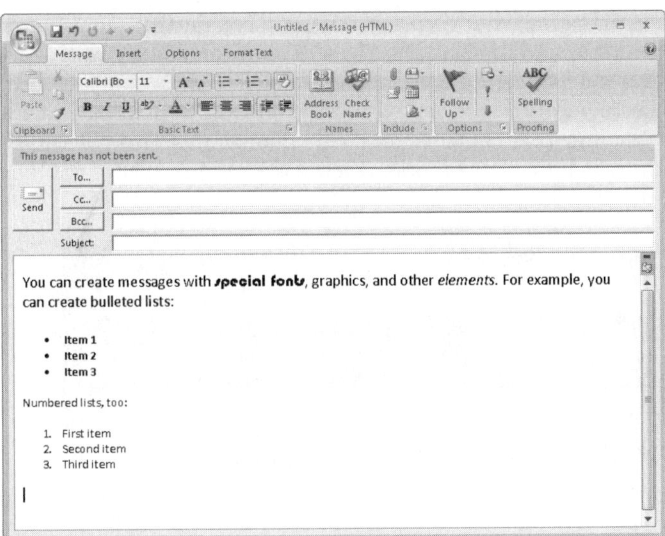

Figure 2-2. Use Outlook 2007 to create rich-text and multimedia messages.

Figure 2-3. Track your personal and work schedules with Outlook 2007.

Organizing your schedule is also one of Outlook 2007's strong suits. You can use categories to categorize appointments, events, and meetings; to control the way they appear in Outlook 2007; and to perform automatic processing. Color labels allow you to identify quickly and visually different types of events on your calendar.

In addition to managing your own schedule, you can delegate control of the schedule to someone else, such as your assistant. The assistant can modify your schedule, request meetings, respond to meeting invitations, and otherwise act on your behalf regarding your calendar. Not only can others view your schedule to plan meetings and appointments (with the exception of items marked personal), but also you can publish your schedule to the Web to allow others to view it over an intranet or the Internet, as shown in Figure 2-4.

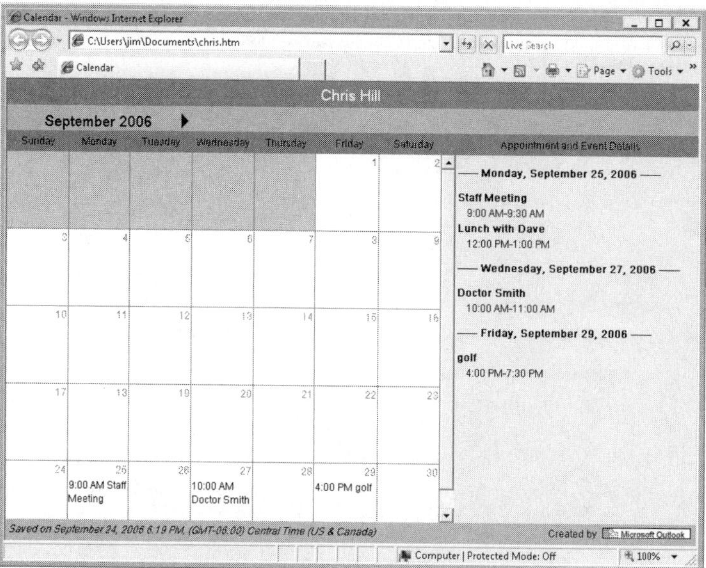

Figure 2-4. You can easily publish your schedule to the Web.

Contact Management

Being able to manage contact information—names, addresses, and phone numbers—is critical to other aspects of Outlook 2007, such as scheduling and messaging. Outlook 2007 makes it easy to manage contacts and offers flexibility in the type of information you maintain. In addition to basic information, you can also store a contact's fax number, cell phone number, pager number, Web page URL, and more, as shown in Figure 2-5. You can even include a picture for the contact.

In addition to using contact information to address e-mail messages, you can initiate phone calls using the contacts list, track calls to contacts in the journal, add notes for each contact, use the contacts list to create mail merge documents, and perform other tasks. The Contacts folder also provides a means for storing a contact's digital certificate, which you can use to exchange encrypted messages for security. Adding a contact's certificate is easy—when you receive a digitally signed message from the contact, Outlook 2007 adds the certificate to the contact's entry. You can also import a certificate from a file provided by the contact.

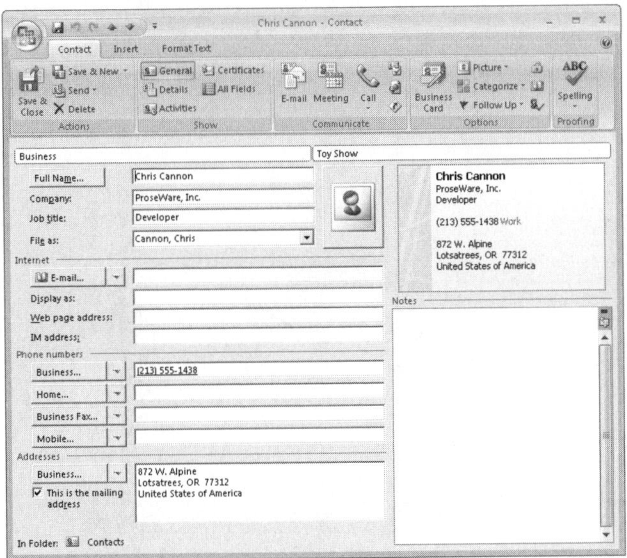

Figure 2-5. You can manage a wealth of information about each contact with Outlook 2007.

For details about digital signatures and encryption, see the section "Message Encryption" later in this chapter. For complete details on how to use the journal, see Chapter 23, "Tracking Documents and Activities with the Journal."

Task Management

Managing your workday usually includes keeping track of the tasks you need to perform and assigning tasks to others. Outlook 2007 makes it easy to manage your task list. You assign a due date, start date, priority, category, and other properties to each task, which makes it easier for you to manage those tasks, as shown in Figure 2-6. As with meetings and appointments, Outlook 2007 keeps you informed and on track by issuing reminders for each task. You control whether the reminder is used and the time and date it's generated, along with an optional, audible notification. You can designate a task as personal, preventing others from viewing the task in your schedule—just as you can with meetings and appointments. Tasks can be one-time or recurring events.

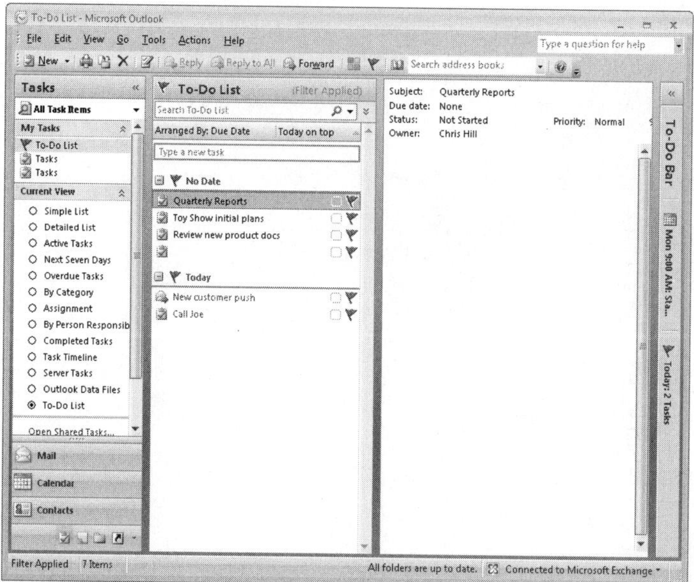

Figure 2-6. Use Outlook 2007 to manage tasks.

If you manage other people, Outlook 2007 makes it easy to assign tasks to other Outlook 2007 users. When you create a task, simply click Assign Task, and Outlook 2007 prompts you for the assignee's e-mail address. You can choose to keep a copy of the updated task in your own task list and receive a status report when the task is complete.

To learn more about how to assign tasks, see "Assigning Tasks to Others" in Chapter 22.

Tracking with the Outlook Journal

Keeping track of events is an important part of managing your workday, and the Outlook 2007 journal makes it simple. The Journal folder allows you to keep track of the contacts you make (phone calls, e-mail messages, and so on), meeting actions, task requests and responses, and other actions for selected contacts, as shown in Figure 2-7. You can also use the journal to track your work in other Microsoft Office system applications, giving you a way to track the time you spend on various documents and their associated projects. You can have Outlook 2007 add journal items automatically based on settings that you specify, and you can also add items manually to your journal.

When you view the journal, you can double-click a journal entry to either open the entry or open the items referred to by the entry, depending on how you have configured the journal. You can also configure the journal to automatically archive items in the default archive folder or in a folder you choose, or you can have Outlook 2007 regularly delete items from the journal, cleaning out items that are older than a specified length of time. Outlook 2007 can use group policies to control the retention of journal entries, allowing administrators to manage journaling and data retention consistently throughout an organization.

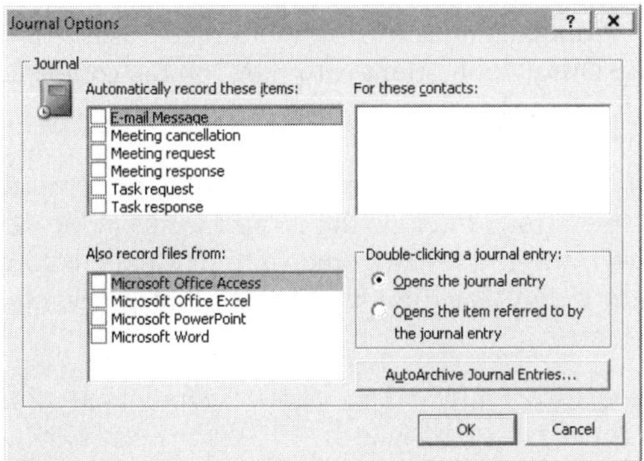

Figure 2-7. Configure your journal using these Outlook 2007 options.

Organizing Your Thoughts with Notes

With Outlook 2007, you can keep track of your thoughts and tasks by using the Notes folder. Each note can function as a stand-alone window, allowing you to view notes on your desktop outside Outlook 2007, as shown in Figure 2-8. Notes exist as individual message files, so you can copy or move them to other folders, including your desktop, or easily share them with others through network sharing or e-mail. You can also incorporate the contents of notes into other applications or other Outlook 2007 folders by using the Clipboard. For example, you might copy a note regarding a contact to that person's contact entry. As you can with other Outlook 2007 items, you can assign categories to notes to help you organize and view them.

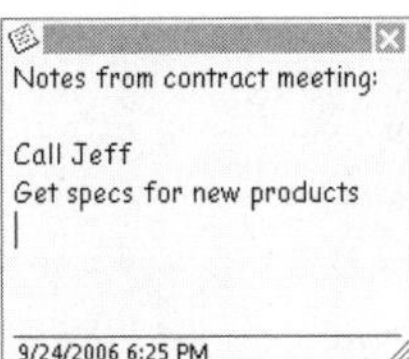

Notes from contract meeting:
Call Jeff
Get specs for new products
9/24/2006 6:25 PM

Figure 2-8. Use notes to keep track of miscellaneous information.

How Outlook Stores Data

If you work with Outlook 2007 primarily as a user, understanding how the program stores data helps you use it effectively to organize and manage your data on a daily basis, including storing and archiving Outlook 2007 items as needed. If you're charged with supporting other Outlook 2007 users, understanding how Outlook 2007 stores data allows you to help others create and manage their folders and ensure the security and integrity of their data. Finally, because data storage is the foundation of all of the Outlook 2007 features, understanding where and how the program stores data is critical if you're creating Outlook 2007–based applications–for example, a data entry form that uses Outlook 2007 as the mechanism for posting the data to a public folder.

For information about creating Outlook 2007–based applications, see Chapter 25, "Using Templates," and the articles, "Programming Forms with VBScript," "Using VBA in Outlook," and, "Integrating Outlook and Other Applications with VBA," on the companion CD.

You're probably familiar with folders (directories) in the file system. You use these folders to organize applications and documents. For example, the Program Files folder in the Microsoft Windows operating system is the default location for most applications that you install on the system, and the My Documents folder (called Documents in Windows Vista) serves as the default location for document files. You create these types of folders in Windows Explorer.

Outlook 2007 also uses folders to organize data, but these folders are different from your file system folders. Rather than existing individually on your system's hard disk, these folders exist within the Outlook 2007 file structure. You view and manage these folders within the Outlook 2007 interface, not in Windows Explorer. Think of Outlook 2007 folders as windows into your Outlook 2007 data rather than as individual elements that exist on disk. By default, Outlook 2007 includes several folders, as shown in Figure 2-9.

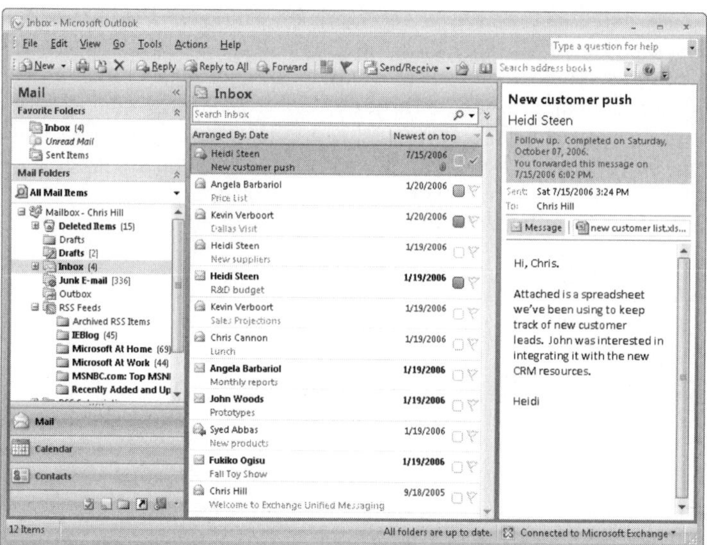

Figure 2-9. Folders organize your data in Outlook 2007.

Personal Folders—.pst Files

If your Outlook 2007 folders aren't stored as individual folders on your system's hard disk, where are they? The answer to that question depends on how you configure Outlook 2007. As in earlier versions of Microsoft Outlook, you can use a set of personal folders to store your Outlook 2007 data. Outlook 2007 uses the .pst extension for a set of personal folders, but you specify the file's name when you configure Outlook 2007.

For example, you might use your name as the file name to help you easily identify the file. The default .pst file contains your Contacts, Calendar, Tasks, and other folders.

You can use multiple .pst files, adding additional personal folders to your Outlook 2007 configuration, as shown in Figure 2-10. For example, you might want to create another set of folders to separate your personal information from work-related data. As you'll learn in Chapter 3, "Advanced Setup Tasks," you can add personal folders to your Outlook 2007 configuration simply by adding another .pst file to your profile.

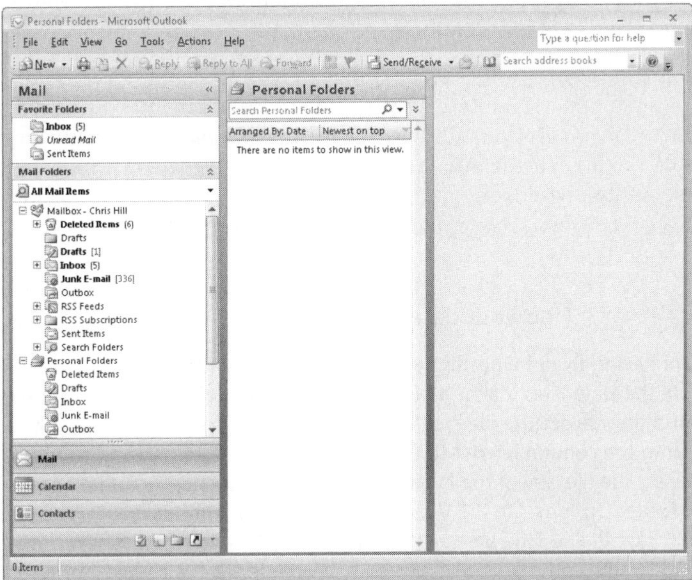

Figure 2-10. You can add multiple sets of folders to your Outlook 2007 configuration.

Options for Working Offline

If you use Outlook 2007 with Exchange Server and do not use local .pst files to store your data, you have two options for working with your mailbox data offline, and these methods differ only in the way synchronization occurs.

An .ost file allows you to work offline. The .ost file acts as an offline copy of your data store on the computer running Exchange Server. When you're working offline, changes you make to contacts, messages, and other Outlook 2007 items and folders occur in the offline store. When you go online again, Outlook 2007 synchronizes the changes between the offline store and your Exchange Server store when you perform a send/receive for the account. For example, if you've deleted messages from your offline store, Outlook 2007 deletes those same messages from your online store when you synchronize the folders. Any new messages in your Inbox on the server are added to your offline store. Synchronization is a two-way process, providing the most up-to-date copy of your data in both locations, ensuring that changes made in each are reflected in the other.

For detailed information about important offline and remote access topics, see Chapter 43, "Working Offline and Remotely." For a discussion of the differences between remote mail and offline use, see Chapter 15, "Receiving Messages Selectively."

Outlook 2007 includes a feature called Cached Exchange Mode. This mode works much the same as offline synchronization with an .ost file. In fact, Outlook 2007 uses an .ost file for Cached Exchange Mode. The main difference is that with Cached Exchange Mode, Outlook 2007 always works from the copy of your mailbox that is cached locally on your computer. Outlook 2007 then automatically handles synchronization between your offline cache mailbox and the mailbox stored on the server. With Cached Exchange Mode, you don't need to worry about synchronizing the two—Outlook 2007 detects when the server is available and updates your locally cached copy automatically.

When you create an Outlook 2007 storage file, Outlook 2007 defaults to a specific location for the file. The default location is the Local Settings\Application Data \Microsoft\Outlook folder of your user profile.

INSIDE OUT Find your data store

If you're having trouble locating your existing storage files, click File, Data File Management. In the Data Files dialog box, shown in Figure 2-11, select the file you want to locate, and then select the file location in the Filename column. If you can't see the entire path, drag the column border to expand the column. Alternatively, to go to the folder containing the file, select the file and click Open Folder. In the folder window, choose Tools, Folder Options. On the View tab of the Folder Options dialog box, select Display The Full Path In The Title Bar to view the fully qualified path to the file. You can also use the Find/Search command in Windows to search for files with a .pst or an .ost extension.

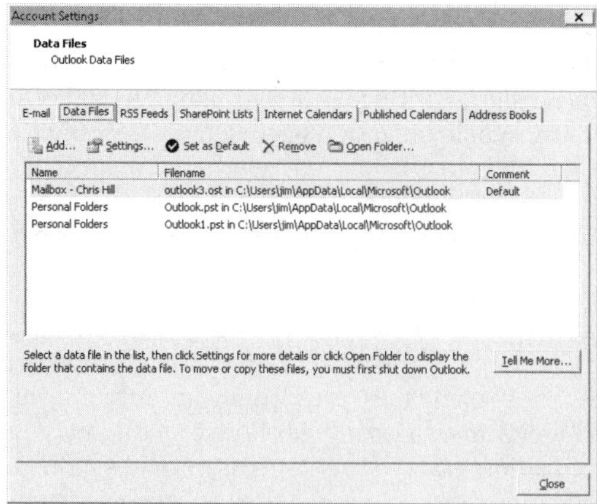

Figure 2-11. Locate your data files by using the Data Files dialog box.

If you use the same computer all the time, it's generally best to store your Outlook 2007 files on a local hard disk. In some situations, however, you will probably want to store them on a network share. For example, you might connect from different computers on the network and use a roaming profile to provide a consistent desktop and user interface regardless of your logon location. (A *roaming profile* allows your desktop configuration, documents, and other elements of your desktop environment to be duplicated wherever you log on.) In this situation, you (or the network administrator) would configure your profile to place your home folder on a network server that is available to you from all logon locations. Your Outlook 2007 files would then be stored on that network share, making them available to you on whichever computer you use to log on to the network. Placing your Outlook 2007 files on a server gives you the added potential benefit of incorporating your Outlook 2007 data files in the server's backup strategy.

TROUBLESHOOTING

You use a roaming profile and logon time is increasing

If you use Outlook 2007 with Exchange Server, your best option is to use your Exchange Server mail store as the storage location for your data instead of using a .pst file. However, if you use a roaming profile, consider turning off Cached Exchange Mode or eliminating the use of an .ost file to reduce the excessive amount of traffic that would otherwise be required to transfer your mailbox data across the network. If you have a situation where you can't use Outlook 2007 to access your mailbox, you can turn to Outlook Web Access or Outlook Anywhere; both enable you to access your mailbox from a Web browser. See Chapter 44, "Accessing Your Outlook Items Through a Web Browser," to learn more about Web-based mailbox access.

Sharing Storage Files

Outlook 2007 provides excellent functionality for sharing information with others. Toward that end, you can share your data using a couple of different methods. Exchange Server users can configure permissions for individual folders to allow specific users to connect to those folders and view the data contained in them. You can also delegate access to your folders to allow an assistant to manage items for you in the folders. For example, you might have your assistant manage your schedule but not your tasks. In that case, you would delegate access for the Calendar folder but not for the Tasks folder.

For a detailed discussion of delegation, see Chapter 35, "Delegating Responsibilities to an Assistant."

Understanding Messaging Protocols

A *messaging protocol* is a mechanism that messaging servers and applications use to transfer messages. Being able to use a specific e-mail service requires that your application support the same protocols the server uses. To configure Outlook 2007 as a messaging client, you need to understand the various protocols supported by Outlook 2007 and the types of servers that employ each type. The following sections provide an overview of these protocols.

SMTP/POP3

Simple Mail Transport Protocol (SMTP) is a standards-based protocol used for transferring messages and is the primary mechanism that Internet-based and intranet-based e-mail servers use to transfer messages. It's also the mechanism that Outlook 2007 uses to connect to a mail server to send messages for an Internet account. SMTP is the protocol used by an Internet e-mail account for outgoing messages.

SMTP operates by default on TCP port 25. When you configure an Internet-based e-mail account, the port on which the server is listening for SMTP determines the outgoing mail server setting. Unless your e-mail server uses a different port (unlikely), you can use the default port value of 25. If you want to use Outlook 2007 for an existing Internet mail account, confirm the SMTP server name and port settings with your ISP.

Post Office Protocol 3 (POP3) is a standards-based protocol that clients can use to retrieve messages from any mail server that supports POP3. This is the protocol that Outlook 2007 uses when retrieving messages from an Internet-based or intranet-based mail server that supports POP3 mailboxes. Nearly all ISP-based mail servers use POP3. Exchange Server also supports the use of POP3 for retrieving mail.

POP3 operates on TCP port 110 by default. Unless your server uses a nonstandard port configuration, you can leave the port setting as is when defining a POP3 mail account.

To learn how to set up an Internet e-mail account for an SMTP/POP3 server, including setting port numbers, see "Using Internet POP3 E-Mail Accounts" in Chapter 7.

IMAP

Like POP3, Internet Message Access Protocol (IMAP) is a standards-based protocol that enables message transfer. However, IMAP offers some significant differences from POP3. For example, POP3 is primarily designed as an offline protocol, which means that you retrieve your messages from a server and download them to your local message store (such as your local Outlook 2007 folders). IMAP is designed primarily as an online protocol, which allows a remote user to manipulate messages and message folders on the server without downloading them. This is particularly helpful for users who need to access the same remote mailbox from multiple locations, such as home and work, using different computers. Because the messages remain on the server, IMAP eliminates the need for message synchronization.

INSIDE OUT **Keep POP3 messages on the server**

IMAP by default leaves your messages on the server. If needed, you can configure a POP3 account in Outlook 2007 to leave a copy of messages on the server, allowing you to retrieve those messages later from another computer. (To learn how to configure a POP3 account, see "Using Internet POP3 E-Mail Accounts" in Chapter 7.) IMAP offers other advantages over POP3. For example, with IMAP, you can search for messages on the server using a variety of message attributes, such as sender, message size, or message header. IMAP also offers better support for attachments because it can separate attachments from the header and text portion of a message. This is particularly useful with multipart Multipurpose Internet Mail Extensions (MIME) messages, allowing you to read a message without downloading the attachments so that you can decide which attachments you want to retrieve. With POP3, the entire message must be downloaded.

Security is another advantage of IMAP, because IMAP uses a challenge-response mechanism to authenticate the user for mailbox access. This prevents the user's password from being transmitted as clear text across the network, as it is with POP3.

IMAP support in Outlook 2007 allows you to use Outlook 2007 as a client to an IMAP-compliant e-mail server. Although IMAP provides for server-side storage and the ability to create additional mail folders on the server, it does not offer some of the same features as Exchange Server or even POP3. For example, you can't store contact, calendar, or other nonmessage folders on the server. Also, special folders such as Sent Items, Drafts, and Deleted Items can't be stored on the IMAP server. Even with these limitations, however, IMAP serves as a flexible protocol and surpasses POP3 in capability. Unless a competing standard appears in the future, it is possible that IMAP will eventually replace POP3. However, ISPs generally like POP3 because users' e-mail is moved to their own computers, freeing space on the mail server and reducing disk space management problems. For that reason alone, don't look for IMAP to replace POP3 in the near future.

For information about other advantages and disadvantages of IMAP and how they affect Outlook 2007, see "Using IMAP Accounts" in Chapter 7. For additional technical information about IMAP, go to *www.imap.org*.

MAPI

Messaging Application Programming Interface (MAPI) is a Microsoft-developed application programming interface (API) that facilitates communication between mail-enabled applications. MAPI support makes it possible for other applications to send and receive messages using Outlook 2007. For example, some third-party fax applications can place incoming faxes in your Inbox through MAPI. As another example, a third-party MAPI-aware application could read and write to your Outlook 2007 Address Book through MAPI calls. MAPI is not a message protocol, but understanding its function in Outlook 2007 helps you install, configure, and use MAPI-aware applications to integrate Outlook 2007.

LDAP

Lightweight Directory Access Protocol (LDAP) was designed to serve with less overhead and fewer resource requirements than its precursor, Directory Access Protocol. LDAP is a standards-based protocol that allows clients to query data in a directory service over a TCP connection. For example, Windows Server uses LDAP as the primary means for querying the Active Directory® directory service. Exchange Server supports LDAP queries, allowing clients to look up address information for subscribers on the server. Other directory services on the Internet employ LDAP to implement searches of their databases.

Like Outlook Express in Windows 2000 and Windows XP and Windows Mail in Windows Vista, Outlook 2007 allows you to add directory service accounts that use LDAP as their protocol to query directory services for e-mail addresses, phone numbers, and other information regarding subscribers.

To learn how to add and configure an LDAP directory service in Outlook 2007, see "Configuring a Directory Service Account in Outlook" in Chapter 17.

NNTP

Network News Transfer Protocol (NNTP) is the standards-based protocol for server-to-server and client-to-server transfer of news messages, or the underlying protocol that makes possible public and private newsgroups. Outlook 2007 does not directly support the creation of accounts to access newsgroup servers but instead relies on Outlook Express or Windows Mail (depending on the operating system) as its default newsreader, as shown in Figure 2-12.

Note

Microsoft Windows 2000 Server and Windows Server® 2003 both include an NNTP service that lets a network administrator set up a news server to host newsgroups that can be accessed by local intranet or remote Internet users. Exchange Server allows the NNTP service to interface with other public or private news servers to pull newsgroups and messages via newsfeeds. Therefore, Windows 2000 Server and Windows Server 2003 by themselves let you set up your own newsgroup server to host your own newsgroups, and Exchange Server lets you host public Internet newsgroups.

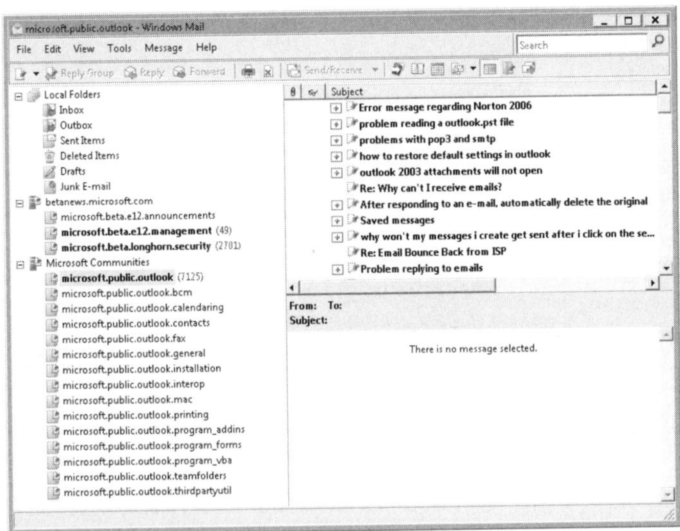

Figure 2-12. Outlook 2007 relies on Outlook Express or Windows Mail for reading and posting to public and private newsgroups.

Using Outlook 2007 Express or Windows Mail, you can download newsgroups, read messages, post messages, and perform other news-related tasks. Other third-party news applications offer extended capabilities.

HTML

HTML is the protocol used most commonly to define and transmit Web pages. Several e-mail services, including Hotmail, provide access to client mailboxes through Web pages and therefore make use of HTML as their message transfer protocol. You connect to the Web site and use the features and commands found there to view messages, send messages, and download attachments.

Outlook 2007 provides enhanced HTML support, which means that you can configure Outlook 2007 as a client for HTML-based mail services. As mentioned earlier in this chapter, Outlook 2007 includes built-in support for Hotmail. HTML support is purely a server-side issue, so HTML-based mail services other than Hotmail have to provide Outlook 2007 support on their own sites. Hotmail accomplishes this support programmatically by means of Active Server Pages (ASP).

INSIDE OUT Find Outlook 2007–based access in Hotmail

The URL for Outlook 2007–based access in Hotmail is *services.msn.com/svcs/hotmail/httpmail.asp*. Outlook 2007 configures the URL automatically when you set up a Hotmail account in Outlook 2007, as shown in Figure 2-13. You can't browse to this URL through your Web browser to retrieve your e-mail, however.

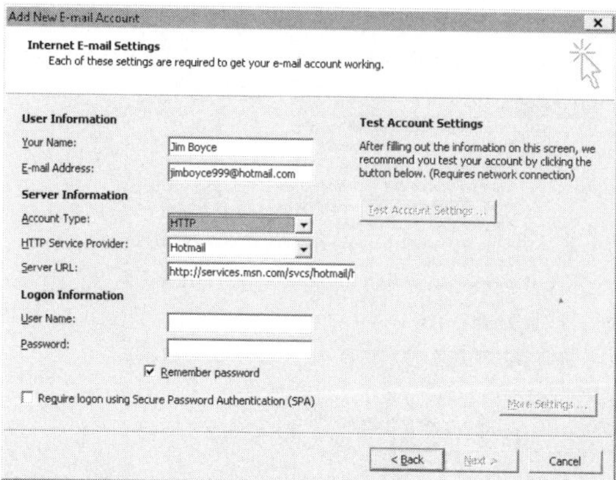

Figure 2-13. Outlook 2007 configures the URL automatically for Hotmail, but you must enter the URL manually for other HTTP-based e-mail services.

INSIDE OUT **Access Exchange Server with HTTP**

Outlook 2007 can connect to an Exchange Server 2003 or Exchange Server 2007 mailbox using HTTP as the protocol, expanding connection possibilities for users and decreasing firewall configuration and management headaches for administrators. See "Establishing a Remote LAN Connection" in Chapter 43 to learn more about using HTTP to connect to Exchange Server.

MIME

Multipurpose Internet Mail Extensions (MIME) is a standard specification for defining file formats used to exchange e-mail, files, and other documents across the Internet or an intranet. Each of the many MIME types defines the content type of the data contained in the attachment. MIME maps the content to a specific file type and extension, allowing the e-mail client to pass the MIME attachment to an external application for processing. For example, if you receive a message containing a WAV audio file, Outlook 2007 passes the file to the default WAV file player on your system.

S/MIME

Secure/Multipurpose Internet Mail Extensions (S/MIME) is a standard that allows e-mail applications to send digitally signed and encrypted messages. S/MIME is therefore a mechanism through which Outlook 2007 permits you to include digital signatures with messages to ensure their authenticity and to encrypt messages to prevent unauthorized access to them.

For a detailed discussion of using Outlook 2007 to send digitally signed and encrypted messages, as well as other security-related issues such as virus protection and security zones, see Chapter 14, "Securing Your System, Messages, and Identity."

MHTML

MIME HTML (MHTML) represents MIME encapsulation of HTML documents. MHTML allows you to send and receive Web pages and other HTML-based documents and to embed images directly in the body of a message instead of attaching them to the message. See the preceding sections for an explanation of MIME.

iCalendar, vCalendar, and vCard

iCalendar, vCalendar, and vCard are Internet-based standards that provide a means for people to share calendar information and contact information across the Internet. The iCalendar standard allows calendar and scheduling applications to share free/busy information with other applications that support iCalendar. The vCalendar standard provides a mechanism for vCalendar-compliant applications to exchange meeting requests across the Internet. The vCard standard allows applications to share contact information as Internet vCards (electronic business cards). Outlook 2007 supports these standards to share information and interact with other messaging and scheduling applications across the Internet.

Security Provisions in Outlook

Outlook 2007 provides several features for ensuring the security of your data, messages, and identity. This section presents a brief overview of security features in Outlook 2007 to give you a basic understanding of the issues involved, with references to other locations in the book that offer more detailed information about these topics.

Protection Against Web Beacons

Many spammers (people who send unsolicited e-mail) use *Web beacons* to validate e-mail addresses. The spammers send HTML-based e-mail messages that contain links to external content on a Web site (the Web beacon), and when the recipient's e-mail client displays the remote content, the site validates the e-mail address. The spammer then knows that the address is a valid one and continues to send messages to it.

Outlook 2007 blocks Web beacons, displaying a red *X* instead of the external image. You can selectively view blocked content on a per-message basis, or you can configure Outlook 2007 to view all content but control access to HTML content in other ways. You can also turn off Web beacon blocking, if you want, and control external HTML content in other ways.

See Chapter 14, "Securing Your System, Messages, and Identity," for an explanation of how to configure HTML message-handling options.

Attachment and Virus Security

You probably are aware that a *virus* is malicious code that infects your system and typically causes some type of damage. The action caused by a virus can be as innocuous as displaying a message or as damaging as deleting data from your hard disk. One especially insidious form of virus, called a *worm*, spreads itself automatically, often by mailing itself to every contact in the infected system's address book. Because of the potential damage that can be caused by viruses and worms, it is critically important to guard against malicious code entering your system.

Outlook 2007 offers two levels of attachment security to guard against virus and worm infections: Level 1 and Level 2. Outlook 2007 automatically blocks Level 1 attachments, a category that includes almost 40 file types known to be potentially harmful to your system—for example, .exe and .vbs files. If you receive a Level 1 attachment, Outlook 2007 displays a paper clip icon beside the message but does not allow you to open or save the attachment. If you try to send a Level 1 attachment, Outlook 2007 displays a reminder that other Outlook 2007 users might not be able to receive the attachment and gives you the option of converting it to a different file type (such as a .zip file) before sending it.

If you receive a Level 2 attachment, Outlook 2007 allows you to save the attachment to disk but not open it directly. You can then process the file with your virus checker before opening it.

CAUTION!

Your virus scanner is only as good as its definition file. New viruses crop up every day, so it's critical that you have an up-to-date virus definition file and put in place a strategy to ensure that your virus definitions are always current.

If you use Exchange Server to host your mailbox, the Exchange Server administrator can configure Level 1 and Level 2 attachments, adding or removing attachment types for each level. In addition, Outlook 2007 allows all users to control the security-level assignments for attachments.

For a detailed discussion of Outlook 2007 virus protection, see "Virus Protection" in Chapter 14.

Macro Viruses

Although viruses were once found almost exclusively in executable files, viruses embedded in documents containing macros have become very common, and Microsoft Office system documents are as subject to them as any other files. However, Outlook 2007 and other Microsoft Office system applications provide a means for you to guard against macro viruses. In Outlook 2007, you can select one of four options for macro security, as shown in Figure 2-14.

To learn how to configure and use macro virus protection, see "Virus Protection" in Chapter 14.

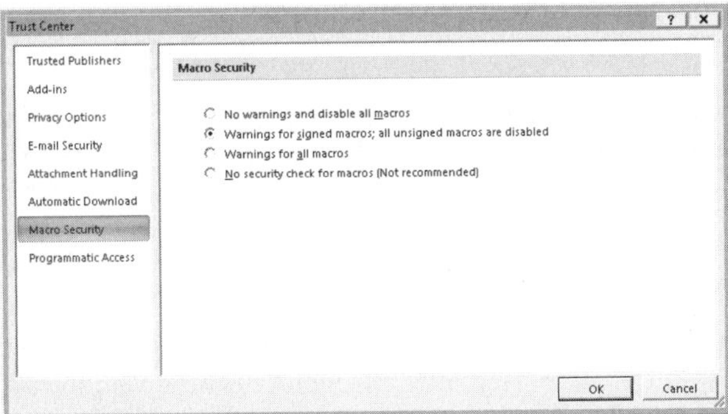

Figure 2-14. Use macro security to prevent macro-borne viruses from affecting your system.

Digital Signatures

Outlook 2007 allows you to add a certificate-based digital signature to a message to validate your identity to the message recipient. Because the signature is derived from a certificate that is issued to you and that you share with the recipient, the recipient can be guaranteed that the message originated with you, rather than with someone trying to impersonate your identity.

For information about how to obtain a certificate and use it to digitally sign your outgoing messages, see "Protecting Messages with Digital Signatures" in Chapter 14.

In addition to signing your outgoing messages, you can also use secure message receipts that notify you that your message has been verified by the recipient's system. The lack of a return receipt indicates that the recipient's system did not validate your identity. In such a case, you can contact the recipient to make sure that he or she has a copy of your digital signature.

> **Note**
>
> Although you can configure Outlook 2007 to send a digital signature to a recipient, there is no guarantee that the recipient will add the digital signature to his or her contacts list. Until the recipient adds the signature, digitally signed messages are not validated, and the recipient cannot read encrypted messages from you.

Message Encryption

Where the possibility of interception exists (whether someone intercepts your message before it reaches the intended recipient or someone else at the recipient's end tries to read the message), Outlook 2007 message encryption can help you keep prying eyes away from sensitive messages. This feature also relies on your digital signature to encrypt the message and to allow the recipient to decrypt and read the message. Someone who receives the message without first having the appropriate encryption key from your certificate installed on his or her system sees a garbled message.

To learn how to obtain a certificate and use it to encrypt your outgoing messages, as well as how to read encrypted messages you receive from others, see "Encrypting Messages" in Chapter 14.

Security Labels

The security labels feature in Outlook 2007 relies on security policies in Windows 2000 Server or later and is supported only on clients running Windows XP or later. Security labels let you add additional security information, such as message sensitivity, to a message header. You can also use security labels to restrict which recipients can open, forward, or send a specific message. Security labels therefore provide a quick indicator of a message's sensitivity and provide control over the actions that others can take with a message.

Understanding Outlook Service Options

If you've been using a version of Outlook earlier than Microsoft Outlook 2002, you're probably familiar with the Outlook 2007 service options. Earlier versions of Outlook supported three service options: No Mail, Internet Mail Only (IMO), and Corporate/Workgroup (C/W). Outlook 2007, like Outlook 2002 and Outlook 2003, uses a *unified mode*. Outlook 2007 unified mode integrates mail services in Outlook 2007, which allows you to configure and use multiple services in a single profile. This means that you can use Exchange Server, POP3, IMAP, and Hotmail accounts all in one profile and at the same time.

To learn how to work with profiles and add multiple accounts to a profile, see "Understanding User Profiles" in Chapter 3. Although Outlook 2007 makes a great e-mail client for a wide range of mail services, you might prefer to use only its contact management, scheduling, and other nonmessaging features and to use a different application (such as Outlook Express or Windows Mail) for your messaging needs. There is no downside to using Outlook 2007 in this configuration, although you should keep in mind that certain features, such as integrated scheduling, rely on the Outlook 2007 messaging features. If you need to take advantage of these features, you should use Outlook 2007 as your primary messaging application.

Options for Starting Outlook

Microsoft Office offers several options to control startup, either through command-line switches or other methods. You can choose to have Outlook 2007 open forms, turn off the Reading Pane (previously called the Preview pane), select a profile, and perform other tasks automatically when the program starts. The following sections describe some of the options you can specify.

Normal Startup

When you install Outlook 2007, Setup places a Microsoft Outlook 2007 icon on the Start menu. You can start Outlook 2007 normally by clicking the icon. You also can start Outlook 2007 by using the Programs menu (choose Start, All Programs, Microsoft Office, Microsoft Office Outlook 2007.)

If more than one profile exists, when Outlook 2007 is started normally, it prompts you for the profile to use, as shown in Figure 2-15. The profile contains your account settings and configures Outlook 2007 for your e-mail servers, directory services, data files, and other settings.

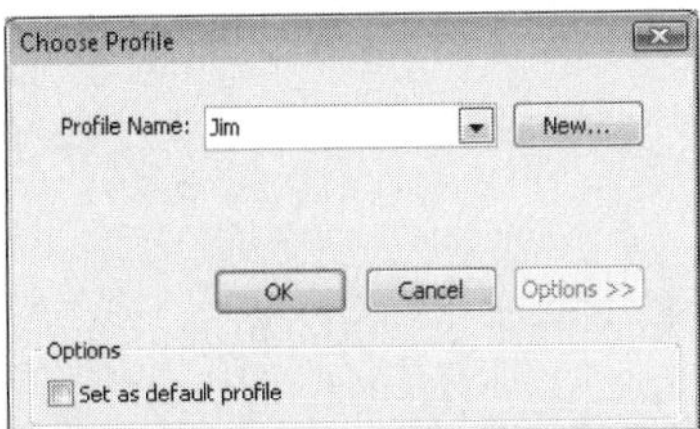

Figure 2-15. Outlook 2007 prompts you to choose a profile at startup.

You can use multiple profiles to maintain multiple identities in Outlook 2007. For example, you might use one profile for your work-related items and a second one for your personal items. To use an existing profile, simply select it in the drop-down list in the Choose Profile dialog box and then click OK. Click New to create a new profile (covered in Chapter 3, "Advanced Setup Tasks"). Click Options in the Choose Profile dialog box, shown in Figure 2-15, to display the option Set As Default Profile. Select this option to specify the selected profile as the default profile, which will appear in the drop-down list by default in subsequent Outlook 2007 sessions. For example, if you maintain separate personal and work profiles and your personal profile always appears in the drop-down list, select your work profile and then choose this option to make the work profile the default.

For an in-depth discussion of creating and configuring profiles, see "Understanding User Profiles" in Chapter 3. The details of configuring service providers (such as for Exchange Server) are covered in various chapters where appropriate—for example, Chapter 7, "Using Internet Mail Accounts," explains how to configure POP3 and IMAP accounts, and Chapter 41, "Configuring the Exchange Server Client," explains how to configure Exchange Server accounts.

Safe Mode Startup

Safe mode is a startup mode available in Outlook 2007 and the other Microsoft Office system applications. Safe mode makes it possible for Microsoft Office system applications to automatically recover from specific errors during startup, such as a problem with an add-in or a corrupt registry setting. Safe mode allows Outlook 2007 to detect the problem and either correct it or bypass it by isolating the source.

When Outlook 2007 starts automatically in safe mode, you see a dialog box that displays the source of the problem and asks whether you want to continue to start the program, bypassing the problem source, or try to restart the program again. If you direct Outlook 2007 to continue starting, the problem items are disabled, and you can view them in the Disabled Items dialog box, as shown in Figure 2-16. To open this dialog box, choose Help and then click Disabled Items. To enable a disabled item, select the item and then click Enable.

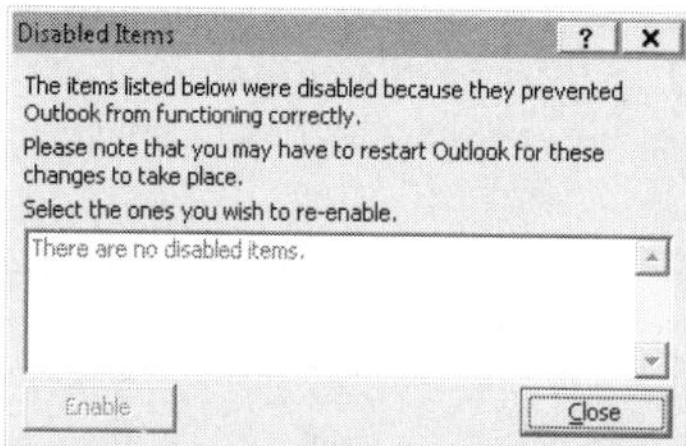

Figure 2-16. Use the Disabled Items dialog box to review and enable items.

In certain situations, you might want to force Outlook 2007 into safe mode when it would otherwise start normally—for example, if you want to prevent add-ins or customized toolbars or command bars from loading. To start Outlook 2007 (or any other Microsoft Office system application) in safe mode, hold down the Ctrl key and start the program. Outlook 2007 detects the Ctrl key and asks whether you want to start Outlook 2007 in safe mode. Click Yes to start in safe mode or No to start normally.

If you start an application in safe mode, you cannot perform certain actions in the application. The following is a summary of these actions (not all of which apply to Outlook 2007):

- Templates can't be saved.
- The last used Web page is not loaded (Microsoft FrontPage®).
- Customized toolbars and command bars are not opened. Customizations that you make in safe mode can't be changed.
- The AutoCorrect list isn't loaded, nor can changes you make to AutoCorrect in safe mode be saved.
- Recovered documents are not opened automatically.
- No smart tags are loaded, and new smart tags can't be saved.

- Command-line options other than */a* and */n* are ignored.
- You can't save files to the Alternate Startup Directory.
- You can't save preferences.
- Additional features and programs (such as add-ins) are not loaded automatically.

To start Outlook 2007 normally, simply shut down the program and start it again without pressing the Ctrl key.

Starting Outlook Automatically

If you're like most Microsoft Office system users, you work in Outlook 2007 a majority of the time. Because Outlook 2007 is such an important aspect of your workday, you probably want it to start automatically when you log on to your computer, saving you the trouble of starting it later. Although you have a few options for starting Outlook 2007 automatically, the best solution is to place a shortcut to Outlook 2007 in your Startup folder.

To start Outlook 2007 automatically when you start Windows, simply drag the Outlook icon from the Start menu or Quick Launch bar to the Startup folder in the Start menu.

INSIDE OUT **Create a new Outlook 2007 shortcut**

If you have no Outlook 2007 icon on the desktop, you can use the Outlook 2007 executable to create a shortcut. Open Windows Explorer, and browse to the folder \Program Files\Microsoft Office\Office12. Create a shortcut to the executable Outlook.exe. Right-click the Outlook.exe file, and then choose Create Shortcut. Windows asks whether you want to create a shortcut on the desktop. Click Yes to create the shortcut.

INSIDE OUT **Change the Outlook Shortcut Properties**

If you want to change the way Outlook 2007 starts from the shortcut in your Startup folder (for example, so you can add command switches), you need only change the shortcut's properties. For details, see "Changing the Outlook Shortcut" in this chapter.

Adding Outlook to the Quick Launch Bar

The Quick Launch bar appears on the taskbar just to the right of the Start menu. Quick Launch, as its name implies, gives you a way to easily and quickly start applications—just click the application's icon. By default, the Quick Launch bar includes the Show Desktop icon as well as the Internet Explorer icon. Quick Launch offers easier application launching because you don't have to navigate the Start menu to start an application.

Note

If you don't see the Quick Launch bar, right-click the taskbar and verify that Lock The Taskbar is not selected on the shortcut menu. If it is, click Lock The Taskbar to deselect it. Then right-click the taskbar again, and click Toolbars, Quick Launch to add the Quick Launch bar to the taskbar.

Adding a shortcut to the Quick Launch bar is easy:

1. Minimize all windows so that you can see the desktop.
2. Using the right mouse button, drag the Microsoft Outlook icon to the Quick Launch area of the taskbar and then release it. If there is no Outlook shortcut on the desktop, right-drag the shortcut from the Start menu, instead.
3. Click Create Shortcut(s) Here.

Note

You can also left-drag the Microsoft Outlook icon to the Quick Launch bar. Windows informs you that you can't copy or move the item to that location and asks whether you want to create a shortcut instead. Click Yes to create the shortcut or No to cancel.

Changing the Outlook Shortcut

Let's assume that you've created a shortcut to Outlook 2007 on your Quick Launch bar or in another location so that you can start Outlook 2007 quickly. Why change the shortcut? By adding switches to the command that starts Outlook 2007, you can customize the way the application starts and functions for the current session. You can also control the Outlook 2007 startup window state (normal, minimized, maximized) through the shortcut's properties. For example, you might want Outlook 2007 to start automatically when you log on, but you want it to start minimized. In this situation, you would create a shortcut to Outlook 2007 in your Startup folder and then modify the shortcut so that Outlook 2007 starts minimized.

To change the properties for a shortcut, locate the shortcut, right-click its icon, and then choose Properties. You should see a Properties page similar to the one shown in Figure 2-17.

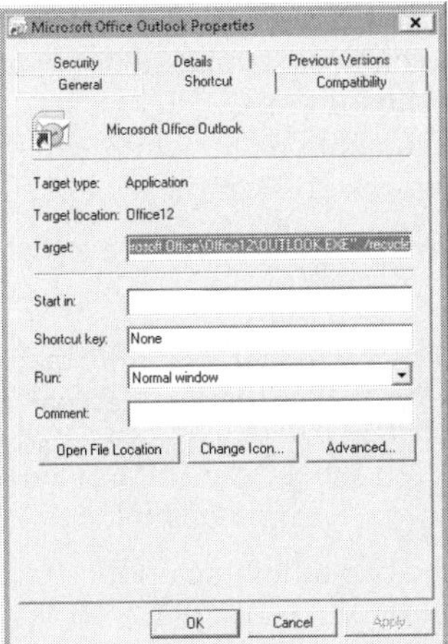

Figure 2-17. A typical Properties page for an Outlook 2007 shortcut.

The following list summarizes the options on the Shortcut tab of the Properties page:

> **Note**
>
> These options have slightly different names depending on which operating system your computer is running. Click Advanced on the Shortcut tab in Windows XP and Windows Vista to view additional settings.

- **Target Type** This read-only property specifies the type for the shortcut's target, which in the example shown in Figure 2-17 is Application.
- **Target Location** This read-only property specifies the directory location of the target executable.
- **Target** This property specifies the command to execute when the shortcut is executed. The default Outlook 2007 command is "C:\Program Files\Microsoft Office\Office12\Outlook.exe" /recycle. The path could vary if you have installed Microsoft Office in a different folder. The path to the executable must be enclosed in quotation marks, and any additional switches must be added to the right, outside the quotation marks. See "Startup Switches" later in this chapter to learn about additional switches that you can use to start Outlook 2007.
- **Start In** This property specifies the startup directory for the application.
- **Shortcut Key** Use this property to assign a shortcut key to the shortcut, which allows you to start Outlook 2007 by pressing the key combination. Simply click in the Shortcut Key box, and then press the keystroke to assign it to the shortcut.
- **Run** Use this property to specify the startup window state for Outlook 2007. You can choose Normal Window, Minimized, or Maximized.

- **Comment** Use this property to specify an optional comment. The comment appears in the shortcut's ToolTip when you position the mouse pointer over the shortcut's icon. For example, if you use the Run As Different User option, you might include mention of that in the Comment box to help you distinguish this shortcut from another that launches Outlook 2007 in the default context.
- **Find Target/Open File Location** Click this button to open the folder containing the Outlook.exe executable file.
- **Change Icon** Click this button to change the icon assigned to the shortcut. By default, the icon comes from the Outlook.exe executable, which contains other icons you can assign to the shortcut. You also can use other .ico, .exe, and .dll files to assign icons. You'll find several additional icons in Moricons.dll and Shell32.dll, both located in the %systemroot%\System32 folder.
- **Advanced** Click this button to access the two following options for Windows XP. (These two options are directly available on the Shortcut tab for Windows 2000 users.)
    - **Run In Separate Memory Space** This option is selected by default and can't be changed for Outlook 2007. All 32-bit applications run in a separate memory space. This provides crash protection for other applications and for the operating system.
    - **Run With Different Credentials** Select this option to run Outlook 2007 in a different user context, which lets you start Outlook 2007 with a different user account from the one you used to log on to the computer. Windows prompts you for the user name and password when you execute the shortcut. This option is named Run As A Different User in Windows 2000.

> **Note**
>
> You also can use the RUNAS command from the Command Prompt window to start an application in a different user context. For more information, see the following section.

When you're satisfied with the shortcut's properties, click OK to close the Properties dialog box.

Using RUNAS to Change User Context

As explained in the preceding section, you can use the option Run As Different User in a shortcut's Properties page to run the target application in a different user context from the one you used to log on to the system. This option is applicable on systems running Windows 2000 or later.

You can also use the RUNAS command from the Command Prompt window in Windows 2000 or Windows XP to run a command–including Outlook 2007–in a different user context. The syntax for RUNAS is

```
RUNAS [/profile] [/env] [/netonly] / user:<UserName>program
```

The parameters for RUNAS can be summarized as follows:

- **/profile** Use this parameter to indicate the profile for the specified user if that profile needs to be loaded.
- **/env** Use the current user environment instead of the one specified by the user's profile.
- **/netonly** Use this parameter if the specified user credentials are for remote access only.
- **/user:<UserName>** Use this parameter to specify the user account under which you want the application to be run.
- **Program** This parameter specifies the application to execute.

Following is an example of the RUNAS command used to start Outlook 2007 in the Administrator context of the domain ADMIN. (Note that the command should be on one line on your screen.)

```
RUNAS /profile / user:admin\administrator
""C:\Program Files\Microsoft Office
\Office12\Outlook.exe" /recycle"
```

It might seem like a lot of trouble to type all that at the command prompt, and that's usually the case. Although you can use RUNAS from the Command Prompt window to run Outlook 2007 in a specific user context, it's generally more useful to use RUNAS in a batch file to start Outlook 2007 in a given predetermined user context. For example, you might create a batch file containing the sample RUNAS syntax just noted and then create a shortcut to that batch file so that you can execute it easily without typing the command each time.

Startup Switches

Microsoft Outlook 2007 supports a number of command-line switches that modify the way the program starts and functions. Although you can issue the Outlook.exe command with switches from a command prompt, it's generally more useful to specify switches through a shortcut, particularly if you want to use the same set of switches more than once. Table 2-1 lists some of the startup switches that you can use to modify the way Outlook 2007 starts and functions.

For an explanation of how to modify a shortcut to add command-line switches, see "Changing the Outlook Shortcut" earlier in this chapter. See "Command-Line Switches for Microsoft Office Outlook 2007" in the Outlook Help content for a complete list of switches.

Table 2-1. Startup Switches and Their Uses

Switch	Use
/a <filename>	Opens a message form with the attachment specified by <filename>
/c ipm.activity	Opens the journal entry form by itself
/c ipm.appointment	Opens the appointment form by itself
/c ipm.contact	Opens the contact form by itself
/c ipm.note	Opens the message form by itself
/c ipm.stickynote	Opens the note form by itself
/c ipm.task	Opens the task form by itself
/c <class>	Creates an item using the message class specified by <class>
/CheckClient	Performs a check to see whether Outlook 2007 is the default application for e-mail, news, and contacts
/CleanFreeBusy	Regenerates free/busy schedule data
/CleanReminders	Regenerates reminders

Choosing a Startup View

When you start Outlook 2007, it defaults to using the Inbox view, as shown in Figure 2-18, but you might prefer to use a different view or folder as the initial view. For example, if you use Outlook 2007 primarily for scheduling, you'll probably want Outlook 2007 to start in the Calendar folder. If you use Outlook 2007 mainly to manage contacts, you'll probably want it to start in the Contacts folder.

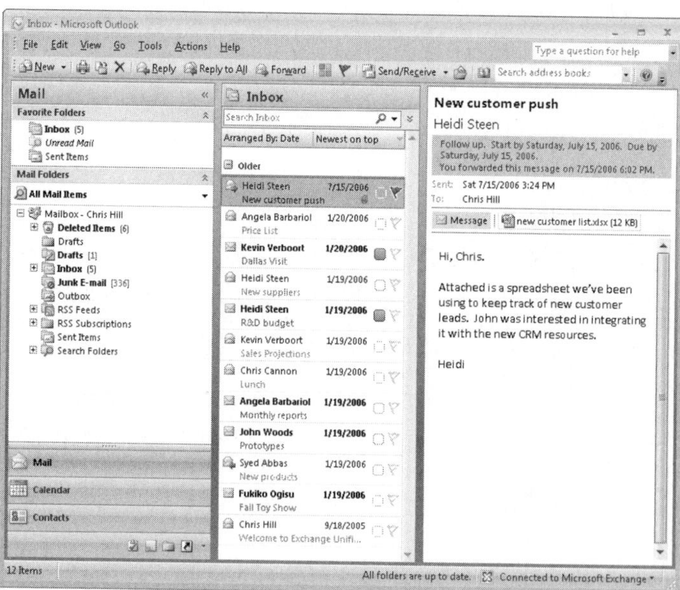

Figure 2-18. Inbox is the default view.

To specify the view that should appear when Outlook 2007 starts, follow these steps:

1. Start Outlook 2007, and then choose Tools, Options.
2. Click the Other tab, and then click Advanced Options to display the Advanced Options dialog box, as shown Figure 2-19.

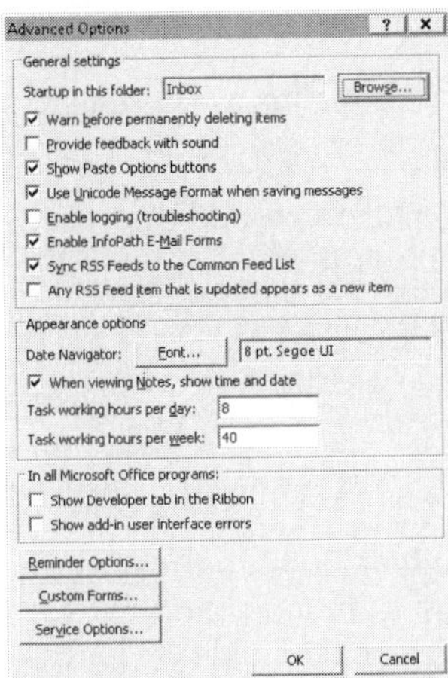

Figure 2-19. Use the Advanced Options dialog box to specify the Startup view.

3. Click Browse, select the folder you want Outlook 2007 to open at startup, and click OK.
4. Click OK, and then close the dialog box.

If you switch Outlook 2007 to a different default folder and then want to restore Outlook Today as your default view, you can follow the preceding steps to restore Outlook Today as the default.

Simply select Outlook Today in the drop-down list or follow these steps with the Outlook Today window open:

1. Start Outlook 2007, and then open the Outlook Today view.
2. Click Customize Outlook Today at the top of the Outlook Today window.
3. In the resulting pane, select When Starting Go Directly To Outlook Today, and then click Save Changes.

Creating Shortcuts to Start New Outlook Items

In some cases, you might want icons on the desktop or your Quick Launch bar that start new Outlook 2007 items. For example, perhaps you would like an icon that starts a new e-mail message and another icon that starts a new appointment item.

Sometimes you need to dash off a quick message, but you have to start Outlook 2007, wait for it to load, compose the message, and then close Outlook 2007 when you've finished. You can simplify the task of sending a new e-mail message by creating a shortcut to a mailto: item on the desktop or on the Quick Launch bar by following these steps:

1. Right-click the desktop, and then choose New, Shortcut.
2. In the Create Shortcut dialog box, type **mailto:** as the item to launch, and then click Next.
3. Type New Mail Message as the shortcut name, and then click Finish.
4. Drag the shortcut to the Quick Launch bar to make it quickly accessible without minimizing all applications.

When you double-click the shortcut, Outlook 2007 actually launches and prompts you for a profile unless a default profile has been set. However, only the new message form appears–the rest of Outlook 2007 stays hidden, running in the background.

You can use the Target property of an Outlook 2007 shortcut to create other types of Outlook 2007 items. Refer to "Changing the Outlook Shortcut" earlier in this chapter to learn how to create an Outlook 2007 shortcut. See Table 2-1 for the switches that open specific Outlook 2007 forms. For example, the following two shortcuts start a new message and a new appointment, respectively:

```
"C:\Program Files\Microsoft Office\Office12\Outlook.exe" /c ipm.note

"C:\Program Files\Microsoft Office\Office12\Outlook.exe" /c ipm.appointment
```

Note

You can use the */a* switch to open a new message form with an attachment. The following example starts a new message and attaches the file named Picture.jpg:

"C:\Program Files\Microsoft Office\Office11\Outlook.exe" /a Picture.jpg

CHAPTER 3

Configuring Outlook Profiles and Accounts

Because Microsoft® Office Outlook® 2007 has so many features, configuring the program—particularly for first-time or inexperienced users—can be a real challenge. However, after you master the basic concepts and experiment with the configuration process, it quickly becomes second nature.

This chapter examines Office Outlook 2007 setup issues, including what you see the first time you start Outlook 2007 and how to use the Add New E-Mail Account Wizard to create, modify, and test e-mail accounts. You'll also learn about user profiles, including how to create and modify them, how to use multiple profiles for different identities, how to copy profiles, and how to configure profile properties.

After you have a solid understanding of profiles, you're ready to tackle configuring the many e-mail and data file services that Outlook 2007 offers. This chapter discusses configuring both online and offline storage and will help you add, modify, and remove personal message stores (personal folders) for a profile.

In addition, you'll learn how to configure Outlook 2007 to maintain an offline copy of your Microsoft Exchange Server mailbox and folders so that you can work with your account while you are disconnected from the network. You'll also learn how to change the storage location for your data and how to set options to control mail delivery.

Understanding the Outlook 2007 Startup Wizard

The first time you run Outlook 2007 after a new installation (as opposed to upgrading from an earlier version of Microsoft Outlook), Outlook 2007 runs the Outlook 2007 Startup Wizard, as shown in Figure 3-1. The wizard guides you through the process of setting up e-mail accounts and *data stores* (the files used to store your Outlook 2007 data). The choices you make using this wizard customize the Outlook 2007 Navigation Pane.

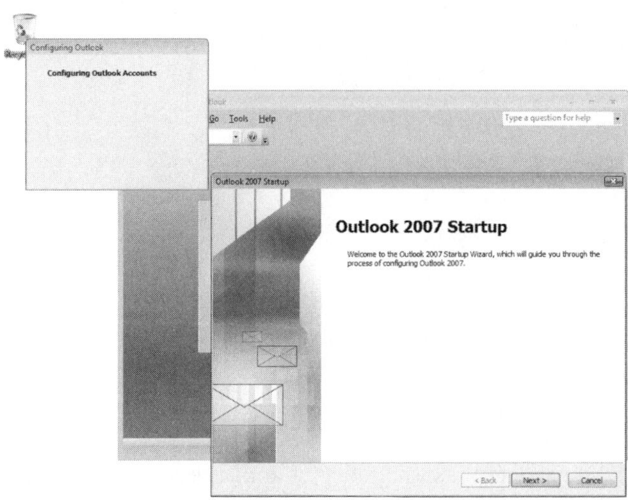

Figure 3-1. Here's what you'll see at first startup after a new installation.

This wizard is very similar to the wizard you use to configure e-mail accounts after Outlook 2007 is installed. You'll add e-mail accounts in the following section.

If you upgraded to Outlook 2007 from an earlier version, Outlook 2007 automatically migrates your accounts, preferences, and data the first time you run it. This means that you don't have to perform any other tasks before working with Outlook 2007, unless you want to add other accounts or take advantage of features not provided by your current profile settings. In the following section, you'll learn how to add other services and accounts to your current Outlook 2007 profile.

Configuring Accounts and Services

Outlook 2007 provides a wizard to help simplify setup and configuration of e-mail accounts, data stores, and directory services. You use the Add New E-Mail Account Wizard to add new e-mail accounts.

Follow these steps to get started in setting up e-mail accounts:

1. Start Outlook 2007. When the Outlook 2007 Startup Wizard appears, click Next. If the wizard does not start automatically, choose Tools, Account Settings, and then click New on the E-Mail tab.
2. On the E-Mail Accounts page, select Yes, indicating that you want to set up an e-mail account, and then click Next.
3. The wizard displays the Add New E-Mail Account wizard, as shown in Figure 3-2. Fill in your e-mail account information to have Outlook 2007 locate your e-mail account automatically.

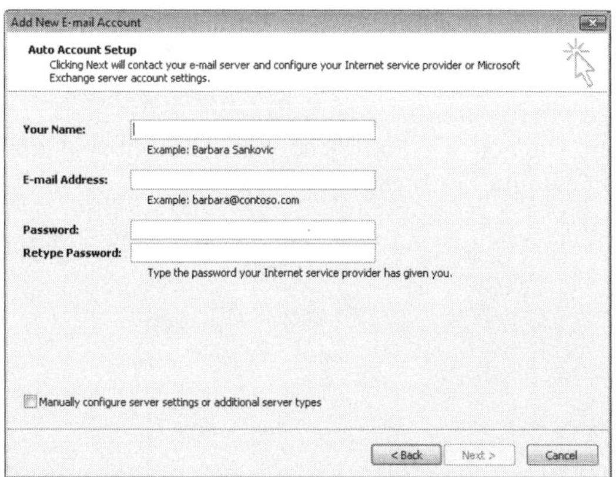

Figure 3-2. Enter the new e-mail account information to add an account to Outlook 2007.

4. Type the password as required, and then click Next.

5. Click Finish on the last page of the wizard.

For a discussion of user profiles and how Outlook 2007 uses them to store your account settings, see "Understanding Profiles" later in this chapter.

Note

If you select Manually Configure Server Settings Or Additional Server Types on the Auto Account Setup page, the wizard prompts you for the e-mail service type. The action that the wizard takes at this point depends on the type of account or server you select. Rather than cover account configuration here, outside the context of using each type of account, this book covers the specifics of each account type in the associated chapter. The following list helps you locate the appropriate chapter and section:

- **Exchange Server** See Chapter 41, "Configuring the Exchange Server Client."
- **Internet E-Mail (POP3, IMAP, or HTTP)** See "Using Internet POP3 E-Mail Accounts" in Chapter 7.
- **Other (Fax Mail Transport or Outlook Mobile Service)** See Chapter 45, "Making Outlook Mobile."

You can easily add an e-mail account to your Outlook 2007 profile after Outlook 2007 is installed. Follow these steps:

1. Right-click the Microsoft Office Outlook icon on the Start menu, choose Properties, and then click E-Mail Accounts. Alternatively, in Outlook 2007, choose Tools, Account Settings.
2. On the E-Mail tab, click New to display the Add New E-Mail Account Wizard, shown in Figure 3-3.

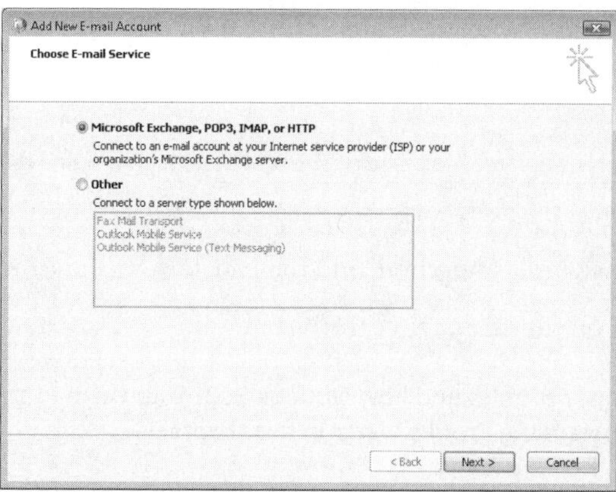

Figure 3-3. Use the Add New E-Mail Account Wizard to add e-mail accounts.

> **Note**
>
> If your system includes multiple profiles, select the one to which you want to add accounts. Right-click the Microsoft Office Outlook icon on the Start menu, and then choose Properties. Click Show Profiles, locate and select your profile, click Properties, and then select E-Mail Accounts.

3. Select the type of e-mail service to add, and then click Next. (As noted earlier, you can refer to other chapters for information about configuring specific account types.)
4. Enter the settings for your account, and then click Next.
5. Click Finish.

TROUBLESHOOTING

Outlook 2007 can't find your e-mail server

If Outlook 2007 can't seem to locate your e-mail server, you can check a handful of settings to determine the problem. First make sure that your computer is connected to the network or the Internet, depending on where the server is located. If you're specifying a server on the Internet, make sure that you have specified the correct, fully qualified domain name (FQDN) of the server, such as *mail.tailspintoys.com*. If you specify the correct name but Outlook 2007 still can't find the server, try pinging the server by name. Open a Command Prompt window, and type the following command, where <server> is the FQDN of the server:

```
PING <server>
```

If this results in an unknown host error, it's likely that the Domain Name System (DNS) is not configured or working properly on your computer (or the host name is wrong). Check the DNS settings for your TCP/IP protocol to make sure that you are specifying the correct DNS server. If you know the IP address of the server, ping the address. If you are able to ping, you definitely have a DNS problem or are specifying the wrong DNS name. If the ping fails, you have a network connectivity or TCP/IP stack problem. At this point, it would be best to consult your network support staff. Your configuration needs to be verified (and changed, if an incorrect value has been specified). If you have faulty hardware, it needs to be replaced.

Understanding Profiles

In Outlook 2007, *profiles* store the configuration of e-mail accounts, data files, and other settings you use in a given Outlook 2007 session. For example, your profile might include an Exchange Server account, an Internet mail account, and a set of personal folders. Outlook 2007 either prompts you to select a profile at startup or selects one automatically, depending on how you've configured it.

In most cases, you'll probably use only one profile and will configure Outlook 2007 to select it automatically. In some situations, however, multiple profiles can be useful. For example, you might prefer to keep your work and personal data completely separate on your notebook computer because of privacy concerns or office policies. In this situation, you maintain two profiles: one for your work data and a second for your personal data. You then configure Outlook 2007 to prompt you to choose a profile at startup. The profile controls which set of data files and configuration settings are used for that specific session. For example, when you're working at the office, you use the office profile, and when you're using the computer at home, you use the personal profile.

It's important to understand that Outlook 2007 profiles have no relationship to the other types of profiles you'll find in a Microsoft Windows® operating system, which include hardware profiles and user profiles. *Hardware profiles* store hardware settings and allow you to switch between different hardware configurations without reconfiguring your system. *User profiles* store the unique working environment (Desktop, My Documents, and so on) that you see when you log on to your computer. Outlook 2007 profiles, in contrast, apply only to Outlook 2007.

> **Note**
>
> Unless otherwise noted, the term *profile* in this book refers to an Outlook 2007 profile.

Each profile can contain multiple accounts and services, which means that you can work with different e-mail servers at one time and use multiple sets of data files (such as a set of personal folders, or .pst file). The following list describes the items stored in an Outlook 2007 profile:

- **Services** These include e-mail accounts and data files, along with their settings. For example, your profile might include an Exchange Server account, two Internet e-mail accounts, a .pst file, and a directory service account. When these accounts are in a single profile, you can use all of them in the same Outlook 2007 session.
- **Delivery settings** The profile specifies the store to which Outlook 2007 should deliver new mail when it arrives. With the exception of Internet Message Access Protocol (IMAP) accounts, which use their own .pst files, all accounts use the same store location. You also can specify the order in which Outlook 2007 processes accounts.

To learn how to configure these delivery properties for a given profile, see "Setting Delivery Options" later in this chapter.

- **Address settings** You can specify which address book Outlook 2007 displays first, where Outlook 2007 should store personal addresses, and the order of the address books that Outlook 2007 uses to check e-mail addresses when the profile includes multiple address books. In earlier versions of Microsoft Outlook, you accessed these settings through the profile properties, but in Outlook 2007, you configure addressing in the Address Book window.

For detailed information about configuring and using address books in Outlook 2007, see Chapter 6, "Using Address Books and Distribution Lists."

The first time you run Outlook 2007, it creates a profile named Outlook even if you don't add any e-mail accounts to the profile. If you do add an e-mail account, Outlook 2007 uses the name you specify in the account settings as the name for the profile.

As mentioned earlier, you can use multiple profiles. The following sections explain how to create new profiles, copy existing profiles to new profiles, and perform related operations.

Creating Profiles

You don't have to be in Outlook 2007 to create a profile–in fact, you *can't* create one in Outlook 2007. You can create profiles from the Start menu or through Control Panel. In addition to specifying a profile name, you can also (optionally) add e-mail and other services to the profile. You can create a profile from scratch or copy an existing profile to create a new one.

Creating a Profile from Scratch

When you have no existing Outlook profile or no profile that contains the accounts or settings you need, you must create a profile from scratch.

Follow these steps to create a new profile:

1. On the Start menu, right-click the Microsoft Office Outlook icon, and then choose Properties. Alternatively, open Control Panel and double-click the Mail icon. If you are using Category view in the Microsoft Windows XP or Windows Vista™ Control Panel, the Mail icon is located in the User Accounts category in Windows XP or in the User Accounts And Family Safety category in Windows Vista.
2. In the Mail Setup dialog box, shown in Figure 3-4, click Show Profiles. If no profiles exist, the Mail dialog box appears; continue with step 3.

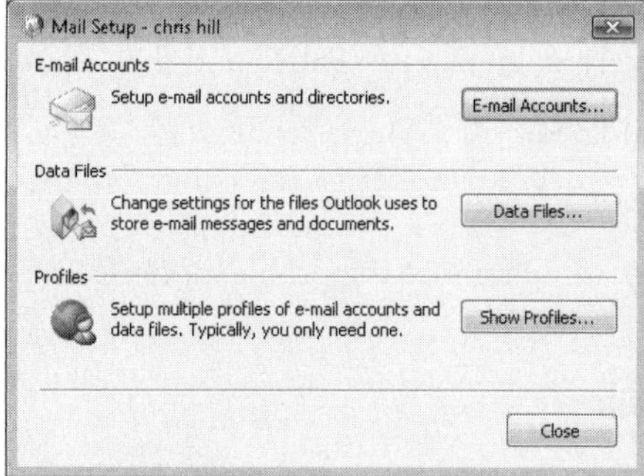

Figure 3-4. You access the current profile's settings as well as other profiles in the Mail Setup dialog box.

3. Click Add, specify a name for the profile in the New Profile dialog box, and then click OK.
4. The Add New E-Mail Account Wizard starts. Add accounts and other services to the profile. Enter requested data such as e-mail address and password. To create a new profile without adding any services (useful if you are not using Outlook 2007 for e-mail), click Cancel, and then click OK. In this situation, Outlook 2007 automatically creates a set of personal folders (a .pst file) to store your Outlook 2007 data.

Copying a Profile

In addition to creating profiles from scratch, you can also copy an existing profile to create a new one. When you copy a profile, Outlook 2007 copies all the settings from the existing profile to the new one, including accounts and data files.

Follow these steps to copy an existing profile:

1. On the Start menu, right-click the Microsoft Office Outlook icon, and then choose Properties. Alternatively, open Control Panel, and then double-click the Mail icon.
2. In the Mail Setup dialog box, click Show Profiles.
3. Select the existing profile that you want to use as the basis for the new profile, and then click Copy.
4. In the Copy Profile dialog box, specify a name for the new profile, and click OK.

Modifying or Removing a Profile

You can modify a profile at any time to add or remove services. You can also remove a profile altogether if you no longer need it.

Follow these steps to modify or remove an existing profile:

1. On the Start menu, right-click the Microsoft Office Outlook icon, and then choose Properties. Alternatively, open Control Panel, and then double-click the Mail icon.
2. In the Mail Setup dialog box, click Show Profiles.
3. Select the profile to be modified or removed.
4. Click Remove if you want to remove the profile, or click Properties to modify the profile settings.

Creating Multiple Profiles

For situations in which you need to create many profiles, such as when you are installing the 2007 Microsoft Office system for multiple users or setting up a server to allow users to install the Microsoft Office system automatically, you can turn to the Microsoft Office Resource Kit for some helpful tools. One of these tools is the Custom Installation Wizard, which helps you customize the Microsoft Office system setup process, apply security settings for Microsoft Office system deployment, and provide the means to create and deploy preconfigured Outlook 2007 profiles.

See the Microsoft Office Resource Kit, available by download from the Microsoft Web site, to learn how to use the Custom Installation Wizard to create custom user profiles and control Outlook with group policy.

Switching Profiles

You can configure Outlook 2007 either to use a specific profile automatically or to prompt you to select a profile at startup. If you want to change profiles, you need to exit Outlook 2007 and then restart, selecting the appropriate profile.

Follow these steps to specify the default profile and use it automatically when Outlook 2007 starts:

1. On the Start menu, right-click the Microsoft Office Outlook icon, and then choose Properties. Alternatively, open Control Panel, and then double-click the Mail icon.
2. In the Mail Setup dialog box, click Show Profiles.
3. In the Mail dialog box, on the General tab, select Always Use This Profile, as shown in Figure 3-5. In the drop-down list, select the default profile that you want Outlook 2007 to use.

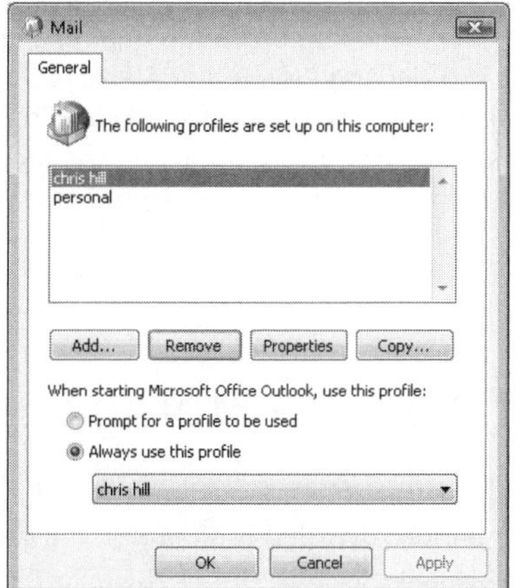

Figure 3-5. You can specify a default profile on the General tab.

4. Click OK.

Specifying the Startup Profile

If you work with multiple profiles and switch profiles relatively often, you'll probably want to configure Outlook 2007 to prompt you to choose a profile at startup. This saves you the trouble of changing the default profile each time you want to switch. For example, assume that you use one profile for your personal accounts and another for your work accounts. Have Outlook 2007 prompt you for the profile when the program starts, rather than configuring the settings each time to specify the default profile.

Follow these steps to configure Outlook 2007 to prompt you to choose a profile:

1. On the Start menu, right-click the Microsoft Office Outlook icon, and then choose Properties. Alternatively, open Control Panel, and then double-click the Mail icon.
2. In the Mail Setup dialog box, click Show Profiles.
3. In the Mail dialog box, select Always Use This Profile, select the profile that you want Outlook 2007 to display as the initial selection in the list, and then select Prompt For A Profile To Be Used.
4. Click OK.

INSIDE OUT **Set the initial profile**

You probably noticed in step 3 of the preceding procedure that you enabled an option and then immediately disabled it by selecting Prompt For A Profile To Be Used. In effect, you've accomplished two tasks: setting the default profile and also configuring Outlook 2007 to prompt you for a profile. In the drop-down list, select the profile you use most often, which saves you the effort of selecting it when prompted at startup.

Configuring Online and Offline Data Storage

The preceding section explained how to add e-mail account services and introduced data stores. This section provides a more detailed look at storage options in Outlook 2007 and shows how to configure those options.

Like earlier versions of Microsoft Outlook, Outlook 2007 offers three options for storing data: your Exchange Server mailbox, .pst files, and offline folder (.ost) files. Outlook 2007 can also use Cached Exchange Mode in conjunction with an .ost file to create a local copy of an Exchange Server mailbox. With Cached Exchange Mode, Outlook 2007 works from the cached local copy of the mailbox and automatically handles synchronization between the local profile and the server. Your mailbox is therefore always available, even when the server is not. When you connect to the network, Outlook 2007 automatically detects server connection status and synchronizes the Outlook 2007 folders.

See Chapter 41, "Configuring the Exchange Server Client," to learn how to configure an Exchange Server client, including enabling and disabling Cached Exchange Mode.

Regardless of its location, a data store holds your Outlook 2007 data, including your Contacts, Calendar, and other folders. You can have only one default store. This means that your e-mail, contacts, schedule, tasks, and other information are all stored in the same set of folders. Outlook 2007 directs all incoming e-mail to your default store. The exceptions to this are IMAP and Hypertext Transfer Protocol (HTTP) accounts, which store their e-mail folders and messages separately from your other data.

For detailed information about configuring and using IMAP accounts and how Outlook 2007 stores IMAP folders and messages, see "Using IMAP Accounts" in Chapter 7.

Although you can have only one default store, you can add other store files to a profile. You can use the other stores to organize or archive your data. For example, if you have a profile with an Exchange Server account and a Post Office Protocol 3 (POP3) account, the profile might be configured to deliver all mail to the Exchange Server mailbox. You might want to add another set of folders (another .pst file) that you can use to separate your Internet mail from your workgroup mail, or perhaps you want to use a different store to separate your personal messages from your work-related messages. Another use for a second store file is to share data with others without exposing your default store. Whatever the situation, you need to decide which type of store is most appropriate for your default store as well as for your additional stores.

Personal Folders and Offline Folders

A .pst file in Outlook 2007 is essentially the same as the default store type in earlier versions of Microsoft Outlook, although the native .pst format of Outlook 2007 is not compatible with Outlook 2002 or earlier. The native Outlook 2003/Outlook 2007 .pst format provides better support for multilingual Unicode data and eliminates the 2-GB file size limit imposed by the Outlook 2002 and earlier .pst format.

You can password-protect .pst files for greater security, although utilities available on the Web can bypass the password security. The .pst files offer encryption, providing an additional level of security. The .pst files do not have a built-in capability for synchronization with an Exchange Server mailbox, although you can work offline if a .pst file rather than the Exchange Server mailbox is configured as the default store location. If the Exchange Server mailbox is your default store (which is recommended), you must use an .ost file to work offline, whether in normal offline mode or in Cached Exchange Mode.

As mentioned earlier, the format for .pst files in Outlook 2007 is different from the format in Outlook 97, Outlook 98, Outlook 2000, and Outlook 2002, which means that those systems cannot share a .pst file created using Outlook 2007. This is a significant consideration if you need to share a local data file with other Microsoft Outlook users who have not yet upgraded to Outlook 2003 or Outlook 2007. However, Outlook 2007 can use .pst files created using earlier versions of Microsoft Outlook.

INSIDE OUT

Make your .pst file available when you're roaming

If you use a roaming Windows profile to provide a common desktop configuration regardless of the computer from which you log on, consider placing the .pst file (if you use one) on a network share that is available from all your logon locations. This eliminates the need to copy your .pst file across the network each time you log on, reducing network utilization and speeding logon time. Microsoft doesn't recommend placing .pst files on a network share because of performance issues, but we have found that this is a workable solution that offers enough advantages to overshadow any performance issues. Naturally, performance depends on the size of a user's mailbox and available network bandwidth. A great alternative is to enable and use Outlook Web Access (OWA) to access your mailbox.

You can choose the format of a .pst file only when you create the .pst file—you can't convert an existing .pst file to the new format. You can, however, simply export all of the items in an existing .pst file to a new .pst file that does use the new format. Start Outlook 2007, choose File, Import And Export, and then follow the wizard's prompts to export to a .pst file. The wizard creates an Outlook 2007 native format .pst file by default.

To decide which .pst file format you should use, consider whether you need to use the .pst file with an earlier version of Microsoft Outlook. If not, the Outlook 2007 native format is the best choice. If you need to export items from an Outlook 2007 .pst file to an earlier version, simply export the items to a .pst file that you created with an earlier version of Microsoft Outlook, or create the pre–Outlook 2003 .pst file in Outlook 2007. To do so, choose the Office Outlook 97-2002 Personal Folders File option when creating the .pst file.

Adding Other Data Stores

Outlook 2007 uses a particular store as your default store to contain your Outlook 2007 data and e-mail, but you can add other store files to help you organize, separate, or archive your data.

Adding another store is easy. Just follow these steps:

1. Right-click the Microsoft Office Outlook icon on the Start menu, choose Properties, and then click Data Files. (Select the profile first, if necessary.) Or, if Outlook 2007 is running, choose Tools, Account Settings, Data Files. The current storage files are listed on the Data Files tab.
2. Click Add, enter the file name, select the type of personal folders file to create, and then click OK.

3. Outlook 2007 next displays the Create Microsoft Personal Folders dialog box, shown in Figure 3-6. Configure settings as necessary based on the following list:

Name Specify the name by which you want the folders to be known in Outlook 2007. This is not the file name for the store file, but you can use the same name for both if you want.

Password Specify an optional password (and type it a second time to verify it) to protect your .pst file from access by others.

Save This Password In Your Password List Select this check box to have Outlook 2007 save the password for your .pst file file in your local password cache. This eliminates the need for you to enter the password each time you open the .pst file. Clear this check box if you want Outlook 2007 to prompt you each time (providing greater security).

Figure 3-6. Use the Create Microsoft Personal Folders dialog box to add a .pst file.

4. Click OK to close the Create Microsoft Personal Folders dialog box.

> **Note**
>
> It's possible for others to gain access to your .pst file and bypass the password, even if you use a compression option. For best security, keep your sensitive data on the computer running Exchange Server rather than in a .pst file. You can also employ NTFS file system permissions to secure the folder where your .pst file is located, granting applicable permissions only to those users who need access to that folder or your .pst file.

INSIDE OUT **Add an existing .pst file to a profile**

You can add an existing .pst file to a profile so that you can work with its contents in Outlook 2007, either permanently or temporarily. For example, you might want to open an archive .pst file to find an old message or two and then "disconnect" the .pst file when you have finished using it. Just start Outlook 2007, choose File, Open, Outlook Data File, and then choose the .pst file. When you have finished using the file, right-click its root in the folder list, and then choose Close to remove the .pst file from the folder list.

Removing Data Stores

Occasionally, you might want to remove a data store from a profile–for example, perhaps you've been using a .pst file as your primary store and are now moving to Exchange Server with an .ost file for offline use.

To remove a data store from a profile, you use steps similar to those you followed to add a store:

1. On the Start menu, right-click the Microsoft Office Outlook icon, choose Properties, and then click Data Files. (Select the profile first, if necessary.) Or, if Outlook 2007 is running, choose Tools Account Settings, Data Files. The current storage files are listed in the Data Files dialog box.
2. Select the data file to remove from the profile, click Remove, and then click Yes to verify the action.
3. Click Close to close the Account Settings dialog box.

When you remove a data file from a profile, Outlook 2007 does not delete the file itself. This means that you can later add the file back to a profile if you need to access its contents. If you don't need the data stored in the file or if you've already copied the data to a different store, you can delete the file. Open the folder where the file is located, and then delete it as you would any other file.

Configuring Offline Storage

Configuring an offline store allows you to continue working with data stored in your Exchange Server mailbox when the server is not available (if your computer is disconnected from the network, for example). As soon as the server becomes available again, Outlook 2007 synchronizes the data either automatically or manually–according to the way in which you have configured Outlook 2007.

For a detailed explanation of folder synchronization, see "Controlling Synchronization and Send/Receive Times" in Chapter 8.

Like earlier versions of Microsoft Outlook, Outlook 2007 supports the use of an .ost file to serve as an offline cache for Exchange Server. This method is compatible with all versions of Exchange Server, including Exchange Server 2000, Exchange Server 2003, and Exchange Server 2007.

Using an .ost File

You can use an .ost file to provide offline capability for your Exchange Server mailbox. You do not need to use a .pst file in conjunction with the .ost file–the .ost file can be your only local store file, if you want. However, you can use other .pst files in addition to your .ost file.

This section assumes that you are working with an Exchange Server account that has not been configured to use Cached Exchange Mode. When you add an Exchange Server account in Outlook 2007, the Add New E-Mail Account Wizard enables Cached Exchange Mode by default. This section helps you create and enable an offline store for a profile that has not had Cached Exchange Mode enabled previously.

> **Note**
>
> The .ost file does not appear as a separate set of folders in Outlook 2007. In effect, the .ost file is hidden and Outlook 2007 uses it transparently when your computer is offline. For more information, see Chapter 43, "Working Offline and Remotely."

Follow these steps to configure offline storage with an .ost file:

1. On the Start menu, right-click the Microsoft Office Outlook icon, choose Properties, and then click E-Mail Accounts. Or, if Outlook 2007 is running, choose Tools, Account Settings.
2. On the E-Mail tab, select the profile, and then click Change.
3. Click More Settings to display the Microsoft Exchange Server dialog box. Click the Advanced tab, and then click Offline Folder File Settings to open the dialog box shown in Figure 3-7.

Figure 3-7. Specify the file name and other settings for the .ost file.

4. Specify a path and name for the .ost file in the File box, and then click OK.

5. Click OK to close the Offline Folder File Settings dialog box.
6. Click Next, and then click Finish.

Configuring Cached Exchange Mode

When you add an Exchange Server account to a profile in Outlook 2007, Outlook enables Cached Exchange Mode by default and creates the .ost file that Cached Exchange Mode will use to store the local copy of the mailbox. If you originally added the Exchange Server account without Cached Exchange Mode, you can still enable it by following these steps:

1. Exit Outlook 2007, and then double-click the Mail icon in Control Panel.
2. Click E-Mail Accounts in the Mail Setup dialog box.
3. Select the Exchange Server account, and then click Change.
4. Select Use Cached Exchange Mode, click Next, and then click Finish.

Outlook 2007 creates the .ost file the next time you start Outlook 2007 and begins the synchronization process if the server is available.

Changing Your Data Storage Location

On occasion, you might need to move a data file from one location to another. For example, perhaps you've been using a local .pst file file and now want to place that file on a network share for use with a roaming profile so that you can access the file from any computer on the network.

Moving a .pst file file is a manual process. You must exit Outlook 2007, move the file, and then reconfigure the profile accordingly.

Follow these steps to move a .pst file:

1. Exit Outlook 2007, right-click the Microsoft Office Outlook icon on the Start menu, and then choose Properties.
2. Select a profile if necessary, and then click Data Files to display the Data Files tab in the Account Settings dialog box, shown in Figure 3-8.

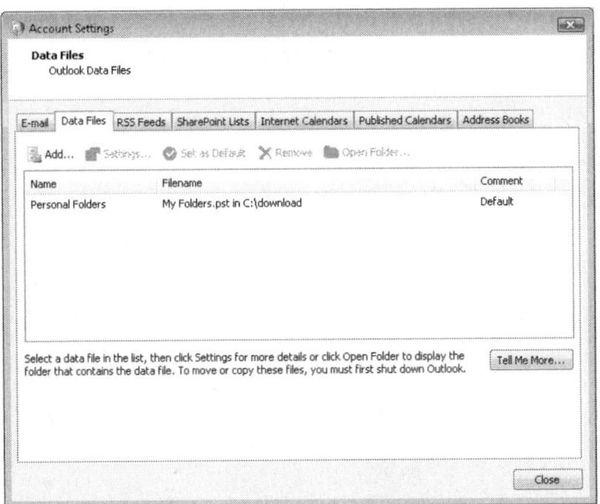

Figure 3-8. Use the Data Files tab to locate the existing .pst file.

3. Select the .pst file you want to move, and then click Open Folder. Outlook 2007 opens the folder where the .pst file is located and selects the file's icon.
4. Drag the file or use the Clipboard to move the file to the desired location, and then close the folder.
5. Back on the Data Files tab, click Settings. Outlook 2007 displays an error message indicating that it can't find the file. Click OK.
6. Browse to the new location of the .pst file, select it, click Open, and then click OK.
7. Click Close to close the Outlook Data Files dialog box, and then click Close again to close the Mail Setup dialog box.

Setting Delivery Options

Outlook 2007 uses one data store location as the default location for delivering messages and storing your other Outlook 2007 items. You can change the store location if needed. You also can specify the order in which Outlook 2007 processes e-mail accounts, which determines the server that Outlook 2007 uses (where multiple servers are available) to process outgoing messages. The order also determines the order in which Outlook 2007 checks the servers for new messages.

For example, assume that you have an Exchange Server account and a POP3 account for your personal Internet mail. If the Exchange Server account is listed first, Outlook 2007 sends messages destined for Internet addresses through Exchange Server. In many cases, however, this might not be what you want. For example, you might want all personal mail to go through your POP3 account and work-related mail to go through your Exchange Server account.

You have two ways to change the e-mail service that Outlook 2007 uses to send a message: you can configure the service order, or you can specify the account to use when you create the message.

Follow these steps to configure the service order for your e-mail:

1. Right-click the Microsoft Office Outlook icon on the Start menu and choose Properties, or in Outlook 2007, choose Tools, Account Settings to display the E-Mail Accounts tab in the Account Settings dialog box, shown in Figure 3-9.

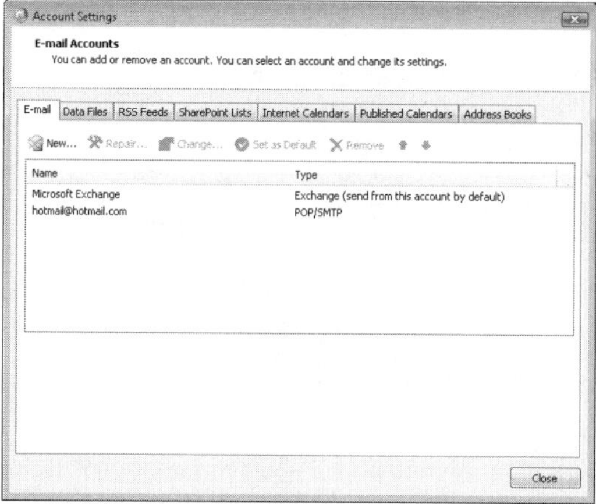

Figure 3-9. Use the E-Mail Accounts tab in the Account Settings dialog box to configure account order.

2. Use the Move Up and Move Down buttons to change the order of the accounts in the list.
3. Click Close.

When you compose a message, you can override the default e-mail service that Outlook 2007 uses to send messages simply by selecting the account before sending the message.

To select the account, follow these steps:

1. Click the Account button in the message window.
2. Select the account you want to use to send the message.
3. Compose the message, make any other changes to options as needed, and then click Send.

CHAPTER 4

Working in and Configuring Outlook

If you've used earlier versions of Microsoft® Outlook®, you'll find that the interface in Microsoft Office Outlook 2007 hasn't changed that much, and you should have no problem getting started. There are, however, some new features and interface enhancements that you will probably like quite a bit. If you're new to Office Outlook 2007 entirely, you need to become familiar with its interface, which is the main focus of this chapter.

Outlook 2007 presents your data using different views, and this chapter shows you how to customize the way those views look. This chapter also examines other standard elements of the interface, including toolbars, the Navigation Pane, the Folder List, and the Reading Pane. You'll also learn how to use multiple Outlook 2007 windows and views and navigate your way through the Outlook 2007 interface.

This chapter looks at the various ways you can configure Outlook 2007, explaining settings that control a broad range of options, from e-mail and spelling to security. In addition, you'll learn about settings in your operating system that affect how Outlook 2007 functions. Where appropriate, the text refers you to other chapters where configuration information is discussed in detail in the context of a particular feature or function.

Web access has been expanded and improved in Outlook 2007, and this chapter examines that Web integration. You'll learn about browsing the Web with Outlook 2007 and about accessing your Microsoft Exchange Server e-mail through a Web browser. Later in the chapter, you'll find a discussion of add-ins, which can enhance Outlook 2007 functionality.

Understanding the Outlook Folders

Outlook 2007 uses a standard set of folders to organize your data. Once you're comfortable working with these standard folders, you'll be able to change their location, customize their appearance, or even create additional folders, as you'll learn throughout this book.

The following list describes the default Outlook 2007 folders:

- **Calendar** This folder contains your schedule, including appointments, meetings, and events.
- **Contacts** This folder stores information about people, such as name, address, phone number, and a wealth of other data.
- **Deleted Items** This folder stores deleted Outlook 2007 items and can contain items of various types (contacts, messages, and tasks, for example). You can recover items from the Deleted Items folder, giving you a way to "undelete" an item if you've made a mistake or changed your mind. If you delete an item from this folder, however, the item is deleted permanently.
- **Drafts** Use this folder to store unfinished drafts of messages and other items. For example, you can use the Drafts folder to store a lengthy e-mail message that you haven't had a chance to finish yet. Or you might start a message, have second thoughts about sending it, and place it in the Drafts folder until you decide whether to send it.
- **Inbox** Outlook 2007 delivers your e-mail to this folder. Keep in mind that, depending on the types of e-mail accounts in your profile, you might have more than one Inbox in locations other than your default information store. For example, if you have an Internet Message Access Protocol (IMAP) account and an Exchange Server account, you'll have an Inbox folder for each.
- **Journal** The Journal folder stores your journal items, allowing you to keep track of phone calls, time spent on a project, important e-mail messages, and other events and tasks.
- **Junk E-Mail** The Junk E-Mail folder contains items that have been placed there by the Outlook Junk E-Mail Filter. This filter is designed to divert the most obvious spam, and you can customize it to suit your needs.
- **Notes** The Notes folder stores and organizes notes. You can move or copy notes to other folders in Outlook 2007 as well as to folders on disk. You can also create shortcuts to notes.
- **Outbox** The Outbox stores outgoing messages until they are delivered to their destination servers. You can configure Outlook 2007 to deliver messages immediately after you send them or have the messages wait in your Outbox until you process them (by synchronizing with the computer running Exchange Server or by performing a send/receive operation through your Post Office Protocol 3 [POP3] account, for example).
- **RSS Feeds and Subscription** These folders store RSS content. Really Simple Syndication (RSS) is a way for content publishers to make news, blogs, and other content available to subscribers.
- **Sent Items** The Sent Items folder stores copies of the messages you have sent. You can configure Outlook 2007 to automatically store a copy of each sent item in this folder.
- **Tasks** The Tasks folder lists tasks that have been assigned to you or that you have assigned to either yourself or others.

Working with the Standard Outlook Views

Before you can become proficient at using Outlook 2007, you need to be familiar with its standard views and other elements of its interface. This section introduces you to the Outlook 2007 standard views and includes information about how to work with these views and customize them to meet your needs.

Outlook Today

Outlook 2007 provides default views of its standard folders as well as one additional view that is a summary of your schedule, tasks, and e-mail for the current day—Outlook Today. To switch to Outlook Today view if you are working in another folder, click the root folder of your mail store in the Navigation Pane. For example, click Personal Folders if your Outlook 2007 data is stored in a personal folders (.pst) file, or click Mailbox if your data is stored in an Exchange Server mailbox. Figure 4-1 shows a typical Outlook Today view. In the Calendar area on the left, Outlook 2007 summarizes your schedule for the current day, showing each appointment with time and title. You can easily view the details of a particular appointment by clicking the appointment time or title to open it.

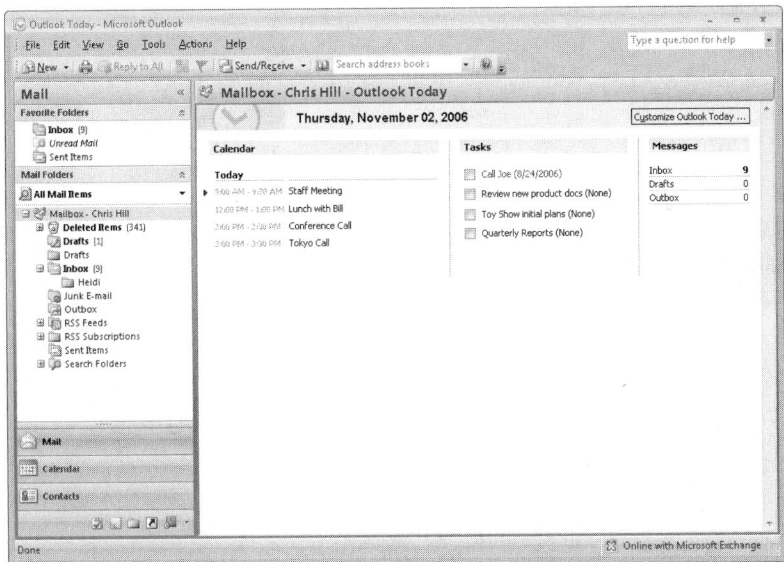

Figure 4-1. Outlook Today lets you see your day at a glance.

In the Tasks area, Outlook Today lists your tasks for the current day, including overlapping tasks with a duration of more than one day. The list includes a title and completion date for each task, along with a check box. You can mark the task as completed by selecting the check box; doing so crosses out the task in the list. If the check box is cleared, the task is incomplete.

In the Messages area, Outlook Today lists the number of messages in your Inbox, Drafts, and Outbox folders. If the number appears in bold, the associated folder contains unread messages.

For details on customizing the Outlook Today view to display additional information (including the use of HTML code in such customization), see Chapter 26, "Customizing the Outlook Interface."

Inbox

The Inbox displays your default message store, as shown in Figure 4-2. For example, if you use an Exchange Server account and store your data on the computer running Exchange Server, the Inbox view shows the Inbox folder on that computer. If you've configured Outlook 2007 to deliver messages to a local store (such as a .pst file), the Inbox view shows the contents of the Inbox folder in that store.

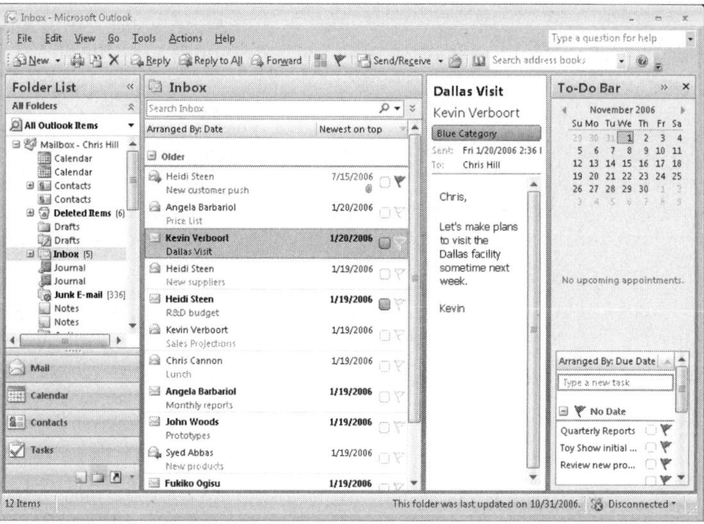

Figure 4-2. The Inbox view shows the contents of the Inbox folder of your default store.

As you can see in Figure 4-2, the Inbox view shows the message header for each message, including such information as sender, subject, and date and time received in various columns. These columns are not always visible, however, because the default configuration includes the Reading Pane on the right in the Outlook 2007 window, which hides many of the columns on a typical display. If you turn off the Reading Pane or move it to the bottom of the window, you can view the message header columns.

You can easily sort messages by clicking on the column header for the column you want to use as the sort criterion. For example, to quickly locate messages from a specific sender, you can click the From column header to sort the list alphabetically by sender. To switch between ascending and descending sort, simply click the column header again. An up arrow next to the column name indicates an ascending sort (such as A to Z), and a down arrow indicates a descending sort (such as Z to A).

To learn how to add and remove columns and change their appearance and order, see "Customizing the Inbox View" later in this chapter.

By default, Outlook 2007 shows the following columns in the Inbox view when the Reading Pane is either off, displayed at the bottom of the window, or taking a minimal amount of space on the right in the window:

- **Importance** This column indicates the level of importance, or priority, that the sender has assigned to a message–Low, Normal, or High. A high-priority message is accompanied by an exclamation point, whereas a down arrow marks a low-priority message. No symbol is displayed for a message of normal importance.

> **Note**
>
> After you've received a message, you can change its priority status by right-clicking the message header, choosing Message Options, and then specifying a new importance level.

- **Icon** The Icon column indicates the type of message and its status. For example, unopened messages are accompanied by a closed envelope icon, and opened messages are accompanied by an open envelope icon.
- **Attachment** The Attachment column displays a paper clip icon if the message includes one or more attachments. Right-click a message and choose View Attachments to view the attachments, or simply double-click an attachment in the Reading Pane.

> **CAUTION!**
>
> Although Outlook 2007 provides protection against viruses and worms by preventing you from opening certain types of attachments, this is no guarantee against infection. Your network administrator might have modified the blocked attachments lists, or you might have modified your blocked attachments list locally, to allow a specific attachment type susceptible to infection to come through. So you should still exercise caution when viewing attachments, particularly from unknown sources. It's a good practice to save attachments to disk and run a virus scan on them before opening them.

- **From** This column shows the name or address of the sender.
- **Subject** This column shows the subject, if any, assigned by the sender to the message.

- **Received** This column indicates the date and time that Outlook 2007 received the message.
- **Size** This column indicates the overall size of the message, including attachments.
- **Categories** This column shows the color indicators for color categories assigned to the message..
- **Flag Status** In this column, you can flag messages for follow-up action. For example, you can flag a message that requires you to place a call, to forward the message, or to respond at a particular time. You specify the action, date, and time for follow-up.

For detailed information about flagging messages for follow-up and other ways to manage and process messages, see "Flagging and Monitoring Messages and Contacts" in Chapter 10.

INSIDE OUT **Time is relative**

The date and time displayed in the Inbox's Received column can be a little deceiving. This data reflects the time the message was placed in your message store. If you're working online with an Exchange Server account, for example, Outlook 2007 shows the time the message was placed in the Inbox folder for your mailbox on the computer running Exchange Server. If the time on your computer isn't coordinated with the time on the server, the time you actually receive the message could be different from the time reflected in the message header. For sent messages (in the Sent Items folder), the time indicated is the time the message was placed in your Outbox. If you're working offline, that time could differ from the time the message is actually sent.

Previewing Messages

Another part of the Inbox view is the Reading Pane, which appears on the right in the Inbox view. You can use the Reading Pane to preview messages without opening them in a separate window. The scroll bar on the right of the Reading Pane lets you scroll through the message. The top of the Reading Pane presents information about the message, such as sender, recipient, subject, and attachments.

You can double-click most of the items in the Reading Pane header to see detailed information about the items. For example, you can double-click the name of the sender to display information about the sender, as shown in Figure 4-3. Use this method to quickly copy contact information about the sender from the message to your Personal Address Book. You can also double-click attachments to open them. Right-clicking an item opens its shortcut menu, on which you can choose a variety of actions to perform on the item—for instance, you can right-click an attachment and choose Save As to save the attachment to disk. Experiment by right-clicking items in the Reading Pane to see which actions you can take for specific items.

Note

The information that Outlook 2007 displays when you double-click the name of the sender of an e-mail message in the Reading Pane depends on whether the sender is in your Contacts folder, in the Global Address List (GAL; Exchange Server accounts), or not in either.

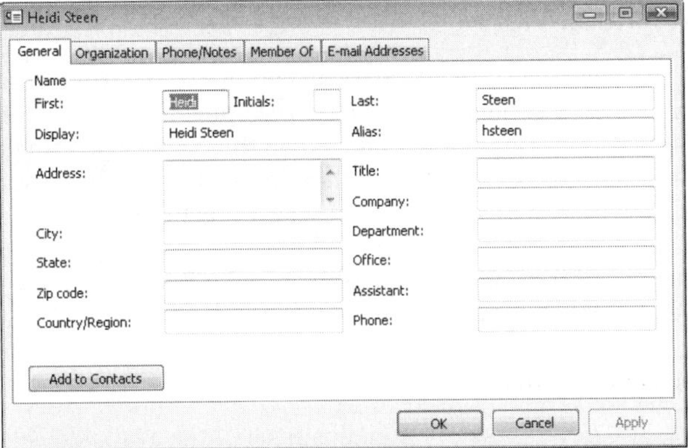

Figure 4-3. After you double-click a sender's address in the Reading Pane, Outlook displays information about the sender.

Note

If a message has been flagged for follow-up, information about the follow-up (the specific action, the date due, and so on) also appears in the Reading Pane header.

Note

To turn the Reading Pane on or off, choose View, Reading Pane, and then choose Right, Bottom, or Off. To change the location of the Reading Pane, choose View, Reading Pane, and then choose Right or Bottom.

For detailed information about using and customizing the Reading Pane in various folders, see "Using the Reading Pane" later in this chapter.

The AutoPreview feature also allows you to preview your messages. With message folders such as the Inbox, AutoPreview displays the first few lines of a message below its message header in the main folder window. This leaves you free to preview the first few lines of a message without opening the message or even selecting it. You can use AutoPreview in conjunction with or instead of the Reading Pane.

For additional information about configuring and using AutoPreview, see "Using AutoPreview" later in this chapter.

Customizing the Inbox View

Outlook 2007 offers a wealth of settings that you can use to control messaging. In addition, you also have quite a bit of control over the appearance of the Inbox and other message folders. For example, you can change the column headings included in the Inbox or add and remove columns. The following sections explore specific ways to customize the Inbox (which apply to other message folders as well).

For detailed information about configuring messaging and other options, see "Configuring Outlook Options" later in this chapter.

Adding and Removing Columns

By default, Outlook 2007 displays only a small subset of the available fields for messages. You can add columns for other fields, such as CC or Sensitivity, to show additional information. However, the Inbox behaves differently depending on the location of the Reading Pane. In most cases, when the Reading Pane is positioned on the right side of the window, the Inbox includes only four columns. The first column shows the sender and message subject. The other three columns list the message received date, color category, and flag status.

Outlook 2007 also provides two column headers above these columns that you can use to change views or change sort order. For example, the default view is Arranged By: Date. You can click this header to choose a different property by which to group the view.

The other column header is either Newest On Top or Oldest On Top, depending on whether the folder is sorted in ascending or descending order. You can click this column to switch between the two.

The number of columns in the message pane depends on the amount of space available in the window. The more space available, the more columns Outlook 2007 displays. For example, continue to drag the left edge of the Reading Pane to the right, and Outlook 2007 eventually shows additional columns. You have to experiment with the size of the Reading Pane to find a layout that suits you, because the amount of available space depends on your system's display resolution. Or simply position the Reading Pane at the bottom of the window to maximize the amount of space available for message pane columns.

To add and remove columns, follow these steps:

1. Open the folder you want to modify, right-click the column header bar, and choose Field Chooser to display the Field Chooser dialog box, shown in Figure 4-4.

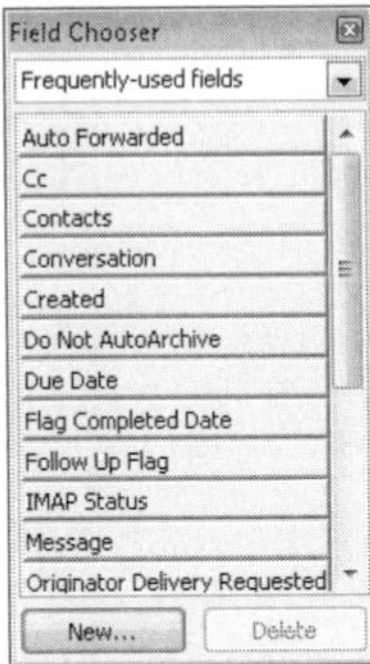

Figure 4-4. Add or remove columns by using the Field Chooser dialog box.

2. Locate the name of the field you want to add, and then drag the field from the Field Chooser dialog box to the desired location on the column header bar. Outlook 2007 displays a red arrow at the top of the column header bar to indicate where the column will be inserted.
3. Add other fields as necessary.
4. To remove a field, drag the field from the column header bar.
5. Close the Field Chooser dialog box.

You can choose other types of fields by selecting a type from the drop-down list at the top of the Field Chooser dialog box. You can also use this dialog box to create custom fields.

Outlook 2007 also provides another method for adding and removing columns in message folders:

1. Choose View, Current View, Customize Current View, and then click Fields to display the Show Fields dialog box, as shown in Figure 4-5.

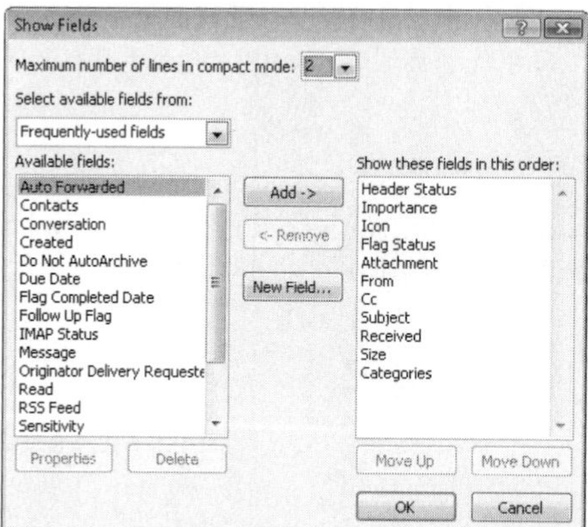

Figure 4-5. You can also use the Show Fields dialog box to add or remove columns.

2. To add a column, select the field in the Available Fields list, and then click Add.
3. To remove a column from the folder view, select the field in the Show These Fields In This Order list, and then click Remove.
4. Click OK to have your changes take effect.
5. Click OK to close the Custom View dialog box.

Changing Column Order

In a message folder, Outlook 2007 displays columns in a specific order by default, but you can easily change the order. The simplest way is to drag a column header to the desired location. You also can right-click the column header bar, choose Customize Current View, click Fields to display the Show Fields dialog box (shown earlier in Figure 4-5), and then use the Move Up and Move Down buttons to change the column order.

Changing Column Names

Outlook 2007 uses a default set of names for the columns it displays in message folders. However, you can change those column names—for example, you might want to rename the From column to Sender.

To change a column name, follow these steps:

1. Right-click the column header bar, and then choose Format Columns to display the Format Columns dialog box, shown in Figure 4-6. If the Format Columns command is not available because of the Reading Pane's location and width, choose View, Arrange By, Custom, and then click Format Columns.

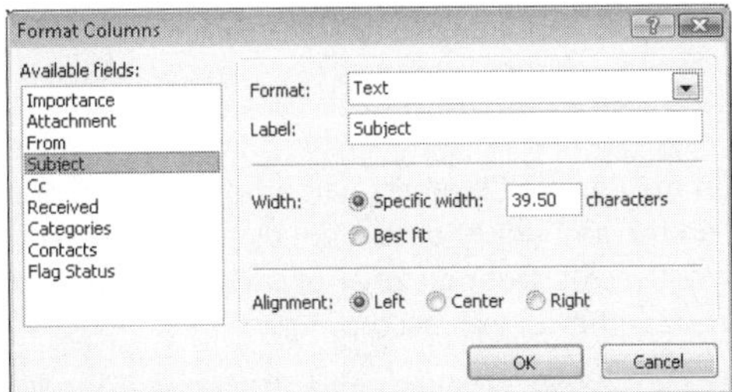

Figure 4-6. You can change several column characteristics, including column header name.

2. In the Available Fields list, select the field for which you want to change the column header.
3. In the Label box, type the label you want displayed in the column header for the selected field.
4. Repeat steps 2 and 3 for the other fields you want to change.
5. Click OK to apply the changes.
6. Click OK to close the Custom View dialog box.

> **Note**
>
> Three columns will not allow you to change the label: Importance, Flag Status, and Attachment. However, you can switch between using a symbol or text in the Importance and Flag Status columns. You can change the Attachment column to display either a paper clip icon or the text True/False, On/Off, or Yes/No, depending on whether the message has an attachment.

Changing Column Width

If a column isn't wide enough to show all the information for the field or if you need to make room for more columns, you might want to change the column width. The easiest way to change the width of a column is to drag the edge of the column header in the column header bar to resize it. Alternatively, you can right-click the column header bar, choose Format Columns, and specify a column width in the Format Columns dialog box (shown earlier in Figure 4-6).

INSIDE OUT **Automatically size columns**

Use the Best Fit option in the Format Columns dialog box to automatically size the selected column based on the amount of data it needs to display. You can also right-click a column and choose Best Fit. Outlook 2007 examines the data for the field in the existing messages and resizes the column accordingly.

Changing Column Alignment

By default, all the columns are left-aligned in message folders, including the Inbox. You can, however, configure the alignment to display the columns as left-justified, right-justified, or centered. For example, you might want to change the format for the Size column to show only numbers and then display the column right-justified. Simply right-click the column header bar and choose Format Columns, or choose View, Arrange By, Custom and then click Format Columns. In the Format Columns dialog box (shown earlier in Figure 4-6), select the column to change, and then under the Alignment option, select Left, Center, or Right, depending on the type of justification you want.

Changing Column Data Format

Each default column in a message folder displays its data using a particular format. For example, the From column shows only the sender, not the recipient. Although in most cases, the specified recipient is you, that isn't the case when the message you've received is a carbon copy. You might then want to change the data format of the From column to also display the person specified in the To field of the message. Other columns also offer different formats. For example, you can change the data format used by time and date fields such as Received or Sent to show only the date rather than date and time.

To change the data format used for a particular column, right-click the column header bar and choose Format Columns, or choose View, Arrange By, Custom and then click Format Columns. In the Format Columns dialog box (shown earlier in Figure 4-6), select the column for which you want to change the format, and then select the format in the Format drop-down list. The available formats vary according to the field selected.

Grouping Messages

Outlook 2007 offers many ways to organize and display your data. A good example of this flexibility is the option of grouping messages based on a hierarchy of criteria. For example, you might want to group messages in your Inbox first by subject, then by sender, and then by date received, as shown in Figure 4-7.

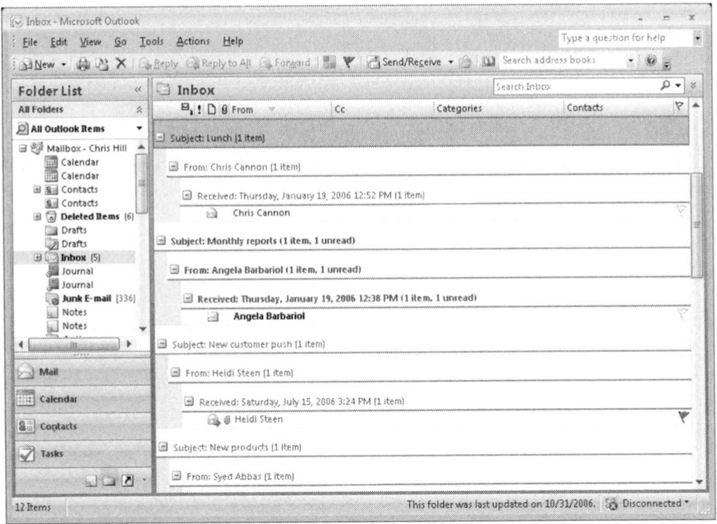

Figure 4-7. These messages are organized by three fields.

To organize your messages based on a particular column, you can simply right-click the column and choose Group By This Field. If the folder is showing the Arranged By column, click this column, and then choose the field by which you want to group the messages.

For more complex groupings, follow these steps:

1. Right-click the column header bar, and then choose Group By Box to display the Group By box above the column header bar.
2. To set up a grouping, drag a column header from the column header bar to the Group By box.
3. To set up an additional level of grouping, drag another column header to the Group By box. Repeat this process until you have as many levels of grouping as you need.

> **Note**
>
> If you are unable to drag an additional column to the Group By box, choose Arrange By on the View menu, and then clear the Show In Groups check box.

4. To remove a grouping, drag the column header from the Group By box to the desired location on the column header bar.

To hide or show the Group By box, right-click the column header bar, and then choose Group By Box again. To expand or collapse your view of a group of messages, click the plus sign (+) or minus sign (–) next to the group or message.

For a detailed explanation of grouping and sorting, along with several other topics that will help you organize your data, see "Grouping Messages by Customizing the Folder View" in Chapter 10.

Calendar

In the Calendar folder, you can look at your schedule in several different ways. By default, Calendar view shows the current day's schedule as well as the Date Navigator (a monthly calendar) in the upper-left corner of the Navigation Pane. It also shows the To-Do Bar, which displays tasks that overlap or fall on the current day, as shown in Figure 4-8. With the To-Do Bar turned on, the Date Navigator moves to the upper-right corner of the To-Do Bar. You can configure the To-Do Bar to show other tasks as well. In addition, the Daily Task List can appear at the bottom of the window in Day and Week views.

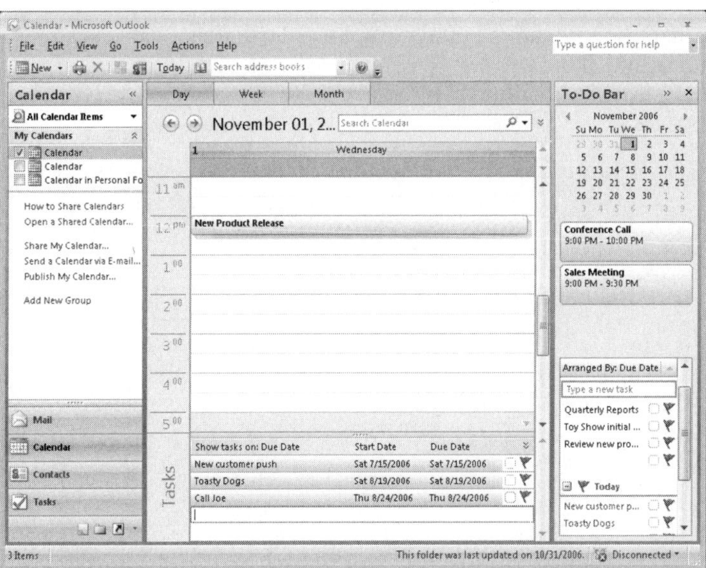

Figure 4-8. The default Calendar view shows your schedule and the Date Navigator, but you can also view tasks, as shown here.

Your schedule shows the subject for each scheduled item—a brief description of a meeting or an appointment, for example—next to its time slot, blocking out the time assigned to the item. Items that overlap in the schedule are displayed side by side, as shown in Figure 4-9.

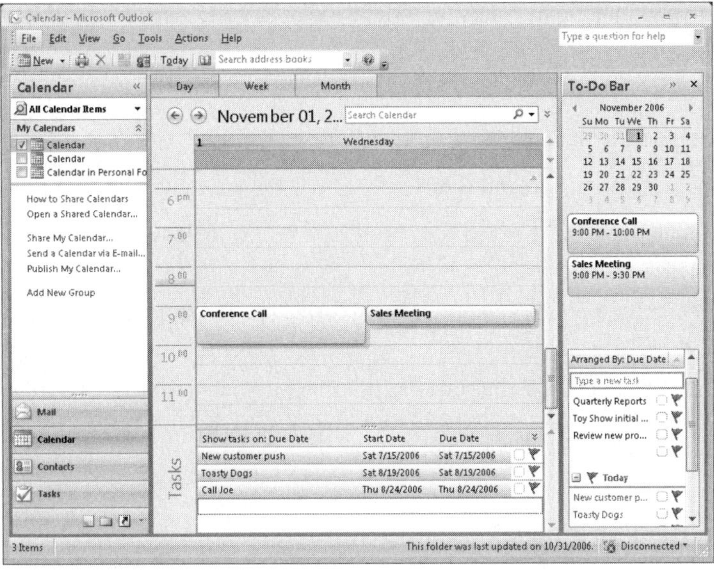

Figure 4-9. Overlapping items appear side by side in your schedule.

Working with the Schedule

Calendar view by default shows only the subject for each item scheduled in the period displayed. You can open the item to modify it or view details about it by double-clicking the item, which opens its form, as shown in Figure 4-10.

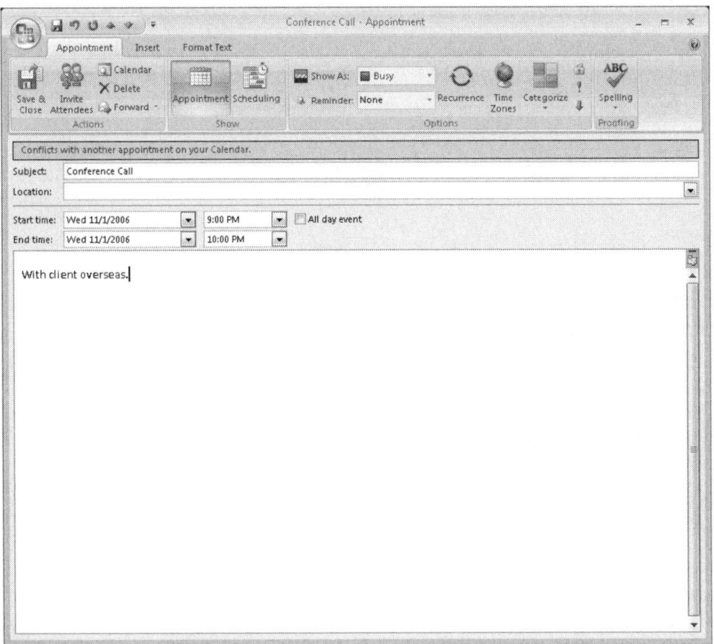

Figure 4-10. A sample appointment form showing details for a selected appointment.

You can add an item to your schedule using one of these methods:

- Double-click the time slot of the start time you want to assign to the item.
- Right-click a time slot, and then choose the type of item to create (an appointment, a meeting, or an event).
- Select a time slot, and then choose File, New to select the item type.
- Click the arrow next to New on the Standard toolbar, and then select the item type.

The first method opens an appointment form. The form opened by the other three methods depends on the type of item you select.

It is also easy to change the start or end time for an item in the schedule. To move an item to a different time without changing its duration, simply drag the item to the new time slot. To change the start or end time only, position the mouse pointer on the top or bottom edge of the item, and then drag it to the desired time.

Using the Calendar's Reading Pane

Like the Inbox and other message views, Calendar view has a Reading Pane that lets you preview appointments and other items in your schedule without opening them. To turn the Reading Pane on or off, choose View, Reading Pane, and then choose either Right, Bottom, or Off. Click the item to display it in the Reading Pane, as shown in Figure 4-11. To display more or less information in the pane, drag the edge of the Reading Pane to resize it. You can also make other changes to the displayed item—such as subject and times—through the Reading Pane.

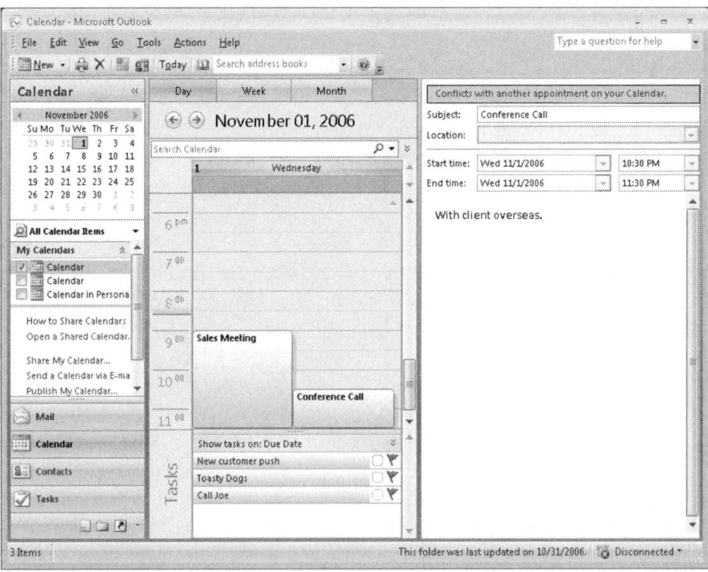

Figure 4-11. Use the Reading Pane in the Calendar view to preview scheduled items.

Using the Task List

The Task List displays a list of your tasks in the To-Do Bar. You can turn the Task List on or off in the To-Do Bar. If the To-Do Bar is not shown, click View, To-Do Bar, and then click Normal or Minimized. By default, the Task List shows the tasks for the current day. As you can in the Inbox and other views, you can change the options and the items displayed in the To-Do Bar: right-click the To-Do Bar column header bar, and then choose the items you want to include, or choose Options to customize how these items are displayed.

For more information about the To-Do Bar and the features Outlook 2007 provides for working with and assigning tasks, see Chapter 22, "Managing Your Tasks."

Using the Date Navigator

The monthly calendars in the upper-right area of the To-Do Bar are collectively called the Date Navigator. When the To-Do Bar is hidden, the Date Navigator appears at the top of the Navigation Pane.

The Date Navigator is useful not only as a calendar but also as a way to provide a fast glance at which days include appointments. Days with a scheduled item appear in bold, and those without scheduled items appear in a normal font. You can view a particular day by clicking it. Click the arrow at the left or right of the Date Navigator to change which months are displayed. You can also click and hold on the column header bar above either month to choose from a shortcut menu which month to view.

INSIDE OUT **Specify the Date Navigator's font**

You can configure the Date Navigator to display all dates in normal text rather than using bold for days that contain items. Choose View, Current View, Customize Current View, and then click Other Settings. Clear the Bolded Dates In Date Navigator Represent Days Containing Items check box, and then click OK. Click OK to close the dialog box.

You can change the number of months displayed by the Date Navigator by resizing the Reading Pane, resizing the Calendar pane, changing the width of the Navigation Pane or the To-Do Bar, or changing the font used by the Date Navigator. Assign a smaller font to show more months. (For details on how to change the Date Navigator's font, see "Setting Advanced Options" later in this chapter.)

Customizing the Calendar View

Although the default Calendar view shows only the subject for a scheduled item, you can configure the view to show additional detail—or you can change the view completely. For example, you can switch from a daily view to one that shows the work week, the calendar week, or the month. You can see examples of Work Week view in Figure 4-12, Week view in Figure 4-13, and Month view in Figure 4-14. To select a particular view, click the Day, Week, or Month button above the Calendar pane. Or choose View, and then choose Day, Work Week, Week, or Month, according to the type of view you want.

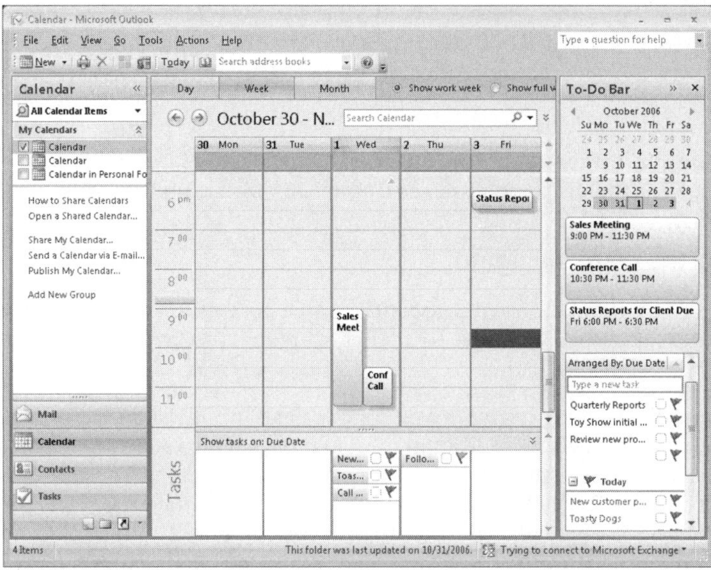

Figure 4-12. Use Work Week view to organize your work schedule.

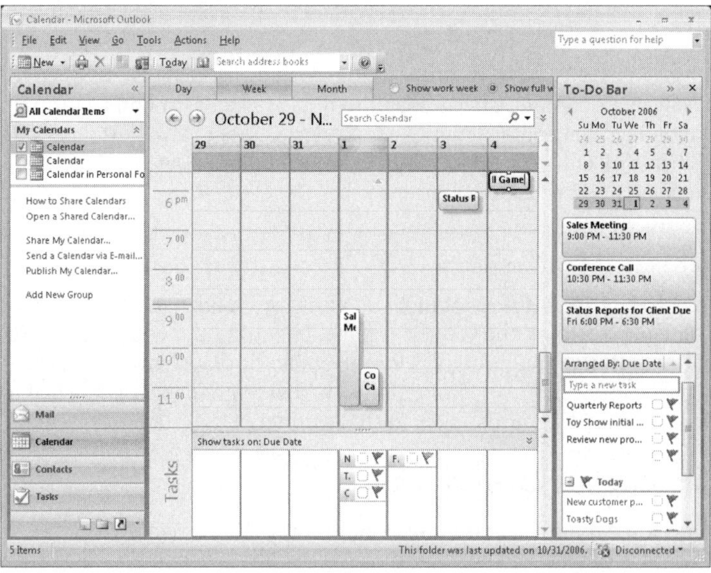

Figure 4-13. Week view can help you plan your entire week, both personal and work time.

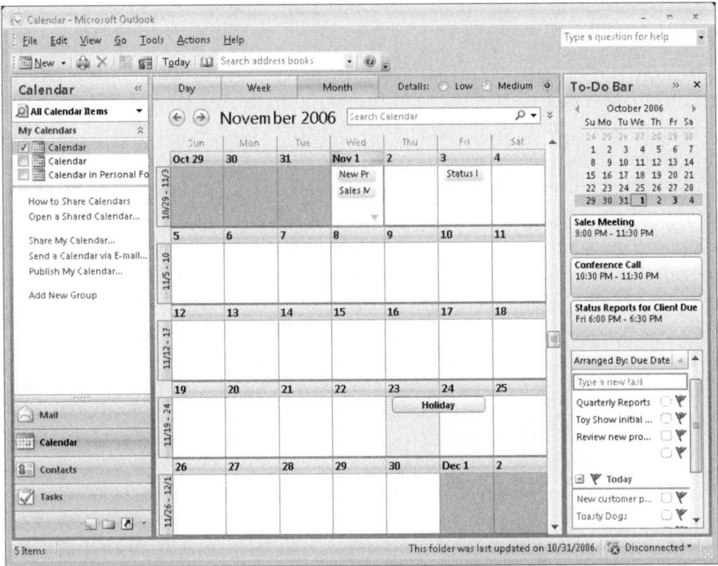

Figure 4-14. Use Month view to plan a broader range of time.

You have additional options for viewing your schedule in the Calendar folder. Choose View, Current View, and then choose one of the following to change the view:

- **Day/Week/Month** Shows the item title only in each view (Day, Work Week, Week, or Month).
- **Day/Week/Month With AutoPreview** Includes AutoPreview in Day and Work Week views. With AutoPreview, Outlook 2007 displays as much of the data for the item as possible in the current view.
- **All Appointments** Shows all appointments.
- **Active Appointments** Shows only active appointments.
- **Events** Shows only events.
- **Annual Events** Shows only annual events.
- **Recurring Appointments** Displays recurring appointments.
- **By Category** Displays scheduled items grouped according to their assigned categories.
- **Outlook Data Files** Displays items organized by the Outlook 2007 data file in which they are stored.

For additional information about customizing the way Outlook 2007 displays information in the various calendar views, see Chapter 20, "Scheduling Appointments."

Contacts

The Contacts folder stores all your contact information. By default, the Contacts folder displays the Business Cards view, shown in Figure 4-15, which shows the name for each contact along with other selected fields (address and phone number, for example). You can view the details for a contact by double-clicking the contact's business card, which opens the contact form, shown in Figure 4-16. Using this form, you can view or make changes to the contact's data or perform other tasks, such as calling the contact, generating a meeting request, or viewing a map of the contact's address. If you have a large number of contact entries stored in the Contacts folder, you can click the buttons at the right edge of the view to select which portion of the contacts list to show.

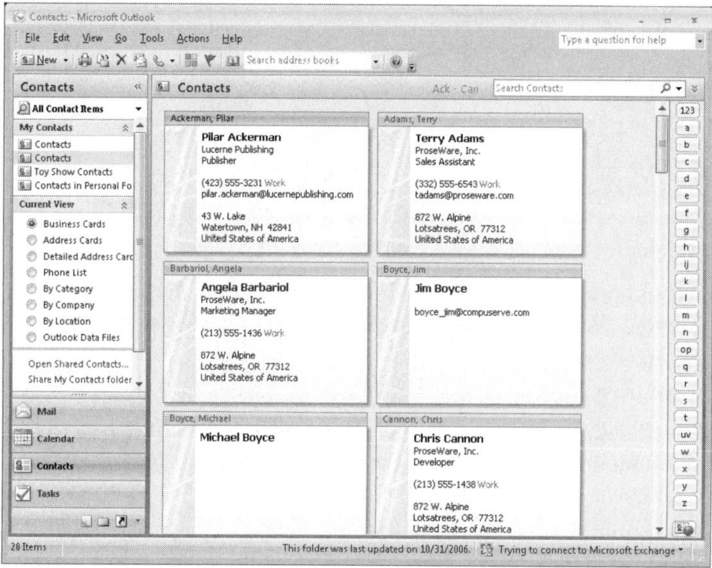

Figure 4-15. By default, the Contacts folder displays Business Cards view.

For a detailed discussion of working with contacts, including the actions you can take with the contact form, see Chapter 18, "Creating and Managing Your Contacts."

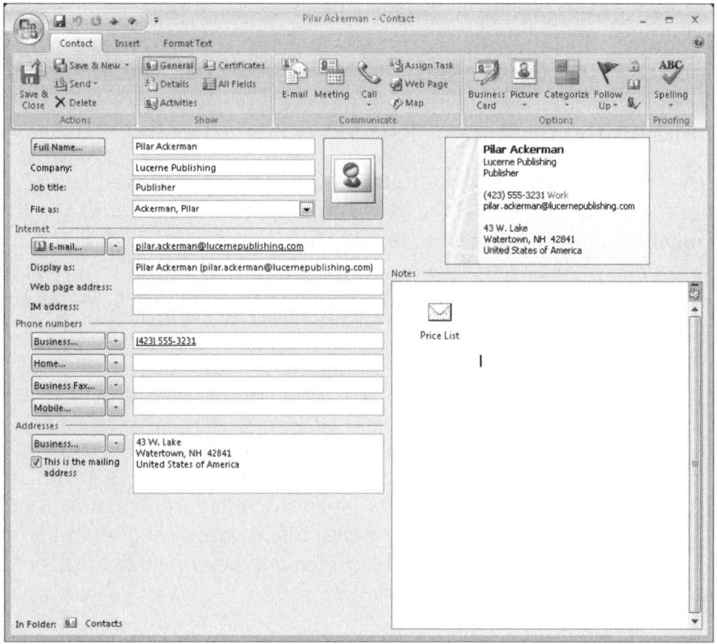

Figure 4-16. When you double-click a contact entry, you can view the contact form for that person.

Outlook 2007 offers several other ways to view the contents of your Contacts folder. Choose View, Current View, and then choose one of the following commands to change the view:

- **Business Cards** Shows the contact information as a virtual business card.
- **Address Cards** Displays the name of each contact along with address and telephone information.
- **Detailed Address Cards** Shows additional detailed information for each contact, including the person's title, the company the person works for, personal notes, and more.
- **Phone List** Displays the contacts as a phone list.
- **By Category** Groups contacts by their assigned categories.
- **By Company** Groups contacts by the company with which they're affiliated.
- **By Location** Groups contacts by country or region.
- **Outlook Data Files** Groups contacts by the Outlook 2007 data file (*.pst) in which the contacts are stored.

Adding contact entries to your Contacts folder is easy: choose File, New and then choose Contact, or click New on the toolbar. Either action opens the contact form, in which you enter the contact's data.

Customizing the Contacts View

Like other views in other folders, the view in the Contacts folder can be customized to suit your needs and preferences. For example, you can adjust the view to display additional fields of information or to remove fields you don't need. You can sort the view based on specific contact criteria or group similar items together based on multiple criteria. For details about customizing the Contacts view, see Chapter 18, "Creating and Managing Your Contacts."

Tasks

The Tasks folder contains your task list. The default Tasks view, shown in Figure 4-17, lists each task in a simple list with subject, due date, and status. Double-click an existing task to open the task form, which displays detailed information about the task, including due date, start date, status, notes, and so on, as shown in Figure 4-18. To add a new task to the list, double-click a blank list entry to open a new task form, where you can enter all the details about the task.

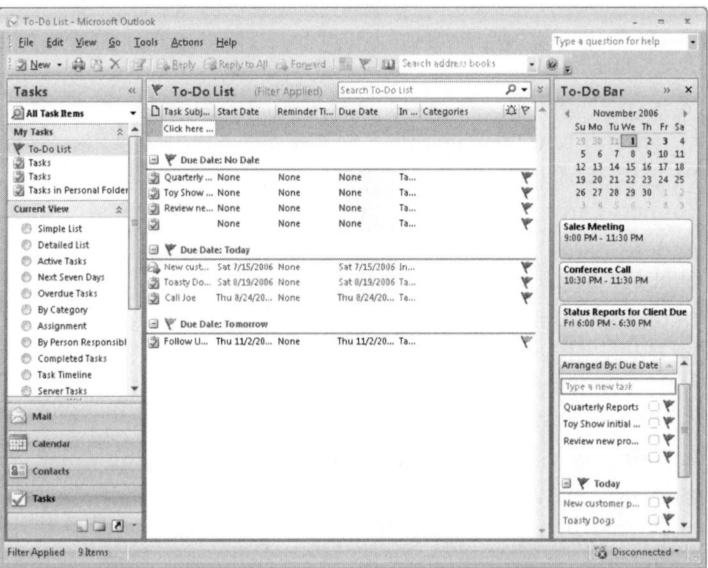

Figure 4-17. By default, the Tasks folder displays this view.

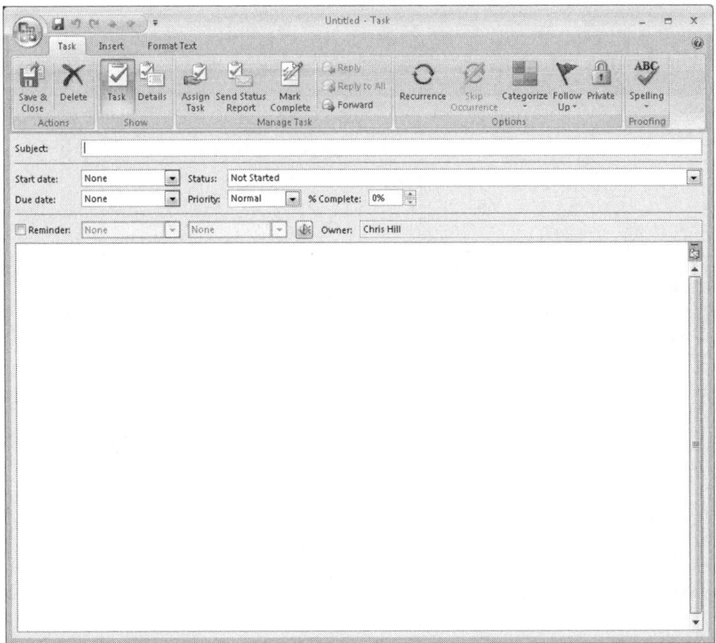

Figure 4-18. Use a task form to create a new task.

The task list shows tasks that you have assigned to others as well as those tasks assigned to you (by yourself or by others). These assignments can be one-time or recurring, and the list shows both in-progress and completed tasks. Additionally, any messages that you have flagged for follow-up appear in your task list.

Like other Outlook 2007 views, Tasks view provides a Reading Pane that you can use to view details for a task without opening the task item. To display the Reading Pane, choose View, Reading Pane, and then specify the location (either Right or Bottom). AutoPreview is also available in the Tasks folder; it displays notes about the task below the task name, as shown in Figure 4-19. To enable AutoPreview, click View, AutoPreview.

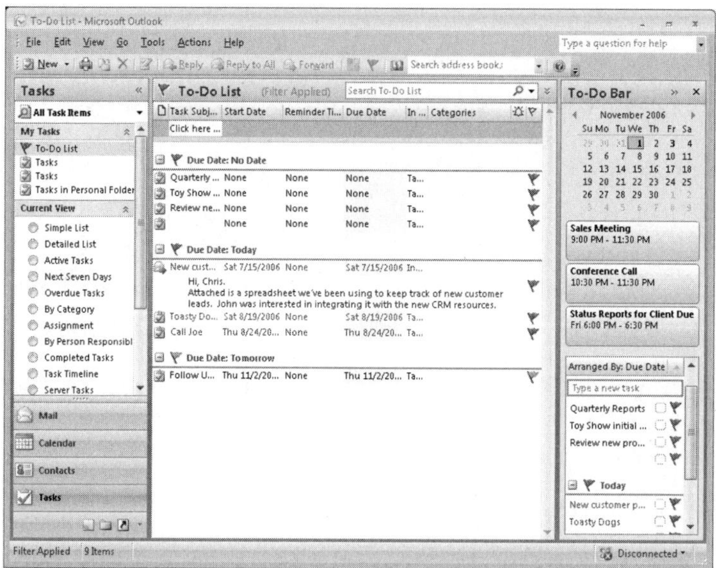

Figure 4-19. AutoPreview displays additional information about a task below the task name in the list.

Customizing the Tasks View

You can customize the view in the Tasks folder in a variety of ways–adding and removing columns, changing column names, or organizing tasks by category or other properties, to list a few. To customize the columns, right-click the column header bar, and then choose Format Columns. The resulting dialog box allows you to select the format for each column, change the name, apply alignment, and so on. To change the order of columns in the view, simply drag the column headers into the desired positions, resizing as needed.

You can also organize your task list in various ways. You can click column headers to sort the columns in ascending or descending order, and you can group the columns based on a particular field or group of fields, just as you can in the Inbox and other Outlook 2007 folders.

You can also choose View, Current View and then choose one of the following commands to change the Tasks view:

- **Simple List** Shows whether the task has been completed, the task name, the folder location of the task, and the due date.
- **Detailed List** Shows status, percent complete, and categories in addition to the information displayed in Simple List view.
- **Active Tasks** Displays tasks that are active.
- **Next Seven Days** Displays tasks scheduled for the next seven days.
- **Overdue Tasks** Displays incomplete tasks with due dates that have passed.

- **By Category** Organizes the task list by the categories assigned to tasks.
- **Assignment** Shows the tasks assigned to specific people.
- **By Person Responsible** Groups the view according to the person responsible for the various tasks.
- **Completed Tasks** Shows only completed tasks.
- **Task Timeline** Displays a timeline of all tasks.
- **Server Tasks** With Exchange Server accounts, helps you view assigned tasks.
- **Outlook Data Files** Displays tasks organized by Outlook 2007 data file location.
- **To-Do List** Displays tasks in the To-Do List with a Reading Pane.

For more information about customizing the view in the Tasks folder, see "Working with the Tasks Folder" in Chapter 22.

Notes

With its Notes feature, Outlook 2007 helps you organize your thoughts and tasks. Each note can function as a stand-alone window, allowing you to view notes on your desktop outside Outlook 2007. The Notes pane provides a look into your Notes folder, where your notes are initially stored. From there, you can copy or move your notes to other locations (such as the desktop) or create shortcuts to them. By default, the initial Notes pane displays the notes as icons, with the first line of the note serving as the title under the note's icon, as shown in Figure 4-20.

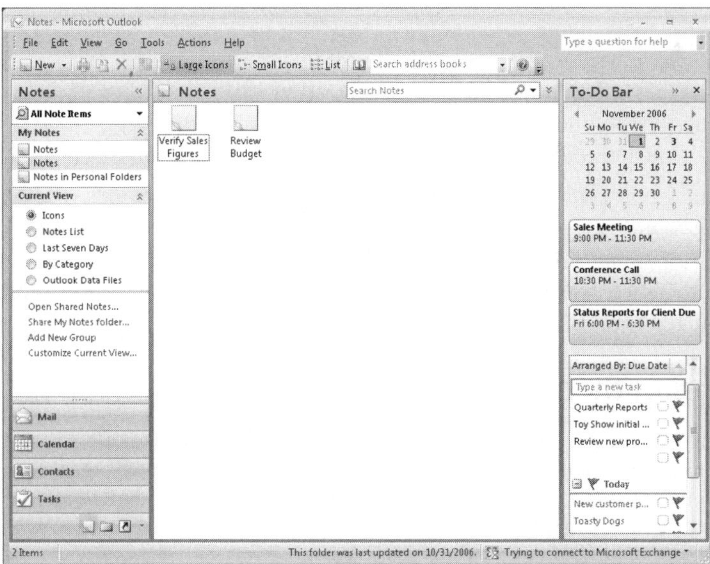

Figure 4-20. The standard Notes pane displays notes as icons.

As it does for other options, Outlook 2007 offers several other ways to view notes. You can select a view by choosing it in the Current View section in the Navigation Pane. You can also choose View, Current View, and then choose one of the following:

- **Icons** Displays an icon for each note, with the first line of the note serving as the icon's description (the default view).
- **Notes List** Displays the notes as a line-by-line list.
- **Last Seven Days** Resembles Notes List view but restricts the display to only the past seven days and is based on the current date.
- **By Category** Groups the notes by their assigned categories.
- **Outlook Data Files** Groups the notes by Outlook 2007 data file location.

You can show the Reading Pane in the Notes folder, displaying the text of a note when you click it in the list. You can also use AutoPreview in Notes List and Last Seven Days views to automatically display the contents of each note. To view the Notes List and Last Seven Days options, choose View, Current View, and then make your selection.

You can customize the views in the Notes folder the same way you can in other folders. You can, for example, drag columns to rearrange them, resize columns, change column names and other properties, add other fields, and group notes based on various criteria.

For a detailed explanation of how to work with the Notes folder, see Chapter 24, "Making Notes."

Deleted Items

The Deleted Items folder contains Outlook 2007 items that you have deleted, and it can include all the Outlook 2007 item types (such as messages, contacts, and appointments). The Deleted Items folder offers a way for you to recover items you've deleted, because the items remain in the folder until you manually delete them from that location or allow Outlook 2007 to clean out the folder. When you delete an item from the Deleted Items folder, that item is deleted permanently.

You can configure Outlook 2007 to automatically delete all items from the Deleted Items folder when you exit Outlook 2007. To do so, choose Tools, Options, and then click Other. Select the Empty The Deleted Items Folder Upon Exiting check box, and then click OK.

Choosing the Startup View

You might want to change the default Outlook 2007 view based on your type of work and the Outlook 2007 folders you use most. Or you might want to use a particular view as the initial view because it presents the information you need right away each morning to start your workday.

You can designate any of the Outlook 2007 folders as your startup view. To do so, follow these steps:

1. In Outlook 2007, choose Tools, Options.
2. Click the Other tab, and then click Advanced Options.
3. Next to the Startup In This Folder text box, click Browse, and then select the folder you want to see by default when Outlook 2007 starts. Click the Mailbox or Personal Folders branch if you want to specify Outlook Today as the default view.
4. Click OK, and then click OK again to close the Options dialog box.

Using Other Outlook Features

In addition to the various folders and views described in this chapter, Outlook 2007 incorporates several other standard components in its interface. The following sections explain these features and how to use them effectively.

> **Note**
>
> This book assumes that you're familiar with your operating system and comfortable using menus. Therefore, neither the Outlook 2007 menu bar nor its individual menus are discussed in this chapter. Specific menus and commands are covered where applicable.

Outlook 2007 uses personalized menus, displaying only those menu items you've used most recently. You can click the double arrow at the bottom of a menu to see all of its commands. Although personalized menus unclutter the interface, they can be annoying if you prefer to see all available commands or are searching for a specific command that isn't displayed. To display all menu commands on a specific menu or toolbar, right-click the menu or toolbar, and then choose Customize. On the Options tab, select Always Show Full Menus.

Using the Navigation Pane

The Navigation Pane appears on the left in the Outlook 2007 window and contains shortcuts to the standard Outlook 2007 folders as well as shortcuts to folders you've created and other important data folders, as shown in Figure 4-21. Just click an icon in the Navigation Pane to open that folder or item. The Navigation Pane gives you quick access not only to Outlook 2007 folders but also to all your data.

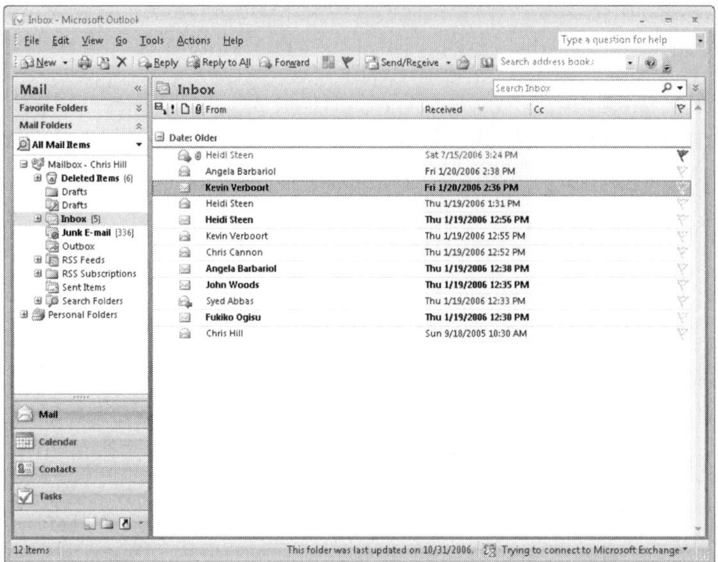

Figure 4-21. The Navigation Pane provides quick access to all Outlook 2007 data and other frequently used resources and folders.

For a detailed discussion of the Navigation Pane, including how to create your own groups and shortcuts, see "Customizing the Navigation Pane" in Chapter 26.

For information about obtaining updates and finding troubleshooting resources for both Outlook 2007 and the 2007 Microsoft Office system, see Article 10, "Updating and Troubleshooting Resources," on the companion CD.

> **Note**
>
> You can create new shortcuts in any of the existing Shortcuts groups in the Navigation Pane, and you can also create your own groups.

Depending on your monitor's resolution and the number of shortcuts in each group, you might not be able to see all the icons in a group. If that's the case, you can use the scroll bar on the right edge of the Navigation Pane to scroll through the icons in the selected group.

Using Objects in the Navigation Pane

Most of the time, you'll probably just click an icon in the Navigation Pane to open its associated folder. However, you can also right-click a view button and use the resulting shortcut menu to perform various tasks with the selected object. For example, you might right-click the Calendar icon and then choose Open In New Window to open a second window showing the calendar's contents. To view a different folder, simply click the folder's button in the Navigation Pane. The content of the upper portion of the Navigation Pane changes according to the folder you select. For example, the Navigation Pane shows the Folder List if you click the Folder List button.

Controlling the Navigation Pane's Appearance

Outlook 2007 shows a selection of view buttons for standard folders in the Navigation Pane. If you don't use certain folders very often, however, you might prefer to remove them from the Navigation Pane to make room for other view buttons. For example, if you never use the Journal or Notes folder, you can remove those view buttons from the Navigation Pane and use the Folder List to access those folders when needed.

To change the view buttons displayed in the Navigation Pane, click Configure Buttons on the lower right in the Navigation Pane, and then choose Add Or Remove Buttons to open the shortcut menu shown in Figure 4-22. Click a folder in the list to either add it to or remove it from the Navigation Pane. Those folders that are selected in the list appear in the pane.

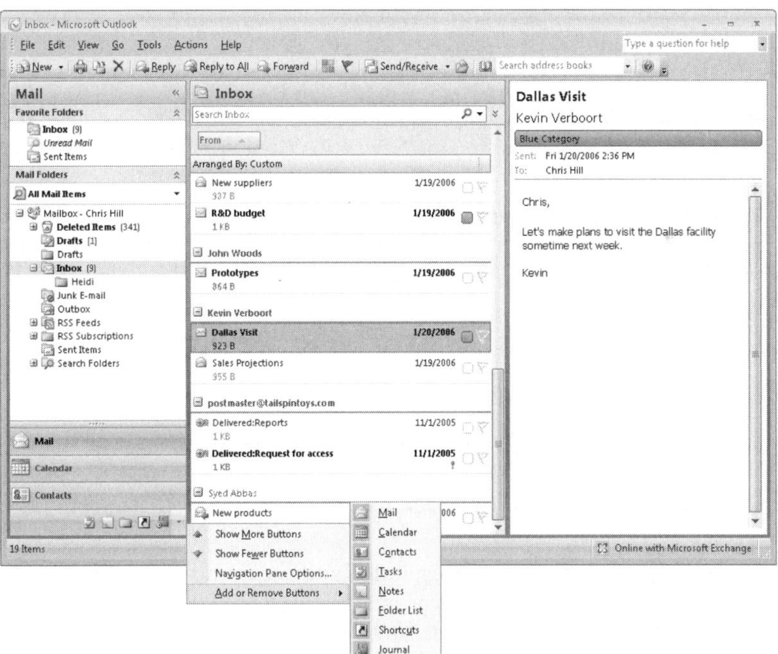

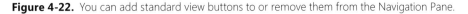

Figure 4-22. You can add standard view buttons to or remove them from the Navigation Pane.

If you need to add or remove more than one folder, click Configure Buttons, and then choose Navigation Pane Options to open the Navigation Pane Options dialog box. Select each folder you want included in the Navigation Pane, and then click OK.

> **Note**
>
> Use the Move Up and Move Down buttons in the Navigation Pane Options dialog box to control the order of buttons in the Navigation Pane.

If you seldom use the Navigation Pane, you can close it or minimize it to make room on the screen for the Folder List or other data. Simply choose View, Navigation Pane, and then choose Off or Minimize to alter the display.

Using the Outlook Toolbars

Outlook 2007 provides a Standard toolbar for the current folder that offers quick access to the tasks and functions you perform most frequently in that folder. Thus, the contents of the Standard toolbar change depending on the folder you have open. Certain items that appear on the toolbar for all folders work in specific ways in the context of the selected folder. For example, when you're working in the Inbox folder, clicking the New toolbar button starts a new e-mail message. With the Contacts folder open, clicking New opens a new contact form. You don't have to accept the default contextual action for these types of toolbar buttons, however; you can click the arrow next to a button to choose a specific command instead, as shown in Figure 4-23. To display the Standard toolbar in a folder, choose View, Toolbars, Standard. Use the same process to turn off the toolbar display.

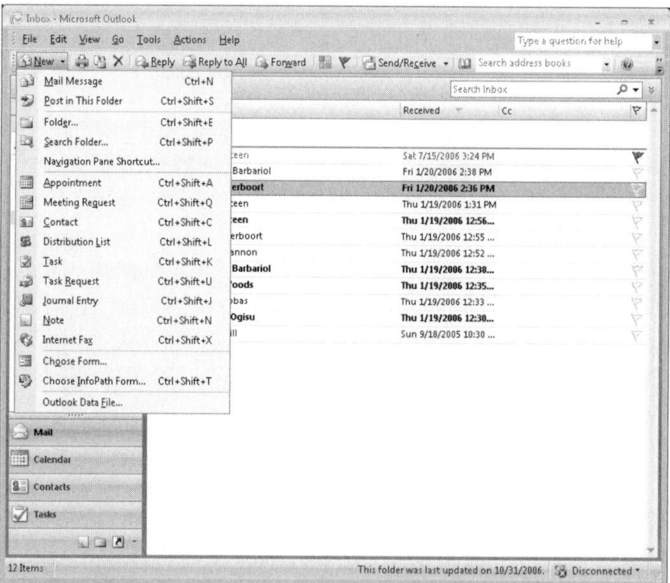

Figure 4-23. Click the arrow next to a toolbar button to view additional command options.

> **Note**
>
> Outlook 2007 and other Microsoft Office system applications refer to both menus and toolbars as *command bars*. However, Outlook 2007 still refers to the individual bars as *toolbars*. This book uses the two terms synonymously.

> **Note**
>
> If you're not sure what function a toolbar button performs, position the mouse pointer over the button to display a ScreenTip explaining the button's purpose.

If your display isn't wide enough to accommodate the entire toolbar, Outlook 2007 displays a double right arrow at the right end of the toolbar. Click this arrow to view the remaining toolbar buttons and to add buttons to or remove buttons from the toolbar.

For more information about customizing the Standard toolbar and other toolbars, see "Customizing Command Bars" in Chapter 26.

The Advanced toolbar, shown in Figure 4-24, provides additional commands and also works in the context of the current folder. In addition to navigation buttons, the Advanced toolbar contains buttons for opening and closing the Reading Pane and the Folder List, printing, setting up rules and alerts, selecting the current view, and more. Turn the Advanced toolbar on or off by choosing View, Toolbars, Advanced.

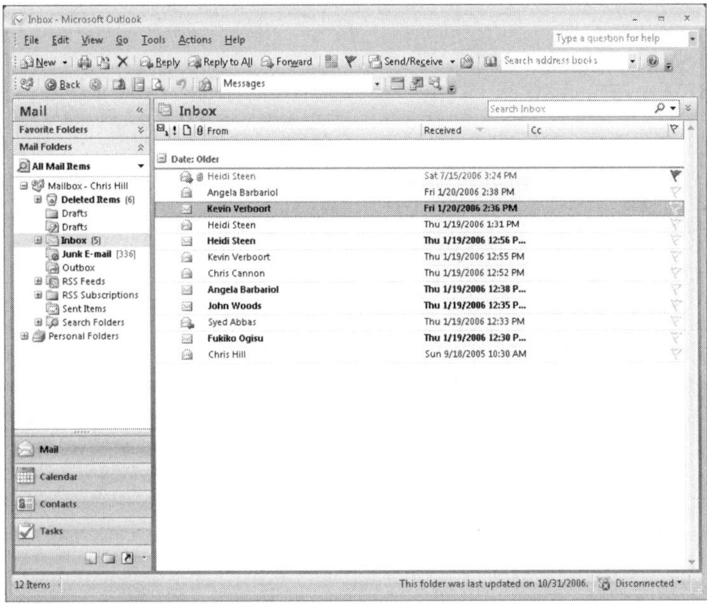

Figure 4-24. The Advanced toolbar lets you change views quickly.

The Web toolbar functions much as the navigation toolbar does in Microsoft Internet Explorer®. It includes Web navigation buttons, a URL address box, buttons for stopping and refreshing the current page, and so on. Choose View, Toolbars, Web to show or hide the Web toolbar.

Using the Ribbon

Unlike some of the other Microsoft Office system applications, the main Outlook 2007 window uses a familiar menu bar and toolbar combination to give you access to commands, options, and tools in Outlook 2007. These other applications, such as Microsoft Office Word 2007, use a new feature called the Ribbon to give you quick access to commonly used features. Outlook 2007 does make use of the Ribbon, but primarily in the individual item forms (message, contact, and so on), as shown in Figure 4-25.

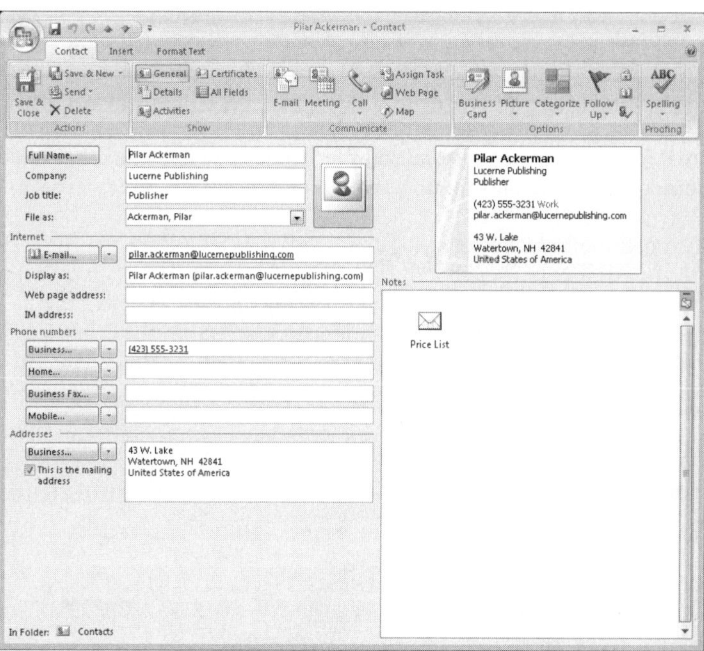

Figure 4-25. The Ribbon provides quick access to context-sensitive commands and features.

The Ribbon is something of a paradigm shift. Rather than provide a linear menu list of commands, the Ribbon divides features onto individual *tabs*, each of which comprises tools with related functions. For example, all of the tools that relate to inserting items into a new message are located together on the Insert tab of the new message form.

Each ribbon tab is divided into *groups*, and each group organizes the features for a specific function. On the Message tab of the new message form, for example, the Basic Text group organizes the tools you use to format text in the message.

Using Multiple Outlook Windows

Although Outlook 2007 opens in a single window, it supports the use of multiple windows, which can be extremely useful. For example, you might want to keep your Inbox open while you browse through your schedule. Or perhaps you want to copy items from one folder to another by dragging them. Whatever the case, it's easy to use multiple windows in Outlook 2007.

When you right-click a folder in the Navigation Pane, the shortcut menu for that folder contains the Open In New Window command. Choose this command to open the selected folder in a new window, keeping the existing folder open in the current window. You also can open a folder from the Folder List (discussed next) in a new window. Simply right-click a folder, and then choose Open In New Window to open that folder in a new window.

Using the Folder List

When you need to switch between folders, you'll probably use the Navigation Pane most of the time. But the Navigation Pane doesn't include shortcuts to all your folders by default, and adding those shortcuts can clutter the pane, especially if you have multiple data stores. Fortunately, Outlook 2007 provides another quick way to navigate your folders: the Folder List.

Click the Folder List button in the Navigation Pane to display the Folder List, as shown in Figure 4-26. In the list, click the folder you want to open. Outlook 2007 hides the Folder List again after you select the folder.

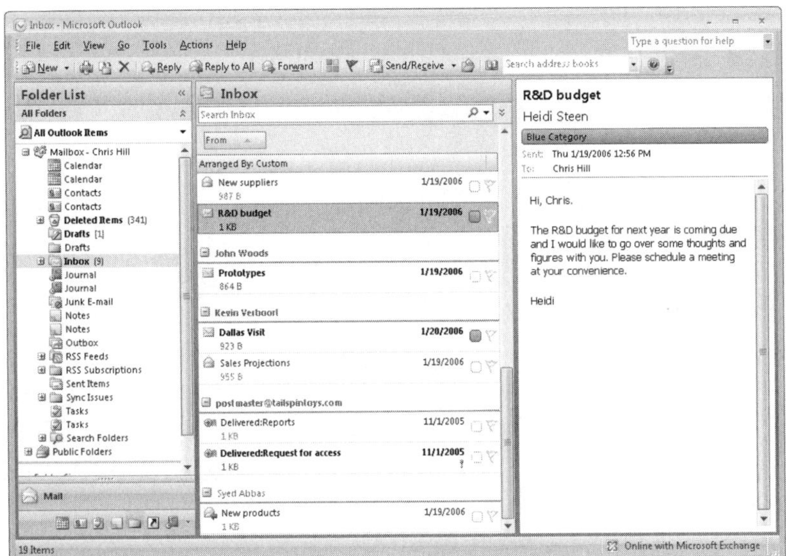

Figure 4-26. Use the Folder List to browse and select other folders.

Using the Status Bar

The status bar appears at the bottom of the Outlook 2007 window, as shown in Figure 4-27, and presents information about the current folder and selected items, such as the number of items in the folder. It can also include other status information, such as the progress of folder synchronization and connection status for Exchange Server. If you don't need the information in the status bar, you can turn it off to gain a little more space for the current folder's display. To turn the status bar on or off, choose View, Status Bar.

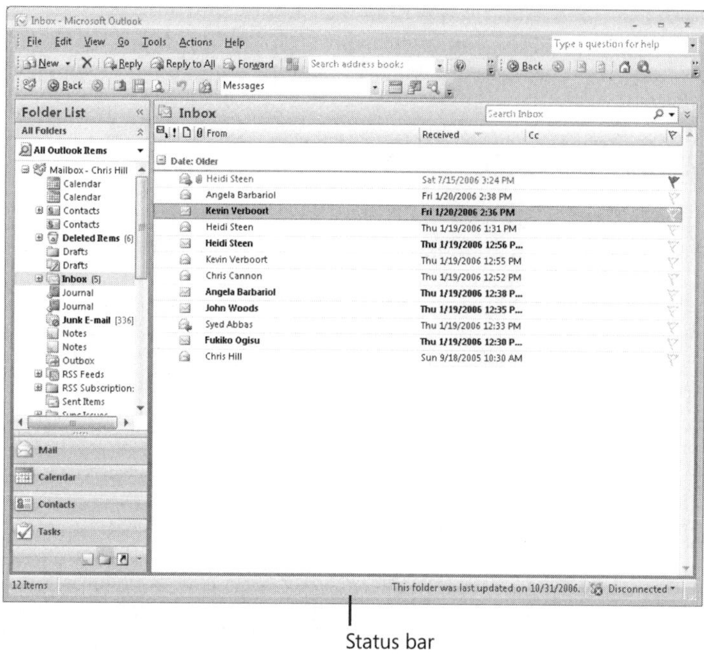

Figure 4-27. The status bar provides useful information, such as the number of items in the selected folder or current connection status to the server.

Using the Reading Pane

In earlier sections of this chapter, you learned about the Reading Pane, which allows you to preview Outlook 2007 items without opening them. For example, you can preview an e-mail message in the Reading Pane simply by clicking the message header. To turn the Reading Pane on or off, choose View, Reading Pane, and then choose Right, Bottom, or Off. You can also click the Reading Pane button on the Advanced toolbar to turn the pane on or off.

To some degree, the way the Reading Pane functions depends on how you configure it. For example, you can set up the Reading Pane to mark messages as read after they've been previewed for a specified length of time. To configure the Reading Pane, choose

Tools, Options, click the Other tab, and then click Reading Pane. Select options based on the following list:

- **Mark Items As Read When Viewed in the Reading Pane** Select this option to have messages marked as read when they've been previewed for the time specified by the following option.
- **Wait *n* Seconds Before Marking Item As Read** Specify the number of seconds a message must be displayed in the Reading Pane before it is marked as read.
- **Mark Item As Read When Selection Changes** Select this option to have the message in the Reading Pane marked as read when you select another message.
- **Single Key Reading Using Spacebar** Selecting this option allows you to use the **Spacebar** to move through your list of messages to preview them. Press **Shift+Spacebar** to move up the list. You also can use the **Up Arrow** and **Down Arrow** keys to move up and down the message list.

The Reading Pane in Outlook 2007 offers some additional functionality, which includes the following:

- In a message, you can double-click an address in the Reading Pane to view details for the address.
- The Reading Pane header displays the message's attachments. You can double-click an attachment to open it or right-click the attachment and choose other tasks on the shortcut menu (such as saving the attachment).
- The Reading Pane displays Accept and Decline buttons so that you can accept or decline a meeting request in the Reading Pane without opening the request.

Using AutoPreview

AutoPreview, which is available in the Inbox, Notes, and Tasks folders, allows you to preview Outlook 2007 items without opening the Reading Pane. For example, with AutoPreview turned on in the Inbox folder, the first three lines of each message appear under the message header. To turn AutoPreview on or off for the current folder, choose View, AutoPreview. The AutoPreview state (on or off) is saved on a folder-by-folder basis, so you can have AutoPreview turned on for the Inbox and turned off for Notes and Tasks.

Using the InfoBar

The InfoBar is the banner near the top of an open e-mail message, appointment, contact, or task. It tells you whether a message has been replied to or forwarded, along with the online status of a contact who is using instant messaging, and so on. The InfoBar in a message form, for example, displays the From, To, Cc, and other fields. In Outlook 2007, as in Outlook 2003, the InfoBar resides in the Reading Pane, as shown in Figure 4-28.

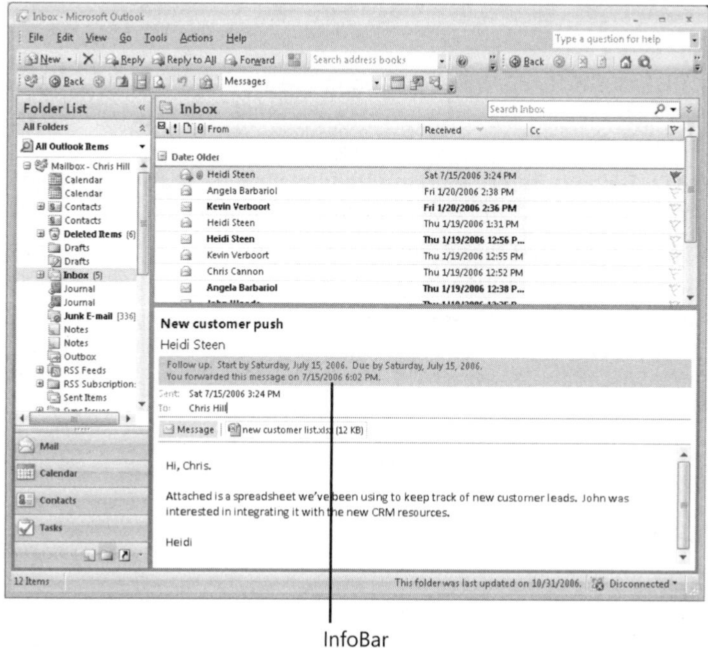

Figure 4-28. The InfoBar appears in the Reading Pane as well as in message and appointment forms. Here the InfoBar indicates that the message is flagged for follow-up.

Some of the fields in the InfoBar simply display information, but others lead to more details. For example, you can double-click a name in the InfoBar to view the associated address and other contact information, or you can double-click attachments to open them.

Configuring Outlook Options

Because Outlook 2007 is a complex application with a broad range of capabilities, you have many options for controlling the way it looks and functions. This portion of the chapter is designed to help you configure Outlook 2007 to perform the way you need it to.

Each of the following sections describes a tab in the Outlook 2007 Options dialog box, providing an overview of the features listed on that tab. Because many of the options in this dialog box are best understood in the context of the feature they control, you'll find more detail about individual options in chapters that focus on a particular Outlook 2007 feature (messaging or scheduling, for example); be sure to consult the cross-references to the applicable chapters for more information.

To open the Options dialog box described here, start Outlook 2007, and then choose Tools, Options.

Preferences Tab

The Preferences tab in the Options dialog box, shown in Figure 4-29, lets you configure general settings for all the Outlook 2007 primary functions, from e-mail to scheduling to contact management.

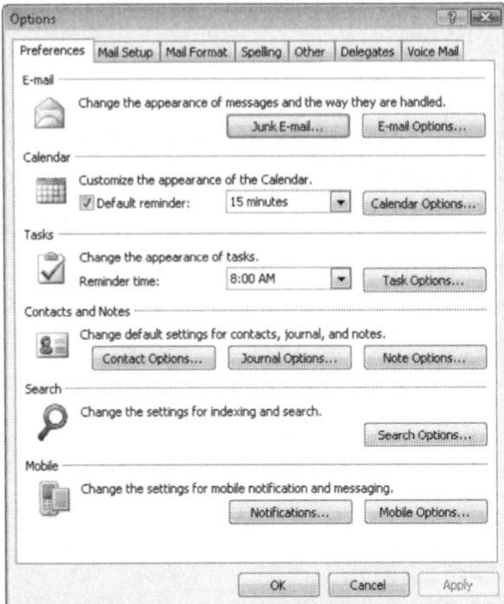

Figure 4-29. Use the Preferences tab in the Options dialog box to configure a broad range of general options.

Each of the option groups on the Preferences tab controls how a specific Outlook 2007 component works. The following list helps you locate specific settings:

- **E-Mail** You can specify how Outlook 2007 handles messages—for example, whether Outlook 2007 keeps a copy of sent items, saves unsent messages, or includes original message content in replies and forwards. You can also configure the Outlook 2007 junk e-mail filter settings. Chapter 8, "Sending and Receiving E-Mail," provides extensive coverage of e-mail configuration options. Chapter 12, "Managing Junk Mail," explains how to block junk e-mail, and Chapter 10, "Finding and Organizing Messages," explains how to filter and sort messages in other ways.
- **Calendar** You can control the look of the Outlook 2007 calendar by, for example, defining the work week, changing the workday start and end times, changing the appearance of the Date Navigator, or setting background color. See Chapter 20, "Scheduling Appointments," for a discussion of options for the Calendar folder.
- **Tasks** You can set the color for completed and overdue tasks, set up reminders for tasks with due dates, and configure other task-related settings. Chapter 22, "Managing Your Tasks," covers task options in detail.
- **Contacts And Notes** You can control the way names are displayed in the Contacts folder, check for duplicate contact entries, configure journal options, and set other options for storing and managing your contact information. See Chapter 19, "Using Business Contact Manager with Outlook," for a complete explanation.

You can also, for example, set the color, size, and font used for notes. Chapter 24, "Making Notes," covers options for notes.

- **Search** Set options to control the way Outlook 2007 indexes and searches information and displays search results.
- **Mobile** Configure settings for Mobile Service options (text messaging).

Mail Setup Tab

On the Mail Setup tab, shown in Figure 4-30, you'll find additional settings that control e-mail accounts and Outlook 2007 messaging functions. For example, you can use the Mail Setup tab to create or modify e-mail accounts and configure how and when Outlook 2007 sends and receives messages.

Figure 4-30. Use the Mail Setup tab to configure e-mail accounts and general messaging properties.

The following list describes the major areas on the Mail Setup tab and directs you to the chapter in which those settings are discussed:

- **E-Mail Accounts** These settings allow you to add, remove, or configure e-mail accounts. See Chapter 3, "Advanced Setup Tasks," and Chapter 7, "Using Internet Mail Accounts," to learn how to configure e-mail accounts.
- **Send/Receive** You can define groups of accounts, which Outlook 2007 then uses to determine when to process messages for specific accounts. You can configure settings separately for each group, providing a high degree of control over when and how Outlook 2007 processes messages. See Chapter 8, "Sending and Receiving E-Mail," for information about send/receive groups and send/receive options.
- **Data Files** These settings let you add, remove, and configure information stores (data files) for Outlook 2007, including setting up offline access. See Chapter 2, "Outlook Overview and Startup," to learn how to manage data files.

- **Dial-Up** Here you can configure a handful of settings that determine how Outlook 2007 handles dial-up connections for sending and receiving messages.

Mail Format Tab

Use the Mail Format tab, shown in Figure 4-31, to control the way your messages look and how you compose those messages. For example, you can use the Mail Format tab to specify either Word 2007 or Outlook 2007 as the default e-mail editor, to choose between plain-text and rich-text options, and to set international formatting options.

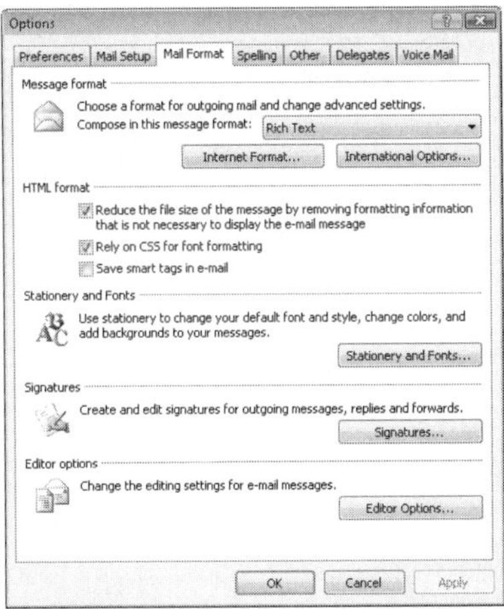

Figure 4-31. Use the Mail Format tab to select the default e-mail editor, mail format, and other properties.

The following list summarizes the option groups on the Mail Format tab. For details about the various settings in each group, consult Chapter 8, "Sending and Receiving E-Mail."

- **Message Format** With these settings, you can choose among HTML, plain text, and rich text for outgoing messages; specify the default e-mail editor; specify the default e-mail viewer for rich-text messages; configure Internet and international options for messages; and set up other messaging features.
- **HTML Format** Set options that determine how Outlook 2007 handles HTML formatting and content for messages.
- **Stationery And Fonts** You can set default stationery (background) for messages, manage stationery, and specify font settings.
- **Signatures** These settings direct Outlook 2007 to add a text signature to all new messages and to replies and forwards. You can configure the two categories of messages separately. (Note that these signatures are different from digital signatures, which allow you to validate the authenticity of and encrypt messages.) Outlook 2007 also has the ability to assign specific signatures to each e-mail account.
- **Editor Options** Change options for the general Outlook 2007 interface (such as color scheme and ScreenTip style).

Spelling Tab

The Spelling tab, shown in Figure 4-32, lets you specify how spelling should be checked in Outlook 2007. The following sections summarize by function the settings available on this tab.

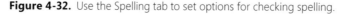

Figure 4-32. Use the Spelling tab to set options for checking spelling.

Checking Spelling

The General Options area of the Spelling tab allows you to set general guidelines for the spelling checker. The two options are:

- **Always Check Spelling Before Sending** Select this option to have Outlook 2007 automatically check spelling before you send a message. You also can check spelling manually.
- **Ignore Original Message Text In Reply Or Forward** Selecting this option specifies that Outlook 2007 will check spelling only in your message text, not in the original message text included in a reply or forward.

Click the Spelling And AutoCorrection button on the Spelling tab to display the following options, which affect all Microsoft Office system programs:

- **AutoCorrect Options** Click this button to specify how Outlook 2007 formats and corrects text as you type.
- **Ignore Words In UPPERCASE** You can instruct the spelling checker to skip words that appear in all uppercase letters. This option is useful, for example, if your document contains numerous acronyms and you don't want the spelling checker to waste time checking them.
- **Ignore Words That Contain Numbers** When you select this option, the spelling checker will not attempt to check the spelling of words that include numbers, such as *some342*.

- **Ignore Internet And File Addresses** When you select this option, the spelling checker will not check URLs or file names, such as *fileforchris.doc*.
- **Flag Repeated Words** Selecting this check box underlines repeated words, even when they are spelled correctly.
- **Enforce Accented Uppercase In French** This option alerts you to French words that contain uppercase letters that are missing an accent mark.
- **Suggest From Main Dictionary Only** When you select this option, words from only the main dictionary that is built into the spelling checker are suggested. Words from your custom dictionaries are not included in the list of suggested words when you check the spelling of a document.
- **Custom Dictionaries** Click this button to load customized dictionaries.
- **Check Spelling As You Type** With this option selected, Outlook 2007 checks spelling as you type messages or any other text in Outlook 2007 and offers suggestions.
- **Use Contextual Spelling** When you select this check box, Outlook 2007 also examines the context of a sentence to determine the use of correctly spelled but misused words–for example, *their* instead of *there*.
- **Mark Grammar Errors As You Type** When you choose this option, Outlook 2007 underlines grammatical errors with green wavy lines.
- **Check Grammar With Spelling** By selecting this check box, you instruct Outlook 2007 to check grammar at the same time as spelling.
- **Show Readability Statistics** If you select this check box, Outlook 2007 displays information about the reading level of the document after completion of spelling and grammar checks.

Using AutoCorrect

Outlook 2007, like other Microsoft Office system applications, supports AutoCorrect, a feature that allows Outlook 2007 to correct common spelling and typing errors and to replace characters with symbols. You also can use AutoCorrect as a shortcut, which means that you can type a small string of characters and have those characters replaced by a longer string. For example, if you frequently type the words **Windows Vista**, you might set up AutoCorrect to replace your shorthand typed phrase **vst** with *Windows Vista*. See the Inside Out sidebar in the "Setting Advanced Options" section later in this chapter for a handy use for smart tags and AutoCorrect entries.

Clicking AutoCorrect Options in the Editor Options dialog box displays the AutoCorrect dialog box, shown in Figure 4-33. You can use this dialog box to add new AutoCorrect entries or change existing entries. Click Exceptions to specify exceptions to AutoCorrect rules.

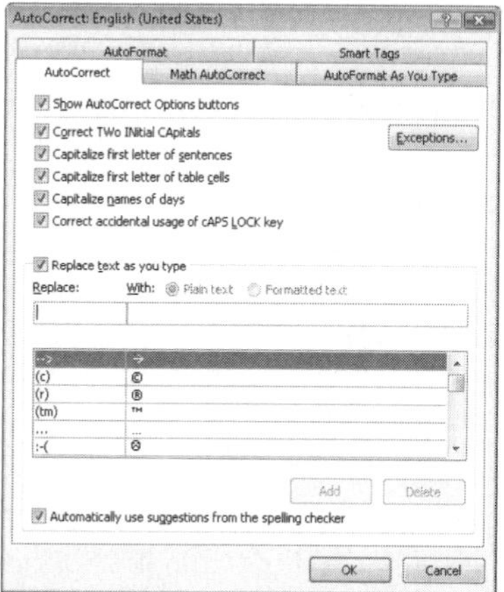

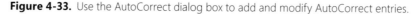

Figure 4-33. Use the AutoCorrect dialog box to add and modify AutoCorrect entries.

Editing a Custom Spelling Dictionary

When Outlook 2007 is checking spelling in a document and finds a word it considers misspelled, the program gives you the option of adding the word to a custom dictionary. This option lets you specify the correct spelling of words not found in the Outlook 2007 standard dictionary. For example, you might want to add your name to the custom dictionary if Outlook 2007 doesn't recognize its spelling. You can also add the correct spelling of special words or terms you use often to the custom dictionary.

INSIDE OUT

Use custom dictionaries throughout the Microsoft Office system

All Microsoft Office system applications use the same spelling features, including the custom dictionary. Words you add to the dictionary from other applications are available in Outlook 2007, and vice versa. This is also true for new dictionaries that you create: if you add another dictionary to Outlook 2007, that new dictionary is available in other Microsoft Office system applications.

Click the Custom Dictionaries button located in the Editor Options dialog box to open the custom dictionary. The Custom Dictionaries dialog box appears. To add new items to your dictionary, click Edit Word List. Type a new word and click Add, or select an existing word and click Delete. The custom dictionary file is stored in the Application Data\Microsoft\UProof folder of your profile folder (which varies according to your operating system).

You can also add other dictionaries to Outlook 2007. To add a new dictionary, follow these steps:

1. Open the Custom Dictionaries dialog box, shown in Figure 4-34, as outlined earlier.

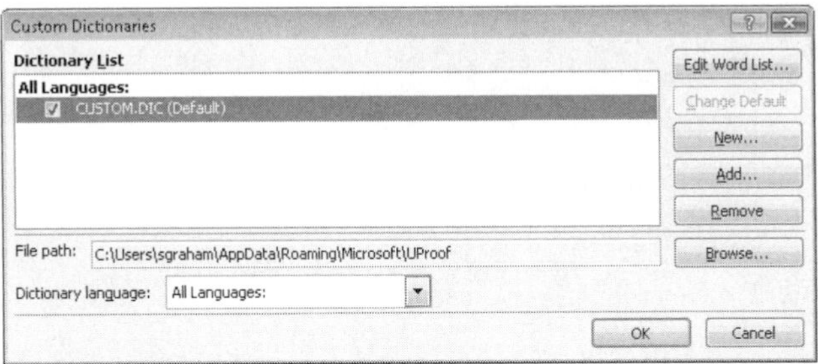

Figure 4-34. Add dictionaries using the Custom Dictionaries dialog box.

2. Click Add.
3. Browse to the desired dictionary file (*.dic), and then click Open. Click OK to close the dialog box.
4. Click OK to close the Editor Options dialog box.

Using International Dictionaries

The Dictionary Language setting in the Customized Dictionaries dialog box allows you to specify the language that Outlook 2007 uses when checking spelling. Simply select the appropriate language in the drop-down list, and then click OK.

Other Tab

The Other tab, shown in Figure 4-35, provides a selection of settings that apply to various aspects of Outlook 2007. The following sections explain how to configure specific features and behavior using this tab.

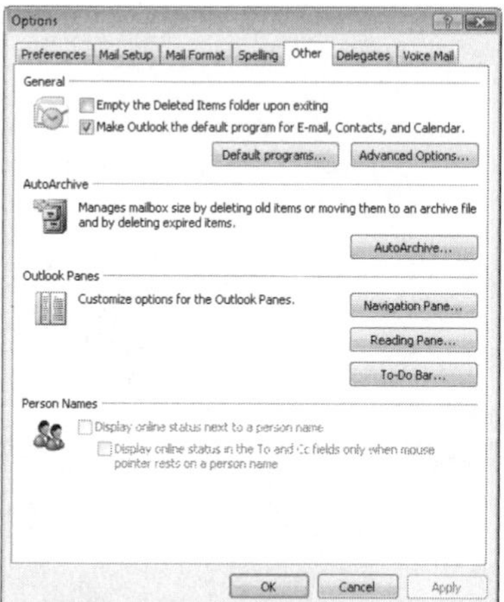

Figure 4-35. The Other tab gives you access to properties for several features.

Defining the Default Program for E-Mail, Contacts, and the Calendar

One setting on the Other tab lets you specify that Outlook 2007 is the default application for creating and viewing e-mail, contacts, and calendar items. Select the Make Outlook The Default Program For E-Mail, Contacts, And Calendar check box if you want Outlook 2007 to start when you open e-mail messages, contact entries, or calendar data from other sources.

Processing Deleted Items

You can use the Other tab to specify how Outlook 2007 processes deleted items. The first of the following two options is located on the Other tab; click Advanced Options to access the second.

- **Empty The Deleted Items Folder Upon Exiting** Select this check box to have Outlook 2007 automatically delete all items from the Deleted Items folder when you exit the program. This action permanently deletes the items.
- **Warn Before Permanently Deleting Items** Click Advanced Options and select this option if you want Outlook 2007 to warn you before it permanently deletes items from the Deleted Items folder.

Setting Up AutoArchive

The options accessed by clicking AutoArchive on the Other tab let you control how Outlook 2007 archives data, processes deleted and expired items, and implements other backup properties, such as the retention policy. See Chapter 30, "Managing Outlook Folders and Data," for more information about backup and archival options and procedures for Outlook 2007.

Customizing Outlook Panes

Clicking Reading Pane on the Other tab provides access to options that specify the way the Reading Pane functions. These options are explained in detail earlier in this chapter; see "Using the Reading Pane."

Click the Navigation Pane button to specify which items appear in the Navigation Pane and their displayed order. For example, if you use the Contacts folder more than the Calendar folder, you might want to move the Contacts folder icon higher in the Navigation Pane.

Click the To-Do Bar button on the Other tab to set options for the To-Do Bar that control which items appear in the To-Do Bar (Date Navigator, appointments, and Task List).

Setting Up Person Names

Use the Person Names area on the Other tab to configure MSN® Messenger and use instant messaging (sending or receiving pop-up messages in communication with other users).

Setting Advanced Options

The Other tab of the Options dialog box lets you access a set of special advanced options for configuring Outlook 2007. Click Advanced Options on the Other tab to display the Advanced Options dialog box, shown in Figure 4-36. You can use the options in this dialog box to configure various aspects of Outlook 2007 behavior and appearance, as described in the following list:

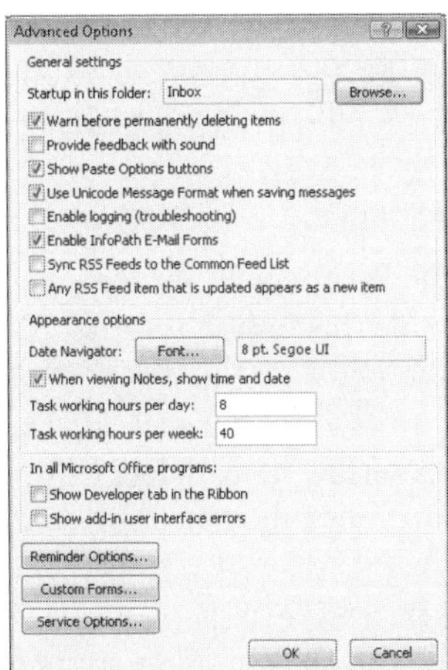

Figure 4-36. The Advanced Options dialog box controls several advanced features.

- **Startup In This Folder** This option lets you specify which folder Outlook 2007 opens by default when you start the program. Click Browse to select the folder.

- **Warn Before Permanently Deleting Items** Enable this option to have Outlook 2007 display a warning before it permanently deletes items.
- **Provide Feedback With Sound** You can direct Outlook 2007 to play a sound when you perform actions such as opening a file or deleting a message.
- **Show Paste Options Buttons** When this option is selected, Outlook 2007 displays a smart tag when you paste data from the Clipboard, allowing you to change the paste format and other paste options. This method of changing these options is faster than using the Edit menu.

INSIDE OUT

Use smart tags to get quick access to features

Smart tags are controls that provide quick access to commands and features without forcing you to browse the application's menu. When you paste data from the Clipboard, for example, Microsoft Office system applications display a smart tag beside the pasted data. You can select other paste formats and fine-tune the data without repasting or using the Edit menu. Smart tags also come in handy with AutoCorrect entries. If you type some text referenced by an AutoCorrect entry, Microsoft Office system applications change the text automatically but add a smart tag beside the modified text so that you can select other changes or undo the correction. Other types of smart tags provide similar quick access to document data and editing.

Use Unicode Message Format When Saving Messages Use the Unicode character set when saving messages to disk.

Enable Logging (Troubleshooting) This option allows Outlook 2007 to log e-mail event status to the OPMLog.log file, which is located in the Temp folder of your profile folder.

Enable InfoPath E-Mail Forms This option allows the controls of a Microsoft Office InfoPath® form to function when received as an e-mail message.

Sync RSS Feeds To The Common Feed List Enable this option to synchronize Really Simple Syndication (RSS) feeds to a common list on the computer running Exchange Server.

Any RSS Feed Item That Is Updated Appears As A New Item Select this option to have updated RSS items appear as new items in your Inbox or designated folder.

Date Navigator Click Font to select the font used by the Date Navigator. Changing the font changes not only the appearance of the Date Navigator but also the number of months displayed. Make the font smaller to show more months or larger to show fewer months.

When Viewing Notes, Show Time And Date You can have Outlook 2007 display the time and date a note was created or last modified at the bottom of the note.

Task Working Hours Per Day and Task Working Hours Per Week These two options define your work week for managing tasks. The default settings are 8 hours and 40 hours, respectively.

Show Developer Tab In The Ribbon Include in the Ribbon the Developer tab, which gives you quick access to the Microsoft Visual Basic® Editor, macro security settings, and other developer-related features.

Show Add-In User Interface Errors Display errors related to Microsoft Office system program add-ins.

> **Note**
>
> The Advanced Options dialog box includes three buttons at the bottom that let you configure a variety of options. Some of these buttons and their options are covered in the following sections. See Chapter 28, "Designing and Using Forms," for information about configuring custom forms.

Configuring Reminder Options

The Reminder Options button in the Advanced Options dialog box opens a simple Reminder Options dialog box that offers two options for configuring Outlook 2007 reminders:

- **Display The Reminder** Choose this option to have Outlook 2007 display reminders in the Reminders window when they come due.
- **Play Reminder Sound** Choose this option to have Outlook 2007 play a sound when a reminder comes due, and choose the sound file you want Outlook 2007 to use.

Custom Forms

Clicking Custom Forms in the Advanced Options dialog box displays the Custom Forms Options dialog box, where you can configure two options:

- **Temporary Storage For Forms** Set the maximum space (in KB) on the hard disk for storage of forms.
- **Allow Forms That Bypass Outlook** Permit forms to run that bypass the Outlook 2007 security model.

Setting Service Options

Clicking Service Options in the Advanced Options dialog box displays the Service Options dialog box, shown in Figure 4-37. This dialog box provides access to two configuration pages.

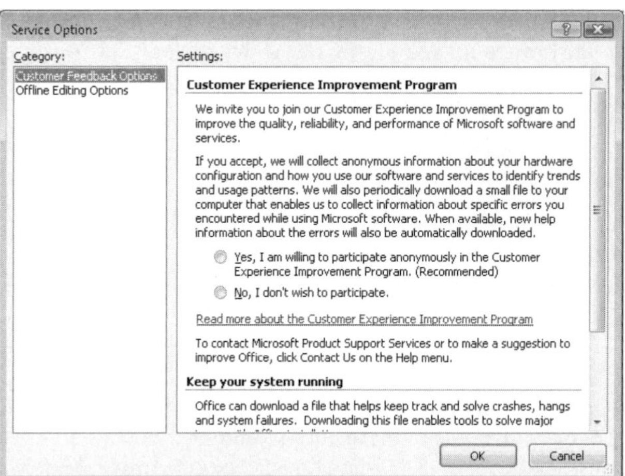

Figure 4-37. Use the Service Options dialog box to configure customer feedback and offline editing options.

- **Customer Feedback Options** The Customer Feedback Options area allows you to enable or disable participation in Microsoft's Customer Experience Improvement Program. When this option is enabled, Microsoft Office system applications submit information about your system and the way you use your applications to Microsoft over the Web, along with information about errors you encounter. Participation is disabled by default. Participating can provide Microsoft with useful information that could ultimately lead to better software, but you can leave this option disabled if you don't want your usage information shared or if providing this information isn't practical because you use a dial-up Internet connection. You can also disable this function in networks with widespread Microsoft Office system deployment to reduce network traffic and reduce data outflow.
- **Offline Editing** The Offline Editing area has two simple configuration options. The first, Server Drafts Location, allows you to set the file location of the server drafts. The second, Offline Editing Options For Document Management Server Files, specifies where such files would be stored for an application, such as Microsoft Office SharePoint® 2007.

Delegates Tab

The Delegates tab in the Options dialog box lets you specify other people who have delegate access to your folders and can send items on your behalf (meeting requests, for example). See Chapter 35, "Delegating Responsibilities to an Assistant," for detailed information about using delegation and specifying delegates.

Voice Mail Tab

The Voice Mail tab appears in the Options dialog box if you are using an Exchange Server account for which Unified Messaging is enabled. The options on the Voice Mail tab let you specify a variety of options that control how you access your mailbox from a phone and how voice mail is handled.

The options on the Voice Mail tab include:

- **Telephone Access Numbers** Specifies the number you use to access voice-enabled features of your Exchange Server mailbox.
- **Reset PIN** Click to reset the personal identification number (PIN) for your voice-enabled mailbox.
- **Choose The Folder To Read When Accessing E-Mail Messages From A Phone** Click Change Folder to choose the mail folder from which you want to listen to mail messages when calling in to the server.
- **Play On Phone Number** Specifies the phone number you use to listen to voice messages as an alternative to playing those messages in Outlook 2007.
- **Voice Mail Greeting** Choose this option to have Exchange Server use your regular greeting for callers.
- **Out Of Office Voice Mail Greeting** Choose this option to have Exchange Server use your Out Of Office greeting for callers.
- **Call** Click to call the Play On Phone Number when you need to play or record a greeting.
- **Send An E-Mail Message To My Inbox When I Miss A Phone Call** Use this option to receive an alert in your Inbox when you miss a call.

Using Outlook on the Web

Outlook 2007 includes several features that integrate its functionality with the Internet. This section explores these features, including a look at browsing the Web with Outlook 2007 and connecting to Exchange Server through the Hypertext Transfer Protocol (HTTP).

Browsing the Web with Outlook

The integration of Outlook 2007 with Internet Explorer allows you to browse the Internet without leaving Outlook 2007. This feature is handy when you need to retrieve a file, view online documents, or otherwise access data on the Web but don't want to open Internet Explorer. The Outlook 2007 ability to browse the Web allows you to continue working in a single interface and avoid switching between open applications.

The Web toolbar includes an Address box in which you can enter the URL for a Web-related resource, such as a File Transfer Protocol (FTP) site or a Web site, as shown in Figure 4-38. To view a site in Outlook 2007, type the URL in the Address box, and then press Enter. Alternatively, you can click the arrow next to the Address box to select a URL that you've visited previously. (Please note that using the Outlook 2007 interface to view a Web site will change the Web site's appearance and content.) The Stop and Refresh buttons on the toolbar perform the same function they do in Internet Explorer.

When you want to go back to working with your Outlook 2007 folders, simply select the folder you need from the Navigation Pane or the Folder List.

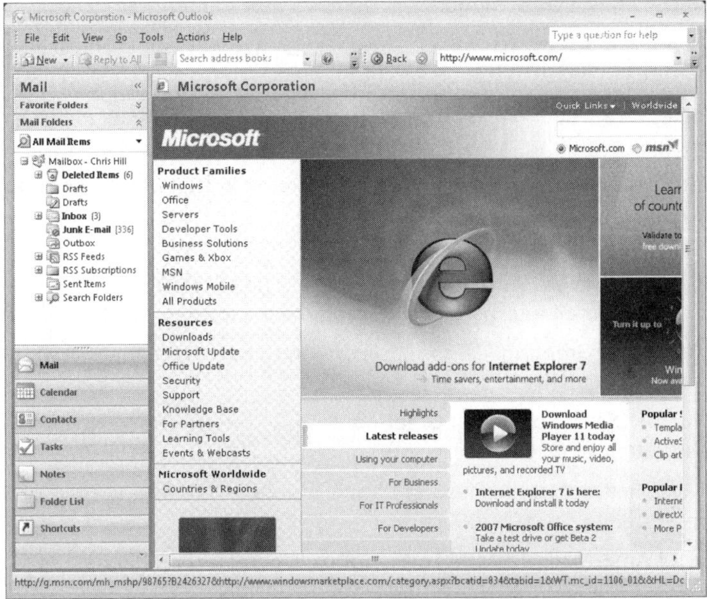

Figure 4-38. You can use Outlook 2007 to browse Web sites and other Web resources.

Connecting to Exchange Server with HTTP

Outlook 2007 includes support for connecting to Exchange Server with HTTP, the standard protocol used to access Web sites. HTTP access to Exchange Server in Outlook 2007 is not the same as using Outlook Web Access (OWA) or Outlook Anywhere (the Exchange Server 2007 name for OWA) to view your mailbox from a Web browser. Instead, Outlook 2007 itself can use HTTP to send and receive messages and interact with your Exchange Server mailbox in other ways.

Using HTTP for access to a computer running Exchange Server provides greater flexibility for remote access with Outlook 2007 and simplifies network security configuration for Exchange Server and network administrators. Remote access and the use of HTTP in Outlook 2007 are covered in Chapter 43, "Working Offline and Remotely."

Accessing Your Mail Through a Browser

Outlook 2007 serves as a great client application for e-mail, but on occasion, you might want to use a simpler method of accessing your messages. For example, you might be out of town unexpectedly, without your computer, and realize that you need to read an important message. Or perhaps you'd like to check your office e-mail from home but don't have your Outlook 2007 configuration installed on your home computer.

Whatever the case, Exchange Server supports access to your Exchange Server mailbox through OWA.

Using OWA or Outlook Anywhere to access your Exchange Server mailbox doesn't require extensive configuration. You simply point your Web browser to the URL on the server that provides access to your mailbox. The URL varies according to how OWA is configured on the server, in addition to a few other considerations.

For a detailed look at using OWA or Outlook Anywhere to access your Exchange Server mailbox, see Chapter 44, "Accessing Your Outlook Items Through a Web Browser."

Configuring Windows Settings for Outlook

Although most of the settings you'll need to configure for Outlook 2007 are configured through the program itself, some settings in the underlying operating system have an impact on the way Outlook 2007 functions and displays your data. This section offers an overview of the settings you might consider reviewing or modifying for use with Outlook 2007.

Display Settings

Because Outlook 2007 packs a lot of information into a relatively small amount of space, your display resolution has some impact on the application's usefulness. You should configure your system for a screen resolution of at least a 1024 × 768 desktop, preferably larger, depending on the size of your monitor. This is particularly important if you're using multiple Outlook 2007 windows at one time.

To configure properties for the display, you use the Display icon in Microsoft Windows® Control Panel. You can also right-click the desktop and choose Properties to open the Display dialog box.

> **Note**
>
> A handful of freeware and shareware applications are available that let you create multiple virtual desktops to expand your available desktop space. A search of your favorite shareware site should turn up at least one or two such utilities. An application we particularly like for managing multiple monitors is UltraMon, from *www.ultramon.com.*

Regional Settings

The regional settings on your computer determine how the operating system displays time, dates, currency, and other localized data. Because Outlook 2007 uses these types of data extensively, configuring your regional settings properly is an important step in setting up for Outlook 2007. This step is especially important for your calendar if you use multiple time zones. To configure regional settings, use the Regional Settings or Regional Options icon in Control Panel.

Time Synchronization

Much of your Outlook 2007 data is time-sensitive. For example, e-mail messages have sent and received times, and meetings are scheduled for specific periods. If your system's clock isn't accurate, some of that data won't be accurate. You should make sure that your clock is set correctly and that the system maintains the accurate time. You can set the time either by using the Date/Time icon in Control Panel or by double-clicking the clock in the system tray.

You also can use synchronization tools to synchronize your computer with a time server. Such tools are available as third-party utilities for use with all Microsoft Windows platforms, and a search of your favorite download site should turn up a few. In addition, Windows XP clients can take advantage of the Windows Time Service (W32Time), which allows client computers to synchronize their time with domain controllers on their network. If you're not familiar with W32Time, check with your system administrator for help in setting it up.

Using Add-Ins

Outlook 2007 provides tremendous functionality right out of the box and could well serve all your needs. However, if you need additional features not provided directly by Outlook 2007, *add-ins* can help to extend Outlook 2007 functionality. Outlook 2007 includes a handful of such add-ins, and third-party developers can produce others.

Outlook 2007 supports two types of add-ins: application-specific (standard) add-ins and Component Object Model (COM) add-ins. Standard add-ins are the type supported by earlier versions of Microsoft Outlook, which allow a developer to add features to one Microsoft Office system application. Standard add-ins are not portable between Microsoft Office system applications. These add-ins are integrated into Outlook 2007 through dynamic-link libraries (DLLs).

COM add-ins use the Microsoft COM to allow shared functionality between the various Microsoft Office system applications. COM add-ins were added as new features in Microsoft Office 2000 and are therefore also available in Microsoft Office 2003 and Outlook 2007. These add-ins are integrated into Microsoft Office system applications, including Outlook 2007, through either DLLs or ActiveX® controls.

You install add-ins when you install the Microsoft Office system; the list of available add-ins depends on which options you select during installation. To view the installed add-ins, choose Tools, Trust Center, and then click the Add-Ins link. Click the drop-down list next to Manage. Choose Exchange Client Extensions to view, install, and enable or disable standard Outlook 2007 add-ins, and click COM Add-Ins to view, install, and enable or disable COM add-ins and control their loading behavior. With your choice selected, click Go to manage the settings.

For more information about different add-ins available for use with Outlook 2007, see "Outlook Add-Ins" on the companion CD.

Using Outlook Effectively

Other chapters in this book include sections that offer best-practice advice on using specific features, such as the calendar. This section of this chapter offers some best-practice advice overall on using Outlook 2007 effectively:

- **Integrate and take advantage of Outlook 2007.** If you have been using Outlook Express, Windows Mail, or another e-mail client instead of Outlook 2007, make the switch to Outlook 2007 for e-mail. Outlook 2007 integrates many of the contact-management and tracking features with e-mail, making it an extremely useful productivity tool. In addition, Outlook 2007 offers some exceptional features for gathering and organizing e-mail (such as search folders), making it an excellent choice for handling all or your e-mail needs.
- **Get organized.** Make extensive use of folders and categories to organize your messages, contacts, appointments, and other Outlook 2007 data. The better you organize your data, the easier it will be to find and work with it, making you that much more efficient. Don't just throw stuff into your Outlook 2007 folders–take the time to manage your data effectively. In particular, make use of categories and search folders to help you manage your e-mail, and use automatic formatting and color categories to organize your calendar.
- **Keep your Inbox cleared out.** Near the end of your workday, allocate a certain amount of time to work through your Inbox and respond to each message. Reply to those you can and move them into appropriate folders for archiving. Those you can't respond to because they require follow-up should be flagged for follow-up. The fewer messages you have in your Inbox at the end of the day, the greater your sense of accomplishment when you leave the office.
- **Take advantage of the Navigation Pane, Reading Pane, and To-Do Bar.** These Outlook 2007 features can help you quickly navigate Outlook 2007 to find the information you need. In Outlook 2007, the capability to minimize the Navigation Pane and To-Do Bar will give you a lot more window space to work with in your Outlook 2007 folders.

For more best-practice advice on using specific Outlook 2007 features, look for the appropriate sections at the end of selected chapters throughout this book.

CHAPTER 5

Creating and Using Categories

One of the primary functions of Microsoft® Outlook® 2007 is to help you organize your data, whether that data is a collection of contacts, a task list, your schedule, or a month's worth of messages. To make this easier, you can use Office Outlook 2007 *categories*, which are a combination of words or phrases and colors that you assign to Outlook 2007 items as a means of organizing the items. For example, you might assign the category Personal to a message from a family member to differentiate that message from your work-related messages and then customize the Inbox view to exclude personal items. A new feature in Outlook 2007 incorporates color with categories, making it easy to identify categories at a glance.

This chapter explains how categories work in Outlook 2007 and shows you how to work with the new color categories, add categories, assign categories to Outlook 2007 items, and use categories to arrange, display, and search Outlook 2007 data.

Understanding Categories

If you've used a personal finance or checkbook program such as Microsoft Money or Intuit Quicken, you're probably familiar with categories. In these programs, you can assign a category to each check, deposit, or other transaction and then view all transactions for a specific category, perhaps printing them in a report for tax purposes. For example, you might use categories to keep track of business expenses and separate them by certain criteria, such as reimbursement policy or tax deductions.

Outlook 2007 categories perform essentially the same function: you can assign categories to Outlook 2007 items and manipulate the data based on those categories. For example, you might use categories to assign Outlook 2007 items such as messages and tasks to a specific project. You could then quickly locate all items related to that project. Or you might use categories to differentiate personal contacts from business contacts. Whatever your need for organization, categories offer a handy and efficient way to achieve your goal.

Note

Outlook 2007 combines colors with categories, giving you the capability to see category assignment at a glance. As you'll learn later in this chapter, you can still use categories without color, simply by assigning the color None to the category.

What can you do with categories? First, with the new integration of color with categories, you can tell instantly what category is assigned to a given item. For example, let's say you create a rule that assigns the Red category to all messages from a particular contact. You can then tell at a glance–without doing anything else–which messages are from that person. Or perhaps you assign the Red category to business messages and Green to personal. Whatever the case, color categories are a great means for visually identifying specific types of messages.

After you assign a category to each relevant Outlook 2007 item, you can sort, search, and organize your data according to the category. Figure 5-1, for example, shows the Advanced Find dialog box after a search for all Outlook 2007 items assigned to the category Toy Show. Figure 5-2 shows the Contacts folder organized by category, displaying all contacts who are involved in the toy show. The ability to search by category makes it easy to find all the items associated with a specific project, contract, issue, or general category.

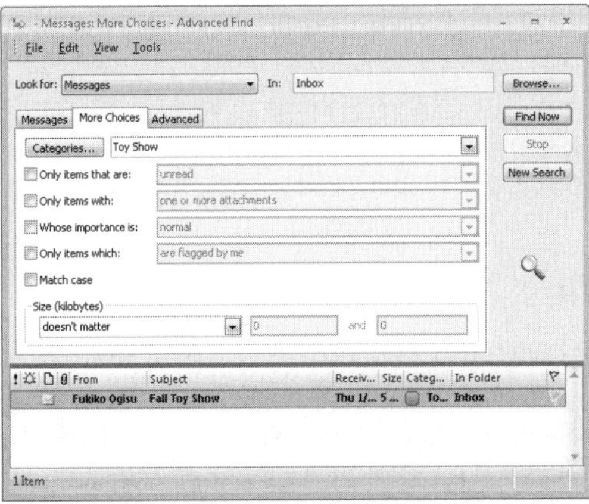

Figure 5-1. The Advanced Find dialog box displays the results of a search for all Toy Show items.

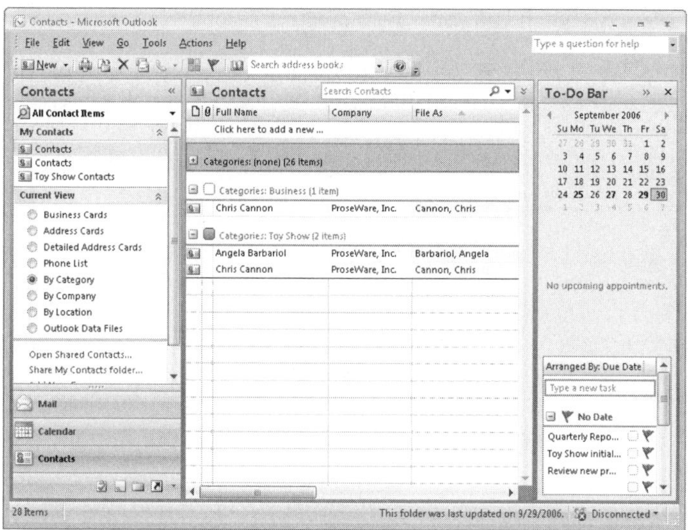

Figure 5-2. You can group contacts by category to list all contacts involved in a particular event or project.

Categories are useful only if you apply them consistently. After you become disciplined in using categories and begin to assign them out of habit, you'll wonder how you ever organized your day without them.

CAUTION!

The Master Category List in earlier versions of Microsoft Outlook has been removed in Outlook 2007. Categories listed in the Master Category List but not assigned to any items are not imported when you upgrade to Outlook 2007.

Customizing Your Category List

Before you assign categories to Outlook 2007 items, you should go through the category list and add the categories you need or tailor the existing categories to suit your needs. To determine which categories to add, spend some time thinking about how you intend to use them, including which colors you want to apply to specific categories. Although you can always add and modify categories later, creating the majority up front not only saves time but also helps you organize your thoughts and plan the use of categories more effectively.

Follow these steps when you're ready to create categories:

1. Open the Color Categories dialog box, shown in Figure 5-3, by selecting any item in Outlook 2007 and choosing Edit, Categorize, All Categories or by right-clicking an item and choosing Categorize, All Categories on the shortcut menu.

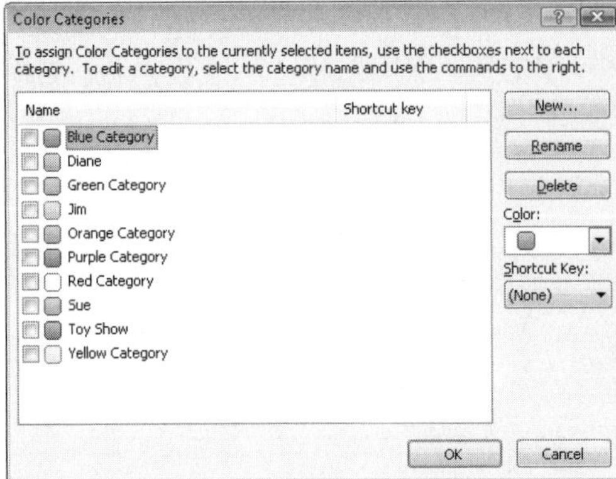

Figure 5-3. You can add a new category in the Color Categories dialog box.

2. Click New to open the Add New Category dialog box.
3. Type the new category name in the Name field, select a color in the Color drop-down list, optionally specify a shortcut key, and then click OK.

Note

Select None in the Color drop-down list if you want a text-only category.

4. Repeat steps 2 and 3 to add other categories as desired, and then click OK to close the Color Categories dialog box.

Note

When you create a new category, Outlook 2007 automatically adds the category to the selected item. You must deselect the category if you don't want it assigned to the selected item. For information about creating new categories while you are assigning categories to an item, see the next section, "Assigning Categories to Outlook Items."

The categories you add to your category list depend entirely on the types of tasks you perform with Outlook 2007, your type of business or organization, and your preferences. The following list suggests ways to categorize business-related data:

- Track items by project type or project name.
- Organize contacts by their type (for example, managers, assistants, technical experts, and financial advisors).
- Keep track of departmental assignments.
- Track different types of documents (for example, drafts, works in progress, and final versions).
- Track contacts by sales potential (for example, 30-day or 60-day).

Organize items by priority. The following list offers suggestions for categorizing personal data:

- Use color to identify critical or urgent issues.
- Organize personal contacts by type (friends, family, insurance agents, legal advisors, and medical contacts, for starters).
- Track items by area of interest.
- Organize items for hobbies.
- Track items related to vacation or other activities.

Assigning Categories to Outlook Items

Assigning categories to items is easy. You can assign multiple categories to each item if needed. For example, a particular contact might be involved in more than one project, so you might assign a category for each project to that contact. If you have a task that must be performed for multiple projects, you might assign those project categories to the task.

With the addition of color in Outlook 2007 categories, assigning multiple categories adds a new dimension. Outlook 2007 will display multiple colors for an item, depending on its type and location. For example, if you assign the Red, Blue, and Green categories to an e-mail message, Outlook 2007 displays each of those three color indicators in the message header, as shown in Figure 5-4. You can resize the Categories column if you want Outlook 2007 to show indicators for all of the assigned categories.

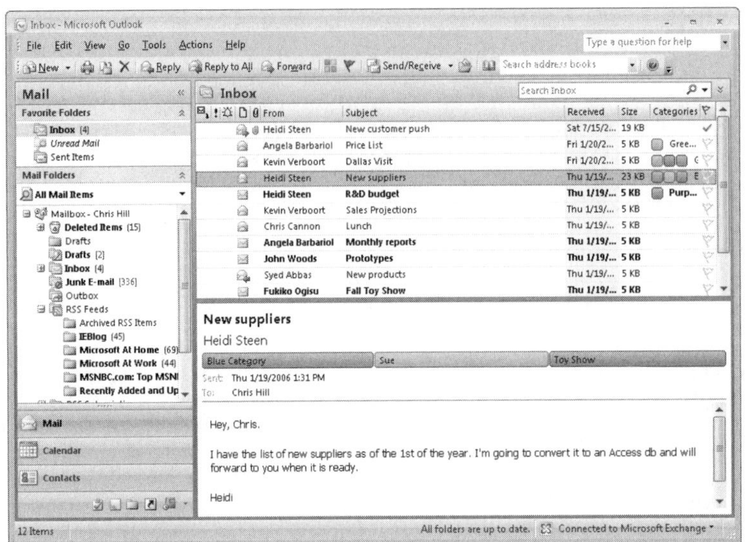

Figure 5-4. Outlook 2007 can show multiple color categories in the message header to indicate multiple categories.

In Calendar view, Outlook 2007 displays the item using the last color you assigned and places as many color indicators as it can in the item label. So if you add the Blue, Green, and Red categories, Outlook 2007 colors the item as Red and puts Blue and Green indicators in the item for the Day and Week views. In Month view, you see only the last color assigned.

To learn how to assign categories to existing items, see the next section, "Assigning Categories to Existing Outlook Items."

Follow these steps to assign categories to a new item:

1. Open the folder in which you want to create the item, and then click New.
2. Use one of the following methods to display the Categories list, depending on the type of item you're creating:

   Message On the Ribbon, click Categorize in the Options group on the Message tab.

   Calendar On the Ribbon, click Categorize in the Options group on the Appointment or Event tab.

   Contact On the Ribbon, click Categorize in the Options group on the Contact tab.

   Task On the Ribbon, click Categorize in the Options group on the Task tab.

> **Note** Click the menu button in the upper-left corner of the note window, and then choose Categorize.

3. Select a single category on the shortcut menu, or click All Categories, and in the Color Categories dialog box, select all the categories that pertain to the item. If you need to add a category, simply click Add.
4. Click OK to close the Color Categories dialog box and continue creating the item.

As you can see in step 3, you can create a category on the fly when you're assigning categories to an item. However, a drawback to creating categories on the fly is that you might not enter the category names consistently. As a result, you could end up with more than one version of a given category. As you might expect, Outlook 2007 treats category names literally, so any difference between two names, however minor, makes those categories different. Searching for one won't turn up items assigned to the other.

Assigning Categories to Existing Outlook Items

Often you will want to add categories to existing Outlook 2007 items. For example, you will likely want to categorize e-mail messages after they arrive. The easiest way to assign a category to an existing item is to right-click the item, choose Categorize, and then choose a category from the shortcut menu, as shown in Figure 5-5. You can use this method for any of the Outlook 2007 items.

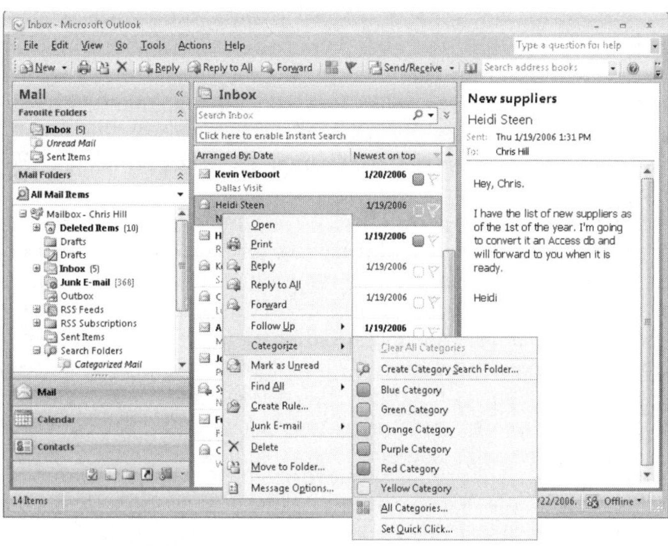

Figure 5-5. Right-click and choose a color category from the shortcut menu.

Assigning a Quick Click Category

Outlook 2007 offers the capability to quickly assign a category with a single click. In message folders, with the Reading Pane displayed on the right, you can click the Category column to assign a Quick Click category. You can also click the Category column in the To-Do Bar to assign a category to tasks in the same way.

Follow these steps to specify the Quick Click category:

1. Choose Edit, Categorize, Set Quick Click to open the Set Quick Click dialog box, shown in Figure 5-6.

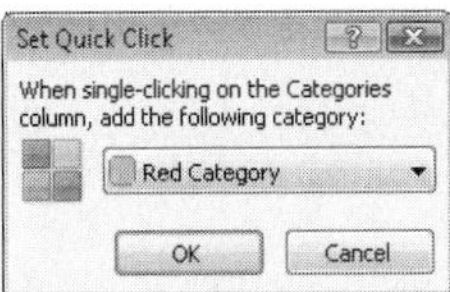

Figure 5-6. Use the Set Quick Click dialog box to specify the Quick Click category.

2. Select a category, and then click OK.

Assigning Categories Automatically

You can easily assign categories when you create an item, but you might prefer to simplify the process for items that will be assigned to the same category (or set of categories). For example, if you frequently create e-mail messages that have specific category assignments, you could bypass the steps involved in adding the categories to each new message. You can accomplish this by using an e-mail template.

For a detailed discussion of templates, see Chapter 25, "Using Templates."

You can use templates for other Outlook 2007 items as well. Simply create the template, assign categories to it as needed, and then save it with a name that will help you easily identify the category assignments or the function of the template. When you need to create a message with that specific set of category assignments, you can create it from the template rather than from scratch. Because the category assignments are stored in the template, new items created from the template are assigned those categories. Using templates to assign categories not only saves you the time involved in adding categories individually but also ensures that the category assignments are consistent. (For example, you won't misspell a name or forget to add a category.)

A more likely possibility is that you want to add categories to e-mail messages when they arrive. You can create a rule to assign one or more categories to messages when they arrive or even when you send them. For example, let's say you subscribe to six newsletters and you want Outlook 2007 to highlight them in the Inbox with the Green category. A great way to do that is to assign the color category to the messages based on the recipient address or other unique characteristics of the messages.

To learn how to create and manage rules in Outlook 2007, see Chapter 11, "Processing Messages Automatically with Rules."

Modifying Categories and Category Assignments

At some point, you'll want to recategorize Outlook 2007 items—that is, you'll want to add, remove, or modify their category assignments. For example, when one project ends and another begins, some of your contacts will move to a different project, and you'll want to change the categories assigned to the contact items. Perhaps you've added some new categories to further organize your data and want to assign those categories to existing items. Or perhaps you made a mistake when you created an item or assigned categories to it, and now you need to make changes. Whatever the case, changing categories and category assignments is easy.

Changing Existing Categories

For one reason or another, you might need to change a category. You might have misspelled the category when you created it, or you might want to change the wording a little. For example, you might delete the category Foes and create a new one named Friends to replace it (assuming that your friends are not really foes). Unlike in earlier versions of Microsoft Outlook, you can change existing categories in Outlook 2007. When you change a category, all items assigned to that category are updated.

For example, assume that you have created a category named Dallas Toy Show and made the category red. You open the Inbox and assign the category to several messages. Then you open the calendar and assign the category to a few meetings. A week later, you discover that the toy show is moving to Seattle. So you open the Color Categories dialog box and rename the category Seattle Toy Show and change the color to blue. When you look in the Inbox, all of the messages with that assigned category now show the new name and color. Likewise, the appointments in the calendar also show the new name and color.

INSIDE OUT **View by category to change categories**

You'll find that one method works well when you want to make the same change to multiple items, such as changing the categories assigned to contacts. That method is to view the items organized by category. For example, assume that you want to view all of the contacts that have the Foes category and then add the Friends category. Choose View, Arrange By, Categories (for some views, you can choose View, Current View, By Category). Find the Foes category, open one contact in the group, and add the Friends category (simply change *Foes* to *Friends*). The item now appears under the Friends category group. Click on the category heading for Foes and drag it to the category heading for Friends. Outlook 2007 adds the Friends category to these contacts.

If you need to change a category globally rather than add one, see "Changing Category Assignments of Multiple Items at One Time" later in this chapter.

Earlier in this chapter, you learned how to create new categories. Changing a category is much like adding a new one.

Follow these steps to modify a category:

1. In Outlook 2007, select any item, and then choose Edit, Categorize, All Categories.
2. In the Color Categories dialog box, click a category to select it.
3. Click Rename, and then type a new name for the category.
4. Select a new color in the Color drop-down list.
5. Click OK to close the Color Categories dialog box.

Changing Category Assignments

You can assign categories to an item at any time, adding and removing the categories you want. To change the categories assigned to a specific item, follow these steps:

1. In Outlook 2007, locate the item for which you want to change the category assignment.
2. Select the item and choose Edit, Categorize, or right-click the item and choose Categorize on the shortcut menu.
3. Select a new category in the drop-down list, or choose All Categories to open the Color Categories dialog box, and then assign or remove multiple categories.

Changing Category Assignments of Multiple Items at One Time

In some cases, you'll want to change the category assignments of several items at one time. For example, assume that you've assigned the category Seattle Toy Show to 50 messages in your Inbox. (You really should do a better job of cleaning out your Inbox!) Now you want to clear the categories on all of those messages. You could change the messages one at a time, or you could hold down Ctrl, select each message, and then change the category. But for a larger number of items, there is an easier way—the trick is to use a view organized by category:

1. Open the folder containing the items whose categories you want to change.
2. Choose View, Arrange By, Categories.
3. Locate the items under the category you want to change.

4. If the category you want to assign to the items has not been assigned yet to any items, assign the category to one item. That item should now show up in the view under its category.

5. Click on the category you are changing, and drag it to the target category.

An important point to understand when using this method to change categories is that Outlook 2007 assigns the target category (the one on which you drop the items) exclusively to the items. For example, assume that you have several items with Red, Blue, and Green category assignments. You drag those items to the Yellow category. All of the items now have *only* the Yellow category. The other categories are removed.

If you want to assign categories to a group of items, you have a couple of different methods from which to choose. If the number of items is relatively small, hold down the Ctrl key, select each item, and then right-click an item and choose Categorize, followed by a category selection. Or choose All Categories to assign multiple new categories.

> **Note**
>
> A list view usually works best when you need to select multiple items.

If you need to change a lot of items, first organize the view by category (choose View, Arrange By, Categories). Then right-click the category whose items you want to change, choose Categorize, and then choose a new category (or choose All Categories to modify multiple categories). Outlook 2007 displays a warning message informing you that the action will be applied to all items in the selected category. Click OK to continue with the change.

Organizing Data with Categories

Now that you've created your personal category list and faithfully assigned categories to all your data in Outlook 2007, how do you put those categories to work for you? Searching for items with given categories is a good example of how you can use categories to organize and sort your data: by specifying those categories in the Advanced Find dialog box, you can compile a list of items to which those categories have been assigned.

You also can sort items by category. To do so, follow these steps:

1. Open the folder containing the items that you want to sort. If the Categories field isn't displayed, right-click the column bar, and then choose Field Chooser.

2. Drag the Categories field to the column bar, and then close the Field Chooser dialog box.

3. Right-click the Categories column, and then choose Group By This Field.

As an alternative to this method, you can use the predefined Categories view. With the folder open, choose View, Arrange By, Categories to display a tabular view sorted by categories.

Note

To clear groupings, right-click the Categories column, and choose Don't Group By This Field.

Viewing Selected Categories Only

In many situations, it's beneficial to be able to restrict a view to show only selected categories. For example, perhaps you want to view all messages that have the Toy Show and Travel Required categories. Whatever the case, you can use a couple of methods to view only items with specific category assignments.

First you can use a custom, filtered view to filter only those items that fit your criteria. Follow these steps to customize a view to show selected categories:

1. Open the Outlook 2007 folder that contains the items you want to view.
2. Choose View, Current View, Customize Current View.
3. In the Customize View dialog box, click Filter.
4. In the Filter dialog box, click the More Choices tab, as shown in Figure 5-7.

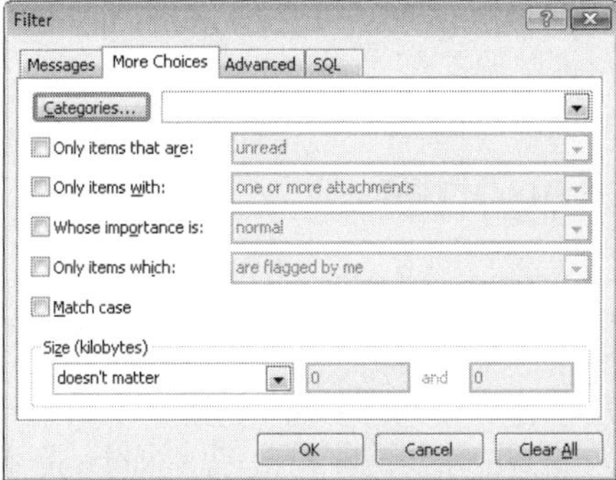

Figure 5-7. Use the More Choices tab in the Filter dialog box to create a custom view.

5. On the More Choices tab, click Categories, select the categories you want to view, and then click OK.
6. Click OK in the Filter dialog box, and then click OK in the Customize View dialog box to view the filtered view.

See Chapter 27, "Creating Custom Views and Print Styles," to learn more about working with custom views.

Chapter 5

Another way to view items with only selected categories, provided you are working with a mail folder, is a search folder. You can create a new search folder that shows only messages with the desired categories. Follow these steps to create the search folder:

1. Right-click Search Folders in the folder list (Navigation Pane), and then choose New Search Folder. Or click the arrow next to New on the Standard toolbar, and then choose Search Folder.
2. In the New Search Folder dialog box, shown in Figure 5-8, scroll to the bottom of the list, select Create A Custom Search Folder, and then click Choose.

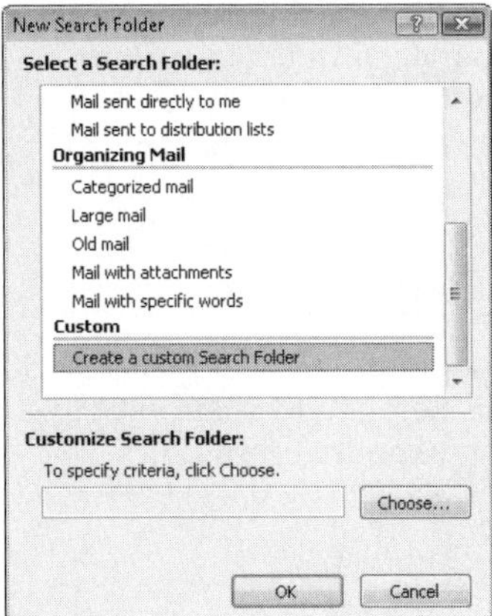

Figure 5-8. Create a custom search folder in the New Search Folder dialog box.

3. In the Custom Search Folder dialog box, shown in Figure 5-9, type a name for the search folder in the Name field.

Figure 5-9. Specify properties in the Custom Search Folder dialog box.

4. Click Criteria to open the Search Folder Criteria dialog box, and then click More Choices.
5. Click Categories, and then select the categories to include in the search folder.
6. Click OK twice to return to the Custom Search Folder dialog box.
7. Click Browse, select the folders to be included in the search, and then click OK.
8. Click OK in the Custom Search Folder dialog box, and then click OK to close the New Search Folder dialog box.

See Chapter 10, "Finding and Organizing Messages," to learn more about creating and using search folders.

Sharing a Category List

If you work in a department, or if you share similar tasks and responsibilities with others, it's helpful to be able to share the same set of categories with those other users. Doing so helps to ensure that everyone is using the same categories, an important point when you're sharing items or receiving items from others that have categories assigned to them. For example, assume that your department is working on a handful of projects. Having everyone use the same project category names helps you organize your Outlook 2007 items and ensures that searches or sorts based on a given project display all items related to the project, including those you've received from others.

Sharing Categories with a Registry File

Outlook 2007 stores your category list in the Calendar folder as a hidden Outlook 2007 item, not in a file. This means that you can't simply share a file to share your categories. Instead, you can create a registry file to share categories.

CAUTION!

An incorrect modification to the registry can prevent Outlook 2007 from running or could even prevent Microsoft Windows® from starting. Be careful when editing the registry.

These steps outline the registry method, which copies categories into the registry:

1. Open Notepad, and then add the following text to the file:

```
Windows Registry Editor Version 5.00

[HKEY_CURRENT_USER\Software\Microsoft\Office\12.0\Outlook\Preferences]
"NewCategories"="Toy Show;New Products;Research"
```

2. In the text string, replace *"Toy Show;New Products;Research"* with your own category names, separating each category from the next with a semicolon.
3. Save the file with a .reg file name extension, and then close Notepad.

At this point, you have a registry file that other Outlook 2007 users can use to import the category list into their systems. Place the .reg file on a network share where the other users can access it, or share it on a CD, a USB drive, or other media. Then have the other users simply double-click the file to add the categories to their registry.

Sharing Categories with E-Mail

Another (and perhaps easier) way to share categories is through e-mail. By default, Outlook 2007 strips categories out of incoming messages so that they are not added automatically to your category list. Outlook 2007 uses a rule to enforce this behavior. If you turn off the rule, categories arrive with incoming messages. However, only the category text arrives; the color is set to None for these categories, but you can modify the categories to add your own color.

Follow these steps to turn off the rule:

1. Choose Tools, Rules And Alerts.
2. In the Rules And Alerts dialog box, clear the Clear Categories On Mail rule.
3. Click OK.

> **Note**
>
> In Microsoft Exchange Server 2007, Clear Categories is enabled by default and is controlled by the server administrator, so the Clear Categories On Mail rule does not appear in the Rules And Alerts dialog box for Exchange Server 2007 accounts. See the Exchange Server 2007 Help documentation for the Set-TransportConfig command to learn how to enable and disable Clear Categories for Exchange Server 2007.

With the rule turned off on the recipients' systems, you can now create a message, assign to it all of the categories you want to share, and then send the message. Follow these steps to add the categories to the outgoing message:

1. Start a new message.
2. In the message form, click the small arrow in the Options area on the Message tab.
3. In the Message Options dialog box, click Categories, and then assign categories to the message as desired.
4. Close the Message Options dialog box, and then send the message.

> **Note**
>
> You can use two registry settings to control whether Outlook 2007 will strip out categories for outgoing and incoming messages. These settings reside in HKEY_CURRENT_USER\Software\Microsoft\Office\12.0\Outlook\Preferences (although the settings do not exist by default). The setting AcceptCategories controls incoming messages, and the setting SendPersonalCategories controls outgoing messages.

Using Categories Effectively

The addition of color categories in Outlook 2007 makes categories even more useful and extends the ways you can use categories to manage your schedule, messages, and other items in Outlook 2007. Like most Outlook 2007 features, categories are not in themselves useful–it's how you use them that makes them useful. Here is a handful of tips for using categories effectively:

- **Create your categories first.** By creating your category list up front before you start assigning categories, you force yourself to take the time to think about what categories you need and how you will use them. What makes sense for someone else might not fit your needs, and vice versa. This doesn't mean that you can't add categories after the fact or change the way you use categories, but some planning up front will help ensure that you get the most out of categorization.
- **Use categories in combination with folders to organize messages.** Categories offer an excellent means for you to organize your Outlook 2007 data. Some people use folders to organize their messages; others use categories exclusively to manage their messages, keeping everything in the Inbox but assigning categories so that they can quickly identify messages. The best approach falls between, with a combination of folders and categories. Use categories to classify messages, but also use folders to organize those messages. For example, you might create a folder named Toy Show to store all messages relating to the upcoming toy show and then use categories to further classify messages in that folder.
- **Use search folders in combination with categories.** After you have categorized your messages, you can use search folders to quickly locate all messages with specified categories. Search folders give you the benefit of potentially searching all of your message folders for specific items, enabling you to quickly locate all items with a specific category, regardless of where they are stored. Take some time to consider which search folders will best suit your needs, and then create them.
- **Rely on colors to help you visually identify items.** Although you can create categories with no color, color will help you tell at a glance that a given message, appointment, or other item fits a specific category. For example, you might color all of your important meetings in red, personal appointments in green, and optional appointments or meetings in yellow. The ability to tell at a glance what an item is will help improve your productivity and effectiveness.
- **Assign color categories to messages using rules.** Although you can certainly assign colors to messages manually, you should also take advantage of rules to assign categories for you automatically. For example, you might categorize messages from specific senders so that you can easily identify them in your Inbox. Or use categories to identify messages from mailing lists, friends, and so on.
- **Identify your most commonly used category.** Determine which category you use the most, and define that category as your Quick Click category. You can then assign that category with a single click of the mouse.

PART 2

E-Mail and Other Messaging

CHAPTER 6
Managing Address Books and Distribution Lists

An e-mail program isn't very useful without the capability to store addresses. Microsoft® Office Outlook® 2007, like other e-mail–enabled applications, has this storage capability. In fact, Office Outlook 2007 offers multiple address books that can help make sending messages easy and efficient.

This chapter explores how Outlook 2007 stores addresses and explains how Outlook 2007 interacts with Microsoft Exchange Server (which has its own address lists) to provide addressing services. You'll learn how to store addresses in the Outlook 2007 Contacts folder and use them to address messages, meeting requests, appointments, and more. You'll also learn how to create distribution lists to broadcast messages and other items to groups of users and how to hide the details of the distribution list from recipients. The chapter concludes with a look at how you can share your address books with others.

> **Note**
>
> Although this chapter discusses the Contacts folder in the context of address lists, it doesn't cover this folder in detail.

For a detailed discussion of using and managing the Contacts folder, see Chapter 18, "Creating and Managing Your Contacts."

Understanding Address Books

As you begin working with addresses in Outlook 2007, you'll find that you can store them in multiple locations. For example, if you're using an Exchange Server account, you have a couple of locations from which to select addresses. Understanding where these address books reside is an important first step in putting them to work for you. The following sections describe the various address books in Outlook 2007 and how you can use them.

Outlook 2007 Address Book

On all installations, including those with no e-mail accounts, Outlook 2007 creates a default Outlook Address Book (OAB). This address book consolidates all your Outlook 2007 Contacts folders. With a new installation of Outlook 2007, the OAB shows only one location for storing addresses: the default Contacts folder. As you add other Contacts folders, those additional folders appear in the OAB, as shown in Figure 6-1. As you'll learn in the section "Removing Contacts Folders from the OAB" later in this chapter, you can configure additional Contacts folders so that they don't appear in the OAB.

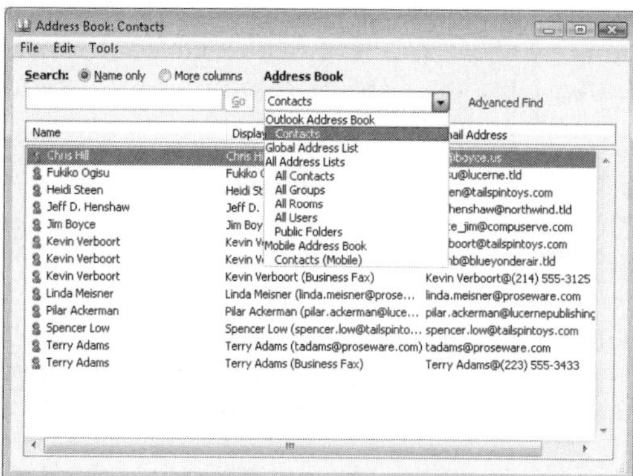

Figure 6-1. The OAB shows all Contacts folders for your profile.

For detailed information on creating and using additional Contacts folders, see "Creating Other Contacts Folders" in Chapter 18.

The OAB functions as a virtual address book collection instead of as an address book because Outlook 2007 doesn't store the OAB as a file separate from your data store. Instead, the OAB provides a view into your Contacts folders.

> **Note**
>
> Earlier versions of Office Outlook enabled users to store addresses in Personal Address Books (PABs), which were kept in separate files from the personal data store. Although PABs are no longer available in Outlook 2007, you can import them into the OAB.

Global Address List (GAL)

When you use a profile that contains an Exchange Server account, you'll find one other address list in addition to the OAB: the Global Address List (GAL). This address list resides on the Exchange Server and presents the list of mailboxes on the server as well as other address items created on the server, including distribution groups and external addresses (see Figure 6-2). However, end users can't create address information in the GAL; only the Exchange Server system administrator can do this.

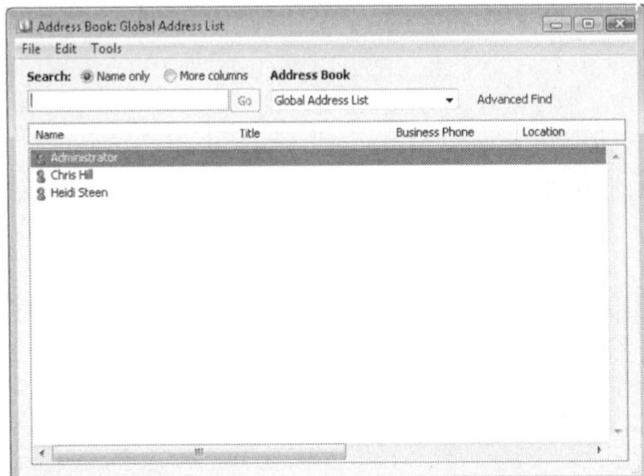

Figure 6-2. The Global Address List shows addresses on the Exchange Server.

LDAP (Internet Directory Services)

Some e-mail addresses are not available in the OAB or GAL but are available using Lightweight Directory Access Protocol (LDAP). This requires network connectivity to the LDAP server.

Details on configuration are found in Chapter 17, "Using LDAP Directory Services."

Other Address Lists

In addition to the OAB, GAL, and LDAP, you might see other address sources when you look for addresses in Outlook 2007. For example, in an organization with a large address list, the Exchange Server system administrator might create additional address lists to filter the view to show only a selection, such as contacts with last names starting with the letter A or contacts external to the organization. You might also see a list named All Address Lists. This list, which comes from Exchange Server, can be modified by the Exchange Server administrator to include additional address lists. The list can also include Public Folders (see Figure 6-3), which can store shared contacts. In addition, the list by default includes All Contacts, All Groups, All Rooms, and All Users, which sort addresses by type.

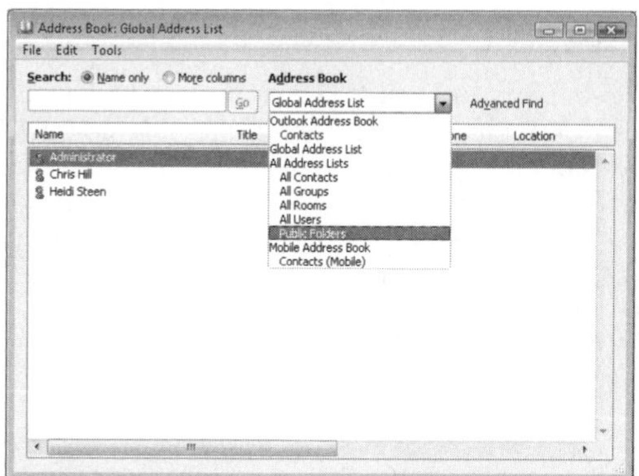

Figure 6-3. Additional address lists can display filtered lists of contacts.

Configuring Address Books and Addressing Options

Outlook 2007 offers a handful of settings you can use to configure the way your address books display contacts and address information. You also can add other address books and choose which address book Outlook 2007 uses by default for opening and storing addresses and processing messages.

Setting the Contacts Display Option for the OAB

You can set only one option for the OAB. This setting controls the order in which Outlook 2007 displays names from the OAB: either First Name, Last Name or Last Name, First Name.

Follow these steps to set this display option:

1. If Outlook 2007 is open, choose Tools, Account Settings, and then select the Address Books tab. If Outlook 2007 is not open, right-click the Outlook icon on the desktop or on the Start menu, choose Properties, click E-Mail Accounts, and then select the Address Books tab.
2. Select Outlook Address Book and click Change to display the Microsoft Office Outlook Address Book dialog box, shown in Figure 6-4.
3. In the Show Names By box, select the display format you prefer. Click Close, and then click Close.

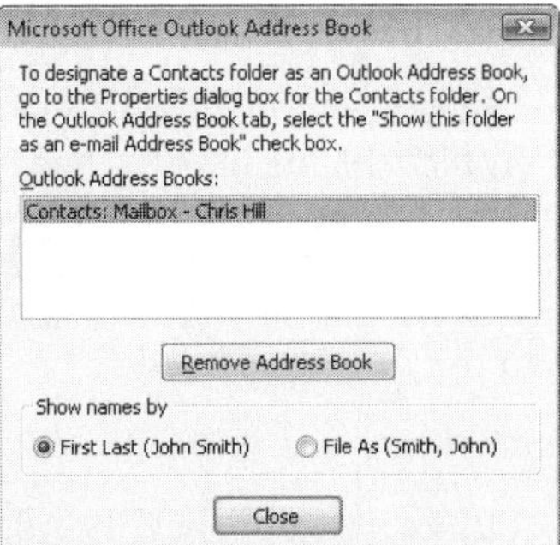

Figure 6-4. Select the display option for Outlook Address Book entries in the Microsoft Outlook Address Book dialog box.

Removing Contacts Folders from the OAB

In most cases, you'll want all your Contacts folders to appear in the OAB. If you have several Contacts folders, however, you might prefer to limit how many folders appear in the OAB or you might simply want to restrict the folders to ensure that specific addresses are used.

You can set the folder's properties to determine whether it appears in the OAB by following these steps:

1. Open Outlook 2007 and open the folders list (or click the Contacts button in the Navigation Pane). Then right-click the Contacts folder in question and choose Properties.
2. Click the Outlook Address Book tab and clear the Show This Folder As An E-Mail Address Book option to prevent the folder from appearing in the OAB.
3. Change the folder name, if necessary, and then click OK.

> **Note**
>
> You can't remove the default Contacts folder from the OAB.

Setting Other Addressing Options

You can configure other addressing options to determine which address book Outlook 2007 displays by default for selecting addresses, which address book is used by default for storing new addresses, and the order in which address books are processed when Outlook 2007 checks names for sending messages. The following sections explain these options in detail.

Selecting the Default Address Book for Lookup

To suit your needs or preferences, you can have Outlook 2007 display a different address list by default. For example, for profiles that include Exchange Server accounts, Outlook 2007 displays the GAL by default. If you use the GAL only infrequently and primarily use your Contacts folders for addressing, you might prefer to have Outlook 2007 show the OAB as the default address list instead of the GAL. Or you might want to display a filtered address list other than the GAL on the server.

Follow these steps to specify the default address list:

1. In Outlook 2007, choose Tools, Address Book or click the Address Book icon on the toolbar. Outlook 2007 displays the Address Book dialog box (see Figure 6-5).

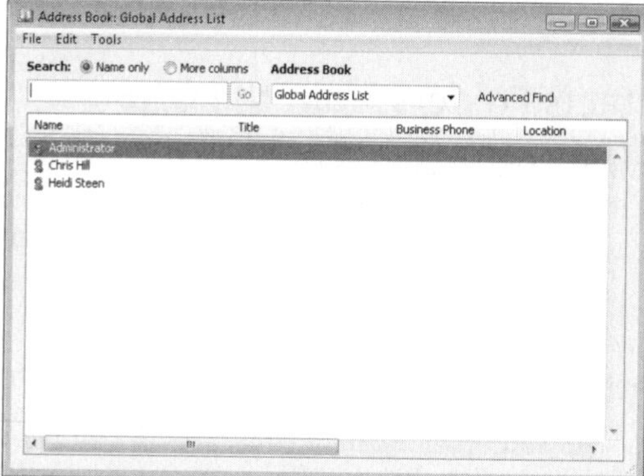

Figure 6-5. You can specify the default address list in the Address Book dialog box.

2. Choose Tools, Options.
3. In the Addressing dialog box, select the default address list from the Show This Address List First drop-down list.
4. Click OK.

Specifying the Default Address Book for New Entries

You can choose which address book you want to use for personal addresses. Although you can't store these addresses in the GAL or other server address books, you can store them in your OAB. When you create a new address in the New Entry dialog box, Outlook 2007 suggests storing the entry in the address book you have chosen as the default. If you want to store a particular address in a different address book, you can do so by clicking the Put This Entry In The option and selecting the address book from the drop-down list (see Figure 6-6).

Figure 6-6. Use the Addressing dialog box to determine where to store addresses.

> **Note**
>
> The OAB is the default location for storing personal addresses. Keep in mind, however, that you don't actually store addresses in the OAB itself. Instead, you store addresses in your Contacts folder, which appears as your OAB.

Follow these steps to specify the default location for storing new personal addresses:

1. Open the Address Book window and choose Tools, Options.
2. Select the default address location for personal addresses from the Keep Personal Address In drop-down list.
3. Click OK.

Specifying How Names Are Checked

When you create a message, you can specify the recipient's name instead of specifying the address. Instead of typing **jim@boyce.us**, for example, you might type **Jim Boyce** and let Outlook 2007 convert the name to an address for you. This saves you the time of opening the address book to look for the entry if you know the name under which it's stored.

When you click Send to process the message, Outlook 2007 checks the address books to determine the correct address based on the name you entered. Outlook 2007 checks names from multiple address books if they are defined in the current profile. For example, Outlook 2007 might process the address through the GAL first, then through your OAB, and then through the LDAP (assuming that all three are in the profile). If Outlook

2007 finds a match, it replaces the name in the message with the appropriate address. If it doesn't find a match or finds more than one, it displays the Check Names dialog box, shown in Figure 6-7, in which you can select the correct address, create a new one, or open the address book to display more names and then select an address.

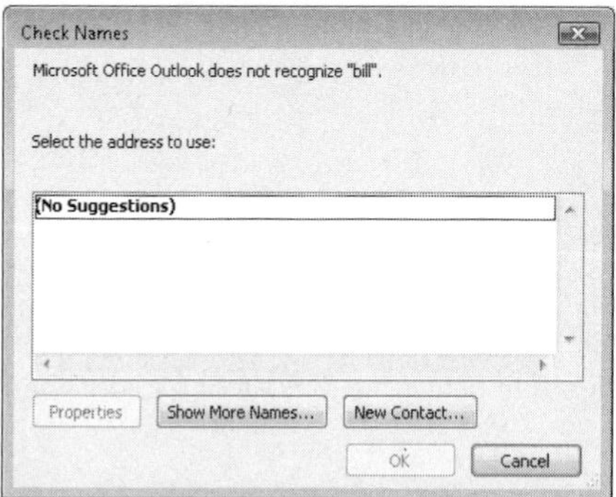

Figure 6-7. The Check Names dialog box helps you resolve address problems before you send a message.

Why change the order in which Outlook 2007 checks your address books? If most of your addresses are stored in an address book other than the one Outlook 2007 is currently checking first, changing the order can speed up name checking, particularly if the address book contains numerous entries.

Here's how to change the address book order:

1. In Outlook 2007, open the Address Book window and choose Tools, Options.
2. Click an address book and then click the up and down arrow buttons that appear with the When Sending Mail list to rearrange the address book order in the list.
3. Click OK to close the dialog box.

Creating Address Book Entries

To quickly create a contact while you're composing a message, type the e-mail address in the To, Cc, or Bcc field, and then press Tab. The e-mail address becomes underlined. Right-click the e-mail address and select Add To Outlook Contacts (see Figure 6-8). You can also create new contacts, distribution groups, and other types of entries from any navigation pane. To do this, select the drop-down arrow next to the New button on the main window's Menu bar and choose the type of item to create.

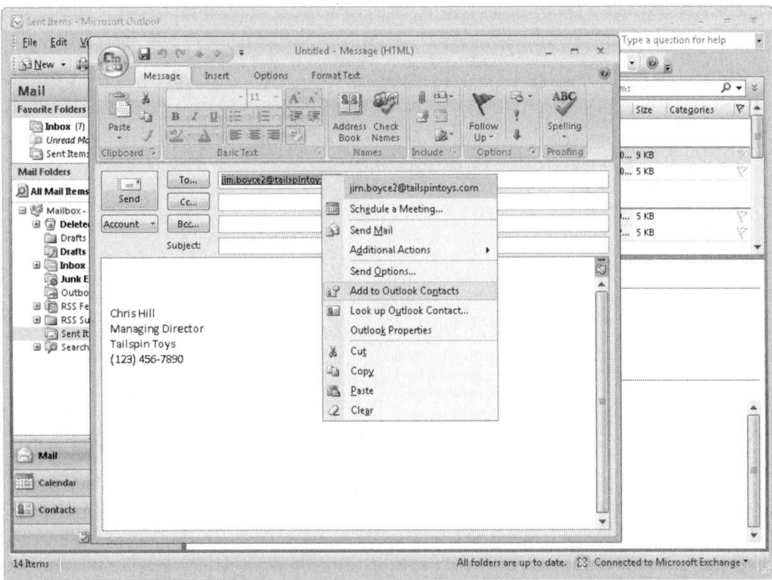

Figure 6-8. Right-clicking an e-mail address gives you extra options.

Modifying Addresses

You can modify any addresses stored in your own address books, as well as in the address books of other users for which you have the appropriate access. You can modify an address while working with an e-mail message or while working directly in the address book. If you're using a message form, click To, Cc, or Bcc. Right-click the address you want to change and click Properties. If you're working in the address book instead, just right-click the address and choose Properties. Outlook 2007 displays the same form you used to create the contact. Make the changes you want and click OK.

Removing Addresses

Removing a contact from the OAB is much easier than creating one. Open the OAB, select the address you want to delete, and click the Delete button on the toolbar or press Delete.

Finding People in the Address Book

If your address book contains numerous addresses, as might be the case in a very large organization, it can be a chore to locate an address if you don't use it often. Outlook 2007 provides a search capability in the address book to overcome that problem, making it relatively easy to locate addresses based on several criteria.

> **Note**
>
> You can simply click in the text box at the top of the Address Book and type a name. Outlook 2007 locates the first address that matches the text you type. If you prefer to see only those items that match the text for which you are searching, you can use the Find dialog box, as described in the following steps.

Follow these steps to locate an address in any address book:

1. Click the Address Book button on the toolbar to open the address book.
2. In the Address Book drop-down list, select the address book you want to search.
3. Choose Tools, Find to display the Find dialog box shown in Figure 6-9 (for Exchange Server address lists) or Figure 6-10 (for the OAB).

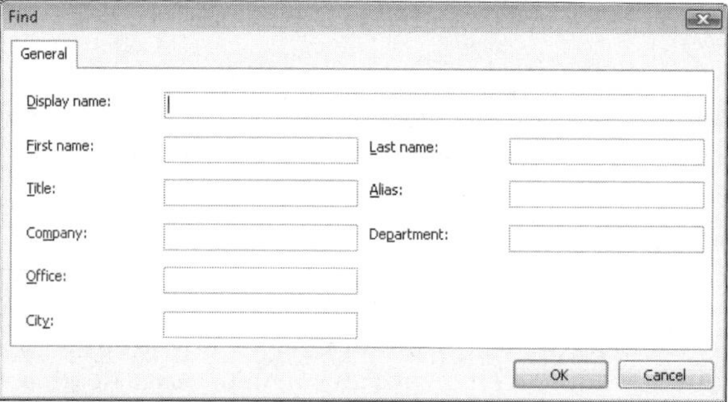

Figure 6-9. Use the Find dialog box to locate people in the Exchange Global Address List.

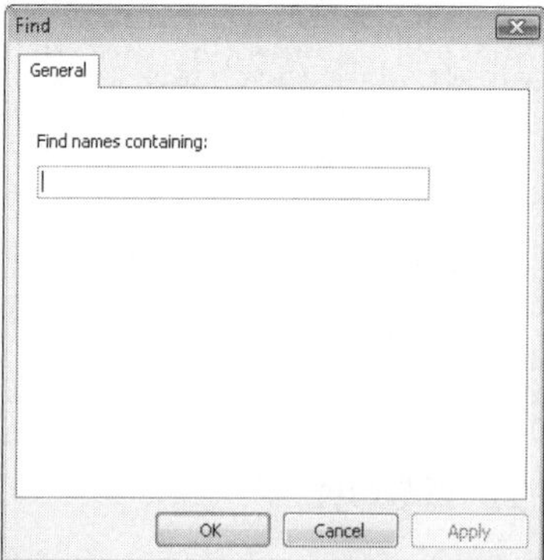

Figure 6-10. The Find dialog box offers only a single search field for Outlook Address Book searches.

4. If you're searching an address list on the Exchange Server, decide which criteria you want to use and enter data in the fields to define the search. If you're searching an OAB, specify the text to search for, which must be contained in the contact's name.
5. Click OK to perform the search.

When you click OK, Outlook 2007 performs a search in the selected address book based on your search criteria and displays the results in the Address Book window. You can revert to the full address book list by selecting the address book from the Address Book drop-down list. Select Search Results from the Address Book drop-down list to view the results of the last search.

INSIDE OUT **Using a directory service**

In addition to searching your address books, you also can search a *directory service* for information about contacts. A directory service is a server that answers queries about data (typically contact information) stored on the server. For detailed information on setting up and using directory services in Outlook 2007, see the section "Configuring a Directory Service Account in Outlook" in Chapter 17.

Using AutoComplete for Addresses

Outlook 2007 automatically keeps track of addresses that you enter in the address fields and stores them in an AutoComplete cache file in your profile folder. When you type an address in the To, Cc, or Bcc fields, Outlook 2007 adds the address to the cache. The cache file has the file name *profile*.nk2, in which *profile* is your Outlook 2007 profile name. The default location for the file is the AppData\Roaming\Microsoft\Outlook folder of your user profile.

When you begin typing in any of these address fields, Outlook 2007 begins matching the typed characters against the AutoComplete cache. If it finds a match, it automatically completes the address. If there is more than one match in the cache, Outlook 2007 displays a drop-down list that contains the names for all the matching entries (see Figure 6-11). Use the arrow keys or mouse to select a name from the list and then press Enter or Tab to add the address to the field.

> **Note**
>
> AutoComplete doesn't check to see whether a particular contact has more than one e-mail address. Instead, it uses whatever address it finds in the cache. If Outlook 2007 has cached one address, but you prefer that it cache a different one, delete the existing cache entry (as explained in the next section). Then address a new message to the contact using the desired e-mail address to cache that address.

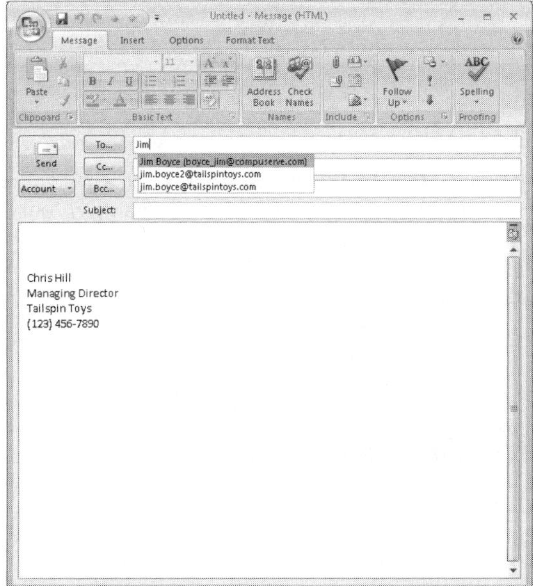

Figure 6-11. Select a name from the AutoComplete cache list offered by Outlook 2007.

You can turn AutoComplete on or off to suit your needs by following these steps:

1. Choose Tools, Options, and click E-Mail Options on the Preferences tab.
2. Click Advanced E-Mail Options.
3. Select or deselect the Suggest Names While Completing To, Cc, And Bcc Fields option to turn AutoComplete on or off, respectively.

> **Note**
>
> You can move your AutoComplete cache file from one computer to another. You can also back it up so you can restore it in the event your computer crashes.

See the section "Backing Up and Restoring Data" in Chapter 31, "Archiving, Backing Up, and Restoring Outlook Data," for details.

Deleting a Name from the AutoComplete Cache

Outlook 2007 caches all entries and moves the lesser-used ones to the bottom of the list, eventually removing ones that are not used.

One common reason to delete a name from the cache is that you either don't use it very often or want to use a different e-mail address for that contact.

It's easy to delete a name from the cache using these steps:

1. Start a new e-mail message and type the first few letters of the name.
2. When Outlook 2007 displays the shortcut menu with the matching entries, select the one you want to delete and press Delete.
3. Repeat this process for any other cached addresses you want to delete.

Deleting the Entire Cache

It's possible, although not common, for the AutoComplete cache to become corrupted, preventing it from working, or causing it to offer incorrect addresses. If you experience this problem, close Outlook 2007 and locate the .nk2 file for your profile, as explained at the beginning of this section. Rename or delete the file and restart Outlook 2007 to create a new AutoComplete cache file (Outlook 2007 creates the file automatically).

Using Distribution Lists

If you often send messages to groups of people, adding all their addresses to a message one at a time can be a real chore, particularly if you're sending the message to many recipients. *Distribution lists* in Outlook 2007 help simplify the process, enabling you to send a message to a single address and have it broadcast to all recipients in the group. Instead of addressing a message to each individual user in the sales department, for example, you could address it to the sales distribution group. Outlook 2007 (or Exchange Server) takes care of sending the message to all the members of the group.

You can create distribution lists in the OAB. You can't create distribution lists in the GAL or other Exchange Server address lists—only the Exchange Server system administrator can create the distribution lists on the server. However, you can modify distribution lists on the Exchange Server computer if you're designated as the owner of the list.

Creating Distribution Lists

Setting up a distribution list in your OAB is a relatively simple procedure. You can create a distribution list using addresses from multiple address books, which means, for example, that you might include addresses from the GAL on the Exchange Server computer as well as personal addresses stored in your Contacts folder. You can also include addresses of different types (for example, Exchange Server addresses, Internet addresses, and X.400 addresses). In general, it's easiest to set up a distribution list if all the addresses to be included already exist, but you can enter addresses on the fly if needed.

Follow these steps to create a distribution list:

1. Open the address book.
2. Choose File, New Entry or right-click in any area of the address list field and click New Entry.
3. Select from the drop-down list the address book in which you want to store the distribution list.
4. In the Select The Entry Type list, select New Distribution List, and then click OK to display the Distribution List dialog box, as shown in Figure 6-12.

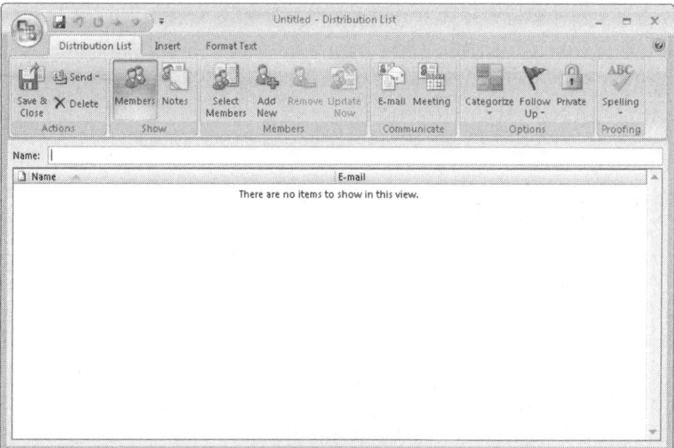

Figure 6-12. Use the Distribution List dialog box for a distribution list in the Contacts folder.

5. In the Name box, specify a name for the list. This is the distribution list name that will appear in your address book.
6. Click Select Members to open the Select Members dialog box (see Figure 6-13).

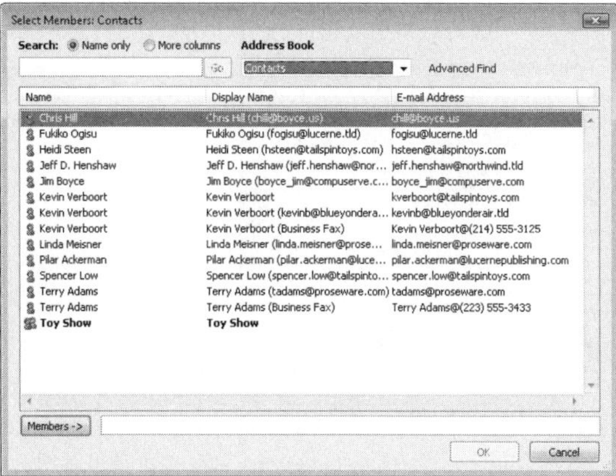

Figure 6-13. Add members to the distribution list using the Select Members dialog box.

7. Add members as needed or manually enter the e-mail address in the Members dialog box to enter new addresses if the addresses don't already exist in one of your address books. Click OK when you finish adding members to the list. Remember to separate each entry by a semicolon if you are adding members manually.
8. Set other options as needed for the distribution list–for example, you can assign categories to the list.
9. Click OK and Save And Close in the Distribution List dialog box.

Note

Select the Advanced Find option in the Distribution List dialog box to search all your address books for members. Enter a name or partial name to display all address book matches to find the desired contact.

Distribution lists appear in the address book with a group icon and a boldface name to differentiate them from individual addresses (see Figure 6-14).

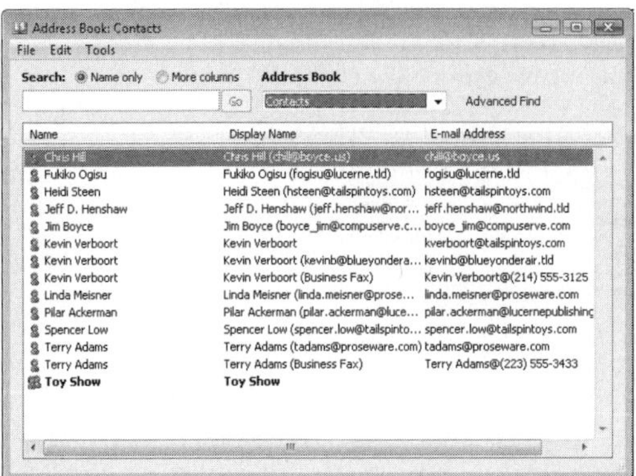

Figure 6-14. Outlook 2007 differentiates between addresses and distribution lists in the address book.

INSIDE OUT **Address types identified**

Outlook 2007 differentiates addresses in the Select Names dialog box as well as the Address Book. When you address an e-mail message, you can tell which address is a fax number and which is an e-mail address. You can also easily differentiate personal addresses from work addresses in both the Select Names and Address Book dialog boxes.

Note

In a Contacts folder, distribution lists look just like addresses, although Outlook 2007 displays a distribution list in the address list with a group icon and with the distribution list name in bold. The distribution list also shows less information than a contact in Address Cards views.

Modifying a Distribution List

Over time, you will add or remove names from your distribution lists. To modify the contents of a list, locate the distribution list in the address book or in your Contacts folder, open the list, and then use the Select Members button to modify the list. You can also remove members from the list by selecting the member and then clicking the Delete button on the toolbar, or by pressing Delete on your keyboard.

Renaming a Distribution List

You can change the name of a distribution list any time after you create it to reflect changes in the way you use the list, to correct spelling, or for any other reason. To rename a distribution list, locate the list in the address book, open it, and then change the name in the Name box. Click Save And Close to apply the change.

Deleting a Distribution List

You can delete a distribution list the same way you delete an address. Locate the distribution list in the address book or Contacts folder, select it, and then click the Delete button on the toolbar or press Delete. Alternatively, you can right-click the list and choose Delete from its shortcut menu.

> **Note**
>
> Deleting a distribution list doesn't delete the addresses associated with the list.

Hiding Addresses when Using a Distribution List

If you include a distribution list in the To or Cc field of a message, all the recipients of your message—whether members of the distribution list or not—can see the addresses of individuals in the list. Outlook 2007 doesn't retain the list name in the address field of the message but instead replaces it with the actual addresses from the list.

In some cases, you might not want to have their addresses made public, even to other members of the list. In these situations, add the distribution list to the Bcc (blind carbon copy) field instead of the To or Cc field. The Bcc field sends copies of the e-mail to all addresses and distribution lists but keeps the addresses hidden from the other recipients.

Distribution Lists for Multiple Address Fields

Regardless of where you create a distribution list, you can't allocate some addresses in the list to the To field and other addresses to the Cc or Bcc field. You can, however, place the distribution list address in either the Cc or Bcc field, if needed.

If you often need to separate addresses from distribution lists into different address fields, you can use a couple of techniques to simplify the process. First, consider splitting the distribution list into two or three separate lists. This approach works well if the To, Cc, and Bcc fields generally receive the same addresses each time. A second approach is to create a template with the addresses already filled in:

1. Start a new mail message.

2. To view the Bcc field, click the Options tab on the ribbon and then click Show Bcc.
3. Fill in the addresses in the appropriate fields as needed.
4. Click the Office button and choose Save As.
5. In the Save As dialog box, choose Outlook Template from the Save As Type drop-down list.
6. Specify a name and location for the template and click Save.

When you need to send a message using the template, browse to the folder in which the template is stored and double-click the file to open the message template. Add any additional addresses, text, or attachments; then send the message as usual.

Using Distribution Lists on a Server

You can use distribution lists on Exchange Server—which are set up by the system administrator—the same way you use local distribution lists to simplify broadcasting messages to multiple recipients. (As mentioned earlier, you can't create distribution lists in the GAL or other Exchange Server address lists from Outlook 2007, although you can modify such a list if you are designated as the list owner.)

You can use a server-side distribution list the same way you use a local distribution list. Select the list from the appropriate address list on the server. The list name is converted to addresses when you send the message, just as a local distribution list is.

Adding a Server-Side Distribution List to Contacts

If you prefer working through your local address books instead of the server address lists, you might want to add a server-side distribution list to your local Contacts folder. You can easily do so through the address book or the list's dialog box. Open the address book, select the distribution list, and then choose File, Add To Contacts.

> **Note**
>
> If you have the list's dialog box open, click Contacts on the General tab. Outlook 2007 then adds the list to your Contacts folder.

When Outlook 2007 displays the distribution list, you can then modify the group, assign categories, send a meeting request or e-mail, mark it as private, or even use the Proof button to run spell-check or use the thesaurus (see Figure 6-15). Make any necessary changes to the distribution list and then click Save And Close.

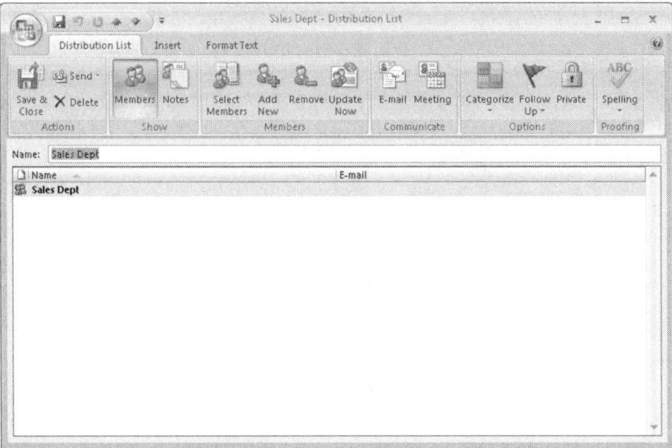

Figure 6-15. You can select various options for distribution lists you store in the Contacts folder.

Automatically Adding Addresses to the Address Book

When you receive a message from a sender whose address you want to save in your local Contacts folder, you can add the address manually. Outlook 2007 also provides an easier method, however. With the message open, right-click the sender's address on the InfoBar and choose Add To Outlook Contacts.

Using the Mobile Address Book

Outlook 2007 adds a new feature for addresses: the Mobile Address Book (MAB), which is added automatically when you add an Outlook 2007 Mobile Service account to your profile. You can also add the MAB manually and use it without an Outlook 2007 Mobile Service account.

See the section "Using Outlook Mobile Service Accounts," in Chapter 45, "Making Outlook Mobile," for more details on Mobile Service accounts.

To add the Mobile Address Book manually, choose Tools, Account Settings. In the Account Settings dialog box, click the Address Books tab and then click New. Choose Additional Address Books and click Next. Choose Mobile Address Book and click Next. Outlook 2007 warns you that the address book will not be available until you stop and restart Outlook 2007. Click OK, Close, and Finish; then restart Outlook 2007.

Like the OAB, the MAB does not actually store addresses. Instead, it searches for and displays existing addresses that have phone numbers in the Mobile contact field (see Figure 6-16). Because the MAB searches for and displays these contacts automatically, you don't have to do anything to add them to the MAB.

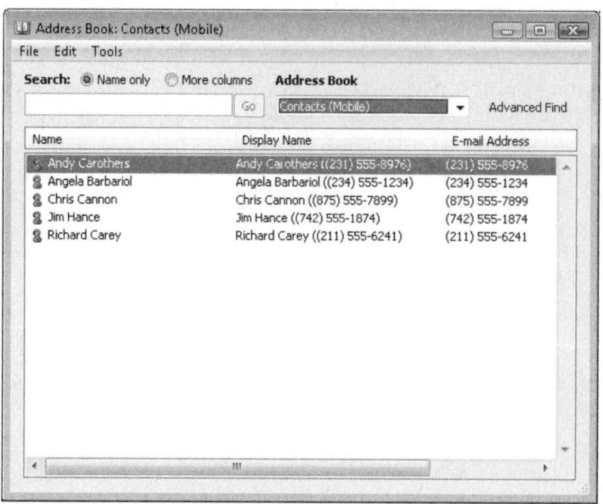

Figure 6-16. You can select various options for distribution lists you store in the Contacts folder.

You can use the MAB as a means to quickly look up mobile numbers for your contacts. Just open the OAB and select Contacts under Mobile Address Book in the drop-down list.

To learn how to work with the MAB in conjunction with an Outlook Mobile Service account, see the section "Using Outlook Mobile Service Accounts" in Chapter 45.

> **Note**
>
> Deleting an entry from the MAB deletes only the number in the Mobile field of the associated contact item; it does not delete the contact itself.

CHAPTER 7

Using Internet Mail Accounts

Not too many years ago, a person with an Internet e-mail address was the exception rather than the rule. Today, however, it seems as though everyone is using Internet e-mail. So it's a good bet that you'll want to use Microsoft® Office Outlook® 2007 to send and receive messages through at least one Internet e-mail account.

This chapter focuses on setting up Office Outlook 2007 to access Internet mail servers and accounts. The chapter also covers topics related to sending and receiving Internet e-mail. You'll learn how to create Internet e-mail accounts, use multiple accounts, and work with e-mail accounts for services such as Microsoft Hotmail® and CompuServe. You'll also learn how to ensure that your messages are available from different locations, what to do if your e-mail service won't accept outgoing mail from your dial-up location, and how to view full message headers in Internet e-mail.

Note

This chapter assumes that your system is already set up to connect to the Internet, either on a broadband connection such as a local area network (LAN), Digital Subscriber Line (DSL), or cable modem or by a dial-up connection. Whatever the situation, your Internet service provider (ISP) or network administrator has likely set up the connection for you. This chapter instead focuses on configuring Outlook 2007 to use the existing connection and setting up specific types of accounts.

For help in creating e-mail accounts and assigning the dial-up connection, see "Configuring Accounts and Services" in Chapter 3.

Using Internet POP3 E-Mail Accounts

Most Internet-based e-mail servers use Simple Mail Transfer Protocol (SMTP) and Post Office Protocol 3 (POP3) to allow subscribers to send and receive messages across the Internet. (A few exceptions, such as CompuServe 2000, use Internet Message Access Protocol [IMAP]; still other services, such as Hotmail and Yahoo!, use Hypertext Transfer Protocol [HTTP]. These other protocols are covered later in this chapter.) If you have an account with a local ISP or other service provider that offers POP3 accounts, or if your office server is a non–Microsoft Exchange Server system that supports only POP3, you can add an Internet e-mail account to Outlook 2007 to access that server.

INSIDE OUT **Configure multiple accounts in one profile**

You can configure multiple Internet e-mail accounts in a single Outlook 2007 profile, giving you access to multiple servers to send and receive messages. For additional information, see "Using Multiple Accounts" later in this chapter.

Follow these steps to add an Internet e-mail account to Outlook 2007:

1. With Outlook 2007 open, choose Tools, Account Settings in Outlook 2007 to add an e-mail account.
2. Accept the default selection Microsoft Exchange, POP3, IMAP, or HTTP, and then click Next.
3. To use the automatic discovery feature to automatically obtain your server configuration information from your existing e-mail server, on the Auto Account Setup page, shown in Figure 7-1, specify the following information:

   Your Name Specify your name as you want it to appear in the From box of messages you send.

   E-Mail Address Enter your e-mail address in the form **<user>@<domain.tld>**, where **<user>** is your user account screen name and **<domain.tld>** is the name of your e-mail domain.

   Password/Retype Password Type your password in the Password field, and then confirm the password in the Retype Password field.

4. Enter your name, e-mail address, and password (twice) for your e-mail account, and then click Next. Outlook 2007 will try to connect to your e-mail server and obtain configuration information via an encrypted connection. If Outlook is able to identify your account settings, the process is complete and you can skip the remaining steps.

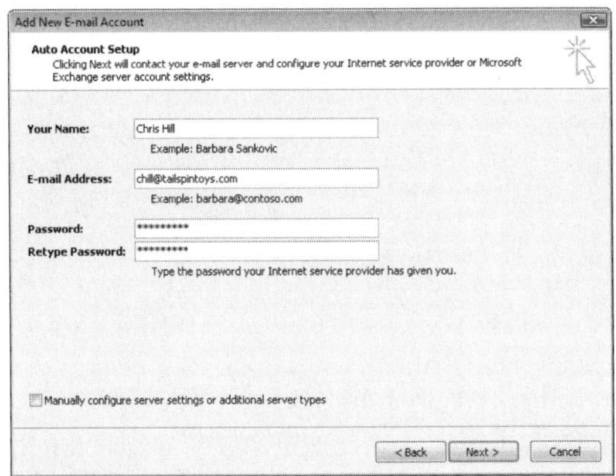

Figure 7-1. Use the Auto Account Setup page to automatically configure the e-mail server settings.

5. If your e-mail server doesn't support encrypted connections, this attempt will fail, and you will be prompted to try an unencrypted connection.

6. If this attempt doesn't complete, you will be prompted to verify the e-mail address and click Retry.

7. If this attempt doesn't complete, the Problem Connecting To Server dialog box is displayed, indicating that you will need to manually configure the settings—the Manually Configure Server Settings check box will be selected automatically. Click Next to continue.

8. In the Choose E-Mail Service dialog box, select Internet E-Mail, and then click Next.

9. On the Internet E-Mail Settings page, shown in Figure 7-2, configure the following settings.

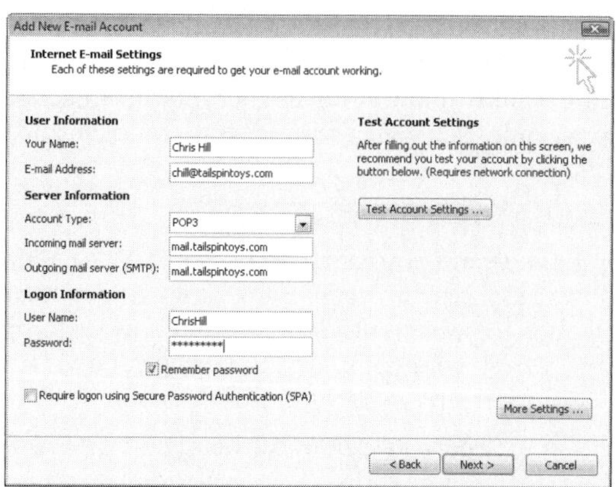

Figure 7-2. Use the Internet E-Mail Settings page to configure the account settings.

Your Name Specify your name as you want it to appear in the From box of messages that others receive from you.

E-Mail Address Specify the e-mail address for your account in the form **<account>@<domain>**—for example, *chill@tailspintoys.com*.

Account Type In the Server Information area, select the Account Type (in this case, POP3) of the e-mail server.

Incoming Mail Server Specify the IP address or Domain Name System (DNS) name of the mail server that processes your incoming mail. This is the server where your POP3 mailbox is located and from which your incoming mail is downloaded. Often, your mail server will use the host name *mail* and your mail server's domain name. So an example of a mail server DNS name might be *mail.tailspintoys.com*. However, this isn't a given rule, so check with your ISP or network administrator for the correct mail server host name.

Outgoing Mail Server (SMTP) Specify the IP address or DNS name of the mail server that you use to send outgoing mail. In many cases, this is the same server as the one specified for incoming mail, but it can be different. Some organizations and many ISPs separate incoming and outgoing mail services onto different servers for load balancing, security, or other reasons.

> **Note**
>
> Many mail servers will not allow outgoing mail unless you connect using the mail server's own network.To learn how to overcome that problem, see the troubleshooting sidebar "My Mail Server Won't Accept Outgoing Messages," later in this chapter.

User Name Specify the user account on the server that you must use to log on to your mailbox to retrieve your messages. In some cases, you should not include the domain portion of your e-mail address. For example, if your address is *chill@tailspintoys.com*, your user name is chill. However, there are mail servers (MSN® and Netscape, for example) that require the full e-mail address as the user name to log on.

Password Specify the password for the user account entered in the User Name box.

Remember Password Select this option to have Outlook 2007 maintain the password for this account in your local password cache, eliminating the need for you to enter the password each time you want to retrieve your mail. Clear this check box to prevent other users from downloading your mail while you are away from your computer. If the check box is cleared, Outlook 2007 prompts you for the password for each session.

Require Logon Using Secure Password Authentication (SPA) Select this option if your server uses SPA to authenticate your access to the server.

10. Click More Settings to display the Internet E-Mail Settings dialog box, shown in Figure 7-3. You can configure these settings based on the information in the following sections.

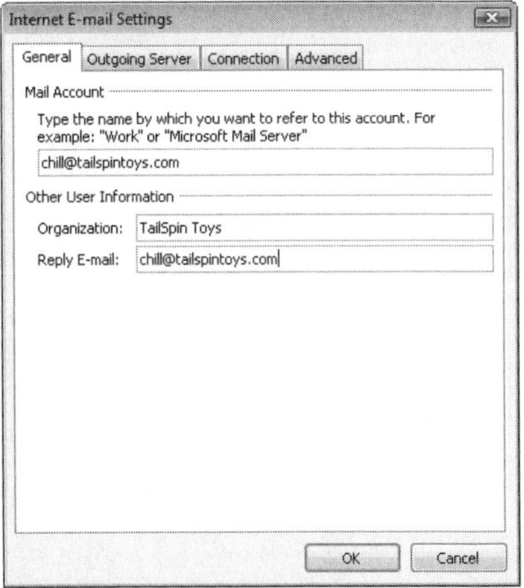

Figure 7-3. Use the General tab to specify the account name, organization, and reply e-mail details.

Configuring General Settings for Internet Accounts

Use the General tab in the Internet E-Mail Settings dialog box (shown earlier in Figure 7-3) to change the account name that is displayed in Outlook 2007 and to specify organization and reply address information as follows:

- **Mail Account** Specify the name of the account as you want it to appear in the Outlook 2007 account list. This name has no bearing on the server name or your account name. Use the name to differentiate one account from another–for example, you might have various accounts named CompuServe, Work, and Personal.

- **Organization** Specify the group or organization name that you want to associate with the account.
- **Reply E-Mail** Specify an e-mail address that you want others to use when replying to messages that you send with this account. For example, you might redirect replies to another mail server address if you are in the process of changing ISPs or mail servers. Enter the address in its full form—**chill@tailspintoys.com**, for example. Leave this option blank if you want users to reply to the e-mail address that you specified in the E-Mail Address box for the account.

Configuring Outgoing Server Settings for Internet Accounts

Use the Outgoing Server tab, shown in Figure 7-4, to configure a handful of settings for the SMTP server that handles the account's outgoing messages. Although in most cases you won't need to modify these settings, you will have to do so if your server requires you to authenticate to send outgoing messages. Some ISPs use authentication as a means of allowing mail relay from their clients outside their local subnets. This allows authorized users to relay mail and prevents unauthorized relay or unauthorized users from sending spam through the server.

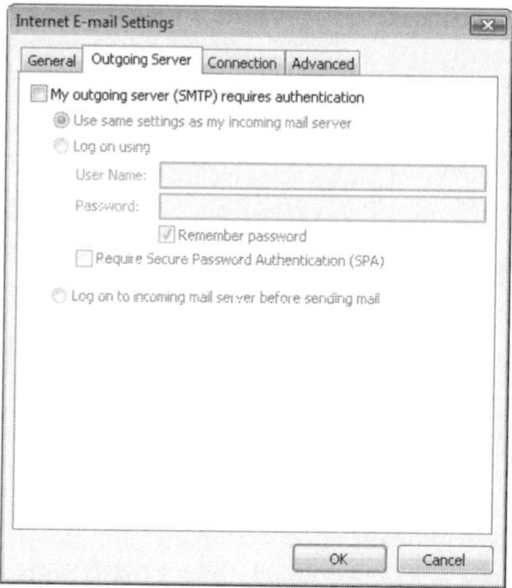

Figure 7-4. Use the Outgoing Server tab to configure authentication and other options for your SMTP server.

The Outgoing Server tab contains the following options:

- **My Outgoing Server (SMTP) Requires Authentication** Select this option if the SMTP mail server that processes your outgoing mail requires authentication. Connections that don't provide valid credentials are rejected. Selecting this option makes several other options on the tab available.
- **Use Same Settings As My Incoming Mail Server** Select this option if the SMTP server credentials are the same as your POP3 (incoming) server credentials.

- **Log On Using** Select this option if the SMTP server requires a different set of credentials from those required by your POP3 server. You should specify a valid account name on the SMTP server in the User Name box as well as a password for that account. In general, you will have to change this setting only if your SMTP and POP3 servers are separate physical servers.
- **Remember Password** Select this check box to have Outlook 2007 save your password from session to session. Clear the check box if you want Outlook 2007 to prompt you for a password each time.
- **Require Secure Password Authentication (SPA)** Select this check box if your server uses SPA to authenticate your access to the server.
- **Log On To Incoming Mail Server Before Sending Mail** Select this option to have Outlook 2007 log on to the POP3 server before sending outgoing messages. Use this option if the outgoing and incoming mail servers are the same server and if the server is configured to require authentication to send messages.

Configuring Connection Settings for Internet Accounts

Use the Connection tab, shown in Figure 7-5, to specify how Outlook 2007 should connect to the mail server for this Internet account. You can connect using the LAN (which includes DSL and cable modem broadband connections), a dial-up connection, or a third-party dialer such as the one included with Microsoft Internet Explorer®.

- **Connect Using My Local Area Network (LAN)** Select the LAN option if your computer is hard-wired to the Internet (LAN, DSL, cable modem, or other persistent connection).
- **Connect Via Modem When Outlook Is Offline** If you use a shared dial-up connection to access the Internet, select this check box if you want Outlook 2007 to attempt a LAN connection first, followed by a dial-up connection if the first attempt fails (for example, when your notebook PC is disconnected from the LAN but a dial-up connection is available).
- **Connect Using My Phone Line** Select this option if you are using a dial-up connection as your default mode of connecting to the Internet or other network hosting your mail server. Select this option to use an existing dial-up networking connection or to create a new dial-up connection. Select the connection from the drop-down list, and then click Properties if you need to modify the dial-up connection. Click Add if you need to add a dial-up connection.
- **Connect Using Internet Explorer's Or A 3rd Party Dialer** Select this option if you want Internet Explorer or another phone dialer application to dial your connection to the network hosting your mail server. If you want to connect to the Internet or to your remote network using the dialer that is included with Internet Explorer or a dialer that is included with a third-party dial-up client, select this option.
- **Use The Following Dial-Up Networking Connection** Select the modem profile to use when dialing your ISP connection.

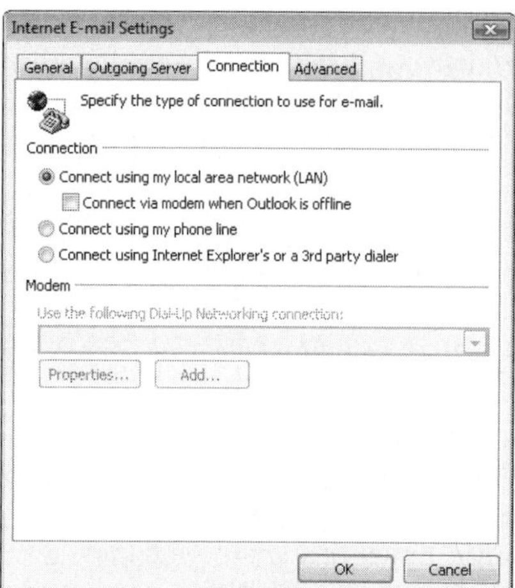

Figure 7-5. Use the Connection tab to specify how Outlook 2007 should connect to the network hosting your mail server.

Configuring Advanced Settings for Internet Accounts

Although you won't normally need to configure settings on the Advanced tab for an Internet account, the settings can be useful in some situations. You can use the options on the Advanced tab, shown in Figure 7-6, to specify the SMTP and POP3 ports for the server, along with time-outs and these other settings.

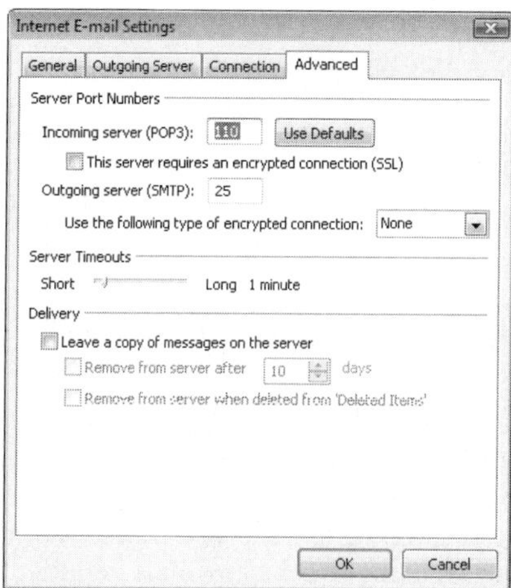

Figure 7-6. Use the Advanced tab to specify nonstandard TCP ports for the server.

- **Incoming Server (POP3)** Specify the TCP port used by the POP3 server. The default port is 110. Specifying a nonstandard port works only if the server is listening for POP3 traffic on the specified port.
- **Outgoing Server (SMTP)** Specify the TCP port used by the SMTP server for outgoing mail. The default port is 25. Specifying a nonstandard port works only if the server is listening for SMTP traffic on the specified port.
- **Use Defaults** Click this button to restore the default port settings for POP3 and SMTP.
- **Use The Following Type Of Encrypted Connection** If your server requires an encrypted connection, use this drop-down list to select the correct type of encryption method–either SSL, TLS, Auto, or None. Select SSL if the server requires the use of a Secure Sockets Layer (SSL) connection, TLS if it requires Transport Layer Security (TLS), and Auto if you want Outlook 2007 to autonegotiate encryption with the mail server. With rare exceptions, public POP3 and SMTP mail servers do not require SSL connections.
- **Server Timeouts** Use this control to change the period of time that Outlook 2007 will wait for a connection to the server.
- **Leave A Copy Of Messages On The Server** Select this check box to retain a copy of all messages on the server, downloading a copy of the message to Outlook 2007. This is a useful feature if you want to access the same POP3 account from different computers and want to be able to access your messages from each one. Clear this check box if you want Outlook 2007 to download your messages and then delete them from the server. Some servers impose a storage limit, making it impractical to leave all your messages on the server.
- **Remove From Server After *n* Days** Select this check box to have Outlook 2007 delete messages from the server a specified number of days after they are downloaded to your system.
- **Remove From Server When Deleted From 'Deleted Items'** Select this option to have Outlook 2007 delete messages from the server when you delete the downloaded copies from your local Deleted Items folder.

Controlling Where Outlook Stores POP3 Messages

When you create a POP3 account, Outlook 2007 needs to know where to store your mail folders. By default, Outlook 2007 stores your POP3 mail folders in whatever location is currently specified as the default delivery location for new mail. For example, if you already have an Exchange Server account with the Exchange Server mailbox designated as the location for e-mail delivery, Outlook 2007 uses the same mailbox location for POP3 mail. Where Outlook 2007 stores the folders also depends on the other services, if any, that you're using with Outlook 2007. The following list summarizes the possibilities:

- **POP3 only or as a first account** When you set up a POP3 account as your only Outlook 2007 e-mail account or as your first account, Outlook 2007 creates a personal folder (.pst) file in which to store your POP3 e-mail folders. Outlook 2007 uses the same .pst file to store your other Outlook 2007 data, such as contacts and calendar information.
- **POP3 added to a profile with an existing Exchange Server account** In this scenario, Outlook 2007 uses the e-mail delivery location specified for your Exchange Server account as the location to deliver POP3 mail. For example, if you currently store your Exchange Server data in your Exchange Server mailbox on the server, your POP3 messages will be placed in your Exchange Server mailbox. In effect, this means that your POP3 messages are downloaded to your computer from your Internet mail account and then uploaded to your Exchange Server mailbox. If you specify a local folder for Exchange Server instead, Outlook 2007 places your POP3 messages in that same local folder.
- **POP3 added after an IMAP account** IMAP accounts are stored only in .pst files, and Outlook 2007 automatically creates a .pst file for the IMAP account. (The file is created when you first open Outlook 2007 using the profile that contains the IMAP account.) Outlook 2007 also creates a .pst file for storing your other Outlook 2007 data, keeping your IMAP data and other Outlook 2007 data separate. Outlook 2007 designates a .pst file as the default location for new mail, even though messages from your IMAP account are delivered to your IMAP-specific .pst file. If you later create a POP3 account, Outlook 2007 uses the same .pst file for your POP3 account by default. This means that your IMAP folders and mail are kept separate from your POP3 and Exchange Server mail. You can change the settings afterward if you want to designate a different file for storing your POP3 messages, but doing so also changes the location of your Contacts folder, Calendar folder, and other Outlook 2007 folders.

Using IMAP Accounts

IMAP is becoming more common on Internet-based e-mail servers because it offers several advantages over POP3. Outlook 2007 support for IMAP means that you can use Outlook 2007 to send and receive messages through IMAP servers as well as through Exchange Server, POP3, and the other mail server types that Outlook 2007 supports.

For more information about IMAP and its differences from POP3, see "IMAP," in Chapter 2.

Configuring an IMAP account is a lot like configuring a POP3 account. The only real difference is that you select IMAP as the account type rather than POP3 when you add the account. You can refer to the preceding section on creating POP3 accounts, "Using Internet POP3 E-Mail Accounts," for a description of the procedure to follow when adding an IMAP account. The one setting you might want to review or change for an IMAP account as opposed to a POP3 account is the root folder path. This setting is located on the Advanced tab of the account's Internet E-Mail Settings dialog box. Open this dialog box, click More Settings, and then click Advanced. Specify the path to the specific folder in your mailbox folder structure that you want to use as the root for your mailbox. If you aren't sure what path to enter, leave this option blank to use the default path provided by the account.

Controlling Where Outlook Stores IMAP Messages

When you create an IMAP account in an Outlook 2007 profile, Outlook 2007 doesn't prompt you to specify the storage location for the IMAP folders. Instead, Outlook 2007 automatically creates a .pst file in which to store the messages. The folder branch for the account appears in Outlook 2007 with the name of the IMAP account as the branch name, as shown in Figure 7-7. Each IMAP account in a profile uses a different .pst file, so all your IMAP accounts are separate from one another and each appears under its own branch in the folders list.

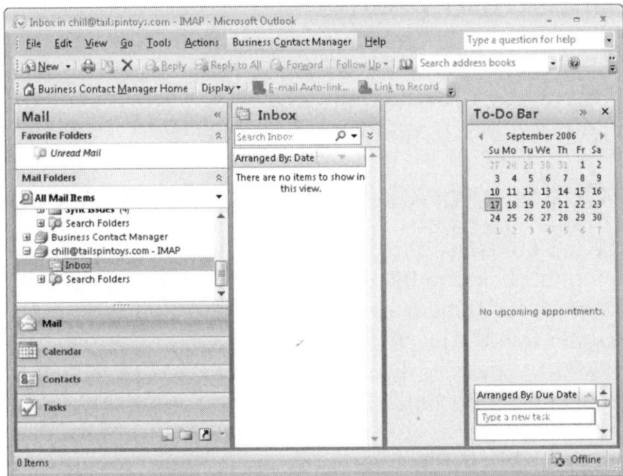

Figure 7-7. An IMAP account uses its own .pst file and appears as a separate folder branch.

How accounts are treated depends on the types of accounts you add to the profile. The following list summarizes the possibilities:

- **IMAP as the first or only account in the profile** Outlook 2007 automatically creates a .pst file to contain the IMAP folder set and a second .pst file (which, for clarity, we'll call a global .pst file) to contain your other Outlook 2007 data such as contacts and calendar information.
- **Multiple IMAP accounts in the profile** Each IMAP account uses a separate .pst file created by Outlook 2007. Outlook 2007 also adds a separate global .pst file to contain your other Outlook 2007 data.

- **IMAP first, followed by non-IMAP accounts** The non-IMAP accounts default to storing their data in the global .pst that is created when you add the IMAP account. The global .pst is defined as the location where new mail is delivered. You can change the location after you set up the accounts, if you prefer. For example, if you add an Exchange Server account, you'll probably want to change the profile's properties to deliver mail to your Exchange Server mailbox instead of to the global .pst file. IMAP mail is unaffected by the setting and is still delivered to the IMAP account's .pst file.
- **Non-IMAP accounts followed by IMAP accounts** The existing accounts maintain their default store location as defined by the settings in the profile. Added IMAP accounts each receive their own .pst file.

Using Outlook with CompuServe

You can use Outlook 2007 to send and receive CompuServe mail through either Classic CompuServe or CompuServe 2000 accounts. The following sections explain the differences between the two and how to configure Outlook 2007 to accommodate them.

Configuring Outlook for Classic CompuServe Accounts

Classic CompuServe accounts use e-mail addresses that end in *@compuserve.com* or *@csi.com*. Classic CompuServe accounts function as POP3 accounts, so configuring them in Outlook 2007 is much the same as configuring other POP3 accounts. However, you need to understand that the logon password you use for your POP3 account is not necessarily the same as the password you use to connect to CompuServe. Your connection password is associated with your user ID, which takes the form *nnnnn,nnnn*—for example, 76516,3403. Your POP3 password is associated with your CompuServe POP3 account name, which is the first part of your CompuServe address (without the domain). In the address *boyce_jim@csi.com*, for example, *boyce_jim* is the user name. Although you can set the two passwords to be the same, they do not have to match.

Before you can begin managing your CompuServe Classic e-mail account through Outlook 2007, you must set your POP3 password. You can do this only by connecting to CompuServe through the CompuServe software. Click Go, type **POPMAIL** as the destination, and press Enter to access the POPMAIL area, where you can set your POP3 password.

For details on configuring POP3 accounts, see "Using Internet POP3 E-Mail Accounts," earlier in this chapter.

After you set the password, create a POP3 account in Outlook 2007 using the settings described in the following list:

- **Your Name** Specify your name as you want it to appear in the From box of messages you send.

- **E-Mail Address** Enter your CompuServe e-mail address in the form **<user>@compuserve.com** or **<user>@csi.com**, where **<user>** is your user account number in dotted format or your POP3 alias. The compuserve.com and csi.com domains are synonymous–you should be able to use either one.
- **Incoming Mail Server** Enter **pop.compuserve.com** as the incoming mail server.
- **Outgoing Mail Server** Enter **smtp.compuserve.com** as the outgoing mail server if you dial a CompuServe access number, or specify the SMTP server name for your local ISP account or for a server on your network that allows mail relay from your computer. To reduce spamming, the smtp.compuserve.com server does not support mail relay from outside the CompuServe network.
- **User Name** Specify your CompuServe account.
- **Password** Specify the password for your CompuServe account.
- **Log On Using Secure Password Authentication (SPA)** Do not select this option (leave it cleared).

Configure the remaining settings as you would for any other POP3 account.

> **Note**
>
> If you use CompuServe only for e-mail, you might not have the CompuServe software installed on your system. You can't use CompuServe 2000 software to configure your POP3 e-mail password because CompuServe Classic and CompuServe 2000 are separate services. You can download the necessary software from *ftp.csi.com/software/windows/cs402/without_ie/cs495bn.exe*. The download is nearly 18 MB, however, so be prepared for a long download if you connect through dial-up.

Configuring Outlook for CompuServe 2000 Accounts

CompuServe 2000 accounts use addresses that end in *@cs.com* and use IMAP instead of POP3. Configure an Outlook 2007 account for CompuServe 2000 by using the following settings in the E-Mail Accounts Wizard when you create the account:

- **Your Name** Specify your name as you want it to appear in the From box of messages you send.
- **E-Mail Address** Enter your CompuServe e-mail address in the form **<user>@cs.com**, where **<user>** is your user account screen name.
- **Incoming Mail Server** Enter **imap.cs.com** as the incoming mail server.
- **Outgoing Mail Server** Enter **smtp.cs.com** as the outgoing mail server if you dial a CompuServe access number, or specify the SMTP server name for your local ISP account or for a server on your network that allows mail relay from your computer. To reduce spamming, the smtp.compuserve.com server does not support mail relay from outside the CompuServe network.

- **User Name** Specify your CompuServe account.
- **Password** Specify the password for your CompuServe account.

Configure the remaining settings as you would for any other IMAP account.

Using Hotmail and Other HTTP-Based Services

Because Outlook 2007 supports the HTTP protocol, you can access your HTTP-based mail services (such as Hotmail) through Outlook 2007 instead of using a Web browser to send and receive messages. Using Outlook 2007 gives you the ability to compose and reply to messages offline, potentially saving you connect charges if you use metered Internet access. HTTP-based mail support also gives you the advantages of Outlook 2007 composition, filtering, and other features that you might not otherwise have when managing your mail with a Web browser.

The following section explains how to set up an account in Outlook 2007 to process your Hotmail account. You can use the same information for almost any HTTP-based account, changing the settings as needed to point to the appropriate URL for the server. Although the following assumes that you're setting up the account for Hotmail, it also provides additional information on configuring other HTTP-based accounts.

Using Outlook with Hotmail Accounts

Because Hotmail is a service owned and operated by Microsoft, it's no surprise that Outlook 2007 includes built-in support for sending and receiving messages through Hotmail.

Follow these steps to configure a Hotmail account in Outlook 2007:

1. In Outlook 2007, click Tools, Account Settings.
2. On the E-Mail tab, click New, accept the Microsoft Exchange, POP3, IMAP, or HTTP option, and then click Next.
3. The Auto Account Setup dialog box is displayed. To automatically configure your Hotmail account in Outlook 2007, provide the following information:

   Your Name Specify your name as you want it to appear in the From box of messages you send.

   E-mail Address Enter your Hotmail e-mail address in the form **<user>@hotmail.com**, where **<user>** is your user account screen name.

   Password and Confirm Password Enter your Hotmail password in the Password field, and then confirm the password in the Retype Password field.
4. After you have entered your name, Hotmail address, and password, click Next. Outlook 2007 will connect to the Hotmail server and download any e-mail that is waiting to be collected.

To manually configure Hotmail server settings in Outlook 2007, in the Auto Account Setup dialog box in step 3 of the preceding procedure, click the Manually Configure Server Settings Or Additional Server Types, and then follow these steps:

1. Click the Internet E-Mail option, and then click Next.

If you want to use multiple profiles and want to learn how to configure settings and accounts for a specific profile, see "Understanding Profiles" in Chapter 3.

2. On the Internet E-Mail Settings page, specify the following information:

   Your Name Specify your name as you want it to appear in the From box of messages that others receive from you.

   E-Mail Address Specify the e-mail address for your Hotmail account, in the form **<account>@hotmail.com**, where **<account>** is your Hotmail account name.

   Account Type In the drop-down list, verify that HTTP is selected.

   HTTP Mail Service Provider After you enter your Hotmail e-mail address, Hotmail will be automatically selected in this drop-down list (or you can select Other if you're configuring Outlook 2007 for a different HTTP-based mail service). If you select Hotmail, Outlook 2007 fills in the Server URL option with the appropriate URL for accessing Hotmail through Outlook 2007.

   Server URL If you are setting up an account for an HTTP-based service other than Hotmail, specify the URL for the server's Web page that provides access to your mail account. This is not necessarily the same URL you would use when accessing your account by using a browser.

   User Name Specify the user account on the server that you must use to log on to your mailbox to retrieve your messages. For a Hotmail account, specify your e-mail address, including the *@hotmail.com* part of the address, such as *Chris.E.Hill@hotmail.com*.

   Password Specify the password for the user account entered in the User Name box.

   Require Logon Using Secure Password Authentication (SPA) Select this check box if your HTTP-based e-mail server uses SPA to authenticate your access to the server. Hotmail does not use SPA, so you can leave this check box cleared for Hotmail accounts.

3. Click OK to accept the settings shown in Figure 7-8, or click More Settings to modify the connectivity settings described in the section "Using Internet POP3 E-Mail Accounts" earlier in this chapter.

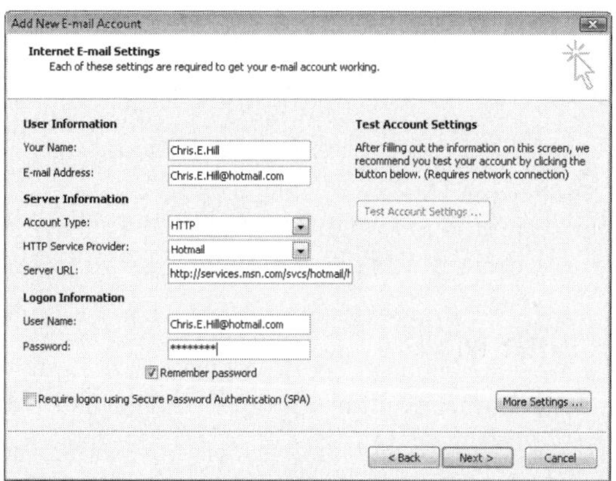

Figure 7-8. Manually configuring settings to set up a Hotmail account.

For more information about configuring properties for HTTP-based accounts, see "Using Internet POP3 E-Mail Accounts" earlier in this chapter. Most of the settings for HTTP and POP3 are the same.

Establishing a Hotmail Account

Hotmail provides several options to establish e-mail accounts, one of which is free (MSN Hotmail), and two of which are paid accounts (MSN Hotmail Plus and MSN Hotmail Premium). Although the free Hotmail account allows for Web-based access via a browser, to use Outlook 2007 to access and manage your e-mail with Hotmail, you must have either an MSN Hotmail Plus or an MSN Hotmail Premium account.

Understanding Where Outlook Stores HTTP Messages

Outlook 2007 stores mail messages for Hotmail and other HTTP e-mail accounts locally, just as it does for POP3. When you add a Hotmail or other HTTP account to a profile, Outlook 2007 creates a .pst file specifically for that account, regardless of whether the profile already includes other accounts. Outlook 2007 delivers new messages to that .pst file, even if the default delivery location is elsewhere. For example, assume that you create a profile with an Exchange Server account as the default delivery location for new mail. You add a POP3 account, and your mail is delivered to your Exchange Server mailbox. You then add a Hotmail account and an IMAP account. Each of these last two accounts gets its own .pst file, and Outlook 2007 delivers new messages for each account to its respective .pst file.

Using Outlook with Prodigy

The Prodigy e-mail service functions as a standard POP3 server. You therefore can use Outlook 2007 to send and receive e-mail through your Prodigy account. Configure the account for *pop.prodigy.net* as the incoming mail server and *smtp.prodigy.net* as the outgoing mail server. Specify your Prodigy account and password for authentication, add a *.pst* if you don't want to use the default delivery location (such as an Exchange Server mailbox), and configure other settings as you would for any other POP3 account.

Using Outlook with MSN

Although MSN mail accounts are available through the Hotmail Web site, you must configure Outlook 2007 with a different URL (not the Hotmail URL) to retrieve your MSN mail. To configure Outlook 2007 to connect to MSN mail servers, start the Add New E-Mail Account Wizard, enter your name and e-mail address (in the form **someone@msn.com**), and then select HTTP as the account type. When the wizard prompts you for the account information, select MSN in the HTTP Service Provider drop-down list, and the Server URL information is automatically filled in. To complete your MSN configuration, specify your MSN account name and password in the Logon Information area of the dialog box, and then click Next. Outlook 2007 creates a .pst file in which to store the messages. In addition, the MSN paid e-mail service (MSN Premium) and ISP service (MSN Dial-Up) include the Microsoft Outlook 2007 Connector, which allows you to manage your MSN account and e-mail offline, as well as synchronize messages, contacts, calendars, notes, and tasks.

For additional information about configuring HTTP account properties, see "Using Outlook with Hotmail Accounts" earlier in this chapter.

Using Multiple Accounts

Although many people still have only one e-mail account, it's becoming much more common to have several. For example, you might have an e-mail account for work, a personal POP3 account with your ISP, and a Hotmail account. Although versions of Microsoft Outlook prior to Outlook 2002 sometimes made it difficult to use multiple accounts, Outlook 2003 and Outlook 2007 accommodate multiple accounts with ease, all in the same profile, which means that you don't need to switch profiles as you use different accounts.

Setting up for multiple accounts is easy—just add the accounts, as needed, to your profile. However, working with multiple accounts in a single profile requires a few considerations, as explained here.

Sending Messages Using a Specific Account

When you send a message, Outlook 2007 will use the default account unless you choose a different one before sending the message, as shown in Figure 7-9. This can sometimes be a problem when you have multiple accounts in your profile. For example, you might want to send a personal message through your personal POP3 account, but if your Exchange Server account is designated as the default, your personal message will go through your office mail server. This might violate company policies or expose your personal messages to review by a system administrator. Additionally, the reply address comes from the account that Outlook 2007 uses to send the message, which means that replies will come back to that account. You might want to check your POP3 mail from home, for example, but you find that replies have been directed to your office account because the original messages were sent under that account.

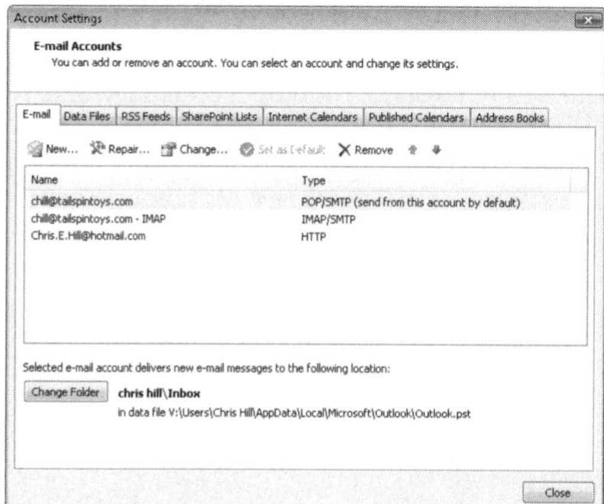

Figure 7-9. Outlook 2007 uses one of your e-mail accounts as the default account for outgoing messages.

Sending messages with a specific account is simple in Outlook 2007. When you compose the message, click Account in the message form, as shown in Figure 7-10, and then select the account you want Outlook 2007 to use to send the current message. Outlook 2007 then uses the reply address and other settings for the selected account for that message.

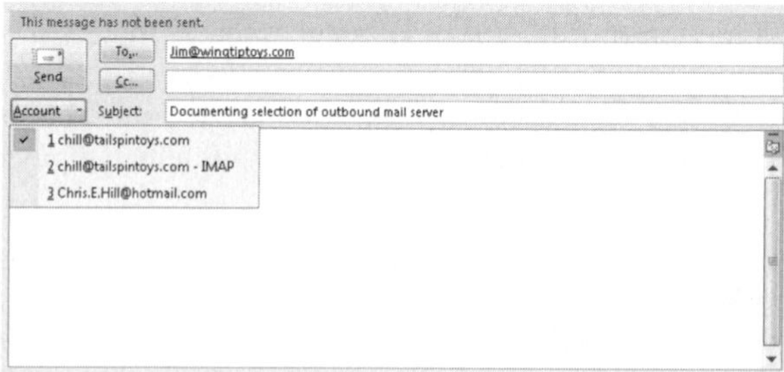

Figure 7-10. Select the account from which you want to send the message by using the Account button in the message form.

Separating Incoming Messages by Account

With the exception of mail for IMAP and HTTP accounts, Outlook 2007 delivers all mail to the default message store. (Outlook 2007 delivers IMAP and HTTP mail to the store associated with the respective accounts.) This can be a problem or an annoyance because all your e-mail could potentially wind up in the same Inbox, regardless of which account it came through. If you manage multiple accounts, it's useful to keep the messages separate. For example, you might want to keep personal messages that come through your POP3 account separate from those that come to your Exchange Server account.

You can separate messages into specific folders or stores using message rules, which allow you to specify actions that Outlook 2007 should take for messages that meet specific criteria, including the account to which they were delivered. For a complete discussion of rules and automatic message processing, see Chapter 11, "Processing Messages Automatically."

INSIDE OUT **Keep messages separate on a shared computer**

If you share a computer with other users, you probably want to keep your messages separate from those of the other users. Although you could use the same logon account and create separate profiles or even use the same profile and set up message rules to separate the incoming messages, neither method is a very good solution. Instead, use different logon accounts on the computer, which keeps your Outlook 2007 profiles separate and therefore keeps your messages separate.

Keeping a Copy of Your Mail on the Server

If you want to be able to retrieve your mail from different computers, you might want to keep a copy of your messages on the mail server. This makes all messages available no matter where you are or which computer you use to retrieve them. For example, if your computer at the office is configured to retrieve messages from your POP3 account every hour and you don't leave a copy of the messages on the server, you'll be able to see only the last hour's worth of messages if you connect from a different computer.

IMAP stores messages on the server by default. POP3 accounts, however, work differently. By default, Outlook 2007 retrieves the messages from the POP3 server and deletes them from the server. If you want the messages to remain on the server, you need to configure Outlook 2007 specifically to do so. Here's how:

1. In Outlook 2007, choose Tools, Account Settings. Alternatively, start the Mail applet in Control Panel (Classic View), and then click E-Mail Accounts.

2. Select the POP3 account, and then click Change.

3. Click More Settings, and then click the Advanced tab.
4. Select Leave A Copy Of Messages On The Server, and then use the two associated options if you want Outlook 2007 to remove the messages after a specific time or after they have been deleted from your local Deleted Items folder.
5. Click OK, click Next, and then click Finish.

TROUBLESHOOTING

My mail server won't accept outgoing messages

Your mail service might not accept mail relay (outgoing messages) unless you connect to the mail server's network. For example, POP3 Classic CompuServe accounts do not support mail relay from other servers. You must dial a special CompuServe number, or point-of-presence, to place your computer on CompuServe's network and establish a connection to CompuServe's outgoing mail server.

Connecting through the server's network isn't always practical, however. For example, if you live in a rural area, you might not have a local access number for your service. In this situation, you might use a local ISP account to connect to the Internet. Your ISP then provides a mail relay that lets you send messages through your account on the ISP's mail server.

To make this work, simply specify your ISP's outgoing mail server instead of the mail server for the remote network, or if you connect through your LAN and your organization provides a mail server with relay capability, specify that server for outgoing mail.

You specify the outgoing mail server through the e-mail account's dialog box by following these steps:

1. In Outlook 2007, choose Tools, Account Settings. Alternatively, right-click the E-Mail (Microsoft Outlook 2007) icon on the Start menu, choose Properties, and then click E-Mail Accounts.
2. Select the POP3 account, and then click Change.
3. Specify the server in the Outgoing Mail Server (SMTP) box, click Next, and then click Finish.

Another option is to use the SMTP service included with Microsoft Windows® XP to send outgoing mail. See the following section for details. Note that Windows Vista™ does not include an SMTP service, so using your own computer as the SMTP server is possible only with Windows XP.

INSIDE OUT **Synchronization with IMAP**

Accessing a POP3 account from more than one computer can cause some real synchronization headaches. Rather than configuring the POP3 e-mail client to leave messages on the POP3 e-mail server so that you can access the messages from other computers, switch to using IMAP instead of POP3 if the server supports IMAP. The messages remain on the server by default, eliminating the need for you to worry about synchronization at all.

Setting Your Own Computer as the Outgoing Mail Server

In some situations, such as the one described in the preceding section, you won't have access to an outgoing mail server for a particular account. Most ISPs, large or small, prevent users from sending mail through their server unless the users are connected to the ISP's network. Dialing in to the ISP provides this connection.

In situations when it isn't practical for you to send outgoing mail through another e-mail server, you can often use your own computer to send the mail. Outlook 2007 isn't capable of this, but the SMTP service included with Windows XP Professional is designed for just that purpose. (The SMTP service is not included with Windows XP Home Edition, nor is it included with Windows Vista.)

Note

Some mail servers do not accept mail from unrecognized servers, so in some instances, you might have problems using your own computer to send mail to certain domains. Even so, the SMTP service can be a very useful tool that handles the majority of your outgoing mail. However, if your computer is connected to a network, check with your network administrator before installing the SMTP service as explained in this section, because adding the service entails some risk.

First, check to see whether the SMTP service is already installed on your computer. The SMTP service requires Microsoft Internet Information Services (IIS), so you need to add IIS as well. In Windows XP:

1. Open Control Panel, and launch Add Or Remove Programs.
2. Click Add/Remove Windows Components, scroll down and select Internet Information Services, and then click Details.
3. Select the SMTP service, and then click OK.

4. Click Next, and then follow the prompts to complete the IIS/SMTP installation. After IIS is installed, open the Internet Information Services console from the Administrative Tools folder, expand the tree and right-click Default Web Site, and then choose Properties.
5. Click the Directory Security tab, click Edit in the Anonymous Access And Authentication Control group, clear the Anonymous Access check box, and then click OK, click Yes, and click OK again to close the Default Web Site Properties dialog box for the Web site.
6. Right-click Default SMTP Virtual Server, choose Properties, and then click the Access tab. Click Authentication, clear the Anonymous Access check box, select the Integrated Windows Authentication option, and then click OK.
7. Click Relay, click Only The List Below, click Allow All Computers Which Successfully Authenticate To Relay, Regardless Of The List Above, and then click OK. Click OK to close the Default SMTP Virtual Server Properties dialog box for the SMTP server.
8. In Outlook 2007, click Tools, Account Settings, and then click Change to open the Change E-Mail Account dialog box for the account for which you need to specify the outgoing mail server, and type **localhost**. (If you are using the SMTP service on a different computer on your network, enter that IP address instead.)
9. Click More Settings to open the Internet E-Mail Settings dialog box, and then click the Outgoing Server tab. Select the My Outgoing Server (SMTP) Requires Authentication option, select the Log On Using option, enter valid credentials (such as your own local logon account) in the User Name and Password fields, and then click OK. Click Next, and then click Finish to complete the changes to the account settings.

Note

If other users on the network will be using the SMTP service on your computer to send outgoing mail or if you are sending through the SMTP service on another computer, select the Log On Using Secure Password Authentication (SPA) option on the Outgoing Server tab in the Outlook 2007 account settings.

In step 5, you disabled anonymous access to Default Web Site, which will help prevent infections by Web-borne viruses and worms. In steps 7 and 8, you restricted access to the SMTP service to only those clients that authenticate to the server, which should prevent spam relay through your computer.

Viewing Full Message Headers

Internet messages include routing information in their headers that specifies the sending address and server, the route the message took to get to you, and other data. In most cases, the header offers more information than you need, particularly if all you're interested in is the body of the message. However, if you're trying to troubleshoot a mail problem or identify a sender who is spamming you, the headers can be useful.

INSIDE OUT Track down spammers

You can't always assume that the information in a message header is accurate. Spammers often spoof or impersonate another user or server—or relay mail through another server—to hide the true origin of the message. The header helps you identify where the mail came from so that you can inform the server's administrator that the server is being used to relay spam. To notify the administrator, you can send a message to *postmaster@<domain>*, where <domain> is the relaying mail server's domain, such as *postmaster@tailspintoys.com*. Most ISPs also recognize an abuse mailbox, such as *abuse@compuserve.com*.

To view the full message header, right-click the message, and then choose Message Options to display the Message Options dialog box, shown in Figure 7-11. The message header appears in the Internet Headers box. You can select the text and press Ctrl+C to copy the text to the Clipboard for inclusion in a note or other message.

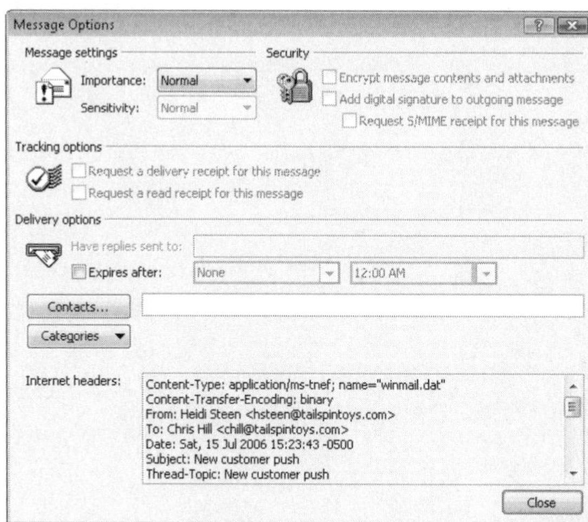

Figure 7-11. View the full message header in the Message Options dialog box.

You can take several steps to reduce the amount of unsolicited e-mail you receive. See Chapter 12, "Managing Junk E-Mail," for details about blocking spam and filtering messages.

CHAPTER 8

Sending and Receiving Messages

Of all the features in Microsoft® Office Outlook® 2007, messaging is probably the most frequently used. Even if you use Office Outlook 2007 primarily for contact management or scheduling, chances are good that you also rely heavily on the Outlook 2007 e-mail and other messaging capabilities. Because many of the Outlook 2007 key features make extensive use of messaging for workgroup collaboration and scheduling, understanding messaging is critical to using the program effectively.

This chapter provides an in-depth look at a wide range of topics related to sending and receiving messages with Outlook 2007. You'll learn the fundamentals–working with message forms, addressing, replying, and forwarding–but you'll also explore other more-advanced topics. For example, this chapter explains how to control when your messages are sent, how to save a copy of sent messages in specific folders, and how to work with attachments.

Working with Messages

This section of the chapter offers a primer to bring you up to speed on the Outlook 2007 basic messaging capabilities. It focuses on topics that relate to all types of e-mail accounts. The Inbox is the place to start learning about Outlook 2007, so launch the program and open the Inbox folder. The next section explains how to work with message forms.

> **Note**
>
> If you haven't added e-mail accounts to your profile, see the appropriate chapter for details. Chapter 7, "Using Internet Mail Accounts," explains how to configure POP3, IMAP, and HTTP accounts; Chapter 41, "Configuring the Exchange Server Client," explains how to configure the Microsoft Exchange Server client.

Opening a Standard Message Form

You can begin a new message in Outlook 2007 by using any one of these methods:

- Choose File, New, Mail Message.
- With the Inbox open, click New on the message form toolbar.
- Click the down arrow beside the New button on the message form toolbar and choose Mail Message.
- With the Inbox open, press **Ctrl+N**.

Outlook 2007 uses a new native e-mail editor that is based on Microsoft Office Word 2007. When you begin a new message, Outlook 2007 displays the Untitled Message form, shown in Figure 8-1.

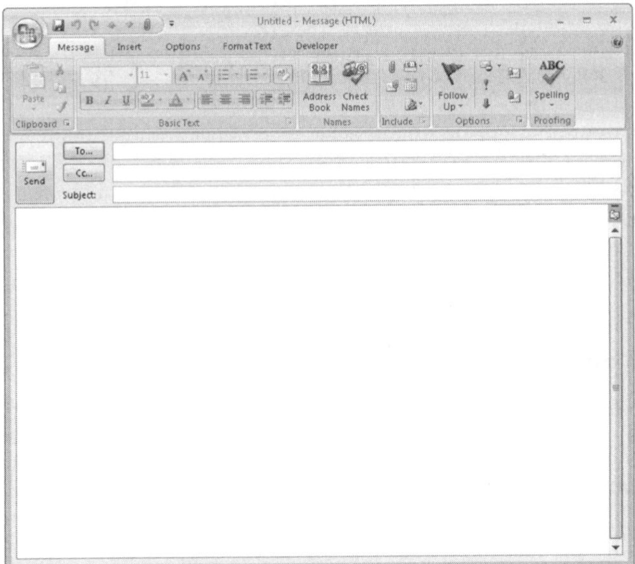

Figure 8-1. You use this standard message form to compose e-mail messages.

Addressing Messages

The Outlook 2007 address books make it easy to address messages. When you want to send a message to someone whose address is stored in your Contacts folder or an address list on the server, you can click in the To box on the message form and type the recipient's name–you don't have to type the entire address. When you send the message, Outlook 2007 checks the name, locates the correct address, and adds it to the message. If multiple addresses match the name you specify, Outlook 2007 shows all the matches and prompts you to select the appropriate one. If you want to send a message to someone whose address isn't in any of your address books, you need to type the full address in the To box.

For more information about Outlook 2007 address books, see Chapter 6, "Managing Address Books and Distribution Lists."

> **Note**
>
> Outlook 2007 can check the names and addresses of message recipients before you send the message. Enter the names in the To box and click the Check Names button on the message form toolbar to perform this action.

To open the address book (see Figure 8-2), click an Address Book icon (To, Cc, or Bcc) beside an address box on the message form. Outlook 2007 opens the Select Names dialog box, which you can use to address the message.

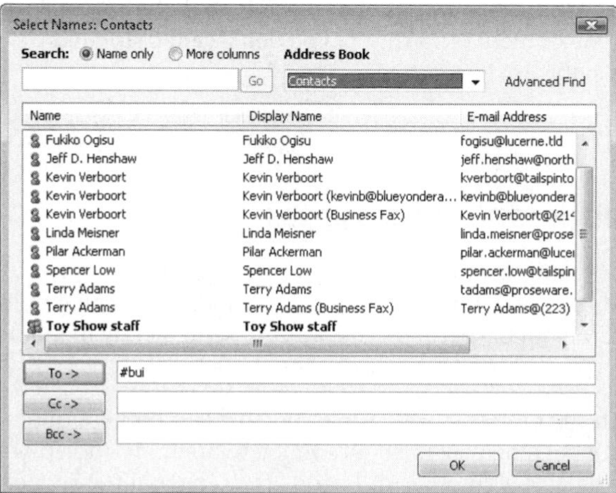

Figure 8-2. In the Select Names dialog box, you can select addresses from the address book.

Follow these steps to select addresses in this dialog box and add them to your message:

1. In the Address Book drop-down list, select the address list you want to view.
2. Select a name from the list, and click To, Cc, or Bcc to add the selected address to the specified address box.
3. Continue this process to add more recipients if necessary. Click OK when you're satisfied with the list.

> **Note**
>
> You can include multiple recipients in each address box on the message form. If you're typing the addresses yourself, separate them with a semicolon.

Including Carbon Copies and Blind Carbon Copies

You can direct a single message to multiple recipients by including multiple addresses in the To box on the message form or by using the Cc (Carbon Copy) and Bcc (Blind Carbon Copy) boxes. The Cc box appears by default on message forms, but the Bcc box does not. To display the Bcc box, on the Options ribbon, in the Fields group, choose Bcc. You use the Cc and Bcc boxes the same way you use the To box: type a name or address in the box, or click the Address Book icon beside the box to open the address book.

INSIDE OUT **Hide addresses when necessary**

The names contained in the To and Cc boxes of your message are visible to all recipients of the message. If you're using a distribution list, Outlook 2007 converts the names on the list to individual addresses, exposing those addresses to the recipients. If you want to hide the names of one or more recipients, or you don't want distribution lists exposed, place those names in the Bcc box.

Copying Someone on All Messages

In some situations, you might want every outgoing message to be copied to a particular person. For example, maybe you manage a small staff and want all employees' outgoing messages copied to you. Or perhaps you want to send a copy of all of your outgoing messages to yourself at a separate e-mail account.

Rules you create with the Outlook 2007 Rules Wizard can process outgoing messages as well as incoming ones. One way to ensure that a recipient is copied on all outgoing messages is to add a rule that automatically adds the recipient to the message's Cc field. Follow these steps to do so:

1. Choose Tools, Rules And Alerts to begin creating the rule.
2. Click New Rule; in the Start From A Blank Rule group, select Check Messages After Sending and click Next.
3. Click Next again without choosing any conditions to cause the rule to be used for all messages. Click Yes in the warning dialog box to confirm that you want the rule applied to all messages.
4. Select the action Cc The Message To People Or Distribution List; then click the underlined link in the Rule Description box and select the addresses where you want to send the carbon copies. These addresses can be from the Global Address List (GAL) or your Contacts folder, or you can type in specific addresses.
5. Click Next, set exceptions as needed, and then click Next.

6. Supply a Name for the rule, verify that the Turn On This Rule check box is selected, and ensure that you are satisfied with the rule settings; then click Finish. Click OK to close the Rules And Alerts dialog box.

For more details about working with message rules, see Chapter 11, "Processing Messages Automatically."

> **Note**
>
> Outlook might display a dialog box informing you that the rule you are creating is client-side only. For information on client-side rules, see the section "Creating Client-Side and Server-Side Rules" in Chapter 11.

Unfortunately, Outlook 2007 doesn't offer a Bcc action for the rule. The add-on Always BCC for Outlook 2007, available at *www.sperrysoftware.com/jcAlwaysBCC.asp*, enables you to automatically add a Bcc recipient. It is designed to work with the Outlook E-Mail Security Update for Outlook 2000 and the same features built into Outlook 2002, Outlook 2003, and Outlook 2007.

Using Templates and Custom Forms for Addressing

A rule is handy for copying all messages—or only certain messages—to one or more people, as explained in the preceding section. Distribution lists are handy for addressing a message to a group of people without entering the address for each person.

If you regularly send the same message to the same people but want to specify some on the To field, others in the Cc field, and still others in the Bcc field, distribution lists and rules won't do the trick. Instead, you can use a template or a custom form to send the message. You create the form or template ahead of time with the addresses in the desired fields; you then open that item, complete it, and send it on its way. Use the following steps to create and use a template for this purpose:

1. In Outlook 2007, start a new message.
2. Enter the e-mail or distribution list addresses as needed in the To, Cc, and Bcc fields.
3. Enter any other information that remains the same each time you send the message, such as subject or boilerplate text in the body of the message.
4. Click the Microsoft Office Button, click Save As and then click Save As.
5. Choose Outlook Template from the Save As Type drop-down list.
6. Enter a name in the File Name field, and if you want to use a location other than your Templates folder, choose a path for the template.

7. Click Save to save the template.
8. Close the message form and click No if prompted to save changes.
9. When it's time to create the message, choose Tools, Forms, Choose Form to open the Choose Form dialog box (see Figure 8-3).
10. Choose User Templates In File System from the Look In drop-down list, choose the template you created in step 7, and click Open.

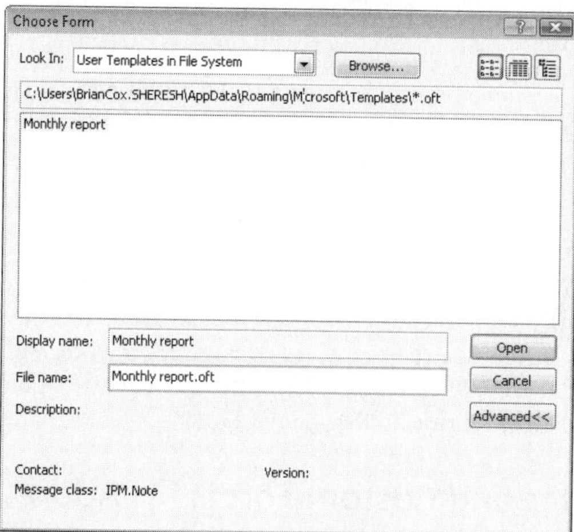

Figure 8-3. Open the template from the Choose Form dialog box.

11. Add any other recipients of message content and click Send to send the message.

> **Note**
>
> If you use the default Template folder for your templates, you don't have to browse for them when you choose the User Templates In File System option.

See Chapter 25, "Using Templates," for more information on using templates in Outlook 2007 and Chapter 28, "Designing and Using Forms," for details on creating and using custom forms.

Specifying Message Priority and Sensitivity

By default, new messages have their priority set to Normal. You might want to change the priority to High for important or time-sensitive messages or to Low for non-work mail or other messages that have relatively less importance. Outlook 2007 displays an icon in the Importance column of the recipient's Inbox to indicate High or Low priority. (For messages with Normal priority, no icon is displayed.)

The easiest way to set message priority is by using the Message ribbon in the message form. In the Options group, click the High Importance button (which has an exclamation point icon) to specify High priority. Click the Low Importance button (which has a down arrow icon) to specify Low priority. To set the priority back to Normal, click the selected priority again to remove the highlight around the button (see Figure 8-4).

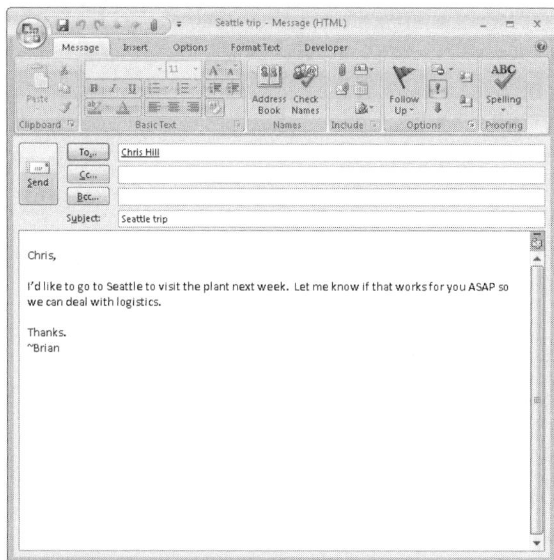

Figure 8-4. Outlook 2007 highlights the appropriate priority button to provide a visual indicator of the message's priority.

You also can specify a message's sensitivity by choosing a Normal (the default), Personal, Private, or Confidential sensitivity level. Setting sensitivity adds a tag to the message that displays the sensitivity level you selected. This helps the recipient see at a glance how you want the message to be treated. To set sensitivity, click the More button in the Options group on the Message ribbon and select the sensitivity level from the Sensitivity drop-down list.

Saving a Message to Send Later

Although you can create some messages in a matter of seconds, others can take considerably longer—particularly if you're using formatting or special features, or if you're composing a lengthy message. If you're interrupted while composing a message or if you simply want to leave the message to finish later, you can save the message in your Drafts folder. Later, when you have time, you can reopen the message, complete it, and send it. Click the Microsoft Office Button and choose Save in the message form to have Outlook 2007 save the message to the Drafts folder (see Figure 8-5). When you're ready to work on the message again, open the Drafts folder and double-click the message to open it.

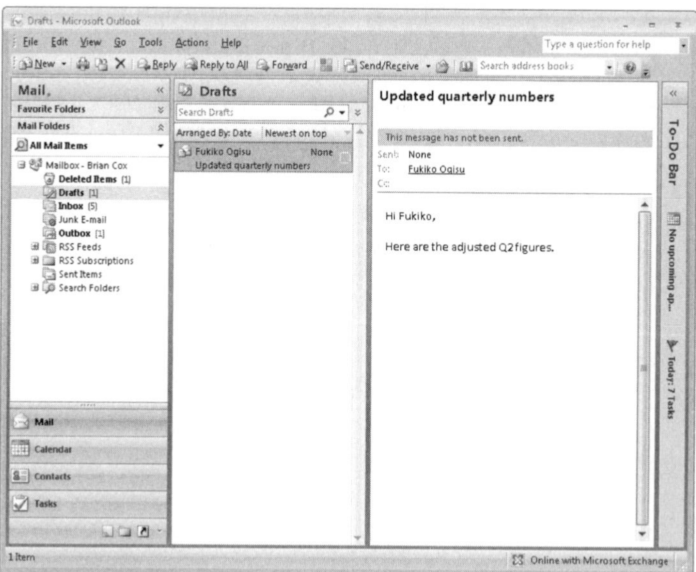

Figure 8-5. Messages in progress are kept in the Drafts folder.

> **Note**
>
> You also can click the Microsoft Office Button and choose Save As to save a message as an HTML document (or in another document format) outside your Outlook 2007 folders.

Setting Sending Options

In the Advanced E-Mail Options dialog box (see Figure 8-6), you can configure various options that affect how Outlook 2007 sends e-mail messages. To open this dialog box, choose Tools, Options and then click E-Mail Options on the Preferences tab. In the E-Mail Options dialog box, click Advanced E-Mail Options.

For details on specifying which account is used to send a message, see the section "Sending Messages Using a Specific Account" in Chapter 7.

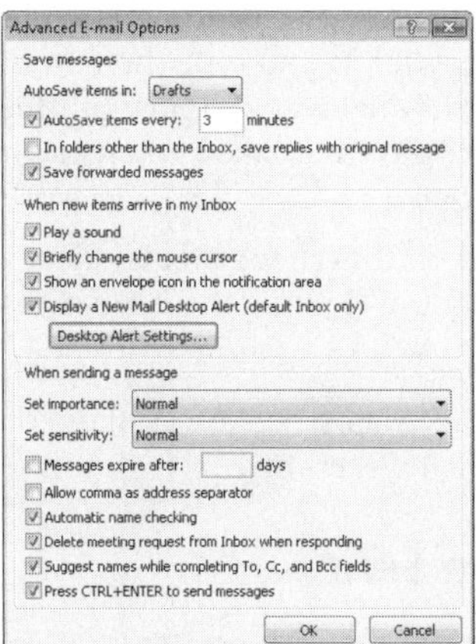

Figure 8-6. You can choose options for sending messages in the Advanced E-Mail Options dialog box.

In the Advanced E-Mail Options dialog box, you can modify the following settings:

- **Set Importance** This option sets the default importance or priority level for all new messages. When you compose a message, you can override this setting by clicking the High Priority button or the Low Priority button on the toolbar in the message form, or by clicking Options on the toolbar and setting the priority in the Message Options dialog box. The default setting is Normal.
- **Set Sensitivity** This option sets the default sensitivity level for all new messages. When you compose a message, you can override this setting by clicking Options on the toolbar and setting the sensitivity level in the Message Options dialog box. The default setting is Normal.
- **Messages Expire After *n* Days** This option causes the messages to expire after the specified number of days. The message appears in strikethrough in the recipient's mailbox at that time. (This setting does not necessarily work with every e-mail client.)
- **Allow Comma As Address Separator** If this check box is selected, you can use commas as well as semicolons in the To, Cc, and Bcc boxes of a message form to separate addresses.
- **Automatic Name Checking** Select this check box to have Outlook 2007 attempt to match names to e-mail addresses. Verified addresses are underlined, and those for which Outlook 2007 finds multiple matches are underscored by a red wavy line. When multiple matches exist and you've used a particular address before, Outlook 2007 underscores the name with a green dashed line to indicate that other choices are available.
- **Delete Meeting Request From Inbox When Responding** Select this check box to have Outlook 2007 delete a meeting request from your Inbox when you respond to the request. If you accept the meeting, Outlook 2007 enters the meeting in your calendar. Clear this check box if you want to retain the meeting request in your Inbox.

- **Suggest Names While Completing To, Cc, And Bcc Fields** When this check box is selected, Outlook 2007 completes addresses as you type them in the To, Cc, and Bcc boxes of the message form. Clear this check box to turn off this automatic completion. See Chapter 5, "Managing Address Books and Distribution Lists," for more information on the address nickname cache and how to work with it.
- **Press Ctrl+Enter To Send Messages** When this check box is selected, Outlook 2007 accepts **Ctrl+Enter** as the equivalent of clicking the Send button when composing a message.

Other options in the Advanced E-Mail Options dialog box are explained in other locations in this book, including in the following sections.

Controlling When Messages Are Sent

To specify when Outlook 2007 should send messages, choose Tools, Options and click Mail Setup to locate the Send Immediately When Connected option. With this option selected, Outlook 2007 sends messages as soon as you click Send (provided that Outlook 2007 is online). If Outlook 2007 is offline, the messages go into the Outbox until you process them with a send/receive operation (which is also what happens if you do not select this option).

Requesting Delivery and Read Receipts

Regardless of which e-mail editor you use, you can request a *delivery receipt* or a *read receipt* for any message. Both types of receipts are messages that are delivered back to you after you send your message. A delivery receipt indicates the date and time your message was delivered to the recipient's mailbox. A read receipt indicates the date and time the recipient opened the message.

Specifying that you want a delivery receipt or read receipt for a message doesn't guarantee that you'll get one. The recipient's mail server or mail client might not support delivery and read receipts. The recipient might have configured the e-mail client to automatically reject requests for receipts or the recipient might answer No when prompted to send a receipt. If you receive a receipt, it's a good indication that the message was delivered or read. If you don't receive a receipt, however, don't assume that the message wasn't delivered or read. A message receipt serves only as a positive notification, not a negative one.

To request receipts for a message you're composing, in the Options group of the Message ribbon, click the More button to display the Message Options dialog box (see Figure 8-7). You'll find the delivery and read receipt options in the Voting And Tracking Options group.

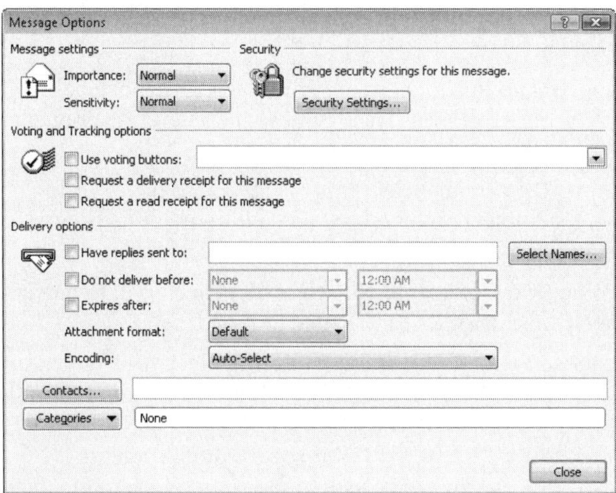

Figure 8-7. Use the Message Options dialog box to request a delivery receipt, a read receipt, or both.

Using Message Tracking and Receipts Options

You can set options to determine how Outlook 2007 handles delivery and read receipts by default. Choose Tools, Options and click E-Mail Options on the Preferences tab. In the E-Mail Options dialog box, click Tracking Options to display the Tracking Options dialog box, shown in Figure 8-8, in which you'll find the options discussed in this section.

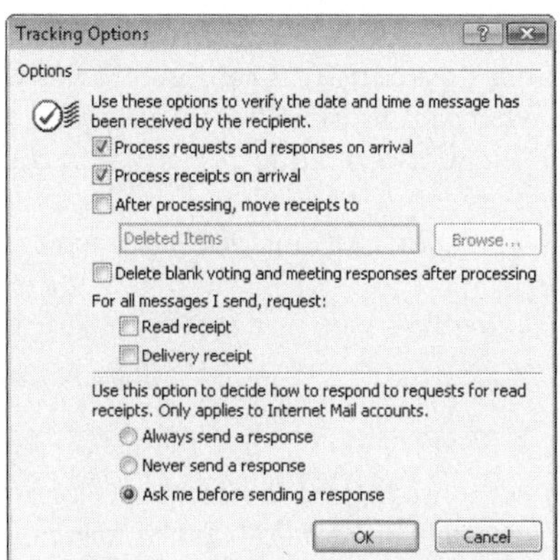

Figure 8-8. Process receipts and responses in the Tracking Options dialog box.

The following options control how Outlook 2007 requests read receipts and how the receipts are processed after they are received:

- **Process Requests And Responses On Arrival** Select this check box to have Outlook 2007 process all message receipt requests and responses when they arrive.
- **Process Receipts On Arrival** Select this check box to have Outlook 2007 generate received/read receipts when messages come in requesting them. Clear this check box to have Outlook 2007 prompt you for each receipt.
- **After Processing, Move Receipts To** Select this check box to have Outlook 2007 move receipts from the Inbox to the specified folder.
- **For All Messages I Send, Request Read Receipt** Select this check box to have Outlook 2007 request a read receipt for each message you send. When you compose a message, you can override this setting; to do so, click the Options button in the Options group of the Message ribbon.
- **For All Messages I Send, Request Delivery Receipt** Select this check box to have Outlook 2007 request a delivery receipt for each message you send.

These three options in the Tracking Options dialog box let you control how Outlook 2007 responds to requests from others for read receipts on messages you receive and apply to Internet mail accounts only:

- **Always Send A Response** When this option is selected, Outlook 2007 always sends a read receipt to any senders who request one. Outlook 2007 generates the read receipt when you open the message.
- **Never Send A Response** Select this option to prevent Outlook 2007 from sending read receipts to senders who request them. Outlook 2007 will not prompt you regarding receipts.
- **Ask Me Before Sending A Response** Selecting this option enables you to control, on a message-by-message basis, whether Outlook 2007 sends read receipts. When you open a message for which the sender has requested a read receipt, Outlook 2007 prompts you to authorize the receipt. If you click Yes, Outlook 2007 generates and sends the receipt. If you click No, Outlook 2007 doesn't create or send a receipt.

> **Note**
>
> The Delete Blank Voting And Meeting Responses After Processing check box, if selected, causes Outlook 2007 to delete voting and meeting requests that contain no comments. Instead, Outlook 2007 processes them automatically.

See the section "Voting in Outlook" in Chapter 42, "Using Outlook with Exchange Server," to learn more about voting. See Chapter 20, "Scheduling Appointments," to learn about the Calendar and scheduling meetings.

Sending a Message for Review

If you compose a message from Office Word 2007 (that is, you started Word 2007 outside Outlook 2007), you have the ability to send the message as a document for review. You might use this feature if you're collaborating on a document with others or incorporating their comments into the final draft. Recipients can review the document and add comments, which they send back to you. They also can incorporate the changes directly into the document, which enables them to take advantage of the Word 2007 revision marks feature.

Before you can send a document for review, you must first add the Send For Review button to the Word 2007 Quick Access Toolbar. To do this, open the document in Word 2007, click the Microsoft Office Button, and choose Word Options. In the Word Options dialog box, select Customize, and then select Commands Not In The Ribbon in the Choose Commands From drop-down list. Select Send For Review and click Add; then click OK. In the document, click the Send For Review button, and then address and send the e-mail message as usual.

For more detailed information on sending documents for review, see *Microsoft Office Word 2007 Inside Out*, by Mary Millhollon and Katherine Murray (Microsoft Press, 2006).

Replying to Messages

When you reply to a message, Outlook 2007 sends your reply to the person who sent you the message. Replying to a message is simple: select the message in the Inbox, and then click the Reply button on the Standard toolbar; choose Actions, Reply; or press **Ctrl+R**. Outlook 2007 opens a message form and, depending on how you have configured Outlook 2007 for replies, can also include the original message content in various formats.

If the message to which you're replying was originally sent to multiple recipients, and you want to send your reply to all of them, click Reply To All; choose Actions, Reply To All; or press **Ctrl+Shift+R**.

For more information about message replies, see the section "Using Other Reply and Forwarding Options" on the next page.

> **Note**
>
> When you use Reply All, Outlook 2007 places all the addresses in the To box. If you don't want the recipients list to be visible, use the Bcc box to send blind carbon copies. To do this, click Reply All, highlight the addresses in the To box, and cut them. Then click in the Bcc box and paste the addresses there.

Forwarding Messages

In addition to replying to a message, you can forward the message to one or more recipients. To forward a message, select the message header in the message folder (Inbox or other), and then click Forward in the Respond group of the Message ribbon or press **Ctrl+F**. Outlook 2007 opens a new message form and either incorporates the original message in the body of the current one or attaches it to the new message.

If you forward a single message, Outlook 2007 forwards the original message in the body of your new message by default, and you can add your own comments. If you prefer, however, you can configure Outlook 2007 to forward messages as attachments instead of including them in the body of your messages.

> **Note**
>
> If you select multiple messages and click Forward, Outlook 2007 sends the messages as attachments instead of including them in the body of your message.

Using Other Reply and Forwarding Options

You can change how Outlook 2007 handles and formats message replies and forwarded messages. These options are found in the E-Mail Options dialog box, shown in Figure 8-9.

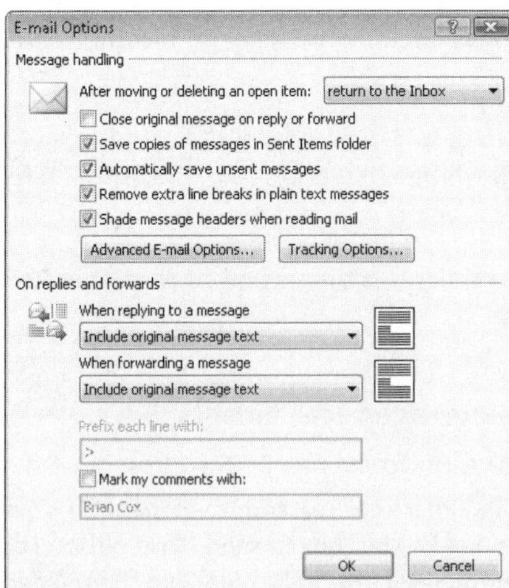

Figure 8-9. You can set options for message replies and forwarded messages in the E-Mail Options dialog box.

To open this dialog box, click Tools, Options; then click E-Mail Options on the Preferences tab. You can then view or set the following options that affect replies and forwards:

- **Close Original Message On Reply Or Forward** Select this check box to have Outlook 2007 close the message form when you click Reply or Forward. Clear this check box to have Outlook 2007 leave the message form open. If you frequently forward the same message with different comments to different recipients, it's useful to have Outlook 2007 leave the message open so that you don't have to open it again to perform the next forward.
- **When Replying To A Message** Use this drop-down list to specify how Outlook 2007 handles the original message text when you reply to a message. You can choose to have Outlook 2007 generate a clean reply without the current message text, include the text without changes, or include but indent the text, for example. Note that you can either include the original message text in the body of your reply or add it to the message as an attachment.
- **When Forwarding A Message** Use this drop-down list to specify how Outlook 2007 handles the original message text when you forward a message. You can, for example, include the message in the body of the forwarded message or add it as an attachment.
- **Prefix Each Line With** If you select Prefix Each Line Of The Original Message in the When Replying To A Message drop-down list or the When Forwarding A Message drop-down list, you can use this box to specify the character Outlook 2007 uses to prefix each line of the original message in the body of the reply or forwarded message. The default is an angle bracket (>) and a space, but you can use one or more characters of your choice.
- **Mark My Comments With** Select this check box and enter a name or other text in the associated box. Outlook 2007 will add the specified text to mark your typed comments in the body of a message that you are replying to or forwarding.

For more details on replying to and forwarding messages, see the sections "Replying to Messages" and "Forwarding Messages" earlier in this chapter.

TROUBLESHOOTING

You can't forward a single message as an attachment

In Outlook 2007, you can send documents from other 2007 Microsoft® Office system applications as attachments, and you can forward multiple messages in Outlook 2007 as attachments. However, sending a single message as an attachment instead of including it in the body of the message in Outlook 2007 requires that you either reconfigure the Outlook 2007 default behavior before forwarding the message or use a workaround.

To change the Outlook 2007 default behavior so that it sends a single message as an attachment when you forward it, choose Tools, Options, E-Mail Options. In the When

Forwarding A Message drop-down list, select Attach Original Message and click OK. This setting now applies to all messages you forward, not just the current one.

If you want to override the Outlook 2007 default behavior for the current message only, use one of these two workarounds. One method is to select *two* messages to forward and then, in the message form, delete the attached message that you don't want to include. A second method is to compose a new message and choose Insert, Item to insert the message (or any other Outlook 2007 item).

Deleting Messages

When you delete messages from any folder other than the Deleted Items folder, the messages are moved to the Deleted Items folder. You can then recover the messages by moving them to other folders, if needed. When Outlook 2007 deletes messages from the Deleted Items folder, however, those messages are deleted from Outlook 2007 permanently.

You can set Outlook 2007 to automatically delete all messages from the Deleted Items folder whenever you exit the program, which helps keep the size of your message store manageable. However, it also means that unless you recover a deleted message before you exit Outlook 2007, that message is irretrievably lost. If you seldom have to recover deleted files, this might not be a problem for you.

To change what happens to items in the Deleted Items folder when you exit Outlook 2007, choose Tools, Options and click the Other tab. Select or clear Empty The Deleted Items Folder Upon Exiting.

Controlling Synchronization and Send/Receive Times

Outlook 2007 uses send and receive groups (or send/receive groups) to control when messages are sent and received for specific e-mail accounts. You can also use send/receive groups to define the types of items that Outlook 2007 synchronizes. Synchronization is the process in which Outlook 2007 synchronizes the local copy of your folders with your Exchange Server message store. For example, assume that while you were working offline you created several new e-mail messages and scheduled a few events. You connect to the Exchange Server and perform a synchronization. Outlook 2007 uploads to your Exchange Server the changes you made locally and also downloads changes from the server to your local store, such as downloading messages that have been delivered to your Inbox on the server.

Send/receive groups enable you to be flexible in controlling which functions Outlook 2007 performs for synchronization. For example, you can set up a send/receive group for your Exchange Server account that synchronizes only your Inbox, not your other folders, for those times when you simply want to perform a quick check of your mail.

Send/receive groups also are handy for helping you manage different types of accounts. For example, if you integrate your personal and work e-mail into a single profile, you can use send/receive groups to control when each type of mail is processed. You might create one send/receive group for your personal accounts and another for your work accounts. You can also use send/receive groups to limit network traffic to certain times of the day. For example, if your organization limits Internet connectivity to specific times, you could use send/receive groups to schedule your Internet accounts to synchronize during the allowed times.

Think of send/receive groups as a way to collect various accounts into groups and assign to each group specific send/receive and synchronization behavior. You can create multiple send/receive groups, and you can include the same account in multiple groups if needed.

Setting Up Send/Receive Groups

To set up or modify send/receive groups in Outlook 2007, choose Tools, Send/Receive, Send/Receive Settings, Define Send/Receive Groups. Outlook 2007 displays the Send/Receive Groups dialog box, shown in Figure 8-10. By default, Outlook 2007 sets up one group named All Accounts and configures it to send and receive when online and offline. You can modify or remove that group, add others, and configure other send/receive behavior in the Send/Receive Groups dialog box.

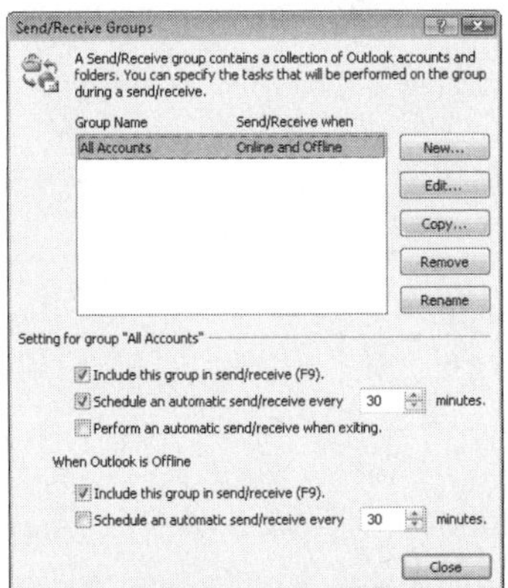

Figure 8-10. You can specify send/receive actions in the Send/Receive Groups dialog box.

When you select a group from the Group Name list, Outlook 2007 displays the associated settings in the Setting For Group area of the dialog box:

- **Include This Group In Send/Receive (F9)** Select this check box to have Outlook 2007 process accounts in the selected group when you click Send/Receive on the message form toolbar or press F9. Outlook 2007 provides this option for both online and offline behavior.

- **Schedule An Automatic Send/Receive Every *n* Minutes** Select this check box to have Outlook 2007 check the accounts in the selected group every *n* minutes (the default is 30 minutes). Outlook 2007 provides this option for both online and offline behavior.
- **Perform An Automatic Send/Receive When Exiting** Select this check box to have Outlook 2007 process the accounts in the selected group when you exit Outlook 2007 from an online session.

Creating New Groups

Although you could modify the All Accounts group to process only selected accounts, it's better to create other groups as needed and leave All Accounts as is for those times when you want to process all your e-mail accounts together.

Follow these steps to create a new group:

1. In Outlook 2007, choose Tools, Send/Receive, Send/Receive Settings, Define Send/Receive Groups.
2. Click New, type the name for the group as you want it to appear on the Send/Receive submenu, and click OK. Outlook 2007 displays the Send/Receive Settings dialog box, shown in Figure 8-11.

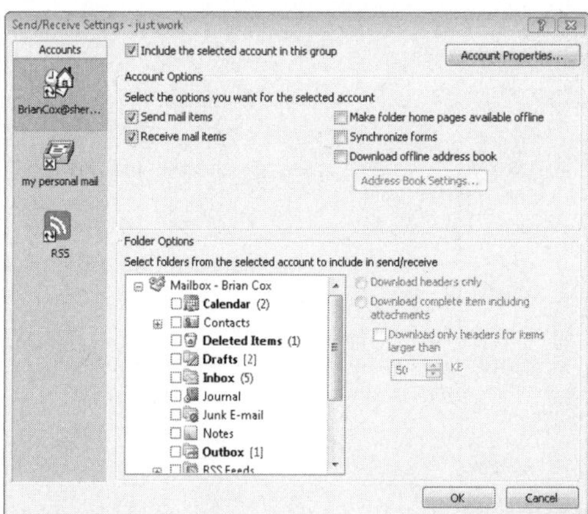

Figure 8-11. You can configure account processing in the Send/Receive Settings dialog box.

3. In the Accounts bar on the left, click the account you want to configure. By default, all accounts in the group are excluded from synchronization, indicated by the red X on the account icon.
4. Select the Include The Selected Account In This Group check box to activate the remaining options in the dialog box and to have the account included when you process messages for the selected group.

5. In the Check Folders From The Selected Account To Include In Send/Receive list, select the check box beside each folder that you want Outlook 2007 to synchronize when processing this group.

6. Select other settings, using the following list as a guide:

   Send Mail Items Select this check box to have Outlook 2007 send outgoing mail for this account when a send/receive action occurs for the group.

   Receive Mail Items Select this check box to have Outlook 2007 retrieve incoming mail for this account when a send/receive action occurs for the group.

   Make Folder Home Pages Available Offline This check box has Outlook 2007 cache folder home pages offline so that they are available to you any time.

   Synchronize Forms Select this check box to have Outlook 2007 synchronize changes to forms that have been made locally as well as changes that have been made on the server.

   Download Offline Address Book When this check box is selected, Outlook 2007 updates the offline address book when a send/receive action occurs for the group.

   Get Folder Unread Count For Internet Message Access Protocol (IMAP) accounts only; you can select this option to have Outlook 2007 get the number of unread messages from the server.

7. If you need to apply filters or message size limits, do so. Otherwise, click OK, and then click Close to close the Send/Receive Groups dialog box.

For information on how to apply message size limits, see the upcoming section "Limiting Message Size."

Other options for the send/receive group are explained in the following sections.

Modifying Existing Groups

You can modify existing send/receive groups in much the same way you create new ones. Choose Tools, Send/Receive, Send/Receive Settings, Define Send/Receive Groups. Select the group you want to modify and click Edit. The settings you can modify are the same as those discussed in the preceding section.

Limiting Message Size

You can also use the Send/Receive Settings dialog box to specify a limit on message size for messages downloaded from the Inbox of the selected Exchange Server account. This provides an easy way to control large messages that arrive in your Exchange Server account. Instead of downloading messages that are larger than the specified limit, Outlook 2007 downloads only the headers. You can then mark the messages for download or deletion, or simply double-click the message to download and open it.

Note

Specifying a message size limit in the Send/Receive Settings dialog box doesn't affect the size of messages that you can receive on the server. It simply directs Outlook 2007 to process them differently.

Follow these steps to specify a message size limit for an Exchange Server 2007 account:

1. Choose Tools, Send/Receive, Send/Receive Settings, Define Send/Receive Groups.
2. Select a group to modify and click Edit.
3. From the Accounts bar, select the Exchange Server account containing the folder for which you want to set a message size limit.
4. Select a folder, as shown in Figure 8-12.

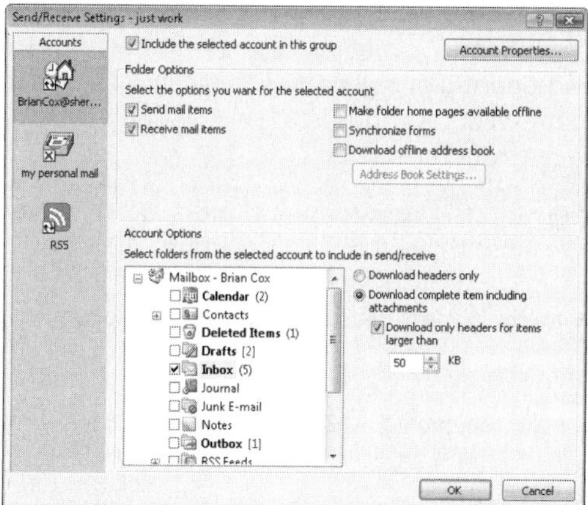

Figure 8-12. Select a folder and then set its parameters in the Send/Receive Settings dialog box.

5. Specify the criteria you want to use to limit message download, based on the following option list, and click OK:

   Download Headers Only Download only the message header, not the message body or attachments.

   Download Complete Item Including Attachments Download the entire message, including body and attachments.

   Download Only Headers For Items Larger Than Download only headers for messages over the specified size.

You can use a similar mechanism to control downloading of large messages from POP3 accounts. In this case, you can choose to download only message headers for messages larger than a specified size.

Follow these steps to configure POP3 message size filtering:

1. Choose Tools, Send/Receive, Send/Receive Settings, Define Send/Receive Groups.
2. Select a group to modify and click Edit.
3. From the Accounts bar, select the POP3 account for which you want to set a message size limit.
4. Select Download Complete Item Including Attachments, select the Download Only Headers For Items Larger Than *Nn* KB check box, specify the size limit, and click OK.

To retrieve a message with a large attachment from a POP3 server, mark the message to be downloaded.

For details on using remote mail with POP3 accounts, see the section "Working with Message Headers" in Chapter 15, "Receiving Messages Selectively."

Scheduling Send/Receive Synchronization

You can schedule synchronization for each send/receive group separately, giving you quite a bit of control over when Outlook 2007 processes your Inbox, Outbox, and other folders for synchronization. You can configure Outlook 2007 to process each send/receive group on a periodic basis and to process specific groups when you exit Outlook 2007. For example, you might schedule the All Accounts group to synchronize only when you exit Outlook 2007, even if you scheduled a handful of other groups to process messages more frequently during the day. Because you can create as many groups as needed and can place the same account in multiple groups, you have a good deal of flexibility in determining when each account is processed.

Simplify with Cached Exchange Mode

If you use an Exchange Server account, configure the account to use Cached Exchange Mode (keep a local copy of the mailbox) and avoid the issue of synchronization altogether. With Cached Exchange Mode enabled, Outlook 2007 handles synchronization on the fly, adjusting to online or offline status as needed.

For a discussion of Cached Exchange Mode, see the section "Configure Cached Exchange Mode" in Chapter 3, "Configuring Outlook Profiles and Account." Also see Chapter 41, "Configuring the Exchange Server Client."

Configuring Send/Receive Schedules

Follow these steps to configure synchronization for each send/receive group:

1. Choose Tools, Send/Receive, Send/Receive Settings, Define Send/Receive Groups.
2. In the Send/Receive Groups dialog box, select the group for which you want to modify the schedule.
3. In the Setting For Group area, select Schedule An Automatic Send/Receive Every *n* Minutes, and then specify the number of minutes that should elapse between send/receive events for the selected group. Set this option for both online and offline behavior.
4. If you want the group to be processed when you exit Outlook 2007, select Perform An Automatic Send/Receive When Exiting.

You can use a combination of scheduled and manually initiated send/receive events to process messages and accounts. For example, you can specify in the Send/Receive Group dialog box that a given group (such as All Accounts) must be included when you click Send/Receive or press F9 and then configure other accounts to process as scheduled. Thus, some accounts might process only when you manually initiate the send/receive event, and others might process only by automatic execution. In addition, you can provide an overlap so that a specific account processes manually as well as by schedule–simply include the account in multiple groups with the appropriate settings for each group.

Disabling Scheduled Send/Receive Processing

On occasion, you might want to disable scheduled send/receive events altogether. For example, assume that you're working offline and don't have a connection through which you can check your accounts. In that situation, you can turn off scheduled send/receive processing until a connection can be reestablished.

To disable scheduled send/receive processing, choose Tools, Send/Receive, Send/Receive Settings, Disable Scheduled Send/Receive. Select this command again to enable the scheduled processing.

Configuring Other Messaging Options

This section of the chapter provides an explanation of additional options in Outlook 2007 that control messaging features and tasks. You can specify how you want to be notified when new mail arrives, configure how Outlook 2007 connects for e-mail accounts that use dial-up networking, and control the formatting of Internet and international e-mail messages.

Setting Up Notification of New Mail

You might not spend a lot of time in Outlook 2007 during the day if you're busy working with other applications. However, you might want Outlook 2007 to notify you when you receive new messages. Outlook 2007 adds new Desktop Alert features to provide you with notification of the arrival of new messages. These options and additional notification options are located in the Advanced E-Mail Options dialog box (refer to Figure 8-6):

- **Play A Sound** Select this option to have Outlook 2007 play a sound when a new message arrives. By using the Change System Sounds option in Control Panel, you can change the New Mail Notification sound to use a .wav file of your choosing.
- **Briefly Change The Mouse Cursor** Select this option to have Outlook 2007 briefly change the pointer to a mail symbol when a new message arrives.
- **Show An Envelope Icon In The Notification Area** Select this option to have Outlook 2007 place an envelope icon in the system tray when new mail arrives. You can double-click the envelope icon to open your mail. The icon disappears from the tray after you read the messages.
- **Display A New Mail Desktop Alert (Default Inbox Only)** Enable this option to have Outlook 2007 display a pop-up window on the desktop when a new message arrives.

If you enable this last option, click Desktop Alert Settings to display the Desktop Alert Settings dialog box (see Figure 8-13). In this dialog box, you specify the length of time the alert remains on the desktop and the alert's transparency value. Click Preview to preview the alert.

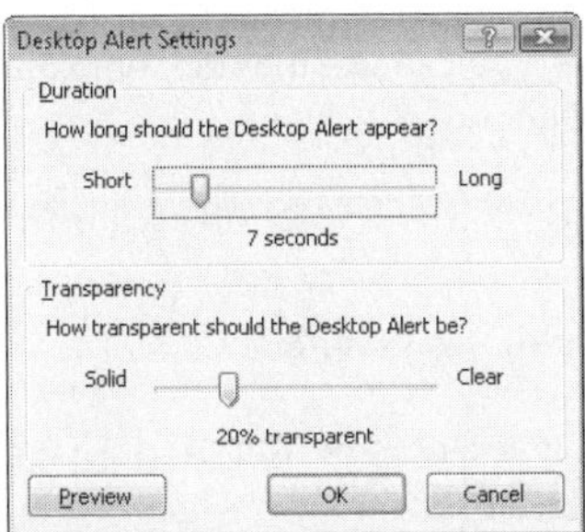

Figure 8-13. Configure alert settings with the Desktop Alert Settings dialog box.

Using Message Alerts

If you enable the Display A New Mail Desktop Alert option, Outlook 2007 displays the alert for each new message. In most cases, that's more than you need. Instead, you probably want Outlook 2007 to alert you only when you receive certain messages, such as those from people in your Contacts folder, from a specific sender, or with certain words in the subject. So instead of enabling this option globally, you might prefer to create a rule that causes the alert to be displayed when the rule fires.

There are two rule actions you can use to generate alerts:

- **Display A Desktop Alert** This action causes Outlook 2007 to display a desktop alert when the rule fires. The alert persists on the desktop for the period of time you have set for the alert in the Outlook 2007 Advanced E-Mail Options dialog box.
- **Display A Specific Message In The New Item Alerts Window** With this action, you can specify a message that appears in the New Item Alerts window (see Figure 8-14). The window persists on the desktop until you close it.

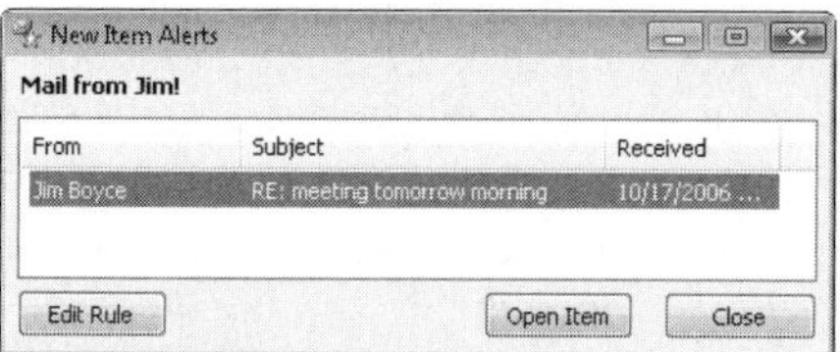

Figure 8-14. The New Item Alerts window displays text you specify.

Which action you use depends on whether you want a custom message to appear for the alert and whether you want the alert to persist until you close it or appear and then go away. To create an alert rule using one (or both) of these actions, create the rule as you would any other and select the alert action you want to use.

> **Note**
>
> To create a rule that displays a New Item Alert, you can use the rule template Display Mail From Someone in the New Item Alert Window.

For more details about working with message rules, see Chapter 11.

If you create an alert rule that uses the Display A Desktop Alert action, it's likely that you will not want Outlook 2007 to display an alert for all messages. You should choose Tools, Options; click E-Mail Options; click Advanced E-Mail Options; and clear the Display A New Mail Desktop Alert option. If you use the Display A Specific Message In The New Item Alert Window option, you might want to leave that enabled, which causes Outlook 2007 to display a desktop alert for all messages and to display the New Item Alerts window for those messages that fire the rule.

Controlling Dial-Up Account Connections

The Mail Setup tab of the Options dialog box (choose Tools, Options) includes options that determine how Outlook 2007 connects when processing mail accounts that use dial-up networking:

- **Warn Before Switching An Existing Dial-Up Connection** Select this option to have Outlook 2007 warn you before it disconnects the current dial-up connection to dial another connection specified by the account about to be processed. This warning gives you the option of having Outlook 2007 use the current connection instead of dialing the other one.
- **Always Use An Existing Dial-Up Connection** Select this option to have Outlook 2007 use the active dial-up connection instead of dialing the one specified in the account settings.
- **Automatically Dial During A Background Send/Receive** When this option is selected, Outlook 2007 dials without prompting you when it needs to perform a background send/receive operation.
- **Hang Up When Finished With A Manual Send/Receive** When this option is selected, Outlook 2007 hangs up a dial-up connection when it completes a manual send/receive operation (one you initiate by clicking Send/Receive).

Formatting Internet and International Messages

The Mail Format tab of the Options dialog box (choose Tools, Options) provides access to settings that control how Outlook 2007 processes Internet and international messages.

Setting Internet Format

To control how Outlook 2007 formats messages sent to Internet recipients, click Internet Format on the Mail Format tab to open the Internet Format dialog box, shown in Figure 8-15.

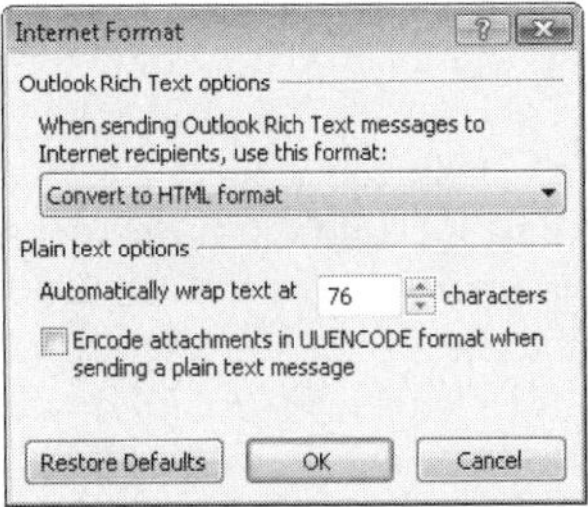

Figure 8-15. Use the Internet Format dialog box to control the format of outgoing Internet messages.

The following list explains the options in the Internet Format dialog box:

- **When Sending Outlook Rich Text Messages To Internet Recipients, Use This Format** Use this drop-down list to specify how Outlook 2007 converts rich-text messages when sending those messages to Internet recipients.
- **Automatically Wrap Text At *n* Characters** In this box, enter the number of characters per line that Outlook 2007 should use for Internet messages.
- **Encode Attachments In UUENCODE Format When Sending A Plain Text Message** When this check box is selected, attachments to messages sent as plain text are encoded within the message as text instead of attached as binary Multipurpose Internet Mail Extensions (MIME) attachments. The recipient's e-mail application must be capable of decoding UUEncoded messages.
- **Restore Defaults** Click this button to restore the Outlook 2007 default settings for Internet messages.

Setting International Options

Click International Options on the Mail Format tab to display the International Options dialog box (see Figure 8-16), which enables you to specify whether Outlook 2007 uses English for message headers and flags and controls the format for outgoing messages.

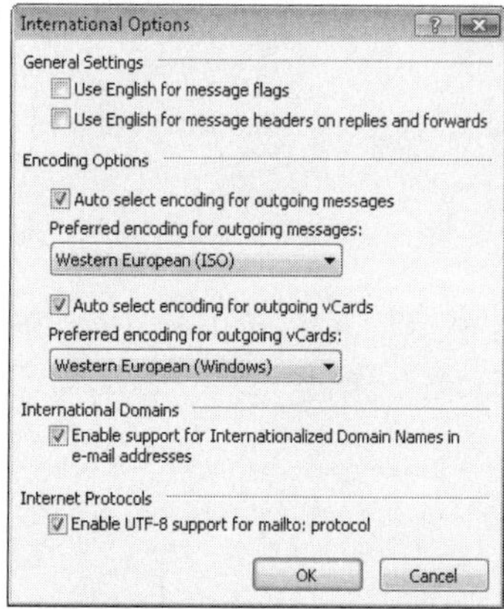

Figure 8-16. Use the International Options dialog box to configure language options for Outlook 2007.

The International Options dialog box includes the following options:

- **Use English For Message Flags** Select this check box to use English for message flag text, such as High Priority or Flag For Follow-Up. If you use a different language and this option is not selected, message flags appear in the selected language instead of in English.

- **Use English For Message Headers On Replies And Forwards** When you're using a non-English version of Outlook 2007, you can select this check box to display message header text–such as From, To, or Subject–in English instead of in the default language.
- **Auto Select Encoding For Outgoing Messages** Select this check box and then choose a preferred encoding option from the drop-down list to specify the encoding character set for outgoing messages. If this check box is not selected, you can choose Encoding in the More Options group of the Options ribbon with a message form open and select the encoding option for the message. If this option is enabled, you cannot change the default encoding for the message.
- **Preferred Encoding For Outgoing Messages** Use this drop-down list to specify the encoding character set Outlook 2007 should use for outgoing messages. Select the setting to take into account the requirements of the majority of messages you send (based on their destination and the language options you use).
- **Auto Select Encoding For Outgoing VCards** Select this check box and then choose a preferred encoding option from the drop-down list to specify the encoding character set for outgoing vCards.
- **Preferred Encoding For Outgoing VCards** Use this drop-down list to specify the encoding character set Outlook 2007 should use for outgoing vCards. Select the setting that meets the requirements of the majority of vCards you send.
- **Enable Support For Internationalized Domain Names In E-Mail Addresses** Select this check box to allow Outlook 2007 to send e-mail to domain names that are in languages other than English.
- **Enable UTF-8 Support For Mailto: Protocol** Selecting this check box causes Outlook 2007 to use UTF-8 encoding for e-mail, enabling the representation of most languages in e-mail messages.

Managing Messages and Attachments

Using the Outlook 2007 e-mail features effectively requires more than understanding how to send and receive messages. This section of the chapter helps you get your messages and attachments under control.

Saving Messages Automatically

You can configure Outlook 2007 to save messages automatically in several ways–for example, saving the current message periodically or saving a copy of forwarded messages. You'll find most of the following options in the E-Mail Options dialog box (see Figure 8-17) and in the Advanced E-Mail Options dialog box (see Figure 8-18).

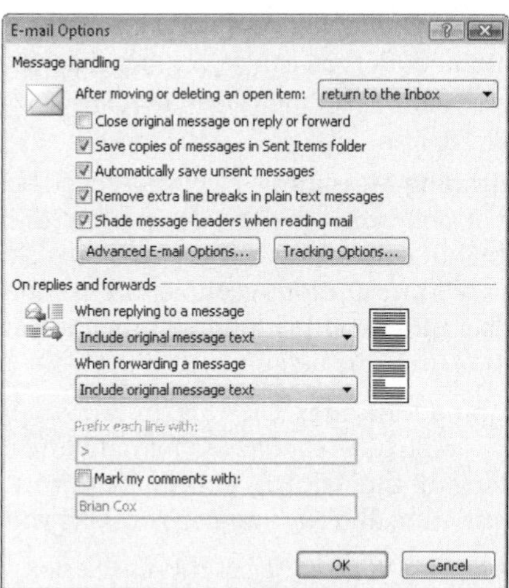

Figure 8-17. In the E-Mail Options dialog box, you can choose whether Outlook 2007 automatically saves unsent messages.

- **Automatically Save Unsent Messages** (in the E-Mail Options dialog box) Use this check box to have Outlook 2007 save unsent messages in the Drafts folder. Outlook 2007 by default saves unsent messages to the Drafts folder every 3 minutes. Clear this check box if you don't want unsent messages saved in this folder.

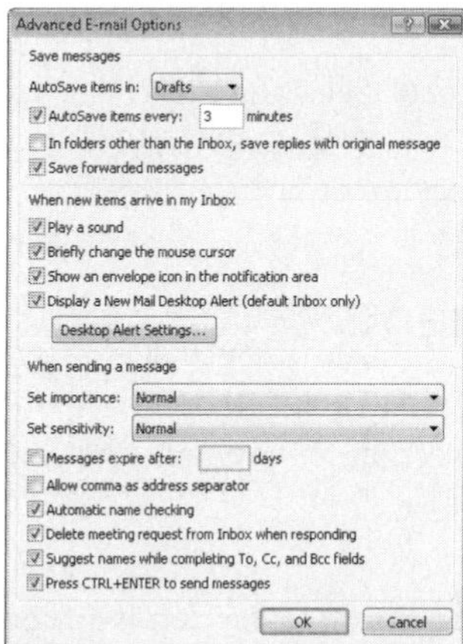

Figure 8-18. In the Advanced E-Mail Options dialog box, you can choose how Outlook 2007 saves copies of messages.

- **AutoSave Items** (in the Advanced E-Mail Options dialog box) Specify the folder in which you want Outlook 2007 to save unsent items. The default location is the Drafts folder.
- **AutoSave Items Every *n* Minutes** (in the Advanced E-Mail Options dialog box) Specify the frequency at which Outlook 2007 automatically saves unsent items to the folder specified by the Save Unsent Items In setting. The default is 3 minutes.

- **In Folders Other Than The Inbox, Save Replies With Original Message** (in the Advanced E-Mail Options dialog box) With this check box selected, Outlook 2007 saves a copy of sent items to the Sent Items folder if the message originates from the Inbox (new message, reply, or forward). If the message originates from a folder other than the Inbox–such as a reply to a message stored in a different folder–Outlook 2007 saves the reply in the same folder as the original. If this option is cleared, Outlook 2007 saves all sent items in the Sent Items folder.

> **Note**
>
> You can also use rules to control where Outlook 2007 places messages. For more information on creating and using rules, see Chapter 11.

- **Save Forwarded Messages** (in the Advanced E-Mail Options dialog box) Select this check box to save a copy of all messages that you forward. Messages are saved in either the Sent Items folder or the originating folder, depending on how you set the previous option.

Retaining a Copy of Sent Messages

Keeping track of the messages you send can often be critical, particularly in a work setting. Fortunately, with Outlook 2007, you can automatically retain a copy of each message you send, providing a record of when and to whom you sent the message.

By default, Outlook 2007 stores a copy of each sent message in the Sent Items folder. You can open this folder and sort the items to locate messages based on any message criteria. You can view, forward, move, and otherwise manage the contents of Sent Items just as you can with other folders.

If you allow Outlook 2007 to save a copy of messages in the Sent Items folder, over time the sheer volume of messages can overwhelm your system. You should therefore implement a means–whether manual or automatic–to archive or clear out the contents of the Sent Items folder. With the manual method, all you need to do is move or delete messages from the folder as your needs dictate.

If you want to automate the archival process, you can do so; for details on how to automatically archive messages from any folder, see the section "Managing Data" in Chapter 30, "Managing Outlook Folders and Data."

Follow these steps to specify whether Outlook 2007 retains a copy of sent messages in the Sent Items folder:

1. Choose Tools, Options and click E-Mail Options on the Preferences tab.
2. In the E-Mail Options dialog box (see Figure 8-17), select the Save Copies Of Messages In Sent Items Folder check box to have Outlook 2007 retain sent

messages. If you want to prevent Outlook 2007 from keeping a copy of sent messages, clear this check box. Click OK. Click OK again to close the Options dialog box.

INSIDE OUT **Overriding default message-saving settings**

If you need to change the Outlook 2007 behavior for a single message, you can override the setting. To choose the folder in which you want to save a message, with the message form open, on the Options tab, in the More Options group, click Save Sent Item, click Other Folder, and then select the folder in which Outlook 2007 should save the message. If you normally save sent messages but do not want to keep a copy of this message, choose Do Not Save from the menu.

Working with Attachments

It's a sure bet that some of the messages you receive include attachments such as documents, pictures, or applications. Outlook 2007 has a new attachment preview feature, which enables you to preview many types of files that you receive in e-mail. In general, you can work with these attachments in Outlook 2007 without saving them separately to disk, although you can do so if needed.

Previewing Attachments

Attachment preview is a new feature of Outlook 2007 that enables you to view the contents of files sent to you in e-mail. You can preview some attachments in the Reading Pane. Outlook 2007 comes with previewers for a variety of file types, including Office 2007 applications, Web pages, and Windows Media® Player, as well as images and text files. Vendors can also make additional file previewers available for download at their Web sites.

To preview a file attachment, follow these steps:

1. In Outlook 2007, with the message selected, click the attachment in the Reading Pane.
2. If the attachment type has a preview handler registered, Outlook 2007 displays a warning about viewing files from untrusted sources (as shown in Figure 8-19). Click Preview File to view the attachment. If there is no preview handler for the attachment file type, Outlook 2007 displays a message indicating this. To view a file for which there is no previewer installed, save the file to disk and open it with the appropriate application.

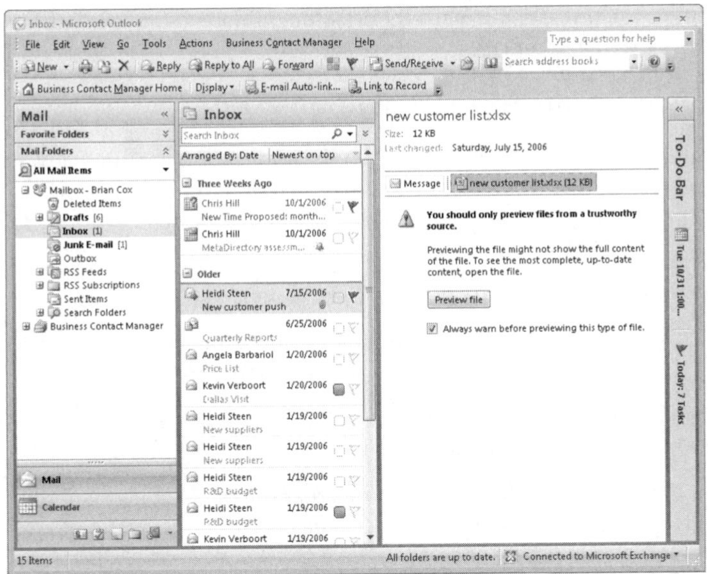

Figure 8-19. Outlook 2007 displays a warning message before previewing an attachment in the Reading pane.

There are limitations on attachment preview, including the following:

- You can preview attachments in HTML and plain text messages, but not those in rich text messages.
- Attachments on received messages can be previewed, but not those in messages you are composing.
- For security reasons, active content (such as macros, scripts, and ActiveX® controls) in the attached files is disabled.

You can configure how attachment previews are handled using the Trust Center. To choose attachment-previewing options, follow these steps:

1. With Outlook 2007 open, select Tools and then Trust Center.
2. In Trust Center, select Attachment Handling.
3. To enable sending replies with edited attachments, select Add Properties To Attachments To Enable Reply With Changes.
4. If you do not want to be able to preview attachments, select Turn Off Attachment Preview.
5. To manage individual previewers, click Attachment And Document Previewers to open the File Previewing Options dialog box. Select all the previewers that you want enabled and clear the check box of any previewer you want to disable. Click OK.

6. When you are satisfied with the attachment previewing configuration, click OK to close the Trust Center.

Viewing Attachments

You might want to view an attachment in the application in which it was created, perhaps to display content that is disabled by the previewer. There are three ways to open a file in the external application directly from Outlook 2007:

- Right-click the message in the Inbox, click View Attachment, and then click the attachment you want to view from the menu.
- Double-click the attachment in the Reading pane when Outlook 2007 is displaying the warning message before previewing the file.
- Double-click the attachment in an open message when Outlook 2007 is displaying the warning message before previewing the file.

In either case, Outlook 2007 displays the Opening Mail Attachment dialog box, prompting you to either Open or Save the file.

Saving Attachments to a Disk

In many instances, however, it's necessary to save attachments to disk. For example, you might receive a self-extracting executable containing a program you need to install. In that case, the best option is to save the file to disk and install it from there.

You can save attachments using either of these methods:

- If you're using the Reading Pane, right-click the attachment in the message and choose Save As.
- Choose File, Save Attachments if you want to save one or more attachments or if the Reading Pane is not available. This option is handy when you want to save all attachments.

Saving Messages to a File

Although Outlook 2007 maintains your messages in your store folders, occasionally you might need to save a message to a file. For example, you might want to archive a single message or a selection of messages outside Outlook 2007 or save a message to include as an attachment in another document. You can save a single message to a file or combine several messages into a single file.

To save one or more messages, open the Outlook 2007 folder in which the messages reside, and then select the message headers. Click File, Save As, Save As; then specify the path, file name, and file format.

When you save a single message, Outlook 2007 gives you the option of saving it in one of the following formats:

- **Text Only** Save the message as a text file, losing any formatting in the original message.
- **Outlook Template** Save the message as an Outlook 2007 template that you can use to create other messages.
- **Outlook Message Format** Save the message in MSG format, retaining all formatting and attachments within the message file.
- **Outlook Message Format–Unicode** Save the message in MSG format with the Unicode character set.
- **HTML** Save the message in HTML format, storing the images in a folder that you can view with a Web browser.
- **MHT files** Save the message in MHT (MIME HTML) format as a single file with all its resources (such as images).

When you save a selection of messages, you can store the messages only in a text file, and Outlook 2007 combines the body of the selected messages in that text file. You can then concatenate the various messages (that is, join them sequentially) into a single text file. You might use this capability, for example, to create a message thread from a selection of messages.

Configuring Message Handling

Outlook 2007 provides several options that enable you to control how Outlook 2007 handles and displays messages. In the E-Mail Options dialog box (refer to Figure 8-18), you can change either of these two settings:

- **After Moving Or Deleting An Open Item** Use this option to control what action Outlook 2007 takes when you move or delete an open item, such as a message. You can set Outlook 2007 to open the previous message, open the next message, or return to the Inbox without opening other messages.
- **Remove Extra Line Breaks In Plain Text Messages** Select this check box to have Outlook 2007 automatically remove extra line breaks from plain-text messages that you receive. Clear the check box to leave the messages as they are.

Moving and Copying Messages Between Folders

Managing your messages often includes moving them to other folders. For example, if you're working on multiple projects, you might want to store the messages related to each specific project in the folder created for that project. The easiest method for moving a message between folders is to drag the message from its current location to the new location. If you want to copy a message instead of moving it, right-click the message, drag it to the folder, and then choose Copy.

If you can't see both the source and destination folders in the folder list or if you prefer not to drag the message, you can use a different method of moving or copying. Select the message in the source folder and choose Edit, Move To Folder or Copy To Folder, depending on which action you need. Outlook 2007 displays a dialog box in which you select the destination folder. You can also select one or more messages, click the Move To Folder button on the toolbar, and then choose a destination folder for the messages.

Note

You can use the shortcut menu to move a message to a specified folder by right-clicking the message and choosing Move To Folder.

CHAPTER 9

Beyond Simple Text Messages

As e-mail has become a more important part of many people's day, the content of e-mail messages has gotten more complex. Whereas text was once adequate, an e-mail message is now likely to contain just about anything: a table, clip art, a photograph, or a link to a Web site. Similarly, the overall look of an e-mail message has evolved with the use of text formatting and stationery. Microsoft® Office Outlook® 2007 has a new native e-mail editor based on Microsoft Office Word 2007 that helps you get your message across clearly and easily.

In this chapter, you'll discover how to add more than just plain text to your messages by working with graphics, hyperlinks, files, attachments, and electronic business cards. As this chapter explains, you can also spruce up your messages by using themes or stationery, which allows you to apply a customized look to your messages. Office Outlook 2007 provides a choice of themes and stationery, or you can create your own. You'll also learn how to automatically attach a text signature or an electronic business card to each message you send.

Formatting Text in Messages

The majority of your messages might consist of unformatted text, but you can use formatted text and other elements to create rich-text and multimedia messages. For example, you might want to use character or paragraph formatting for emphasis, add graphics, or insert hyperlinks to Web sites or other resources. The following sections explain how to accomplish these tasks.

Formatting text in messages is easy, particularly if you're comfortable with Microsoft Word. Even if you're not, you should have little trouble adding some snap to your messages with character, paragraph, and other formatting.

Outlook 2007 introduces a native e-mail editor, based on Office Word 2007, with a rich palette of tools for you to use in creating and formatting messages. For example, you can apply paragraph formatting to indent some paragraphs but not others, create bulleted and numbered lists, and apply special color and font formatting. These options are simple to use. Understanding the underlying format in which your messages are sent, however, requires a little more exploration. Outlook 2007 supports three formats for e-mail messages:

- **HTML format** Lets you create multimedia messages that can be viewed directly in a Web browser and an e-mail client.
- **Rich-text format (RTF)** Lets you add paragraph and character formatting and embed graphics and other nontext media in your message. RTF can be used when sending e-mail to people using Microsoft Exchange Server and earlier versions of Outlook, but it is converted to HTML when sent to an Internet address.

> **Note**
>
> You can specify how Outlook 2007 handles rich-text messages sent to the Internet by choosing Tools, Options. On the Mail Format tab, click Internet Format. In the Internet Format dialog box, under Outlook Rich Text Options, select the format you prefer in the drop-down list. You can choose to have Outlook 2007 send messages as HTML, plain text, or rich text.

- **Plain-text format** Doesn't allow any special formatting, but it offers the broadest client support—every e-mail client can read plain-text messages.

By default, Outlook 2007 uses HTML as the format for sending messages. HTML format lets you create multimedia messages that can be viewed directly in a Web browser and an e-mail client. Depending on the capabilities of the recipient's e-mail client, however, you might need to use a different format.

> **Note**
>
> Using HTML format for messages doesn't mean that you need to understand HTML to create a multimedia message. Outlook 2007 takes care of creating the underlying HTML code for you.

The Ribbon on the new message form provides many options for formatting messages. To choose the format for the current message, on the Options tab, in the Format group, select Plain Text, HTML, or Rich Text. To set the default message format for all new messages, choose Tools, Options on the Outlook 2007 menu bar, and then click the Mail Format tab in the Options dialog box, as shown in Figure 9-1. Select the format in the Compose In This Message Format drop-down list.

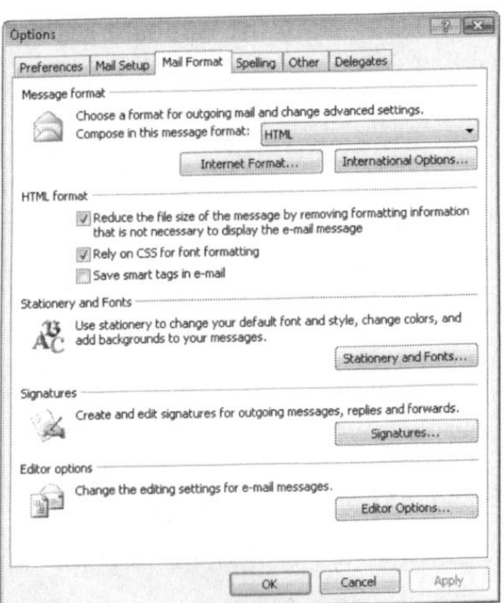

Figure 9-1. Use the Mail Format tab to set the default message format.

On the Mail Format tab, you can click Stationery And Fonts to display the Signatures And Stationery dialog box, shown in Figure 9-2. Use the options in this dialog box to control which fonts Outlook 2007 uses for specific tasks, such as composing new messages, replying to or forwarding a message, and composing or reading plain-text messages. You can specify the font as well as the font size, color, and other font characteristics. You can also select Pick A New Color When Replying Or Forwarding to have Outlook 2007 choose a color that has not yet been used in that message for text you add to a message when replying or forwarding it. This is useful when you are replying inline to someone else's message and want your text to be easily distinguishable.

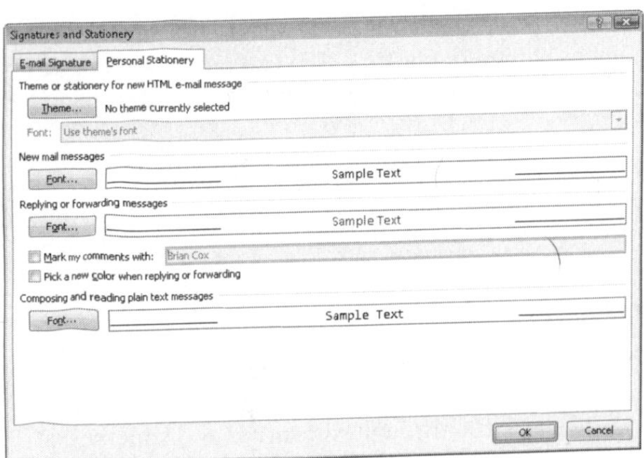

Figure 9-2. Use the Signatures And Stationery dialog box to control the appearance of fonts in Outlook 2007 for specific tasks.

For more information about stationery, see "Customizing the Appearance of Your Messages" later in this chapter.

Outlook 2007 has a number of text formatting controls that are distributed over a number of groups on multiple tabs. The most commonly used formatting commands are on the Message tab, in the Basic Text group, for convenient access, as shown in Figure 9-3. You can specify the font face, size, color, style (bold, italic, or underline), and highlight. Settings for bulleted or numbered lists are also available in this group.

Figure 9-3. Use the Basic Text group on the Message tab for common text formatting options.

INSIDE OUT The appearance of the Ribbon changes

The exact appearance of the Ribbon varies depending on the width of the message window. A command might have an icon with a text label in full screen, appear as just an icon when the window is narrower, and then disappear altogether when the window is narrower still! If a particular command is not immediately apparent, you should resize the window to see whether the command becomes visible.

When you select some text in your message, a transparent mini-toolbar pops up next to your mouse pointer, as shown in Figure 9-4. If you move the mouse pointer over the toolbar, it becomes opaque, and you can choose formatting options to apply to the highlighted text.

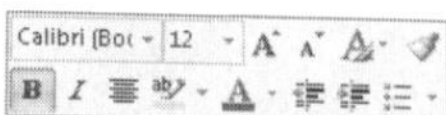

Figure 9-4. The mini-toolbar gives you immediate access to the most commonly used text formatting options.

Extensive text formatting capabilities are provided on the Format Text tab, shown in Figure 9-5, which has font and paragraph formatting as well as style-related options. In addition to the options found in the Basic Text group on the Message tab, you can apply character formatting such as strikethrough, subscript, and superscript. Finer paragraph control is provided with options such as line spacing, borders, and background shading. More complex multilevel lists are also available on this tab. You can also sort text using the Sort option in the Paragraph group.

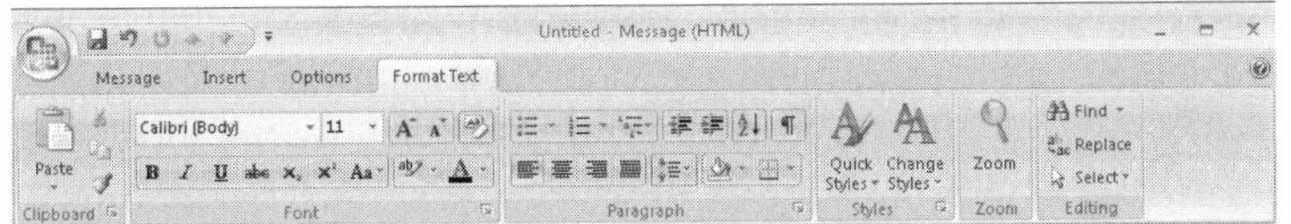

Figure 9-5. The Format Text tab has a wide range of text formatting options.

Several special text options like WordArt, drop caps, and text boxes are available on the Insert tab, in the Text group, shown in Figure 9-6. You can also insert Quick Parts (prewritten sections of text), text boxes, or the date and time (with optional automatic update).

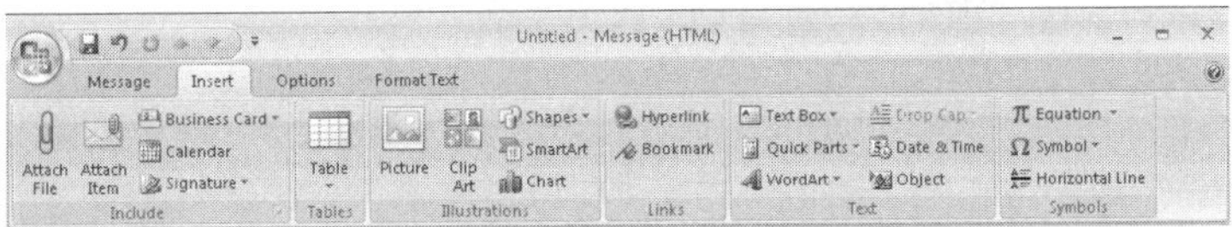

Figure 9-6. The Insert tab has text options that provide special effects.

Themes are configured on the Options tab, in the Themes group, shown in Figure 9-7, where you can select a theme or change individual parts of your current theme. The message format is also set on the Options tab, in the Format group.

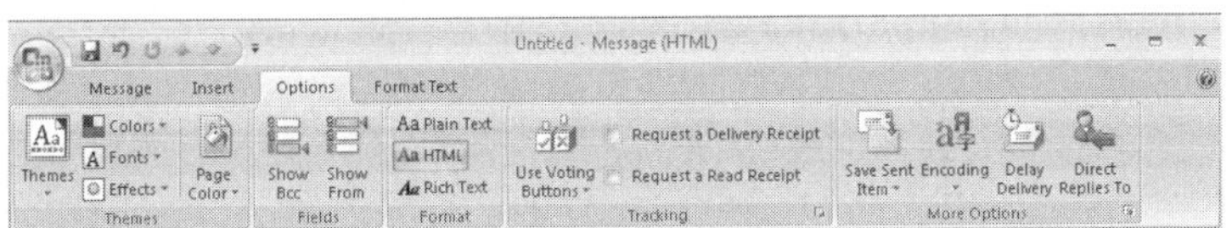

Figure 9-7. Use the Options tab to choose and configure a theme and set the message format.

Formatting Lists

Outlook 2007 provides three types of lists: bulleted, numbered, and multilevel. Although each type of list looks different, the basic procedures used to create them are the same. Each type of list has a library of preconfigured styles, and you can define your own list styles if you want. All three types of lists are available in the Paragraph group on the Format Text tab; bulleted and numbered lists are also found on the Message tab, in the Basic Text group.

To format a bulleted list, follow these steps:

1. With the message open, select the text that you want formatted as a list.
2. On the Format Text tab, in the Paragraph group, select Bullets. To select a different style for the list, click the arrow next to Bullets, and then select a style from the library.
3. If you want to change the text to a different level, select Change List Level, and then choose the new level from the menu.

4. To create a new style for the list, select Define New Bullet to display the Define New Bullet dialog box, shown in Figure 9-8. Click Symbol, Picture, or Font, select the new bullet character in the resulting dialog box, and then click OK. Click OK again to close the Define New Bullet dialog box.

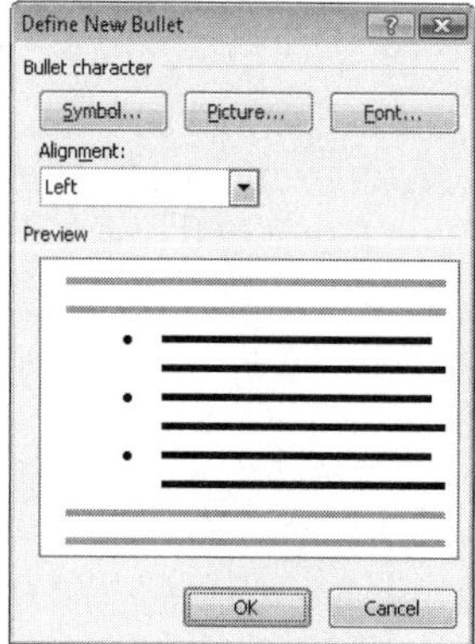

Figure 9-8. Choose the new bullet style in the Define New Bullet dialog box.

Numbered lists are created in much the same way as bulleted lists, letting you choose the number style (roman, arabic, and so on) and related options. Multilevel lists have many additional options that you can configure, as shown in Figure 9-9, allowing you to create highly customized lists if needed.

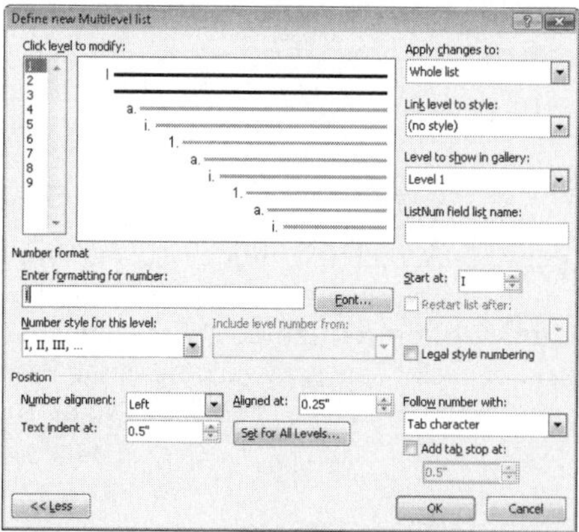

Figure 9-9. You can modify many options for multilevel lists in the Define New Multilevel List dialog box.

Options on the Format Text Tab

You can access only a portion of the text formatting options in the Basic Text group on the Message tab. A number of other options are available on the Format Text tab, including the following:

- **Character Formatting** Additional character styles include strikethrough, subscript, and superscript.
- **Shading** This option lets you apply a color to the background of the selected text.
- **Borders And Shading** You can choose options for adding borders, gridlines, and shading to selected paragraphs.
- **Line Spacing** You can set the spacing between lines and paragraphs. You can also open the Paragraph dialog box, which has settings for indentation, line breaks, and page breaks, as well as control over text flow over page breaks (widow/orphan control, keeping lines together, and so on).
- **Sort** Orders the selected paragraphs based on the criteria you specify in the Sort Text dialog box.
- **Show/Hide** You can toggle the display of normally hidden formatting characters such as paragraph marks.

Working with Styles

Outlook 2007 lets you choose from a gallery of styles to easily format text using a number of predefined looks. Each theme has its own complete set of font styles, created based on the colors and fonts that you specify for the theme. You can also define your own custom style sets if you prefer to use styles that are not defined by the current theme.

The Quick Styles gallery, shown in Figure 9-10, displays the most commonly used styles, giving you an easy way to format the text in your message. When you define custom styles, they are also displayed in the Quick Styles gallery.

Styles shown in the Quick Styles gallery include:

- Normal
- List Paragraph
- Strong (bold)
- Headings (levels 1 and 2)
- Titles (title, subtitle, and book title)
- Emphasis (several italicized styles)
- Quotes (regular and bold)
- References (regular and bold)

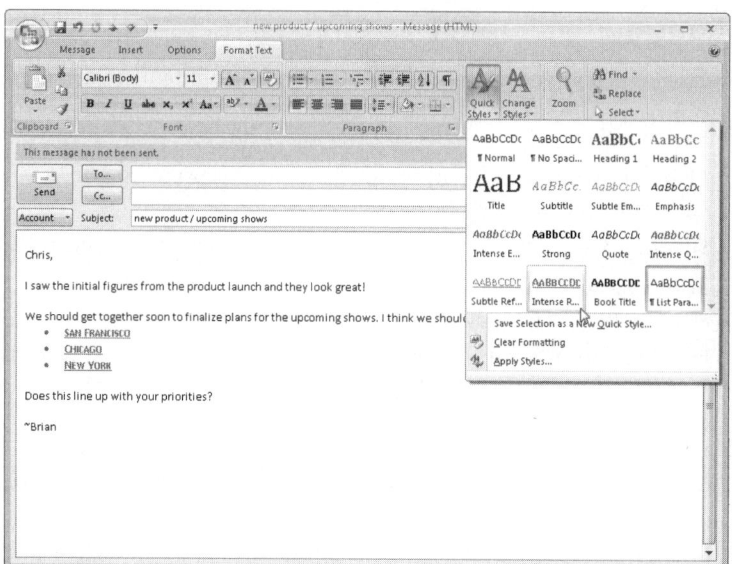

Figure 9-10. The Quick Styles gallery has a number of predefined styles for a variety of uses.

To apply a style using the Quick Styles gallery, follow these steps:

1. With a message open, select the text you want to format.
2. On the Format Text tab, in the Styles group, click Quick Styles to display the Quick Styles gallery.

> **Note**
>
> If the Ribbon is wide enough, a selection of Quick Styles will be displayed instead of the Quick Styles button. In this case, click the More button to view the Quick Styles gallery.

3. Point to a style you are considering to see a Live Preview of the style applied to the selected text. In Figure 9-10, the bulleted text has been selected, and Live Preview has applied the Intense Reference Quick Style. Select the style that you want to apply.

You can create new styles that will be available in the Quick Styles gallery. To create a new Quick Style, first format some text as you want the new style to appear. Next, on the Format Text tab, in the Styles group, click Quick Styles, and then click Save Selection As A New Quick Style. The Create New Style From Formatting dialog box is displayed, in which you can give the style a name. You can also click Modify to change the style if you want.

To remove a style from the Quick Styles gallery, right-click the Quick Style in the gallery, and then choose Remove From Quick Styles gallery. The deletion is immediate, without a confirmation message box, but it can be undone using the Undo command.

To display the complete list of styles, on the Format Text tab, in the Styles group, click the Styles dialog box launcher. You can format your message in the same way as with Quick Styles, by selecting some text and then choosing the style to apply from the Styles window.

New styles can be created, and the formatting of text in messages can be examined, by using the Style Inspector from the Styles window. The complete set of styles can be configured by clicking Manage Styles and using the Manage Styles dialog box. (There are approximately 300 styles available!) To configure options for the Styles window, click Options.

> **Note**
>
> When you change the theme, custom fonts are not changed unless they use a theme color—in which case, the color is updated. Resetting font styles is done by reapplying a style set.

You can change the fonts and colors used to determine the current Quick Styles. To change these options, on the Format Text tab, in the Styles group, click Change Styles, and then select one of the following options:

- **Style Set** This setting specifies the font face used for the Quick Styles. You can choose from several options or create your own style set from the existing message (saved as a Word 2007 template).
- **Colors** You can select a set of theme colors to use for the font color set or create a custom set of theme colors.
- **Fonts** This option lets you pick a font set from an existing theme or create your own font set by selecting a body font and a heading font.
- **Set As Default** Choosing this option sets the current configuration (theme, style set, and any customized settings except background) as the default for new messages.

Using Style Sets

A style set consists of a number of font styles, initially created from the theme settings, but customizable after that. Style sets can be created, saved, and applied independent of theme-related font changes and will override theme settings.

To work with style sets, with a new message open, on the Format Text tab, in the Styles group, click Change Styles, and then click Style Set. You can then choose from the following actions:

- To apply a style set, select the style set from the menu.
- To set the font styles back to the new message default, choose Reset To Quick Styles From Template.
- To set the font styles back to the Outlook 2007 default font styles, choose Reset Document Quick Styles.
- To create a new style set, select Save As Quick Style Set. The Save Quick Style Set dialog box will be displayed, allowing you to name the style set.

Creating a Custom Style Set

To customize font styles, follow these steps:

1. Type some text, and then format it as you want the updated style text to appear. (In this example, we will change the Title style.) Select the text, and on the Format Text tab, in the Styles group, click Quick Styles (or click More in the Quick Styles gallery).
2. In the Quick Styles gallery, right-click Title, and then choose Update Title To Match Selection.
3. Repeat for each font style you want to define.
4. When you have finished customizing the font styles, delete all of the text in your message. (This leaves the styles you created intact but creates the new message without unwanted text content.)
5. To save the style set you created, on the Format Text tab, in the Styles group, click Change Styles, Style Set, Save As Quick Style Set.
6. In the Save Quick Style Set dialog box, specify a file name for the style set, and then click Save. The style set is saved as a Word 2007 template file.

Using Tables

Using Outlook 2007, you can easily add a variety of tables to your e-mail messages. You can use a Word 2007 table for textual information or a Microsoft Office Excel® 2007 spreadsheet with its support for mathematical operations. You can easily apply a style to your table by selecting it from the visual gallery of built-in and custom styles.

Inserting a Table in a Message

You can add a table to your e-mail quickly with one of several methods provided by Outlook 2007. To insert a table in a message, follow these steps:

1. With a message open, position the insertion point where you want the table to appear. (You can nest tables by setting the insertion point inside a table cell.)
2. On the Insert tab, in the Tables group, click Table to display the Insert Table menu. You can create a table using one of the following methods:
   - To draw a table, use the mini-table grid on the Insert Table menu. As you move your mouse over the table grid on the menu, you get a preview of the table in the body of your message, as shown in Figure 9-11. Click the lower-right cell of the desired table grid to insert it in the message.

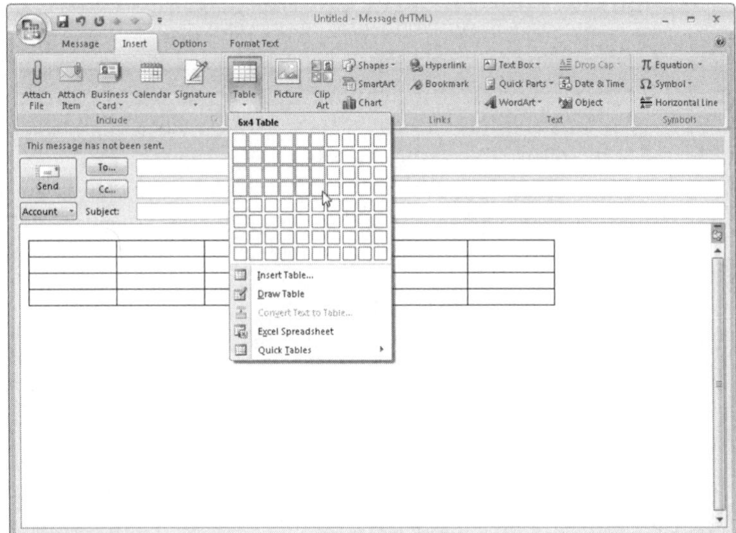

Figure 9-11. You can preview a table before you insert it in your message by using Table Live Preview.

   - Select Insert Table on the Insert Table menu to open the Insert Table dialog box, shown in Figure 9-12, and specify the table size and AutoFit behavior. Selecting the Remember Dimensions For New Tables check box makes these settings the default for new tables.

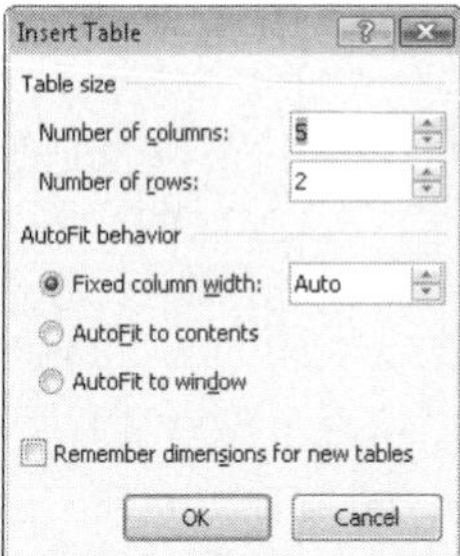

Figure 9-12. You choose the settings for a new table in the Insert Table dialog box.

- Selecting Draw Table lets you draw a single table cell in the message window. If needed, you can then split the cell or add cells to the table. When you finish editing the table, you can click anywhere else in your message to return to editing the text.
- Selecting Excel Spreadsheet creates an Office Excel 2007 table in the message and displays the Excel 2007 commands on the Ribbon. When you finish editing the spreadsheet, you can click anywhere else in your message to return to editing the text.
- Selecting Quick Tables displays a gallery that lets you select a previously saved table design. Outlook 2007 does not have any Quick Tables by default, so this option is usable only after you have created some Quick Tables of your own.

For information about creating Quick Tables, see "Working with Quick Tables" later in this chapter.

Working with Tables

When you select a table in an e-mail message, the Microsoft Office system Ribbon displays two additional Table Tools tabs. The Design tab lets you control visual style effects and configure settings such as header rows. The Layout tab has commands that let you add and remove table cells and work with cell properties.

INSIDE OUT Limitations on styling Excel 2007 spreadsheets

Although Excel 2007 tables provide a lot of additional functionality, you are limited in your ability to do page layout on an Excel 2007 object in your message. Neither of the Table Tools tabs (Design and Layout), which contain commands used to apply styles to tables, are available when an Excel 2007 object is selected. If you want to use the tools in Outlook 2007 to format your tables, you can create an Excel spreadsheet with your data and then copy the completed information to an appropriately sized Outlook 2007 table. You can then apply the Outlook 2007 built-in styling effects to the table.

Chapter 9

On the Design tab, shown in Figure 9-13, specify the table style, colors, borders, and options, such as whether a header row is used, as described here:

- **Table Style Options** You can apply specific effects to individual rows, such as Header Row, Total Row, First Column, or Last Column. You can also choose to have rows, columns, or both banded in alternating colors to make your data stand out.
- **Table Styles** You can select a visual table style from the built-in gallery, modify the current style, or create a new table style. Shading and Borders effects can be applied to a selection of cells.
- **Draw Borders** This group contains commands to format the Line Style, Line Weight, and Pen Color. You can also draw a new table or erase existing table cells and content. You can also click the dialog box launcher to display the Borders And Shading dialog box and configure these options.

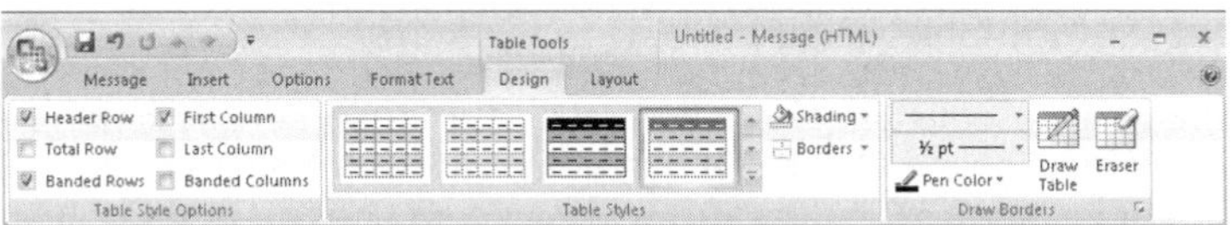

Figure 9-13. You can apply a variety of style options to a table by using the Design tab commands.

You can use the commands on the Layout tab, shown in Figure 9-14, to insert and delete cells and configure how the data is displayed inside table cells.

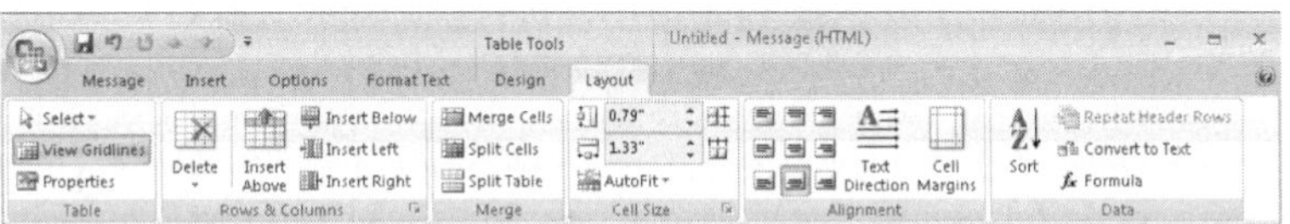

Figure 9-14. Use the Layout tab to manage cells and format the information they contain.

The Layout tab contains these command groups:

- **Table** You can select all or part of the table, view gridlines (or turn them off), and display the Table Properties dialog box.
- **Rows & Columns** Rows and columns can be inserted and deleted using these commands. Clicking the Insert Cells dialog box launcher lets you specify the direction to shift existing cells when inserting new ones.
- **Merge** These commands let you merge cells, split cells, or split the table into multiple tables.
- **Cell Size** You can specify the size of individual cells, distribute rows or cells evenly, or choose AutoFit. Click the dialog box launcher to display the Table Properties dialog box, and then set the size, alignment, text wrapping options, and margins for the cell.
- **Alignment** You can choose from nine preset alignment options (top left, top right, center, bottom right, and so on) for the selected table text. Text can be

written from left to right, top to bottom, or bottom to top using the Text Direction command. Cell margins for the entire table can be set here as well.

- **Data** You can sort the table information, convert the table to text, or insert a formula using those commands. To have the header row repeat on tables that span multiple pages, select the header row in the table, and then click Repeat Header Rows.

Working with Quick Tables

The Quick Tables gallery is your personal gallery of tables that you can quickly insert into your messages. This can be simply an empty table formatted exactly the way you want or a complete table with not only a custom look but data as well. Once you have customized the appearance of a table, you can save it as a Quick Table so that you can easily re-create the format and style of frequently used tables.

To create a Quick Table, follow these steps:

1. Insert a table into a message, format it, and then enter any content you want to be contained in your Quick Table (headings, for example).
2. Select the table (or part of it), and on the Insert tab, in the Table group, click Table, choose Quick Tables, and then click Save Selection To Quick Tables Gallery.
3. In the Create New Building Block dialog box, give the table a name, and then click OK. The Quick Table is now listed in the Quick Tables gallery for easy use. If you want the table to appear in a different gallery, such as Text Box or Quick Parts, select the gallery name in the Gallery drop-down list. (Some galleries are available only in the Building Blocks Organizer, shown in Figure 9-15.) You can assign a category to the table in the Category drop-down list. (This category is visible only in the Building Blocks Organizer.) The Options drop-down list selections have no effect on Quick Tables.

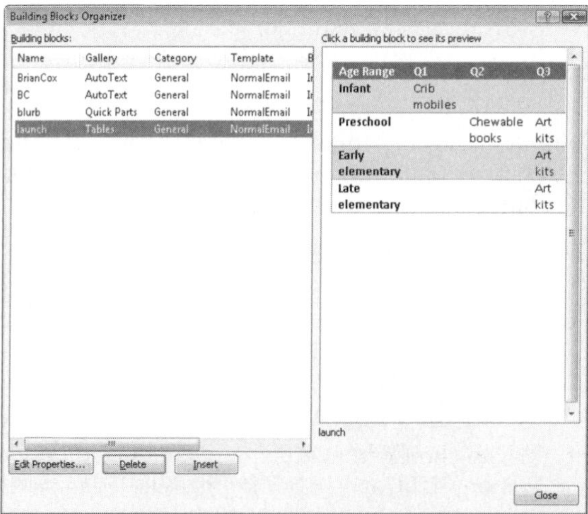

Figure 9-15. Use the Building Blocks Organizer to remove a Quick Table.

To remove a Quick Table from the gallery, open the gallery, right-click the table, and then choose Organize And Delete to open the Building Blocks Organizer, shown earlier in Figure 9-15. Select the table you want to remove, click Delete, and then click OK.

INSIDE OUT **Add the Building Blocks Organizer to the Quick Access Toolbar**

You can manage the entire range of building blocks, such as Quick Tables, Quick Parts, Text Boxes, and so on, in the Building Blocks Organizer. It is also the only way to insert Quick Tables that have been added to custom galleries. If you use the Building Blocks Organizer often, you might want to add an icon to the Quick Access Toolbar to give you quicker access. To add the Building Blocks Organizer to the Quick Access Toolbar, follow these steps:

1. With a new message open, click the Microsoft Office Button, and then select Editor Options.
2. In the Editor Options dialog box, choose Customize.
3. In the Choose Commands From drop-down list, select Commands Not In The Ribbon. Select Building Blocks Organizer, click Add, and then click OK.

Using Special Text Features

Outlook 2007 includes a number of text options and text objects that you can insert into your e-mail messages. If you repeatedly type the same text in multiple messages, for example, you can save the text for reuse. You can apply decorative text effects such as drop caps and WordArt as well. These options are available on the Insert tab, in the Text group.

Quick Parts

Quick Parts are chunks of reusable content (text, graphics, and so on) that you can insert into a message with a click of your mouse. You can create a Quick Part for anything that you commonly have to enter into a message such as contact information, directions and a map, and so on.

To save a Quick Part, follow these steps:

1. Create a message with the content that you want to reuse, and then select the content.
2. On the Insert tab, in the Text group, click Quick Parts, and then select Save Selection To Quick Parts Gallery. You can select a gallery in the Gallery drop-down list. (Remember, some galleries are available only in the Building Blocks Organizer.) You can assign a category to the table in the Category drop-down list.

By default, a Quick Part is inserted in its own paragraph; if you want to insert the Quick Part without inserting a line break first, select Content Only from the Options drop-down list.

Once you have saved the Quick Part, using it is easy. To use the Quick Part, on the Insert tab, in the Text group, click Quick Parts, and then select the Quick Part from the gallery.

Drop Cap

You can use a drop cap to create a special look at the beginning of a paragraph. When you select a drop cap, Outlook 2007 creates a small text box and inserts a single, specially formatted character. (This character is still treated like part of the paragraph, not as a separate text box.) To create a drop cap, follow these steps:

1. Open the message, and then position the insertion point in the paragraph that should get the drop cap.
2. On the Insert tab, in the Text group, click Drop Cap, as shown in Figure 9-16.

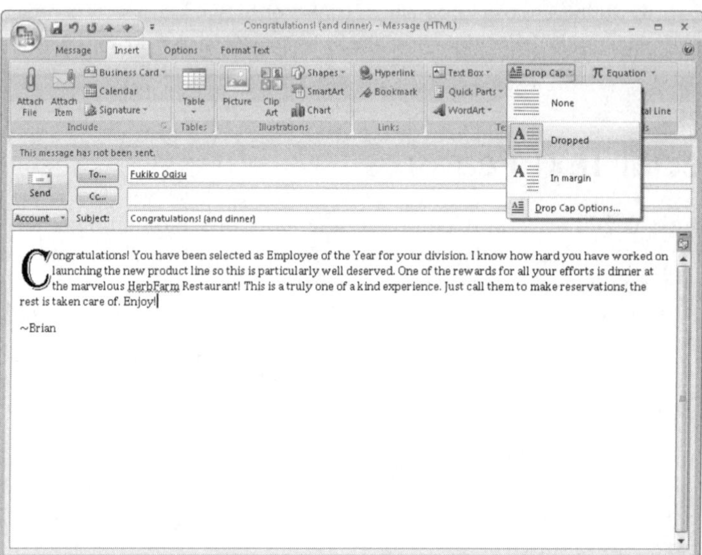

Figure 9-16. You can quickly add drop caps to your messages.

3. Select Dropped or In Margin to create a drop cap. To format the drop cap, choose Drop Cap Options.
4. In the Drop Cap dialog box, you can specify the position, font, number of lines to drop, and distance from text. When you have finished, click OK.

Date & Time

To insert the date and time, follow these steps:

1. With a message open, on the Insert tab, in the Text group, click Date & Time.
2. In the Date And Time dialog box, select the format you want in the Available Formats list. Select the Update Automatically check box if you want the time to be updated to the current time automatically, and then click OK.

Some of the options in the Text group operate more like objects than text. Options such as WordArt are inserted by creating an object; a tab is then added to the Ribbon for related Word Art commands. In contrast with normal text, you can move such objects to any location in the message (in the same way that you can position a graphic) for layout purposes.

Text Box

To create a text box, follow these steps:

1. With a message open, on the Insert tab, in the Text group, click Text Box, and then select Draw Text Box.
2. The Text Box Tools Format tab will be displayed, as shown in Figure 9-17, allowing you to style the box (shape, shadows, colors, and so on) and specify layout options (text wrapping, layering, grouping).

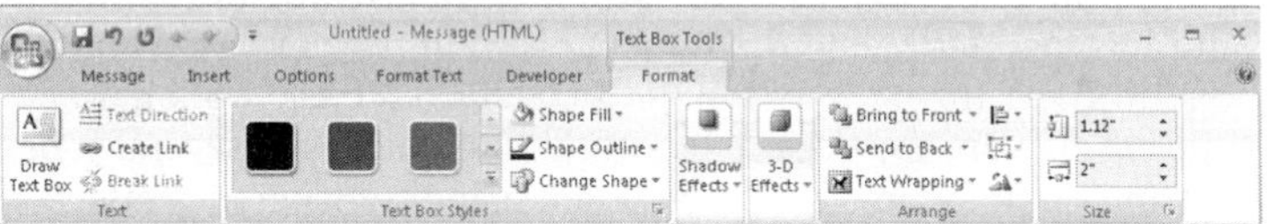

Figure 9-17. Use the Text Box Tools Format tab to apply styles to a text box.

3. Enter your text in the text box. This text can be formatted in the usual ways using the tools on the Format Text tab.
4. To move the text box, you can drag it with the mouse or select it and nudge it with the keyboard.

WordArt

To create WordArt, follow these steps:

1. With a message open, on the Insert tab, in the Text group, click WordArt.
2. Select a style for your WordArt from the gallery.
3. In the Edit WordArt Text dialog box, enter your text, configure the font format options, and then click OK.

To format your WordArt, click the WordArt object to display the WordArt Tools Format tab, shown in Figure 9-18, and then apply the desired effects to your WordArt. When you have finished, click outside the WordArt box to return to editing the rest of your message.

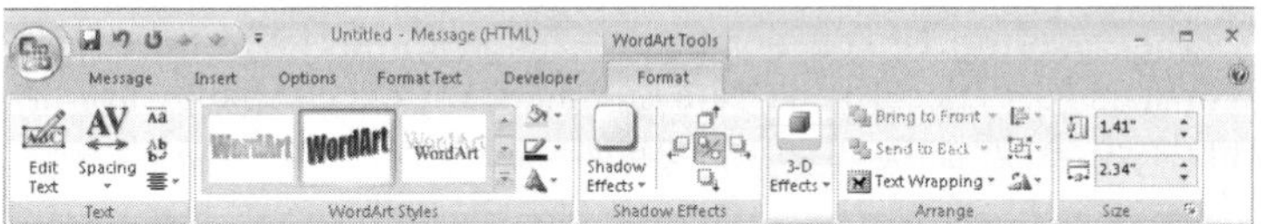

Figure 9-18. Format WordArt using the commands on the WordArt Tools Format tab.

Object

The last option in the Text group is Object, which lets you insert an object into your message. You can use an existing object or create a new one. To insert an object, with a message open, on the Insert tab, in the Text group, click Object. In the Object dialog box, select the object type or file name, and then click OK.

Including Illustrations in Messages

Outlook 2007 provides a variety of illustration types that you can use to enhance your e-mail. You can add pictures, clip art, shapes, charts, and SmartArt (new to Outlook 2007). You control page layout, so you can place illustrations in any location in your message and then format them in a number of ways, including adding borders, shadows, and three-dimensional (3-D) effects. (Exact options vary between illustration types.) You can wrap your text around illustrations in several styles and even layer text and graphics on top of each other, using transparency effects to make everything visible.

Each type of illustration has one or more groups of commands specific to it, providing the controls needed for that kind of illustration. They also share a number of groups of commands on the Ribbon and operate in much the same way. We will examine the process of inserting a picture in some detail in the next section, describing the common commands. Following that, we will highlight the differences between the other types of illustration.

Your ability to insert graphics in a message depends in part on which message format you use. With the new Outlook 2007 editor, you can insert embedded graphics when using HTML (the default) or RTF, with minor differences in layout options. You can't insert embedded graphics in a message that uses plain-text format.

INSIDE OUT **Attach graphics files to plain-text messages**

Although you can't insert embedded graphics in a plain-text message, you can attach a graphic (or other) file to plain-text e-mail. To attach a graphic to a plain-text message, follow these steps:

1. In the message form, on the Insert tab, in the Include group, click Attach File.
2. In the Insert File dialog box, locate the file you want to attach, and then click Insert.

TROUBLESHOOTING

Commands on the Design tab are missing or disabled

Commands on the Design tab might be missing or always unavailable. This is because some commands work only with certain types of illustrations or when the message uses a particular format. For example, the Group command is always shown on the Design tab, in the Arrange group, even though its use is limited to only one type of illustration: shapes. If the message is in rich-text format, the Arrange group, which controls some aspects of text and graphics layout, is not displayed at all. You can still use a subset of those commands, however, by right-clicking the image and choosing the command from the shortcut menu.

Inserting a Picture from a File

Follow these steps to insert a picture in a message:

1. On the Insert tab, in the Illustrations group, click Picture to display the Picture dialog box.
2. In the Picture dialog box, select the graphics file to insert in the message, and then click Insert. (To insert a link to the image, click the arrow next to Insert, and then select Link To File or Insert And Link.)
3. In the message, when the picture is selected, Outlook 2007 displays the Picture Tools Format tab with tools used to format the picture, as shown in Figure 9-19.

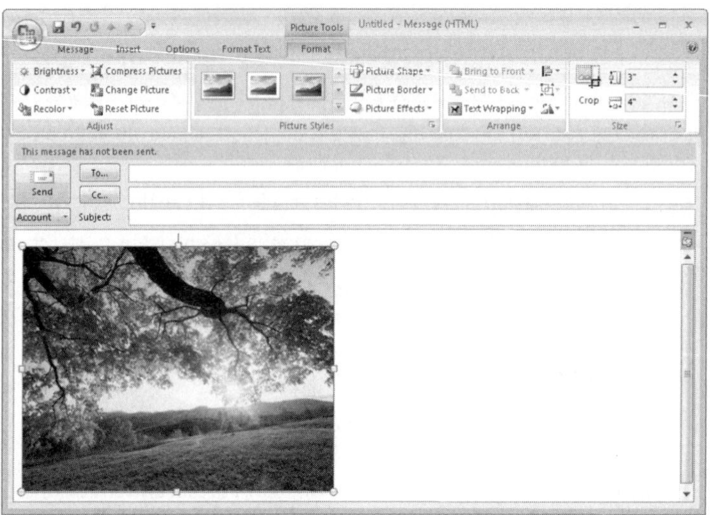

Figure 9-19. You can adjust the appearance of the picture as well as format how the picture is displayed in the e-mail message.

To adjust the appearance of the picture, under Picture Tools, click the Format tab, and then in the Adjust group, use the appropriate tools, as follows:

Brightness and Contrast You can increase or decrease the brightness or contrast in 10 percent increments by selecting a value on the menu. Choose Picture Correction Options to display the Format Picture dialog box, and then set an exact amount to adjust the Brightness and Contrast settings.

Recolor You can apply a tinted filter to the picture, changing it to be similar to a grayscale, but done with shades of a single color.

Compress Pictures Outlook 2007 can compress the images in your e-mail messages to minimize message size. When you select Compress Picture, you are given the option of compressing one picture or all of the images in the message. You can click Options in the Compress Pictures dialog box to set the automatic compression option, choose whether to delete cropped areas of images, and determine the picture quality.

Change Picture This option lets you replace the current image while keeping the object formatting and size settings intact.

Reset Picture You can reset the picture to the original image as inserted from a file, discarding all changes you have made.

4. You can customize how the picture appears in the message by using the options in the Picture Styles group, as described here:

Quick Styles You can choose from a number of framing and perspective options to set the overall look of the picture.

Picture Shape Select a shape for the picture to be displayed in, and Outlook 2007 will automatically crop the image to fit. The Picture Shapes gallery contains a number of shapes in several categories, including rectangles, arrows, flowchart objects, banners, and callouts.

Picture Border You can add an optional border around the graphic, with a specified pixel width and pattern, and using the colors from your theme or custom colors. To configure additional border settings, choose More Lines on the Weight menu to display the Format Picture dialog box, shown in Figure 9-20, and then configure the Line Style settings.

Figure 9-20. You can customize many aspects of the picture border in the Format Picture dialog box.

Picture Effects You can apply a number of effects to a picture to produce just the look you want for your message. The available effects are Shadow, Reflection, Glow, Soft Edges, Bevel, and 3-D Rotation. The Preset option has some preconfigured effects that you can choose from.

5. You can specify how you want the image aligned in the message and how text will flow with the graphic using the options in the Arrange group. The commands operate as described here:

   Bring To Front/Send To Back These options specify which layer the picture is in.

   Text Wrapping You can choose how the text wraps relative to the picture, selecting from having the image in line with text, behind text, or in front of text or having the text only at the top and bottom of the picture or wrapped around a square. To drag a picture to a new location in the message, you must first select it and then choose either Behind Text or In Front of Text.

> **Note**
>
> If the message uses RTF format, you can access the Bring To Front, Send To Back, and Text Wrapping commands by right-clicking the image and then choosing the command from the shortcut menu.

   Align You can line up multiple pictures (or other objects) by selecting them (using **Shift**-click) and then clicking Align. You can choose to align the edges or centers of the selected objects.

   Group This command is unavailable when you are working with pictures.

   Rotate You can change the orientation of the picture by selecting Rotate Right 90°, Rotate Left 90°, Flip Vertical, or Flip Horizontal. To have finer control over image orientation, choose More Rotation Options on the Rotate menu to open the Size dialog box, and then set the exact degree of rotation. (You can also resize and crop images in the Size dialog box.)

6. The picture can be resized and cropped with the settings in the Size group. To crop the image, select Crop, and then drag the cropping handles on the image. To resize the image, enter the new size in the Shape Height and Shape Width fields. (If Outlook 2007 is configured to constrain the aspect ratio of pictures, you need to enter only one of these options, not both.)

7. If you want to set Alternate Text (which is displayed in place of the picture for recipients whose e-mail clients don't show graphics), right-click the picture, and then choose Size on the shortcut menu. In the Size dialog box, select the Alt Text tab. Enter your text in the Alternative Text box, and then click Close.

8. To add a hyperlink to the picture, right-click on the picture, and then choose Hyperlink on the shortcut menu. (For detailed instructions on working with hyperlinks, see "Working With Hyperlinks" later in this chapter.)

Some, but not all, of the formatting and graphical effects are cumulative, and you might have to experiment to get exactly the effect you want. As an example, Figure 9-21 shows a picture that has had a number of things done to it in order to achieve this effect. After the picture was inserted and resized, Text Wrapping was set to Behind Text. Next the

Bevel Rectangle option was selected from the Quick Styles gallery to give the picture a new shape. Brightness was set to 40 percent to give the picture a semitransparent look. Last Preset 10 was applied from the Presets gallery to apply the rotation and other effects.

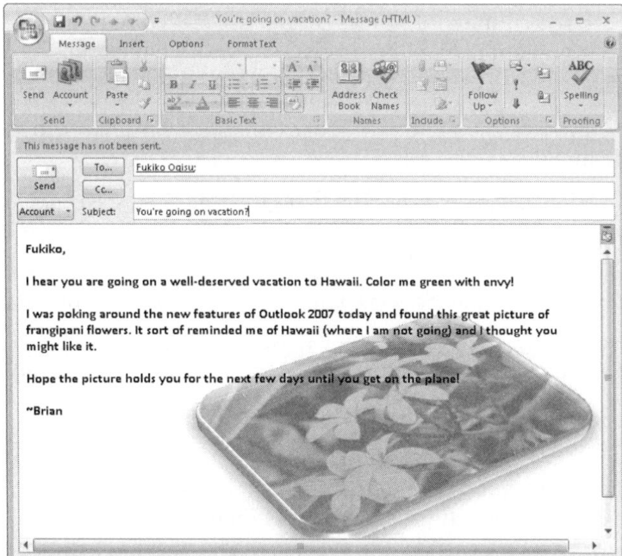

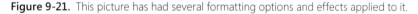

Figure 9-21. This picture has had several formatting options and effects applied to it.

INSIDE OUT **Find previous versions of your picture files**

Outlook 2007 can search for previous versions of a picture file when you are inserting it into a message. Windows Vista™ creates these previous versions in one of two ways: when Windows Vista creates a restore point or when you use the Back Up Wizard. (See the Windows Vista Help Center for more information about creating previous versions of files.) If you have previous versions of your picture files, you can have Outlook 2007 search for them in the Insert Picture dialog box by clicking the arrow next to Insert and selecting Show Previous Versions. Outlook 2007 will display all previous versions of that image.

Inserting Clip Art

Inserting a clip art image launches the Clip Art task pane, which lets you search for the clip art image you want to use. You can enter search terms and specify the collections to search, as well as limit the file types that are returned in the results. Once the clip art has been inserted, under Picture Tools, on the Format tab, use the commands as described in the preceding section.

Inserting Shapes

Outlook 2007 includes a library of shapes (previously called AutoShapes) from which you can select just the right one to illustrate your words. Shape types include lines, basic shapes (square, cylinder, and so on), arrows, flowchart objects, callouts, stars, and banners.

To insert a shape into a message, follow these steps:

1. With a message open, on the Insert tab, in the Illustrations group, select Shapes.
2. Choose a shape from the Shapes gallery.
3. Click and drag across the message where you want to create the shape.
4. With the shape selected, the Drawing Tools Format tab will be displayed, as shown in Figure 9-22, providing you with these options for formatting the shape:

   Insert Shapes You can select a shape to create, edit a shape, or edit text with the commands in this group.

   Shape Styles This group provides a Quick Styles gallery of frame and fill effects, shape fill, shape outline, and shape changing effects.

   Shadow Effects This group provides control over the shape's shadow effects, toggles the shadow on or off, and lets you nudge the shadow. You can also choose the shadow color.

   3-D Effects This group contains the 3-D Effects gallery, and you can turn 3-D effects on or off and set tilting options. Menu options include 3-D Color (themes or custom), Depth (in points), Direction (perspective), Lighting (direction and type), and Surface (select a surface finish: matte, plastic, metal, or wire frame).

   Arrange This group controls how the shape is aligned in the message and how text flows with the graphic. You can move the shape to the front or back layer, control text wrapping, align multiple shapes, group shapes together, and control rotation of the shape. If the message uses RTF format, you can access the Bring To Front, Send To Back, and Text Wrapping commands by right-clicking the image and then choosing the command on the shortcut menu.

   Size This group lets you set the shape height and shape width.

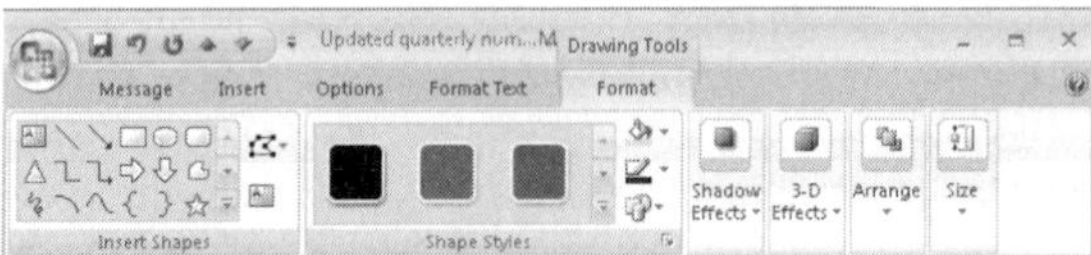

Figure 9-22. You can work with shapes using the commands on the Drawing Tools Format tab.

INSIDE OUT **Insert a new drawing**

To insert a blank drawing, with a message open, on the Insert tab, in the Illustrations group, click Shapes, and then click New Drawing Canvas. This will insert a blank drawing object in your message in which you can draw using the Outlook 2007 built-in drawing tools.

Inserting a Chart

When you choose a chart as the illustration type to insert, the Insert Chart dialog box opens, allowing you to select the type of chart you want to use. When you click OK, an Excel 2007 workbook is opened with a small amount of data entered. After you have entered your data, click the Microsoft Office Button, and then click Close to update the chart and return to Outlook 2007. On the Ribbon, under Chart Tools, there are three tabs with quite a few commands allowing you fine control over the appearance of your chart, as described in the following sections.

Design Tab

The Chart Tools Design tab contains groups of commands that let you choose the type, style, and layout of the chart as well as the data it contains, as shown in Figure 9-23.

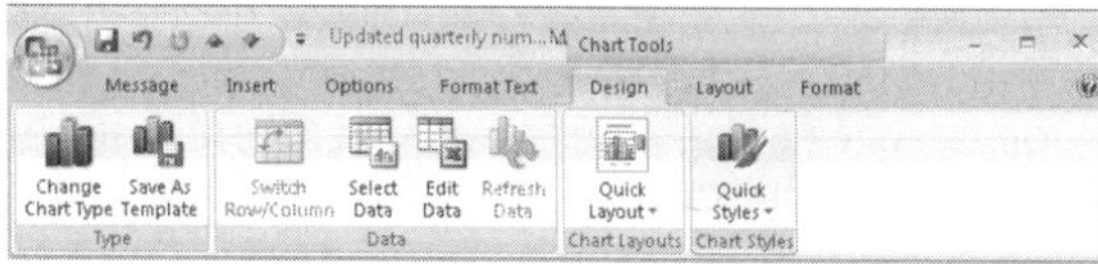

Figure 9-23. You can control the style and data for your chart using the Chart Tools Design tab.

The Design tab has these groups:

- **Type** You can select the chart type (pie, bar, area, and so on) and save the current chart as a template.
- **Data** This group has commands that let you manipulate your data in Excel 2007.
- **Chart Layouts** You can choose from the Quick Layout gallery using various arrangements of the chart, legend, title, and other text.
- **Chart Styles** This group consists of a Quick Styles gallery with a selection of colors, outlines, and effects.

Layout Tab

The Chart Tools Layout tab, shown in Figure 9-24, has groups of commands that control the appearance of many aspects of the chart such as grid, labels, and background.

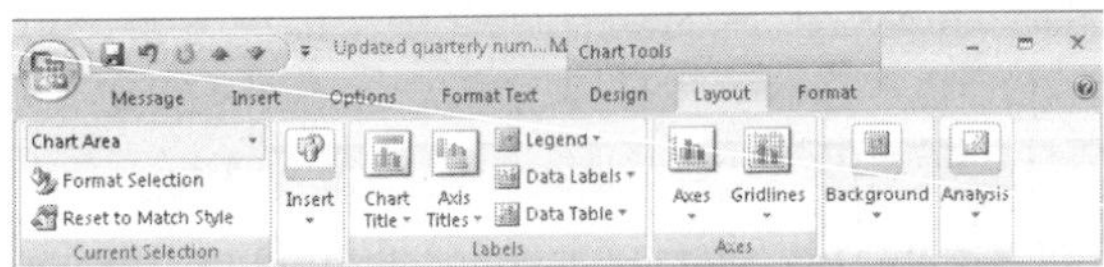

Figure 9-24. You can control the display of data and labels and add analysis tools to charts with the commands on the Chart Tools Layout tab.

The Layout tab contains these groups of commands:

- **Current Selection** You can select a chart element and format the selection.
- **Insert** You can insert a picture or shape or draw a text box inside your chart.
- **Labels** These commands let you turn titles, legends, and data labels on and off. You can also format the style and placement of these labels.
- **Axes** The Axes command controls the display of the horizontal and vertical axes; the Gridlines command does the same for the chart gridlines.
- **Background** You can turn on the display of a background color on the Plot Area, Chart Floor, and Chart Wall and also control the 3-D rotation of the chart.
- **Analysis** The commands in the Analysis group can add additional data to your charts. Each analysis option works with only certain types of charts. You can select a Trendline (most chart types), Drop Lines (area and line charts), High-Low Lines (2-D line chart), Up/Down bars (line chart), and Error Bars with Standard Error, Percentage, or Standard Deviation (most chart types).

Format Tab

The Chart Tools Format tab, shown in Figure 9-25, provides you with the tools you need to customize the appearance of your charts. You can control colors, styles, and effects and the page layout of your chart using these commands.

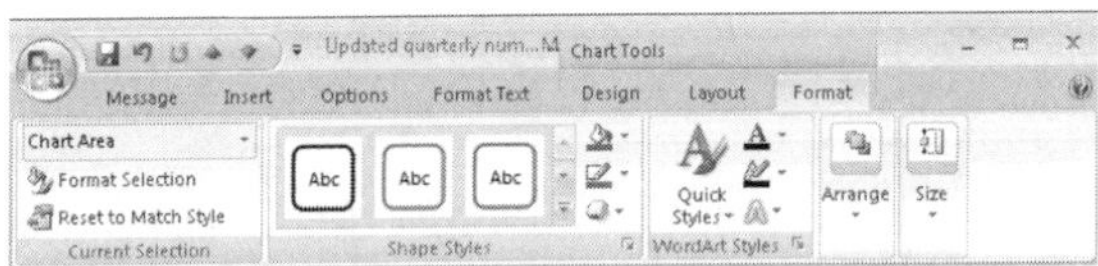

Figure 9-25. You can customize the appearance of your chart with the commands on the Chart Tools Format tab.

The Format tab contains these groups:

- **Current Selection** You can select a chart element and format the selection.
- **Shape Styles** This group provides a Quick Styles gallery with frame and fill effects, shape fill, shape outline, and shape effects options.
- **WordArt Styles** These commands control the text used in text labels, axes, titles, and legends. (WordArt commands are available only if a suitable chart component is selected.)

- **Arrange** This group contains the text wrapping, layering, and alignment commands. (This group is not available if your message is in RTF format.)
- **Size** This group specifies the shape height and shape width.

Inserting SmartArt

SmartArt is a type of reusable object designed as a means of displaying complex information in an easy-to-understand graphical format. Outlook 2007 includes a gallery of SmartArt graphics in formats that represent things such as a list, a hierarchy (like an organizational chart), a process (like a flowchart), or a relationship (such as a Venn diagram).

To insert a SmartArt graphic into a message, follow these steps:

1. With a message open, on the Insert tab, in the Illustrations group, select SmartArt.
2. In the Choose A SmartArt Graphic dialog box, shown in Figure 9-26, select a SmartArt graphic, and then click OK.

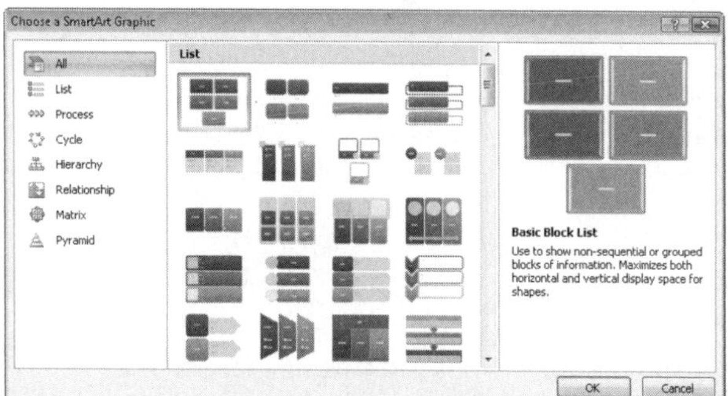

Figure 9-26. You can select the style of SmartArt graphic you want in the Choose A SmartArt Graphic dialog box.

Once the SmartArt graphic is inserted in the message, you can add text and format the graphic. The two SmartArt Tools tabs are described in the following sections.

Design Tab

The SmartArt Tools Design tab, shown in Figure 9-27, contains groups of commands that let you work with the SmartArt content, adding and customizing shapes and changing layout and styles.

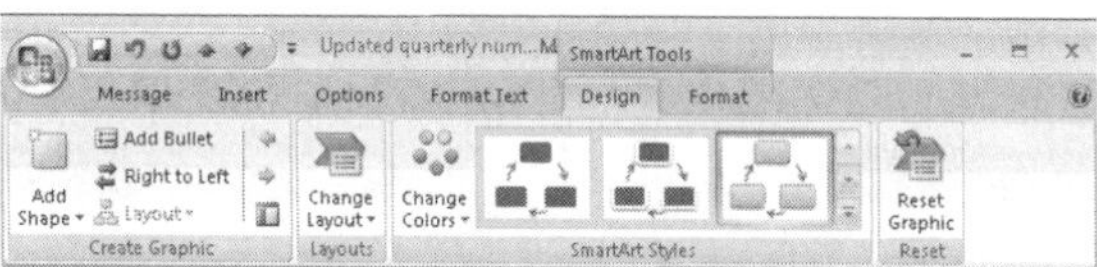

Figure 9-27. You can work with the graphics components and layout of SmartArt using the SmartArt Tools Design tab.

The groups available on the Design tab are:

- **Create Graphic** You can add a shape, bullet, or text pane to the SmartArt graphic and manipulate the text layout inside the SmartArt shapes with this set of controls.
- **Layouts** This group lets you change the SmartArt type either from the gallery or in the Choose A SmartArt Graphic dialog box.
- **SmartArt Styles** You can change the colors used in the SmartArt and the effects used in the SmartArt style.
- **Reset** The Reset Graphic command lets you quickly remove all custom formatting from the selected object.

Format Tab

The SmartArt Tools Format tab, shown in Figure 9-28, has the commands you need to style the SmartArt and control its placement in the message.

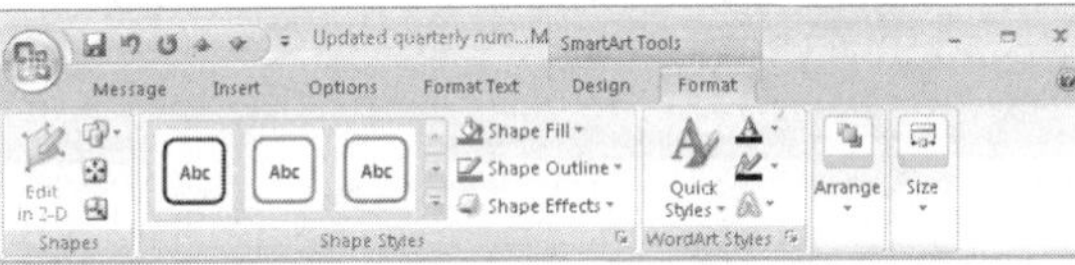

Figure 9-28. You can change the appearance of the SmartArt text, frame, and background using the SmartArt Tools Format tab.

The groups available on the Format tab are:

- **Shapes** You can choose the shapes to use as SmartArt elements and then resize those shapes.
- **Shape Styles** This group provides frame and fill effects, shape fill, shape outline, and shape changing effects.
- **WordArt Styles** You can format the text used in SmartArt objects, selecting a style from the gallery, Text Fill, Text Outline, and Text Effects. Each of these options has additional menu selections for fine-grained control over text format.
- **Arrange** This group contains the text wrapping, layering, and alignment commands. (This group is not displayed when a message is in RTF format.)
- **Size** This group lets you specify the shape height and shape width.

Using Symbols in a Message

A few other options are available on the Insert tab for you to use in your e-mail messages. You can also insert math equations, symbols (such as © or ™), and horizontal lines used for visual separation.

Inserting an Equation

To insert an equation in a message, follow these steps:

1. On the Insert tab, in the Symbols group, click Equation to create an empty equation box in your message.
2. Use the commands on the Equation Tools Design tab, shown in Figure 9-29, to create the equation, as follows:

   Tools You can specify how the equation is displayed: Linear is one-dimensional for easy editing, whereas Professional is two-dimensional for display. (These two commands are unavailable until you have entered some data in the equation.) You can enter plain text by clicking Normal Text. Clicking Equation displays the Equation gallery and lets you save new equations to it. Click the dialog box launcher to view the Equation Options dialog box.

   Symbols To add a symbol to the equation, click the symbol. (Click the More arrow to display the entire gallery.)

   Structures You can easily insert a number of mathematical structures into your equation by selecting a structure from the Structures group. You can choose a structure from these sets: Fraction, Script, Radical, Integral, Large Operator, Bracket, Function, Accent, Limit And Log, Operator, and Matrix. Each set has a number of selections, including many commonly used options.

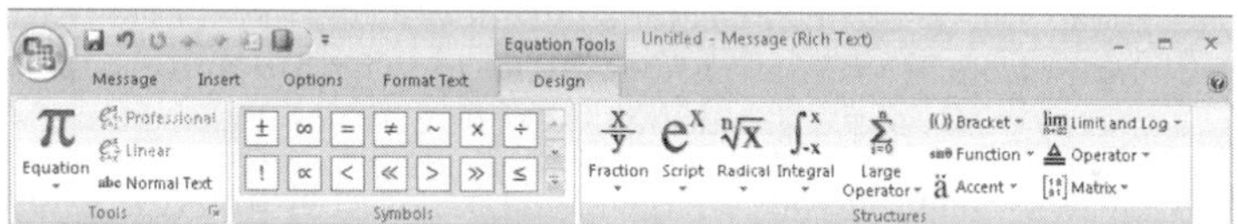

Figure 9-29. You can use the Equation Tools Design tab to complete your equation.

Inserting a Symbol

On the Insert tab, in the Symbols group, click Symbol. Select the symbol from the display of commonly used symbols, or click More Symbols to open the Symbol dialog box. In the Symbol dialog box, select the symbol, click Insert, and then click Close. (You can insert multiple symbols by clicking Insert after selecting one, then selecting the next symbol and clicking Insert again, and so on.)

Inserting a Horizontal line

On the Insert tab, in the Symbols group, click Horizontal Line. Outlook 2007 will insert a line at the insertion point location. To format the line, right-click it, and then choose Format Horizontal Line. In the Format Horizontal Line dialog box, shown in Figure 9-30, you can set the size, color, and alignment of the line. (Outlook 2007 uses the most recent settings in this dialog box when you create new lines.)

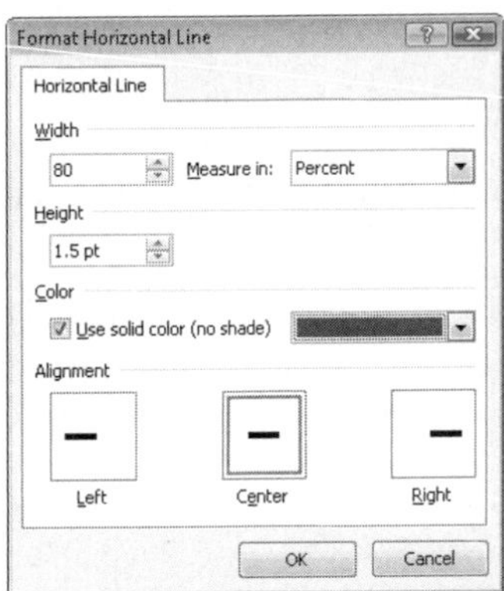

Figure 9-30. You can set the properties of horizontal lines in the Format Horizontal Line dialog box.

Working with Hyperlinks

You can easily insert hyperlinks to Web sites, e-mail addresses, network shares, and other items in a message. When you type certain kinds of text in a message, Outlook 2007 automatically converts the text to a hyperlink, requiring no special action from you. For example, if you type an e-mail address, an Internet URL, or a Universal Naming Convention (UNC) path to a share, Outlook 2007 converts the text to a hyperlink. To indicate the hyperlink, Outlook 2007 underlines it and changes the font color.

When the recipient of your message clicks the hyperlink, the resulting action depends on the type of hyperlink. With an Internet URL, for example, the recipient can go to the specified Web site. With a UNC path, the remote share opens when the recipient clicks the hyperlink. This is a great way to point the recipient to a shared resource on your computer or another computer on the network.

INSIDE OUT **Follow a hyperlink**

You can't follow (open) a hyperlink in a message you're composing by clicking the hyperlink. This action is restricted to allow you to click the hyperlink text and edit it. To follow a hyperlink in a message you're composing, hold down the Ctrl key and click the hyperlink.

Inserting Hyperlinks

You have another option for inserting a hyperlink in a message:

1. Position the insertion point where you want to insert the hyperlink.

2. On the Insert tab, in the Links group, click Hyperlink to display the Insert Hyperlink dialog box, shown in Figure 9-31. (If you select text to use for the link, that text is automatically inserted in the Text To Display box.)

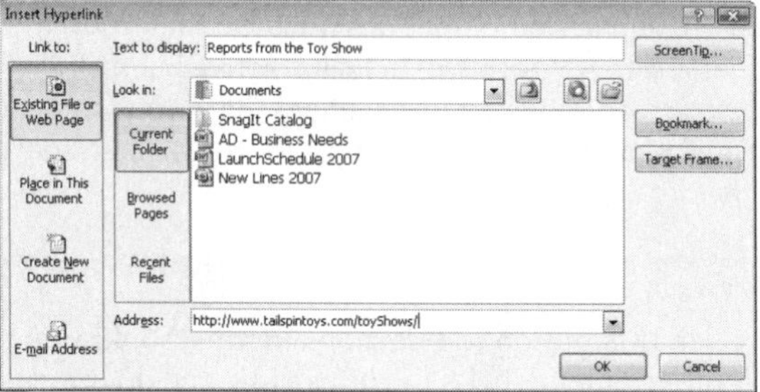

Figure 9-31. Use the Insert Hyperlink dialog box to insert a hyperlink and configure link settings.

The options displayed in the Insert Hyperlink dialog box vary according to the type of hyperlink you're inserting, as explained in the following sections.

Inserting Hyperlinks to Files or Web Pages

To insert a hyperlink to a file or Web page, select Existing File Or Web Page in the Link To bar. Then provide the following information in the Insert Hyperlink dialog box:

- **Text To Display** In this box, type the text that will serve as the hyperlink in the message. Outlook 2007 underlines this text and changes its color to indicate the hyperlink.
- **Look In** In this area, you can specify the location that Outlook 2007 should display the contents of. You can choose from these options:

  Current Folder If you are linking to a file, select Current Folder, and then use this drop-down list to locate and select the file on the local computer or on the network.

  Browsed Pages To insert a hyperlink to a page you've recently viewed in your Web browser, click Browsed Pages. The document list in the dialog box changes to show a list of recently browsed pages.

  Recent Files If you want to insert a hyperlink to a file you've used recently, click Recent Files to view a list of most recently used files in the document list of the dialog box.

- **Address** Type the local path, the Internet URL, or the UNC path to the file or Web site in this box.
- **ScreenTip** Click this button to define an optional ScreenTip that appears when the recipient's mouse pointer hovers over the hyperlink (when viewed in Microsoft Internet Explorer® version 4.0 or later).

INSIDE OUT View custom ScreenTips

Even though you can add custom ScreenTips using Outlook 2007, they cannot be seen in e-mail messages. Custom Screen Tips actually require Internet Explorer (version 4.0 or later). To see the ScreenTips you add in Outlook 2007, you have to use Outlook Web Access (OWA) with Exchange Server or first save the e-mail message as an HTML file and then view it in Internet Explorer.

- **Bookmark** Click this button to select an existing bookmark in the specified document. When the recipient clicks the hyperlink, the document opens at the bookmark location.
- **Target Frame** Click this button to specify the browser frame in which you want the hyperlink to appear. For example, choose New Window if you want the hyperlink to open in a new window on the recipient's computer.

TROUBLESHOOTING

Recipients of your messages can't access linked files

If you're setting up a hyperlink to a local file, bear in mind that the recipient probably won't be able to access the file using the file's local path. For example, linking to C:\Docs\Policies.doc would cause the recipient's system to try to open that path on his or her own system. You can use this method to point the recipient to a document on his or her own computer. However, if you want to point the recipient to a document on your computer, you must either specify a UNC path to the document or specify a URL (which requires that your computer function as a Web server).

The form of the UNC path you specify depends on the operating system of the recipient. In Microsoft Windows 2000 and later versions, you can specify a deep UNC path, such as \\<server>\<share>\<subfolder>\<sub-subfolder>\<document>.doc, where <server> is the name of the computer sharing the resource, <share> is the share name, <subfolder> is the name of a folder in the path to the file, and <document> is the name of the document to open. Microsoft Windows® 95, Microsoft Windows 98, Microsoft Windows Me, and Microsoft Windows NT® are limited to \\<server>\<share>\<document>. In order for the deep hyperlink to work properly, however, the recipient must be using Windows 2000 or later.

Inserting a Hyperlink to a Place in the Current Message

If you click Place In This Document in the Link To bar, the Insert Hyperlink dialog box changes, as shown in Figure 9-32. The Select A Place In This Document area shows the available locations in the open document: headings, bookmarks, and the top of the document. Select the location to which you want to link, provide other information as necessary (the text to display in the hyperlink, for example, or perhaps a ScreenTip), and then click OK.

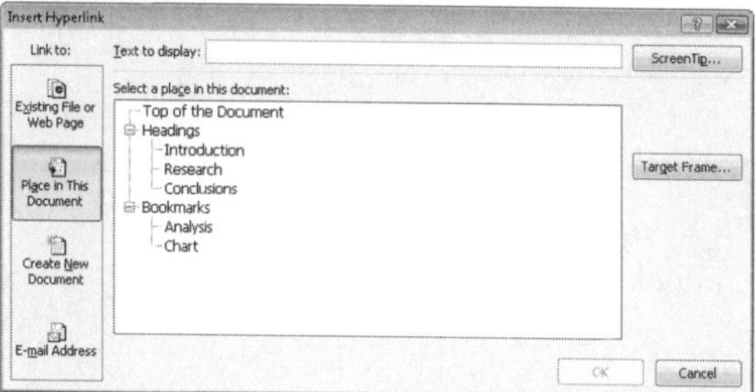

Figure 9-32. You can easily link to a location in the current document.

> **Note**
>
> This method is commonly used when you have opened a document in Word 2007 and are inserting a hyperlink in that document rather than in a separate e-mail message.

Inserting a Hyperlink to a New Document

If you select Create New Document in the Link To bar of the Insert Hyperlink dialog box, you can specify the path to a new document and choose to either edit the document now or insert the hyperlink for later editing. You'll most often use this method for inserting hyperlinks in a Word 2007 document rather than in an e-mail message.

Inserting a Hyperlink to an E-Mail Address

If you select E-Mail Address in the Link To bar, you can easily insert an e-mail address as a hyperlink in a message. When recipients click the hyperlink, their e-mail programs will open a new e-mail message addressed to the person you have specified in the hyperlink. Although you can simply type the e-mail address in the message and let Outlook 2007 convert it to a mailto: link, you might prefer to use the Insert Hyperlink dialog box instead. As Figure 9-33 shows, you can use this dialog box to enter an e-mail address or select from a list of e-mail addresses you have recently used on your system and to specify the subject for the message.

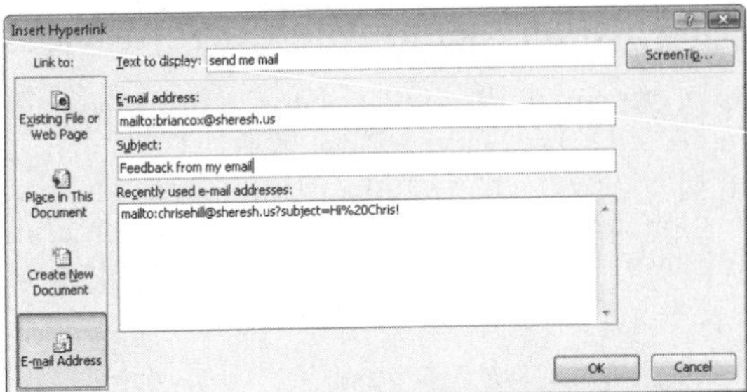

Figure 9-33. You can insert a mailto: hyperlink in your e-mail message.

Removing a Hyperlink

To remove a hyperlink, right-click the hyperlink, and then choose Remove Hyperlink on the shortcut menu. Outlook 2007 retains the underlying text but removes the hyperlink.

Inserting Bookmarks

A *bookmark* is an internal reference used to locate a specific place in a document and link to it by name. When you insert a bookmark in Outlook 2007, it is then available in the Insert Hyperlink dialog box as a linkable location. This is particularly useful if you have a lengthy e-mail message, or one with sections or illustrations that you want the reader to be able to find quickly. To insert a bookmark in a message, follow these steps:

1. With a message open, select the text (or picture, chart, and so on) that you want the bookmark to reference. On the Insert tab, in the Links group, click Bookmark.
2. In the Bookmark dialog box, shown in Figure 9-34, enter a name in the Bookmark Name box, click Add, and then click OK.

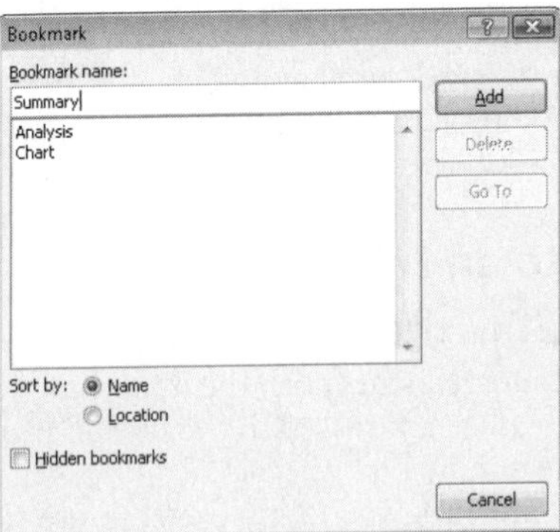

Figure 9-34. You can manage bookmarks using the Bookmark dialog box.

To remove a bookmark, on the Insert tab, in the Links group, click Bookmark. Select the bookmark you want to remove, click Delete, and then click Close.

Including Other Items in a Message

You might also want to include things such as files and other Outlook 2007 items in your mail messages at times. Outlook 2007 makes it easy for you to insert a calendar, a business card, or another item in your e-mail message.

Attaching Files

To attach a file to a message, follow these steps:

1. Position your insertion point where you want to insert the file, and on the Insert tab, in the Include group, select Attach File to open the Insert File dialog box.
2. Locate and select the file to insert, and then click Insert.

Alternatively, you can click the paper clip icon on the toolbar to insert a file as an attachment, or you can simply drag the file into the message window.

Inserting Files in the Body of a Message

Occasionally, you'll want to insert a file in the body of a message rather than attaching it to the message. For example, you might want to include a text file, a Word 2007 document, or another document as part of the message. To insert a file in the body of the message, you can use the steps described in the preceding section for attaching a file, with one difference: in step 2, click the button next to Insert, and then click Insert As Text.

INSIDE OUT **Use the Clipboard to insert a file**

In some cases, you'll find it easier to use the Clipboard to insert a file in a message, particularly if the file is already open in another window. (Just select the file, and then copy and paste or cut and paste it into the message.) You can also use the Clipboard when you need to insert only a portion of a file, such as a few paragraphs from a document.

Including an Outlook 2007 Item

You might want to include other Outlook 2007 items in a message you are sending. To include another Outlook 2007 item, follow these steps:

1. While creating a message, on the Insert tab, in the Include group, click Attach Item.
2. In the Insert Item dialog box, shown in Figure 9-35, locate and select the item or items you want to include.

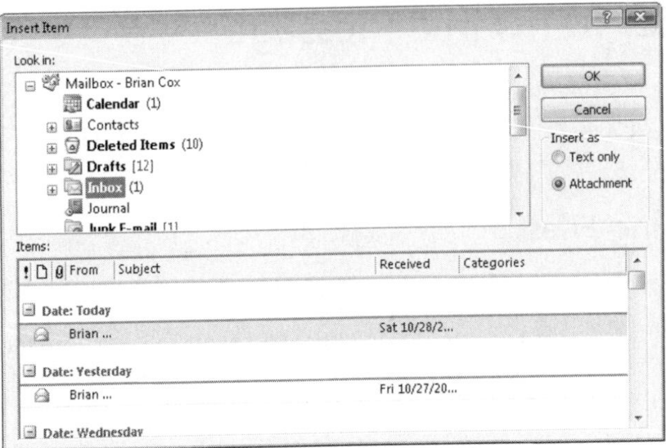

Figure 9-35. Select the Outlook 2007 items to include in a message in the Insert Item dialog box.

3. Select Attachment or Text Only, and then click OK.

> **Note**
>
> If the message is in RTF format, you also have the option to insert a shortcut to the item in the message.

Attaching a Business Card to a Message

With Outlook 2007, you can send a copy of a contact item in vCard format, a standard format for exchanging contact information. This allows the recipient to import the contact data into a contact management program, assuming that the recipient's program supports the vCard standard (as most do).

Here's how to share your contact information with others using a vCard:

1. In Outlook 2007, open the Contacts folder, and then select the contact item you want to send.
2. Choose Actions, Send As Business Card. Outlook 2007 inserts the vCard into the message.
3. Complete the message as you normally would, and then click Send.

You can also include a business card in a message from the new message form. On the Insert tab, in the Include group, click Business Card. If the contact is displayed in the recently used contacts list on the menu, you can select the contact. Otherwise, choose Other Business Cards to open the Insert Business Card dialog box, and then select a name from the complete Contacts list.

INSIDE OUT Send data as an Outlook 2007 item

If you know that the recipient uses Outlook 2007, you can right-click the contact and choose Send Full Contact, In Outlook Format (or select the contact and choose Actions, Send Full Contact, In Outlook Format) to send the contact data as an Outlook 2007 contact item. Outlook 2007 users can also use vCard attachments.

For more details on using and sharing vCards, see "Sharing Contacts" in Chapter 18.

Including a Calendar

To send a calendar in e-mail, follow these steps:

1. While composing a message, on the Insert tab, in the Include group, click Calendar to open the Send A Calendar Via E-mail dialog box, as shown in Figure 9-36.

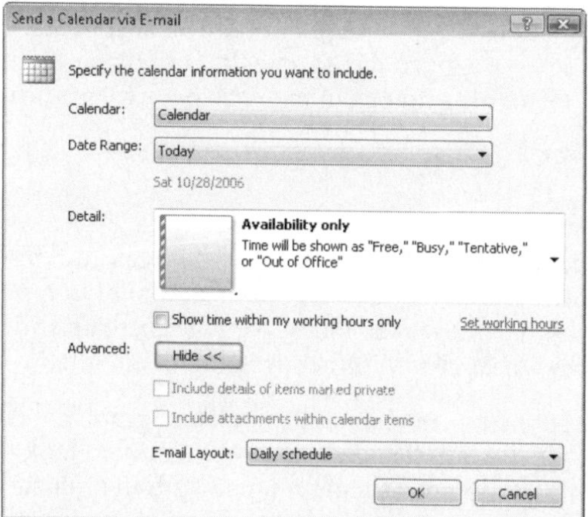

Figure 9-36. You can select the information you want to include when sending a calendar via e-mail.

2. Choose the Calendar, Date Range, Detail level, and other parameters for the calendar. Click OK.

See Chapter 36, "Sharing Calendars," for more information about sharing your calendar using Outlook 2007.

> **Note**
> We will discuss the use of signatures in the section "Using Signatures" later in this chapter.

Customizing the Appearance of Your Messages

By default, Outlook 2007 uses no background or special font characteristics for messages. However, it does support the use of themes and, to a lesser degree, stationery, so you can customize the look of your messages. Outlook 2007 has two types of themes as well as stationery, each of which functions a bit differently from the others. It helps to understand the differences between these options before you get started using them.

Understanding How Outlook Formats Messages

The appearance of an Outlook 2007 e-mail message is the result of a complex behind-the-scenes interaction between a number of settings. A single message is likely to draw some of its formatting information from several different sources. While much of the process of determining how a given message looks is invisible to you, it helps to understand what goes into formatting an e-mail message before you start working with these settings.

Office Themes

Themes apply a single, customizable look to your messages (and more, since they can be shared across 2007 Microsoft Office system applications) by combining several settings to create a specific look. Themes make it easy for you to create and implement a unified look and feel for all of your Microsoft Office system documents.

A theme has a set of font faces, coordinated colors, and graphical effects that are combined to create a palette of styles that gives you a unified look for all of the elements of your messages. Each portion of a theme can use built-in or custom settings that you create, giving you an endless number of combinations to work with. The components of a theme are:

- **Colors** A set of eight colors that are applied consistently across all of the graphical elements in your e-mail. You can use built-in color sets or create your own.
- **Fonts** Two fonts—one for body text and another for heading text—are used as the basis for the gallery of font styles used by that theme. Outlook 2007 has a number of built-in theme fonts, or you can create a custom set.
- **Effects** An effect is a particular look for graphical objects created by using different values for lines, fills, and 3-D effects to create varying end results. Effects are selected from a built-in gallery. You cannot create custom effects.

- **Page Color** The page background can be a solid color, gradient, pattern, texture, or picture, or it can be left blank.

> **Note**
>
> Although you can save a theme that includes a background set by using the Page Color command, the background is not applied when you use that theme in Outlook 2007. To set a default background, you must use stationery or a legacy theme.

Office Themes are created in Outlook 2007, Word 2007, Excel 2007, and PowerPoint 2007. In Outlook 2007, you create and apply these themes within an e-mail message. (Microsoft Office PowerPoint® 2007 has the widest range of theme creation options.) Themes are stored as .thmx files under your user profile.

Legacy Themes

Outlook 2007 can also use themes from earlier versions of Microsoft Outlook to apply a background (color or image), a set of colors, and a few styled items, such as fonts and bulleted lists. While you can set one of these themes to be the default for new Outlook 2007 messages in the Signatures And Stationery dialog box, you have to use Microsoft FrontPage® 2003 to edit them. For most people, this limits the use of these themes to the built-in set. It's easier to create an Office Theme or stationery if you want the functionality it supplies than to work with legacy themes. These themes are stored as a set of files (Microsoft Office system theme file [.elm], setup file [.inf], and graphics files) in C:\Program Files\Common Files\microsoft shared\THEMES12.

Stationery

Stationery creates a customized look for your e-mail using a background image and font formatting. With most of the Microsoft Office system document formatting moving to themes, stationery is mostly a legacy feature with only a background image and a few font styles, but it is the simplest way to get a background into new messages by default. Stationery is stored as HTML files in C:\Program Files\Common Files\microsoft shared\Stationery, with supporting graphics in an associated folder. If you create or modify stationery using Word 2007, graphics and any other files that you use in the stationery are saved in a subfolder of the directory where you save the template.

> **Note**
>
> To use themes or stationery, you must use RTF or HTML format for the message.

Style Sets

A *style set* is a working set of font styles used for messages: normal, heading, title, and so on. Outlook 2007 creates a style set by applying the theme colors to the body and heading fonts to configure the actual font styles. You can customize the display of the fonts in a message and save it as a custom style set. Style sets are saved as Word 2007 templates.

Outlook 2007 combines these settings to configure the exact look of each message you create. When you create a new message, the collective default settings for new messages that you have configured are applied, as described in Table 9-1. Backgrounds can come from legacy themes or stationery, while font and graphical styling information comes from the currently saved default settings (which is usually a theme). If you have customized font styles, those are loaded from the template that you created.

Table 9-1 Message Style Components

Component	Controlled By	To Set
Backgrounds	Stationery or legacy theme	Choose Tools, Options, and on the Mail Format tab, select Stationery And Fonts. On the Personal Stationery tab, under Theme Or Stationery To Use For New HTML Messages, choose Theme, and then select a theme.
Colors, fonts, and effects	Office Themes	When composing a message, on the Options tab, in the Themes group, click one of the Themes options.
Custom font styles	Style set	When composing a message, on the Format Text tab, in the Styles group, click Change Styles, and then choose Style Set.

Using Themes to Customize Your Messages

You can select a theme from the Themes gallery, shown in Figure 9-37, which displays built-in Office Themes and custom themes that you create. If you don't find a theme you like in the Themes gallery, you can look for others, either locally (on your hard disk or network) or using Microsoft Office Online.

To select a theme, with a message open, on the Options tab, in the Themes group, click Theme, and then select a theme from the Themes gallery.

You can also choose to Reset To Theme From Template, which causes new Outlook 2007 messages to use the Office Theme that is the default for new messages.

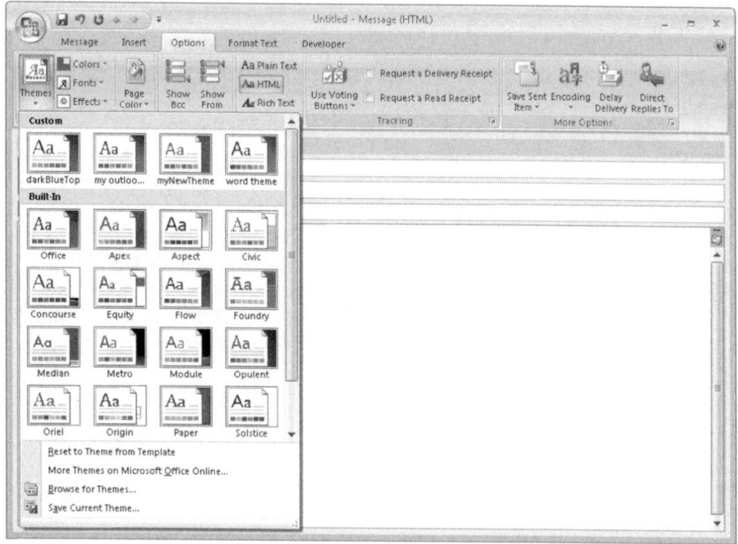

Figure 9-37. You can select a theme or save the current theme using the Themes command.

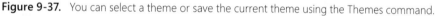

To look for additional themes, select More Themes On Microsoft Office Online.

If you have additional themes saved locally, you can select Browse For Themes to find them on your hard disk or in a network location.

INSIDE OUT Find your custom themes quickly

Outlook 2007 saves custom themes you create in the <profile>\AppData\Roaming\Microsoft\Templates\Document Themes folder. When you browse for additional themes, however, Outlook 2007 starts you in the <profile>\Documents folder. You need to change to the correct folder to see your themes. If you have saved a theme recently, you might be able to select the folder that contains the themes by clicking the Previous Locations arrow in the Choose Theme Or Themed Document dialog box. If not, select Save Current Theme on the Themes menu, select the path to the folder in the Address box, press **Ctrl+C**, and then click Cancel. You can then select Browse For Themes, paste the path into the Address Bar, and then press **Enter** to quickly go to the correct location and find your themes.

You can also choose Save Current Theme.

Colors

You can choose a set of colors to use for the text and other style options, or you can create a new set of custom colors. To select a color, with a message open, on the Options tab, in the Themes group, click Color. Select a set of theme colors in the Colors gallery, as shown in Figure 9-38.

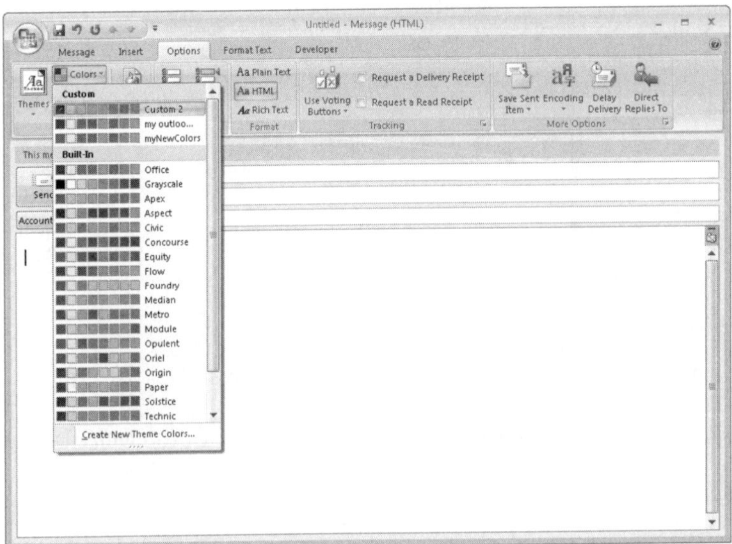

Figure 9-38. You can select a set of colors for your theme using the Colors gallery.

To create a new set of theme colors, follow these steps:

1. With a message open, on the Options tab, in the Themes group, click Color, and then click Create New Theme Colors.
2. In the Create New Theme Colors dialog box, shown in Figure 9-39, select the colors you want, enter a name for the theme colors in the Name box, and then click Save. You can then select the theme colors from the Colors gallery.

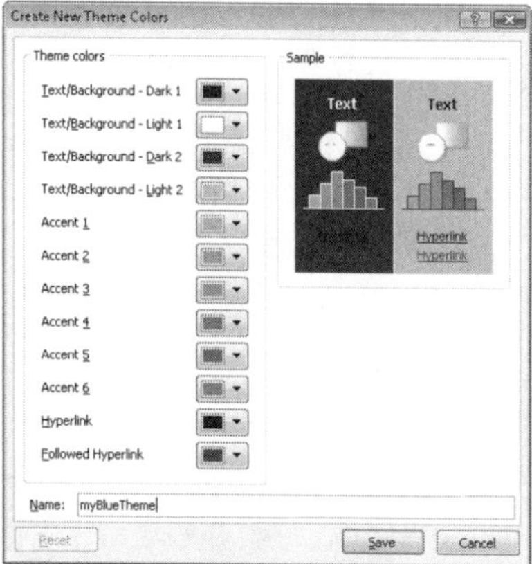

Figure 9-39. You can select a set of colors for your theme in the Create New Theme Colors dialog box.

Fonts

Themes use two font selections, in combination with colors and other settings, to create a range of Quick Styles for the fonts in your message. You choose a font for the headings and a font for the body text, and Outlook 2007 does the rest. You can control the font styles more precisely by saving stationery or saving a message form or using the options on the Ribbon, on the Format Text tab, in the Style group.

To select fonts, with a message open, on the Options tab, in the Themes group, click fonts. Select a font pair from the Fonts gallery, as shown in Figure 9-40.

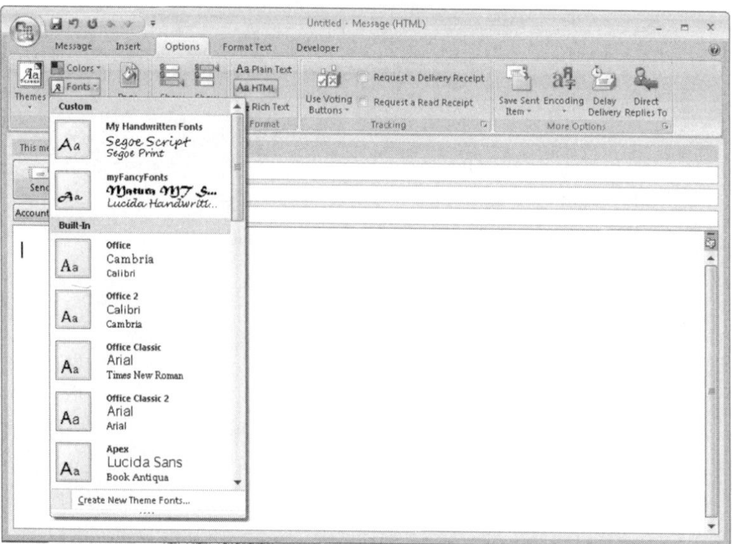

Figure 9-40. You can select the theme fonts in the Fonts gallery.

Chapter 9

If you want to choose two specific fonts rather than a preset pair, follow these steps:

1. On the Fonts menu, choose Create New Theme Fonts.
2. In the Create New Theme Fonts dialog box, shown in Figure 9-41, select a heading font and a body font. Give the theme fonts a name, and then click Save.

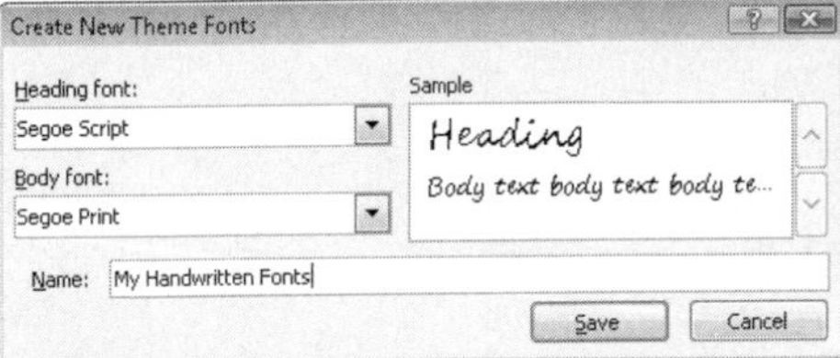

Figure 9-41. You can select one font for the body text of your messages and another for the headings in the Create New Theme Fonts dialog box.

Effects

Outlook 2007 themes use effects for creating a particular look in the graphical elements (such as SmartArt and charts) that you insert in your e-mail. Effects vary in the weight of the lines they use and the opacity, glow, and texture of the surfaces on the objects that Outlook 2007 creates. The Effects gallery provides previews of the effects, but you should try out various effects on an e-mail message with some graphical elements in it to see the various effects in action.

To select an effect for your messages, open a message, and on the Options tab, in the Themes group, click Effects, and then select an effect in the Effects gallery, shown in Figure 9-42.

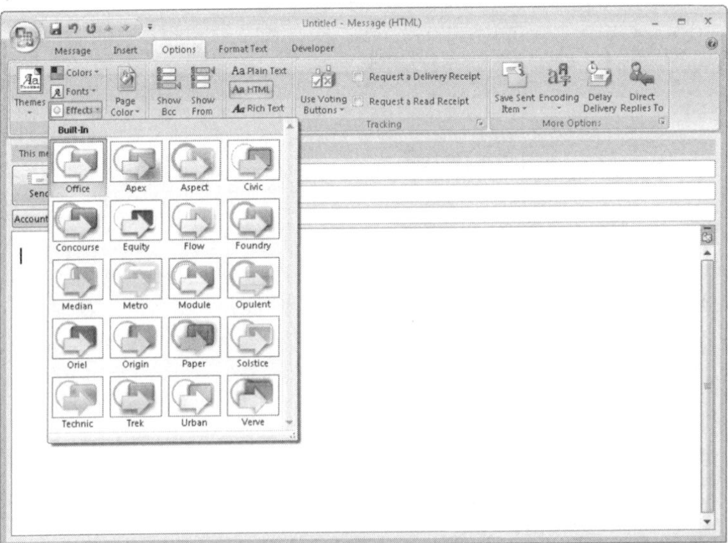

Figure 9-42. You can choose from a number of effects for the graphical elements of your messages.

Page Color

The Page Color option lets you select a background for the e-mail message you are composing. Outlook 2007 lets you choose from colors, gradients, textures, patterns, and pictures for your message background.)

To select a page color, in Outlook 2007, with a new, blank e-mail message open, on the Options tab, in the Themes group, select Page Color and do one of the following:

- To use a color that is displayed on the Page Colors menu, click the color. The Theme Colors area displays the theme colors on the top line and light-to-dark variations of each color in a vertical bar below the color. You can also choose a standard (VGA) color or no color.
- If you want to choose a different solid color, click More Colors to open the Colors dialog box. Select the color you want to use, and then click OK.
- Select Fill Effects to use a gradient, texture, pattern, or picture as the message background. The Fill Effects dialog box has several tabs:

  Gradient The Gradient tab, shown in Figure 9-43, gives you several options to create a shaded background. Choose the number of colors to use, and then select the colors in the Color 1 and Color 2 drop-down lists. Choose a shading style, and then click a variant. The Sample area gives you a preview of the current settings. When you have finished, click OK.

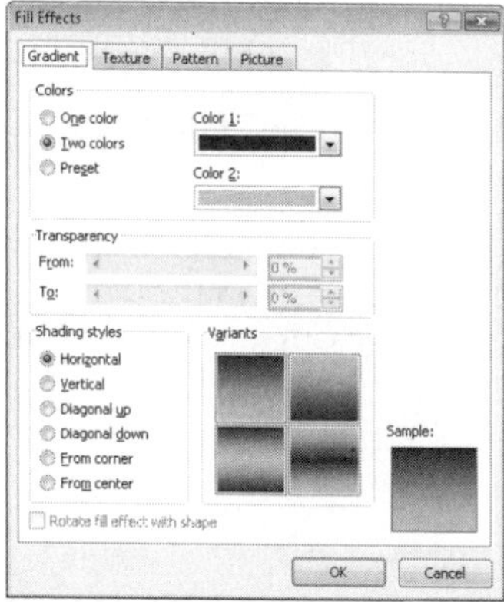

Figure 9-43. You can create your own shaded background on the Gradient tab in the Fill Effects dialog box.

  Texture Has a selection of small images that are tiled on the message background. Select a texture you like, or click Other Texture to select a different graphics file to use as the texture.

  Pattern Has a number of patterns to select from and lets you set the Foreground and Background colors to configure the final look of the pattern.

  Picture Lets you choose a picture to use as the background by clicking Select Picture and locating the image you want to use.

INSIDE OUT **Use a background image automatically on new messages**

Although you can add a background image to an e-mail message using the Page Color command in the Theme group on the Options tab, a saved theme will not load the background image in an e-mail message. You can use existing stationery, however, or a legacy theme, to apply a background image to your new e-mail messages by default. The only way to choose your own background image for e-mail messages is by creating new stationery, which allows you to apply a background and font styles to new messages.

Creating a Custom Theme

You can use these commands to create a customized theme that you can share across your Microsoft Office system documents. To create your own theme, follow these steps:

1. In Outlook 2007, with a new, blank e-mail message open, on the Options tab, in the Themes group, click Page Color, select a background, and then click OK.
2. On the Options tab, in the Themes group, click Colors, and then select a set of colors to use.
3. On the Options tab, in the Themes group, click Fonts, and then select a pair of fonts to use.
4. On the Options tab, in the Themes group, click Effects, and then select a style of effects to use.
5. Once you are satisfied with the configuration of the theme, save it so that you can apply it easily later on. To save the theme, on the Options tab, in the Themes group, click Themes, and then click Save Current Theme. Name the theme, and then click Save.

Note

Outlook 2007 saves custom themes to <profile>\AppData\Roaming\Microsoft\Templates\Document Themes.

When you load this theme, it will set the message colors, fonts, and effects but not the background settings. To save the background, you must create either stationery or a form. If you want to configure the theme settings as well as the background image, save a form. If you want to specify only the background image and font styles that you manually format, create stationery.

For information about customizing all aspects of a new message, see "Creating a Custom Message Appearance" on the next page.

Using Stationery to Customize Your Messages

With Outlook 2007 stationery, you use a set of characteristics that define the font style, color, and background image for messages. In effect, stationery can give your messages a certain look and feel, as shown in Figure 9-44. Stationery provides more limited customization than themes, and Outlook 2007 uses stationery very little. There are several built-in stationery options, although the only way to use them is to assign them as the default message format. In addition, you cannot create new stationery or customize existing stationery directly in Outlook 2007; you must use another program such as Word 2007.

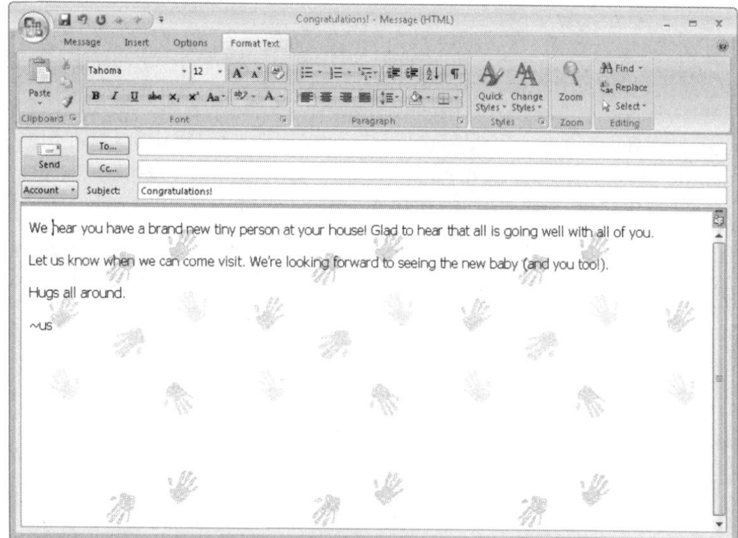

Figure 9-44. Stationery gives your messages a customized look.

You can assign a default stationery to be used in all your messages. To do so, follow these steps:

1. In Outlook 2007, choose Tools, Options, and then select the Mail Format tab.
2. On the Mail Format tab, click Stationery And Fonts to display the Signatures And Stationery dialog box.
3. On the Personal Stationery tab of the Signatures And Stationery dialog box, click Theme.
4. In the Theme Or Stationery dialog box, shown in Figure 9-45, choose the default stationery in the Choose A Theme list, and then click OK. If you have default

stationery selected and no longer want your messages to use any stationery, follow the same procedure but set the default stationery to No Theme.

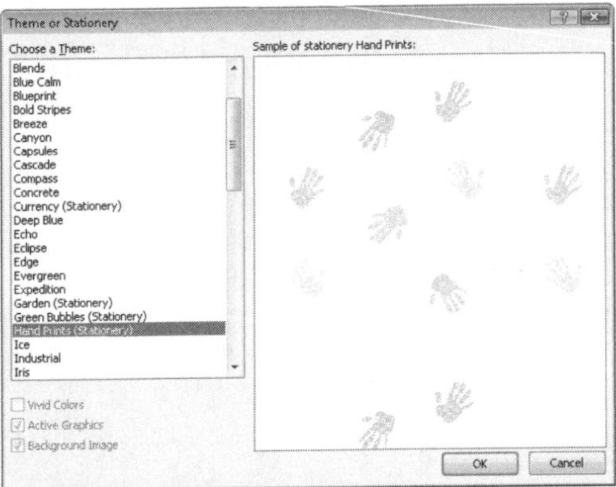

Figure 9-45. Use the Theme Or Stationery dialog box to preview and select stationery.

5. If you want to use fonts that are different from those in the stationery you just chose, in the Signatures And Stationery dialog box, in the Font drop-down list, under Theme Or Stationery For New HTML E-Mail Message, select either Use My Font When Replying And Forwarding Messages or Always Use My Fonts.

6. In the Signatures And Stationery dialog box, click the Font button for each font you want to customize, configure the options in the Font dialog box, and then click OK.

7. When you have finished setting the new message defaults, click OK to close the Signatures And Stationery dialog box.

INSIDE OUT **Create new stationery**

You can create new stationery in Word 2007 to use with Outlook 2007. To do this, create a new document in Word 2007, select the picture that you want to use as a background, and then format any font style that you want to use with Outlook 2007. Save the file as HTML in the C:\Program Files\Common Files\microsoft shared\Stationery folder. You can then choose this stationery as the default for new messages in the Signatures And Stationery dialog box.

Creating a Custom Message Appearance

As you've seen, each customization method supports different aspects of a new e-mail message's format. While you can set a default background for new messages using stationery, the new message will take on the default Office Theme colors and effects as well as most font settings. Similarly, while you can specify two fonts and a set of colors in a theme, Microsoft Office system controls the interaction of your choices to create the actual font styles, so if you want to control a font style yourself, you have to use stationery.

If you want to predefine every aspect of a new e-mail message, you might have to take a few steps to create the default new message settings you want. Although you can manually configure any number of settings, optimally you will have already created all of the subparts of the new message format already. If not, it's a good idea to do so before you get started, to give yourself easily reusable settings. Then you just have to choose a few settings and save the message format as the default.

> **Note**
>
> Before starting this process, you need stationery that uses your background image. For information about creating custom stationery, see "Using Stationery to Customize Your Messages" earlier in this chapter.

To create your customized default new message, follow these steps:

1. To set a background for new messages, click Tools, Options, and then on the Mail Format tab, click Signatures And Fonts. In Theme Or Stationery For New HTML Message, choose the stationery containing the background you want to use.
2. Open a new, blank e-mail message, and then verify that the background specified in the stationery is applied.
3. On the Options tab, in the Themes group, select the theme that contains the settings you want to use. Alternatively, you can manually configure any theme settings that you want to customize.
4. Select a style set (or format any text styles you want to customize).
5. When you are satisfied with the settings for new messages, on the Format Text tab, in the Styles group, click Change Styles, and then click Save As Default.

Using Signatures

Outlook 2007 supports two types of signatures that you can add automatically (or manually) to outgoing messages: standard signatures and digital signatures. This chapter focuses on standard signatures, which can include text and graphics, depending on the mail format you choose.

To learn about digital signatures, which allow you to authenticate your identity and encrypt messages, see "Protecting Messages with Digital Signatures" in Chapter 14.

Understanding Message Signatures

Outlook 2007 can add a signature automatically to your outgoing messages. You can specify different signatures for new messages and for replies or forwards. Signatures can include both text and graphics as well as vCard attachments. Both rich-text and HTML formats support business cards and graphics in messages. If your signature contains graphics and you start a new message using plain-text format, the graphics are removed, although any text defined by the signature remains. When you start a message using plain-text format, business cards are attached but not included in the body of the message.

Why use signatures? Many people use a signature to include their contact information in each message. Still others use a signature to include a favorite quote or other information in the message. Regardless of the type of information you want to include, creating and using the signature is easy.

INSIDE OUT **Use multiple signatures**

You can create a unique signature for each e-mail account, and use one signature for new messages and a different one when you reply to or forward a message. When you send a message, Outlook 2007 appends the appropriate signature to the outgoing message.

Defining Signatures

To define a signature, you use the Outlook 2007 Mail Format options. If you want to include a graphic, check before you start to ensure that you already have that graphic on your computer or that it's available on the network.

Follow these steps to create a signature:

1. In Outlook 2007, choose Tools, Options, and then select the Mail Format tab.
2. Click Signatures to open the Signatures And Stationery dialog box, and then click New.
3. In the New Signature dialog box, specify a name for the signature as it will appear in Outlook 2007, and then click OK.
4. In the Signatures And Stationery dialog box, click the signature you just created in the Select A Signature To Edit list.
5. In the Edit Signature area, type the text you want to include in the signature, and then use the toolbar to format the text, as shown in Figure 9-46.

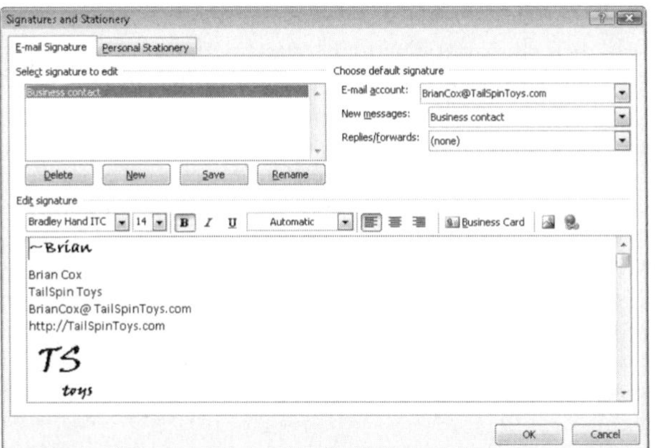

Figure 9-46. Format the text of your signature in the Edit Signature area of the Signatures And Stationery dialog box.

- To attach a vCard from an Outlook 2007 contact item, click Business Card. In the Insert Business Card dialog box, select the contact item, and then click OK.
- To insert a picture, click the Picture icon. In the Insert Picture dialog box, select the picture, and then click Insert.
- To insert a hyperlink, click the Hyperlink icon. In the Insert Hyperlink dialog box, select the location to link to, type the text to display (if needed), and then click Insert.

6. When you have finished with the signature, click Save.
7. Create other signatures if desired, and then click OK to close the Signatures And Stationery dialog box.

Adding Signatures to Messages

The signature Outlook 2007 adds to new messages and the signature it adds to replies and forwards don't have to be the same. To set up different signatures for these different kinds of messages, choose Tools, Options, select the Mail Format tab, and then click Signature.

In the Choose Default Signature area, select an account in the E-Mail Account drop-down list. Select a signature in the New Messages drop-down list and one in the Replies/Forwards drop-down list.

INSIDE OUT Specify the default message format

Keep in mind that the signature data Outlook 2007 adds to the message depends on the message format specified on the Options tab. Set the message format to HTML or rich text if you want to create or edit signatures that contain graphics.

Other than letting you specify the signature for new messages or for replies and forwards, Outlook 2007 does not give you a way to control which signature is attached to a given message. For example, if you want to use different signatures for personal and business messages, you must switch signatures manually. However, Outlook 2007 does store signature options separately for each account, so you can control signatures to some degree just by sending messages through a specific account.

You can change the signature when composing a message. On the Insert tab, in the Include group, click Signature, and then select the signature on the menu. If you want a new signature, choose Signatures on the menu to open the Signatures And Stationery dialog box, and then create a new signature to use.

INSIDE OUT **Outlook 2007 uses only one signature per message**

Unlike Outlook 2003, which lets you insert multiple signatures in the same message, Outlook 2007 erases the current signature when you choose a new one on the Signatures menu in a message. If you are used to adding snippets of content to your messages using signatures with Outlook 2003, you can use Quick Parts to accomplish this (and more). More information about Quick Parts is available in the section "Using Special Text Features" earlier in this chapter.

Backing Up Your Signatures

You should back up your signatures when you finish creating them and after you add a significant number of new ones. Signatures are stored in <profile>\AppData\Roaming\Microsoft\Signatures as a set of files (text, HTML, and rich text) and a corresponding folder of files containing pictures, XML files, and theme data.

There is no provision for backing up your signature inside Outlook 2007. To back up your signatures, you should back up the contents of <profile>\AppData\Roaming\Microsoft\Signatures.

Using the Proofing and Research Tools

From the old standby spelling and grammar check to research and translation tools, Outlook 2007 has a number of tools to help you get your message across clearly. You can perform searches across a wide variety of sources, from electronic reference books such as Microsoft Encarta® to Web sites. A number of research options are installed by default, and you can add more to customize your searches. The default research options include reference books such as Encarta and thesauruses in multiple languages; general-purpose research Web sites, including Encarta Encyclopedia and MSN® Research and Business; and Financial Web sites such as MSN Money Stock Quotes and Thomson Gale Company Profiles.

On the Message tab, in the Proofing group, you can click Spelling and then select from the following options:

- **Spelling & Grammar** Performs a spelling and grammar check in accordance with the current configuration.
- **Research** This option performs a search across the sources you select. You can choose categories to search (for example, All Reference Books) or individual data sources (for example, Microsoft Encarta).

See "Configuring Research Options" later in this chapter for details on customizing the services used for searches.

- **Thesaurus** You can select English, French, or Spanish as the thesaurus language in the drop-down list.
- **Translate** The translation feature lets you translate small amounts of text between a number of common languages. To translate text in a message, select the text, and then on the Message tab, in the Proofing group, click Translate. Select the text's current language in the From drop-down list and the language you want the text translated to in the To drop-down list. The translated text is displayed in the Translation area of the Research pane, as shown in Figure 9-47. if you want to use the translated text in your message, select the text in the Research pane, and then press **Ctrl+C** to copy it to the Clipboard.

Figure 9-47. You can translate text between a number of languages using the Research pane.

INSIDE OUT Switch research modes

Once you have opened the Research pane by selecting Research, Thesaurus, or Translate, you can switch between the three research modes by selecting different data sources to search in the drop-down list. Selecting a thesaurus from the Reference Books list is the same as clicking Thesaurus in the Proofing group. Selecting Translation in the drop-down list gives you these options for translating text:

- **Translation ScreenTip** Selecting this option causes Outlook 2007 to display a ScreenTip with a brief translation of a word when you point to the word with the mouse, as shown in Figure 9-48.

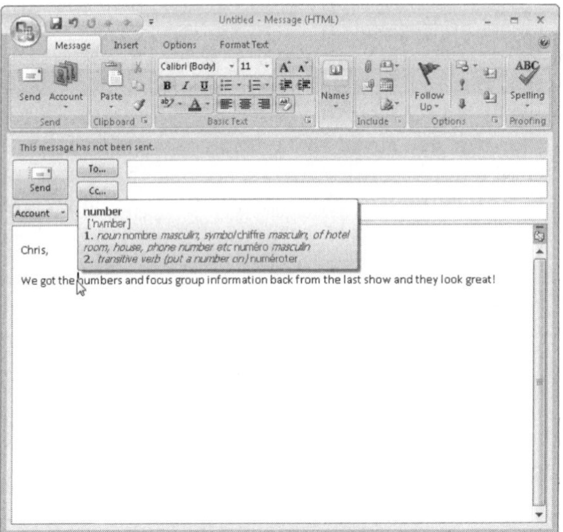

Figure 9-48. Translation ScreenTips give you a quick translation of an individual word.

- **Set Language** You can set the language to be used for proofing specific sections of text in a message, letting you check the spelling and grammar of multilanguage messages. The default setting is Detect Language Automatically, which should work in most cases. If Outlook 2007 is having a difficult time recognizing text in a particular language, you can select the text and then select Set Language to mark the language.
- **Word Count** This selection displays the statistics for the message, including number of words, lines, paragraphs, pages, and characters. You can choose to include the contents of footnotes, endnotes, and text boxes in the statistics.

Configuring Research Options

The list of services that Outlook 2007 uses when doing various forms of research can be customized to meet your individual needs. To configure the reference books and research sites that Outlook 2007 searches, on the Message tab, in the Proofing group, click Research. In the Research pane, select Research Options. You can select from the following options:

- **Services** Activate services and resources that are installed by selecting the check box in the Services list. To deactivate a service, clear its check box.
- **Add Services** To add more services, select Add Services, and then select the provider in the Advertised Services list. To add a new provider, enter the location of the service in the Address box.
- **Update/Remove** To manage installed services, select Update/Remove to display the Update Or Remove Services dialog box. To update a service, select it in the Currently Installed Services, Grouped By Provider list, and then click Update to reinstall the provider for that service. To remove a service, select the provider in the list, and then click Remove. (You cannot remove installed options such as dictionaries and thesauruses.) Click Close when you have finished updating services.
- **Parental Control** If you want to provide filtered access to research services, click Parental Control to open the Parental Control dialog box. You can then choose Turn On Content Filtering To Make Services Block Offensive Results. You can also opt to Allow Users To Search Only The Services That Can Block Offensive Results. These settings can also be protected with a password.

> **Note**
>
> You must be logged on with an Administrator account to configure Parental Control settings.

CHAPTER 10

Finding and Organizing Messages

Without some means of organizing and filtering e-mail, most people would be inundated with messages, many of which are absolutely useless. Fortunately, the Microsoft® Office Outlook® 2007 junk e-mail filters can take care of most, if not all, of the useless messages. For the rest, you can use several Office Outlook 2007 features to help you organize messages, locate specific messages, and otherwise get control of your Inbox and other folders.

This chapter shows you how to customize your message folder views, which will help you organize your messages. You'll also learn about the Outlook 2007 search folders, which give you a great way to locate messages based on conditions that you specify and to organize messages without adding other folders to your mailbox. This chapter also explains how to use categories and custom views to organize your messages.

Finding and Organizing Messages with Search Folders

The Outlook 2007 search folders are an extremely useful feature for finding and organizing messages. A *search folder* isn't really a folder but rather a special view that functions much like a separate folder. In effect, a search folder is a saved search. You specify conditions for the folder, such as all messages from a specific sender or all messages received in the last day, and Outlook 2007 displays in that search folder view those messages that meet the specified conditions.

In a way, a search folder is like a rule that moves messages to a special folder. However, although the messages seem to exist in the search folder, they continue to reside in their respective folders. For example, a search folder might show all messages in the Inbox and Sent Items folders that were sent by Jim Boyce. Even though these messages appear in the Jim Boyce search folder (for example), they are actually still located in the Inbox and Sent Items folders.

Using Search Folders

It isn't difficult at all to use a search folder. The Folder List includes a Search Folders branch, as shown in Figure 10-1, that lists all of the search folder contents. Simply click a search folder in the Folder List to view the headers for the messages it contains.

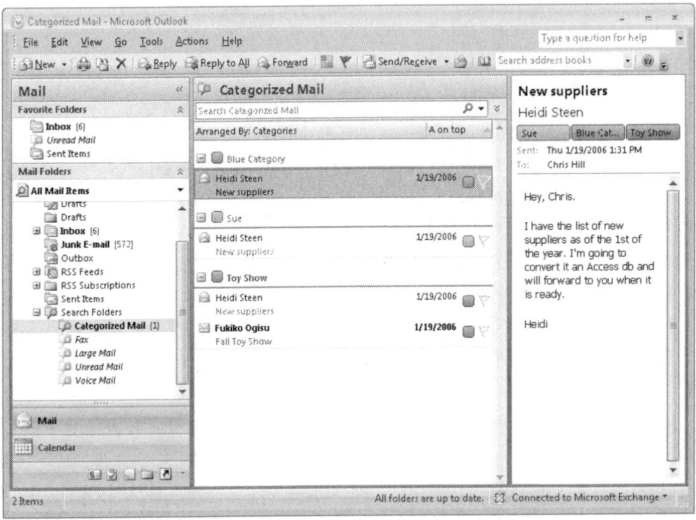

Figure 10-1. Search folders appear under their own branch in the Folder List. This folder shows all messages that are categorized.

Customizing Search Folders

Outlook 2007 includes five search folders by default, which you can use as is or customize to suit your needs:

- **Categorized Mail** This search folder shows all messages that have categories assigned to them.
- **Fax** If you are connected to a Microsoft Exchange Server 2007 mailbox with unified messaging enabled, this search folder will enable you to see all received faxes in your mailbox.
- **Large Mail** This search folder shows all messages that are 100 KB or larger.
- **Unread Mail** This search folder shows all messages that are unread.
- **Voice Mail** If you are connected to an Exchange Server 2007 mailbox with unified messaging enabled, this search folder shows all received voice-mail messages.

In addition, if you have migrated from Microsoft Outlook 2003, you might also have these search folders in your mailbox:

- **For Follow Up** This search folder shows all messages that are flagged for follow-up.
- **Important Mail** This search folder shows all messages that are marked as Important.

You can customize these existing search folders as well as those you create yourself. For example, you might increase the value in the Large Mail search folder from 100 KB to 200 KB if you frequently receive messages larger than 100 KB that you don't want included in the Large Mail search folder.

To customize an existing search folder, open the Folder List, right-click the folder, and then choose Customize This Search Folder to open the Customize dialog box, similar to the one shown in Figure 10-2.

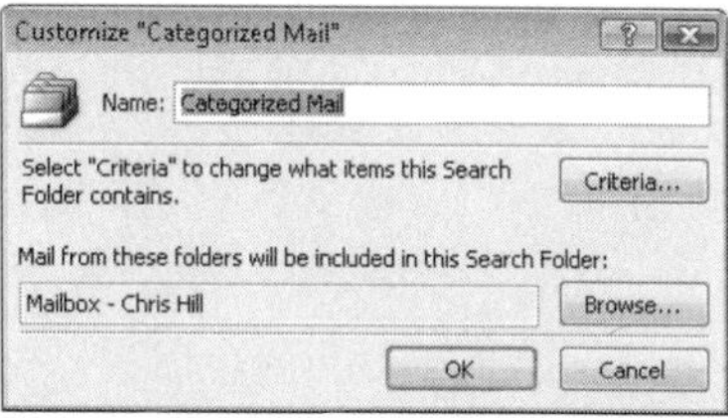

Figure 10-2. Set the criteria or folders to include for a search folder in the Customize dialog box.

You can change the name of the search folder in the Name box in the Customize dialog box. To change the criteria for the search folder, click the Criteria button to display a dialog box that enables you to change your selection. The dialog box that appears depends on the criteria you used when you created the folder. For example, if you are modifying a search folder that locates messages from a specific sender, Outlook 2007 displays the Select Names dialog box so that you can specify a different person (or additional people).

Note

You can change the criteria of only two of the default search folders, the Large Mail and Categorized Mail folders. The criteria for the other three can't be changed. However, you can change the folders to be included in the search for all of the default search folders.

To change which folders are included in the search folder, click Browse in the Customize dialog box to open the Select Folder(s) dialog box. Select each folder that you want to include, or select the Personal Folders or Mailbox branch to include all folders in the mail store in the search. Select the Search Subfolders option to include in the search all subfolders for a selected folder. When you have finished selecting folders, click OK, and then click OK again to close the Customize dialog box.

Creating a New Search Folder

If the default search folders don't suit your needs, you can create your own search folder with the criteria and included subfolders that locate the messages you want. To create a search folder, right-click the Search Folders branch, and then choose New Search Folder to open the New Search Folder dialog box, shown in Figure 10-3.

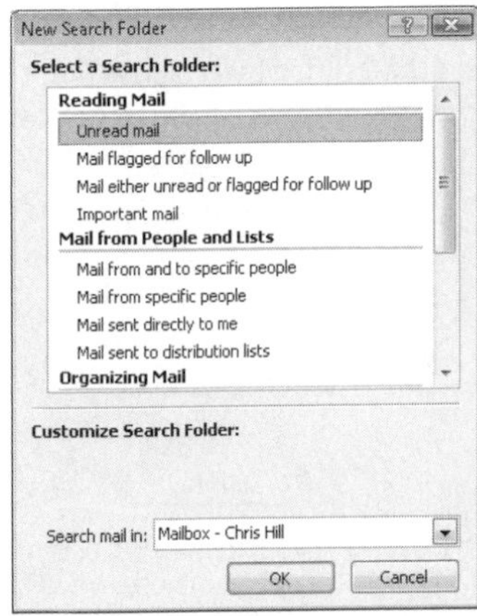

Figure 10-3. Create a new search folder with the New Search Folder dialog box.

The New Search Folder dialog box provides several predefined search folders, and you can easily create a custom search folder by choosing one from the list. If the search folder you select requires specifying additional criteria, click the Choose button to open a dialog box in which you specify the criteria. Then, in the New Search Folder dialog box, select an account in the Search Mail In drop-down list to search that account.

> **Note**
>
> The Choose button appears in the New Search Folder dialog box only if the selected search folder requires additional configuration, such as the sender's name.

If the predefined search folders won't do the trick, scroll to the bottom of the Select A Search Folder list, select Create A Custom Search Folder, and then click Choose to open the Custom Search Folder dialog box to specify a custom criterion for the search folder, a search folder name, and subfolders to include.

Flagging and Monitoring Messages and Contacts

Outlook 2007 allows you to *flag* a message to draw your attention to the message and display an optional reminder when the follow-up action is due. The flag appears in the message header, as shown in Figure 10-4.

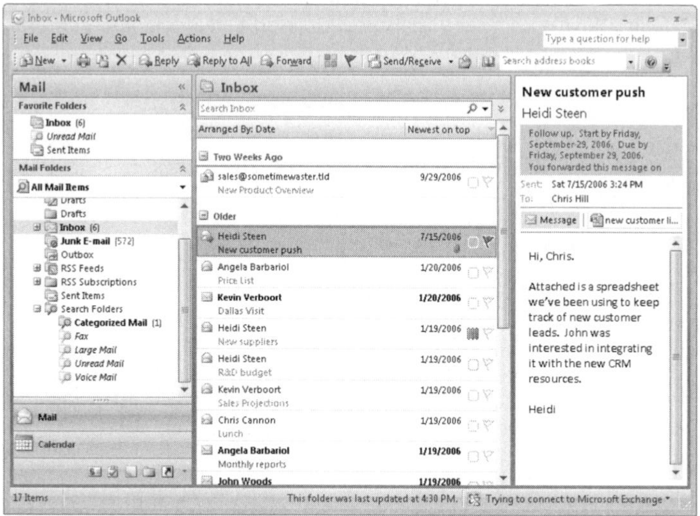

Figure 10-4. You can flag a message to highlight it or to include additional information.

Outlook 2003 offered six flag types, compared with just one in earlier versions. In Outlook 2007, colored flags are replaced by color categories, reducing follow-up flag colors to red and a few shades of pink. You can choose from one of five predefined flags or choose a custom flag. The predefined flags have date specifications of Today, Tomorrow, This Week, Next Week, and No Date. If you choose the custom flag option, you can specify any date you want. The predefined dates therefore give you a quick and easy way to assign a general follow-up date, while the custom option lets you specify a specific date.

See Chapter 5, "Creating and Using Categories," to learn more about color categories.

Flagging Received and Previously Sent Messages

You can flag messages that you've received from others, as well as those you've sent. This capability gives you a way to flag and follow up messages from your end. You can flag messages in any message folder, including the Sent Items folder.

INSIDE OUT **Add notes to received messages**

You can use flags to add notes to messages you receive from others, giving yourself a quick reminder of pending tasks or other pertinent information. Outlook 2007 can generate a reminder for you concerning the flagged item. To set up Outlook 2007 to do so, right-click the message, choose Follow Up, Add Reminder, and then set a due date and time.

Follow these steps to flag a message you have received (or a message that resides in the Sent Items folder):

1. Locate the message you want to flag.
2. Right-click the message, choose Follow Up, and then select a follow-up period from the cascading menu (Today, Tomorrow, and so on), or to specify a custom date, choose Custom.
3. If you chose Custom, enter the follow-up action text in the Flag To field or select an existing action from the drop-down list, and then specify a start date and an end date.
4. Click OK.

Flagging Outgoing Messages

With Outlook 2007, you can flag outgoing messages for follow-up for yourself, the recipient, or both. So, the capability to flag an outgoing message lets you set a reminder on the message to follow up on the message yourself. For example, you might send an e-mail message to a coworker asking for information about a project. The follow-up flag could remind you in a week to follow up if you haven't had a response. You can also flag a message to generate a reminder on the recipient's computer.

Use the following steps to flag a message you send:

1. With the message form open prior to sending the message, on the Message tab on the Ribbon, in the Options Group, click Follow Up, and then click Add Reminder to open the Custom dialog box, shown in Figure 10-5.
2. In the Flag To drop-down list, select the text you want to include with the flag, or type your own text in this box.
3. If you want to include a due date and a subsequent reminder, select the date in the Due Date drop-down list, which opens a calendar that you can use to select a date. Alternatively, you can enter a date, day, time, or other information as text in the Due Date box.

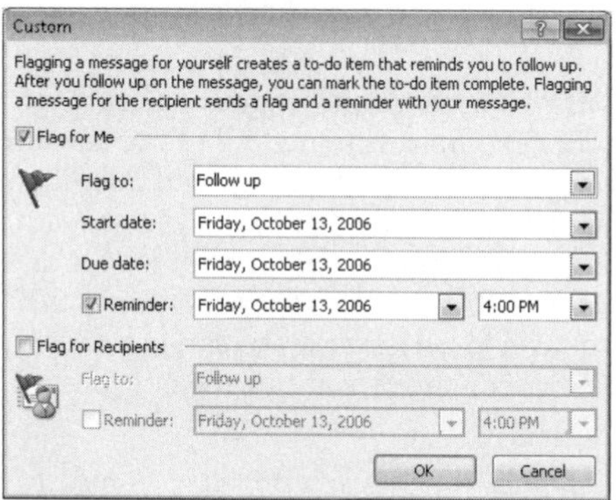

Figure 10-5. Select the flag text or type your own message in the Custom dialog box.

4. Click OK, and then send the message as you normally would.

Follow these steps to flag a message for follow-up on the recipient's computer:

1. Open a new message form, and then click Follow Up in the Options group on the Message tab.
2. Choose Flag For Recipients to open the Custom dialog box.
3. Verify that the Flag For Recipients option is checked, and then select the follow-up action in the Flag To drop-down list.
4. Specify a reminder, and then click OK.
5. Complete the message, and then send it.

Viewing and Responding to Flagged Messages

A flag icon appears next to the message header for flagged messages in the message folder. If you have configured Outlook 2007 to display the Reading Pane, the flag text appears in the InfoBar. The flag icons also help you to identify flagged messages regardless of whether the Reading Pane is displayed. You can sort the view in the folder using the Flag column, listing all flagged messages together to make them easier to locate. To view the flag text when the Reading Pane is turned off, simply open the message. The flag text appears in the message form's InfoBar.

Outlook 2007 has no special mechanism for processing flagged messages other than the reminders previously discussed. You simply call, e-mail, or otherwise respond based on the flag message. To change the flag status, simply click the flag, or right-click a flagged message and then choose Flag Complete. To remove the flag from the message, right-click a flagged message, and then choose Clear Flag.

Flagging Contact Items

You can flag contact items as well as messages, marking them for follow-up or adding other notations to an item. For example, you might flag a contact item to remind yourself to call the person by a certain time or date or to send documents to the contact. A flag you add to a contact item shows up in all contacts views, but it isn't always readily apparent–for instance, the flag shows up as text in Address Cards and Detailed Address Cards views, as shown in Figure 10-6. In other views, Outlook 2007 uses a flag icon, as shown in Figure 10-7. As you can for messages, you can use one of the Outlook 2007 predefined flags to mark a contact item, or you can specify your own flag text.

> **Note**
>
> The flag icon does not appear in Business Cards view. In some of the other views, you can use the Field Chooser to add the Follow Up Flag field to the view.

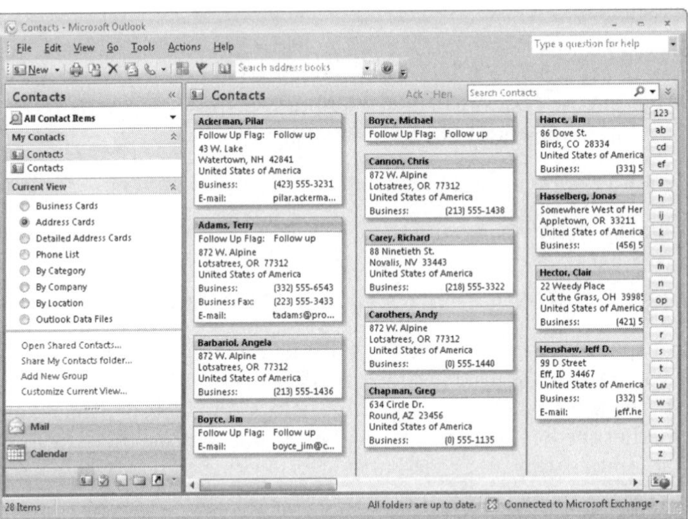

Figure 10-6. You can flag contacts as well as messages.

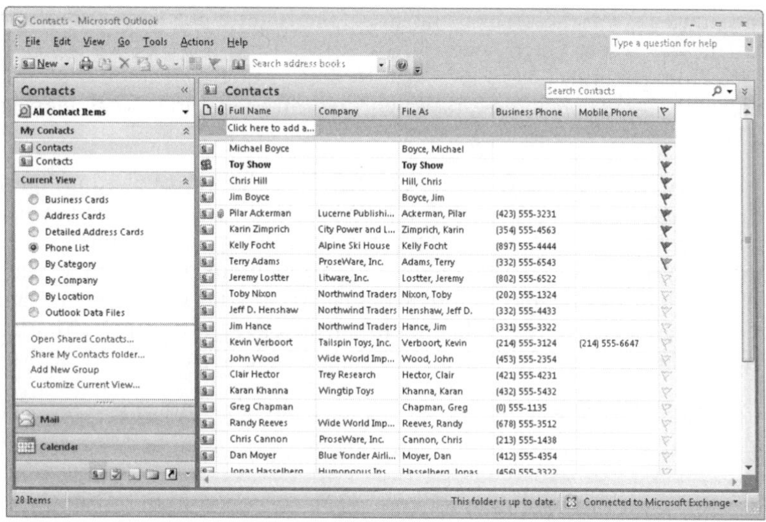

Figure 10-7. You can list items in the Contacts folder by flag.

Flagging a contact is easy—just right-click the contact, choose Follow Up, and then select a follow-up date. To assign a custom flag to a contact item, follow these steps:

1. Right-click the contact item, choose Follow Up, and then choose Custom.
2. In the Custom dialog box, select the flag type in the Flag To drop-down list, or type in your own text.
3. Specify the due date and time.
4. If desired, add a reminder, and then click OK.

Outlook 2007 uses the same icons for flagged contact items as it does for messages. A red flag icon indicates a pending action, and a check mark indicates a completed action. To change the flag status for a contact item, right-click the item, and then choose Mark Complete or Clear Flag.

Grouping Messages by Customizing the Folder View

To help you organize information, Outlook 2007 allows you to customize various message folder views. By default, Outlook 2007 displays only a small selection of columns for messages, including the From, Subject, Received, Size, Flag, Attachment, and Importance columns.

For details on how to add and remove columns from a folder view to show more or less information about your messages, see "Working with the Standard Outlook Views" in Chapter 4.

You can easily sort messages using any of the column headers as your sort criterion. To view messages sorted alphabetically by sender, for example, click the column header of the From column. To sort messages by date received, click the column header of the Received column. Click the Attachment column header to view all messages with attachments.

In addition to managing your message view by controlling columns and sorting, you can *group* messages based on columns. Whereas sorting allows you to arrange messages in order using a single column as the sort criterion, grouping allows you to display the messages in groups based on one or more columns. For example, you might group messages based on sender, and then on date received, and finally on whether they have attachments. This method helps you locate messages more quickly than if you had to search through a message list sorted only by sender.

Grouping messages in a message folder is a relatively simple process:

1. In Outlook 2007, open the folder you want to organize.
2. Right-click the column header, and then choose Group By This Field if you want to group based only on the selected field. Choose Group By Box if you want to group based on multiple columns.

Filtering a View Using Categories

As explained in Chapter 5, "Creating and Using Categories," the addition of color categories in Outlook 2007 makes it very easy to identify specific messages or types of messages. For example, you might categorize messages you receive from specific people so that you can see at a glance that a message is from a particular person.

In some situations, you might want to customize a view so that you see only messages that have certain categories. For example, assume that you have categorized messages for two projects, each with a unique category. Now you want to view all messages from both projects. The easiest way to do that is to filter the view so that it shows only messages with those two categories assigned to them. You can do that using a custom view or a search folder. Both of these methods are explained in the section "Viewing Selected Categories Only" in Chapter 5.

Managing E-Mail Effectively

Before we offer tips on effective e-mail management, let's ask the question, "Why bother?" If you receive a large number of messages, the answer is probably staring you in the face–a chaotic Inbox full of messages. With a little bit of planning and effort, you can turn that Inbox into...well...an empty Inbox! When you leave the office at the end of the day with an empty Inbox, you'll be amazed at the sense of accomplishment you'll feel.

Here are some tips to help you get control of your mailbox:

- **Categorize, categorize, categorize.** Categorizing your messages offers several benefits. First, with the introduction of color categories in Outlook 2007, assigning categories to messages will help you quickly identify specific types of messages. Second, you'll be able to search for messages by category with filtered views, search folders, and the search features built into Outlook 2007. You can assign categories manually or assign them automatically with rules. Whatever the case, the more diligent you are in assigning categories, the more useful they will be for finding messages and organizing your mailbox.
- **Organize with folders.** Although you could simply leave all messages in the Inbox, moving messages into other folders will unclutter your Inbox and help you locate messages when you need them. There is no right or wrong way to structure your message folders—use whatever structure and number of folders suits the way you work. What is important is that you organize in a way that suits you.
- **Organize with rules.** Use rules to move messages into other folders, assign categories, and otherwise process messages when they arrive in your Inbox. Rules enable you to organize your messages automatically, potentially saving you an enormous amount of time.
- **Let search folders organize for you.** Search folders are an extremely useful feature in Outlook 2007. With a search folder, you can organize messages based on almost any criteria without actually moving the messages from their current locations. Search folders take very little effort to set up and offer you the benefit of being able to search your entire mailbox for messages that fit the search criteria. You can bring together in one virtual folder all messages in your mail store that fit the search criteria.

CHAPTER 11

Processing Messages Automatically

If you receive a lot of messages, you might want to have the messages analyzed as they come in, to perform actions on them before you read them. For example, you can have all messages from a specific account sent to a specific folder. Perhaps you want messages that come from specific senders to be assigned high priority. Microsoft® Office Outlook® 2007 lets you manipulate your incoming messages to achieve the results you want. This chapter shows you how, starting with an overview of message rules.

Understanding Message Rules

A *message rule* defines the actions that Office Outlook 2007 takes for a sent or received message if the message meets certain conditions specified by the rule. For example, you might create a rule that tells Outlook 2007 to move all messages from a specific Post Office Protocol 3 (POP3) account into a specified folder rather than leaving them in your default Inbox. Or you might want Outlook 2007 to place a copy of all outgoing high-priority messages in a special folder.

In Outlook 2007, you use one or more *conditions* for defining a message rule. These conditions can include the account from which the message was received, the message size, the sender or recipient, specific words in various fields or in the message itself, the priority assigned to the message, and a variety of other conditions. In addition, you can combine multiple actions to refine the rule and further control its function. For example, you might create a rule that moves all your incoming POP3 messages to a folder other than the Inbox and also deletes any messages that contain certain words in the Subject field. Although not a complete list, the following are some of the most common tasks you might perform with message rules:

- Organize messages based on sender, recipient, or subject.
- Copy or move messages from one folder to another.
- Flag messages.
- Delete messages automatically.

- Reply to, forward, or redirect messages to individuals or distribution lists.
- Respond to messages with a specific reply.
- Monitor message importance (priority).
- Print a message.
- Play a sound.
- Execute a script or start an application.

For details on how to generate automatic replies to messages, see "Creating Automatic Responses with the Out Of Office Assistant" and "Creating Automatic Responses with Custom Rules" in Chapter 13.

Whatever your message processing requirements, Outlook 2007 probably offers a solution through a message rule, based on either a single condition or multiple conditions. You also can create multiple rules that work together to process your mail. As you begin to create and use message rules, keep in mind that you can define a rule to function either when a message is received or when it is sent. When you create a rule, you specify the event to which the rule applies.

You create all message rules in the same way, regardless of the specific purpose of the rule. Rather than focusing on defining rules for specific tasks, this chapter explains the general process of creating rules. With an understanding of this process, you should have no problem setting up rules for a variety of situations. In fact, creating message rules is relatively easy, thanks to the Outlook 2007 Rules Wizard.

In Outlook 2007, choose Tools, Rules And Alerts. You'll first see the Rules And Alerts dialog box, shown in Figure 11-1. The E-Mail Rules tab contains all the existing rules that you have defined. Outlook 2007 applies the rules in the order in which they are listed, an important fact to consider when you're creating rules. To start the Rules Wizard, click New Rule.

You might use certain rules all the time but use others only at special times. Each rule includes a check box beside it. Select this check box when you want to use the rule; clear it when you want to disable the rule.

Note

You can't open the Rules And Alerts dialog box if you are working offline with a Microsoft Exchange Server account.

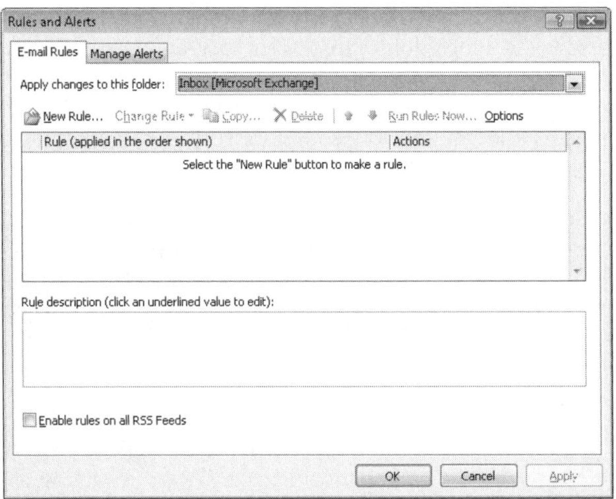

Figure 11-1. The Rules And Alerts dialog box displays existing rules and allows you to create and modify message rules.

For more information about determining the order in which message rules execute, see "Setting Rule Order" later in this chapter.

TROUBLESHOOTING

Rules don't work for some of your accounts

If some of your rules work only for certain accounts and not for others, the problem could be that some of those accounts are Hypertext Transfer Protocol (HTTP)–based mail accounts. The message rules in Outlook 2007 do not process messages sent to or received from HTTP-based mail accounts, such as Microsoft Hotmail®, nor can you manually apply rules to process messages in the Inbox sent from HTTP accounts after the messages have been received. Check with your HTTP mail service provider to determine whether it offers server-side message rules that you can use in place of the Outlook 2007 message rules to process your messages.

Creating and Using Rules

In Outlook 2007, you can create either *client-side* or *server-side* rules. Outlook 2007 stores client-side rules locally on your computer and uses them to process messages that come to your local folders, although you also can use client-side rules to process messages on computers running Exchange Server. A client-side rule is needed when you're moving messages to a local folder instead of to a folder on the computer running Exchange Server. For example, if messages from a specific sender that arrive in your Exchange Server Inbox must be moved to one of your personal folders, the rule must function as a client-side rule, because the computer running Exchange Server is not able to access your personal folders.

Server-side rules reside on the computer running Exchange Server instead of on your local computer, and they can usually process messages in your Exchange Server mailbox whether or not you're logged on and running Outlook 2007. The Out Of Office Assistant is a good example of how server-side rules can be used. It processes messages that come into your Inbox on the server even when your computer is turned off and you're a thousand miles away. As long as Exchange Server is up and functioning, the server-side rules can perform their intended function.

When you create a rule, Outlook 2007 examines the rule's logic to determine whether it can function as a server-side rule or a client-side rule. If it can function as a server-side rule, Outlook 2007 stores the rule on the computer running Exchange Server and treats it as a server-side rule. If the rule must function as a client-side rule, Outlook 2007 stores it locally and appends *(client-only)* after the rule name to designate it as a client-side rule. Figure 11-2 shows two rules in Outlook 2007, one of which functions as a client-side rule and another that functions as a server-side rule.

> **Note**
>
> If you don't use an Exchange Server account, all rules you create are client-side rules.

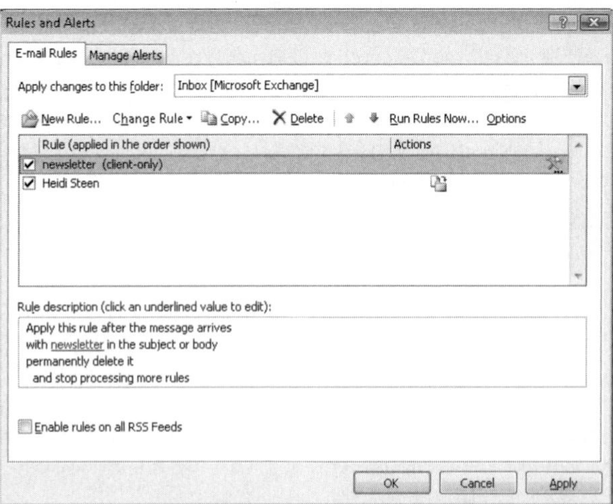

Figure 11-2. Outlook 2007 supports server-side rules as well as client-side rules.

TROUBLESHOOTING

Your server-side rules don't execute

Server-side rules, which process messages arriving in your Exchange Server Inbox, usually can execute when Outlook 2007 isn't running. In some cases, however, server-side rules can't function unless Outlook 2007 is running and you're connected to the server.

When a server-side rule is unable to process a message because Outlook 2007 is offline (or for other reasons), the computer running Exchange Server generates a deferred action message (DAM), which it uses to process the message when Outlook 2007 comes back online. When Outlook 2007 goes online, it receives the DAM, performs the action, and deletes the DAM.

For information about how to apply client-side rules to specific folders or to all accounts, see "Applying Rules to Specific Folders or All Folders" later in this chapter.

Creating New Rules

When you create a message rule, you must first specify whether you want to create the rule from a predefined template or from scratch. Because the templates address common message processing tasks, using a template can save you a few steps. When you create a rule from scratch, you set up all the conditions for the rule as you create it. You can use many different conditions to define the actions the rule performs, all of which are available in the Rules Wizard. With or without a template, you have full control over the completed rule and can modify it to suit your needs. The Outlook 2007 templates are a great way to get started, however, if you're new to using Outlook 2007 or message rules.

Let's look first at the general procedure for creating rules and then at more specific steps. The general process is as follows:

1. Select the Inbox in which the rule will apply. For example, if you have an Exchange Server account and an Internet Message Access Protocol (IMAP) account, you must choose the Inbox to which the rule will apply.

Note

If you have only one account, or an Exchange Server account and one or more POP3 accounts, you have only one Inbox to choose as the target for the rule. IMAP accounts, however, use their own Inbox folders, meaning that you can apply rules to these accounts separately from your Exchange Server and POP3 accounts. For example, if you have an Exchange Server account, two POP3 accounts, and an IMAP account in the same profile, you'll see two Inboxes listed as possible targets for the rule: one for the Exchange Server and POP3 accounts and one for the IMAP account.

2. Specify when the rule applies–that is, when a message is received or when it is sent.
3. Specify the conditions that define which messages are processed–for example, account, sender, priority, or content.
4. Specify the action to take for messages that meet the specified conditions–for example, move, copy, or delete the message; change its priority; flag it for follow-up; or generate a reply.
5. Create other message rules to accomplish other tasks as needed, including possibly working in conjunction with other rules.
6. Set the order of rules as needed.

TROUBLESHOOTING

You have conflicting message rules

Outlook 2007 support for multiple accounts, combined with the ability to use both client-side and server-side rules, can pose certain problems. For example, assume that you have a POP3 account that delivers messages to your Exchange Server mailbox rather than to a local store. Also assume that you create a client-side rule to process certain POP3 messages but that you also have a server-side rule for processing messages. The server-side rule takes precedence because the client-side rule doesn't execute until the message arrives in the Inbox, even though the message came through your computer before it was placed in your Exchange Server mailbox. Thus the message is processed by the server-side rule, potentially bypassing the local rule. If the server-side rule deletes the message, for example, the message will never make it to your personal folders to allow the client-side rule to act on it.

The order of rule precedence is important for the same reason—two rules, even on the same side, can perform conflicting actions. Keep this in mind when you're creating rules and working with non–Exchange Server accounts that store messages in your Exchange Server mailbox.

Note

When you specify multiple conditions for a rule, the rule combines these conditions in a logical AND operation—that is, the message must meet all of the conditions to be considered subject to the rule. You also can create rules that use a logical OR operation, meaning that the message is subject to the rule if it meets any one of the conditions. For details, see "Creating Rules That Use OR Logic" later in this chapter.

The following steps guide you through the more specific process of creating a message rule:

1. In Outlook 2007, choose Tools, Rules And Alerts to display the Rules And Alerts dialog box.
2. In the Apply Changes To This Folder drop-down list, select the folder to which you want to apply the rule. If you have only one Inbox, you don't need to make a selection.
3. Click New Rule to display the wizard page shown in Figure 11-3.

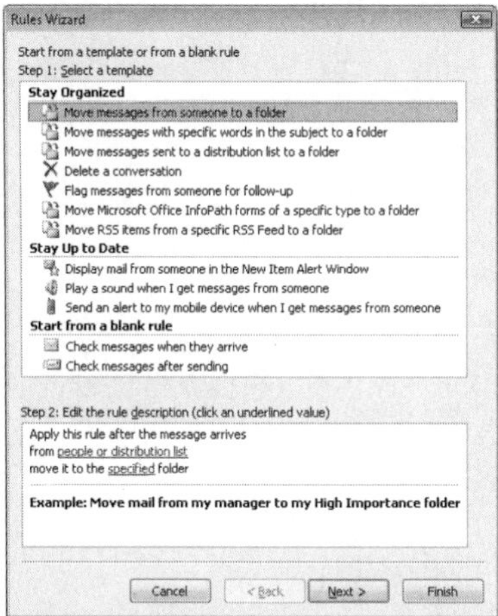

Figure 11-3. To create a rule, you can use a template or start from scratch.

4. If you want to use a template to create the rule, select the template from the list, and then click Next. To create a rule from scratch, choose Check Messages When They Arrive or Check Messages After Sending, and then click Next.
5. In the Step 1: Select Condition(s) list in the top half of the wizard page shown in Figure 11-4, select the conditions that define the messages to which the rule should apply. For template-based rules, a condition is already selected, but you can change the condition and add others as necessary.
6. In the Step 2: Edit The Rule Description area of the wizard page (see Figure 11-4), click the underlined words that specify the data for the conditions. For example, if you're creating a rule to process messages from a specific account, click the word *specified*, which is underlined, and then select the account in the Account dialog box. Click OK, and then click Next.

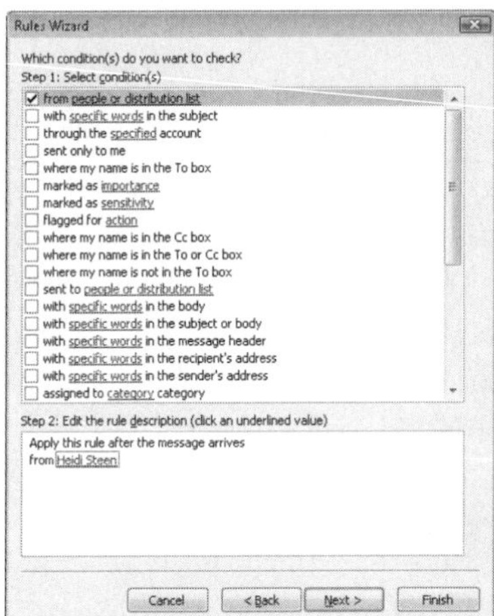

Figure 11-4. Select the conditions to define the messages to which the rule will apply.

7. In the Step 1: Select Action(s) area of the new wizard page, select the actions that you want Outlook 2007 to apply to messages that satisfy the specified conditions. For example, Figure 11-5 shows a rule that moves messages to a specified folder if they meet the rule condition.

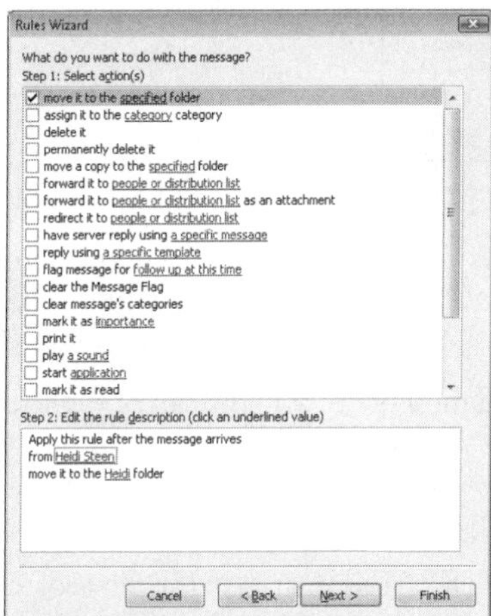

Figure 11-5. Select the actions that Outlook 2007 should take for messages that meet the rule's conditions.

8. In the Step 2: Edit The Rule Description area of the wizard page, click each underlined value needed to define the action, and then specify the data in the resulting dialog box. Click OK to close the dialog box, and then click Next.

9. In the Step 1: Select Exception(s) (If Necessary) area of the wizard page, select exceptions to the rule if needed, and specify the data for the exception conditions, as shown in Figure 11-6. Click Next.

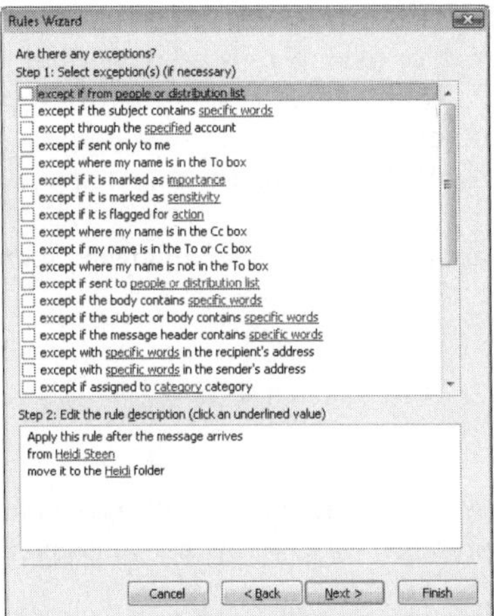

Figure 11-6. You can specify exceptions to the rule to fine-tune message processing.

10. On the final page of the Rules Wizard, shown in Figure 11-7, specify a name for the rule as you want it to appear in Outlook 2007.

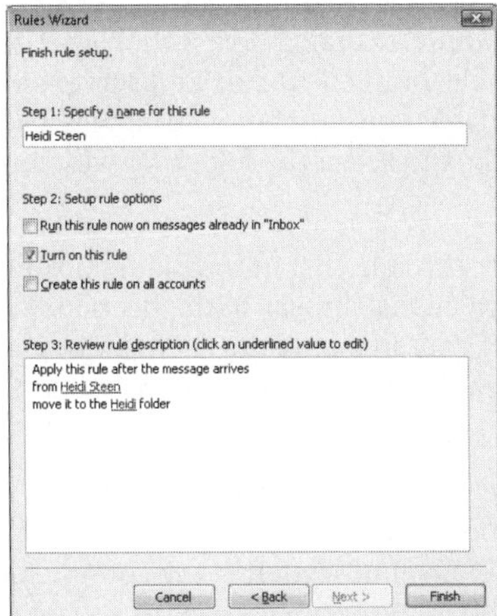

Figure 11-7. Configure a name and options for the rule.

11. Select options according to the following list, and then click Finish:
    - **Run This Rule Now On Messages Already In "Inbox"** Select this check box if you want Outlook 2007 to apply the rule to messages that you have already received and that currently reside in the Inbox folder in which the rule applies. For example, if you have created a rule to delete messages from a specific recipient, any existing messages from the recipient are deleted after you select this check box and click Finish to create the rule.
    - **Turn On This Rule** Select this check box to begin applying the rule you have created.

- **Create This Rule On All Accounts** Select this check box to apply the rule to all applicable folders. For example, if you have three folders listed in the Apply Changes To This Folder drop-down list at the top of the initial Rules Wizard page, selecting this check box causes Outlook 2007 to apply the rule to all three folders instead of only the selected folder.

For more details on using rules in various folders, see the following section, "Applying Rules to Specific Folders or All Folders."

> **Note**
>
> To create a rule that operates on all messages, don't specify a condition that Outlook 2007 must check. Outlook 2007 prompts you to verify that you want the rule applied to all messages.

Applying Rules to Specific Folders or All Folders

When you first open the Rules And Alerts dialog box, it displays the rules that have already been defined for your profile, both client-side and server-side, as shown earlier in Figure 11-2. You might recall that you use the Apply Changes To This Folder drop-down list at the top of the dialog box to select the folder for which you want to create or modify a rule.

Regardless of the folder you select, the rules list in the dialog box always displays your server-side rules. The client-side rules that appear in the list depend on the folder you select. The list for a selected folder contains only the client-side rules for that particular folder, unless you've copied a rule to multiple folders or created a rule expressly for all folders.

To apply a rule to a specific folder, select that folder in the Apply Changes To This Folder drop-down list when you begin creating the rule. To apply a rule to all folders, select the Create This Rule On All Accounts option at the completion of the wizard (as explained in the preceding section).

Copying Rules to Other Folders

By default, Outlook 2007 doesn't create rules for all folders; instead, it creates the rule only for the selected folder. If you have created a rule for one folder but want to use it in a different folder, you can copy the rule to the other folder.

Follow these steps to do so:

1. Choose Tools, Rules And Alerts to open the Rules And Alerts dialog box.

Note

If necessary, choose the target folder from the Apply Changes To This folder list.

2. Select the rule that you want to copy, and then click Copy.
3. When you're prompted in the Copy Rules To dialog box, select the destination folder for the rule, and then click OK.

For details on sharing rules with other Outlook 2007 users, see "Sharing Rules with Others" later in this chapter.

Creating Rules Based on Existing Messages

In some situations, it's easier to create rules from specific messages. For example, if you frequently receive unwanted messages from a particular sender, you might want to delete the messages without downloading them. You can specify the address when you begin to create a rule in the Rules Wizard, but in this case, it would be easier to create the rule from the message instead, saving you the trouble of typing the sender's name or address. Or perhaps the subject of a particular group of messages always contains a unique string of text, and you want to build the rule around that text. Rather than typing the text yourself, you can create the rule from one of the messages.

Here's how to create a rule from a specific message:

1. In Outlook 2007, open the folder containing the message.
2. Right-click the message header, and then choose Create Rule.
3. Outlook 2007 displays a Create Rule dialog box that reflects the properties of the selected message–sender and subject, for example–as shown in Figure 11-8. Select an action from the Do The Following area in the dialog box. Or click Advanced Options to open the Rules Wizard to choose additional actions. Select a condition, and then complete the rule as you normally would if you were creating it from a template or from scratch.

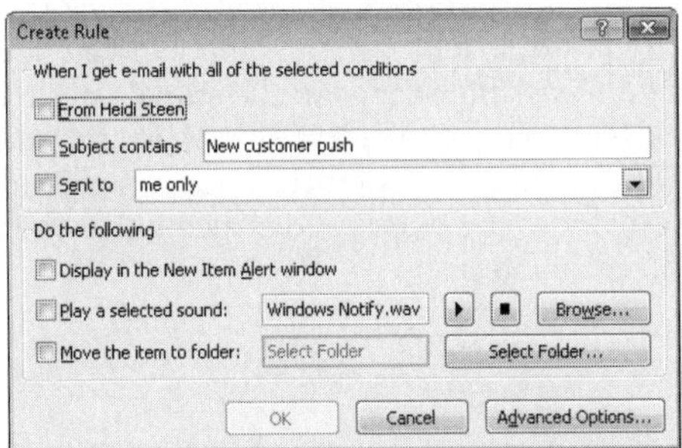

Figure 11-8. Use the Create Rule dialog box to specify basic rule conditions and actions.

Chapter 11

Note

Remember that HTTP accounts don't support Outlook 2007 rules. If you right-click a message stored in a folder for an HTTP-based mail account, you'll see that the Create Rule command is not available. Also, rules are always created in the Inbox, not in other folders. You can, however, run rules manually in other folders.

Creating Rules That Use OR Logic

Up to now, you've explored relatively simple rules that function based on a single condition or on multiple AND conditions. In the latter case, the rule specifies multiple conditions and applies only to messages that meet all the conditions. If a rule is defined by three AND conditions, for example, Outlook 2007 uses it only on messages that meet condition 1, condition 2, and condition 3.

You also can create rules that follow OR logic. In this case, a rule specifies a single condition but multiple criteria for that condition. The rule will then act on any message that meets at least one of the criteria for the condition. For example, you might create a rule that deletes a message if the subject of the message contains any one of three words. If one of the conditions is met (that is, if the subject of a message contains at least one of the three words), Outlook 2007 deletes that message.

With Outlook 2007, you can create several rules that use OR logic within a single condition, but you can't create a single rule that uses OR logic on multiple conditions. For example, you might create a rule that deletes a message if the message contains the phrase *MLM*, *Free Money*, or *Guaranteed Results*. However, you can't create a message rule that deletes the message if the subject of the message contains the words *Free Money* (condition 1), or if the message is from a specific sender (condition 2), or if the message is larger than a given size (condition 3). OR must operate within a single condition. When you create a rule with multiple conditions, Outlook 2007 always treats multiple conditions in the same rule using AND logic. You would have to create three separate rules to accommodate the latter example.

If you have a situation where you need to check for more than one piece of data in a single condition, you can do so easily enough; however, when you create the rule and define the condition, specify multiple items. For example, if you need a rule that processes messages based on four possible strings in the subject of the messages, click Specific Words in the rule description area of the Rules Wizard, where you specify rule conditions. In the Search Text dialog box, enter the strings separately. As you can see in Figure 11-9, the search list includes the word *or* to indicate that the rule applies if any one of the words appears in the subject.

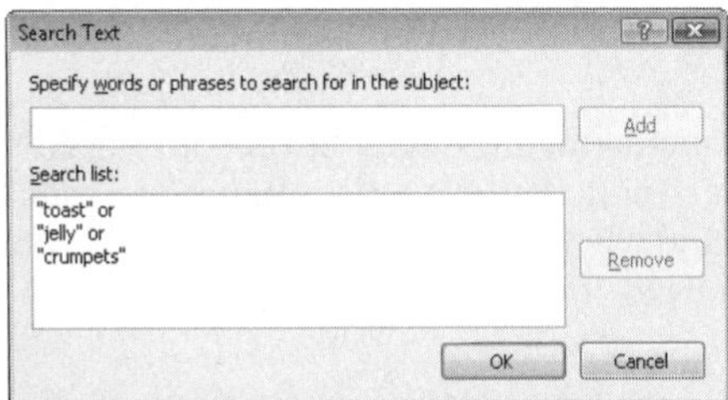

Figure 11-9. Specify data separately to create a rule that uses OR logic.

Although you can't create a single rule with OR logic operating on multiple conditions in Outlook 2007, you can create rules that combine AND and OR logic. For example, you might create a rule that applied if the message arrived at a specific account and the subject contained the words *Free Money* or *Guaranteed Results*. Keep in mind that you must specify two conditions—not one—to build the rule. The first condition would check for the account, and the second would check for the words *Free Money* or *Guaranteed Results*.

Consider the following example:

1. Choose Tools, Rules And Alerts.
2. In the Rules And Alerts dialog box, click New Rule.
3. Click Check Messages When They Arrive, and then click Next.
4. Select Through The Specified Account.
5. Select With Specific Words In The Subject Or Body.
6. At the bottom of the dialog box, click Specified, and then in the Account dialog box, select the e-mail account and click OK.
7. Click Specific Words at the bottom of the dialog box to open the Search Text dialog box.
8. Type **Free Money**, and then click Add.
9. Type **Guaranteed Results**, click Add, and then click OK.

Look at the rule conditions in the Step 2 area of the dialog box. The rule indicates that it will act on messages that are from the specified account and that have the text *Free Money* or *Guaranteed Results* in the message.

Modifying Rules

You can modify a rule at any time after you create it. Modifying a rule is much like creating one. To modify a rule, choose Tools, Rules And Alerts to open the Rules And Alerts dialog box. Select the rule that you want to modify, and then click Change Rule to display a menu of editing options. If you choose Edit Rule Settings on the menu, Outlook 2007 presents the same options you saw when you created the rule, and you can work with them the same way. Click Rename Rule to change the name of the rule, or click an action to add the selected action to the rule (retaining any existing actions).

Controlling Rules

Rules can be an effective tool for managing messages, but you also need to manage your rules to make them effective overall. For example, you need to consider the order in which rules run, control how and when rules run, and even disable or remove rules. The following sections explain how to control your rules.

Setting Rule Order

Outlook 2007 executes rules for incoming messages when they arrive in the Inbox, whether on the server or locally (depending on whether the rules are client-side or server-side). Outlook 2007 executes rules for outgoing messages when the messages arrive in the Sent Items folder.

As mentioned earlier, the order in which rules are listed in Outlook 2007 determines how Outlook 2007 applies them. In some situations, the sequence could be important. Perhaps you have one rule that moves high-priority messages to a separate folder and another rule that notifies you when high-priority messages arrive. For the latter rule to work properly, it needs to execute before the one that moves the messages, because the notification rule won't execute if the messages are no longer in the Inbox.

You can control the order of Outlook 2007 rules easily by taking the following steps:

1. In Outlook 2007, choose Tools, Rules And Alerts to open the Rules And Alerts dialog box.
2. Select a rule to be moved.
3. Use the Move Up and Move Down buttons to change the order in the list, as shown in Figure 11-10. Rules execute in the order listed, with the rule at the top executing first and the one at the bottom executing last.

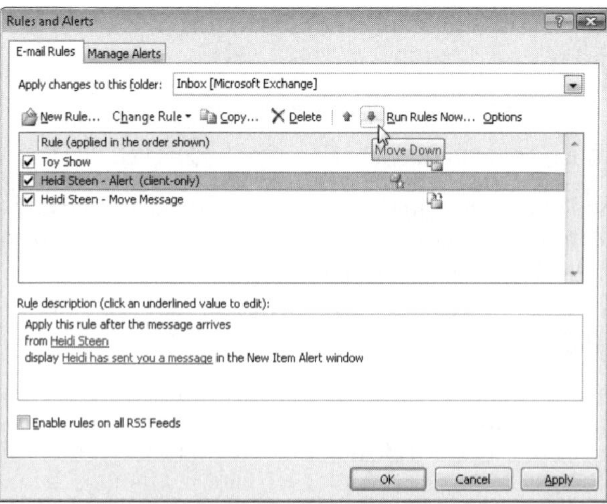

Figure 11-10. You can control execution order for rules by rearranging the rules list.

Stopping Rules from Being Processed

In certain cases, you might want your message rules to stop being processed altogether. Perhaps someone has sent you a very large message that is causing your dial-up connection to time out or is taking a long time to download. You would like to create a rule to delete the message without downloading it, but you don't want any of your other rules to execute. In this case, you would place a new rule at the top of the list and define it so that the last action it takes is to stop processing any other rules. In effect, this allows you to bypass your other rules without going through the trouble of disabling them.

You can also use the Stop Processing More Rules action to control rule execution in other situations. To stop Outlook 2007 from executing other rules when a message meets a specific condition, include Stop Processing More Rules as the last action for the rule. You'll find this action in the What Do You Want To Do With The Message list in the Rules Wizard.

Disabling and Removing Rules

In some cases, you might want to turn off message rules so that they don't execute. Perhaps you use a rule to do routine cleanup on your mail folders but don't want the rule to run automatically. Or perhaps you want to create a rule to use only once or twice but you would like to keep it in case you need it again later. In those cases, you can disable the rule. Choose Tools, Rules And Alerts, and then clear the check box for that rule in the list. Only those rules with check boxes that are selected will apply to incoming or outgoing messages.

Because the amount of space allocated for message rules in Outlook 2007 is finite, removing unused rules can make room for additional rules, particularly if you have several complex rules. If you don't plan to use a rule again, you can remove it by choosing Tools, Rules And Alerts, selecting the rule, and then clicking Delete.

Sharing Rules with Others

By default, Outlook 2007 stores server-side rules on the computer running Exchange Server and stores client-side rules on your local system. Regardless of where your message rules are stored, you can share them with others by exporting the rules to a file. You can then send the file as an e-mail attachment or place it on a network share (or a local share) to allow other users to access it. You can also export the rules to create a backup of them for safekeeping or in the event that you need to move your Outlook 2007 rules to a new computer, as explained in the next section.

Follow these steps to export your message rules to a file:

1. In Outlook 2007, choose Tools, Rules And Alerts.
2. In the Rules And Alerts dialog box, click Options.

3. In the Options dialog box, shown in Figure 11-11, click Export Rules, and then select a path for the file in the resulting Save Exported Rules As dialog box (a standard file save dialog box).

Figure 11-11. Use the Options dialog box to import and export rules.

4. To save the rules using Microsoft Outlook 2002, Outlook 2000, or Outlook 98 format, select the appropriate format in the Save As Type drop-down list. Otherwise, leave the selection at Rules Wizard Rules to save for Outlook 2007.
5. Click Save.

You can export your rules in any of four formats, depending on the version of Microsoft Outlook used by the people with whom you want to share your rules. If you need to share with various users, export using the earliest version of Microsoft Outlook. Later versions will be able to import the rules because they are forward-compatible.

> **Note**
>
> If you are sharing rules with someone else, at this point, you have a rules file that you can send to the other person. The following section explains how to restore rules, which is the process the other person would use to import your rules.

Backing Up and Restoring Rules

Outlook 2007 stores server-side rules in your Exchange Server mailbox, so in principle, there is no reason to back up your server-side rules. We say "in principle" because that point of view assumes that the Exchange Server administrator is performing adequate backups of your mailbox so that you won't lose your messages or your rules. It's still a good idea to back up server-side rules just in case, using the method explained in the preceding section, "Sharing Rules with Others."

Outlook 2007 stores client-side rules in the default mail store–that is, the .pst file defined in your Outlook 2007 profile as the location for incoming mail. Storing the rules in the .pst file simplifies moving your rules to another computer, because you are also likely to move your .pst file to the other computer to retain all of your Outlook 2007 items. To make this process work, however, you need to add the .pst file to the second computer in a certain way.

Outlook 2007 checks the default mail store .pst file for the rules, but it doesn't check any other .pst files you might have added to your profile. So if you added an e-mail account to the profile and then added the .pst file from your old system, you won't see your rules.

One of the easiest methods for making sure things get set up correctly is to add the .pst file to your profile before you add the e-mail account. Then when you add the account, Outlook 2007 uses the existing .pst file as the default store. The result is that your rules will be available without any additional manipulation.

Here's how to make it happen:

1. Right-click the Outlook icon on the Start menu, and then choose Properties. Or click the Mail icon in Control Panel.
2. In the Mail Setup dialog box, click Show Profiles.
3. Click Add, type a name for the profile, and then click OK.
4. Click Cancel. When asked whether you want to create a profile with no e-mail accounts, click OK.
5. Click Properties to open the newly created profile.
6. Click Data Files to display the Data Files tab in the Account Settings dialog box.
7. Click Add, and then click OK in the New Outlook Data File dialog box.
8. In the Create Or Open Outlook Data File dialog box, browse to and select the .pst file that contains your rules, and then click OK.
9. Click OK in the Personal Folders dialog box.
10. In the Account Settings dialog box, click the newly added data file, and then click Set As Default.
11. Add your e-mail accounts to the profile.
12. Click Close, click Close again, and then click OK to close the profile properties.

When you start Outlook 2007, you should now have access to the rules stored in the .pst file, plus all of your existing Outlook 2007 items.

Using the Organize Pane to Create Rules

The Rules Wizard isn't the only method you can use to manage messages in Outlook 2007. Using the Organize pane provides an easier way to create certain types of rules, making it an attractive alternative for novice users. With this method, however, you do have fewer options and less flexibility.

When you choose Tools, Organize with the Inbox open, Outlook 2007 changes the view to include the Organize pane at the top of the view, as shown in Figure 11-12. The Organize pane includes three modes:

- **Using Folders** Use this mode to move selected messages into a specified folder.
- **Using Colors** Use this mode to apply a specified color to messages with a specific sender or recipient. Outlook 2007 changes the color of the message header in the Inbox accordingly. You can also color messages sent only to you.
- **Using Views** Use this mode to choose a view for the Inbox.

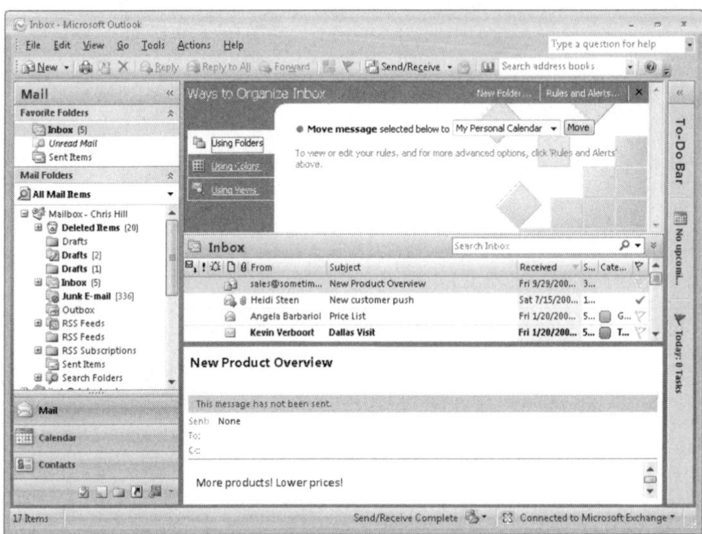

Figure 11-12. Use the Organize pane to manage messages with folders, colors, and views.

Managing messages with the Organize pane is generally self-explanatory; it's included here only to identify it as an alternative to the Rules Wizard. If you provide support for other Outlook 2007 users, you might want to recommend the Organize pane to those users you think might have difficulty using the Rules Wizard.

Using Rules to Move Messages Between Accounts

One common task users often want to perform is to move messages between accounts. Assume that you have two accounts: an Exchange Server account for work and a POP3 account for personal messages. You have specified the Exchange Server mailbox as the delivery location for new mail, so all your POP3 messages go into your Exchange Server Inbox. However, you now want those messages to go into an Inbox in a local .pst file instead of your Exchange Server mailbox. In this case, it's a simple matter to move the personal messages from the Exchange Server Inbox to the POP3 Inbox. Just create a rule that moves messages that meet the specified conditions to your POP3 Inbox.

Note

Before you run through these steps to create a rule for moving messages based on their account, create a folder to contain the messages.

Here's how to accomplish this:

1. In Outlook 2007, choose Tools, Rules And Alerts to open the Rules And Alerts dialog box.
2. Click New Rule, and in the Rules Wizard, select Check Messages When They Arrive and then click Next.
3. Select Through The Specified Account. In the rule description area, click the underlined word *specified*, select your POP3 account, and then click OK and Next.
4. Select Move It To The Specified Folder, and then click the underlined word *specified* in the rule description area.
5. Select the folder in your .pst file to which the messages should be moved, and then click OK and Next.
6. Specify any exceptions to the rule, and then click Next again.
7. Specify a name for the rule and other options as needed, and then click Finish.

Running Rules Manually and in Specific Folders

Normally you use message rules to process messages when they arrive in your Inbox or are placed in the Sent Messages folder. However, you also can run rules manually at any time. Perhaps you have created a rule that you want to use periodically to clean out certain types of messages or move them to a specific folder. You don't want the rule to operate every time you check mail; instead, you want to execute it only when you think it's necessary. In this case, you can run the rule manually.

You might also want to run a rule manually when you need to run it in a folder other than the Inbox. For example, assume that you've deleted messages from a specific sender and now want to restore them, moving the messages from the Deleted Items folder back to your Inbox. In this situation, you could create the rule and then execute it manually in the Deleted Items folder.

It's easy to run a rule manually and in a specific folder following these steps:

1. Choose Tools, Rules And Alerts.
2. Click Run Rules Now. Outlook 2007 displays the Run Rules Now dialog box.
3. Select the rule that you want to run in the list, as shown in Figure 11-13. By default, Outlook 2007 will run the rule in the Inbox unless you specify otherwise.

Click Browse to browse for a different folder. If you also want to run the rule in subfolders of the selected folder, select the Include Subfolders check box.

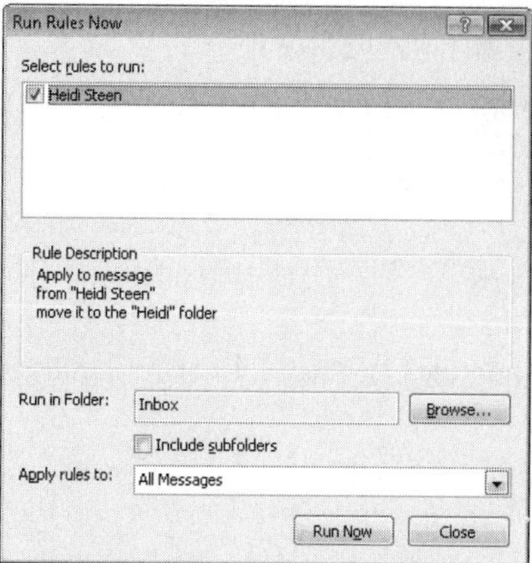

Figure 11-13. Use the Run Rules Now dialog box to run a rule manually in a specified folder.

4. In the Apply Rules To drop-down list, select the type of messages on which you want to run the rule (All Messages, Read Messages, or Unread Messages).
5. Click Run Now to execute the rule, or click Close to cancel.

CHAPTER 12

Managing Junk E-Mail

Tired of wading through so much junk e-mail? Anyone with an e-mail account these days is hard-pressed to avoid unsolicited ads, invitations to multilevel marketing schemes, or unwanted adult content messages. Fortunately, Microsoft® Office Outlook® 2007 offers several features to help you deal with all the junk e-mail coming through your Inbox.

Office Outlook 2007 improves on the junk e-mail and adult content filters in earlier versions of Microsoft Outlook to provide much better anti-junk-mail features. Anti-phishing measures have been added too, scanning e-mail for suspicious content and automatically disabling it. The Junk E-Mail folder restricts certain e-mail functionality, displaying e-mail messages as plain text and preventing replies to messages contained in the folder, as well as blocking attachments and embedded links.

Outlook 2007 offers four levels of junk e-mail protection, with Safe Senders and Safe Recipients lists to help you identify valid messages. It also provides a Blocked Senders list to help you identify e-mail addresses and domains that send you junk e-mail, which enables you to exclude those messages from your Inbox. E-mail can also be blocked based on the originating top-level domain or language encoding used.

How Outlook 2007 Junk E-Mail Filtering Works

If you're familiar with the junk e-mail filters in earlier versions of Outlook 2007, you already know a little about how Outlook 2007 filters junk e-mail. However, Outlook 2007 adds some new features to expand junk e-mail filtering. Before you start configuring Outlook 2007 to filter your junk e-mail, you should have a better understanding of how it applies these filters.

Outlook 2007 provides four filter modes. To specify the filter mode, choose Tools, Options, and then click Junk E-Mail on the Preferences tab to display the Junk E-Mail Options dialog box, shown in Figure 12-1. The following sections explain the four filter modes.

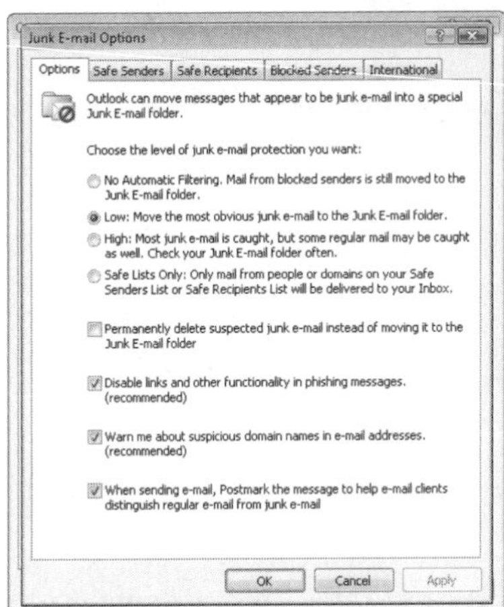

Figure 12-1. Use the Junk E-Mail Options dialog box to quickly configure Outlook 2007 to filter unwanted messages.

No Automatic Filtering

This option protects only against mail from individuals and domains in your Blocked Senders list, moving it to the Junk E-Mail folder. All other mail is delivered to your Inbox.

Low

This option functions essentially like the junk e-mail and adult content filters in earlier versions of Outlook 2007. Outlook 2007 uses a predefined filter to scan the body and subject of messages to identify likely spam.

You can't specify additional filter criteria for subject or content checking for this junk e-mail filter, although you can create your own custom junk e-mail rules to block messages using additional criteria.

High

This level uses the same filtering as the Low level, but it also uses additional message scanning logic to determine whether a message is spam. Outlook 2007 scans the message body and message header for likely indications that the message is spam. You do not have any control over this scanning, other than to enable it by choosing the High scanning level.

If you choose the High option, you should not enable the option to delete junk e-mail messages rather than move them to the Junk E-Mail folder. Although Outlook 2007 will catch most spam, it will also generate false positives, blocking messages that you expect or want. You should review the Junk E-Mail folder periodically and mark any valid messages as not being junk e-mail. Marking messages in this way is explained in "Marking and Unmarking Junk E-Mail" later in this chapter.

Safe Lists Only

This level provides the most extreme message blocking. Only messages originating with senders in your Safe Senders and Safe Recipients lists are treated as valid messages, and all others are treated as junk e-mail.

Although this protection level offers the most chance of blocking all of your junk mail, it also offers the most chance of blocking wanted messages. To use this level effectively, you should allow Outlook 2007 to place messages in the Junk E-Mail folder and review the folder periodically for valid messages. When you find a valid message, add the sender to your Safe Senders list.

Understanding How Outlook 2007 Uses the Filter Lists

Outlook 2007 maintains three lists: Safe Senders, Safe Recipients, and Blocked Senders. Figure 12-2 shows a Blocked Senders list, which blocks all messages from these senders. Messages originating from an address or a domain on the list are filtered out. Entering a domain in the Blocked Senders list blocks all messages from that domain, regardless of the sender. Add *wingtiptoys.com* to the list, for example, and Outlook 2007 would block messages from *joe@wingtiptoys.com*, *jane@wingtiptoys.com*, and all other e-mail addresses ending in *@wingtiptoys.com*.

Figure 12-2. Use the Blocked Senders list to block messages by address or domain.

The Safe Senders and Safe Recipients lists identify senders and domains that Outlook 2007 should not filter, regardless of subject or content. Use the Safe Senders list to identify valid messages by their originating address. Use the Safe Recipients list to identify valid messages by their target address. For example, if you participate in a mailing list, messages for that list are sometimes addressed to a mailing list address rather than your own address, such as *list@wingtiptoys.com* rather than *jim@wingtiptoys.com*. Add the mailing list address to the Safe Recipients list to prevent Outlook 2007 from treating the mailing list messages as junk e-mail.

You have two options for adding entries to each of the three filter lists: specify an e-mail address, or specify a domain. As mentioned earlier, if you specify a domain, Outlook 2007 blocks all messages from that domain, regardless of sender. However, Outlook 2007 is rather selective in blocking. Specify *@wingtiptoys.com*, for example, and Outlook 2007 will block messages from *joe@wingtiptoys.com* and *jane@wingtiptoys.com* but will not block messages from *joe@sales.wingtiptoys.com*. You must specify the subdomain explicitly in a list to either accept or block that subdomain. For example, to block the subdomain *sales.wingtiptoys.com*, enter **sales.wingtiptoys.com** in the Blocked Senders list.

INSIDE OUT **Simplify management of filter lists**

Outlook 2007 recognizes wildcard characters, so you can simply enter ***.<domain>** to block all messages from a domain and its subdomains. For example, use ***.wingtiptoys.com** to block *sales.wintiptoys.com*, *support.wingtiptoys.com*, and all other subdomains of *wingtiptoys.com*. You can import and export a filter list, which enables you to move a list between computers or share the list with others. The filter list is simply a text file with a single e-mail address on each line, making it easy to create and manage the list.

Outlook 2007 also lets you specify a set of top-level domains and language encodings to block as part of its junk e-mail filtering. These options are set on the International tab by selecting the desired domains and encodings from the provided lists.

Deleting Instead of Moving Messages

Outlook 2007 by default moves junk e-mail to the Junk E-Mail folder, which it creates in your mailbox. The Junk E-Mail folder gives you the capability to review your junk e-mail messages before deleting them. If you prefer, you can configure Outlook 2007 to delete messages instead of placing them in the Junk E-Mail folder. As a general rule, you should configure Outlook 2007 to automatically delete messages only after you have spent a month using the Junk E-Mail folder, adding senders to your Safe Senders list and otherwise identifying to Outlook 2007 valid messages that have generated false positives.

Postmarking Messages

Postmarks are a method of adding a "cost" to each e-mail message as a means of discouraging spammers. When you send a message, a unique postmark is generated using information from that specific piece of e-mail, such as recipients and the time that it was sent. This costs a certain amount of computational power and time, although not really enough for the typical Outlook 2007 user to notice. A spammer sending thousands of messages an hour, however, would definitely see a performance hit—in theory, enough to require additional computers for processing—and thus be discouraged from using postmarks.

When a mail client that supports Outlook 2007 e-mail postmarking receives a message, it includes the presence (or lack) of a postmark in its junk e-mail evaluation process. E-mail with a postmark is seen as much less likely to be spam.

Even when you have enabled this feature by selecting When Sending E-Mail, Postmark The Message To Help E-Mail Clients Distinguish Regular E-Mail From Junk E-Mail on the Options tab, not all outgoing messages are postmarked. For example:

- If a message does not contain any of the characteristics of spam, when evaluated by the Outlook 2007 Junk E-Mail filter, the postmark is determined to be unnecessary and is not added.
- When Outlook 2007 is used with Microsoft Exchange Server, e-mail to recipients with entries in the Microsoft Exchange Global Address List (GAL) is not postmarked.

Junk Filtering with Exchange Server

The junk filtering technology in Outlook 2007 works in most situations. However, to take advantage of junk filtering with an Exchange Server account hosted on a computer running Microsoft Exchange 2000 Server or earlier, you must use Cached Exchange Mode to create a locally cached copy of your mailbox. Filtering is not available in Outlook 2007 with Exchange 2000 Server when you are working online unless you configure your Exchange Server account to deliver messages to a local .pst file instead of the mailbox on the server. Outlook 2007 does scan messages if they are delivered to a .pst file. Junk filtering does work with Microsoft Exchange Server 2003 and later in both online mode and Cached Exchange Mode.

How Outlook 2007 Phishing Protection Works

Phishing is an attempt to fraudulently obtain personal information by luring you to a Web site and asking you to disclose things like passwords, credit card numbers, and so on. This Web site is *spoofed*, or pretending to be a trusted site—sometimes remarkably well—when it is actually a fake setup to help steal your personal information. Phishing is often done by sending e-mail that directs you to the spoofed site. With the widespread use of HTML e-mail, it's easier to disguise the actual destination of a link, and accordingly harder for you to detect the misdirection.

Fortunately, Microsoft has added anti-phishing features to Outlook 2007, to help protect you from suspicious Web sites and e-mail addresses. E-mail messages are evaluated as they arrive, and messages that appear to be phishing are delivered to the Inbox, not the Junk E-Mail folder, but are otherwise treated much like junk e-mail, with a number of functions disabled.

- **Disable Links And Other Functionality In Phishing Messages** If Outlook 2007 determines that a message appears to be phishing, the message is delivered to the Inbox, but attachments and links in the message are blocked and the Reply and Reply All functions are disabled.
- **Warn Me About Suspicious Domain Names In E-Mail Addresses** This option warns you when the sender's e-mail domain uses certain characters in an attempt to masquerade as a well-known, legitimate business. Leaving this functionality enabled protects you against phishing attacks using spoofed e-mail addresses.

> **Note**
>
> Phishing protection is functional even when the No Automatic Filtering option is selected and other junk e-mail protection options are disabled.

Enabling and Configuring Junk E-Mail Filtering

To begin filtering out unwanted messages, start Outlook 2007 and follow these steps:

1. Choose Tools, Options, and then click the Junk E-Mail button on the Preferences tab to open the Junk E-Mail Options dialog box (shown earlier in Figure 12-1).
2. Choose a level of protection on the Options tab, as explained earlier.
3. If you want to delete messages rather than move them to the Junk E-Mail folder, select the Permanently Delete Suspected Junk E-Mail Instead Of Moving It To The Junk E-Mail Folder check box.
4. Select the Disable Links And Other Functionality In Phishing Messages check box to protect against common phishing schemes.
5. If you want to be warned when a domain name appears to be spoofed, select Warn Me About Suspicious Domain Names In E-Mail Addresses.
6. To enable postmarks on your outbound e-mail, select When Sending E-Mail, Postmark The Message To Help E-Mail Clients Distinguish Regular E-Mail From Junk E-Mail.
7. Click OK to apply the filter changes.

To configure the lists that Outlook 2007 uses in filtering junk e-mail, start Outlook 2007 and follow these steps:

1. Choose Tools, Options, and then click the Junk E-Mail button on the Preferences tab to open the Junk E-Mail Options dialog box.
2. Click the Safe Senders tab, and then click Add and enter the e-mail address or domain of the sender that you want Outlook 2007 to deliver to your Inbox, regardless of content or subject. Click OK, and then repeat this for each sender you want to add.
3. On the Safe Senders tab, select the Also Trust E-Mail From My Contacts check box if you want Outlook 2007 to always accept e-mail from senders in your Contacts folder, regardless of content or subject. You can also choose to select the Automatically Add People I E-Mail To The Safe Senders List check box.
4. Click the Safe Recipients tab, and add the target addresses or domains for which Outlook 2007 should allow messages (used typically to accept e-mail sent to a mailing list).
5. Click the Blocked Senders tab, and add the addresses or domains of junk e-mail senders whose messages you want Outlook 2007 to explicitly block.
6. Click the International tab, and select the top-level domains and types of language encoding that Outlook 2007 should always block.
7. Click OK to apply the filter changes.

Controlling Automatic Downloads

Images and other online content present another potential hazard in e-mail, because you usually, at minimum, confirm that your e-mail address is valid when you download this content. Content from unknown sources can also be malicious, containing Trojan horses, viruses, and so on.

The new Trust Center, shown in Figure 12-3, lets you decide when Outlook 2007 should download external content in e-mail messages, Really Simple Syndication (RSS) items, and Microsoft Office SharePoint® discussion boards. The Safe Senders and Safe Recipients lists can be used to determine downloading settings, as can Security Zones.

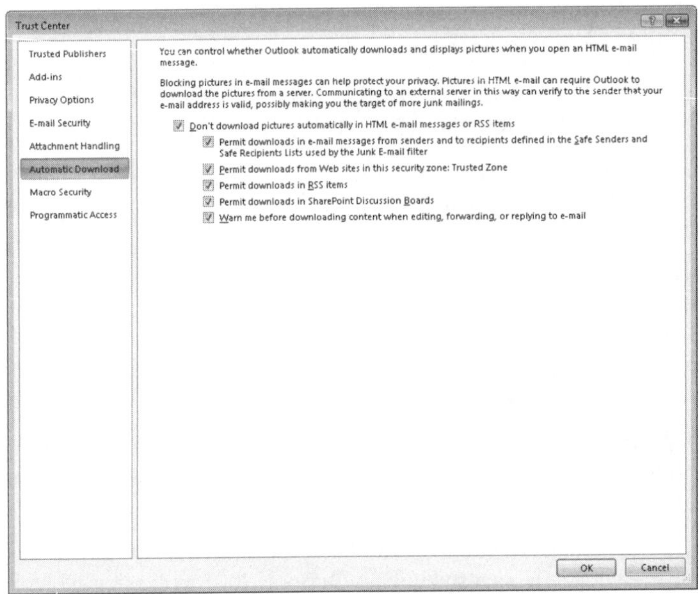

Figure 12-3. Configure Automatic Download options in the Trust Center.

The Automatic Download options are described in the following list:

- **Don't Download Pictures Automatically In HTML E-Mail Messages Or RSS Items** This setting prevents images from downloading to your computer automatically, except as directed by additional settings in this screen. Blocking automatic image downloads protects you from spammers who use your connection to their server to verify your identity as well as from malicious content (a Trojan horse disguised as an image, for example).
- **Permit Downloads In E-Mail Messages From Senders And To Recipients Defined In The Safe Senders And Safe Recipients Lists Used By The Junk E-Mail Filter** You can tell Outlook 2007 to use the safe lists that you have created to determine which images it will download automatically. This lets you see images from those sources that you have already decided you trust while blocking other images.
- **Permit Downloads From Web Sites In This Security Zone: Trusted Zone** Content that resides on a Web site that is included in the Trusted Security Zone is downloaded automatically when this setting is enabled. This lets you receive images and other content from trusted sources such as corporate servers or partners based on a common list, reducing the amount of configuration needed.
- **Permit Downloads In RSS Items** Control over images downloading in RSS feeds is configured separately, allowing you to block images in RSS feeds without affecting e-mail messages.

- **Permit Downloads In SharePoint Discussion Boards** You can configure whether to download content from SharePoint discussion boards separately, offering you finer control over the content that is downloaded to your computer.
- **Warn Me Before Downloading Content When Editing, Forwarding, Or Replying To E-Mail** If this setting is enabled, Outlook 2007 will warn you before downloading content in messages that you are replying to, forwarding, or editing. If you choose to not download the images and continue with your actions, Outlook 2007 will remove the images from the message, and the recipient will not be able to retrieve them. This is an improvement over Microsoft Outlook 2003, in which you could complete your operation only if you downloaded the images.

Configuring Automatic Downloading of External Content

To configure image downloading, start Outlook 2007, and then follow these steps:

1. Choose Tools, Trust Center, and then select Automatic Download to view the options for handling image downloads (shown earlier, in Figure 12-3).
2. To stop Outlook 2007 from automatically downloading images, select the Don't Download Pictures Automatically In HTML E-Mail Messages Or RSS Items check box.

> **Caution**
>
> If this check box is not selected, all other options on this screen will be unavailable, and all images will be displayed, creating potential security risks.

3. If you want to view images from sources you trust, select the Permit Downloads In E-Mail Messages From Senders And To Recipients Defined In The Safe Senders And Safe Recipients Lists Used By The Junk E-Mail Filter check box.
4. To allow sites you trust to download images, select Permit Downloads From Web Sites In This Security Zone: Trusted Zone.
5. If you want to view images in RSS feeds, select Permit Downloads In RSS Items.
6. To view images from SharePoint sites, select Permit Downloads In SharePoint Discussion Boards.
7. If you want Outlook 2007 to alert you that images are being downloaded when you take action on an e-mail message, select Warn Me Before Downloading Content When Editing, Forwarding, Or Replying To E-Mail.
8. Apply the changes by clicking OK.

Marking and Unmarking Junk E-Mail

The junk e-mail filters in Outlook 2007 might not catch all of the messages you consider to be junk. You can easily mark and unmark messages as junk mail without opening the Junk E-Mail Options dialog box. When you receive a message that is junk but that Outlook 2007 does not place in the Junk E-Mail folder (or delete), right-click the message, choose Junk E-Mail, and then choose the list to which you want the sender added. You can add the sender to the Blocked Senders, Safe Senders, or Safe Recipients list as needed, according to the message's content. You can also add the sender's domain to the Safe Senders list.

If Outlook 2007 marks a message as junk mail and moves it to the Junk E-Mail folder but you don't want the message treated as junk mail, you can mark the message as not junk (essentially, unmark the message). Open the Junk E-Mail folder, right-click the message, and choose Junk E-Mail, Mark As Not Junk. Outlook 2007 displays a Mark As Not Junk dialog box. If you click OK without taking any other action, Outlook 2007 moves the message back to the Inbox. Select the Always Trust E-Mail From option to also have the sender's e-mail address added to the Safe Senders list. Any address that message was sent to can also be added to the Safe Recipients List.

Note

If the message is from a sender inside your organization, you do not have the option of adding that sender to the Safe Senders List either from the shortcut menu or from the Mark As Not Junk dialog box.

Creating Other Junk E-Mail Rules

Once you configure it and make adjustments for false positives, the filtering technology built into Outlook 2007 can be an effective tool for waging your daily fight against junk e-mail. The filtering technology in Outlook 2007 isn't perfect, however, so you might need to handle junk e-mail in other ways. One technique is to create your own rules to handle exceptions that the built-in filters can't adequately address.

You can create rules that look explicitly for keywords or phrases in the subject or body of a message or look for specific other criteria and then move those messages to the Junk E-Mail folder (or delete them). See Chapter 11, "Processing Messages Automatically," for details on creating and working with rules.

Reply or Unsubscribe?

Although you might be tempted to have Outlook 2007 automatically send a nasty reply to every piece of spam you receive, resist the urge. In many cases, the spammer's only way of knowing whether a recipient address is valid is when a reply comes back from that address. You make your address that much more desirable to spammers when you reply, because they then know that there's a person at the other end of the address. The best course of action is to delete the message without looking at it.

In the past, many spammers also used unsubscribe messages to identify valid addresses, which made unsubscribing to a particular spammer a hit-or-miss proposition. In some cases, the spammer would delete your address, and in others, simply add your address to the good e-mail address list. With state and federal laws like CAN-SPAM and individuals and companies becoming more litigious, spammers more often than not heed unsubscribe requests. Just a few years ago, we would have recommended that you not bother unsubscribing to spam. Today, you will likely have at least a little better luck unsubscribing to spam without generating a flood of new messages. However, you should still approach the problem cautiously.

Other Spam Filtering Solutions

The spam blocking features in Outlook 2007 can help considerably in blocking unwanted messages, but there are other options you should consider in addition to the Outlook 2007 filtering technologies.

Filtering in Exchange Server

If your company or organization uses Exchange Server, you can perform some spam filtering tasks right at the server without adding third-party software. Exchange 2003 Server and Exchange Server 2007 both support domain filtering for virtual Simple Mail Transfer Protocol (SMTP) servers.

Exchange Server 2007 offers some additional features not included in Exchange 2003 Server, making it potentially more effective for blocking spam. One server in an organization is designated as the Edge Transport server and is responsible for mail flow and control between internal e-mail servers and the Internet. By default, only unauthenticated, inbound e-mail from the Internet is filtered, although internal e-mail can also be filtered if desired.

Exchange Server 2007 can filter e-mail based on a number of different criteria, including:

- **Content** E-mail messages are examined to see whether they have characteristics of spam and are checked against a safe list aggregated from the Safe Sender lists of Outlook 2007 users within the organization.

- **Attachment** Attachments can be filtered based on either the Multipurpose Internet Mail Extensions (MIME) type of the file or the file name. Administrators can choose to strip the attachment and deliver the message or reject the message, either with a failure message to the sender or silently.
- **Connection** E-mail is evaluated based on the IP address of the server that is attempting to send the message using a variety of safe and blocked lists to determine whether the message should be delivered.
- **Recipient** The addresses that the e-mail is sent to are compared to a local directory and an administrator-managed blocked list to determine what to do with the e-mail.
- **Sender** Like the Recipient filter, this filter uses a locally maintained blocked list to block certain addresses from sending e-mail to the organization.
- **Sender ID** The sending system's Domain Name System (DNS) server is queried to determine whether the IP address of the system that originated the message is authorized to send e-mail from that domain. This verification process protects you against spoofed e-mail addresses, a ploy commonly used by spammers and phishers alike.
- **Sender Reputation** This feature collects information about e-mail senders and evaluates incoming e-mail based on a number of characteristics to assign a Spam Confidence Level (SCL) rating. This rating determines whether the message is delivered, and the rating is passed to other computers running Exchange Server when the message is sent to them.

If you are responsible for administering a computer running Exchange Server, you will find additional information in the Help files provided with Exchange Server.

Using Third-Party Filters

Several third-party antispam solutions are available that you can consider for your organization. For example, Symantec's MailSecurity for Microsoft Exchange provides content scanning and filtering capabilities. MailSecurity filters incoming messages for content, spyware, adware, and attachment file types (not just file name extensions).

MailSecurity is available for Exchange Server, Domino, and SMTP servers. You'll find more information about MailSecurity at *www.symantec.com/Products/enterprise?c=prodcat&refId=1011*.

Another product to consider is GFI Mail Essentials (*www.gfi.com/mes*). Mail Essentials provides several levels of content filtering with support for blocked lists, safe lists, and additional header checking options, as shown in Figure 12-4, that enable it to detect and block spam based on a broad range of criteria.

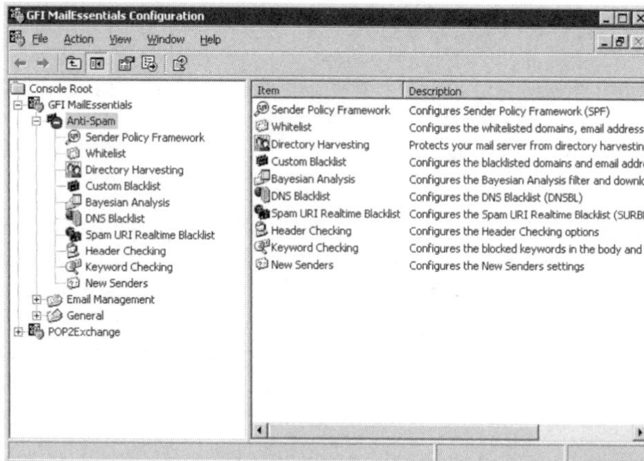

Figure 12-4. GFI Mail Essentials provides an excellent set of filtering features.

Mail Essentials works with Exchange 5.5 or later, Lotus Notes, and any SMTP e-mail server. In addition to spam filtering, Mail Essentials supports the automatic addition of message disclaimers, mail archiving, inbound and outbound mail monitoring, automatic replies, and a Post Office Protocol 2 (POP2) Exchange service that downloads messages from POP3 servers and delivers them to Exchange Server mailboxes.

These are just a few of the solutions available for filtering and managing messages. Many mail servers offer their own filtering capabilities, and many other products provide filtering services for existing mail servers.

One of the most prevalent spam filtering solutions is SpamAssassin, based on an open-source heuristic scanning application developed originally for UNIX-based servers. You can find information about open-source SpamAssassin at *www.spamassassin.org*.

Depending on your existing mail server platform and the development expertise within your organization, you might be able to implement your own filtering solution based on SpamAssassin. There are commercial implementations of SpamAssassin, as well. For example, the Network Associates suite of SpamKiller products is based on SpamAssassin. You can find more information about SpamKiller at *www.mcafee.com/us/enterprise/products/anti_spam/*.

Managing Junk E-Mail Effectively

E-mail is a critical tool for most people, but it can also be a frustration when you feel overwhelmed by junk e-mail. By using the features provided in Outlook 2007 and taking a few additional steps, you can greatly reduce the amount of junk e-mail you receive and the corresponding risks:

- **Use the Outlook 2007 junk e-mail filters and phishing protection.** The default option of Low on the Options tab in the Junk E-Mail Options dialog box provides some protection, but it might not be enough. You might want to raise the level to High and check your Junk E-Mail folder regularly to ensure that Outlook 2007 is not sending legitimate messages there. Use the International tab in the Junk E-Mail Options dialog box to block top-level domains from which you never want to receive messages or to block messages in specific languages.
- **Use the Safe Senders list and Blocked Senders lists.** Building both your blocked and safe lists will make a considerable difference in how well Outlook 2007 can filter your e-mail.
- **Update the Outlook 2007 junk e-mail filters regularly.** Updates for Outlook 2007 can be obtained by choosing Help, Check For Updates. You can also download updated filters from office.microsoft.com/en-us/officeupdate/.
- **Disable functionality that can inadvertently confirm your identity.** Features like read and delivery receipts and automatic acceptance of meeting requests can confirm your identity to a spammer. Outlook 2007 lets you configure receipt processing for Internet e-mail differently from messages within your corporate network so that you can leave receipts on for your business contacts while disabling them for messages from outside the organization.
- **Guard your primary e-mail address.** Many people have a secondary e-mail address—often from a free public provider such as Microsoft Hotmail®—that they use when posting on message boards, newsgroups, and so on. Even so, you might want to change your e-mail address when posting it in public by changing the @ to AT or inserting extra characters (such as *chrisHillREMOVE@wingtiptoys.com*). This can help prevent automated gathering of your address by spammers' robots.
- **Don't reply to spam.** Even a seemingly simple unsubscribe message confirms that your e-mail address is valid, so unless you know the sender, just delete the message.
- **Don't automatically download images and other online content.** Spammers can verify your e-mail address when you connect to the server to download the external content in a message. Online content is blocked by default, and it's a good idea to leave it that way. You can download content for an individual message by right-clicking the message box telling you that the content has been blocked and then selecting Download Pictures.
- **Don't forward chain e-mail.** These messages clutter up inboxes, expose e-mail addresses, and are all too often hoaxes. If you absolutely must forward a message, send it to only the few people who will definitely be interested, and use the BCC option for their e-mail addresses.

- **Never provide personal information in e-mail.** Even with a trusted correspondent, you should avoid sending critical data such as credit card or social security numbers in unencrypted e-mail.
- **Don't provide personal information to links you get in e-mail.** If you get e-mail that appears to be from a company you do business with, don't assume it actually is. Most e-mail that provides a link and asks for personal data is spoofed in an attempt to get you to disclose this information. If you think the e-mail might be valid, type the URL of the business into your browser rather than clicking the link in the e-mail message to be sure you end up at the correct site.
- **Read each Web site's privacy policies.** Get in the habit of checking privacy policies before providing your e-mail address. Sure, this can take a minute or two, but it takes more than that to delete the spam you will get if they misuse or sell your e-mail address. Most Web sites explain what they do with the information they collect; you might want to carefully consider whether to provide any information to those that do not.
- **Keep antivirus, spyware, and firewall protection up to date.** Outlook 2007 can help you avoid most junk e-mail and the associated threats, but the most effective protection is a multilayered approach. You should also install firewall and antivirus software and make sure that it is kept up to date. You might also want to obtain utilities that protect against spyware and other malicious software.

CHAPTER 13

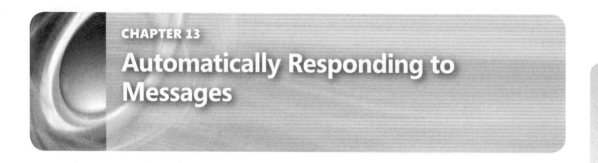

Automatically Responding to Messages

Most of the time, you probably answer your own messages, but no doubt, there are times when you would like Microsoft® Office Outlook® 2007 to reply to messages for you automatically. For example, when you are out of the office on vacation, you probably want people who send you messages to receive an automatic reply that you are out but will respond to them when you return.

There are other reasons to set up automatic replies. For example, maybe you are selling something from a Web site and want people to receive a price list when they send a message to one of your e-mail accounts. Or perhaps you want to send a response when coworkers submit time sheets or other reports to you.

Whatever the case, Office Outlook 2007 offers several handy features to automate replies. Let's take a look at the easiest to use—the Out Of Office Assistant.

Creating Automatic Responses with the Out Of Office Assistant

One of the key features in Outlook 2007 that makes it a great e-mail client is the Out Of Office Assistant, which lets you automatically generate replies to incoming messages when you aren't in the office. For example, if you're going on vacation for a couple of weeks and won't be checking your e-mail, you might want to have the Out Of Office Assistant send an automatic reply to let senders know that you'll respond to their messages when you get back. Or you might do something similar when you are traveling for the day.

The Out Of Office Assistant is a Microsoft Exchange Server feature. To learn how to create automatic responses with custom rules for use with other e-mail servers, see "Creating Automatic Responses with Custom Rules" later in this chapter.

Before you start learning about the Out Of Office Assistant, take a few minutes to consider a few other issues that relate to managing e-mail when you're out of the office.

First, the Out Of Office Assistant is a server-side component for Exchange Server. This means that you can use it to process mail sent to your Exchange Server account but not your Post Office Protocol 3 (POP3), Internet Message Access Protocol (IMAP), Hypertext Transfer Protocol (HTTP), or other e-mail accounts, unless those accounts deliver incoming messages to your Exchange Server Inbox. You can create rules to process your other accounts and simulate the function of the Out Of Office Assistant, but you must do this by creating custom rules.

Second, because the Out Of Office Assistant functions as a server-side component, it processes your messages even when Outlook 2007 isn't running (a likely situation if you're scuba diving off the Great Barrier Reef for a couple of weeks). To process your other accounts with custom Out Of Office rules, Outlook 2007 must be running and checking your messages periodically. If you have a direct Internet connection, you can configure the rules, configure your send/receive groups to allow Outlook 2007 to periodically check messages for the non–Exchange Server accounts, and leave Outlook 2007 running. If you have a dial-up connection to these accounts, you'll have to also configure Outlook 2007 to dial when needed and disconnect after each send/receive operation.

CAUTION!

Be sure to configure your dial-up connection to disconnect after a reasonable idle period, such as 15 minutes. Otherwise, if your Internet access is metered, you might come back from two weeks of sun and fun to find that your dial-up connection has been connected continuously for the last two weeks. Most Internet service providers (ISPs) implement an idle cutoff, but any activity on the line can cause your dial-up connection to remain connected, so it's important to configure the behavior from your side as well. Also be sure to configure Outlook 2007 to disconnect after the send/receive operation is completed.

If you use RPC-over-HTTP to connect to Exchange Server, Outlook 2007 will keep the connection alive. If you will be away from your computer for a while, close Outlook 2007 to prevent this.

Understanding Out Of Office Assistant Features

The features available in the Out Of Office Assistant depend on the version of Exchange Server that your account resides on. In Exchange Server 2003 and earlier, you turn on the Out Of Office Assistant, and as soon as you do, Exchange Server responds to received messages by replying with your specified Out Of Office reply.

It continues to send Out Of Office replies until you turn off the Out Of Office Assistant. Exchange Server 2007, on the other hand, lets you specify the time period when you will be out. You don't have to turn on or turn off the assistant–just specify the start date and end date for the time you will be out of the office, and during that time, Exchange Server will respond with Out Of Office replies.

Another difference in Exchange Server 2007 is the capability to specify different behavior for external and internal Out Of Office messages. For example, you might want to offer more information in the Out Of Office message you send to coworkers, such as who will be handling issues while you are gone, but omit that information from replies sent to people outside your organization. You or your Exchange Server administrator can control how replies are sent to specific external domains. For example, your organization might want to allow Out Of Office replies to go to business partners in specific companies but not to other senders or specific domains, such as Microsoft Hotmail®, Yahoo!, and so on. The Exchange Server 2007 Out Of Office Assistant can also be configured not to send replies to junk mail. Plus you can now use fonts, colors, and formatting in your replies.

> **Note**
>
> Because the Out Of Office Assistant is a server-side feature, you can take advantage of Exchange Server 2007 Out Of Office Assistant features from Outlook 2003 as well as Outlook 2007.

Using the Out Of Office Assistant is easy. Here's the process in a nutshell:

1. Specify the text you want Outlook 2007 to use for automatic replies when you're out of the office.
2. If necessary, create custom rules for the computer running Exchange Server to use to process incoming messages during your absence.

For information about custom Out Of Office rules, see "Creating Custom Out Of Office Rules" later in this chapter.

3. Turn on the Out Of Office Assistant, which causes the Out Of Office Assistant to start responding to incoming messages. Or if you are using an Exchange Server 2007 account, you can specify the Out Of Office Assistant startup time, and Exchange Server will respond accordingly.
4. When you get back, turn off the Out Of Office Assistant so that it stops processing messages.

Note

When you start Outlook 2007, it checks to see whether the Out Of Office Assistant is turned on. If it is, Outlook 2007 asks whether you want to turn it off. After the Out Of Office Assistant is set up and functioning, messages that arrive in your Inbox receive an Out Of Office response with the message text you've specified. Exchange Server keeps track of the send-to list and sends the Out Of Office response the first time a message comes from a given sender. Subsequent messages from that sender are sent to your Inbox without generating an Out Of Office response. This procedure cuts down on the number of messages generated and keeps the senders from becoming annoyed by numerous Out Of Office replies.

Note

Exchange Server deletes the send-to list for Out Of Office responses when you turn off the Out Of Office Assistant from Outlook 2007.

Using the Out Of Office Assistant with Exchange Server 2003 and Earlier

Follow these steps to specify the text for automatic replies and to tell the computer running Exchange Server 2003 or earlier that you're out of the office:

1. In Outlook 2007, select the Exchange Server Inbox, and then choose Tools, Out Of Office Assistant.
2. In the Out Of Office Assistant dialog box, shown in Figure 13-1, type the body of your automatic message reply in the AutoReply box. While the Out Of Office Assistant is active, Exchange Server uses this message to reply to incoming messages.

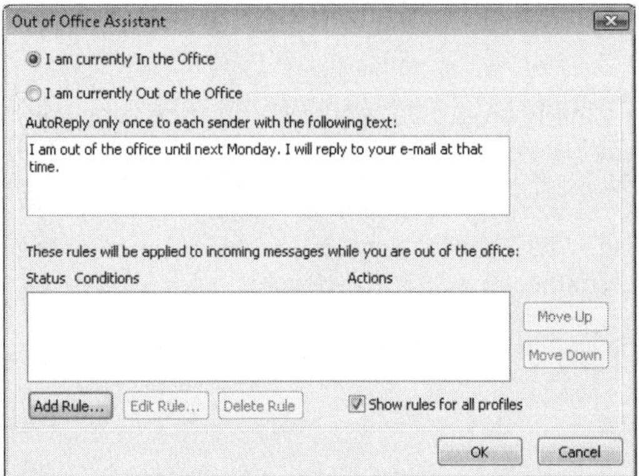

Figure 13-1. Use the Out Of Office Assistant dialog box to specify your automatic message reply.

3. Select I Am Currently Out Of The Office, and then click OK.

Using the Out Of Office Assistant for Exchange Server 2007

Follow these steps to specify the text for automatic replies and to tell Exchange Server 2007 or earlier that you're out of the office:

1. In Outlook 2007, select the Exchange Server Inbox, and then choose Tools, Out Of Office Assistant.
2. In the Out of Office Assistant dialog box, shown in Figure 13-2, click Send Out Of Office Auto-Replies.

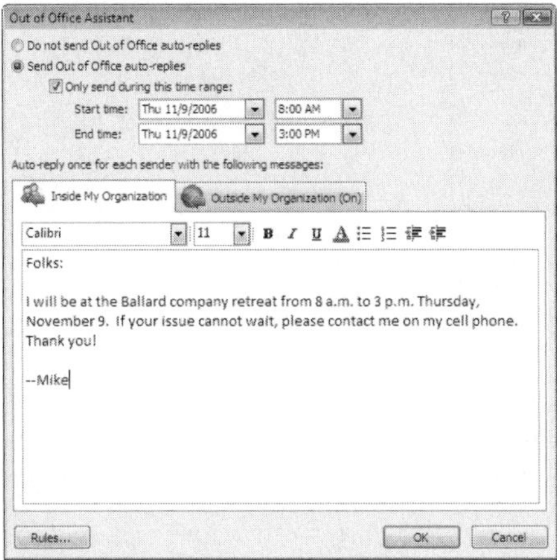

Figure 13-2. You can create custom rules to use with the Out Of Office Assistant.

3. Use the Start Time drop-down list to specify the starting date and time when you will be out of the office.

4. Use the End Time drop-down list to specify the date and time you will return to the office.

5. Click in the Inside My Organization box, and then type your Out Of Office reply. If you want to enhance your message, use fonts and other options from the formatting tools on the Out Of Office toolbar.

6. Click the Outside My Organization tab, and then specify the message you want sent to people outside your organization.

7. When you are satisfied with the message(s), click OK.

> **Note**
>
> If you want to turn off Out Of Office replies, choose Out Of Office Assistant on the Tools menu, click the Do Not Send Out Of Office Auto-Replies option, and then click OK.

Creating Custom Out Of Office Rules

With the Out Of Office Assistant, you can create custom rules to use in addition to the basic automatic reply. To create a custom rule, open the Out Of Office Assistant, click Rules, and then click Add Rule to display the Edit Rule dialog box, shown in Figure 13-3.

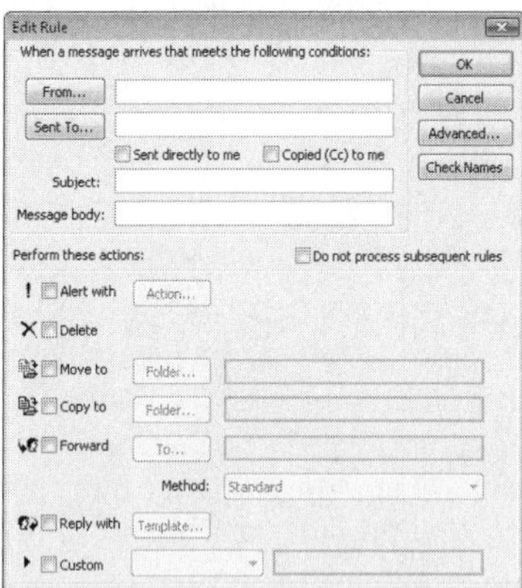

Figure 13-3. You can create custom rules to use with the Out Of Office Assistant.

The options in the Edit Rule dialog box are straightforward, particularly if you're experienced at creating rules. Specify the conditions that the incoming messages should meet, and then specify the action that Exchange Server should perform if a message meets those conditions.

If you need more help creating and using rules, see Chapter 11, "Processing Messages Automatically."

When you define the conditions, keep in mind that the Out Of Office Assistant conditions can be met by either full or partial matches. For example, you could type **yce** in the Sent To box, and the rule would apply if the address contained *Joyce*, *Boyce*, or *Cayce*. If you want the condition to be met only if the full string is found, enclose the text in quotation marks—for example, type **"yce"**.

Creating Automatic Responses with Custom Rules

The Out Of Office Assistant is great for generating automatic replies to messages that arrive in your Inbox when you're out of the office. However, the Out Of Office Assistant sends an Out Of Office response only the first time a message arrives from a given sender. Subsequent messages go into the Inbox without generating an automatic response.

In some cases, you might want Outlook 2007 to generate automatic replies to messages at any time or for other types of accounts that do not use Exchange Server. Perhaps you've set up an Internet e-mail account to take inquiries about a product or service you're selling. You can create a rule to automatically send a specific reply to messages that come in to that account. Or you might want people to be able to request information about specific products or topics by sending a message containing a certain keyword in the subject line. In that case, you can create a rule to generate a reply based on the subject of the message.

Note

In Web jargon, applications or rules that create automatic responses are often called *autoresponders*.

You create automatic responses such as these not by using the Out Of Office Assistant, but by creating custom Outlook 2007 rules with the Rules Wizard. As with other rules, you specify conditions that incoming messages must meet to receive a specific reply. For example, you might specify that an incoming message must contain the text *Framistats* in its subject to generate a reply that provides pricing on your line of gold-plated framistats.

Note

You aren't limited to specifying conditions only for the subject of an incoming message. You can use any of the criteria supported by the Outlook 2007 rules to specify the conditions for an automatic response.

Setting Up the Reply

When you use a custom rule to create an automatic response, you don't define the reply text in the rule. Rather, you have two options: specifying a template on your local computer or setting up a specific message on the server. If you opt to use a template on your local computer, you create the message in Outlook 2007 and save it as a template file.

Follow these steps to create the template:

1. Begin a new message, and then enter the subject and body but leave the address boxes blank.

> **Note**
>
> Include an address in the Bcc field if you want a copy of all automatic responses sent to you or to a specific address.

2. Click the Microsoft Office Button, and then choose Save As.
3. In the Save As dialog box, specify a path and name for the file, select Outlook 2007 Template (*.oft) in the Save As Type drop-down list, and then click Save.

Using a template from your local system causes the rule to function as a client-side rule. As a result, Outlook 2007 can use the rule to process accounts other than your Exchange Server account (such as a POP3 account), but Exchange Server can't generate automatic responses when Outlook 2007 isn't running or is offline.

TROUBLESHOOTING

Your autoresponse rule executes only once

When you create a rule using the Reply Using A Specific Template rule action, Outlook 2007 executes the rule only once for a given sender in each Outlook 2007 session. Outlook 2007 keeps track of the senders in a list and checks incoming messages against the list. For the first message from a given sender that matches the rule conditions, Outlook 2007 generates the response; for subsequent messages, Outlook 2007 doesn't generate the response. This prevents Outlook 2007 from sending repetitive responses to a person who sends you multiple messages that satisfy the rule conditions. Closing and restarting Outlook 2007 refreshes the sender list, and the next message from that sender that meets the criteria generates a response. The Out Of Office Assistant uses the same process—and this behavior is by design.

If you create a server-side rule that uses Have Server Reply Using A Specific Message, Exchange Server creates an autoresponse for all messages that meet the specified conditions, regardless of whether the message is the first from a particular sender.

Creating Automatic Responses from Local Templates

Follow these steps to create a client-side rule that responds to incoming messages with a reply from a template stored locally on your computer:

1. Using Outlook 2007 as your e-mail editor, compose the reply message and save it as a template (.oft) file.
2. Choose Tools, Rules And Alerts to open the Rules And Alerts dialog box.
3. Click New Rule.
4. Select Check Messages When They Arrive, and then click Next.
5. Specify the conditions for the rule (such as Sent Only To Me or Where My Name Is In The To Box), and then click Next.
6. Select Reply Using A Specific Template, and then in the rule description area, click the A Specific Template link.
7. In the Select A Reply Template dialog box, shown in Figure 13-4, select the template that you want to use for the reply, and then click Open.

> **Note**
>
> Use the Look In drop-down list to choose the location where the template is stored. You can open templates stored in Outlook or in the file system (including from a network file server).

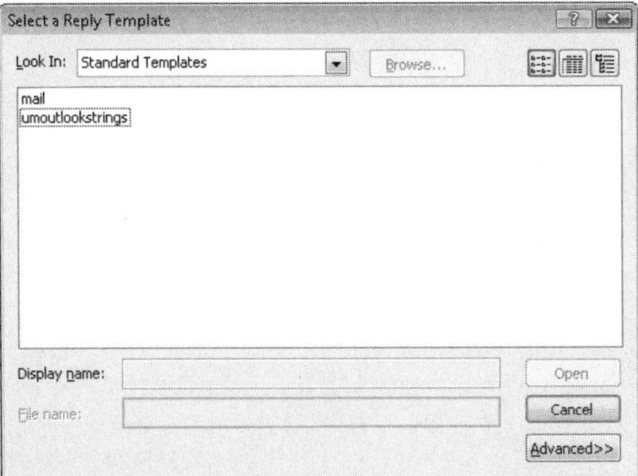

Figure 13-4. Select the message template to use as the reply.

8. Click Next, and then specify exceptions, if any, for the rule.
9. Click Next, specify final options for the rule, specify a name for the rule, and then click Finish.

Note

By default, Outlook turns on the rule. You can clear the Turn On Rule check box prior to clicking Finish if you don't want the rule enabled right away.

Creating Automatic Responses from the Server

Follow these steps to create a server-side rule to generate automatic responses using a message stored on the server:

1. Choose Tools, Rules And Alerts to open the Rules And Alerts dialog box.
2. Click New Rule.
3. Select Check Messages When They Arrive, and then click Next.
4. Specify the conditions for the rule, and then click Next.
5. Select Have Server Reply Using A Specific Message, and then in the rule description area, click the A Specific Message link.
6. Create the message using the resulting message form, specifying the subject and text but no addresses (unless you want to copy the reply to a specific address), and then click Save and Close.
7. Click Next, and then specify exceptions, if any, for the rule.
8. Click Next, specify final options for the rule, and then click Finish.

CHAPTER 14

Securing Your System, Messages, and Identity

Microsoft® Office Outlook® 2007 includes features that can help protect your system from computer viruses and malicious programs, prevent others from using e-mail to impersonate you, and prevent the interception of sensitive messages. Some of these features—such as the ability to block specific types of attachments—were first introduced in Office Outlook 2002. Other security features—such as the ability to block external images in HTML-based messages—were introduced in Office Outlook 2003. This feature enables Outlook to block HTML messages sent by spammers to identify valid recipient addresses. These messaging security features are extended and enhanced in Office Outlook 2007.

This chapter begins with a look at the settings you can use to control HTML content. Because HTML messages can contain malicious scripts or even HTML code that can easily affect your system, the capability to handle these messages in Outlook 2007 is extremely important.

This chapter also discusses the use of both digital signatures and encryption. You can use a digital signature to authenticate your messages, proving to the recipient that a message indeed came from you, not from someone trying to impersonate you. Outlook 2007 enables you to encrypt outgoing messages to prevent them from being intercepted by unintended recipients; you can also read encrypted messages sent to you by others. In this chapter, you'll learn how to obtain and install certificates to send encrypted messages and how to share keys with others so that you can exchange encrypted messages.

Configuring HTML Message Handling

Spammers are always looking for new methods to identify valid e-mail addresses. Knowing that a given address actually reaches someone is one step in helping spammers maintain their lists. If a particular address doesn't generate a response in some way, it's more likely to be removed from the list.

One way spammers identify valid addresses is through the use of *Web beacons*. Spammers often send HTML messages that contain links to external content, such as pictures or sound clips. When you display the message, your mail program retrieves the remote data to display it, and the remote server then validates your address. These external elements are the Web beacons.

Note

Nonspammers also frequently include external content in messages to reduce the size of the message. So external content isn't a bad thing per se (depending on how it is used).

Since Outlook 2003, Outlook blocks external content from HTML messages by default, displaying a red X in the place of the missing content. The result is that these Web beacons no longer work because the external content is not accessed when the message is displayed. Messages that fit criteria for the Safe Recipients and Safe Senders lists are treated as exceptions—the external content for these messages is not blocked.

Note

You can rest the mouse pointer on a blocked image to view the descriptive alternate text (if any) for the image.

When you preview an image in the Reading Pane for which Outlook 2007 has blocked external content, Outlook 2007 displays a message in the InfoBar, indicating that the blocking occurred (see Figure 14-1). You can click the InfoBar and choose Download Pictures to view the external content. Outlook 2007 then downloads and displays the content in the Reading Pane. The same is true if you open a message; Outlook 2007 displays a warning message, telling you that the content was blocked (see Figure 14-2). You can click the warning message and choose Download Pictures to download and view the content. Outlook 2007's blocking of external content for messages in this way lets you take advantage of content blocking without using the Reading Pane.

If you edit, forward, or reply to a message containing blocked content (from an open message or a message displayed in the Reading Pane), Outlook 2007 displays a warning dialog box indicating that the external content will be downloaded if you continue. You can click OK to download the content and continue with the reply or forward, click No to tell Outlook 2007 to forward the content as text without downloading the content, or click Cancel to not open the message or download the content (see Figure 14-3). Thus, you can now reply to or forward a message without downloading the external content (which wasn't possible with previous versions of Outlook).

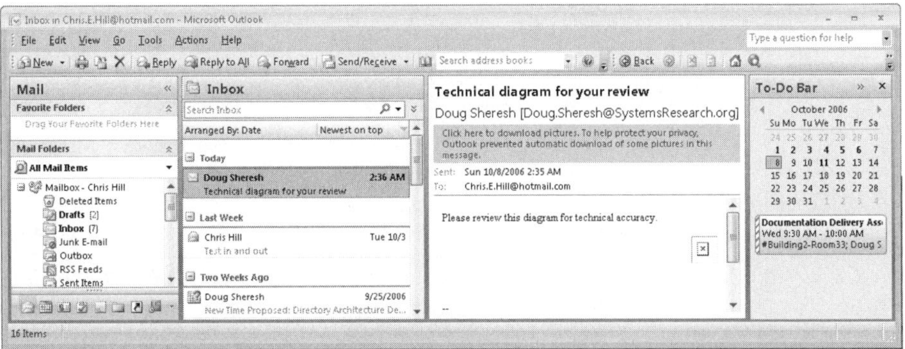

Figure 14-1. Click the InfoBar in the Reading Pane to view external content for a selected message.

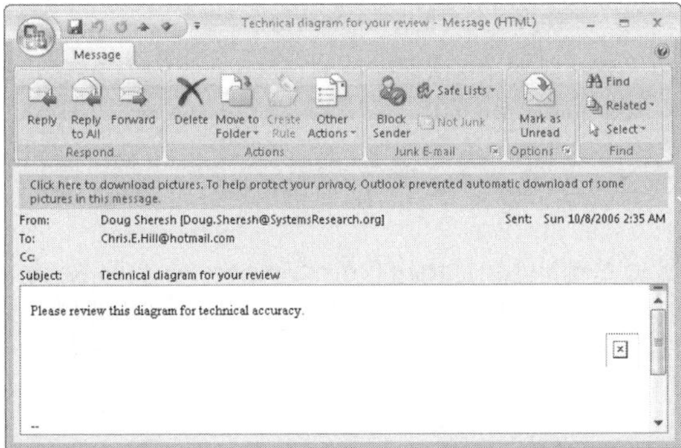

Figure 14-2. You can access blocked content when you open a message by clicking the InfoBar and selecting Download Pictures.

Figure 14-3. You can now forward or reply to a message with blocked content without downloading the content.

Outlook 2007 provides a few options to control the way content blocking works. To configure these options, choose Tools, Trust Center, and then click the Automatic Download page. Figure 14-4 shows the resulting Automatic Download settings page.

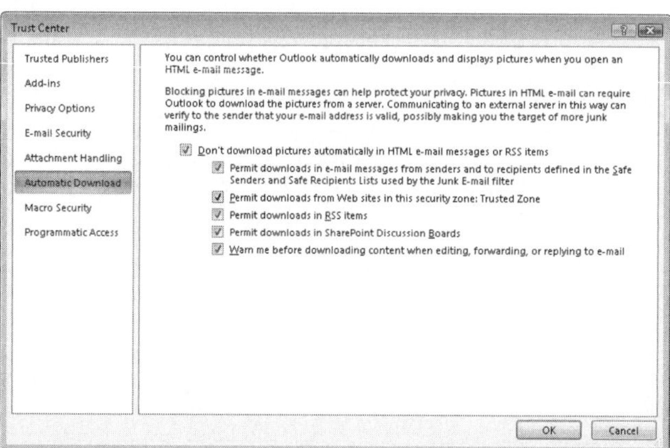

Figure 14-4. Configure content blocking with the Automatic Download settings page.

Configure content blocking using the following options:

- **Don't Download Pictures Automatically In HTML E-Mail Or RSS Items** Select this check box to allow Outlook 2007 to block external picture content with the exception of messages that fit the Safe Senders and Safe Recipients lists. When selected, this check box enables the five check boxes below it to further refine content blocking.
- **Permit Downloads In E-mail Messages From Senders And To Recipients Defined In The Safe Senders And Safe Recipients List Used By The Junk E-Mail Filter** Select this check box to allow Outlook to download content if the message is from a sender in your Safe Senders list or is addressed to a recipient in your Safe Recipients list.
- **Permit Downloads From Web Sites In This Security Zone: Trusted Zone** Select this check box to allow external content from sites in Microsoft Windows® Security Center/Internet Explorer® Trusted Sites zone.
- **Permit Downloads In RSS Items** Select this check box to allow external content included in RSS feeds.
- **Permit Downloads In SharePoint Discussion Boards** Select this check box to allow external content included in SharePoint® Discussion Boards.
- **Warn Me Before Downloading Content When Editing, Forwarding, Or Replying To E-Mail** Select this check box to receive a warning about external content when you edit, reply to, or forward a message for which external content has been blocked.

To take advantage of the exceptions for external content, you must add the message's originating address to the Safe Senders list, add the recipient address to the Safe Recipients list, or add the remote domain to the Trusted Sites zone in Internet Options (in the Windows Security Center).

For more details on configuring the Safe Recipients and Safe Senders lists, see "Enabling and Configuring Junk E-Mail Filtering" in Chapter 12.

Protecting Messages with Digital Signatures

Outlook 2007 supports the use of *digital signatures* to sign messages and validate their authenticity. For example, you can digitally sign a sensitive message so that the recipient can know with relative certainty that the message came from you and that no one is impersonating you by using your e-mail address. This section of the chapter explains digital certificates and signatures and how to use them in Outlook 2007.

Understanding Digital Certificates and Signatures

A *digital certificate* is the mechanism that makes digital signatures possible. Depending on its assigned purpose, you can use a digital certificate for a variety of tasks, including the following:

- Verifying your identity as the sender of an e-mail message
- Encrypting data communications between computers–between a client and a server, for example
- Encrypting e-mail messages to prevent easy interception
- Signing drivers and executable files to authenticate their origin

A digital certificate binds the identity of the certificate's owner to a pair of keys, one public and one private. At a minimum, a certificate contains the following information:

- The owner's public key
- The owner's name or alias
- A certificate expiration date
- A certificate serial number
- The name of the certificate issuer
- The digital signature of the issuer

The certificate can also include other identifying information, such as the owner's e-mail address, postal address, country, or gender.

The two keys are the aspect of the certificate that enables authentication and encryption. The private key resides on your computer and is a large unique number. The certificate contains the public key, which you must give to recipients to whom you want to send authenticated or encrypted messages.

Think of it as having a "read content key" and a "create content key:" one key (the private key) lets you create encrypted content, and the other key (the public key) lets others read the content encrypted with the first key.

Outlook 2007 uses slightly different methods for authenticating messages with digital signatures and for encrypting messages, as you'll see later in the chapter. Before you begin either task, however, you must first obtain a certificate.

Obtaining a Digital Certificate

Digital certificates are issued by certificate authorities (CAs). In most cases, you obtain your e-mail certificate from a public CA such as VeriSign or Thawte. However, systems based on Windows servers running Certificate Services can function as CAs, providing certificates to clients who request them. Check with your system administrator to determine whether your enterprise includes a CA. If it doesn't, you need to obtain your certificate from a public CA, usually at a minimal cost. Certificates are typically good for one year and must be renewed at the end of that period.

If you need to obtain your certificate from a public CA, point your Web browser to the CA Web site, such as *www.verisign.com* or *www.thawte.com*. Follow the instructions provided by the site to obtain a certificate for signing and encrypting your e-mail (see Figure 14-5, for example). The certificate might not be issued immediately; instead, the CA might send you an e-mail message containing a URL that links to a page where you can retrieve the certificate. When you connect to that page, the CA installs the certificate on your system.

> **Note**
>
> Alternatively, in Tools, Trust Center, click E-Mail Security, and then click on Get A Digital ID to display a page from the Microsoft Web site that includes links to several certificate authorities. Select a vendor under Available Digital IDs (such as Verisign) and click the link to its Web site to obtain a certificate.

Figure 14-5. You can use the Web to request a digital certificate from a public CA.

If you're obtaining a certificate from a CA on your network, the method you use depends on whether the network includes an enterprise CA or a stand-alone CA.

If you're using Windows Vista™ as a domain client on a network with an enterprise CA, follow these steps to request a certificate:

1. Select the Windows button; in the Start Search box, type **MMC**. Click OK.
2. In the Microsoft Management Console (MMC), choose File, Add/Remove Snap-In.
3. In the Add Standalone Snap-In dialog box, select Certificates, and then click Add.
4. In the Certificates Snap-In dialog box, select My User Account, and then click Finish.
5. Click OK to return to the MMC.
6. Expand the Certificates–Current User branch.
7. Expand the Personal branch, right-click Certificates, and choose All Tasks, Request New Certificate. You can also right-click the Personal branch and choose All Tasks, Request New Certificate.
8. Follow the prompts provided by the Certificate Request Wizard and the enterprise CA to request your certificate. The certificate should install automatically.

To request a certificate from a stand-alone CA on your network (or if your computer is part of a workgroup), point your Web browser to *http://*<server>*/certsrv*, where <server> is the name or IP address of the CA. The CA provides a Web page with a form that you must fill out to request the certificate (see Figure 14-6). Follow the CA prompts to request and obtain the certificate. The site includes a link that you can click to install the certificate.

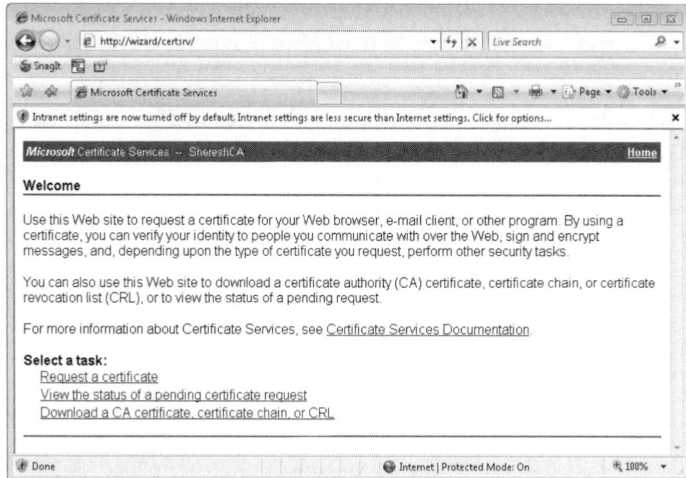

Figure 14-6. A Windows-based CA presents a Web form that you can use to request a certificate.

Copying a Certificate to Another Computer

You can copy your certificate from one computer to another, which means that you can use it on more than one system. The process is simple: you first export (back up) your certificate to a file, and then import the certificate into the other system. The following sections explain how to export and import certificates.

> **Note**
>
> As you use the Certificate Import Wizard and the Certificate Export Wizard (discussed in the following sections), you might discover that they don't precisely match the descriptions presented here. Their appearance and operation might vary slightly, depending on the operating system you're running and the version of Microsoft Internet Explorer you're using.

Backing Up Your Certificate

Whether you obtained your certificate from a public CA or from a CA on your network, you should back it up in case your system suffers a drive failure or if the certificate is lost or corrupted. You also should have a backup of the certificate so that you can export it to any other computers you use on a regular basis, such as a notebook computer or your home computer. In short, you need the certificate on every computer from which you plan to digitally sign or encrypt messages. To back up your certificate, you can use Outlook 2007, Internet Explorer, or the Certificates console (available in Microsoft Windows 2000, Microsoft Windows XP, and Windows Vista). Each method offers the same capabilities; you can use any one of the three.

Follow these steps to use Outlook 2007 to back up your certificate to a file:

1. In Outlook 2007, choose Tools, Trust Center, and then click the E-Mail Security page.
2. Click Import/Export to display the Import/Export Digital ID dialog box, shown in Figure 14-7.

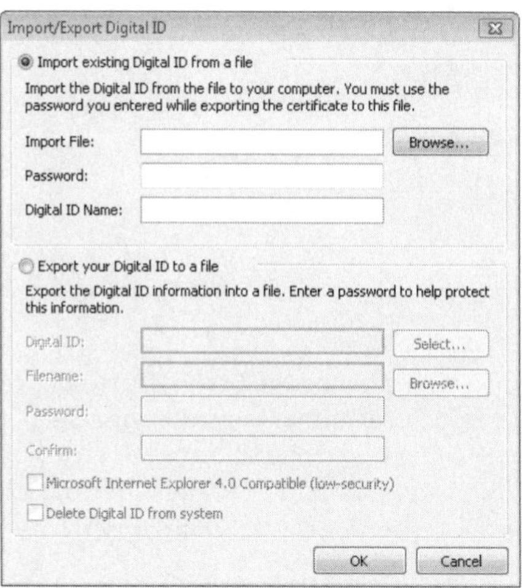

Figure 14-7. You can export certificates in the Import/Export Digital ID dialog box.

3. Select the Export Your Digital ID To A File option. Click Select, choose the certificate to be exported, and click OK.
4. Click Browse and specify the path and file name for the certificate file.
5. Optionally, you can enter and confirm a password (using a password is a good idea because you are also exporting your private key).
6. If you plan to use the certificate on a system with Internet Explorer 4, select the Microsoft Internet Explorer 4.0 Compatible (Low-Security) check box. If you use Internet Explorer 5 or later, clear this check box.
7. If you want to remove this Digital ID from this computer, select the check box next to Delete Digital ID From System.
8. Click OK to export the file. The Exporting Your Private Exchange Key dialog box is displayed. Click OK to complete the export process.

If you want to use either Internet Explorer or the Certificates console to back up a certificate, use the Certificate Export Wizard, as follows:

1. If you're using Internet Explorer, begin by choosing Tools, Internet Options. Click the Content tab, and then click Certificates. In the Certificates dialog box, shown in Figure 14-8, select the certificate you want to back up and click Export to start the wizard. If you're using the Certificates console, begin by opening the console and expanding Certificates–Current User/Personal/Certificates. Right-click the certificate to export, and then choose All Tasks, Export to start the wizard.

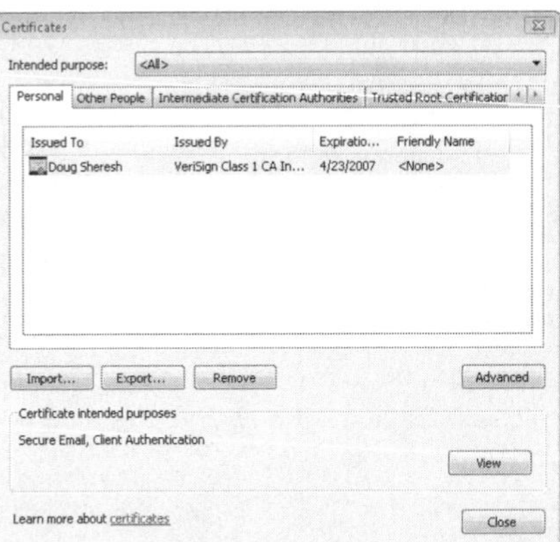

Figure 14-8. You can use the Certificates dialog box to export a certificate.

2. In the Certificate Export Wizard, click Next.
3. On the wizard page shown in Figure 14-9, select Yes, Export The Private Key; then click Next.

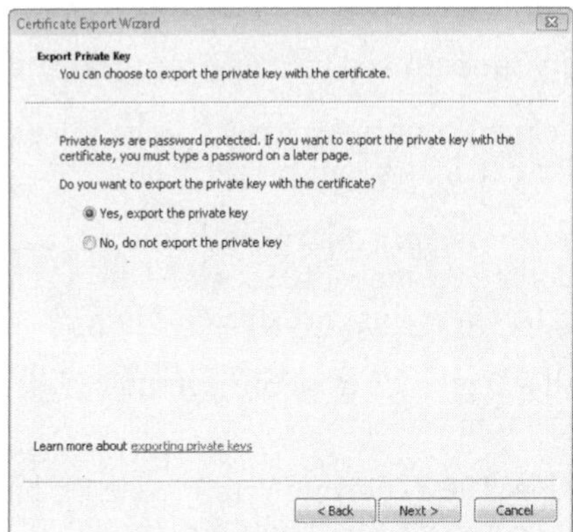

Figure 14-9. This wizard enables you to export the private key.

4. Select Personal Information Exchange; if other options are selected, clear them unless needed. (If you need to include all certificates in the certification path, remove the private key on export, or export all extended properties, and then select that option.) Click Next.
5. Specify and confirm a password to protect the private key and click Next.
6. Specify a path and file name for the certificate and click Next.
7. Review your selections and click Finish.

TROUBLESHOOTING

You can't export the private key

To use a certificate on a different computer, you must be able to export the private key. If the option to export the private key is unavailable when you run the Certificate Export Wizard, it means that the private key is marked as not exportable. Exportability is an option you choose when you request the certificate. If you request a certificate through a local CA, you must select the Advanced Request option to request a certificate with an exportable private key. If you imported the certificate from a file, you might not have selected the option to make the private key exportable during the import. If you still have the original certificate file, you can import it again—this time selecting the option that will enable you to export the private key.

Installing Your Certificate from a Backup

You can install (or reinstall) a certificate from a backup copy of the certificate file by using Outlook 2007, Internet Explorer, or the Certificates console. You must import the certificate to your computer from the backup file.

The following procedure assumes that you're installing the certificate using Outlook 2007:

1. In Outlook 2007, choose Tools, Trust Center, and then click the E-Mail Security page.
2. Click Import/Export to display the Import/Export Digital ID dialog box, shown earlier in Figure 14-7.
3. In the Import Existing DigitalID From File section, click Browse to locate the file containing the backup of the certificate.
4. In the Password box, type the password associated with the certificate file.
5. In the Digital ID Name box, type a name by which you want the certificate to be shown. Typically, you'll enter your name, mailbox name, or e-mail address, but you can enter anything you want.
6. Click OK to import the certificate.

You can also import a certificate to your computer from a backup file using either Internet Explorer or the Certificates console, as explained here:

1. If you're using Internet Explorer, begin by choosing Tools, Internet Options. Click the Content tab, click Certificates, and then click Import to start the Certificate Import Wizard. If you're using the Certificates console, begin by opening the console. Right-click Certificates–Current User/Personal, and then click All Tasks, Import to start the wizard.
2. In the Certificate Import Wizard, click Next.

3. Browse and select the file to import, and then click Open. (If you don't see your certificate file, check the type of certificates shown in the Open dialog box by clicking the drop-down list to the right of the file name field.) After your certificate is selected in the File To Import dialog box, click Next.
4. If the certificate was stored with a password, you are prompted to enter the password. Provide the associated password and click Next.
5. Select the Automatically Select The Certificate Store Based On The Type Of Certificate option and click Next.
6. Click Finish.

Signing Messages

Now that you have a certificate on your system, you're ready to start digitally signing your outgoing messages so that recipients can verify your identity. When you send a digitally signed message, Outlook 2007 sends the original message and an encrypted copy of the message with your digital signature. The recipient's e-mail application compares the two versions of the message to determine whether they are the same. If they are, no one has tampered with the message. The digital signature also enables the recipient to verify that the message is from you.

> **Note**
>
> Because signing your e-mail requires Outlook 2007 to send two copies of the message (the unencrypted message and the encrypted copy), the signed e-mail message is larger.

Understanding S/MIME and Clear-Text Options

Secure/Multipurpose Internet Mail Extensions (S/MIME), an Internet standard, is the mechanism in Outlook 2007 that enables you to digitally sign and encrypt messages. The e-mail client handles the encryption and decryption required for both functions.

Users with e-mail clients that don't support S/MIME can't read digitally signed messages unless you send the message as clear text (unencrypted). Without S/MIME support, the recipient is also unable to verify the authenticity of the message or verify that the message hasn't been altered. Without S/MIME, then, digital signatures are relatively useless. However, Outlook 2007 does offer you the option of sending a digitally signed message as clear text to recipients who lack S/MIME support. If you need to send the same digitally signed message to multiple recipients—some of whom have S/MIME-capable e-mail clients and some of whom do not—digitally signing the message allows those with S/MIME support to authenticate it, and including the clear-text message allows the others to at least read it.

The following section explains how to send a digitally signed message, including how to send the message in clear text for those recipients who require it.

Adding Your Digital Signature

Follow these steps to digitally sign an outgoing message:

1. Compose the message in Outlook 2007.
2. On the Message tab in the Options group, click the Message Options Dialog Box Launcher (in the lower-right corner) to open the Message Options dialog box.
3. Click Security Settings to open the Security Properties dialog box, as shown in Figure 14-10.

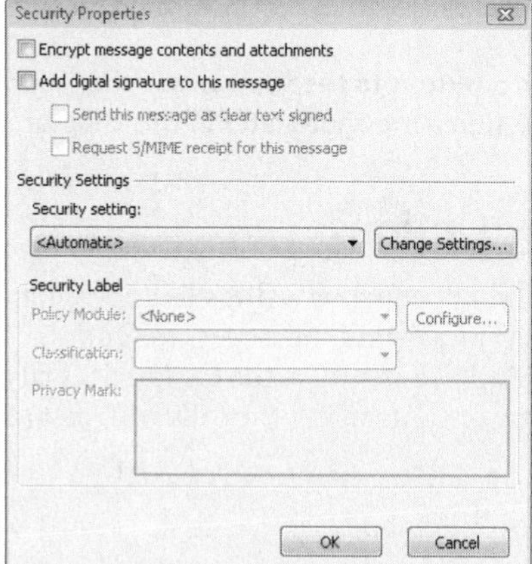

Figure 14-10. You can add a digital signature using the Security Properties dialog box.

4. Select Add Digital Signature To This Message, and then select other check boxes as indicated here:

   Send This Message As Clear Text Signed Select this check box to include a clear-text copy of the message for recipients who don't have S/MIME-capable e-mail applications. Clear this check box to prevent the message from being read by mail clients that don't support S/MIME.

   Request S/MIME Receipt For This Message Select this check box to request a secure receipt to verify that the recipient has validated your digital signature. When the message has been received and saved, and your signature is verified (even if the recipient doesn't read the message), you receive a return receipt. No receipt is sent if your signature is not verified.

5. If necessary, select security settings in the Security Setting drop-down list. (If you have not yet configured your security options, you can do so by clicking Change Settings.)

For details on security option configuration, see the section "Creating and Using Security Profiles" later in this chapter.

6. Click OK to add the digital signature to the message.

> **Note**
>
> If you send a lot of digitally signed messages, you'll want to configure your security options to include a digital signature by default; see the following section for details. In addition, you might want to add a button to the toolbar to let you quickly sign the message without using a dialog box.

For details about how to add such a button to the toolbar, see the Troubleshooting sidebar "You need a faster way to digitally sign a message" later in this chapter.

Setting Global Security Options

To save time, you can configure your security settings to apply globally to all messages, changing settings only as needed for certain messages. In Outlook 2007, choose Tools, Trust Center, and then click E-Mail Security. On the E-Mail Security page, shown in Figure 14-11, you can set security options using the following list as a guide.

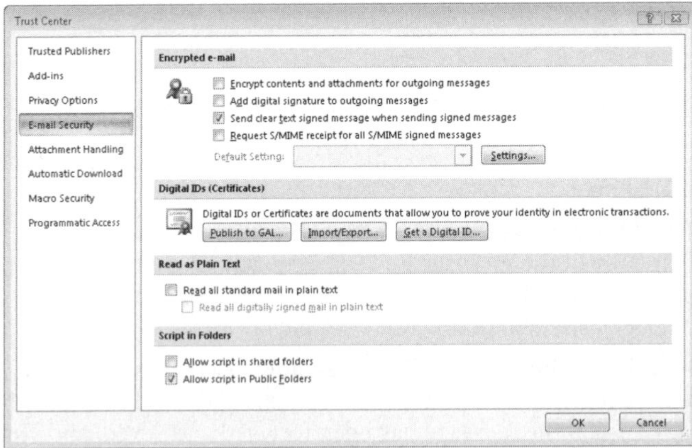

Figure 14-11. Use the E-Mail Security page of the Trust Center to configure options for digital signing and encryption.

- **Encrypt Contents And Attachments For Outgoing Messages** If most of the messages you send need to be encrypted, select this check box to encrypt all outgoing messages by default. You can override encryption for a specific message by changing the message's properties when you compose it. Clear this check box if the majority of your outgoing messages do not need to be encrypted.

For information about encryption, see the section "Encrypting Messages" later in this chapter.

- **Add Digital Signature To Outgoing Messages** If most of your messages need to be signed, select this check box to digitally sign all outgoing messages by default. Clear this check box if most of your messages do not need to be signed; you will be able to digitally sign specific messages as needed when you compose them.
- **Send Clear Text Signed Message When Sending Signed Messages** If you need to send digitally signed messages to recipients who do not have S/MIME capability, select this check box to send clear-text digitally signed messages by default. You can override this option for individual messages when you compose them. In most cases, you can clear this check box because most e-mail clients support S/MIME.
- **Request S/MIME Receipt For All S/MIME-Signed Messages** Select this check box to request a secure receipt for all S/MIME messages by default. You can override the setting for individual messages when you compose them. A secure receipt indicates that your message has been received and the signature verified. No receipt is returned if the signature is not verified.
- **Settings** Click Settings to configure more-advanced security settings and create additional security setting groups. For details, see the following section, "Creating and Using Security Profiles."
- **Publish To GAL** Click this button to publish your certificates to the Global Address List (GAL), making them available to other Exchange Server users in your organization who might need to send you encrypted messages. This is an alternative to sending the other users a copy of your certificate.

Creating and Using Security Profiles

Although in most cases you need only one set of Outlook 2007 security settings, you can create and use multiple security profiles. For example, you might send most of your secure messages to other Exchange Server users and only occasionally send secure messages to Internet recipients. In that situation, you might maintain two sets of security settings: one that uses Exchange Server security and another that uses S/MIME, each with different certificates and hash algorithms (the method used to secure the data).

You can configure security profiles using the Change Security Settings dialog box, which you access through the Settings button on the E-Mail Security page of the Trust

Center dialog box. One of your security profiles acts as the default, but you can select a different security profile any time it's needed.

Follow these steps to create and manage your security profiles:

1. In Outlook 2007, choose Tools, Trust Center, and then click the E-Mail Security page.
2. Click Settings to display the Change Security Settings dialog box, shown in Figure 14-12. Set the options described in the following section as needed. If you are creating a new set of settings, start by clicking New prior to changing settings because selecting New clears all other setting values.

   Security Settings Name Specify the name for the security profile that should appear in the Default Setting drop-down list on the Security tab.

   Cryptographic Format In this drop-down list, select the secure message format for your messages. The default is S/MIME, but you also can select Exchange Server Security. Use S/MIME if you're sending secure messages to Internet recipients. You can use either S/MIME or Exchange Server Security when sending secure messages to recipients on your Exchange Server.

   Default Security Setting For This Cryptographic Message Format Select this check box to make the specified security settings the default settings for the message format you selected in the Cryptography Format drop-down list.

   Default Security Setting For All Cryptographic Messages Select this check box to make the specified security settings the default settings for all secure messages for both S/MIME and Exchange Server security.

   Security Labels Click to configure security labels, which display security information about a specific message and restrict which recipients can open, forward, or send that message. Security labels rely on security policies implemented in Windows 2000 or later.

   New Click to create a new set of security settings.

   Delete Click to delete the currently selected group of security settings.

   Password Click to specify or change the password associated with the security settings.

   Signing Certificate This read-only information indicates the certificate being used to digitally sign your outgoing messages. Click Choose if you want to choose a different certificate. Once you choose a signing certificate, all the fields in the Certificates and Algorithms are automatically populated.

You assign the default signing and encryption certificates through Outlook 2007's global security settings; for information, see the section "Setting Global Security Options" earlier in this chapter.

Hash Algorithm Use this drop-down list to change the hash algorithm used to encrypt messages. Hash algorithm options include MD5, SHA1, SHA256, SHA384, and SHA512. For more information on these hashing algorithms, see the following article:

"The .Net Developers Guide Cryptography Overview" (http://windowssdk.msdn.microsoft.com/en-us/library/92f9ye3s.aspx.)

Encryption Certificate This read-only information indicates the certificate being used to encrypt your outgoing messages. Click Choose if you want to specify a different certificate.

Encryption Algorithm Use this drop-down list to change the encryption algorithm used to encrypt messages. The encryption algorithm is the mathematical method used to encrypt the data.

Send These Certificates With Signed Messages Select this check box to include your certificate with outgoing messages. Doing so allows recipients to send encrypted messages to you.

3. Click OK to close the Change Security Settings dialog box.

Figure 14-12. Configure your security profiles in the Change Security Settings dialog box.

4. In the Default Setting drop-down list on the E-Mail Security page, select the security profile you want to use by default and then click OK.

INSIDE OUT You need a faster way to digitally sign a message

If you don't send a lot of digitally signed messages, you might not mind the steps for getting to the Security Properties dialog box to sign a message you compose. However, if you frequently send digitally signed messages, but don't want to configure Outlook 2007 to sign all messages by default, all the clicking involved in signing the message can be onerous. To digitally sign your messages faster, consider adding a toolbar button that lets you toggle a digital signature with a single click by following these steps:

1. Open the Inbox folder in Outlook 2007.
2. Click New to display the message form for a new message.
3. In the message form, choose the Customize Quick Access Toolbar drop-down list (at the end of the Quick Access Toolbar) and click More Commands.
4. In the Choose Commands From drop-down list, select All Commands.
5. In the All Commands list, shown in Figure 14-13, select Digitally Sign Message and click Add, then OK to close the dialog box. The Digitally Sign Message icon will be added to the end of the Quick Access Toolbar. If you later want to switch security profiles, you can select the profile you want to use in the Default Setting drop-down list on the E-Mail Security page in the Trust Center dialog box.

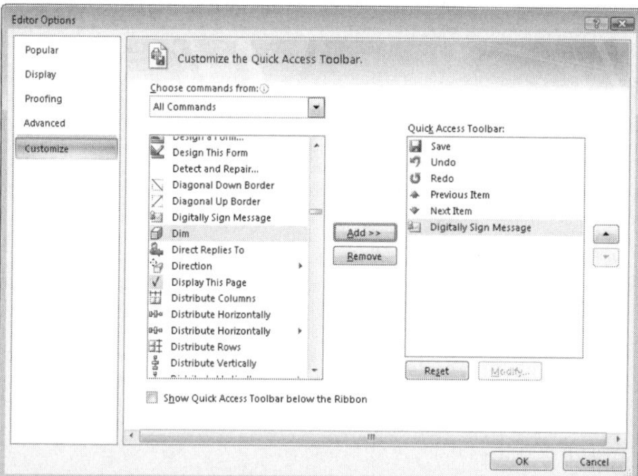

Figure 14-13. Use the Customize The Quick Access Toolbar to add the Digitally Sign Message command to the toolbar.

The Digitally Sign Message and Encrypt icons are also added to the Options group on the Message tab when you add a DigitalID to Outlook 2007. Click Close and then close the message form.

Now whenever you need to digitally sign or encrypt a message, you can click the appropriate button on the Quick Access Toolbar or in the Options group on the Ribbon when you compose the message. Outlook 2007 displays an outline around the button to indicate that the command has been selected, so you can tell at a glance whether the message will be signed, encrypted, or both.

Reading Signed Messages

When you receive a digitally signed message, the Inbox displays a Secure Message icon in place of the standard envelope icon (see Figure 14-14) and shows a Signature button in the Reading Pane. The message form also includes a Signature button (see Figure 14-15). You can click the Signature button in either the Reading Pane or the form to display information about the certificate.

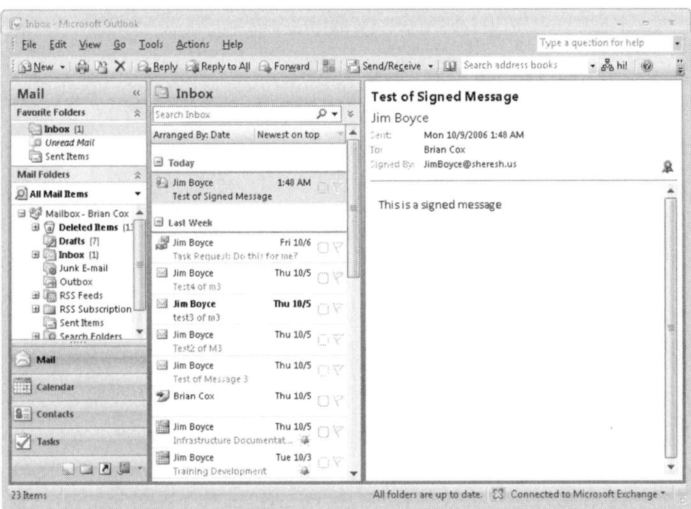

Figure 14-14. Outlook 2007 displays a different icon in the Inbox for secure messages.

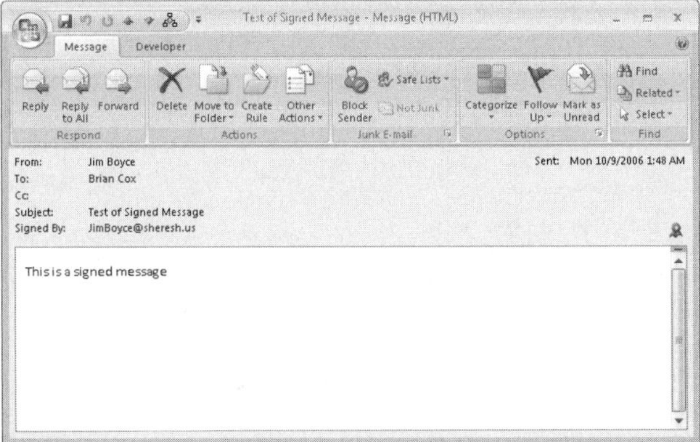

Figure 14-15. Click the Signature button on the message form to view information about the certificate.

Because Outlook 2007 supports S/MIME, you can view and read a digitally signed message without taking any special action. How Outlook 2007 treats the message, however, depends on the trust relationship of the associated certificate. If the certificate is not explicitly distrusted, Outlook 2007 displays the message in the Reading Pane.

If the certificate is explicitly not trusted, you'll see only an error message in the Reading Pane header, as shown in Figure 14-16. When you open the message, you are alerted that there's a problem with the sender's certificate and the text of the message is not displayed. Outlook 2007 displays a dialog box that notes the error when you open the message (see Figure 14-17).

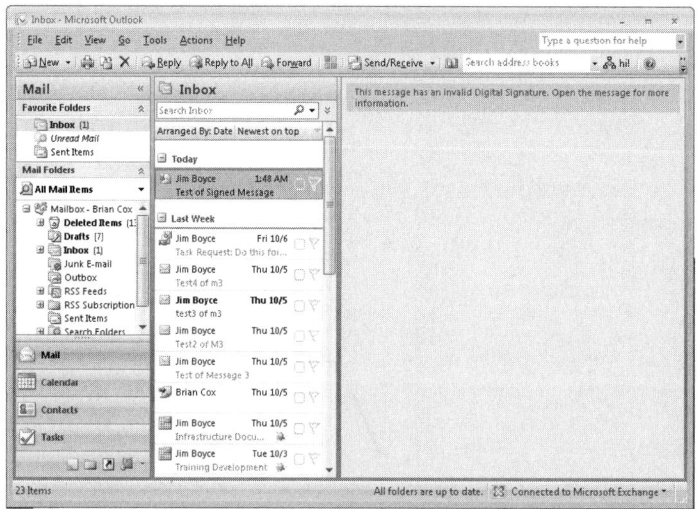

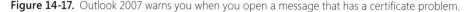

Figure 14-16. Outlook 2007 displays an error message if the digital signature of an incoming message is not trusted.

Figure 14-17. Outlook 2007 warns you when you open a message that has a certificate problem.

There is no danger in opening a message with an invalid certificate. However, you should verify that the message really came from the person listed as the sender and is not a forged message.

Changing Certificate Trust Relationships

To have Outlook 2007 authenticate a signed message and treat it as being from a trusted sender, you must add the certificate to your list of trusted certificates. An alternative is to configure Outlook 2007 to inherit trust for a certificate from the certificate's issuer. For example, assume that you have a CA in your enterprise. Instead of configuring each sender's certificate to be trusted explicitly, you can configure Outlook 2007 to inherit trust from the issuing CA–in other words, Outlook 2007 will implicitly trust all certificates issued by that CA.

Follow these steps to configure the trust relationship for a certificate:

1. In Outlook 2007, select the signed message. If the Reading Pane displays an error message, or if you aren't using the Reading Pane, open the message and click the Secure Message button to view the Message Security Properties dialog box (see Figure 14-18). Otherwise, click the Secure Message button in the Reading Pane.

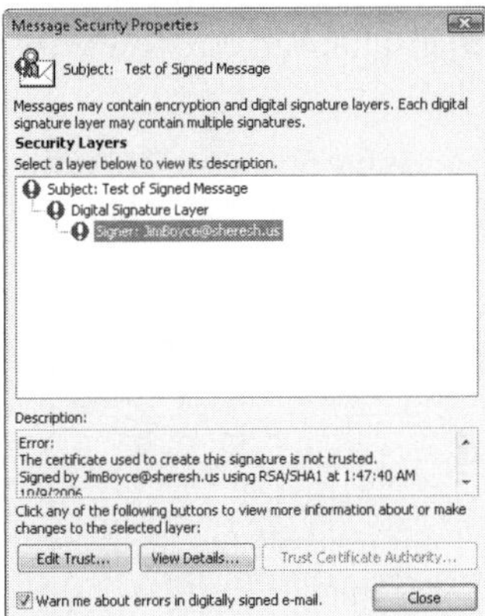

Figure 14-18. Use the Message Security Properties dialog box to view status and properties of the certificate.

2. Click Details, and in the Message Security Properties dialog box, click the Signer line, and then click Edit Trust to display the Trust tab of the View Certificate dialog box, as shown in Figure 14-19.

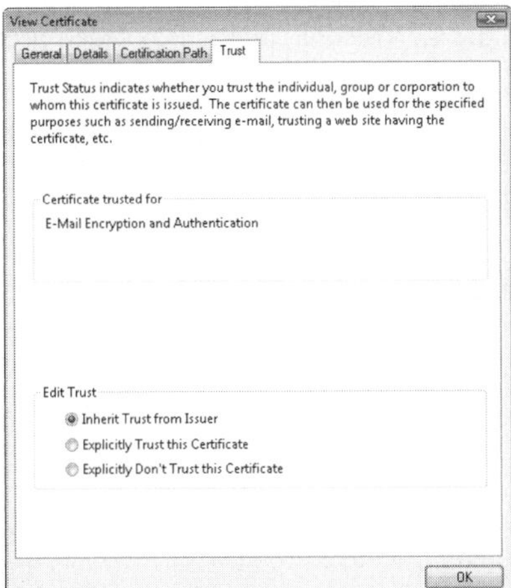

Figure 14-19. Use the Trust tab to configure the trust relationship for the certificate.

3. Select one of the following options:

   Inherit Trust From Issuer Select this option to inherit the trust relationship from the issuing CA. For detailed information, see the following section, "Configuring CA Trust."

   Explicitly Trust This Certificate Select this option to explicitly trust the certificate associated with the message if you are certain of the authenticity of the message and the validity of the sender's certificate.

   Explicitly Don't Trust This Certificate Select this option to explicitly distrust the certificate associated with the message. Any other messages that you receive with the same certificate will generate an error message in Outlook 2007 when you attempt to view them.

4. Click OK, click Close to close the Message Security Properties dialog box, and click Close again to close the Digital Signature dialog box.

For information on viewing a certificate's other properties and configuring Outlook 2007 to validate certificates, see "Viewing and Validating a Digital Signature" later in this chapter.

Configuring CA Trust

Although you might not realize it, your computer system by default includes certificates from several public CAs (typically VeriSign, Thawte, Equifax, GTE, or several others), which were installed when you installed your operating system. By default, Outlook 2007 and other applications trust certificates issued by those CAs without requiring you to obtain and install each CA's certificate.

The easiest way to view these certificates is through Internet Explorer:

1. In Internet Explorer, choose Tools, Internet Options and click the Content tab.
2. Click Certificates to open the Certificates dialog box (see Figure 14-20). Click the Trusted Root Certification Authorities tab, which contains a list of the certificates.

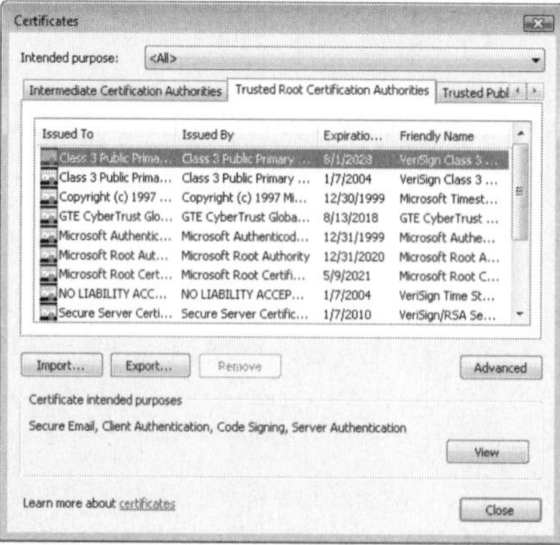

Figure 14-20. You can view a list of certificates in Internet Explorer's Certificates dialog box.

If you have a personal certificate issued by a specific CA, the issuer's certificate is installed on your computer. Messages you receive that are signed with certificates issued by the same CA inherit trust from the issuer without requiring the installation of any additional certificates. If you're working in a large enterprise with several CAs, however, you'll probably receive signed messages containing certificates issued by CAs other than the one that issued your certificate. Thus you might not have the issuing CA's certificate on your system, which prevents Outlook 2007 from trusting the certificate. In this case, you need to add that CA's certificate to your system.

If you need to connect to a Windows-based enterprise CA to obtain the CA's certificate and install it on your system, follow these steps:

1. Point your Web browser to *http://*<machine>*/certsrv*, where <machine> is the name or IP address of the CA.
2. After the page loads, select Download A CA Certificate, Certificate Chain, Or CRL.
3. Select Download CA Certificate, and then choose to Open (at this point you could also Save it to your computer if you want to save the certificate file for later use).
4. Click Install Certificate to install the CA's certificate on your system. This will launch the Certificate Import Wizard. Click Next.
5. In the Certificate Store dialog box, select Automatically Select The Certificate Store Based Upon The Type Of Certificate. Click Next and then click Finish to add the CA certificate. You will be notified that the import was successful and will have to click OK twice to close the dialog boxes.

The procedure just outlined assumes that the CA administrator has not customized the certificate request pages for the CA. If the pages have been customized, the actual process you must follow could be slightly different from the one described here.

> **Note**
>
> If you prefer, you can download the CA certificate instead of installing it through the browser. Use this alternative when you need to install the CA certificate on more than one computer and must have the certificate as a file.

Configuring CA Trust for Multiple Computers

The process described in the preceding section is useful when configuring CA trust for a small number of computers, but it can be impractical with a large number of computers. In these situations, you can turn to group policy to configure CA trust in a wider area such as an organizational unit (OU), a domain, or an entire site.

You can create a certificate trust list (CTL), which is a signed list of root CA certificates that are considered trusted, and deploy that CTL through Group Policy. This solution requires that you be running the Active Directory® directory service with Windows XP, and/or Windows Vista clients as domain members.

Follow these steps to create and deploy the CTL:

1. Log on to a domain controller and open the Active Directory Users And Computers console.
2. Create a new Group Policy Object (GPO) or edit an existing GPO at the necessary container in Active Directory, such as an OU.
3. In the Group Policy Editor, expand the branch User Configuration\Windows Settings\Security Settings\Public Key Policies\Enterprise Trust.
4. Right-click Enterprise Trust and choose New, Certificate Trust List to start the Certificate Trust List Wizard.
5. Click Next, and then specify a name and valid duration for the CTL (both optional), as shown in Figure 14-21. Select one or more purposes for the CTL in the Designate Purposes list (in this example, choose Secure Email), and then click Next.

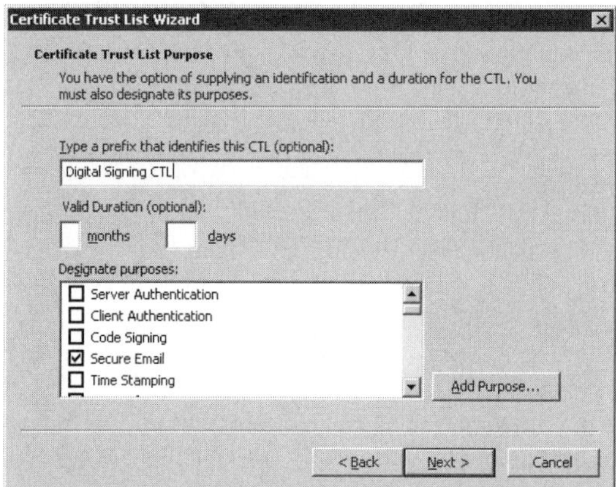

Figure 14-21. Select a purpose for the CTL and other properties, such as a friendly name for easy identification.

6. On the Certificates In The CTL page (see Figure 14-22), click Add From Store to add certificates to the list from the server's certificate store. Choose one or more certificates and click OK.

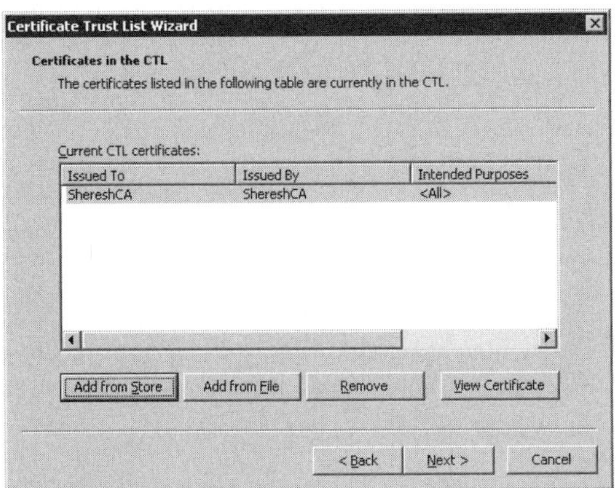

Figure 14-22. Add certificates to the CTL.

7. If the certificates are stored in an X.509 file, Microsoft Serialized Certificate Store, or PKCS #7 certificate file, click Add From File, select the file, and click Open.
8. Back on the Certificates In The CTL page, click Next. On the Signature Certificate page, select a certificate to sign the CTL. The certificate must be stored in the local computer certificate store instead of the user certificate store. Click Next after you select the certificate.
9. You can optionally choose the Add A Timestamp To The Data option and specify a timestamp service URL if one is available. Otherwise, click Next.
10. Optionally, enter a friendly name and description for the CTL to help identify it, click Next, and click Finish.

Viewing and Validating a Digital Signature

You can view the certificate associated with a signed message to obtain information about the issuer, the person to whom the certificate is issued, and other matters.

To do so, follow these steps:

1. Open the message and click the Signature button in either the Reading Pane or the message form; then click Details to display the Message Security Properties dialog box, which provides information about the certificate's validity in the Description box.
2. Click Signer in the list to view additional signature information in the Description box, such as when the message was signed (see Figure 14-23).

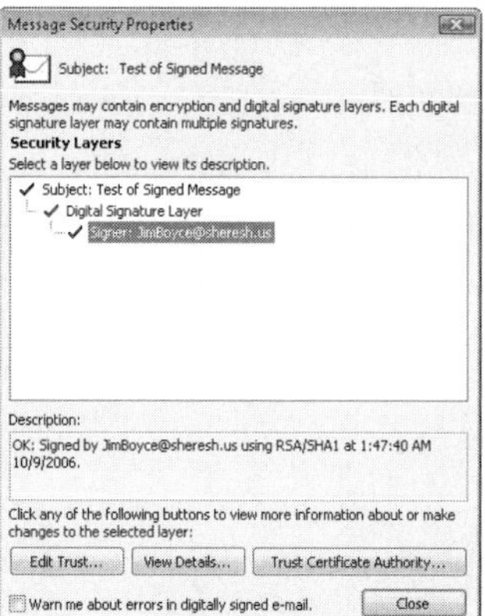

Figure 14-23. The Description box offers information about the validity of the certificate.

3. Click View Details to open the Signature dialog box, shown in Figure 14-24, which displays even more detail about the signature.

Figure 14-24. Use the Signature dialog box to view additional properties of the signature and to access the certificate.

4. On the General tab of the Signature dialog box, click View Certificate to display information about the certificate, including issuer, certification path, and trust mode.

5. Click OK, click Close to close the Message Security Properties dialog box, and click Close again to close the Digital Signature dialog box.

The CA uses a certificate revocation list (CRL) to indicate the validity of certificates. If you don't have a current CRL on your system, Outlook 2007 can treat the certificate as trusted, but can't validate the certificate and will indicate this when you view the signature.

You can locate the path to the CRL by examining the certificate's properties as follows:

1. Click the Signature button for the message, either in the Reading Pane or in the message form, and then click Details..
2. In the Message Security Properties dialog box, click Signer and then click View Details.
3. On the General tab of the Signature dialog box, click View Certificate and then click the Details tab (see Figure 14-25).

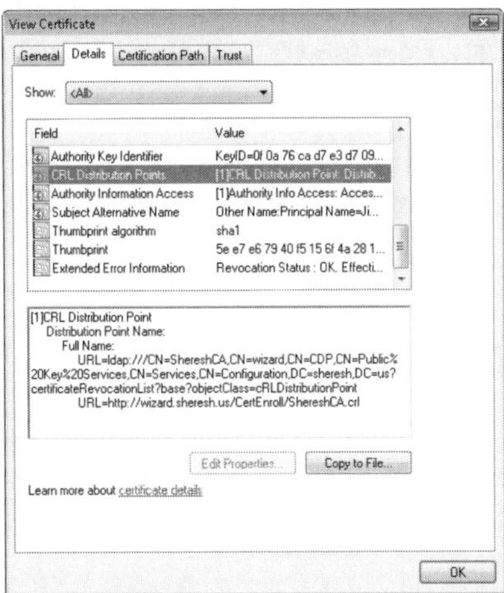

Figure 14-25. Use the Details tab to view the CRL path for the certificate.

4. Scroll through the list to find and select CRL Distribution Points.
5. Scroll through the list in the lower half of the dialog box to locate the URL for the CRL.

When you know the URL for the CRL, you can point your browser to the site to download and install the CRL. If a CA in your enterprise issued the certificate, you can obtain the CRL from the CA.

To obtain and install the CRL, follow these steps:

1. Point your browser to *http://*<machine>*/certsrv*, where <machine> is the name or IP address of the server.
2. Select the Retrieve The CA Certificate Or Certificate Revocation List option and click Next.
3. Click Download Latest Certificate Revocation List and save the file to disk.
4. After downloading the file, locate and right-click the file, and then choose Install CRL to install the current list.

Encrypting Messages

You can encrypt messages to prevent them from being read by unauthorized persons. It is, of course, true that with significant amounts of computing power and time any encryption scheme can probably be broken. However, the chances of someone investing those resources in your e-mail are pretty remote. So you can be assured that the e-mail encryption Outlook 2007 provides offers a relatively safe means of protecting sensitive messages against interception.

Before you can encrypt messages, you must have a certificate for that purpose installed on your computer. Typically, certificates issued for digital signing can also be used for encrypting e-mail messages.

For detailed information on obtaining a personal certificate from a commercial CA or from an enterprise or stand-alone CA on your network, see "Obtaining a Digital Certificate," earlier in this chapter.

Getting Ready for Encryption

After you've obtained a certificate and installed it on your system, encrypting messages is a simple task. Getting to that point, however, depends in part on whether you're sending messages to an Exchange Server recipient on your network or to an Internet recipient.

Swapping Certificates

Before you can send an encrypted message to an Internet recipient, you must have a copy of the recipient's public key certificate. To read the message, the recipient must have a copy of your public key certificate, which means you first need to swap public certificates.

> **Note**
>
> When you are sending encrypted messages to an Exchange Server recipient, you don't need to swap certificates. Exchange Server takes care of the problem for you.

The easiest way to swap certificates is to send a digitally signed message to the recipient and have the recipient send you a signed message in return, as outlined here:

1. In Outlook 2007, choose Tools, Trust Center, and then click the E-Mail Security page.
2. Click Settings to display the Change Security Settings dialog box.

3. Verify that you've selected S/MIME in the Cryptography Format drop-down list.
4. Select the Send These Certificates With Signed Messages option and click OK.
5. Click OK to close the Trust Center dialog box.
6. Compose the message and digitally sign it. Outlook 2007 will include the certificates with the message.

When you receive a signed message from someone with whom you're exchanging certificates, you must add the person to your Contacts folder to add the certificate by following these steps:

1. Open the message, right-click the sender's name, and then choose Add To Outlook Contacts. If the Reading Pane is displayed, you can right-click the sender's name in the pane and choose Add To Outlook Contacts.
2. Outlook 2007 displays the Contact tab of the contact form (see Figure 14-26). Fill in additional information for the contact as needed.

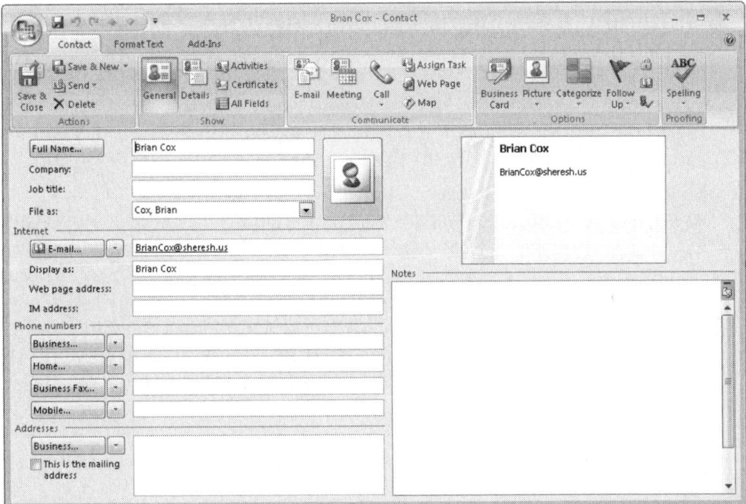

Figure 14-26. Use the contact form to add the sender's certificate to your system.

3. Click the Certificates button (in the Show group). You should see the sender's certificate listed (see Figure 14-27), and you can view the certificate's properties by selecting it and clicking Properties. If no certificate is listed, contact the sender and ask for another digitally signed message.

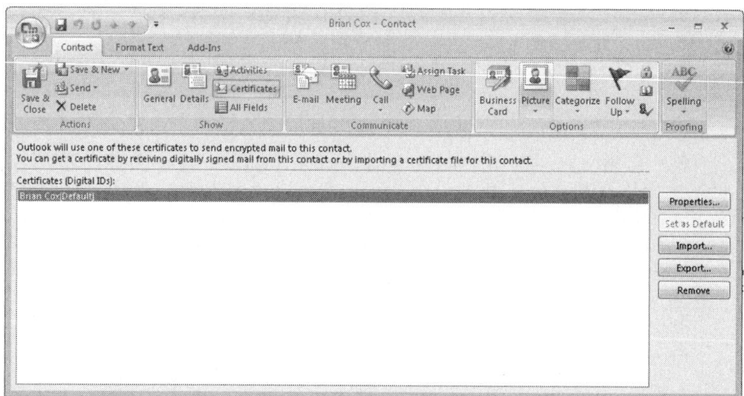

Figure 14-27. The Certificates button on the contact form displays the sender's certificate.

4. Click Save & Close to save the contact item and the certificate.

Obtaining a Recipient's Public Key from a Public CA

As an alternative to receiving a signed message with a certificate from another person, you might be able to obtain the person's certificate from the issuing CA. For example, if you know that the person has a certificate from VeriSign, you can download that individual's public key from the VeriSign Web site. Other public CAs offer similar services. To search for and download public keys from VeriSign (see Figure 14-28), connect to *https://digitalid.verisign.com/services/client/index.html*. Check the sites of other public CAs for similar links that enable you to download public keys from their servers.

The process for downloading a public key varies by CA. In general, however, you enter the person's e-mail address in a form to locate the certificate, and the form provides instructions for downloading the certificate. You should have no trouble obtaining the public key after you locate the certificate on the CA (there is a link to download the public key certificate from the CA to a file on your computer).

Save the public key to disk, and then follow these steps to install the key:

1. Open the Contacts folder in Outlook 2007.
2. Locate the contact for whom you downloaded the public key.
3. Open the contact item, and then click the Certificates button.
4. Click Import. Browse to and select the certificate file obtained from the CA and click Open.
5. Click Save & Close to save the contact changes.

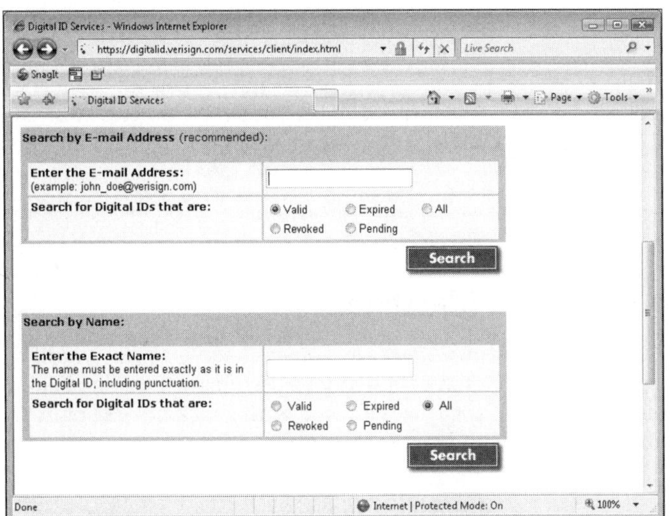

Figure 14-28. VeriSign, like other public CAs, provides a form you can use to search for and obtain public keys for certificate subscribers.

Sending Encrypted Messages

When you have everything set up for sending and receiving encrypted messages, it's a simple matter to send one:

1. Open Outlook 2007 and compose the message.
2. In the message form, click the Encrypt icon in the Options group (on the Message tab).

Alternatively, do the following:

1. On the Message tab, click the Message Options Dialog Box Launcher in the Options group that displays the Message Options dialog box, and then click Security Settings.
2. Select Encrypt Message Contents And Attachments, and then click OK.
3. Click Close, and then send the message as you normally would.
4. If the message is protected by Exchange Server security, you can send it in one of three ways, depending on your system's security level:
   - If the security level is set to Medium (the default), Outlook 2007 displays a message informing you of your security setting. Click OK to send the message.
   - If the security level is set to Low, Outlook 2007 sends the message immediately, without any special action on your part.
   - If the security level is set to High, type your password to send the message.

> **Note**
>
> To make it easier to encrypt a message, you can add the Encrypt command to the Quick Access Toolbar in the message form. For details about the process involved in doing this, see the Troubleshooting sidebar "You need a faster way to digitally sign a message," earlier in this chapter.

Reading Encrypted Messages

When you receive an encrypted message, you can read it as you would read any other message, assuming that you have the sender's certificate. Double-click the message to open it. Note that Outlook 2007 uses an icon with a lock instead of the standard envelope icon to identify encrypted messages.

> **Note**
>
> You can't preview encrypted messages in the Reading Pane. Also, the ability to read encrypted messages requires an S/MIME-capable mail client. Keep this in mind when sending encrypted messages to other users who might not have Outlook 2007 or another S/MIME-capable client.
>
> You can verify and modify the trust for a certificate when you read a message signed by that certificate. For information on viewing and changing the trust for a certificate, see the section "Changing Certificate Trust Relationships" earlier in this chapter.

Importing Certificates from Outlook Express

If you have used Microsoft Windows Mail or Microsoft Outlook Express to send and receive secure messages, your Windows Mail Contacts (or Outlook Express address book) contains the public keys of the recipients. You can import those certificates to use in Outlook 2007 if they are not already included in the Contacts folder. Unfortunately, Windows Mail/Outlook Express doesn't export the certificates when you export its address book; instead, you must export the certificates one at a time.

Follow these steps to move certificates from Windows Mail or Outlook Express to Outlook 2007:

1. Open Windows Mail and select Tools, Windows Contacts (or, if using Outlook Express, choose Tools, Address Book).

2. In Windows Contacts (for Windows Mail) or the Address book (for Outlook Express), double-click the name of the person whose certificate you want to export.
3. Click the IDs tab in Windows Mail (or the Digital IDs tab in Outlook Express).
4. Select the certificate to export and click Export.
5. Save the certificate to a file. (Windows Mail and Outlook Express use the CER file extension.)
6. Open Outlook 2007, open the Contacts folder, and open the contact item for the person who owns the certificate you're importing.
7. Click the Certificates button, click Import, select the file created in step 5, and click Open.
8. Save and close the contact form.

Protecting Data with Information Rights Management

In response to market demands for a system with which companies can protect proprietary and sensitive information, Microsoft has developed an umbrella of technologies called Information Rights Management (IRM). Outlook 2007 incorporates IRM, enabling you to send messages that prevent the recipient from forwarding, copying from, or printing the message. The recipient can view the message, but the features for accomplishing these other tasks are unavailable.

> **Note**
>
> IRM is an extension for the Microsoft Office system applications of Windows Rights Management. For information on using IRM with other Office applications, see *2007 Microsoft Office System Inside Out*, from Microsoft Press.

There are two paths to implementing IRM with the Microsoft Office system. Microsoft offers an IRM service that, as of this writing, is free. This path requires that you have a Microsoft Passport to send or view IRM-protected messages. You must log in to the service with your Passport credentials to download a certificate, which Outlook 2007 uses to verify your identity and enable the IRM features. The second path is to install Microsoft Windows Server 2003 running the Rights Management Service (RMS) on Windows Server 2003. With this path, users authenticate on the server with NTLM or Passport authentication and download their IRM certificates.

The first path provides simplicity because it does not require that organizations deploy an RMS server. The second path provides more flexibility because the RMS administrator can configure company-specific IRM policies, which are then available to users. For example, you might create a policy template requiring that only users within the company domain can open all e-mail messages protected by the policy. You can create any number of templates to suit the company's data rights needs for the range of Microsoft Office system applications and document types.

Not everyone who receives an IRM-protected message will be running Outlook 2003 or Outlook 2007, so Microsoft has developed the Rights Management Add-On for Internet Explorer, which enables these users to view the messages in Internet Explorer. Without this add-on, recipients cannot view IRM-protected messages. With the add-on, recipients can view the messages, but the capability to forward, copy, or print the message is disabled, just as it is in Outlook 2007.

This chapter explains how to configure and use IRM in Outlook 2007 with the Microsoft IRM service. As of this writing, Windows Rights Management Services is available for Windows Server 2003 by download (currently as a Service Pack 2 release). Check *www.boyce.us* and *www.microsoft.com/windowsserver2003/technologies/rightsmgmt/default.mspx* periodically for additional information on RMS as it becomes available.

Using Microsoft's IRM Service

To configure Outlook 2007 to use the IRM service and send IRM-protected messages, follow these steps:

1. Open Outlook 2007 and start a new message. With the message form open, choose Microsoft Office Button, Permission, Do Not Forward.
2. If you do not have the IRM add-on installed, Outlook 2007 displays the dialog box shown in Figure 14-29. Choose Yes, I Want To Sign Up For This Free Trial Service From Microsoft and click Next.

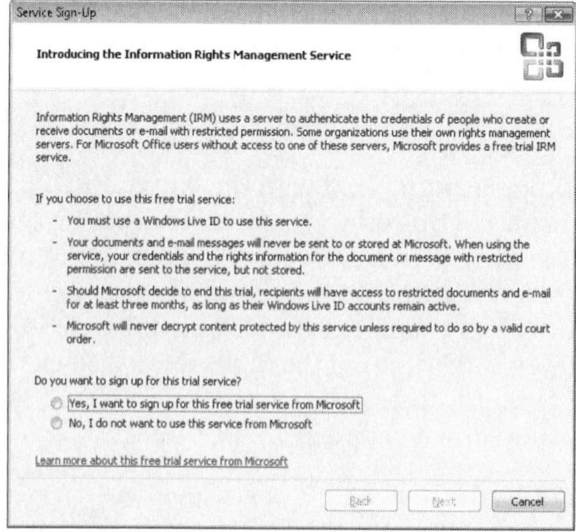

Figure 14-29. Choose Yes and click Next to start the enrollment process.

3. The wizard asks if you already have a Microsoft Passport. If so, choose Yes and click Next to open a sign-in dialog box and enter your Passport credentials. If not, choose No and click Next; then follow the prompts to obtain a Microsoft Passport.

4. After you obtain a Passport and click Next, Outlook 2007 displays the page shown in Figure 14-30. Choose Standard to obtain a certificate that you can use on your own computer. Choose Temporary if you need a certificate only for a limited time, such as when you are working from a public computer. Then click Next, Finish to complete the process.

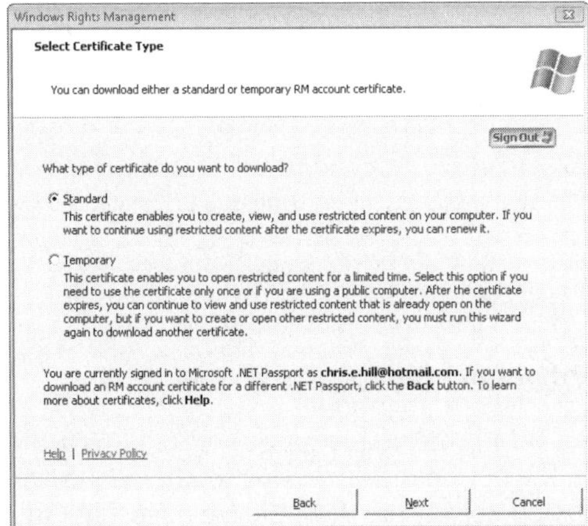

Figure 14-30. You can choose between a standard certificate and a temporary one.

> **Note**
>
> You can download a certificate for a given Passport 25 times or to 25 computers.

5. After the IRM certificate is installed on your computer, Outlook 2007 returns you to the message form. The InfoBar in the form displays a Do Not Forward message, as shown in Figure 14-31, indicating that the message is protected by IRM.

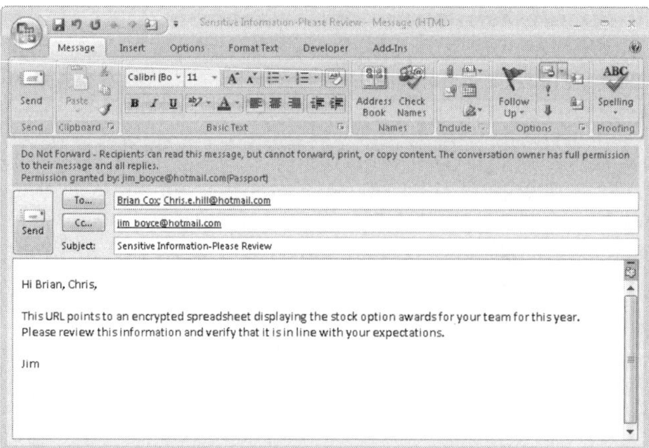

Figure 14-31. The InfoBar indicates when a message is protected by IRM.

6. Address the message and add the message body and attachments, if any, as you would for any other message. Then send the message.

Viewing IRM-Protected Messages

If you attempt to view an IRM-protected message without first obtaining a certificate, Outlook 2007 gives you the option of connecting to Microsoft's service to obtain one. After the certificate is installed, you can view the message, but Outlook 2007 indicates in the InfoBar (both Reading Pane and message form) that the message is restricted (see Figure 14-32). The commands for forwarding, copying, and printing the message are disabled.

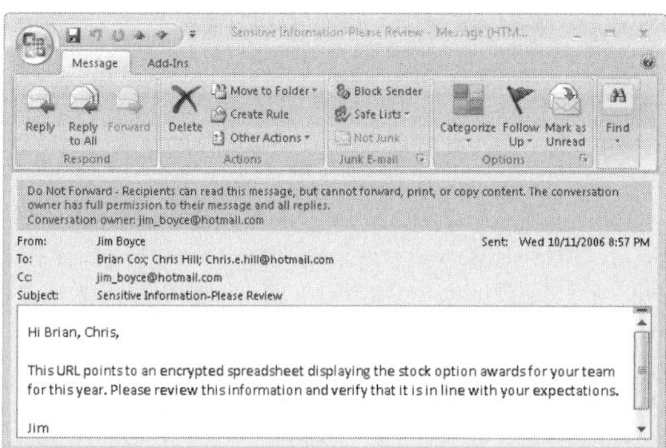

Figure 14-32. The InfoBar in the Reading Pane indicates that a message is restricted.

Working with Multiple Accounts

It's possible that you use more than one Microsoft Passport. If you have more than one Passport and need to choose between them when you send or view an IRM-protected message, open the message form for sending or viewing and choose Microsoft Office Button, Permission, Manage Credentials to open the Select User dialog box, as shown in Figure 14-33. Choose an account and click OK to use that account for the current message.

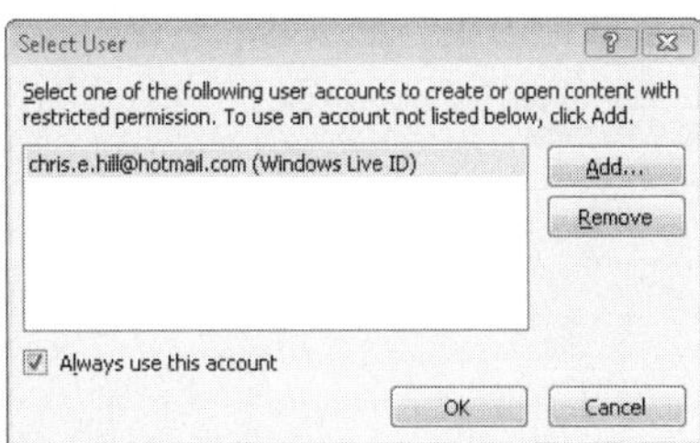

Figure 14-33. You can select from multiple accounts to restrict messages or view restricted messages.

If you have only one account configured on the computer and want to add another account, click Add to start the Service Sign-Up Wizard and download a certificate for another e-mail address and corresponding Microsoft Passport.

CHAPTER 15

Receiving Messages Selectively

Like earlier versions of Microsoft® Outlook®, Microsoft Office Outlook 2007 includes a feature called *remote mail* that allows you to manage your e-mail messages without downloading them from the server. Although you might not believe that you need yet another way to retrieve your messages, remote mail offers advantages that you'll come to appreciate over time.

Originally, remote mail was primarily a feature for Microsoft Exchange Server, but other e-mail accounts can take advantage of similar capabilities (which, for the sake of simplicity, this chapter refers to generically as *remote mail*). For example, with Post Office Protocol 3 (POP3), Internet Message Access Protocol (IMAP), and Hypertext Transfer Protocol (HTTP) accounts, you can download just message headers to review your messages before downloading the message bodies and attachments. The process is similar for all these types of accounts, although POP3 and Exchange Server accounts offer additional options.

This chapter focuses specifically on using remote mail for non–Exchange Server accounts. It explains how to set up your system to use remote mail for IMAP, HTTP, and POP3 accounts; how to manage your messages through remote mail; and how to use alternatives to remote mail, such as send/receive groups.

For detailed information about configuring and using the remote mail feature for Exchange Server accounts, see "Using Remote Mail" in Chapter 43.

Understanding Remote Mail Options

The primary advantage of using remote mail is the ability to work with message headers of waiting messages without downloading the messages themselves. You can simply connect to the e-mail server, download the headers for new messages, and disconnect. You can then take your time reviewing the message headers to decide which messages to download, which ones to delete without reading, and which ones to leave on the server to handle later. After you've made your decisions and marked the headers accordingly, you can connect again and download those messages you've marked to retrieve, either leaving the others on the server or deleting them.

Remote mail is extremely useful when you're pressed for time but have a message with a large attachment waiting on the server. You might want to retrieve only your most critical messages without spending the time or connect charges to download that message and its attachment. To accomplish this, you can connect with remote mail and select the messages you want to download, leaving the one with the large attachment on the server until a less busy time when you can download it across the network or through a broadband Internet connection.

Remote mail is also useful when you discover a corrupt message in your mailbox, a message with a very large attachment, or a message that you suspect could be infected with a virus, and the message might otherwise prevent Outlook 2007 from downloading your messages. You can connect with remote mail, delete the offending message without downloading it, and then continue working normally.

> **Note**
>
> With the exception of Microsoft Hotmail® accounts, which require a paid account for POP3 access, remote mail works only for the Inbox; you can't use it to synchronize other folders. With a Hotmail account, you can download headers for the Inbox, Deleted Items, Junk Mail, and Sent Items folders.

Remote Mail in a Nutshell

Outlook 2007 offers remote mail for several types of accounts, with differing capabilities. All of the following accounts allow you to download and mark message headers without downloading the messages themselves:

- **Exchange Server** By marking the message headers, you can indicate which messages to download and which to delete from the server. In addition, you can specify conditions that determine which messages are downloaded–for example, those with particular subjects, those from certain senders, those smaller than a specified size, or those without attachments. You can mark messages offline.

See "Using Remote Mail" in Chapter 43 to learn more about remote mail features for Exchange Server accounts.

- **POP3** By marking the message headers, you can indicate which messages should be moved from the server to your system, which messages should be downloaded with a copy left on the server, and which messages should be deleted from the server without being downloaded. You also can specify a size limit and download only messages that are smaller than the specified size; for messages that exceed the size limit, you can download headers only. You can mark messages offline.
- **IMAP and HTTP** By marking the message headers, you can indicate which messages to download and which to delete from the server. Both types of accounts

store mail on the server, so marking to download a copy isn't relevant (as it is for a POP3 account), because a copy of the message stays on the server anyway. With an HTTP account, you must be online to mark message headers for deletion; IMAP accounts allow you to mark for deletion while offline. You don't have any special options for selective or conditional processing with either type of account.

Using Remote Mail with Hotmail

Remote mail is a good choice for managing your POP3, IMAP, or Exchange Server mailbox remotely. With Hotmail accounts, remote mail doesn't offer any real advantage because Hotmail accounts download the headers without the full messages anyway; the message bodies are downloaded only when you view the messages. However, you can't delete messages from Hotmail without being online, although you can delete unread messages without downloading them as long as you don't have the Reading Pane turned on. You also can connect through your Web browser to Hotmail to delete messages without downloading them.

Setting Up for Remote Mail

Non-Exchange Server accounts generally deliver messages to a personal folders (.pst) file, although you can configure POP3 accounts to download messages from the POP3 server and place them in your Exchange Server Inbox. If your POP3 account delivers mail to your Exchange Server mailbox, you can use remote mail with the account as long as you're connected to the Exchange Server while you're using remote mail on the POP3 account. For example, assume that you connect over the local area network (LAN) to the Exchange Server but connect to a POP3 account by modem. In that scenario, you'd be able to use remote mail through the Exchange Server for the POP3 account.

In another scenario, assume that you dial into your LAN to work with your Exchange Server account, and the remote access server also provides connectivity to the Internet. Your POP3 account delivers mail to your Exchange Server mailbox. In this case, you can use remote mail for both accounts because you have access to your mail store. The key is that to use remote mail, you must have access to your mail store so that Outlook 2007 has a place to deliver the downloaded message headers.

If you don't use Exchange Server, you don't need to do anything special to configure your system to use remote mail. Because your mail store is local, you have access to it all the time (unless the server at your ISP is down or offline).

To use remote mail, you need a connection to the remote server. Generally, this takes the form of a dial-up connection, either to the server's network or to the Internet. If you haven't already done so, you'll need to set up a dial-up connection to the appropriate point.

Working with Message Headers

The following sections explain the specific steps to follow as you perform various tasks with message headers through remote mail. You'll learn how to download the headers, how to selectively mark them, and how to process them.

Downloading Message Headers

When you want to process messages selectively, you first download the message headers and then decide what action you want to perform with each message, based on its header. Downloading message headers for an account is easy. In Outlook 2007, choose Tools, Send/Receive, <Account> Only, Download Inbox Headers, where <Account> is the name of the account whose headers you want to process.

After you choose the Download Inbox Headers command, Outlook 2007 performs a send/receive operation but downloads only message headers from the specified account. If you want to save on connect charges, you can then disconnect from the server to review the headers and decide what to do with each message.

Outlook 2007 displays the downloaded message headers in the Inbox. Outlook 2007 displays an icon in the Header Status column to indicate that the message has not yet been downloaded, as shown in Figure 15-1. A message header that has not been marked for download shows a sheet of paper with the corner folded over. A message marked for download shows the same icon but with an arrow at the bottom.

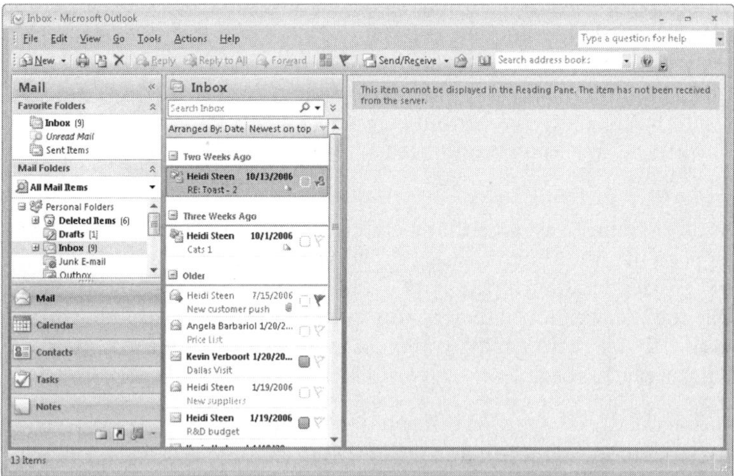

Figure 15-1. Outlook 2007 places an icon in the Header Status column to indicate that the message itself has yet to be downloaded.

Marking and Unmarking Message Headers

After you download the headers, you can decide what to do with each message: retrieve it, download a copy, or delete it.

Marking to Retrieve a Message

With a POP3 account, you can mark a message header to have Outlook 2007 retrieve the message, remove it from the server, and store it in your local store. With IMAP or HTTP mail accounts, you can mark a message header to have Outlook 2007 download the message, but those accounts continue to store the message on the server until you delete it.

To mark a message to be downloaded from the server to your local store, select the message header, right-click it, and choose Mark To Download Message(s). Alternatively, you can choose Tools, Send/Receive, Mark To Download Message(s).

> **Note**
>
> To select multiple message headers quickly, hold down the Ctrl or Shift key while you click the message headers.

Marking to Retrieve a Copy

In some cases, you might want to download a copy of a message but also leave the message on the server—for example, you might need to retrieve the same message from a different computer. To mark a message header to have Outlook 2007 retrieve a copy, select the message header, right-click it, and choose Mark To Download Message Copy. Alternatively, you can select the message header and choose Tools, Send/Receive, Mark To Download Message Copy. Outlook 2007 indicates in the Header Status column of the Inbox that the message is marked for download by changing the message icon accordingly, as shown in Figure 15-2.

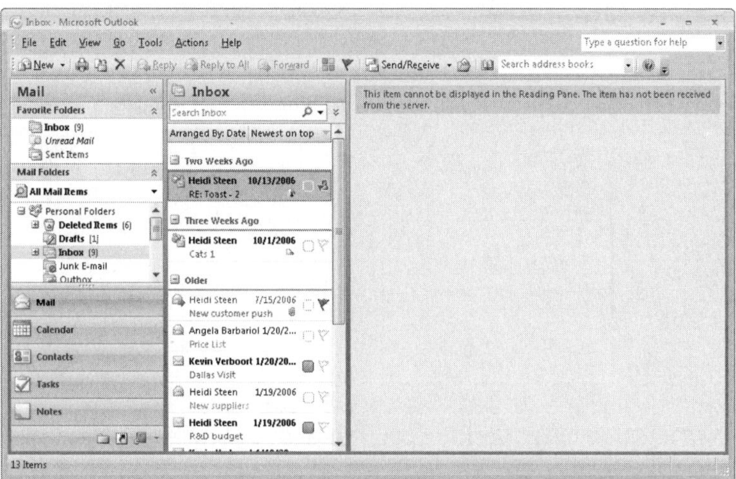

Figure 15-2. This message is marked to have Outlook 2007 retrieve a copy.

> **Note**
>
> As explained earlier, it isn't necessary to download a copy from an IMAP or HTTP server, as those servers continue to store a copy of the message on the server. Downloading a copy is applicable only to POP3.

> **Note**
>
> So that you can easily identify the pending action, Outlook 2007 displays different icons in the Header Status column of the Inbox for messages marked to download and messages marked to download a copy.

Marking to Delete a Message

You also can mark messages to be deleted from the server without downloading. You might do this for junk mail or messages with large attachments that you don't need and don't want choking your download session.

To mark a message for deletion, select the message header, right-click it, and choose Delete or press the **Delete** key. Outlook 2007 strikes through the message header and changes the download icon to indicate that the message will be deleted the next time you process messages, as shown in Figure 15-3.

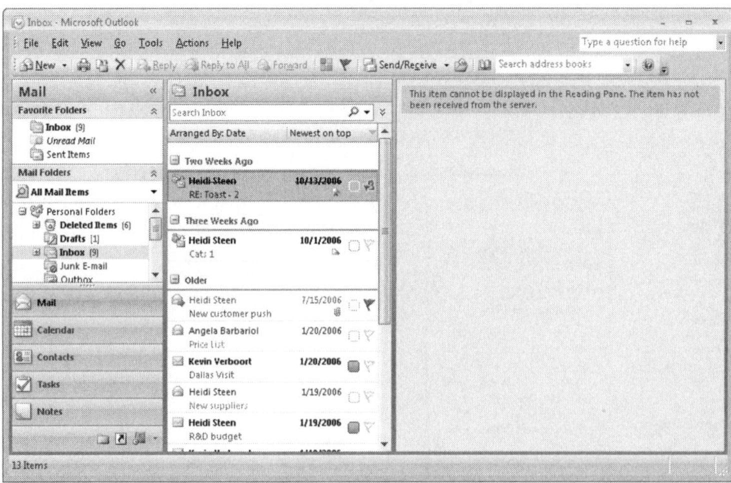

Figure 15-3. Strikethrough indicates that the message will be deleted without downloading.

Unmarking a Message

As you work with message headers, you'll occasionally change your mind after you've marked a message. In that case, you can unmark the message. Select the message header, right-click it, and then choose Unmark Selected Headers. Alternatively, you can choose Tools, Send/Receive, Unmark Selected Headers.

You also can unmark all message headers, clearing all pending actions. To do so, choose Tools, Send/Receive, Unmark All Messages.

Processing Marked Headers

After you've reviewed and marked the message headers, you can process the messages to apply the actions you've chosen. When you do so, for example, messages marked for download are downloaded to your system, and messages marked for deletion are deleted from the server.

To process all marked messages, choose Tools, Send/Receive, Process All Marked Headers. You can also choose Process Marked Headers In This Folder to process only the current folder or choose Tools, Send/Receive, Account Only, Process Marked Headers to process only a specific account. After you choose a command, Outlook 2007 connects and performs the specified actions, as shown in Figure 15-4.

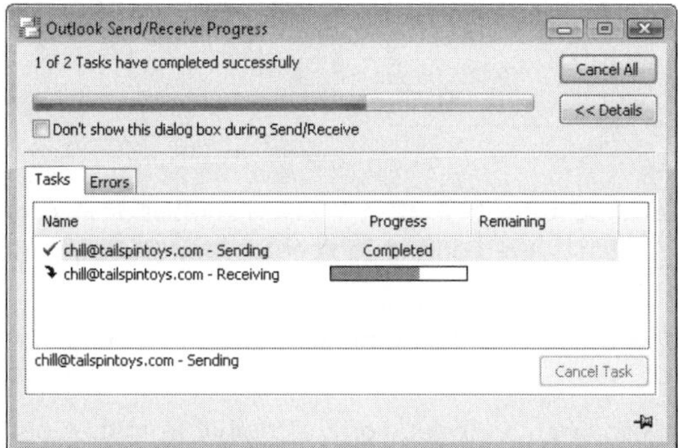

Figure 15-4. Outlook 2007 displays this dialog box to indicate progress status for remote mail, as it does for other send/receive operations.

TROUBLESHOOTING

You can't find the remote mail commands

As you work with remote mail, you'll probably wish for an easier, faster way to access the remote mail commands. These commands are buried on the Tools menu, making it difficult to locate them quickly. Outlook 2007 also doesn't provide a toolbar for remote mail commands. Fortunately, you can create your own toolbar if you find remote mail useful.

Follow these steps to create your own toolbar for remote mail:

1. In Outlook 2007, choose View, Toolbars, Customize (or right-click a toolbar and then choose Customize) to open the Customize dialog box. Click the Toolbars tab, shown in Figure 15-5.

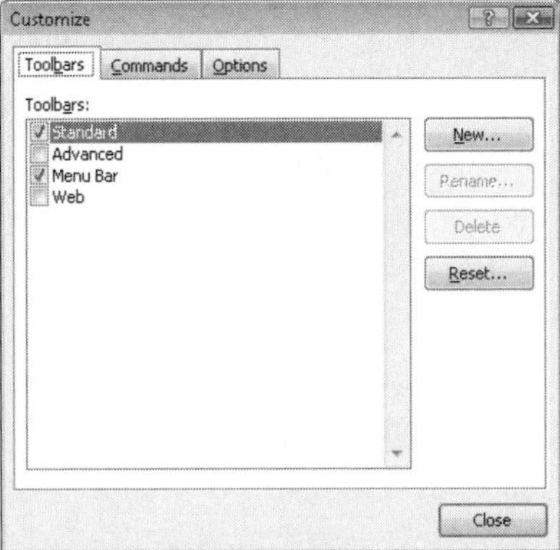

Figure 15-5. Use the Toolbars tab to create your own toolbar for remote mail.

2. Click New. Type the name **Remote Mail** in the New Toolbar dialog box, and then click OK. The new toolbar is listed on the Toolbar tab, and Outlook 2007 opens an empty toolbar.
3. In the Customize dialog box, click the Commands tab, and then in the Categories list, select Tools.
4. Drag the commands you want to include on the toolbar from the Commands list to the new toolbar. At a minimum, the following commands are useful:
   - Download Headers In This Folder
   - Mark To Download Message(s)
   - Mark To Download Message Copy
   - Delete (located in the Edit Categories list)
   - Unmark Selected Headers
   - Unmark All Headers
   - Process All Marked Headers
   - Process Marked Headers In This Folder

Chapter 15

Selective Downloading for POP3 Using Send/Receive Groups

Using send/receive groups in Outlook 2007 gives you additional options for selective message processing with POP3 accounts. You can configure a POP3 account in a send/receive group to download only headers, for example, or to download only those messages smaller than a specified size while retrieving only headers for larger messages. If you prefer to process your POP3 account selectively—perhaps because you connect over a dial-up connection, or because you want to delete unwanted messages before they arrive in your Inbox, or because you need to control which messages are downloaded—you can use a send/receive group to process the account.

For details on setting up send/receive groups, see "Controlling Synchronization and Send/Receive Times" in Chapter 8.

Let's assume that your profile includes two POP3 accounts, a Hotmail account, and an Exchange Server account. You want to process messages normally for the Hotmail and Exchange Server accounts but would like to process the POP3 accounts selectively. You can configure a send/receive group (either the default All Accounts group or another that you create) to perform a send/receive operation for the other accounts that processes all messages. You can also configure the POP3 accounts in the send/receive group to download only message headers. When you perform a send/receive operation with the group, the POP3 accounts download only headers, and the other accounts download messages.

> **Note**
>
> You can't use send/receive groups for selective processing with Hotmail and HTTP accounts.

You can configure multiple send/receive groups, using different settings for each (although some settings, such as Exchange Server filters, apply to all send/receive groups to which the folder belongs). For example, you might configure your POP3 accounts in the All Accounts send/receive group to download message bodies and attachments but create a second send/receive group named POP3 Remote that processes only message headers for your POP3 accounts when that group is executed.

Retrieving Only Message Headers

After you decide which combination of send/receive groups makes the most sense for you, follow these steps to configure a POP3 account to retrieve only message headers and then process the headers:

1. In Outlook 2007, choose Tools, Send/Receive, Send/Receive Settings, Define Send/Receive Groups.
2. Select the existing send/receive group in which you want to configure POP3 accounts for headers only (or create a group for that purpose), and then click Edit.
3. In the Accounts list in the Send/Receive Settings dialog box, shown in Figure 15-6, click the POP3 account.

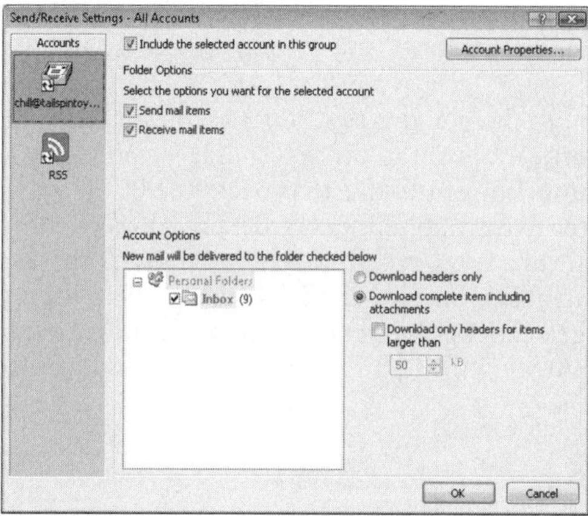

Figure 15-6. You can configure a POP3 account to download only headers.

4. If you are creating a new group, select the Include The Selected Account In This Group check box.
5. Select the Download Headers Only option.
6. If you don't want the group to send messages from the selected POP3 account, clear the Send Mail Items check box.
7. Click OK, and then close the Send/Receive Groups dialog box.
8. Choose Tools, Send/Receive, and select the group to have Outlook 2007 process it according to the settings you specified in the preceding steps. Outlook 2007 then downloads message headers.
9. Review and mark the downloaded message headers, and then process the group again. Alternatively, choose Tools, Send/Receive, Process All Marked Headers.

Retrieving Based on Message Size

You can configure a POP3 account in a send/receive group to specify a message size limit. Messages that meet or are below the specified size limit are downloaded in their entirety, complete with attachments. For messages larger than the specified size, only headers are downloaded. This is an easy way to restrict the volume of incoming POP3 mail and keep large messages from choking a low-bandwidth connection such as a dial-up connection.

Follow these steps to configure a POP3 account in a send/receive group to download headers only for messages over a specified size:

1. In Outlook 2007, choose Tools, Send/Receive, Send/Receive Settings, Define Send/Receive Groups.
2. Select or create the send/receive group, and then click Edit.
3. Select the POP3 account in the Accounts list in the Send/Receive Settings dialog box, and then select the Download Complete Item Including Attachments option.
4. Select Download Only Headers For Items Larger Than *n* KB, as shown in Figure 15-7.

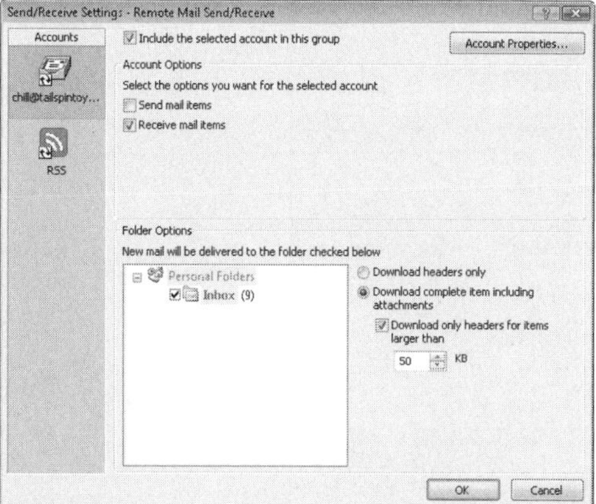

Figure 15-7. You can specify a message size limit to control connect time and mail volume.

5. Enter a value to define the message size limit, and then click OK.
6. Click Close to close the Send/Receive Groups dialog box.

Keeping Messages on the Server

Often you'll want to keep a copy of your messages on the server and download a copy. For example, you might be checking your messages from the office but want to be able to retrieve them from home or from your notebook computer. Or perhaps you're using remote mail to process a few important messages and want to leave copies on the server for safekeeping. You can configure the account to leave a copy of all messages on the server, allowing you to retrieve the messages again from another system.

When you configure a POP3 account to retain messages on the server, you also can specify that the messages must be removed after they've been on the server for a designated period of time. Alternatively, you could have Outlook 2007 delete the messages from the server when you delete them from your Deleted Items folder, which prevents the messages from being downloaded again from the server after you've deleted your local copies.

Here's how to configure these options for POP3 accounts:

1. In Outlook 2007, choose Tools, Account Settings, or right-click the Outlook 2007 icon on the Start menu, choose Properties, and then click E-Mail Accounts.
2. Select the E-Mail tab.
3. Select the POP3 account, and then choose Change.
4. Click More Settings, and then click the Advanced tab, shown in Figure 15-8.

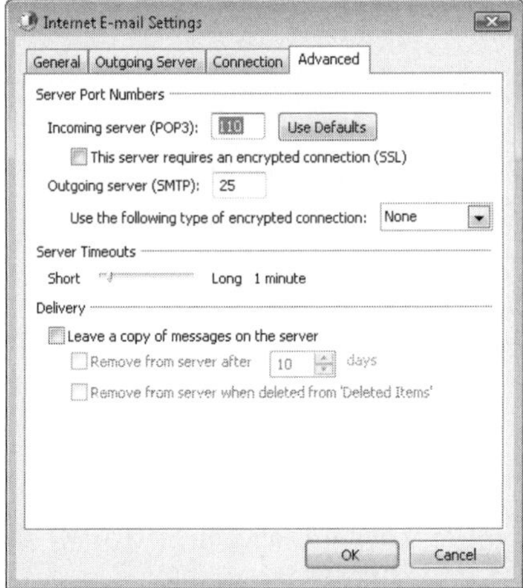

Figure 15-8. Use the Advanced tab to configure the account to leave messages on the server.

5. Select the Leave A Copy Of Messages On The Server check box, and then select one of the two associated check boxes if needed. Click OK.
6. Click Next, and then click Finish.

CHAPTER 16

Using RSS Feeds

This chapter explains one of the new features in Microsoft® Office Outlook® 2007: Really Simple Syndication (RSS)—the ability to integrate external information provided by content publishers (such as news Web sites) into a folder in Office Outlook 2007. The information is transmitted in a particular XML format (described as an *RSS feed*). To use this information, you configure Outlook 2007 to subscribe to the RSS feeds that provide the stories or information you want. These stories (or other RSS-provided information) are stored in a feed-specific folder under the RSS Feeds folder in Outlook 2007.

Understanding RSS

RSS is essentially an XML-based means to format news stories and other dynamically changing Web content so that RSS-aware software applications can access and retrieve this content automatically. Many Web browsers, such as Microsoft Internet Explorer®, have a built-in RSS-aware component (sometimes called a *news aggregator* or a *news reader*) that can connect to RSS feed locations and retrieve RSS-formatted content.

As the RSS format was developed, there have been multiple (sometimes competing) specifications for RSS, with multiple vendors and industry groups disagreeing on which specification to use. Fortunately for Outlook 2007 users, dealing with the different specifications is an issue for application developers—in Outlook 2007, you simply paste in the URL to the RSS feed that you want to retrieve, and Outlook 2007 takes care of the rest.

RSS is also referred to as *Web content syndication*, where users subscribe to the content they want from news sites (and other Web sites providing dynamic information). In this case, a subscription is not like signing up for a newsletter, where you have to provide an e-mail address for the information to be sent to. Rather, to subscribe to RSS feeds, you only have to locate the URL for the specific feed that you want and configure your RSS reader (in this case, Outlook 2007) to connect to that URL. The RSS reader will automatically retrieve the information (news articles, or other dynamic content) from the site.

> **Note**
>
> Some RSS feeds might require you to log in to an account with a user name and password to retrieve the RSS feed.

Configuring RSS

Setting up RSS feeds in Outlook 2007 is very easy to do—simply decide which sites you want to get RSS feeds from, determine the appropriate URL for the RSS feed from that site, and provide that URL to Outlook 2007. It would be simple and convenient if all sites formatted their RSS feed URLs the same way, such as *www.domain.com/rss.xml*, yet each Web site creates its own URL format for delivering RSS content. Consider the following examples of RSS feed URLs:

- **Microsoft MSDN® Web site:** *msdn.microsoft.com/rss.xml*
- **Seattle Times:** *seattletimes.nwsource.com/rss/home.xml*
- **Google News:** *news.google.com/nwshp?hl=en&tab=wn&q=&output=rss*
- **CNN Top Stories:** *rss.cnn.com/rss/cnn_topstories.rss*

Adding RSS Feeds to Outlook

To add a new RSS feed from a site to your Outlook 2007 RSS Feeds folder, you will first have to determine the appropriate URL for the site or for the specific feed from the site (as many sites have more than one RSS feed). Some sites use an RSS icon (such as the Seattle Times), an XML icon (such as CNN), or another specific icon denoting a specific feed of articles or information available via RSS. The MSDN site, for example, uses a little red icon with curved lines to indicate that the content is available via RSS.

To add a new RSS feed to Outlook 2007:

1. Right-click the RSS Feeds folder in the Navigation Pane, and then select Add A New RSS Feed, as shown in Figure 16-1.

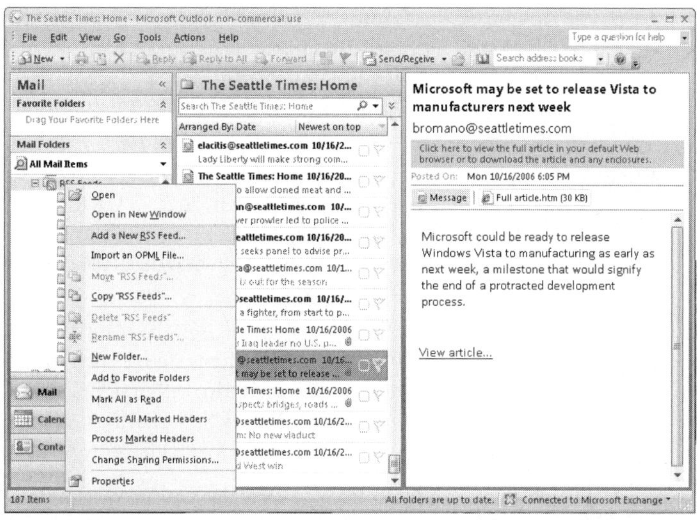

Figure 16-1. Right-click the RSS Feeds folder to begin adding a new feed.

2. The New RSS Feed dialog box is displayed, as shown in Figure 16-2. This is the location to type (or paste) the URL of the RSS feed that you want to add. In this example, the URL for the MSDN Web site RSS feed is used. Click Add to add the URL of the new RSS feed.

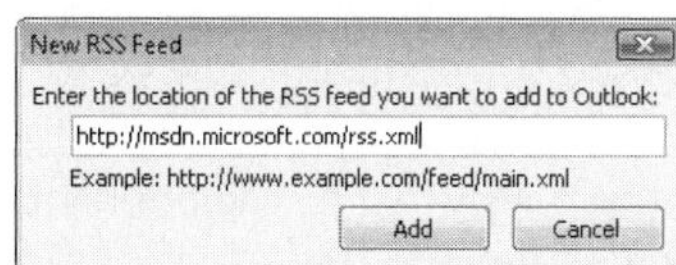

Figure 16-2. Enter the URL of the new RSS feed that you want to add.

3. You are then asked to confirm whether to add this URL as a new RSS feed and warned that you should add RSS feeds only from sources you trust, as shown in Figure 16-3. Clicking Yes adds the RSS feed using default values.

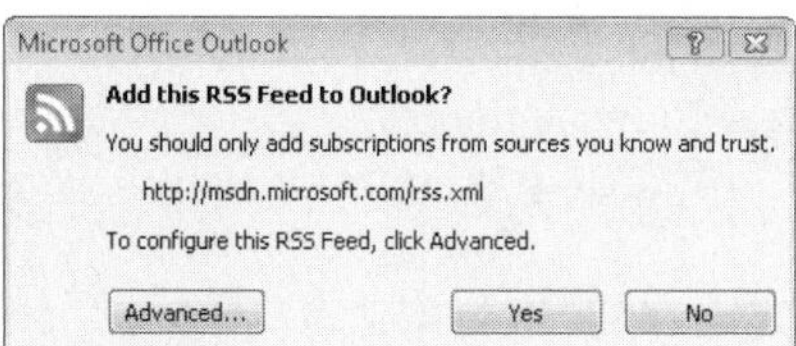

Figure 16-3. A verification is requested, with an Advanced option for additional control over the RSS feed.

4. Click the Advanced button to access further control over the RSS feed. A transient dialog box is displayed, indicating that Outlook 2007 is contacting the source of the RSS feed for further information. Once the site is accessed, the RSS Feed Options dialog box is displayed, as shown in Figure 16-4, enabling you to change the following aspects of the RSS feed:

   General The General area displays the name of the feed (as shown in Outlook 2007), the Channel Name, the Location (the URL entered to access the RSS feed), and the Description provided by the RSS feed source. The Feed Name box lets you change the name of the feed as displayed in the Outlook 2007 RSS Feeds folder.

   Delivery Location The Delivery Location area displays the location within the Outlook 2007 mailbox as well as the path on the drive and the file name of the Outlook 2007 data file storing the folder. Clicking the Change Folder button in this area opens the New RSS Feed Delivery Location dialog box, which lets you create a new folder or select a new Outlook 2007 data file to store the RSS feeds in.

   Downloads The Downloads area includes two options specifying how Outlook 2007 deals with downloading RSS information (both are not selected by default): The Automatically Download Enclosures For This Feed option enables the automatic downloading of attachments connected to articles in this feed. The Download The Full Article As An .html Attachment To Each Item option instructs Outlook 2007 to automatically handle the articles in this RSS feed by downloading the complete articles as .html attachments.

   Update Limit The Update This Feed With The Publisher's Recommendation check box in the Update Limit area (selected by default) sets the timing of updates to the RSS feed to be controlled by the publisher, using the update time specified by the source of the RSS feed.

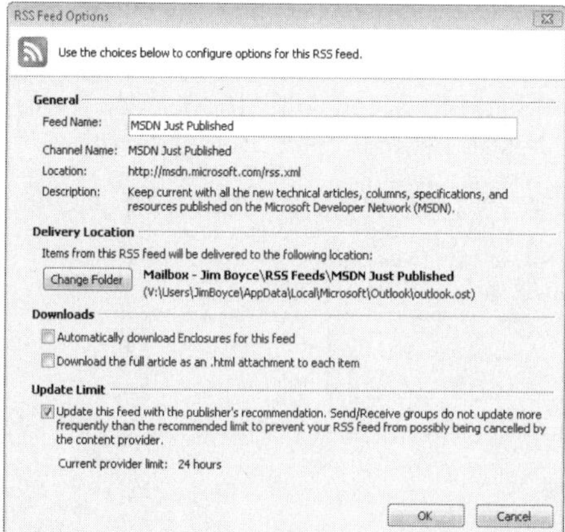

Figure 16-4. The RSS Feed Options dialog box lets you set the name, location, and update limit as well as control what is downloaded in the RSS feed.

5. After you have completed setting the options in the RSS Feed Options dialog box, click OK to return to the confirmation dialog box shown earlier in Figure 16-3. Click Yes to confirm the addition of the RSS feed. If you haven't yet chosen to synchronize your RSS feeds between Outlook 2007 and Internet Explorer, the message box shown in Figure 16-5 is displayed, asking whether you want to set this synchronization option at this time. Click Yes to synchronize the Outlook 2007 and Internet Explorer RSS feeds, click No to decide not to synchronize the feeds, and click Remind Me Later to postpone making the decision about synchronizing the RSS feeds.

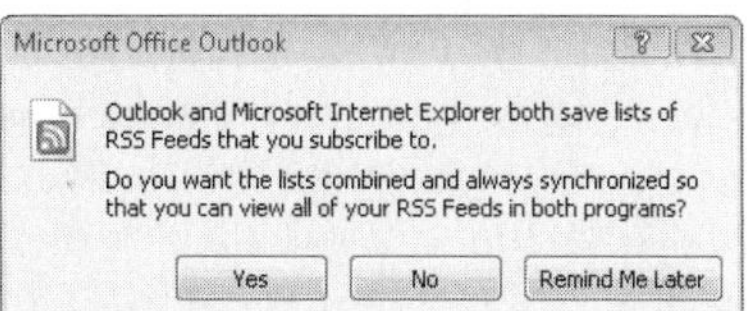

Figure 16-5. You can elect to synchronize Outlook 2007 RSS feeds with Internet Explorer.

Using Your RSS Feeds

After the RSS feeds have been added, you can begin to use them to access the information provided in the feed. To get to the RSS-provided information, click the Folder icon at the bottom of the Navigation Pane, and then scroll down to the RSS Feeds folder. The sites that you have configured to get RSS feeds from will appear under the RSS Feeds folder, as shown in Figure 16-6, and will display the title of the feed and the number of unread articles in parentheses following the title.

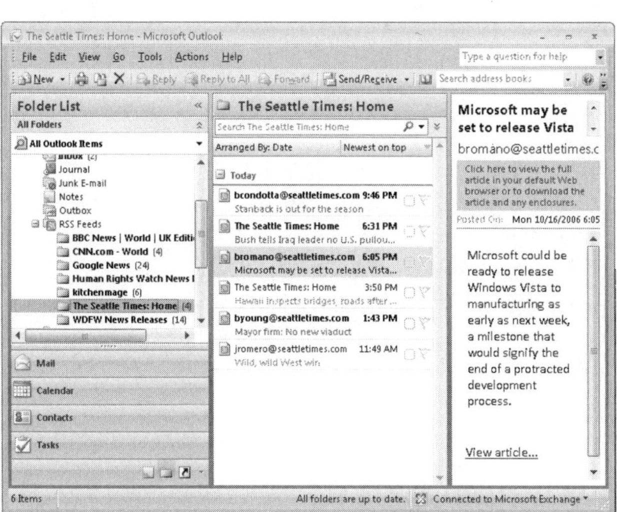

Figure 16-6. Selecting a particular RSS feed displays a list of downloaded articles from that site.

Selecting the specific RSS feed that you are interested in will display the list of articles. Selecting a specific article will display the summary of the article in the Reading Pane with links to the complete article. You can either click the InfoBar at the top of the article that states "Click here to view the full article in your default Web browser or to download the article and any enclosures" or click the View Article link at the bottom of the summary in the Reading Pane. Clicking the InfoBar displays a shortcut menu offering two options:

- **View Full Article** Choosing View Full Article loads the entire article in the default browser (commonly Internet Explorer).
- **Download/Update All Content** The Download/Update All Content option contacts the source of the RSS feed and downloads the content and any associated enclosures (such as images). Once downloaded, the display in the Reading Pane changes, showing new information under the InfoBar with a Message tab, a Full Article.htm tab showing the size of the article, as shown in Figure 16-7, and a tab that displays associated pictures (if any).

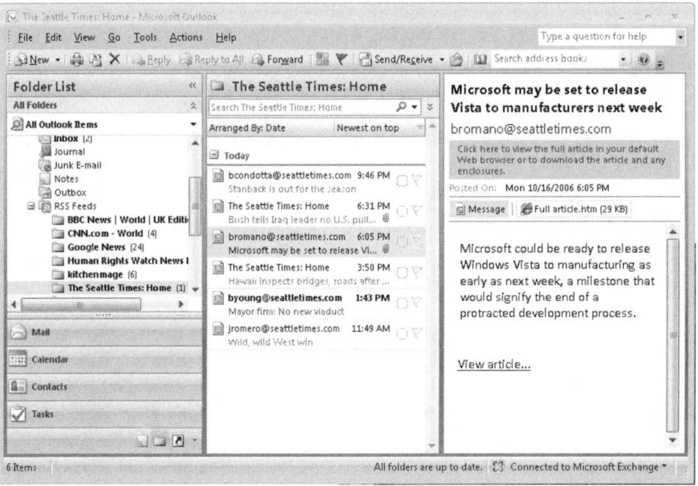

Figure 16-7. Choosing the Download/Update All Content option links to an article summary and full article content.

Selecting the Full Article.htm tab activates the preview for the article and displays a warning about previewing files only from trusted sources, as shown in Figure 16-8. The Full Article.htm preview warning provides a Preview File button to load the file and a check box allowing you to enable or disable the warning.

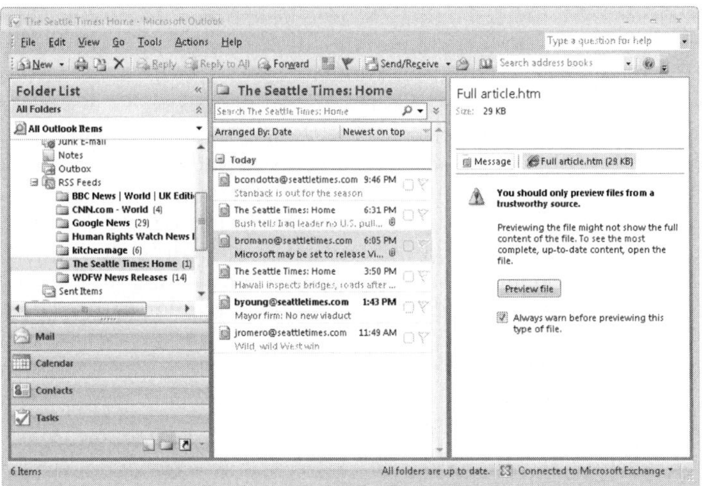

Figure 16-8. After viewing the warning, click the Preview File button to load the article in the Reading Pane.

When loading an article in the Reading Pane, Outlook 2007 will block images and links, preventing the activation of content during the preview, as shown in Figure 16-9. If you know that the site is trustworthy and that the article is safe, you can open the article in your browser (by choosing the View Full Article option on the InfoBar shortcut menu in the initial Reading Pane display of the article summary).

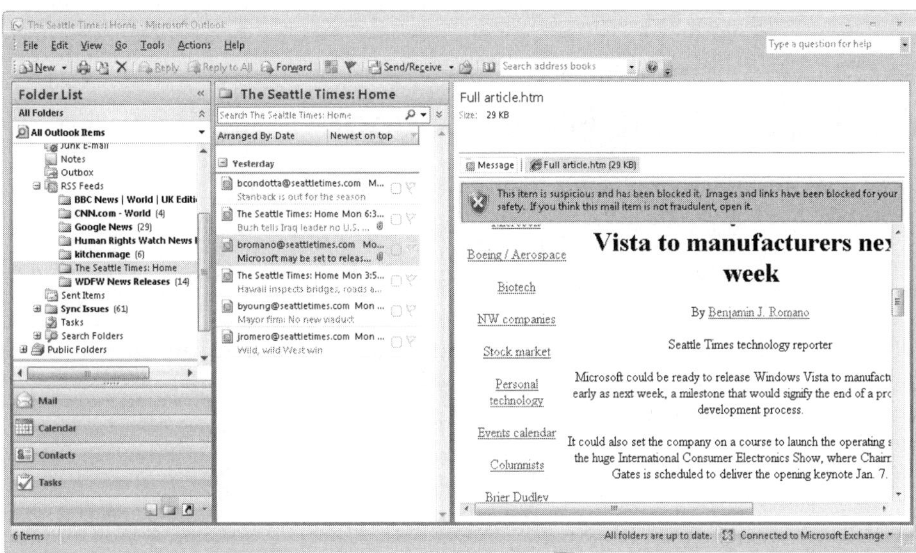

Figure 16-9. When you preview the article in the Reading Pane, the InfoBar displays a message about blocking images and links.

Viewing the article provided in the RSS feed by opening the message presents additional options, as shown in Figure 16-10. You can forward the article to others or even share the specific RSS feed with other people (sending them the RSS feed URL) by clicking Share This Feed in the Respond group. Clicking Download Content in the Options group gives you the option to update the article content—Outlook 2007 contacts the source of the RSS feed and obtains an updated version of the article. Clicking Other Actions lets you save attachments, forward the article as an attachment, change the encoding format, toggle the message header, view the source, view the article in the browser, and set the zoom (magnification) level. In addition to these RSS-specific options are common message options, such as Categorize, Follow Up, and Mark As Unread, as well as Find, Related, and Select options.

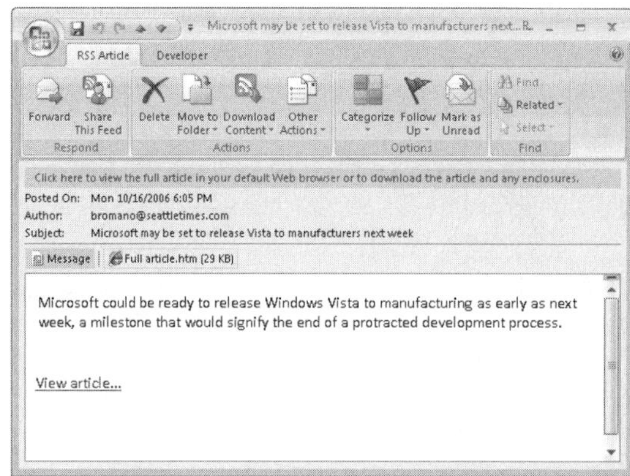

Figure 16-10. Options to forward and share the article are available when viewing an RSS article.

Adding an OPML File to Outlook

Outline Processor Markup Language (OPML) is a popular means of exchanging lists of RSS feeds, enabling sites to provide a set of RSS feeds to subscribers in a single file. OPML is another XML-based format, one specifically designed to handle information structured as an outline, yet it also has been successfully used to handle lists of RSS feeds.

To add an OPML-based list of RSS feeds to Outlook 2007, follow these steps:

1. Right-click the RSS Feeds folder in the Navigation Pane, and then choose Import An OPML File, as shown in Figure 16-11.

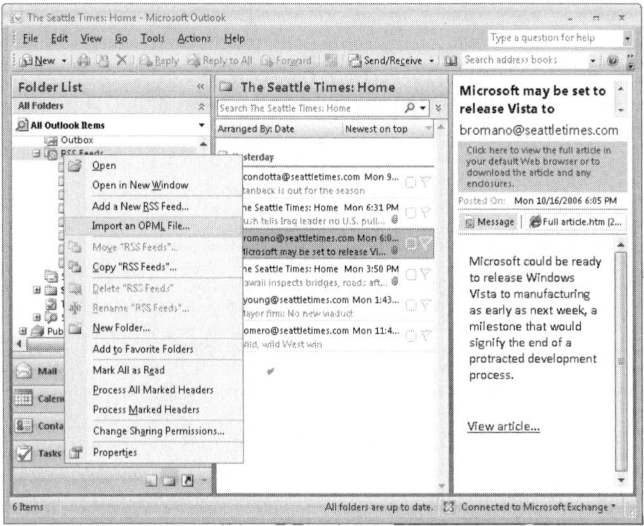

Figure 16-11. Importing a list of RSS feeds via an OPML file.

2. The Import An OPML File Wizard is displayed, as shown in Figure 16-12. Browse to the location on your computer or network that contains the OPML file with the list of RSS feeds, select the file, and then click OK.

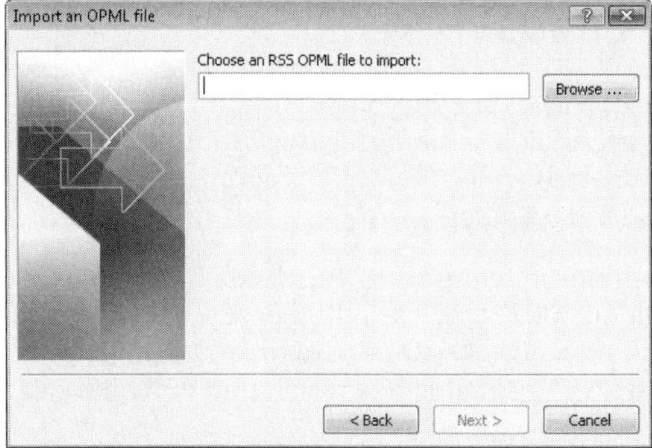

Figure 16-12. Select the OPML file containing the RSS feeds.

3. After selecting the OPML file, the Import An OPML File Wizard displays a list of RSS feeds that the OPML file contains, as shown in Figure 16-13, and enables the selection of each RSS feed to be added to your Outlook 2007 RSS Feeds folder. Select each desired RSS feed in the list by clicking the check box next to the feed (or click the Select All button to select all of them). After you have selected all the RSS feeds you want, click Next.

Figure 16-13. Select the OPML file containing the RSS feeds.

4. Just as when you add an individual RSS feed, if you haven't opted to synchronize your Outlook 2007 and Internet Explorer RSS feeds, you will be prompted to select whether to integrate them now. The Import An OPML File Wizard will now display the list of RSS feeds that you selected earlier, explaining that those RSS feeds have been added to Outlook 2007. Click the Finish button to return to Outlook 2007, and then go to the RSS Feeds folder to review the new RSS feeds added through the OPML file.

Managing Your RSS Feeds

Once you have your RSS feeds set up, you might want to change aspects of how the RSS feeds are configured, such as changing the URL that the RSS feed is derived from, changing how it downloads enclosures, or changing how other users can access a particular RSS feed on your computer.

You can configure options for controlling RSS feeds in Outlook 2007 in several ways. To control how Outlook 2007 handles all RSS Feeds, choose Tools, Options, select Other, and then click Advanced Options to display the Advanced Options dialog box, shown in Figure 16-14. In this dialog box, you'll find two options that affect RSS feeds:

- Sync RSS Feeds To The Common Feed List
- Any RSS Feed Item That Is Updated Appears As A New Item

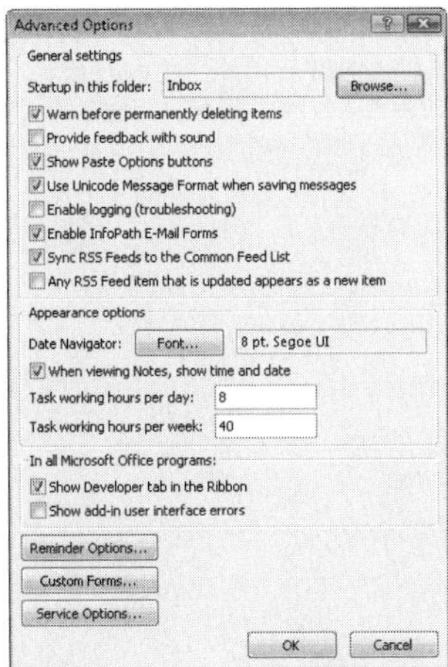

Figure 16-14. Configure handling of RSS feed items and synchronization in the Advanced Options dialog box.

To change the configuration of an RSS feed once it has been set up, choose Tools, and then choose Account Settings. In the Account Settings dialog box, click the RSS Feeds tab, shown in Figure 16-15, select the RSS feed that you want to modify, and then click Change.

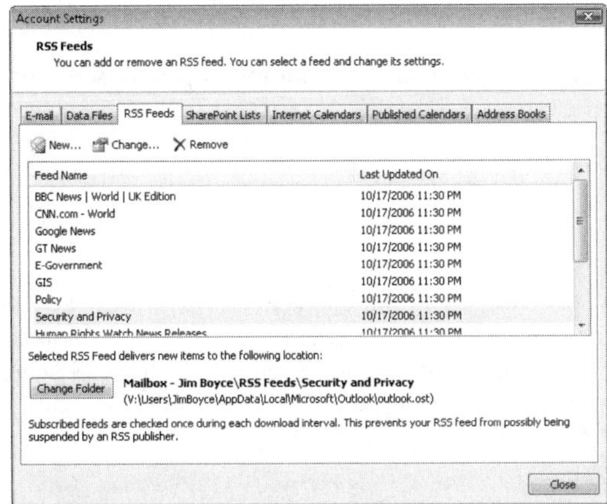

Figure 16-15. Select the RSS Feeds tab to change an RSS feed configuration.

The name of the RSS feed can be modified in the RSS Feed Options dialog box, shown in Figure 16-16, and the Channel Name, Location, and Description are displayed. You can change the mailbox folder as well as the mail storage file in which the RSS feed is contained by clicking the Change Folder button. The Downloads area includes controls for how RSS downloads are handled, including whether to Automatically Download Enclosures For This Feed and whether to Download The Full Article As An .html Attachment To Each Item. Although the Update Limit option to use the publisher's recommendation for update frequency is selected, this option can be disabled, allowing you to update the feed manually. For more information about configuring these options, see "Adding RSS Feeds to Outlook" earlier in this chapter.

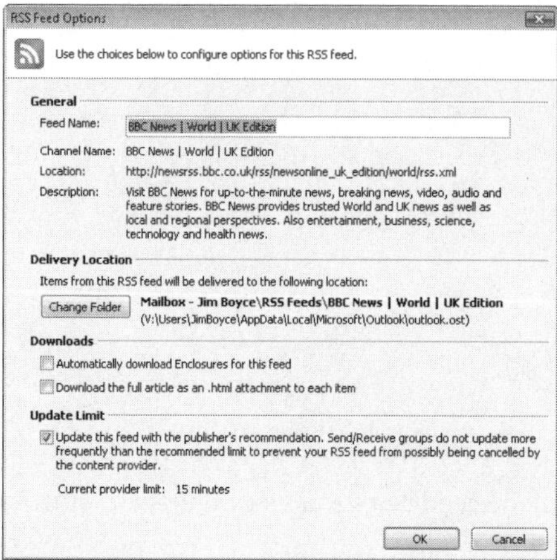

Figure 16-16. The RSS Feed Options dialog box lets you control the name, the storage location, and how the RSS download is managed.

You can also enable or disable downloads in RSS feeds in the Trust Center, on the Automatic Downloads page, where you can select or clear the Permit Downloads In RSS Items check box.

For more information about setting these RSS configuration options, see "Adding RSS Feeds to Outlook" earlier in this chapter.

Chapter 16

Setting RSS Properties

A core set of configuration controls for RSS feeds is available on the seven tabs of the Properties dialog box accessible in the RSS Feeds folder (and all RSS folders created under it). To set these RSS configuration options, right-click the RSS Feeds folder (or the desired subfolder), and then choose Properties.

> **Note**
>
> If your Outlook 2007 configuration does not include an Exchange Server account, only five tabs will be displayed in the Properties dialog box.

The General tab is displayed, as shown in Figure 16-17, enabling you to set the name of the RSS folder and the description, as well as whether to display the number of all items or just unread items. In addition, you can configure the form used in posting to the RSS folder, display the folder size (on both the local computer and the server), and specify whether to automatically generate Microsoft Exchange views. Clicking the Clear Offline Items button removes the data from the offline data store.

Figure 16-17. The General tab of the RSS Feeds Properties dialog box enables setting RSS folder properties.

The Home Page tab, shown in Figure 16-18, lets you set the default page URL of the folder and specify whether to Show Home Page By Default For This Folder. Clicking the Browse button opens the File Web Files dialog box, where you can select a new default Web page; clicking the Restore Defaults button resets the default Web page and options to the default values.

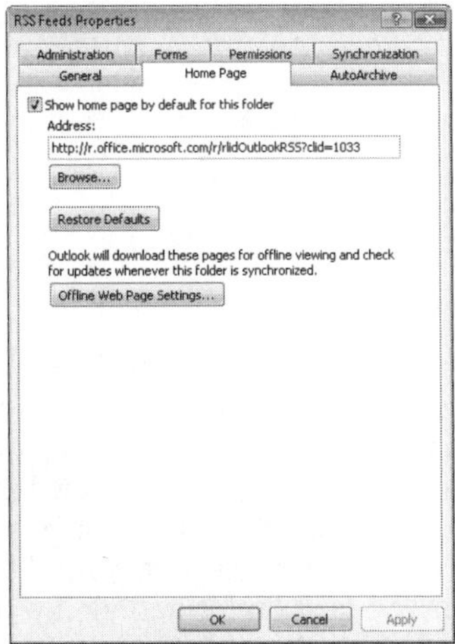

Figure 16-18. You can set the default URL and display settings on the Home Page tab.

Clicking the Offline Web Page Settings button lets you configure the offline settings for the RSS feed, including a check box on the Web Document tab that specifies whether Outlook 2007 will make this page available offline. The Schedule tab synchronization setting defaults to Only When I Choose Synchronize From The Tools Menu, as shown in Figure 16-19.

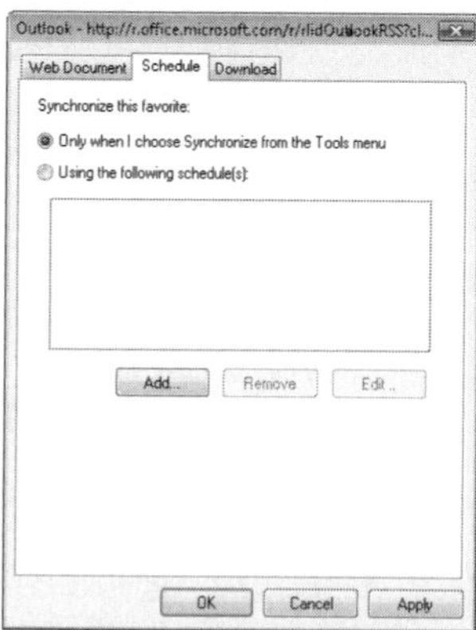

Figure 16-19. Synchronization defaults to manual, but you can schedule synchronization periods.

By selecting Using The Following Schedule(s) and then clicking the Add button, however, you can set the schedule for synchronizing an RSS feed in the New Schedule dialog box. The synchronization can be set to a specific time of day, as shown in Figure 16-20, a descriptive name can be applied, and you can elect to have the computer automatically connect to the network if it is not connected when the synchronization begins.

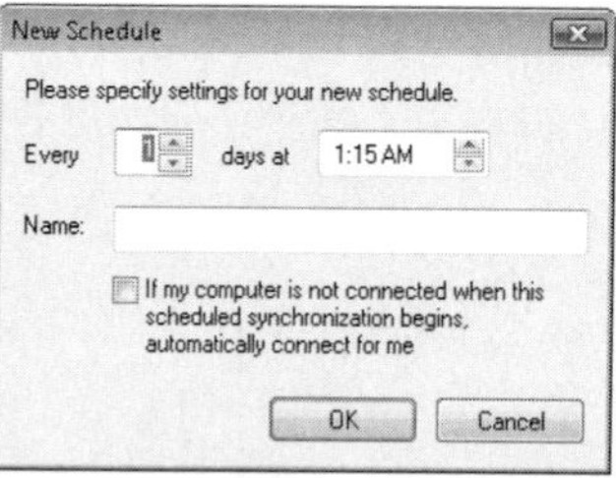

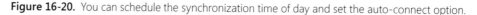

Figure 16-20. You can schedule the synchronization time of day and set the auto-connect option.

The Download tab, shown in Figure 16-21, lets you configure the depth of content to download, reserved disk space, content change alerts, and site login. Set the Download Pages *n* Links Deep From This Page option to the number of links deep of content that you want to download for this specific RSS feed. You can select Follow Links Outside Of This Page's Website to have Outlook 2007 download external content. By configuring the Limit Hard-Disk Usage For This Page To option, you can control how much hard drive space you want to reserve to store this RSS feed's information. If you want to be alerted about content change, select the When This Page Changes, Send E-Mail To option, and provide your E-Mail Address and Mail Server (SMTP) information. For RSS feeds that require credentials, click the Login button, and then provide your user name and password. Click OK to accept your changes and return to the RSS Feeds Properties dialog box.

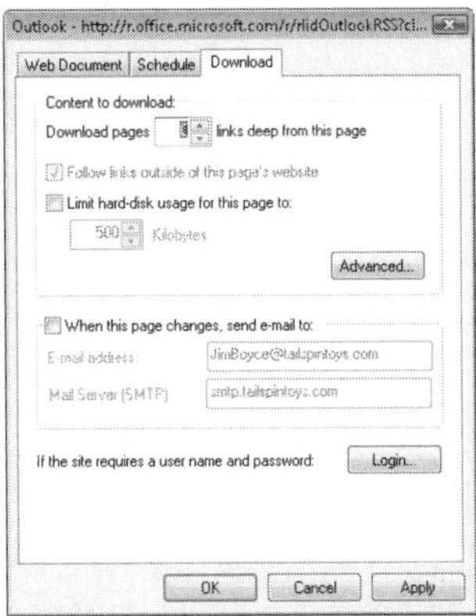

Figure 16-21. Set the download, notification, and login settings for this RSS feed.

To control the archiving of RSS feeds, you select the AutoArchive tab in the RSS Feeds Properties dialog box, shown in Figure 16-22, and then configure the archiving settings to your preference. The default is to not archive the RSS items, but you can configure the Archive This Folder Using These Settings option to set the time limit (the point at which Outlook 2007 cleans out items older than the set period). After you have set the archive time limit, you can configure where archived items are moved to.

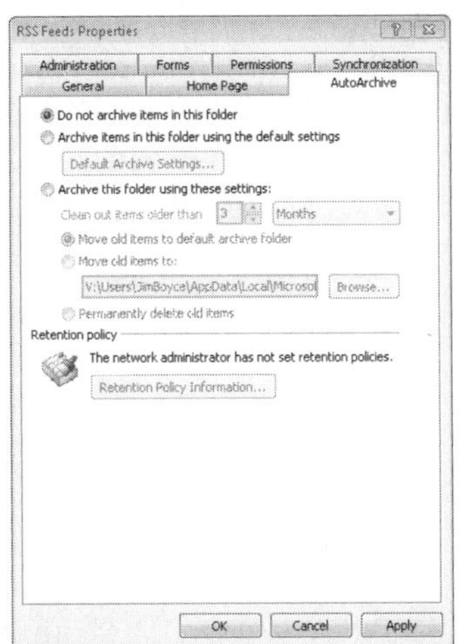

Figure 16-22. Set the archive option, time limit, and archive location for this RSS feed.

You can set the initial folder view on the Administration tab, configuring the view to Normal (the default), Group By From, Group By Subject, Group By Conversation Topic, Unread By Conversation, or Messages. Other options include specifying whom this folder is available to—either All Users With Access Permissions or Owners Only.

To associate custom forms with this RSS feed, select the Forms tab, shown in Figure 16-23, to configure the Forms Associated With This Folder option. After you have specified one or more custom forms to use with this RSS feed, in the Allow These

Forms In This Folder area, select Only Forms List Above, Forms Listed Above And The Standard Forms, or Any Form.

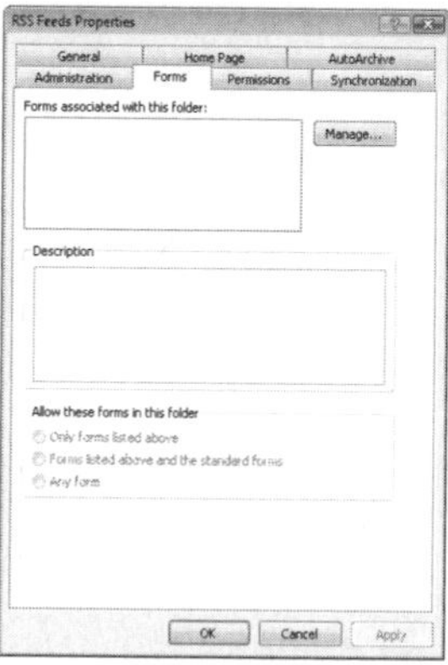

Figure 16-23. You can manage the association of forms with an RSS Feed.

To control who has access to view or modify this RSS feed, click the Permissions tab, shown in Figure 16-24, and then specify the permission levels for the Default, Anonymous, and Owner accounts. The Owner account has full permissions by default; the Anonymous and Default accounts have none. If you want to provide specific users access to this RSS feed, click Add, and then select the appropriate user accounts. To allow anonymous access to this RSS feed, select Anonymous, and then, in the Permission Level drop-down list, select the desired level of access for anonymous users.

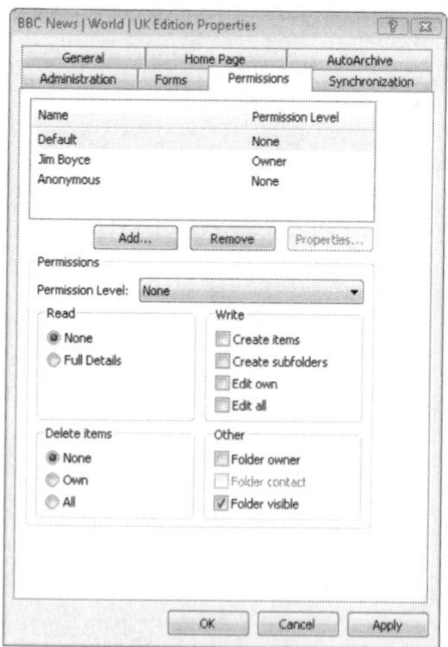

Figure 16-24. You can set the permissions to control access to this RSS feed.

The Synchronization tab lets you set the synchronization filter for the RSS feed. Click the Filter button to display the Filter dialog box, and then select the filter criteria to apply to the offline copy of the RSS items associated with this folder.

CHAPTER 17

Using LDAP Directory Services

Lightweight Directory Access Protocol (LDAP) is a standard method for querying directory services. For example, you can query LDAP servers for the address, phone number, or other information associated with an entry in the directory. Microsoft® Windows® 2000 Server (and later versions of Windows Server) use LDAP as the primary mechanism for accessing the Active Directory® directory service. Servers running Microsoft Exchange Server can also act as LDAP servers, allowing users to look up addresses and associated information in the directory.

This chapter explores LDAP and explains how to configure LDAP directory service accounts in Microsoft Office Outlook® 2007 and Microsoft Windows Mail.

Overview of LDAP Services

LDAP was designed to require less overhead and fewer resources than its predecessor, Directory Access Protocol (DAP), which was developed for X.500, a standards-based directory service. LDAP is a standards-based protocol that allows clients to query data in a directory service over a TCP connection. Microsoft Active Directory, Novell eDirectory, IBM WebSphere, and directory services on the Internet such as Bigfoot, InfoSpace, and Yahoo! all employ LDAP to implement searches of their databases.

For additional information about Microsoft's early strategies for implementing LDAP as part of Active Directory, refer to "MS Strategy for Lightweight Directory Access Protocol (LDAP)," available in the Microsoft Windows NT® Server Technical Notes section of Microsoft TechNet or on the Web at *www.microsoft.com/technet/archive/winntas/plan/ldapcmr.mspx*. **Although the material is now archived, it is still relevant for planning an LDAP-based directory service for use with Active Directory.**

Configuring a Directory Service Account in Outlook

In addition to supporting e-mail accounts, Office Outlook 2007 also allows you to add LDAP-based directory service accounts that enable you to query for subscriber information in the remote server's directory. The LDAP server might be internal to your organization, hosted by another company, or one of several LDAP directories located on the Internet. With an LDAP account in your profile, you can look up names, addresses, and other information stored in the directory.

To set up and configure an LDAP account in Outlook 2007, follow these steps:

1. Right-click the Outlook 2007 icon on the Start menu, choose Properties, and then click E-Mail Accounts (and select the profile if necessary). Alternatively, if Outlook 2007 is already started, choose Tools, Account Settings.
2. Select the Address Books tab, and then click New.
3. Select Internet Directory Service (LDAP), and then click Next.
4. On the Directory Service (LDAP) Settings page of the Add New E-Mail Account wizard, shown in Figure 17-1, type the server name or the IP address in the Server Name box.

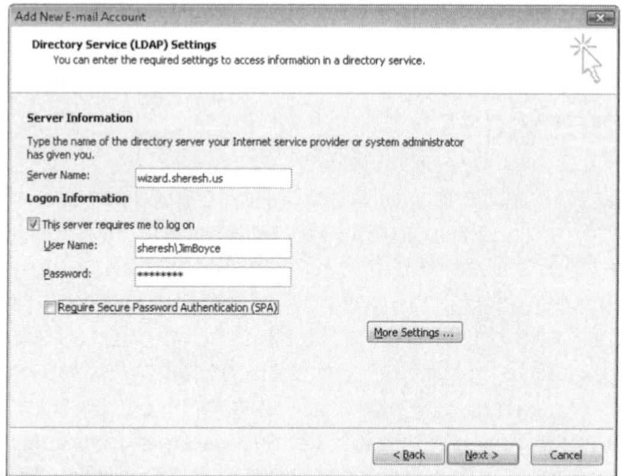

Figure 17-1. Specify the server name, and supply logon credentials if the server requires authentication.

5. If the server requires authentication, select the This Server Requires Me To Log On check box. Specify the logon credentials in the User Name and Password boxes. If you're authenticating on a Windows Server domain controller, include the domain by entering <domain>\<user> in the User Name box, where <domain> is the domain name and <user> is the user account.

Chapter 17

INSIDE OUT Add the domain for LDAP authentication

Failing to include the domain in the authentication string will result in the authentication error message "Failed to connect to <server> due to invalid authentication." If you clear the This Server Requires Me To Log On check box and the server requires authentication, you'll receive the error message "No entries were found. You may need to supply authentication information in order to be able to access the directory." Clear this check box only if the server allows anonymous LDAP queries.

6. Click More Settings to open the Microsoft LDAP Directory dialog box, shown in Figure 17-2.

Figure 17-2. Change the display name, port, and other properties as needed.

7. Change the name in the Display Name box to the name you want Outlook 2007 to display in the address book for the directory service.
8. In the Port box, type the port number required by the LDAP server. The default port is 389, although you can use 3268 for most searches in an Active Directory global catalog (GC).

INSIDE OUT Use two ports

Port 3268 is the default port for the Active Directory GC. Certain types of data are available through one specific port, whereas other types of data are accessed through the other. For example, read-only copies of data from other domains are available only through the GC port. For that reason, you might create two directory services, one for each port.

9. You can select the Use Secure Sockets Layer (SSL) check box to connect to the LDAP server through SSL. In most cases, SSL won't be required. This option works only if the server allows an SSL connection.

10. In the Microsoft LDAP Directory dialog box, click the Search tab, shown in Figure 17-3.

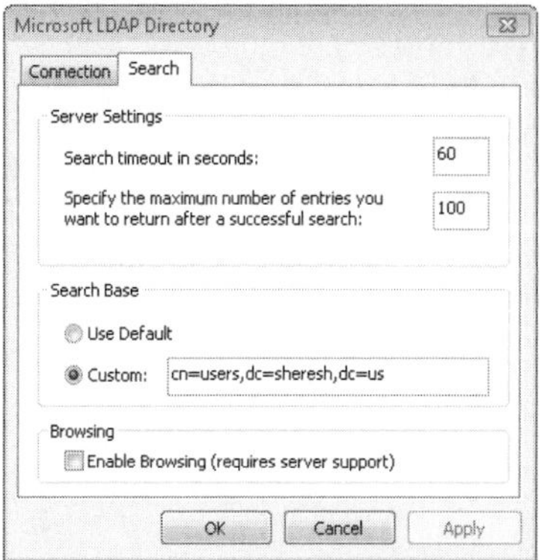

Figure 17-3. Use the Search tab to configure the time-out, number of hits to return, and the search base.

11. Specify the search time-out and the maximum number of entries you want returned in a search. In the Search Base box, either select Use Default (the Users container) or type the root for your search in the directory. If you're searching Active Directory, for example, you might enter **dc=**<domain>**,dc=**<suffix>, where <domain> is your domain name (without the domain suffix). Specify the domain suffix (net, com, org, or us, for example) as the last data item. (See "Setting the Search Base" on the facing page for more details.) To be able to browse the directory, select the Enable Browsing (Requires Server Support) check box. The Active Directory domain controller must allow browsing for this feature to work.

12. Click OK to close the dialog box, and then click Next and click Finish to complete the account setup.

Note

Queries to Active Directory using SSL should be directed to port 636. GC queries using SSL should be directed to port 3269.

You can use the directory service accounts created in Outlook 2007 to perform LDAP queries from within Outlook 2007. Microsoft Windows Mail accounts can also be used for these types of searches. However, you can't use these accounts from the search/find feature of your operating system.

> **Note**
>
> You can make changes to a directory service account in Outlook 2007 and query using the new settings without restarting Outlook 2007.

Setting the Search Base

The search base for an LDAP query specifies the container in the directory service where the query will be performed. When querying against Active Directory on a server running Windows, specifying no search base causes Outlook 2007 to return all items in the directory that have an e-mail address. Often, this means that you see many system-level objects, as shown in Figure 17-4. These additional objects often confuse casual users, and even users familiar with Active Directory generally don't want to see these system-level objects. You can set the search base to more closely target the information you're trying to find, but to do so, you must understand what the search base really is.

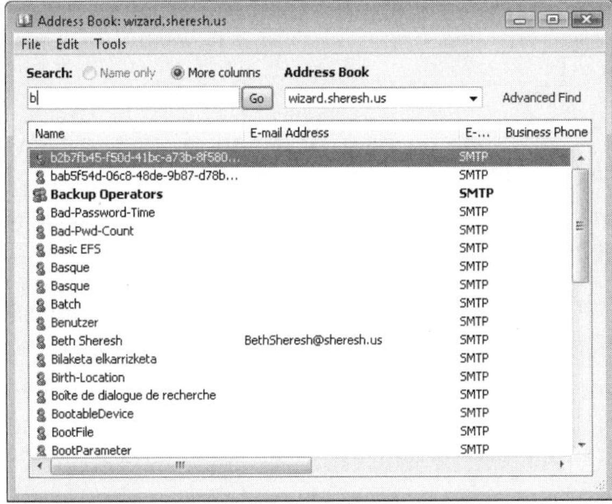

Figure 17-4. A query with no search base returns all objects with e-mail addresses.

Each entry in the directory has a Distinguished Name (DN), which is a fully qualified name that identifies that specific object. Relative Distinguished Names (RDNs) are concatenated to form the DN, which uniquely identifies the object in the directory. RDNs include the following:

- **cn=** common name
- **ou=** organizational unit
- **o=** organization
- **c=** country
- **dc=** domain

> **Note**
>
> Active Directory drops the *c=* attribute and adds the *dc=* attribute.

For example, assume that you want to search the Users container in the domain boyce.us. The search base would be as follows:

cn=users,dc=boyce,dc=us

Notice that the domain is represented by two *dc* attributes. If the domain you are searching is microsoft.com, you would use *dc=microsoft,dc=com* instead.

In some cases, the part of the directory you want to search will be in a specific organizational unit (OU). Or you might be setting up multiple LDAP accounts in Outlook 2007, each configured to search a specific OU. For example, perhaps your company has Sales, Marketing, Support, External Contacts, and a handful of other OUs, and you want to configure an LDAP query for each one. One solution is to add an LDAP service for each and configure the search base accordingly. For example, let's say we're configuring an LDAP service account to query the Support OU in the boyce.us domain. The search base would be as follows:

ou=support,dc=boyce,dc=us

Keep the following points in mind when deciding on a search base:

- Specifying no search bases causes Outlook 2007 to retrieve objects from the entire directory.
- Specifying a search base sets the branch of the directory to search in the directory tree.

If you decide to include a search base, determine the common name for the object or OU, and then add the domain. You can't specify just the *ou* or *cn* attribute without the domain, but you can specify the domain by itself to perform a top-down search of the domain.

> **Note**
>
> If you need to search different branches of the directory tree, you can add multiple LDAP service accounts to your profile, each with the appropriate search base. Or add only one LDAP service account, and then simply change its search base when you need to query a different branch.

TROUBLESHOOTING

Your LDAP query returns this error message: "There are no entries in the directory service that match your search criteria"

Sooner or later, you'll attempt to query an LDAP server that you know contains at least one item meeting your search criteria, but you'll receive an error message telling you that no entries in the directory service match your criteria. One possible cause of this problem is that the search option specified at the LDAP server might be preventing the query from completing successfully. For example, you might be issuing an "any" query, but the server is configured to treat such queries as initial queries.

You might also receive this error message if you've incorrectly set the LDAP directory service account properties—for example, you might have configured the account to use port 389 when the server requires SSL. Check your directory service account settings to ensure that you have specified the proper server name or address, port, and search base.

Configuring a Directory Service Account in Windows Mail

You can use Windows Mail as well as Outlook 2007 to perform LDAP searches. This capability can be handy when you're working on a system that does not have Outlook 2007 installed, such as a notebook computer that you use infrequently. You can access LDAP queries by using the Windows Mail Contacts list or by using the search/find feature of your operating system.

To configure Windows Mail LDAP directory services, follow these steps:

1. In Windows Mail, choose Tools, Accounts.
2. In the Internet Accounts dialog box, click Add. The Add Internet Account Wizard starts. On the Select Account Type page, shown in Figure 17-5, click Directory Service, and then click Next.

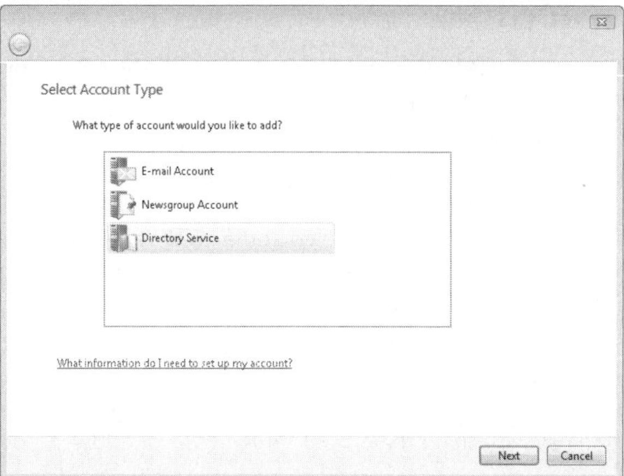

Figure 17-5. Select Directory Service to add a directory service account.

3. On the Internet Directory Server Name page, shown in Figure 17-6, type the Domain Name System (DNS) name or the IP address of the LDAP server in the Internet Directory (LDAP) Server box. If the server requires authentication, select the My LDAP Server Requires Me To Log On check box, and then click Next.

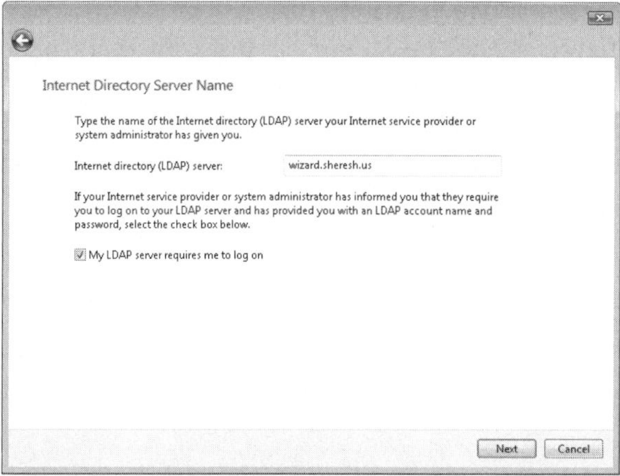

Figure 17-6. Enter the DNS or IP address of the LDAP server, and select the logon option.

4. If you selected authentication, the Internet Directory Server Logon page is displayed. Specify the account name and password for the directory server. If you're authenticating using a domain account outside your current domain, enter the account in the form <domain>\<account>. Specify the password, and then click Next.
5. The wizard next asks whether you want to check addresses using this directory service. Choose Yes, and then click Next.
6. Click Finish to complete the account setup.

7. In the Internet Accounts dialog box, select the account you just created, and then click Properties to display the General tab of the Properties dialog box for the account, shown in Figure 17-7.

Figure 17-7. The General tab lists the entries made in the Add Internet Accounts Wizard and lets you modify name, server location, and other LDAP server properties.

8. Click the Advanced tab, shown in Figure 17-8, specify the port you want to use, the search time-out, and the search base, and then click OK.

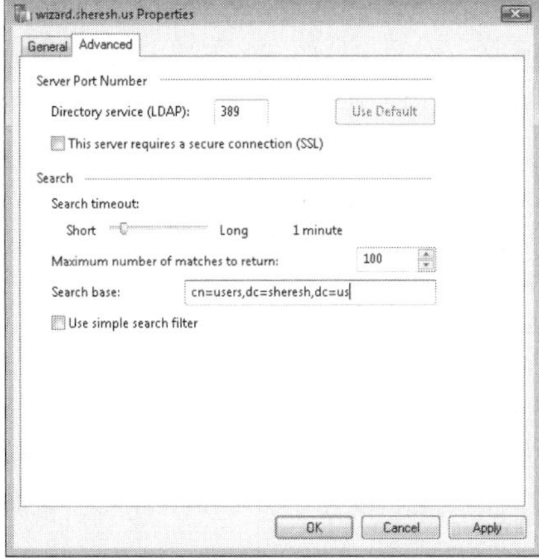

Figure 17-8. Use the Advanced tab to configure the port and other search properties.

9. Close the Internet Accounts dialog box.

You can also perform LDAP searches in Outlook Express. The process is very similar to LDAP searching in Windows Mail.

Using LDAP to Find People

LDAP directory services that you create within Outlook 2007 can be searched through the Outlook 2007 Address Book only. Windows Mail comes preconfigured with LDAP directory service accounts. You can also query Active Directory services using the Find option in Windows Mail or in Windows Vista™ using the Search Active Directory feature on the Network page.

You can perform LDAP queries in Outlook 2007 by using directory service accounts you add to Outlook 2007. Follow these steps to perform an LDAP query with an LDAP server in Outlook 2007:

1. In Outlook 2007, click the Address Book icon on the toolbar to open the Address Book window. Alternatively, you can choose Tools, Address Book.
2. In the Outlook Address Book, select the directory service in the Address Book drop-down list. Depending on how the directory service account is configured (whether or not Enable Browsing is enabled), Outlook 2007 might display the contents of the directory immediately in the Address Book. When browsing is enabled, Outlook can automatically access directory information and display it in the Address Book. For information about how to enable browsing, see "Configuring a Directory Service Account in Outlook" and Figure 17-3 earlier in this chapter. If Enable Browsing is not selected, no names will be listed, and you will be prompted with "Type your search keywords and click 'Go' to perform a search."
3. To search using specific criteria, click the Advanced Find link or choose Tools, Find. Either action opens the Find dialog box, shown in Figure 17-9.

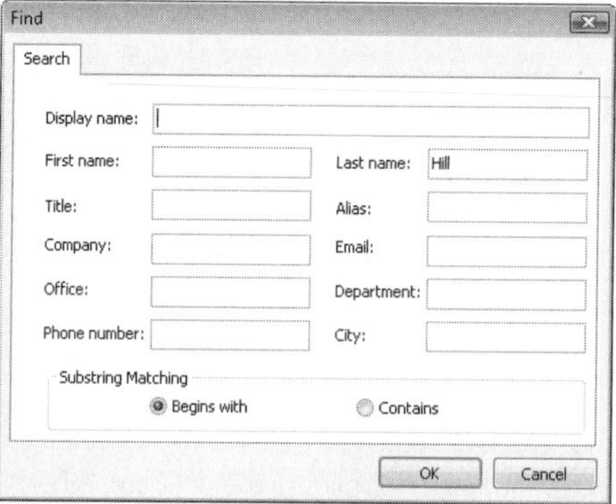

Figure 17-9. Use the Find dialog box to specify the criteria for the LDAP query.

4. Specify the criteria for the search, and then click OK. If objects meeting the search criteria exist within the LDAP directory, the results will show a list of all matching objects.

Searching from Windows Mail

You can perform queries from within Windows Mail using LDAP directory service accounts you create in Windows Mail.

Follow these steps to do so:

1. In Windows Mail, click the arrow next to the Find icon on the main toolbar and then select People, or in the main window or in the message window, choose Edit, Find, and then select People to open the Find People dialog box, shown in Figure 17-10.

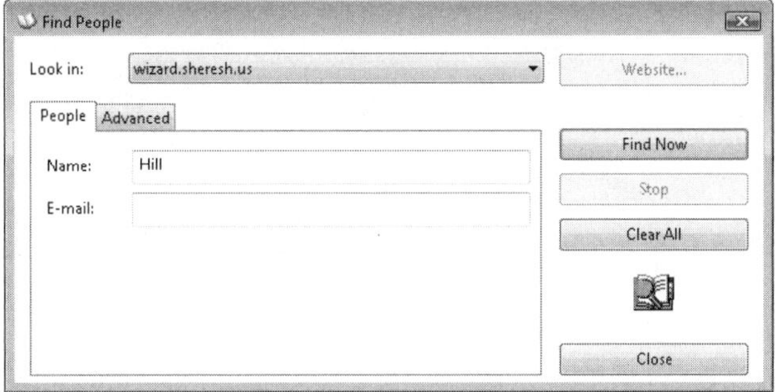

Figure 17-10. Use the Find People dialog box to perform LDAP queries in Windows Mail.

2. In the Look In drop-down list, select the directory service account to use.
3. Specify the criteria for the search (such as name or e-mail address), click the Advanced tab to specify additional parameters if needed, and then click Find Now.

PART 3

Working with Contacts

CHAPTER 18

Creating and Managing Your Contacts

The Contacts folder in Microsoft® Office Outlook® 2007 is an electronic tool that can organize and store the thousands of details you need to know to communicate with people, businesses, and organizations. You can use the Contacts folder to store e-mail addresses, street addresses, multiple phone numbers, and any other information that relates to a contact, such as a birthday or an anniversary date.

From a contact entry in your list of contacts, you can click a button or choose a command to have Office Outlook 2007 address a meeting request, an e-mail message, a letter, or a task request to the contact. If you have a modem, you can have Outlook 2007 dial the contact's phone number. You can link any Outlook 2007 item or 2007 Microsoft Office system document to a contact to help you track activities associated with the contact.

Outlook 2007 allows you to customize the view in the Contacts folder to review and print your contact information. You can sort, group, or filter your contacts list to better manage the information or to quickly find entries.

Outlook 2007 integrates well with Microsoft Windows® SharePoint® Services (WSS) and SharePoint Portal Server, both of which provide the means for users to share documents, contacts, messages, and other items through a Web-based interface. You can import contacts from Outlook 2007 to a WSS site, or vice versa.

Outlook 2007 also supports the use of vCards, the Internet standard for creating and sharing virtual business cards. You can save a contact entry as a vCard and send it in an e-mail message. You can also add a vCard to your e-mail signature.

This chapter discusses contact management in Outlook 2007. The Outlook 2007 Contacts feature provides powerful tools to help you manage, organize, and find important contact information.

Working with the Contacts Folder

The Contacts folder is one of the Outlook 2007 default folders. This folder stores information such as name, physical address, phone number, and e-mail address for each contact. You can use the Contacts folder to quickly address e-mail messages, place phone calls, distribute bulk mailings through mail merge (in Microsoft Office Word 2007), and perform many other communication tasks. The Contacts folder is not, however, the same as your address book. Your Outlook Address Book lets you access the Contacts folder for addressing messages, but the Address Book also lets you access addresses stored in personal address books and Microsoft Exchange Server address lists.

For detailed information about working with address books in Outlook 2007, see Chapter 6, "Managing Address Books and Distribution Lists."

You can open the Contacts folder either by clicking the Contacts button in the Navigation Pane or by opening the Folder List and clicking Contacts. When you open the folder, you'll see its default view, Business Cards, which displays contact entries as virtual business cards that show name, address, phone number, and a handful of other items for each contact, as shown in Figure 18-1. Outlook 2007 provides several predefined views for the Contacts folder that offer different ways to display and sort the contacts list.

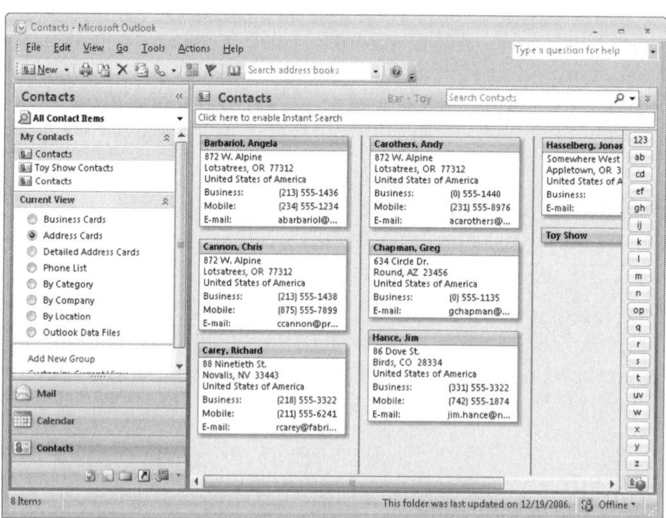

Figure 18-1. Use the Contacts folder to manage contact information such as address, phone number, and fax number for your business associates and friends.

For details about the available views in the Contacts folder and how to work with them, see "Viewing Contacts" later in this chapter.

> **Note**
>
> You can use the alphabet index on the right in the folder window to quickly jump to a specific area in the Contacts folder. For example, click the M button to jump to the list of contacts whose names begin with M.

When you double-click an entry in the Contacts folder, Outlook 2007 opens a contact form similar to the one shown in Figure 18-2. This multitabbed form lets you view and modify a wealth of information about the person. You also can initiate actions related to the contact. For example, you can click the Call button in the Communicate group on the Contact tab on the Ribbon to dial the contact's phone number. You'll learn more about these tasks throughout the remainder of this chapter. The following section explains how to create a contact entry and also introduces the tabs on the Ribbon to help you understand the types of information you can store.

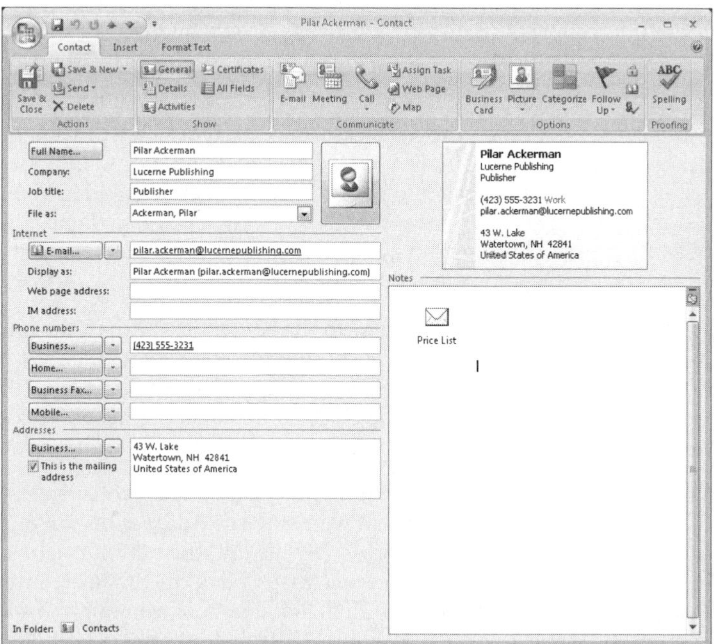

Figure 18-2. The General page of a contact form shows address, phone, and other information about the contact.

Creating a Contact Entry

To create a contact entry, you can start from scratch, or you can base the new entry on a similar existing entry—for example, the entry for a contact from the same company.

You can open a contact form and create a new entry from scratch in any of the following ways:

- Choose File, New, Contact.
- Right-click a blank area in the Contacts folder (not a contact entry), and then choose New Contact.
- With the Contacts folder open, click New or press **Ctrl+N**.
- In any other folder view (such as Messages), click the arrow next to the New button on the toolbar, and then choose Contact.

When the contact form opens, type the contact's name in the Full Name box and enter the information you want to include for the contact, switching tabs as needed. To save the entry, click Save & Close. To save this entry and continue to add contacts, click Save And New.

Filling in the information on the contact form is straightforward. You might find a few of the features especially useful. For example, the File As drop-down list allows you to specify how you want the contact to be listed in the Contacts folder. You can choose to list the contact in either Last Name, First Name format or First Name, Last Name format; to list the contact by company name rather than personal name; or to use a combination of contact name and company name.

You can also store more phone numbers in the contact entry than the four that are displayed on the form. When you click the down arrow next to a phone number entry, as shown in Figure 18-3, you see a list of possible phone numbers from which you can select a number to view or modify; the checked items on the list are those that currently contain information. When you select a number, Outlook 2007 shows it on the form.

In addition to storing multiple phone numbers for a contact, you also can store multiple physical addresses. Click the down arrow next to the Address button on the form to select a business, home, or other address. (By default, the button is labeled Business.) The E-Mail box can also store multiple addresses; click the down arrow to choose one of three e-mail addresses for the individual. For example, you might list both business and personal addresses as well as a Hypertext Transfer Protocol (HTTP)–based address (such as a Microsoft Hotmail® address) for the contact. The Details page of the contact form, shown in Figure 18-4, lets you add other information, such as the contact's department, office number, birthday, and anniversary. Internet Free/Busy is a feature of Outlook 2007 that allows you to see when others are free or busy so that you can efficiently schedule meetings. Outlook 2007 users have the option to publish their free/busy information to a user-specified URL file server, which you can enter in the Address box.

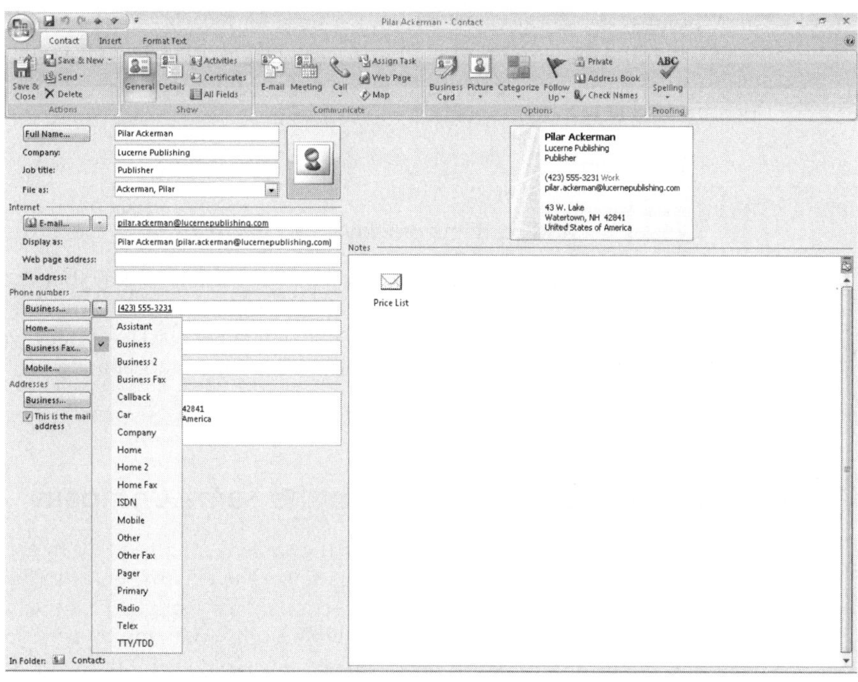

Figure 18-3. You can store multiple phone numbers for a contact, but only four appear on the form at one time.

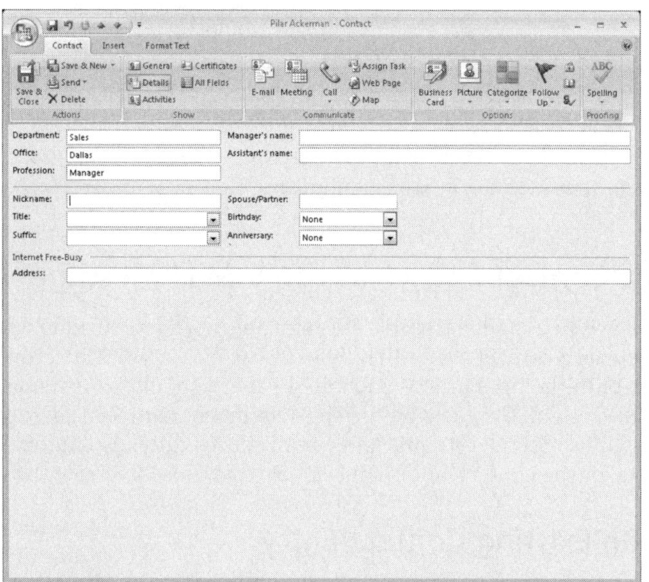

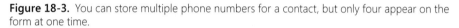

Figure 18-4. The Details page stores additional information—both business and personal—about the contact.

The Activities page of the contact form is useful for locating e-mail messages, logged phone calls, and other items or activities associated with a specific contact. For information about using the Activities page, see "Associating a Contact with Other Items and Documents" later in this chapter.

INSIDE OUT **Add contacts quickly**

When you use one of the table views (such as Phone List) to display your Contacts folder, you'll see a row at the top of the list labeled Click Here To Add A New Contact. This is a handy way to enter a contact's name and phone number quickly—simply type the information directly in the row, and Outlook 2007 adds the contact entry to the folder.

Creating Contact Entries from the Same Company

If you have several contacts who work for the same company, you can use an existing contact entry to create a new entry. Simply select the existing entry in Business Cards or Address Cards view, and then choose Actions, New Contact From Same Company. Outlook 2007 opens a new contact form with all the company information (name, address, and phone numbers) supplied–all you have to do is fill in the personal details for that individual.

Note

You can also use a template to create multiple contact entries that share common data such as company affiliation. For information about working with templates in Outlook 2007, see Chapter 25, "Using Templates."

Creating a Contact Entry from an E-Mail Message

When you receive an e-mail message from someone you'd like to add to your contacts list, you can create a contact entry directly from the message. In the From box of the message form or in the InfoBar in the Reading Pane, right-click the name, and then choose Add To Outlook Contacts on the shortcut menu. Outlook 2007 opens a new contact form with the sender's name and e-mail address already entered. Add any other necessary data for the contact, and then click Save & Close to create the entry.

Copying an Existing Contact Entry

In some cases, you might want to create a copy of a contact entry. For example, although you can keep both personal and business data in a single entry, you might want to store the data separately. You can save time by copying the existing entry rather than creating a new one from scratch.

To copy a contact entry in the Contacts folder, right-click and drag the entry to an empty spot in the folder, and then choose Copy. Outlook 2007 displays the Duplicate Contact Detected dialog box. Click Add New Contact, and then click Add to create a new entry containing all the same information as the original. You also can copy contact information to another folder. Open the folder where the contact entry is stored, and then locate the destination folder in the Navigation Pane or in the Folder List. Right-click and drag the contact entry to the destination folder, and then choose Copy on the shortcut menu.

Creating Other Contacts Folders

In addition to providing its default Contacts folder, Outlook 2007 allows you to use multiple contacts folders to organize your contacts easily. For example, you might use a shared contacts folder jointly with members of your workgroup for business contacts and keep your personal contacts in a separate folder. Or you might prefer to keep contact information you use infrequently in a separate folder to reduce the clutter in your main Contacts folder. The process of creating a contact entry in any contacts folder is the same regardless of the folder's location—whether it is part of your Exchange Server account or in a personal folders (.pst) file, for example.

To create a new folder for storing contacts, follow these steps:

1. Choose File, New, Folder, or right-click the Folder List and choose New Folder to open the Create New Folder dialog box, shown in Figure 18-5.

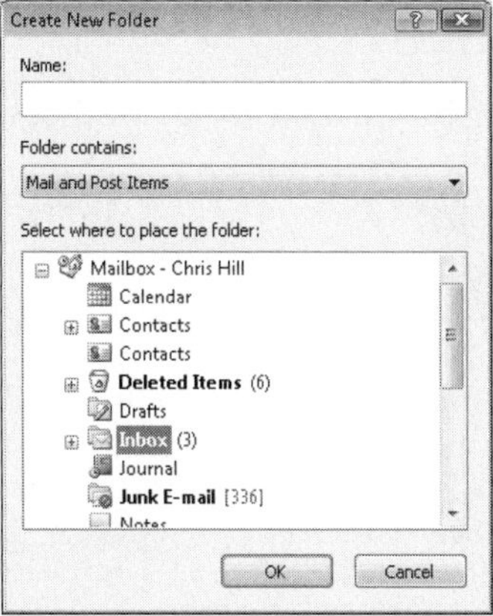

Figure 18-5. Use the Create New Folder dialog box to create new Outlook 2007 folders.

2. In the Name box, type a name for the folder. This is the folder name that will be displayed in Outlook 2007 (in the Navigation Pane and in the Folder List, for example).

3. Select Contact Items in the Folder Contains drop-down list.
4. In the Select Where To Place The Folder list, select the location for the new folder.
5. Click OK.

When you create a new contacts folder using this method, Outlook 2007 sets up the folder using default properties for permissions, rules, description, forms, and views. If you want to create a new contacts folder that uses the same custom properties as an existing folder, you can copy the folder design, as explained in the following section.

Copying the Design of a Folder

Another way to set up a new contacts folder is to copy the design of an existing contacts folder to the new one. Folder design properties include permissions, rules, description, forms, and views.

> **Note**
>
> You can copy a folder design as described here only for folders that are contained in an Exchange Server mailbox.

To copy the design of an existing contacts folder, follow these steps:

1. In the Folder List, click the contacts folder to which you want to copy the folder properties.
2. Choose File, Folder, Copy Folder Design.
3. In the Copy Design From dialog box, shown in Figure 18-6, select the folder with the design you want to copy.

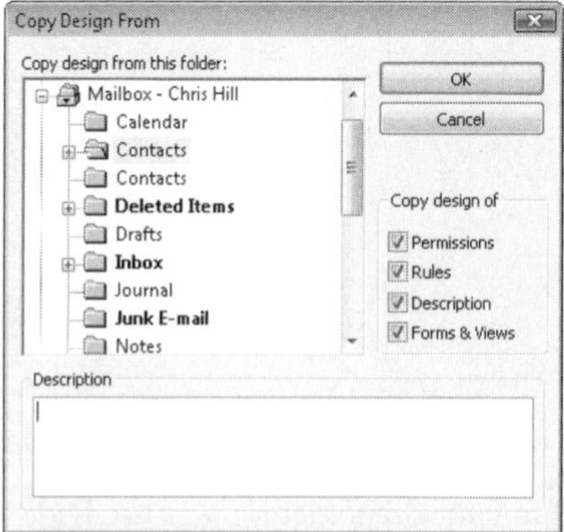

Figure 18-6. In the Copy Design From dialog box, select the folder with the design you want to copy.

4. In the Copy Design Of area, select the specific properties you want to copy.
5. Click OK. An Outlook 2007 prompt warns you that the existing properties of the current folder will be replaced with properties from the source folder. Click Yes to perform the copy, or click No to cancel.

Copying a folder's properties this way does not copy the contents of the folder–it copies only the selected properties. It is also different from copying the folder itself, which copies the contents of the folder to a new location.

For more information about copying folders, see "Using and Managing Folders" in Chapter 30.

Working with Contacts

You can do much more with your Outlook 2007 contacts list than just view address and phone information. Outlook 2007 provides a set of tools that make it easy to phone, write, e-mail, or communicate with contacts in other ways. This section explains these tools.

Associating a Contact with Other Items and Documents

As you work with contacts, it's useful to have e-mail messages, appointments, tasks, documents, or other items related to the contact at your fingertips. You can relate items to a contact by inserting one Outlook 2007 item in another. For example, if you create a task to call several of your contacts, you can use the Attach Items button on the Insert tab to insert those contacts in the task:

1. With the task open, click Attach Item on the Insert tab.
2. Select the contacts in the resulting Insert Item dialog box, shown in Figure 18-7.
3. Click OK to insert the item.

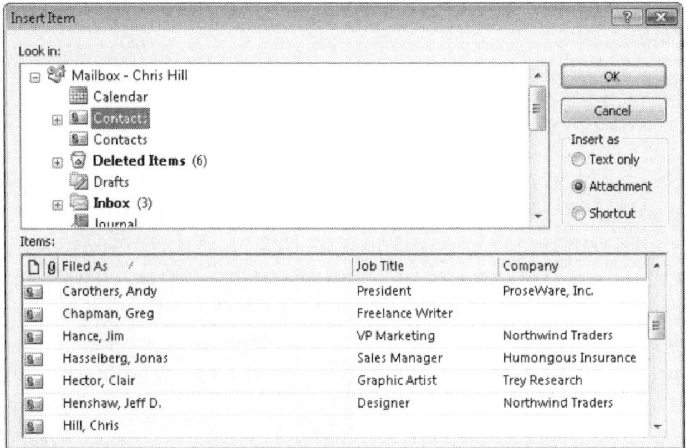

Figure 18-7. Use the Insert Item dialog box to associate contacts with a task.

For details on setting up tasks, see "Working with Tasks in the Tasks Folder" in Chapter 22.

E-mail messages that you send to a contact are automatically associated to that contact and appear on the Activities page of the contact form (discussed shortly). In addition, most items you create using the Actions menu are automatically associated with the contact entry and appear on the Activities page. For example, if you choose Actions, New Task For Contact to create a new task for a contact, Outlook 2007 associates the task with the contact.

On the Contact tab of the Ribbon of any contact form, clicking the Activities button in the Show group displays all the items associated with that contact, as shown in Figure 18-8. Outlook 2007 searches for links to items in the main Outlook 2007 folders, including Contacts, e-mail (Inbox and other message folders), Journal, Notes, Tasks, and Calendar.

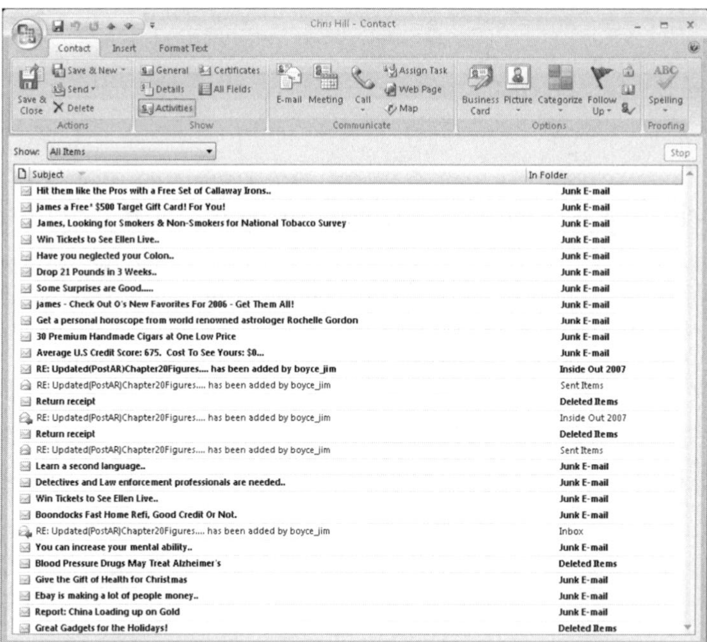

Figure 18-8. The Activities page shows all items linked to the contact.

What good is the Activities page? It's extremely useful for finding items associated with a specific contact. For example, you could sort the Inbox by sender to locate an e-mail message from a particular person, or you could use the Activities page of his or her contact form to achieve the same result. You could also view a list of the tasks assigned to an individual by checking the Activities page. Although you can view these associations in other folders, the Activities page not only offers an easier way to view the links but also lets you see all linked items, not just specific types of items.

Associating Contacts and Documents

In many cases, you might want to insert one or more documents in a contact. For example, assume that you manage contracts for several individuals or companies. You can insert a contract document into the contact covered by the contract to make it easier to open the document from the contact form. With this association, you don't need to remember the document name if you know the name of the contact with whom it is associated.

Follow these steps to insert a document in a contact:

1. Open the Contacts folder, open the contact item, and then click the Insert tab.
2. Click Attach File.
3. Locate the files you want to associate with the contact, and then click Insert.
4. The link now appears in the Notes area of the contact details.
5. Click the Contact tab, and then click Save & Close to create the link.

When you want to open the document, simply open the contact form and click the link in the Notes section.

In the preceding example, you actually inserted the document in the contact item. An alternative is to insert a hyperlink to the document in the contact item. The advantage to this method is that you are not duplicating the document–it remains in its original location on disk. When you need to open the document, you can click the hyperlink in the contact item. Or you can open the document from its location on disk.

Linking a document in a contact is easy. In step 3 of the preceding example, rather than click Insert, click the down arrow next to the Insert button, and then select Insert As Hyperlink.

Removing a Link

Occasionally, you'll want to remove a link between a contact and another item. For example, perhaps you've accidentally linked the wrong document to a contact, or perhaps the contact who had been associated with a particular project has taken a different job.

To remove a link from a contact to an item, follow these steps:

1. Open the contact item, and then on the Contact tab, in the Show group, click Activities.
2. Right-click the link to the item you want to remove, and then choose Delete.

> **Note**
>
> Although you can remove the contact association in a task, doing so removes the task from the contact's Activities page only if the task is assigned to someone other than the linked contact. If the contact owns the task, the task continues to be listed on the Activities page even after the task is marked as completed.

Assigning Categories to Contacts

A *category* is a keyword or a phrase that helps you keep track of items so that you can easily find, sort, filter, or group them. Use categories to keep track of different types of items that are related but stored in different folders. For example, you can keep track of all the meetings, contacts, and messages for a specific project when you create a category named after the project and then assign items to it.

Categories also give you a way to keep track of contacts without putting them in separate folders. For example, you can keep business and personal contacts in the same contacts folder and use the Business and Personal categories to sort the two sets of contacts into separate groups.

One quick way to assign categories to a contact is to right-click the contact item, choose Categorize, and then click a category. If the category you want doesn't appear in the category list, choose All Categories on the shortcut menu. Then, in the Color Categories dialog box, you can select the check boxes next to the categories you want to assign to the contact. Alternatively, you can open the contact item, click the Categorize button on the contact form, and select a category, or click All Categories to open the Color Categories dialog box. This dialog box is useful not only for assigning categories but also for reviewing the categories you've already assigned to an item.

For more information about how to assign a category to a contact; how to use categories to sort, filter, and group contact items; and how to create your own categories, see Chapter 5, "Creating and Using Categories."

Resolving Duplicate Contacts

If you create a contact entry using the same name or e-mail address as an entry that already exists in your Contacts folder, Outlook 2007 displays the Duplicate Contact Detected dialog box, in which you can choose to either add the new contact entry or update your existing entry with the new information, as shown in Figure 18-9.

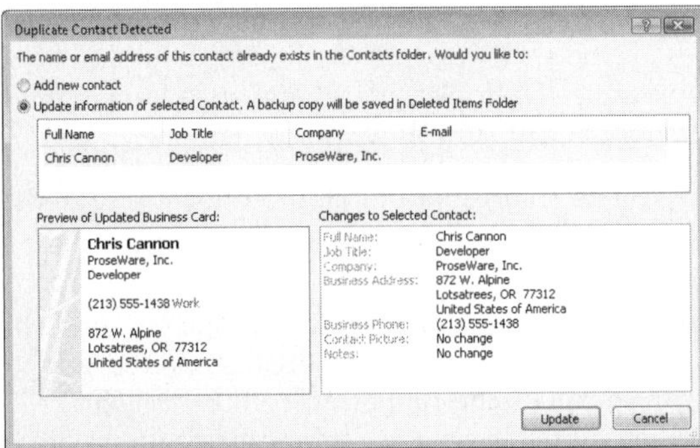

Figure 18-9. Use the Duplicate Contact Detected dialog box to tell Outlook 2007 how to handle a duplicate contact.

If you select the first option, Outlook 2007 adds the new contact to your Contacts folder, and you'll now have two entries listed under the same name or e-mail address. In that case, you'll probably want to add some information to the contact forms—perhaps company affiliation or a middle initial—to distinguish the two entries.

If you select the second option, to update the existing entry with information from the new one, Outlook 2007 compares the fields containing data in both entries and copies the data from the new entry into any fields that have conflicting data. For example, if you have a contact named Chris Ashton whose phone number is 555-5655, and you create a new contact entry for Chris Ashton with a new phone number, Outlook 2007 copies the new number into the existing entry and leaves the other fields the same.

Not all data is simply copied, however. Outlook 2007 does not copy any categories you've assigned to the new entry or any text that appears in the message box of the new entry. If you want to copy data from these fields from a new entry into an existing entry, you must copy that data manually. Likewise, if you've added links to items other than contacts on the Activities page of the new contact form (links to tasks or appointments, for example), Outlook 2007 does not copy them. Certificates and links to contacts on the Activities page are copied from the new entry and added to the existing entry without replacing the original information.

In case you need to revert to the information in the original contact entry, a copy of the original entry is stored in your Deleted Items folder whenever Outlook 2007 copies new data.

> **Note**
>
> If you are adding many contacts, Outlook 2007 can save the information faster if you do not require the program to detect duplicates. To turn off duplicate detection, choose Tools, Options. Click Contact Options, and then clear the Check For Duplicate Contacts check box.

Phoning a Contact

If you have a modem, you can use Outlook 2007 to dial any phone number you specify, including phone numbers for contacts in your contacts list.

To make a phone call to a contact using Outlook 2007, follow these steps:

1. Open the Contacts folder.
2. Right-click a contact item, and then choose Call Contact to open the New Call dialog box with the contact's phone number already entered, as shown in Figure 18-10. You can also click the Dial button on the toolbar, or if the contact form is open, click the Call button in the Communicate group on the Contact tab of the Ribbon.

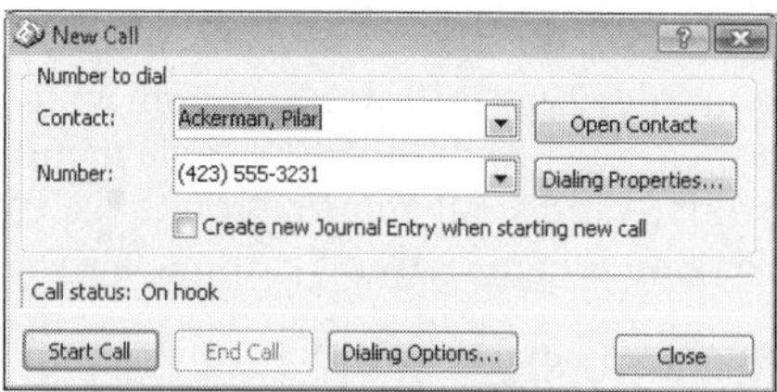

Figure 18-10. Select the number to call and other options in the New Call dialog box.

   - If you want Outlook 2007 to use a phone number associated with a different contact, type the contact's name in the Contact box, and then press **Tab** or click in the Number box. Alternatively, you can simply type the phone number in the Number box.
   - If the contact entry for the person you're calling already includes phone numbers, select the phone number in the Number box. If the contact entry doesn't specify a phone number, type the number in the Number box.

3. To keep a record of the call in the journal, select the Create New Journal Entry When Starting New Call check box. If you select this check box, a journal entry opens with the timer running after you start the call. You can type notes in the text box of the journal entry while you talk.
4. Click Start Call.
5. Pick up the phone handset, and begin the call.
6. If you created a journal entry for the call, click Pause Timer to stop the clock when you've finished the call, and then click Save & Close.
7. Click End Call, and then hang up the phone.

INSIDE OUT **Keep track of phone calls**

If you want to time a call and type notes in Outlook 2007 while you talk, you can create a journal entry for the call as you dial. The journal entry form contains a timer that you can start and stop and also provides space to type notes. For example, you might want to use this option if you bill clients for time spent on phone conversations. For more information about using the journal for phone calls, see Chapter 23, "Tracking Documents and Activities."

Note

If you omit the country code and area code from a phone number, the automatic phone dialer uses settings from the Dialing Properties dialog box, which you can access through the Phone And Modem Options icon in Control Panel or by clicking Dialing Properties in the New Call dialog box. If you include letters in the phone number, the automatic phone dialer does not recognize them.

Setting Up Speed Dial Entries

If you make frequent calls to particular phone numbers, you can create a speed dial list of those phone numbers and quickly make calls from the list. Before you become enamored with the idea of the Outlook 2007 speed dialing feature, however, you should understand that it suffers from a flaw that renders it only moderately useful. Although you can add names and numbers to the speed dial list, Outlook 2007 keeps only the numbers and loses the names. If you remember whom a particular number belongs to, this isn't a problem. However, if you have more than a few numbers on the list, the speed dial feature won't do you much good.

Follow these steps to create entries in the speed dial list:

1. Open the Contacts folder, and then choose Actions, Call Contact, New Call to open the New Call dialog box. Alternatively, you can click the Dial button on the Standard toolbar.
2. Click Dialing Options to display the Dialing Options dialog box.
3. If the person's contact information is stored in the Contacts folder, type the name in the Name box, and then press Tab to move to the Phone Number box, where Outlook 2007 automatically fills in the phone number from the contact entry. If you need to use a different number, select it from the drop-down list or type the number in the Phone Number box.
4. Click Add to add the entry to the speed dial list, shown in Figure 18-11.

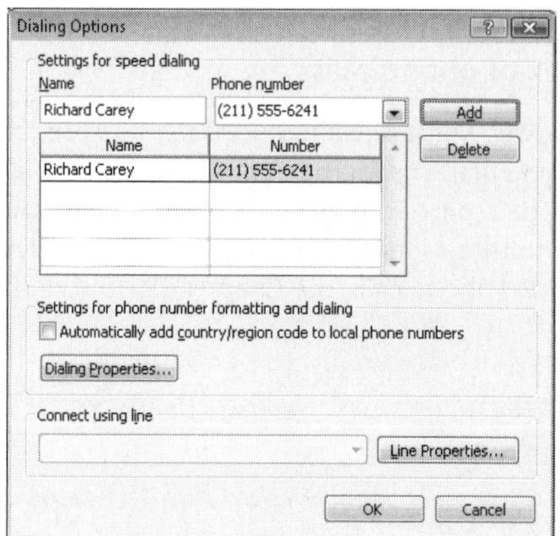

Figure 18-11. Use the Dialing Options dialog box to add speed dial numbers.

5. Repeat these steps to add other numbers as needed, and then click OK.
6. Click Close to close the New Call dialog box.

> **Note**
>
> To dial a speed dial number, click the arrow next to the Call button on the Standard toolbar, click Speed Dial, and then click a speed dial entry in the corresponding list.

Redialing Recently Dialed Numbers

In addition to using the speed dial list, you also can select a phone number from a list of numbers you've recently dialed. To do so, choose Actions, Call Contact, Redial, and then choose the number you want to dial on the menu.

Sending an E-Mail Message to a Contact

If you're working in the Contacts folder, you can send an e-mail message to one of your contacts without switching to the Inbox folder. This is a handy feature that can save a lot of time in an average work day.

Here's how to send a message from the Contacts folder:

1. In the Contacts folder, select the contact item, click Actions, Create, and then select New Message To Contact. Or simply right-click the contact, click Create, and then click New Message To Contact.
2. In the Subject box, type the subject of the message.

3. In the message body, type the message.
4. Click Send.

Connecting to a Contact's Web Site

It seems everyone has a Web site these days, whether it's a company's site or a collection of family photos. If you have the URL for a contact's Web page recorded in the contact entry, you can connect to that site directly from Outlook 2007. This is particularly handy for linking to business sites from a company contact entry—for example, you might create a link to the company's support or sales page. Associating Web sites with contacts is often more meaningful than simply storing a URL in your Favorites folder.

With the contact item open, you can connect to the contact's Web site by performing one of the following actions:

- Click on Web Page in the Communicate group on the Contact tab.
- Press **Ctrl+Shift+X**.
- Click the hyperlink that appears in the Web Page Address box in the contact entry.

Scheduling Appointments and Meetings with Contacts

Many Outlook 2007 users believe that the Calendar folder is the only place you can easily schedule a new appointment or meeting, but that's not the case. You can schedule an appointment or a meeting in any Outlook 2007 folder. The Contacts folder, however, is a logical place to create new appointments and meetings because those events are often associated with one or more contacts stored in the Contacts folder.

Scheduling a Meeting with a Contact

Meetings differ from appointments in that they are collaborative efforts that involve the schedules of all the attendees. When you set up a meeting, Outlook 2007 creates and sends meeting requests to the individuals you want to invite. You can create meeting requests for any number of contacts through the Contacts folder, saving the time of switching folders.

To send a meeting request to one or more of your contacts from the Contacts folder, follow these steps:

1. Open the Contacts folder, and then select the contact entries for those people you want to invite to the meeting. (To select multiple entries, hold down the **Ctrl** key and click the entries.)
2. Choose Actions, Create, and then select New Meeting Request To Contact.
3. In the Subject box, type a description of the proposed meeting.

4. In the Location box, type the location.
5. Enter the proposed start and end times for the meeting.
6. Select any other options you want.
7. Click Send.

For details about setting up meetings and sending meeting requests, see Chapter 21, "Scheduling Meetings and Resources."

Assigning a Task to a Contact

The Tasks folder in Outlook 2007 offers a handy way to keep track of your work and the work you delegate to others. For example, if you manage a group of people, you probably use the Tasks folder to assign tasks to the people who work for you. However, if you need to assign a job to one of your contacts, you can do this directly from the Contacts folder. Doing so adds the contact's name to the Contacts box in the task request.

Follow these steps to assign a task to a contact:

1. In the Contacts folder, select the contact, choose Actions, Create, and then select New Task For Contact. Or simply right-click the contact, choose Create, and then select New Task For Contact.
2. Outlook 2007 opens a new task form. Enter the subject and other information about the task, and then click Assign Task. Outlook 2007 adds the contact's e-mail address in the To box. Enter other information as needed, such as start and stop dates for the task.
3. Click Send to send the task request.

Flagging a Contact for Follow-Up

You can flag a contact item for follow-up to have Outlook 2007 remind you to call or e-mail the contact. For example, suppose that you want to make a note to yourself to call a colleague at 10:00 A.M. tomorrow to ask about the status of a project. You could create a note in the Notes folder, create a task, or add an appointment to your schedule—but an easy way to create the reminder is to add a follow-up flag to the contact entry in the Contacts folder. Flagging a contact item adds an additional field to the contact data. The flag text appears in the contacts list, as shown in Figure 18-12, and shows up as a message on the contact form, as shown in Figure 18-13. You can also organize the view in the Contacts folder to show contacts sorted by flag: choose View, Current View, By Follow-Up Flag to view contacts organized by follow-up flag.

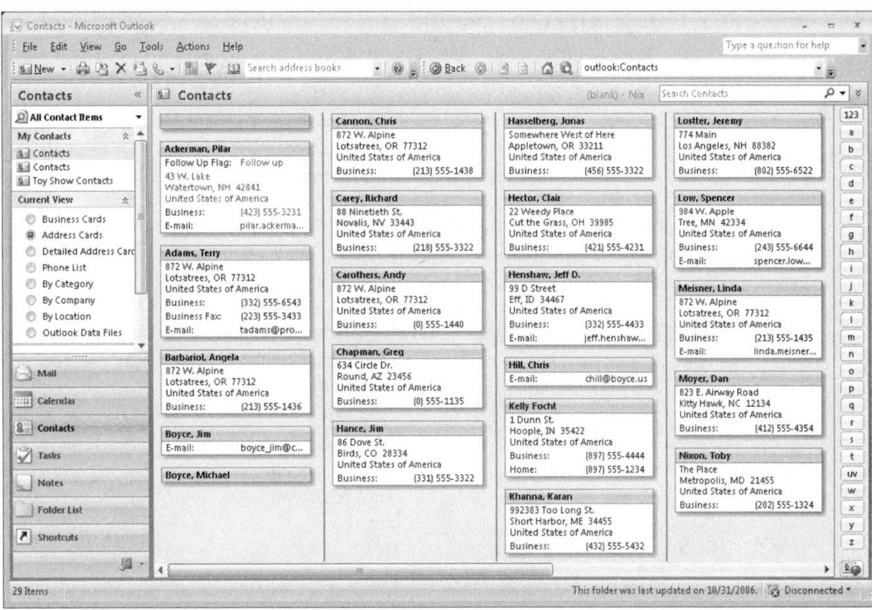

Figure 18-12. The follow-up flag appears in the contacts list.

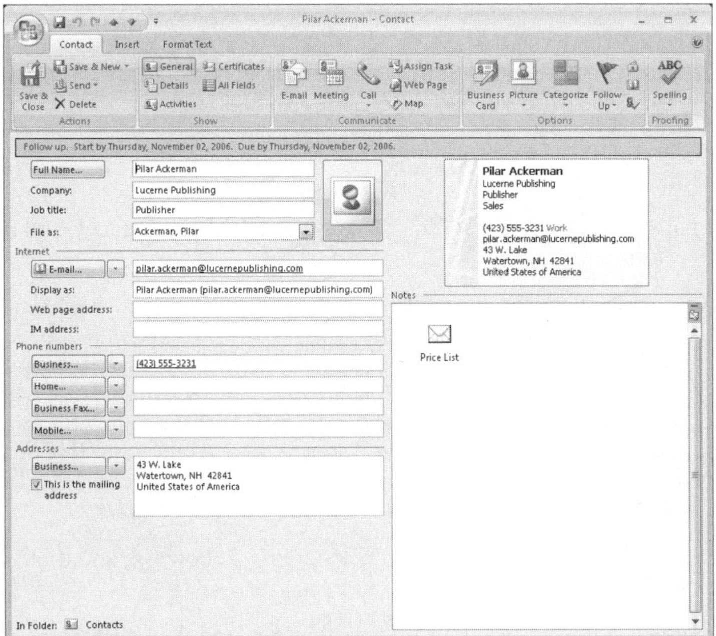

Figure 18-13. Outlook 2007 displays a message on the contact form indicating that a follow-up is needed for the contact.

If you specify a particular date and time for follow-up when you add the flag, Outlook 2007 generates a reminder at the appointed time. Adding a reminder helps ensure that you don't forget to follow up with the contact at the appropriate time.

Follow these steps to flag a contact for follow-up:

1. In the Contacts folder, select the contact that you want to flag, and then choose Actions, Follow Up. Or right-click the contact, and then choose Follow Up.
2. If one of the default follow-up time options suits you, click it. If not, click Custom to open the Custom dialog box.
3. In the Flag To box of the Custom dialog box, shown in Figure 18-14, select the flag text you want Outlook 2007 to use, or type your own flag text.

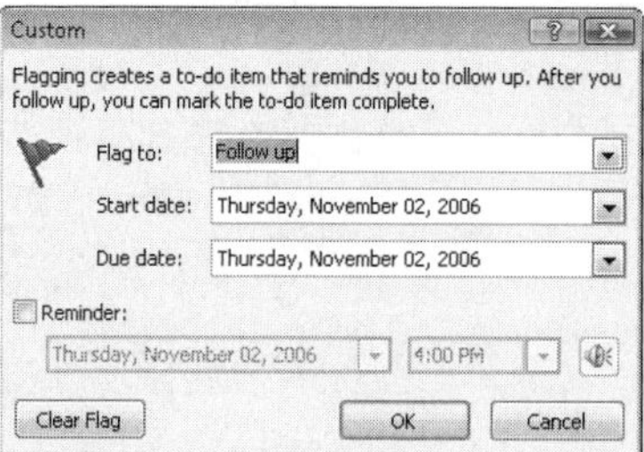

Figure 18-14. Use the Custom dialog box to specify the flag text and set an optional reminder.

4. Select a start date in the Start Date drop-down list, and then select a due date in the Due Date drop-down list.
5. If you want a reminder, click the Reminder option, select a date, and then specify a time.
6. Click OK. Outlook 2007 adds the flag text to the contact item and adds an entry to your task list.

When you have completed your follow-up action, you can remove the flag from the contact item (clear the flag) or mark the follow-up as completed. If you clear the flag, Outlook 2007 removes it from the contact item and the task list. If you prefer to have the flag remain, you can mark the follow-up as completed. In this case, the flag remains, but the contact form includes a message indicating that the follow-up was accomplished (and the date). When you choose View, Arrange By, Current View, By Follow-Up Flag to view the Contacts folder sorted by flag, the completed items are grouped together. Use one of the following methods to mark a follow-up flag as completed:

- Select the flagged contact item, click Actions, Follow Up, and then click Mark Complete.
- Right-click the contact item, click Follow Up, and then click Mark Complete.

Use one of the following methods to clear a flag, which removes it from the contact item:

- Select the contact item, click Actions, Follow Up, and then click Clear Flag.
- Right-click the contact item in the Contacts folder, click Follow Up, and then click Clear Flag.

Finding Contacts

If you store only a small list of contacts, finding a particular contact is usually not a problem. As the number of contacts grows, however, it becomes more and more difficult to locate information, especially if you aren't sure about a name. For example, you might remember that a person works for a certain company but can't recall the person's name. Outlook 2007 provides features to help you quickly and easily locate contact information.

Perhaps the easiest method of locating a contact if you know the name is to type the name in the Search Address Books box on the Outlook 2007 Standard toolbar and then press **Enter**. Outlook 2007 locates the contact and displays the contact form. If more than one contact matches the data you've entered, Outlook 2007 displays the Choose Contact dialog box, which lists all the matches to allow you to select the appropriate one, as shown in Figure 18-15.

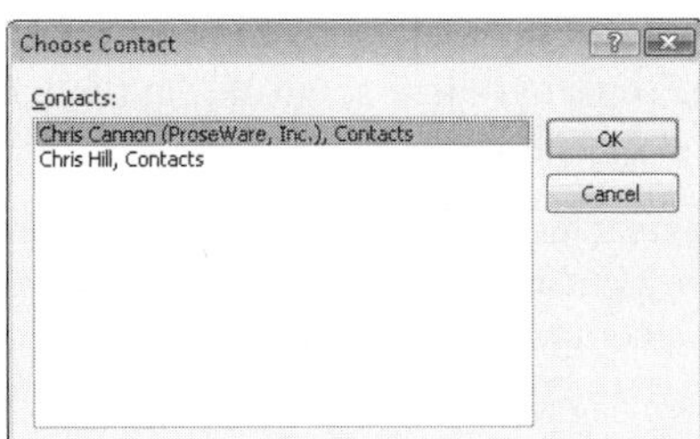

Figure 18-15. Use the Choose Contact dialog box to select the correct contact after a search returns multiple items.

Finally, if you need to perform an advanced search, choose Tools, Instant Search, Advanced Find to open the Advanced Find dialog box, shown in Figure 18-16. You can use this dialog box to perform more complex searches based on multiple conditions, such as searching for both name and company.

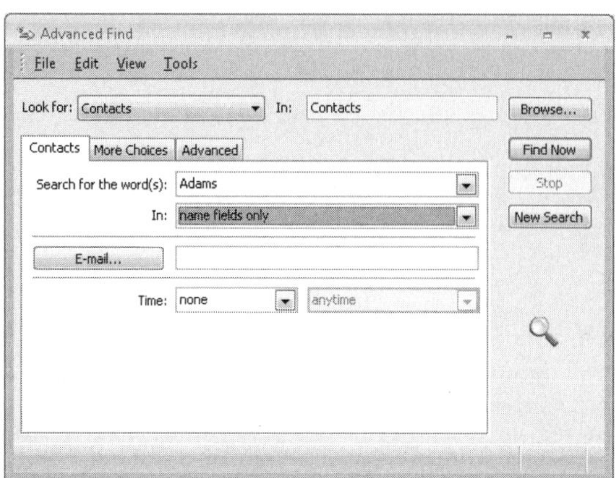

Figure 18-16. Use the Advanced Find dialog box to perform more complex searches using multiple conditions.

For a detailed discussion of how to perform both simple and complex searches in Outlook 2007, see Chapter 33, "Finding and Organizing Outlook Data."

Making a Common Change to Multiple Contacts

Making changes to a single contact doesn't take long, but making the same change to several contacts can take a lot of time. You can relieve some of that time drain by propagating a change for a single contact to multiple contacts.

For example, let's say that your Contacts folder includes contacts for several people who work for the same organization. The organization's fax number has changed, and now you need to make that change for each contact. Propagating the change to other contacts is a simple drag-and-drop action with the Outlook 2007 capability to group items in the Contacts folder view.

Here's how to make it happen:

1. Open the folder containing the contacts to be changed.
2. In the Navigation Pane, click the view that best displays the information you need to change. In this example, choose By Company because its table view includes the fax number. Then click View, Arrange By, Custom.

> **Note**
>
> Only table views give you the option of grouping. The Business Cards, Address Cards, and Detailed Address Cards views do not.

3. Click Group By, and in the Group Items By drop-down list, select the item you want to change (in this example, Business Fax). Figure 18-17 shows By Company view grouped by Business Fax.

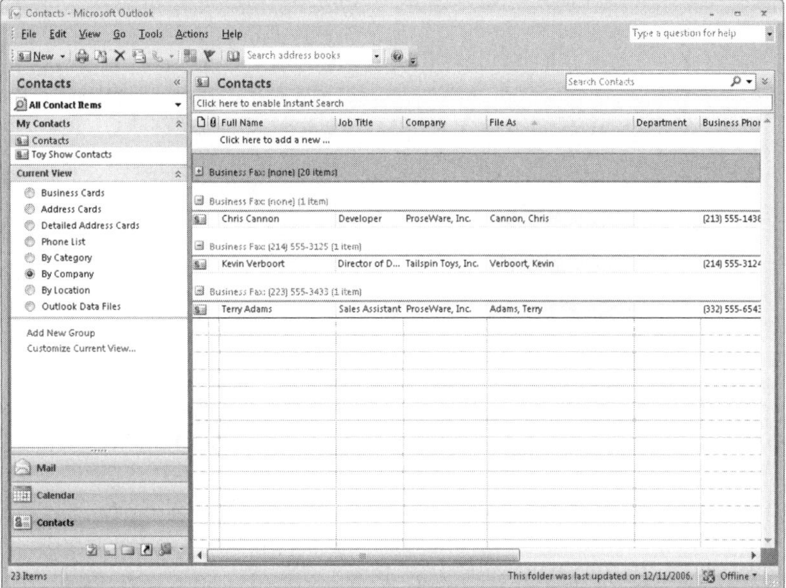

Figure 18-17. By Company view has been grouped by the Business Fax field.

4. In the Expand/Collapse Defaults drop-down list, select All Collapsed. Click OK twice to return to the view you just created.

5. Expand the group that includes the item you want to change.

6. Open one of the contacts, make the needed change, and then save and close the contact. This contact now appears by itself under a different group.

7. To propagate the change, drag the gray grouping bar for the unchanged contacts to the grouping bar for the modified contact. Outlook 2007 makes the change to the other contacts automatically.

Changing multiple items at one time is easy as long as you remember that you need to first display a table view and then group it by the item you want to change. You can either customize an existing view or create a new one. If you customize an existing standard view, you can restore it to its default condition by clicking View, Arrange By, Current View, Define Views, selecting the view, and then clicking Reset.

Viewing Contacts

Outlook 2007 provides predefined views for reviewing your contacts list in the Contacts folder. For example, Address Cards view displays names and addresses of contacts in small blocks that look like address labels. This view is a convenient way to look up a contact's mailing address. In Phone List view, Outlook 2007 displays contact entries in table rows with details such as phone, job title, and department name in columns. This view is helpful for quickly finding a contact's phone number or job title. You can customize the various standard views to control the amount of detail or to help you organize and analyze information.

Using Standard Views in the Contacts Folder

The Contacts folder offers several standard formats for viewing contacts. To change views, select a view in the Navigation Pane or click View, Current View, and then select the view that you want to use. Two of the standard formats are card views and the rest are table views, as described in the following list:

- **Business Cards** This view shows the contacts in a business card format.
- **Address Cards** This view displays contact entries as individual cards with name, one mailing address, and business and home phone numbers.
- **Detailed Address Cards** This view also displays individual cards, which show name, business and home addresses, phone numbers, and additional details such as job title, company, and Web address.
- **Phone List** This table view displays a list with the contact's name, the company name, business phone number, business fax number, home phone number, mobile phone number, categories, and a check box to enable or disable journaling for the contact.
- **By Category** This view groups contacts by their assigned categories.
- **By Company** This view groups contacts by company, which is helpful when you're trying to find a contact who works for a particular company.
- **By Location** This view groups contacts by country or region.
- **Outlook Data Files** This view shows contacts grouped by their storage location.

> **Note**
>
> You can easily resize address cards by dragging the vertical separator between columns, which changes the width of all card columns.

Customizing Contacts View

The methods of customizing the view in Outlook 2007 folders are generally the same for all folders. This section examines some specific ways you might customize the Contacts folder to make it easier to locate and work with contacts. For example, you might use a specific color for contacts who work for a particular company. You can also change the fonts used for the card headings and body, specify card width and height, and automatically format contact entries based on rules.

Chapter 27, "Creating Custom Views and Print Styles," covers additional ways to customize views.

Filtering Contacts View

You can filter the view in the Contacts folder to show only those contacts that meet the conditions you specify in the filter. For example, you can use a filter to view only those contacts who work for a particular company or who live in a particular city.

Follow these steps to set up a view filter in the Contacts folder:

1. Open the Contacts folder, click View, Current View, and then Customize Current View.
2. Click Filter in the Customize View dialog box.
3. In the Filter dialog box, specify the conditions for the filter. If you don't see the items you need to specify for the condition, use the Field drop-down list on the More Choices or Advanced tab to select the necessary field.
4. Click OK to close the Filter dialog box, and then click OK in the Customize View dialog box to apply the filter.

When you want to view the entire contents of the folder again, you can remove the filter, as detailed here:

1. Click View, Current View, and then select Customize Current View.
2. Click Filter.
3. In the Filter dialog box, click Clear All, and then click OK.
4. Click OK to close the View Summary dialog box.

> **Note**
>
> If you want to reset the view to its default properties, click Reset Current View in the Customize Current View dialog box.

Configuring Fonts and Card Dimensions

You can change the font used for card headings and the card body text in the card views (Address Cards view and Detailed Address Cards view). You can also change the font style, size, and script, but not the color.

Follow these steps to change the font for card headings and body text:

1. Click View, Current View, and then select Customize Current View.
2. In the Customize View dialog box, click Other Settings to display the Format Card View dialog box, shown in Figure 18-18.

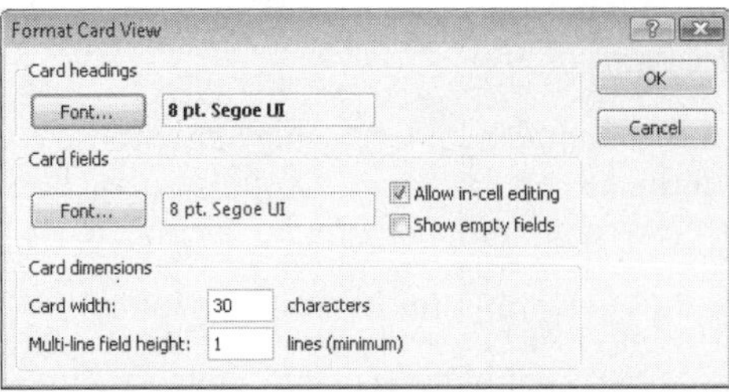

Figure 18-18. Use the Format Card View dialog box to specify the font for card headings and body text.

3. Click Font in the Card Headings or Card Fields area of the dialog box to open a standard Font dialog box in which you can select font characteristics.
4. Make your font selections, and then click OK.
5. Specify options according to the following list, and then click OK:

   Allow In-Cell Editing Selecting this check box allows you to modify contact data by clicking a field in the view without opening the contact form.

   Show Empty Fields Select this check box if you want to show all fields for all contacts, even if the fields are empty. Clear this check box to simplify the view of your Contacts folder. Note that when this check box is selected, Outlook 2007 displays all fields defined for the view, not all contact fields.

   Card Width Set the card width (in number of characters) using this option.

   Multi-Line Field Height Use this option to specify the number of lines you want to display on the card for multiline fields.

6. Click OK to close the Customize View dialog box.

Using Automatic Formatting

Outlook 2007 performs some limited automatic formatting of data in the Contacts folder. For example, it uses bold for distribution list items, regular font for unread contacts, and red for overdue contacts (contact entries with an overdue follow-up flag). You can make changes to these automatic formatting rules, and you can even create your own rules. For example, you might want to display overdue contacts in blue rather than in red, or you might want to use a particular color for all contacts who work for a certain company.

Follow these steps to modify the formatting for an existing rule or to create a new rule:

1. Open the Contacts folder. Click View, Current View, and then Customize Current View.
2. Click Automatic Formatting in the Customize View dialog box to display the Automatic Formatting dialog box, shown in Figure 18-19.

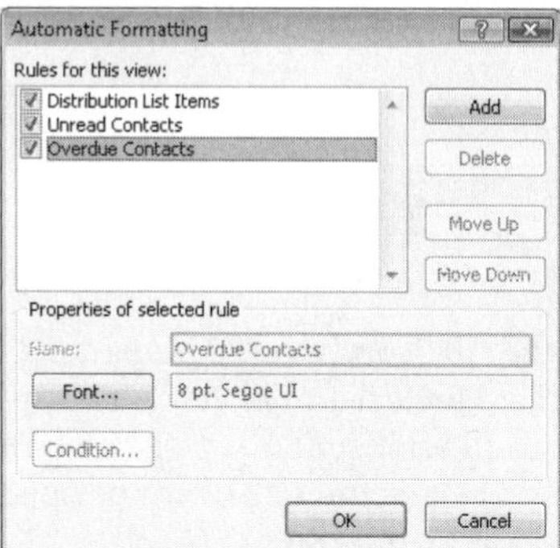

Figure 18-19. Use the Automatic Formatting dialog box to create custom rules that control how Outlook 2007 displays contacts.

3. If you want to modify an existing rule, select the rule, and then click Font to change the font characteristics or click Condition to modify the condition for the rule. If you are changing the condition, skip to step 6. Otherwise, skip to step 7.

> **Note**
>
> You can modify a rule condition only for rules that you have created. You cannot change the condition for the three predefined rules.

4. Click Add if you want to add a new rule. Outlook 2007 creates a new rule named Untitled.
5. Type a new name in the Name field, click Font and specify font characteristics, and then click Condition to open the Filter dialog box, shown in Figure 18-20.

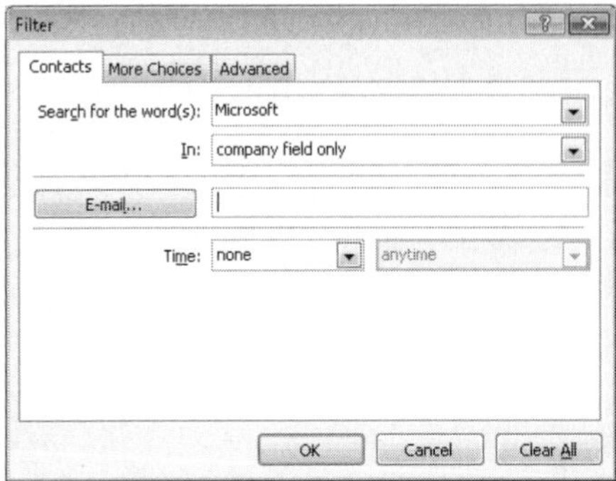

Figure 18-20. You can specify complex conditions using the Filter dialog box.

6. Specify the criteria to define the rule condition. For example, click Advanced, click Field, click Frequently Used Fields, and click Company. Then select Contains in the Condition drop-down list and type a company name in the Value box. This will automatically format all contacts from the specified company using the font properties you specify in the next step.
7. Click OK to close the Filter dialog box, click Font in the Automatic Formatting dialog box, specify the font properties, and then click OK.
8. Close the Automatic Formatting and Customize View dialog boxes to view the effects of the new rule.

> **Note**
>
> Automatic formatting rules follow the hierarchy in the list shown in the Automatic Formatting dialog box. Use the Move Up and Move Down buttons to change the order of rules in the lists and thereby change the order in which they are applied.

Filtering Contacts with Categories

Categorizing contacts allows you to organize your contacts into groups that you create. For example, categories provide an easy way to distinguish all of your personal contacts from business contacts. Categorizing also gives you the ability to group people from different companies who are all involved in the same project. Outlook 2007 provides an easy way for you to categorize your contacts, using color coding to distinguish the categories from each other. You can also define custom labels for categories so that you can identify the category by both color and label.

You can define your categories either by using a color category for the first time or by using the Color Categories dialog box. Outlook 2007 offers three ways to open the Color Categories dialog box:

- Click the Categorize button on the Standard toolbar, and then click All Categories.
- Click Actions, Categorize, and then click All Categories.
- Right-click any contact item, and then choose Categorize, All Categories.

> **Note**
>
> When you use a color category for the first time, Outlook 2007 displays a Rename Category dialog box that lets you change the text associated with the category.

To create a new category and assign a color to it, follow these steps:

1. In the Color Categories dialog box, click New.
2. Type an appropriate name for the category, and and then select a color in the drop-down color palette.
3. Click OK.

> **Note**
>
> For quick category assignment, assign a unique shortcut key to each of the categories you use most often. You can assign the shortcut key through the Color Categories dialog box.

You should now see the category you just created in your category list. To assign these categories to your contacts, follow these steps:

1. In the Contacts folder, right-click any item in the contacts list.
2. Click Categorize on the shortcut menu.
3. Select the category you just added in the list.

Now that you have categorized your contacts, it's time to view them. Outlook 2007 has already provided a filter to show your contacts grouped in the way you selected. To view your contacts by category, use one of the following methods:

- In the Navigation Pane, under Current View, select By Category.

- Click View, Current View, and then By Category.
- In the Navigation Pane, select Customize Current View, and then select Filter. Click More Choices, and then click the Category button. Select the category or categories you want to display, and then click OK. Click OK twice more to exit the dialog boxes.

For more information about categories, see Chapter 5, "Creating and Using Categories."

Printing Contacts

As an experienced user of Windows, you probably need little if any explanation of how to print. So rather than focusing on basic printing commands, this section offers some insight into why you might print from the Contacts folder and what your options are when you do print.

Why print? If you're like most people, you probably try to work from your computer as much as possible and reduce the amount of paper you generate. The completely paperless office is still a distant goal for most people, however, and there will be times when you want to print your contacts list. For example, you might need to take a copy of your contacts with you on a business trip, but you don't have a notebook computer. A hard copy of your contacts is the solution.

Outlook 2007 supports several predefined styles that allow you to print contact information using various formats, including preprinted sheets for several popular day planners. You can print a single contact entry, a selection of entries, or all entries. To print a selection (one or more), first select the contact entries to print by holding down the **Ctrl** key and clicking each one. If you want to print all contacts, choose Edit, Select All, and then choose File, Print to open the Print dialog box, shown in Figure 18-21.

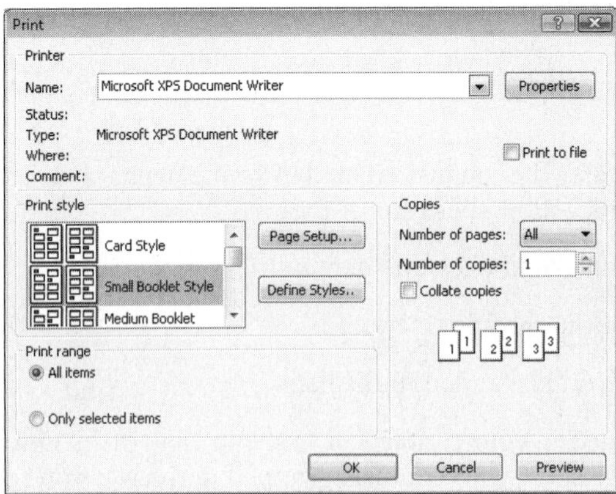

Figure 18-21. You can select several predefined styles in the Print dialog box.

In the Print Style area of the Print dialog box, you can select one of five print styles, each of which results in a different printed layout. You can use the styles as listed, modify them, or create new styles. To modify an existing style, select the style, and then click Page Setup to display the Page Setup dialog box, which resembles the one shown in Figure 18-22.

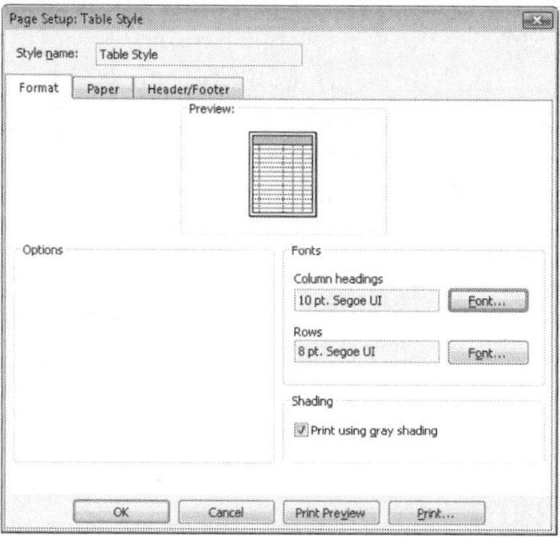

Figure 18-22. Modify a print style in the Page Setup dialog box.

Use the Format tab of this dialog box to specify fonts and shading and to set options such as printing a contact index on the side of each page, adding headings for each letter, and setting the number of columns. Use the Paper tab to select the type of paper, such as a preprinted sheet for your day planner, as well as to set up margins, paper source, and orientation. Use the Header/Footer tab to add a header, a footer, or both to the printout.

If you need a custom layout but don't want to modify the existing styles, you can create your own style. In the Print dialog box, click Define Styles to display the Define Print Styles dialog box, shown in Figure 18-23. Select a style to use as the basis for your new style, and then click Copy to open the Page Setup dialog box. Modify settings as needed, and then click OK to save the new style. Outlook 2007 uses the same name but prefixes the name with *Copy Of* (Copy Of Card Style, for example). You can change the name in the Style Name box in the Page Setup dialog box.

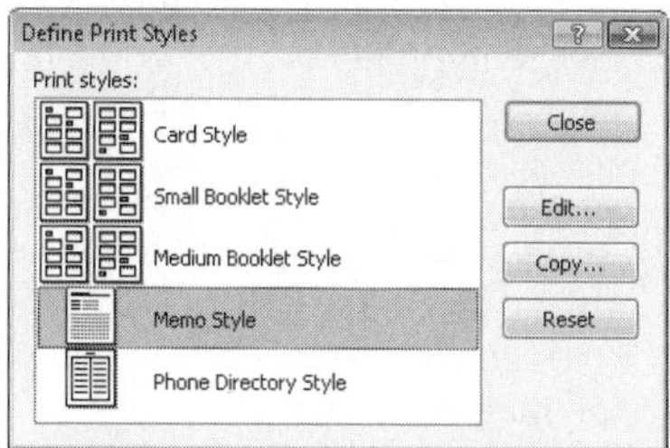

Figure 18-23. Select a style to copy in the Define Print Styles dialog box.

For a detailed discussion of printing in Outlook 2007 and creating custom print styles, see "Printing in Outlook" in Chapter 27.

Custom Contact Printing with Word

Although Outlook 2007 provides several features for printing, your capability to customize the way the printed documents look is rather limited. You can overcome this limitation by using Office Word 2007 rather than Outlook 2007 to print contacts. You have considerable control over how a Word 2007 document looks and is printed, making Word 2007 an excellent tool for custom printing. You can copy data from Outlook 2007 to Word 2007 manually, but it's much more efficient to use a macro to automate the process and make custom contact printing a one-click process. Because the process requires macros and macros haven't yet been covered in detail, refer to Chapter 27, "Creating Custom Views and Print Styles," which includes a section that explains how to print contacts using Word 2007. It also includes sample macro code that you can tailor to your specific needs.

Working with Distribution Lists

A distribution list is a collection of contacts. It provides an easy way to send messages to a group of people. For example, if you frequently send messages to the marketing team, you can create a distribution list named Marketing Team that contains the names of all members of this team. A message sent to this distribution list goes to all recipients who belong to the list. Outlook 2007 converts the address list to individual addresses, so recipients see their own names and the names of all other recipients in the To box of the message instead of seeing the name of the distribution list. You can use distribution lists in messages, task requests, and meeting requests.

INSIDE OUT **Use nested distribution lists**

Distribution lists can contain other distribution lists as well as individual addresses. For example, you might create a distribution list for each of seven departments and then create one distribution list containing those seven others. You could use this second list when you need to send messages to all seven departments.

You can create distribution lists in your Contacts folder using your contacts list. You can store addresses from any available source (the Global Address List [GAL], a personal address book, a contacts list, and so on). In general, you should create your distribution lists in the location where you store the majority of your addresses.

Creating a Personal Distribution List

Follow these steps to create a new distribution list in the Contacts folder:

1. Click File, New, and then select Distribution List to open a distribution list form, as shown in Figure 18-24.

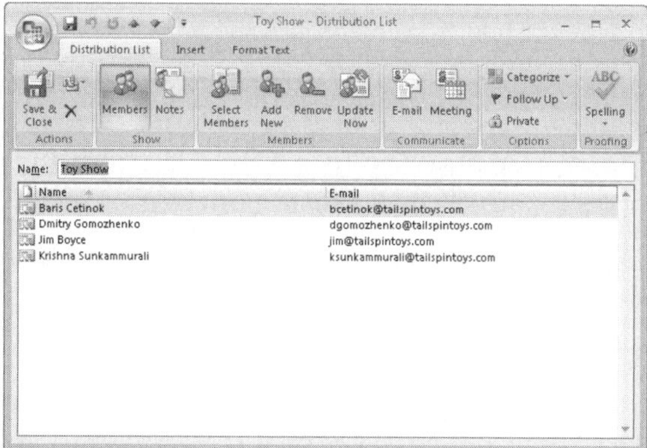

Figure 18-24. Add members to and remove members from a distribution list on the distribution list form.

2. Type the name for your distribution list in the Name box. This is the name by which the list will appear in your Contacts folder. If you're creating a distribution list for the marketing department, for example, use the name Marketing.

3. In the Members group, click Select Members to open the Select Members dialog box, shown in Figure 18-25.

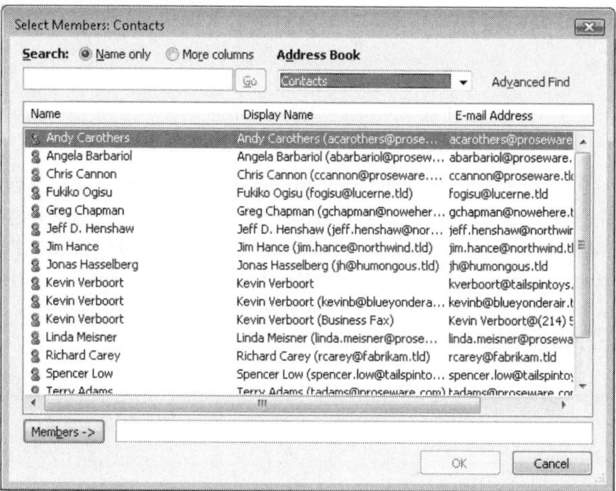

Figure 18-25. Use the Select Members dialog box to select addresses to include in the list.

4. In the Address Book drop-down list, select the location from which you want to select addresses (for example, the Global Address List or the Contacts folder).

5. In the Search box, type a name that you want to include, which locates the name in the list, or select the name in the Name list, and then click Members.
6. Repeat steps 4 and 5 to add all addressees to the list, and then click OK when you've finished.
7. If you want to add a longer description of the distribution list, click the Notes button and type the text.
8. Click Save & Close. The new distribution list is added to your contacts list.

Adding or Deleting Names in a Distribution List

You can easily add and delete names in a distribution list. For example, perhaps your department has added a few new employees and you need to add their addresses to the department distribution list.

Follow these steps to add or remove names in a distribution list:

1. In your Contacts folder, open the distribution list to display the distribution list form.
2. Perform one or more of the following actions:
   - To add an address from an address book or a contacts folder, click Select Members.
   - To add an address that is not in a contacts folder or an address book, click Add New.
   - To delete a name, click the name, and then click Remove.
3. Click Save & Close.

INSIDE OUT **Fine-tune distribution lists**

You can assign categories to a distribution list, mark it as private, or add notes to it by using the distribution list form. You can also update addresses in a distribution list if their source addresses have changed. For example, if you've changed a colleague's e-mail address in the contact entry and now want to update the corresponding address in the distribution list, you can open the distribution list, select the address, and click Update Now on the distribution list form.

Sharing Contacts

Outlook 2007 lets you share contacts with others by sending vCards through e-mail or by sharing your Contacts folder. The former method lets you share contacts with people who don't use Outlook 2007 or who don't have access to your network or to your Exchange Server. The latter method–sharing your Contacts folder–is a good solution when you need to provide access to contacts for others on your network. This section explains how to share contacts through vCards, offers a brief overview of sharing the Contacts folder, and explains how to share contacts from a public folder.

Note

You can use Windows SharePoint Services (WSS) to share contacts and even integrate those contacts within Outlook 2007. See Chapter 40, "Collaboration with Outlook and Windows SharePoint Services," to learn how to work with and share contacts from a WSS site.

Sharing Your Contacts Folders

If you're running Outlook 2007 with Exchange Server 2000 or later, you can assign permissions to a folder stored in your Exchange Server mailbox to give other users access to that folder. You can grant permissions on a group basis or a per-user basis. Outlook 2007 provides two groups by default–Anonymous and Default–that you can use to assign permissions on a global basis. You also can add individual users to the permissions list and use distribution lists to assign permissions.

Outlook 2007 offers two methods to set permissions on a folder. Here is the easiest method:

1. Open the Folder List, right-click the Contacts folder, and then choose Share Contacts.
2. Outlook 2007 displays a Sharing Invitation message, as shown in Figure 18-26, on the next page.
3. Click To, and then select the people to whom you want to grant access.
4. If you also want to request access to the recipients' calendars, select the Request Permission To View Recipient's Contacts Folder check box.

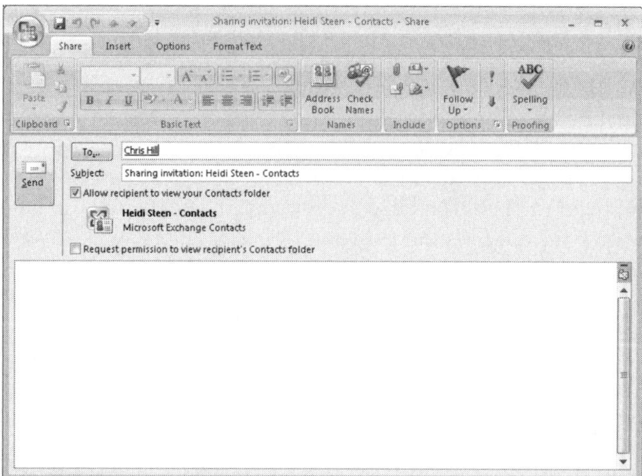

Figure 18-26. You can share your Contacts folder using a simple sharing message.

5. Click Send.

6. Outlook 2007 prompts you to confirm that you want to grant Reviewer (read-only) access to the folder. Click Yes.

The message that the recipients receive informs them that they have been granted access to the folder and can click Open in the message header to open your Contacts folder in Outlook, as shown in Figure 18-27.

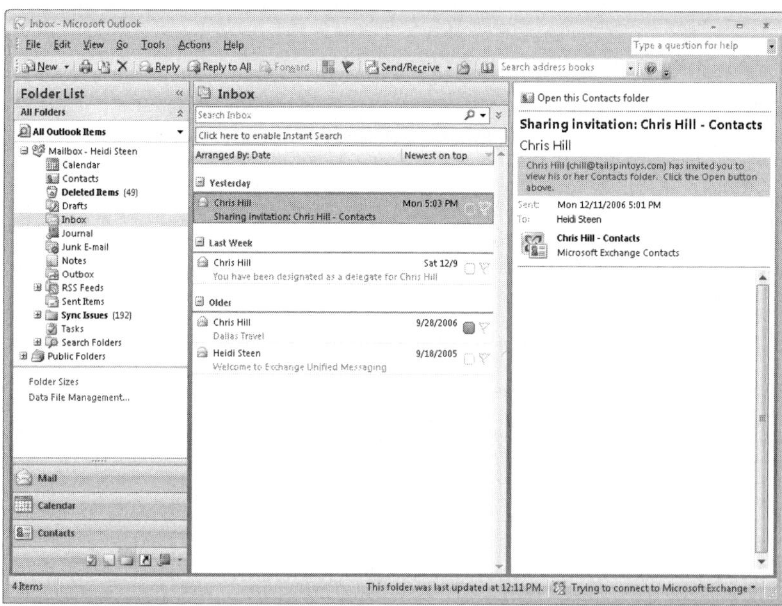

Figure 18-27. Users who receive the sharing message can simply click Open This Contacts Folder in the message header to open the shared folder.

You can also set permissions directly on the folder, which is useful when you want to specify permissions other than Reviewer. Follow these steps to set permissions on your Contacts folder to allow other users access to your contacts:

1. Open the Folder List, right-click the Contacts folder, and then choose Properties on the shortcut menu to display the Contacts Properties dialog box for the folder.
2. Click the Permissions tab, as shown in Figure 18-28.

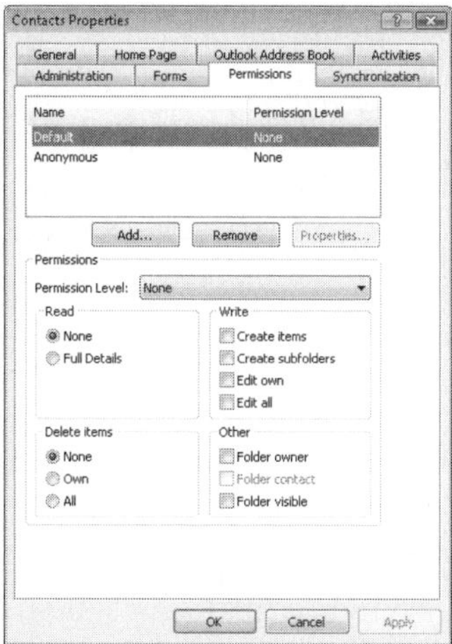

Figure 18-28. Configure permissions on the Permissions tab.

3. Click Add to display the Add Users dialog box.
4. Select the person for whom you want to configure permissions, and then click Add. Click OK to return to the Permissions tab.
5. In the Name box, select the name of the person you just added.
6. In the Permission Level drop-down list, select a level of permission according to the tasks that the user should be able to perform with your Contacts folder. When you select a permission level, Outlook 2007 selects one or more individual permissions in the Permissions area. You also can select or clear individual permissions as needed.
7. Click OK to save the permission changes.

You can grant several permissions for a folder, and you can assign them in any combination you need. See "Sharing Your Calendar" in Chapter 36 to learn more about sharing permissions for Outlook folders.

For a complete explanation of permissions and folder sharing, see "Granting Access to Folders" in Chapter 35.

Sharing Contacts with vCards

A vCard presents contact information as an electronic business card that can be sent through e-mail. vCards are based on an open standard, allowing any application that supports vCards to share contact information. In addition to sending a vCard as an attachment, you also can include it with your message signature.

When you receive a message with a vCard attached, a paper clip icon appears in the Reading Pane to indicate the attached vCard. Use one of the following methods to add the data in the vCard as a contact entry:

- In the Reading Pane, select the paper clip icon, and then click the file name that appears.
- If you've opened the message, right-click the business card icon in the message, and then choose Open.

After you can view the information sent in the vCard, click Save & Close to add the information to your contacts list.

> **Note**
>
> You can drag a vCard from a message to your Contacts folder to add the contact information.

Creating a vCard from a Contact Entry

As mentioned earlier, one way to send contact information to someone else is to attach the contact entry to a message as a vCard. You can use this method to share your own contact information or to share one or more other contact entries with another person.

Follow these steps to attach a vCard to a message:

1. In the Contacts folder, select the contact item you want to send as a vCard.
2. Choose Actions, Send Full Contact, In Internet Format (vCard). Outlook 2007 opens a new message form with the contact entry attached as a vCard.
3. Specify an address, complete the message as you would any other, and then click Send to send it.

Including a vCard with Your Signature

The second method of sharing a contact is useful when you want to share your own contact information. Rather than attaching it to a message, you can have Outlook 2007 send it along with your message signature. This ensures that the vCard is sent with all outgoing messages.

Note

You can attach text (such as a favorite quote) and graphics to each outgoing message as part of your signature. For complete details on using signatures with Outlook 2007, see "Using Signatures" in Chapter 9.

Follow these steps to add your contact information as a vCard to your message signature:

1. Create your own contact entry if you have not already done so.
2. Click Tools, Options.
3. Click Mail Format and then Signatures.
4. Click New.
5. Enter a name for your signature.
6. Click Business Card.
7. Browse to your own business card, and then click OK.
8. In the Signatures And Stationery dialog box, shown in Figure 18-29, add other information as needed.

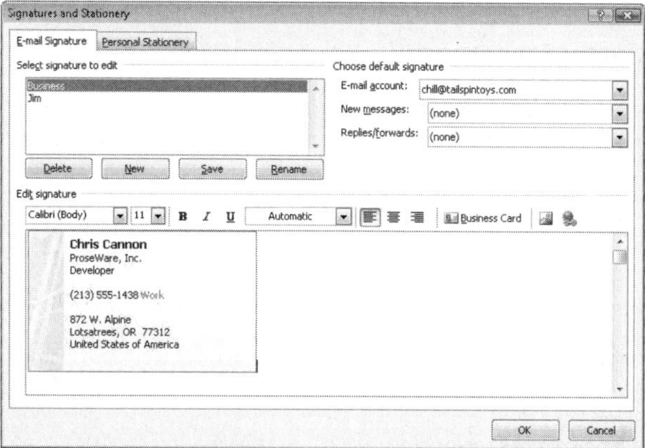

Figure 18-29. Use the Signatures And Stationery dialog box to add text, graphics, and a vCard to your outgoing messages automatically.

9. Click OK twice.

From now on, your contact information will be attached to outgoing messages.

> **Note**
>
> To prevent signatures from being added to your outgoing messages, choose Tools, Options, and then click the Mail Format tab. Select None in the New Messages drop-down list.

Saving a Contact Entry as a vCard

In addition to sending vCards as e-mail attachments, Outlook 2007 allows you to save a contact entry to a file as a vCard. You might do this if you want to link to vCards on a Web site so that others can download the vCards directly rather than receiving a message with the vCards attached. Or perhaps you want to save a large number of contacts as vCards and send them to someone on a Zip disk or other removable media rather than through e-mail.

Follow these steps to save a contact item as a vCard file:

1. Open the contact item that you want to save as a vCard.
2. In Windows Vista™, click the Microsoft Office Button, click Save As, and then click Export To vCard File. In Microsoft Windows XP, click File, Save As. In the Save As type drop-down list, select vCard Files (*.vcf).
3. Type a name in the File Name box, and then click Save.

Saving a vCard Attachment in Your Contacts Folder

When you receive a message containing a vCard attachment, you'll probably want to save the vCard as a contact item in your Contacts folder. Follow these steps to do so:

1. Open the message containing the attached vCard.
2. Double-click the attachment to open it.
3. In the open contact form, click Save & Close. The information in the vCard is saved in your Contacts folder by default.

Setting Contact Options

Outlook 2007 provides several options that control how it stores and displays contacts. To view these options, choose Tools, Options, and then click Contact Options on the

Preferences tab. In the Contact Options dialog box, shown in Figure 18-30, you can configure the following options:

- **Default "Full Name" Order** This option specifies how Outlook 2007 creates the Full Name field when you click Full Name in the new contact form and enter the contact's first, middle, and last names, along with suffix and title.
- **Default "File As" Order** This option specifies the name that Outlook 2007 uses in the card title. Outlook 2007 uses the information you specify for first, middle, and last name—as well as company—to create the card title based on how this option is set.
- **Check For Duplicate Contacts** Select this check box if you want Outlook 2007 to check for duplicate contacts when you create new contacts.

Figure 18-30. Configure options for contacts in the Contact Options dialog box.

Using Contacts Effectively

Contacts can be a very powerful tool in Outlook 2007. As with any Outlook 2007 feature, you can use them in different ways to suit your needs, and how you use them might not be the most effective way for someone else. However, there are some things you can do to make contacts more useful:

- **Be complete.** The more information you can include for each contact, the more useful your contacts will be. For example, fill in as many of the phone number fields as you can; this will give you more options when using Outlook 2007 to dial a contact.
- **Use categories to your advantage.** Assigning categories to your contacts will help you organize them more effectively—for example, keeping your personal contacts separated from your business contacts.

- **Enter the company name for your business contacts.** Entering the company name in the contact will enable you to group your contacts by company, making it easier not only to locate contacts but also to modify contacts globally when a company change occurs (such as a phone number or company name change).
- **Work from the contact.** If you work in the Contacts folder a lot, keep in mind that you can initiate certain actions from the Contacts folder, such as issuing a new meeting request, assigning a task, creating a new journal entry, or calling the contact. This can save you the trouble of switching to a different folder to initiate these actions.
- **Don't forget the picture.** The capability to add a picture can be very useful. For example, if your organization is growing rapidly or is already large, providing pictures in contacts for employees can help your staff get to know everyone.

CHAPTER 19

Using Microsoft Business Contact Manager

Microsoft® Business Contact Manager is an add-on for Microsoft Office Outlook® 2007 that builds on the customer management features already in Office Outlook 2007 to create a system for managing clients, sales opportunities, and other business data. Business Contact Manager doesn't replace Outlook 2007 but instead adds new item types, additional folders, and features for managing these items to help you keep track of accounts, customers, and business opportunities more efficiently.

This chapter explores Business Contact Manager and explains how to install the software, create accounts and contacts, generate reports, and use its other features. By the end of this chapter, you'll have a solid background in using Business Contact Manager and can begin taking advantage of it to manage your business contacts and accounts.

Understanding What Business Contact Manager Can Do

Business Contact Manager is a customer resource management (CRM) tool that integrates with Outlook 2007. By itself, Outlook 2007 enables you to manage contacts, e-mail, a calendar, and tasks. Business Contact Manager extends those capabilities to add accounts, business contacts, and business opportunities (such as sales) to your Outlook 2007 data. These items appear under their own Business Contact Manager branch in the folder list, as shown in Figure 19-1.

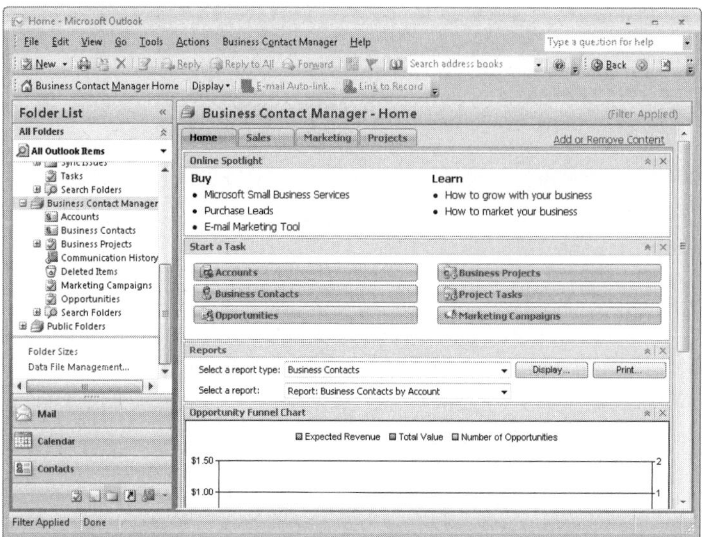

Figure 19-1. Business Contact Manager adds folders and item types to Outlook 2007.

The main benefit of using Business Contact Manager is that it gives you the means to easily integrate all information about a customer account in one place (see Figure 19-2). You can easily link e-mail, contacts, notes, documents, and other items related to an account and then view and manage those items from a single point. The result is the capability to organize all account data in one location, quickly find information, and improve customer response, which ultimately should mean cost savings and potentially more revenue.

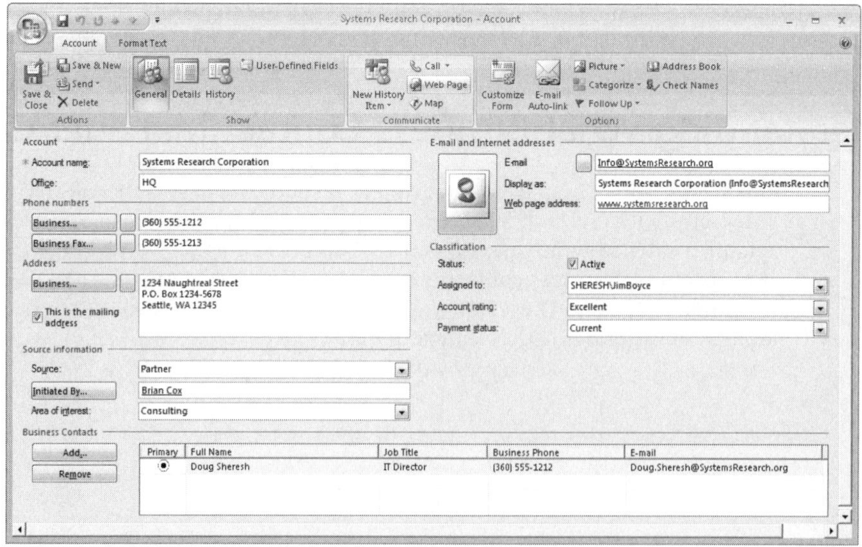

Figure 19-2. Account items enable you to manage information about a customer account.

Business Contact Manager also enables you to keep track of sales opportunities and the product information associated with those sales from initial contact through after-sale customer support. The Opportunity item type, shown in Figure 19-3, stores information about a sales contact, potential or actual orders, product items, and other details related to the potential sale.

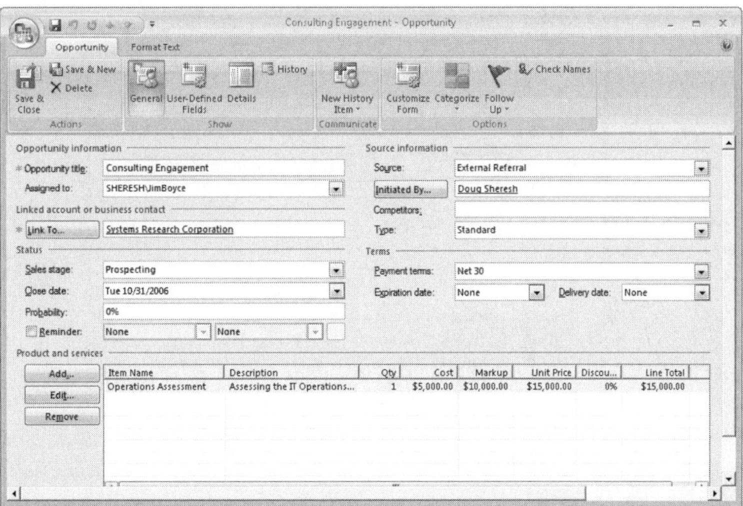

Figure 19-3. Use Opportunity items to record potential or actual sales and related information.

The Communication History folder (see Figure 19-4) is a Journal folder that keeps track of events associated with each contact, account, or opportunity. By automatically journaling items, the Communication History folder makes it relatively easy to search for and locate these items.

In addition to these special-purpose folders, Business Contact Manager also adds reporting capabilities to Outlook 2007 to help you manage and analyze the information you've stored about your accounts, contacts, and sales. They include several predefined reports for each item type, which you can use as is or modify to suit your needs.

This section has provided a brief overview of what Business Contact Manager can do. In a nutshell, the program adds new item types and folders to Outlook 2007 to give you a set of tools for managing your business accounts, contacts, and sales opportunities. As you begin to experiment with Business Contact Manager through the remaining chapters, you'll develop a better understanding of how Business Contact Manager can fit in with your business practices. Before you can start, however, you need to have Business Contact Manager installed.

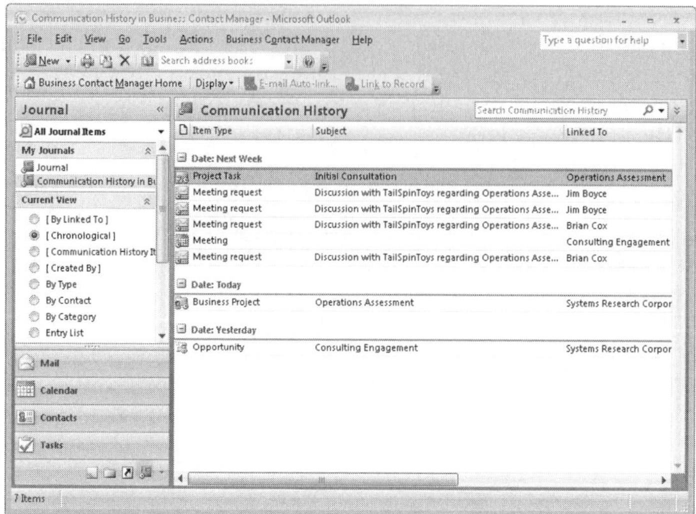

Figure 19-4. Use the Communication History folder to quickly locate items.

> **Note**
>
> You can assign categories to each of the Business Contact Manager item types, just as you can for standard Outlook 2007 items. Categories help you organize and search for data. This chapter doesn't cover categories.

See Chapter 5, "Creating and Using Categories," for details on creating and working with categories. See Chapter 10, "Finding and Organizing Messages," to learn how to create and use search folders with Business Contact Manager to organize and locate items.

Configuring Business Contact Manager

The first time you run Outlook 2007 after installing Business Contact Manager, you'll be presented with the option to begin using the software with Outlook 2007. (If this option is not automatically displayed, you can initiate it by selecting Configure Business Contact Manager on the Outlook Help menu.) If you decide to use it, Business Contact Manager automatically creates a new database in which to store your Business Contact Manager data (if one does not already exist). If Business Contact Manager detects a database, it gives you the option of selecting an existing database or creating a new one (see Figure 19-5). To create a new database, choose Create A New Database and click Next. To use an existing database, such as one you copied from another computer, choose Select An Existing Database, select the database from the drop-down list, and click Next. After the database is created, click Finish and you're ready to start setting up your business items, as explained in the section "Working with Business Contacts" later in this chapter. First, however, you might want to know a little more about Business Contact Manager.

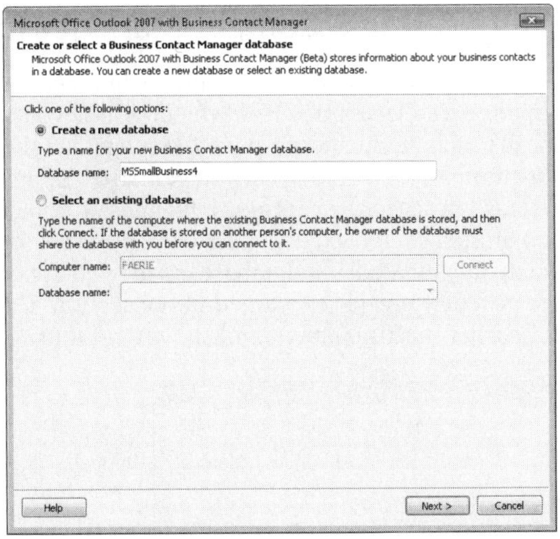

Figure 19-5. You have the option of creating a new database or using an existing one.

Where Is Business Contact Manager?

As you first start to use Business Contact Manager, you might not need to know where it's located on your computer. But as time goes on, and you need to perform other tasks such as backing up your database, you'll want to know where its files are located.

Setup installs Business Contact Manager by default into the \Program Files\Microsoft Small Business\Business Contact Manager folder. This main folder stores the Business Contact Manager core executables and dynamic-link libraries (DLLs), as well as support files such as templates, scripts, icons, and documentation. The following subfolders contain additional items:

- **HomePage** This folder contains the default HTML page, icons, and graphic files used in the Business Contact Manager home page.
- **ImportUtility** This folder contains the files that support import and export operations between Business Contact Manager and other business management applications such as Act! and QuickBooks.
- **SetupBootstrap** This folder contains the setup program for Business Contact Manager.
- **<language>\WelcomeMessage** This folder contains the HTML information page that Business Contact Manager displays when first selected.

The Business Contact Manager database, however, is stored within the user profile information:

- **Business Contact Manager database** This database is stored in the user profile account, specifically in the \Users\<username>\AppData\Local\Microsoft\Business Contact Manager folder, which also contains the Cache, Config, and Logs folders.

Adding and Removing Business Contact Manager for a Profile

When Business Contact Manager is installed on a computer, you receive a Startup page asking whether you want to enable it (see Figure 19-6) the first time you open Outlook 2007 with a profile that doesn't include Business Contact Manager. (If the Startup page shown in Figure 19-6 is not automatically displayed, you can also initiate the Business Contact Manager Startup wizard by selecting Configure Business Contact Manager on the Outlook Help menu.) Simply click Next and follow the prompts. If no database already exists, one is automatically created; if a database exists, you are prompted to select an existing one or create a new one (as explained in the section "Configuring Business Contact Manager," earlier in this chapter, and shown in Figure 19-5).

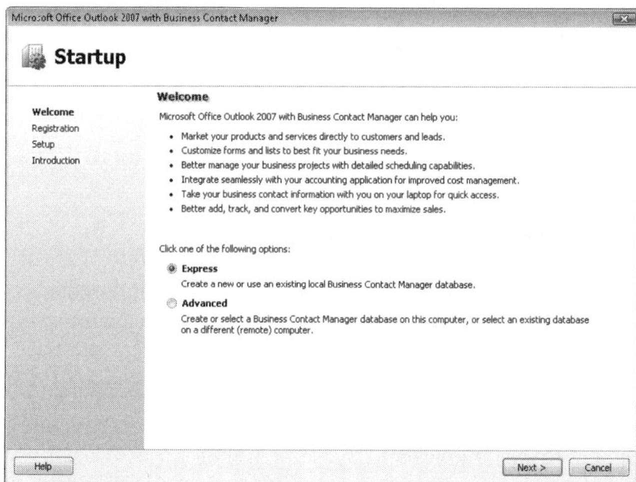

Figure 19-6. Business Contact Manager prompts you to select either Express or Advanced installation.

If you decide you don't want to use Business Contact Manager with a particular profile after it is enabled, you can close Business Contact Manager easily enough. Open the folder list (by clicking the Folder List icon at the bottom of the Navigation Pane), right-click the Business Contact Manager branch, and choose Close Business Contact Manager. Outlook 2007 removes the folders from the folder list and removes the Business Contact Manager–related commands from the Outlook 2007 menu. This method affects only the current profile; it does not remove Business Contact Manager entirely from the computer, nor does it affect other profiles.

Perhaps you are creating a new Outlook 2007 profile and want to explicitly add a Business Contact Manager database to the profile. Or, after you remove Business Contact Manager from a profile, you might decide you want it back again.

You can add a Business Contact Manager database to a new profile or to an existing one. If you choose the former approach, simply create a new Outlook 2007 profile that contains your existing Outlook 2007 data. When you start Outlook 2007 with that profile, Outlook 2007 asks if you want to use Business Contact Manager. Click Yes to add it to the profile.

If you click No, Outlook 2007 will not add a database to the profile. However, you can add one manually. To add or restore a Business Contact Manager database to an existing profile, follow these steps:

1. Open the Mail tool from Control Panel (Classic View) or right-click the E-Mail (Microsoft Office Outlook) icon on the Start menu and choose Properties.
2. Click Show Profiles and select the profile to which you want to add Business Contact Manager; then click Properties.
3. Click Data Files and in the Outlook Data Files dialog box, click Add.
4. Select Business Contact Manager Database and click OK.
5. To add an existing database, select Use An Existing Database and select the database previously used with the profile. To create a new database, choose the Create A New Database option. Then click Next and click Close.
6. Click Close and click OK to close the remaining dialog boxes. Start Outlook 2007 and verify that your Business Contact Manager data and folders are now available in Outlook 2007.

Using the Business Contact Manager Interface

The Business Contact Manager in Office Outlook 2007 is a bit different from earlier versions, so this chapter starts with explaining the new interface. Business Contact Manager has a set of folders relating to its core components and items: Accounts, Business Contacts, Business Projects, Communication History, Project Tasks, Opportunities, and Marketing Campaigns. These folders and the Home page are the starting point for working with Business Contact Manager.

Business Contact Manager Folders

The Business Contact Manager folders are displayed in the Outlook 2007 Navigation Pane, although sometimes most of the subfolders are hidden. To display all the subfolders of the Business Contact Manager, start by clicking the Folders List icon in the Navigation Pane, and then select Business Contact Manager (as shown in Figure 19-7). When you select the Business Contact Manager folder, the default Home page is displayed.

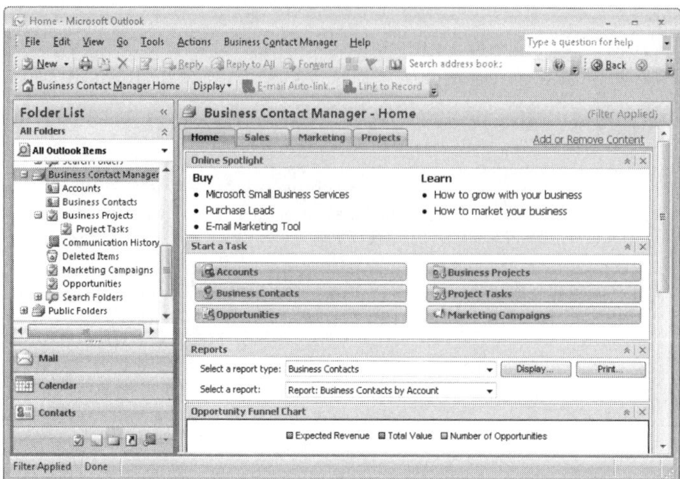

Figure 19-7. The Business Contact Manager folder displays all subfolders and the Home page.

> **Note**
>
> You can configure Outlook so that it starts up on the Business Contact Manager Home page when it opens. To do this, follow these steps:
>
> 1. Click Tools, Options, and select the Other tab.
> 2. Click Advanced Options.
> 3. Next to Startup In This Folder, click Browse, and then select the Business Contact Manager folder from the folder list.

Home Page

The Business Contact Manager Home page, shown in Figure 19-7, provides links to tutorials and services (in the Online Spotlight section) that you can use in combination with Business Contact Manager. The Start A Task section of the page contains options corresponding to the related Business Contact Manager items:

- Accounts
- Business Contacts
- Opportunities
- Business Projects
- Project Tasks
- Marketing Campaigns

Selecting one of these options is effectively the same as clicking the folder of the same name in the Navigation Pane–the same item-related page is loaded (that is, clicking on Accounts loads the Accounts page). (The content and use of each of these folders are covered in their respective sections later in this chapter.) Below these folder options, the page includes a section to select and configure reports and displays opportunity summaries.

Sales Page

Clicking the Sales tab displays the Sales page, shown in Figure 19-8, which contains the same Spotlight section providing links to the tutorial and services. This page consolidates sales-related links of Business Contact Manager items such as the following:

- **New Account** Opens a new account form
- **New Opportunity** Opens a new opportunity form
- **New Business Contact** Opens a new business contact form
- **Set Up Connection To Accounting** Opens a dialog box with links explaining how you can interconnect your accounting software and Business Contact Manager

The Sales page includes a Reports section as well as a section linking sales-related accounts information.

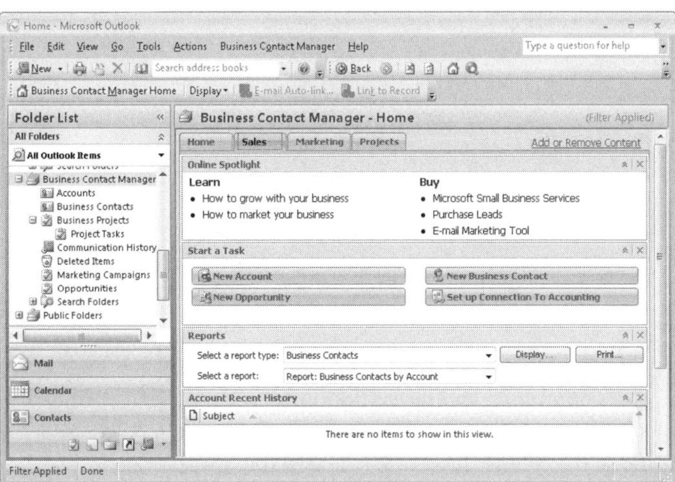

Figure 19-8. The Sales page centralizes links to sales-related operations.

Marketing Page

To assist you with coordinating your marketing efforts, Business Contact Manager's Marketing page (see Figure 19-9) links you to options to starting and monitoring a Marketing Campaign. In addition to the standard Spotlight section, the Start A Task section supplies links to the following:

- **New Marketing Campaign** Opens the new Marketing Campaign form, assisting you with starting your new marketing efforts
- **New E-Mail Marketing Service Campaign** Opens the new Marketing Campaign form with the List Builder selected as the delivery option

Below the standard Reports section, the Marketing Campaigns section displays the status of all your ongoing Marketing Campaigns.

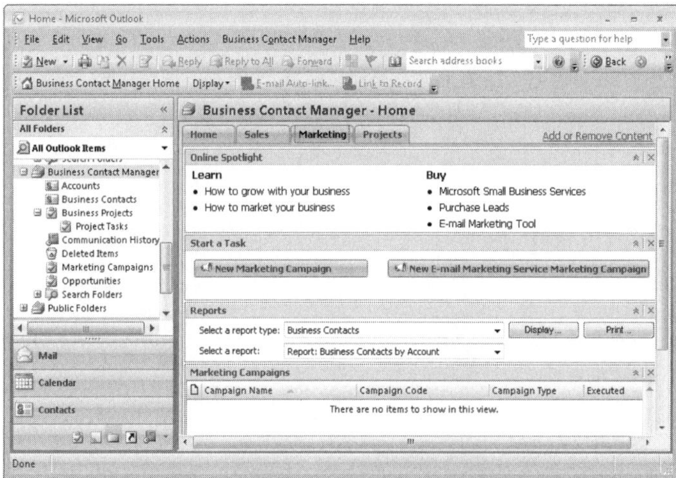

Figure 19-9. The Marketing page unifies access to new and ongoing Marketing Campaigns.

Projects Page

In addition to the standard Spotlight and Reports sections, the Projects page provides links to start new projects and project tasks. It also displays the status of current projects in the Open Business Projects section (see Figure 19-10).

As described in this section, the Home, Sales, Marketing, and Projects pages come with default selections and displays, yet you can add items to the display of a page using the Add Or Remove Content link. The Add Or Remove Content dialog box enables you to select any of the available content information items and set the order in which they appear in the page display (see Figure 19-11).

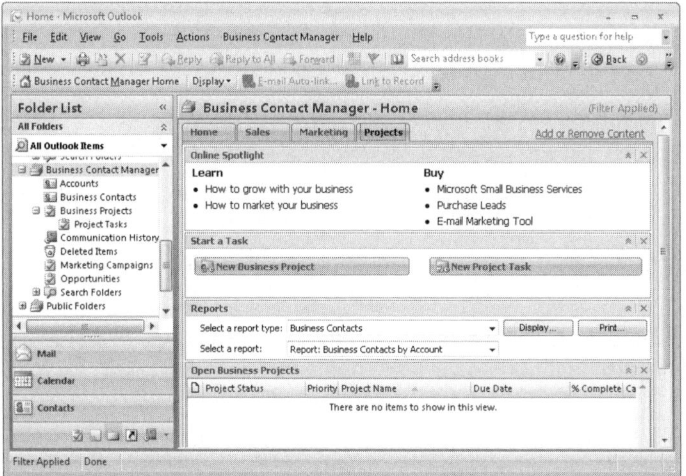

Figure 19-10. Quick access to new and ongoing projects is provided in the Projects page.

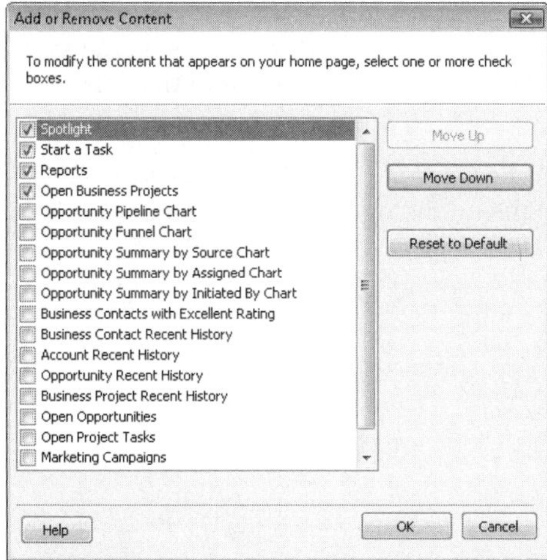

Figure 19-11. You can add or remove content from the default Business Content Manager pages.

Using this dialog box, you can add the Business Project Recent History to the Projects page, for example. Thus, in addition to the Open Business Projects information, you can review the recent tasks related to the projects.

Business Contact Manager Menu

In addition to the options available in the Business Contact Manager folders or the Home, Sales, Marketing, and Projects pages, you can select these and other options from the Business Contact Manager menu on the Outlook 2007 toolbar (see Figure 19-12).

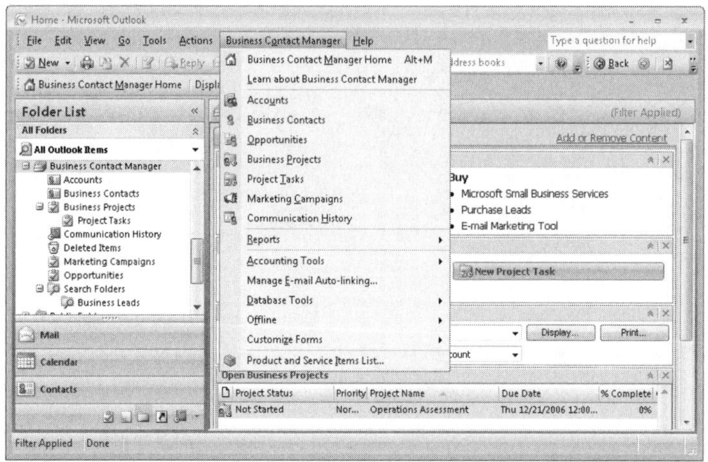

Figure 19-12. You can select Business Content Manager options from the menu on the Outlook 2007 toolbar.

The Accounts, Business Contacts, Opportunities, Business Projects, Project Tasks, Marketing Campaigns, and Communication History options do the same thing as clicking the folder by the same name—that is, taking you to the default display for that item.

The Reports option links you to the array of reports available in Business Contact Manager. These reports include the following categories:

- Accounts
- Activity
- Business Contacts
- Leads
- Opportunities
- Business Projects
- Marketing Campaigns

Each category of reports can be printed according to different sort criteria—the Accounts report, for example, can be printed by City, Rating, Payment Status, Source of Lead, and so on, as shown in Figure 19-13.

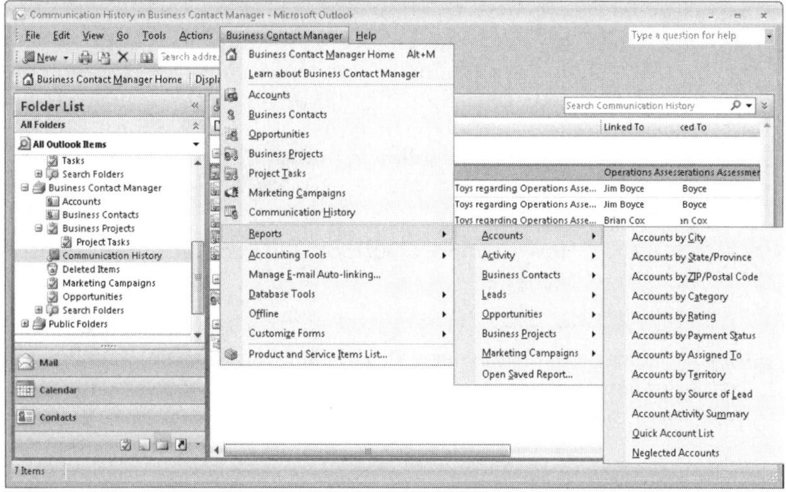

Figure 19-13. There is a range of reports that Business Content Manager can print, and you can select the sort criteria.

Working with Business Contacts

One of the first tasks you will want to accomplish after installing Business Contact Manager is to add business contacts. It makes sense to add contacts before you add accounts because each account probably has at least one contact associated with it. If the contact has been created, you can simply assign it to an account when you create the account.

> **Note**
>
> Business Contact Manager can import data from several different sources. If you currently use another contact management application and want to move its data to Business Contact Manager, see the section "Importing and Exporting Information" later in this chapter for details.

Copying Existing Contacts

You can copy existing contacts from your Contacts folder (or other contacts folders) to the Business Contacts folder. To do so, open the folder list, open the Contacts folder, and then scroll down to locate the Business Contacts folder under the Business Contact Manager branch. Right-click a contact from the Contacts folder and drag and drop it on the Business Contacts folder; then choose Copy from the shortcut menu. To move the contact instead of copying it, choose Move from the menu or simply drag the contact to the Business Contacts folder.

A business contact item includes additional fields not found in a standard Outlook 2007 contact item, such as the account they are linked to or the representative in your company to which they are assigned. After you copy or move the item to the Business Contacts folder, you will likely want to edit the contact to include additional information. Double-click the contact to open it; then add or edit information in it according to the information provided in the following section.

> **INSIDE OUT** **How to import Outlook 2007 contacts to Business Contact Manager**
>
> If you have many contacts in your Outlook 2007 Contacts folder that you want to copy to your Business Contacts folder, you can simply select multiple contacts and drag them to the Business Contacts folder. An alternative is to import your contacts from Outlook 2007 into Business Contact Manager.

See the section "Importing Contacts or Accounts" later in this chapter for details on how to import contacts into Business Contact Manager.

Creating New Business Contacts

You create a new business contact item in much the same way as you create a standard Outlook 2007 contact item. Double-click a blank area of the Business Contacts folder or open the folder and click New on the toolbar (or choose File, New, Business Contact). Figure 19-14 shows a business contact item with many of its fields filled in.

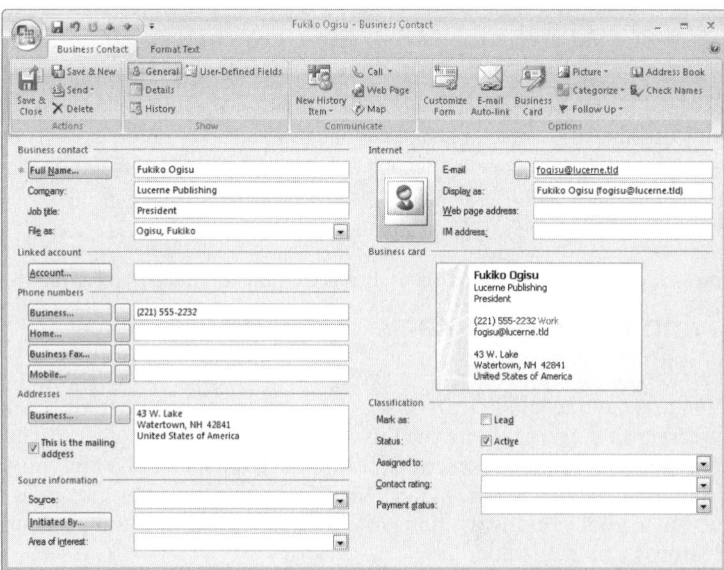

Figure 19-14. A business contact item includes several fields not found in a standard contact item.

Most of the fields on the General page are the same as those found in a standard Outlook 2007 contact item.

See Chapter 18, "Creating and Managing Your Contacts," if you need more information on working with contacts and these standard fields.

A new set of fields on the General page for a business contact item is grouped under the Classification section, which provides check boxes and drop-down lists that enable you to specify information about the contact's status:

- **Mark As** Use this option to specify whether the contact is a lead for a sales follow-up. This field can be useful in reports to separate active sales leads from other business contacts.
- **Status** Use this option to specify whether the contact is active or inactive. You can use this field in reports to separate active from inactive contacts.
- **Payment Status** Use this option to choose between Current and Overdue for the contact's account status.
- **Contact Rating** Use this option to select an overall financial rating for the contact from this drop-down list.
- **Payment Status** Use this option to select the current payment status for the contact from this drop-down list.

There are other new fields on the General page grouped under the Source Information section:

- **Source** Use this option to specify how the contact was made (Advertisement, Direct Mail, and so on). This field can be useful in reports to assess marketing efforts.
- **Initiated By** Use this option to select the Account, Business Contact, or Marketing Campaign responsible for initiating the business contact.
- **Areas Of Interest** Use this option to select interests shared with this business contact, such as products, services, joint marketing efforts, or any other share interest category you have configured.

This section of the chapter focuses on creating and working with business contact items.

See the section "Attaching Items" later in this chapter for details on linking items to your contacts.

The Details page for a business contact item, shown in Figure 19-15, provides several additional fields you can use to track various items of information about a business contact.

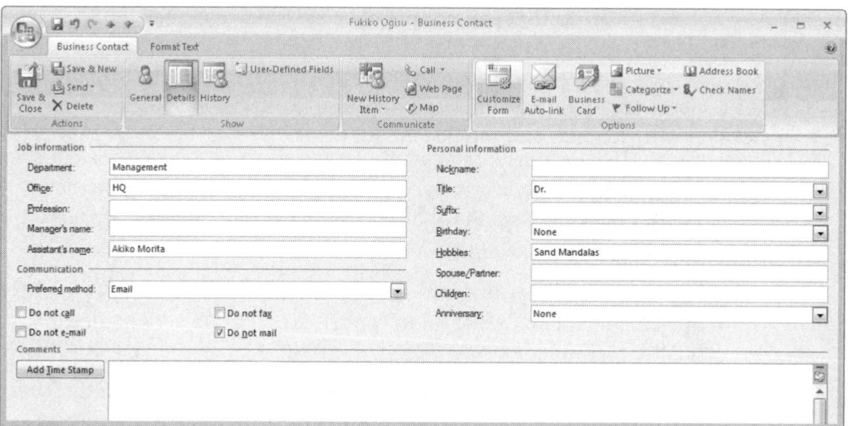

Figure 19-15. Use the Details page to add more information to the contact.

The fields on the Details page are generally self-explanatory. Note that the four check boxes under the Preferred Method drop-down list (Do Not Call, Do Not E-Mail, Do Not Fax, and Do Not Mail) are informational fields only and do not actually prevent these actions. If you select the Do Not E-Mail check box for the contact, for example, Outlook 2007 does not honor that setting if you attempt to send an e-mail. The message will go through without any prompts to the contrary. You can, however, use these fields to filter your contacts list prior to sending an e-mail to the contacts list.

The History page, shown in Figure 19-16, shows all the items that are linked to the contact, including e-mail messages, notes, opportunities, tasks, appointments, phone logs, and files. Some of these items you must link yourself through the contact item, whereas others are linked automatically. For example, if you send an e-mail to a business contact, Business Contact Manager automatically links the e-mail to the contact and includes it in the Communication History list. The View drop-down list enables you to see these History items according to the following sort criteria: By Linked To, Chronological, Communication History Item List, and Created By.

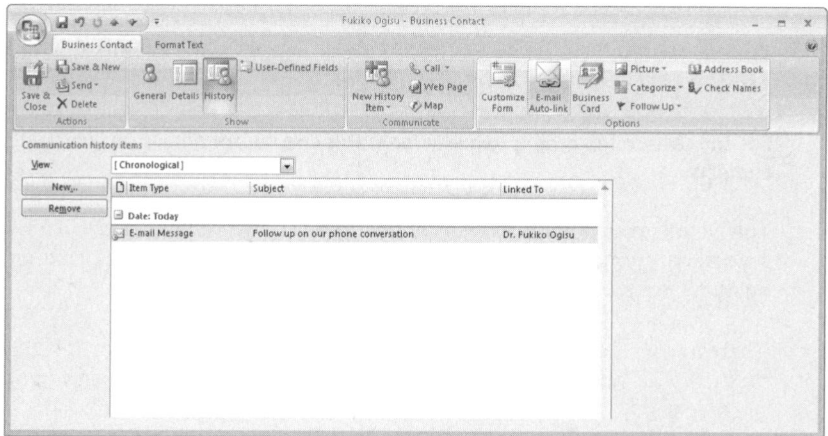

Figure 19-16. Use the History page to review interaction with the contact.

INSIDE OUT How to use views to honor contact settings

If you want to honor the intent represented by these fields (for example, not calling someone if Do Not Call is selected for their contact item), you should make it a habit of checking them before taking the actions specified by them. An alternative is to create a custom view that filters the items based on the pertinent field. Chapter 27, "Creating Custom Views and Print Styles," discusses how to create custom views, but it is briefly discussed here because these fields are user-defined fields, which are not specifically mentioned in Chapter 27.

The following example shows how to create a view that shows only those contacts whose Do Not Call check box is cleared:

1. In Business Contact Manager, open the Business Contacts folder and click View, Current View, and then Define Views.
2. In the Custom View Organizer dialog box, click New. Enter the name **OK to Call**, select Table from the Type Of View list, and click OK.
3. In the Customize View dialog box, click Filter, and then click Advanced to show the Advanced tab, shown in Figure 19-17.

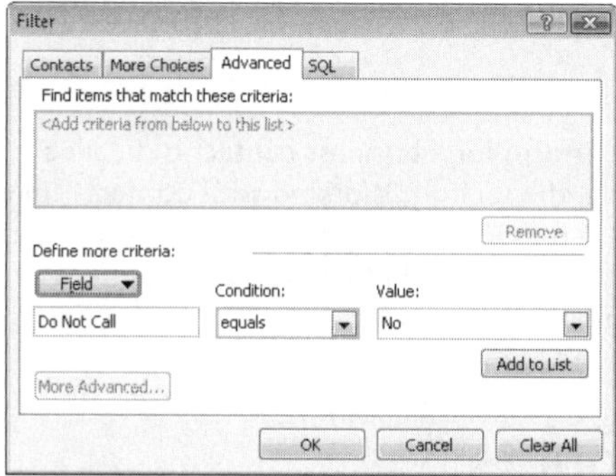

Figure 19-17. Add filter criteria for the view on the Advanced tab.

4. Click Field, click User-Defined Fields In Folder, and then click Do Not Call. Select a different field if you want to filter based on that field instead.
5. Make sure that the Condition drop-down list is set to Equals and choose No from the Value drop-down list. Then click Add To List.
6. Click OK, OK, and Apply View to show the view you just created.

Using Contacts

There are several actions you might take with a business contact, including sending an e-mail, calling, faxing, sending a letter, or adding a note. When you perform many of these tasks, Business Contact Manager adds the item to the contact's history. For example, send an e-mail to a contact, and Business Contact Manager links that e-mail to the contact. This linking happens automatically in most cases. In the case of an e-mail, you don't even have to go through the Business Contacts folder to have the e-mail linked to the contact. With the Inbox folder open, simply send the contact a message. Outlook 2007 checks the recipient; if it is one of your business contacts, Outlook 2007 automatically links the e-mail to that contact.

Note

In some cases, changing contact information in Business Contact Manager negates this crossover between the Contacts folder and the Business Contacts folder. If you apply a title (Dr., Mr., and so on) to a contact in the Business Contacts folder and then go to your Inbox and send e-mail to the contact (using the Contacts folder addressing), the contact in the Business Contacts folder does not show the e-mail in the History page.

You can initiate actions for a business contact in different ways. For example, select a contact in the Business Contacts folder; choose Actions, Create; followed by the action you want to perform, such as New Business Note For Business Contact. You can also right-click a contact in the folder, click Create, and then click an action from the resulting context menu.

Each of the actions you can perform for a business contact is detailed elsewhere in this book where applicable. For example, the section "Working with Contacts" in Chapter 18 explains several actions such as sending e-mail, calling, and sending a letter. Chapter 20, "Scheduling Appointments," and Chapter 21, "Scheduling Meetings and Resources," explain how to schedule appointments and meetings with contacts.

Creating and Using Accounts

Business Contact Manager also adds *accounts* as a new type of Outlook 2007 item. An account is generally synonymous with a customer, but you might have different accounts for a single customer. To create a new account, double-click in an empty area of the Accounts folder. You can also click New on the toolbar with the Accounts folder open or choose File, New, Account.

As Figure 19-18 shows, the General page for an account includes a name to identify the account, address, phone numbers, and several other items. An account also includes the same Classification information as a contact, including the name of the primary contact assigned to the account. It also enables you to associate multiple contacts with the account. Finally, the General page includes an Account History area that lists all the items (e-mail, tasks, notes, and so on) that are linked to the account.

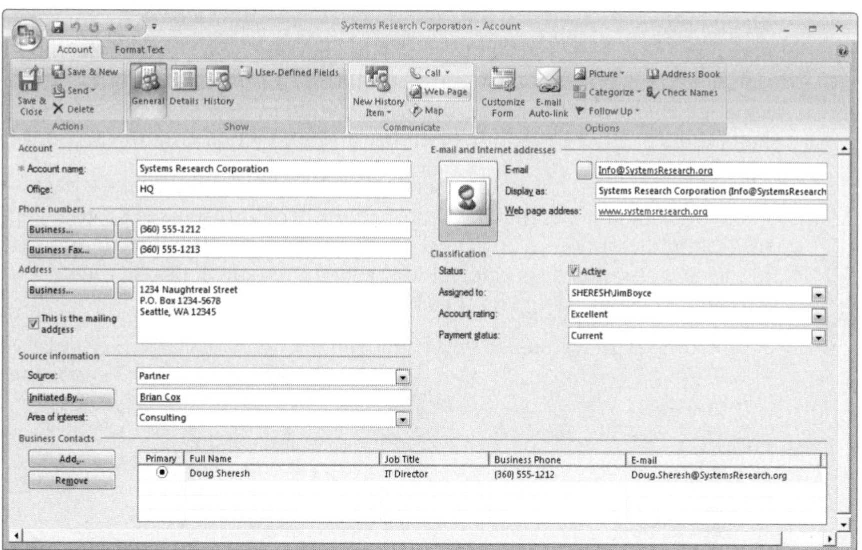

Figure 19-18. Use the General page to set account name, primary contact, and other general fields.

> ### Note
>
> When you send an e-mail to any contact associated with an account, Business Contact Manager links the e-mail to the contact. The list on the account's History page shows all items linked to all the account's contacts, not just for the primary contact. This automatic tracking is one of Business Contact Manager's most useful features.

The Details page, shown in Figure 19-19, provides additional fields to track other information about the account, such as Type Of Business and Territory, and provides a comments field in which you can record comments about the account.

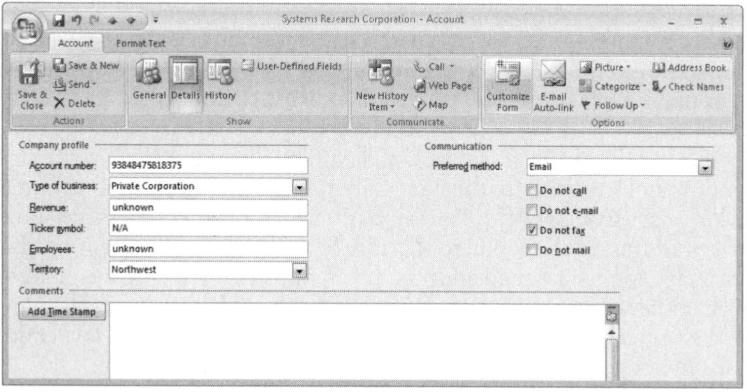

Figure 19-19. Specify additional information and comments on the Details page.

Many of the fields are the same for an account as they are for a contact. For example, contacts and accounts both have Address fields, Phone Number fields, and Classification fields. However, the fields are unique. For example, the Phone Number field for an account can be different from the Phone Number field of the contact assigned as the primary contact for the account. Keep this in mind when creating accounts and contacts.

The History page for accounts (see Figure 19-20), like the History page for business contacts, tracks the items that are linked to the account, such as projects, opportunities, tasks, and meetings. If you set up a business project or define an opportunity related to the account, Business Contact Manager automatically links the items to the account and includes it in the list on the History page.

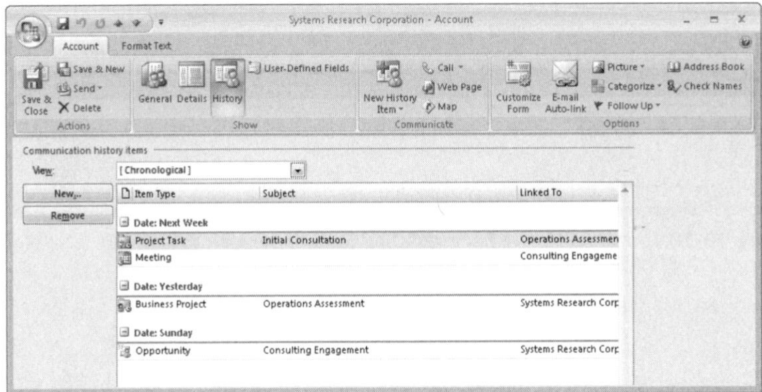

Figure 19-20. Projects, opportunities, and other items are automatically added to the History page of an account.

Performing Actions with Accounts

You can also perform many of the same actions for an account as you can for a contact. For example, you can right-click an account and choose Call Account to open the New Call dialog box with the account phone number displayed. Or you might right-click an account, select Create, and choose New Message To Account to start a new e-mail message to the address specified in the account's E-Mail field.

As with a contact, you can access these actions from the Actions menu or by right-clicking an account and choosing the desired action. However, understand that Business Contact Manager performs the action using the information associated with the account, not with the contacts that are linked to the account. For example, if you right-click an account and choose Call Contact, Business Contact Manager shows the account's phone number in the New Call dialog box, not the phone number assigned in the Primary Contact field. The same is true for an e-mail message–Business Contact Manager addresses the e-mail to the address specified in the account's E-Mail field, not the primary contact's e-mail address. If you need to work with a contact's information instead, either open the contact directly from the Business Contacts folder or double-click the contact in the Business Contacts area on the account's form and then use the Actions menu in the resulting contact form to perform the action.

Creating and Using Business Projects

The Business Projects form is the base for tracking information related to projects that your business is engaged in. You can create a new Business Project form by clicking the Business Projects folder (or choosing the Business Contact Manager menu on the toolbar and selecting Business Projects) and then double-clicking on an empty line in the Business Project folder. Alternatively, you can create a new Business Projects form by selecting the New Business Project in the Projects page of the Business Contact Manager Home page.

Using this form, you assign a name to the project, note the person it is assigned to, and define the type of project, such as fixed fee, hourly, or a custom billing schedule. In addition to this basic project information, you define the account or business contact to which the project is linked and can add any related accounts or business contacts (see Figure 19-21). You specify the Start Date, Due Date, and Priority, as well as configuring the Project Status and % Complete throughout the project to reflect the current state of completion. In addition, you can review or create the related Project Tasks that make up the elements of the project. The Details page provides a Comments field to enable you to put in related project information along with a date/time stamp, and the History page (similar to the History pages in the Business Contacts and Accounts forms discussed earlier in this chapter) maintains a list of communications and scheduling items related to this project.

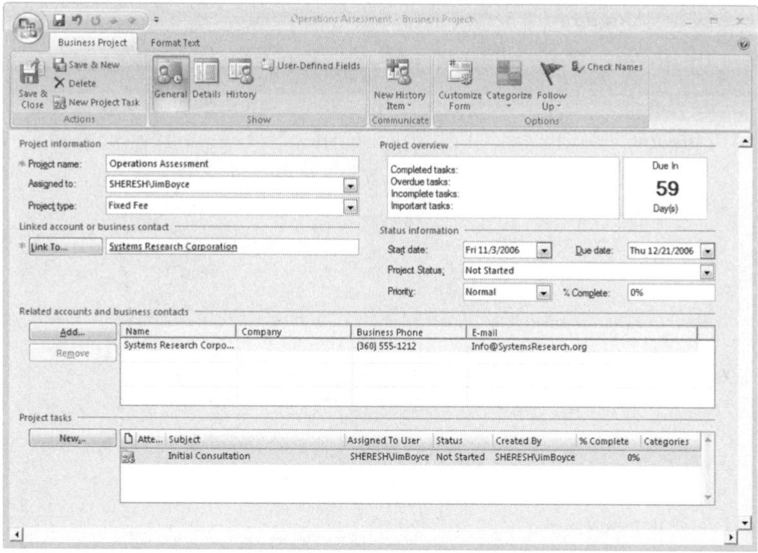

Figure 19-21. The Business Project form enables you to centrally track the information related to a project.

Working with Project Tasks

To track the individual tasks related to each Business Project, the Project Tasks form provides the means to store key information related to each task. You can start a new Project Task form by selecting the Project Tasks folder (or selecting the Business Contact Manager menu and choosing Project Tasks) and then double-clicking an empty line in the Project Tasks folder. You can also create a new Project Tasks form by clicking the New Project Tasks in the Projects page of the Business Contact Manager default page.

You begin monitoring a Project Task by defining the task name in the Subject field and specifying the representative that it is assigned to (see Figure 19-22). Next, you link the task (in the Linked Project section) to the Business Project that the task is related to, so that all related Project Tasks are displayed in the appropriate Business Project. You then modify the Project Task Settings to reflect the operational requirements for the specific task, including the Start Date, Due Date, Status, and % Complete fields. There is also an Attention Required field, which is particularly useful when sorting Project Tasks, enabling you to sort those tasks that require attention to the top of the list. In addition, you can set the Project Task Priority as well as setting the time for a Reminder. The Comment field provides a place to collect the salient details about each task, specifying details that help you manage or complete the task.

The Details page of the Project Tasks form further supports task monitoring and billing efforts by enabling you to track the following fields:

- **Date Completed** The date on which the task-related work is finished
- **Total Work** The total amount of time that completing the task required
- **Actual Work** The amount of time considered billable for the task
- **Mileage** The amount of mileage accrued in completing the task

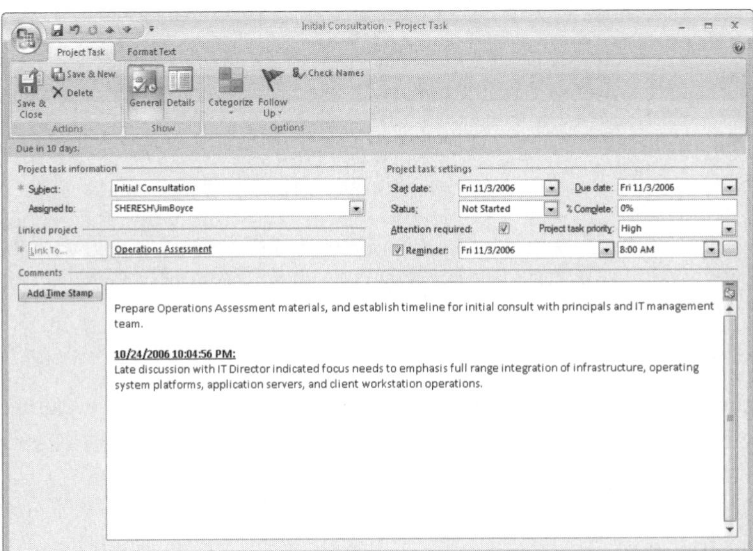

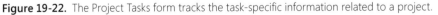

Figure 19-22. The Project Tasks form tracks the task-specific information related to a project.

Creating and Using Opportunities

Business Contact Manager is geared primarily to people in sales, and the inclusion of the Opportunity item type illustrates that focus. You can use opportunities to track sales leads at various stages, from the initial inquiry through to the placement of the order.

To create a new opportunity, open the Opportunities folder and click New on the toolbar; or chose File, New, and then Opportunity. As Figure 19-23 illustrates, the General page for an Opportunity item includes a name for the opportunity, source for the lead, stage of the sale, and product list, among other sales-related fields. The User-Defined Fields page enables you to include additional fields to specify additional information in your Opportunities form, and the Details page provides a place to add comments.

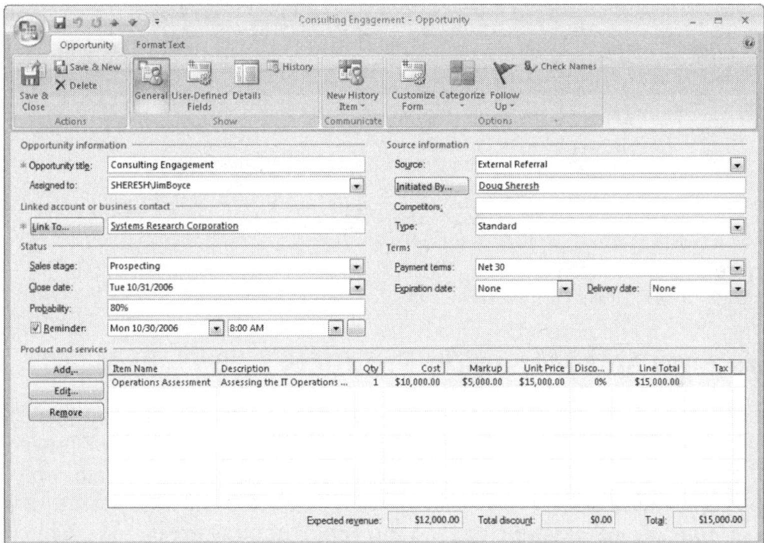

Figure 19-23. An Opportunity item defines a sale or a potential sale.

Like the other forms discussed in this chapter, the Opportunity form starts with you specifying a title describing the nature of the opportunity, and then choosing to whom the opportunity is assigned. Each opportunity must be associated with an account or a business contact by the Link To options on the opportunity's General page, just under the Opportunity title.

Business Contact Manager displays the Link To An Account Or A Business Contact dialog box (see Figure 19-24), in which you can either Search (using the Search box) or select a category—either Accounts or Business Contacts under the Folder heading. After you have selected a category (Accounts or Business Contacts), select a name from the list for the opportunity to be linked to. Alternatively, you can choose to create a new account or business contact by clicking New and completing the information for the account or business contact. Choose the desired Account or Business Contact and click Link To and then click OK to link it to the opportunity.

If you choose the command to create a new account or contact, Business Contact Manager prompts you to enter the name and related information for the account or contact. After you enter the name and click OK, Business Contact Manager creates a new item of the selected type and associates it with the opportunity.

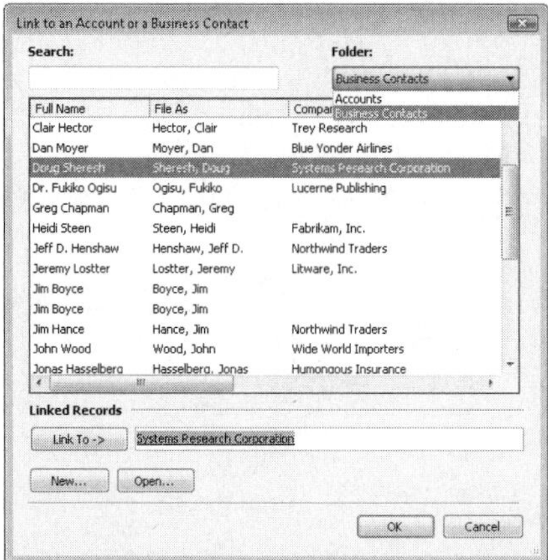

Figure 19-24. Use the Link To An Account Or A Business Contact dialog box to choose a contact or account to associate with the opportunity.

Creating and Managing Products

In addition to the general information included in an opportunity, you can also track specific sale-related information, including products and services. Business Contact Manager creates a product and service database in which you maintain your company's line of products and services, and you can add items to the opportunity from this database. You can add existing items to the opportunity or create new items in the database as needed.

To manage this product and services list, from the Outlook 2007 toolbar, choose Business Contact Manager, Product And Service Items list to open the Products And Services dialog box (see Figure 19-25). This dialog box lists the existing product items in the database and enables you to add, edit, or delete products or services or import a list of products and services from another source.

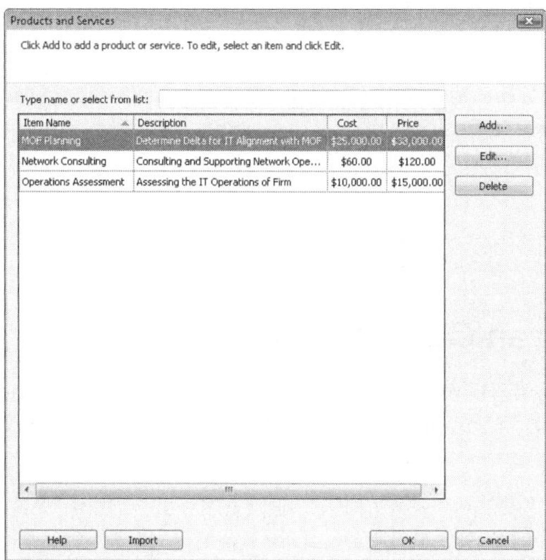

Figure 19-25. Use the Products And Services dialog box to add or modify products in the database.

To add a new item, click Add to display the Add Product Or Service dialog box or click Edit to display the Edit Product Or Service dialog box, shown in Figure 19-26. Enter information in the Item Name, Description, Default Quantity, Unit Cost, and Unit Price fields; select the check box next to Taxable if the item is a taxable transaction; and then click Save to add the information to the database. Repeat the process to edit or add other items to the product database.

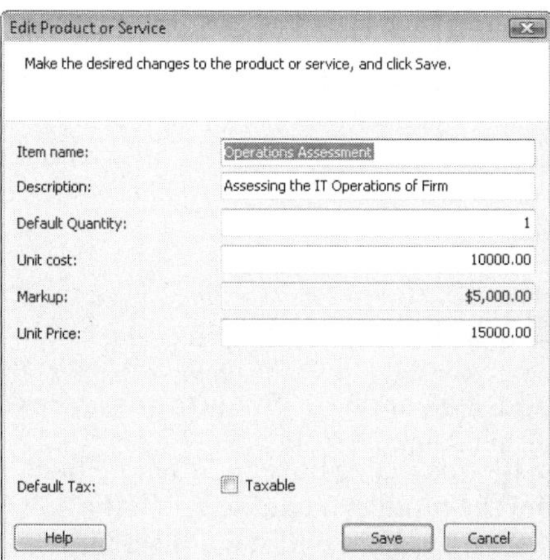

Figure 19-26. Enter a new item or edit an existing item to manage your Products And Services database.

Note

You probably already have a product database outside Business Contact Manager. If so, you can import the database to Business Contact Manager, instead of re-creating all the entries, and save a lot of time and effort. See the section "Importing Products" later in this chapter to learn how.

Adding Products to an Opportunity

As you learned earlier, an opportunity can include a list of products to be included in the sale. To add products, open the opportunity; on the General page, in the Product And Services section, click Add.

Business Contact Manager displays an Add Product Or Service dialog box that is similar to the Add Product Or Service dialog box you use to create products in the database, but as Figure 19-27 illustrates, you can enter additional information, including Quantity, Line Total (Before Discount), and Discount (%). The dialog box also shows the subtotal (Line Total) for the item.

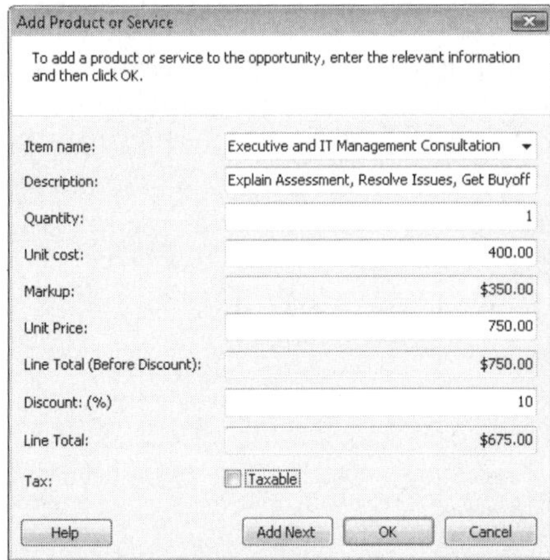

Figure 19-27. Add a product, set quantity, line total, and other items with the Add Product Or Service dialog box.

You can create an item on the fly with this dialog box, but it's more likely you will want to select an existing item from the product database. Click the down arrow in the Item Name field to edit a product. Business Contact Manager imports the product information from the database, and you can then set the Quantity, Line Total (Before Discount), or Discount (%) as needed. Click OK to close the dialog box and return to the Opportunity form, or click Add Next to add the current item, clear the form, and add another item.

Creating Marketing Campaigns

Another feature of Business Contact Manager is the capability to create, launch, and manage marketing campaigns. The integration of marketing campaigns into Business Contact Manager enables you to leverage your existing information on business contacts, accounts, and sales leads to directly communicate your marketing efforts with clients and potential customers and to track the results.

It is easy to create a new marketing campaign. You can start by clicking the Marketing Campaigns folder (or choosing Business Contact Manager on the toolbar and selecting Marketing Campaigns) and then double-clicking an empty spot in the Marketing Campaigns folder. You can also create a new Marketing Campaign form by clicking the New Marketing Campaign in the Marketing page of the Business Contact Manager default page.

You start a marketing campaign by following the five steps laid out in the Marketing Campaign form.

Step 1: What Is This Marketing Campaign For?

First, you establish the Title and Campaign Code, and then you select the Campaign Type from the following:

- **E-Mail** This option enables you to use all or portions of your list of accounts, business contacts, or leads by sending an e-mail message with your marketing information to those contacts you select.
- **Direct Mail Print** You can use your list of accounts, business contacts, or leads in your marketing efforts by mail-merging this list with your Microsoft Office Word 2007 template you create to communicate your marketing focus.
- **Telemarketing** This option does not let you select a list or delivery method, assuming that you will use your own telemarketing script file and enable the option to Use Existing File in step 4.
- **Printed Flyer, Seminar/Conference, Mass Advertisement, and Other** These options prevent the selection of recipients and delivery method but enable the option to Use Existing File in step 4.

Next, you establish the start date and end date and set the budgeted cost allocated for the marketing campaign, and then you enter any relevant comments.

Step 2: Who Will See It?

In this section, you can create a list from your accounts, business contacts, and leads to determine who the recipients will be.

- All Accounts
- All Business Contacts And Leads
- All Business Contacts
- All Leads
- Search Folder
- Existing Campaign
- New List

The preceding options that enable you to choose from items (All Accounts, All Business Contacts, All Business Contacts And Leads, and All Leads) in the Business Contact Manager database are self-explanatory. The Search Folder option enables you to pick a different folder from which you can pull your recipients. The Existing Campaign option enables you to leverage the list of recipients from a marketing campaign you already created. The New List option enables you to create a filter of the Business Contacts list and review the results of applying the filter, so that you can, for example, exclude all those business contacts who do not have an e-mail address on file.

Step 3: How Will They Get It?

For all campaign types other than E-Mail and Direct Mail Print, the Delivery Method is set to Other. For E-Mail campaigns, the Delivery Method is set to Outlook; for Direct Mail Print, the Delivery Method is set to Word Mail Merge.

Step 4: What Will They Get?

For all campaign types other than E-Mail, step 4 is set to Use Existing File. For E-Mail campaigns, the field is set to E-Mail Subject, and you can click Create to create new e-mail containing your marketing message.

Step 5: Are You Ready to Launch the Marketing Campaign?

After you complete the first four steps of the Marketing Campaign form, the Launch button is enabled (it is disabled by default), and you can choose to begin the marketing campaign. If you are not yet ready to launch the campaign, you can click Save & Close in the Actions group to save the information without launching the campaign.

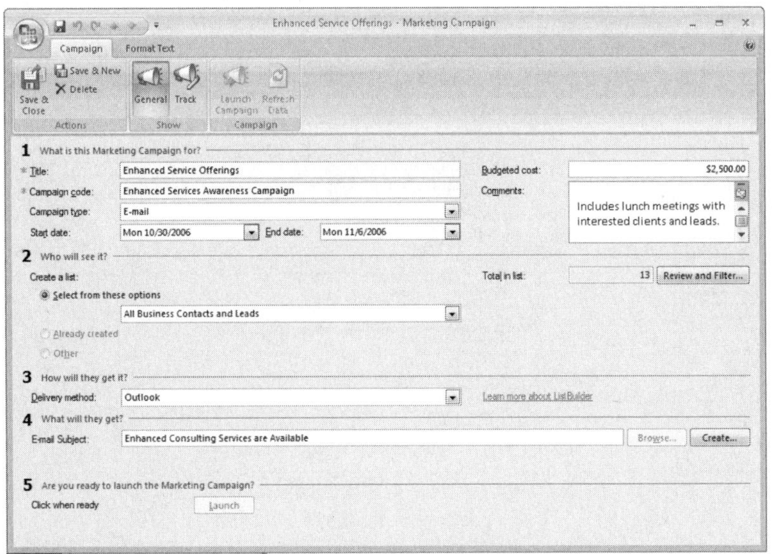

Figure 19-28. You can create a marketing campaign by specifying the marketing information and budget.

The Business Contact Manager is particularly agile when you choose to implement a marketing campaign by e-mail. After you complete the first three steps of the Marketing Campaign form, you then create the e-mail to send to the select group of accounts, business contacts, or leads. When you click Create, the e-mail form shown in Figure 19-29 is displayed, and then you construct the marketing materials you want to send to all the recipients. Note the lack of the To: and Cc: fields in this form because the addresses are already selected in the Marketing Campaign form.

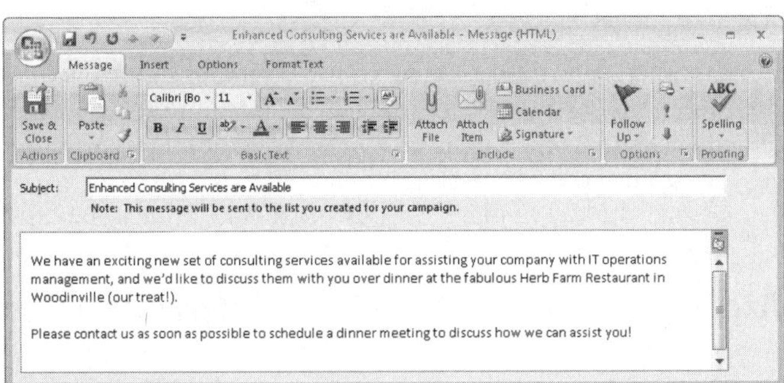

Figure 19-29. To implement a marketing campaign by e-mail, create the message to advertise your offerings.

After you have completed your e-mail, you can click Launch, which implements your selected mailing list and then takes you to the Track page (see Figure 19-30). The Track page displays the results of the mailings, listing any errors in e-mail addresses, and noting all of them in the lists that were sent.

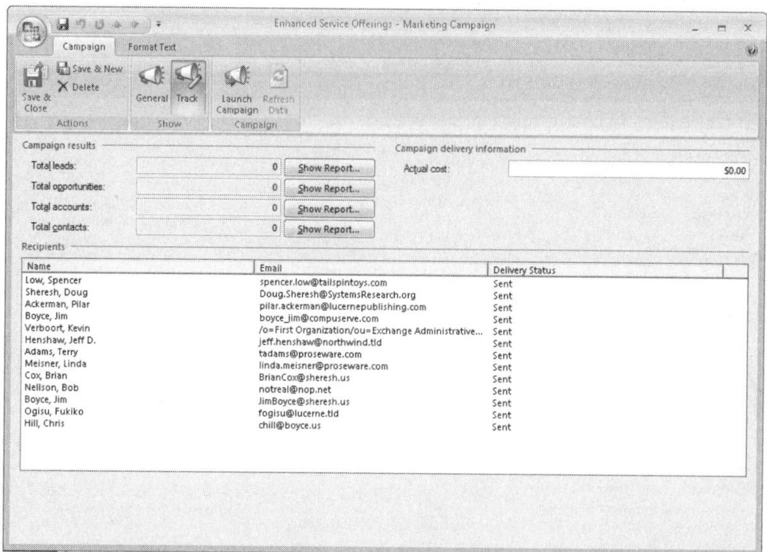

Figure 19-30. After launching the marketing campaign, the Track page is displayed, showing the status of the marketing efforts and costs to date.

Tracking Item History

The Communication History folder provides a place for you to view all the events and items that are linked to accounts, business contacts, and opportunities in your Business Contact Manager database. The Communication History folder is much like the Journal folder in your other Outlook 2007 folders in that it automatically tracks events such as e-mail messages and meetings.

The Communication History folder shows all linked items and is useful when you need a global view of all items. As with other folders, the Communication History folder provides predefined views that you can use to change the way its information is displayed. For example, you can use the Chronological view (the default), shown in Figure 19-31, to see all the messages linked to items in your Business Contact Manager database in chronological order.

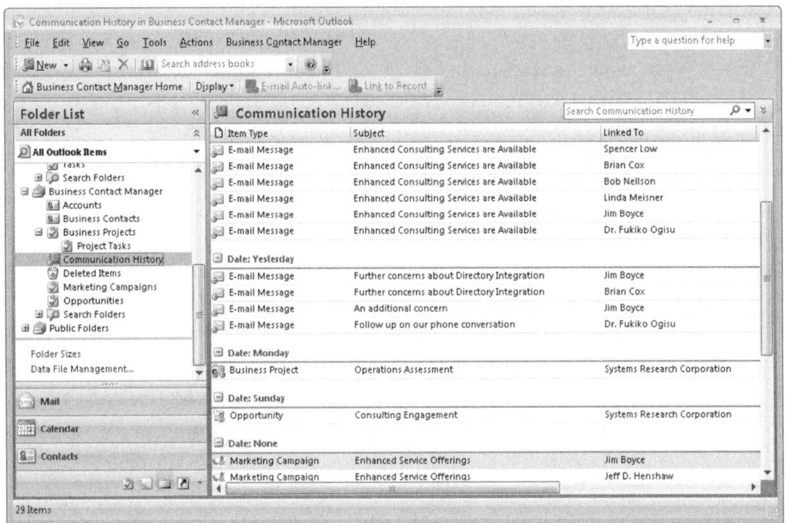

Figure 19-31. The Communication History folder includes a handful of predefined views, including the Chronological view.

Other predefined views include the By Linked To, Communication History Item List, and Created By views.

You can also create your own views as needed to organize the folder's items in other ways. For example, you might create a custom view that shows messages only from a specific sender or that are associated with a particular account.

Chapter 27, "Creating Custom Views and Print Styles," explains in detail how to create and use custom views.

The following steps illustrate an example of how to create a view of the Communication History folder that shows all items for a specific account:

1. Open the Communication History folder and choose View, Current View, Define Views.
2. In the Custom View Organizer dialog box, click New.
3. Enter the name **Wingtip Toys**, choose Table, and click OK.
4. Click Filter in the Customize View dialog box, and then click the Advanced tab (see Figure 19-32).

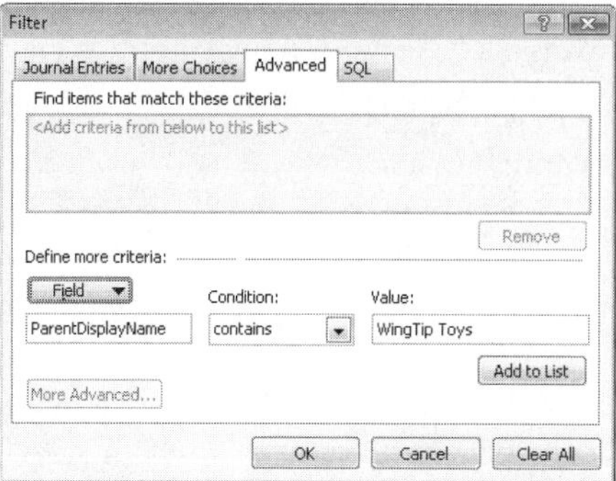

Figure 19-32. Use the Advanced tab to create a filtered view of the Communication History folder.

5. Click Field, User-Defined Fields In Folder, and ParentDisplayName.
6. Click in the Value field and type **Wingtip Toys**, click Add To List, and click OK.
7. Click OK, and then click Apply View to view all items associated with the Wingtip Toys account.

> **Note**
>
> Because the Communication History folder shows all items by default, it's not usually the best place to go to find items associated with a particular business contact, account, or opportunity. Although you can create custom views that will locate these items for you, a better approach is to simply open the account, contact, or opportunity, and view the associated items there. Viewing the links from the item's form saves you the trouble of creating a view to locate the linked items.

Attaching Items

In most cases, Business Contact Manager adds items to the Communication History folder automatically. For example, send an e-mail to a business contact; Business Contact Manager links the e-mail to the contact, and it shows up in the Communication History folder. Or create a Call Contact task for a contact, and Business Contact Manager adds that to the contact.

You can also link items manually. For example, you might want to add a phone log item to an account when you receive a call from one of the account's contacts, attach a document to the account, or schedule an appointment for a contact. You can add the following to each of the Business Contact Manager item types (except project tasks and marketing campaigns) by right-clicking the item and selecting Create:

- **Business Note** Use this option to add a note containing a subject, comments, and information about who created the note and when it was created.
- **Task** Use this option to add a standard Outlook 2007 task to the selected item.
- **Appointment** Use this option to add a standard Outlook 2007 appointment to the selected item.
- **Phone Log** Use this option to add to the item a phone log entry that includes call start time, duration, subject, and comments. The Business Phone Log form includes a timer you can start and pause during the call to time the call.
- **Linked File** Use this option to add any type of file to the selected item. For example, you might add an Office Word 2007 document, a Microsoft Office Excel® 2007 worksheet, or a brochure in Portable Document Format (PDF) format.

You can also add the following to business contacts and accounts:

- **Mail Message** Use this option to send a mail message to the business contact or to the e-mail address specified in the account's properties.
- **Opportunity** Use this option to add a new sales Opportunity item to the business contact or account.
- **Business Project** Use this option to add a new Business Project item to the business contact or account.
- **Marketing Campaign** Use this option to add a new Marketing Campaign item to the business contact or account.

To add an item to an account or business contact, select that item from its folder, right-click it, and then select Create. Choose from the menu the type of item to add. Business Contact Manager opens a form that varies depending on the type selected. Enter the needed information in the form and click Save & Close to associate it with the selected item. The linked item then shows up in the Communication History folder.

Creating Reports

What would a CRM system be without reports? Business Contact Manager includes a range of predefined reports that you can use as is or customize to suit specific needs. There are reports for accounts, business contacts, business projects, opportunities, leads, and marketing campaigns, as well as activity reports by account, business contact, and opportunity.

To create a report, click the Business Contacts Manager menu, choose Reports, and then choose the report category and specific report you want to view. A report window opens and displays the report, as shown in Figure 19-33.

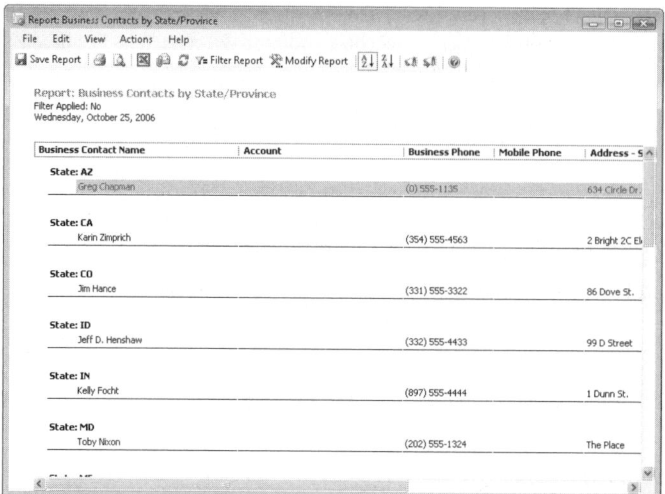

Figure 19-33. Business Contact Manager includes several reports for analyzing information in your database.

The report window shows the first page of the report. You can scroll through the report using the scrollbars or sort the report using the ascending or descending sort button on the toolbar to change the order of information displayed.

Modifying Reports

You can modify reports to change the way they appear or change the information displayed in them. For example, you might want to make relatively minor changes, such as changing the report title, adding other information to the header, or turning off page numbers. Or you might want to make more extensive changes, such as changing which columns of information are displayed in the report.

Click the Modify Report button on the toolbar to open the Report dialog box shown in Figure 19-34. The toolbar contains several options that control the information that appears in the report, such as the Filter Report, Modify Report, and sort order buttons. You can also use the results of the report to start a marketing campaign by clicking one of the Open Marketing Campaign buttons. The Modify Report pane provides the following options to control which information is displayed:

- **Columns** This option enables you to select the specific columns of information that is shown in the report.
- **Fonts And Numbers** You can select the fonts used for Column Labels, Row Labels, Report Body text, Subtotal, and Total.

- **Header And Footer** This option enables you to control what information is displayed in the headers and footers in the report. You can set the Company Name, Company URL, Report Title, Subtitle, Filter Text, Date Created, Notes, and Footer; and you can select the font for each of these items.

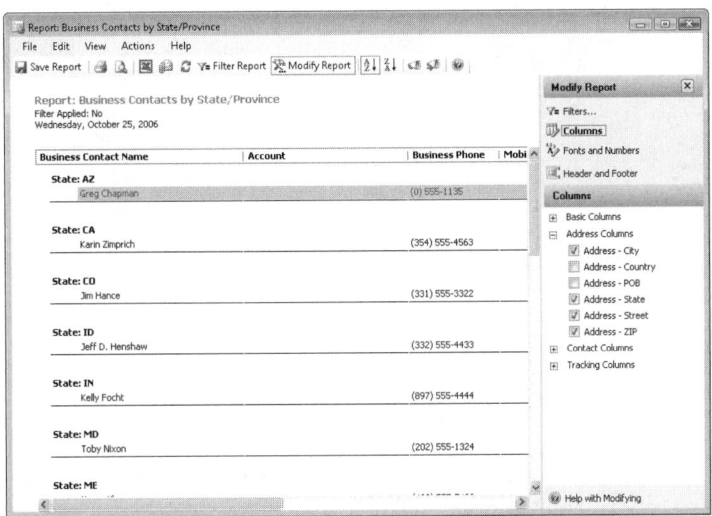

Figure 19-34. Use the Modify Report options to control the information included on a report.

Filtering Reports

You can filter the reports to change which of the possible range of items are displayed in the report. For example, assume that you open the Business Contacts By State/Province report and want to view the entries that have a Contact Status of Active. To filter the report based on this criterion (or any other criteria), select the Filter Report button on the report toolbar, and clear the Inactive check box under Contact Status (see Figure 19-35). The Simple Filter tab provides a number of additional predefined filters, such as which items to include, payment status, rating, source of lead, and to whom it is assigned. For more detailed specification of a filter based on fields and criteria you select, click the Advanced Filter tab. To preview the effect of your filter, click the Review Results tab.

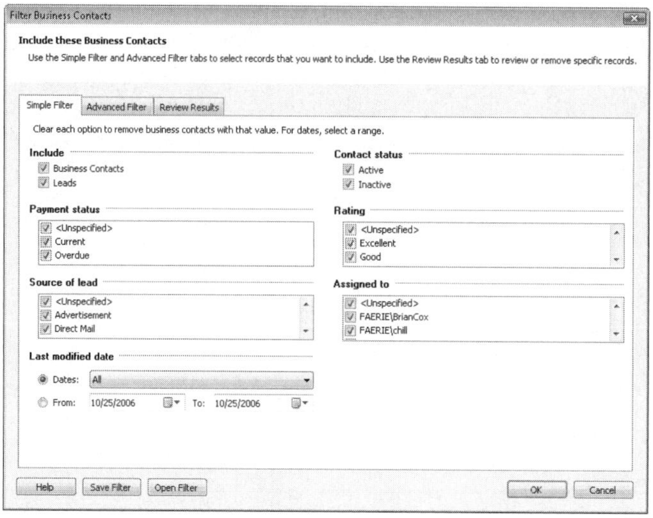

Figure 19-35. Use the Filter option on the toolbar to filter the report.

To further refine the filtering of report information, you can use the Advanced Filter tab (see Figure 19-36) to select which records are included in the report and to set up filters that include or exclude information. The capability to filter the report is an important tool to tailor the information included in the report. You'll find that setting filters is easy, particularly if you have used the filter capabilities in Outlook 2007 views, which are similar.

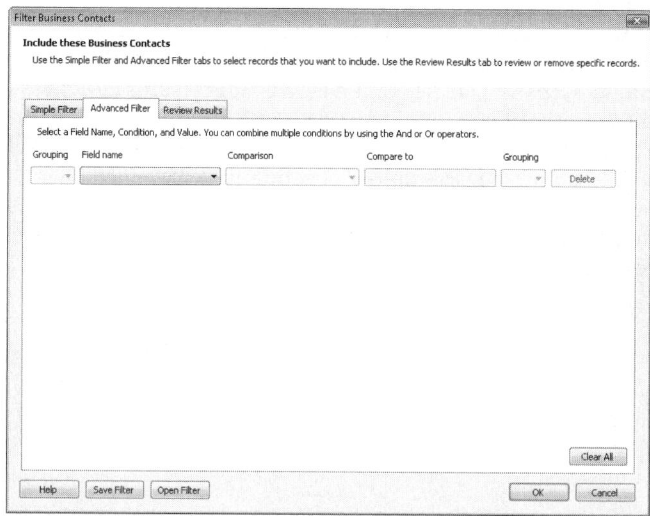

Figure 19-36. Use the Advanced Filter tab to include or exclude records in the report.

Note

You can use AND or OR logic for a filter condition. Choose AND when you want the condition to apply in addition to the previous conditions; for example, to display contacts with names that start with B and who are located in Texas. Use OR to display contacts with names that start with B or who live in Texas. In this example, if you used the OR logic, a contact would appear in the report if the last name started with B, or lived in Texas, or both.

The following example filters the business contacts to include only those contacts with last names that start with B and a home state of TX.

1. Choose Business Contact Manager, Reports, Business Contacts, Quick Business Contacts List to create a phone list report.
2. In the report window, click Filter Report on the toolbar, and then click the Advanced Filter tab.
3. In the Field Name drop-down list, select Last Name, choose Begins With from the Comparison drop-down list, and enter **B** in the Compare To text box.
4. Accept the logical operator AND; in the second row Field Name list, choose Home State/Province. In the Comparison drop-down list choose Equals, and then enter **TX** in the Compare To text box.
5. Click OK to refresh the report based on the new filter criteria.

Note

You can save a report to a Word 2007 document or an Office Excel 2007 document and edit the report in those applications. The next section explains how.

Saving Reports

After you create a report, you can print it, but you might also want to save the report to disk so you can edit it, send it to someone else, or put it in on a Web site. Business Contact Manager can save reports only as a .bcr (a Business Contact Manager Report) format. However, you can export the report to Excel 2007 format. You can also send the report to someone else in e-mail as an Excel 2007 worksheet.

To save a report as an Excel 2007 file, click the Excel icon (Export To Excel) on the Report toolbar, and Business Contact manager opens a new Excel 2007 worksheet containing the report information. To save this worksheet to disk, click the Microsoft Office Button, select Save As, specify a file name, and then click Save.

To send the report in e-mail as an Excel file, click the icon on the toolbar that looks like a paper clip and envelope (with a ScreenTip that displays Send E-Mail With Report As Excel Attachment). Business Contact Manager opens a new e-mail message and attaches the report as an Excel (.xls) file.

Printing Reports

At some point, you will probably want to print a report. Business Contact Manager gives you the capability to print reports, although the options are somewhat limited. To print a report, open the report; modify it as needed; and choose File, Print or click the Print button on the toolbar. Business Contact Manager opens a standard Print dialog box you can use to select a printer and set the number of copies to print. Just click OK to print the report to the selected printer.

Importing and Exporting Information

If you are just starting to organize your business information in electronic format, you probably have to enter most of it manually in Business Contact Manager—creating contacts, accounts, and sales opportunities yourself. If you've been using other solutions to keep track of this information and now want to move to Business Contact Manager, you can import data from those other applications to Business Contact Manager and save quite a bit of time.

Importing Contacts or Accounts

Business Contact Manager can import data from other applications. You can import data from Act!, Excel 2007, Microsoft Office Access 2007, Microsoft List Builder Contacts, Microsoft Sales Leads, QuickBooks, Outlook Contacts, other Business Contact Manager databases, or any application that can export to a comma-separated value (.csv) file. All options except the Act! 4.0, 5.0 Database option prompt you to specify a file from which to import. Importing from Act! requires that you have Act! installed on your computer.

To import data, choose Business Contact Manager, Database Tools, Import And Export to open the Business Data Import And Export Wizard. Click Import a File and click Next. Choose the data source (see Figure 19-37) and click Next.

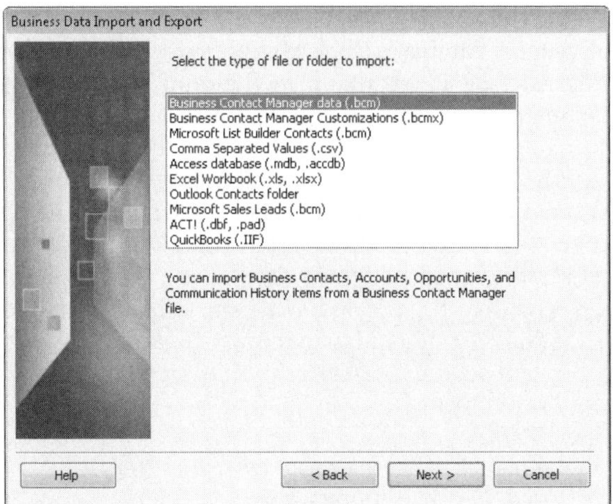

Figure 19-37. Choose the source for importing data to Business Contact Manager.

The following example imports contacts from an Office Access 2007 database:

1. Choose Business Contact Manager, Database Tools, Import And Export to open the Business Data Import And Export Wizard. Click Import A File and click Next.
2. Choose Access Database and click Next; then click Browse to locate and select the Access 2007 database (.mdb or .accdb) file containing your contact list and click Open. Specify how you want duplicates handled, and then click Next.
3. In the Business Data Import And Export Wizard page, shown in Figure 19-38, select the table from which you want to import data, select Business Contacts as the destination to import the contacts as business contacts, or choose Accounts to import the contacts as accounts.

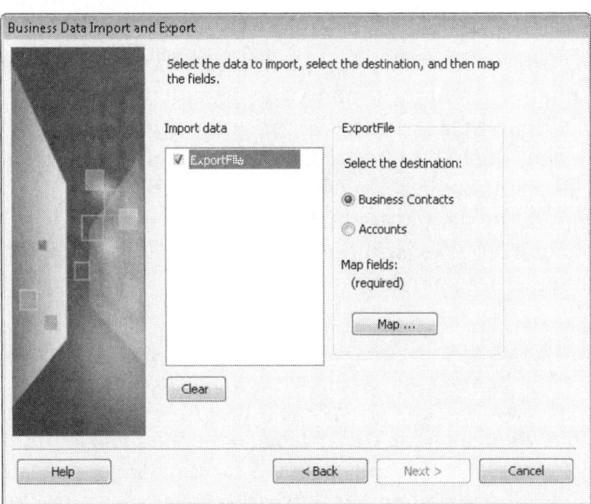

Figure 19-38. Select the destination for the incoming data.

4. You also have to map the fields in the Access 2007 database to the related fields in the Business Contacts database. Click Map to open the Map Fields dialog box, shown in Figure 19-39. Fields that have the same name in the Access 2007 database and the Business Contacts database will automatically be mapped. To map outstanding fields, drag the fields from the left pane to the right pane, dropping them on the fields to which you want them mapped. For example, drag the Job-Title field in the left pane to the Job Title field in the right pane for a contact. Ignore (do not map) those fields that you do not want imported into Business Contact Manager.

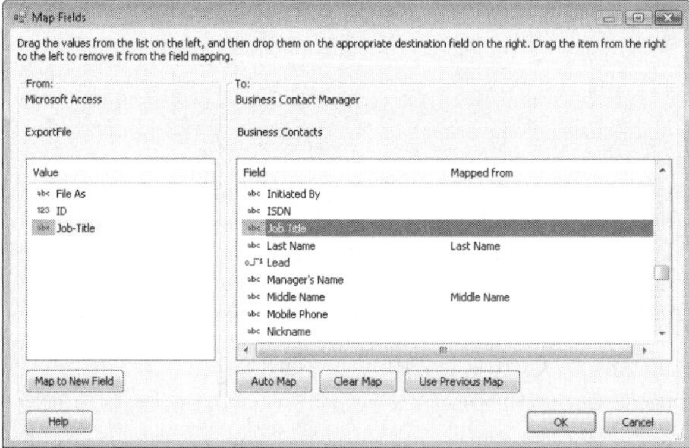

Figure 19-39. Map fields from the source to the destination.

5. After you have mapped all the desired fields, click OK, click Next, and click Next again to start the import process.

Importing Products

In addition to importing contacts and accounts, you can also import a list of products and services into Business Contact Manager. Business Contact Manager imports products only from a comma-delimited (.csv) text file, which means that you must first export the data from its current location to a .csv file. It also means that you might need to tweak the existing database format before you export the data to make sure that it is in the right format. Business Contact Manager requires three fields in this sequence: Product Name, Description, and Unit Price. The database can include additional fields, but when you export the data, you must export it so these three fields (or the ones that correspond to them in your existing product database) are exported as the first three fields and in the sequence specified.

> **Note**
>
> To change field order in an Access 2007 table, open the table in Design view, place the cursor at the left edge of a row, and when the cursor changes to a left-facing arrow, click and drag the row into the desired position in the table.

Note

The Product And Services List dialog box does not show the Default Quantity field, but it is included in the Business Contact Manager Products And Services database and is accessible in the Add Product Or Service and Edit Product Or Service dialog boxes.

The following steps explain how to export a table from an Access 2007 database to a .csv file. For details on exporting from other applications, check the application's Help documentation.

1. Open Access 2007, click More under Recent Databases, browse to and select the database that contains your products and services list, and click Open.
2. Right-click the products and services table and choose Copy.
3. Right-click in the left pane and choose Paste to open the Paste Table As dialog box (see Figure 19-40). Enter a unique name for the table, choose Structure and Data, and click OK.

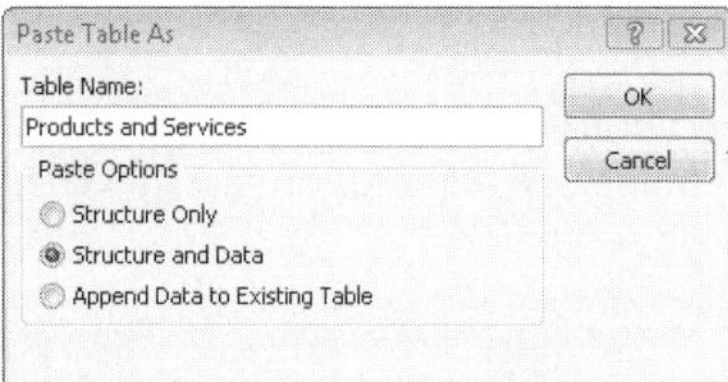

Figure 19-40. Paste the table into the database as a copy.

4. Right-click the copy of the table you created in step 3, select Design view, and adjust the order of the fields so that from top to bottom the fields are Product Name, Description, and Unit Price. Close the table and save changes to its layout.
5. Select the External Data page on the Ribbon and select Text File in the Export group to open the Export-Text File dialog box. Enter the file name **My Products and Services.csv** (or another unique file name that does not already exist) and click OK.
6. In the Export Text Wizard (see Figure 19-41) accept (or select) Delimited and verify that the fields are listed in the correct order without any additional fields in front of the product name field. Click Finish to accomplish the export.

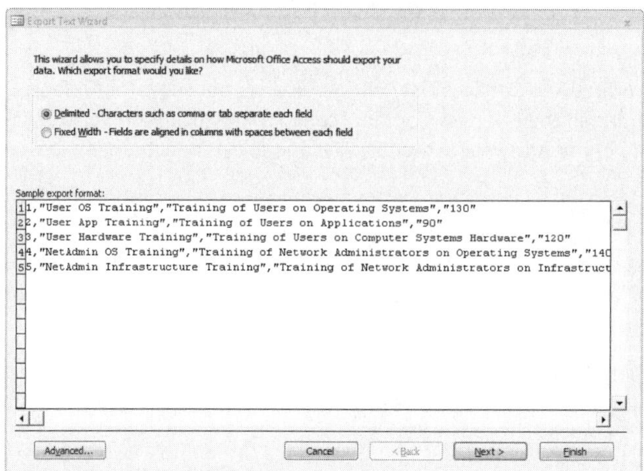

Figure 19-41. Use the Export Text Wizard to export from Access to a .csv file.

> **Note**
>
> The default settings in Access 2007 for exporting to a .csv file are correct for exporting to Business Contact Manager. These include a quotation mark (") character as the text qualifier and a comma (,) as the field separator.

With the table exported to a .csv file, you're ready to import the product list into Business Contact Manager by following these steps:

1. In Outlook 2007, choose Business Contact Manager, Product And Services Items List to open the Products And Services dialog box.
2. Click Import to open the Import Product And Service Items dialog box, shown in Figure 19-42.

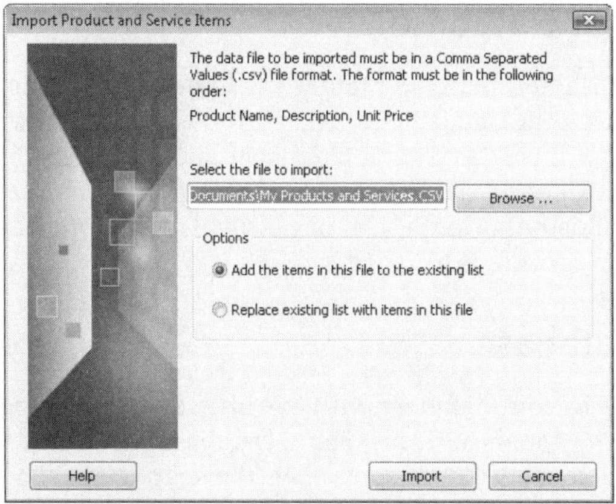

Figure 19-42. Import product items in the Import Product And Service Items dialog box.

3. To replace any existing product list, choose the Replace Existing List With Items In This File option. To append the incoming data to your existing Business Contact Manager products and services list, choose the Add The Items In This File To The Existing List option.
4. Click Browse and select the .csv file (previously created in step 5) that contains your products and services list; then click Import to import the data. The products should now appear in the Products And Services list dialog box. Click OK to close the dialog box.

With your product list now imported into Business Contact Manager, you can begin associating products with opportunities, as explained in the section "Adding Products to an Opportunity" earlier in this chapter.

Managing Your Business Contact Manager Data

After you go through the time and trouble of setting up accounts, contacts, opportunities, and your product list, you certainly don't want to have to go through it all again if your system crashes. So you should regularly back up your Business Contact Manager database. If your system does crash, or if the database is lost for some other reason, you can recover the database from the backup copy.

Business Contact Manager adds database management tasks to the Business Contact Manager menu, as explained in the next few sections.

Cleaning Up the Database

One of the tasks you should perform regularly is to defragment the database to improve performance and check the database for errors. You accomplish both of these tasks in one operation. Choose Business Contact Manager and select Database Tools, Manage Database. Click Check For Errors to open the Check For Errors dialog box. Click Start to start the process. Business Contact Manager displays the progress in the dialog box. Click Close when the process is finished.

Sharing the Database

You can share access to your database with coworkers by selecting Business Contact Manager and choosing Database Tools, Share Database. The Share Your Business Contact Manager Database dialog box displays the shared/not shared status of your database and enables you to choose whether or not to share it. Select I Want To Share My Data to share your database and select I Do Not Want To Share My Data to stop sharing your database. Select the desired option and click Next.

If you are electing to share your database, the Share Database dialog box (as shown in Figure 19-43) enables you to select the users that you want to provide access to your Business Contact Manager database. To select specific users, click the check box next to their name. You can also add new users to the list, but you must be an administrator to do so.

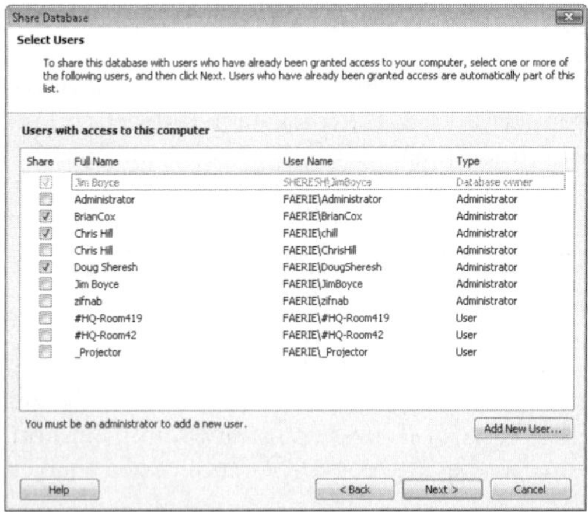

Figure 19-43. Select the users with whom you want to share your Business Contact Manager database.

Backing Up the Database

As a precaution against a lost or corrupted database, you should frequently back up your Business Contact Manager databases. To back up a database, choose Business Contact Manager, Database Tools, Manage Database. On the Backup/Restore tab, click Back Up Database to display the Database Backup dialog box, shown in Figure 19-44. Click Browse and specify the location and file name for the database, and then click Save. Optionally, enter a password to protect the database, and then click OK. Business Contact Manager creates a compressed backup of the database file. When Business Contact Manager displays its completion message, click OK.

Figure 19-44. Click Browse to specify the backup location and file name.

> **Note**
>
> For best recoverability, place backup copies of your database on a network server or copy them to a CD. This procedure enables you to recover the files if your local hard disk fails.

Restoring the Database

To restore a database, choose Business Contact Manager, Database Tools, Manage Database. On the Backup/Restore tab, click Restore Database to display the Restore Backup dialog box. Click Browse to locate and select the backup file, and then click Open. Enter a password if the backup is password-protected, and then click OK to start the restore.

Deleting Databases

You can delete a Business Contact Manager database if you no longer need it. A typical database can take up a lot of space, so deleting databases that you no longer need helps you conserve disk space.

CAUTION!

To delete a database, first make sure that you don't need it and you know specifically which ones (by name) can be deleted. As a precaution, you should back up the database and copy it to CD before deleting it. When you're ready to delete it, use Windows Explorer to go the \Users\AppData\Local\Microsoft\Business Contact Manager folder, right-click the database files (MSSmallBusiness.mdf and MSSmallBusiness.ldf), and select Delete.

INSIDE OUT Remove a database associated with the current profile

You can't delete a database that is associated with the current profile. To remove it from the profile, right-click the Business Contact Manager branch in the folder list and click Close Business Contact Manager. You can also choose Tools, Account Settings. On the Data Files tab, click Business Contact Manager, and then click Remove to remove the file. If you share your computer with someone else, make sure that you aren't removing someone else's Business Contact Manager data.

PART 4

Managing Your Time and Tasks

CHAPTER 20

Scheduling Appointments

For most of us, a calendar is a basic tool for organizing our lives, both at work and at home. With the calendar in Microsoft® Office Outlook® 2007, you can schedule regular appointments, all-day and multiday events, and meetings. You can view your schedule almost any way you want. In addition, you can share your calendar with others, which is a big help when scheduling organizational activities.

This chapter first describes the calendar and explains how to work with the basic Calendar folder view. Then you'll learn how to schedule and work with appointments and events. You'll also find information about the more advanced view options for the calendar and about how to share your calendar and free/busy information and view different time zones.

Both this chapter and the next focus on the features available in the Office Outlook 2007 Calendar folder. This chapter covers appointments and events; the following chapter discusses meetings and resources.

Calendar Basics

The Outlook 2007 Calendar folder provides a central location for storing vast amounts of information about your schedule. Figure 20-1 shows a basic one-day view of a calendar. You see this view when you first click the Calendar icon in the Navigation Pane to open the folder. This example calendar contains no appointments yet, and no tasks are listed in the Daily Task List.

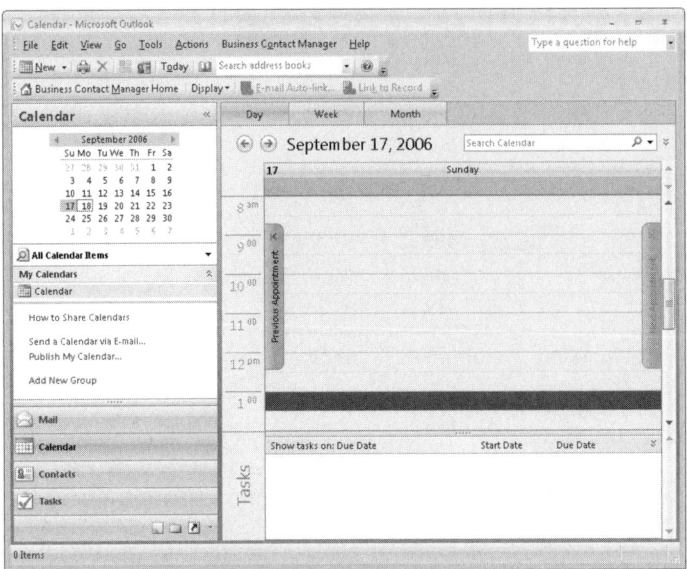

Figure 20-1. The default one-day view of the Outlook 2007 calendar.

Understanding Calendar Items

The Outlook 2007 calendar can contain three types of items: appointments, events, and meetings.

- An *appointment*, which is the default calendar item, involves only your schedule and time and does not require other attendees or resources. The calendar shows appointments in the time slots corresponding to their start and end times.
- When an appointment lasts longer than 24 hours, it becomes an *event*. An event is marked on the calendar not in a time slot, but in a banner at the top of the day on which it occurs.
- An appointment becomes a *meeting* when you invite other people, which requires coordinating their schedules, or when you must schedule resources. Meetings can be in-person meetings established through Outlook 2007 meeting requests. (Meetings can also be set up online using Microsoft Office Live Meeting, which is a separate application.) In this chapter and in Chapter 21, we'll look at meeting requests in Outlook 2007.

For in-depth information about meetings initiated in Outlook 2007, see Chapter 21, "Scheduling Meetings and Resources." For information about online meetings, see "Using Microsoft Office Live Meeting" in Chapter 39.

You can create an appointment in any of these ways:

- Choose File, New, Appointment.
- When the Calendar folder is open, click the New button on the Standard toolbar.
- When any other Outlook 2007 folder is open, click the arrow next to New on the toolbar, and then choose Appointment.
- Click a time slot on the calendar, and simply type the subject of the appointment in the time slot.

For detailed information about creating appointments and using the appointment form, see "Working with One-Time Appointments" later in this chapter.

Using the Time Bar

When you choose a calendar display of 14 or fewer days, the Time Bar appears, displaying 30-minute time increments by default. Figure 20-2 shows the Time Bar set to 30-minute increments, with a 30-minute appointment on the calendar.

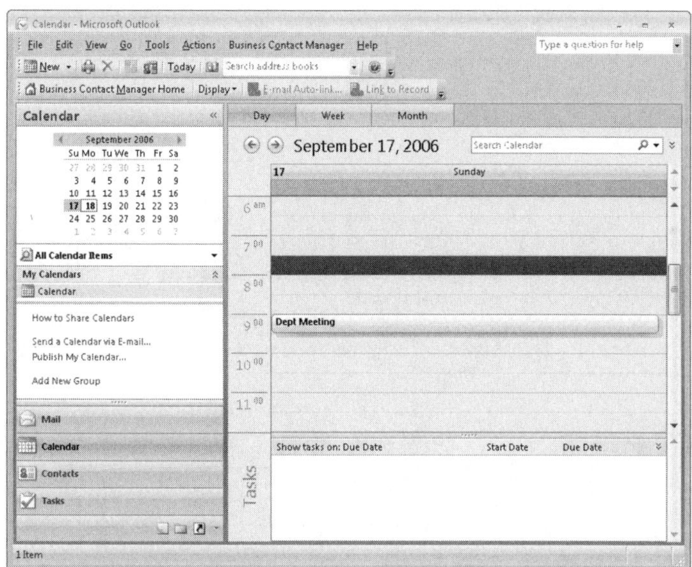

Figure 20-2. By default, the Time Bar is set to display 30-minute increments.

You can set the Time Bar to display different time increments. To do so, begin by right-clicking the Time Bar to display the shortcut menu shown in Figure 20-3.

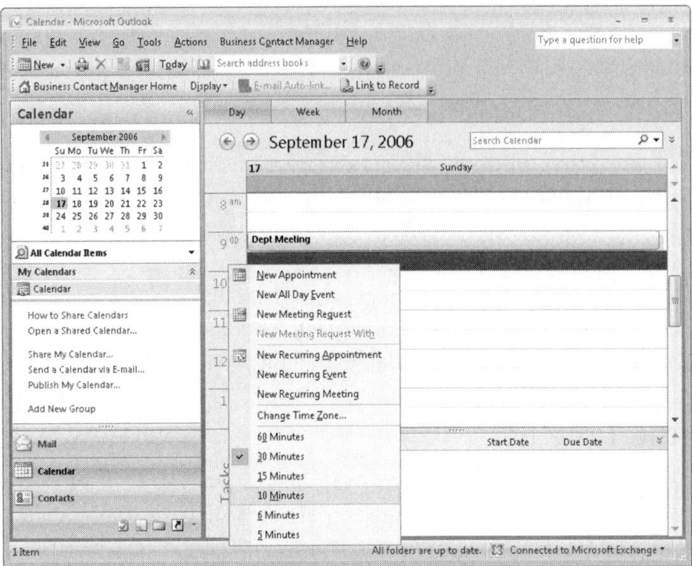

Figure 20-3. Use the Time Bar shortcut menu to change the time increment.

If you want to change the time scale to 10 minutes, select 10 Minutes; subsequently, the 30-minute appointment takes up three time intervals instead of one, as shown in Figure 20-4.

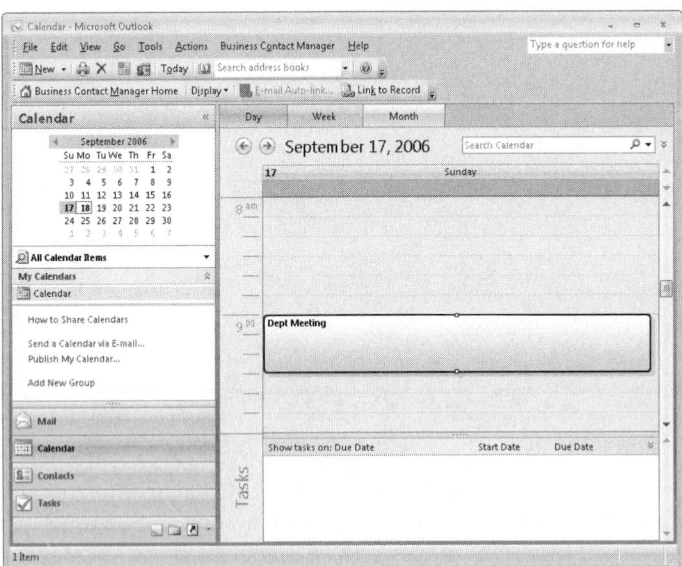

Figure 20-4. The Time Bar has been changed to display 10-minute increments.

To choose a 60-minute interval, right-click the Time Bar, and then select 60 Minutes; Figure 20-5 shows the result. Note that when an appointment takes up less than a full Time Bar increment, as in this example, the scheduled time of the appointment is displayed as a ScreenTip when you hover the mouse pointer over the appointment subject on the calendar.

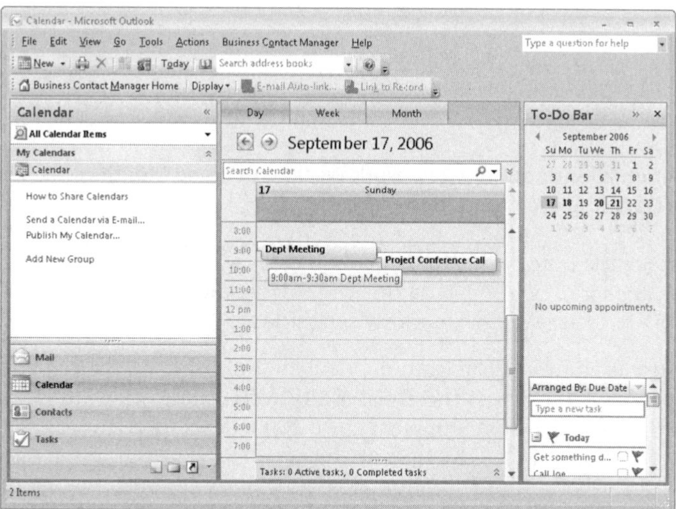

Figure 20-5. The Time Bar is set to 60-minute intervals and the time is displayed when you hover the mouse pointer over the appointment.

Outlook 2007 places appointments side by side on the calendar when they are scheduled in the same time interval (as shown in Figure 20-5).

Using the Date Navigator

The Date Navigator is shown as a small calendar at the top of the Navigation Pane. It has several important uses. For example, you can use it to select the day to view on the calendar–in effect, jumping from one date to another. When you click a day in the Date Navigator, Outlook 2007 displays that day according to how you have set the view (by using the Day, Work Week, or Week tabs:

- In Day view, the selected day is displayed.
- In Work Week view (five days by default–configurable by choosing Tools, Options, Calendar Options), Outlook 2007 displays the week containing the day that you clicked in the Date Navigator.
- In Full Week view (seven days), the calendar switches to a one-day view for the date you click.

> **Note**
>
> When the To-Do Bar is displayed, the Date Navigator appears at the top of the To-Do Bar. When you close the To-Do Bar, the Date Navigator moves to the top of the Navigation Pane.

By clicking the right and left arrows next to the month names in the Date Navigator, you can scroll forward and backward through the months.

For more information about the Day, Work Week, Week, and Month views, see "Setting the Number of Days Displayed" on the facing page.

Another use of the Date Navigator is to denote days that contain scheduled items. Those days appear in bold type; days with no scheduled items appear as regular text. This allows you to assess your monthly schedule at a glance.

Last, you can use the Date Navigator to view multiple days on the calendar. In the Date Navigator, simply drag across the range of days you want to view; those days will all appear on the calendar. For example, Figure 20-6 shows what happens when you drag across three days in the Date Navigator. You can also view multiple consecutive days by clicking the first day and then holding down the **Shift** key and clicking the last day. To view multiple nonconsecutive days, click the first day that you want to view and then hold down the **Ctrl** key and click each day that you want to add to the view.

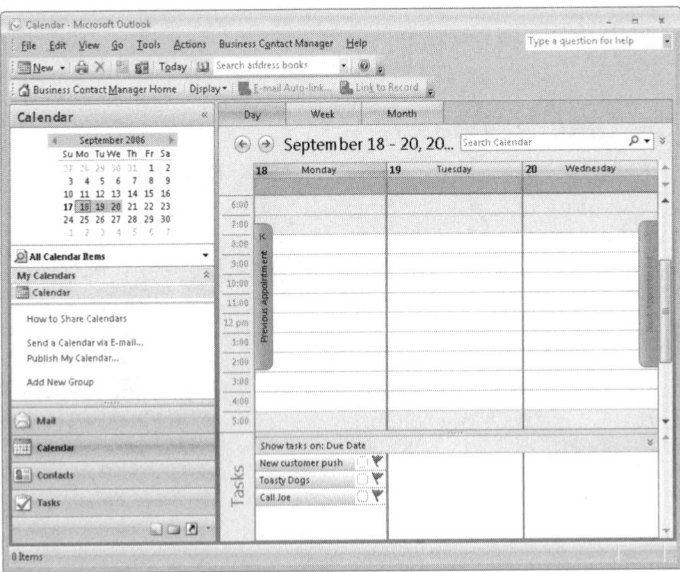

Figure 20-6. You can view multiple days by selecting them in the Date Navigator.

Using the To-Do Bar

The To-Do Bar replaces the old Microsoft Outlook TaskPad and offers an easy way of working with tasks from the Calendar folder. The To-Do Bar is not turned on by default, but it can be enabled using the To-Do Bar command on the View menu. The To-Do Bar displays existing tasks from the Tasks folder and also allows you to add new tasks. Adding a new task is as simple as clicking in the Task List area of the To-Do Bar and typing the task subject. Double-click the task item to open the task form if you'd like to add more details. When you create a task in the To-Do Bar, Outlook 2007 automatically adds it to the Tasks folder.

One of the main advantages of having the To-Do Bar in the Calendar folder is that it enables you to assess your schedule and fit in tasks where appropriate. When you drag a task from the Task List to the calendar, an appointment is added. When you double-click the appointment, the appointment form appears, with the task information filled in. You need only set the schedule information for the appointment and save it to the calendar (as explained in "Working with One-Time Appointments" on the next page).

Setting the Number of Days Displayed

You can set the number of days displayed in the calendar in several ways. One way is to use the Date Navigator, as discussed earlier. The easiest way, however, is to use the appropriate tab in Calendar view. To select the number of days to view, click the Day, Week, or Month tab.

When the calendar displays 14 or fewer days, the days are shown side by side with the Time Bar (as shown earlier in Figure 20-6, for example). Figure 20-7 shows the calendar with seven days displayed.

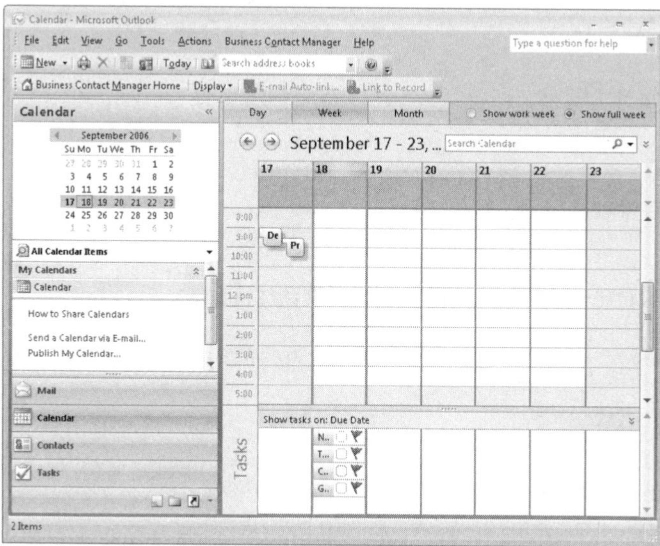

Figure 20-7. The calendar display changes depending on the number of days you are viewing.

When you click the Month tab in Calendar view, the view is different from the view you see when you select more than seven days in the Date Navigator. However, the Date Navigator and the To-Do Bar can optionally appear in Month view, as shown in Figure 20-8. This behavior is different from earlier versions of Microsoft Outlook, which do not include the Date Navigator or To-Do Bar in Month view.

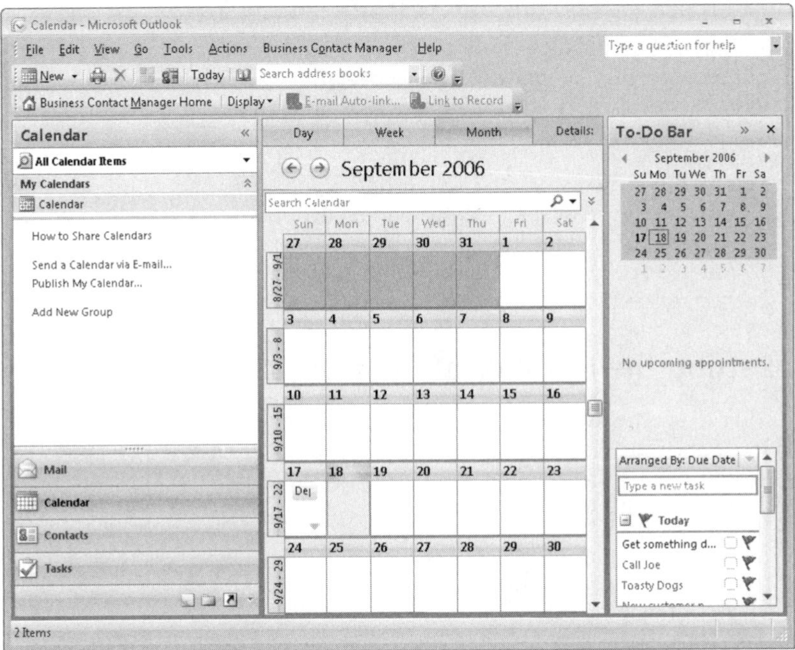

Figure 20-8. Month view can include the Date Navigator and the To-Do Bar.

Selecting a Date

You can select a date in two ways. The first is by using the Date Navigator, as described earlier. The second way is to click the Today button on the toolbar; this action takes you to the current day.

Working with One-Time Appointments

The most basic calendar item is the one-time appointment. You can create a one-time appointment in several ways:

- If the Calendar folder is not open, choose File, New, Appointment or click the arrow next to New on the toolbar and then choose Appointment. The appointment defaults to the next full 30 minutes.
- If the Calendar folder is open, select a time in the calendar and then click New on the toolbar, or alternatively, right-click the calendar and choose New Appointment. The appointment is scheduled for the time selected in the calendar.

- Right-click a date in Month view, and then choose New Appointment. The appointment defaults to your specified start-of-workday time and runs for 30 minutes.

When you take any of these actions, Outlook 2007 opens the appointment form, shown in Figure 20-9, where you can specify information for the new item.

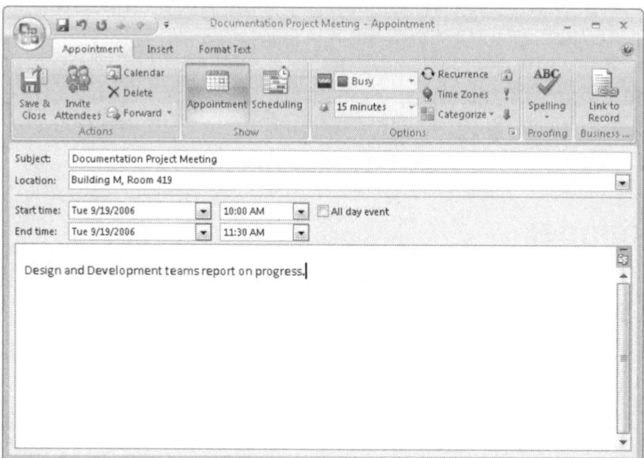

Figure 20-9. Use the appointment form to create a new appointment.

> **INSIDE OUT** Create an appointment quickly
>
> To quickly create an appointment, you can click a blank time slot on the calendar and type the subject of the appointment. When you use this method, however, Outlook 2007 doesn't automatically open a new appointment form. To add details to the appointment, you must double-click the new appointment to open the form. Note that if you click a blank date in Month view and type a subject, Outlook 2007 creates an all-day event rather than an appointment.

Specifying the Subject and Location

Type the subject of an appointment in the Subject box at the top of the appointment form. Make the subject as descriptive as possible because it will appear on the calendar.

If you want, you can type a location for the appointment in the Location box. To view a list of all previously typed locations, click the Location drop-down arrow; you can select a location in this list. Outlook 2007 will display the location you specify next to the appointment subject in Calendar view (and in parentheses next to the subject in ScreenTips when you hover the mouse pointer over the scheduled appointment).

Specifying Start and End Times

You set the start and end times of the appointment by typing the date and time in the Start Time and End Time boxes or by clicking the drop-down arrows beside each box. If you click a drop-down arrow for a date, a calendar appears. Click a drop-down arrow for time, and a list of potential start and end times in 30-minute increments appears. The End Time drop-down list shows how long the appointment will be for each given end time. You can also click in these fields and type a value. For example, you might use this method when you want to create a 15-minute appointment when Outlook 2007 is set to use a 30-minute default appointment duration. If you select an appointment time that conflicts with another appointment, a bar above the Subject line will display the message "Conflicts with another appointment on your Calendar."

Setting a Reminder

You can set a reminder for an appointment by clicking the Reminder arrow in the Options group on the Appointment tab. In the Reminder drop-down list, you can specify when the reminder should appear; the default is 15 minutes before the appointment. By default, a reminder both plays a sound and displays a reminder window, as shown in Figure 20-10. If you don't want the reminder to play a sound, or if you want to use a different sound, click the Sound option at the bottom of the Reminder drop-down list to change the settings.

Note

To change the default behavior of appointment reminders, choose Tools, Options, and then click Preferences. In the Calendar area of the Preferences tab, you can select (or clear) the default reminder and set the default reminder time.

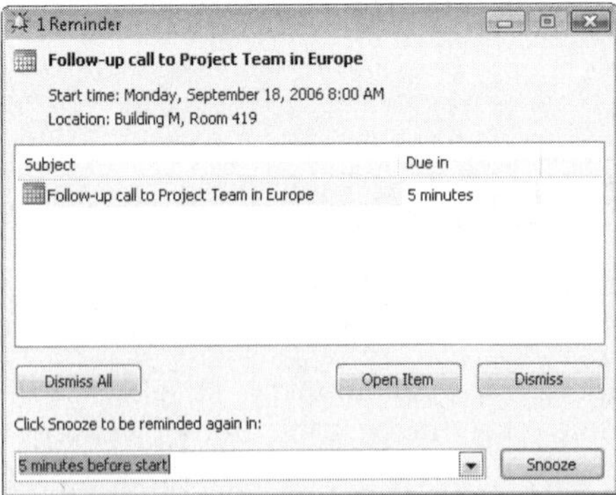

Figure 20-10. You can dismiss a reminder by clicking Dismiss or postpone it by clicking Snooze.

Classifying an Appointment

Outlook 2007 uses color and patterns to indicate free/busy information for appointments. In the calendar itself, Outlook 2007 does not show an indicator next to appointments marked Busy. It uses the following bars at the left edge of the appointment to indicate status:

- Free (white)
- Tentative (shaded with diagonal lines)
- Out Of Office (shaded dark purple)

> **Note**
>
> When you are scheduling a meeting or viewing a group schedule, Outlook 2007 shows busy time using a blue bar.

The indicator (a small bar to the left of the appointment) appears on your local calendar and is also displayed when other users view the free/busy times for that calendar. By default, the time occupied by an appointment is classified as Busy. To reclassify an appointment, select the indicator in the Show As drop-down list in the Options group, as shown in Figure 20-11.

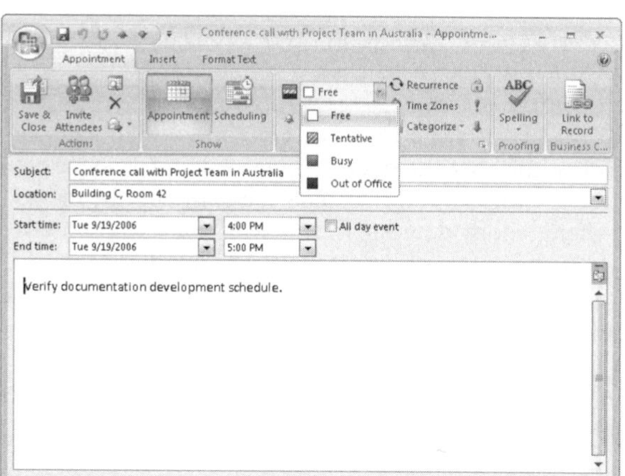

Figure 20-11. Use this drop-down list to select a classification for your appointment, which specifies how the appointment is displayed on your calendar.

Adding a Note

Sometimes an appointment requires more detail. You might need to remind yourself about documents that you need to bring to the appointment, or perhaps you need to write down directions to an unfamiliar location. When that's the case, you can add a note by typing your text in the large text area of the form, as shown in Figure 20-12.

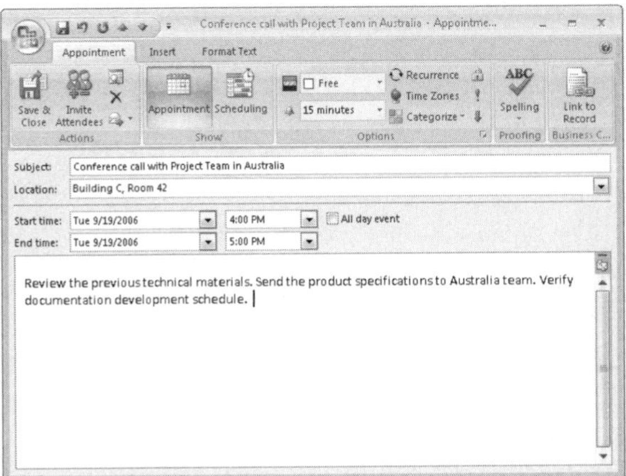

Figure 20-12. You can write a note on the appointment form.

Categorizing an Appointment

Assigning a category to an appointment is simply another method of organizing your information. Outlook 2007 provides a number of default categories associated with colors, and you can customize the names for each category. The color association enables you to more easily identify the categories of appointments within your calendar. You can create additional categories as desired and associate each with a specific color. Outlook 2007 allows you to categorize your appointments so that you can then filter or sort them before viewing. In this way, you can get an overview of all Outlook 2007 items based on a particular category. For example, you could view all appointments, meetings, messages, contacts, and tasks that have been assigned the same category—perhaps all the items related to a specific work project or objective.

For more information about working with categories in Outlook 2007, see Chapter 5, "Creating and Using Categories."

To assign a category to an appointment, click Categorize in the Options group of the appointment form. To assign a single category to the appointment, simply select the category in the drop-down list, as shown in Figure 20-13. To select multiple categories, modify existing categories, or create new categories, select the All Categories option at the bottom of the drop-down list.

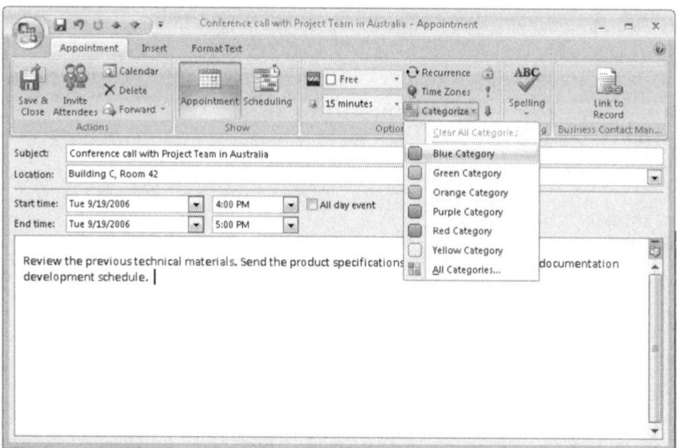

Figure 20-13. You can assign color categories to your appointment.

When you select All Categories, the Color Categories dialog box is displayed, as shown in Figure 20-14, enabling you to manage the categories. In this dialog box, you can select one or more categories and then click OK to assign them to the appointment. You can also rename or delete any of the existing categories and change the color association, as well as assigning a shortcut key for each category.

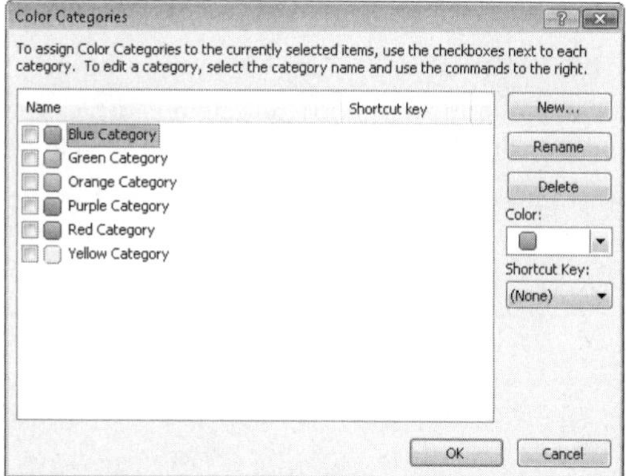

Figure 20-14. You can assign multiple categories to your appointment and configure a category label, color, and shortcut key.

Saving an Appointment

You can save an appointment in several ways. The most basic method is to click the Save & Close button on the Ribbon. This saves the appointment in the Calendar folder and closes the appointment form. If you want to save the appointment but keep the form open, click the Microsoft Office Button, and then click Save.

A more complex way to save appointments allows them to be transferred to other users (who might or might not use Outlook 2007) and opened in other applications. To save your appointments in any of a number of file formats, click the Microsoft Office Button, and then choose Save As to display the Save As dialog box, shown in Figure 20-15.

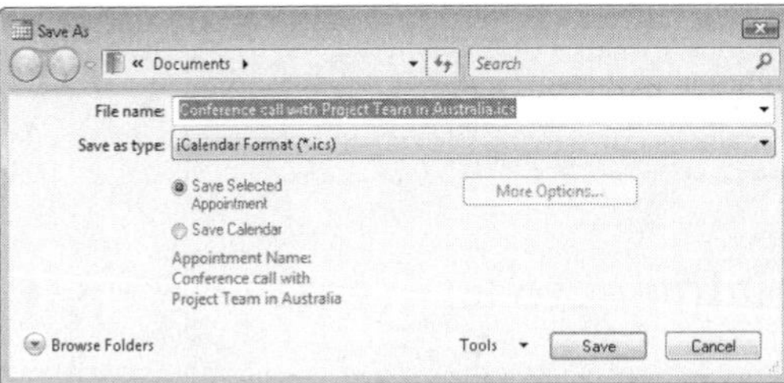

Figure 20-15. You can save your appointment in any of several formats so that the appointment can be opened with another application. You can also save the calendar or any date range portion of it.

The following formats are available:

- **Rich Text Format and Text Only** These formats save the appointment in a file that text editors can read. Figure 20-16 shows an example of an appointment saved in Rich Text Format and then opened in WordPad.

> **Note**
>
> You can create a new appointment from an Outlook 2007 Template file by choosing File, New, Choose Form and then selecting User Templates In File System in the Look In list.

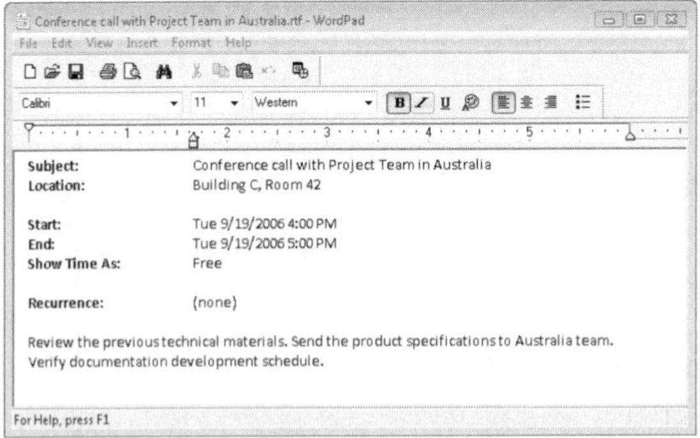

Figure 20-16. An appointment saved in Rich Text Format or Text Only can be displayed in any application that supports those file types.

- **Outlook 2007 Template** This format allows you to save an appointment and use it later to create new appointments.

- **Outlook Message Format** Saving an appointment in this format is almost the same as saving an appointment to the calendar, except that the appointment is saved in a file in case you want to archive the file or move it to another installation of Outlook 2007. You can view the file in Outlook 2007, and the data appears as it would if you had opened the item from the calendar.
- **iCalendar Format and vCalendar Format** These formats are used to share schedule items with people who use applications other than Outlook 2007. iCalendar is a newer version of the standard (maintained by the Internet Mail Consortium) and should be used if possible.

Changing an Appointment to an Event

To change an appointment to an event, select the All Day Event check box on the appointment form. When an appointment is converted to an event, the start and end times are removed and only the start and end dates are left because events by definition last all day. The event appears in the banner area of the calendar.

Working with One-Time Events

An event is an appointment that lasts for one or more entire days. You can create an event by right-clicking the calendar and then choosing New All Day Event. Unlike appointments, events are not shown in time slots on the calendar. Instead, events are displayed as banners at the top of the calendar day. Figure 20-17 shows the calendar with a scheduled event–in this case, a trade show.

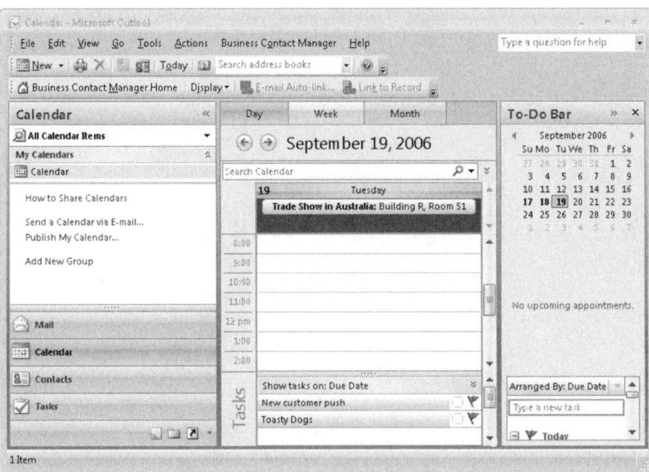

Figure 20-17. Outlook 2007 displays events as banners on the calendar.

> **INSIDE OUT** **Create an event quickly**
>
> A simple way to add an event is to click the banner area of the calendar and start typing the subject of the event. When you add an event this way, the event is automatically set to last for only the selected day. Or, in Month view, click a date and then type the subject to create a one-time event on that date. To add details and change the duration of the event, you must use the event form.

Using the Event Form

You can use an Event form in much the same way you use an Appointment form, with a few exceptions:

- You can set the start and end times only as dates, not times. (If you select times, the form changes from an event form to an appointment form, and the All Day Event check box is cleared.)
- The default reminder is set to 18 hours.
- The time is shown by default as Free, as opposed to Busy.

The event form and the appointment form look the same except that the All Day Event check box is selected on the event form. You can open an event form by right-clicking the time in Calendar view and then choosing New All Day Event.

To create an event using the event form, type the subject, specify the start and end dates, add any optional information, and then click Save & Close in the Actions group. Figure 20-18 shows the event form for a trade show event.

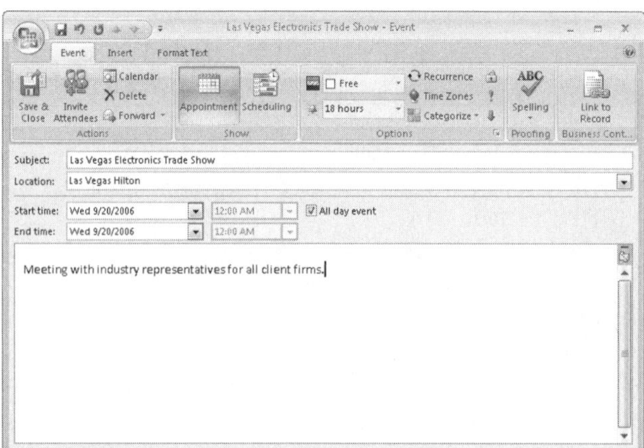

Figure 20-18. Use the event form to specify the details of an event to be added to your calendar.

Changing an Event to an Appointment

To change an event to an appointment, clear the All Day Event check box on the event form. The boxes for start and end times reappear, and the event will now be displayed in time slots on the calendar, not in the banner area.

Creating a Recurring Appointment or Event

When you create a recurring appointment or a recurring event, Outlook 2007 automatically displays the recurrences in the calendar. A recurring appointment could be something as simple as a reminder to feed your fish every day or pay your mortgage every month. You can create a recurring calendar item by right-clicking the calendar and then choosing New Recurring Appointment or New Recurring Event. Alternatively, you can open a normal (nonrecurring) item and then click the Recurrence button in the Options group. Either method displays the Appointment Recurrence dialog box, shown in Figure 20-19.

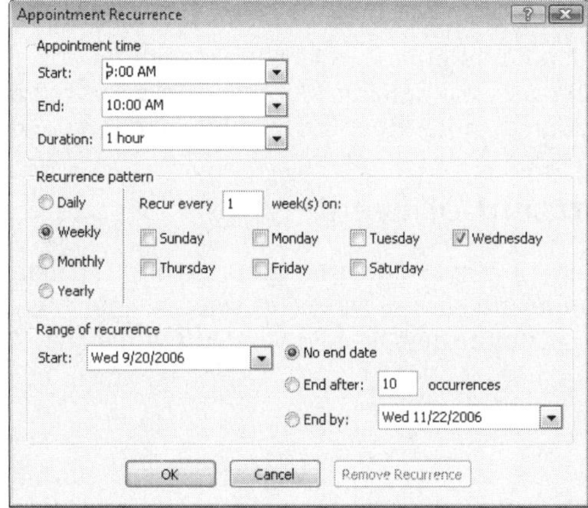

Figure 20-19. You can specify criteria that direct Outlook 2007 to display an appointment or event multiple times in the calendar.

In the Appointment Time area, you set the appointment time and duration. If you're creating the recurrence from an existing nonrecurring appointment, the time of that appointment is listed by default.

The Recurrence Pattern area changes depending on whether you select the Daily, Weekly, Monthly, or Yearly option, as follows:

- **Daily** Specify the number of days or every weekday.
- **Weekly** Specify the number of weeks and the day (or days) of the week.
- **Monthly** Specify the number of months as well as the day of the month (such as the 27th) or the day and week of the month (such as the fourth Wednesday).
- **Yearly** Specify the date (such as December 27th) or the day and week of the month (such as the fourth Wednesday of each December).

At the bottom of the Appointment Recurrence dialog box is the Range Of Recurrence area. By default, the start date is the current day, and the recurrence is set to No End Date. You can choose to have the appointment recur a specified number of times and then stop, or you can set it to recur until a specified date and then stop—either method has the same effect. For example, to set a recurring appointment that starts on the first Monday of a month and continues for four Mondays in that month, you could either set it to occur four times or set it to occur until the last day of the month.

Modifying an Appointment or Event

There are many reasons you might need to change a scheduled appointment or event—an event could be rescheduled, an appointment could be moved to a better time, or the topical focus could be added to or changed. In each case, you will need to modify the existing appointment or event, updating information or changing the date or time.

Changing an Appointment or Event

Modifying an existing appointment or event is easy. First open the appointment or event by locating it in the calendar and then either double-clicking or right-clicking it and choosing Open. Make the necessary changes in the form, and then click Save & Close on the Ribbon. The updated appointment or event is saved in the Calendar folder.

Deleting an Appointment or Event

You can delete an appointment or event in several ways. To send the item to the Deleted Items folder, right-click the item and choose Delete, or select the item and press the **Delete** key. To permanently delete the item, hold down **Shift** while choosing Delete or pressing the **Delete** key.

CAUTION!

You cannot recover an item that has been deleted using the Shift key unless you are using Microsoft Exchange Server and your administrator has configured the server for a retention period.

Using Categories and Colors

You can use color as a tool to identify appointments and events. In Outlook 2003, the assignment of colors and categories was separate from that of other categories, but in Outlook 2007 these have been combined. The easiest way to assign color to an appointment is to use the Categorize drop-down list on the appointment form. You can also create rules that direct Outlook 2007 to assign color labels automatically via the Edit, Automatic Formatting menu option in Outlook 2007.

Assigning Color Categories to an Appointment Manually

The Categorize drop-down list on the appointment form shows the different color labels (associated with categories) that you can assign to an appointment as a visual cue to indicate the topic of the appointment. Categories can also reflect appointment importance or requirements. Simply select a color in the drop-down list when you fill in the appointment form. In Figure 20-20, the appointment shown is a business one, and it will be displayed on the calendar in the specified color. To set colors independently of categories, use the automatic formatting rules described in the next section.

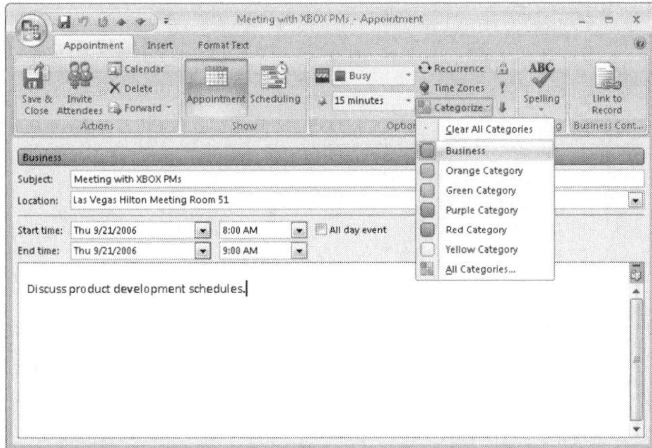

Figure 20-20. You can assign a color category label to your appointment.

You can assign a category to an appointment without associating a color with it, by defining a category and selecting None for the color. Categories without colors will not provide the visual cue that enables you to quickly identify the nature of an appointment, but they still are useful—for example, when you filter your Calendar view by category.

> **Note**
>
> Manual color category settings always override automatic settings, even when the category color setting is set to None.

Assigning Color to an Appointment Automatically

To have Outlook 2007 automatically assign a color label to an appointment, you can create automatic formatting rules.

To create a Color rule, do the following:

1. Choose Edit, Automatic Formatting to display the Automatic Formatting dialog box.
2. Click Add to add a new rule.
3. Type a name and assign a label to the new rule. Figure 20-21 shows a rule to automatically color all Important appointments with the red color.

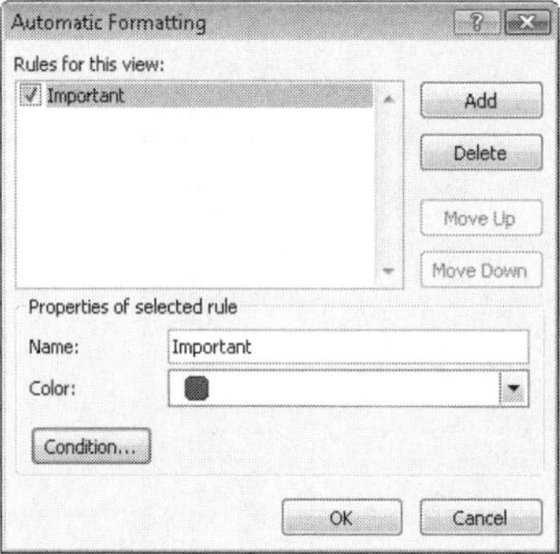

Figure 20-21. This new rule automatically assigns the red color to all Important appointments.

4. Click Condition to open the Filter dialog box, shown in Figure 20-22, where you specify the condition for the rule.

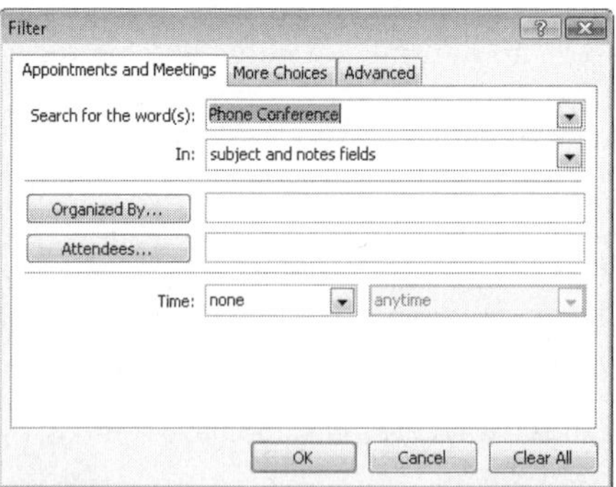

Figure 20-22. The Filter dialog box lets you set a filter that defines the condition on which the automatic color rule works.

For details about using filters, see "Customizing the Current Calendar View" on the opposite page.

5. In this dialog box, assign a condition to the rule. For example, you might use the most basic type of filter and search for a word or phrase in all appointments. In this case, Outlook 2007 will search for the words *Phone Conference* in the Subject and Notes fields and will apply the rule to mark these appointments as Important (red) if *Phone Conference* is found.

> **Note**
>
> The More Choices and Advanced tabs in the Filter dialog box enable you to select other criteria, such as categories, read status, attachments, size, or matching fields.

6. Click OK to assign the condition to the new rule.
7. Click OK twice, once to close the Automatic Formatting dialog box and again to close the Customize View dialog box. A rule is now in effect that all appointments with the phrase *Phone Conference* in their Subject or Notes field will be assigned the red color, designating them as Important.

Printing Calendar Items

You can print calendar items in two ways. The simplest method is to right-click the item and then choose Print on the shortcut menu. This method prints the item using the default settings.

The other way to print an item is to first open it by double-clicking it or by right-clicking it and choosing Open. You can then click the Microsoft Office Button and click Print to display the Print dialog box, or click the arrow next to Print and select Quick Print to print using the default settings.

You can make selections in the Print dialog box to change the target printer, the number of copies, and the print style, if necessary. The print style defines how the printed item will look. Click Page Setup to change the options for the selected style. In the Page Setup dialog box, use the Format tab to set fonts and shading; the Paper tab to change the paper size, orientation, and margin settings; and the Header/Footer tab to add information to be printed at the top and bottom of the page.

Customizing the Current Calendar View

In addition to setting the number of days displayed, configuring the Time Bar, and color-coding your appointments, you can customize the standard view of the Calendar folder in other ways. You can redefine fields, set up filters that define which items are displayed on your calendar, and control fonts and other view settings. To configure the view, begin by choosing View, Current View, Customize Current View to open the Customize View dialog box, shown in Figure 20-23.

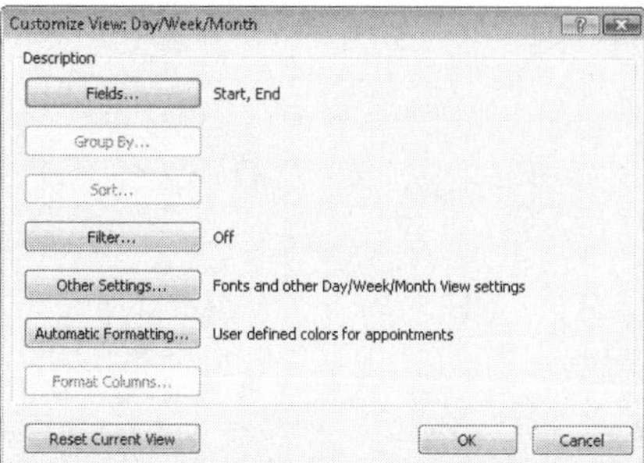

Figure 20-23. Use the Customize View dialog box to change view settings.

INSIDE OUT **Customize additional views**

You can also customize views other than the current one. To do so, choose View, Current View, Define Views. Select the view in the Custom View Organizer dialog box, and then click Modify. This displays the Customize View dialog box, where you can change the options for the selected view.

Redefining Fields

Only two of the fields used for calendar items can be redefined: the Start and End fields. The values in these fields determine an item's precise location on the calendar–that is, where the item is displayed. By default, the value contained in the Start field is the start time of the appointment and the value contained in the End field is the end time of the appointment, which means that the item is displayed on the calendar in the time interval defined by the item's Start and End values.

To redefine either the Start or the End value, click Fields in the Customize View dialog box to open the Date/Time Fields dialog box. In the Available Date/Time Fields list, select the field that you want to use for the Start field, and then click Start. Use the End button to change the End field. For example, if you redefine the Start field to Recurrence Range Start and the End field to Recurrence Range End, all recurring calendar items will be displayed as a single item that starts on the date of the first occurrence and ends on the date of the last occurrence. This can be handy if you want to view the entire recurrence range for a given item graphically.

Filtering Calendar Items

You can filter calendar items based on their content, their assigned category, or other criteria. By filtering the current view, you can determine which calendar items are displayed on your calendar—for example, all items related to one of your work projects, all items that involve a specific coworker, or items with a particular importance level.

To filter calendar items, follow these steps:

1. Choose View, Current View, Customize Current View to open the Customize View dialog box.
2. Click Filter to open the Filter dialog box.
3. If the Appointments And Meetings tab isn't displayed, as shown in Figure 20-24, click it to bring it to the front.

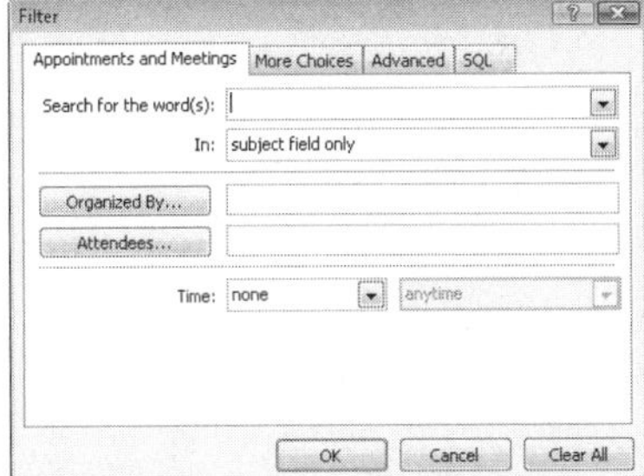

Figure 20-24. You can filter calendar items based on a specified word or phrase.

4. In the Search For The Word(s) box, type the word or phrase you want to use as the filter.
5. In the In drop-down list, select which areas of the calendar item to search—for example, you might have Outlook 2007 look only in the Subject field of your appointments.
6. Click OK. Outlook 2007 displays on your calendar only those calendar items that contain the specified word or phrase.

To set additional criteria, you can use the three other tabs in the Filter dialog box—More Choices, Advanced, and SQL—as follows:

- **More Choices** On this tab, you can click Categories to select any number of categories. After you click OK, only calendar items belonging to the selected categories are displayed on the calendar. Using the check boxes on the More Choices tab, you can filter items based on whether they are read or unread, whether they have attachments, or their importance setting. The final check box on the tab enables or disables case matching for the word or phrase specified on the Appointments And Meetings tab. You can also filter items depending on size.

- **Advanced** This tab allows an even wider range of filter criteria. You can specify any field, adding a condition such as Contains or Is Not Empty or a value for conditions that require one. Clicking Add To List adds the criteria to the list of filters.
- **SQL** This tab has two purposes. In most cases, it displays the SQL code for the filter, based on the filter criteria you select on the other three tabs. If the Edit These Criteria Directly check box is selected, however, you can manually type the SQL code for filtering calendar items directly on the SQL tab. This flexibility allows you to fine-tune your filters with a great degree of precision.

Controlling Fonts and Other View Settings

You can use the Customize View dialog box (shown earlier in Figure 20-23) to make additional changes to the current view. In the Customize View dialog box, click Other Settings to display the Format Day/Week/Month View dialog box, shown in Figure 20-25.

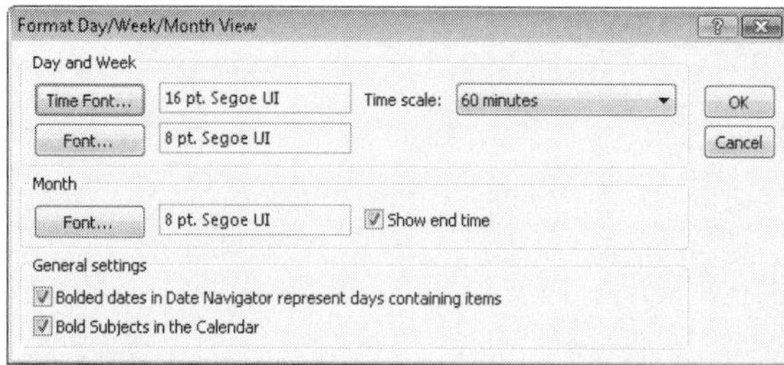

Figure 20-25. You can use the Format Day/Week/Month View dialog box to set font preferences for the Calendar folder as well as other options.

In the Format Day/Week/Month View dialog box, you can do the following:

- Set the fonts used in Calendar view.
- Set the calendar's time increments by selecting an option in the Time Scale drop-down list. This sets the amount of time represented by each interval in the Time Bar.
- Specify whether days with scheduled items should appear in bold in the Date Navigator.
- Specify whether Subjects in the calendar should appear in bold.

Creating a Custom View

Up to now, we have looked only at the customization of existing views, but you can also create completely new views and copy and modify views. If your current view is one you use often but nevertheless must change frequently to filter calendar items or modify fields, you might find it easier to create a new view.

To create a view or to see a list of already defined views, choose View, Current View, Define Views to open the Custom View Organizer dialog box, shown in Figure 20-26.

Note

To work with the Outlook 2007 calendar views, you must open the Calendar folder.

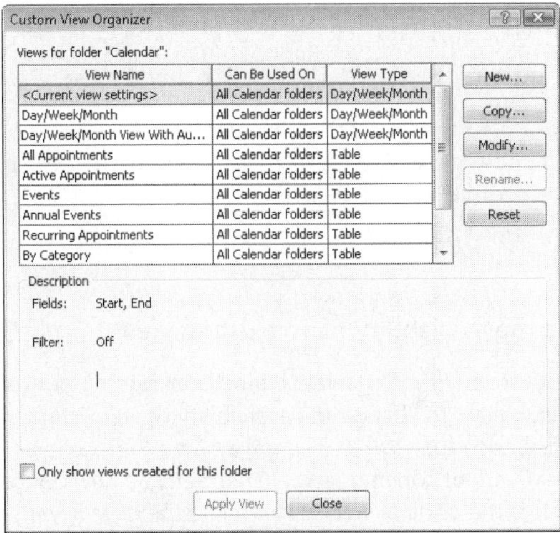

Figure 20-26. The Custom View Organizer dialog box allows you to see and work with the currently defined views as well as create new ones.

Creating a New View

To create a view, follow these steps:

1. Click New in the Custom View Organizer dialog box to open the Create A New View dialog box, shown in Figure 20-27.

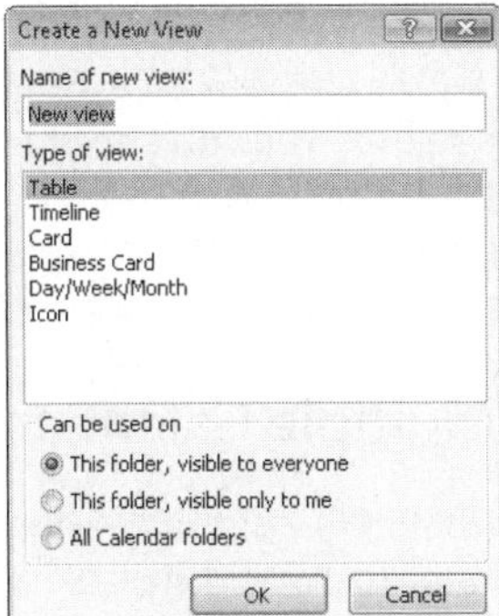

Figure 20-27. You can use the Create A New View dialog box to specify a name, a view type, the folder to which the view applies, and who is allowed to see the view.

2. Name the new view, and then select a view type. In the Can Be Used On area, specify the folder to which the view applies and who is allowed to see the view. You can select one of the following options:

   This Folder, Visible To Everyone Limits the view to the current folder and makes it available to any user.

   This Folder, Visible Only To Me Limits the view to the current folder but makes it available only to the current user.

   All Calendar Folders Allows the view to be used in any Calendar folder by any user.

3. Click OK to create the new view. The Customize View dialog box appears, in which you can set the options for the new view.

INSIDE OUT **Change the availability of an existing view**

The Modify option in the Custom View Organizer dialog box does not let you change the availability of an existing view. To change the availability of an existing view or who is allowed to see a view, first copy the view and assign a name to the copy. (See the next section for more information about copying views.) Then select a new option in the Can Be Used On area. Last, delete the original view and rename the new view using the name of the deleted view.

For information about setting view options in the Customize View dialog box, see "Customizing the Current Calendar View " earlier in this chapter.

Copying a View

If you want to modify an existing view but also want to keep the original, you can make a copy of the view. To copy a view, select it in the Custom View Organizer dialog box, and then click Copy. In the Copy View dialog box, you can specify the name of the new view, the folder to which the view will apply, and who is allowed to see the view. Click OK to create the copy, which is added to the list in the Custom View Organizer dialog box and the list on the View, Current View menu.

Using Overlay Mode to View Multiple Calendars in One

There are times when you need to view and compare multiple schedules to identify related items, such as workflow dependencies within a project, as well as to find and alleviate scheduling conflicts. For example, you might want to view your personal calendar in contrast to your departmental calendar to compare scheduling and task overlaps. Outlook 2007 adds a new capability to view multiple calendars in overlay mode, as shown in Figure 20-28.

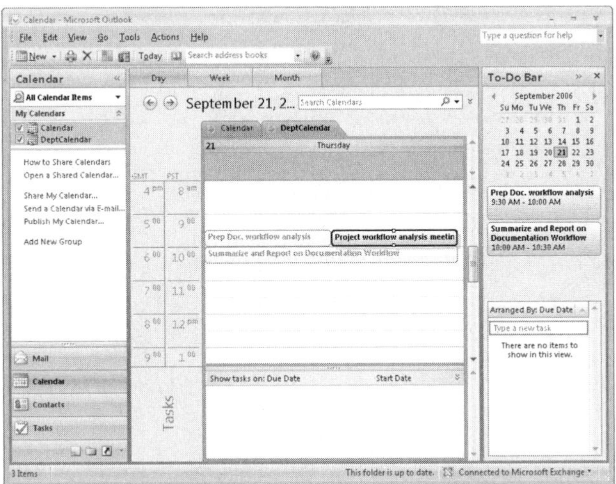

Figure 20-28. You can overlay multiple calendars to view related or conflicting schedules.

To view multiple calendars in overlay mode:

1. Select multiple calendars by selecting the check boxes next to the calendars in the Navigation Pane.
2. Under My Calendars, right-click one of the calendars in the Navigation Pane, and then choose View In Overlay Mode.

> **Note**
>
> You can click the left arrow icon at the left edge of the calendar's name tab to overlay the calendar with the leftmost calendar. Click the right arrow icon to move the selected calendar out of overlay mode.

Backing Up Your Schedule

To back up items in your Calendar folder, you must export the data to a personal folders (.pst) file. To do so, follow these steps:

1. Choose File, Import And Export to start the Import And Export Wizard.
2. Click Export To A File, as shown in Figure 20-29, and then click Next.

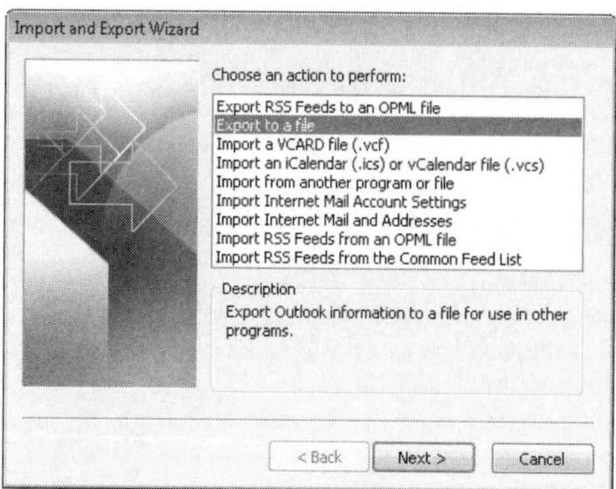

Figure 20-29. To back up calendar items, start the Import And Export Wizard, and then select Export To A File.

3. On the Export To A File page, shown in Figure 20-30, select Personal Folder File (.pst), and then click Next.

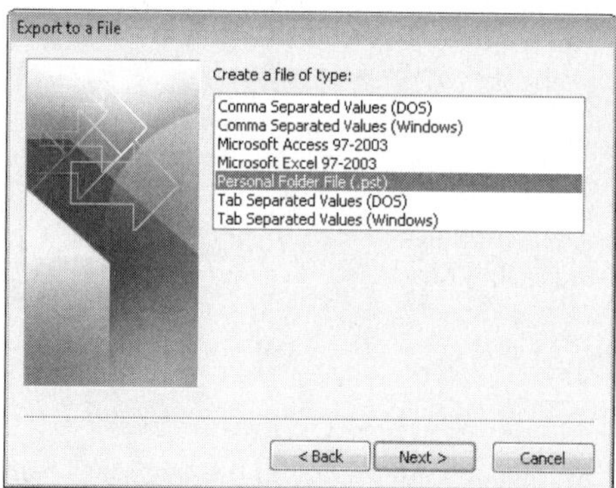

Figure 20-30. Calendar items should be backed up to a .pst file.

4. In the Export Personal Folders dialog box, select the folder to export (the Calendar folder in the example shown in Figure 20-31). If you select the Include Subfolders check box, any subfolders of the selected folder are exported as well.

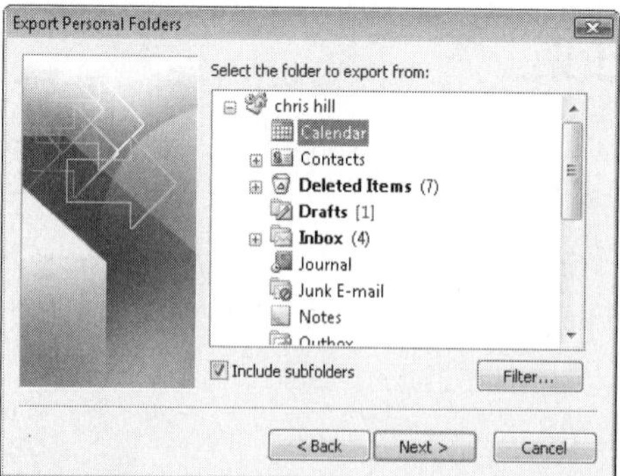

Figure 20-31. You use the Export Personal Folders dialog box to specify the folder to export to a file.

5. Click Filter to open the Filter dialog box, in which you can specify the items to be exported. You can use the Filter dialog box if you want to export only specific items from your Calendar folder. If you choose not to use the Filter dialog box, all items will be exported. Click Next to continue.

For details about using the Filter dialog box, see "Filtering Calendar Items" earlier in this chapter.

6. Specify the exported file and the export options. The export options control how Outlook 2007 handles items that have duplicates in the target file. You can choose to overwrite duplicates, create duplicates in the file, or not export duplicate items.
7. Click Finish. The Create Microsoft Personal Folders dialog box, shown in Figure 20-32, displays the selected file name.

Figure 20-32. Type a password and verify the password before creating the .pst file.

8. Specify a descriptive name for the .pst file. You can also set a password for the file.
9. Click OK to create the file.

To restore data backed up to the .pst file, follow these steps:

1. Choose File, Import And Export to start the Import And Export Wizard.
2. Select Import From Another Program Or File, and then click Next.
3. Select Personal Folder File (.pst), and then click Next.
4. On the Import Personal Folders page, specify the backup file and how Outlook 2007 should handle duplicate items. You can choose to overwrite duplicates, create duplicate items, or not import duplicates. Then click Next. If you assigned a password to the backup file, you will be prompted to enter it at this point.
5. Select the folder within the .pst file to be imported (the Calendar folder in this case), decide whether to include subfolders, and select the target folder. (By default, the target folder is the folder with the same name in the current mailbox, as shown in Figure 20-33.) You can also click Filter to specify in the Filter dialog box which items are to be imported.

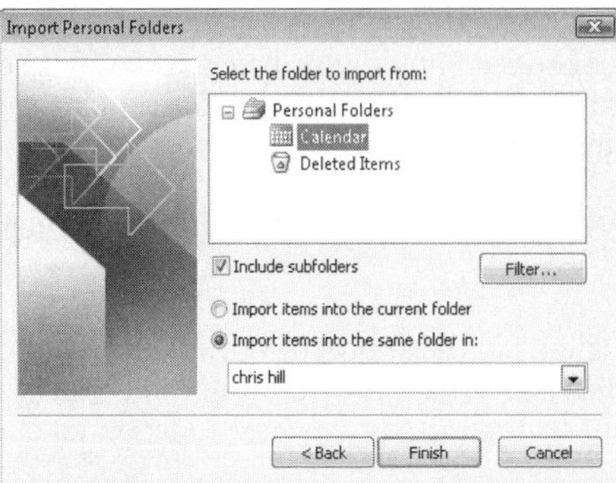

Figure 20-33. When you're importing items, you must select the folder to be imported from the .pst file, whether to include subfolders, and the target folder.

6. Click Finish to complete the import process.

Managing Time Zones

Outlook 2007 gives you a great deal of flexibility when it comes to time zones on your calendar. You can change time zones easily and even add a second time zone to the calendar. If you work for a corporation that has multiple offices in different time zones, being able to quickly reference your calendar with various zones can make scheduling simpler.

Changing the Time Zone

To work with time zones, use the Time Zone dialog box, shown in Figure 20-34. To open this dialog box, right-click the Time Bar and choose Change Time Zone. (Alternatively, choose Tools, Options, click Calendar Options, and then click Time Zone.)

Figure 20-34. You can set the current time zone and display a second time zone.

In the Time Zone dialog box, you can specify a label for the current time zone, which is displayed above the Time Bar on your calendar. You can also set the time zone you want to use by selecting it in the Time Zone drop-down list, and you can specify whether to automatically adjust for daylight saving time.

> **Note**
>
> Changing the time zone in the Time Zone dialog box has the same effect as changing the time zone by using the Date And Time dialog box through Control Panel (Classic View).

When you change the time zone, the time of your appointments adjusts as well. Your appointments stay at their scheduled time in the original time zone but move to the appropriate time in the new time zone. For example, an appointment scheduled for 10:00 A.M. in the GMT+2 time zone will move to 8:00 A.M. if the time zone is changed to GMT (Greenwich Mean Time). Appointments are scheduled in absolute time, regardless of the time zone.

Using Two Time Zones

To add a second time zone to your calendar, follow these steps:

1. In the Time Zone dialog box, select the Show An Additional Time Zone check box.
2. Assign a label to the second time zone. This step is not necessary, but it can help to avoid confusion later on. (If your first time zone does not already have a label, adding one now will allow you to easily distinguish between the two.)
3. In the second Time Zone drop-down list, select the second time zone.
4. Select the Adjust For Daylight Saving Time check box if you want Outlook 2007 to make this adjustment.
5. Click Swap Time Zones to swap the current time zone with the second time zone. This feature is useful if you travel between corporate offices in different time zones.

Figure 20-35 shows the calendar after these changes have been applied.

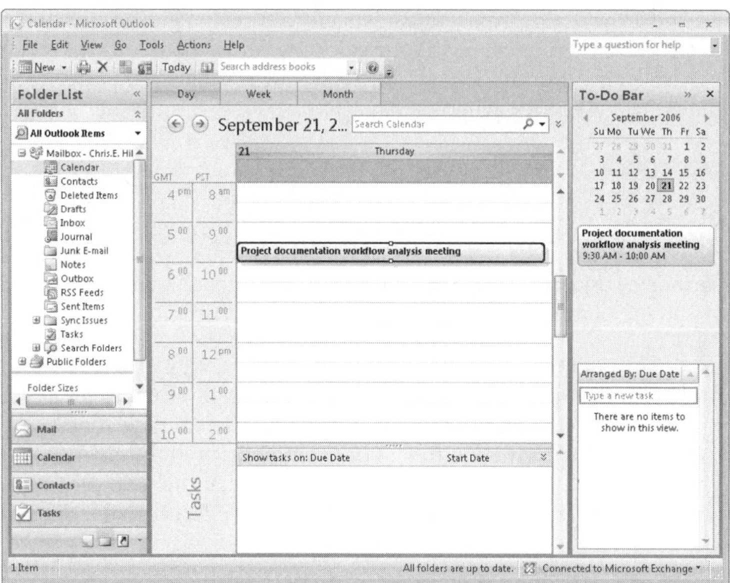

Figure 20-35. The calendar displays both time zones in the Time Bar under their respective labels.

Managing Your Calendar Effectively

Your Outlook 2007 calendar can help you track your appointments and events and facilitate your collaboration with coworkers, vendors, and clients. To maximize the value of the Outlook 2007 calendar, you will want to provide as much detail in the information you enter as you can. In addition to simply marking the dates and times of scheduled appointments and events, the calendar information will serve as a quick reference to key points in your workflow, projects, and goals. In addition, the interface features (such as Categories and Automatic Formatting) can provide valuable visual and cognitive cues to the nature and importance of your calendar information.

- **Use color categories for quick identification.** Outlook 2007 has combined color and category labeling of appointments and events and allows you to define the name of each category and the color associated with it. By defining a set of categories that fits the categories of events, appointments, and information you will be storing in your calendar, you can make it easy to mark (and later identify) the nature and significance of items in your calendar at a glance. These user-defined color categories can provide you with visual cues that help you identify calendar items, tasks, and e-mail that are related—such as a departmental project or role-based recurring activities. The color categories in Outlook 2007 are contained in your default data file; thus for users of Microsoft Exchange Server, your color categories are available regardless of which computer you log on from.
- **Use automatic formatting to format items based on user-selectable criteria.** In addition to color categories, you can use automatic formatting to assign a color

to appointments, events, and so on in your calendar based on criteria that you define. This can be particularly useful in that you can provide specific words, phrases, or other criteria that Outlook 2007 will use to automatically tag the appointment or event with a specific color. You can use automatic formatting, for example, to find the phrase *Phone Conference* in the Subject or Notes field of appointments and automatically color all those items in your calendar (with a color you select) to provide you with visual cues that the item involves a phone conference.

For specific information about how to assign colors automatically, see the section "Assigning Color to an Appointment Automatically" earlier in this chapter.

- **Delegate calendar update responsibilities.** In managing your calendar, scheduling appointments and events, and communicating your schedule information effectively, you can make use of the abilities to delegate access and degrees of editing and authoring control to team members, assistants, and key people involved in ongoing projects.

Note

To delegate control over your calendar (or other functions of Outlook 2007), you and the person you are delegating to must both be using Microsoft Exchange for your mail servers.

For network environments using Microsoft Exchange, however, the ability to delegate differential levels of control can be a useful way to turn schedule management into a cooperative effort. Even without providing other users with the ability to send e-mail messages as you, you can nevertheless enable them to read your schedule, create new items or subfolders, edit and delete their own additions to your schedule, and even edit all calendar content. When you are working closely with an associate or a team member on a mutual project, that person could add schedule items on your behalf that address his or her area (documentation, code development, marketing) of responsibility.

- **Share your calendar information.** In addition to those environments where you can directly delegate access to read information from and write information to your calendar, in all cases you can post your calendar information to the external or internal Web servers so that management, team, and project members can view your schedule information. In some cases, you might want to publish only the free/busy portion of your schedule information–for example, when publishing your schedule on the Internet. But when publishing your schedule to internal corporate Web servers, you will want to provide access to more detail so that co-workers and managers stay up to date. The Outlook 2007 Publish To Internet options let you specify the date range and level of detail published, determine access (everyone or just those you invite), and select calendar update frequency. You can also share your calendar via e-mail with the selected group of e-mail recipients for whom your calendar is relevant by using the Send Via E-Mail option. This option also lets you choose the date range and level of detail sent so that you can control how much of your calendar information you are providing.

For detailed information about sharing calendars, see Chapter 36, "Sharing Calendars."

- **Use views to manage your calendar.** The various views of your calendar provide a built-in way for you to quickly assess your schedule–simply switching between the Day, Week, and Month tabs reminds you of your scheduled activities. Using the built-in views enables you to see your schedule laid out as a timeline (which you can view on a daily, weekly, or monthly basis). Other default views enable you to see all of your scheduled items as a list that you can sort by date, type of appointment or event, subject, category, and a range of other criteria. Using these views can help you quickly find events and appointments of current topical interest and provide reminders of upcoming scheduled obligations. When specific view and filter criteria are particularly useful for you, creating a custom view using these criteria will provide you with an instant ability to see your schedule information in that format.
- **Use Overlays to Compare Calendars.** For everyone in a work environment, the scheduling of appointments and events has interdependencies with coworkers, teams, project groups, and departments. To avoid scheduling conflicts, it can be very helpful to align your schedule with schedules from other people or groups you are working with. Using Outlook 2007 to bring in additional calendars (from coworkers or groups) and review them in overlay mode greatly facilitates the comparing of schedules.

CHAPTER 21

Scheduling Meetings and Resources

Before the introduction of workgroup software such as Microsoft® Exchange and Microsoft Office Outlook® 2007, scheduling a meeting could be a difficult task. Now all it takes is a few simple steps to avoid those endless e-mail exchanges trying to find a suitable meeting time for all invitees. Office Outlook 2007 provides you with a single place to schedule both people and resources for meetings. You can take advantage of these features whether or not you use Exchange Server.

Chapter 20, "Scheduling Appointments," tells you all about scheduling appointments. Meetings and appointments are similar, of course: both types of items appear on your calendar, and you can create, view, and store them in your Outlook 2007 Calendar folder. An appointment, however, involves only your schedule and time, whereas a meeting involves inviting others and coordinating their schedules. Another difference is that a meeting often requires you to schedule resources, such as a conference room or an overhead projector.

You can schedule meetings with other Outlook 2007 users as well as those who use any e-mail or collaboration application that supports the vCalendar or iCalendar standard. (For more information, see "iCalendar, vCalendar, and vCard" in Chapter 2.) This chapter takes you through the process of scheduling meetings and lining up resources.

Sending a Meeting Request

To schedule a meeting, you begin by selecting your calendar in Outlook 2007 and sending a meeting request. Choose File, New, Meeting Request or click the arrow next to New on the toolbar and choose Meeting Request. The meeting form opens, as shown in Figure 21-1.

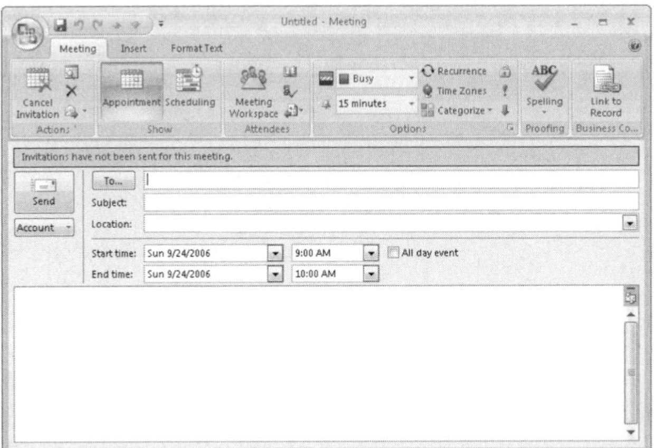

Figure 21-1. You use the meeting form to schedule meetings and send meeting requests.

A meeting request is like an appointment item but with a few additional details–and you can work with it in much the same way you work with an appointment. This chapter describes only the parts of a meeting request that differ from an appointment.

For details about creating and working with appointments in the Outlook 2007 Calendar folder, see Chapter 20, "Scheduling Appointments."

Selecting Attendees

To invite people to your meeting, start by selecting their names on either the Appointment page or the Scheduling page of the Meeting tab. To select them on the Appointment page, you can type each name in the To box, separating the names with a semicolon. When you enter the names manually, Outlook 2007 considers each person a required attendee. Alternatively, you can click To to open the Select Attendees And Resources dialog box, shown in Figure 21-2. In this dialog box, select a name in the Name list, and then click Required or Optional to designate whether that person's attendance is critical. (This choice will be reflected in the meeting request you send to these individuals.) After you have finished adding names, click OK to close the dialog box.

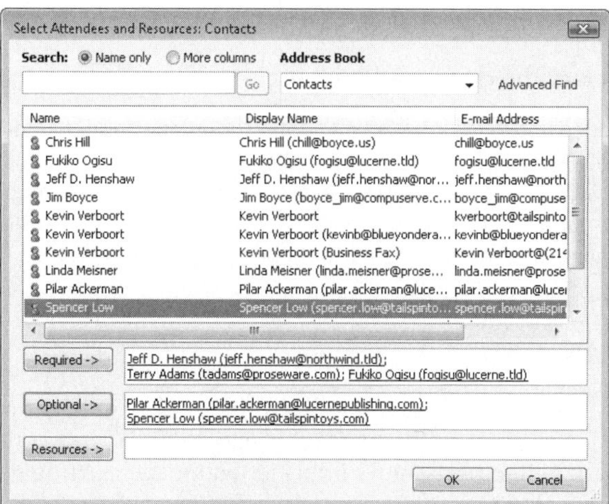

Figure 21-2. In the Select Attendees And Resources dialog box, you can add the names of the individuals you're inviting to your meeting.

Clicking Scheduling on the Meeting tab displays the Scheduling page, shown in Figure 21-3. You can click in the designated box in the All Attendees column and type a name or an e-mail address. Alternatively, you can click Add Others and select the location from which you want to add the names. For example, if you want to add individuals from the Global Address List (GAL), click Add Others, and then select Add From Address Book to open the Select Attendees And Resources dialog box. As before, select a name, click Required or Optional, and then click OK.

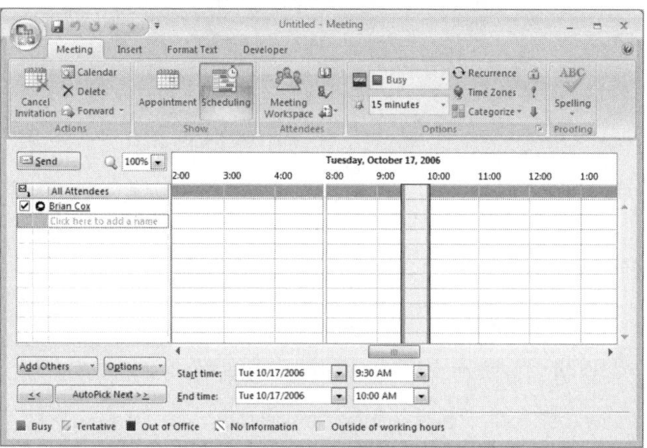

Figure 21-3. You can use the Scheduling page to add meeting attendees and view their schedules.

INSIDE OUT **Select the correct address list**

Can't find the attendee you're looking for, and you know that attendee is in the address book? Make sure that the correct address list is selected in the Address Book drop-down list. By default, the GAL, which shows all names from your Exchange Server organization, is selected (if you're running Outlook 2007 with Exchange Server). It is possible to change the default address list, however, and yours could be set to something else.

Scheduling a Meeting

After you have added the names of the individuals you want to invite, the Scheduling page on the meeting form displays free/busy information for all the people you selected. In Figure 21-4, the Scheduling page shows information for the meeting organizer (you), required attendees, and optional attendees.

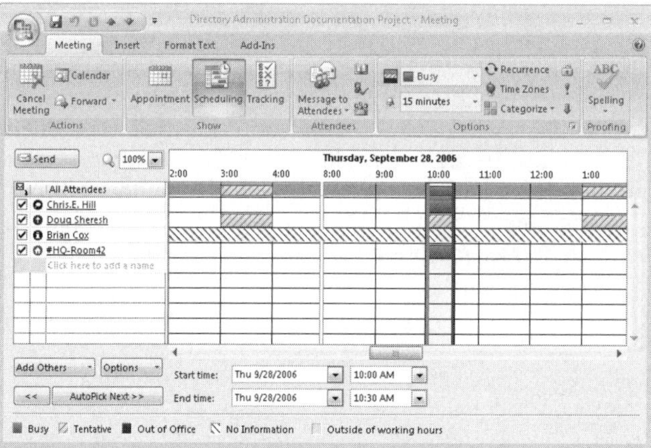

Figure 21-4. The Scheduling page shows the attendees you selected along with their free/busy times.

The icons you see beside each name have the following meanings:

Icon	Description
(magnifying glass icon)	The magnifying glass icon indicates the meeting organizer.
(arrow icon)	The arrow icon indicates a required attendee.
(i icon)	The icon containing the letter *i* indicates an optional attendee.
(building icon)	The building icon indicates a scheduled resource.

INSIDE OUT Specify free/busy server location

Outlook 2007 queries the free/busy time of each attendee based on the settings you have configured for that purpose. As you'll see in Chapter 36, "Sharing Calendars," you can configure Outlook 2007 to check Microsoft Office Online, another globally specified free/busy server, and individual servers specified with each contact. These all work in conjunction with Exchange Server, if it is present.

After you have identified a time slot that fits everyone's schedules, you can schedule the meeting for a particular time slot using the Meeting Start Time and Meeting End Time drop-down lists.

If you want Outlook 2007 to fit the meeting into the next available time slot, click AutoPick Next. By default, AutoPick selects the next time slot in which all attendees and at least one resource are free.

INSIDE OUT Configure the AutoPick feature

To change the default actions of AutoPick, click Options on the Scheduling page, and then make your choices on the AutoPick menu. You can set AutoPick to select the next time slot in which all attendees and all resources are free, the next time slot in which all attendees and at least one resource are free (the default), a time slot in which only required attendees are free, or a time slot in which required attendees and at least one resource are free.

You can specify whether the Scheduling page's display of free/busy information should show only working hours (the default) or the entire day. To define working hours for your calendar, choose Tools, Options, and then click Calendar Options. To set displayed hours for a meeting, click the Options button on the Scheduling page and set or clear the Show Only My Working Hours option. Working hours are a way of displaying your time in the Calendar folder and controlling which hours are displayed on the Scheduling page. In most cases, including nonworking hours on the Scheduling page would become unmanageable.

After you have selected all the attendees, found an available time slot, and filled in all the necessary details on the message form, click Send on the form to send the meeting request to the attendees.

Scheduling a Meeting from the Contacts Folder

If it's more convenient, you can initiate meeting requests from the Contacts folder instead of the Calendar folder. Right-click the contact entry for the person you want to invite to a meeting, and then choose Create, New Meeting Request To Contact. The meeting form opens, with the contact's name in the To box. From here, you can select more attendees and enter meeting details such as subject and location.

If the contact entry contains an address for an Internet free/busy server (on the Details tab of the contact entry, in the Address box of the Internet Free/Busy area), you can download the contact's free/busy information by clicking Options on the Scheduling page and then selecting Refresh Free/Busy Information. You can also download the contact's free/busy information from Microsoft Office Online, if the contact uses that service, or from another free/busy server if one is specified in the Free/Busy Options dialog box. (This will be explained in detail in Chapter 36, "Sharing Calendars.")

For details about Microsoft Office Online, see "Managing Your Free/Busy Information" in Chapter 36.

Changing a Meeting

To change any part of a meeting request, including attendees, times, or other information, first double-click the meeting item in the Calendar folder to open it, and then make your changes. Click the Save icon on the Quick Access Toolbar to save the changes to the Calendar folder, or click Send Update to send an updated meeting request to the attendees. If you make changes that affect the other attendees, such as adding or removing attendees or changing the time or location, you should click Send Update so that the attendees get the new information.

Sending a Meeting Request with Scheduling Assistant

When you are using Outlook 2007 with Microsoft Exchange Server 2007, you have an enhanced tool for scheduling meetings called Scheduling Assistant. In many ways, scheduling a meeting with Scheduling Assistant is similar to how you schedule meetings using Microsoft Exchange Server 2003—to schedule a meeting, you begin by sending a meeting request. Choose File, New, Meeting Request, or click the arrow next to New on the toolbar and choose Meeting Request. The meeting form opens, as shown in Figure 21-5.

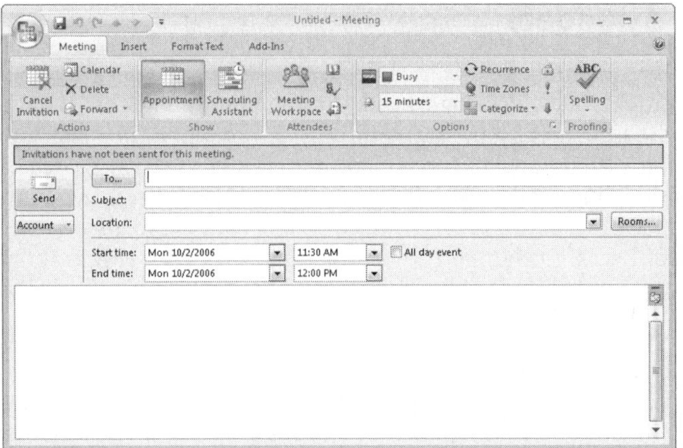

Figure 21-5. The meeting form with Scheduling Assistant includes an option to select rooms.

When you request a meeting using Scheduling Assistant, in addition to the standard meeting or appointment forms, you can select one or more rooms to reserve for the meeting by clicking the Rooms button to the right of the Location box (as shown in Figure 21-5). When you click the Rooms button, the Select Rooms dialog box is displayed, as shown in Figure 21-6. To select a room, click the room (or hold down the **Ctrl** key and click to select multiple rooms), click the Rooms button at the bottom of the dialog box to add the rooms to your meeting request, and then click OK.

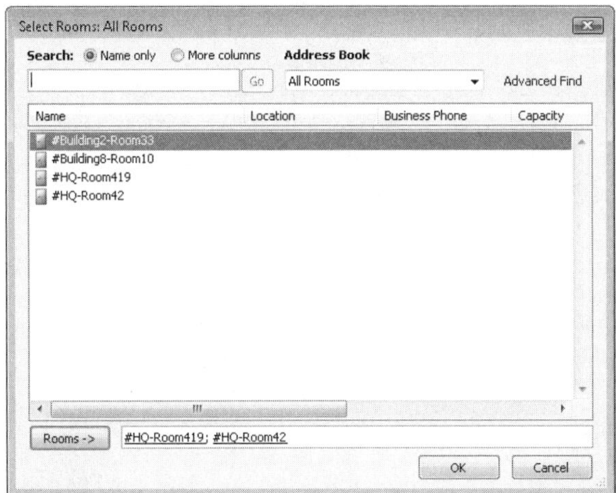

Figure 21-6. The Select Rooms dialog box lets you add one or more rooms to the meeting request.

For details about creating and working with meetings using Microsoft Exchange Server 2000/2003, see "Scheduling a Meeting" earlier in this chapter.

Selecting Attendees

In the same way you invite people to your meeting using the Scheduling option, when using Scheduling Assistant, you start by selecting names on either the Appointment page or the Scheduling Assistant page on the Meeting tab. Using the Appointment option, you can type each name in the To box (separating the names with a semicolon); each name entered manually is a required attendee. Alternatively, you can click the To button to open the Select Attendees And Resources dialog box (shown in Figure 21-7 for Outlook 2007 with Exchange 2007 and in Figure 21-2 for earlier versions), select a name, click Required or Optional to designate that person's attendance status, and then click OK.

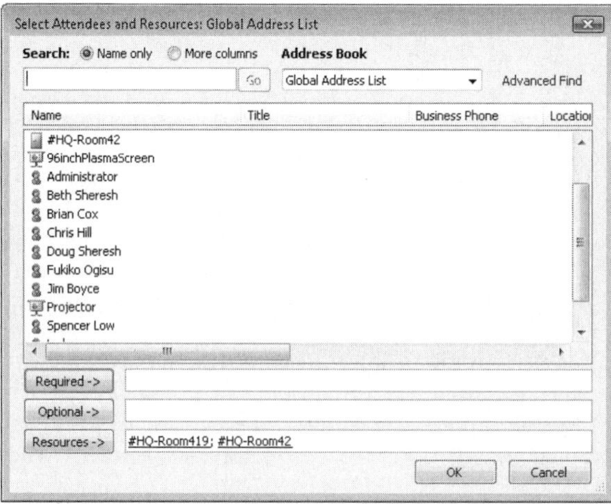

Figure 21-7. The Select Attendees And Resources dialog box lets you request one or more people to attend the meeting.

To add names using Scheduling Assistant, shown in Figure 21-8, you can click in the designated box in the All Attendees column and then type a name or an e-mail address. Alternatively, you can click Add Attendees to open the Select Attendees And Resources dialog box. As before, select a name, click Required or Optional, and then click OK. Similarly, you can click the Add Rooms button to open the Select Rooms dialog box, select one or more rooms, click Add Rooms, and then click OK.

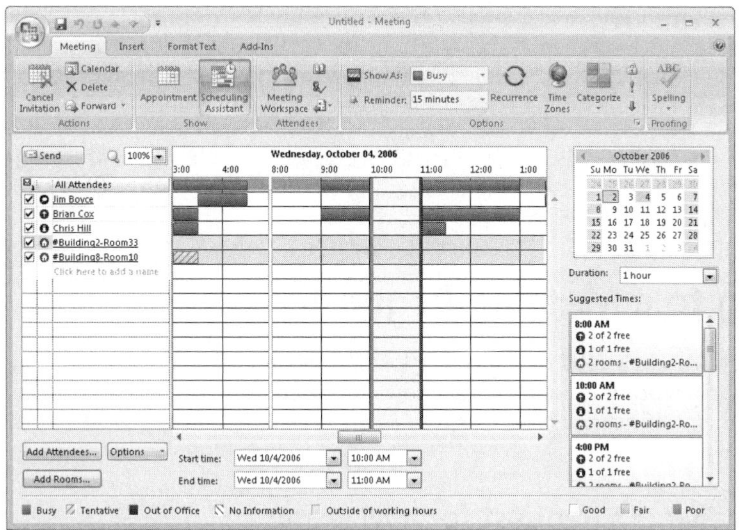

Figure 21-8. Scheduling Assistant.

Scheduling a Meeting Using Scheduling Assistant

Scheduling Assistant not only displays free/busy information for all the people you selected but also shows suggested times when people and resources are available. Scheduling Assistant lets you modify the duration of the meeting (shown in Figure 21-8) and then shows the suggested times when people can meet and the rooms (or other resources) are available. Instead of having to find a time slot that fits everyone's schedules, you can click one of the suggested times to schedule the meeting and then select the specific room that you want for the meeting, as shown in Figure 21-9.

Figure 21-9. You can use Scheduling Assistant to pick a meeting time and select a room for the meeting.

You can specify whether the display of free/busy information on the Scheduling page should show only working hours (the default) or the entire day. To define working hours for the calendar, choose Tools, Options, and then click Calendar Options. To set the display of working hours for a particular meeting, click the Options button on the

Scheduling page, and set or clear the Show Only My Working Hours option. Working hours are a way of displaying your time in the Calendar folder and controlling which hours are displayed on the Scheduling page. In most cases, including nonworking hours on the Scheduling page would become unmanageable.

After you have selected all the attendees, found an available time slot, and filled in all the necessary details on the message form, click Send on the form to send the meeting request to the attendees.

Responding to a Meeting Request

When you click Send on a meeting form, a meeting request e-mail message is sent to the invited attendees. This message allows the attendees to accept, tentatively accept, or reject the meeting invitation; propose a new time for the meeting; and include a message in the reply.

Receiving a Request for a Meeting

The attendees you've invited to your meeting will receive a meeting request message similar to the one shown in Figure 21-10. When an attendee clicks Calendar, a copy of his or her calendar opens, showing the meeting tentatively scheduled.

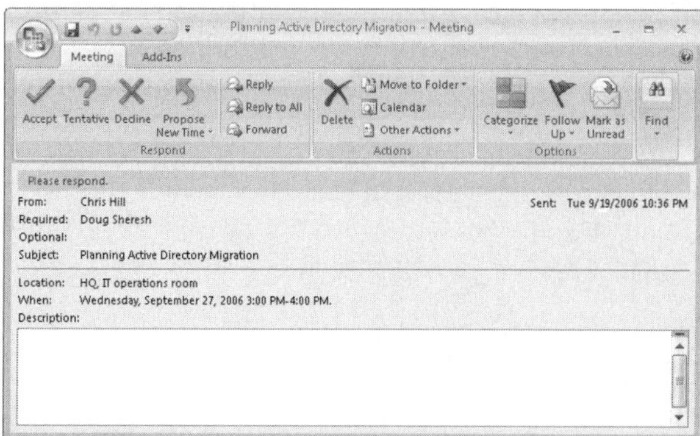

Figure 21-10. A meeting request received by an invited attendee.

An invited attendee has four options when replying to a meeting request:

- Accept the meeting outright.
- Tentatively accept the meeting.
- Decline the meeting.
- Propose a new time for the meeting.

When an attendee chooses to accept, tentatively accept, or decline a meeting request, he or she is presented with three options: send the response immediately (which sends the default response), edit the response before sending (which allows the attendee to send a message with the response), or send no response.

To propose a new meeting time, the attendee can click Propose New Time. The Propose New Time dialog box that appears is essentially the same as the Scheduling page of the meeting form. From here, the attendee can select a new time for the meeting and propose it to the meeting organizer by clicking Propose Time.

TROUBLESHOOTING

You've lost a meeting request

When you respond to a meeting request in e-mail, the original request message is automatically deleted from your Inbox. Outlook 2007 automatically adds the meeting information to your Calendar folder when you receive the e-mail message. If you respond to the meeting request from your calendar, however, the e-mail message is not deleted from your Inbox.

If you need to retrieve any of the data in the e-mail message, check your Deleted Items folder for the meeting request itself and your Calendar folder for the meeting information.

To have Outlook 2007 keep meeting request messages in your Inbox even after you've responded, follow these steps:

1. Choose Tools, Options, and then click E-Mail Options.
2. Click Advanced E-Mail Options.
3. Clear the Delete Meeting Request From Inbox When Responding check box.

Receiving a Response to Your Request

When an invited attendee responds to a meeting request, a message is returned to you, the meeting organizer. This message contains the response, including any message the attendee chose to include. In the meeting request response shown in Figure 21-11, the attendee has accepted the meeting and included a message. Notice that the response also lists the attendees who have accepted, tentatively accepted, and declined up to this point.

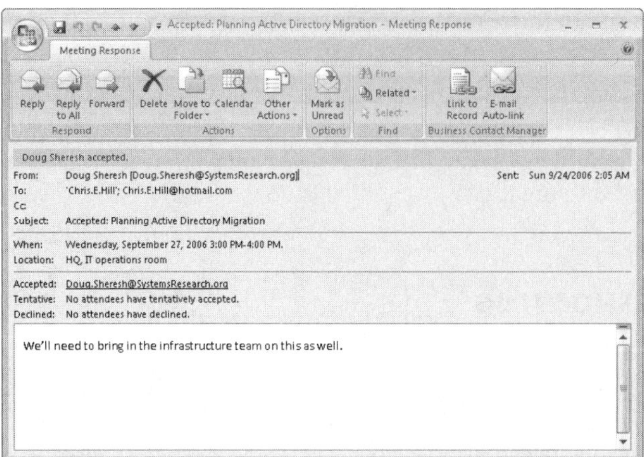

Figure 21-11. A response to a meeting request shows the acceptance status of the request and any message from the attendee.

Figure 21-12 shows a response in which the attendee has selected the Propose A New Time option on a meeting request.

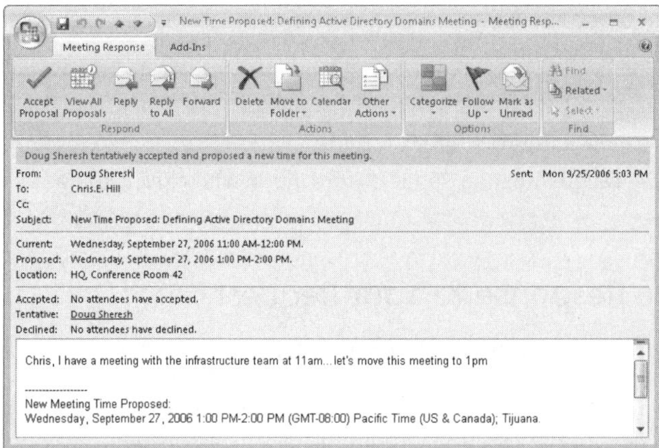

Figure 21-12. When an invited attendee proposes a new time for the meeting, the response to the meeting organizer looks like this.

When you receive a response proposing a new meeting time, you have two choices:

- Click Accept Proposal to accept the new time and open the meeting form. Verify any changes, and then click Send Update to send the new proposed time to the attendees.
- Click View All Proposals to open the Scheduling page of the meeting form, which displays a list of all proposed new times for the meeting suggested by any of the attendees, as shown in Figure 21-13. You can select a new time from the list of proposed times and then click Send to send the new time to the meeting attendees.

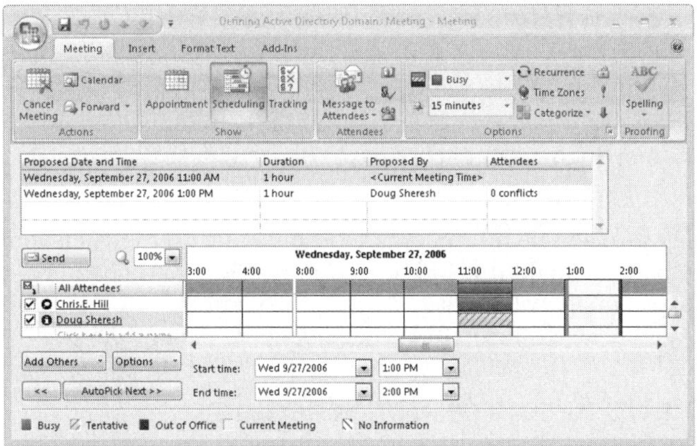

Figure 21-13. You can view the meeting times proposed by all attendees.

Checking Attendees

After you send a meeting request, you can check which attendees have accepted or declined by opening the meeting form in the Calendar folder and clicking the form's Tracking button in the Show group on the Meeting tab, as shown in Figure 21-14. (The Tracking button is not displayed on the initial meeting form; Outlook 2007 adds it after the meeting request has been sent.) The Tracking button shows each invited attendee and indicates whether their attendance is required or optional and the status of their response. The meeting organizer is the only person who can view the status of attendees.

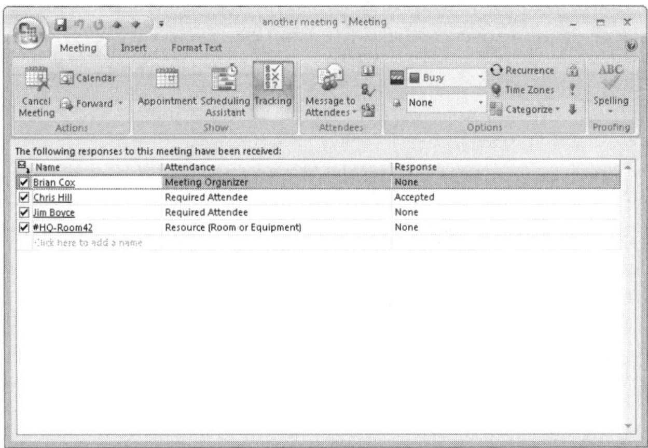

Figure 21-14. Only the person who scheduled the meeting can view the status of the attendees.

Scheduling Resources

To successfully plan and carry out a meeting, you'll usually need to schedule resources as well as people. *Resources* are items (such as computers and projectors) or locations (such as a meeting room) that are required for a meeting. You select resources in much the same way you select attendees.

The ability to schedule resources is typically most useful when you need to set up a meeting, but you might find other occasions when this capability comes in handy. For example, you might want to schedule laptop computers for employees to take home for the weekend or schedule digital cameras to take to building sites.

Setting Up Resources for Scheduling

You schedule a resource by sending a meeting request, adding the resource as a third type of attendee. (The other two types of attendees are Required and Optional, as previously mentioned; see "Selecting Attendees" earlier in this chapter.) Because a resource is scheduled as a type of attendee, it must have a mailbox and a method of accepting or rejecting meeting requests. When you use Outlook 2007 and Exchange Server 2003, a resource is almost identical to any other Exchange Server user except that it is configured to allow another user (the resource administrator) full access to its mailbox. In Exchange Server 2007, unlike user mailbox accounts, all resource mailbox accounts are automatically disabled (yet are still accessible as resources from within Outlook 2007).

The first step in setting up a resource for scheduling is to create (or have your system administrator create) a mailbox and an account for the resource. In many cases, resource account names are preceded by a symbol, such as # or &, so that the names, when alphabetized, appear as a group at the top or bottom of the GAL.

How resources are assigned on the mail server running Microsoft Exchange Server is dependent on which version of Exchange Server you are using. When you set up resource accounts on a server running Exchange Server 2003, you have to go into Active Directory Users And Computers (within the domain in which the server running Exchange is operating) and create and configure user accounts and the subsequent mailboxes. You then have to modify the Mailbox Rights and assign Full Mailbox Access to the resource administrator. The resource administrator has to create a new profile and use the profile to access the mailbox and configure (using the Scheduling Resources option) the Automatically Accept Meeting Requests And Process Cancellations option, which allows the resource scheduling to work. To avoid schedule conflicts, it's also necessary to select Automatically Decline Conflicting Meeting Requests.

When you are using Exchange 2007, you can use new features to schedule both room and equipment resources. In Exchange 2007, instead of using the Active Directory Users And Computers console to add users and their mail accounts, you use the Exchange Management Console. To add a user account and mailbox to Exchange 2007, you browse to the Recipients Configuration container and then select the New Mailbox link. The New Mailbox dialog box provides four options for mailbox creation:

- **User Mailbox** The User mailbox is associated with a user account, enabling the user to send, receive, and store e-mail messages, calendar items, tasks, and other Outlook 2007 items.

- **Room Mailbox** The Room mailbox is reserved as a resource-type mailbox, and the associated account in the Active Directory® directory service is disabled.
- **Equipment Mailbox** The Equipment mailbox is also reserved as a resource-type mailbox, and the associated account in Active Directory is disabled.
- **Linked Mailbox** The Linked mailbox is employed for users that will access the mailbox from a separate trusted forest.

To assign resources for use in Outlook 2007, you add a new mailbox, select the resource type (either Room or Equipment), and then complete the required information (which is essentially the same information you would provide for any user account–name, logon name, password, and alias). After you have created a Room mailbox, for instance, when you click the Rooms button in an Outlook 2007 meeting form, all of the rooms associated with Room mailboxes will be displayed. Equipment resources (as well as rooms) are displayed in the Select Attendees And Resources list and can be included in the meeting request by selecting the desired equipment and clicking the Resources button.

Using the Configured Resources

To schedule a resource after you have configured it, create a meeting request and fill in the details. When you add attendees to the meeting request using the Select Attendees And Resources dialog box, select the resource you want to add from the list, and then click Resources, as shown in Figure 21-15. Resources are added to the Resources box instead of to the Required or Optional box. When you have finished adding resources, click OK. Then complete and send the meeting request as you normally would.

For details about creating and sending meeting requests, see "Sending a Meeting Request" earlier in this chapter.

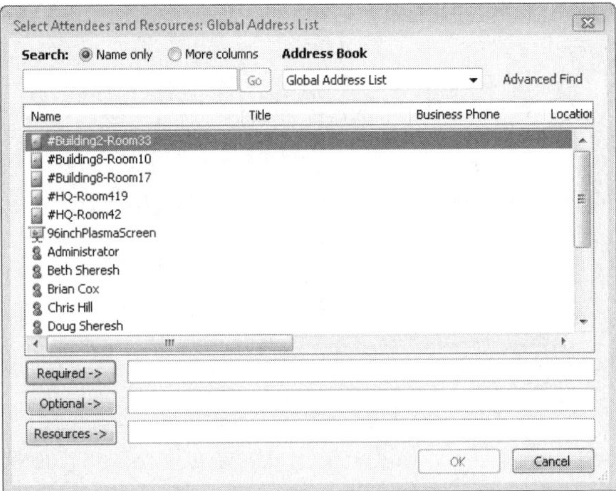

Figure 21-15. Add a resource by selecting it from the list and clicking Resources.

After you send the meeting request, Outlook 2007 (when used in an Exchange Server 2003 environment) responds with a message about the resource's availability. If the resource is available during the time slot proposed for the meeting, Outlook 2007 notifies you that the resource has been booked successfully, as shown in Figure 21-16.

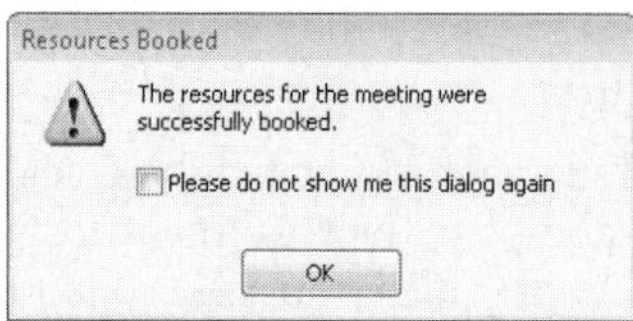

Figure 21-16. Outlook 2007 notifies you if the resource was successfully booked.

Figure 21-17 shows the message that appears when you try to book a resource in a time that overlaps with an existing meeting in that resource's calendar (when in an Exchange Server 2003 environment). Click OK to return to the meeting form, where you must reschedule the meeting or choose a different resource.

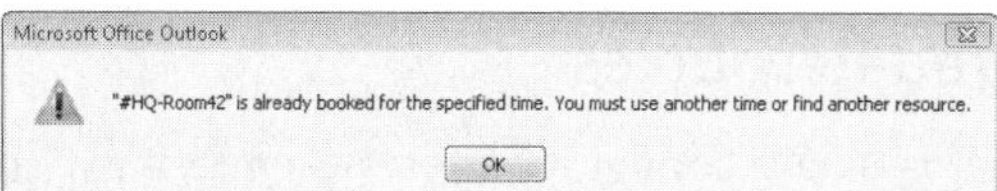

Figure 21-17. When resources are already booked, you must change the meeting time or choose another resource.

Figure 21-18 shows the calendar for the resource being scheduled in the preceding examples. The meeting shown has been scheduled automatically.

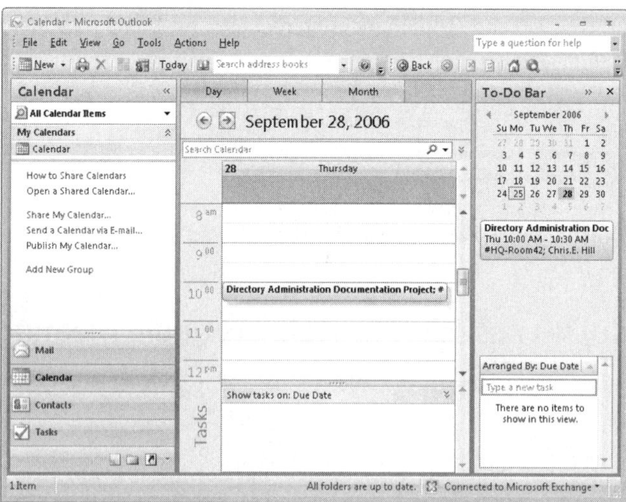

Figure 21-18. The meeting shown on the resource's calendar was booked automatically.

Managing Meetings Effectively

Meetings are an essential part of working in a corporate business environment. While necessary, they are not necessarily always the most effective use of your time. Using the scheduling tools in Outlook 2007 can help you expedite the scheduling of meetings, remind you in advance of upcoming meetings, and help you complete your meetings on time. Using the Outlook 2007 meeting scheduling capability can help improve the quality of your meetings as well. By planning the meeting and notifying all participants of the agenda (in the content of the meeting request), you give them (and yourself) time to prepare notes, documents, and other presentation materials ahead of time. This also allows participants an opportunity to present questions, concerns, and additions to the agenda prior to the meeting, thus ensuring a more comprehensive meeting that isn't distracted by unforeseen complications. You should also keep in mind the specific characteristics of the people invited to each meeting, anticipate aspects (people who show up late, are too verbose, or are easily distracted) that can impair meeting efficiency, and plan your meeting strategy to avoid such issues.

Find the Best Time for the Meeting

When you schedule a meeting in your Outlook 2007 calendar, you can use Outlook 2007 to review the free/busy time on the schedules of the other people you invite to the meeting, thus enabling you to pick times that are available for all attendees when you initially schedule the meeting. To view free/busy information when scheduling a meeting (adding a new meeting request), click Scheduling in the Show group on the Meeting tab. After you have added all attendees, their free/busy information will be retrieved and displayed in a timeline, showing the status of the schedules for each period in the timeline. In addition, resources (such as reserved rooms) will be displayed, showing you which times are available to use the resources. You can refresh the free/busy information by clicking Options and then selecting Refresh Free/Busy. You can also use AutoPick to select a meeting time. Outlook 2007 will select the next available meeting time based on your AutoPick criteria—such as All People, One Resource to pick the first time when all of the attendees are free and one resource (such as a conference room) is available. The AutoPick criteria can be set on the Options, AutoPick menu, which lets you specify whether to require all or some attendees and whether one or more resources have to be available.

Use Scheduling Assistant to Help Schedule Meetings

If you have Outlook 2007 set up as a client to Exchange Server 2007, the scheduling functionality is expanded—the Location box on the Appointment page on the Meeting tab has a Rooms button that facilitates meeting room selection, and the Scheduling Assistant page on the Meeting tab (if you're working in an Exchange Server 2007 environment, the page is labeled Scheduling Assistant) provides further capability to review free/busy information and find available meeting times. In addition to the Free/Busy grid displaying the available times for a meeting (see Figure 21-8), the Suggested Times pane (on the right) shows the Date Navigator, with color-coded dates for possible meeting days (the darker the color, the lower the possibility of scheduling a meeting with the selected attendees). Below the Date Navigator is the selected Duration setting for the meeting, followed by a list of suggested times and showing how many of the requested attendees are free to attend.

Using these features, you can reliably schedule meetings where all people and resources are available, and without a flurry of back-and-forth e-mail to determine availability for a particular date and time.

Set a Sufficient Reminder to Enable You to Make Meetings on Time

Using the Outlook 2007 reminders can facilitate your getting to your meetings on time. You can assess your own work pattern and determine the best default time for Outlook 2007 to remind you of upcoming meetings. Choose Tools, Options to open the Options dialog box, where you can set the default reminder time in the Calendar area to alert you at the best time prior to the meeting. You can also set reminders for specific meetings to provide an additional reminder (perhaps closer to the start of the meeting) by selecting the reminder time in the Options group on the Appointment page for each meeting.

Schedule Meeting End Times with a Reminder to Help Meetings Stay on Schedule

You can use the Outlook 2007 reminders to help you keep meetings running on schedule. To have Outlook 2007 send you notification of the impending end of the allotted meeting time, schedule an appointment to occur at the end time of the meeting, and then in the appointment, set the reminder to occur 5 to 10 minutes before the meeting end. Having such end-of-meeting reminders can give you the time to effectively wrap up the meeting, reminding people of tasks assigned during the meeting and summarizing critical details.

CHAPTER 22

Managing Your Tasks

Microsoft® Office Outlook® 2007 offers a broad selection of tools to help you manage your workday, including techniques for handling e-mail; a way to manage appointments, meetings, and events; a handy method of creating quick notes; and a journal for tracking projects, calls, and other items. All these tools are often related to creating and completing tasks. For example, writing this book was a long string of tasks to be completed: drawing up the outline, writing each chapter, and reviewing edits, for starters.

In your job, your tasks during the average day are no doubt different. Perhaps they include completing contracts, making sales calls, writing or reviewing documents, completing reports, developing Web sites, or developing program code. Some tasks take only a little time to complete, whereas others can take days, weeks, or even months.

Office Outlook 2007 provides the means not only to track your own tasks but also to manage those tasks you need to assign to others. This feature is a much more efficient and effective way to manage tasks than using a notebook, sticky notes, or just your memory. You can set reminders and sort tasks according to category, priority, or status to help you view and manage them.

This chapter examines the Tasks folder and its related features. In addition to learning how to manage your own tasks, you'll also learn to assign tasks to and manage tasks assigned to others.

Working with Tasks in the Tasks Folder

Outlook 2007 provides several ways for you to create and manage tasks. You can create one-time tasks or recurring tasks, set up reminders for tasks, and assign tasks to others. In this section, you'll see how to create tasks for yourself and how to use Outlook 2007 to manage those tasks effectively.

The default view in the Tasks folder is the To-Do List, shown in Figure 22-1, which organizes the tasks by Due Date. Depending on the amount of space available in the view, Outlook 2007 shows additional columns in the To-Do List view, such as Start Date, Reminder Time, Due Date, the folder in which the tasks are located, and Categories.

If you prefer to see a less cluttered view, you can choose the Simple List view, which shows the following columns:

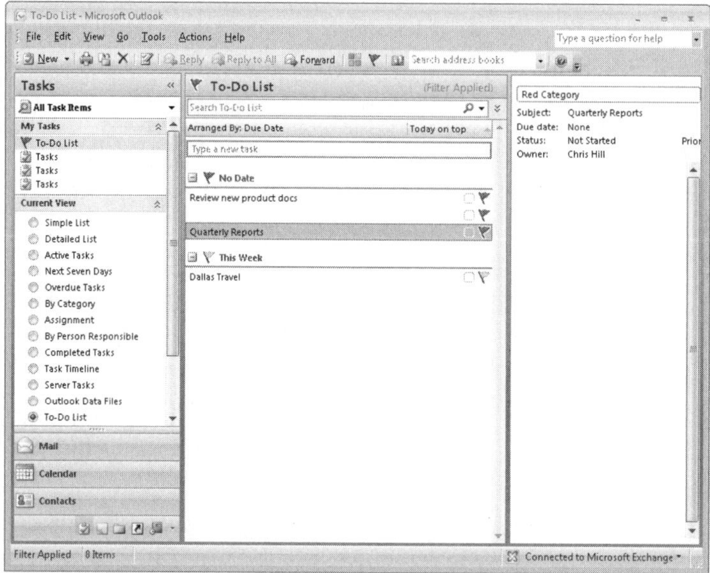

Figure 22-1. Outlook 2007 uses a simple list as the default Tasks folder view.

- **Icon** The Icon column indicates one of two states: either that the task is yours or that it's assigned to another person. The clipboard icon with a check mark indicates that the task is your own. A hand under the icon indicates that the task is assigned to someone else.
- **Complete** Use this check box to indicate that a task has been completed. A check in the box indicates a completed task. Outlook 2007 strikes through the task's subject and due date when you mark the task as completed, offering another visual cue to help you distinguish completed tasks from those that are still outstanding.
- **Subject** You can enter any text in the Subject column, but generally this text should describe the task to be performed. You can also add notes to each task to further identify the purpose or goal of the task.
- **Due Date** This column indicates the due date for the task and by default shows the day and date. You can specify different date formats if you want.
- **In Folder** This column shows the folder in which the task is located.

For details on customizing the Tasks folder view, see "Viewing and Customizing the Tasks Folder" later in this chapter. For additional information about features in Outlook 2007 that can help you use and manage views, see "Using Other Outlook Features" in Chapter 4.

You can view all the details of a task by double-clicking the task item. Doing so opens the task form, the format of which varies depending on whether the task is yours or is assigned to someone else. Figure 22-2 shows the form for a task that belongs to you. Figure 22-3 shows the Task page of a form for a task assigned to someone else.

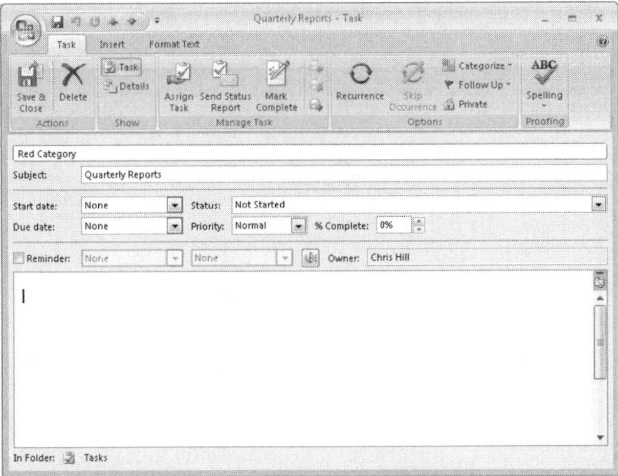

Figure 22-2. Create a new task with this standard task form.

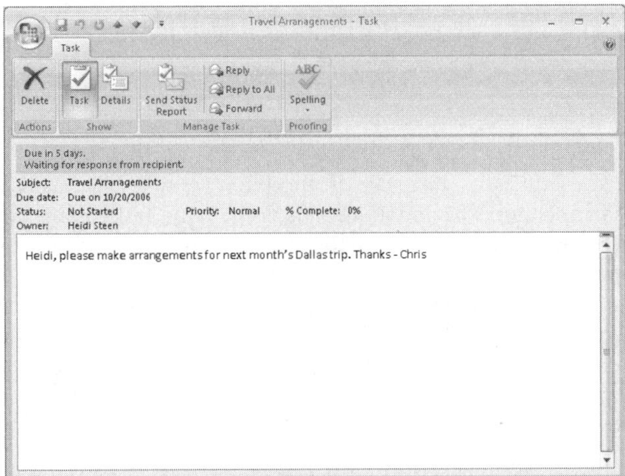

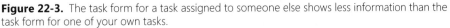

Figure 22-3. The task form for a task assigned to someone else shows less information than the task form for one of your own tasks.

The Details page of the task form, shown in Figure 22-4, shows additional information about the task such as date completed, total work required, actual work performed, and related background information.

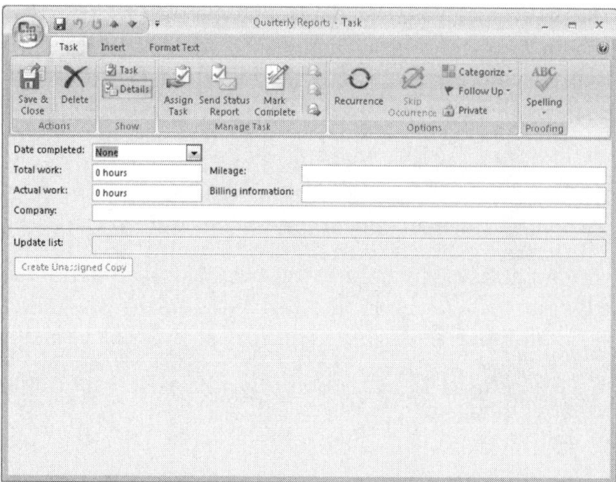

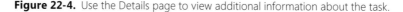

Figure 22-4. Use the Details page to view additional information about the task.

Note

Press **Ctrl+Tab** to switch between pages in any multipaged dialog box or form, including the task form.

Browsing Tasks Quickly

Although you can open tasks by double-clicking them in the Tasks folder, you might prefer to cycle through your tasks right in the task form. For example, when you want to review several tasks, opening and closing them from the task list one after another is a waste of clicks and effort. Instead, you can use the Next Item and Previous Item buttons on the form's Quick Access Toolbar to display tasks in forward or reverse order (relative to the listed order in the Tasks folder). The list doesn't cycle from end to beginning or beginning to end, however, so clicking a button when you're at either of those points in the list closes the task form.

Creating a Task

Creating a task is mechanically much the same as creating any item in Outlook 2007. Use any of the following methods to create a new task:

- Between the column header bar and the first task in the list is a new task entry line labeled Click Here To Add A New Task. In the To-Do Bar, the box is labeled

Type A New Task. Click the line and start typing if you want to specify only the subject for the task, without initially adding details or selecting options. You can open the task at any time afterward to add other information.

- Double-click in an empty area of the task list.
- Right-click in an empty area of the task list, and then choose New Task.
- With the Tasks folder open, click New on the Standard toolbar.
- With any Outlook 2007 folder open, click the arrow next to the New button on the Standard toolbar, and then choose Task. This allows you to create a new task when another folder such as the Inbox or the Calendar folder is displayed.

The options on the task form are straightforward. Simply select the options you want and set the task properties (such as start date and due date). Opening the Due Date or Start Date drop-down list displays a calendar that you can use to specify the month and date for the task. If no specific date is required for the task, you can leave the default value None selected. If you currently have a date selected and want to set the date to None, select None in the drop-down list.

INSIDE OUT **Specify total work and actual work**

As you'll learn a little later in this section, you can specify values for Total Work and Actual Work on the Details page of the task form. Total Work indicates the total number of hours (days, weeks, and so on) required for the task; Actual Work lets you record the amount of work performed to date on the task. Unfortunately, the % Complete value on the Task page is not tied to either of these numbers. Thus, if Total Work is set to 40 hours and Actual Work is set to 20 hours, the % Complete box doesn't show 50 percent complete. Instead, you must manually specify the value for % Complete.

Note

The % Complete value is tied to the Status field on the Task page. If you set % Complete to 100, Outlook 2007 sets the status to Completed. If you set % Complete to 0, Outlook 2007 sets the status to Not Started. Any value between 0 and 100 results in a status of In Progress. Selecting a value in the Status drop-down list has a similar effect on % Complete. Select Not Started, for example, and Outlook 2007 sets the % Complete value to 0.

In addition to entering information such as the percentage of work that's completed, the priority, and the status, you can also set a reminder for the task. As it does for other Outlook 2007 items, such as appointments, Outlook 2007 can display a reminder window and play a sound as a reminder to start or complete the task. You can set only one reminder per task, so it's up to you to decide when you want Outlook 2007 to remind you about the task. Click the speaker button on the task form to select the audio file that you want Outlook 2007 to use for the reminder.

One key task setting is the Owner setting. When you create a task, you own that task initially. Only the owner can modify a task. Task ownership is relevant only to assigned tasks—that is, tasks that you assign to others to perform.

For details about task ownership, see "Assigning Tasks to Others" later in this chapter.

Other information that you can specify on the Task tab of the task form's Ribbon includes categories and the private or nonprivate status of the task. The ability to assign categories to tasks can help you organize your tasks. You can assign multiple categories to each task as needed and view the Tasks folder sorted by category. For example, you might assign project categories to tasks to help you sort the tasks according to project, allowing you to focus on the tasks for a specific project.

For details on working with categories, see "Assigning Categories to New Items" in Chapter 5.

The private or nonprivate status of a task allows you to control whether others who have delegate access to your folders can see a specific task. Tasks marked as private aren't visible unless you explicitly grant permission to the delegate to view private items. To control the visibility of private items, choose Tools, Options, and then click the Delegates tab. Double-click a delegate, and in the Delegate Permissions dialog box, shown in Figure 22-5, select or clear the Delegate Can See My Private Items check box. Repeat the process for any other delegates as needed.

Figure 22-5. Use the Delegate Permissions dialog box to control the visibility of private items.

> **Note**
>
> The Delegates option is available only if you're using Microsoft Exchange Server.

The Details page of the task form (shown earlier in Figure 22-4) allows you to specify additional information about the task. The options on the Details page include the following:

- **Date Completed** Use this calendar to record the date the task is completed. This is the actual completion date, not the projected completion date.
- **Total Work** Specify the total amount of work required for the task. You can enter a value in minutes, hours, days, or weeks by entering a value followed by the unit, such as 3 days.
- **Actual Work** Record the total amount of work performed on the task to date. You can enter the data using the same units as in the Total Work box.
- **Company** List any companies associated with the task such as suppliers, customers, or clients.
- **Mileage** Record mileage associated with the task if mileage is reimbursable or a tax-deductible expense.
- **Billing Information** Record information related to billing for the task, such as rate, person to bill, and billing address.
- **Update List** This option applies to tasks assigned to others. It shows the person who originally sent the task request and the names of all others who received the task request, reassigned the task to someone else, or elected to keep an updated copy of the task on their task list. When you send a task status message, Outlook 2007 adds these people as recipients of the status message.
- **Create Unassigned Copy** Use this button to create a copy of an assigned task that you can send to another person.

For details on working with the update list, assigned tasks, and unassigned copies, see "Assigning Tasks to Others" later in this chapter.

TROUBLESHOOTING

Others can't see your tasks

For others to see your tasks, you must share your Tasks folder. If you're using Exchange Server as your mail server, you can also allow others to see your tasks by granting them delegate access to your Tasks folder. The two methods are similar with one major difference: Granting delegate access to others allows them to send messages on your behalf. Sharing a folder simply gives others access to it without granting send-on-behalf-of permission.

To share your Tasks folder without granting send-on-behalf-of permission, right-click the Tasks folder icon in the Folder List in the Navigation Pane, and then choose Properties. Click the Permissions tab, and then add or remove users and permissions as needed.

For additional details on sharing folders and setting permissions, see "Granting Access to Folders" in Chapter 35. To learn how to set up delegate access to your folders, see "Delegating Responsibilities to an Assistant" also in Chapter 35.

Creating a Recurring Task

Earlier in this chapter, you learned several ways to create a task that occurs once. You can also use Outlook 2007 to create recurring tasks. For example, you might create a recurring task for reports you have to submit on a weekly, monthly, or quarterly basis. Perhaps you perform backup operations once a week and want Outlook 2007 to remind you to do this.

You create a recurring task much the same way you create a single-instance task, except that when the task form is open, you click the Recurrence button on the Task tab of the Ribbon to display the Task Recurrence dialog box, shown in Figure 22-6.

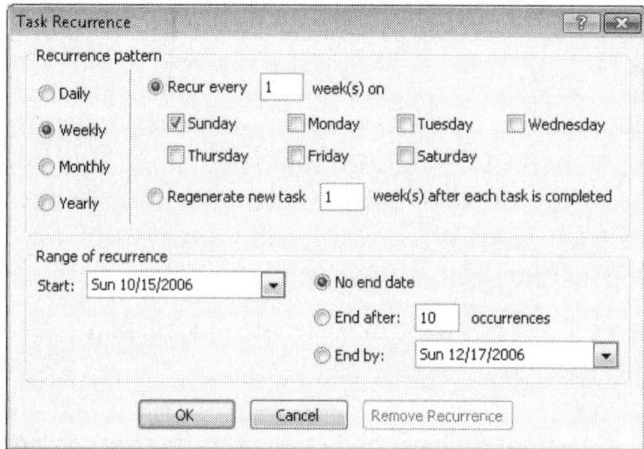

Figure 22-6. Create recurring tasks by using the Task Recurrence dialog box.

You can select daily, weekly, monthly, or yearly recurrence. Selecting one of these four options in the dialog box changes the options available in the dialog box, allowing you to select the recurrence pattern. For example, select Weekly, and then select the days of the week on which you want the task to occur.

When you create a recurring task, one of the decisions you must make is whether you want the task to recur at a specified period regardless of the task's completion status. You can also choose to regenerate a new task after the existing task is completed. For example, you can create a task that recurs every Friday. The task will recur whether or not you marked the previous instance as completed. If you need to complete the previous task before the next task is generated, however, you should configure the recurrence so that the new task is created only after the previous one is completed. For example, perhaps you run a series of reports, but each relies on the previous report being completed. In this situation, you would probably want to set up the task to regenerate only after the preceding one was completed.

The Regenerate New Task option in the Task Recurrence dialog box allows you to configure the recurrence so that the new task is generated a specified period of time after the previous task is completed. Select the Regenerate New Task option, and then specify the period of time that should pass after completion of the task before the task is regenerated.

Other options for a recurring task are the same as those for a one-time task. Specify subject, details, contacts, categories, and other information as needed. Remember to set up a reminder for the task if you want Outlook 2007 to remind you before the task's assigned completion time.

Adding a Reminder

You can add a reminder to a task when you create the task or after you create it. As with reminders for appointments, you specify the date and time for the reminder as well as an optional sound that Outlook 2007 can play along with the reminder.

To add a reminder, follow these steps:

1. Open the task, and then select Reminder on the Task page.
2. Use the calendar in the drop-down list next to the Reminder check box to select the date, and then select a time for the reminder. You can select a time in half-hour increments in the drop-down list or specify your own value by typing it in the box.
3. Click the speaker button to open the Reminder Sound dialog box, in which you select a WAV file to assign to the reminder.
4. Click OK, and then close the task form.

> **Note**
>
> Outlook 2007 uses a default time of 8:00 A.M. for the reminder. You can change this default value by choosing Tools, Options and then setting the Reminder Time option on the Preferences tab.

Setting a Task Estimate

When you create a task, you might also want to estimate the time it will take to complete the task. You can enter this estimate in the Total Work box on the Details page of the task form. As the task progresses, you can change the Total Work value to reflect your changing estimate or leave it at the original value to track time overruns and underruns for the task. For example, assume that you propose a 40-hour task to a client. As you work through the task, you continue to update the Actual Work box to reflect the number of hours you've worked on the task. You reach 40 hours of work on the task and haven't completed it. You then have to make a decision: do you update the Total Work value to show a new estimate for completion and bill the client accordingly, or do you leave it as is and absorb the cost overrun?

Unfortunately, the Total Work and Actual Work fields are simple, nonreactive data fields. Outlook 2007 provides no interaction between the two to determine an actual Percent Complete value for the task. For that reason—and because Outlook 2007 can't calculate job costs based on charge rates and the amount of work completed—Outlook 2007 by itself generally isn't a complete job tracking or billing application. You should investigate third-party applications to perform that task or develop your own applications using the 2007 Microsoft Office system as a development platform.

For details on how to get started developing your own Microsoft Office system applications, see Articles 1, 2, and 3 on the companion CD.

Marking a Task as Completed

Logically, the goal for most tasks is completion. At some point, therefore, you'll want to mark tasks as completed. When you mark a task as completed, Outlook 2007 strikes through the task in the task list to provide a visual cue that the task has been finished. The easiest way to mark a task as completed is to place a check in the Complete column, which by default is the second column from the left in the Simple List view. You can also mark a task as completed on the Task page. Simply select Completed in the Status drop-down list or set the % Complete box to 100.

Outlook 2007 by default sorts the task list by completion status. If you've changed the list to sort based on a different column, simply click that column header. For example, clicking the Complete column header sorts the task list by completion status. If you want to view only completed tasks, click Completed Tasks in the Navigation Pane or choose View, Current View, Completed Tasks. Viewing only incomplete tasks is just as easy: click Active Tasks in the Navigation Pane or choose View, Current View, Active Tasks.

For additional details on customizing the Tasks folder view, see "Viewing and Customizing the Tasks Folder" later in this chapter.

Assigning Tasks to Others

In addition to creating tasks for yourself in Outlook 2007, you can also assign tasks to others. For example, you might manage a staff of several people and frequently need to assign them projects or certain tasks in a project. The main benefit of using Outlook 2007 to assign those tasks is that you can receive status reports on assigned tasks and view these status reports in your Tasks folder. Outlook 2007 automates the process of sending task requests and processing responses to those requests. You'll learn more about assigning tasks in the sections that follow. First, however, you need to understand task ownership.

About Task Ownership

When you create a task, you initially own that task. Only a task's owner can make changes to the task. This means that you can modify the properties (the percent complete, the status, the start date, and so on) of all tasks that you create and own. When you assign a task to someone else and that person accepts the task, the assignee becomes the owner of the task. You can then view the task's properties, but you can no longer change them. Similarly, you become the owner of tasks assigned to you when you accept them, and you can then make changes to those tasks.

A task's Owner property is a read-only value, which appears in the Owner box on the Task page. You can click the value, but you can't change it directly. The only way to change owners is to assign the task and have the assignee accept it.

Making or Accepting an Assignment

Assigning a task to someone else is a simple process. In general, you create the task, add details, and specify options for the task. Then you tell Outlook 2007 to whom you want to assign the task, and Outlook 2007 takes care of generating the task request and sending it to the assignee.

Follow these steps to assign a task to someone else:

1. In Outlook 2007, open the Tasks folder, and create a new task.
2. Add information and set options for the task such as start date, due date, status, and priority.
3. On the Task tab, in the Manage Task group, click Assign Task. Outlook 2007 changes the form to include additional options, as shown in Figure 22-7.

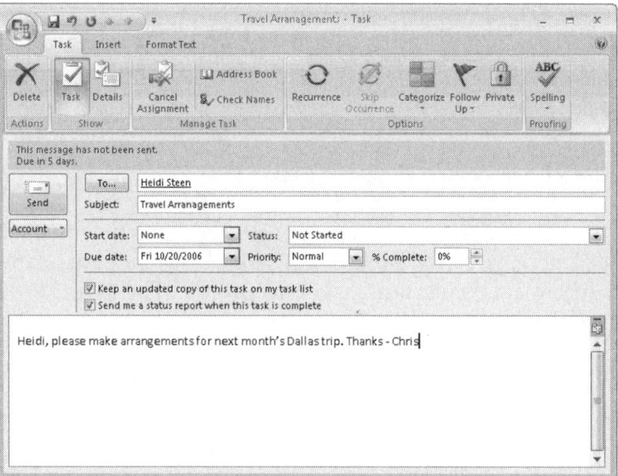

Figure 22-7. Outlook 2007 offers additional options when you assign a task to someone else.

4. In the To box, enter the address of the person to whom you're assigning the task, or click To to browse the Address Book for the person's address.

5. Outlook 2007 automatically selects the following two check boxes. Set them as you want, and then click Send to send the task request to the assignee.

   Keep An Updated Copy Of This Task On My Task List Select this check box if you want to keep a copy of the task in your own task list. You'll receive updates when the assignee makes changes to the task, such as a change in the % Complete status. If you clear this check box, you won't receive updates, nor will the task appear in your task list.

   Send Me A Status Report When This Task Is Complete Select this check box if you want to receive a status report on completion. The status report comes in the form of an e-mail message that Outlook 2007 generates automatically on the assignee's system when the assignee marks the task as completed.

For information about task updates and status reports, see "Tracking the Progress of a Task" later in this chapter.

> **Note**
>
> Click Cancel Assignment on the Ribbon to cancel an assignment and restore the original task form.

When you click Send, Outlook 2007 creates a task request message and sends it to the assignee. If you open the task, you'll see a status message indicating that Outlook 2007 is waiting for a response from the assignee, as shown in Figure 22-8. This message changes after you receive a response and indicates whether the assignee accepted the task.

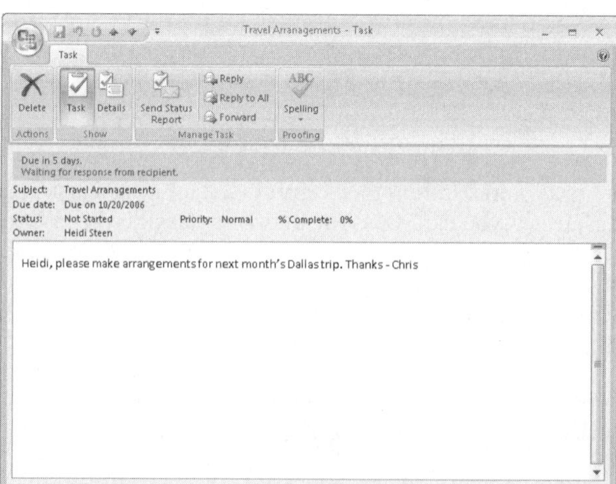

Figure 22-8. Outlook 2007 indicates that it is waiting for a response to a task request for a selected task.

When you receive a task request from someone who wants to assign a task to you, the message includes buttons that allow you to accept or decline the task. Figure 22-9 shows the buttons on the InfoBar when the Reading Pane is displayed.

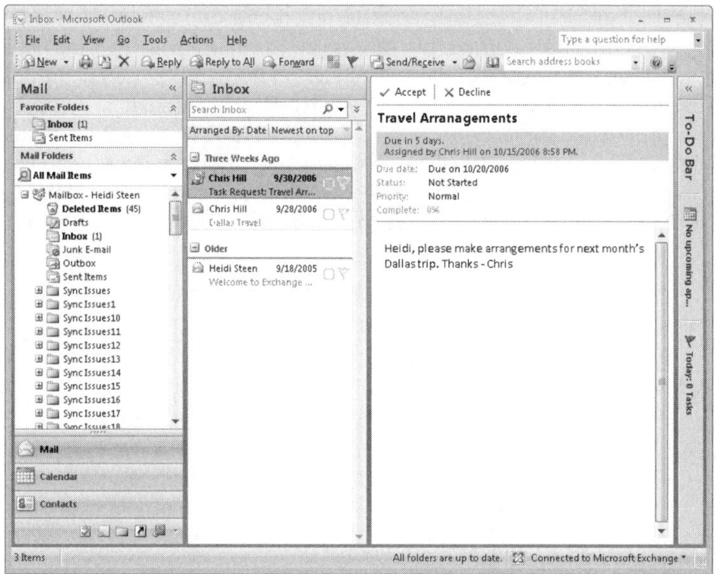

Figure 22-9. You can easily accept or decline a task request by clicking the Accept or Decline button on the Reading Pane InfoBar.

You can click either Accept or Decline to respond to the request. If the Reading Pane isn't visible, you can open the message and then click Accept or Decline in the Respond group on the message form's Ribbon. When you do so, Outlook 2007 displays either an Accepting Task or a Declining Task dialog box, giving you the option of sending the accept or decline message as is or editing it. For example, you might want to add a note to the message that you'll have to change the due date for the task or that you need additional information about the task. Select Edit The Response Before Sending in the dialog box if you want to add your own comments; select Send The Response Now if you don't want to add comments. Then click OK to generate the message. The next time you synchronize your Outbox with the server, the message will be sent.

You have one more option in addition to accepting or declining a task request that's waiting for your response—you can "pass the buck" and assign the task to someone else. For example, assume that you manage a small group of people. Your supervisor assigns a task to you, and you want to assign it to one of the people under you. When you receive the task request, open it, click Assign Task, and then select the person to whom you want to assign the task. Outlook 2007 creates a task request and sends it to the assignee. When the assignee accepts the task, his or her copy of Outlook 2007 sends an acceptance notice to you and adds both the originator's address and your address to the update list on the Details page of the task form. This means that changes to the task by the assignee are updated to your copy of the task and to the originator's copy.

TROUBLESHOOTING

Task requests keep disappearing

After you accept or decline a task, Outlook 2007 automatically deletes the task request from your Inbox. Unlike meeting requests, task requests are always deleted—Outlook 2007 doesn't provide an option that allows you to control this behavior. Outlook 2007 does, however, keep a copy of the task request in the Sent Items folder. Outlook 2007 also deletes task update messages after you read them. These messages are generated automatically when someone modifies an assigned task. Outlook 2007 sends the task update message to the people listed in the update list on the Details page of the task form. Although you can manually move these update messages out of the Deleted Items folder, Outlook 2007 provides no way to prevent them from being deleted.

When a response to a task assignment reaches you, Outlook 2007 doesn't automatically act on the response. For example, if someone accepts a task that you assigned, Outlook 2007 doesn't consider the task accepted until you open the response. Until that point, the InfoBar in the Reading Pane still indicates that Outlook 2007 is waiting for a response. When you open the response, the InfoBar in the message form indicates whether the task has been accepted or declined, depending on the assignee's action. Outlook 2007 deletes the response when you close the message. You have no options for controlling this behavior–Outlook 2007 always deletes the response.

If an assignee declines your task request, you can easily assign the task to someone else (or reassign it to the same individual). Open the response, and click Assign Task on the form's toolbar just as you would when assigning a new task.

Reclaiming Ownership of a Declined Task

Your tasks won't always be accepted–you're bound to receive a rejection now and then. When you do, you have two choices: assign the task to someone else, or reclaim ownership so that you can modify or complete the task yourself. To reclaim a task, open the message containing the declined task request, and then choose Actions, Return To Task List.

Note

When you assign a task, the assignee becomes the temporary owner until he or she accepts or rejects the task. Reclaiming the task restores your ownership so that you can modify the task.

Assigning Tasks to Multiple People

In some situations, you'll no doubt want to assign a task to more than one person. As a department manager, for example, you might need to assign a project to the people in your department or at least to a small group. Outlook 2007 is somewhat limited in task management: it can't track task status when you assign a task to more than one person. You can certainly assign the task, but you won't receive status reports.

What's the solution? You must change the way you assign tasks, if only slightly. Rather than assigning the whole project as a single task, for example, break the project into separate tasks and assign each one individually, or break a specific task into multiple tasks. Use a similar name for each task to help you recognize that each one is really part of the same task. For example, you might use the names Quarterly Report: Joe and Quarterly Report: Jane to assign the preparation of a quarterly report to both Joe and Jane.

INSIDE OUT **Working around limitations**

Although the Outlook 2007 task management features are certainly useful, a more comprehensive set of tools for distributing and managing tasks within a project would be a great addition to the program. For example, the ability to subdivide a task automatically would be helpful, as would the ability to assign a task to multiple people and still receive updates without having to subdivide the task. You can, however, work around this by adjusting the way you assign and manage tasks.

Assigning Multiple Tasks Through an Assistant or a Group Leader

If you manage more than one group, task assignment becomes a little more complex because you probably have more than one group or department leader under you. Ideally, you would assign a task to a group leader, and the group leader would then delegate portions of the task to members of his or her group. How you accomplish that delegation depends on whether you want to receive status updates directly from group members or only from the group leader.

If you want to receive updates from group members, divide the overall task into subtasks and assign them to the group leader. The leader can then assign the tasks as needed to individuals in the group. Task updates are then sent to both you and the group leader. If you prefer to receive updates only from the group leader, create a single all-encompassing task and assign it to the group leader, who can then divide the project into individual tasks to assign to group members as needed.

Tracking the Progress of a Task

When you assign a task, you can choose to keep an updated copy of the task in your task list. This copy allows you to track the status of the task. As the assignee adds or changes task information—such as changing the Total Work value—that assignee's copy of Outlook 2007 generates an update and sends it to the addresses listed in the task's update list (on the Details page of the task form). Typically, the update list includes only one name—the name of the person who assigned the task. If the task was delegated (passed on from one person to another), the update list shows all persons in the assignment chain.

> **Note**
>
> If you assign a task to multiple people, Outlook 2007 can no longer track task status. This limitation is one reason to subdivide a task, as explained in the preceding section.

As mentioned, Outlook 2007 sends task status messages to the update list addresses when an assignee makes changes to a task. When you receive a status message, Outlook 2007 updates your copy of the task when you read the status message. Outlook 2007 then deletes the status message, with one exception: when the assignee marks the task as completed, Outlook 2007 sends a Task Completed message to the update list addresses. When you receive and read the message, Outlook 2007 marks your copy of the task as completed but does not delete the task completed message. Figure 22-10 shows a Task Completed message.

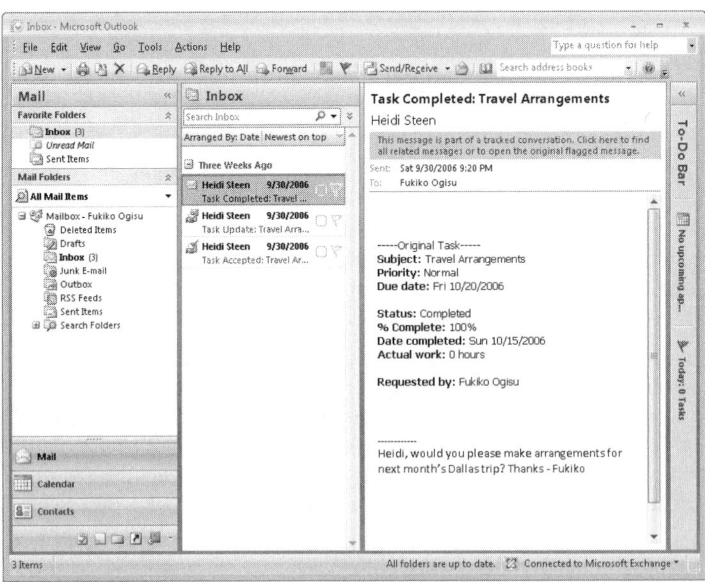

Figure 22-10. Outlook 2007 generates a Task Completed message when an assignee marks a task as completed.

Sending a Task Status Report

As you work on an assigned task, you'll probably want to send status updates to the person who assigned the task to you. Sending task status reports is more than easy—it's automatic. Outlook 2007 generates the updates each time you modify the task, such as when you change the % Complete value. Because you can't force another update without changing the task, you might want to make a small change in one of the task's properties—for example, increasing the % Complete value by 1 percent—to generate an update.

Creating an Unassigned Copy of an Assigned Task

Outlook 2007 allows you to create an unassigned copy of a task that you have assigned to someone else. This unassigned copy goes into your task list with you as the owner. You can then work on the task yourself or assign it to someone else. For example, suppose that you assigned a task to someone but you want to work on it too. You can create a copy and then work on the copy, changing its dates, completion status, and other information as you go.

Creating an unassigned copy has one drawback, however: You will no longer receive updates for the assigned task. This makes it more difficult to track the other person's progress on the assigned task.

Follow these steps to create an unassigned copy of a task:

1. In Outlook 2007, open the Tasks folder, and then click the assigned task.
2. Click the Tasks tab on the Ribbon, click Details, and then click Create Unassigned Copy.
3. Outlook 2007 displays a warning that creating the copy will prevent you from receiving updates to the assigned task. Click OK to create the copy or Cancel to cancel the process.
4. Outlook 2007 replaces the existing task with a new one. The new task has the same name except that the word *copy* is appended to the name in the Subject box. Make changes as needed to the task, and then choose Save & Close to save the changes.

Viewing and Customizing the Tasks Folder

As mentioned at the beginning of this chapter, Outlook 2007 uses the To-Do List view as the default Tasks folder view. Several other predefined views are also available, including those described in the following list. To use any of these views, choose View, Arrange By, Current View, and then select the view you want.

- **Simple List** Shows the task name, the due date, and whether the task is completed. This is the default view for the Tasks folder.

- **Detailed List** Shows not only the information in a simple list but also status, percent complete, and categories.
- **Active Tasks** Shows tasks that are active (incomplete).
- **Next Seven Days** Shows tasks for the next seven days.
- **Overdue Tasks** Shows incomplete tasks with due dates that have passed.
- **By Category** Organizes the task list by the categories assigned to tasks.
- **Assignment** Shows tasks assigned to specific people.
- **By Person Responsible** Groups the view according to the person responsible for a task.
- **Completed Tasks** Shows only completed tasks.
- **Task Timeline** Shows a timeline of all tasks.
- **Server Tasks** Shows tasks stored on a server running Microsoft SharePoint®.
- **Outlook Data Files** Shows tasks organized by the data file in which they are stored.
- **To-Do List** Shows the To-Do List.

Outlook 2007 provides several ways to customize the view of the Tasks folder. These methods are the same as those for other Outlook 2007 folders. For details on sorting, grouping by various columns, adding and removing columns, and customizing the folder view in other ways, see "Customizing the Inbox View" in Chapter 4.

For information about using filters to locate and display specific tasks, such as those with certain text, dates, or other properties, see "Using Advanced Find" in Chapter 33.

In addition to using the customizing methods described in Chapter 4, "Working In and Configuring Outlook," you might also want to change the way Outlook 2007 displays certain items in the Tasks folder. For example, you could change the font or character size for the column names or change the color that Outlook 2007 uses to display overdue tasks (red by default). The following sections explain how to make these types of changes in the Tasks folder.

Changing Fonts and Table View Settings

Outlook 2007 by default uses an 8-point Segoe UI font for column headings, rows, and AutoPreview text. You can select a different font or different font characteristics (point size, italic, color, and so on). You also can change the style and color for the gridlines in list views and specify whether to show the Reading Pane.

Follow these steps to customize your view settings:

1. Right-click the column header bar and then choose Customize Current View, or choose View, Current View, Customize Current View.
2. In the Customize View dialog box, click Other Settings to display the Other Settings dialog box, shown in Figure 22-11.

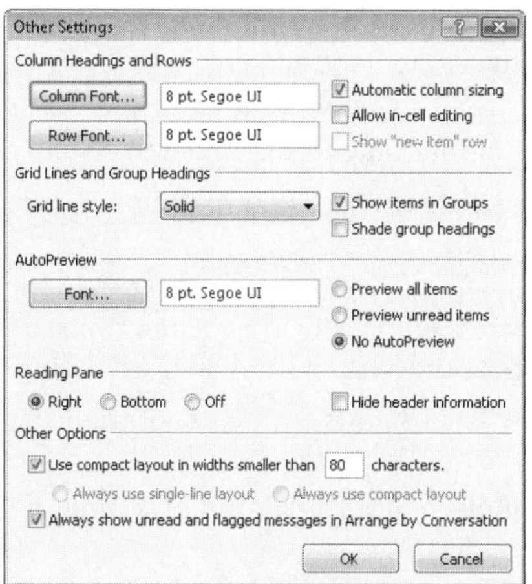

Figure 22-11. Configure font properties for the Tasks folder in the Other Settings dialog box.

3. Click Column Font or Row Font in the Column Headings And Rows area of the dialog box, or click Font in the AutoPreview area to open a standard Font dialog box that you can use to configure font, size, and other settings for the specified text.

> **Note**
>
> You can change color only for the AutoPreview text. Row and column text is displayed in a fixed color.

4. Use the options in the Grid Lines And Group Headings area to specify the line type and color you want Outlook 2007 to use for list views.
5. Set the other options, using the following list as a guide:

   Automatic Column Sizing Sizes columns automatically and fits them to the display's width. Clear this check box to specify your own column width (by dragging each column's header), and use a scroll bar to view columns that don't fit the display.

   Allow In-Cell Editing Allows you to click in a cell and modify the contents. If this check box is cleared, you must open the task to make changes.

   Show "New Item" Row Displays a row at the top of the list for adding new tasks. The New Item row appears only if in-cell editing is selected.

   Show Items in Groups Group items together (such as by date).

   Shade Group Headings Adds shading to headings when you view items in a grouped table view (where items are grouped by column value, such as all tasks with the same due date).

Preview All Items Turns on AutoPreview and causes Outlook 2007 to display the first three lines of the contents of all items.

Preview Unread Items Turns on AutoPreview and causes Outlook 2007 to display the first three lines of the contents of unread items only.

No AutoPreview Displays only the headings for items and does not display AutoPreview text.

Reading Pane The options in this area control the location of the Reading Pane. Click the Off button to hide the Reading Pane. You also can choose View, Reading Pane to select the location or turn the Reading Pane on or off.

Hide Header Information Choose this option to not show header information in the Reading Pane.

Other Options These options control a handful of settings that determine view layout.

6. Click OK to close the Other Settings dialog box, and then click OK to close the Customize View dialog box.

Using Automatic Formatting

Outlook 2007 can perform automatic text formatting in the Tasks folder just as it can for other folders. For example, Outlook 2007 displays overdue tasks in red and uses gray strikethrough for completed and read tasks. Outlook 2007 has five predefined automatic formatting rules, and you can create additional rules if you want to set up additional automatic formatting. For example, you might create a rule to show in red all tasks that haven't been started and are due within the next seven days.

To create automatic formatting rules, choose View, Current View, Customize Current View, and then click Automatic Formatting to display the Automatic Formatting dialog box, shown in Figure 22-12.

Figure 22-12. Modify or create custom automatic formatting rules in the Automatic Formatting dialog box.

Follow these steps to create a new rule:

1. In the Automatic Formatting dialog box, click Add. This creates a new rule named Untitled.
2. Type a title for the rule, and then click Font. Use the resulting Font dialog box to specify the font characteristics you want Outlook 2007 to use for tasks that meet the rule's conditions. Click OK to close the Font dialog box.
3. Click Condition to open the Filter dialog box, shown in Figure 22-13. Specify the criteria for the condition. For example, select Due in the Time drop-down list, and then select In The Next 7 Days. This specifies that you want Outlook 2007 to use the font selections from step 2 to format any tasks that are due within the next seven days.

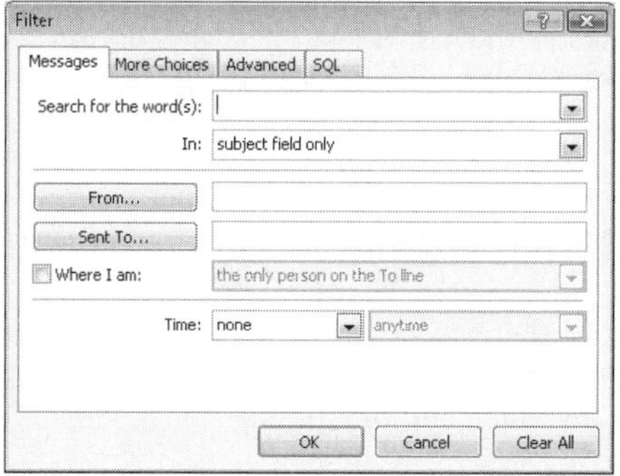

Figure 22-13. Use the Filter dialog box to specify conditions for the formatting rule.

4. Use the More Choices and Advanced tabs to set other conditions as needed, and then click OK.
5. Add other rules as needed. Click OK to close the Automatic Formatting dialog box, and then click OK to close the Customize View dialog box.

You can create fairly complex rules using the Filter dialog box, which can help you organize and identify specific types of tasks. Also note that you can change the order of the rules in the Automatic Formatting dialog box by using the Move Up and Move Down buttons. Outlook 2007 applies the rules in order from top to bottom, so it's possible for one rule to override another.

Setting General Task Options

Outlook 2007 provides a few options that control the appearance of items in the Tasks folder, reminders, and other task-related elements. To set these options, choose Tools, Options. On the Preferences tab of the Options dialog box, the Reminder Time option specifies the default reminder time for tasks. This option is set to 8:00 A.M. by default, but you can change the time if you want—perhaps you'd prefer to see reminders at 10:00 A.M. instead. Keep in mind that this setting is the default that Outlook 2007 uses for task reminders when you create a task, but you can change the reminder time for individual tasks as needed.

If you click Task Options, Outlook 2007 displays the Task Options dialog box, which includes the following options:

- **Overdue Task Color** Select the color you want Outlook 2007 to use to display overdue tasks.
- **Completed Task Color** Select the color you want Outlook 2007 to use to display completed tasks.
- **Keep Updated Copies Of Assigned Tasks On My Task List** Select this option to have Outlook 2007 keep a copy of assigned tasks in your Tasks folder and update their status when assignees make changes to the tasks.
- **Send Status Reports When Assigned Tasks Are Completed** Select this option to have Outlook 2007 send status reports to you when tasks that you assigned to someone else are completed.
- **Set Reminders On Tasks With Due Dates** Select this option to have Outlook 2007 set a reminder on tasks with due dates. Outlook 2007 bases the timer on the task's due date and the reminder time specified in the Options dialog box.

Working with Tasks in Other Ways

Outlook 2007 provides a few other ways to work with tasks in addition to the Tasks folder. The following sections explain how to set up and track tasks in the task list area of the To-Do Bar, the Daily Task List, and in Outlook Today view.

Working with Tasks in the To-Do Bar

The To-Do Bar is a new interface feature in Outlook 2007, and the task list is a component of the To-Do Bar. Figure 22-14 shows the To-Do Bar with the task list at the bottom.

By default, Outlook 2007 shows only subject, category color indicators, and flag status for tasks in the task list, but as you expand the width of the To-Do Bar, other columns appear. You can add and remove columns as needed. To do so, right-click the column header bar above the task list, and then choose Custom. In the Customize View dialog box, click Fields to open the Show Fields dialog box, where you can specify the columns to include in the view and their order.

You can modify tasks directly in the task list just as you can in the Tasks folder, depending on the view settings you've specified. For example, if you've turned on in-cell editing, you can make changes to a task simply by clicking it and typing the needed changes. You can mark a task as completed, change the Actual Work value, change the due date, and so on. The task list is, in this respect, no different from the Tasks folder. The primary benefit of the task list is that it allows you to work with your tasks in a single window along with the other tools in the view.

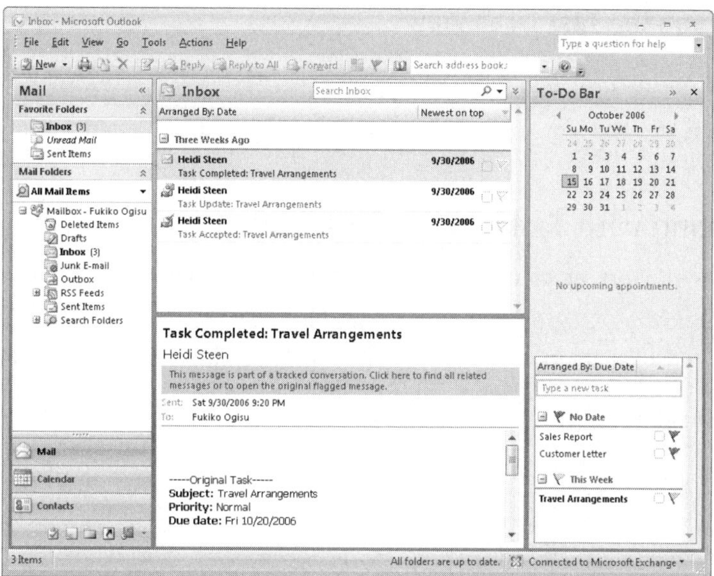

Figure 22-14. The task list appears at the bottom of the To-Do Bar.

INSIDE OUT **Show and hide the task list**

To show or hide the task list in the To-Do Bar, choose To-Do Bar from the View menu, and then choose Task List from the cascading menu.

You can use the same methods that you use to create tasks in the Tasks folder to create a new task in the task list. Right-click in the empty area of the task list, and then choose New Task or New Task Request, depending on whether you're creating the task for yourself or assigning it to someone else. If both the Show New Item Row option and in-cell editing are enabled, you can click the Type A New Task row between the first task in the list and the column header to create a new task. Alternatively, you can click the arrow next to the New button on the Standard toolbar and then choose Task to create a new task.

Changing the Task List's View

Outlook 2007 offers six views for the task list, and you can create custom views, as well. To change the view, right-click in an empty area of the task list, choose Arrange By, and then select a view. You can also click on a column header in the task list and choose a view.

Working with Tasks in Outlook Today

Chapter 4, "Working In and Configuring Outlook," explains how Outlook Today gives you quick access to a useful selection of data. Outlook Today view is shown in Figure 22-15. The Calendar area displays meetings and events scheduled for the current day (and for subsequent days, if space allows). The Messages area indicates the number of unread messages in your Inbox, messages in the Drafts folder, and unsent messages in the Outbox. The Tasks area lists your tasks.

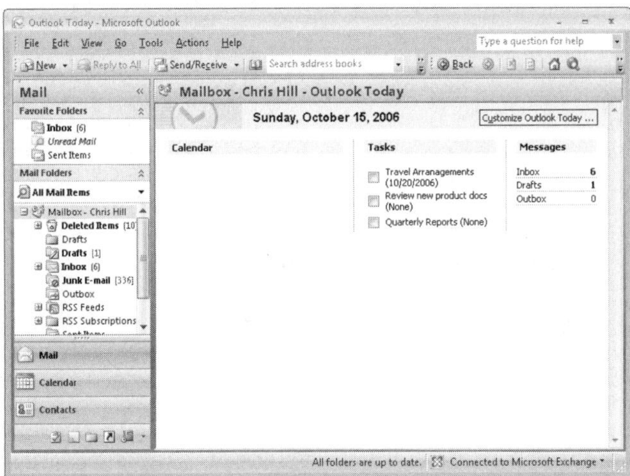

Figure 22-15. Outlook Today offers quick access to a range of information.

For more information about using Outlook Today, see "Working with the Standard Outlook Views" in Chapter 4.

You can't create a task by clicking in the Tasks area of Outlook Today, but you can click the arrow next to the New button on the toolbar and then choose Task to create a new task. To modify a task, click the task's name in the list to open the task form. Mark a task as completed by selecting the check box next to its name.

Using the Daily Task List

Outlook 2007 adds a new way to manage tasks through the Daily Task List, which optionally appears at the bottom of the calendar, as shown in Figure 22-16. The Daily Task

List shows the list of tasks that are due on the selected day. You can work with the tasks in the Daily Task List much as you can with the tasks in the To-Do Bar.

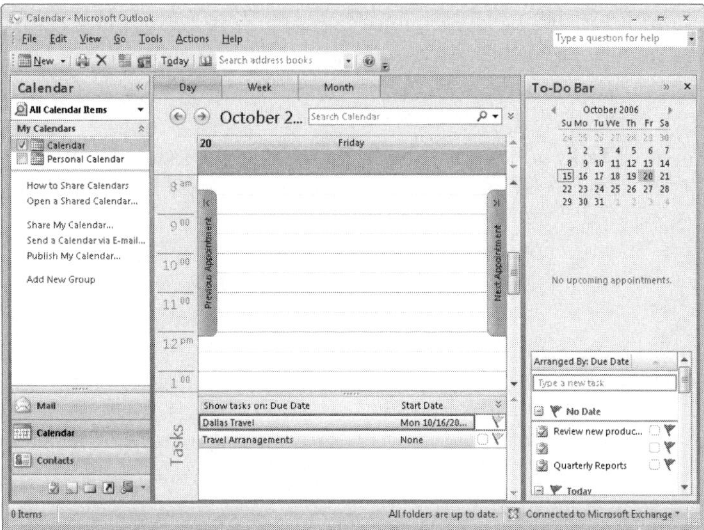

Figure 22-16. The Daily Task List resides at the bottom of the calendar.

To turn the Daily Task List on or off, choose Daily Task List on the View menu, and then choose Normal or Minimized to show the list. When the Daily Task List is displayed, you can click the Minimize button at the far-right edge of the Daily Task List column bar to minimize it. Likewise, when the Daily Task List is minimized, click the Restore button to display it.

Managing Tasks Effectively

Tasks are one of the Outlook 2007 features that many people overlook, spending their time instead primarily in the Inbox, Contacts, and Calendar folders. Nevertheless, tasks can be extremely useful and a powerful productivity and workflow tool. If you haven't used tasks before, spend the time to become familiar with them. When you are comfortable using tasks, the following tips will help you make the most of them:

- **Really use them.** Tasks won't do you much good if you just put a few on your task list and then don't really use them. Instead, use tasks in Outlook 2007 for all of your daily, weekly, and monthly tasks. Make sure to set progress status as you go along and mark tasks as complete when you complete them.
- **Use task assignment.** Outlook 2007 tasks can be a great tool for helping you organize your day and get your job done. Task assignment extends that benefit across your team or workgroup. Get your group in the habit of using tasks, and then start using task assignment across the group to manage tasks.

- **Use realistic due dates.** Setting realistic due dates for your tasks and working on the tasks accordingly will help you integrate tasks into your daily work schedule. The keys to being successful using Outlook 2007 tasks are to be diligent about how you use them and to integrate them into your workday and workflow.
- **Use reminders.** By assigning reminders to your tasks, you'll be able to keep track of when the tasks are coming due. Assign a reminder period sufficiently long to enable you to complete the task by its due date.
- **Keep the tasks at hand.** Make use of the task list in the To-Do Bar and the Daily Task List in the Calendar folder to keep your tasks visible at all times so that you can work with them easily and see their status.

CHAPTER 23

Tracking Documents and Activities with the Jounal

Remembering everything that you've done during the course of a busy day—e-mail messages sent, phone calls made, appointments set up—can be difficult. However, the Journal feature in Microsoft® Office Outlook® 2007, which records your daily activities, can help you keep track of it all. In addition to tracking Office Outlook 2007 items such as e-mail messages and appointments automatically, you can use the journal to monitor every 2007 Microsoft Office system document you create or modify. You can also manually record an activity that occurs away from your computer—a phone conversation, for example, or a handwritten letter that you mailed or received.

The Journal folder provides a single place to track all your work and your daily interactions. For example, you can use the journal to list all items related to a specific contact: e-mail messages sent and received, meetings attended, and tasks assigned. You can track all the hours you've spent on activities related to a particular project. Or you can use the journal to retrieve detailed information based on when you performed an action—for example, if you know that you worked on a Microsoft Office Excel® 2007 document last Tuesday but can't remember the path to the file, you can quickly look up the document if you've configured the journal to automatically record work on Office Excel 2007 files.

This chapter shows you how to record your work in the journal both automatically and manually. You'll also learn how to view and print your journal in standard and customized views.

Understanding the Outlook Journal

The Journal folder, shown in Figure 23-1, provides you with tools to track and record daily activities. Although other components of Outlook 2007 provide similar note-keeping capabilities, only the journal provides a full (and optionally automatic) means to date and time stamp an activity, log the entry type (for example, a phone call or a meeting request), and even track the time spent on an activity for billing purposes.

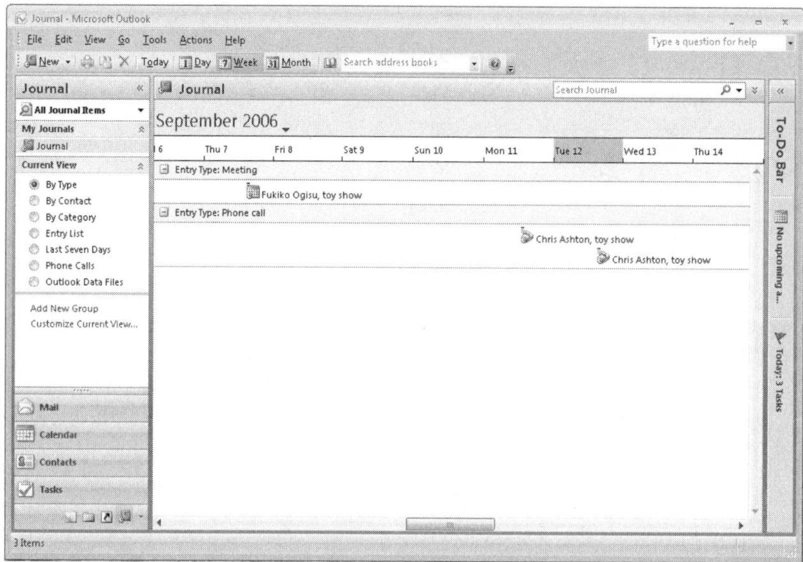

Figure 23-1. Use the journal as an electronic diary of events, phone calls, tasks, and other daily items.

Outlook 2007 records entries in your Journal folder based on when an action occurs. For example, a Microsoft Office Word 2007 document is recorded on the journal timeline when you create or modify the document. You can organize journal entries on the timeline into logical groups—such as e-mail messages, meetings, phone calls, or any items related to a specific project. You also can assign categories to journal items and organize the folder view by category. For example, you could assign a project name as a category to all journal items associated with that project, which would allow you to easily group journal entries by project.

You can open a journal entry form, as shown in Figure 23-2, and review details about an activity, or you can use the journal entry as a shortcut to go directly to the Outlook 2007 item or the file referred to in the journal entry.

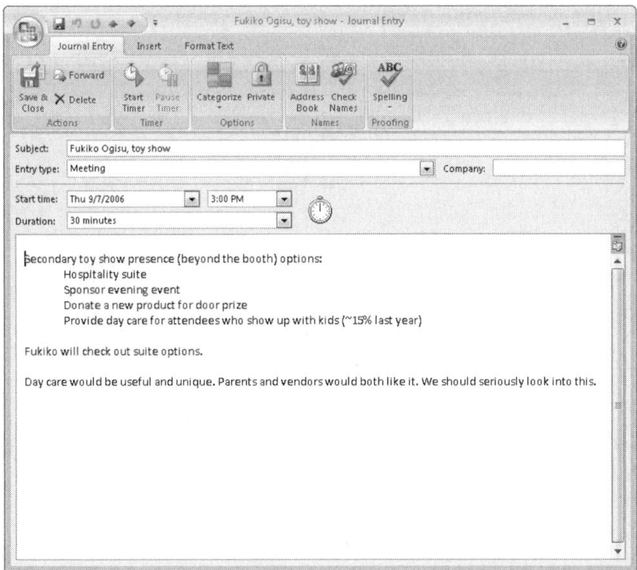

Figure 23-2. The journal entry form contains many fields to help you organize, store, and find your journal entries.

The Outlook 2007 journal is an electronic diary. Everything that you normally write in your calendar or day planner (what you did, when you did it, and all the details you want to remember) you can record in the journal.

To open the Journal folder, click the Journal icon in the Navigation Pane. Figure 23-1 shows the journal By Type view, which you see the first time you open the journal. Figure 23-3 shows Entry List view, another way of organizing your Journal folder.

For information about the views available to organize your Journal folder, see "Viewing the Journal" later in this chapter.

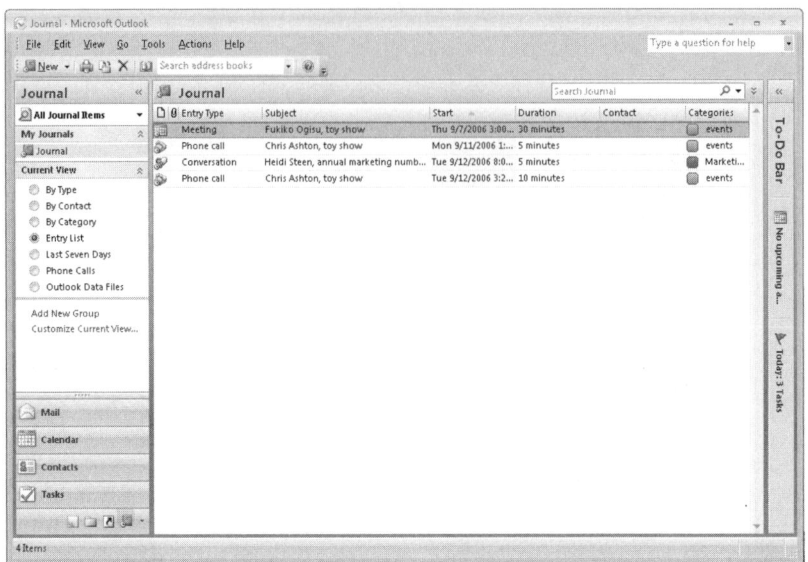

Figure 23-3. You can switch to the Entry List view of the Journal folder.

Using Automatic Journaling

You can have Outlook 2007 create automatic journal entries for a wide range of items, including e-mail messages (both sent and received), task requests, and files you create or open in other Microsoft Office system applications. In fact, you can use automatic journaling to record activities based on any contact, Microsoft Office system document, or Outlook 2007 item you select.

For example, suppose that you routinely exchange important e-mail messages with a business associate, and you want to track all exchanges for reference. Incoming messages from this associate arrive in your Inbox. You read them, reply to them, and then archive the incoming messages to another folder. Now, however, your associate's messages are stored in one folder and your replies are in another. (By default, replies are stored in the Outlook 2007 Sent Items folder.) Configuring the journal to automatically track all of your e-mail exchanges with your associate places a record of all messages relating to this contact (both received and sent) in one convenient location. Instead of hunting for your response to your associate's question from two weeks ago, you can open the journal and find the entry associated with the message. Double-click the link embedded in the journal entry, and Outlook 2007 takes you to the message containing your response. Figure 23-4 shows a journal entry automatically added from an e-mail message.

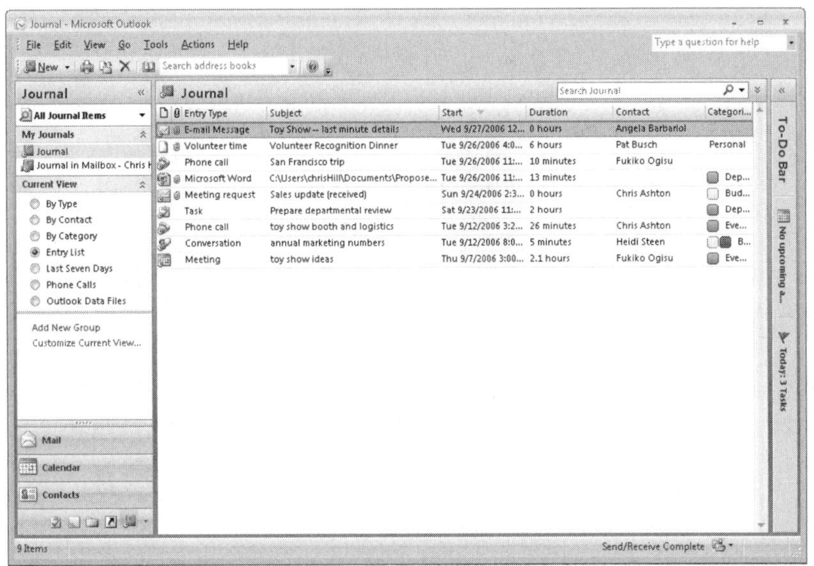

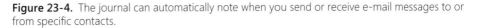

Figure 23-4. The journal can automatically note when you send or receive e-mail messages to or from specific contacts.

INSIDE OUT Organize messages using search folders

Search folders are another useful tool for organizing messages. You might set up a search folder that lists all of the messages to or from a specific contact to help you quickly find those messages. See Chapter 10, "Finding and Organizing Messages," for a complete discussion of search folders.

INSIDE OUT Find e-mail items quickly

To find e-mail items in the journal more quickly, select Entry List view, and then click the Contact column to sort the view according to contact. This helps you see all journal items associated with a specific contact, including those items created automatically from e-mail messages.

As another example, consider a writer who uses Office Word 2007 every day to make a living. Turning on automatic document tracking for this application could provide some interesting insight into how the writer's workday is allocated and which documents are the most demanding. The same holds true for other Microsoft Office system applications that you use frequently.

If you use document tracking in such a scenario, however, you should be aware of the distinction between how Outlook 2007 tracks a document and how Word 2007 itself records editing time. (In Word 2007, you can click the Microsoft Office Button and then choose Prepare, Properties to open the Document Properties panel. Click Document Properties, select Advanced Properties in the drop-down list, and click the Statistics tab to locate the Total Editing Time field.) Outlook 2007 tracks the time a document is open, whereas Word 2007 tracks the time spent physically editing a document (that is, pressing keys). The Outlook 2007 journal automatically records the entire span of time a document is open, even if you are away from your desk tending to other matters.

If a record of the actual time spent working on a document is important to you (whether you're mulling a paragraph, reading a lengthy section, or editing or entering new text), the journal offers a more realistic record. However, if you fail to close the document when you move on to other things, you'll end up adding time to the document's journal entry that wasn't really spent on the document. It's best to use a combination of the Word 2007 Total Editing Time field and the Outlook 2007 journal's tracking to get a realistic picture of how you spend your time.

Overall, the best choice is usually to use automatic tracking for your critical contacts and for specific applications that benefit from an automatic audit trail. You can place other items in the journal manually as required.

Note

After you set it up, the journal's automatic tracking is always on. A piece of Outlook 2007 code runs in the background and monitors the Microsoft Office system applications you've selected to track—even if Outlook 2007 itself is closed.

Another issue to consider in relation to journaling is latency. When you use automatic tracking for documents, you'll often notice a significant lag between the time you close a document and the time the entry appears (or is updated) in the journal. Also keep in mind that if you've opened the document previously, the most recent tracking entry doesn't appear at the top of the list. By default, journal entries are ordered according to start date, which in this case would be the first time the document was opened or created, not the most recent time.

> **Note**
>
> Using automatic journaling can have a significantly negative impact on the performance of your applications because of the added overhead involved in journaling. This might not be apparent on your system, depending on its capabilities and the types of documents you use. However, if you see a significant decrease in performance after turning on automatic journaling and can't afford the performance drop, you'll need to stop automatic journaling and resort to adding journal entries manually.

Setting Journal Options

The journal has many options that allow you to control what is recorded, how it is recorded, and when it is recorded. To set journal options, choose Tools, Options. On the Preferences tab, click Journal Options to open the Journal Options dialog box, shown in Figure 23-5. The choices you make in this dialog box determine how your journal is set up and what it tracks.

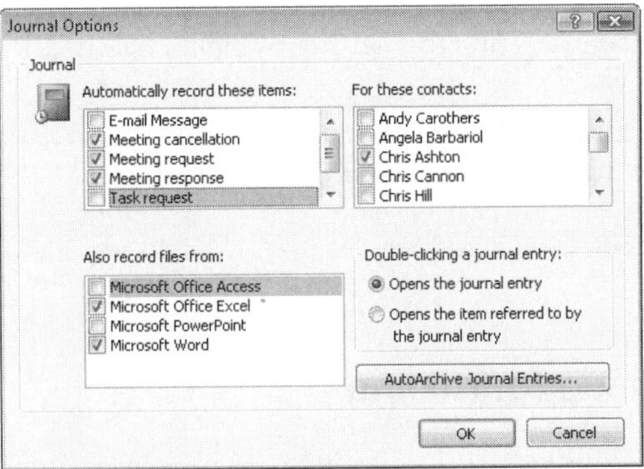

Figure 23-5. The Journal Options dialog box contains customization choices for the journal.

The following list summarizes the options in the Journal Options dialog box:

- **Automatically Record These Items** Select from a list of Outlook 2007 items that can be tracked as journal entries. All options here involve three forms of messaging: regular e-mail, meeting notifications, and task delegation. Item types selected in this list are tracked for the contacts you specify in the For These Contacts list. Selecting an item to track without choosing an associated contact has no effect for that tracking option.
- **For These Contacts** Here you link items you want to track with those contacts you want to track them for–task requests from your boss, for example. Outlook 2007 then automatically creates journal entries for the selected contacts and related items. Only contacts in your main Contacts folder can be selected for automatic journaling. You'll need to move (or copy) contact entries from subfolders to the main Contacts folder if you want to track items for them.

- **Also Record Files From** Outlook 2007 creates an automatic journal entry every time a Microsoft Office system application selected in this list creates or accesses a document. The selections available depend on which Microsoft Office system applications are installed on your system. Documents from Microsoft Office Access, Office Excel, Office PowerPoint®, Office Word, and Office Project can be tracked.

CAUTION!

When you set up automatic tracking for a particular document type (for example, Word 2007 documents), this setting applies to all documents you create, open, close, or save with the selected application. Thus automatic tracking can also create many journal entries filled with information you might not need to preserve. Make this selection with care.

- **Double-Clicking A Journal Entry** Double-clicking a journal entry can open either the entry itself or the item referred to by the entry, depending on your selection in this area of the dialog box. Use this option to specify which action you prefer as the default. You can later override this setting by right-clicking the journal entry in any journal view.
- **AutoArchive Journal Entries** Click to open the Journal Properties dialog box and configure archive settings for the Journal folder.

For details on archiving Outlook 2007 items, see Chapter 31, "Archiving, Backing Up, and Restoring Outlook Data."

Turning Off Automatic Journaling

You won't find a one-click solution when you want to turn off automatic journaling. To turn off this feature, you must open the Journal Options dialog box and clear all the check boxes in the Automatically Record These Items and Also Record Files From lists. It's not necessary to clear contacts selected in the For These Contacts list. Because automatic journaling consists of tracking specific Outlook 2007 events for a contact as well as when specific types of Microsoft Office system files are accessed, breaking the link for items to track is enough.

TROUBLESHOOTING

Automatic journaling is causing delays

Automatic journaling can cause very long delays during manual or automatic save operations as well as when you exit the application. Although it might appear that the application has stopped responding, in fact it is simply saving the journal information. If your system stops responding during these procedures, check Outlook 2007 to see whether automatic journaling is turned on for the specific application involved. If so, wait a minute or two to give the application a chance to save your data, and then turn off automatic journaling if it has become too inconvenient to use. You can continue to add journal items manually for the application, if needed.

Automatically Recording E-Mail Messages

Recording e-mail to and from colleagues in the journal is a great way to keep track of discussions and decisions concerning a project, and it's easy to locate those messages later.

To record e-mail messages exchanged with a specific contact, follow these steps:

1. In Outlook 2007, choose Tools, Options, and then click Journal Options on the Preferences tab to open the Journal Options dialog box.
2. In the Automatically Record These Items list, select the E-Mail Message check box.
3. In the For These Contacts list, select the contact whose e-mail you want to record.
4. Click OK twice to close both dialog boxes.

Automatically Recording Contact Information

You can configure your journal to automatically keep track of your interactions with any one of your contacts. If you're working with a colleague on a specific project, for example, you might want to monitor your progress by recording every e-mail message, meeting, and task that involves this colleague.

To set up your journal to keep such a record based on the name of the contact, follow these steps:

1. In Outlook 2007, choose Tools, Options, and then click Journal Options on the Preferences tab to open the Journal Options dialog box.
2. In the Automatically Record These Items list, select the types of Outlook 2007 items you want to record in the journal.

3. In the For These Contacts list, select the relevant contact. (You can select more than one.)
4. Click OK twice to close both dialog boxes.

Automatically Recording Document Activity

Suppose you create and maintain custom Excel 2007 workbooks for the different divisions in your corporate enterprise. In the course of a busy day, it's easy to forget to write down which files you worked on and for how long. There's a better way than keeping track on paper: you can have the journal automatically record every Microsoft Office system file you open, including when and how long you had each file open. Outlook 2007 can monitor your files and create a journal entry for every document you open and work on from other Microsoft Office system applications such as Microsoft Office Visio®, Office Word, Office Excel, Office Access, Office PowerPoint, and Office Project.

> **Note**
>
> Although the journal can automatically record work only in these Microsoft Office system programs, you can enter your work from other programs manually.

Follow these steps to automatically record files you create or open:

1. In Outlook 2007, choose Tools, Options, and then click Journal Options on the Preferences tab to open the Journal Options dialog box.
2. In the Also Record Files From list, select the programs for which you want to automatically record files in your journal. When you create, open, close, or save a document from any of the selected programs, the journal will record a new entry.
3. By default, double-clicking an icon on the journal timeline opens the journal entry. If you'd rather be able to open the associated file when you double-click the icon, select the Opens The Item Referred To By The Journal Entry option.

> **Note**
>
> Regardless of which option you choose to be the default in the Journal Options dialog box, you can always right-click an icon on the journal timeline and then choose either Open Journal Entry or Open Items Referred To on the shortcut menu.

4. Click OK twice to close both dialog boxes.

INSIDE OUT Add items manually

If you've set up automatic journaling for all entries created by an application (Excel 2007, for example), every document you create in that application generates a journal entry. If you right-click an entry and choose Open Item Referred To, Outlook 2007 opens the document that created the journal entry. However, this behavior can change. If you add a document item manually to the entry and the icon for that item appears before the original document's icon in the entry, Outlook 2007 opens the manually added document. In other words, Outlook 2007 always opens the first document referenced in the entry when you choose Open Item Referred To on the entry's shortcut menu. This can be confusing because the subject continues to reference the original document. In addition, the manually added document does not appear in the View Attachments list on the entry's shortcut menu unless you inserted it as a file instead of as a shortcut. So when you add entries manually, make sure to place the icon for the document added manually after the original document's icon and insert the document as a file.

INSIDE OUT How the journal handles changes to tracked items

Because journal entries contain links to your documents instead of copies of the actual documents, the entries might reference documents that no longer exist on your system. The journal has no way to record the deletion, moving, or renaming of files, so while the journal entries for the deleted objects still exist, the referenced objects don't open.

Similarly, the journal can't find e-mail messages that have been moved from the Inbox to another folder. If you change the text on the subject line of a tracked e-mail message, the journal entry keeps the old subject line, but it can still find and open the message.

Adding Journal Items Manually

Automatic journaling can be tremendously useful, but what if some of the work you need to track is done in applications other than Microsoft Office system applications? You can't record the files automatically in your journal, but you can record them manually. Or what if you want to track your work only in a specific Word 2007 file rather than in every Word 2007 document? Instead of turning on automatic recording for all Word 2007 files, you can manually record your work in only specified files.

Likewise, if you want to record a nonelectronic event in your journal—a chat at the water cooler, a box of chocolates sent to a client, or your approval of a printed proposal—you can add a journal entry manually. You can also use this method if you'd prefer to pick and choose which documents, messages, meetings, and task requests are entered in the journal rather than having Outlook 2007 routinely record all such items.

Recording Work in a File Manually

To keep a record of when and how long you worked in a file (along with any extraneous notes to yourself), follow these steps:

1. Locate the file you want to work in. You can browse to the folder that contains the file using any technique you like, such as browsing My Computer or My Documents.
2. Drag the file icon in the folder window to the Journal icon in the Navigation Pane. It's easiest to drag the file if you resize both the Outlook 2007 window and the folder window so that you can clearly see both.
3. Click Start Timer to begin recording your working hours, as shown in Figure 23-6, and then double-click the file shortcut icon to open the file. At any time, you can enter notes to yourself in the area where the shortcut icon is located.

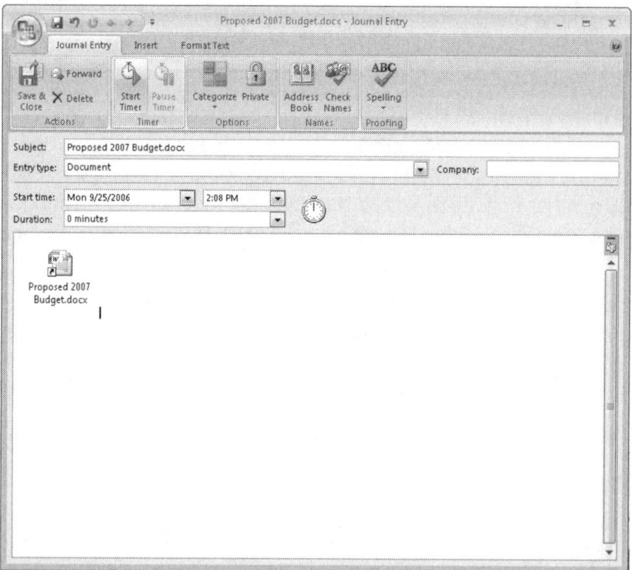

Figure 23-6. Click Start Timer to start recording time spent on a document.

4. When you finish working in the file, remember to stop the journal timer by clicking Pause Timer and then clicking Save & Close.

> **Note**
>
> If you need to take a temporary break in your work, click Pause Timer. When you return to work on the file, click Start Timer to continue recording your working hours.

Recording Outlook Items Manually

Recording an Outlook 2007 item such as a task in the journal is even easier than recording a file: open the Outlook 2007 window where the item is listed, and then drag the item to the Journal icon in the Navigation Pane. For example, suppose that you want to record how much time you spend cleaning out your filing cabinets, a task you've entered in the Tasks folder. Open the Tasks folder, and then drag the task item to the Journal icon in the Navigation Pane. Click Start Timer and go to work. Then click Pause Timer to take a break. When you finish, click Save & Close.

Recording Other Activities Manually

Any activity you want to record can be entered in your journal. For example, you can monitor the time you spend on the Internet (which can be considerable) as well as recording any Web page addresses you want to save and other notes you need to jot down.

To do so, follow these steps:

1. Double-click a blank area in your Journal folder. A new journal entry form opens.
2. In the Subject box, type a description of your activity.
3. In the Entry Type box, select an appropriate entry type for the activity. You can't create your own entry type on this screen, but you can choose among several available types. For example, you could classify an Internet search as Remote Session. Type any notes, including hyperlinks, in the body of the journal item.

For information about custom entry types, see "Creating and Using Custom Entry Types" later in this chapter.

4. Click Start Timer to begin recording your activity.
5. When you've finished with your activity, click Pause Timer to stop the timer, and then click Save & Close to close the journal entry.

Manually Recording Phone Calls

When you use automatic dialing to call a contact, you can time the phone call, type notes in Outlook 2007 while you talk, and create a journal entry for the call. This feature can come in handy if, for example, you bill clients for your time spent on phone conversations.

Follow these steps to keep a record of an outgoing call in the journal:

1. Open the Contacts folder, and select the contact entry for the person you want to call.
2. Click the Dial button on the Standard toolbar, or if the Contact window is open for the contact, click the Call button in the Communicate group on the Contact tab to open the New Call dialog box, as shown in Figure 23-7.

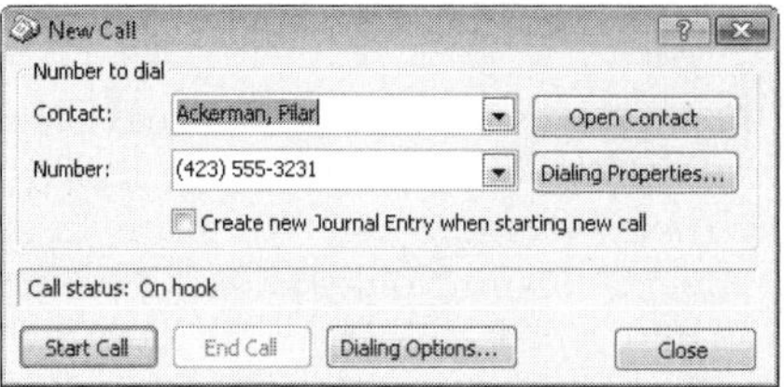

Figure 23-7. You can automatically start a new journal entry from the New Call dialog box.

3. Select the Create New Journal Entry When Starting New Call check box, and then click Start Call. A journal entry opens with the timer running. You can type notes in the body of the journal entry while you talk.
4. When you've finished with the call, click Pause Timer to stop the clock, and then click Save & Close.

You also can create journal entries for incoming calls, although Outlook 2007 currently offers no means of automatically creating the journal entries when you pick up the phone and start talking. Instead, when you answer the call and realize that you want to track it, you can open the journal as you begin the conversation, start a new journal item, and click Start Timer. Make notes as needed, and click Pause Timer when you hang up. Add any necessary details to the journal entry form, and then click Save & Close to create the item.

INSIDE OUT Use the journal as an inexpensive stopwatch

You can start a new journal item and use the timer to time any activity, assuming that you don't need to-the-second timing. Just stop the timer and close the form without saving it unless you actually want to save the information in the journal.

For information about setting up automatic phone dialing and making calls from the Contacts folder, see "Working with Contacts" in Chapter 18.

Creating and Using Custom Entry Types

You can assign categories to all Outlook 2007 items to provide a means of sorting and organizing those items. The journal is no exception: each journal item can have multiple categories assigned to it. Journal items, however, can also be classified by *entry type*, which defines the purpose of the journal item. In many respects, entry types are like categories, because you can use them to sort and search for journal items.

When you create a journal item manually, Outlook 2007 assumes that you're creating a phone call journal entry and automatically selects Phone Call as the entry type. However, you can select a different entry type in the Entry Type drop-down list. Figure 23-8 shows some of the available entry types.

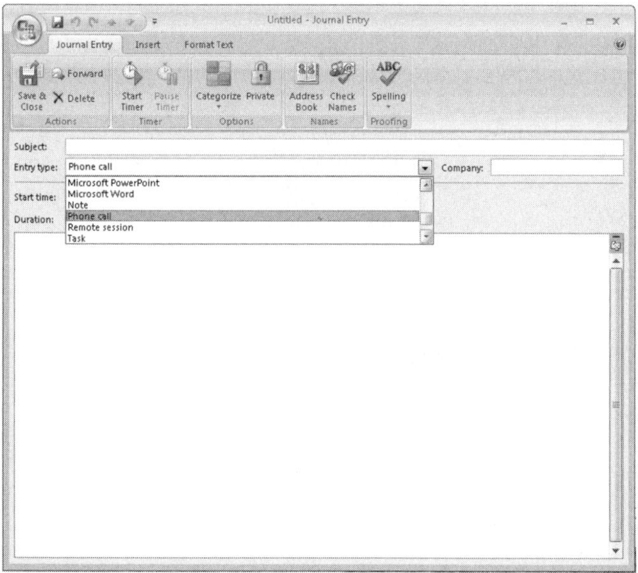

Figure 23-8. You can select entry types from a predefined list.

Unlike categories, which you can create on the fly, journal entry types are limited to those types found in the predefined list in Outlook 2007. Although the default entry types cover a lot of bases, they don't offer much flexibility. For example, you might want to use the journal to track your activity in an application that isn't included in the list, or you might need to keep track of trips to the doctor, school programs, or other events. Although you don't have the ability to add entry types directly when you create a journal entry, you can modify the registry to add journal entry types. You can use these user-defined entry types for journal items that you enter manually.

Here's how:

1. Open the Registry Editor by choosing Start, clicking in the Search box, typing **regedit**, and then pressing **Enter**. (In Microsoft Windows® XP, click Run, type **regedit** in the Open box, and then press **Enter**.)

2. Open the key HKEY_CURRENT_USER\Software\Microsoft\Shared Tools\Outlook\Journaling.
3. Right-click Journaling, and then choose New, Key.
4. Rename the key based on what the new entry type will be. For example, you might name the type **Volunteer Time**.
5. Right-click the key you just created, and then choose New, String Value. Rename the string value **Description**.
6. Double-click the Description value just created, and then set its value to the text you want to appear in the Entry Types drop-down list, such as **Volunteer time.**
7. Close the Registry Editor.

After you have edited the registry to add the new entry type, it appears on the journal entry form in the Entry Type drop-down list, as shown in Figure 23-9.

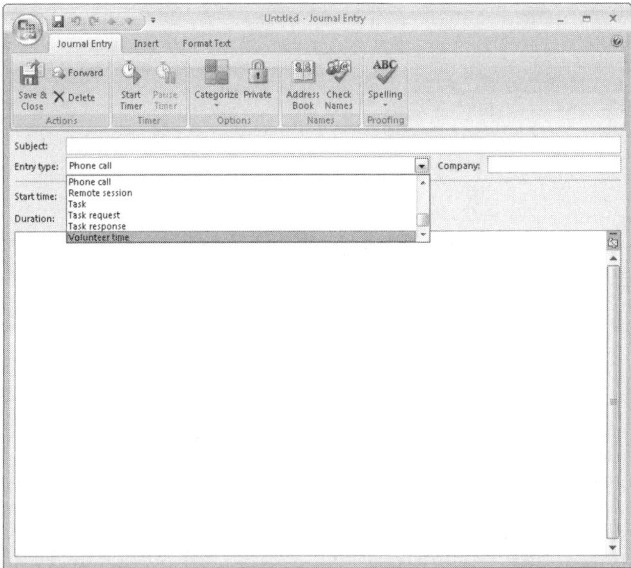

Figure 23-9. Your custom entry type appears in the drop-down list.

Changing Journal Entries

You can modify any details of a journal entry–for example, adding more notes to yourself, adding a contact's names or categories, or changing the duration of your activity. You can also move the entry to a different position on the journal timeline if you entered the wrong start date or time when you began recording the activity.

For information about timeline views in the Journal folder, see "Viewing the Journal" later in this chapter.

Modifying an Entry

Suppose that in the middle of your department budget meeting, you realize that you didn't stop the journal timer when you stopped working on a spreadsheet to come to the meeting. You know that you worked on the spreadsheet for about three hours, however, so you can change the journal entry to reflect your actual work time.

To change the duration or any other property of an existing journal entry, follow these steps:

1. Open the Journal folder, and double-click the entry to open it.
2. Select the information you want to change, and then enter the correct data. For example, to change an incorrect record of how long you spent on an activity, click in the Duration box, change the value, and press **Enter**.
3. Make other changes as needed in the journal entry form.
4. Click Save & Close.

Moving an Entry on the Timeline

Suppose that you belatedly created a journal entry for a phone call you made yesterday and inadvertently entered the wrong date. When you later notice that the journal entry is in the wrong spot on the timeline, you can move the entry to the correct date.

Follow these steps to do so:

1. Open the Journal folder, and double-click the entry to open it.
2. In the Start Time box, type or select a date.
3. Click Save & Close. Outlook 2007 then moves the entry to the correct spot on the timeline.

Deleting an Entry

Deleting a single entry from your journal timeline is easy: Either click the entry's icon to select it and then press **Delete**, or right-click the entry's icon and choose Delete on the shortcut menu.

What if you've been automatically recording your work in Excel 2007 workbooks but have also been experimenting with Excel 2007, creating several test workbooks that you don't want to save or track? Now you have numerous useless entries cluttering up your Journal folder. You can delete them one at a time, but it's faster to switch to a table view of your entries, sort them so that all the useless entries are in one group, and delete them all at once.

For information about the various views in the Journal folder, including table views and timeline views, see "Viewing the Journal" later in this chapter.

Follow these steps to delete a group of entries:

1. In the Navigation Pane, under Current View, select Entry List. The view switches to a table view of all your journal entries.
2. To sort the entries so that all the ones you want to delete appear together, click the Entry Type column header. To sort specific entries by subject within a group of entry types, hold down the **Shift** key while you click the Subject column header.

> **Note**
>
> You can sort by as many as four categories using this method of holding down the **Shift** key while you click column headers. Clicking the Contact or Categories header will group the journal items by that category and clear the other sort settings. Once the list is grouped, you can sort on multiple categories as described earlier.

3. To select and delete multiple journal entries, press **Shift** or **Ctrl** while you select the entries you want to delete, and then click the Delete button on the toolbar. (Alternatively, you can press the **Delete** key to delete selected entries or right-click any of the selected entries and choose Delete on the shortcut menu.)
4. When you finish deleting the journal entries that you don't want, you can select the view you were using previously on the Current View list in the Navigation Pane.

> **Note**
>
> It's easy to turn on Group By This Field inadvertently when working with the Entry List view but not quite so easy to turn it off. To turn off this option, choose View, Arrange By, and then deselect Show In Groups.

Connecting Journal Activities to Individual Contacts

If you work on a project with a colleague, you can associate your journal entries for the project with that colleague's contact entry. All the journal entries that are associated with the contact will appear when you select Activities view on the contact form.

Although you can see the contacts associated with a journal item in the list views (as shown earlier in Figure 23-4), the Contacts field is no longer displayed by default when the journal item is opened. You can add contacts by clicking Address Book in the Names group on the Journal Entry tab, but contacts cannot be deleted or viewed that way. To enable the Contacts field, choose Tools, Options, click the Contact Options button, select the Show Contact Linking On All Forms check box, and then click OK twice. The Contact field will then be visible in journal items when they are open.

For example, Figure 23-10 shows a journal entry for a Word 2007 letter to an associate. To connect a journal entry and document to a contact, click Contacts at the bottom of the journal entry form. In the resulting Select Contacts dialog box, click the names of the contacts with whom the journal entry should be associated, and then click OK. The selected names will appear in the Contacts box at the bottom of the journal entry form.

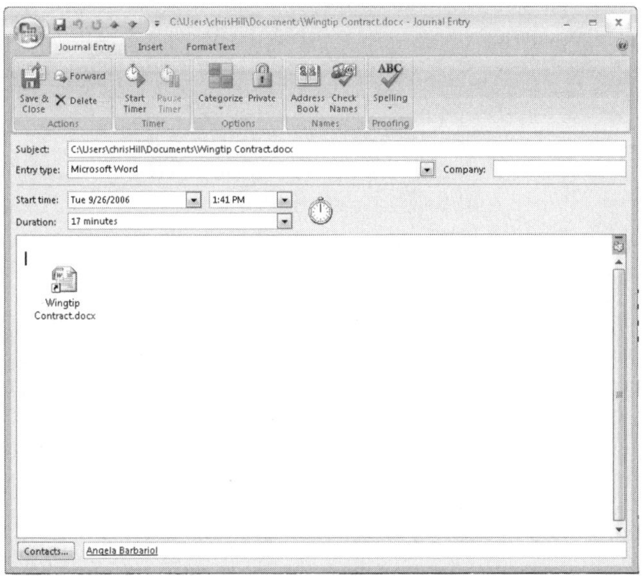

Figure 23-10. This journal entry shows a Word 2007 document associated with a contact.

So what does this do for you? When you open the contact entry for an associated contact and click Activities in the Show group on the Contact tab, as shown in Figure 23-11, you'll see a list of every Outlook 2007 item associated with that contact. You can open any of these items by double-clicking it. This is just one more way Outlook 2007 keeps all your information interconnected.

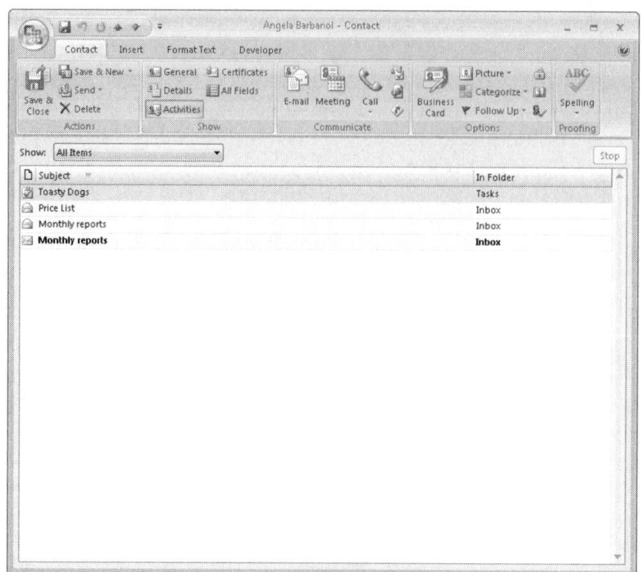

Figure 23-11. The Activities page shows all items associated with the selected contact.

Viewing the Journal

When you look at the Journal folder in a monthly timeline view, you get a good overall picture of your recorded activities, but you must point to an individual icon to identify the activity. (When you point to an icon, a subject label appears.) You can make a few changes to a journal timeline view—for example, you can choose to always display the subject labels for icons in a monthly view, or you can specify a more useful length for the labels. You can also show week numbers in the timeline heading, which is useful for planning in some industries.

Because the Outlook 2007 journal creates a record of your activities, the six standard views available in the Journal folder differ considerably from the views in other types of Outlook 2007 folders. The following sections introduce you to each of the Journal folder views.

> **Note**
>
> You can choose whether to view a timeline in a journal view in day, week, or month increments by clicking the Day, Week, or Month button on the toolbar. These buttons are available only in the journal views that show a timeline and are not available in list views.

Using By Type View

The default view for the Journal folder is By Type view, shown in Figure 23-12. In this view, the journal entries are arranged in a timeline and are categorized by the entry type. To select By Type view, choose Current View, By Type in the Navigation Pane.

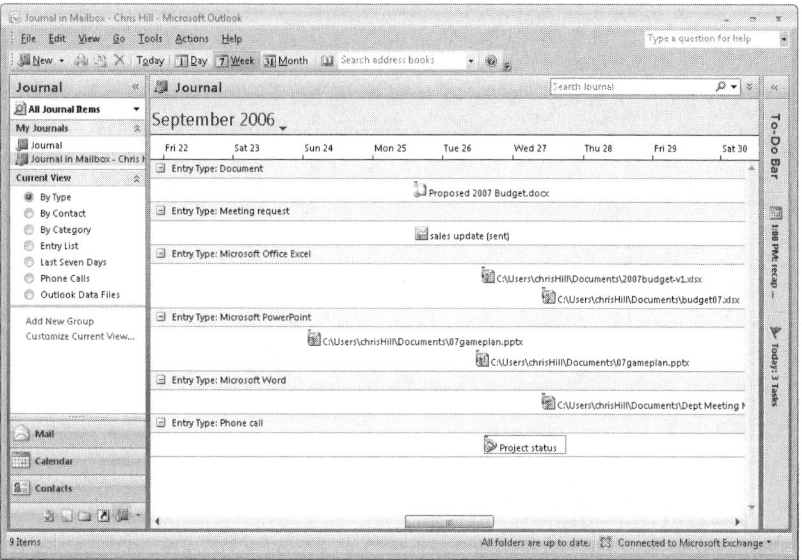

Figure 23-12. By Type view is the default Journal folder view.

Each entry type is indicated in a title bar. You can click the small box on the left in the title bar to expand or contract the type. A plus sign (+) in the box means that the type is collapsed, whereas a minus sign (–) indicates that the type is expanded. You might need to use the vertical scroll bar to see the complete list. When you expand a type, you can view any journal entries for that type in the area below the title bar.

> **Note**
>
> If you're surprised to find no entries when you expand a particular entry type, that's because Outlook 2007 displays the entries as a timeline. If no entries for the selected entry type were created recently, you might need to use the horizontal scroll bar to find the most recent entries.

By Type view is most useful if you want to find out which documents you worked on during a specific period. This view is not particularly useful for locating documents based on any other criteria. For example, you wouldn't want to use By Type view to locate all documents relating to a particular contact.

Using By Contact View

In By Contact view, shown in Figure 23-13, journal entries are also arranged in a timeline and are categorized by the contact associated with the entries.

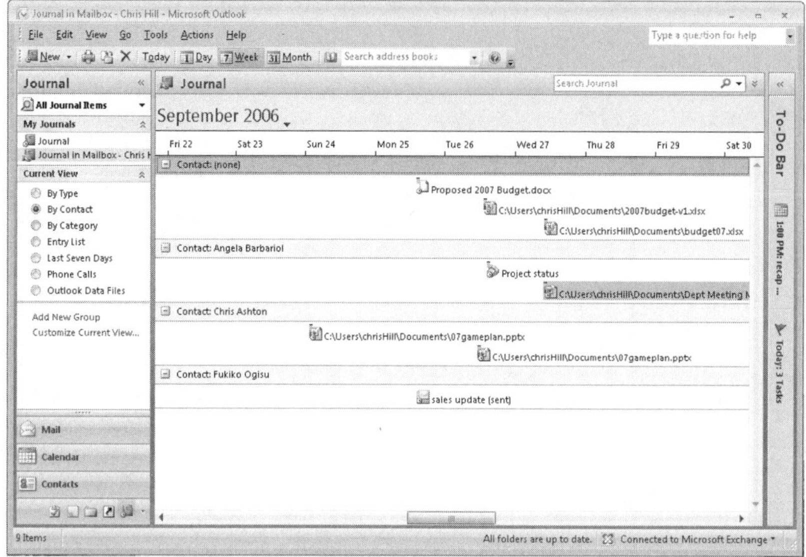

Figure 23-13. Use By Contact view to organize the journal by the contacts associated with each journal entry.

Each contact is indicated by a title bar that shows the contact's name. Click the small box to expand or collapse the contact. You might also need to use the horizontal scroll bar to view all items from a given contact.

By Contact view makes it easy to find all documents and other journal items related to a specific contact. Any type of document can appear in the list, as can phone calls and other items associated with specific contacts.

Using By Category View

In By Category view, shown in Figure 23-14, journal entries are also arranged in a timeline and are organized by the categories you've assigned to them.

> **Note**
>
> A journal item will appear in more than one location in the list if you assign multiple categories to it.

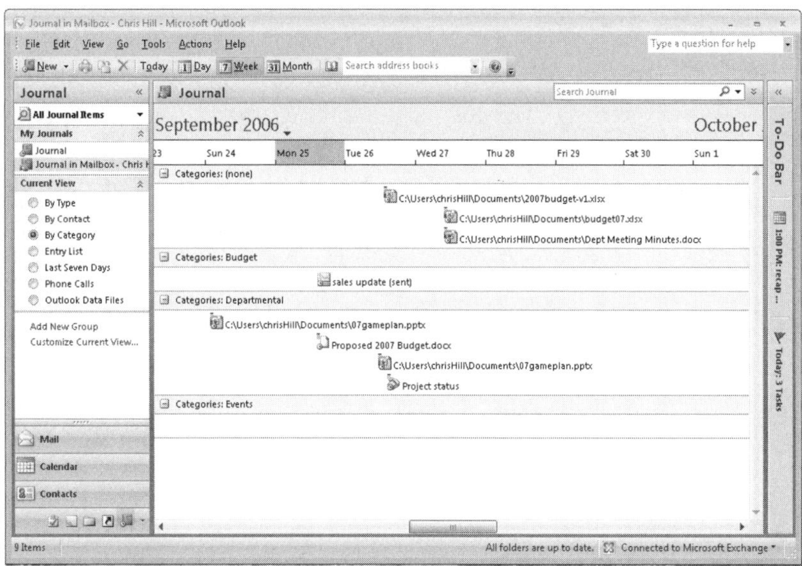

Figure 23-14. Use By Category view to organize the Journal folder based on the categories assigned to each journal item.

By Category view can be handy if you create categories that break down journal entries by project. This view can be almost useless, however, unless you take the time to assign categories when you create documents. Outlook 2007 doesn't assign any categories by default. You can assign categories using the standard list in Outlook 2007, or you can create your own categories.

For information about assigning categories and creating custom categories, see Chapter 5, "Creating and Using Categories."

INSIDE OUT **Assign categories to multiple entries**

You can access the Categories dialog box by right-clicking the journal entry and then choosing Categorize. To assign a category to multiple journal entries, select them all (by holding down the Shift or Ctrl key as you select), right-click the selection, and then choose Categorize.

Using Entry List View

Entry List view, shown in Figure 23-15, might be the most useful view of all. This view dispenses with the timeline and instead displays all journal entries in a table.

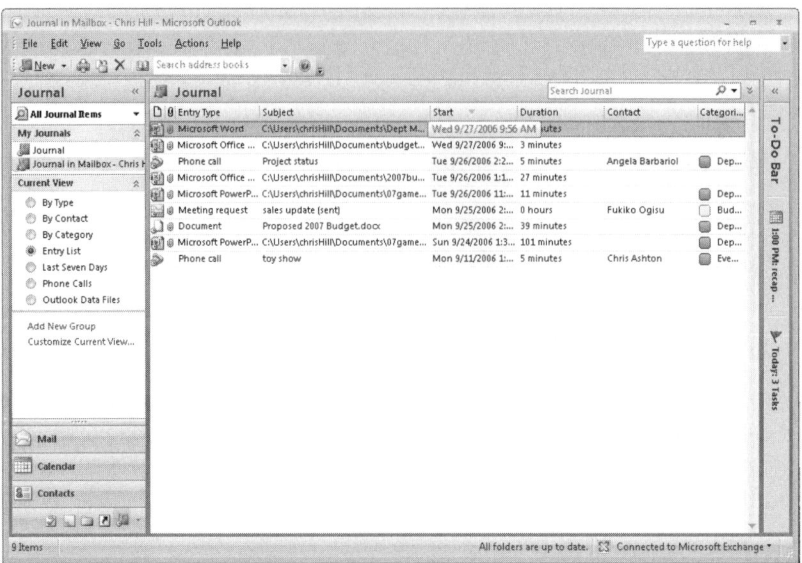

Figure 23-15. Entry List view displays journal entries in a table instead of on a timeline.

Because Entry List view does not use the timeline to display entries, it's much easier to view the list of entries—you don't have to use the horizontal scroll bar to locate the items. By default, this view is sorted in descending order based on the start date, but you can quickly sort the list using any of the column headers. Simply click a column header to sort the list; click the header a second time to reverse the sort order.

The paper clip icon in the second column of Entry List view indicates that an entry is a document. If this icon isn't displayed, the entry is a log of an activity that occurred within Outlook 2007, such as an e-mail message.

Using Last Seven Days View

Last Seven Days view resembles Entry List view. This view is useful when you need to locate items you've worked on recently—especially if you can't quite remember the file name, contact, or category.

When you look closely at Last Seven Days view, you might notice that something doesn't look quite right: the dates shown for the journal entries clearly span much more than a week. The explanation is that the dates shown are the start dates for the journal entries, not the dates when the items were last accessed. Outlook 2007 is displaying the journal entries that have been created, accessed, or modified within the past week. Each entry shown in this view was accessed in some way during the past week, although the original entries might have been created quite some time ago.

INSIDE OUT **Change the period of time shown in Last Seven Days view**

You can customize Last Seven Days view to specify a different time period, such as the past month. To do so, choose Customize Current View in the in the Navigation Pane, click Filter in the Customize View dialog box, and then select the new time condition and duration in the Time drop-down list.

Using Phone Calls View

Phone Calls view, shown in Figure 23-16, displays only journal items that are associated with phone calls. Tracking phone calls and viewing them in the Journal folder can be extremely helpful. You can, for example, monitor the time you spend on billable calls. Even if you don't bill for your time, you'll find that phone call journal entries make it easier to recall phone conversations.

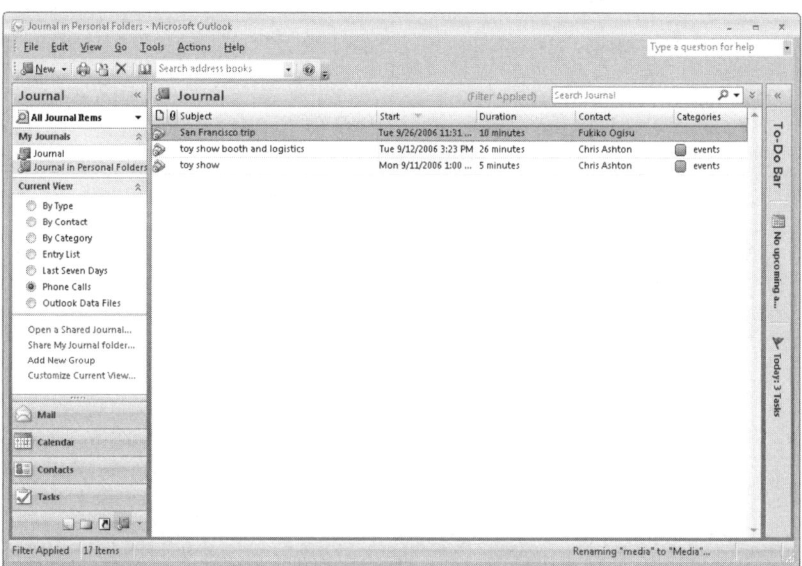

Figure 23-16. Use Phone Calls view to organize the Journal folder according to journal items associated with phone calls.

Outlook 2007 creates journal entries for phone calls automatically only if you use the AutoDialer to begin the call. If you create the journal entry at the time you place the phone call, you can use the Timer to track the time you spend on the phone. Otherwise, you must specify the duration yourself by entering the appropriate time on the phone call journal entry form. You can do so by selecting a time in the Duration drop-down list or by entering a time (in minutes).

Note

Remember to link your phone call journal entries to the appropriate contacts so that it will be easier to find all entries relating to specific contacts.

Customizing Journal Views

All the standard views in the Journal folder are customizable in a variety of ways. The changes you make to these views are persistent, however, so proceed with care. If you end up mangling a standard view beyond repair, it can be restored to its default by using the Reset button in the Define Views dialog box, which you can open by choosing Customize Current View in the Navigation Pane. (No such option exists for custom views.)

For information about creating custom views in Outlook 2007, see Chapter 27, "Creating Custom Views and Print Styles."

Displaying Item Labels on the Monthly Timeline

Displaying the subject line of each journal item in a timeline view gives you additional information about those items without requiring you to point to each item with your mouse to display the ScreenTip-style label.

To display item labels on a monthly timeline, follow these steps:

1. In a timeline view, right-click in an empty area of the Journal folder, and then choose Other Settings on the shortcut menu.
2. In the Format Timeline View dialog box, select the Show Label When Viewing By Month check box.

Note

By default, the label width is 80 characters, but if you find that your labels are too short or too long, return to this dialog box and change the number in the Maximum Label Width box. The label width applies to the labels in the day and week timeline as well as the month timeline. To also hide the display of week numbers, you can clear the Show Week Numbers check box.

3. Click OK to close the dialog box.

Showing Week Numbers

In some industries, it's important to know schedules based on weeks of the year. You can show week numbers in your timeline view by following these steps:

1. With the journal displayed in a timeline view, right-click in an empty area of the Journal folder, and then choose Other Settings on the shortcut menu.
2. In the Format Timeline View dialog box, select the Show Week Numbers check box.
3. Click OK to close the dialog box. In a monthly timeline, week numbers replace dates. In week and day views, both the week number and dates are displayed in the timeline header.

Printing Journal Items

The options available when you print from the Journal folder depend on whether a timeline view or a table (list) view is currently open. In a table view, you can open and print individual items, print the entire list, or print only selected rows. Printing the table is useful if you want a snapshot of the journal for a specific period of time. You can print list views using either Table Style or Memo Style print styles (explained shortly).

> **Note**
>
> You don't have to open an item to print it. Simply right-click the item, and then choose Print from the shortcut menu.

In a timeline view, you can print individual journal items or several items at a time (hold down the Ctrl key and click to select multiple items). You can print one or more items, each on an individual page, in Memo Style, and you can print attached files along with the journal entry details. To print the attached files, select the Print Attached Files check box in the Print dialog box.

For more information about printing views in Outlook 2007 and creating custom print styles, see Chapter 28, "Designing and Using Forms."

Table Style, shown in Figure 23-17, is available from any table view. It prints the selected view just as you see it in Outlook 2007: each item on a separate row, with the fields displayed as columns. Table Style has limited configuration options.

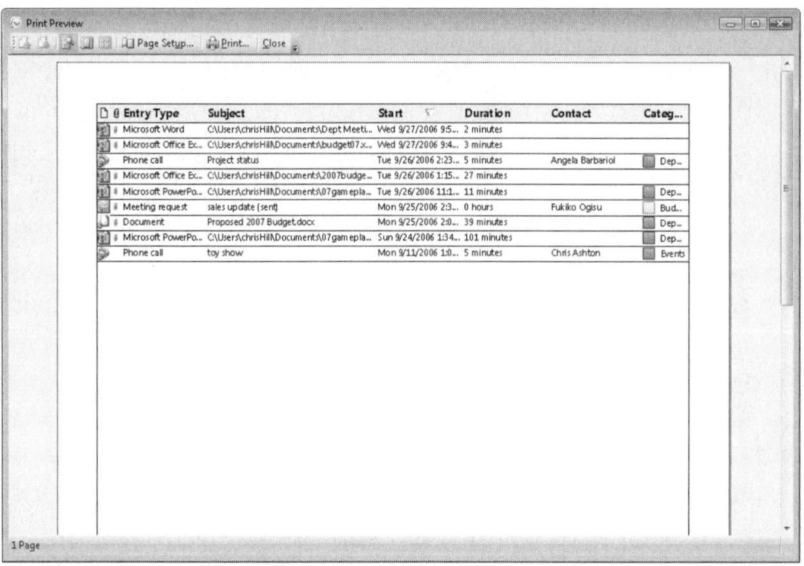

Figure 23-17. Table Style prints journal entries in a table.

Memo Style, shown in Figure 23-18, prints one item per page, with your name as the title and the details of the record following. Memo Style is a simple and quick one-item-at-a-time print style. You can specify the title and field fonts, paper options, and the contents and fonts used by the header and footer.

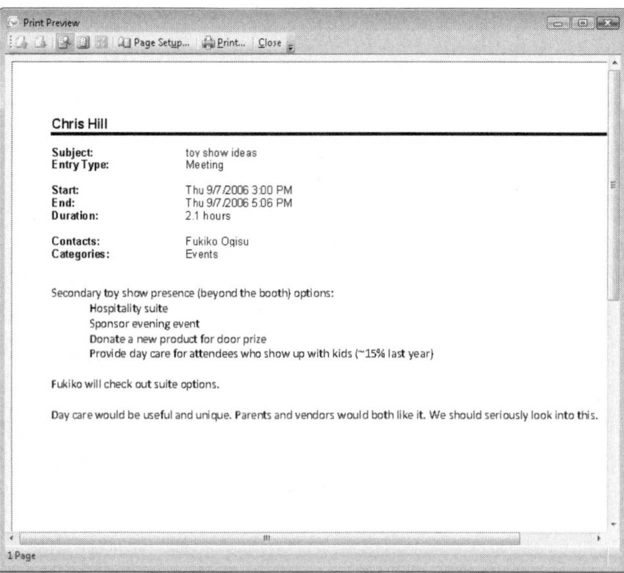

Figure 23-18. Memo Style prints a single journal item per page.

Printing from the Journal folder is not a particularly difficult task for anyone who has used and printed from any Windows-based application. However, you might be wondering how you can print just a selection of a table view. For example, you might need to print only the items that fall within a specific range or those associated with a particular contact.

Follow these steps to print a selection of a table view:

1. Open the table view.
2. Click columns as needed to sort the data to help you locate the items you want to print. For example, click the Start column header to locate items that fall within a certain time range, or click the Contact column header to locate items associated with a specific contact.
3. Select the first item in the range, hold down the **Shift** key, and then select the last item in the range.
4. Choose File, Print to open the Print dialog box.
5. Select Table Style in the Print Style area, and then select the Only Selected Rows option.
6. Set other print options as needed, and then click OK.

Sharing Journal Information

Because the Outlook 2007 journal keeps track of activities using a timeline, you might find that it is one of the most useful of the Outlook 2007 folders to share. If you're working on a project with several people, a shared Outlook 2007 Journal folder might be just what you need to make certain everyone is on track.

If you and all the people with whom you want to share the Journal folder use Microsoft Exchange Server, you can share the Journal folder as a public folder on the computer running Exchange Server.

Follow these steps to share a personal Journal folder:

1. In Outlook 2007, open the Folder List.
2. Right-click the Journal folder, and then choose Change Sharing Permissions to open the Permissions tab of the Journal Properties dialog box, as shown in Figure 23-19.

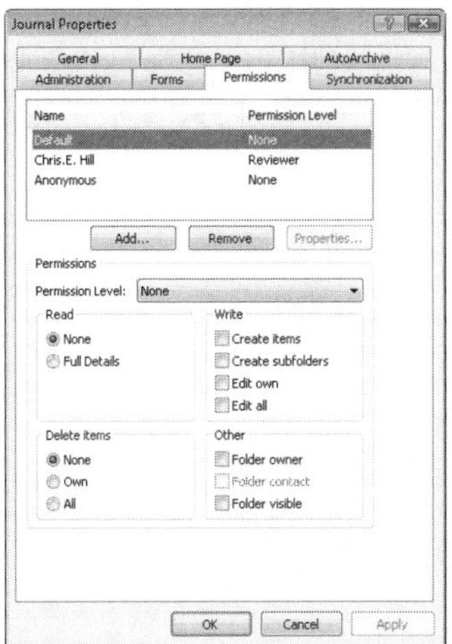

Figure 23-19. Share a Journal folder by using the Permissions tab in the Journal Properties dialog box.

3. Click Default, and then select options in the Permissions area to specify the types of tasks all users can perform if they have no explicit permissions set.
4. Click Add to open the Add Users dialog box, select a user (or more than one), click Add, and then click OK to return to the Permissions tab.
5. With the user selected in the Name list, select permissions in the Permissions area to specify the tasks that the user can perform. You can select a Permission Level and then customize the permissions as needed.
6. Click OK to apply the permissions.

For details about sharing folders, see "Granting Access to Folders" in Chapter 35.

If you want to invite specific people to share your journal, you can send them an e-mail message to let them know that you have granted them permission to view your journal. You can also request to share their journals as part of this message. The permissions that you set control the types of access that will be allowed. The recipients of the message can accept or decline the invitation to share your journal and also decide whether to share their journals with you.

To invite someone to share your journal, follow these steps:

1. In Outlook 2007, open the Folder List.
2. Right-click the Journal folder, and then choose Share "Journal" to create a Sharing Invitation e-mail message.
3. Select the recipients, and then click Send to send the message.

4. If the recipients share their journals with you, there will be an Open This Journal option on the Sharing tab of the Ribbon. When you view another person's journal, a new group named People's Journals is created in the Navigation Pane, and a link to the other journal is added to it.

Using the Journal Effectively

The journal can be a useful tool, helping you track how you spend your time over the course of the workday. This information, collected over time, can be used for a range of things such as reporting, billing, and staffing allocation. You can analyze your work activities to get a clearer picture of which projects and activities occupy your time and then use that data to optimize your time and productivity.

Make Using the Journal a Habit

The more information a journal item contains, the more useful it is. Get in the habit of entering critical information when you create a journal item, especially contacts, categories, and the contents of other fields used for organization and retrieval of journal items. It takes only a minute to make notes or update the time spent on an activity while it's fresh in your mind, and by providing as much information as possible, you ensure that you have all of the information you might need.

By regularly using the journal, you will also become more familiar with how it operates and what sort of data it is recording. Although the journal can accumulate a lot of information, both automatically and manually, it's unlikely that it will store exactly what you want right after you start using it. Taking a few minutes on a regular basis to fine-tune your journal settings will pay off when it comes time to analyze the accumulated data. If you find yourself deleting a specific sort of entry more often than not, stop automatically recording it.

Use the Journal's Automatic Recording Features

The journal offers automatic recording of certain Outlook 2007 activities and time spent editing Microsoft Office system documents. Enabling automatic tracking of those items provides you with quite a bit of data with no additional effort. These options should be used judiciously, however, to ensure against collecting so much information that it becomes difficult to find the important items among the unneeded ones.

INSIDE OUT **Set up automatic journaling for a new contact**

When you create a new contact entry in your Outlook 2007 Contacts folder, click All Fields on the Contact tab. In the Select From drop-down list, select Frequently Used Fields, and then set the Journal field to Yes. This is the same as selecting the contact in the Journal Options dialog box; the journal will then record the types of activities that you selected.

Use the Journal Only for Those Things You Need to Track

It might be tempting to turn on all of the automatic recording options for the journal so that you collect the maximum possible amount of information. Although you can do this, you might discover that doing so introduces a lot of unnecessary journal items. Outlook 2007 automatically records e-mail messages, journal items, notes, and upcoming tasks and appointments for each entry in the Contacts folder, so in general you don't need to record these items in the journal. You can view these items by opening the Contacts folder and selecting Activities in the Show group.

> **Note**
>
> If you want to export a file containing records of items like e-mail messages and notes to work with in an Excel 2007 workbook or an Access 2007 database, you must track these items using the journal. Although these activities can be viewed on the Activities page for a contact, you cannot export information to a file from there.

Similarly, you might want to be careful about automatically recording all work that you do in a certain type of document. If most of your work in Excel 2007 is on projects that you want to track with the journal, turning on automatic recording for Excel 2007 files is a good idea; you can delete the occasional unneeded journal item. If, on the other hand, most of your time in Word 2007 is spent on projects or tasks that don't need to be tracked, you should manually create journal items for those few Word 2007 documents that actually need them.

Add Addresses to Your Primary Contacts Folder

The automatic recording feature of the journal works only with the contents of your primary Contacts folder, not with the Exchange Server Global Address List (GAL) or any secondary Contacts folders. If you want to automatically record journal items associated with people whose e-mail addresses are in a secondary Contacts folder or provided by the GAL, you must first add them to your primary Contacts folder.

To copy or move contacts between folders, open the Outlook 2007 Contacts folder, and then select the source folder in the My Contacts list in the Navigation Pane. Right-click an entry and drag it to the destination Contacts folder (by default, the primary Contacts folder is the top one in the list), and then select Move or Copy.

Create Custom Entry Types to Meet Your Individual Needs

Although there are a number of entry types in the default journal configuration, there are likely to be additional entry types that you would find useful. You might want the ability to track things such as travel time or research as discrete entry types to make billing for those activities easier and more accurate. You should add custom entry types so that your journal reflects how you spend your time in greater detail. See "Creating and Using Custom Entry Types" earlier in this chapter for detailed information about creating additional entry types.

Time Management Using the Journal

Once you have started to use the journal to track your activities, you can analyze your current time usage to find ways to increase your productivity. You are likely to discover some unexpected time leaks—things that consume an inordinate amount of your time. Identifying these time leaks is the first step in correcting them and getting better control over your work time.

By examining journal items in a variety of views, you can assess how much time a given project, client, and activity is currently taking. If you need more extensive analysis and reporting functionality, journal information can be exported to a file for use with external programs.

Using Views to Analyze Time Usage

Choosing the right view for the job will make it easier for you to understand and use the information collected by the journal. There are a number of predefined views available, allowing you to choose the view that makes it easiest to review a particular set of items.

The journal provides two types of views by default:

- **Timeline views** Journal items are displayed on a timeline, which can be set to show a single day, a week, or a month at a time, with items grouped by Entry Type, Contact, or Category. Timeline views are particularly good for looking at the specific tasks that occupied a given period of time and can be used to assess time usage and predict time allocation needs.
- **List views** These views display journal items in a simple tabular format, making them useful for reviewing a large amount of data quickly. Entry List view displays all journal items, Last Seven Days view limits the display to the past week, and Phone Calls view shows only that type of entry.

Using Custom Views of the Journal

Although the existing journal views provide a number of ways to look at your journal, you will probably want your own customized views of the information. To create a custom view, on the View menu, choose Current View, Define Views. In the Custom View Organizer dialog box, select New. Give the view a name, specify where the view can be used and to whom it will be visible, and then click OK. In the Customize View dialog box, configure the available options for your custom view, and then click OK.

For detailed information about creating custom views in Outlook 2007, see Chapter 27, "Creating Custom Views and Print Styles."

Exporting Journal Items to Other Programs

You might want to analyze the information contained in the journal using a database or a spreadsheet application, each of which offers certain capabilities not available in Outlook 2007. If you need to perform mathematical calculations on your journal data, for example, you can export the information to Excel 2007. For database style analysis and reporting, you can create an Access 2007 database from journal information.

To export your journal, follow these steps:

1. In Outlook 2007, on the File menu, choose Import And Export to open the Import And Export Wizard.
2. In the Choose An Action To Perform list, select Export To A File, and then click Next.
3. In the Create A File Of Type list, select the Microsoft Office Access or Microsoft Office Excel file format, and then click Next.
4. In the Select A Folder To Export From list, select the Journal folder, and then click Next.
5. Enter a name for the exported file, and then click Next.

At this point, you can either click Finish to create the exported file or select Map Custom Fields if you want to customize the field mappings for the exported data. If you select Map Custom Fields, the Map Custom Fields dialog box will open, as shown in Figure 23-20, allowing you to drag a value from Outlook 2007 to a field in the exported document. To change the name of a mapped field, click the Field name in the To box and type the new name. After you have completed mapping the fields, you can click the Next button and review individual journal entries to verify that the mapping is correct. When you are satisfied with the field mappings, click OK to return to the Export To A File dialog box, and then click Finish to create the file.

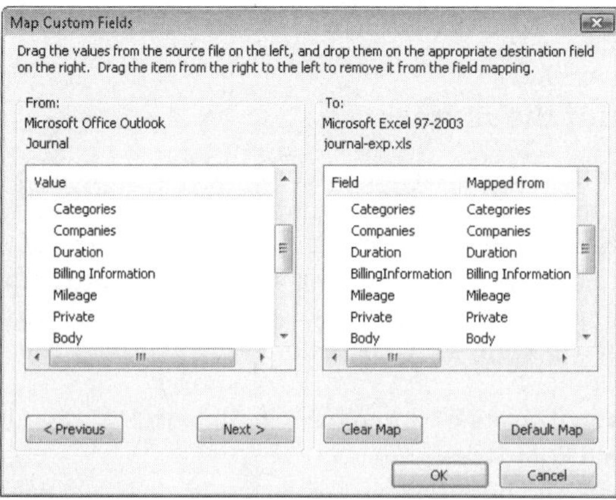

Figure 23-20. Connect journal fields to fields in the exported file in the Map Custom Fields dialog box.

CHAPTER 24

Making Notes

If you're like most people, there's at least one note stuck to your monitor, lying on your desk, or tucked in a drawer, keeping some critical piece of information relatively safe until you need it again—safe, that is, until you lose the note. If you're looking for a better way to keep track of all the small bits of information you receive every day, you can use Microsoft® Office Outlook® 2007 to create electronic notes for quick to-do lists, phone numbers, shopping lists—you name it. Notes reside in the Notes folder by default, but you can copy or move notes to other Office Outlook 2007 folders, use them in documents, place them on the desktop, or place them in your other file system folders. This chapter examines notes and explores how to use them effectively in Outlook 2007 as well as how to integrate them in your other applications.

Understanding Outlook Notes

You can use Outlook 2007 notes to keep track of any kind of text-based information. For example, you might make a note as a reminder to call someone, to pick up a few things from the store on the way home, or to jot down a phone number. Outlook 2007 notes are really just simple text files, which you can create and view in the Outlook 2007 Notes folder, as shown in Figure 24-1.

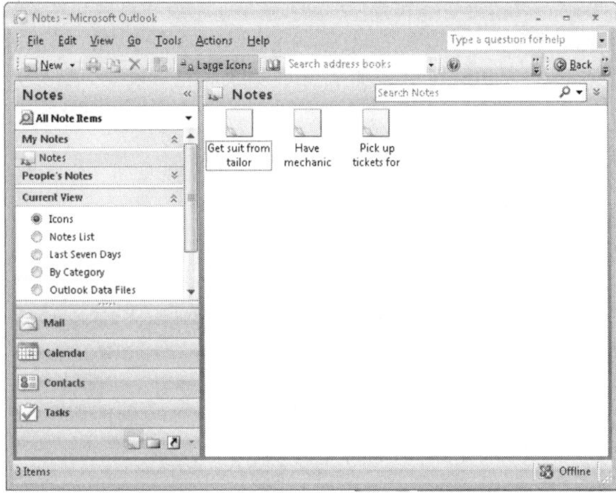

Figure 24-1. You can create and view your notes in the Notes folder.

When you create a new note, Outlook 2007 opens a window similar to the one shown in Figure 24-2. The Note window is essentially a text box. As you type, the text wraps, and the window scrolls to accommodate the text. At the bottom of the Note window, Outlook 2007 displays the date and time you created the note.

Figure 24-2. To create a new note, type in a Note window.

You don't have to save the note explicitly—just close the Note window, and Outlook 2007 adds the note you've created to the Notes folder. You can copy or move a note to another Outlook 2007 folder or to a file system folder (such as your desktop), copy the text to the Clipboard for inclusion in another document, or save the note to a text file. The following sections explain not only how to perform these actions, but also how to use notes in other ways.

INSIDE OUT Choose the best feature for the job

Although you can use notes in Outlook 2007 to keep track of just about any kind of information, a note is not always the best approach. Be sure you're not using the note in place of a more effective Outlook 2007 feature. For example, if you need to remind yourself to make a casual phone call at some time during the day, a note might suffice. However, if you need to set up an important conference call, it's better to create an appointment or a task and have Outlook 2007 provide a reminder at the appropriate time. Likewise, the Contacts folder is the best place to keep track of contact information rather than recording it on scattered notes. Notes are great when you need speed and convenience, but when another Outlook 2007 feature is suitable, you should view a note as a stopgap. For example, you might create a note for a quick to-do list now and then add each item as a task in your Tasks folder later when you have the time. As you become more familiar with notes, take a look at how you use them to make sure you're working effectively.

Configuring Note Options

Before you start creating notes, you might want to take a few minutes to configure the options that control the default appearance of notes.

To set these options, follow these steps:

1. Start Outlook 2007, and choose Tools, Options.
2. On the Preferences tab, under Contacts And Notes, click Note Options to display the Notes Options dialog box, shown in Figure 24-3.

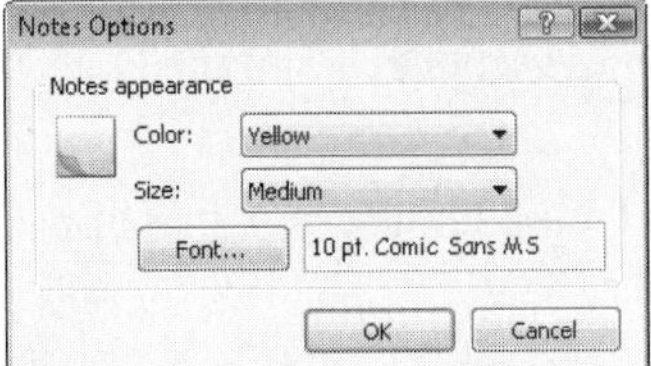

Figure 24-3. Use the Notes Options dialog box to control the size and color of the Note window and the font used for notes.

3. Set the various options in this dialog box to configure the default color for notes (the color of the Note window), the default size of the window, and the font used for the note text, and then click OK.

You can change the window size of any individual note by dragging the border of the Note window. You also can change the color of an existing note at any time (as explained in the following section).

> **Note**
>
> Because Outlook 2007 stores the date and time created for each note, you should check to make sure that your system time is accurate before creating a note.

Working with Notes

Of all the Outlook 2007 features, notes are by far the easiest to use. The following sections explain how to create notes, change their color, copy them to other folders, and more.

Adding a Note

You create notes in the Notes folder. To open this folder, click the Notes icon at the bottom of the Navigation Pane.

After you've opened the folder, follow these steps to create a note:

1. Right-click in the Notes folder and choose New Note on the shortcut menu, or simply double-click in the folder window. Either action opens a blank Note window.
2. Type your note directly in the window.
3. Click the Close button in the upper-right corner of the Note window to close and save the note.

If the current view is set to Icons, Outlook 2007 uses the first approximately 26 characters in the note as the title and displays the title under the icon for the note in the Notes folder.

Reading and Editing a Note

To read a note, you can double-click it to open the Note window or point to or click the icon for the note and read the text under the icon. Switching to Notes List view (on the View menu, choose Current View, Notes List) shows more contiguous content. To change the content of a note, open it as just described, and then edit it the same way you would edit a text file. Keep in mind, however, that you have no formatting options, so your notes are limited to plain text. To save your changes, simply close the Note window.

After you have opened a note, a note icon appears in the upper-left corner of the Note window, which provides a menu of editing options, as follows:

- **New Note** Creates a new note.
- **Save As** Saves the current note as a new note.
- **Delete** Deletes the current note (without confirmation).
- **Forward** Forwards the note as an attachment to a new e-mail message.
- **Cut** Cuts the selected text in the current note.
- **Copy** Copies the selected text in the current note.
- **Paste** Pastes the cut or copied text in the current note.
- **Categorize** Enables you to assign categories to the note.
- **Contacts** Lets you assign a contact to the note.
- **Print** Prints the note to the selected printer.
- **Close** Closes the Note window.

Forwarding a Note

Although you'll probably create notes mainly for your own use, you might need to forward a note to someone. For example, a colleague might request a phone number or other contact information that you've stored in a note. The easiest way to share the information is to forward the note as an e-mail message. Because Outlook 2007 sends the note as an attachment, the recipient can easily copy the note to his or her own Notes folder, place it on the desktop, or use the Clipboard to copy the data to a new contact entry.

To forward a note, follow these steps:

1. Open the Notes folder, right-click the note, and choose Forward on the shortcut menu. Outlook 2007 opens a standard message form. If you are using Outlook 2007 as your e-mail editor, the note is shown as an attachment to the message, as shown in Figure 24-4. If you are sending a note in a Rich Text message, Outlook 2007 embeds the note as an icon in the body of the message.

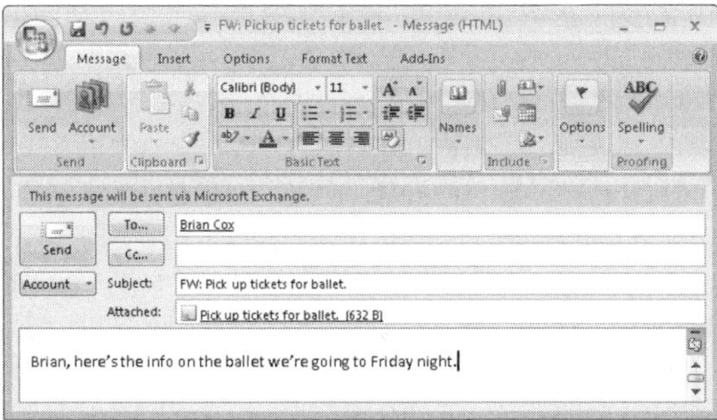

Figure 24-4. When you forward a note, Outlook 2007 attaches it to the message.

2. Complete and send the message as you would any other message.

You can send notes in e-mail messages using other methods too—you're not limited to embedding the note in the message or attaching it. For example, if you first click in the Folder List at the bottom of the Navigation Pane, you can open the Notes folder and then use the right mouse button to drag the selected note to the Inbox. The resulting shortcut menu allows you to create a message with the note as text in the body of the message, as a shortcut, or as an attachment.

Adding a Note Sent to You

When someone else sends you a note in an e-mail message, you can work with the note directly in the message. The note appears as an attachment to the message, as shown in Figure 24-5. You can open the message and double-click the note to open it in a Note window, but you'll probably prefer to copy the note to your own Notes folder.

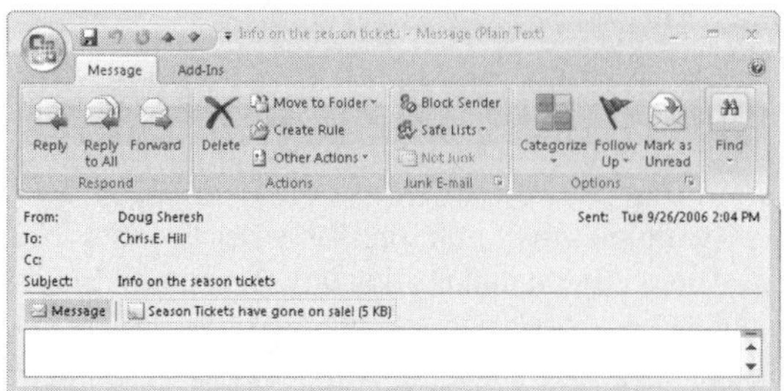

Figure 24-5. When a note is embedded in an e-mail message, you can open the note by double-clicking it.

To copy a note you've received to your Notes folder, follow these steps:

1. Open the Navigation Pane (if it is not already open), click the Folder List icon, and then scroll down so that the Notes folder is visible.
2. Open your Inbox, locate the note, and drag it to the Notes folder in the Navigation Pane. If the Reading Pane in the Inbox is open, you can drag the note from there; otherwise, open the message and drag the note.

Using a Note to Create a Task or an Appointment

If you've made a note about a task you must perform or an appointment you must keep, you can easily create an Outlook 2007 task or appointment directly from the note. To do so, drag the note to the Tasks icon or the Calendar icon in the Navigation Pane, as appropriate. Alternatively, you can click the Folder List icon in the Navigation Pane and then select the note and drag it to the Tasks folder or Calendar folder. Outlook 2007 opens a new task form or a new appointment form with the note contents as the subject and contents of the task or appointment.

Moving and Copying Notes

You can move and copy notes to other folders. How Outlook 2007 treats the note depends on the destination folder itself. For example, if you copy a note to another notes folder, Outlook 2007 treats it as a note. But if you copy a note to the Calendar or Tasks folder, Outlook 2007 uses the note to create a new appointment or a new task.

If you use the right mouse button to drag a note to the Contacts icon (or Contacts folder, if the Folder List is open) in the Navigation Pane, Outlook 2007 creates a new contact and gives you several options for how to handle the note text. Outlook 2007 can add the text to the contact, add it as an attachment, or add it as a shortcut, depending on your selection. You can also copy the note as a journal entry by using the right mouse button to drag it to the Journal icon in the Navigation Pane. You can then choose to create the journal item with the note as an attachment or as a shortcut.

Note

Copying a note within the Notes folder is easy. Just use the right mouse button to drag the note to a new location in the folder, release the mouse button, and choose Copy.

You can move or copy notes by dragging. To move a note to another Notes folder, drag the icon for the note to the destination folder. To copy a note instead of moving it, hold down the **Ctrl** key while dragging the note.

Note

Dragging a note to a non-notes folder always copies the note rather than moving it—the original note remains in the Notes folder.

Copying a Note to the Clipboard

If you want to use the text of a note in another application or another Outlook 2007 folder, you can copy the note text to the Clipboard. For example, you might copy a phone number from a note to a contact entry in the Contacts folder. To copy information from inside a note, open the note, select the desired text, and then press **Ctrl+C**. To copy the entire contents of a note from an e-mail attachment to the Clipboard, right-click the note, and then choose Copy. If you're working with the note in the Notes folder, you can select the note and then choose Edit, Copy or press **Ctrl+C**. Start the application or open the form in which you want to use the note text, and then choose Edit, Paste or press **Ctrl+V** to paste the data from the Clipboard. By default, this process will copy the text of the note down to the end of the first paragraph (the first place you pressed **Enter** in the note). To copy the entire contents of a note, open the note and select all the text (or right-click and choose Select All), and then right-click and select Copy.

Note

If you copy a note from an e-mail message and then paste the note into another message, Outlook 2007 copies the note as an embedded OLE object rather than as text.

Copying a Note to the Desktop or Another Folder

In addition to moving and copying notes inside Outlook 2007, you also can move or copy notes to your desktop or to another file system folder. Outlook 2007 creates an .msg file (an Outlook 2007 message file) to contain the note when you copy or move it outside Outlook 2007. After you have copied or moved the note, you can double-click the file to open it.

To copy a note to the desktop or a file system folder, you need only drag it from the Notes folder to the desired destination. To move the note instead of copying it, hold down the **Shift** key while dragging.

> Note
>
> You can also move or copy a note from the desktop or a file system folder to your Notes folder. Just drag the note from its current location to the Notes folder.

Changing Note Color

By default, Outlook 2007 notes are yellow; however, you can change the default color in the Notes Options dialog box. To change the default color of Notes, choose Tools, Options, click on Note Options, and then select one of the five available colors (blue, green, pink, yellow, or white) in the Color drop-down list as your default.

You can change the color of an individual note at any time by changing its category and thus the color it is associated with (see the next section).

For information about the Notes Options dialog box, see "Configuring Note Options" earlier in this chapter.

Assigning Color Categories to Notes

You can assign categories to notes, just as you can to any other Outlook 2007 item. Categorizing helps you organize your notes, particularly if you choose to view your Notes folder by category. By default, notes are not assigned to any category. (When displayed by category, unless otherwise assigned to a specific category, the notes show up under None.) You can assign multiple categories to each note. For example, you might assign a project category to a note as well as an Urgent category.

You assign colors to notes in Outlook 2007 by selecting a category and thus the color associated with it. You can have a category with no color association and assign that category to a note, but this will effectively color the note white. You can have up to 25 colors associated with categories, and you can have more than one category using the same color; thus, there is a bit of flexibility in color and category assignment. You might, for example, decide to color all of your marketing communications green and so set up a general Marketing category, a Sales Calls category, and a New Client Meetings category all associated with the color green. In this way, you provide yourself with the visual cue (the color green) that the notes (appointments, meetings, e-mail messages, and so on) colored green are related to marketing efforts, and yet you can still differentiate the nature of the item (general marketing, sales call, new client meeting, and so on) when you sort them by category.

For information about By Category view, see "Viewing Notes" later in this chapter.

To assign categories to a note, follow these steps:

1. Right-click the note and choose Categorize, or select the note and choose Edit, Categorize.
2. On the Categorize menu, shown in Figure 24-6, choose the applicable category.

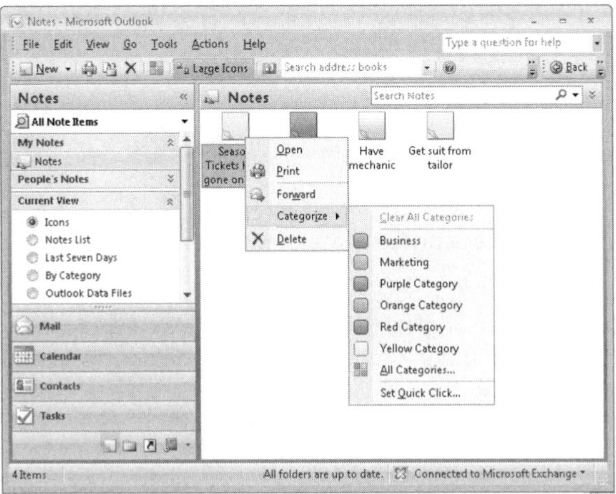

Figure 24-6. Use the Categorize menu to assign categories to notes.

3. If you don't see the categories you need, or if you want to select multiple categories for the note, click All Categories to display the Color Categories dialog box, click New to create the required category and to associate a color, and then click OK.
4. Click OK in the Color Categories dialog box to close the dialog box and assign the selected categories.

You can view the categories assigned to notes by using any one of several methods. For example, you can choose View, Current View, By Category (or Notes List or Outlook Data Files) to view the Notes folder organized by category. You can choose File, Print Preview to view all notes with category information. To show one note and the categories assigned to it, you can select a note and then choose File, Print Preview—the printout contains the note's categories.

For detailed information about working with categories, see Chapter 5, "Creating and Using Categories."

Printing a Note

To print a note, select the note, and then choose File, Print. Alternatively, you can right-click the note and choose Print on the note's shortcut menu. Outlook 2007 prints your name at the top of the page, followed by the date the note was created or last modified, the categories assigned to the note (if any), and the body of the note text. You also can choose File, Print Preview to preview the note.

Date and Time Stamping Notes

Outlook 2007 stamps each note with the date and time you created it and displays this information at the bottom of the Note window. This date and time remain until you modify the note by adding or removing text. Outlook 2007 then replaces the original date and time with the date and time you modified the text and stores this information with the note.

INSIDE OUT **Change a note's time stamp**

Simply opening and reading a note does not change its time stamp. If you need to modify the note but retain the original time stamp, create a copy of the note and modify the copy. Drag the note to another location in the Notes folder to create the copy.

Deleting a Note

If you no longer need a note, you can delete it. Deleting a note moves it to the Deleted Items folder. What happens to it from there depends on how you have configured Outlook 2007 to process deleted items. If Outlook 2007 clears out the Deleted Items folder each time you exit the program, for example, the note is permanently deleted at that time. You can delete a note in any of the following ways:

- Right-click the note, and then choose Delete.
- Select the note, and then press the Delete key.
- Select the note, and then choose Edit, Delete.
- Drag the note to the Deleted Items folder in the Navigation Pane.

Viewing Notes

Outlook 2007 provides five predefined views for the Notes folder. To switch to a different view, choose View, Current View. You can use any of the following predefined views:

Icons This default view displays an icon for each note with the first line (25 characters) of the note text serving as the icon's description.

Notes List This view displays the notes as a line-by-line list showing the entire contents of the note (with AutoPreview on).

Last Seven Days This view is similar to Notes List view and displays the entire contents of the notes (with AutoPreview on), but only those notes created or modified within the past seven days, based on the current date.

By Category This view groups the notes as a list by their assigned categories and displays the first line of text in each note. If more than one category is assigned to a single note, the note appears in each category group.

Outlook Data Files This view groups the notes as a list by their associated Outlook 2007 data file and displays the entire contents of the note (with AutoPreview on).

You can use the Reading Pane with the Notes folder (choose View, Reading Pane, and then choose Right or Bottom) to display the text of a note when you click the note. When you use Notes List view, Last Seven Days view, By Category view, or Outlook Data Files view in the Notes folder, you can also use AutoPreview, which automatically displays the contents of each note in the list. AutoPreview can be turned on or off by right-clicking in the Notes folder and selecting or clearing the AutoPreview option. In addition, AutoPreview options as well as font type, size, and color can be set in the Other Settings dialog box (right-click in the Notes folder and then choose Other Settings).

You can customize any of the views in the Notes folder the same way you customize the standard views in other folders. You can, for example, drag columns to rearrange them, resize columns, change column names and other properties, add other fields, and group notes based on various criteria.

For details about creating your own custom views, see Chapter 27, "Creating Custom Views and Print Styles."

Creating New Notes Folders

You can easily create a new folder for notes in Outlook 2007 in a couple of ways. If you click the Folder List icon at the bottom of the Navigation Pane, you can then right-click the Notes folder and choose New Folder. When you provide a name for the new folder, it is added below the current Notes folder. Alternatively, you can select the Notes folder, choose File, New, and then choose New Folder. After you name the new folder and click OK, the new folder is saved as a subfolder of the Notes folder.

PART 5

Customizing Outlook

CHAPTER 25
Using Templates

If you use Microsoft® Office Word frequently, you're probably familiar with templates. These useful tools can help you quickly and easily create documents that share standard elements—for example, boilerplate text, special font and paragraph formatting, and paragraph styles.

You can also use templates in Microsoft Office Outlook® 2007 to streamline a variety of tasks. There is nothing magical about these templates; they are simply Office Outlook 2007 items that you use to create other Outlook 2007 items. For example, you might create an e-mail template for preparing a weekly status report that you send to your staff or management. Perhaps you use e-mail messages to submit expense reports and would like to use a template to simplify the process.

This chapter not only discusses e-mail templates but also explores the use of templates for other Outlook 2007 items. For example, you'll learn how to use templates to create appointments, contact entries, task requests, and journal entries. The chapter also suggests some ways of sharing templates with others.

Working with E-Mail Templates

An e-mail template is really nothing more than a standard e-mail message that you have saved as a template. Here are some suggested uses for e-mail templates:

- Create an expense report form.
- Send product information to potential clients.
- Create status reports for ongoing projects.
- Send messages to specific groups of recipients.
- Create a form for information requests or product registration.

When you need to send similar messages frequently, creating a message template can save you quite a bit of time, particularly if the message contains a great deal of frequently used text, graphics, or form elements. You also reduce potential errors by reusing the same message each time rather than creating multiple messages from scratch. You can use the template to provide the bulk of the message, filling in any additional information required in each particular instance.

Creating an E-Mail Template

Creating an e-mail template is as easy as creating an e-mail message. You can start by opening a new message form, just as you would if you were sending a new message to a single recipient or group.

To create an e-mail template from scratch, follow these steps:

1. With the Inbox folder open, click the New button on the toolbar to open a new mail message form. Enter the boilerplate text and any information that you want to include every time you send a message based on this template. For example, you can specify the subject, address, other headings, bullets, lists, and tables.

2. Click the Microsoft Office Button, and then click Save As in the message form.

3. In the Save As dialog box, shown in Figure 25-1, specify a name for the file. Select Outlook Template in the Save As Type drop-down list. Outlook 2007 adds an .oft file name extension to the file name. You can specify a path if you want to save the file in a different location.

   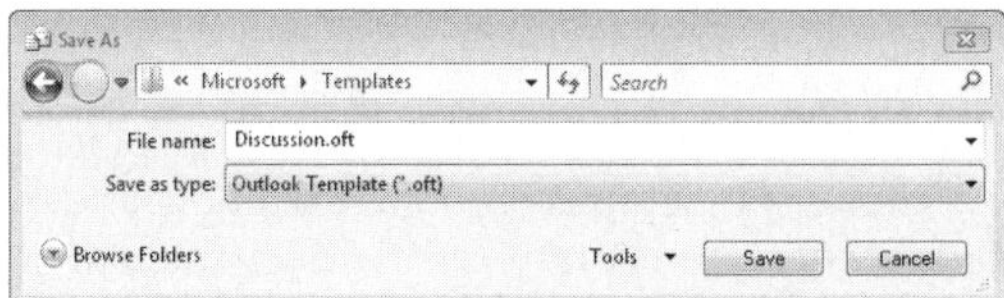

   Figure 25-1. Save your newly created template as an .oft file.

   Outlook 2007 opens your My Documents folder with the file type corresponding to the current item (HTML, Rich Text Format, or Text Only). The default location for user templates, however, depends on your operating system version. On Microsoft Windows XP, the location is the <profile>\Application Data\Microsoft\Templates folder, and on Windows Vista™, it is the <profile>\AppData\Roaming\Microsoft\Templates folder, where <profile> is your user profile folder (which is Documents And Settings\<user> on most Windows XP systems but is Users\<user> on Windows Vista systems). When you select Outlook Template as the file type, Outlook 2007 automatically switches to your Templates folder.

4. Click Save to save the template. Close the message form, and then click No when asked whether you want to save changes.

You can create as many e-mail templates as you need, storing them on your local hard disk or on a network server. Placing templates on a network server allows other Microsoft Outlook users to use them as well.

Using an E-Mail Template

After you create an e-mail template, it's a simple matter to use the template to create a message by following these steps:

1. In Outlook 2007, click the arrow next to New on the Standard toolbar, and then click Choose Form. Alternatively, choose File, New, Choose Form. Outlook 2007 opens the Choose Form dialog box, as shown in Figure 25-2.

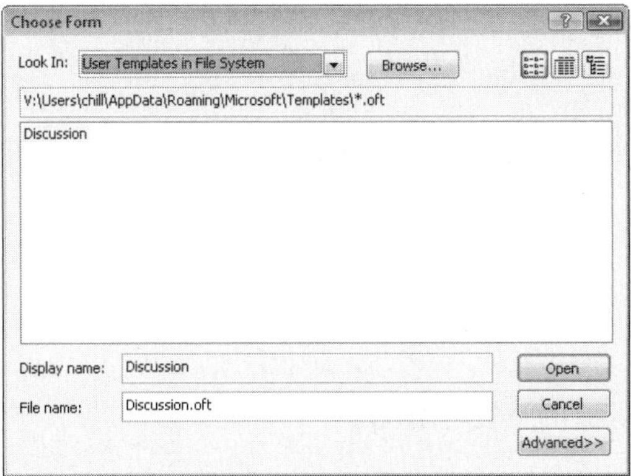

Figure 25-2. Select the template in the Choose Form dialog box.

2. In the Look In drop-down list (which is set to Organizational Forms Library by default), select the location where the template is stored. In this example, the template is stored in the user default template folder. To use this template, select User Templates In File System.

3. Select the template from the list, and then click Open to display a message form based on the template data.

4. Fill in the message form to include any additional or modified information, and then send the message as you would any other.

Using a Template with a Distribution List

You can easily send messages to recipients in a distribution list without using a template: Simply start a new message, select the distribution list from the address book, and send the message. If the messages you send to the members of the list are different each time you use the list, you don't need a template. However, if the messages contain much the same information time after time, they're good candidates for templates. For example, you might need to submit weekly reports to a group of administrators or managers, send task lists to people who work for you, or broadcast regular updates about products or services.

You create a template for a distribution list the same way you create any other e-mail template. The only difference is that you store the list of recipients within the template. To do so, simply select the distribution list in the appropriate address box when you create the template. If you don't want the various members of the group to see the addresses of other members on the list, be sure to insert the distribution group in the Bcc box rather than in the To or Cc box.

For more information about working with distribution lists, see Chapter 6, "Using Address Books and Distribution Lists."

Using Other Outlook Template Types

E-mail messages are not the only Outlook 2007 item you can create from a template. In fact, you can create a template for any type of Outlook 2007 item. This section of the chapter explores some common situations in which you might use specific types of templates.

Appointments and Meetings

You might find it useful to create templates for setting up certain types of appointments and meetings. If you prefer to use a set of appointment properties that differ from the Outlook 2007 default properties, you can use a template that contains your preferred settings and then create each new appointment or meeting from that template. For example, if you have regular meetings with the same group of people, you can set up a template in which those individuals are already selected on the Scheduling page so that you don't have to assemble the list each time you schedule a meeting. Perhaps you prefer to have Outlook 2007 issue a reminder an hour before each appointment rather than the default of 15 minutes.

You can create templates for appointments and meetings the same way you create e-mail templates. Open a new appointment form or meeting request, and then fill in all the data that will be standard each time you use the template. Then click the Microsoft Office Button, click Save As, and save the file as an Outlook Template. When you want to use the template, choose File, New, Choose Form, and then follow the steps outlined in "Using an E-Mail Template" earlier in this chapter. You can also click the arrow next to New on the Standard toolbar and select Choose Form to select a form.

For more information about using appointment forms and their settings, see Chapter 20, "Scheduling Appointments." For details about meeting requests, see Chapter 21, "Scheduling Meetings and Resources."

Contacts

In your Contacts folder, you're likely to add contact entries for people who work in or belong to the same organization, business, department, or other entity. These contacts might share the same company name, address, or primary phone number. In such a case, why not create a template to save yourself the trouble of entering the information for each contact entry separately (and potentially getting it wrong)? Or, for example, you might use the same conferencing URL for all of your online meetings hosted by Microsoft Office Live Meeting. Why not create a template that specifies the URL, eliminating the chore of setting it each time you create a new contact?

As with other templates, you create a contact template by opening a new contact form and filling in the standard data. Then click the Microsoft Office Button, click Save As, and save the contact as an Outlook Template.

For more information about creating contact entries and working in the Contacts folder, see Chapter 18, "Creating and Managing Your Contacts."

INSIDE OUT **Create contacts from the same company**

You can create contact entries that share common company information by selecting a contact item and choosing Actions, New Contact From Same Company. However, this might not give you the results you need in all cases. For example, the New Contact From Same Company command uses the same address, company name, business phone number, business fax number, and Web page address for the new contact as for the selected one. If you also want to use the same directory server, categories, notes, or other properties for the new contacts, it's best to create a contact entry, save it as a template, and then create other contact entries from the template.

Tasks and Task Requests

If you perform the same task frequently, you can create a basic task as a template and then modify it as needed for each occurrence of the task. You also can create a task template with a specific set of properties and then use it to create various tasks. For example, you could create all of your tasks with the status specified as In Progress rather than the default Not Started. Or perhaps you need to create many tasks with the same set of categories assigned to them.

In addition to creating task items from templates, you might also want to use templates to create task requests. A task request template is handy if you manage a group of people to whom you need to assign similar or identical tasks. Set up a template that incorporates the common elements, and then create each task request from the template, filling in or modifying the unique elements and addressing the request to the specific person assigned to the task.

You use the same methods described earlier for e-mail templates to create and open templates for tasks and task requests.

For more information about creating tasks and task requests, see Chapter 22, "Managing Your Tasks."

Journal Entries

You can use the Outlook 2007 journal to keep track of activities such as phone calls, remote sessions, or other actions that you want to record. Why use journal templates? Any time you find yourself adding a manual journal entry for the same type of activity with the same or similar properties, consider creating a template for the action. Perhaps you frequently record journal entries for phone calls to a particular individual, account, or company that contain the same phone number or company name or log the same duration. Rather than creating a journal entry from scratch each time, create a template and use the template instead.

For more information about working with the Outlook 2007 journal, see Chapter 23, "Tracking Documents and Activities."

Editing Templates

Outlook 2007 stores templates as .oft files when you save them to disk. You can modify any template to make changes as needed.

To modify a template, follow these steps:

1. Choose Tools, Forms, Choose Form.
2. Outlook 2007 displays the Choose Form dialog box (shown earlier in Figure 25-2). In the Look In drop-down list, select the location where the template is stored.
3. Select the template, and then click Open.
4. Make changes as needed, and then choose Save and Close (or click the Microsoft Office Button and then click Save) to save the changes.

Note

To find templates you've created so that you can edit them, choose User Templates In File System from the Look In drop-down list in the Choose Form dialog box, and then browse to the folder where you saved the template.

Sharing Templates

In some situations, you might find it useful to share templates with other users. For example, assume that you're responsible for managing several people who all submit the same type of report to you on a regular basis through e-mail. In that situation, you might create an e-mail template with the appropriate boilerplate information and your address in the To box and then have the staff use that template to generate the reports. This ensures that everyone is providing comparable information. In addition, whenever you need a different set of data from these employees, you need only modify the template.

When Outlook 2007 is running on Windows Vista, Outlook 2007 stores your template files in the AppData\Roaming\Microsoft\Templates folder of your profile. On a new installation of Windows Vista, this folder would be \Users\<user>\AppData\Roaming\Microsoft\Templates.

With Windows XP, Outlook 2007 stores your template files in the Application Data\Microsoft\Templates folder of your user profile. On a new installation of Microsoft Windows XP, for example, this folder would be \Documents And Settings\<user>\Application Data\ Microsoft\Templates, where <user> is your user name. On systems upgraded from Microsoft Windows NT® Workstation, the folder would be located in \Winnt\Profiles\<user>\Application Data\Microsoft\Templates.

The easiest way to find the location where Outlook 2007 stores your templates is to save a template or at least go through the motions of saving it. Open a form, click the Microsoft Office Button, click Save As, and then select Outlook Templates. Outlook 2007 displays the path to the folder just above the file name field. (Click the arrow next to Microsoft Templates, or hold the mouse pointer over the Refresh icon to the right to see the path displayed in a ScreenTip.)

Why do you need to know where Outlook 2007 stores your templates? To share a template, you need to share the template file. This means placing the template in a shared network folder, sharing your template folder, or sending the template file to other users (the least desirable option). For any of these options, you need to know the location of the template file you want to share. After you locate the file, you can share the folder that contains it, copy the template to a network share, or forward it to other users as an attachment.

INSIDE OUT **Share a template using a network share**

Probably the best option for sharing a template is to create a network share and place the template in that share. Configure permissions for the share so that you have full control and other users have read-only access to the folder. This allows you to make changes to the template, while allowing others to use but not modify the template. If other users need to create and manage templates in the same folder, give all users the permissions necessary to create and modify files in the folder, and then use file-level NTFS file system permissions for individual template files to control which users can modify them.

Using Templates Effectively

The ability to use templates for Outlook 2007 e-mail, meetings, appointments, tasks, and even journal entries provides you with the means to implement shortcuts in creating new items. Consider how much of your work involves repeatedly sending out e-mail messages, meeting requests, and so on that are essentially the same information structure even though the details differ from day to day.

- **Look at items you use repeatedly and create templates for them.** Imagine if every time you found yourself creating meetings, tasks, or e-mail messages that contained common, repeated elements, instead of simply creating yet another individual meeting invitation (with your latest agenda and required materials), you created a template with only the common elements (meeting topic, agenda list, required materials, and meeting goals). Within a short time, you would have a catalog of templates available that corresponded to your specific Outlook 2007 items. Then when you needed to schedule such a meeting, you could use the template to shortcut the process of producing the meeting request. Examples of this could include the following:
    - Meeting templates for team meetings, general department meetings, budget meetings, and project meetings (a different one for each project)

- E-mail templates for regular team notices (work schedules, weekly meetings, team building, and so on), submitting travel or expense reports, project-related updates (a different one for each project), responding to information requests, and client/customer communications (a different one for each client)
- Appointment templates for phone conferences, job interviews, client interviews, and offsite sales presentations
- Task templates for weekly reports, weekly and monthly to-do lists, project tasks (a different template for each project), and quarterly and annual reports

Your own uses of templates will exceed and differ from those in the preceding list, and yet you can see how the use of templates can speed up many Outlook 2007 operations that you perform repeatedly.

- **Share your templates with others in your organization.** Each organization has many people who perform similar (if not the same) activities, tasks, and operations. Thus it is likely that templates that you create to facilitate your own work will also apply to the activities of your coworkers. Every team in your organization, for example, has (at least structurally) similar weekly/monthly status reports, and every employee has the same annual/semiannual review reporting requirements. As you create templates to ease your workflow, assess and identify the other people or groups within your organization that could benefit from the template (or a closely related derivation).
- **Store templates where they are easily accessible.** After you have created templates that are useful to other people in your organization, you need to store the templates in a location that is accessible to everyone who could use them. The default location for templates on your system is not the best place to share them from, because your system might not be online at all times that others need access to the templates. You also might have templates in the default folder that you don't actually want to share.

  It is more useful to create a folder on a commonly accessible file server (or Distributed File System [DFS] share) and copy all of the templates that you want to share to this location. On this file share, you can set sharing permissions to allow other users appropriate permissions. For example, if any other users should be able to add or modify templates, you can grant Change permission to the Everyone group (or the Domain Users group); however, if no one should be able to modify or add templates, you can set share permissions to Read. You can also use NTFS file system permissions to further control access and the ability to add, modify, or delete the templates on a per-template basis. Once the share has been created, the templates have been uploaded, and the appropriate share-level and file-level permissions have been applied, you should send e-mail messages to the relevant groups and users to inform them of the template location, access, and restrictions.

CHAPTER 26

Customizing the Outlook Interface

Microsoft® Office Outlook® 2007 has an easy-to-use yet powerful interface that serves most users well right out of the box. However, you probably perform certain tasks that are not readily available through the standard Office Outlook 2007 interface. For example, perhaps you use remote mail frequently and want quick access to the remote mail functions rather than having to scroll through menus to find them.

As all 2007 Microsoft Office system applications do, Outlook 2007 provides a way to tailor the interface to your needs. You can customize the Navigation Pane to add your own shortcuts, customize the To-Do Bar, customize Outlook Today view and other standard views, and customize the way Outlook 2007 displays your folders. You can also create custom toolbars.

This chapter focuses on the various ways you can fine-tune Outlook 2007 to the way you work. Some of the changes covered are minor; others are more significant. All of them can enhance your experience with Outlook 2007 and make it a more useful tool for bringing efficiency to your workday.

Customizing the Navigation Pane

Most people browse through Outlook 2007 folders using the Navigation Pane. This section explains how you can customize the Navigation Pane to suit your preferences.

A Quick Tour of the Navigation Pane

The Navigation Pane, which appears on the left side of the Outlook 2007 window, was introduced in Microsoft Outlook 2003 and replaces the Outlook Bar that was a staple of the Microsoft Outlook interface prior to Outlook 2003. The Navigation Pane gives you quick access to all of your Outlook 2007 folders. Outlook 2007 adds a great new feature to the Navigation Pane—the capability to minimize the Navigation Pane to gain more window space for the current folder view but still open the Navigation Pane quickly when you need it.

The Navigation Pane contains buttons that serve as shortcuts to your Outlook 2007 folders, as shown in Figure 26-1. The Navigation Pane also includes shortcuts to a few common items, including Outlook Today view and the Microsoft Office Online Web site. You can access these shortcuts by clicking the Shortcuts icon at the bottom of the Navigation Pane.

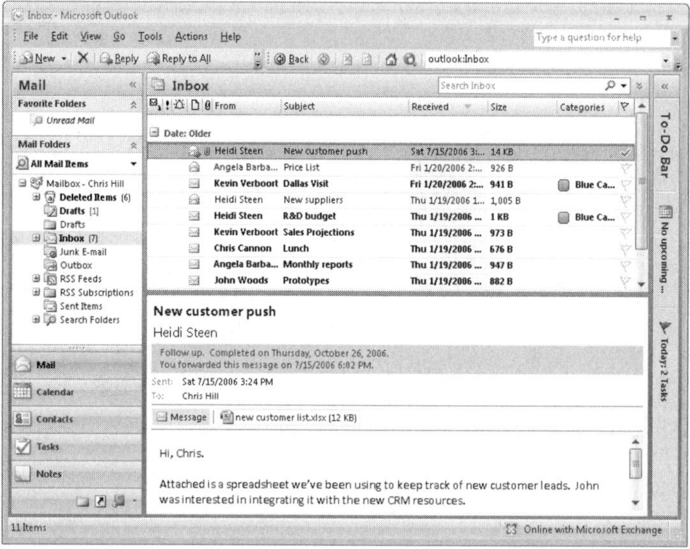

Figure 26-1. The Navigation Pane provides shortcuts to Outlook 2007 folders and other objects.

You can make several changes to the Navigation Pane, including adding and removing groups, adding and removing shortcuts, and changing the appearance of its icons. The following sections explain these changes.

> **Note**
>
> You can change the width of the Navigation Pane by dragging its border.

Showing and Hiding the Navigation Pane

If you use the Navigation Pane often, you'll probably want it to remain open all the time, but if you work with a particular Outlook 2007 folder most of the time, you might prefer to have the additional space for your favorite folder view or the Reading Pane. In Outlook 2007, you now have the capability to minimize the Navigation Pane to gain more window space but easily restore it when you need it, as shown in Figure 26-2. To minimize the Navigation Pane, choose View, Navigation Pane, and then choose Minimize. When the Navigation Pane is minimized, you'll find an Expand The Navigation Pane button in the upper-right corner of the Navigation Pane. Just click this button to expand the Navigation Pane. The button changes to a Minimize The Navigation Pane button, which when clicked minimizes the Navigation Pane.

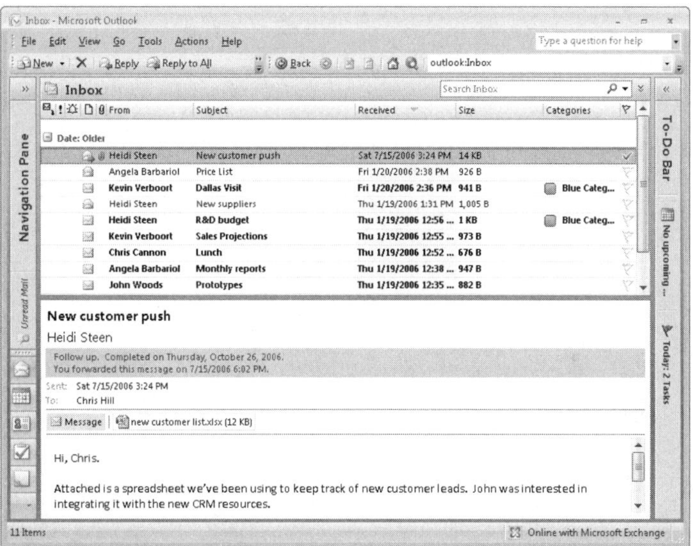

Figure 26-2. The Navigation Pane now has a minimized state.

Outlook 2007 also allows you to turn on or turn off the Navigation Pane as needed. Choose View, Navigation Pane, and then choose Off to turn it off.

> **Note**
>
> Press **Alt+F1** to quickly show or hide the Navigation Pane. Outlook 2007 cycles through off, minimized, and normal Navigation Pane states when you press **Alt+F1**.

Changing the Number of Buttons on the Navigation Pane

Outlook 2007 can display up to eight buttons in the bottom portion of the Navigation Pane, and these include a button for each of the standard Outlook 2007 folders, the Folder List, and Shortcuts. The number of buttons displayed depends on the size of the Outlook 2007 window and how many buttons you choose to show. If you need more space for the Folder List, for example, you can simply drag the bar above the Mail button to resize the lower portion of the Navigation Pane, which changes the number of buttons shown. You can show or hide buttons by clicking the double arrow at the bottom of the Navigation Pane and choosing Show More Buttons or Show Fewer Buttons, as shown in Figure 26-3.

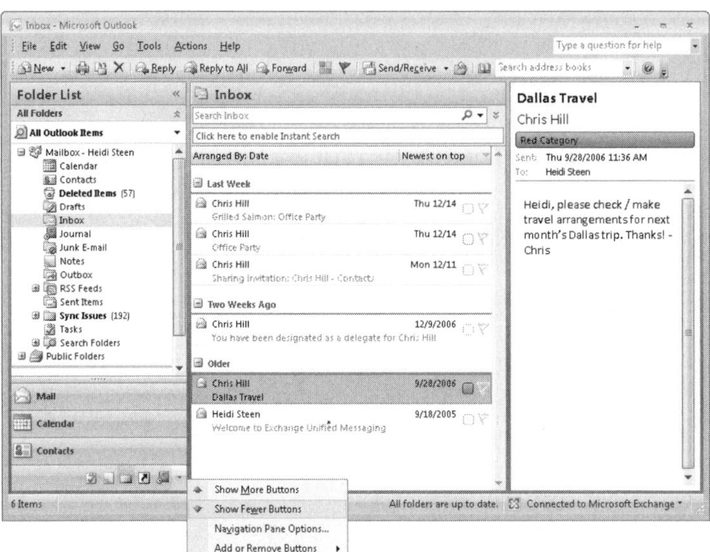

Figure 26-3. Use this menu to show or hide buttons.

Outlook 2007 does not by default show all of the available buttons in the Navigation Pane. For example, the Journal button doesn't appear by default in the Navigation Pane. To add or remove buttons, click Configure Buttons (the double arrow) at the bottom of the Navigation Pane, click Add Or Remove Buttons, and then select the button that you want to add or remove.

> **Note**
>
> If you want to add or remove more than one folder, right-click a folder button in the Navigation Pane, and then choose Navigation Pane Options to open a dialog box that you can use to add and remove buttons.

Adding a Shortcut to an Outlook Folder or a Public Folder

The Navigation Pane includes buttons for each of the built-in Outlook 2007 folders, and the Folder List provides quick access to all other Outlook 2007 folders and public folders (which are available only with Microsoft Exchange Server). You can easily add shortcuts to any folder by following these steps:

1. Click the Shortcuts button at the bottom of the Navigation Pane to open the Shortcuts pane.
2. Click Add New Shortcut to open the Add To Navigation Pane dialog box, shown in Figure 26-4.

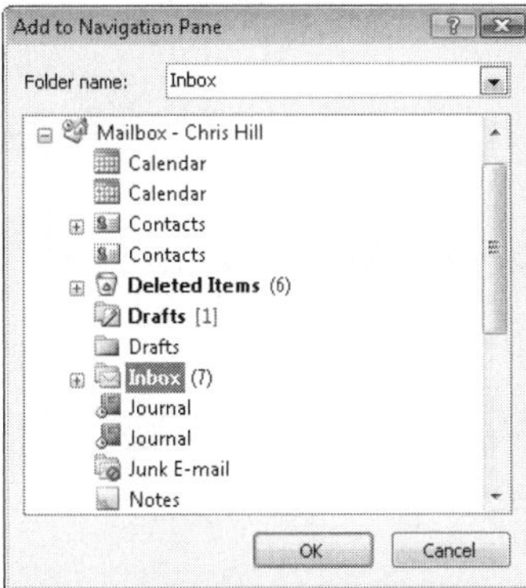

Figure 26-4. Select the folder for which you want to add a shortcut.

3. Select a folder in the list, and then click OK. Outlook 2007 adds the shortcut to the Shortcuts group.
4. Drag the shortcut to a different group, if desired.

Adding a File Folder or Document to the Navigation Pane

You can create shortcuts to file system folders or Outlook 2007 folders and add them to existing Navigation Pane groups or to new groups that you create. For example, if you use a particular document folder often, you might want to add that folder to one of your Navigation Pane shortcut groups.

The process is similar, regardless of the type of shortcut you're adding:

1. In Outlook 2007, open the group in which you want to create the shortcut.
2. Click the Shortcuts button in the Navigation Pane to open the Shortcuts pane.
3. In Microsoft Windows®, open the folder containing the folder or file for which you want to create a shortcut, and then position the folder and the Outlook 2007 window so that you can see both, as shown in Figure 26-5.

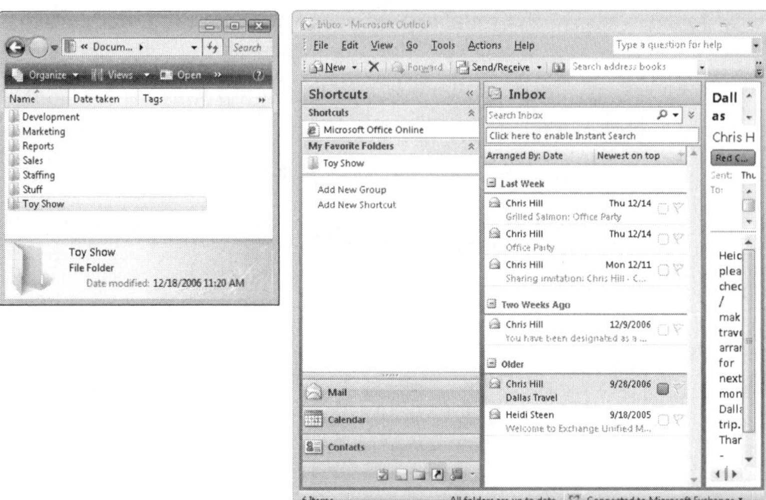

Figure 26-5. Drag a shortcut, folder, or document from Windows to the Navigation Pane to create a shortcut.

4. Drag the folder or document from the folder window to the shortcut group name where you want to add it.

INSIDE OUT **Create shortcuts to network shares you use often**

You can specify Universal Naming Convention (UNC) paths in addition to mapped drives. A UNC path takes the form \\<server>\<share>, where <server> is the computer sharing the folder and <share> is the folder's share name. You can specify longer UNC paths, such as \\<server>\Documents\Contracts\Completed. To use network shortcuts in Outlook 2007, first create the shortcut on the desktop and then drag it to a shortcut group in the Navigation Pane.

Adding a Web Site to the Navigation Pane

You can add shortcuts to Web sites to the Navigation Pane. This lets you quickly open a site from Outlook 2007 to do research, check stock quotes, view news, and so on.

To add a Web site shortcut to the Navigation Pane, first create the shortcut on the desktop or in another folder. Open the Navigation Pane shortcut group in which you want to place the shortcut, and then simply drag the existing shortcut to the Navigation Pane. You can also copy shortcuts from your Favorites menu easily. Position your Web browser so that you can see it and the Navigation Pane. Open the Favorites menu, and then drag the shortcut from the browser to the shortcut group in the Navigation Pane.

INSIDE OUT **Create new Web shortcuts**

You can create new Web shortcuts on the desktop or in a file system folder (such as My Documents) by right-clicking the location and choosing New, Shortcut. On the first page of the Create Shortcut Wizard, type the URL to the Web page, File Transfer Protocol (FTP) site, or other Internet resource. Use **http://** as the URL prefix for Web pages, use **ftp://** for FTP sites, or use **https://** for secure sites that use Secure Sockets Layer (SSL).

Removing a Shortcut from the Navigation Pane

If you decide you no longer want a particular shortcut in the Navigation Pane, you can remove it easily. Simply right-click the shortcut, and then choose Delete Shortcut. Click Yes to remove the shortcut or No to cancel.

Renaming a Shortcut in the Navigation Pane

In some cases, you'll want to change the name that Outlook 2007 assigns to a shortcut in the Navigation Pane. For example, when you add a Web site shortcut, its name is the URL, which typically doesn't fit very well in the Navigation Pane. Perhaps you simply want to change the shortcut's name to something more descriptive.

To change the shortcut name, right-click the shortcut, and then choose Rename Shortcut. Type the new name, and then press Enter.

Working with Groups in the Navigation Pane

Outlook 2007 creates one group by default, named Shortcuts, in the Navigation Pane. You can also add your own groups, remove groups, and rename them. This section explains these tasks.

Adding a Group to the Navigation Pane

At some point, you might want to add your own groups of shortcuts to the Navigation Pane to help you reorganize existing shortcuts or organize new shortcuts. For example, you might want to create a group to contain all your Web shortcuts.

Adding a new group is easy. Click the Shortcuts button in the Navigation Pane, and then click Add New Group. Outlook 2007 adds a new group named New Group and highlights the group name so that you can change it, as shown in Figure 26-6. Type the group name, and then press **Enter**. Then begin adding shortcuts or moving shortcuts to the group from your other groups.

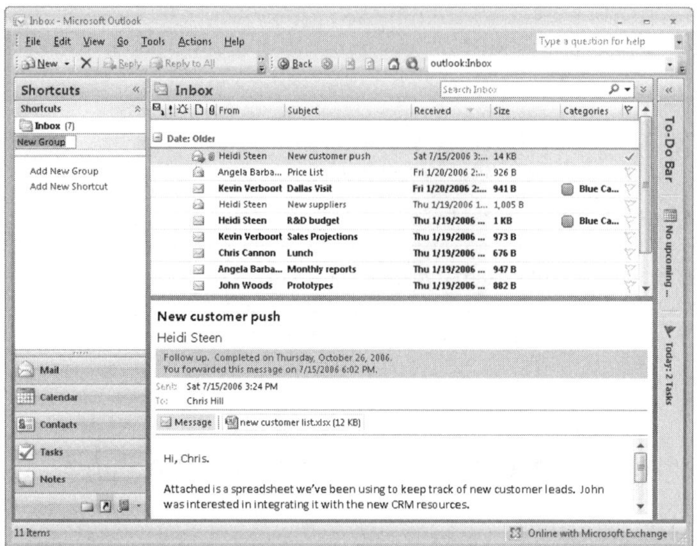

Figure 26-6. Type a name for the new group.

Renaming a Group in the Navigation Pane

You can rename a group as easily as you rename a shortcut. Start Outlook 2007, right-click the group name in the Navigation Pane, and then choose Rename Group. Type a new name for the group, and then press **Enter**.

Removing a Group from the Navigation Pane

If you decide that you want to remove a group from the Navigation Pane, you can do so at any time. Simply right-click the group name in the Navigation Pane, and then choose Remove Group. Click Yes to remove the group or No to cancel.

> **Note**
>
> If the group you remove contains shortcuts that you've copied from other locations (such as the desktop), removing the group does not affect those shortcuts. Only the group is removed from the Navigation Pane; the shortcuts remain in their other locations. Shortcuts that exist only in that group, however, are deleted.

Customizing the To-Do Bar

The To-Do Bar combines the Date Navigator, appointments, and the task list. The To-Do Bar sits at the right side of the Outlook 2007 window, as shown in Figure 26-7. As with the Navigation Pane, you can minimize the To-Do Bar to make more window space available for your Outlook 2007 folders or for the Reading Pane but still access the To-Do Bar quickly when you need it.

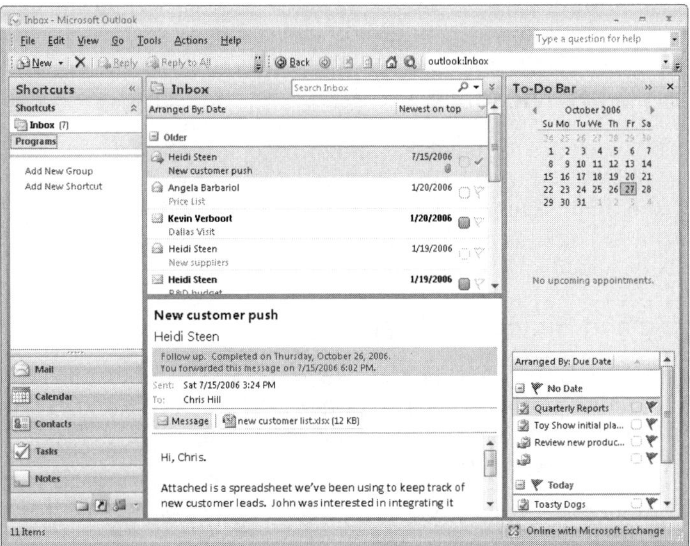

Figure 26-7. The To-Do Bar combines the Date Navigator, appointments, and the task list.

> **Note**
>
> To display the To-Do Bar, choose View, To-Do Bar, and then choose Normal.

You can control which of these three items appears in the To-Do Bar. To customize the To-Do Bar, choose To-Do Bar on the View menu, and then select or clear the Date Navigator, Appointments, or Task List options. To control other options for the To-Do Bar, choose View, To-Do Bar, and then choose Options. In the resulting To-Do Bar Options dialog box, shown in Figure 26-8, you can specify the number of month rows in the Date Navigator and the number of appointments shown in the Appointments area.

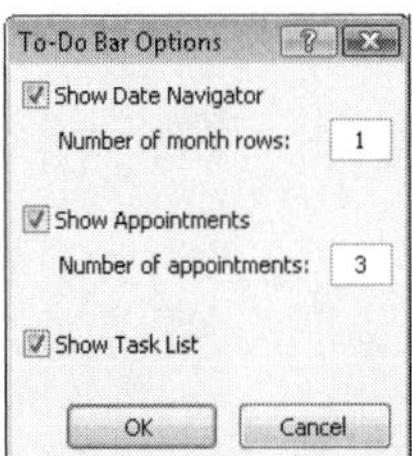

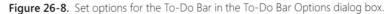

Figure 26-8. Set options for the To-Do Bar in the To-Do Bar Options dialog box.

Customizing Toolbars

You can work with toolbars as they're provided in Outlook 2007, or you can customize their location and contents to suit your preferences. This section explains how to relocate toolbars, add and remove commands, and configure custom options.

Working with Toolbars

Outlook 2007 includes the menu bar and three toolbars by default: Standard, Advanced, and Web. You can also create your own toolbars (see "Creating Custom Toolbars" later in this chapter). Outlook 2007 makes it easy to rearrange your screen by displaying or hiding toolbars. You also can move toolbars to different locations in the Outlook 2007 window.

Displaying and Hiding Toolbars

You probably use the same one or two toolbars on a regular basis but sometimes need to display or hide a particular toolbar. By default, Outlook 2007 always displays the menu bar–you can't turn it off. Outlook 2007 also displays the Standard toolbar by default, although you can turn it off if you don't use it.

To display or hide a toolbar, choose View, Toolbars, and then select the toolbar in question.

> **Note**
>
> You can right-click the menu bar or any toolbar and then turn toolbars on or off by using the shortcut menu.

Moving and Docking Toolbars

All Outlook 2007 toolbars–including the menu bar–are *dockable*. This means that you can attach the toolbar to any of the four sides of the Outlook 2007 window. You can also float a toolbar. Figure 26-9 shows toolbars docked at the left and right edges of the Outlook 2007 window. Figure 26-10 shows a toolbar floating on the desktop.

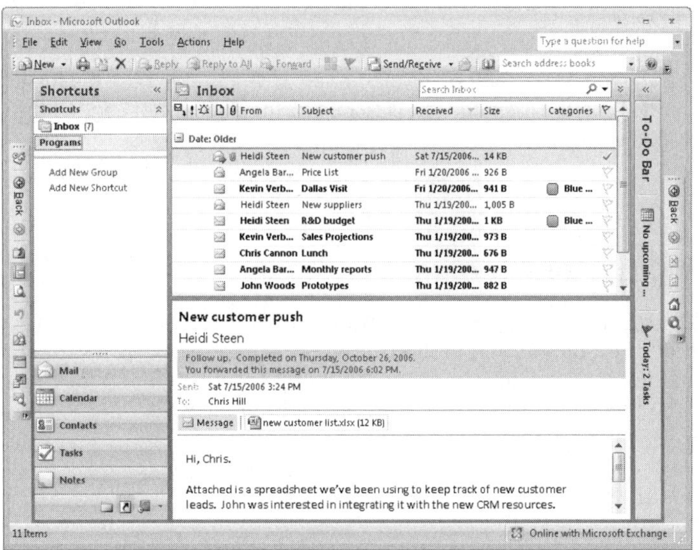

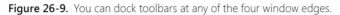

Figure 26-9. You can dock toolbars at any of the four window edges.

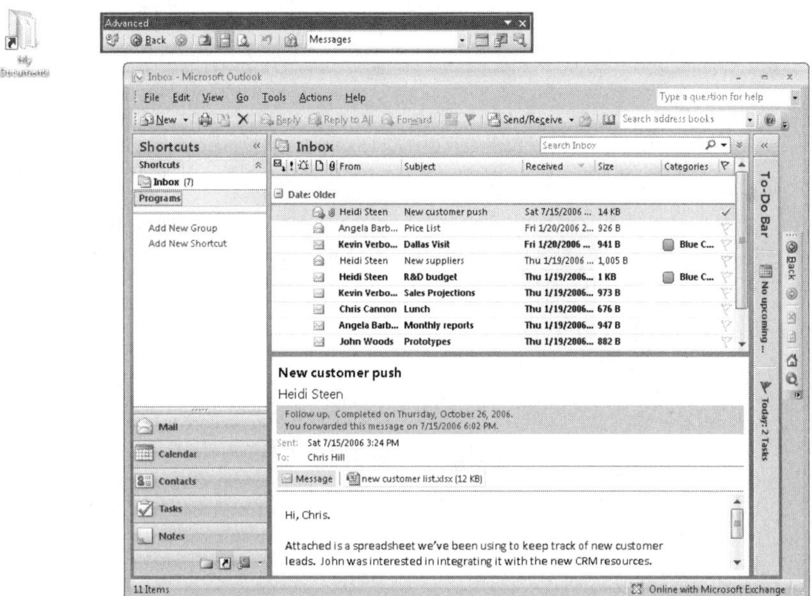

Figure 26-10. Toolbars can also float on the desktop.

On the left in each toolbar (if the toolbar is displayed at the top or bottom of the Outlook 2007 window) or at the top (if the toolbar is docked at the right or left edge of the window) is an anchor that you can use to move the toolbar. Just click and drag the toolbar to the desired location.

> **Note**
>
> If you need more vertical room in your folder views and don't use the menu bar often, consider docking the menu bar and toolbars at the right or left edge of the Outlook 2007 window.

Creating Custom Toolbars

Outlook 2007 gives you considerable control over the appearance and content of its toolbars. Because menus and toolbars are very similar, you use a similar process to modify menus and toolbar items. The following sections explain how to make several types of changes to your toolbars, including adding new ones.

> **Note**
>
> If you wreak havoc with the default toolbars in your zeal to customize them, you can restore them with relative ease. For details, see "Recovering the Default Toolbars" later in this chapter.

You can modify the existing toolbars, but in many cases, you'll probably want to create your own. For example, you might want to create a toolbar for remote mail. Perhaps you use another group of commands to which you'd like quick access.

After you add a new toolbar, you can add buttons and menus to it (as explained in the following section). Because menus and toolbars are both considered toolbars in Outlook 2007, the process for creating a menu is the same as the one for creating a toolbar.

Follow these steps to create a toolbar:

1. In Outlook 2007, right-click any toolbar, and then choose Customize to open the Customize dialog box. Alternatively, choose View, Toolbars, Customize.
2. In the Customize dialog box, click the Toolbars tab, and then click New.
3. Type a name for the toolbar, and then click OK. Outlook 2007 opens a blank toolbar.

In the following section, you'll learn how to add commands to your new toolbar.

Adding Items

The default toolbars provided in Outlook 2007 cover the most commonly used commands, but they are not all-inclusive. Therefore, you might want to add frequently used commands to the existing toolbars or create custom toolbars.

In either case, you need to know how to add buttons to a toolbar. Just follow these steps:

1. In Outlook 2007, right-click any toolbar, and then choose Customize to open the Customize dialog box. Alternatively, choose View, Toolbars, Customize.
2. Click the Commands tab, shown in Figure 26-11.

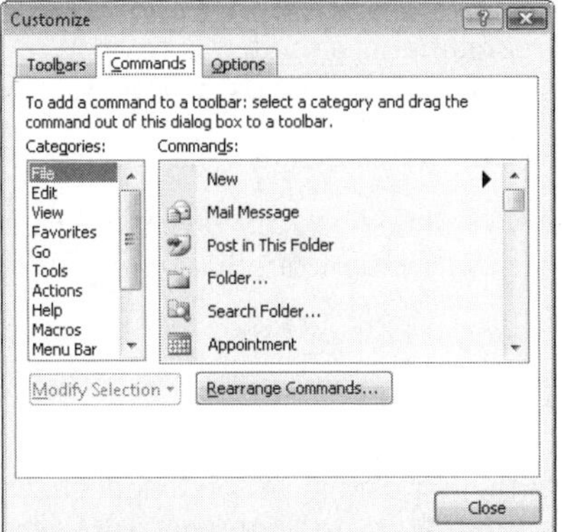

Figure 26-11. Use the Commands tab to add commands to your toolbars.

3. In the Categories list, select the command category containing the command you want.
4. In the Commands list, locate the command and drag it to the appropriate toolbar.
5. Repeat steps 3 and 4 to add other commands as needed, and then click Close to close the Customize dialog box.

Note

You can add a combination of menus and buttons to any toolbar.

Removing Items

If you don't use certain commands on a toolbar, you might want to remove them to make room for others or to simplify the Outlook 2007 window.

To remove a button, follow these steps:

1. In Outlook 2007, open the Customize dialog box.
2. With any tab of the Customize dialog box displayed, drag the button off its toolbar. You can release the button as soon as you see a small *X* appear by the mouse pointer.
3. Click Close to close the Customize dialog box.

Reorganizing Items

You can also rearrange the buttons on a toolbar. The key point to understand is that whenever the Customize dialog box is open, any action you take on a toolbar modifies that toolbar. For example, if you drag a button or command off the toolbar, Outlook 2007 removes that button or command.

Therefore, the basic method of reorganizing a toolbar is to open the Customize dialog box and then simply drag the buttons or commands, as follows:

1. In Outlook 2007, open the Customize dialog box.
2. With any tab in the Customize dialog box displayed, drag an item on a toolbar from one location to another on the same toolbar or on a different toolbar.
3. Click Close to close the Customize dialog box.

Modifying Toolbar Items

Outlook 2007 inserts items on a toolbar using a set of default characteristics. However, you can change these characteristics for any toolbar item. For example, you can change the name of a menu, its shortcut key, or the icon assigned to a button. Following is a list of the modifications you can make:

- Change an item's name, reset it to its default properties, or delete the item.
- Modify the button image assigned to a toolbar item by selecting a different image or editing the existing image.
- Change the style of the item so that it appears as text only, image only, or a combination of image and text.
- Assign a hyperlink to an item. When you click the item in Outlook 2007, the document or site referenced by the link opens.

Follow these steps to modify an existing toolbar item:

1. In Outlook 2007, open the Customize dialog box.
2. Right-click the command button or menu item that you want to change. Outlook 2007 presents a shortcut menu from which you can choose one of the following commands:

   Reset Resets the item to its default properties.

   Delete Removes the item from the toolbar.

   Name Changes the name of the item. Precede with an ampersand (&) the key that you want to use as the keyboard shortcut (the key you press instead of clicking the item). Note that some objects do not display their names by default.

Copy Button Image Copies the button image of the selected item to the Clipboard for use on a different button or in another program (or for documentation).

Paste Button Image Pastes the contents of the Clipboard on the item for use as the button image.

Reset Button Image Resets the button to display its default image.

Edit Button Image Opens the Button Editor dialog box, shown in Figure 26-12, so that you can edit the button image.

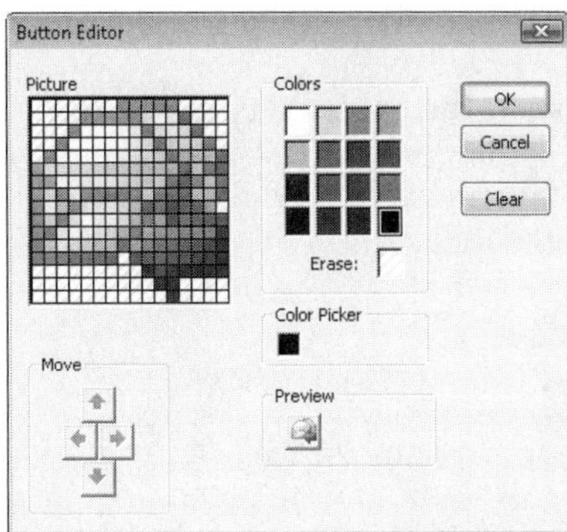

Figure 26-12. Use the Button Editor dialog box to edit the image assigned as a button's icon.

Change Button Image Selects a different button image from a set of predefined images.

Default Style Resets the button to its default style, such as image only or text only.

Text Only (Always) Shows the item as text without an image regardless of whether the item is on a toolbar or a menu.

Text Only (In Menus) Shows the item as text only (without an image) if it's used on a menu.

Image And Text Shows the item as an icon with a text description beside it.

Begin A Group Inserts a separator above a selected menu item or to the left of a selected toolbar button.

Edit Hyperlink Assigns to the selected item a hyperlink that opens the linked site or document when you select the toolbar item in Outlook 2007.

3. Click Close to close the Customize dialog box.

Changing the Width of the Drop-Down List

Some Outlook 2007 toolbar items use a drop-down list to display a list of information or to allow you to type information such as a search phrase or an address. If the drop-down list isn't wide enough to adequately display its information, you can widen it. You can also shrink lists that are too wide.

Here's how to change the width of a drop-down list:

1. In Outlook 2007, open the Customize dialog box.
2. Select the drop-down list that you want to modify.
3. Drag the left or right border of the drop-down list to resize it as needed.
4. Click Close to close the Customize dialog box.

Changing the Button Size

You can configure toolbars to display their buttons using either small icons (the default) or large icons. If your monitor is configured for a relatively high resolution, which can make the toolbar buttons hard to distinguish, configuring the toolbars for large icons can considerably improve their readability.

Follow these steps to configure button size:

1. In Outlook 2007, open the Customize dialog box.
2. Click the Options tab, shown in Figure 26-13.

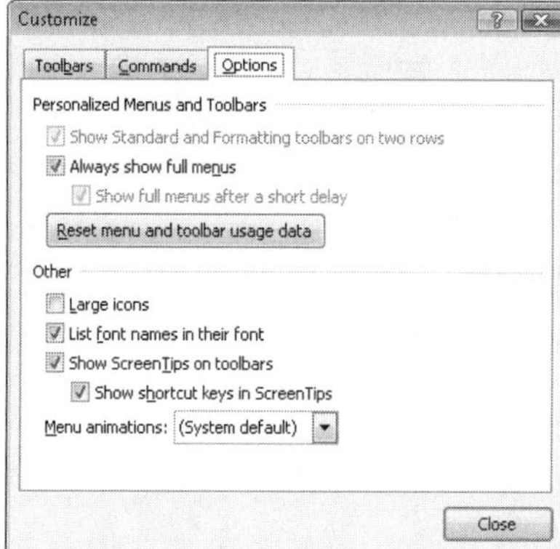

Figure 26-13. Configure icon size on the Options tab.

3. Select the Large Icons check box to turn on large icons, or clear the check box if you want to use the default small icon size. The change occurs immediately when you select or clear the option.
4. Click Close to close the Customize dialog box.

TROUBLESHOOTING

Add or Remove Separators on Toolbars

Toolbars can include separators between groups of toolbar buttons. Separators are purely an aesthetic element—they serve no other purpose than to provide a visual separation between items on a toolbar or menu.

No obvious feature in the user interface gives you the ability to drag separators into position or remove them. Actually, adding and removing them is easy, but you have to know the secret.

Follow these steps to add or remove a separator on a toolbar:

1. In Outlook 2007, open the Customize dialog box.
2. Locate the two items that you want to separate. Drag the item on the right slightly to the right. Outlook 2007 inserts a separator to the left of the item you dragged.
3. To remove a separator, drag the item just to the right of the separator slightly to the left.
4. Click Close to close the Customize dialog box.

You can also add a separator to a toolbar by using an item's shortcut menu. Open the Customize dialog box, right-click an item, and choose Begin A Group. Outlook 2007 inserts a separator to the left of the item.

Follow these steps to add or remove a separator on a menu:

1. In Outlook 2007, open the Customize dialog box.
2. Locate the two menu items that you want to separate. Drag the lower of the two items slightly downward. Outlook 2007 inserts a separator just above it.
3. To remove a separator, drag the menu item just below the separator slightly upward.
4. Click Close to close the Customize dialog box.

Resetting Individual Toolbars

If you've made quite a few changes to the default toolbars, the time might come when you want to reset them to their default state.

You can do so easily, as the following steps illustrate:

1. In Outlook 2007, open the Customize dialog box.
2. Click the Toolbars tab.
3. Select the toolbar that you want to reset, and then click Reset. Outlook 2007 prompts you to verify that you want to reset the selected toolbar.
4. Click OK to reset the toolbar or Cancel to cancel the task.

Renaming a Custom Toolbar

Although Outlook 2007 doesn't allow you to rename the default toolbars, you can rename any custom toolbars that you've created.

Follow these steps to rename a custom toolbar:

1. In Outlook 2007, open the Customize dialog box.
2. Select the toolbar that you want to rename, and then click Rename.
3. Type a new name, and then click OK.
4. Click Close to close the Customize dialog box.

Deleting a Custom Toolbar

You can turn off any toolbar to hide it. However, if you no longer need a custom toolbar that you've created, you probably want to delete it.

Follow these steps:

1. In Outlook 2007, open the Customize dialog box.
2. Click the Toolbars tab.
3. Select the toolbar to delete, and then click Delete.
4. Click OK to verify that you want to delete the toolbar or Cancel to cancel the task.

Sharing a Custom Toolbar

Outlook 2007 stores your toolbar definitions in the Outcmd.dat file. The data stored there includes changes that you make to the default toolbars as well as custom toolbars that you create. Outlook 2007 maintains a separate Outcmd.dat file for each user. If you share your computer with others who also use Outlook 2007, there are probably multiple Outcmd.dat files stored on the system. By default, Outlook 2007 stores the file in the Application Data\Microsoft\Outlook folder of your profile (Windows XP) or AppData\Roaming\Microsoft\Outlook (Windows Vista™).

If you've spent quite a bit of time customizing the toolbars and want to share those changes with others, you can do so by sharing your Outcmd.dat file by e-mail, file share, or similar method. If someone else has customized such a file for you, you can easily install it on your system. Just keep in mind that if you import someone else's Outcmd.dat file, you will lose any customized toolbars that you have created previously on your computer.

If you've received a customized Outcmd.dat file from another user, follow these steps to install it on your system:

1. Obtain the customized Outcmd.dat file from the other user (or if you're sharing yours, give the file to others who need its customized toolbars).

2. Exit Outlook 2007, and then locate the Outcmd.dat file in your profile folder on your system.
3. Rename the existing Outcmd.dat file as **Outcmd.old**.
4. Copy the other user's Outcmd.dat file to your profile folder where the original Outcmd.dat file was located.
5. Restart Outlook 2007.

CAUTION!

If you made changes to your toolbars before installing the other user's Outcmd.dat file, you'll lose those changes after installing the new file.

Recovering the Default Toolbars

As mentioned, Outlook 2007 stores toolbar customization settings in the Outcmd.dat file. If your Outcmd.dat file becomes corrupted, you can restore the default toolbars by deleting or renaming the existing Outcmd.dat file. This process is also handy when you've made extensive changes to your toolbars and want to restore them to their defaults.

Follow these steps:

1. Exit Outlook 2007.
2. Locate the Outcmd.dat file for your profile.
3. Rename the file **Outcmd.old**.
4. Restart Outlook 2007. You should now see only the default toolbars.

Controlling Toolbar Appearance and Behavior

Outlook 2007 lets you configure a handful of properties that control the way your toolbars appear and function. To set these properties, start Outlook 2007, and then choose View, Toolbars, Customize. Click the Options tab in the Customize dialog box (shown earlier in Figure 26-13).

The Options tab provides the following settings:

- **Show Standard And Formatting Toolbars On Two Rows** Shows the Standard and Formatting toolbars on two rows when both toolbars are displayed.
- **Always Show Full Menus** Turns off *adaptive menus* (those that show only the most frequently used commands) and shows all menu items. Clear this option to turn on adaptive menus.

- **Show Full Menus After A Short Delay** Shows all menu items after you position the mouse pointer on a menu for a short delay period.
- **Reset Menu And Toolbar Usage Data** Resets the usage data for adaptive menus. This command has no effect on the location of a toolbar or on customized toolbars (that is, toolbar modifications remain as they are).
- **Large Icons** Shows large toolbar icons.
- **List Font Names In Their Font** Displays font names in their actual font to give you a sample of the font.
- **Show ScreenTips On Toolbars** Shows ScreenTips when you position the mouse pointer over a toolbar button.
- **Show Shortcut Keys In ScreenTips** Includes with the ScreenTip text the shortcut key (such as a function key), if any, assigned to each toolbar item.
- **Menu Animations** Lists a menu on which you can select a menu animation effect for Outlook 2007 to use when you open a menu. Select the (System Default) option to use your operating system's default menu effect.

Note

You can configure the operating system's menu animation effect on the Effects tab in the Display dialog box. Right-click the desktop, and then choose Properties to display this dialog box. Click the Appearance tab, click Effects, and then configure the system for no animation to turn off animations in Outlook 2007.

Customizing Outlook Today View

Outlook 2007 uses Outlook Today view as its default view. Outlook Today combines your most commonly used Outlook 2007 data into a single view, summarizing your schedule, tasks, and key e-mail folders for the current day, as shown in Figure 26-14. You can work with the view as is or modify it to suit your needs. This section explores how to customize Outlook Today view.

For a basic description of how to use Outlook Today view, see the next section, "Configuring Outlook Today."

Although Outlook Today presents useful information, it might not show all the information you want or need to really keep track of your workday. You can customize Outlook Today view to show additional information and use HTML to present a truly customized interface. The following sections explain how.

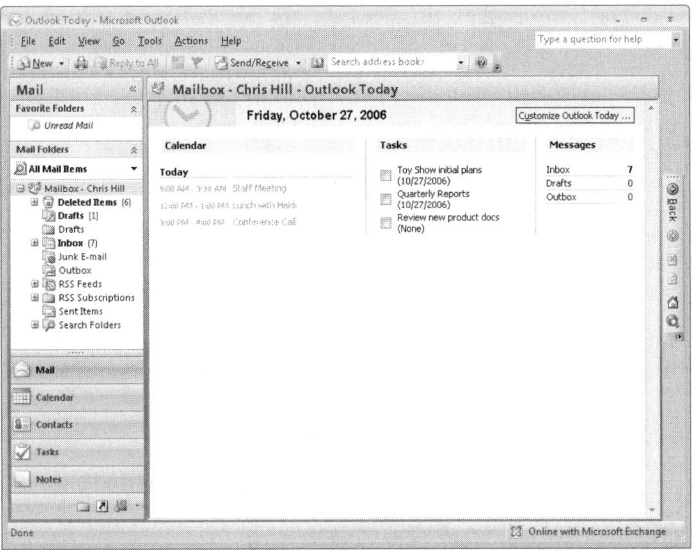

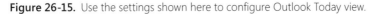

Figure 26-14. Outlook Today, which is the default Outlook 2007 view, summarizes your current day.

Configuring Outlook Today

You can configure several options that control how this view looks as well as the data it displays. To configure the view, click the Customize Outlook Today link in Outlook Today view (in the upper-right corner of the view). The Customize Outlook Today page shown in Figure 26-15 appears.

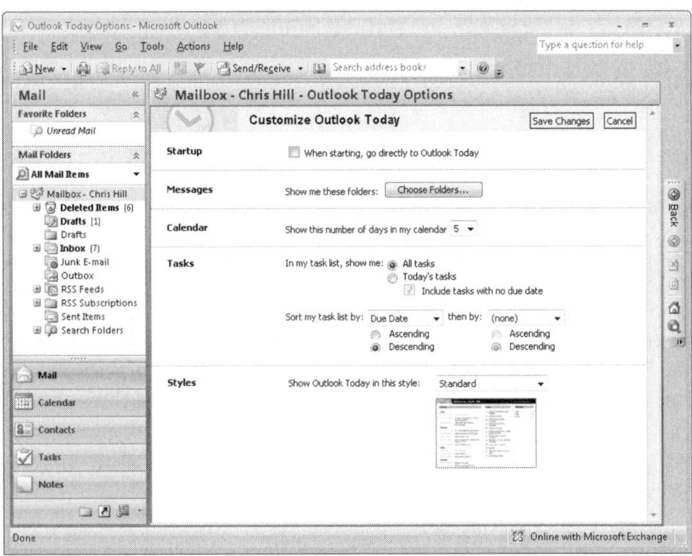

Figure 26-15. Use the settings shown here to configure Outlook Today view.

The following sections explain the changes you can make to Outlook Today view on this page. When you're satisfied with the changes, click Save Changes in the Customize Outlook Today title bar, or click Cancel to close the page without applying the changes.

Specifying the Startup View

If you select the When Starting, Go Directly To Outlook Today check box, Outlook 2007 opens Outlook Today view when you first start the program.

You also can specify the startup folder by using Outlook 2007 options, as explained here:

1. In Outlook 2007, choose Tools, Options.
2. Click Other.
3. Click Advanced Options.
4. In the Startup In This Folder drop-down list, select Outlook Today.
5. Click OK twice to close the dialog boxes.

The Startup In This Folder drop-down list specifies the folder that Outlook 2007 will use by default when you start Outlook 2007. Choosing Outlook Today in the list has the same effect as selecting When Starting, Go Directly To Outlook Today.

Note

If Outlook Today is configured as the default view and you clear the When Starting, Go Directly To Outlook Today check box without specifying a different startup folder in the Options dialog box, Outlook 2007 makes your Inbox the startup folder.

Specifying Folders to Show

Outlook Today view shows the Drafts, Inbox, and Outbox folders. If you seldom use the Drafts folder, you might prefer to remove it from Outlook Today. Or perhaps you want to add other folders to the view, such as Tasks and Contacts, to give you a quick way to open those folders without using the Navigation Pane.

To configure the folders that Outlook Today displays, click Choose Folders on the Customize Outlook Today page to open the Select Folder dialog box, shown in Figure 26-16. Select each folder that you want to display, and then click OK.

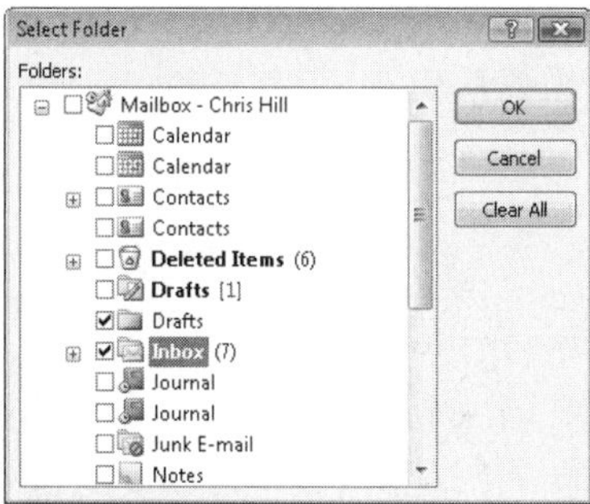

Figure 26-16. Use the Select Folder dialog box to choose the folders you want Outlook Today to display.

Setting Calendar Options

The Calendar portion of Outlook Today view displays a certain number of days from your calendar based on the current date. You can specify the number of days displayed by using the Show This Number Of Days In My Calendar option. Select a number from 1 to 7.

Setting Task Options

The Tasks area of the Customize Outlook Today page lets you configure how Outlook Today displays your tasks. The following list summarizes these options:

- **All Tasks** Shows all tasks regardless of the status or completion deadline.
- **Today's Tasks** Shows overdue tasks and incomplete tasks that are due today.
- **Include Tasks With No Due Date** Shows tasks for which you've assigned no due date.
- **Sort My Task List By *criteria* Then By *criteria*** Sort your task list according to the task's importance, due date, creation time, and start date. You can specify two sort conditions and also choose between ascending or descending sort order for both conditions.

Using Styles

By default, Outlook Today displays its information using three columns on a white background. Outlook 2007 provides additional styles that you can select to change the overall appearance of Outlook Today view. Use the Show Outlook Today In This Style drop-down list to select a style. The Customize Outlook Today page shows a sample of the style after you select it.

CHAPTER 27

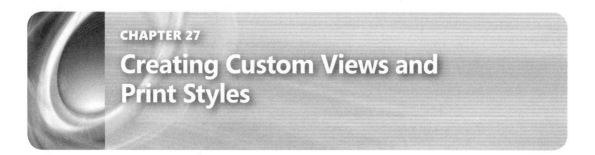

Creating Custom Views and Print Styles

Earlier chapters discussed the standard views that Microsoft® Office Outlook® 2007 provides for its many folders and data types. Those chapters also discussed customizing standard views by grouping and sorting items and by adding and removing columns, changing column order and properties, filtering the view, and so on.

In this chapter, you'll learn how to create custom views in Office Outlook 2007 to present the information you want in a format that suits your needs. Because generating a printed version of your data is often a byproduct of creating a view, this chapter also focuses on how to create custom print styles in Outlook 2007. For those situations in which the Outlook 2007 custom views and print styles won't give you the results you need, you can turn to scripts and Microsoft Office Word 2007 to accomplish custom printing tasks.

For more information about customizing existing views, see "Working with the Standard Outlook Views" in Chapter 4. You'll also find information about specific views in the chapters that cover them. For example, for more information about working with and customizing views in the Contacts folder, see "Viewing Contacts" in Chapter 18.

Creating and Using Custom Views

If the options for customizing existing Outlook 2007 views don't provide the information view you need, you can create your own views. You have two options for doing so: modifying an existing view or creating a new view from scratch.

Basing a New View on an Existing View

You can create a new, custom view from an existing view if the existing one offers most of the view elements you need. This is usually the easiest method because it requires the least amount of work.

Follow these steps to create a new, custom view from an existing view:

1. Open the folder for which you want to modify the view, and then select the view to display it.
2. Choose View, Current View, Define Views to open the Custom View Organizer dialog box, shown in Figure 27-1.

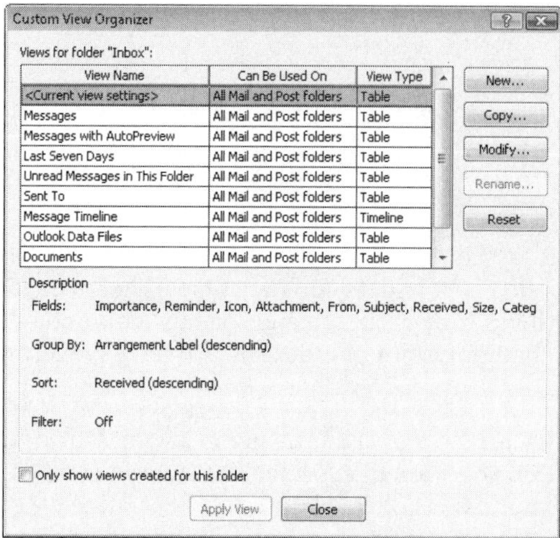

Figure 27-1. Use the Custom View Organizer dialog box to create a new view.

3. In the Views For Folder list, select the view you want to use as the basis for your new view, and then click Copy.
4. In the Copy View dialog box, type a name in the Name Of New View box, and then select one of the following options:
   - **This Folder, Visible To Everyone** Makes the view available only in the folder from which it was created. Anyone with access to the specified folder can use the view.
   - **This Folder, Visible Only To Me** Makes the view available only in the folder from which it was created. Only the person who created the view can use it.
   - **All Type Folders** Makes the view available in all folders that match the specified folder type. For example, when you create a custom view based on the Inbox, this option becomes All Mail And Post Folders, and Outlook 2007 makes the view available from the Inbox, Outbox, Drafts, Sent Items, and other message folders. If you base the new view on the Contacts folder, this option becomes All Contact Folders and makes the view available from all contacts folders.

5. Click OK to create the copy. The Customize View dialog box opens, as shown in Figure 27-2.

Figure 27-2. The Customize View dialog box lets you access the functions you can use to define your custom view.

6. Use the options provided in the Customize View dialog box to customize the view.

For details on all the options that you can configure in the Customize View dialog box, see "Customizing a View's Settings" later in this chapter.

7. After you've modified the settings as needed, click OK to close the Customize View dialog box and apply the view changes.

Creating a New View from Scratch

You can create an Outlook 2007 view from scratch if the view you want doesn't have much in common with any of the existing views. For example, perhaps you want to create an Inbox view that displays your messages as icons rather than headers, as shown in Figure 27-3. You can't modify a standard message view to display messages as icons, so you need to create the view from scratch.

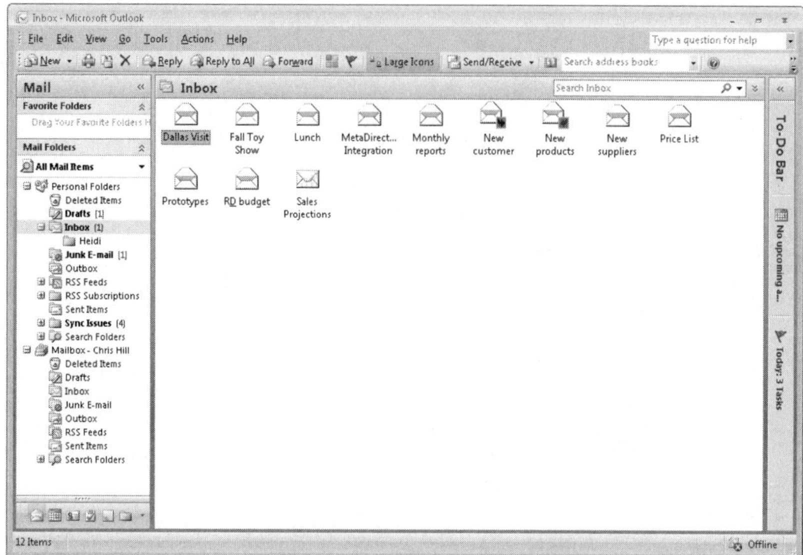

Figure 27-3. This Inbox view shows message icons rather than headers.

The process for creating a view from scratch is much like the process of modifying an existing view. When you create a new view, however, you have additional options for specifying the view.

Follow these steps to create a view from scratch:

1. In Outlook 2007, open the folder or folder type for which you want to create a custom view.
2. Choose View, Current View, Define Views to open the Define Views dialog box.
3. Click New to open the Create A New View dialog box, shown in Figure 27-4.

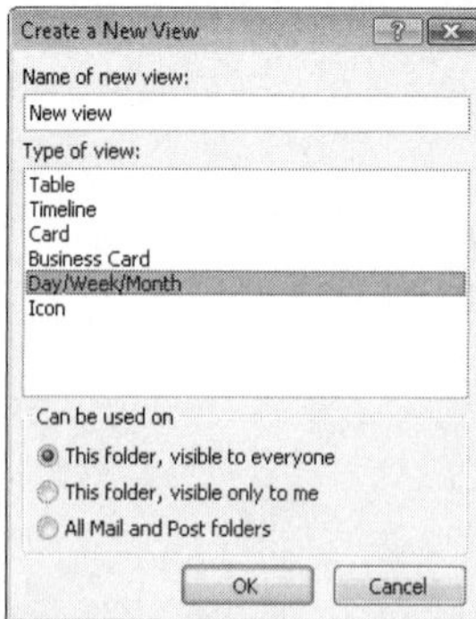

Figure 27-4. You can create several types of new views.

4. In the Name Of New View box, type a name for your new view.

5. In the Type Of View list, select the type of view you want to create, as follows:

   Table Presents information in tabular form with one item per row and columns according to your selections. The default Inbox view is an example of a table view.

   Timeline Displays items on a timeline based on the item's creation date (such as the received date for a message or the event date for a meeting). You might find this view type most useful for the Calendar folder.

   Card Displays information using cards, as in Address Cards view (the default view in the Contacts folder).

   Business Card Displays information using customizable, graphical business cards, similar to Detailed Address Cards view.

   Day/Week/Month Displays days in the left half of the window and monthly calendars in the right half. The actual view depends on the type of folder for which you create the view. Figure 27-5 shows a Day/Week/Month view created for the Inbox folder.

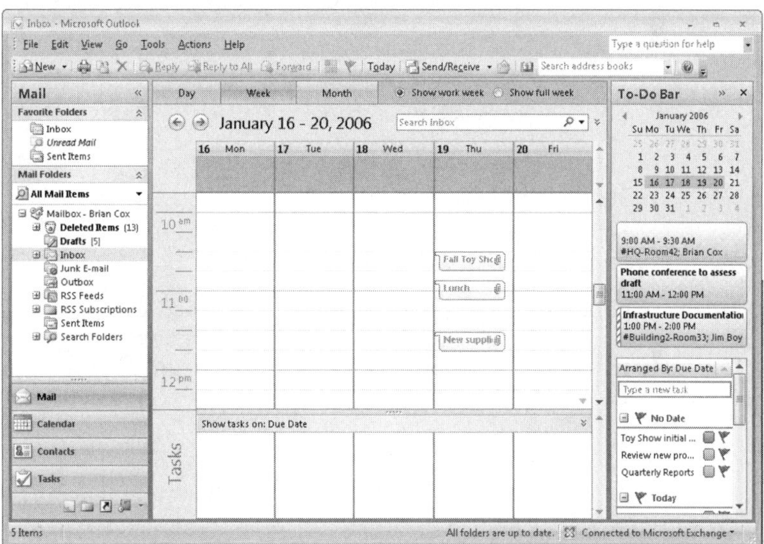

Figure 27-5. This Day/Week/Month view was created for the Inbox folder.

   Icon Displays the items as icons, much as a file system folder does.

6. In the Can Be Used On area, select an option as described in the preceding section, and then click OK. The Customize View dialog box opens.

7. Customize the view as needed, and then click OK.

8. Click Apply View to apply the view, or click Close to close the dialog box without applying the view.

For details on all the options you can configure in the Customize View dialog box, see "Customizing a View's Settings" below.

Modifying, Renaming, or Deleting a View

You can easily modify, rename, and delete custom views. For example, perhaps you want to apply a filter to a view in the Contacts folder to show only those contacts who work for a particular company. Maybe you want to have Outlook 2007 apply a certain label to appointments that have specified text in the subject.

To modify, rename, or delete a view, follow these steps:

1. Choose View, Current View, Define Views to open the Define Views dialog box.
2. In the Views For Folder list, select the view that you want to change, and then do one of the following:
   - To modify the view, click Modify. Use the options in the Customize View dialog box to apply changes to the view (as explained in the following section).
   - To rename the view, click Rename, and then type the new name.
   - To delete the view, click Delete. The Reset button changes to Delete if you select a custom view.
3. Click Close.

Customizing a View's Settings

Outlook 2007 gives you considerable control over the appearance and contents of a view. When you define a new view or modify an existing view, you end up in the Customize View dialog box, shown earlier in Figure 27-2. You can open this dialog box in the following ways:

- Choose View, Current View, Customize Current View.
- Choose View, Current View, Define Views, and then select a view and click Modify.
- Choose Customize Current View in the Navigation Pane when viewing the Contacts, Journal, Notes, or Tasks folder.

The options available in the Customize View dialog box change according to the folder selected. For example, the options for the Contacts folder differ in some respects from the options for the Inbox. The same general concepts hold true for each type of folder, however. The following sections explain the various ways you can use these dialog box options to customize a view.

Configuring Fields

Clicking Fields in the Customize View dialog box in most cases opens the Show Fields dialog box, shown Figure 27-6, in which you can select the fields that you want to include in the view. (Exceptions to this behavior are discussed later.) For example, you might use the Show Fields dialog box to add the Cc or Sensitivity field to the view.

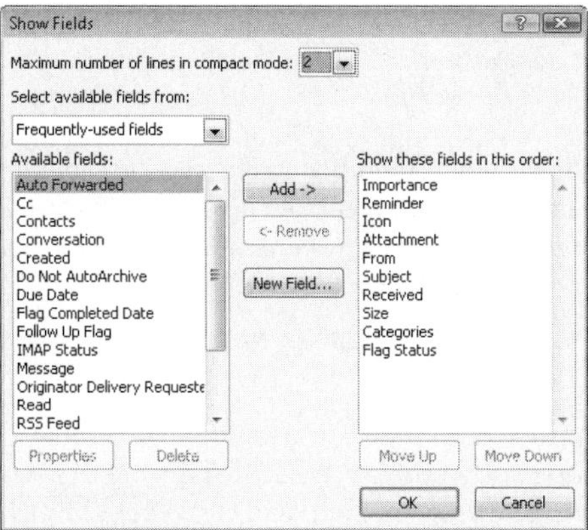

Figure 27-6. Use the Show Fields dialog box to add fields to or remove fields from the view.

Adding fields in the Show Fields dialog box is easy. The available fields (those not already in the view) appear in the list on the left, and the fields already displayed appear in the list on the right. Select a field in the Available Fields list, and then click Add to add it to the view. To remove a field from the view, select the field in the Show These Fields In This Order list, and then click Remove. Use the Move Up and Move Down buttons to rearrange the order in which the fields are displayed in the view.

TROUBLESHOOTING

You need to restore a view to its original settings

You've customized a view, and now you've decided that you need the old view back again. For the future, remember that you can copy an existing view. Rather than modifying an existing view, you can copy a view and then modify the copy. This way you'll still have the original view if you need it.

It's easy to restore a standard view to its previous settings, however. Choose View, Current View, Define Views. Select the view you want to restore, and then click Reset. Click OK when prompted to confirm the action.

> **Note**
>
> You can rearrange the order in which fields are displayed in a table view by dragging the column header for a field to a new location on the column header bar.

> **Note**
>
> You can click New Field in the Show Fields dialog box to create a custom field. For additional information about creating and using custom fields, see Chapter 28, "Designing and Using Forms," and Article 1, "Programming Forms with VBScript," on the companion CD.

In some cases, clicking Fields in the Customize View dialog box opens a Date/Time Fields dialog box similar to the one shown in Figure 27-7. This occurs when you're working with a view that shows time duration, such as Day/Week/Month view in the Calendar folder, By Type view in the Journal folder, or Task Timeline view in the Tasks folder–in effect, nontable views that show time duration graphically.

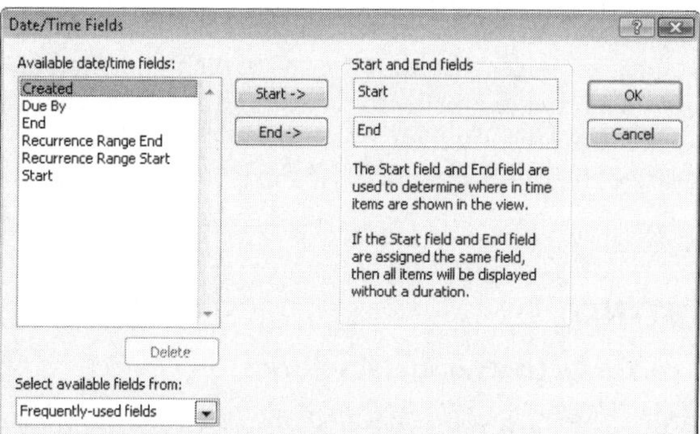

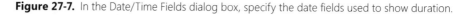

Figure 27-7. In the Date/Time Fields dialog box, specify the date fields used to show duration.

You use the Date/Time Fields dialog box to specify the fields that Outlook 2007 will use to show item duration in the view. The default settings vary but are typically either Start and End or Start Date and Due Date. As an example, you might use the Date/Time Fields dialog box to change the Task Timeline view in the Tasks folder to show the Date Completed field for the task's end rather than the Due Date field.

Grouping Data

Sometimes it's helpful to be able to group items in an Outlook 2007 folder based on specific data fields. For example, you might want to group tasks by owner so that you can see at a glance the tasks assigned to specific people. Perhaps you want to organize contacts by country or region. In these and similar cases, you can modify an existing view or create a new one to organize the view based on the most pertinent data. To group data in a view, click Group By in the Customize View dialog box to open the Group By dialog box, shown in Figure 27-8.

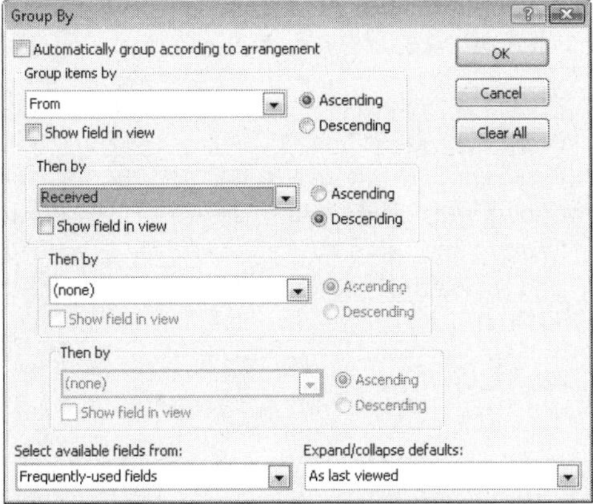

Figure 27-8. Use the Group By dialog box to specify criteria for grouping items in a view.

Follow these steps to group data in a view:

1. In the Group By dialog box, clear the Automatically Group According To Arrangement check box.
2. Select a field type in the Select Available Fields From drop-down list at the bottom of the dialog box. This selection controls the fields that appear in the Group Items By drop-down list.
3. Select a field in the Group Items By drop-down list, and then select either Ascending or Descending, depending on the sort order you want to use. Select the Show Field In View check box to display the field in the view.
4. If you want to create subgroups under the main group, select a field in the Then By drop-down list. (The dialog box contains three such lists, providing three additional grouping levels.) For example, you might group tasks by Owner and then by Due Date.
5. After you've specified all the grouping levels you need, use the Expand/Collapse Defaults drop-down list to specify how you want Outlook 2007 to treat the groups. Use the following list as a guide:

   As Last Viewed Collapses or expands the group according to its state in the previous session.

   All Expanded Expands all items in all groups.

   All Collapsed Collapses all items in all groups.

6. When you're satisfied with the group settings, click OK to close the Group By dialog box. Then click OK to close the Customize View dialog box.

Sorting Data

Sorting data in a view is different from grouping data. For example, you might group the Tasks folder by owner. Each group in the view then shows the tasks assigned to a particular person. You can then sort the data within the group as needed. For example, you might sort the tasks based first on due date and then on subject. Figure 27-9 shows the Tasks folder grouped by owner and sorted by due date.

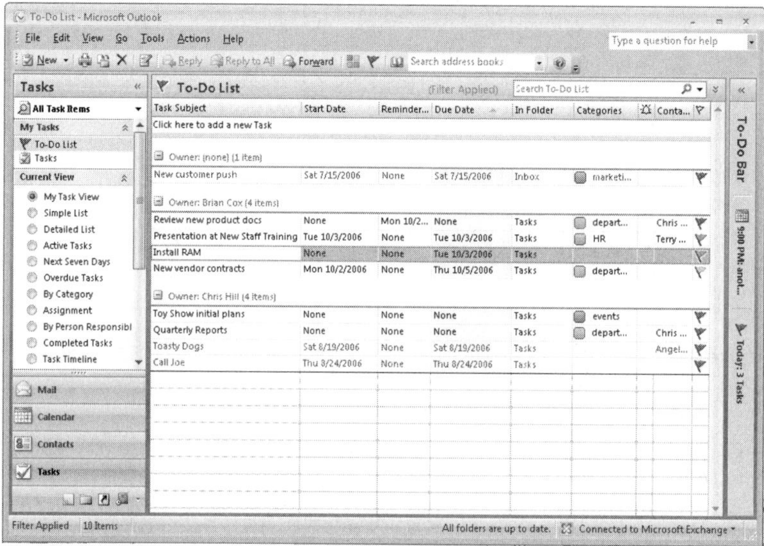

Figure 27-9. In this view, tasks are grouped by owner and then sorted by due date.

Sorting doesn't rely on grouping—you can sort a view whether or not it is grouped. For example, you might sort the Inbox based on the Received field to show messages in the order in which you received them.

> **INSIDE OUT** **Sort table views quickly**
>
> You can quickly sort a table view by clicking the column header for the field by which you want to sort the view. Click the header again to change between ascending and descending sort order.

To create a sort order when you customize or define a view, click Sort in the Customize View dialog box to open the Sort dialog box, shown in Figure 27-10.

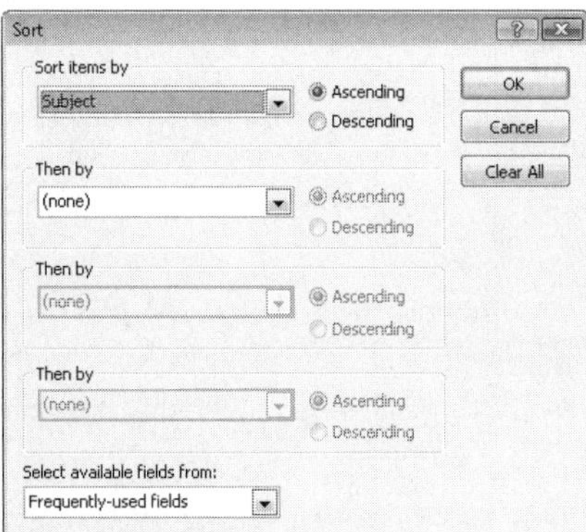

Figure 27-10. Configure a sort order for the view in the Sort dialog box.

To configure sorting in the Sort dialog box, follow these steps:

1. In the Select Available Fields From drop-down list, select the type of field the sort should be based on.
2. In the Sort Items By drop-down list, select the specific field by which you want to sort the view.
3. Select Ascending or Descending, depending on the type of sort you need.
4. Use the Then By lists to specify additional sort levels, if necessary.
5. Click OK to close the Sort dialog box, and then click OK to close the Customize View dialog box.

Applying Filters to the View

In Outlook 2007, the ability to filter a view is an extremely powerful feature that gives you considerable control over the data displayed in a given view. For example, you might have hundreds of messages in your Inbox and need to filter the view to show only those messages from a particular sender. You could simply sort the Inbox by the From field and scan the list of messages, but you might want to refine the search a little, perhaps viewing only messages from a specific sender that have an attachment and were sent within the previous week. Filters allow you to do just that.

To configure a filter, click Filter in the Customize View dialog box to open the Filter dialog box, shown in Figure 27-11. This multitabbed dialog box lets you specify multiple conditions to define which items will appear in the view.

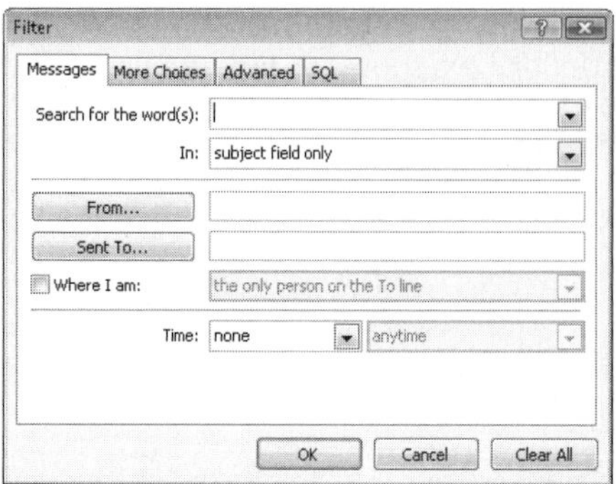

Figure 27-11. Use the Filter dialog box to specify multiple conditions that determine what data appears in the view.

Note that the first tab in the Filter dialog box varies according to the current folder type. For a contacts folder, for example, the first tab is labeled Contacts and offers options for creating filter conditions that apply to contacts. For a message folder, the first tab is labeled Messages and provides options for creating filter conditions specific to messages.

The various tabs in the Filter dialog box include a broad range of options that let you specify multiple conditions for the filter. You can use conditions from more than one tab. For example, you might enter words to search for and a sender on the Messages tab, select categories on the More Choices tab, and specify a particular field and value on the Advanced tab.

> **Note**
>
> The Advanced tab of the Filter dialog box gives you access to all available fields and several criteria (Contains, Doesn't Contain, and Is Empty, for example), making it the place to go to configure conditions not available on the other tabs. To define filter criteria, select a field in the Field drop-down list, select an option in the Condition drop-down list, type a value, and then click Add. Use the SQL tab to perform Structured Query Language (SQL) queries to retrieve data from the folder to show in the custom view.

Configuring Fonts and Other General Settings

When you click Other Settings in the Customize View dialog box, Outlook 2007 opens a dialog box that lets you configure some general settings for the custom view. These options vary from one folder type to another—the Contacts folder, the Inbox, and the Calendar folder, for example, all use different options. You can change such properties as the font used for column headers and row text, the grid style and shading for table views, and a handful of other general options.

Creating Rules for Automatic Formatting of Text

Click Automatic Formatting in the Customize View dialog box to display the Automatic Formatting dialog box, similar to the one shown in Figure 27-12. This dialog box lets you create rules that cause Outlook 2007 to automatically format data in the view based on the criteria you specify. For example, you might create an automatic formatting rule that has Outlook 2007 display in blue all tasks that you own and display all other tasks in black. Or perhaps you may create a rule to display in green all contacts from a specific company.

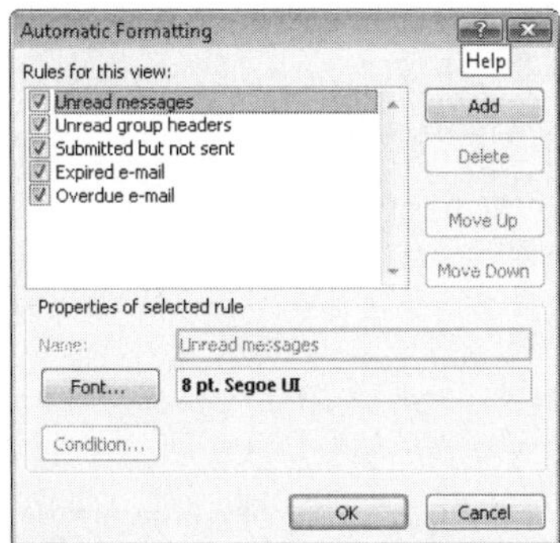

Figure 27-12. Use the Automatic Formatting dialog box to create rules that automatically format text in views based on the conditions you specify.

As you're working in the Automatic Formatting dialog box, keep in mind that you can't create task-oriented rules, as you can with the Rules Wizard. For example, you can't create a rule in this dialog box that moves messages from one folder to another. The rules you create in the Automatic Formatting dialog box control only the appearance (color, font, and font styles) of data in the view.

For information about the Rules Wizard see Chapter 11, "Processing Messages Automatically."

You can't modify the conditions for predefined rules, but you can specify the font characteristics to use for the rule. You can also create your own rules and change the order in which rules are applied to achieve the results you need.

To set up an automatic formatting rule for text, follow these steps:

1. Click Add in the Automatic Formatting dialog box to add a new rule named Untitled.
2. Click Font to open a standard Font dialog box in which you specify the font, font style, and color that will apply to text that meets the rule's condition.
3. Close the Font dialog box, and then click Condition to open the Filter dialog box, shown in Figure 27-13. This dialog box offers three tabs you can use to specify the condition for the rule. You can specify multiple conditions from multiple tabs, if needed.

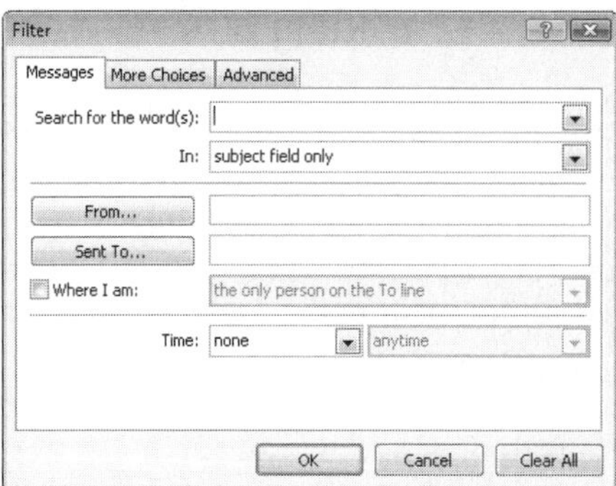

Figure 27-13. Specify conditions for the rule in the Filter dialog box.

4. Click OK when you're satisfied with the filter condition.

TROUBLESHOOTING

You need to restrict the available views

In some situations, you might want to restrict the available views to only the custom views you've created, hiding the standard views that Outlook 2007 provides. For example, perhaps you created a custom calendar view that you want all employees to use instead of the standard calendar views because your custom view includes additional information that the standard views don't contain. When you restrict the Outlook 2007 views to only custom views, the standard views no longer appear on the View menu.

You must configure each folder separately. For example, you might restrict the Calendar folder views without restricting the Inbox folder views. This would give users the ability to choose one of the standard Outlook 2007 views in the Inbox folder but would limit their choices to only custom views in the Calendar folder.

Follow these steps to restrict the views that Outlook 2007 provides on the View menu:

1. In Outlook 2007, select the folder for which you want to restrict views.
2. Choose View, Current View, Define Views to open the Define Views dialog box.
3. Select the Only Show Views Created For This Folder check box, and then click Close.
4. Repeat steps 2 and 3 to restrict other folders as necessary.

Note

The option to tell Outlook 2007 to use only custom views for a folder is not available in the Tasks folder.

Printing in Outlook

Many users work in Outlook 2007 and never print any of the items they store in the program. For other users, however, the ability to print from Outlook 2007 is important. For example, if you use a hard-copy day planner rather than a notebook computer or a Personal Digital Assistant (PDA) to keep track of your daily schedule, you might prepare the schedule in Outlook 2007 and then print it for insertion in the day planner.

This section examines the options and methods for printing your Outlook 2007 data. It also explains how to customize the print styles provided by Outlook 2007 to create custom styles that better suit your preferences or needs.

Overview of Print Styles

Outlook 2007 offers several predefined print styles that you can use to print information from various Outlook 2007 folders. The most common print styles are Table and Memo, as indicated in Table 27-1, which lists the standard print styles in Outlook 2007.

Table 27-1 Outlook 2007 Print Styles by Folder Type

Folder Type	View	Print Styles
Calendar	Day/Week/Month Day/Week/Month with AutoPreview	Daily, Weekly, Monthly, Tri-Fold, Calendar Details, Memo
	Active Appointments All Appointments Events Annual Events Recurring Appointments By Category Outlook Data Files	Table, Memo
Contacts	Business Cards Address Cards Detailed Address Cards	Card, Small Booklet, Medium Booklet, Memo, Phone Directory
	Phone List By Category By Company By Location Outlook Data Files	Table, Memo
Inbox	All except Message Timeline	Table, Memo
	Message Timeline	Prints individual items only
Journal	By Type By Contact By Category	Prints individual items only

Folder Type	View	Print Styles
	Entry List Last Seven Days Phone Calls Outlook Data Files	Table, Memo
Notes	Icon	Memo
	All except Icon	
Tasks	All except Task Timeline	Table, Memo
	Task Timeline	Prints individual items only

Note

Most views that have just Table and Memo styles available have only the Table style available if no item is selected.

INSIDE OUT **Printing a timeline**

As Table 27-1 indicates, you can print only individual items when you're working with a timeline view. However, if you're scheduling a major project, a printout of a timeline view would be useful. If you need that capability, consider using Microsoft Office Project 2007 instead of Outlook 2007. For details about how you can use Outlook 2007 to enhance your work in Office Project 2007, see Chapter 39, "Integrating Microsoft Outlook and Microsoft Project."

Printing from Outlook

Printing from Outlook 2007 is just as easy as printing from any other application. Simply select the view or item you want to print, and then choose File, Print (or if you have an item open, click the Microsoft Office Button, and then click Print) to print the document or choose File, Print Preview (or click the Microsoft Office Button, and then click Print, Print Preview) to preview it.

If you click the Microsoft Office Button and then click Print, Outlook 2007 displays a Print dialog box similar to the one shown in Figure 27-14. The contents of the dialog box vary according to the type of view from which you're printing.

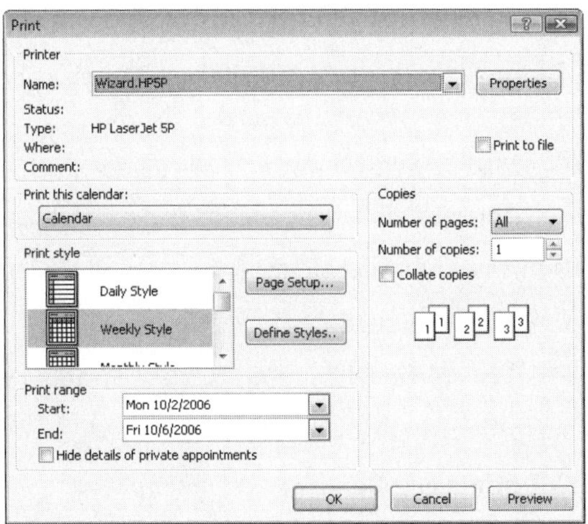

Figure 27-14. You can select an existing print style in the Print dialog box.

In the Print Style list, select a print style. For example, select Phone Directory Style for the Contacts folder to print a phone list, or select one of the two booklet styles to print contact entries for a day planner. If you need to fine-tune the print settings, click Page Setup to display a Page Setup dialog box similar to the one shown in Figure 27-15.

For additional details on printing contacts and using different print styles with the Contacts folder, see "Printing Contacts" in Chapter 18.

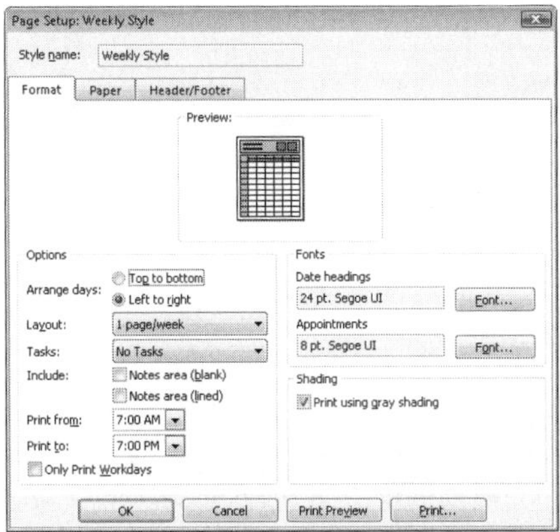

Figure 27-15. Use the Page Setup dialog box to modify print options for the selected style.

Use the Format tab of the Page Setup dialog box to specify the layout, fonts, and other general properties for the job. The options on the Format tab vary from one folder type to another. For example, you can use the Format tab to set the following options, some of which are specific to particular folder types:

- Whether Outlook 2007 keeps sections together or starts a new page for each section

- The number of columns per page
- The number of blank forms to print at the end of the job (such as blank contact forms)
- Whether Outlook 2007 prints a contact index on the page edge
- Whether letter headings for each alphabetic section of a contact list are included
- The font used for headings and for body text
- Whether Outlook 2007 adds gray shading to headings
- Whether the Daily Task List, To-Do Bar, or notes areas are printed with a calendar
- Whether weekends are printed in a calendar view
- Whether Outlook 2007 prints one month of a calendar per page

Use the Paper tab, shown in Figure 27-16, to configure the page type, size, source, and other properties. For example, in the Type list on the Paper tab, you can select the type of day planner you use so that Outlook 2007 prints using that style.

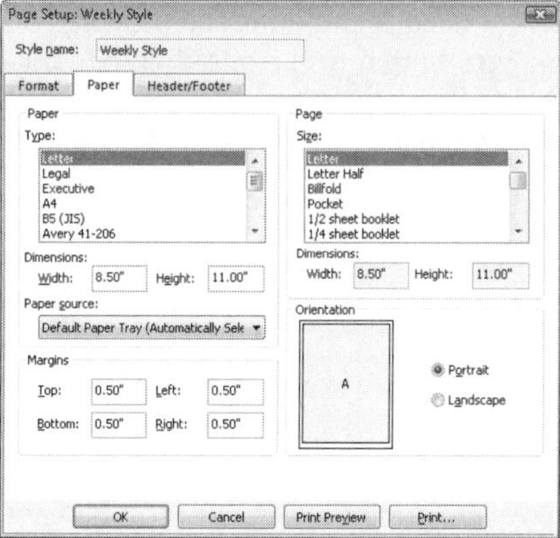

Figure 27-16. Use the Paper tab to configure the paper source, size, type, and other paper settings.

Use the Header/Footer tab, shown in Figure 27-17, to specify the items that you want printed in the header and the footer. This tab provides three boxes for the header and three for the footer. The left box specifies items that print on the left side of the page, the middle box specifies items that print in the middle of the page, and the right box specifies items that print on the right side of the page. You can enter text manually or use the buttons near the bottom to insert specific data such as page numbers, the user, the time, and other dynamic data.

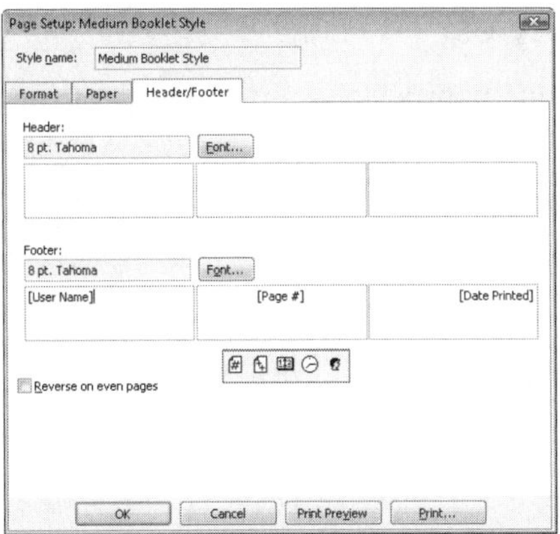

Figure 27-17. Use the Header/Footer tab to enter header and footer data.

After you select the page setup options, you can return to the Print dialog box or preview the document. The Print dialog box offers a handful of options that can help you further refine the printed data. For example, use the Start and End lists to specify a range of data to print. Select the Hide Details Of Private Appointments check box if you don't want the details of your private appointments printed. Set printer properties, the number of copies to print, and other general print settings, and then click OK to print or click Preview to preview the document.

Calendar Printing Assistant for Outlook

The Outlook 2007 calendar is an excellent tool for managing your schedule, but its printing options are somewhat limited. This can be frustrating if you, like many people, want to print a customized view of your calendar to take with you when you're away from your computer.

To meet this need, Microsoft has created the Calendar Printing Assistant, which offers a simple way of creating custom views of your calendar for printing and distribution. With the Calendar Printing Assistant, you can:

- Choose from dozens of templates, with views ranging from a day to a year.
- Fully customize the formatting, including styles and images.
- Use the same themes as other 2007 Microsoft Office system applications such as Office PowerPoint® 2007, Office Word 2007, and Office Excel® 2007, including any custom themes you have created.
- Integrate information from multiple calendars, tasks, and to-do lists into a single view.
- Publish your custom calendar as an .xps document, allowing you to use Information Rights Management (IRM) to control access and distribution.

The Calendar Printing Assistant for Microsoft Office Outlook 2007 is available at *www.microsoft.com/office/preview/programs/outlook/cpa.mspx*.

Creating Custom Print Styles

Outlook 2007 provides a broad range of print styles, so it's likely that they will fit most of your needs. When these print styles don't quite offer what you need, however, you can create a custom print style.

> **Note**
>
> If you find yourself using an existing print style but frequently making the same option changes before printing, modify the existing print style to create a custom print style.

You can either modify an existing print style or copy a style and then modify it to incorporate the changes you need. If you always use the same modifications on a particular print style, you might prefer to simply modify that existing style rather than creating a new one. If you use the default style occasionally but modify its properties for most other print jobs, consider creating a custom print style based on the existing one so that both are available.

Follow these steps to modify or create a new print style:

1. In Outlook 2007, open the view for which you want to modify the print style or on which you want to base your custom print style.
2. Choose File, Page Setup, Define Print Styles to open the Define Print Styles dialog box, shown in Figure 27-18.

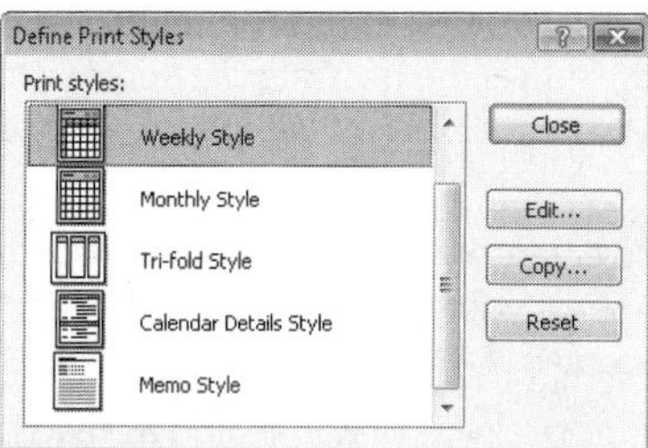

Figure 27-18. Use the Define Print Styles dialog box to modify and copy print styles.

3. If you want to create a new style, select an existing style, and then click Copy. Otherwise, select an existing style, and then click Edit. In either case, Outlook 2007 displays a Page Setup dialog box similar to the one shown in Figure 27-19.

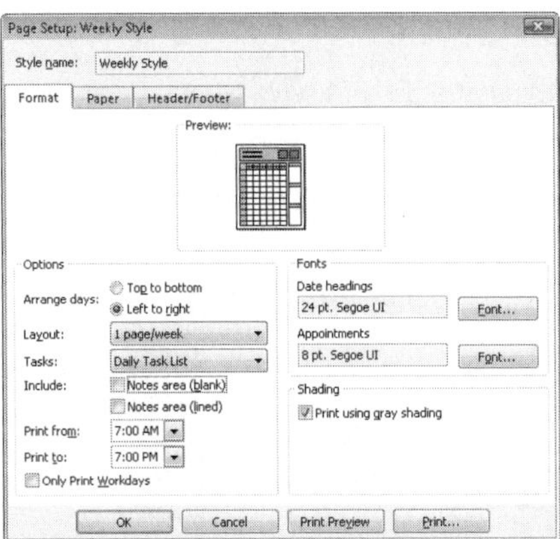

Figure 27-19. Use the Page Setup dialog box to specify properties for the print style.

4. Specify options as needed in the dialog box, and then click OK to apply the changes.
5. In the Define Print Styles dialog box, click Close.

When you want to print using a particular style, open the view from which you want to print, and then choose File, Print. In the Print dialog box, select the style in the Print Style list, set other properties as necessary, and then click OK to print.

Deleting Print Styles

If you've created some custom print styles but no longer use them, or if you've been experimenting with print styles and have a few samples you want to delete, removing them is a simple matter.

Follow these steps to remove a print style:

1. Choose File, Page Setup, Define Print Styles to open the Define Print Styles dialog box.
2. Select the style you want to remove, and then click Delete.
3. When you have finished deleting print styles, click Close.

Resetting Print Styles

You can't delete the standard print styles provided in Outlook 2007, but you can restore them to their default state. For example, suppose that you made several changes to the default Small Booklet style for the Contacts folder. Now you want to restore the print style to its default settings, but you don't remember what they are. Fortunately, Outlook 2007 remembers them for you.

To reset a print style, follow these steps:

1. Choose File, Page Setup, Define Print Styles to open the Define Print Styles dialog box.
2. Select the style you want to reset, and then click Reset. Outlook 2007 prompts you to verify the action.
3. Click OK to reset the style or Cancel to cancel the operation.
4. Click Close.

Custom Printing with Scripts and Word

The existing print styles in Outlook 2007 and the capability to define custom styles accommodate the needs of most users. In some situations, however, these built-in printing features are not enough. With a little custom scripting and Word 2007, however, you can overcome these limitations.

Word 2007 offers almost unlimited print layout capabilities, making it a great tool for laying out almost any type of document. For example, assume that you're not satisfied with the way Outlook 2007 prints messages from mail folders. When you print a message, the recipient's name appears in large, bold type at the top of the page, as shown in Figure 27-20. You are likely printing your own messages, so you might want different information–such as the message subject–displayed on the first line.

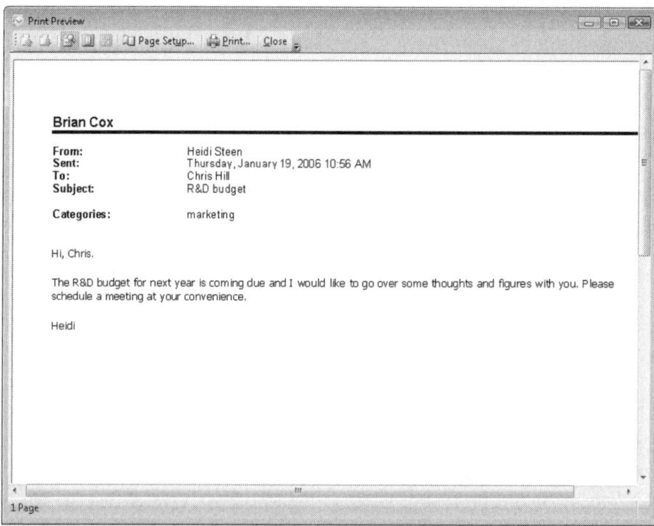

Figure 27-20. The standard message layout.

Although you can make minimal changes to the print layout such as adding headers or footers, you can't do much in Outlook 2007 to change the way most items are printed.

You can, however, copy Outlook 2007 items to Word 2007, format the document as needed, and then print it (from Word 2007). You might think that moving the data from Outlook 2007 to Word 2007 is a time-consuming task, but you can make it happen in less than a second—provided you create a script to accomplish the task for you.

Using a Custom Contact Style

In this first example, assume that you want to create a specific layout for contacts that prints the contact name in bold, places the contact's picture in the upper-right corner, and then includes selected contact information such as address, phone, e-mail, and other properties underneath. Figure 27-21 illustrates this custom print layout.

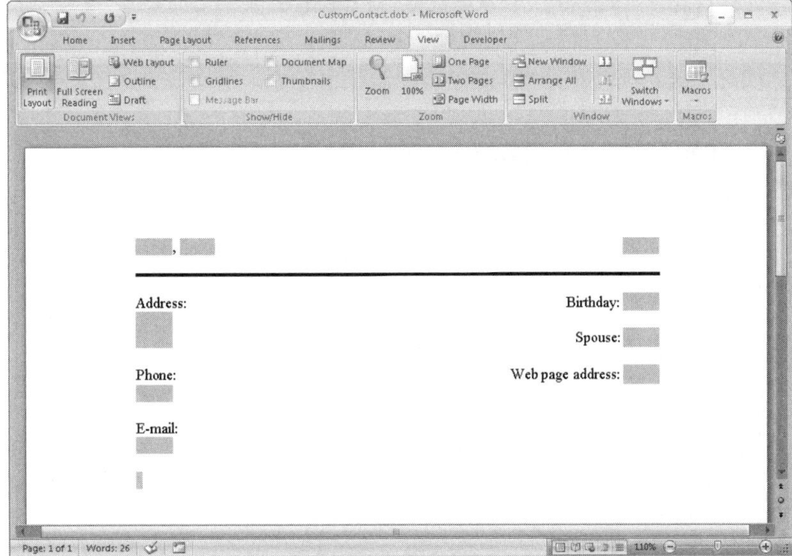

Figure 27-21. This contact style presents selected information in a specific layout.

The first step in creating this custom contact style is to create the document layout in Word 2007. In a nutshell, this means creating a document template that contains a text form field for each contact item that you want included on the printout and then following these steps:

> **Note**
>
> The companion CD contains two sample templates named CustomContactPrint.dotx and CustomMessagePrint.dotx that you can customize to suit your needs or simply use as samples for this example. The code for the macros used in this section is also included (CustomContact.txt and CustomMessagePrint.txt). Create a folder named myMail in the root of the C drive, and then copy these files into that folder so that the macros can locate them.

1. In Word 2007, open a new document. Click the Microsoft Office Button, and then click Word Options. On the Popular tab, select the Show Developer Tab On The Ribbon check box, and then click OK.
2. Enter labels for the Outlook 2007 fields. Then position the insertion point after the first label, and on the Developer tab, in the Controls group, select the Rich Text content control to insert a field to contain the data that will come from the Outlook 2007 contact.
3. Select the first text form field, press the **Spacebar** to delete the default text, and on the Insert tab, in the Links group, choose Bookmark. In the Bookmark dialog box, shown in Figure 27-22, type a name for the bookmark that identifies the field (such as **LastName**), and then click Add.

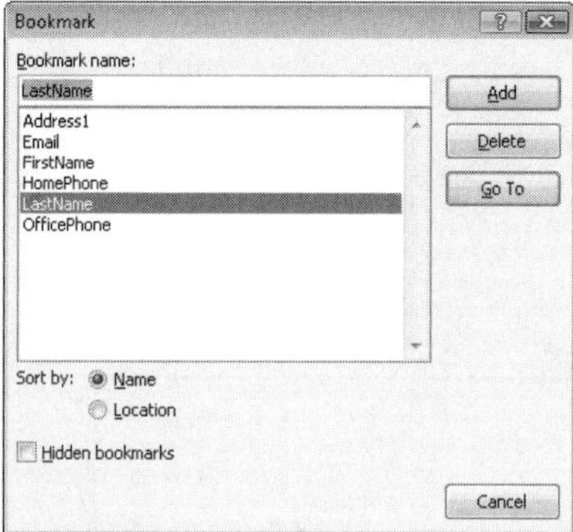

Figure 27-22. Add a bookmark for each text form field.

4. Select the remaining fields and add bookmarks for them, naming the bookmarks according to the information the field will contain, such as FirstName, Email, Phone, and so on.
5. Select the Title field, format it using a larger font, and then add any other characteristics such as bold type.
6. Draw a line separating the name and other information, if desired.
7. Click the Microsoft Office Button, click Save As, Word Template, specify the path C:\myMail and the name CustomContact.dotx, click Save, and then exit Word 2007.

You now have a template that is ready to be filled in by Outlook 2007. The next step is to create a macro in Outlook 2007 that copies the desired information from the current contact item to the form and then prints the form. The following sample macro accomplishes these tasks. However, this sample does not provide extensive error checking, so consider this a starting point for your own macro. For example, you might want to add code that verifies that the current item is a contact item, and if not, displays an error message and exits.

Getting Ready to Use Macros

Outlook 2007 has tighter security settings than earlier versions, so before you can run macros, you have to set the macro security level to allow unsigned macros to execute. You also have to configure Outlook 2007 to display the Developer tab on the Ribbon so that you can access macro commands from an open Outlook 2007 item.

To configure macro security, in Outlook 2007, choose Tools, Trust Center. In the Trust Center, select Macro Security (or choose Tools, Macros, Security). Choose Warnings For All Macros, and then click OK. If you prefer not to have Outlook 2007 warn you when a macro is trying to execute, you can select No Security Check For Macros, but be careful, because this allows any macro to execute without your knowledge.

To access the Developer tab, in any Outlook 2007 folder, double-click an item to open it. Click the Microsoft Office Button, and then click Editor Options. On the Popular tab, select the Show Developer Tab On The Ribbon check box, and then click OK.

The following macro is included on the companion CD in the file CustomContactPrint.txt. Before using this macro, you need to create a folder named myMail in the root of the C drive. Copy the Word 2007 templates that are included on the companion CD into that folder so that the macros can locate them.

Choose Tools, Macro, Macros, type **CustomContactPrint** in the Macro Name field, and then click Create. Enter the following code:

```
Sub CustomContactPrint()
    'Set up objects
    Dim strTemplate As String
    Dim objWord As Object
    Dim objDocs As Object
    Dim objApp As Application
    Dim objItem As Object
    Dim objAttach As Object
    Dim numAttach As Integer
    Dim objNS As NameSpace
    Dim mybklist As Object
    Dim x As Integer
    Dim pictureSaved As Boolean
    Dim myShape As Object
    'Dim ContactAddress
    'Create a Word document and current contact item object
    Set objApp = CreateObject("Outlook.Application")
    Set objNS = objApp.GetNamespace("MAPI")
    'Check to ensure Outlook item is selected
    If TypeName(objApp.ActiveInspector) = "Nothing" Then
        MsgBox "Contact not open. Exiting", vbOKOnly + vbInformation, "Outlook Inside 
Out"
        Exit Sub
    End If
```

```
    Set objItem = objApp.ActiveInspector.CurrentItem
    Set objWord = CreateObject("Word.Application")
    strTemplate = "c:\myMail\CustomContact.dotx
    Set objDocs = objWord.Documents
    objDocs.Add strTemplate
    Set mybklist = objWord.activeDocument.Bookmarks
    'Fill in the form
    objWord.activeDocument.Bookmarks("LastName").Select
    objWord.Selection.TypeText CStr(objItem.LastName)
    objWord.activeDocument.Bookmarks("FirstName").Select
    objWord.Selection.TypeText CStr(objItem.FirstName)
    If objItem.HasPicture = True Then
        Set objAttach = objItem.Attachments
        numAttach = objAttach.Count
        For x = 1 To numAttach
            If objAttach.Item(x).DisplayName = "ContactPicture.jpg" Then
                objAttach.Item(x).SaveAsFile "C:\myMail\" & _
                objAttach.Item(x).DisplayName
                pictureSaved = True
            End If
        Next x
        If pictureSaved = True Then
            objWord.activeDocument.Bookmarks("Picture").Select
            Set myShape = objWord.activeDocument.Shapes.AddPicture("c:\myMail\
ContactPicture.jpg", False, True, 432, -25)
            objWord.activeDocument.Shapes(1).Left = 432 - objWord.activeDocument.
Shapes(1).Width
        End If
    End If
    objWord.activeDocument.Bookmarks("Address1").Select
    objWord.Selection.TypeText CStr(objItem.BusinessAddressStreet)
    objWord.activeDocument.Bookmarks("Address2").Select
    objWord.Selection.TypeText CStr(objItem.BusinessAddressCity)
    objWord.Selection.TypeText ", "
    objWord.Selection.TypeText CStr(objItem.BusinessAddressState)
    objWord.Selection.TypeText " "
    objWord.Selection.TypeText CStr(objItem.BusinessAddressPostalCode)
    objWord.activeDocument.Bookmarks("Spouse").Select
    objWord.Selection.TypeText CStr(objItem.Spouse)
    objWord.activeDocument.Bookmarks("Phone1").Select
    objWord.Selection.TypeText CStr(objItem.BusinessTelephoneNumber)
    objWord.activeDocument.Bookmarks("WebPage").Select
    objWord.Selection.TypeText CStr(objItem.BusinessHomePage)
    objWord.activeDocument.Bookmarks("Email1").Select
    objWord.Selection.TypeText CStr(objItem.Email1Address)
    'Print and exit
    objWord.PrintOut Background:=True

    'Process other system events until printing is finished
    While objWord.BackgroundPrintingStatus
        DoEvents
    Wend
```

```
    objWord.Quit SaveChanges:=wdvbaDoNotSaveChanges
    Set objApp = Nothing
    Set objNS = Nothing
    Set objItem = Nothing
    Set objWord = Nothing
    Set objDocs = Nothing
    Set mybklist = Nothing
End Sub
```

If you examine this macro code, you'll see that it uses named bookmarks to locate the position in the document where each contact element will be inserted. Also notice that the lines in the macro that insert specific contact items reference those items by their Outlook 2007 object model names, such as Email1Address, BusinessTelephoneNumber, BusinessHomePage, and so on. If you want to modify this macro to insert other contact items, you'll need to know the item names. To view contact item properties, choose Tools, Macro, Visual Basic Editor, and then choose Help, Microsoft Visual Basic Help. Select Outlook Object Model Reference, and then click ContactItem Object. Click the Properties link, and then scroll through the list of properties to locate the one you need.

This macro also determines whether the contact has a picture associated with it. If so, the macro cycles through the attachments to locate the picture (which is always named ContactPicture.jpg) and saves it to disk. The macro then inserts the picture in the Word 2007 document. Although ContactPicture.jpg is always the first attachment, regardless of the order in which items are attached or their names, this macro checks each attachment anyway to accommodate future changes in Outlook 2007 regarding picture attachments.

Note

The macro saves the picture file in the folder you created for the Word 2007 templates, C:\myMail\. You can change the macro code to save and load the picture from any path. You can also change the path location for the Word 2007 document template as needed.

To run the macro and print a contact in this format, in the Contacts folder, open the contact you want to print. On the Developer tab, in the Code group, select Macros. (If you have not added the Developer tab to the Ribbon, press **Alt+F8**.) Select the CustomContactPrint macro, and then click Run. The macro will run and print the open contact on the default printer.

Using a Custom Message Style

You can use a method similar to the one in the preceding section to print messages from Outlook 2007 using Word 2007. For example, assume that you want to print e-mail messages with the subject in large, bold type at the top of the page and with other message content printed below that. Figure 27-23 shows a sample form in Word 2007. Use the same general steps detailed in the preceding section to create a

Word 2007 template that contains the form text fields and bookmarks needed to hold the message items.

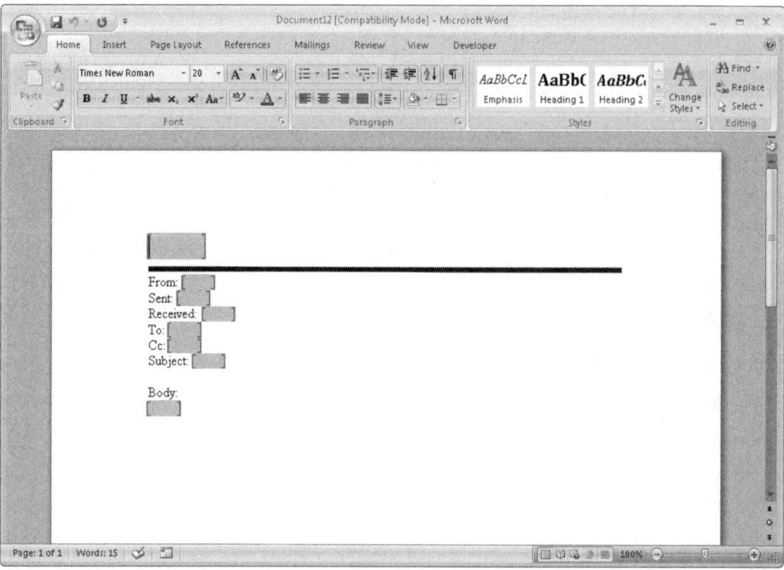

Figure 27-23. A sample form in Word 2007 for printing messages.

After you create the document template in Word 2007 and save it, open the Microsoft Visual Basic® Editor and create the following macro:

This sample macro is contained on the companion CD as CustomMessagePrint.txt.

```
Sub CustomMessagePrint()
    'Set up objects
    Dim strTemplate As String
    Dim objWord As Object
    Dim objDocs As Object
    Dim objApp As Application
    Dim objItem As Object
    Dim objNS As NameSpace
    Dim mybklist As Object
    'Create a Word document and current message item object
    Set objApp = CreateObject("Outlook.Application")
    Set objNS = objApp.GetNamespace("MAPI")
    'Check to ensure Outlook item is selected
    If TypeName(objApp.ActiveInspector) = "Nothing" Then
        MsgBox "Message not open. Exiting", vbOKOnly + vbInformation, "Outlook Inside
Out"
        Exit Sub
    End If
    Set objItem = objApp.ActiveInspector.CurrentItem
    Set objWord = CreateObject("Word.Application")
```

```
    strTemplate = "c:\myMail\prnmsg.dotx"
    Set objDocs = objWord.Documents
    objDocs.Add strTemplate
    Set mybklist = objWord.activeDocument.Bookmarks
    'Fill in the form
    objWord.activeDocument.Bookmarks("Title").Select
    objWord.Selection.TypeText CStr(objItem.Subject)
    objWord.activeDocument.Bookmarks("From").Select
    objWord.Selection.TypeText CStr(objItem.SenderName)
    objWord.activeDocument.Bookmarks("Sent").Select
    objWord.Selection.TypeText CStr(objItem.SentOn)
    objWord.activeDocument.Bookmarks("Received").Select
    objWord.Selection.TypeText CStr(objItem.ReceivedTime)
    objWord.activeDocument.Bookmarks("To").Select
    objWord.Selection.TypeText CStr(objItem.To)
    objWord.activeDocument.Bookmarks("Cc").Select
    objWord.Selection.TypeText CStr(objItem.CC)
    objWord.activeDocument.Bookmarks("Subject").Select
    objWord.Selection.TypeText CStr(objItem.Subject)
    objWord.activeDocument.Bookmarks("Body").Select
    objWord.Selection.TypeText CStr(objItem.Body)
    'Print and exit

    objWord.PrintOut Background:=True
    'Process other system events until printing is finished
    While objWord.BackgroundPrintingStatus
        DoEvents
    Wend
    objWord.Quit SaveChanges:=wdvbaDoNotSaveChanges
End Sub
```

As with the CustomContactPrint macro, you can customize this macro and document template to accommodate different or additional message fields as needed.

Custom Printing with Excel

Office Excel 2007 is another solution to custom printing requirements, particularly for Outlook 2007 table views. For example, assume that you want to print all of your Outlook 2007 contacts but you want to arrange them in a different order from what the Table style offers in Outlook 2007 and use different formatting for some of the columns. The solution is to simply copy the contacts to Excel 2007, format and rearrange as needed, and print by following these steps:

1. Open the Outlook 2007 folder containing the items you want to print, and then choose a table view. This example uses the Phone List view, as shown in Figure 27-24.
2. Select the items that you want included in the printed document, and then press **Ctrl+C** or choose Edit, Copy to copy the items to the Clipboard.

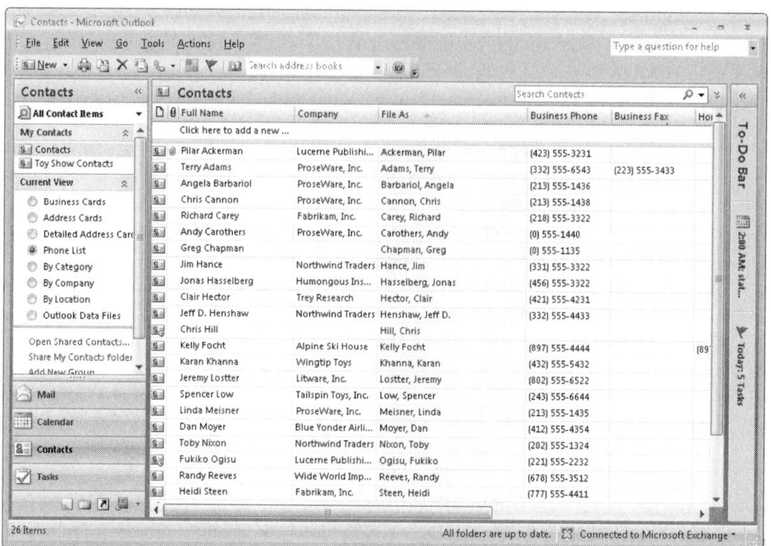

Figure 27-24. You can easily copy data from an Outlook 2007 table view to Excel 2007.

3. Start Excel 2007, and then press **Ctrl+V** or choose Edit, Paste to paste the data into Excel 2007, as shown in Figure 27-25.

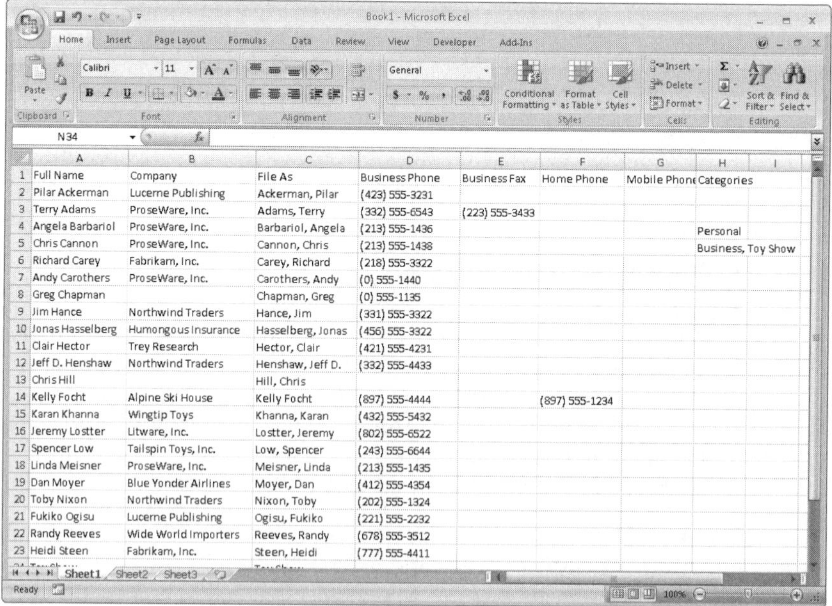

Figure 27-25. Copy data to Excel 2007, and then arrange, format, and print.

4. Rearrange columns, apply formatting, and otherwise adjust the layout as needed, and then print the worksheet.

CHAPTER 28

Designing and Using Forms

Even without any custom programming, Microsoft® Office Outlook® 2007 provides an excellent set of features. In fact, many organizations don't need anything beyond what Office Outlook 2007 offers right out of the box. Others, however, have special needs that are not addressed adequately by Outlook 2007—perhaps because of the way these organizations do business or because of specific requirements in their particular industries. In such cases, you have ample opportunity to extend the functionality of Outlook 2007 through custom design and programming.

For example, you might need to add some fields to your message forms or your meeting request forms. Perhaps you need an easier way for users to perform mail merge operations with Microsoft Office Word 2007 and Outlook 2007 contacts lists. Maybe you simply want to fine-tune your forms to add your company logo, special instructions, or warnings for users.

Whatever your situation, you can easily make changes to the existing Outlook 2007 forms, or you can even design new ones. The changes you make can be simple or complex: you might add one or two fields to the standard contact form, or you might add a considerable amount of program code to allow Outlook 2007 to perform custom tasks or interact with other 2007 Microsoft Office system applications. This chapter starts you on the right path by explaining how Outlook 2007 uses forms and how you can customize them to suit your needs. If you aren't comfortable programming with Microsoft Visual Basic® for Applications (VBA), don't worry—you can accomplish a lot with custom forms without ever writing a single line of program code.

Forms are such a normal part of everything we do on computers that we sometimes take them for granted. It's still true, however, that a lot of programs used all over the world can be accessed only with screens that provide monochrome text and puzzling menus with strange codes and submission sequences. With their versatility and ease of use, forms offer a revolutionary approach—and you can unlock their power with several mouse clicks and some solid planning. This chapter discusses using Outlook 2007 forms as part of a software solution for individual computing needs. It also examines the types of forms you can modify and create and how the forms are created, published, and stored.

With Outlook 2007, you can employ two basic strategies for form development. The first is to use or modify a standard form. The second is to create your own form from scratch. With either strategy, it's important to remember that you're programming events that are specifically associated with the item involved, not with the Outlook 2007 application generally. In other words, when you put code behind your form, you're dealing with events related to the item that's represented by the form. For example, if you were to design a form to create a custom e-mail message, you'd probably program a common event named *Item_Send*, which occurs when the item (the message) is sent. You couldn't program the form to respond to an event that fires (that is, occurs or executes) when the item is specifically sent from the Outbox to another user's Inbox or when the user's view changes from one folder to another. This is because in form development, you can access only the events associated with the item in question.

Overview of Standard Forms, Item Types, and Message Classes

Outlook 2007 uses a combination of forms, item types, and message classes as its fundamental components. Although you don't need to understand much about any of these three components to use Outlook 2007, a developer must understand them reasonably well. Obviously, the more you know, the more powerful your Outlook 2007–based solution will be.

Outlook Forms

Outlook 2007 provides numerous predefined forms that you can use as the foundation of your form-based solution. These standard forms include the following:

- Appointment form
- Contact form
- Journal entry form
- Meeting request form
- Message form
- Post form
- Task form
- Task request form
- RSS article form

As this list of Outlook 2007 forms indicates, the basic item types available in a typical Outlook 2007 with Microsoft Exchange Server application are each represented by a corresponding form. The Outlook 2007 forms in this list match the ones you are used to working with on a daily basis, so you are not starting with a blank slate when you want to customize a form for your own use.

Each of these forms comes with built-in user interface elements and corresponding functionality. For example, the appointment form shown in Figure 28-1 has interface elements and functions that relate to setting appointments, such as generating reminders and controlling the calendar display. The contact form, in contrast, is designed to permit the addition or modification of contact information.

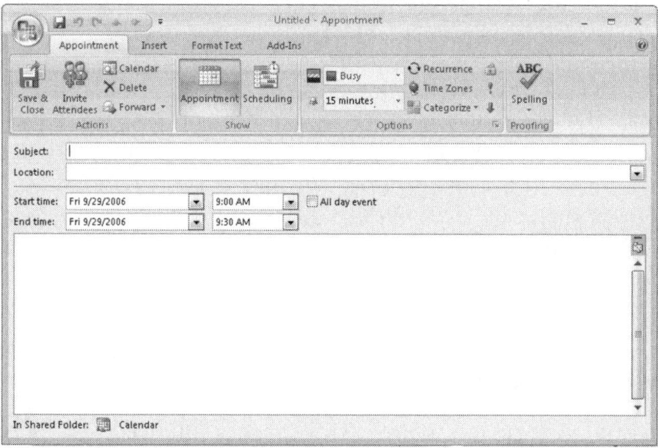

Figure 28-1. The appointment form is one of the standard forms that you can use in Outlook 2007.

Outlook Item Types

Several basic item types are part of an Outlook 2007 installation. Among the 2007 Microsoft Office system VBA item types that you can use are the following ones specific to Outlook 2007:

- MailItem
- ContactItem
- TaskItem
- AppointmentItem
- PostItem
- NoteItem

> **Note**
>
> Other item types are built into Outlook 2007, including the JournalItem and DistListItem types. This book does not cover these additional types, but you can find information about them by consulting the Microsoft MSDN® Web site (*http://msdn.microsoft.com*) and searching on these item types.

These item types represent built-in functionality. If you have ever used Outlook 2007 to create an e-mail message or to add an appointment to your calendar, you have benefited from this functionality. Of particular importance, this functionality is accessible to you as you develop custom solutions with Outlook 2007. Outlook 2007 provides corresponding forms for each of these item types, and these standard forms are designed with behaviors that directly relate to the item types they represent. You can extend the behaviors of these forms and leverage all the functions and properties of the item types, some of which are not exposed in the standard forms. In addition, you can reach beyond Outlook 2007 to incorporate the functionality of other Microsoft Office system applications such as Microsoft Office Word 2007, Microsoft Office Excel® 2007, Microsoft Office InfoPath® 2007, Microsoft Office PowerPoint® 2007, Microsoft Office Project 2007, Microsoft Office Visio® 2007, and any application or control that exposes a programmatic Component Object Model (COM) interface.

Outlook Message Classes

Although forms and item types are the basic elements you need to understand to create a custom Outlook 2007 solution, it's helpful to know what a message class is and how it relates to Outlook 2007 form development. A message class represents to Outlook 2007 internally what an item type represents to a user or developer externally. In other words, when a user opens an e-mail message from the Inbox, that message is a MailItem. Internally, however, Outlook 2007 calls it by a different name, IPM.Note. IPM (interpersonal message) is a holdover from earlier generations of Microsoft's messaging legacy. All messages in Outlook 2007 are representations of an IPM of some sort. An appointment calendar item, for example, is an IPM.Appointment. The list of default message classes includes the following:

- IPM.Note
- IPM.Contact
- IPM.Appointment
- IPM.Task
- IPM.Post
- IPM.Activity

- IPM.Schedule.Meeting.Request
- IPM.POST.RSS
- IPM.Task.Request

Again, unless you're developing a fairly sophisticated collaborative solution, these message classes won't surface often. However, understanding what they mean to Outlook 2007 will help as you progress in your use of the program and in developing Outlook 2007 solutions.

Creating Custom Forms from Standard Forms

A standard form is a great point of departure for developing a custom solution. For example, have you ever sent an e-mail message with an attached document to someone and forgotten to include the attachment? In a large company, this rather common error could amount to hundreds, if not thousands, of extra e-mail messages being sent each day as users send follow-up messages containing the omitted attachments. If the attachment was a document needed for review, there is the potential for significant time loss as well. By adding a small script to the standard mail message form, you can avoid this problem. You can programmatically assess whether an attachment has actually been added to the e-mail message and prompt the user to add one if needed.

To begin working with the standard forms, click Tools, Forms, and then select Design A Form to display the Design Form dialog box, shown in Figure 28-2. You can simply select one of the standard forms listed in this dialog box and begin working with the form in design mode. Later sections in this chapter discuss how to save and publish the forms you modify or create.

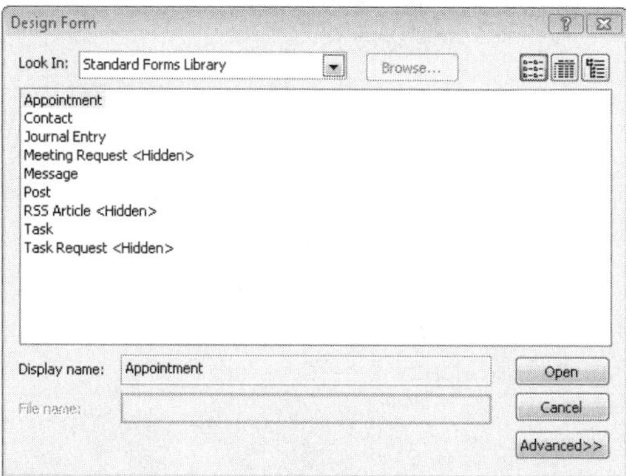

Figure 28-2. In the Design Form dialog box, you can choose the type of form you want to create.

INSIDE OUT **Avoid scripts when opening forms for design**

When you choose to redesign an existing form, that form might have a script with event handlers that will fire when you open the form in design mode. Usually, however, you don't want to have code firing when you're trying to design a form. To keep this from happening, hold down the Shift key as you click the form to open it for design. The code will still be present and will run when you debug the form, but it will not run while you open, design, and save the form.

Compose vs. Read

One of the most basic processes in Outlook 2007 is sending and receiving messages and documents. Although this is a fairly simple process, it requires a close look. In nearly all cases, the form a sender employs to compose an e-mail message is not the exact form that the receiver of that message uses to read the message. For example, although a user can edit the Subject field when composing a message, the recipient can't, under normal circumstances, edit the subject. This is because the standard forms have Compose and Read areas.

Figure 28-3 shows a message being composed; Figure 28-4 shows the same message after it has been received.

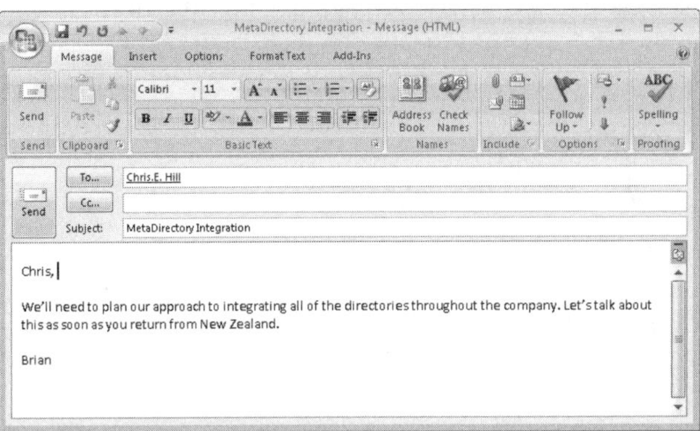

Figure 28-3. Compose a message using a standard message form.

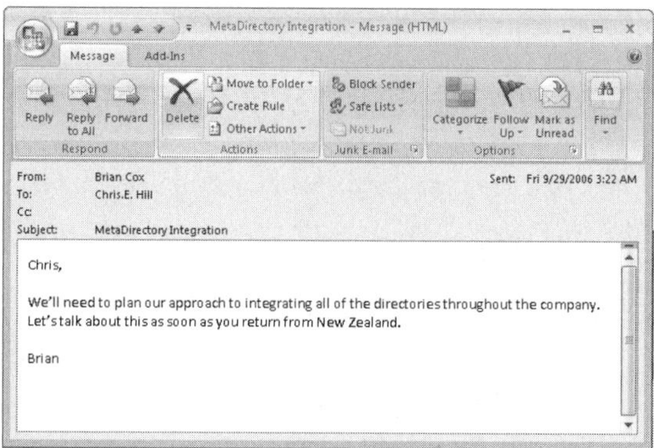

Figure 28-4. Here is the same message shown in Figure 28-3, after it has been received. Notice that some fields can no longer be modified.

Notice that some of the fields, such as Subject and To, can't be modified by the recipient in the Read version. It is, however, entirely possible to configure a form with identical Compose and Read areas. Whether this makes sense for your Outlook 2007 solution is up to you.

To work with a standard form, choose Tools, Forms, select Design A Form to display the Design Form dialog box (shown earlier in Figure 28-2), and then select a Message type form. When you're working with a standard form in design mode, you can switch between the Compose and Read pages by clicking the Edit Compose Page and Edit Read Page buttons in the Design group on the Developer tab. You can select these options by clicking the arrow in the Design group, as shown in Figure 28-5, and then clicking the Edit Compose Page or Edit Read Page button.

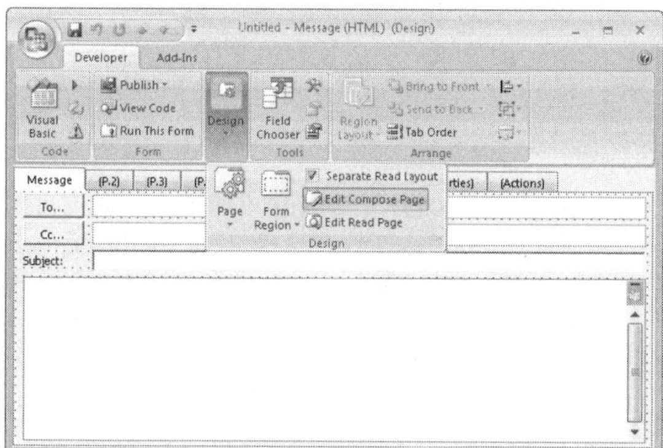

Figure 28-5. Use the Edit Compose Page and Edit Read Page buttons located in the Design group to switch between compose and read views of the form.

In Figure 28-6, the Compose page of the standard message form is ready for editing. When you click Edit Read Page, the Read area of the form appears for editing, as shown in Figure 28-7.

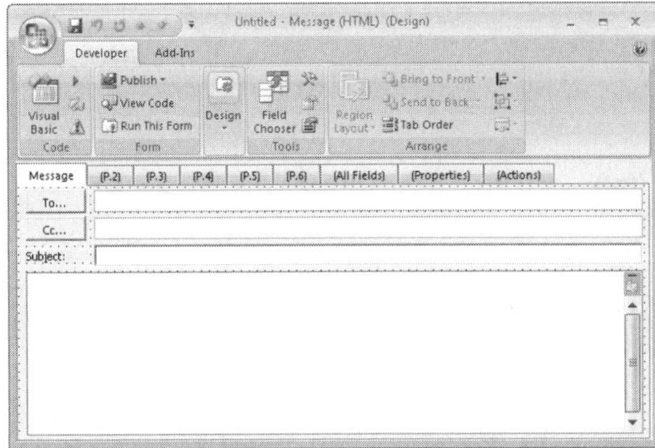

Figure 28-6. This standard Compose area is ready for editing.

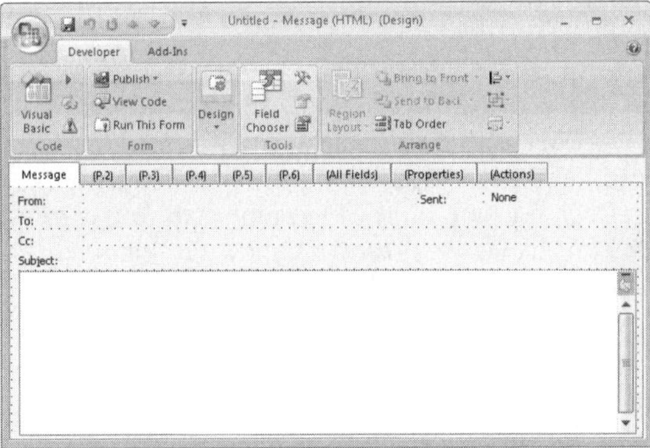

Figure 28-7. The Read area for a message item looks similar to the Compose area.

Because this is a standard form, a number of controls are already on the form. For example, the text box control for the body of the message is the largest element on the form. This control is bound to an Outlook 2007 field. The following section examines fields and what they mean to an Outlook 2007 solution; working with controls is discussed in "Adding and Arranging Controls" later in this chapter.

Outlook Fields

An Outlook 2007 field represents a discrete unit of information that is intelligible to Outlook 2007, such as the Bcc and To fields in an e-mail message. You don't need to tell Outlook 2007 that e-mail messages have these fields–they are already included in the standard form. Outlook 2007 provides a number of fields that you can use, and you can also add new fields. In theory, an unlimited number of fields are available, but the most common practice is to use a generous number of the built-in fields and a judicious number of new, user-defined properties. For now, this discussion focuses on the fields already available to you.

Because it provides so many built-in fields, Outlook 2007 groups them to make it easier to find the ones you need. For example, some fields, such as To, From, Subject, Importance, Expires, Due By, Created, Size, and Attachment, are particular to e-mail messages. Other fields, such as City, Children, and Birthday, are associated with Outlook 2007 contacts. You can, however, use fields from other forms to suit your needs on any form you're designing–for example, Outlook 2007 doesn't prevent you from adding a Birthday field to an e-mail form.

You can find more information about user-defined fields in the Microsoft Knowledge Base article "How to Work with User-Defined Fields in Solutions in Outlook 2002," at *support.microsoft.com/kb/290656*. Although this article was written for an earlier version of Microsoft Outlook, the information in the article applies to later versions, including Outlook 2007.

When you work with a form, you can view the available fields in the Field Chooser, shown in Figure 28-8. To display the Field Chooser (if closed), click the Field Chooser button to the right of the Edit Read Page button; clicking this button shows or hides the Field Chooser. In the Field Chooser, the fields are organized by categories and displayed in a list. You can choose a category in the drop-down list and then search in the body of the Field Chooser for the fields you need.

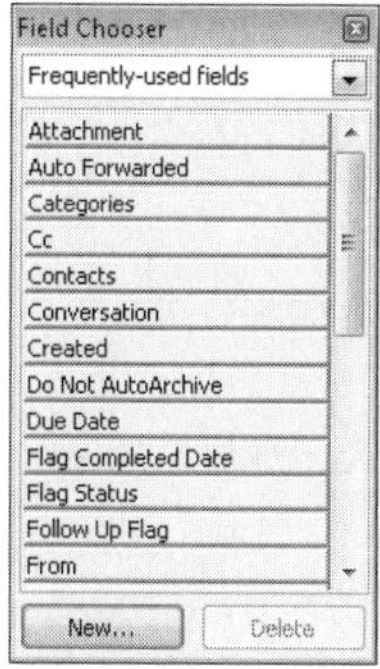

Figure 28-8. The Field Chooser allows you to view and choose the fields available for use.

Item Types and Fields

The scrollable list of fields shown in the Field Chooser in Figure 28-8 contains all the fields available for a form published in a certain folder. The standard item types come with a number of fields already defined. For example, a mail message comes with To, Subject, Body, and Sent fields already defined. Although you have the full range of fields available as you modify or create a form, you can speed your development time and decrease your effort by carefully selecting a standard form that most closely corresponds to the solution you're developing. This way, you can leverage as many built-in fields as possible. You'll learn how to represent these fields on your form using controls in the section "Adding and Arranging Controls" later in this chapter.

Creating Custom Forms from Scratch

Working with standard forms is great if you want to build a solution that is directly related to one of the Outlook 2007 item types. However, you might need an Outlook 2007 form that isn't based on an item type at all. For example, you might want to create a form that allows users to report their work hours or initiate a purchase order. Although you could base these examples on a standard form, they could just as easily require a completely new form that you need to create.

The good news is that creating a completely new form is easier than it sounds. In fact, Outlook 2007 doesn't really permit you to create forms completely from scratch, although you can certainly achieve the same effect. You have two ways to create a form that doesn't contain any built-in form elements:

- Modify a standard form by deleting all built-in interface elements from the form and adding your own.
- Modify a standard form by hiding the page that contains built-in interface elements and showing a new page that contains elements that you add.

You'll learn how to add pages to forms in the next section. First let's look at how to break down a standard form to a blank form by removing built-in interface controls.

The following steps show how to turn a standard post form (a form that is used to post a note into a folder) into a blank form:

1. Choose Tools, Forms.
2. Select Design A Form.
3. Select the Post form, and then click Open. The form opens in design mode with the Message page selected.
4. Click each control (TextBox, Label, Button, and so on) on the Message page and delete it.
5. With the Message page still selected, click Page in the Design group, and then select Rename Page.
6. Type a new name in the dialog box and then click OK.

The form now looks similar to the form shown earlier in Figure 28-7, but with some changes. The figure shows a modified (blank) Compose area for this form, but you can also modify the Read area (via Edit Read Page). Of course, you'll also want to make these pages do something, but for now, you at least have a blank form to work with. To have this blank form available as a template, click the Microsoft Office Button, choose File, Save As, and then select Outlook Template in the Save As Type drop-down list.

Creating Multipage Forms

A multipage form allows you to fit a great deal of information on one form while also reducing confusion for the user. For example, you could create a form on which employees could both report their time for the week and report any expenses for which they need reimbursement. By using two pages, one form can serve both needs.

Any form can be a multipage form; all possible pages are already on the form you create or modify. However, these pages are not automatically visible. If you look closely at the names on the page tabs shown previously in Figure 28-7, you'll see that except for the first name in the list, the name of each page is enclosed in parentheses, indicating that the page is not visible. To change the Visible property of a page, click its tab, click Design, Page, and then select Display This Page.

> **Note**
>
> You can make all pages visible, but you cannot make all pages invisible. If you try to do so, Outlook 2007 tells you that at least one page must be visible on the form.

The first (default) page of a form, which is initially visible, has Compose and Read capabilities already available, as mentioned earlier. The additional pages on a form, which are initially invisible, don't have these capabilities until you add them. To do so, select one of these pages, and then choose Separate Read Layout in the Design group, which activates the Edit Compose Page and Edit Read Page buttons.

Adding and Arranging Controls

The real power of forms comes from the controls you place on them. To construct a robust Outlook 2007 forms solution, you need to carefully plan what the form is supposed to do; what pieces of information it will display, modify, save, or send; which controls will display these information units; and how the controls will be laid out. You can put two types of controls on a form: a control bound to an Outlook 2007 field and a control that is not bound. This section looks first at field-bound controls. Field-bound controls are bound to specific control types, such as drop-down lists, text boxes, command buttons, labels, or check boxes.

To display a field on your form, follow these steps:

1. Display the Field Chooser, and then select a field category in the drop-down list.
2. In the scrollable list in the Field Chooser, select the field that you want, and then drag it onto the form.
3. Format the control as needed.

INSIDE OUT **Work with the users of the form**

You can place any number of controls on a form, but it's a good idea to plan your form with an eye toward usability. Work closely with those individuals who will be using the form to ensure that it corresponds to their real needs. Find out how the users want the forms to be laid out, and listen to their suggestions about how the information should flow. No matter how much work you put into your solution, it won't be useful unless people actually use it.

You can resize, move, or rename a control, and you can change a number of its properties. To resize the control, select the control by clicking it, and position the mouse pointer over one of the control handles, which are represented by small boxes. When a small arrow appears, you can drag the handles in the appropriate direction to resize the control.

To move a control to a new location, simply drag it. Notice that the form's canvas is covered with a grid. Each point on the grid is a possible location for a corner or other relevant point on a control. You can choose to have controls snap to the grid points by right-clicking on the grid and selecting Snap To Grid. You can define the distances between the points on this grid. This is important, because the greater the scale of the grid (the greater the distance between points on the grid), the fewer places you can locate a control on your form. Conversely, the smaller the scale, the more you can refine the positioning of your controls.

To change the grid, follow these steps:

1. In the Arrange group, click the Align button.
2. Click Set Grid Size.
3. Type a number (of pixels) for the height and width spacing.
4. Click OK.

The smaller the number you use for spacing, the smaller the scale. This means that more points on the grid will appear, and you can have more control over where your objects fit on the grid. The default is 8, but 3 is a good number to choose for greater positioning control.

INSIDE OUT **Limiting controls on your forms**

When you're using controls on forms, you can be tempted to make one form do too much. Although there's no precise limit for the number of controls that can be included on one form, the recommendation is using fewer than 300. However, experience with custom forms development suggests that even 200 is excessive. You should try to keep the number of controls down to a few dozen or so when possible. Forms that try to do too much usually become confusing to users, and these forms often do not perform well. Keeping your forms focused and giving them a crisp design makes them easier to code and debug too. If you find that your form is overloaded, consider creating a COM add-in to allow a broader application context, or develop a stand-alone application that handles all of your information needs.

Properties

Controls have a number of properties that you can view and modify. To find out what these properties are, right-click a control, and then choose Properties on the shortcut menu to display the Properties dialog box. Figure 28-9 shows a Properties dialog box for a text box control.

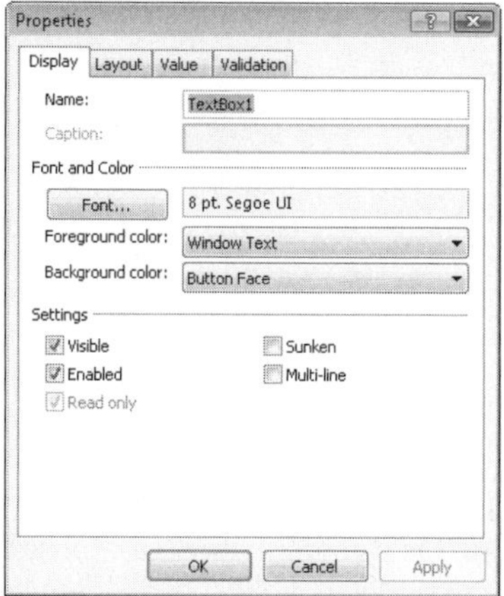

Figure 28-9. You can use the Properties dialog box to modify the properties of a control.

Display

The Display tab of a control's Properties dialog box (a text box example is shown in Figure 28-9) lists the most commonly used properties of the particular control. Changing the setting of a property in this dialog box enables the Apply button; clicking Apply or OK sets the value of that property for the selected control.

The default names of controls are rather generic, such as TextBox1 or CheckBox1. You'll want to change these to names that are more descriptive for your solution, such as txtFirstName or chkHasVacation.

You can learn more about naming conventions for controls by visiting the Microsoft MSDN Web site at msdn.microsoft.com and searching for *Visual Basic Coding Conventions Overview.*

Layout

The Layout tab in the Properties dialog box lets you set the position of the field within the form. The position settings are set in pixels offset from the top and left of the form. You can specify the height and width of the field as displayed in the form by setting the Height and Width values. You can also configure the field to automatically resize as the form size is being changed by selecting the Resize With Form check box in the Automatic Layout area, as shown in Figure 28-10.

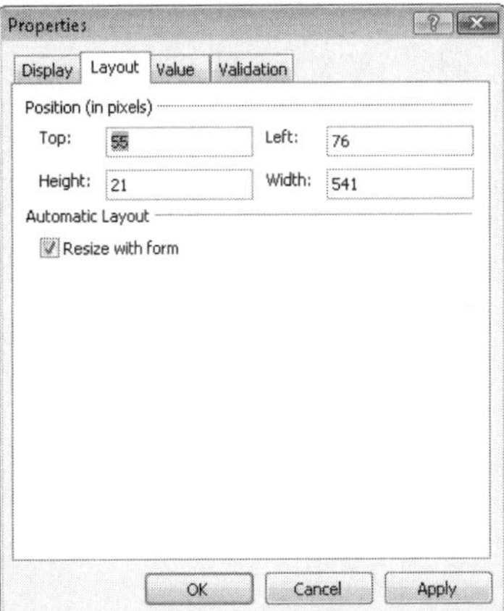

Figure 28-10. Use the Layout tab to set the position and size of a control.

Value

The Value tab in the Properties dialog box, shown in Figure 28-11, contains a number of settings that relate to the field value that the control represents. As mentioned, each control in the Field Chooser list is bound to an Outlook 2007 field. When you modify the properties of a control, you can change the field to which the control is bound.

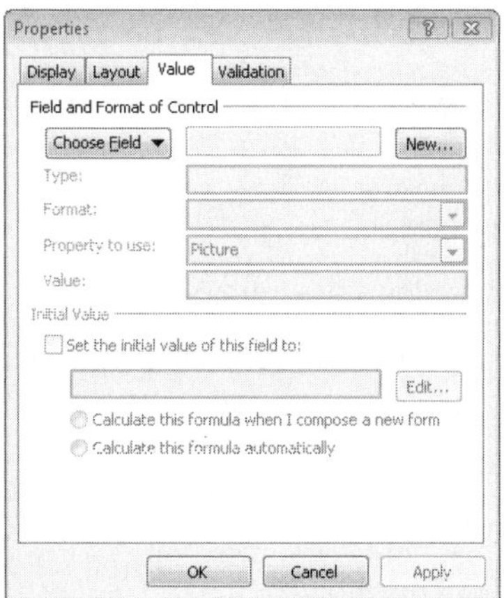

Figure 28-11. Use the options on the Value tab to set the field and format for a control.

To change the bound-field property, click Choose Field, and then select the field to which you want to bind the control in the drop-down list. Make sure that the field value is bound to the correct property of your control. Normally, the field value is tied to the control's *Value* property; this is rarely changed. However, you can change this setting so that, for example, the value of a field is tied to your control's *Enabled* property. In this case, if the value of the field is *True*, the control is enabled; if the value is *False*, the control is not enabled.

You can also set the initial value of your control to display a default value. Select the Initial Value Of This Field To check box, and then type an initial value in the text box. This value doesn't have to be a predetermined one–you can have it correspond to a dynamic value, such as the current day or the concatenation of Subject field and the current date. To make the initial value more dynamic, click Edit to open the Initial Value For dialog box; an example is shown in Figure 28-12.

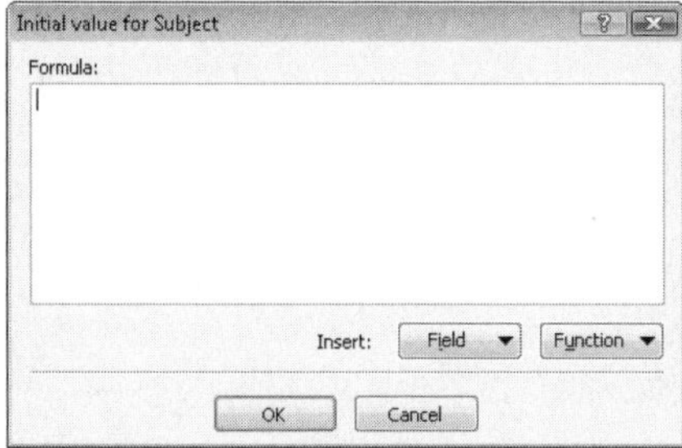

Figure 28-12. Use this dialog box to customize the initial value for a control.

In this dialog box, you establish a formula for the initial value of your control. For example, you can simply insert a built-in function, such as *Date( )*, for the formula.

To insert a built-in function—the *Date( )* function, in this example—follow these steps:

1. Click the Function button.
2. Click Date/Time, and then click Date( ).
3. The function appears in the Formula text box.
4. Click OK, and then click OK again to close the Properties dialog box.

When you run the form, the text box control will contain the current date as its initial value. Your users can always change the control's initial value unless you set the control to Read Only (on the Display tab).

Validation

The Validation tab in the Properties dialog box allows you to set certain properties that relate to how (or whether) the value of the control is validated. For example, if you create a form for a purchase order, you might want to ensure that users indicate the quantity of parts they want to order. The order processing department will send you many thanks for requiring certain values before the purchase order gets to them, as it reduces the amount of information traffic and busywork needed to process an order.

Suppose that you've added a control to your form that requires a value for a text box, and that value is required to be less than or equal to 10 characters. If the user fails to enter a valid value, Outlook 2007 will display a message that prompts the user to enter a correct value.

To set the properties on the Validation tab that will be necessary for this example, as shown in Figure 28-13, follow these steps:

1. Display the Properties dialog box, and then click the Validation tab.
2. Select the A Value Is Required For This Field check box.
3. Select the Validate This Field Before Closing The Form check box.
4. Click the Edit button located to the right of the Validation Formula text box.
5. Click Function.
6. Click Text, Len(string), and then click OK. The *Len(string)* function appears in the Validation Formula text box.
7. In the Validation Formula text box, type **<=10** after the function, and then click OK.
8. In the Display This Message If The Validation Fails text box, type the following text (including the quotation marks):

   "Please enter a value between 1 and 10 characters."

   Alternatively, you can click the Edit button, type the message without quotation marks, and then click OK.

9. Click OK to close the Properties dialog box.

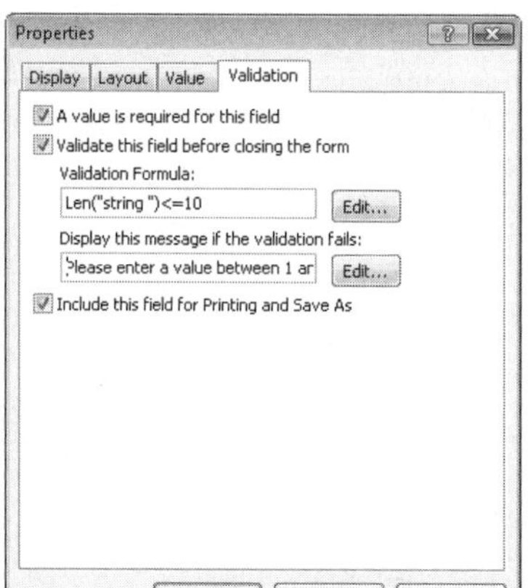

Figure 28-13. Use the Validation tab to require and verify the value entered in a control.

In the example exercise, when a user works with your form, the text box that requires validation must contain a value, and the value must be less than or equal to 10 characters. If the value the user enters is 11 characters or more, Outlook 2007 will display a message box containing the validation text you provided when the user tries to send the form. The user can then make the appropriate changes to the text box value and attempt to resend the form.

Standard Controls

This chapter has thus far concentrated on controls that are bound to Outlook 2007 fields and that appear in the Field Chooser. However, these aren't the only controls you can add to a form. This section takes a brief look at some of the standard controls that are available in Outlook 2007 as well as controls that come as part of the Microsoft Office system.

Controls appear in a Control Toolbox, which is a small, resizeable window made visible when you click the button next to the Field Chooser button on the form. Figure 28-14 shows the Toolbox.

Figure 28-14. The Control Toolbox allows you to add controls to your form.

As you hold the mouse pointer over the control icons in the Toolbox, the name of each control appears. To add one of these controls to your form, drag the control icon onto the form. You can then resize and reposition the control or set its properties, as discussed earlier.

Refer to *Programming Microsoft Outlook and Microsoft Exchange 2003, Third Edition*, by Thomas Rizzo (Microsoft Press, 2003), to learn more about the properties, methods, events, and possible uses of the standard controls.

These standard controls are useful but limited. As your skills in developing Outlook 2007–based solutions progress, you'll find that you need functionality that transcends the abilities of the standard controls provided in the Toolbox. Fortunately, you can add other controls and make them accessible via the Toolbox window. For example, if you design a number of forms that work with Microsoft Office PivotTables®, you can add a PivotTable control to the Control Toolbox.

Follow these steps to add the PivotTable control to the Toolbox:

1. Right-click an empty area of the Toolbox window.
2. Choose Custom Controls.
3. Scroll down the Available Controls list, and then click the box next to Microsoft Office PivotTable 11.0.
4. Click OK. The control appears in the Custom Controls dialog box.

You can now add this control to a form and work with its specific properties and behaviors just as you did for the standard controls.

Custom controls can make your Outlook 2007 solution extremely robust and powerful. However, be aware that the control you're using might not exist on the computer of the person receiving the message. In other words, although you might have the PivotTable control on your computer, the person who uses your form to compose a message or receives a message composed on your form might not have the PivotTable control installed. For your solution to work, you need to ensure that the custom controls you use are properly distributed and installed on other users' computers.

Note

Methods of distributing custom controls vary widely. Some controls come without an installing package, many use Microsoft Installer, and others use a third-party installation mechanism. You should read the documentation that accompanies your custom control or consult the manufacturer to determine the best method for distributing your control.

After creating your form, you can test it to see what it looks like when it is run. With the new form open, choose Run This Form in the Form group. This won't cause the form to close or disappear. Instead, Outlook 2007 produces a new form based on the form you've just created. The newly created form is an actual running form that you can send and read, and any included functions or scripts are also run when the form is opened.

Adding Graphics to Forms

Although developing solutions in Outlook 2007 can require much thought and effort, users might not necessarily share your enthusiasm and excitement about the forms you've created. One way to increase acceptance and usability is to add some pleasing graphics to the forms. These graphics can come in a variety of formats, such as JPG, GIF, WMF, EMF, and ICO.

One way to add a graphic to your form is to use the image control from the Control Toolbox. Initially, the control will appear as a gray square. You can resize it, just as you can resize any of the standard controls, although it's a good idea to place the picture in the control before you resize it. Set the picture source for the image control by using the Properties dialog box, shown in Figure 28-15. Double-click the Picture property, and then select the desired picture in the Load Picture dialog box.

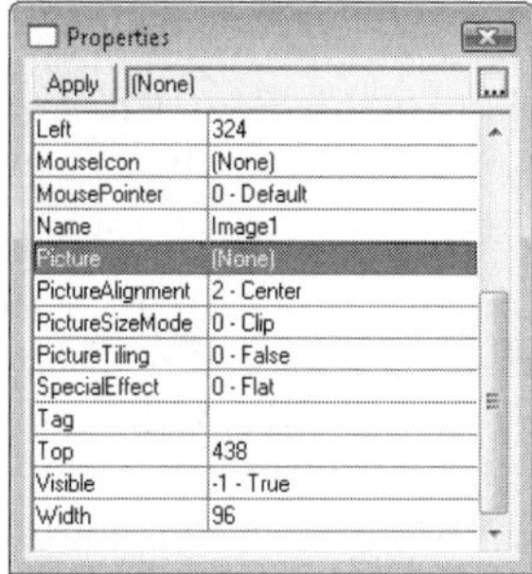

Figure 28-15. Use the Properties dialog box to select a picture to insert into the image control.

Follow these steps to insert a picture in your control:

1. Right-click the image control that you placed on your form.
2. Click Advanced Properties.
3. In the list of properties, scroll down to the Picture property.
4. Select the Picture property and then click the ellipsis button (...) at the top of the form, or simply double-click the Picture property.
5. In the Load Picture dialog box, navigate to the picture you want to appear in the image control, and then click Open.
6. Close the Advanced Properties dialog box, and then verify that the control now contains the picture you chose.

INSIDE OUT **Change your images at run time**

As is the case with all the controls you use on a custom form, you can change the values of many of their properties when the form is running. For example, you can create a form with an image that changes based on certain criteria. You can add code to your form that alters the setting of the control's *Picture* property and thus loads an image into the control that is different from the image you specified at design time.

Another way to make your forms more attractive and usable is to add an icon to buttons on the forms. You can configure the command button available in the Toolbox to display both a text caption and a graphic. For example, if your button sends a custom message to a recipient when clicked, you could add an envelope image to the button to convey the notion of sending a message. To have the button display an image, set the *Picture* property for the button just as you would for an image control. You can also set the *Picture* property for other controls, such as text boxes and labels.

In addition, you can display a custom icon in the form's title bar. Outlook 2007 always displays a default icon in the upper-left corner of a form, indicating whether it is a task form, an appointment form, and so on. You can change this icon by clicking the Properties tab of your form when you're working in design mode. Click Change Large Icon or Change Small Icon, and then navigate to the .ico file you want to use. The Large Icon setting tells Outlook 2007 which image to display when a user displays the properties of the form. The Small Icon setting specifies the title bar image and the image that is shown when the form is displayed in an Outlook 2007 folder.

Adding User-Defined Fields

There are times when the types of data that you need to share, gather, or track with forms exceed the Outlook 2007 default field definitions. You might want to have your contact form display the hire date and review date, for example, but these fields don't exist in the Outlook 2007 field list.

You can define new fields that contain information that is relevant to your use of Outlook 2007. These user-defined fields can be bound to a control in the same way that you bind a preexisting field to controls in Outlook 2007 forms.

When you want to implement a new field in a form, start by opening the Design Form dialog box (choose Tools, Form, Design A Form). To create a new form field, you can either open the Field Chooser and click the New button or click the All Fields tab and then click the New button.

The New Field dialog box will prompt you for the field name, data type, and display format for the new field. In the Name box, type the name of the new field, such as Hire Date, and then select the data type for the field in the Type drop-down list–in this case,

Date/Time. In the Format drop-down list, select the display format for the date (or day, time, and date) layout that you want for the field.

The new field is added to the Select From drop-down list, and you can find the new field in the User Defined Fields In Inbox item. The field can be selected in the Field Chooser and on the All Fields tab. To use your new field, drag it onto your form. You will need to remember to add the field to both the Edit Compose Page and the Edit Read Page, and commonly you will want to set the properties of the field in the Edit Read Page to read-only (on the Display tab).

Using Office Documents to Create Outlook Forms

If you have installed Outlook 2007, you probably also have Word 2007, Excel 2007, and PowerPoint 2007 installed. These other programs provide an even more powerful Outlook 2007 form solution: You can use documents, spreadsheets, and slide presentations as the form of a message. For example, suppose that you created a form that required a user to enter several values and send the form to someone else. The recipient then has to type those values into an Excel 2007 spreadsheet. Wouldn't it make more sense to have the first user type the values directly into the spreadsheet at the outset? If your company already uses an Excel 2007 spreadsheet for expense reimbursements, you can leverage this by letting employees use the spreadsheet as they always have–the only difference is that each employee will now set a recipient or a public folder as the spreadsheet's destination.

Although you could have the users open the document, make changes, and then choose File, Send To, Mail Recipient to mail the document, you might prefer to incorporate the document into a standard form. For example, perhaps you want to broadcast an Excel 2007 spreadsheet to a group of users to show sales status or other data. You can create a standard message form, but in place of (or in addition to) the message body, add an Excel 2007 custom control that pulls the spreadsheet data from a server, updating the data when the user opens the form from his or her Inbox.

Covering this type of form development falls outside the scope of this chapter, but you might need only a nudge in the right direction to begin adding these custom controls to your own forms.

Here's how:

1. In Outlook 2007, choose Tools, Forms, Design A Form to open the Design Form dialog box.
2. Select Message in the Standard Forms Library, and then click Open.
3. Resize the message body control to make room for the Spreadsheet control.
4. Click the Control Toolbox icon, right-click the Control Toolbox, and then choose Custom Controls to open the Additional Controls dialog box.

5. Scroll through the Available Controls list to locate and then select the Microsoft Office Spreadsheet 11.0 control. Click OK to add the Spreadsheet control to the Control Toolbox.

6. Drag the spreadsheet control onto your form. Figure 28-16 shows a Spreadsheet control added to a message form.

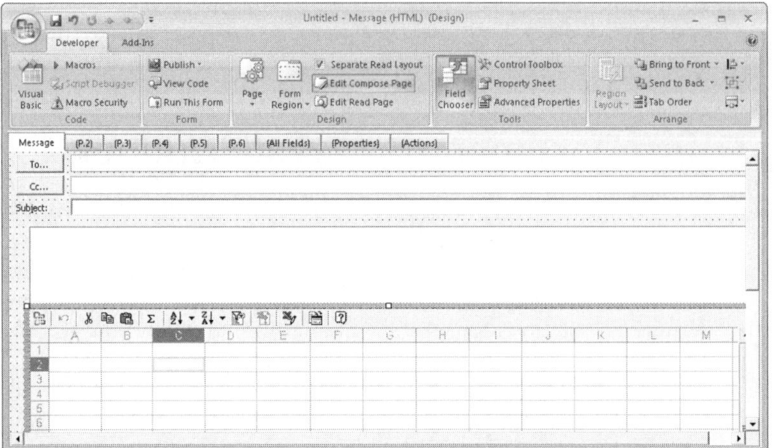

Figure 28-16. You can add custom Microsoft Office system controls to a form to publish or accept data input.

7. Resize the Spreadsheet control to fit the form as needed. Right-click the toolbar portion of the control, and then click Advanced Properties.

8. Use the properties in the control's Properties dialog box to specify the data location and to define the data.

9. Make other design changes as needed to the form, and then save (by clicking the Microsoft Office Button and then clicking Save As) or publish the form (by clicking Publish in the Form group). For more information about publishing forms, see "Publishing and Sharing Forms" later in this chapter.

If you browse through the Additional Controls dialog box, you'll find a wide range of additional controls you can add to your forms. You can add charts, PivotTables, database forms, and many other controls to create powerful and useful forms.

A Word About Form Regions

Outlook 2007 provides enhancements to the ability to develop custom forms, enabling you to define form regions that can be added to existing forms or as entirely separate regions. Earlier versions of Microsoft Outlook provided restricted functionality when creating custom forms—if you wanted to add a few fields to an existing form, Microsoft Outlook required you to develop a new custom form. Further, customized forms could not be displayed in the Reading Pane, a common way for Microsoft Outlook users to review their mail. These factors presented limitations on developing messaging solutions based on Microsoft Outlook.

In Outlook 2007, however, there is a new ability to define and use *form regions*—a defined section of a form that can contain controls and information from external applications and data sources.

These new form regions can be classified into types of regions: Adjoining, Separate, Replace, or Replace All. Adjoining regions provide the ability to add a region to an existing built-in or custom form. Thus if you want to customize an existing form, just adding new fields, information, or controls, you can use an Adjoining region. You also have the option to display an Adjoining region in the Reading Pane. When you want to replace one or more tabs on a form, you need to use Separate regions. Using a Separate region that replaces the default (first) page of a form enables your form to be displayed in the Reading Pane. Using Separate regions, you can add information in the middle of a form or customize the entire form to meet your requirements. A Replace region replaces the default page, and a Replace All region replaces all of the pages in the specific form, effectively creating a new form of the designated message class.

One disadvantage of using form regions is that they require that both the sender and the recipient have the same add-in component used in the form region installed on their computers. Senders and recipients of forms using form regions, however, are not dependent on having shared access to Exchange Server public folders.

Custom form development frequently requires creating custom code to process the associated business logic, which in earlier versions of Microsoft Outlook left you programming Microsoft Visual Basic Scripting Edition (VBScript) in Notepad to develop the necessary coding. With form regions, however, your coding can be developed in your preferred Integrated Development Environment (IDE) and is installed and implemented as an add-in to Outlook 2007. Thus, your code can access data from sources other than Outlook 2007, listen for events on controls, and monitor and react to other Outlook 2007 data.

To create a form region, start as you would to design a form. Choose Tools, Form, Design A Form, and then select a form of the message class that you want to use as the base for your new form. In the Design group on the Developer tab, click the Form Region button to display the New Form Region and Open Form Region options, as shown in Figure 28-17.

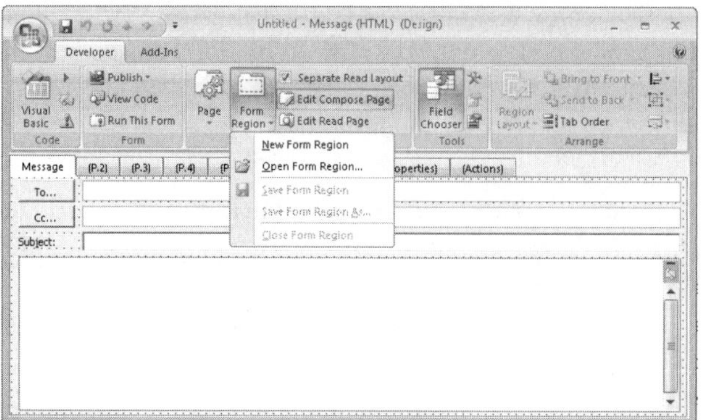

Figure 28-17. You can add control form content and functionality by creating form regions in a form.

When you choose to create a new form region, Outlook 2007 creates a new tab named Form Region, as shown in Figure 28-18, where you can specify fields, controls, and properties for the region.

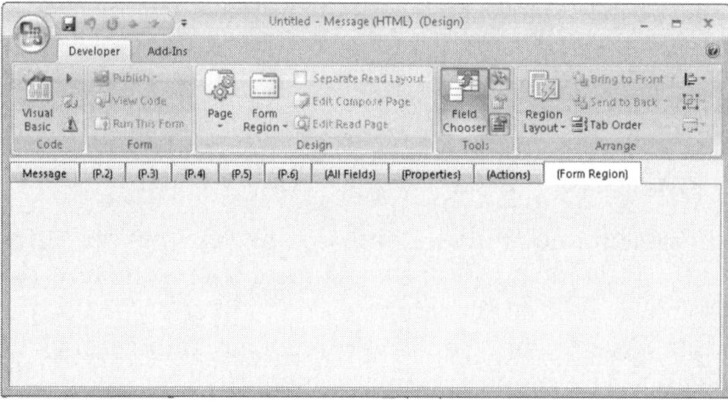

Figure 28-18. Adding a new form region creates a new tab in the form.

Implementing form regions, however, requires the development of an add-in and a related XML file as well as registering the add-in in the registry. As a result, using form regions demands a bit of software development as well as the creation of related files.

The details of developing solutions using form regions is beyond the scope of this book. The Microsoft Developer Network site (*www.msdn.com*) includes a number of articles explaining how to use Microsoft Visual Studio® Tools for Office to create the requisite add-in and support files. See the information at the following URLs for specific information about creating and implementing form regions in Outlook 2007:

- Building an Outlook 2007 form region with a managed add-in: *hmsdn2.microsoft.com/en-us/library/ms788695.aspx*.
- A development environment to create add-ins: Visual Studio Tools for Office, at *msdn.microsoft.com/office/tool/vsto/*.

- A tutorial that provides instruction on creating and implementing a form region add-in: "Outlook 2007 Add-In: Form Region Add-In," at *www.microsoft.com/downloads/details.aspx?familyid=932b830f-bf8f-41fc-9962-07a741b21586&displaylang=en.*

Publishing and Sharing Forms

After you create your form and define its behaviors, properties, and settings, you'll want to make it available to users. First, however, you'll need to preserve your form in one of these two ways:

- Save the form as a file.
- Publish the form to a folder or other location.

Saving Forms

You can save a form from the Form design dialog box by clicking the Microsoft Office Button and then clicking Save As. In the Save As dialog box, select the file name and location. The form file is saved as an Outlook Template file (.oft).

Publishing Forms

Publishing a form is a lot like saving the form. When you finish your form, you can publish it to a specific folder location. You can publish it to your Inbox or another folder in your mailbox, a public folder, the Organizational Forms Library (Exchange Server), or your Personal Forms Library.

Follow these steps to publish a form to a folder or forms library:

1. Click Tools, Forms, and then select Design A Form.
2. In the Design Form dialog box, select the location (such as User Templates In File System) containing the form that you want to publish.
3. Select the form that you want to publish, and then click Open.
4. In the Form group, click Publish, and then click Publish Form As to open the Publish Form As dialog box. (The first time you use the Publish Form button, the Publish Form As dialog will be displayed, but after a form has been saved once, the Publish Form button will simply save the existing form, overwriting the previous version.)
5. In the Look In drop-down list, select the folder or forms library where you want to publish the form. (The default is the Personal Forms Library.)
6. Type the display name and the form name.
7. Click Publish to save the form in the selected location.

INSIDE OUT **Create a staging area for your forms**

When you're creating a form, it's a good idea to keep the production version of the form separate from the development version. Create a staging folder where you publish the forms you're working on. When you complete a form design, publish your form in this staging folder at regular intervals so that you don't lose the modifications you've made to the form. Only people designing and testing forms for your organization should have access to this folder.

After you publish a form, the folder in which you publish it contains the form itself and all the underlying information that another person's instance of Outlook 2007 needs to understand the form.

Choosing Forms

After you have created a custom form and saved or published it for common use, you will need to select the form in order to use it. Custom forms are normally stored in a location related to their expected use. Custom forms intended for common use, for example, are usually stored in an accessible network location. If you have a custom form intended for your own use, however, you would store it in the Personal Forms Library. Or if you want to use a form that you have saved to a folder on your local hard disk, you would store it using the User Templates In File System location.

In each of these cases, to locate your custom form, you select the appropriate location in the Look In drop-down list of the Choose Form dialog box, shown in Figure 28-19.

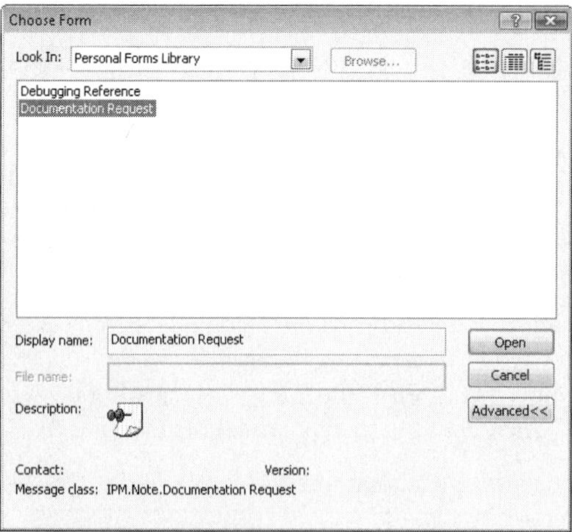

Figure 28-19. Select a custom form in the Choose Form dialog box by first selecting its location.

To use a custom form from these (or any other) locations, follow these steps:

1. Choose Tools, Forms, and then select Choose A Form.
2. In the Choose Form dialog box, select the location in which your custom form is stored (such as the Personal Forms Library).
3. Select the custom form that you want to use.
4. Click Open.

TROUBLESHOOTING

Users can't access your custom form

After you've completed and published your custom form, you might hear from a user who reports receiving this message when trying to access the form: "The custom form could not be opened, and Outlook 2007 will use an Outlook 2007 form instead. The object could not be found." You should first make sure that your form is properly published. If the form is not published so that Outlook 2007 can find it, or if an .oft file is not available, Outlook 2007 won't be able to open the file.

Sometimes, however, Outlook 2007 reports this error even when the form is available. The cause might be a corrupted file named Frmcache.dat. The Frmcache.dat file contains information that Outlook 2007 uses to prevent multiple instances of the same form from being loaded. Outlook 2007 checks the cache to see whether a form using the same message class name is in the cache before attempting to display a form. Outlook 2007 copies the form definition to the cache if the definition does not exist or loads the definition already in the cache, and then Outlook 2007 displays the form. In addition, if a change has been made to a form, Outlook 2007 copies the new form definition to the cache. The file is located in Users\<profile name>\AppData\Local\Microsoft\FORMS on a computer running Windows Vista™, or in Documents And Settings\<profile name>\Local Settings\Application Data\Microsoft\Forms on a computer running Windows XP, or at Windows\Forms on computers running earlier versions of Windows.

If this file is corrupted, reinstalling Outlook 2007 can solve the problem, but there is a simpler way. You could try closing Outlook 2007 and then deleting Frmcache.dat. Or you can locate an instance of Outlook 2007 that displays the form properly and copy that profile's instance of Frmcache.dat to the profile of the offending instance, thus overwriting the file.

Publishing to local folders or to the Personal Forms Library is perfectly acceptable, but you might find that many of your solutions are destined for a wider audience that, in an Exchange Server environment, can be reached only through public folders.

For More Information About VBScript and Outlook

This chapter has presented a brief introduction to programming Outlook 2007 solutions. Because the skills you acquire as you learn to use and extend Outlook 2007 will pay off for a long time, you'll undoubtedly want to deepen your understanding. There are numerous additional sources you can consult to do so.

Microsoft supplies a copious amount of documentation about Outlook 2007 and about building collaborative solutions around Outlook 2007. The online documentation for Outlook 2007 and the Microsoft Office Developer Center documentation (*http://msdn2.microsoft.com/en-us/office*) are probably the best in the industry for any product. Although the MSDN Web site (*http://msdn.microsoft.com*) has an overwhelming but well-organized body of documentation, you might want to consider using Microsoft Visual Studio 2005 Tools For Office Second Edition as well. Visual Studio 2005 Tools For Office not only offers more specific documentation than MSDN but also contains extremely useful code samples and other materials.

The 2007 Microsoft Office Resource Kit and a wide selection of Microsoft Press books can aid you in learning about VBScript, Microsoft Office system, and Microsoft Exchange Server development. Visit the Microsoft Press Web site at *http://www.microsoft.com/learning/books/* to find the latest releases that discuss the most current technologies.

Using Forms Effectively

Each of the forms in Outlook 2007 serves the same purpose–to present information in a specific format. Outlook 2007 forms provide access to all Outlook 2007 items–messages, notes, meetings, tasks, journal entries, and so on–and enable you to create custom forms using any of the available fields. By creating custom forms that align with your workflow, you can ease the communication of information as well as the transfer of data important to your business.

In creating custom forms, you begin by selecting a default form that most closely resembles the form and function you want for your new forms. You can then choose to add or delete fields on the default page and/or create additional pages containing fields to display or gather further information.

- **Know when not to use forms.** Outlook 2007 form creation can give you the capability to customize e-mail messages, meeting requests, and other Outlook 2007 items, but if existing forms provide the functionality you need, it is easier and more effective to use the existing forms. When you consider creating a new form, start by asking "Is the functionality I need already present in an existing form?" Consider that in addition to the time needed to create a custom form, there are distribution logistics (how you get the form to all who would need it), as well as training needed to enable people to effectively use the new form.

When you are communicating to customers, vendors, and others outside your organization, you'll need to determine whether they are using Outlook 2007 (with Rich Text Format [RTF] support enabled) or some other e-mail application. For Outlook 2007 forms to work, the recipient must also be using Outlook 2007 as an e-mail client and must have RTF support.

- **Keep forms simple but comprehensive.** Once you have decided that a new form is necessary, evaluate the information that you need the form to display, transmit, or gather, and then limit the form information to the minimum data required to fulfill your operational or organizational needs. You can create a custom form with multiple pages containing an exhaustive array of fields, yet the complexity of using such a form could easily outweigh any hoped-for benefits. Keep in mind that each custom form you create is intended to facilitate the communication of information. The easier it is for people to use the custom form to exchange information, the more likely it is that people will use the form, and thus the more value it will have for your organization.

  Consider a custom form created to enhance customer relationship management by including 15 fields of concise contact information, key project assessment, and a project status summary vs. a custom form that includes five pages containing 200 fields of exhaustive contact information, step-by-step project notes, milestones and timelines, equipment reserved, travel time, technical assessments, customer evaluation, and so on. The first option with 15 fields is much more likely to be used. When you actually have a need to gather 200 fields' worth of information, you'll want to consider subdividing the data into related sets and then creating separate forms for each set.

- **Use user-defined fields to store information not included by default in Outlook.** Although Outlook 2007 contains fields for the data it uses in contacts, e-mail, meeting requests, tasks, and so on, there are invariably additional pieces of information that your organization could benefit by having included that are not part of the Outlook 2007 default field set. Consider additions to the meeting form that could be useful when you're scheduling meetings with coworkers. For example, to identify who will be leading the meeting, you could add a Presenter field to the custom meeting request form. Likewise, you might consider adding Food Preferences and Food Allergies fields to a custom appointment form for those appointments with clients or staff that involve dining out or food being brought in or catered.

  You might want to add information in your contacts list that isn't shared but that assists you in working with others or relating to their personal interests. You could, for example, create a custom contact form to enable you to track the specialized knowledge or favorite sports of each of the people in your contacts list. Then when you want to find a coworker, for example, who just happens to know how IPv6 actually works, you can search on *IPv6* and display the names of every person in your contacts list who is fluent in IPv6. (Searching on user-defined fields requires you to select the Query Builder and then add your custom form and fields to the query criteria.)

CHAPTER 29

Automating Common Tasks

Microsoft® Office Outlook® 2007 is a feature-rich product and, as such, has an option, a wizard, or a graphical tool for accomplishing nearly anything you require from a personal information manager. If something does come up that the folks at Microsoft haven't planned for, however, you also have the option of customizing Office Outlook 2007 by using its built-in support for Microsoft Visual Basic® code additions. Through the use of flexible Visual Basic for Applications (VBA) scripting options and built-in security controls, you can easily simplify and automate common tasks.

In this chapter, you'll learn how to create and use a macro. This includes creating the macro, stepping through a macro to test it, and deleting macros you no longer need. In addition, you'll find out about implementing security options for macros.

This chapter explores macros in general. For a more complete discussion of developing custom applications and automating tasks with Visual Basic, see Article 7, "Using VBA in Outlook," and Article 8, "Integrating Outlook and Other Applications with VBA," on the companion CD.

Understanding Automation Options

Outlook 2007 has a number of built-in automation options that allow the application to perform certain tasks for you. For example, the Rules Wizard automatically moves, copies, and forwards e-mail messages; and the Organize pane automatically color-codes e-mail messages and deals with junk and adult e-mail messages. The Out Of Office Assistant acts as an answering service when you're away.

For information about these examples of built-in automation options, see Chapter 11, "Processing Messages Automatically ," and "Creating Automatic Responses with the Out Of Office Assistant" in Chapter 13.

If a built-in option can accomplish the automated task you require, it should be your first choice. By using a built-in option instead of a custom one, you minimize problems that can occur if you need to reinstall Outlook 2007 or use Outlook 2007 on multiple machines. Using standardized options also guards against compatibility problems with upgrades to Outlook 2007.

If none of the automation options does the trick, however, you can accomplish just about any customization by using VBA. This chapter focuses on the use of VBA procedures known as macros to automate common tasks.

For detailed information about using VBA with Outlook 2007, see Article 7, "Using VBA in Outlook," and Article 8, "Integrating Outlook and Other Applications with VBA," on the companion CD.

Understanding Macros

So just what is a *macro*? In general terms, a macro is a number of commands grouped together to execute a particular task. Macros are like small programs that operate within other programs. Macros have been around for a long time, and all 2007 Microsoft Office system products support them at some level. In Outlook 2007, macros are implemented as VBA procedures that are not linked to a particular form and are available from anywhere in Outlook 2007. In Outlook 2007, you manage macros in one of two ways: by using the Tools menu, which contains a Macro submenu, or by using commands in the Code area on the Developer tab. To display the Developer tab, open an Outlook 2007 item, click the Microsoft Office Button, and then click Editor Options. On the Popular page, select Show Developer Tab In The Ribbon, and then click OK.

Using Macros

Macros are most useful for tasks that must be performed repeatedly without change. Even so, because a macro contains Visual Basic code, it can be flexible and can respond to variables or user input. With the power of scripting, a macro can accomplish a task in the most efficient way in response to specific conditions.

CAUTION!

Macros can be extremely powerful. This power can be a great asset for you, but it can also mean that any problems can become serious ones. Like many other things, macros can be dangerous when used improperly. Inexperienced programmers should take great care when writing and using macros in Outlook 2007.

Following are the three basic programming elements you can work with in an Outlook 2007 macro:

- **Object** An object is a particular part of a program, such as a button, a menu item, or a text field. Objects make up any element of Outlook 2007 that you can see or work with. An object has properties, and how you set these properties determines how the object functions.

- **Property** Any part of an object–its color, its width, and its value–is part of the set of attributes that make up its properties.
- **Method** A method is a task that an object carries out, such as showing a form or reading file information. Methods can be modified based on user input or the value of certain properties.

In general, a VBA macro either determines or modifies the value of an object property or calls a method. Macros, then, are nothing more than simple programs that use VBA to access or modify Outlook 2007 information.

> **Note**
>
> Before you can work with macros, you might need to configure macro security settings. For information about configuring macro security, see "Setting Macro Security" later in this chapter.

> **Note**
>
> In Microsoft Office Excel® 2007 and Microsoft Office Word 2007, you can simply record your mouse movements and keystrokes using the Macro Recorder, and the computer plays them back when you execute the macro. Outlook 2007 doesn't include a macro recorder, so you have to create macros by writing the macro code yourself. Therefore, users familiar with programming basics and VBA will have a head start in learning to create Outlook 2007 macros.

Creating a Macro from Scratch

The process for creating an Outlook 2007 macro is simple. The process for creating a *useful* macro, on the other hand, is more complex. Because of that, any serious discussion of VBA is left for articles on the companion CD. In this chapter, we'll fall back on the most basic of functions, the Hello World message box macro. This macro creates a function that displays a message box containing the text *Hello World*. Clicking OK (the only button) closes the message box and ends the macro.

To create this macro, follow these steps:

1. Choose Tools, Macro, Macros to open the Macros dialog box.
2. In the Macro Name box, type a descriptive name for your new macro (no spaces are allowed). In Figure 29-1, the macro is titled *HelloWorldMsgBox*.

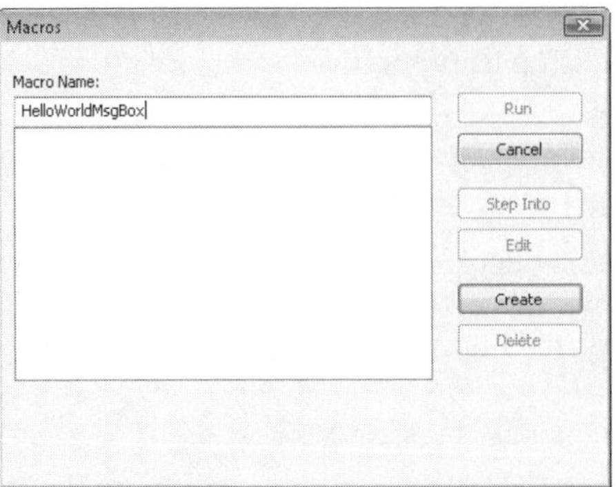

Figure 29-1. Enter the name for a new macro in the Macro Name box.

3. Click Create. Microsoft Visual Basic starts, which allows you to add functionality to your macro. For those who are not programmers, creating VBA code might seem daunting, but simple tasks are actually quite easy. (Note that if you have macros, they will be displayed in this window, each in its own section of the project file.)

4. The first line of the macro starts with *Sub* and contains the macro name–in this case, *HelloWorldMsgBox*. On the next line, type the following, as shown in Figure 29-2:

   MsgBox ("Hello World")

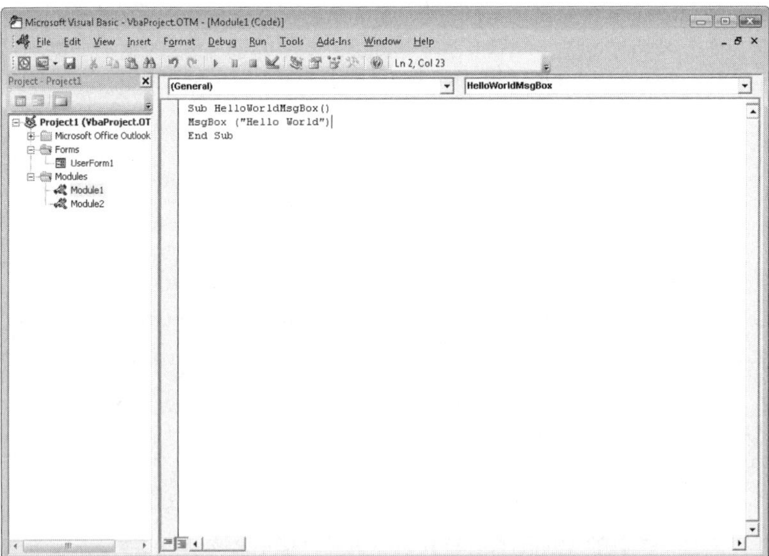

Figure 29-2. You add code between the first and last lines of a macro.

5. To test the code, choose Run, Run Sub/UserForm, or click the Run Sub/UserForm button on the toolbar. The message box shown in Figure 29-3 appears.

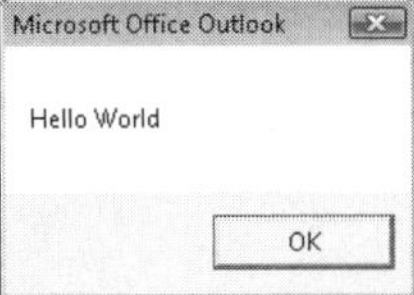

Figure 29-3. The Hello World message box appears when you run the macro.

> **Note**
>
> If you get a message saying macros are not enabled, you should check your macro security settings. To learn how to configure macro security, see "Setting Macro Security" later in this chapter.

6. Choose File, Save. (The file name, which cannot be changed here, is Project1.)
7. Close the Visual Basic Editor.

Running a Macro

After you save a macro, it is available for use. Choose Tools, Macro, Macros, and then select the *HelloWorldMsgBox* macro. When you click Run, the message box appears as it did when you tested the macro in the Visual Basic Editor. Running a macro this way is inconvenient, however. If you'll be using the macro often, you might want to add it as an item on your toolbar for easier access.

The procedure to add a button to the Outlook 2007 toolbar varies depending on where you want the button to appear. You can add a macro command to any of the toolbars in the Outlook 2007 main window or to the Quick Access Toolbar that is displayed when you are viewing an open item, such as a message or a contact. To add the macro to a toolbar in the Outlook 2007 main window, follow these steps:

1. Choose View, Toolbars, Customize to open the Customize dialog box. Verify that the toolbar you want to modify is selected in the list on the Toolbar tab.
2. Click the Commands tab.
3. In the Categories list, select Macros. The *HelloWorldMsgBox* macro appears on the right, as shown in Figure 29-4.

Figure 29-4. Locate the macro, and then add it to the toolbar.

4. Drag the *HelloWorldMsgBox* macro to a location on the toolbar. Outlook 2007 adds a button to the toolbar, and clicking the button runs the macro immediately.

Macros used with individual items (messages, meetings, and so on) are added to the Quick Access Toolbar that is displayed when viewing an open item. Additions to the Quick Access Toolbar appear for only items of that type—for example, macros added to a calendar item are shown only while viewing other Calendar items.

To add the macro to the Quick Access Toolbar, follow these steps:

1. Click the Customize Quick Access Toolbar button, and then choose More Commands to open the Editor Options dialog box.
2. In the Choose Commands From drop-down list, select Macros. The *HelloWorldMsgBox* macro appears in the list below, as shown in Figure 29-5.
3. Click Add to add the *HelloWorldMsgBox* macro button to the Quick Access Toolbar.
4. Click OK to close the Editor Options dialog box.

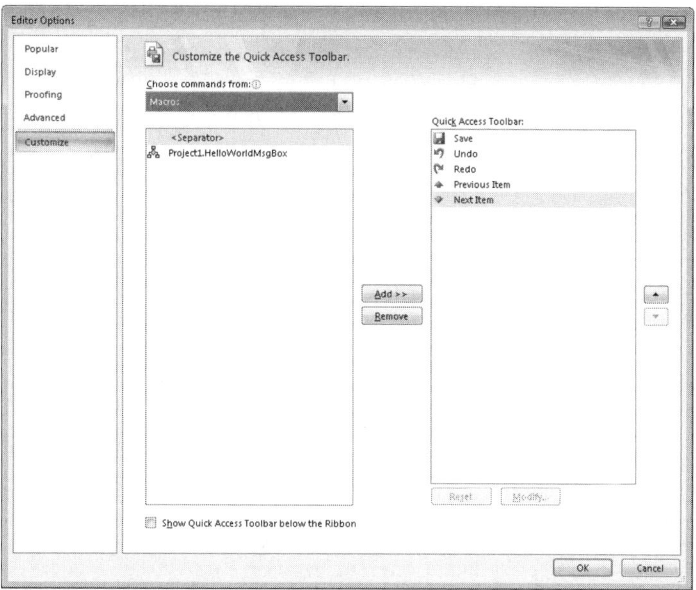

Figure 29-5. Add a button for the macro to the Quick Access Toolbar.

Editing a Macro

After you create a macro, you can edit it by returning to the Macros dialog box:

1. In the Macros dialog box, select the *HelloWorldMsgBox* macro, and then click Edit. The Visual Basic Editor starts and displays the selected macro.
2. Modify the macro so that it matches the following:

```
Sub HelloWorldMsgBox()
MsgBox ("Click OK to create a new message")
Set newMsg = Application.CreateItem(0)
    newMsg.Subject = "Sample Message from a Macro"
    newMsg.Body = "You can even add text automatically."
    newMsg.Display
End Sub
```

3. Verify that the changed macro works properly by clicking the Run Sub/UserForm button on the Microsoft Visual Basic toolbar. Instead of showing a simple message box as before, the macro should now present you with an e-mail message window. (This window might be hidden behind the Microsoft Visual Basic window.) The message should have information automatically filled in in the subject and body fields, as shown in Figure 29-6.

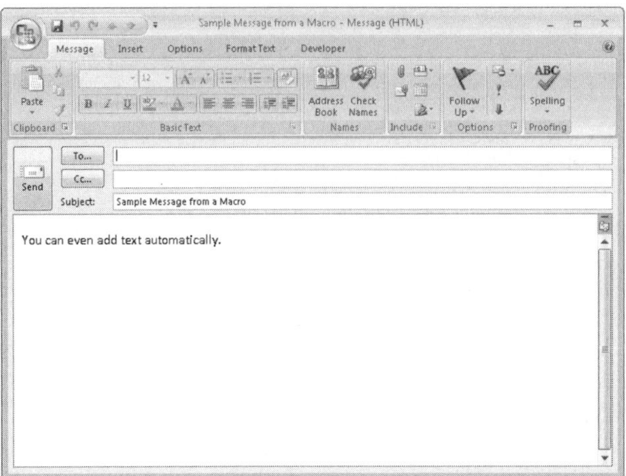

Figure 29-6. The modified macro displays an e-mail message window.

4. Save the changes to your Visual Basic project, and then close Microsoft Visual Basic. Close the e-mail message you created.
5. When you return to the Macros dialog box, select the modified macro, and then click Run. You should see the same e-mail message that you saw in Figure 29-6. Close the e-mail message.

> **Note**
>
> When you edit a macro, you'll eventually want to save it and test the changes. To ensure that you can return to the original macro in case of trouble, first export the project so that you can retrieve it later. For information about exporting, see "Sharing Macros with Others" later in this chapter.

Stepping Through a Macro

When you're creating a macro, it's often helpful to step through the code, which allows you to watch each line as it is being processed and see problems as they occur. To do this, open the *HelloWorldMsgBox* macro for editing (as described in the preceding section), and then press F8. Alternatively, open the Macros dialog box, select a macro, and then choose Step Into. The first line of the macro is highlighted, and its code is processed. To process the next line, press F8 again.

Step through the rest of the macro using the F8 key. Notice that clicking OK merely closes the message box rather than creating the e-mail message. This is because later steps are not followed automatically. The new e-mail message is created only after you press F8 through the line of the subprocedure that creates it—in this case, the last line of the macro.

Note

You can step through a macro only when it is being edited. When macros are executed from within Outlook 2007, they automatically move through all procedures.

TROUBLESHOOTING

Your macro doesn't run properly

If you are having problems getting a macro to run properly, you can try several approaches to determine the source of the problem. The most common problem is incorrect syntax in your code. Finding errors in code can be a vexing job, but using the step-through process generally helps to find the line that is causing you problems.

If your syntax is correct, the problem might have to do with the way you're running the macro. Among the problems you should check are the security settings on the macro and the security settings on the computer. Also, if the macro has been deleted but a toolbar button still remains, you might be trying to run a macro that no longer exists.

Deleting a Macro

Sometimes a macro outlives its usefulness. To delete a macro you no longer need, choose Tools, Macro, Macros. In the Macros dialog box, select the macro you want to remove, and then click Delete. When you're prompted to verify that you want to permanently delete the macro, click Yes to remove the macro from the list, making its code unavailable to Outlook 2007.

Note

If you have created a toolbar button for a macro that you subsequently delete, you must locate the button and remove it in a separate operation.

Sharing Macros with Others

If you're creating macros for use by a group of people, or even an entire organization, the macros must be installed separately for each user. Unfortunately, although the Macros dialog box has options for creating and deleting macros, it has no option for adding macros from other places. You can't share macros the same way you share files. Instead, sharing macros with other users is generally a two-step process: the user who creates the macro must export the macro code, and the other user must import the code. To share a macro, follow these steps:

1. Choose Tools, Macro, Visual Basic Editor.
2. In Microsoft Visual Basic, choose File, Export File to open the Export File dialog box, shown in Figure 29-7.

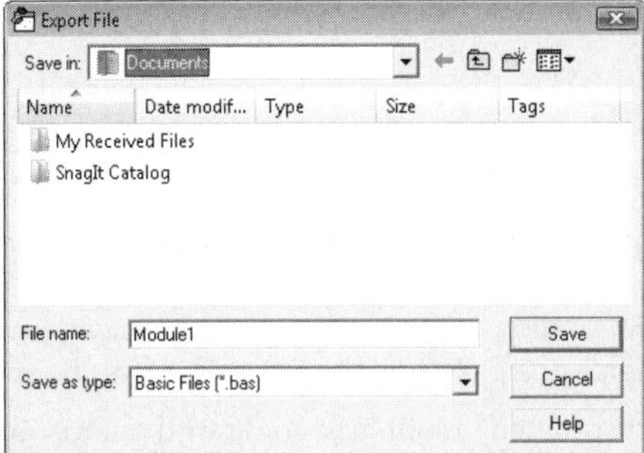

Figure 29-7. A macro file is exported so that it can be shared.

3. In the Save As Type box, save the project as a .bas file. (By doing so, you can then e-mail the file to another user or make it available on the network.)

Once another user has access to the .bas file, that user can install the macro by following these steps:

1. Choose Tools, Macro, Visual Basic Editor.
2. In the Visual Basic Editor, choose File, Import File.
3. Browse to the file, open it, and then save it.

The user can now access the macro through the Macros dialog box.

Setting Macro Security

Macros have several advantages, including their power, their flexibility, and their ability to run automatically, even without your knowledge. These advantages have a dark side, however, and poorly written or malicious macros can do significant damage to an Outlook 2007 message store. Because of the potential danger that macros pose, the Outlook 2007 Tools menu offers four security levels for Outlook 2007 macros:

- **No Warnings and Disable All Macros** Macros are totally disabled, and Outlook 2007 does not display any warning that a macro is attempting to run.
- **Warnings For Signed Macros; All Unsigned Macros Are Disabled** Your system can run only macros that are digitally signed. This means that some macros—even benign and potentially useful ones—are not available.
- **Warnings For All Macros** You will be prompted as to whether you want to run any macros.
- **No Security Check For Macros (Not Recommended)** Macros run automatically, regardless of their signature. This is the most dangerous setting.

For information about digital signatures, see "Protecting Messages with Digital Signatures" in Chapter 14.

Using Security Levels

To view or change the security level, choose Tools, Macro, Security to open the Trust Center, and then click Macro Security, as shown in Figure 29-8. (You can also access the Trust Center by opening an Outlook 2007 item and, on the Developer tab, in the Code group, clicking Macro Security.) The default setting is Warnings For Signed Macros; All Unsigned Macros Are Disabled, which is probably the best choice for most users.

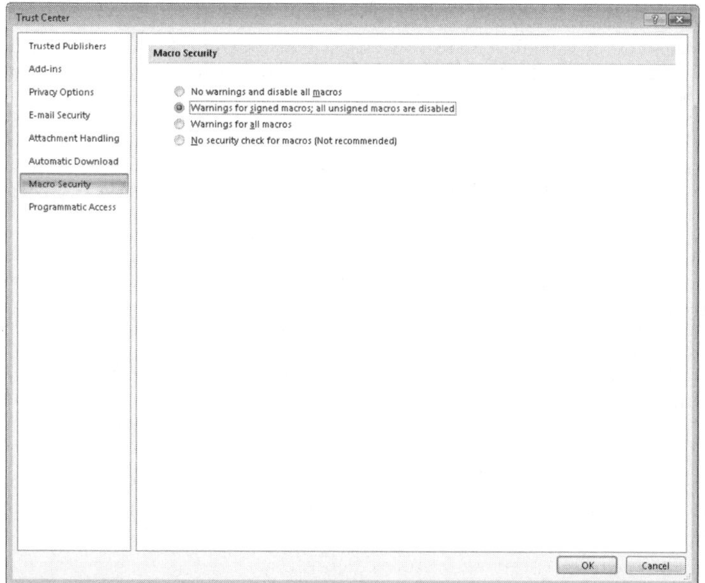

Figure 29-8. You can set the security level for macros in the Trust Center.

INSIDE OUT **Security and user-created macros**

When you create your own macros, they are not controlled by the security settings. User-created macros do not need to be signed and will run regardless of the security setting you have selected—even if you choose no warnings and disable all macros! This is nice for purposes of design and editing, but it assumes that you realize exactly what a macro will do. Moreover, it means that when you want to test macro security settings, you must run Outlook 2007 under a different user account.

Specifying Trusted Sources

To reduce the number of times you're prompted about whether to run a macro (if you've set the security level to Warnings For Signed Macros; All Unsigned Macros Are Disabled) or to be able to run macros at all (if you've set the security level to Warnings For All Macros), you can specify a trusted source.

When a digitally signed macro runs, Outlook 2007 displays the certificate attached to the macro. In addition to choosing whether to run the macro, you're also given the choice of adding the certificate holder (the organization or individual who created the macro) to your list of trusted sources. Once the holder of the certificate is trusted, any macros signed with that certificate run without prompting at the Warnings For Signed Macros; All Unsigned Macros Are Disabled security setting. To view the list of trusted certificates or to remove a trusted source, choose Tools, Trust Center. Click Trusted Publishers to view the sources. To remove a trusted source, select the source, and then click Remove.

Signing Your Macros to Avoid Security Warnings

Macro security in Outlook 2007 gives you control over when macros can run, which helps prevent malicious code from affecting an Outlook 2007 user's system. When macro security is set to Warnings For Signed Macros; All Unsigned Macros Are Disabled in Outlook 2007, only digitally signed macros from trusted sources can run. A setting of Warnings For All Macros causes Outlook 2007 to prompt you whether to enable and allow macros to run. A setting of No Security Check For Macros allows all macros to run, which poses significant risks from malicious code.

If you create your own macros, you probably would like to digitally sign your macros so that they will run on other people's computers without triggering Outlook 2007 macro security warnings. Outlook 2007, like all versions since Microsoft Outlook 2000, provides the means to sign VBA projects.

To create a self-signing certificate, follow these steps:

1. Choose Start, All Programs, Microsoft Office, Microsoft Office Tools, and then select Digital Certificate For VBA Projects.
2. Type a descriptive name for your certificate, such as **Outlook 2007 Code Signing Certificate**, in the Your Certificate's Name dialog box, and then click OK.
3. Click OK to confirm creation of the certificate.

To sign a macro, follow these steps:

1. In Outlook 2007, choose Tools, Macro, Macros, to open the Macros dialog box.
2. Select a macro, and then click Edit to open the Visual Basic Editor.
3. Choose Tools, Digital Signature to open the Digital Signature dialog box.
4. Click Choose, select your code-signing certificate, and then click OK. Click OK again, and then close the Visual Basic Editor.

On the computer that will be running the macro, verify that you have configured Outlook 2007 macro security for either Warnings For Signed Macros; All Unsigned Macros Are Disabled or Warnings For All Macros settings, and then attempt to run a macro. When Outlook 2007 asks whether you want to trust the macro publisher, click Yes. Your custom macros should now run on that computer without triggering the Outlook 2007 security warnings.

PART 6

Managing and Securing Outlook

CHAPTER 30

Managing Outlook Folders and Data

Like any system, Microsoft® Office Outlook® 2007 can become overloaded with messages, contact information, appointments, and other data. If you can't manage all this data, you'll be lost each time you try to find a particular item. Office Outlook 2007 helps you manage information by providing folders for storing your data. You also can create your own folders, move data between folders, and set folder properties.

This chapter focuses on managing your Outlook 2007 folders and their contents. You'll learn how to create new folders to store e-mail messages, contact information, and other files. You'll also learn how to set up Outlook 2007 folders to use Web views so that you can display Web pages inside folders. In addition, you'll find out what it takes to archive your data when you want to archive data on the spot.

Understanding Outlook Folders

Outlook 2007 folders are used like the folders you use in Microsoft Windows® Explorer or My Computer. You use Outlook 2007 folders to store items you work with, such as e-mail messages and attachments, contact entries, journal entries, tasks, appointments, and notes. Outlook 2007 includes default folders for each type of item—for example, the Calendar, Contacts, Journal, Inbox, RSS Feeds, and Tasks folders. Along with these item-type folders are other default folders, such as Deleted Items, Drafts, Junk E-Mail, Outbox, and Sent Items.

These folders are all part of your personal folders (.pst) file, so they are private. If you are running Outlook 2007 with Microsoft Exchange Server, others on your network to whom you've assigned rights can view and manage items stored in these folders if you make the folders public.

> **Note**
>
> In addition to the folders listed here, in an Exchange Server 2003 environment, your Exchange Server administrator can set up public folders that appear in your Folder List but are stored on the computer running Exchange Server. You and others who have rights to these public folders will see a Public Folders icon in your Folder List. If you have the necessary rights, you can create and delete these public folders, store and manage items in them, and see content added to them by other users. In an Exchange Server 2007 environment, the use of public folders has been superseded by the functionality provided in Microsoft Office SharePoint® 2007.

Working with the Folder List

If you move between folders frequently, you might want to navigate by using a combination of the Navigation Pane and the Folder List. The Navigation Pane gives you quick access to the Outlook 2007 folders that the majority of people use most often. However, you might use different Outlook 2007 folders, or you might want to access certain file system folders from Outlook 2007. For example, suppose that you have an Exchange Server account but also use a set of personal folders to store personal messages and contacts or other data. Because Outlook 2007 doesn't automatically add shortcuts in the Navigation Pane for your other folders, the best way to access these folders is usually through the Folder List, as shown in Figure 30-1.

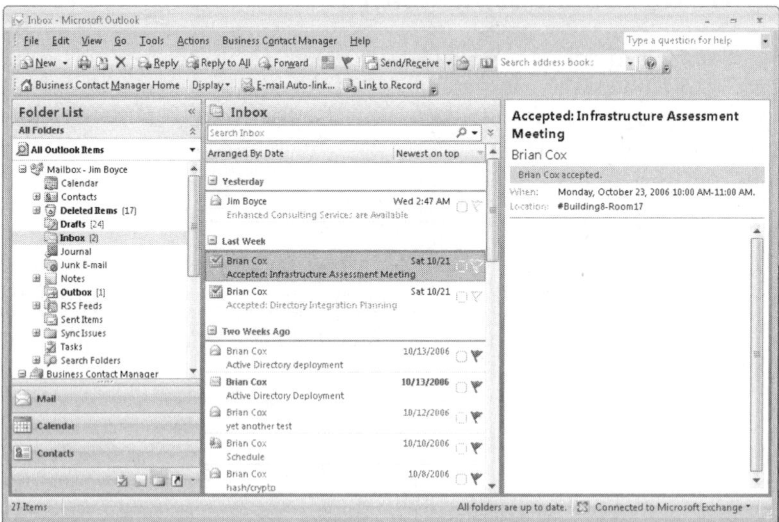

Figure 30-1. Use the Folder List to move between folders not listed in the Navigation Pane or to see which folders are included in a given store.

You can display the Folder List in two ways:

- Choose Go, Folder List.
- Click the Folder List button at the bottom of the Navigation Pane.

The behavior of the Folder List has changed from earlier versions of Microsoft Outlook. In earlier versions (pre-Outlook 2003), the Folder List automatically hid itself after you selected a folder from it. In Outlook 2007 (and in Outlook 2003), the Folder List remains visible in the Navigation Pane until you click one of the Outlook 2007 folder buttons below the Folder List. Clicking a folder in the Folder List itself does not cause the Folder List to disappear.

> **Note**
>
> You can right-click a folder in the Folder List to display the folder's shortcut menu, which gives you access to specific actions that you can perform on the folder. Many of these actions, such as opening and deleting folders, are explained in the following sections.

Using and Managing Folders

When you perform an action in Outlook 2007, you do so inside a folder. Outlook 2007 provides a handful of actions that you can perform with folders to change their behavior, location, appearance, and so on, as described in the following sections.

Using a Folder

When you're ready to work with information in Outlook 2007, you first go to the folder in which that information is stored. For example, to read a new e-mail message downloaded to your Inbox folder, you must open the Inbox folder and then select the message to read. To open a folder, click its button in the Navigation Pane or click the folder name in the Folder List.

When you open the folder, its contents are displayed in the main Outlook 2007 window. To see the contents of a particular folder item, you must open the item using one of these methods:

- Double-click the item in the main Outlook 2007 window.
- Right-click the item, and then choose Open.
- Click the item, and then press **Enter**.
- Click the item, and then choose File, Open, Selected Items.
- Click the item, and then press **Ctrl+O**.

Depending on the type of folder you open, the Reading Pane might be available. The Reading Pane displays the contents of the currently selected item without requiring you to open a separate window for the folder item. The Reading Pane is handy because it provides a quick view and can help keep your desktop tidier. To display the Reading Pane, choose View, Reading Pane and then select Right or Bottom, or simply click the Reading Pane button on the Advanced toolbar.

By default, the Reading Pane appears on the right in the main Outlook 2007 window, as shown in Figure 30-2. You can resize this pane by dragging the edge. To see an item in the Reading Pane, simply select the item in the folder.

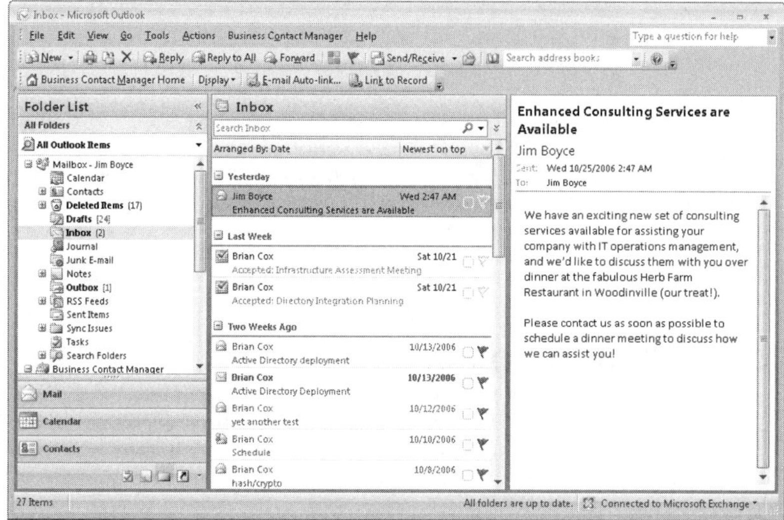

Figure 30-2. You can view the contents of a folder item in the Reading Pane.

For more information about working with the Reading Pane, see "Working with the Standard Outlook Views" in Chapter 4.

> **Note**
>
> Only one item can be open in the Reading Pane at any given time. If you want to open additional items, you must double-click them to display them in separate windows.

Creating a Folder

As you know, Outlook 2007 provides a basic set of folders in which you can store certain types of data, such as the Contacts folder for storing contact information. As you use Outlook 2007 more, you'll want to add other folders to organize your data. For example, you might add other message folders to store particular kinds of messages.

Each Outlook 2007 folder you add has a specific *type* based on the type of data it stores. For example, a mail folder differs from a contacts folder because the former stores messages and the latter stores contact entries. Similarly, a calendar folder stores appointments and events, and a notes folder stores notes. When you add a folder, you specify the folder type. You also specify the name of the folder and its location.

Follow these steps to create a folder:

1. Take one of the following actions to display the Create New Folder dialog box:
   - Choose File, New, Folder.
   - Choose File, Folder, New Folder.
   - Right-click a folder in the Folder List, and then choose New Folder.
   - Press **Ctrl+Shift+E**.
   - Click the arrow next to the New button on the Standard toolbar, and then choose Folder.
2. In the Name box, type a name for the folder, shown in Figure 30-3.

Figure 30-3. Use the Create New Folder dialog box to specify folder type, location, and other properties of the new folder.

3. In the Folder Contains drop-down list, choose the type of item you want to store in this new folder.
4. In the Select Where To Place The Folder list, select the location for the new folder. Selecting the Inbox, for example, places the new folder as a subfolder of the Inbox.
5. Click OK.

Adding a Folder Shortcut to the Navigation Pane

If you have a frequently used folder that isn't listed in the Navigation Pane, you can create a shortcut to the folder in the Shortcuts area of the Navigation Pane, as explained here:

1. At the bottom of the Navigation Pane, click Shortcuts .
2. In the Shortcuts pane, click Add New Shortcut to display the Add To Navigation Pane dialog box, shown in Figure 30-4.

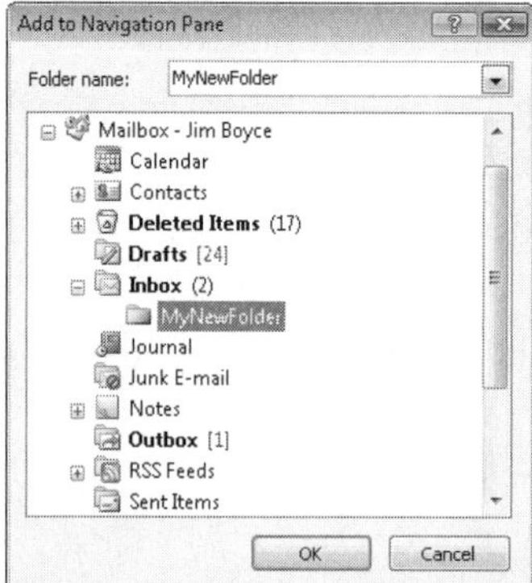

Figure 30-4. Add folders to the Shortcuts pane with the Add To Navigation Pane dialog box.

3. Select a folder in the list, and then click OK.

You can also create your own shortcut groups. Click the Add New Group shortcut. Outlook 2007 creates a new shortcut and highlights the name so that you can change it. Type a new name, and then press **Enter**. You can easily move shortcuts from one group to another simply by dragging them.

> **Note**
>
> You can drag folders, documents, and Web shortcuts to a group in the Shortcuts pane to quickly create shortcuts to those items. If you have several URLs in your Microsoft Internet Explorer® Favorites folder that you want to copy to Outlook 2007 shortcuts, open the Favorites folder, and drag the URLs to an Outlook 2007 shortcut group. Internet Explorer running under Windows Vista™ will initially display the Internet Explorer Security dialog box, citing the restriction against dragging Web content outside of Protected Mode without prior approval. Click Allow to let the Web URL be dragged into the Outlook 2007 shortcut group. If you want to allow this to occur every time with prompting, click the Always Allow Web Content To Be Copied To This Program check box before clicking Allow.

When you want to remove a shortcut, right-click it, choose Delete Shortcut, and then click Yes.

TROUBLESHOOTING

Folder and content remains when shortcut is removed

When you remove a folder shortcut from the Navigation Pane, you remove only the shortcut. You do not remove the folder from Outlook 2007, nor do you delete the folder's contents. For information about deleting a folder and its contents, see "Deleting a Folder" later in this chapter.

If you decide that a folder shortcut should be renamed, follow these steps:

1. Right-click the folder shortcut you want to rename.
2. Choose Rename Shortcut.
3. Type a new name, and then press **Enter**.

Note

When you rename the folder shortcut, the folder name in the Folder List does not change; only the shortcut name changes.

Working with Favorite Folders

A feature in Outlook 2007 is the favorite folders pane in the Navigation Pane for each of the Outlook 2007 folder types. When you click the Mail button in the Navigation Pane, for example, Outlook 2007 displays a Favorite Folders list at the top of the Navigation Pane. This list, by default, includes three of the most commonly used mail folders: the Inbox, Unread Mail, and Sent Items folders, as shown in Figure 30-5.

Note that the naming convention isn't consistent across Outlook 2007 folder types for the favorite folders pane. The favorite folders panes for the other folders are named My Calendars, My Contacts, My Tasks, My Journals, and My Notes. All but My Calendars appear at the top of the Navigation Pane when you open the folder. My Calendars appears below the Date Navigator in the Navigation Pane when you open the Calendar folder.

You can easily add folders to and remove folders from their respective favorites lists. For example, if you use a separate folder for your personal contacts, you might add the folder to the My Contacts list to make it readily available without the need to open the Folder List. To add a folder to its favorites list, open the Folder List, right-click the folder, and then choose Add To Favorite Folders (for a Mail folder). For other folder types such as Contacts, the folder is placed in your My Contacts list (or My Calendars for Calendar type folders, My Notes for Notes type folders, and so on) automatically. To remove a mail folder from its favorites list, right-click the folder in the Folder List or in the favorites list, and then choose Remove From Favorite Folders. For other folder types, right-click the folder you want to remove, and then select Delete <folder name>, where <folder name> is the name of the folder you created.

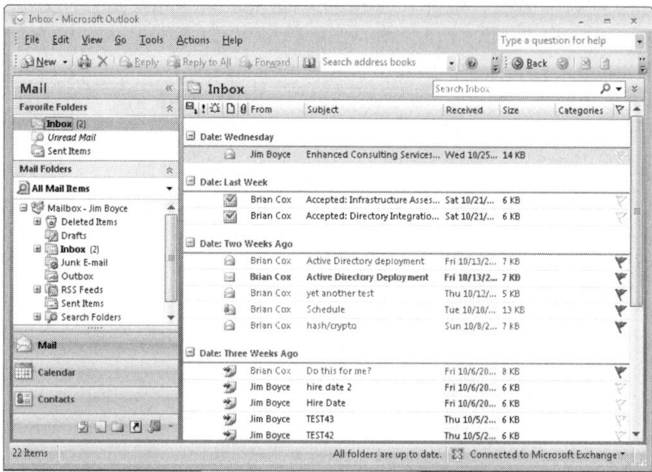

Figure 30-5. Use the Favorite Folders list to quickly open frequently used folders.

You can also change the order of favorite folders in the list. Right-click the folder in the list and choose Move Up In List or Move Down In List, or simply drag the folder to the desired location in the list.

INSIDE OUT Deletion of favorite folders is not consistent

Adding and removing mail folders is different from adding and removing other folder types. When you add a mail folder to your favorites using Add To Favorite Folders, you are including a link to an existing folder. When you right-click on that folder in the Favorite Folders list and select Remove From Favorite Folders, only the link to the original folder is removed (leaving the original folder intact). If you right-click the mail folder in the Favorite Folders list and choose Delete, however, the mail folder is actually deleted. Similarly,when you create a new contacts folder, the folder is automatically added to your My Contacts list, and when you right-click it and choose Delete (there is no Remove From Favorite Folders menu option), the folder is actually deleted. This is true for the Calendar, Notes, Tasks, and Journal folder types.

Renaming a Folder

Sometimes you need to change a folder's name, perhaps as a result of project modifications or a company name change. Unfortunately, you can't rename the default folders created by Outlook 2007. You can, however, change the names of folders you create. To rename a folder, begin with one of these actions:

- Open the Folder List, right-click the folder, and then choose Rename.
- Select the folder, and then click the folder name to highlight it.
- Select the folder, and then choose File, Folder, Rename.

After taking one of these actions, simply type the new name and then press **Enter** to have the change take effect.

Another way to change a folder's name is through its Properties dialog box, as shown in Figure 30-6, which you can display by right-clicking the folder in the Folder List and choosing Properties. On the General tab, type a new name in the top box. Click OK to save the name and to return to the Folder List.

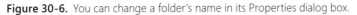

Figure 30-6. You can change a folder's name in its Properties dialog box.

> **Note**
>
> When you change a folder's name, shortcuts to the folder in the Navigation Pane are updated to reflect the change.

Copying and Moving a Folder

Occasionally, you might need to move or copy a folder from one location to another. For example, suppose that you've created some message folders in your Inbox to organize messages, but now you want to move those folders to a folder other than the Inbox. Or maybe you want to copy the Contacts folder from your Exchange Server mailbox to a set of personal folders.

Moving or copying folders is easy. Open the Folder List, right-click the folder you want to move or copy, and choose either Move or Copy on the shortcut menu. Outlook 2007 displays a Move Folder dialog box, as shown in Figure 30-7, or a Copy Folder dialog box. Select the folder in which you want to store the moved or copied folder and click OK, or choose New to create a new folder in which to store the moved or copied folder.

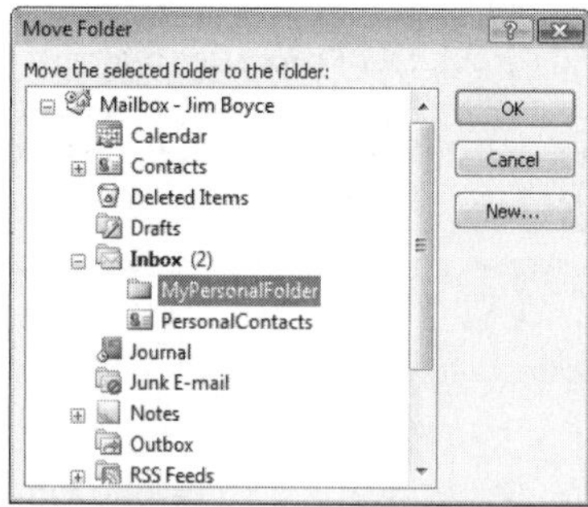

Figure 30-7. To move a folder, select its new location in the Move Folder dialog box.

Another way to move a folder is to drag it to a new location. You can copy a folder using a similar technique; just hold down the **Ctrl** key while dragging.

You can move one type of folder so that it becomes a subfolder of another type of folder. For example, suppose that you receive e-mail messages containing contact information. You can store these messages in a folder named, say, Contact Info. You then can store the Contact Info folder as a subfolder of Contacts. The type of data you can store in the subfolder is the type you originally established for that folder. (For example, when a mail-type folder becomes a subfolder of a contacts-type folder, neither folder changes its type.)

If you want to move or copy a folder to the root of the folder store, move or copy the folder to the topmost folder in the list (such as Personal Folders). If you use the Edit, Cut or Edit, Copy commands to move or copy, select the topmost folder and then choose Edit, Paste.

Deleting a Folder

You can delete an Outlook 2007 folder the same way you delete a folder in Windows Explorer or My Computer. When you delete an Outlook 2007 folder, it's removed from the Folder List and placed in the Deleted Items folder. This way, if you decide you want the folder back, you can retrieve it from the Deleted Items folder.

When you delete a folder, you delete the contents of the folder as well. The contents move with the folder to the Deleted Items folder and can be retrieved along with the folder later. (The items can be retrieved only until the Deleted Items folder is emptied.) You also can retrieve individual items from the Deleted Items folder, even if those items were deleted as part of a folder deletion. For example, if you delete a message folder named Project Alpha containing three messages, you can retrieve one, two, or all three messages individually without retrieving the Project Alpha folder. To retrieve a folder from the Deleted Items folder, click Deleted Items, and then select the folder to retrieve. Move that folder from the Deleted Items folder to its original location or to another location.

Although you can't delete any of the default folders (the folders that Outlook 2007 provides), you can delete folders you've added.

To do so, follow these steps:

1. Make sure that the folder doesn't contain any data you need to keep or any data that you have not archived or backed up.
2. Open the Folder List, right-click the folder, and then choose Delete.
3. Click Yes to confirm the deletion or No to cancel.

INSIDE OUT **Automatically delete items matching a specific date**

Outlook 2007 can automatically remove items in a folder that match a specified date. If Outlook 2007 is configured to empty the Deleted Items folder on a certain date or whenever you quit the program, however, you might lose important items that you accidentally or prematurely sent to that folder. To see the deletion date of a folder, right-click the folder, and then choose Properties. On the AutoArchive tab, if the Archive This Folder Using These Settings option is selected, look to see whether the Permanently Delete Old Items option is also selected. If it is, the time in the Clean Out Old Items Older Than option specifies how much time you have to retrieve an item from that folder. Don't assume that the folder you deleted last year will still be around today.

Setting Folder Properties

Folders have several properties that control the way they appear and function, as well as others that control archiving, administration, and other activities. To view or set these properties, open the Folder List, right-click the folder, and then choose Properties to open a Properties dialog box for the folder. The following sections explain the options on each of the tabs in the Properties dialog box.

Configuring General Folder Properties

You can use the General tab, shown in Figure 30-8, to locate information about a folder, name the folder, add a descriptive comment, and set other properties.

Figure 30-8. Use the General tab of a folder's Properties dialog box to view information about the folder and set a few general properties.

The options on the General tab are described in the following list:

- **Name** In the top box, specify the name for the folder as you want it to appear in Outlook 2007.
- **Type** This read-only property specifies the type of content the folder contains.
- **Location** This read-only property specifies the location in the folder hierarchy for the selected folder.
- **Description** Use this box to type an optional description of the folder. The description appears only in the folder's Properties dialog box.
- **Show Number Of Unread Items** Use this option with message folders to cause Outlook 2007 to display, in the Folder List and favorite folders pane, the number of unread messages in the folder. Outlook 2007 displays the folder name in bold if the item contains unread messages and includes the number of unread items in parentheses to the right of the folder name.
- **Show Total Number Of Items** Use this option with all folder types to show the total number of items in the folder. Outlook 2007 shows the folder name in bold if it contains items and displays the total number of items in parentheses to the right of the folder name. This option can be particularly useful with search folders to show the total number of items that match the search folder's criteria.

- **When Posting To This Folder, Use** This drop-down list includes two selections. One is the default type of item you can store in the folder, such as Contacts for a contacts folder. The other is Forms. If you select Forms in the list, Outlook 2007 opens the Choose Form dialog box, shown in Figure 30-9. Here you can select the form that the folder should use for new items added to the folder. For example, you might want to use a custom appointment form for a calendar folder.

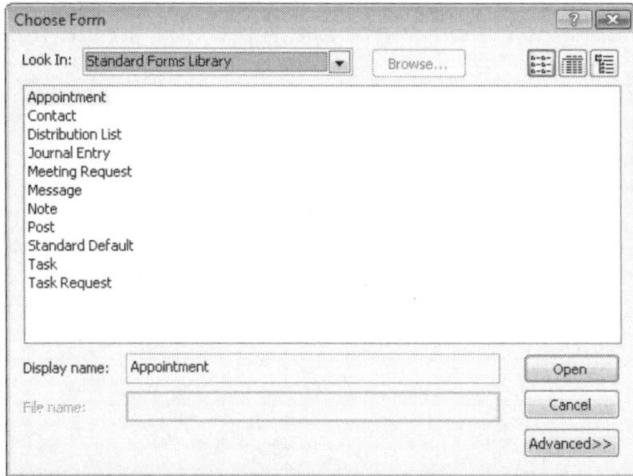

Figure 30-9. Specify the type of form to be used by the folder.

- **Automatically Generate Microsoft Exchange Views** Select this check box to have Outlook 2007 create views of public folders so that Microsoft Exchange Server users can view the folders.
- **Folder Size** Click this button to view information about the amount of space a folder and its subfolders use.
- **Clear Offline Items** The Clear Offline Items button removes all items from your offline store.

TROUBLESHOOTING

Assigning a form to a folder fails

The option to select Forms in the When Posting To This Folder, Use This drop-down list enables you to select a custom designed form (of the correct type) to control entry of items into the folder. There is a constraint, however—what you select when you choose Forms and then select a form type from the Standard Forms Library or Personal Forms Library has to match the object type of the folder. If you create a new mail folder, for example, the form selected has to also be of the IPM.Post type. Likewise, if you create a calendar folder, the form selected has to be of the IPM.Appointment type. If the type doesn't match, you get an error message stating, "You cannot create an item of this type in this folder."

Configuring Home Page Properties for a Folder

The Home Page tab lets you assign a Web page as the default home page for a folder, as shown in Figure 30-10. By default, the Address field is blank and the Show Home Page By Default For This Folder check box is not selected (which is different from how the tab appears in Figure 30-10). The Restore Defaults button resets the selections on the tab to the default values. Once a Web page is assigned, however, the Offline Web Page Settings button is enabled, to check for updates and download the selected pages for offline viewing.

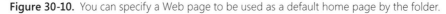

Figure 30-10. You can specify a Web page to be used as a default home page by the folder.

Configuring AutoArchive Properties for a Folder

Outlook's AutoArchive feature automatically archives items after a specified period, which can help you avoid having folders cluttered with old messages, tasks, and so on. You configure archival properties on the AutoArchive tab of a folder's Properties dialog box. For details, see "Configuring Automatic Archiving" in Chapter 31.

Configuring Administration Properties for a Folder

Outlook 2007 provides options for setting administration properties for each folder. To change these properties for a public folder, you must have owner permissions for that folder. In addition, for all but the Initial View On Folder option, you must be running Outlook 2007 with Exchange Server. The following options are available on the Administration tab:

- **Initial View On Folder** You can specify the view you see when you open a folder. Your choices are Normal, Group By Form, Group By Subject, Group By Conversation Topic, and Unread By Conversation. The default view is Normal.
- **Drag/Drop Posting Is A** This option lets you specify an item's format when you drag the item to a public folder.

- **Add Folder Address To** You can choose to have Outlook 2007 add the folder address to your Personal Address Book. You can then send e-mail directly to the folder.
- **This Folder Is Available To** You can specify the users who can access the folder. You can select all users who have access permissions, or you can limit access to the owner.
- **Folder Assistant** While working online, you can modify processing rules for new items posted to the public folder.
- **Moderated Folder** This option allows you to select moderators for this moderated folder.
- **Folder Path** You can specify the location of the folder.

Configuring Form Properties for a Folder

Outlook 2007 items are based on forms, which standardize how information is distributed to other users and stored in Outlook 2007. One example of a form is the contact form that Outlook 2007 provides when you create a new contact entry.

For more information about forms, see Chapter 28, "Designing and Using Forms."

On the Forms tab of the Properties dialog box, you can set or view the following form properties for a folder:

- **Forms Associated With This Folder** This item shows a list of forms in the Folder Forms Library associated with the folder. By default, this item is blank.
- **Manage** You can specify a form that you want to move to the Folder Forms Library, thereby listing it in the Forms Associated With This Folder list. You also can click Manage to set up a new form in the Folder Forms Library.
- **Description** Add a description of a form you select in the Forms Associated With This Folder list. You can change the description by clicking Manage, selecting the form, selecting Properties in the Forms Manager dialog box, and then changing the text in the Comments field in the Form Properties dialog box. Click OK twice to save your changes.
- **Allow These Forms In This Folder** You can specify the types of forms you allow in the folder. (The folder must be a public folder.) You can specify that only forms from this list (Only Forms Listed Above) be allowed in the folder, or you can specify that Forms Listed Above And The Standard Forms or Any Form be allowed in the folder. If you select the Forms Listed Above And The Standard Forms option, forms such as messages, tasks, and even documents (for example, Microsoft Office Word 2007 files or Microsoft Office Excel® 2007 worksheets) can be stored in the folder.

Note

If you run Outlook 2007 with Exchange Server 2003, your folders might have public folders set up by system administrators or others who have folder creation privileges. In that case, you can administer permissions properties for these folders using the Permissions tab. For information about folder permissions, see "Granting Access to Folders" in Chapter 35.

Configuring Permissions for a Folder

You can control access to folders in Outlook 2007 by selecting the Permissions tab and specifying the users that will be granted access and the type of access they will be granted. The default permissions provide full control to the owner of the folder, as shown in Figure 30-11, and assign no permissions to access or modify content to the Default and Anonymous groups. To add users to the Permissions list, click Add, and then select the user to include in the list. Once a user has been added, select the user, and use the drop-down list next to Permission Level to set the general permission level (Owner, Publishing Editor, Editor, Publishing Author, Author, Non-Editing Author, Reviewer, Contributor, or None). You can further refine the permission level by selecting options in the Read, Write, Delete Items, and Other areas.

Figure 30-11. To control access to a folder, set permission levels for users accessing the folder.

Configuring Synchronization Properties for a Folder

The Synchronization tab lets you filter the content that is synchronized with a folder. To establish a filter, click Filter, and in the Filter dialog box, shown in Figure 30-12, configure the criteria that you want the filter to use when downloading new items. The Filter dialog box simply sets the filter criteria; it does not perform the synchronization. To synchronize folder content, click on Send/Receive on the Standard toolbar.

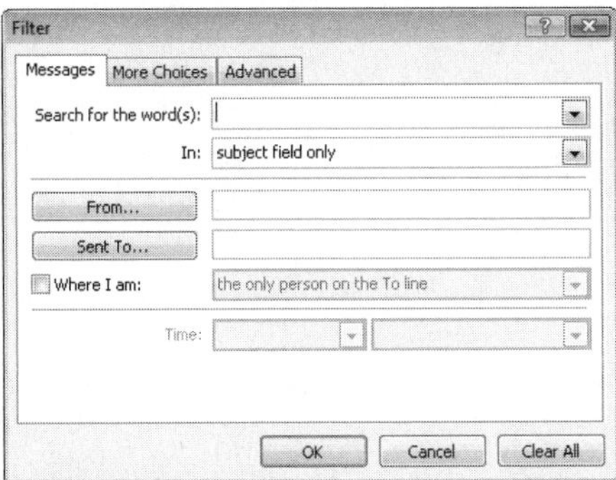

Figure 30-12. Set the criteria to filter the content that is downloaded when the folder is synchronized with the server.

Configuring Properties for a Contacts Folder

The Contacts folder has additional properties that you can control. When configuring properties for a Contacts folder, you can set the following address book options on the Outlook Address Book tab:

- **Show This Folder As An E-Mail Address Book** Select this option to have Outlook 2007 display contacts in a way that lets you select e-mail addresses from the Address Book dialog box. (This is automatically selected for the default Contacts folder.)
- **Name Of The Address Book** Specify the address book name.

You can also configure the default view for the activity items linked to a contact in the Contacts folder by using the Activities tab of the folder's Contacts Properties dialog box, shown in Figure 30-13. Selecting an option in the Default Activities View drop-down list causes the selected view to appear by default when you click the Activities button in the Show group of a contact. You can also select additional folders that can be chosen dynamically or selected by default for display on a contact's Activities page.

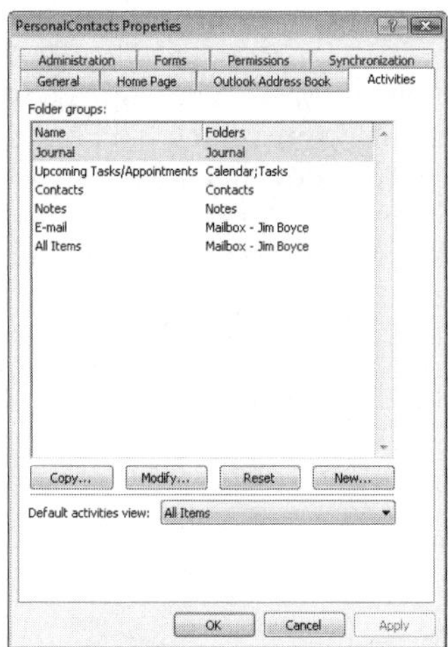

Figure 30-13. Use the Activities tab settings to set the default view that appears on a contact's Activities page.

The options on the Activities tab are listed here:

- **Folder Groups** You can select the group of folders that might contain activities related to contacts.
- **Copy, Modify, Reset, New** Click the appropriate button to add folder groups to or modify folder groups in the Folder Groups list.
- **Default Activities View** You can select the default view that appears on the Activities tab of a contact form when you open a contact entry. The other options (that are not the default) can be selected in the Show drop-down list on the contact's Activities page.

Using Web Views with Folders

The popularity of the Internet and its usefulness to businesses and individuals make it almost imperative that software include features for accessing Web pages. Outlook 2007 offers such features, providing ways for users to access the Web without switching to a different program. This section describes how you can access the Web by specifying a Web page as a home page for a folder.

Why Use Web Views?

When you assign a Web page as a home page for a folder, you make it convenient and easy to access intranet or Internet resources. The primary reason to use a Web view in a folder is to access a Web site or an intranet resource without leaving Outlook 2007. As shown in Figure 30-14, you can open a folder that includes a Web page as a home page and then access another page from there. You no longer have to start a separate Web browser, such as Internet Explorer, to open the Web page.

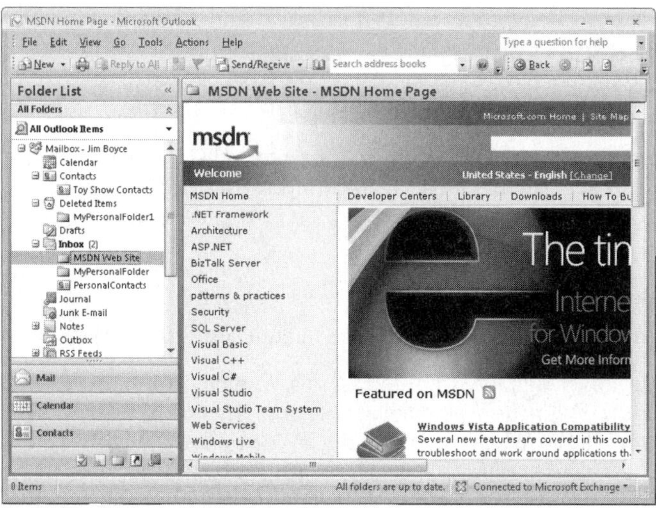

Figure 30-14. You can view a Web page without leaving Outlook 2007.

Assigning a Web Page to a Folder

You can assign a Web page to any folder in your Folder List.

To assign a Web page, follow these steps:

1. Right-click a folder in the Folder List, and then choose Properties.
2. Click the Home Page tab, as shown in Figure 30-15.

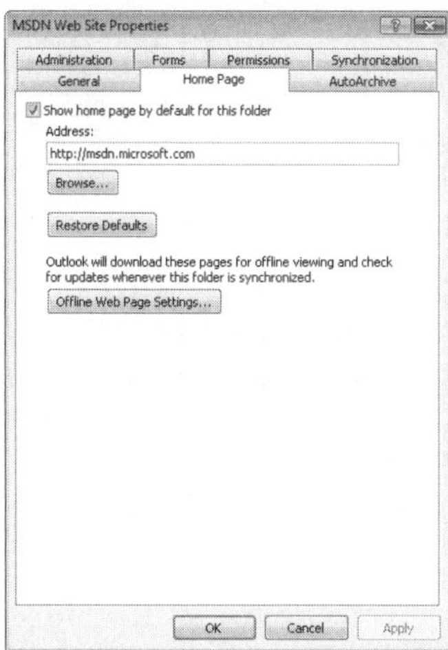

Figure 30-15. Specify a Web page view for a folder using this dialog box.

3. Set Web page view properties as necessary, using the following options:

   Show Home Page By Default For This Folder Select this check box if you want Outlook 2007 to display the Web page rather than the existing default folder view.

   Address Specify the URL of a local or remote HTML page or another Internet resource, such as a File Transfer Protocol (FTP) site. In this example, the following URL for the MSDN® Web site is specified:

   http://msdn.microsoft.com

   Browse Click to browse for a URL.

   Restore Defaults Click to restore the default settings (no Web page).

4. For your folder that you want to assign a Web page to, type the URL (Internet or local address) for the Web page you want to display. You also can click Browse and then select a Web page in the Find Web Files dialog box. Click OK after selecting a page to return to the Home Page tab.

5. Click OK.

Removing a Web Page from a Folder

After a while, you might tire of using a Web view in a folder, or the Web page might become obsolete.

To remove a Web page from a folder, follow these steps:

1. Right-click the folder in the Folder List, and then choose Properties.
2. Click the Home Page tab.
3. Clear the Show Home Page By Default For This Folder check box.
4. Click OK.

Using a Folder's Web Page

Each time you open a folder with a Web page view, Outlook 2007 displays the specified Web page according to the Home Page options you selected. If the Web page includes hyperlinks, you can click them to navigate to other pages or sites. In addition, you can type a different URL in the Address box in Outlook 2007 and then press **Enter** to display a new Web page inside the Outlook 2007 folder.

INSIDE OUT **Create shortcuts to Web pages**

You can create shortcuts to Web pages by clicking the Shortcuts icon at the bottom of the Navigation Pane to open the Shortcut pane and then dragging a URL link (from Internet Explorer or another browser) to the Shortcut pane. An alternative to creating shortcuts is to create Outlook 2007 folders and then assign them a home page. This method has the advantage of making the pages available from the Folder List—just click on the folder in the Folder List to navigate to the associated Web page or FTP folder.

Using Multiple Personal Folders

Items you create and receive in Outlook 2007 are stored in personal folder (.pst) files. The default location for .pst files is \Users\<user>\AppData\Local\Microsoft\Outlook.

If you don't use Outlook 2007 with Exchange Server, you use personal folders for storing your Outlook 2007 information and data. (With Exchange Server, your messages, calendar, and other items are stored centrally on the server, although you can use .pst files in conjunction with an Exchange Server account.)

You can create multiple personal folders to help you organize your data. For example, you can store e-mail messages associated with a project or a client in one folder and store other messages and items in a more general folder. Another useful way to set up multiple .pst files is to use one for archiving. This can help you back up your data more consistently, and Outlook 2007 can prompt you at different intervals to ensure that your archive is up to date. Outlook 2007 even includes the Archive.pst file, in which you can archive items.

Note

As Outlook 2007 copies items to the archive file, it removes them from their original location. As a result, the archiving of Outlook 2007 items is essentially a "move" process.

You can also use a .pst file to share information with other users on your network. The users must have read/write permissions to open the file.

After you create a .pst file, it appears in the Folder List automatically. You can add it to a Shortcuts group in the Navigation Pane just as you can with any other folders. You then can access the .pst file simply by clicking its shortcut.

For information about adding a folder shortcut, see "Adding a Folder Shortcut to the Navigation Pane" earlier in this chapter.

Adding a Personal Folder

A personal folder can have any name you give it. By default, the names take the form Personal Folder(1).pst, Personal Folder(2).pst, and so on. At the top of the Folder List, you can see the name of the active personal folder, which by default appears as Personal Folders.

To add a personal folder, follow these steps:

1. Choose Tools, Account Settings, click the Data Files tab, and then click Add to open the New Outlook Data File dialog box, shown in Figure 30-16.

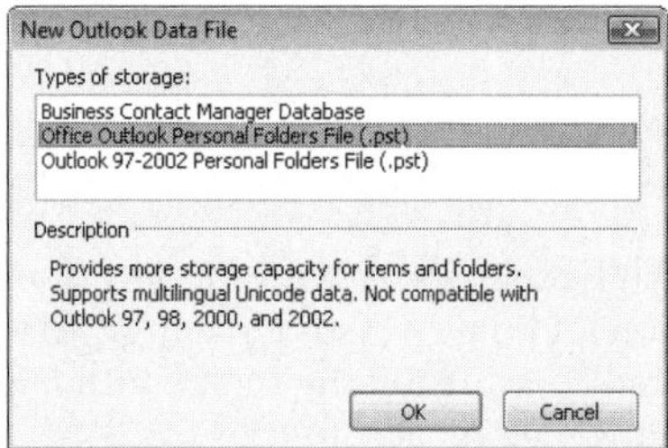

Figure 30-16. Click a Personal Folders File (.pst) option to create a personal folder.

2. Select Office Outlook Personal Folders File (.pst) if you will not be using the .pst file with an earlier version of Outlook. Choose Outlook 97-2002 Personal Folders File (.pst) if you need to use the .pst file with an earlier version of Outlook.
3. Click OK. The Create Or Open Outlook Data File dialog box appears.
4. In the File Name box, type a name for the new personal folders file.
5. Click OK. The Create Microsoft Personal Folders dialog box appears, as shown in Figure 30-17.

Figure 30-17. Use the Create Microsoft Personal Folders dialog box to set the .pst file's properties.

6. In the Name box, type a name for the folder. This name appears in the Folder List after you create the folder.
7. If you want to protect your .pst file further, type a password in the Password box, and then retype it in the Verify Password box. Each time Outlook 2007 starts, you'll be prompted to enter this password to access your .pst file. If you want, you can click the check box to save the password in your password list so that Outlook 2007 can retrieve the password when it starts.

Note

If you want to limit who can access your .pst file, you should not save your Outlook 2007 password in the password list.

8. Click OK.
9. The new personal folders item appears in the Data Files list. Click Close in the Account Settings dialog box, and the new personal folder (named earlier in step 6) is accessible in the Folder List.

Removing a Personal Folder

If you no longer need a set of personal folders (contained in a .pst file), you can remove the file from the Data Files list in the Account Settings dialog box, which removes the file from your profile. Removing a set of personal folders from your profile does not delete the .pst file–it remains intact, and you can add it back to the profile or add it to a different profile, if needed.

When you are ready to remove a .pst file, follow these steps to remove it using the Data Files list:

1. Choose Tools, Account Settings, and then click the Data Files tab (or choose File, Data File Management).
2. Select the .pst file you want to remove.
3. Click Remove.
4. When prompted about removing the .pst file, click Yes to remove it or No to cancel. If you click Yes, Outlook 2007 removes the .pst file from your profile and from the Folder List but does not delete it from the file system.
5. Click Close.

> **Note**
>
> You can also remove a set of personal folders through the Folder List. Right-click Personal Folders in the list, and then choose Close. Note that the command name reflects the name of the folders, so if you named your folder My Personal Stuff, the command reads Close "My Personal Stuff." Using this process to close personal folders (and the related .pst file) has the same effect as removing the folders using the Data Files process just described. In either case, the .pst file containing the mail items is not deleted from the file system; it is only removed from the Outlook 2007 profile.

Managing Data

As you use Outlook 2007, you'll find that folders will become full of messages, appointments, and other items. One way to manage this data is to copy or move it between folders so that the data is organized according to how you work. In addition, you need to make sure that your data is backed up and archived properly in case you accidentally delete data or a system failure occurs.

In this section, you'll learn how to copy and move data between folders, how to archive data automatically and manually, and how to restore data in case of a system failure or a reinstallation of Outlook 2007.

Copying and Moving Data Between Folders

Occasionally, you might need to move or copy data from one location to another. For example, perhaps you've received an e-mail message from a client connected with a project you're managing. Instead of keeping that message in the Inbox folder, where it might get lost with all the other messages you receive every day, you can move it to a folder devoted to that particular project.

To move data to another folder, follow these steps:

1. Open the Folder List, and then click the folder that includes the message or other item you want to move.
2. After the folder opens, right-click the message or other item, and then choose Move To Folder to open the Move Items dialog box, shown in Figure 30-18.

> **Note**
>
> Choose Edit, Undo Move if you need to move the item back to its original location. This command is effective only immediately after you've performed the move and before you do anything else.

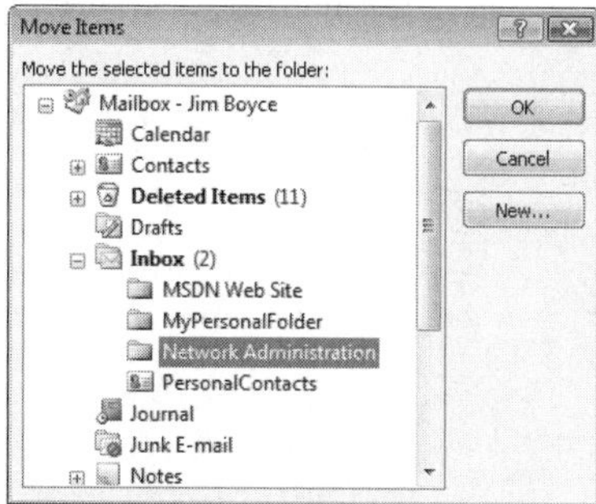

Figure 30-18. Use the Move Items dialog box to move data to a different location.

3. Select an existing folder and click OK, or click New to create a folder in which to store the moved data.
4. Click OK. The data is moved to the selected location.

Another way to move data is to select it in the folder and drag it to a new location. Similarly, you can copy data by holding down the **Ctrl** key while you drag. Alternatively, you can right-click an item, drag it to a new location, and then release the right mouse button and select either Move or Copy.

Storing Items in the Personal Folders or Mailbox Branch

If you move an item to the root of the data store by choosing Personal Folders or Mailbox in the Folder List, Outlook 2007 dutifully moves the item to the root of your mail store. If the destination was a secondary set of personal folders, you can view the items simply by clicking the Personal Folders branch in the Folder List.

However, Outlook 2007 displays Outlook Today view when you click the primary Personal Folders or Mailbox branch in the Folder List, effectively hiding any items stored there. You can perform a search to locate and display the items, but an easier method is to simply turn off Outlook Today view temporarily (or permanently if you never use it).

Open the Folder List, right-click Personal Folders or Mailbox, depending on your account type, and choose Properties. Click the Home Page tab, clear the Show Home Page By Default For This Folder check box, and then click OK. You can now view and work with the items that are located in the root of your mail store. To restore Outlook Today view, select the Show Home Page By Default For This Folder check box.

> **Note**
>
> After you remove items from a .pst file, the file size of the .pst file is not reduced. To reduce the size, you must use the Compact command. To do this, choose Tools, Account Settings and click the Data Files tab (or choose File, Data File Management), and then select your .pst file. Choose Settings, and then click Compact Now in the Personal Folders dialog box.

CHAPTER 31

Archiving, Backing Up, and Restoring Outlook Data

Over time, your Microsoft® Office Outlook® 2007 data store can become overloaded with messages, contact information, appointments, and other data. If you can't manage all this data, you'll be lost each time you try to find a particular item. What's more, the more data in your data store, the larger your .pst file (if you're using one) or your Microsoft Exchange Server mailbox. Many companies impose mailbox size limits to help manage disk use on the servers. So the size of your mailbox can become a problem.

This chapter focuses on managing your Office Outlook 2007 folders and their contents. You'll learn how to archive your data, both manually and automatically, using AutoArchive. You'll also learn how to back up your data and recover it when needed.

Archiving Your Outlook Data

Over time, you will likely want to move some of your Outlook 2007 items to a separate location because you no longer need them but don't want to delete them. For example, perhaps you want to keep copies of all of the messages in your Sent Items folder so that you can refer to them later if needed, but you don't want them to stay in Sent Items. In these situations, you can use the Outlook 2007 AutoArchive feature to move out those old items.

The Outlook 2007 AutoArchive feature archives data automatically according to settings you configure for each folder or all your folders. You might want to archive every day if you receive new data that you don't want to take the chance of losing overnight. Or you might want to set AutoArchive to run once a week.

To set up a folder to automatically archive using the default AutoArchive settings, follow these steps:

1. Right-click a folder in the Folder List, choose Properties, and then in the Properties dialog box, click the AutoArchive tab.

2. Select Archive Items In This Folder Using The Default Settings, as shown in Figure 31-1.

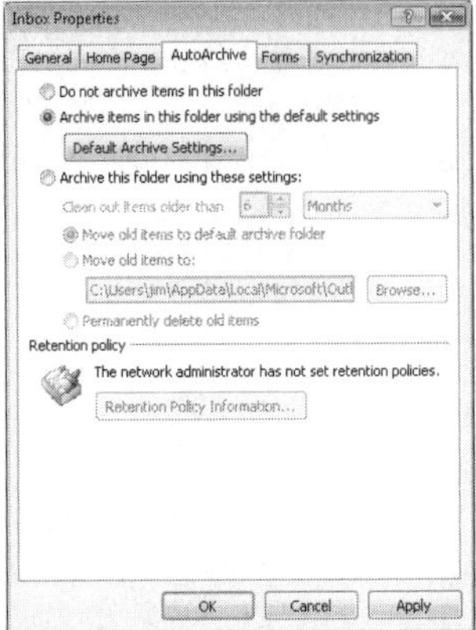

Figure 31-1. Use the AutoArchive feature to archive the data in your folders.

3. Click OK.
4. Repeat these steps for each folder you want to archive.

By default, Outlook 2007 starts AutoArchive every 14 days and archives your data in the selected folder to the Archive.pst personal folders file.

For information about changing the default AutoArchive settings, see "Configuring Automatic Archiving" later in this chapter.

You can also specify custom AutoArchive settings for a folder. Open the Properties dialog box for the folder, click the AutoArchive tab, and then select the Archive This Folder Using These Settings option. Then specify settings on the AutoArchive tab as desired for the folder. See the section "Configuring Automatic Archiving" later in this chapter for details about each of the available settings.

From this point on, the folder for which you have enabled automatic archiving will be archived when Outlook 2007 performs its next automatic archive operation. However, you can also initiate an archive operation any time you need. The next section explains how.

Archiving Your Data Manually

You can archive data not only automatically but also manually—for example, before leaving on vacation or when you need to move your files to a new machine.

To archive data manually, perform these steps:

1. Choose File, Archive.

2. In the Archive dialog box, shown in Figure 31-2, select one of the following options:

   Archive All Folders According To Their AutoArchive Settings Use this option to archive all folders using preset AutoArchive settings. When you select this option, the remaining options in this dialog box become unavailable. Go to step 7.

   Archive This Folder And All Subfolders Select this option if you want to archive individual folders and their subfolders. Go to step 3.

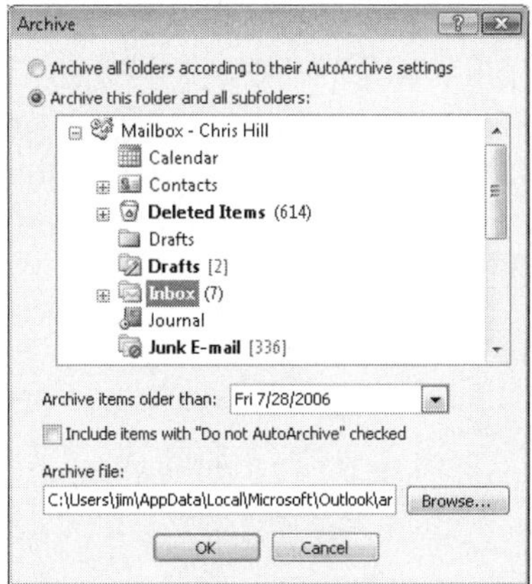

Figure 31-2. Select the way you want to archive data in all or selected folders.

3. Select the folder you want to archive. If the folder includes subfolders, those folders are archived as well.

4. In the Archive Items Older Than drop-down list, specify the latest date from which Outlook 2007 should start archiving data. For instance, if you want to archive data older than today's date, select that date. Otherwise, all your data in the selected folder will not be archived.

5. If you have specified that a folder should not be archived automatically but you want to archive this folder now, select the Include Items With "Do Not AutoArchive" Checked check box.

6. To change the personal folders file that will store your archive, click Browse, and then specify the file and folder where the archive will be stored. You also can type the path and file name in the Archive File box if you know this information.

7. Click OK.

Outlook 2007 begins archiving your data. If the folder contains a large amount of data, archiving might take several minutes (or longer, depending on the speed of your computer and other factors). You can watch the status of the archiving by looking at the right side of the Outlook 2007 status bar. When the process has finished, the Archive.pst file (or whichever archive file you specified in step 6) will contain the data that Outlook 2007 just archived.

Restoring Data After a System Failure or a Reinstallation

Suppose that you've worked on a project for six months and you've been diligent about archiving messages and other items from the project. You come into work one day and find that your system has failed and Outlook 2007 has lost all your data. You need the archived data to get back all your lost information and continue working. How do you get it back?

You can restore data from an archive file in two ways: drag items from a .pst file to a folder, or import a .pst file.

The following steps show you how to drag data from a .pst file:

1. After restoring your computer and, if necessary, reinstalling Outlook 2007, choose File, Open, Outlook Data File to open the Open Outlook Data File dialog box, shown in Figure 31-3.

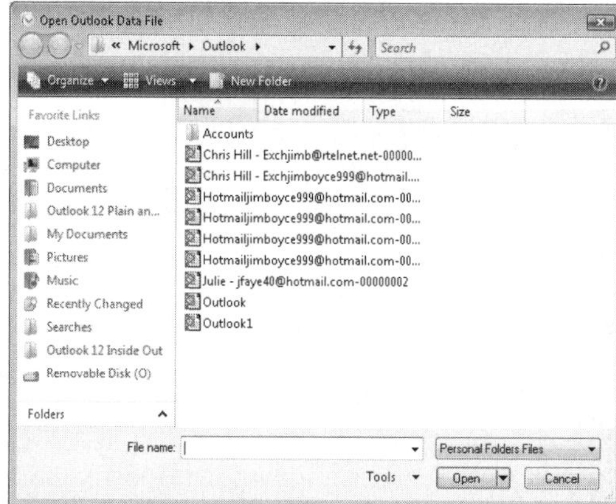

Figure 31-3. Select the .pst file that contains the data you want to restore.

2. Select the file that contains the archived items you want to restore.

3. Click OK. The archive folder (named Archive Folders by default) now appears in your folder list.

4. Click the plus sign (+) next to Archive Folders (or the name you've given this folder) to expand the folder. Expand subsequent folders if necessary until your data is in the pane on the right.

5. Drag the folder or item to the original folder in which the data was stored.

6. Continue dragging items until they all are restored. To drag multiple items at one time, hold down the **Ctrl** key, select the items, and then drag them to the destination.

To restore items by importing a .pst file, follow these steps:

1. Choose File, Import And Export to open the Import And Export Wizard.
2. Select Import From Another Program Or File, and then click Next.
3. Select Personal Folder File (.pst), and then click Next.
4. On the Import Personal Folders page, shown in Figure 31-4, type the name of the file you want to import in the File To Import box, or click Browse to locate the file using the Open Personal Folders dialog box.

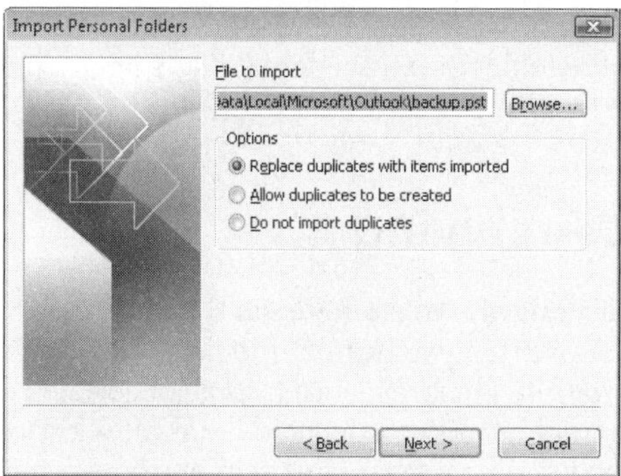

Figure 31-4. On the Import Personal Folders page, specify the name of the file you want to import.

5. Select one of the following import options pertaining to duplicate data:

   Replace Duplicates With Items Imported Replaces duplicate items that might be in your folders during import.

   Allow Duplicates To Be Created Lets Outlook 2007 create duplicates in the destination folders.

   Do Not Import Duplicates Outlook 2007 will not create duplicate items.

6. Click Next.
7. Select the folder from which you want to import data.
8. If the archived folder includes subfolders you want to import as well, select the Include Subfolders option.
9. To filter data, click Filter. You can filter by using search strings, Structured Query Language (SQL), and other advanced querying methods. Click OK after filling in your filter information.

10. Select one of the following destination options:

    Import Items Into The Current Folder Select this option to import data into the current folder–that is, the folder currently selected.

    Import Items Into The Same Folder In Choose this option to import data into the destination folder of the same name as the source folder (such as from the Inbox to the Inbox). Then, in the drop-down list under this last option, select the destination personal folders or mailbox.

11. Click Finish.

Outlook 2007 displays a window showing you the progress of the import process. The archive folder appears in the folder list (if the folder list is open), but it is removed when the operation is completed.

Configuring Automatic Archiving

Outlook 2007 provides several ways to configure and manage your data-archiving settings. For example, suppose that you want Outlook 2007 to run AutoArchive every day, but you want to be prompted before it starts. You can configure AutoArchive to do just that. In addition, you might want to delete old items after a specific date (say, after a message sits in the Inbox for six months). This section shows you how to configure AutoArchive to handle many of your archiving needs.

To set AutoArchive options, choose Tools, Options, click the Other tab, and then click Auto-Archive to open the AutoArchive dialog box. The following sections explain the options that you'll find in the AutoArchive dialog box.

Run AutoArchive Every *n* Days

Outlook 2007 allows you to run AutoArchive on a per-day cycle. For example, if you want to run it each day, set it to run every 1 day. To archive every other day, set AutoArchive to run every 2 days, and so on.

> **Note**
>
> Outlook 2007 has different aging periods for different types of items. Calendar, Notes, Journal, Drafts, and Inbox folders have a default of six months. Outbox is three months, and Sent Items and Deleted Items are two months. Contacts folders do not have an AutoArchive option, so you must manually archive them.

To set the length of time between AutoArchive sessions, set the Run AutoArchive Every *n* Days option to the number of days you want between archiving sessions, as shown in Figure 31-5. The number you enter must be between 1 and 60.

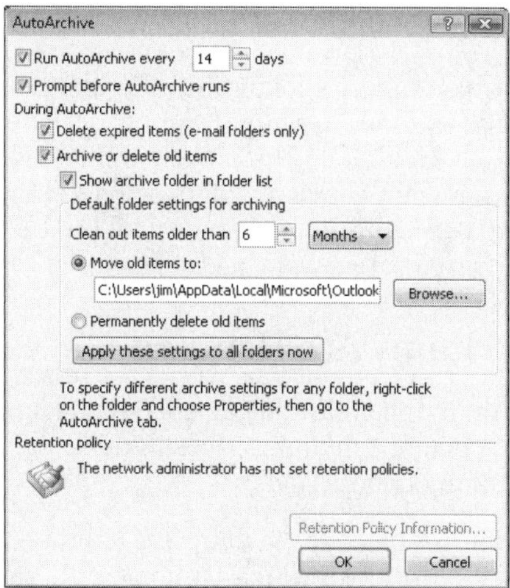

Figure 31-5. Set up Outlook 2007 to run AutoArchive at specified intervals.

Prompt Before AutoArchive Runs

You can have Outlook 2007 display a message before it starts an AutoArchive session. The message includes a Cancel button to let you cancel the AutoArchive session for that day.

To activate this option, select the Prompt Before AutoArchive Runs check box in the AutoArchive dialog box.

Delete Expired Items

In your message folders, AutoArchive can delete messages if they are older than a specified amount of time. To set this option, select the Delete Expired Items check box. Also make sure that the Archive Or Delete Old Items check box is selected.

In the Default Folder Settings For Archiving area, set the amount of time you want to elapse before AutoArchive automatically deletes e-mail messages. The default is six months, but you can set this to as high as 60 months or as low as one day.

Archive Or Delete Old Items

If you want AutoArchive to archive or delete old Outlook 2007 items, select the Archive Or Delete Old Items check box. Then set the amount of time that should elapse before old items are archived or deleted. Again, the default is six months, but you can set this to as high as 60 months or as low as one day.

Show Archive Folder In Folder List

If you want Outlook 2007 to display your archive folder in the Folder List, select the Show Archive Folder In Folder List check box. You might want to select this check box if you think you'd like to be able to see which items have been archived. Also, you might find that some items are removed from your working folders (such as Inbox or Calendar) before you want them removed. By showing the archive folder in the Folder List, you can quickly and easily move items back to a working folder.

Specifying How Archived Items Are Handled

In the Default Folder Settings For Archiving area, you can specify the number of days, weeks, or months that should elapse before e-mail messages or other items are archived or deleted (as described in the preceding two sections).

In addition, this area includes options for the way old items are handled. With the Move Old Items To option, you can specify a .pst file to which Outlook 2007 should move archived items. Click Browse to identify a different location and the .pst file in which you want to store archives.

On the other hand, if you want to delete archived items, select Permanently Delete Old Items, and Outlook 2007 will delete items during the AutoArchive sessions. This option is probably not a good choice if you want to retain information for long periods of time.

Applying Settings to All Folders

If you want these AutoArchive settings to apply to all your folders, click Apply These Settings To All Folders Now. Any settings you establish for individual folders (see the next section) are not overridden by the default settings in the AutoArchive dialog box.

Using AutoArchive Settings for Individual Folders

When you configure AutoArchive settings, you can use the default settings just described, or you can specify options for individual folders.

To take the latter approach, open the Properties dialog box for the folder, click the AutoArchive tab, and then click Archive This Folder Using These Settings. Then set the following options:

- **Do Not Archive Items In This Folder** Specify that the current folder should not be archived.
- **Archive This Folder Using These Settings** Direct Outlook 2007 to archive items in the folder based on the custom settings you specify in the dialog box.
- **Clean Out Items Older Than *n*** This option lets you specify the number of days, weeks, or months that should pass before AutoArchive removes items in the selected folder.
- **Move Old Items To Default Archive Folder** You can have Outlook 2007 move old items to the folder specified for default AutoArchive settings.

- **Move Old Items To** This option lets you specify a different folder in which to archive old items. Click Browse to locate a different folder or file.
- **Permanently Delete Old Items** You can direct Outlook 2007 to delete items in this folder during archiving.

Setting Retention Policy

Your system administrator might enforce company retention policies for your mailbox. If you are running Outlook 2007 with Exchange Server, your administrator can set retention polices that you can't override with AutoArchive settings. For example, your company might require that all e-mail messages be saved and archived to backup tapes or disks and then retained for seven years. As much as you try, you can't change these settings without having the appropriate permissions. To view retention policy settings, click Retention Policy Information on the AutoArchive tab.

Backing Up and Restoring Data

An important part of working with a computer system is ensuring that you protect any critical data against loss. You protect your data by making a *backup*, a copy of the information that you can store on another disk or on a backup tape. In the event of a critical failure, you can then use this copy to replace or restore any lost information.

Outlook 2007 stores information in two primary ways: in a set of personal folders or in an Exchange Server mailbox, which resides in a shared database on the computer running Exchange Server. With an Exchange Server mailbox, your message store is located on the server. The network administrator is generally responsible for backing up the server, and with it, the Exchange Server database that contains all the users' information.

If you don't use Exchange Server, Outlook 2007 stores your data in a .pst file, a set of personal folders. In this scenario, each user has his or her own .pst file or even multiple personal folder files. These .pst files can be located either on the local hard disk of your computer or in a home directory on the server. Although server-based .pst files and local .pst files are identical from a functional standpoint, they aren't identical from a backup perspective. Generally, the network administrator regularly backs up server-based user home directories, so if the .pst files are in your home directory, you shouldn't have to do backups on your own (although you can, of course).

With local message stores, however, normal network backup strategies do not apply. Most networks don't back up every hard disk on every machine. It simply isn't efficient. Similarly, if you're a home user, you probably don't have a server to which you can save data or a network administrator to watch over the server. In such cases, you need to take steps on your own to protect your data. Individual backup and restore scenarios apply to these kinds of cases.

Backing Up Your Outlook Data

Three primary options are available for backing up Outlook 2007 data:

- Exporting some or all information to a backup .pst file
- Copying the .pst file to another disk
- Using a backup program to save a copy of the .pst file to tape, another hard disk, or optical media such as CD-R/CD-RW or DVD-R/DVD-RW

Table 31-1 lists the features available in each backup option.

Table 31-1. Backup Options in Outlook 2007

Backup Type	Export	Copy	Backup
Complete backup	Yes	Yes	Yes
Partial backup	Yes	No	No
Automated backup	No	Yes	Yes

The following sections focus on the use of backup programs and .pst copies.

Backing Up Your Personal Folders

If you store your Outlook 2007 data in one or more sets of personal folders, the data resides in a .pst file. This file is usually located on your local hard disk, but it could also be stored on a shared network folder. The first step in backing up your personal folders is to determine where the .pst file is located.

If you are not sure whether you use an Exchange Server account, follow these steps to check your e-mail settings:

1. Click the Mail icon in Control Panel, or right-click the Outlook icon on the Start menu and then choose Properties.
2. In the Mail Setup dialog box, click Show Profiles, choose your profile, and then click Properties. Then click E-Mail Accounts to open the E-Mail Accounts dialog box.

If the E-Mail Accounts list includes only Microsoft Exchange Server, your Outlook 2007 data is stored in your Exchange Server mailbox on the server, and you need to talk to your Exchange Server administrator about backups or use the Export method described in "Exporting Data" in Chapter 32. If the E-Mail Accounts list shows an Exchange Server account along with other accounts, look at the mail delivery location specified at the bottom of the dialog box. This area shows where incoming mail is delivered. If it specifies a mailbox, your incoming mail is delivered to your Exchange Server mailbox. If it references a set of personal folders, your incoming mail is stored in a .pst.

If the E-Mail Accounts list shows more than one e-mail account, it's possible that your Outlook 2007 data is stored in more than one set of personal folders. For example,

Internet Message Access Protocol (IMAP) and Hypertext Transfer Protocol (HTTP) accounts store their data in their own .pst files. If you want to back up everything in this situation, you need to back up multiple .pst files.

To determine whether you are using more than one .pst file, choose File, Data File Management to open the Data Files tab of the Account Settings dialog box, shown in Figure 31-6. The path and file name for the .pst are generally long, so it's unlikely that you'll be able to read the full name. Click the vertical bar at the right of the Filename column and drag it to the right until you can view the entire path. Or simply click Open Folder, which opens the folder where the .pst file is stored and highlights the .pst file in the folder.

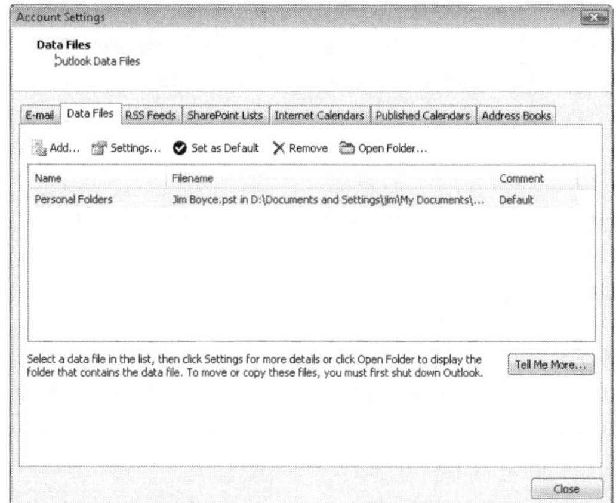

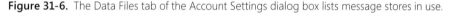

Figure 31-6. The Data Files tab of the Account Settings dialog box lists message stores in use.

After you have verified that the message store is not being backed up elsewhere and is stored in a .pst file, you need to choose which kind of backup to do. Both of the following methods work well, and each has its advantages. Back up each of the .pst files listed in the Data Files tab of the Account Settings dialog box using one of these methods.

Backing Up Using File Copy

Personal folders or archive files can be extremely large—often hundreds of megabytes—so simply saving a .pst file to a floppy disk isn't an option anymore. As files have grown, however, so have the methods available for moving them around. Any of the following options would be acceptable to use with a file backup method:

- Recordable (CD-R) or rewritable (CD-RW) CD drive
- Recordable (DVD-R) or rewritable (DVD-RW) DVD drive
- Zip drive or some other large-capacity storage disk
- Network server drive
- A drive on another computer on the network
- A separate hard disk in the machine where the .pst file is stored

INSIDE OUT **Check network backup policies**

Be certain to check with your network administrator about the recommended policy for backing up .pst files in your organization. If, for example, .pst files are not allowed on your network because of resource allocation, you'll want to know this and choose another backup method, rather than copying your .pst file to the network only to find it deleted the next week. Remember that whatever the merits of a particular backup method, it's critical that your IT staff support it.

If you are saving to a CD or DVD, you can probably use the software that was included with the drive to copy the file. If you're using a Zip (or similar) drive or a network location, simply drag the file to your chosen backup location. Make sure to exit Outlook 2007 before starting the backup copy process.

INSIDE OUT **Don't move the .pst file**

When copying, be careful not to accidentally *move* the .pst file instead. If you move it, you'll find no message store when you restart Outlook 2007. If you do accidentally move your .pst file, you simply need to copy the file back to the correct location. To avoid this potential problem, automate the copy.

Backing Up Using the Microsoft Backup Utility

Both Microsoft Windows® XP and Windows Vista™ include a backup application. You can use these applications to identify files for archiving; they offer the following enhancements over a standard file copy:

- Allow simple setup of a backup plan by using wizards
- Have options for verifying the backup
- Have built-in restore and scheduling options

Note

If you have not used a backup utility in Windows before, take some time to scan through the program's Help content to learn about the program's ins and outs.

Restoring Your Data

Anyone who works with computers long enough will eventually experience a critical error. A drive will become corrupted, a virus will get through your virus software's protection, or you'll accidentally delete something you need. This is the point when all the time and trouble you've invested in backing up your data will pay dividends.

Depending on how you created your backup file, you will have one of two options: you can simply recopy your backup .pst file from the backup location where you copied it, or you can run the backup utility and use the Restore tab to bring back the missing file or files. From there, you can select the backup file that contains the .pst file and then determine which files to restore and where to put them.

Note

By default, the backup utility restores a file to its original location. This is generally the best choice, because if the .pst file isn't restored to the proper location, Outlook 2007 won't be able to find it.

Whichever method you use, be certain to carefully check the drive for errors and viruses before you restore your data. You don't want to restore the file only to see it destroyed again a few hours later.

INSIDE OUT Familiarize yourself with the restore process

It's important to be familiar with the restore process before a disaster recovery process is under way. You should occasionally try restoring your backed-up .pst file to another computer to verify that your backups work. This will help to ensure that the restore process will work and that you know how to perform the necessary tasks.

Using the Offline Folders Option

If you use an Exchange Server account and want to have a backup of your message store available locally, one possible option is to use offline folders. Offline folders allow you to access your message store when your computer is not connected to the server, such as when you're away from the office. To use offline folders, you must create an offline folder (.ost) file, which is stored on the local drive of your computer. If you configure the Exchange Server account to use Cached Exchange Mode, Outlook 2007 creates an .ost file for you automatically and stores your data in that .ost file.

In a sense, .ost files provide backup in reverse: instead of saving data to a server to back it up, the offline process saves the information from the server to the workstation. Although offline folders don't offer a standard backup, an occasional synchronization to an offline store is an easy way to create a second copy of Outlook 2007 data. (With Cached Exchange Mode, Outlook 2007 always works from the .ost file and synchronizes with the Exchange Server mailbox automatically.) If the Exchange Server mailbox is lost, you need only start Outlook 2007 and choose to work offline to access the lost data. At that point, you can export the data to a .pst file to create a backup.

For more information about setting up and using offline folders, see "Working Offline with Outlook and Exchange Server" in Chapter 43.

Backing Up Additional Outlook Data

You should consider including some other items in your regular Outlook 2007 backup scheme in addition to your mailbox and personal folders. The following list identifies these additional items:

- **Outcmd.dat** This file stores customized toolbar and menu settings.
- **<profile>.xml** This file stores customized Navigation Pane settings (shortcuts and shortcut groups). Replace <profile> with the name of your Outlook 2007 profile.
- **<profile>.nk2** This file stores nicknames for AutoComplete (shortcut names for e-mail addresses that you have typed in the recipient fields). Replace <profile> with the name of your Outlook 2007 profile.
- **<name>.srs** This file stores send/receive groups. Replace <name> with the name of the send/receive group.

Note

The .dat, .xml, .nk2, and .srs files are all located by default in the Application Data\Microsoft\Outlook folder of your Windows user profile (such as \Documents and Settings\jim\Application Data\Microsoft\Outlook). To back up these files, exit Outlook 2007, and then back up these files to the same location where you back up your .pst file(s).

In addition to backing up these files on a regular basis, you should also back up your signature files, if you use signatures in Outlook 2007. Signature files are stored in the Application Data\Microsoft\Signatures folder of your Windows user profile, such as \Documents and Settings\<user>\Application Data\Microsoft\Signatures, where <user> is your Windows logon name. Outlook 2007 creates three files for each signature, one each in .txt, .htm, and .rtf format. For example, if you create a signature named Knowledge, Outlook 2007 creates the files Knowledge.txt, Knowledge.htm, and Knowledge.rtf. The simplest way to back up all your signatures is to back up the entire folder.

CHAPTER 32

Moving Data in and out of Outlook with Import/Export

To be truly useful, your data needs to be portable. You need to be able to move it between applications. For example, maybe you want to copy all of your contacts from Microsoft® Office Outlook® 2007 to Microsoft Office Excel® 2007 or Microsoft Office Access 2007. Maybe you need to bring data from Office Excel 2007 into Office Outlook 2007. Whatever the case, your Outlook 2007 data is portable, thanks to the import and export features built into the program.

This chapter explains the features in Outlook 2007 that enable you to move data out of Outlook 2007 to other programs and to import data into Outlook 2007 from other programs.

Exporting Data

Sooner or later, you might want to make copies of part or all of the message store for use in other applications. You can do this by using the export process, in which you save information to a different .pst file or transform data for use in Microsoft Office Word 2007, Access 2007, or other programs. (The reverse process, importing data, is covered in the next section.)

The export process in Outlook 2007 is extremely straightforward. It allows you to use a wizard to send copies of information from the Outlook 2007 message store. This section looks at three export options in some depth: exporting messages, exporting addresses, and exporting data to a file.

Exporting Outlook Data to a .pst File

You can copy messages and other items into a new or an existing set of personal folders. Unlike backing up, this option lets you choose which items you want to export and which you want to exclude. You can use this method whether your mail is stored in a Microsoft Exchange Server mailbox or in a set of personal folders.

You might already know how to use the AutoArchive feature to move messages out of your message store and into a long-term storage location in another .pst file. You can use the Import And Export Wizard to export messages to a file. Using the Import And Export Wizard to export messages works in a similar way to AutoArchive; the major difference is that when messages in the store are exported, they aren't removed; instead, they are copied, as they are during backup.

For information about using AutoArchive, see "Archiving Your Outlook Data" in Chapter 31.

To export some or all of your Outlook 2007 data, follow these steps:

1. Choose File, Import And Export to start the Import And Export Wizard, as shown in Figure 32-1.

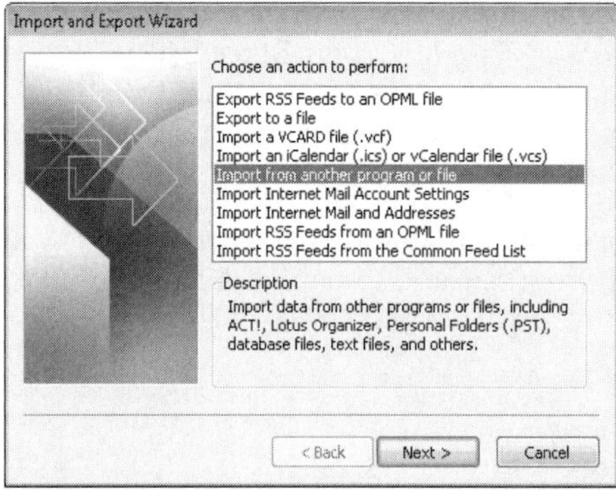

Figure 32-1. Use the Import And Export Wizard to export data to a file.

2. Select Export To A File, and then click Next.

3. The options available on the next wizard page break down into three basic types: text files, databases, spreadsheets, and a personal folders file. Figure 32-2 shows most of the formats available for exporting. Although you can export your messages in any of these formats, you'll probably find .pst files the most useful. For this example, select Personal Folder File (.pst), and then click Next.

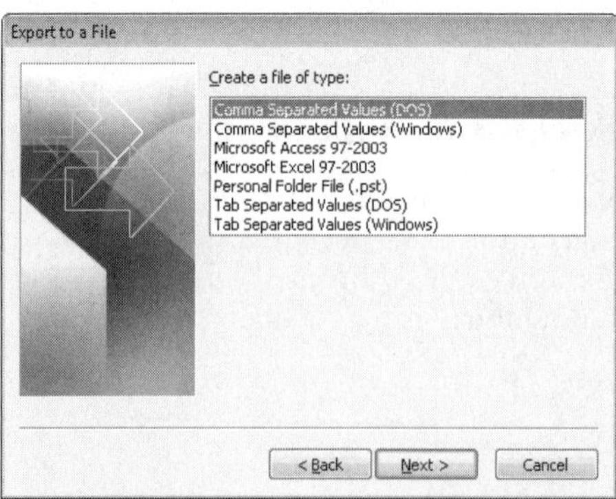

Figure 32-2. You can choose one of these file types for exporting.

4. On the Export Personal Folders page, select the folder you want to export. To include subfolders of the selected folder, select the Include Subfolders option. To export all of your Outlook 2007 data, select the Mailbox or Personal Folders branch, and then select the Include Subfolders option.

> **Note**
>
> It isn't easy to export just a selection of folders. If you want to export only the Inbox and the Sent Items folders, for example, you must run the export twice: once for the Inbox and then again for Sent Items, specifying the same backup .pst location each time.

5. If you want to specify a filter, click Filter. Figure 32-3 shows the Filter dialog box. By using a filter, you can specify that only certain items be exported. This option could be useful, for example, if you need to send all correspondence with representatives of Wingtip Toys to a new sales representative who will be dealing with that firm. You could export the relevant messages to a .pst file that you could send to the new rep, who could then import them. After you've specified any needed filters, click OK to close the Filter dialog box and return to the wizard page, and then click Next.

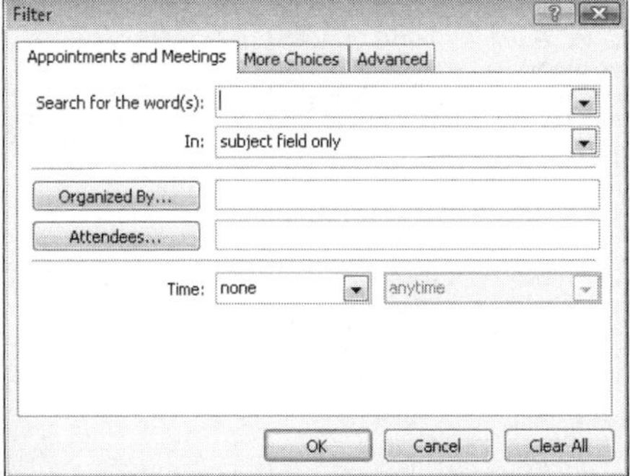

Figure 32-3. Use the Filter dialog box to export only those messages that fit certain criteria.

6. On the final wizard page, specify the location where you want to save exported information, and then specify how duplicate items should be handled. If no export file exists, specify the path and name of the file to be created. If an export file does exist, browse to the file you want to use. When you click Finish, the wizard creates the personal folders file (if it is new), runs the export, and then closes the file.

Exporting Addresses

You can also export address lists out of Outlook 2007 for use elsewhere. Exporting addresses is similar to exporting messages: you use the same Import And Export Wizard. The difference is that addresses are sometimes exported to a database or a spreadsheet to allow easier access to phone numbers, addresses, and other information.

To export the address list to Microsoft Access, for example, first start the Import And Export Wizard. As you work through the wizard, select Export To A File, and then select Microsoft Access. Select the Contacts folder, and then provide a name for the Microsoft Access database that will be created for the exported addresses.

The primary difference between exporting to a personal folders file and exporting to a database lies in mapping out the fields for the database itself. From the wizard, you can click Map Custom Fields to open the Map Custom Fields dialog box, shown in Figure 32-4. If you are mapping to an existing database rather than a new one, you can map fields in Outlook 2007 to specific fields in the database. For example, assume that your existing target database includes fields named *fName* and *lName*, and you want to map the *First Name* field to *fName* and the *Last Name* field to *lName*. The Map Custom Fields dialog box enables you to do just that.

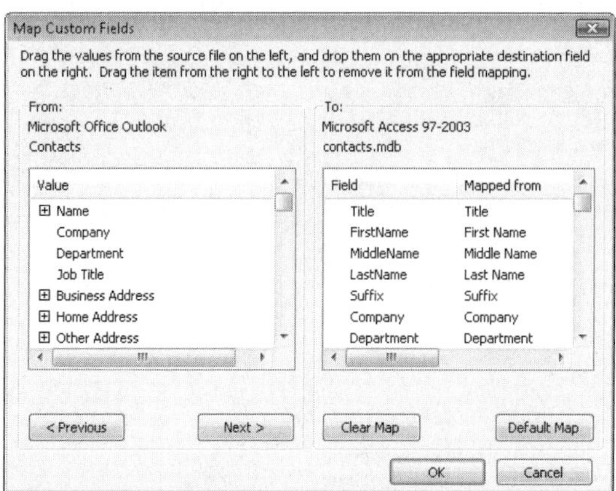

Figure 32-4. Use the Map Custom Fields dialog box to map fields for export into a Microsoft Access database.

After you've finished the field mapping, click OK, and then click Finish to create the new database file and export the contact information into it.

> **Note**
>
> When you're exporting to a database, you don't have a filter option. Therefore, if you're exporting only certain records, you should create a subfolder to contain the contacts you want to export. Copy the contacts to this new subfolder, export the subfolder, and then delete the duplicate contacts and the folder containing them.

Exporting Data to a File

Occasionally, data in .pst format simply isn't usable for a particular task. Outlook 2007 gives you a number of options for other export formats, such as Excel, Access, or various text file formats. For example, if you need to export information from Outlook 2007 into a third-party software package, or if you want to use the information in any capacity for which a direct export path is not available, your best option might be to export the needed information to a basic text file, either tab-delimited or comma-delimited. Figure 32-5 shows a text file that was exported from Outlook 2007.

Figure 32-5. This contact information has been exported into a basic text file.

Exporting data to a text file is an easy process:

1. In Outlook 2007, choose File, Import And Export.
2. Choose Export To A File, and then click Next.
3. To export to a comma-delimited file, select Comma Separated Values (Windows). To export to a tab-delimited file, select Tab Separated Values (Windows). Then click Next.
4. Specify a file name for the export file, and then click Next.
5. If you want to change the way fields are mapped, click Map Custom Fields (shown earlier in Figure 32-4). When you have finished mapping fields, click OK, and then click Finish.

Importing Data

Data transfer is a two-way street, of course, and any discussion of how to take information out of Outlook 2007 would be incomplete without a discussion of how to bring information back in as well. Far more options are available for bringing information in than for sending information out.

Importing Data into Outlook

The process of importing data into your Outlook 2007 message store is the same regardless of whether you're importing information into a personal folder or an Exchange Server mailbox. You begin the process by identifying exactly what type of information you want to import and whether Outlook 2007 can properly access and import the data.

The next sections examine some examples of importing information into Outlook 2007. To begin the import process for any of the examples discussed in these sections, use the Import And Export Wizard.

Importing Internet Mail Account Settings

When upgrading an e-mail system to Outlook 2007, you can often save time and avoid configuration problems by importing the Internet mail settings from the previous system. This process does not bring over any messages or addresses; it simply transfers any existing Internet e-mail account information to the current Outlook 2007 profile. This option works only if the computer on which Outlook 2007 is installed had previously been using a different e-mail client, such as Outlook Express or Eudora.

To start the wizard to import your settings, choose File, Import And Export. Select Import Internet Mail Account Settings, and then click Next. The wizard is very straightforward, taking you through all the steps of verifying and reestablishing the account. Fields are filled with information taken from the detected settings; you can modify them as needed during the import process. After you have imported the information, the new service will often require you to exit, log off, and restart Outlook 2007 before it will be active. At that point, you should be able to receive and send Internet e-mail through Outlook 2007.

Importing Internet Mail and Addresses

In addition to importing Internet e-mail configuration settings, as just discussed, the other step involved in migrating e-mail data to Outlook 2007 is to bring in any address lists or saved messages that were stored in the previous system. To import an existing message store, follow these steps:

1. Choose File, Import And Export. When the wizard starts, select Import Internet Mail And Addresses, and then click Next.

2. On the Outlook Import Tool page of the wizard, specify the program from which you are migrating the data. After you select the application, you must specify what to import: messages (Import Mail), addresses (Import Address Book), or both. Then click Next.

3. On the Import Addresses page, specify how Outlook 2007 should handle duplicates. The default entry, Allow Duplicates To Be Created, can create a bit of cleanup work (deleting the duplicate entries that might be created for certain contacts), but it guards against accidental information loss from overwriting the wrong contact entry. Replace Duplicates With Items Imported causes Outlook 2007 to overwrite any existing contacts in Outlook 2007 with matching items from your other mail program. Select Do Not Import Duplicate Items if you want Outlook 2007 to skip any duplicate addresses.

4. Click Finish. The wizard runs the import and then displays the Import Summary dialog box. If the import has gone well, you'll see an indication that all the messages have been imported. If you see that only a portion of the total messages have been imported, you'll know that a problem occurred and not all the information was transferred.

5. In the Import Summary dialog box, click Save In Inbox if you want to save the summary message to your Outlook Inbox folder. Click OK if you just want to close the dialog box.

Importing a vCard File

One of the handiest ways to share contact information is by using vCards, which are a form of electronic business card. When you receive a vCard from someone, you can import the card into your Contacts folder for later use. Start the Import And Export Wizard, select Import A vCard File (.vcf), and then click Next. Browse to the directory where you saved the .vcf file, select the file, and then click Open. The file will be imported as a new contact entry in your Contacts folder.

For details about using vCards to share contact information, see "Sharing Contacts" in Chapter 18.

> **Note**
>
> If you receive the .vcf file as an e-mail attachment, you can double-click the .vcf file icon to import the card into your Contacts folder.

Importing an iCalendar or a vCalendar File

Numerous options, including iCalendar and vCalendar files, are available to users who want to share calendar information. Although they're used for much the same purpose, iCalendar and vCalendar work in different ways.

> **Note**
>
> iCalendar is a newer standard that is gradually replacing vCalendar. Both are still commonly used, however.

You use iCalendar to send calendar information out across the Web to anyone using an iCalendar-compatible system. Users who receive an iCalendar meeting invitation simply accept or decline the meeting, and the information is automatically entered into their calendars. An import process is generally not necessary.

In contrast, you use vCalendar files much as you use vCards: they allow you to create a meeting and send it out as an attachment to other attendees. Attendees can then double-click the attachment or use the import process to bring this meeting into their schedules. If necessary, users can also import iCalendar meetings the same way.

Importing iCalendar and vCalendar files is easy. Choose File, Import And Export to start the Import And Export Wizard. Select Import An iCalendar (.ics) Or vCalendar File (.vcs), and then click Next. Select the file, and then click OK to complete the import.

> **Note**
>
> The file name extension used for vCalendar files is .vcs; iCalendar files use an .ics file name extension.

Importing from Another Program File

You've now seen most of the common import options. However, you'll also occasionally encounter situations in which you might need to import other types of information, such as third-party data, text files, and so on. Perhaps the most important of these other possibilities is importing information from another .pst file. This could involve bringing back information from an archive, restoring lost messages from a backup, or even completing the process in the example discussed earlier, in which you need to give a new sales rep copies of all messages sent to or received from Wingtip Toys. If three or four other employees had all exported messages to .pst files, the easiest option for the new rep would be to import the messages back into his or her own message store for easy access.

The following steps describe the process of importing from an existing .pst file. Keep in mind that other file import options are similar, although the particular data and formatting of each file will dictate certain changes in the import process.

To import from an existing .pst file, perform the following steps:

1. Start the Import And Export Wizard. Select Import From Another Program Or File, and then click Next.
2. In the list of file types, select Personal Folder File (.pst).
3. Browse to the .pst file you want to import. (If you want to import multiple .pst files, you must import each one separately.) Specify how to handle duplicates on the same page, and then click Next.

> **Note**
>
> As mentioned earlier, allowing Outlook 2007 to create duplicates minimizes the risk of overwriting data, but it does increase the size of the store. If you're importing a number of .pst files that might have overlapping data (if many recipients were copied on the same messages, for example), it's often better to avoid importing duplicates.

4. On the Import Personal Folders page of the wizard, shown in Figure 32-6, select the folders to import–either the entire store or only a particular folder or set of folders.

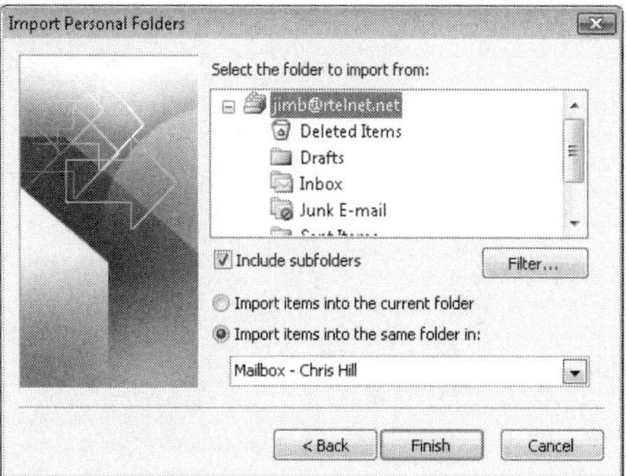

Figure 32-6. Select the folder on the Import Personal Folders page.

5. The wizard allows you to filter the data you're importing the same way you filter exported data. Click Filter to open the Filter dialog box, and then add any filters you need.
6. Specify the folder into which the data should be imported.
7. Click Finish to begin the import.

Note

Our fictional sales rep could create a subfolder named Wingtip under the Inbox and then select that folder before starting the Import And Export Wizard. Note that by choosing to import only from the .pst file's Inbox and selecting Import Items Into The Current Folder, the sales rep could bring all the messages from the .pst file into his or her message store without flooding the Inbox with old Wingtip information. Creating subfolders for importing and exporting can be a good way to keep track of where information is coming from and what you are sending out.

CHAPTER 33

Finding and Organizing Outlook Data

Although some people use Microsoft® Office Outlook® 2007 only for e-mail, the majority of people use all the personal information manager (PIM) features the program has to offer. Because a PIM is only as good as its ability to help you search for and organize data, Office Outlook 2007 offers a solid selection of features to help you do just that.

This chapter shows you how to perform simple and advanced searches to locate data. You'll learn how to search using Instant Search as well as the Find A Contact feature and Advanced Find. This chapter also explores various ways you can organize your Outlook 2007 data–for example, by creating additional folders for storing specific types of messages.

Using Instant Search

Microsoft redesigned the search functionality used by Windows Vista™ and the 2007 Microsoft Office system with a focus on performance and ease of use. The resulting Instant Search feature of the Microsoft Office system provides a simple, unified search interface that is the same across all of the Outlook 2007 folders. Instant Search relies on the Windows Vista Windows Desktop Search, which indexes Outlook 2007 mail folders to deliver search results faster.

Searching in Outlook 2007 is as simple as typing your search terms in the Instant Search box at the top of the Inbox. Outlook 2007 displays results as you type, automatically filtering out older results when there are a large number of items. To focus searches, Outlook 2007 searches only the folder that you have open, although you can easily choose to search all of your folders instead.

When you start a search, you first determine the scope of your search. Outlook 2007 sets the search scope as the folder that is selected in the Navigation Pane. To change the search scope, you click a different folder in the Navigation Pane.

As you type text in the Instant Search box, the search results are displayed in the pane below the Instant Search box. To refine your search and get fewer results, type more text. To widen your search, delete some text. You can also build custom queries based on a wide range of criteria.

Note

If you prefer to use the tools provided in earlier versions of Microsoft Outlook, you still can. Advanced Find and the Find A Contact feature remain available as options for those who prefer a familiar interface.

Note

Instant Search requires Windows Desktop Search, which is part of Windows Vista and is available as a download for Microsoft Windows® XP. For more information about Windows Desktop Search, you can visit the Windows Desktop Search site at *www.microsoft.com/windows/desktopsearch/*.

Using Instant Search with Windows XP

Because Windows Desktop Search is not included with Windows XP, you install Instant Search just a bit differently on a computer that is running Windows XP. You must download and install the Windows Desktop Search software so that you can install it either when you first start Outlook 2007 or later. Once you restart Outlook 2007, Instant Search is enabled. Other than that, Instant Search operates the same way on a computer running Windows XP as on one running Windows Vista.

Configuring Instant Search

While the default configuration of Instant Search should work in most circumstances, you might need to fine-tune things just a bit to optimize Instant Search for how you use Outlook 2007. Using Instant Search might require configuring a few different options, most of which are found in Outlook 2007, although a few options are set with Indexing Options in the Control Panel.

Turning Instant Search On and Off

You turn Instant Search on and off differently depending on whether you are using Windows Vista or Windows XP.

- **Enabling Instant Search on a Computer Running Windows Vista** Instant Search is enabled by default on computers running Windows Vista. If you have turned Instant Search off, you can enable it by clicking the arrow next to the Instant Search box and then selecting Search Options. Under Index Messages In These Data Files, select the files you want Instant Search to index and search. You must exit and restart Outlook 2007 for this change to take effect.
- **Enabling Instant Search on a Computer Running Windows XP** On computers running Windows XP, you are prompted to download the Windows Desktop Search software the first time you start Outlook 2007. Once the software is downloaded and installed, you must restart Outlook 2007 to complete the installation process and use Instant Search.

  If you have chosen not to install Windows Desktop Search and enable Instant Search, you can always change your mind. To turn on Instant Search, click the Click Here To Enable Instant Search option under the Instant Search box.

Note

Microsoft must validate your copy of Windows XP before you are allowed to download Windows Desktop Search. If you have not yet installed the validation ActiveX® control, you will be prompted to install it. Right-click the information bar, and then choose Install. A security warning dialog box will appear; click Install again. Once the ActiveX control is installed, you will be returned to the download screen.

Note

If your computer is running Windows XP and you have not downloaded the Windows Desktop Search software, you are prompted repeatedly to install it. If you don't want to see these prompts, you can disable them. To do so, on the Tools menu, choose Options. Choose Other, and then click Advanced Options. In the Advanced Options dialog box, clear the Show Prompts To Download Windows Desktop Search check box, and then click OK.

- **Disabling Instant Search** To turn off Instant Search, click the arrow next to the Instant Search box, and then select Search Options. Under Index Messages In These Data Files, deselect all of the files. You must exit and restart Outlook 2007 for this change to take effect.

Choosing Search Options

You can determine the initial scope of searches as well as how Outlook 2007 handles results in the Search Options dialog box.

To configure Instant Search, follow these steps:

1. Click the arrow next to the Instant Search box, and then select Search Options. (You can also select Tools, Options, and then on the Preferences tab, click Search Options.)
2. In the Search Options dialog box, shown in Figure 33-1, configure the search settings as described here.

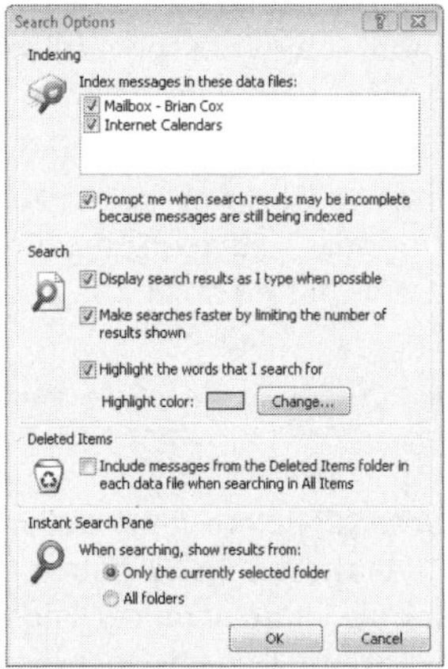

Figure 33-1. You can configure Instant Search using the Search Options dialog box.

- To specify which Outlook 2007 data files are indexed, and thus searched using Instant Search, under Index Messages In These Data Files, select the files you want indexed and deselect those you do not.
- To have Outlook 2007 show you search results as you type, in the Search area, select Display Search Results As I Type When Possible. If this option is cleared, Outlook 2007 does not start searching until you click the Search button or press **Enter**.
- When your search has a large number of results, Outlook 2007 by default limits the number of items it displays by filtering for the most recent. To view all results of your searches, no matter the number, clear the Make Searches Faster By Limiting The Number Of Results Shown check box.
- To have Outlook 2007 highlight your search terms where they appear in the results, select Highlight The Words That I Search For. You can also set the highlight color.

- If you want Outlook 2007 to search mail items that have been moved to the Deleted Items folder but not yet actually deleted, select Include Messages From The Deleted Items Folder In Each Data File When Searching In All Items.
- To set the default scope of Instant Search, under When Searching, Show Results From, choose either Only The Currently Selected Folder or All Folders.

3. Click OK when you have finished configuring the Instant Search options.

Controlling Which Data Files Are Searched

If you have multiple Outlook 2007 data files, you can tell Outlook 2007 to include only specific data files in an Instant Search without removing them from the list of files that are indexed. This allows you to stop a file from being searched without having to re-create the index for the file when you want it included again—a much faster option. You might use this technique to segregate project or client files, or perhaps to exclude a large archive file from searches most of the time, yet be able to easily include the file when you need to.

To change which data files Outlook 2007 searches, follow these steps:

1. In the Navigation Pane, under Mail Folders, click the arrow next to All Mail Items, as shown in Figure 33-2.

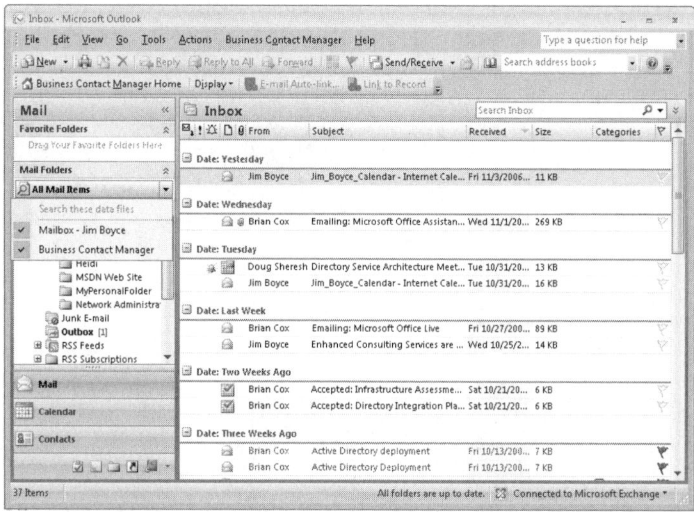

Figure 33-2. You can choose which files are included in Instant Search.

2. Select the Outlook 2007 data files that you want included in searches by default. At least one data file must be selected, but you can choose additional files to search as well.

You can also specify whether your Outlook 2007 files are indexed in the Indexing Options item in the Control Panel. For information about using Indexing Options, see "Configuring Indexing Options" later in this chapter.

Performing a Search

Instant Search looks at most fields of Outlook 2007 items when performing searches, making it easy for you to find what you are looking for. This means that you can type almost anything that you think might be in the item you're looking for, even if the item is in an attachment. To search for a message or other Outlook 2007 item, follow these steps:

1. Click in the Instant Search box (or press **Ctrl+E**), and then type your search text.
2. Outlook 2007 will display the search results as you type, with the search terms highlighted. To narrow the search results, type more text. To widen the results, delete some text.
    - If you do not see the items you want, you can broaden your search scope by clicking the arrow next to the Instant Search box and then selecting Search All Folders. You can also click the Try Searching All Folders link in the results pane.
    - If your search returns a large number of results, Outlook 2007 might display only the most recent results. If you see a message in the InfoBar similar to the one shown in Figure 33-3, click it to show all results, including the older items.

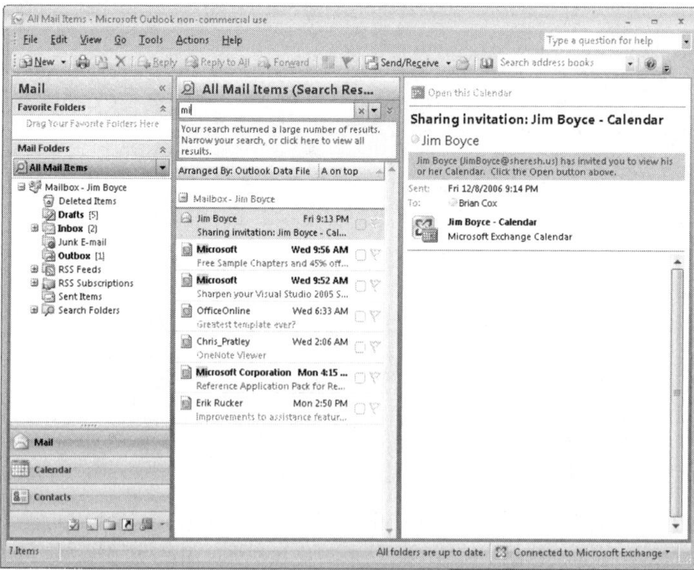

Figure 33-3. Click the message in the InfoBar to display the complete set of search results.

To clear the search and start over, click the X to the right of the Instant Search box.

To repeat a search you have performed recently, click the arrow next to the Instant Search box, and then choose Recent Searches. Select the search you want to repeat in the list.

Note

You might find that the results of some of your searches include an item that really doesn't seem to belong there, and in which you can't find the words you searched for. This might be because the item has an attachment that contains the search term.

TROUBLESHOOTING

You don't get any search results

If you repeatedly get fewer results than you expect, or you get no results at all, you should try disabling Instant Search and repeating the search. If you do get results with Instant Search disabled, you might be having problems with Windows Desktop Search indexing.

Check your indexing status by clicking the arrow next to the Instant Search box and selecting Indexing Status. If a message appears stating that Outlook 2007 is currently indexing your files, note the number of items remaining to be indexed. Check back in a while to see whether the numbers are different. If the numbers are unchanged, you should rebuild the index. For information about rebuilding the index, see "Configuring Indexing Options" later in this chapter.

Using the Query Builder

The Query Builder shows you a number of extra fields that you can search within to refine your search results. Each type of folder (Mail, Contacts, and so on) displays the most commonly used fields for that type of folder, so each one shows a different list of fields by default. You can also add fields, even those in custom forms, to the Query Builder to support searches for exactly the data you want.

1. To display the Query Builder, click the Expand The Query Builder button next to the Instant Search box. This will open a pane showing the default fields for that type of folder, as shown in Figure 33-4.

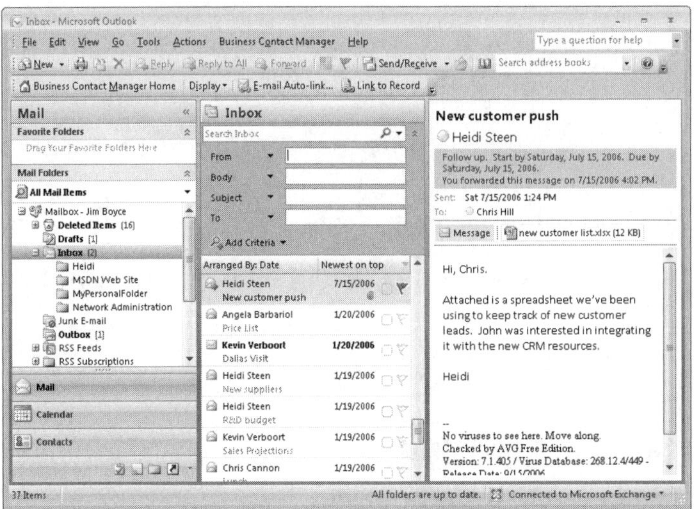

Figure 33-4. Each folder shows a different list of fields in the Query Builder.

2. If you want to show additional fields, click Add Criteria, and then select the fields in the list. To add a field from a custom form, click the form name, and then click the field name.

Making Fields from Custom Forms Available

To add a custom form to the Query Builder list, follow these steps:

1. Click the Expand The Query Builder button.
2. Click Add Criteria, and then click Add Form.
3. In the Select Enterprise Forms For This Folder dialog box, choose the type of forms you want to select from.
4. In the list in the left pane, select the form you want to add, and then click Add. Repeat this for each form you want to add. (To display form groups by category, select Show Categories.)
5. Click Close.

How Indexing Impacts Instant Search

If Outlook 2007 is still indexing files, your search results might be empty or incomplete. If your mail files have not been indexed completely, when you perform a search, Outlook 2007 displays a message, as shown in Figure 33-5, explaining that the search results might be incomplete.

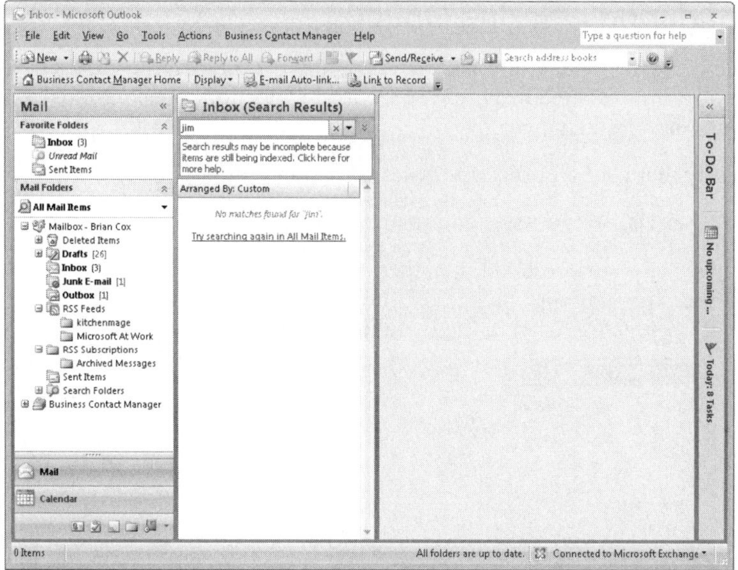

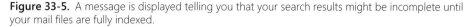

Figure 33-5. A message is displayed telling you that your search results might be incomplete until your mail files are fully indexed.

If you click the message in the InfoBar, a message box will be displayed, as shown in Figure 33-6, telling you how many items remain to be indexed.

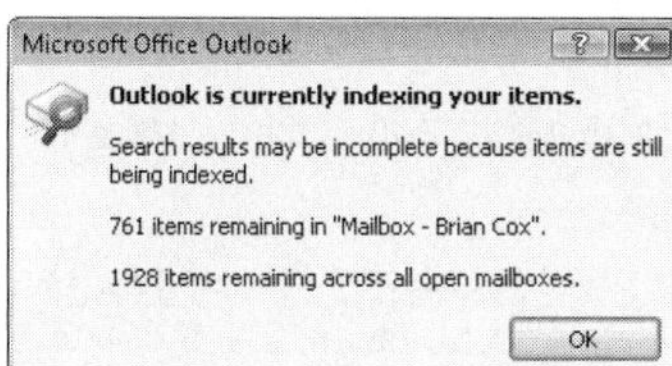

Figure 33-6. You can view the current indexing status in this message box.

> **Note**
>
> When you are using Instant Search and your mail files are not completely indexed, Outlook 2007 should display a warning that your search results might be incomplete. This warning might have been disabled in the Search Options dialog box (and sometimes simply fails to appear), making it seem as if you have no matching items when you actually do.

Configuring Indexing Options

While indexing is generally self-maintaining, you can control some settings using the Indexing Options item in Windows Control Panel. Indexing Options is part of the System And Maintenance group.

To verify that your Outlook 2007 files are being indexed, follow these steps:

1. Click the Start button, and then click Control Panel.
2. Click Systems And Maintenance, and then click Indexing Options. In the Indexing Options dialog box, shown in Figure 33-7, verify that your Outlook 2007 files are listed in the Included Locations list.

Figure 33-7. You can see the status of indexing across the entire system in the Indexing Options dialog box.

3. If your Outlook 2007 files are not listed, click Modify to display the Indexed Location dialog box. Under Change Selected Locations, select the Microsoft Office Outlook check box to include the files in the locations that should be indexed. (Outlook 2007 files belonging to other users are visible but are disabled.) Click OK.

TROUBLESHOOTING

Troubleshooting indexing problems

You might need to rebuild the index due to problems such as empty search results when you know that there are items that match your search. Rebuilding an index takes a while, perhaps even several hours, and is significantly slower if you are also using the computer at the same time. Because of this, you will want to rebuild the index only when you are experiencing ongoing problems with Instant Search and preferably when you will be away from the computer for a while.

You can rebuild the search index by opening the Indexing Options item in Control Panel and then clicking Advanced. Under Troubleshooting, click Rebuild. Once the index is rebuilt, restart Outlook 2007 to have it use the new index.

If this does not resolve your problems, the next step is to restore the original index settings and re-create the indexes. To do this, open the Indexing Options item in Control Panel, and then click Advanced. Under Troubleshooting, click Restore Defaults. This will remove any custom settings you configured and delete existing index information. When the computer is restarted, Windows will delete the index and rebuild it using the default configuration. Like rebuilding the index, this operation takes a considerable amount of time, so you should do it only when you really need to and can afford the impact on your computer's performance.

Searching for Contacts

If you're like most Outlook 2007 users, your Contacts folder will grow to contain a lot of contact entries—typically, too many to allow you to browse through the folder when you need to quickly find a particular contact. You're also likely to encounter situations in which, for example, you need to locate contact information but can't remember the person's last name. Fortunately, Outlook 2007 makes it easy to locate contact data, providing two convenient ways to search contacts: Instant Search and the Search Address Books box on the Standard toolbar.

Instant Search works the same way across all of the Outlook 2007 folders, so to locate a contact, begin typing the contact's name in the Search Contacts box. If you click the Expand The Query Builder button, the default search fields are:

- Business Phone
- Company
- E-Mail
- Full Name
- Mailing Address
- Mobile Phone

If you want to add more fields, you can click Add Criteria and then select the fields in the list.

You can also use the Search Address Books box on the Standard toolbar, shown in Figure 33-8, to search for contacts. Type the search criterion (such as a first name, last name, or company), and then press **Enter**.

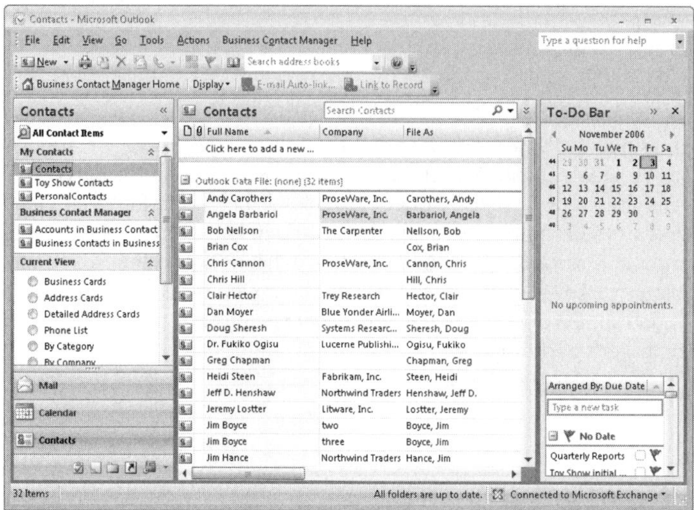

Figure 33-8. The Search Address Books box allows you to find a contact entry quickly.

If Outlook 2007 finds only one contact that matches the search criteria, it opens the contact entry for that person. Otherwise, Outlook 2007 displays the Choose Contact dialog box, shown in Figure 33-9, in which you can select the contact entry to open.

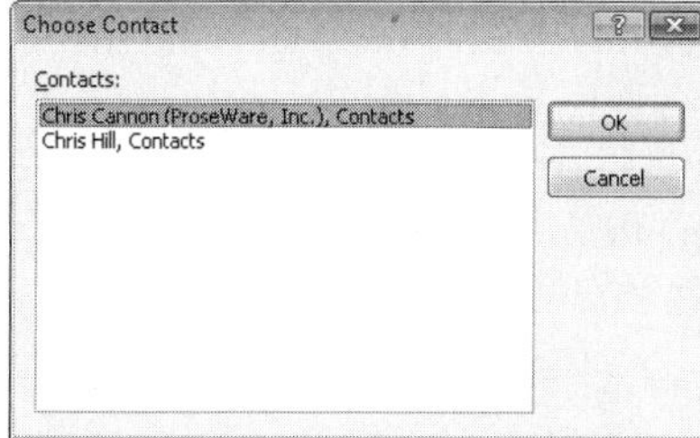

Figure 33-9. Select a contact when Outlook 2007 finds more than one that fits your search.

> **Note**
>
> The Search Address Books box can be useful when you need to perform a quick search for a contact based on a limited amount of data. To locate contacts and other Outlook 2007 items based on multiple search conditions, use Instant Search or Advanced Find.

Using Advanced Find

In addition to Instant Search, Outlook 2007 still provides the Advanced Find feature for performing advanced searches that require specifying multiple search conditions.

The Advanced Find Dialog Box

To open the Advanced Find dialog box, shown in Figure 33-10, choose Tools, Instant Search, Advanced Find or press Ctrl+Shift+F. You can use this dialog box to search for any type of Outlook 2007 item using multiple search conditions.

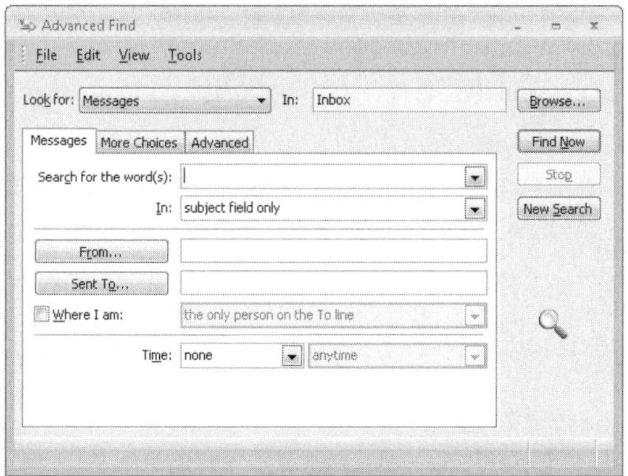

Figure 33-10. Use the Advanced Find dialog box when you need to search using multiple conditions.

The options provided in the Advanced Find dialog box change depending on the type of item you select in the Look For drop-down list. If you select Contacts, for example, the options change to provide specialized search criteria for contacts, such as restricting the search to a name, a company, or an address. Selecting Messages in the drop-down list changes the options so that you can search the subject field of messages, search the subject and message body, or specify other search criteria specific to messages.

> **Note**
>
> When you select a different item type in the Look For drop-down list, Outlook 2007 clears the current search and starts a new one. Outlook 2007 does, however, prompt you to confirm that you want to clear the current search.

On the Messages tab in the Advanced Find dialog box (refer to Figure 33-10), you specify the primary search criteria. The following list summarizes all the available options (although not all options appear at all times):

- **Search For The Word(s)** Specify the word, words, or phrase for which you want to search. You can type words individually or include quotation marks around a phrase to search for the entire phrase. You also can select from a previous set of search words.
- **In** Specify the location in the Outlook 2007 item where you want to search, such as only the subject of a message. The options available in this list vary according to the type of item you select in the Look For drop-down list.
- **From** Specify the name of the person who sent you the message. Type the name or click From to browse the address book for the name.
- **Sent To** For messages, specify the recipients to whom the message was sent.
- **Attendees** Specify the people scheduled to attend a meeting.
- **Organized By** Specify the person who generated the meeting request.
- **E-Mail** Browse the address book to search for contacts by their e-mail addresses.
- **Named** Specify the file name of the item for which you're searching. You can specify a single file name or use wildcard characters to match multiple items. The Named box appears if you select Files or Files (Outlook/Exchange) in the Look For drop-down list.
- **Of Type** Choose the type of file for which to search when using the Files or Files (Outlook/Exchange) options.
- **Journal Entry Types** Specify the journal entry type when searching the journal for items.
- **Contact** Browse for a contact associated with an item for which you're searching.
- **Where I Am** When searching for messages, specify that you are the only person on the To line, on the To line with others, or on the Cc line with others.
- **Status** Search for tasks based on their status. You can select Doesn't Matter, Not Started, In Progress, or Completed.
- **Time** Specify the creation or modification time, the start or end time, or other time properties specific to the type of item for which you are searching.

Specifying Advanced Search Criteria

You use the More Choices tab in the Advanced Find dialog box, shown in Figure 33-11, to specify additional search conditions to refine the search.

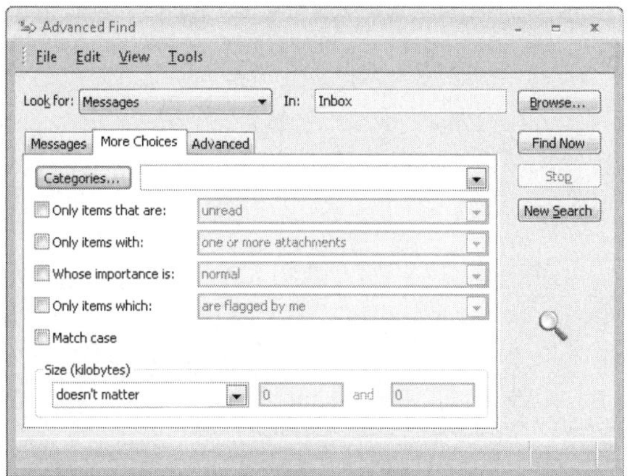

Figure 33-11. Use the More Choices tab to refine the search.

The following options are available on the More Choices tab:

- **Categories** Specify the category or categories associated with the items for which you are searching. You can type the categories separated by commas, or you can click Categories to open the Categories dialog box and then select categories.
- **Only Items That Are** Search for items by their read status (read or unread).
- **Only Items With** Search for items by their attachment status (one or more attachments or no attachments).
- **Whose Importance Is** Specify the importance (High, Normal, or Low) of the items for which you are searching.
- **Only Items Which** Specify the flag status of the items for which you are searching.
- **Match Case** Direct Outlook 2007 to match the case of the text you entered as the search criterion. Clear this check box to make the search case-insensitive.
- **Size** Specify the size criterion for the items in your search. You can select one of several options to define the size range in which the item must fall to match the search.

The More Choices tab is the same for all Outlook 2007 items except the Files search item. With Files selected in the Look For drop-down list, the Only Items With option is not available.

You can use the Advanced tab in the Advanced Find dialog box, shown in Figure 33-12, to create more complex searches. On this tab, select the fields to include in the search as well as the search conditions for each field. You can build a list of multiple fields.

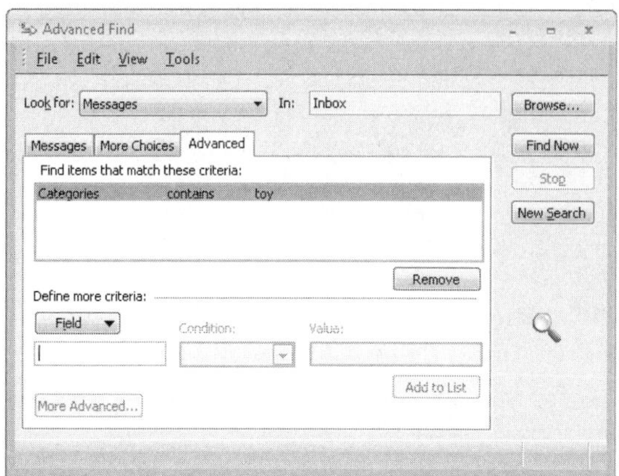

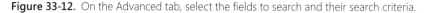

Figure 33-12. On the Advanced tab, select the fields to search and their search criteria.

Organizing Data

Searching for data and organizing data usually go hand in hand. One of the main motivations for organizing your data is that you want to be able to find it easily. Even with perfect organization, however, you'll still need to perform searches now and then because of the sheer amount of data that might be involved. Outlook 2007 provides several ways to organize your data. Whereas other chapters focus on specific ways to organize your Outlook 2007 items, this section provides an overview of ways you can organize certain types of items and points you to the appropriate chapters for additional information.

Organizing Your E-Mail

E-mail messages probably make up the bulk of your Outlook 2007 data. For that reason, organizing your messages can be a challenge. Outlook 2007 offers several features that will help you organize your messages so that you can find and work with them effectively and efficiently.

Search Folders

Search folders are the best means in Outlook 2007 to quickly organize messages without moving those messages around to different folders. A search folder looks and acts like a folder, but it's really a special type of view that displays in a virtual folder view all messages that fit the search condition for the search folder. Search folders offer two main benefits: They can search multiple folders, and they organize messages without requiring that the messages be moved from their current folder.

See "Finding and Organizing Messages with Search Folders" in Chapter 10 to learn more about search folders.

Using Folders

Another great way to organize your e-mail messages is to separate them in different folders. For example, if you deal with several projects, consider creating a folder for each project and moving each message to its respective folder. You can create the folders as subfolders of your Inbox or place them elsewhere, depending on your preferences. You might even create a folder outside the Inbox named Projects and then create subfolders for each project under that folder.

For more information about creating and managing folders, see Chapter 30, "Managing Outlook Folders and Data."

Using Rules

Rules are one of the best tools you have in Outlook 2007 for organizing messages. You can apply rules to selectively process messages—moving, deleting, copying, and performing other actions on the messages based on the sender, the recipient, the account, and a host of other message properties. You can use rules in combination with folders to organize your e-mail messages. For example, you might use rules to automatically move messages for specific projects to their respective folders. You can apply rules to messages when they arrive in the Inbox or any time you need to rearrange or organize.

For a detailed discussion of rules, see Chapter 11, "Processing Messages Automatically with Rules."

Using Color Categories

Outlook 2007 uses color categories to help organize your e-mail messages. If you create rules to apply certain color categories to specified e-mail messages, the color can provide a visual indicator of the sender, the subject, the priority, or other properties of the message. In this way, you can see at a glance whether a particular message meets certain criteria. You can also use automatic formatting in a view to apply color categories.

For more information about color categories, see Chapter 5, "Creating and Using Categories."

Using Views

Views give you another important way to organize your Outlook 2007 data. The default views organize specific folders using the most common criteria. You can customize Outlook Today view using HTML to provide different or additional levels of organization. You can also create custom views of any Outlook 2007 folder to organize your data to suit your preferences.

For more information about customizing views, see "Customizing Outlook Today View" in Chapter 26 and "Creating and Using Custom Views" in Chapter 27.

Using the Organize Pane

You can organize your Inbox and other folders manually, or you can use the Organize pane, which gives you quick access to some of the organizational features that Outlook 2007 provides. Open a folder, and then choose Tools, Organize to view the Organize pane, shown in Figure 33-13. Using this feature to organize your e-mail folders is relatively easy.

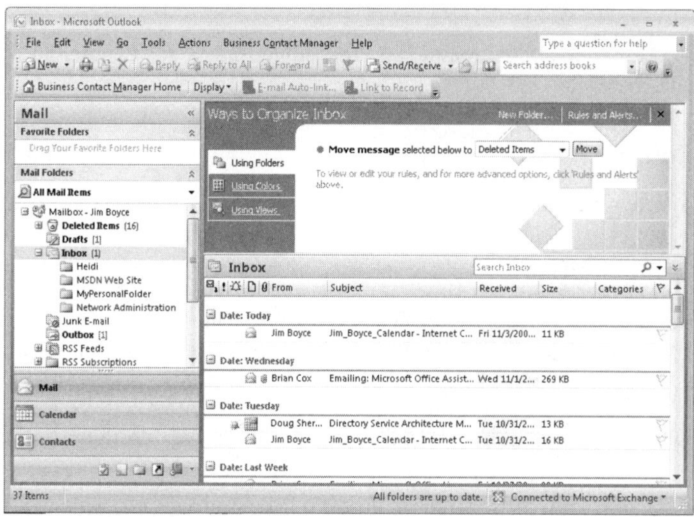

Figure 33-13. Use the Organize pane to create rules and organize your message folder in other ways.

The Organize pane gives you four options for organizing the current folder. Clicking the link for a particular option changes the options displayed in the Organize pane. The following list describes the types of actions that you can perform with each option (not all options appear in every folder):

- **Using Folders** Moves selected messages to other folders.
- **Using Colors** Colors messages sent to or from an individual. You can also specify that messages sent only to you be displayed in a specific color.
- **Using Categories** Adds categories to selected items and creates new categories.
- **Using Views** Selects from several predefined views.

You'll find additional information about the Organize pane in "Using the Organize Pane to Create Rules" in Chapter 11.

Organizing Your Calendar

You can use the Organize pane in your Calendar folder, as shown in Figure 33-14, to organize items in your calendar.

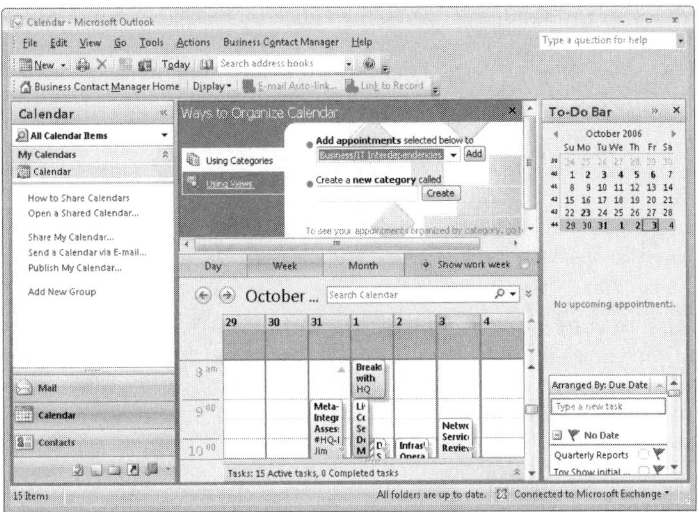

Figure 33-14. Use the Organize pane in the Calendar folder to apply categories to calendar items and select a view.

To assign categories to calendar items, click the Using Categories link. Select the items, select the category you want in the drop-down list, and then click Add. You can also use the Organize pane to create a category.

For a detailed discussion of categories, including how to share categories with others, see Chapter 5, "Creating and Using Categories."

You can change the calendar view from the Organize pane, which allows you to switch to a view that organizes your data the way you want. To change your view, click the Using Views link in the Organize pane, and then select an existing view in the list. (This is the same as choosing View, Current View, followed by the view you want to use. Changing the view this way, however, closes the Organize pane, whereas choosing the option in the Organize pane does not.)

Organizing Contacts, Tasks, and Notes

Like your other Outlook 2007 folders, the Contacts, Tasks, and Notes folders have an Organize pane that you can use to organize your contacts, tasks, and notes. The Organize pane gives you three options for organizing contacts and tasks:

- **Using Folders** Use this option to move selected items to another folder, which you can select from a drop-down list in the Organize pane (refer to Figure 33-13).
- **Using Categories** Click this link to assign selected items to one or more categories and create new categories.
- **Using Views** Click this link to select a view. This is the same as choosing View, Current View, followed by the view you want to use, but unlike that method, this link leaves the Organize pane open.

The Notes folder provides only the Using Folders and Using Views options and does not let you specify categories in its Organize pane. You can assign categories to a note, however, by right-clicking the note and then choosing Categorize.

Organizing Your Outlook Items Effectively

It's far too easy to get swamped in e-mail, but you can make it less of a probability if you learn to use the options that Outlook 2007 offers to help you stay organized. Here are a few tips to get you started:

- **Clean out your inbox every day.** There is a very real psychological boost when you can leave your office at the end of the day with your Inbox empty—and it's a pretty nice way to start your morning too. A habitually empty Inbox also means that any mail that is in the Inbox is still unread, so it's easy to tell what you still need to read.
- **Handle each e-mail message only once.** Many time management systems share a similar mantra regarding handling each e-mail message exactly once. Open it, read it, decide what you have to do about the message and do it. *Right now*. For most people, a lot of their mail requires no action beyond reading it. If that's the case, delete (or file) mail items immediately. Move any items that require action to a folder other than the Inbox, assigning a color category to make it easier to locate or set a follow-up flag to remind you of a deadline if needed.
- **Turn off the Reading Pane if you have a hard time emptying your Inbox.** While the Reading Pane makes it easy to read a piece of mail quickly, the Reading Pane also makes it easy to read mail without dealing with it.
- **Use rules to sort mail that you don't need to read immediately into folders as it arrives.** You can also assign categories using rules as mail arrives, providing additional information that you can use to locate that mail later.
- **Use a combination of folders and categories to manage your mail.** Create folders to contain large groups of mail, and then categorize the messages to display a manageable subset of messages.
- **Use search folders to create customized views of your Outlook 2007 items.** Search folders automatically filter the contents of a list of folders you specify based on the set of criteria found in the Advanced Find dialog box. This lets you see specific sets of messages by simply selecting a folder.
- **Create custom views of messages.** Custom views that filter Outlook 2007 items are another powerful tool, letting you quickly switch between various subsets of messages. Because views can be used in multiple folders, you can create a view once and reuse it in many places.
- **If you have lots of e-mail, consider using multiple .pst files to separate disparate information into discrete data stores.** In addition to segregating data storage, this makes it easy to select specific data sets for Instant Search by clicking the arrow next to All Mail Items in the Navigation Pane.

CHAPTER 34

Security and Virus Protection

If you use Microsoft® Office Outlook® 2007 on a daily basis to manage e-mail, appointments, and contacts, losing the information that you've stored in Office Outlook 2007 could cause significant problems. Outlook 2007 data can be lost in a number of ways, from accidental deletion to file corruption to hard disk failure. In addition, a user who purchases a new computer might leave behind information when transferring data to the new machine.

This chapter examines virus protection for both the server and workstation to help you understand how to protect yourself and your network from e-mail-borne viruses. Outlook 2007 provides features to protect against viruses in attachments, and there are several steps you can and should take to add other forms of virus protection.

Providing Virus Protection

Hardware and software failures are by no means the only source of anguish for the average user or administrator. Viruses and worms have become major problems for system administrators and users alike. When a major virus or worm outbreak hits, companies grind to a halt, systems shut down, system administrators turn off mail servers, and general chaos ensues.

The effects of a particularly virulent virus or worm can be devastating for a company. A virus or worm can bring your mail servers to a quick halt because of the load it imposes on them with the sheer amount of traffic it generates. Bandwidth, both local and across wide area network (WAN) links, is affected as multiple copies of infected messages flood the network. Files can become infected, rendering them unusable and subjecting users to reinfection. This means that you must recover the files from backups, making an adequate backup strategy even more important than usual.

One often overlooked effect that viruses have on a company is the public relations nightmare they can create. How would your customers react if they received a flood of infected messages from your company that brought their mail servers to a screeching halt and damaged their production files? Forget for a moment the ire of your customers' system administrators. Could your company survive the ill will generated by such a catastrophe?

At the least, your company would probably suffer serious consequences. Therefore, developing and implementing an effective virus protection strategy is as important—perhaps more so—than developing a backup strategy. When you examine your antivirus needs, approach the problem from two angles: protecting against outside infection and preventing an outgoing flood of infected messages. You can approach the former through either client-side or server-side solutions, but the latter typically requires a server-side solution.

Implementing Server-Side Solutions

Whether or not your organization uses Microsoft Exchange Server, your first line of defense against viruses and worms should reside between your local area network (LAN) and the Internet. Many antivirus solution vendors offer server-side products that monitor traffic coming from the Internet and detect and block viruses in real time. One such product is McAfee WebShield SMTP from McAfee (*www. mcafee.com*). WebShield is part of the Network Associates Active Virus Defense product, which also includes client antivirus software and an antivirus solution for Exchange Server. Another solution that filters viruses before they get to your network is Panda Software's Panda Antivirus + Firewall 2007, which works in conjunction with any firewall that supports Content Vectoring Protocol (CVP) to allow the firewall and the antivirus product to interact. You might also consider Symantec's AntiVirus Gateway Solution, which provides antivirus, antispam, and other filtering functionality at the Internet gateway.

Stopping viruses before they get into your LAN is a great goal, but even the best products sometimes miss. If your organization uses Exchange Server, you should also consider installing an Exchange-based antivirus solution. Microsoft Antigen (formerly from Sybari) protects Exchange Server 2000 and Exchange Server 2003 and has been rebranded as Microsoft Forefront Security for Exchange Server for use with Exchange Server 2007. McAfee offers GroupShield Exchange, and Panda Software offers Panda BusinesSecure 2006 Exchange with TruPrevent Technologies. A third solution is Symantec Mail Security for Microsoft Exchange. Each of these applications works at the application programming interface (API) level with Exchange Server to provide real-time virus detection and removal/quarantine. Other companies also offer antivirus solutions for Exchange Server.

In addition to detecting and removing viruses from network and Exchange Server traffic, you also should implement a solution that provides real-time virus detection for your network's file servers. These solutions scan the server for infected files as files are added or modified. For example, a remote user might upload a file containing a virus to your File Transfer Protocol (FTP) server. If local users open the file, their systems become infected and the virus begins to spread across your LAN. Catching and removing the virus as soon as the file is uploaded to the FTP server is the ideal solution.

Consider all these points as you evaluate server-side antivirus products. Some might be more important to you than others, so prioritize them and then choose an antivirus suite that best suits your needs and priorities.

Implementing Client-Side Solutions

In addition to blocking viruses and worms at the server, you should also provide antivirus protection at each workstation, particularly if your server-side virus detection is limited. Even if you do provide a full suite of detection services at the server, client-side protection is a vital piece of any antivirus strategy. For example, suppose that your server provides virus filtering, scanning all e-mail traffic coming from the Internet. Even so, the server might miss a new virus in a message with an attached file, perhaps because the virus definition file has not yet been updated. A user opens the infected file and infects his or her system, and the worm begins replicating across the LAN. If the user has a client-side antivirus solution in place, the worm is blocked before it can do any damage.

Use the following criteria to evaluate client-side antivirus solutions:

- **Are frequent updates available?** On any given day, several new viruses appear. Your antivirus solution is only as good as your virus definition files are current. Choose a solution that offers daily or (at most) weekly virus definition updates.
- **Can updates be scheduled for automatic execution?** The average user doesn't back up documents on a regular basis, much less worry about whether antivirus definition files are up to date. For that reason, it's important that the client-side antivirus solution you choose provide automatic, scheduled updates.
- **Does the product scan a variety of file types?** Make sure that the product you choose can scan not only executables and other application files but also Microsoft Office system documents for macro viruses.

You'll find several client-side antivirus products on the market. Microsoft has two offerings that might be of interest: Microsoft Windows Live™ OneCare includes antivirus protection in its suite of services for home and small business computer users, and Microsoft Forefront Security for Clients offers similar protection for computers in an enterprise environment, although it *does not* scan e-mail. Other popular products include Symantec Norton AntiVirus (*www.symantec.com*), Network Associates VirusScan (*www.nai.com*), and Panda Antivirus for Servers and Desktops (*www.pandasecurity.com*). Many other products are available that offer comparable features.

Virus Protection in Outlook

Virus protection is an important feature in Outlook 2007. You can configure Outlook 2007 to automatically block specific types of attachments, thus helping prevent virus infections. Outlook 2007 provides two levels of attachment protection, one for individual users and one for system administrators.

Outlook 2007 provides features to help protect your system against viruses and other malicious system attacks. For example, Outlook 2007 supports attachment virus protection, which helps protect against viruses you might receive through infected e-mail attachments. Outlook 2007 offers protection against Microsoft Office system macro viruses, letting you choose when macros run. Control over programmatic access is also configurable, allowing management of how applications interact with the security features in Outlook 2007 as well as their ability to send e-mail.

For information about protecting against malicious HTML-based messages, see "Configuring HTML Message Handling" in Chapter 14.

Protecting Against Viruses in Attachments

In the old days, infected boot floppy disks were the most common way computer viruses were spread. Today, e-mail is by far the most common infection mechanism. Viruses range from mostly harmless (but irritating) to severe, sometimes causing irreparable damage to your system. Worms are a more recent variation, spreading across the Internet primarily through e-mail and by exploited operating system flaws. Worms can bog down a system by consuming the majority of the system's resources, and they can cause the same types of damage as viruses.

Outlook 2007 provides protection against viruses and worms by letting you block certain types of attachments that are susceptible to infection. This prevents users from opening attached files that could infect their systems and execute malicious code on a user's system to damage or steal data. Executable programs (.exe, .com, and .bat files) are also good examples of attachments that are primary delivery mechanisms for viruses. Many other document types are equally susceptible–HTML documents and scripts, for instance, have rapidly become favorite delivery tools for virus terrorists. Outlook 2007 provides two levels of protection for attachments, Level 1 and Level 2. The following sections explain these two levels, the file types assigned to each, and how to work with attachments.

Level 1 Attachments

Level 1 attachments are those that are common vectors for infection, such as executable (.exe) files. When you receive a message containing an attachment in the Level 1 group, Outlook 2007 displays the paper clip icon next to the message header, indicating that the message has an attachment, just as it does for other messages with attachments. When you click the message header, Outlook 2007 displays a message indicating that it has blocked the attachment.

You cannot open Level 1 attachments that are blocked by Outlook 2007. You can open and view the messages, but Outlook 2007 disables the interface elements that otherwise would allow you to open or save the attachments. Outlook 2007 displays a message in the InfoBar informing you that the attachment has been blocked and cannot be opened, as shown in Figure 34-1. If you forward a message with a blocked attachment, Outlook 2007 strips the attachment from the forwarded message.

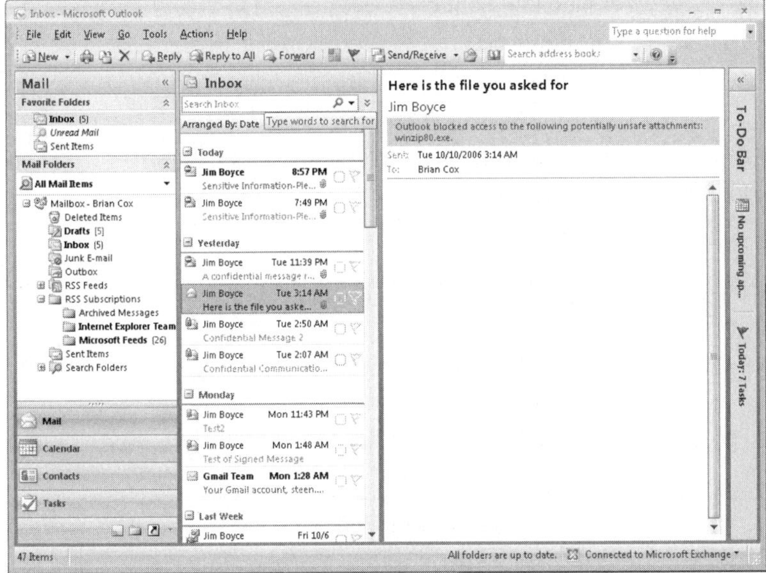

Figure 34-1. Outlook 2007 displays a message informing you that it has blocked the attachment.

For details on how to open attachments that have been blocked by Outlook 2007, see "Opening Blocked Attachments" later in this chapter.

Table 34-1 lists the file name extensions for Level 1 attachments.

Table 34-1. Level 1 Attachments

File Name Extension	Description
.ade	Access project extension
.adp	Access project
.app	Executable application
.asp	Active Server Page
.bas	BASIC source code
.bat	Batch processing
.cer	Internet security certificate file
.chm	Compiled HTML help
.cmd	DOS CP/M command file; command file for Windows NT®
.com	Command

File Name Extension	Description
.cpl	Windows® Control Panel extension
.crt	Certificate file
.csh	csh script
.der	DER encoded X509 certificate file
.exe	Executable file
.fxp	FoxPro compiled source
.hlp	Windows Help file
.hta	Hypertext application
.inf	Information or setup file
.ins	Internet Information Services (IIS) Internet communications settings
.isp	IIS Internet service provider (ISP) settings
.its	Internet document set; Internet translation
.js	JavaScript source code
.jse	JScript® encoded script file
.ksh	UNIX shell script
.lnk	Windows shortcut file
.mad	Microsoft Access module shortcut
.maf	Microsoft Access file
.mag	Microsoft Access diagram shortcut
.mam	Microsoft Access macro shortcut
.maq	Microsoft Access query shortcut
.mar	Microsoft Access report shortcut
.mas	Microsoft Access stored procedures
.mat	Microsoft Access table shortcut
.mau	Media attachment unit
.mav	Microsoft Access view shortcut
.maw	Microsoft Access data access page
.mda	Microsoft Access add-in; Microsoft MDA Access 2 workgroup
.mdb	Microsoft Access application; Microsoft MDB Access database
.mde	Microsoft Access MDE database file
.mdt	Microsoft Access add-in data
.mdw	Microsoft Access workgroup information
.mdz	Microsoft Access wizard template

File Name Extension	Description
.msc	Microsoft Management Console snap-in control file
.msh	Microsoft shell
.msh1	Microsoft shell
.msh2	Microsoft shell
.mshxml	Microsoft shell
.msh1xml	Microsoft shell
.msh2xml	Microsoft shell
.msi	Microsoft Windows Installer file
.msp	Microsoft Windows Installer update
.mst	Microsoft Windows SDK setup transform script
.ops	Microsoft Office system profile settings file
.pcd	Microsoft Visual Test
.pif	Windows program information file
.plg	Microsoft Developer Studio® build log
.prf	Windows system file
.prg	Program file
.pst	Microsoft Exchange address book file; Outlook personal folder file
.reg	Registration information/key for Windows 95/98; registry data file
.scf	Windows Explorer command
.scr	Windows screen saver
.sct	Windows script component; FoxPro screen
.shb	Windows shortcut into a document
.shs	Shell scrap object file
.ps1	Windows PowerShell
.ps1xml	Windows PowerShell
.ps2	Windows PowerShell
.ps2xml	Windows PowerShell
.psc1	Windows PowerShell
.psc2	Windows PowerShell
.tmp	Temporary file/folder
.url	Internet location
.vb	Visual Basic Scripting Edition (VBScript) file; any Visual Basic source
.vbe	VBScript encoded script file

File Name Extension	Description
.vbs	VBScript script file; Visual Basic for Applications (VBA) script
.vsmacros	Microsoft Visual Studio® .NET binary-based macro project
.vsw	Microsoft Visio® workspace file
.ws	Windows script file
.wsc	Windows script component
.wsf	Windows script file
.wsh	Windows script host settings file
.xnk	Exchange public folder shortcut

Level 2 Attachments

Outlook 2007 also supports a second level of attachment blocking. Level 2 attachments are defined by the administrator at the server level and therefore apply to Exchange Server accounts, not to Post Office Protocol 3 (POP3), Internet Messsage Access Protocol (IMAP), or Hypertext Transfer Protocol (HTTP)–based accounts. Because the Level 2 list is empty by default, no attachments are blocked as Level 2 attachments unless the Exchange Server administrator has modified the Level 2 list.

You can't open Level 2 attachments directly in Outlook 2007, but Outlook 2007 does allow you to save them to disk, and you can open them from there.

Configuring Blocked Attachments

Attachment blocking is an important feature in Outlook 2007 to help prevent viruses from infecting systems. Although you can rely on the default Outlook 2007 attachment security, you can also choose a centrally managed method of customizing attachment handling for Outlook 2007. You can configure attachment blocking in three ways:

- **Using Group Policy** With Outlook 2007, you can use Group Policy to control how Outlook 2007 handles security, including attachments and virus prevention features. The use of Group Policy also allows the application of these customized security settings in environments without public folders, such as a computer running Exchange Server 2007 or with clients running Outlook 2007 that are not using Exchange Server. Using Group Policy does, however, require that you be using the Active Directory® directory service to manage your network.
- **Using the Exchange Security Form** Earlier versions of Microsoft Outlook used the Exchange Security Form, which provides essentially the same options as the Group Policy settings now do. The Exchange Security Form relies on Exchange Server shared folders, however, which limits the use of these configuration options to only organizations using Exchange Server. You can still use the

Exchange Security Form with Exchange Server 2007, for example, to support legacy Microsoft Outlook clients.

- **At the user's workstation** If neither of the preceding options is available to you, a limited amount of customization can be done on an individual workstation. For example, you can modify the client's registry to change the Level 1 list (as explained in the section "Configuring Attachment Blocking Directly in Outlook" later in this chapter). These modifications also affect non–Exchange Server accounts.

Configuring attachment blocking centrally, either via Group Policy or on a computer running Exchange Server, is the most effective and efficient method; it gives you, as an administrator, control over attachment security. It also allows you to tailor security by groups within your Windows domains.

Note

Because this book focuses on Outlook 2007 used with Exchange Server 2007, the use of the Exchange Security Form is not covered. For detailed information about using the Exchange Security Form, see the Office 2003 Resource Kit, available at *office.microsoft.com/en-us/ork2003/*.

In addition to specifying when Outlook 2007 blocks attachments, you can configure other aspects of Outlook 2007 security via Group Policy (or using the Exchange Security Form), letting you limit the behavior of custom forms and control programmatic access to Outlook 2007.

INSIDE OUT Keep systems safe

Apparently Microsoft's theory for Level 2 attachments is that the user has a client-side antivirus solution in place that will scan the file automatically as soon as the user saves the file to disk. Or perhaps the theory is that you can rely on the user to manually perform a virus check on the file. Neither of these scenarios is a sure bet by any means. Even if the user has antivirus software installed, it might be disabled or have an outdated virus definition file. That's why it's important to provide virus protection at the network and server levels to prevent viruses from reaching the user at all.

It's also important to educate users about the potential damage that can be caused by viruses and worms. Too often these infect systems through user ignorance—users receive an attachment from a known recipient, assume that it's safe (if they even consider that the file could be infected), and open the file. The result is an infected system and potentially an infected network.

Configuring Attachments in Exchange Server

Attachment blocking in Exchange Server can be configured in two ways:

- Group Policy is used by Exchange Server 2007, enabling the configuration of these settings without reliance on public folders, which are optional in Exchange Server 2007, or registry entries on each of the client computers.
- The Exchange Security Form, which is configured via an adminstrative template stored in a public folder, is used in earlier versions of Exchange Server. While the Exchange Security Form can be used only in environments that have public folders, such as Exchange Server 2003, it is still available for configurations, such as using down-level clients, where it is required.

The settings that are configurable in Group Policy and those set via the Exchange Security Form are largely the same, as described in the following section. Whether you choose to use one or the other, or both, depends on the versions of Exchange Server and Microsoft Outlook that you need to support. Table 34-2 shows which methods can be used by various e-mail servers.

Table 34-2. Security Methods and Types of E-Mail Servers

	Security Method	
E-Mail Server	**Group Policy**	**Exchange Security Form**
Exchange Server 2007 (no public folders)	Yes	No
Exchange Server 2007 (with public folders)	Yes	Yes
Exchange Server 2003	Yes	Yes
Non–Exchange Server	Yes	No

Outlook 2007 clients can use any of these methods, depending on the Outlook Security Mode set in Group Policy. When you use only Group Policy settings, clients running Outlook 2003 or earlier use the default security settings. If an Exchange Security Form is also available, clients running Outlook 2003, Outlook 2002, and Outlook 2000 (with the security update) will use it. Table 34-3 describes the specific behavior of each client with each security method.

Table 34-3. Security Methods and Versions of Microsoft Outlook

		Security Method	
Microsoft Outlook Version	**Group Policy**	**Exchange Security Form**	**Both**
Outlook 2007	Uses Group Policy settings (by default)	Uses ESF if set in Group Policy (Outlook Security Settings)	Depends on configuration (Group Policy can override ESF, and vice versa)

Microsoft Outlook Version	Security Method Group Policy	Exchange Security Form	Both
Outlook 2003, Outlook 2002, and Outlook 2000 with security update	Uses default settings	Uses Exchange Security Form settings	Uses Exchange Security Form settings
Outlook 2000 without the security update and earlier	Uses default settings	Uses default settings	Uses default settings

Outlook Security Mode is set in Group Policy to specify how clients running Outlook 2007 apply security settings. Outlook 2007 can use Group Policy settings, use the Exchange Security Form stored in one of two public folders (Outlook Security Settings or Outlook 10 Security Settings), or use the Outlook 2007 default security settings.

> **Note**
>
> Using both Group Policy settings and the Exchange Security Form supports the widest range of clients and is particularly useful during upgrades from Outlook 2003 to Outlook 2007 or Exchange Server 2003 to Exchange Server 2007. Outlook 2007 clients can retrieve their security information from the appropriate location transparently.

Using Outlook Security Settings

There are three categories of settings you can configure using Group Policy, controlling attachments, forms, and programmatic access to Outlook 2007. These settings are described in the following sections.

> **Note**
>
> This section covers the settings as described in Group Policy; settings in the Exchange Security Form are similar, even if worded slightly differently.

Attachment Security Settings

A number of options are available for customization of attachment handling, including making changes to the blocked attachment lists, specifying when prompts appear, and controlling users' ability to configure their own attachment management.

- **Display Level 1 Attachments** This option allows Outlook 2007 users to see and open Level 1 attachments.
- **Allow Users To Demote Attachments To Level 2** Enabling this option allows Outlook 2007 users to demote Level 1 attachments to Level 2, which lets a user save the attachments to disk and then open them.
- **Do Not Prompt About Level 1 Attachments When Sending An Item** This setting disables the warning that normally appears when a user tries to send a Level 1 attachment. The warning explains that the attachment could cause a virus infection and that the recipient might not receive the attachment (because of attachment blocking on the recipient's server).
- **Do Not Prompt About Level 1 Attachments When Closing An Item** You can disable the warning that normally appears when the user closes a message, an appointment, or another item that contains a Level 1 attachment.

> **Note**
>
> Disabling warning prompts for Level 1 attachments does not change how Outlook 2007 deals with them. Even without a warning, users are not able to view or open Level 1 attachments in Outlook 2007 items when a setting that disables warning prompts is enabled.

- **Allow In-Place Activation Of Embedded Ole Objects** This option allows Outlook 2007 users to open embedded OLE objects (such as Microsoft Office Excel® 2007 spreadsheets, Access 2007 databases, and other documents) by double-clicking the object's icon.
- **Display Ole Package Objects** Enable this option to show embedded OLE objects in e-mail messages. Hiding the objects prevents the user from opening them.
- **Add File Extensions To Block As Level 1** Use this setting to modify the Level 1 attachment list. You can enter a list of file name extensions to add to the list.
- **Remove File Extensions Blocked As Level 1** You can specify a list of file name extensions to remove from the Level 1 attachment list.
- **Add File Extensions To Block As Level 2** Use this setting to modify the Level 2 attachment list. You can enter a list of file name extensions to add to the list.
- **Remove File Extensions Blocked As Level 2** You can specify a list of file name extensions to remove from the Level 2 attachment list.

- **Prevent Users From Customizing Attachment Security Settings** This Group Policy setting is used in earlier versions of Microsoft Outlook to specify whether users can add files to (or remove files from) the Level 1 and Level 2 attachment lists that you have configured. This option overrides other settings; if it is enabled, users cannot configure the lists even if other settings would normally allow them to.
- **Allow Access To E-Mail Attachments** This setting also is for earlier versions of Microsoft Outlook. You can create a list of file types that are to be removed from the default Level 1 attachment list. This is functionally equivalent to the Remove File Extensions Blocked As Level 1 setting, just for legacy clients.

Custom Form Security Settings

There are several options that control the actions that can be taken by scripts and controls in custom forms:

- **Allow Scripts In One-Off Outlook Forms** Enabling this option allows scripts to be executed if the script and the form layout are contained in the message.
- **Set Outlook Object Model Custom Actions** This setting determines the action Outlook 2007 takes if a program attempts to execute a task using the Outlook 2007 object model. For example, a virus could incorporate a script that uses the Outlook 2007 object model to reply to a message and attach itself to that message, bypassing the Outlook 2007 security safeguards. Prompt User causes Outlook 2007 to prompt the user to allow or deny the action. Automatically Approve allows the program to execute the task without prompting the user. Automatically Deny prevents the program from executing the task without prompting the user. Prompt User Based On Computer Security uses the Outlook 2007 security settings.
- **Set Control Itemproperty Prompt** This setting determines the action Outlook 2007 takes if a user adds a control to a custom Outlook 2007 form and binds that control to any address information fields (To or From, for example). You can select Prompt User to have Outlook 2007 ask the user to allow or deny access to the address fields when the message is received, Automatically Approve to allow access without prompting the user, Automatically Deny to deny access without prompting the user, or Prompt User Based On Computer Security to use the Outlook 2007 security settings.

> **Note**
>
> You can control which applications can access Outlook 2007 programmatically, to send e-mail or retrieve Outlook 2007 information, using Group Policy. For detailed information about how to do this, see "Enabling Applications to Send E-Mail with Outlook" later in this chapter.

Configuring Security Using Group Policy

There are two steps involved in configuring Outlook 2007 attachment security using Group Policy. First, you configure the security settings for attachments and custom forms. Once you are satisfied with the configuration, you configure Group Policy as the method that Outlook 2007 uses to obtain security information.

> **Note**
>
> Security settings applied via Group Policy do not take effect immediately. Changes will be made after the computer receives a Group Policy update (usually at the next logon) and consequently starts Outlook 2007. Even when a computer receives refreshed Group Policy automatically, settings will not apply to Outlook 2007 until the next time it is started.

You manage Outlook 2007 attachment security using the Outlook 2007 administrative template (Outlk12.adm) which is found in the Admin Pack (adminpak.msi) and the Group Policy Editor.

For detailed information about using Group Policy templates, go to: *support.microsoft.com/kb/924617.*

To install the administrative template, follow these steps:

1. Create a folder on the local computer to contain the template files. (The steps outlined here assume that you're creating a folder named AdminPak for the files.)
2. Download the administrative templates from *www.microsoft.com/downloads/details.aspx?familyid=92d8519a-e143-4aee-8f7a-e4bbaeba13e7*. Save the file in the AdminPak directory.
3. Open a Command Prompt window, and switch to the AdminPak folder.
4. Type **adminTemplates /extract:\adminPak**, and then press **Enter**.
5. Follow the prompts to extract the administrative templates.

To add the administrative template to Group Policy, follow these steps:

1. On a server with the Windows Server administrator tools installed, click Start, Run, type **gpedit.msc** in the Open box, and then press **Enter**.
2. In the Group Policy editor, browse to User Configuration/Administrative Templates.
3. Right-click Administrative Templates, and then select Add/Remove Template.

4. In the Add/Remove Templates dialog box, click Add.
5. Browse to the AdminPak directory. Select outlk12.adm, and then click Open.
6. In the Add/Remove Templates dialog box, click Close.

To configure the Outlook 2007 attachment security settings, follow these steps:

1. On a server with the Windows Server administrator tools installed, run Group Policy by clicking Start, Run, typing **gpedit.msc**, and then pressing **Enter**.
2. Browse to User Configuration\Administrative Templates\Classic Administrative Templates (ADM)\Microsoft Office Outlook \Security\Security Form Settings\Attachment Security.
3. Configure the settings using this list as a guide. The default setting is Not Configured for all items in this policy:
    - Enable Display Level 1 attachments if you want to allow Outlook 2007 users to see and open Level 1 attachments, effectively setting the attachments to Level 2.
    - To allow Outlook 2007 users to change Level 1 attachments to Level 2, enable Allow Users To Demote Attachments To Level 2.
    - If you want to surpress the warning that usually appears when a Level 1 attachment is sent, enable Do Not Prompt About Level 1 Attachments When Sending An Item.
    - To disable the warning that normally appears when the user closes an item that contains a Level 1 attachment, enable Do Not Prompt About Level 1 Attachments When Closing An Item.
    - If you want to let Outlook 2007 users open embedded OLE objects (such as Microsoft Office Word 2007 documents, Excel 2007 spreadsheets, and other documents), enable Allow In-Place Activation Of Embedded Ole Objects.
    - Enable Display Ole Package Objects to show embedded OLE objects in e-mail messages and allow users to open them.
    - You can block additional file types by enabling Add File Extensions To Block As Level 1. Specify a list of file name extensions, without periods and separated by semicolons (;), in the Additional Extensions field.
    - You can specify a list of file name extensions to remove from the Level 1 attachment list by enabling Remove File Extensions Blocked As Level 1 and entering the list in the Additonal Extensions field.
    - To add file types to the Level 2 list, enable Add File Extensions To Block As Level 2, and then enter a list of extensions.
    - Enable Remove File Extensions Blocked As Level 2, and then specify a list of file name extensions to remove from the Level 2 attachment list.

To configure the Custom Form Security settings, follow these steps:

1. In Group Policy, go to User Configuration\Administrative Templates\Classic Administrative Templates (ADM)\Microsoft Office Outlook 2007\Security\Security Form Settings\Custom Form Security.
2. Select Allow Scripts In One-Off Outlook Forms if you want scripts to be executed when the script and the form layout are contained in the message.
3. Set the Outlook object model Custom Actions execution prompt to specify the action that Outlook 2007 takes if a program attempts to execute a task using the Outlook 2007 object model. Select Prompt User to have Outlook 2007 prompt the user to allow or deny the action. Select Automatically Approve to allow the program to execute the task without prompting the user. Select Automatically Deny to prevent the program from executing the task without prompting the user. Select Prompt User based On Computer Security to use the Outlook 2007 security settings.
4. You can select Set Control Itemproperty Prompt and then configure the action that Outlook 2007 takes if a user adds a control to a custom Outlook 2007 form and binds that control to an address information field (such as To or From). Select Prompt User to have Outlook 2007 ask the user to allow or deny access to the address fields when the message is received. Select Automatically Approve to allow access without prompting the user. Select Automatically Deny to deny access without prompting the user. Select Prompt User Based On Computer Security to use the Outlook 2007 security settings.

To configure legacy Microsoft Outlook settings, follow these steps:

1. In Group Policy, go to User Configuration\Administrative Templates\Classic Administrative Templates (ADM)\Microsoft Office Outlook 2007\Security.
2. If you do not want users to modify the Level 1 and Level 2 attachment lists, select Prevent Users From Customizing Attachment Security Settings.
3. To remove file types from the default Level 1 attachment list, select Allow Access To E-Mail Attachments, and then provide a list of file name extensions (without a period) in the List Of File Extensions To Allow field. You can enter multiple file name extensions separated by semicolons.

Setting the Outlook Security Mode

After you have configured the Outlook 2007 security settings, you have to enable the use of those settings by enabling Exchange Server security and selecting the Outlook Security Mode. You do this using the same administrative template that you used to configure the security settings. To select the security mode for Outlook 2007, follow these steps:

1. Run Group Policy, and then open Outlk12.adm. Go to User Configuration\Administrative Templates\Classic Administrative Templates (ADM)\Microsoft Office Outlook 2007\Security\Security Form Settings.

2. Double-click Outlook Security Mode, and then select Enabled. Select Use Outlook Security Group Policy in the drop-down list, and then click OK.

Configuring Attachment Blocking Directly in Outlook

The preceding sections explained how to configure attachment blocking for Exchange Server users. Non–Exchange Server users can also control attachment blocking, although the method for modifying the attachment list is different. So if you use Outlook 2007 in a workgroup or on a stand-alone computer without Exchange Server, you can still control which attachments Outlook 2007 prevents you from opening. You simply have fewer options for controlling and applying security settings.

> **Note**
>
> If you modify the registry settings that affect the Level 1 list, you must restart Outlook 2007 for the changes to take effect.

Removing Blocked File Types from the Level 1 List

To change the Level 1 attachment list, you must modify a registry setting on your local computer. You can remove file types from the list, as well as add them. To apply the changes across multiple computers, distribute a registry script file. You can distribute this file through a logon script, place it on a network share for users to access, or send users a message containing a shortcut to the file. (For information about how to deploy registry files using a logon script, see the Windows Server help file.)

Follow these steps to create the necessary registry settings and optionally export them as a .reg file for other users:

1. On a system with Outlook 2007 installed, choose Start, Run, and then type **regedit** in the Run dialog box.
2. In the Registry Editor, open the key HKEY_CURRENT_USER\Software\Microsoft\Office\12.0\Outlook\Security.
3. In that key, add a string value named **Level1Remove**.
4. Set the value of Level1Remove to include the file name extensions of those files you want removed from the Level 1 attachment list, without leading periods and separated by semicolons. The following example removes Microsoft Installer (.msi) files and Help (.hlp) files from the list:

   msi;hlp
5. If you want to share the customized registry with other users, choose Registry, Export Registry File. Select a location for the .reg file, and then click Save. You can then distribute the .reg file to the other users, as noted earlier.

Adding Blocked File Types to the Level 1 List

Outlook 2007 is aggressive about which attachments it blocks, but you might want to add other attachment types to the Level 1 list so that Outlook 2007 will block them. Using the same method as in the preceding procedure, add the registry value HKEY_CURRENT_USER\Software\Microsoft\Office\12.0\Outlook\Security\Level1Add. Set the value of Level1Add to include the file name extensions that you want added to the Level 1 list. You can add multiple file types separated by semicolons. See the preceding section for options for propagating the change to other users.

Opening Blocked Attachments

Although it's useful to block attachments in general, there will undoubtedly still be a occasional legitimate attachment that ends up blocked by Outlook 2007. Fortunately, even though attachments are blocked, you can still access them using a few other approaches. The attachment file type (Level 1 or Level 2) and the other e-mail programs available to you determine the best method for opening the file.

Allowing Level 1 Attachments

You can configure Outlook 2007 to allow certain Level 1 attachments (essentially removing them from the Level 1 list) by modifying the registry. (See "Configuring Attachment Blocking Directly in Outlook" earlier in this chapter for instructions.) You might want to do this if you find yourself repeatedly having to deal with the same type of blocked Level 1 attachment. If you are using Exchange Server, your ability to do this may be controlled by the administrator as described in "Configuring Blocked Attachments" earlier in this chapter.

Allowing Level 2 Attachments

Outlook 2007 also uses a list of Level 2 attachments, which are defined by the administrator at the server level (and therefore apply to Exchange Server accounts). You can't open Level 2 attachments in Outlook 2007, but you can save them to disk and open them from there. To open a Level 2 attachment this way, follow these steps:

1. Open the message, click the Microsoft Office Button, and then click Save As, Save Attachments. Select the attachment that you want to save.
2. In the Save Attachment dialog box, specify the folder in which you want to save the file, and then click Save.
3. Outside Outlook 2007, browse to the folder where you saved the attachment, and then open the file.

Because the Level 2 list is empty by default, no attachments are blocked as Level 2 attachments unless the Exchange Server administrator has modified the Level 2 list.

For detailed information about configuring attachment blocking under Exchange Server, see "Configuring Blocked Attachments" earlier in this chapter.

Protecting Against Office Macro Viruses

Like other Microsoft Office system applications, Outlook 2007 allows you to use macros to automate common tasks. Macros have become an increasingly popular infection mechanism for viruses because most inexperienced users don't expect to have their systems infected by the sort of Office documents they regularly work with. However, Office macros can contain viruses that cause just as much damage as any other virus. Protecting yourself against macro viruses is an important step in safeguarding your system overall.

You can guard against macro viruses by implementing a virus scanner on your computer that checks your documents for macro viruses, by installing an antivirus solution on your e-mail server, or by using both methods. Another line of protection is to control how and when macros are allowed to run. Outlook 2007 provides four security levels for macros that determine which macros can run on the system. To set the level, in Outlook 2007, choose Tools, Macro, Security, and then select one of these levels:

- **No Warnings And Disable All Macros** Macros are totally disabled, and Outlook 2007 does not display any warning that a macro is attempting to run.
- **Warnings For Signed Macros; All Unsigned Macros Are Disabled** Your system can run only macros that are digitally signed. This means that some macros—even benign and potentially useful ones—are not available.
- **Warnings For All Macros** You will be prompted as to whether you want to run any macros.
- **No Security Check For Macros (Not Recommended)** Macros run automatically, regardless of their signature. This is the most dangerous setting.

For additional information about configuring macro security and specifying trusted sources, see "Setting Macro Security" in Chapter 29.

To learn how to add a digital signature to your macros so that they don't generate a security warning, see "Signing Your Macros to Avoid Security Warnings" in Chapter 29.

Enabling Applications to Send E-Mail with Outlook

Some applications interact with Outlook 2007, most typically using the Address Book to address and send a message. In most cases, these applications will generate a security warning dialog box. The warning is built into Outlook 2007 to help you identify when unauthorized applications are attempting to access your Outlook 2007 data. For example, a worm that propagates itself by e-mail would likely generate the warning.

The section "Configuring Attachments in Exchange Server" earlier in this chapter explained how Exchange Server administrators can use Group Policy to configure security settings for Outlook 2007 users. That section covered how to configure attachment blocking. You can also use Group Policy to configure the behavior of specific types of applications in relation to the security features in Outlook 2007, as well as specify dynamic-link libraries (DLLs) that should be explicitly trusted and allowed to run without generating a security warning.

If you have not already configured Group Policy to manage security settings, see "Configuring Attachments in Exchange Server" earlier in this chapter to learn how.

Configuring Programmatic Access

Just as with the other security settings that can be configured in Exchange Server, you can control programmatic access to Outlook 2007 via either Group Policy or the Exchange Security Form.

Configuring Programmatic Access Using Group Policy

To configure the settings that determine how Outlook 2007 security features handle various types of applications, follow these steps:

1. Run Group Policy, and then go to User Configuration\Administrative Templates\Classic Administrative Templates (ADM) Microsoft Office Outlook 2007\Security\Security Form Settings\Programmatic Security settings.
2. Configure the Outlook 2007 object model–related settings as desired. Each of these policy items has the same Guard behavior options. Select Prompt User to have Outlook 2007 prompt the user to allow or deny the action. Select Automatically Approve to allow the program to execute the task without prompting the user. Select Automatically Deny to prevent the program from executing the task without prompting the user. Select Prompt User Based On Computer Security to use the Outlook 2007 security settings.

   Configure Outlook Object Model Prompt When Sending Mail Specifies the action that Outlook 2007 takes when an application tries to send mail programmatically with the Outlook 2007 object model.

   Configure Outlook Object Model Prompt When Accessing An Address Book Specifies the action that Outlook 2007 takes when an application tries to access an address book with the Outlook 2007 object model.

   Configure Outlook Object Model Prompt When Reading Address Information Specifies the action that Outlook 2007 takes when an application tries to access a recipient field, such as To or Cc, with the Outlook 2007 object model.

Chapter 34

Configure Outlook Object Model Prompt When Responding To Meeting And Task Requests Specifies the action that Outlook 2007 takes when an application tries to send mail programmatically by using the Respond method on task and meeting requests.

Configure Outlook Object Model Prompt When Executing Save As Specifies the action that Outlook 2007 takes when an application tries to programmatically use the Save As command to save an item.

Configure Outlook Object Model Prompt When Accessing The Formula Property Of A Userproperty Object Specifies the action that Outlook 2007 takes if a user has added a Combination or Formula custom field to a custom form and bound it to an Address Information field. Blocking access can prevent an application from indirectly retrieving the value of the Address Information field through its Value property.

Configure Outlook Object Model Prompt When Accessing Address Information Via UserProperties.Find Specifies the action that Outlook 2007 takes when an application tries to search mail folders for address information using the Outlook 2007 object model.

3. Configure the Simple MAPI settings next as desired. Each of these policy items has the same set of options. You can select Prompt User to have Outlook 2007 prompt the user to allow or deny the action. Select Automatically Approve to allow the program to execute the task without prompting the user. Select Automatically Deny to prevent the program from executing the task without prompting the user.

   Configure Simple MAPI Sending Prompt Specifies the action that Outlook 2007 takes when an application tries to send mail programmatically with Simple MAPI.

   Configure Simple MAPI Name Resolution Prompt Specifies the action that Outlook 2007 takes when an application tries to access an address book with Simple MAPI.

   Configure Simple MAPI Message Opening Prompt Specifies the action that Outlook 2007 takes when an application tries to access a recipient field, such as To or Cc, with Simple MAPI.

4. When you have finished configuring programmatic settings, close Group Policy.

Part of the battle in getting an application past the Outlook 2007 security prompts is understanding what method it is using to access your Outlook 2007 data. If you're not sure, you can simply change one setting, test, and if the change doesn't enable the application to bypass the security prompts, change a different setting. This trial-and-error method isn't the most direct, but it won't take much time to test each of the possibilities. Remember that you must refresh Group Policy and then start Outlook 2007 for these changes to be applied.

Trusting Applications

In addition to (or as an alternative to) configuring security settings to allow various types of applications to bypass the Outlook 2007 security prompts, you can also identify specific applications that can bypass the Outlook 2007 security prompts. These applications must be specifically written to use the Outlook 2007 security trust model.

Using Group Policy to Trust Applications

Before an unsigned application (for example, a noncommercial application) can be added to the trusted add-ins list, you must generate a hash key value to use when setting the Group Policy. The Outlook 2007 Security Hash Generator Tool is available from Microsoft by going to *office.microsoft.com/downloads/* and searching for *Outlook 2007 Security Hash Generator Tool*. Once you have downloaded the hash generator, you have to install and register it before using it to create hash keys.

To install the hash generator, follow these steps:

1. On a computer running Windows XP, run OutlookSecHashGen.exe to start installation. Specify a folder for the extracted files, and then click OK.
2. Open a Command Prompt window, and then go to the folder with the extracted files.
3. Type **CreateHash.bat /register**, and then press Enter.

To register an add-in, follow these steps:

1. Open a Command Prompt window, and then go to the folder with the extracted files.
2. Type **CreateHash.bat <filename>.dll** (using the name of your file).
3. When the hash value is displayed, copy and paste it into the value field in Group Policy (or save it in a text file).

To add a trusted application, follow these steps:

1. Copy, to a location accessible to the computer where you will be modifying the Outlook 2007 security settings, the DLL or other executable file that loads the application to be trusted.
2. Generate a hash key, and note the value for use during installation.
3. Run Group Policy, and then go to User Configuration\Administrative Templates\Classic Administrative Templates (ADM)\Microsoft Office Outlook 2007\Security\Security Form\Programmatic Security\Trusted Add-ins.
4. Select Enabled, and then click the Show button. In the Show Contents dialog box, click Add.

5. In the Add Item dialog box, fill in the Enter The Name Of The Item To Be Added field, enter the hash value you generated in the Enter The Value Of The Item To Be Added field, and then click OK.
6. Repeat the process for any other applications you want to add to the trusted list, and then close Group Policy.

Tips for Securing Your System

As you have seen, Outlook 2007 has several ways to help keep your system more secure, but there are additional steps that you can take to further ensure that you don't fall victim to viruses or other malicious software.

Make sure that your antivirus protection is kept up to date. The threat from viruses changes on a daily basis, and virus definitions need updating just about as quickly. Set your antivirus software to check for updates automatically, and check it occasionally to make sure that it's doing so.

Create exceptions to the standard rules with discretion. Although there are a number of ways around the virus protection measures provided in Outlook 2007, you should be careful deciding when you use them. Just because you can demote all Level 1 attachments to Level 2 to get past the Outlook 2007 built-in filtering doesn't mean you should.

If you need to send a file that you know will be blocked by Outlook 2007 on the recipient's end, you can rename the file to change the file name extension. Changing an .exe file to an .exx file will get it past the Outlook 2007 filters, and because it's not an actual executable file, it can't be executed accidentally.

Get in the habit of storing the file in an archive, such as a compressed (zipped) folder, created using Windows Explorer (or a program such as WinZip) before sending. Since files with a .zip extension are not blocked by Outlook 2007, you can be sure that your attachment will arrive, allowing the recipient to save it and extract the contents.

Note

To create a zipped folder, in a Windows Explorer window, select the file(s) you want to zip, and then right-click and choose Send To, Compressed (Zipped) Folder. A compressed file will be created in the current folder.

If you have access to a location where you can upload files, such as a file server or an FTP site, upload your files there and send e-mail with a link to the site rather than sending the file as an attachment. This method has advantages beyond avoiding unwanted attachment blocking: Mail files are smaller without large attachments, for example, and multiple people can download a file from a single location.

When it comes to computer security, a little common sense goes a long way. Pay attention to what you do in e-mail. Don't open unexpected attachments or those from unknown sources.

PART 7

Collaboration

CHAPTER 35

Delegating Responsibilities to an Assistant

Microsoft® Office Outlook® 2007, when used with Microsoft Exchange Server, provides features that allow you to delegate certain responsibilities to an assistant. For example, you might want your assistant to manage your schedule, setting up appointments, meetings, and other events for you. Or perhaps you want your assistant to send e-mail messages on your behalf.

This chapter explains how to delegate access to your schedule, e-mail messages, and other Office Outlook 2007 data, granting an assistant the ability to perform tasks in Outlook 2007 on your behalf. This chapter also explains how to access folders for which you've been granted delegate access.

Delegation Overview

Why delegate? You could simply give assistants your logon credentials and allow them to access your Exchange Server mailbox through a separate profile on their systems. The disadvantage to that approach is that your assistants then have access to all your Outlook 2007 data. By using the Outlook 2007 delegation features, however, you can selectively restrict an assistant's access to your data.

You have two ways of delegating access in Outlook 2007. First, you can specify individuals as delegates for your account, which gives them send-on-behalf-of privileges. This means that the delegated individuals can perform such tasks as sending e-mail messages and meeting requests for you. When an assistant sends a meeting request on your behalf, the request appears to the recipients to have come from you. You can also specify that delegates should receive copies of meeting-related messages that are sent to you, such as meeting invitations. This is a necessity if you want an assistant to be able to handle your calendar.

The second way you can delegate access is to configure permissions for individual folders, granting various levels of access within the folders as needed. This does not give other users send-on-behalf-of privileges but does give them access to the folder and its contents. The tasks they can perform in the folder are subject to the permission levels you grant them.

Note

When a message is sent on your behalf, the recipient sees these words in the From box: *<delegate> on behalf of <owner>*, where <delegate> and <owner> are replaced by the appropriate names. This designation appears in the header of the message form when the recipient opens the message but doesn't appear in the header in the Inbox. The Inbox shows the message as coming from the owner, not the delegate.

Assigning Delegates and Working as an Assistant

You can assign multiple delegates so that more than one individual can access your data with send-on-behalf-of privileges. You might have an assistant who manages your schedule and therefore has delegate access to your calendar and another delegate–your supervisor–who manages other aspects of your workday and therefore has access to your Tasks folder. In most cases, however, you'll probably want to assign only one delegate.

Adding and Removing Delegates

You can add, remove, and configure delegates for all your Outlook 2007 folders through the same interface.

Follow these steps to delegate access to one or more of your Outlook 2007 folders:

1. Choose Tools, Options to open the Options dialog box.
2. Click the Delegates tab, as shown in Figure 35-1.

Figure 35-1. The Delegates tab shows the current delegates, if any, and lets you add, remove, and configure delegates.

Chapter 35

3. Click Add to open the Add Users dialog box.
4. Select one or more users, and then click Add.
5. Click OK. Outlook 2007 displays the Delegate Permissions dialog box, shown in Figure 35-2.

Figure 35-2. Configure delegate permissions in the Delegate Permissions dialog box.

6. For each folder, select the level of access you want to give the delegate based on the following list:

   None The delegate has no access to the selected folder.

   Reviewer The delegate can read existing items in the folder but can't add, delete, or modify items. Essentially, this level gives the delegate read-only permission for the folder.

   Author The delegate can read existing items and create new ones but can't modify or delete items.

   Editor The delegate can read existing items, create new ones, and modify existing ones, including deleting them.

7. Set the other options in the dialog box using the following list as a guide:

   Delegate Receives Copies Of Meeting-Related Messages Sent To Me Sends copies of all meeting-related messages to the delegate.

   Automatically Send A Message To Delegate Summarizing These Permissions Sends an e-mail message to the delegate informing him or her of the access permissions you've assigned in your Outlook 2007 folders, as shown in Figure 35-3.

   Delegate Can See My Private Items Allows the delegate to view items you've marked as private. Clear this option to hide your private items.

8. Click OK to close the Delegate Permissions dialog box.
9. Add and configure other delegates as you want, and then click OK.

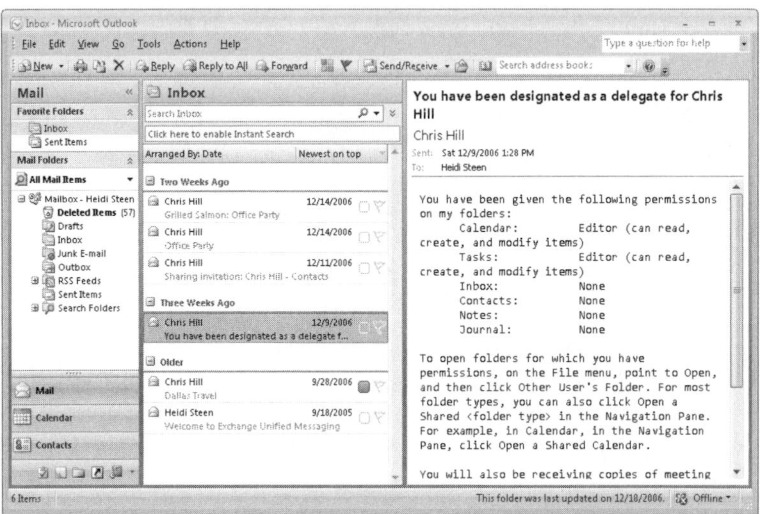

Figure 35-3. Outlook 2007 sends a message to delegates regarding their access privileges.

If you need to modify the permissions for a delegate, select the Delegates tab, select the delegate in the list, and then click Permissions to open the Delegate Permissions dialog box. Change the settings as needed, just as you do when you add a delegate. If you need to remove a delegate, select the delegate on the Delegates tab, and then click Remove.

> **Note**
>
> If the Permissions button appears dimmed or you are unable to assign delegate permissions for some other reason, the problem could be that you have designated a local .pst file as the default delivery location for your profile. Make sure that you configure your profile to deliver mail to your Exchange Server mailbox instead. See "Configuring Online and Offline Data Storage" in Chapter 3 for details.

Taking Yourself out of the Meeting Request Loop

If your assistant has full responsibility for managing your calendar, you might want all meeting request messages to go to the assistant rather than to you. That way, meeting request messages won't clog your Inbox.

Taking yourself out of the request loop is easy. Here's how:

1. With any folder open, choose Tools, Options.
2. Click the Delegates tab.
3. Select the My Delegates Only option, and click OK.

> **Note**
>
> The My Delegates Only option appears dimmed if you haven't assigned a delegate.

Opening Folders Delegated to You

If you are acting as a delegate for another person, you can open the folders to which you've been given delegate access and use them as if they were your own folders, subject to the permissions applied by the owner. For example, suppose that you've been given delegate access to your manager's schedule. You can open his or her Calendar folder and create appointments, generate meeting requests, and perform the same tasks you can perform in your own Calendar folder. However, you might find a few restrictions. For example, you won't be able to view the contents of personal items unless your manager has configured permissions to give you that ability.

Follow these steps to open another person's folder:

1. Start Outlook 2007 with your own profile.
2. Choose File, Open, Other User's Folder to display the Open Other User's Folder dialog box, as shown in Figure 35-4.

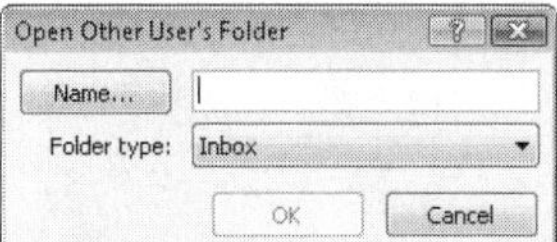

Figure 35-4. Use the Open Other User's Folder dialog box to open another person's Outlook 2007 folder.

3. Type the person's name or click Name to browse the address list, and then select a name.
4. In the Folder Type drop-down list, select the folder you want to open, and then click OK. Outlook 2007 generates an error message if you don't have the necessary permissions for the folder; otherwise, the folder opens in a new window.

If you don't currently have access to the selected folder, Outlook 2007 asks whether you want to request access. If you click yes, Outlook 2007 opens the message form shown in Figure 35-5. Add a note to the person whose calendar you want to access, and then click Send. The other person receives the message and can click Allow or Deny to either allow or deny access to his or her calendar, as shown in Figure 35-6.

> **Note**
>
> If you want to share your calendar with the other person, select the Allow Recipient To View Your Calendar option.

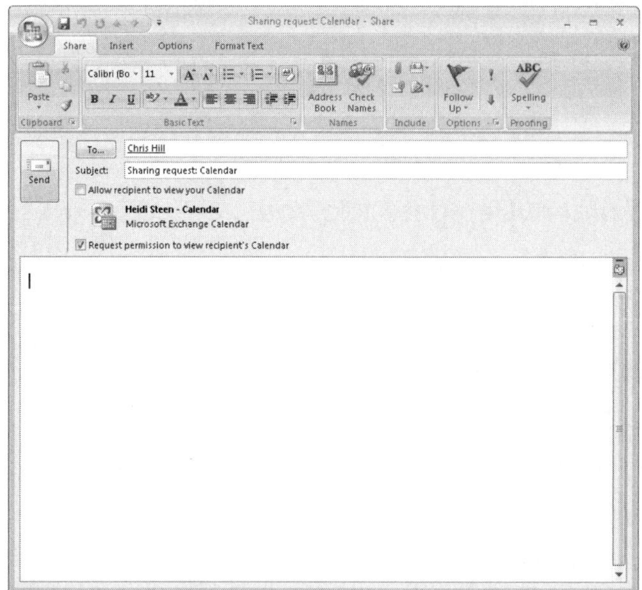

Figure 35-5. You can request access to another person's folder with an e-mail message.

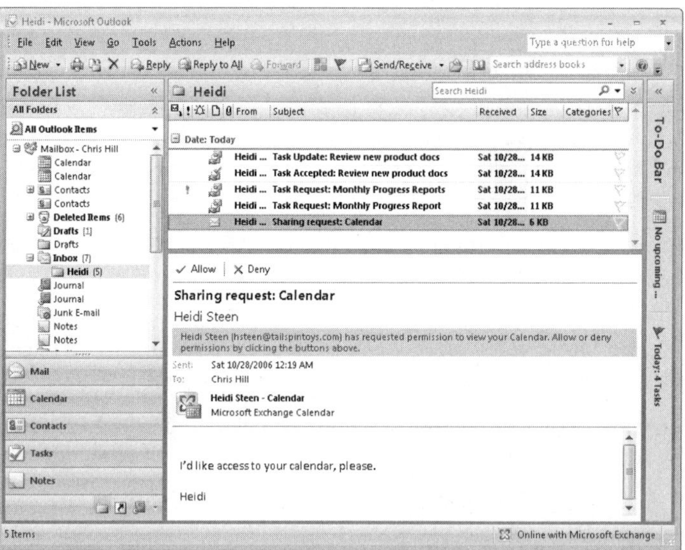

Figure 35-6. The recipient can either allow or deny the request directly in the e-mail message.

Depending on the permissions set for the other person's folder, you might be able to open the folder but not see anything in it. If someone grants you Folder Visible permission, you can open the folder but not necessarily view its contents. For example, if you are granted Folder Visible permission for a Calendar folder, you can view the other person's calendar. If you are granted Folder Visible permission for the Inbox folder, you can open the folder, but you can't see any headers. Obviously, this latter scenario isn't useful, so you might need to fine-tune the permissions to get the effect you need.

> **Note**
>
> When you click File, Open, the menu lists other users' folders that you've recently opened. You can select a folder from the list to open it.

When you've finished working with another person's folder, close it as you would any other window.

Scheduling on Behalf of Another Person

If you've been given delegate privileges for another person's calendar, you can schedule meetings and other appointments on behalf of that person.

To do so, follow these steps:

1. Start Outlook 2007 with your own profile.
2. Click File, Open, and then select Other User's Folder. Type the user name in the text box or click Name and select the user name from the Global Address List (GAL). In the Folder Type drop-down list, select Calendar, and then click OK.
3. In the other person's Calendar folder, create the meeting request, appointment, or other item as you normally would for your own calendar.

As mentioned earlier, a meeting request recipient sees the request as coming from the calendar's owner, not the delegate. When the recipient opens the message, however, the header indicates that the message was sent by the delegate on behalf of the owner. Responses to the meeting request come back to the delegate and a copy goes to the owner, unless the owner has removed himself or herself from the meeting request loop.

For details about how to have meeting request messages go to the delegate rather than to the owner, see "Taking Yourself out of the Meeting Request Loop" earlier in this chapter.

Sending E-Mail on Behalf of Another Person

If you've been given Author or Editor permission for another person's Inbox, you can send messages on behalf of that person. For example, as someone's assistant, you might need to send notices, requests for comments, report reminders, or similar messages.

To send a message on behalf of another person, follow these steps:

1. Start Outlook 2007 with your own profile.

2. Start a new message. If the From field isn't displayed, click Options, and then select Show From.
3. In the From field, type the name of the person on whose behalf you're sending the message.
4. Complete the message as you would any other, and then send it.

Granting Access to Folders

You can configure your folders to provide varying levels of access to other users according to the types of tasks those users need to perform within the folders. For example, you might grant access to your Contacts folder to allow others to see and use your contacts list.

Granting permissions for folders is different from granting delegate access. Users with delegate access to your folders can send messages on your behalf, as explained in earlier sections. Users with access permissions for your folders do not have that ability. Use access permissions for your folders when you want to grant others certain levels of access to your folders but not the ability to send messages on your behalf.

Configuring Access Permissions

Several levels of permissions control what a user can and cannot do in your folders. These permissions include the following:

- **Create Items** Users can post items to the folder.
- **Create Subfolders** Users can create additional folders inside the folder.
- **Edit Own** Users can edit those items they have created and own.
- **Edit All** Users can edit all items, including those they do not own.
- **Folder Owner** The owner has all permissions for the folder.
- **Folder Contact** The folder contact receives automated messages from the folder such as replication conflict messages, requests from users for additional permissions, and other changes to the folder status.
- **Folder Visible** Users can see the folder and its items.
- **Delete Items** Depending on the setting you choose, users can delete all items, only those items they own, or no items.
- **Free/Busy Time** For the calendar, users can see your free/busy time.
- **Free/Busy Time, Subject, Location** For the calendar, users can see your free/busy time, as well as the subject and location of calendar items.
- **Full Details** For the calendar, users can see all details of items.

Outlook 2007 groups these permissions into several predefined levels, as follows:

- **Owner** The owner has all permissions and can edit and delete all items, including those he or she doesn't own.
- **Publishing Editor** The publishing editor has all permissions and can edit and delete all items but does not own the folder.
- **Editor** Users are granted all permissions except the ability to create subfolders or act as the folder's owner. Editors can edit and delete all items.
- **Publishing Author** Users are granted all permissions except the ability to edit or delete items belonging to others and the ability to act as the folder's owner.
- **Author** This level is the same as the Publishing Author level except authors can't create subfolders.
- **Nonediting Author** Users can create and read items and delete items they own, but they can't delete others' items or create subfolders.
- **Reviewer** Users can view items but can't modify or delete items or create subfolders.
- **Contributor** Users can create items but can't view or modify existing items.
- **Free/Busy Time** Users can see your free/busy time.
- **Free/Busy Time, Subject, Location** Users can see your free/busy time, as well as the subject and location for items on your calendar.
- **None** The folder is visible, but users can't read, create, or modify any items in the folder.

Follow these steps to grant permissions for a specific folder:

1. Start Outlook 2007, open the Folder List, right-click the folder, and then choose Properties.
2. Click the Permissions tab, shown in Figure 35-7.

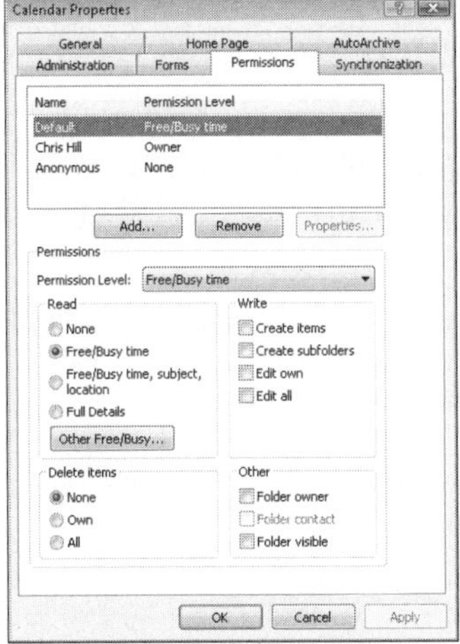

Figure 35-7. Use the Permissions tab to configure access permissions for the folder.

3. Select Default, and then set the permissions you want users to have if they are not explicitly assigned permissions (if their names don't appear in the Name list).
4. Click Add to add a user with explicit permissions. Select the name in the Add Users list, click Add, and then click OK.
5. In the Name list, select the user you just added, and then set specific permissions for the user.
6. Click OK to close the folder's Properties dialog box.

As you can see in Figure 35-7, you can remove users to remove their explicit permissions. Just select the user, and then click Remove.

To view (but not modify) a user's address book properties, as shown in Figure 35-8, select the user, and then click Properties.

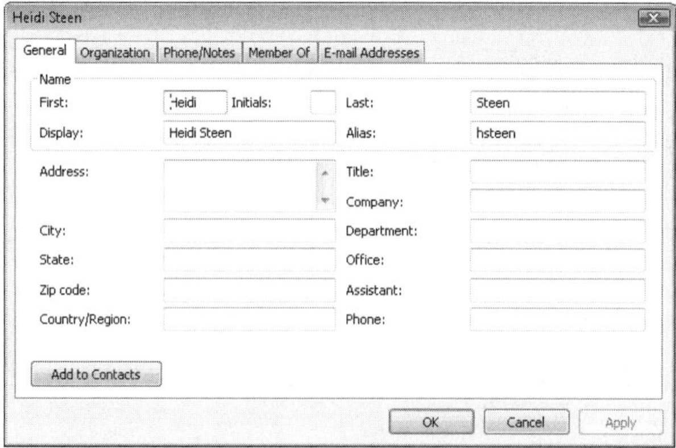

Figure 35-8. You can view a user's address book properties.

Accessing Other Users' Folders

After you've been granted the necessary permissions for another user's folder, you can open the folder and perform actions according to your permissions. For example, if you have only read permission, you can read items but not add new ones. If you've been granted create permission, you can create items.

To open another user's folder, choose File, Open, Other User's Folder. Type the user's name in the text box, or click Name, select the user in the GAL, and then click OK. Select the folder you want to open in the Folder Type drop-down list, and then click OK.

For more information about opening and using another person's folder, see "Opening Folders Delegated to You" earlier in this chapter.

CHAPTER 36
Sharing Calendars

Microsoft® Office Outlook® 2007 provides a number of ways for you to share your calendar information with others. In addition to using Microsoft Exchange Server to share your calendar with other Exchange Server users, you can also publish your calendar to the Web and invite others to share access to it. You can publish your calendar to Microsoft Office Online or to any Web Distributed Authoring and Versioning (WebDAV) server. You can also send your calendar to someone else via e-mail, save the calendar as a Web page and then send it, or post the calendar to a Web server.

Sharing Your Calendar

If you use Exchange Server, you can allow other users to access your entire calendar or selected calendar items. To share your calendar and its items, you must set permission levels for various users. In most cases, permissions are set by using built-in roles, as described in Table 36-1, but you can also set custom permissions for the rare cases when the built-in role does not fit the situation. Some permissions allow users only to view your calendar; others allow users to add or even edit items.

Table 36-1. Folder Permissions

Permission	Description
Owner	The Owner role gives full control of the calendar. An Owner can create, modify, delete, and read folder items; create subfolders; and change permissions on the folder.
Publishing Editor	The Publishing Editor role has all rights granted to an Owner except the right to change permissions. A Publishing Editor can create, modify, delete, and read folder items and create subfolders.
Editor	The Editor role has all rights granted to a Publishing Editor except the right to create subfolders. An Editor can create, modify, delete, and read folder items.

Permission	Description
Publishing Author	A Publishing Author can create and read folder items and create subfolders but can modify and delete only folder items that he or she creates, not items created by other users.
Author	An Author has all rights granted to a Publishing Author but cannot create subfolders. An Author can create and read folder items and modify and delete items that he or she creates.
Nonediting Author	A Nonediting Author can create and read folder items but cannot modify or delete any items, including those that he or she creates.
Reviewer	A Reviewer can read folder items but nothing else.
Contributor	A Contributor can create folder items but cannot delete items.
Free/Busy Time, Subject, Location	A user with these access rights can view the free/busy information as well as the subject and location.
Free/Busy Time	A user with these access rights can view only the free/busy information.
None	The None role has no access to the folder.

The first step in sharing a calendar is to right-click it in the Navigation Pane and then choose Properties. Click the Permissions tab to view the current permissions for the folder. Figure 36-1 shows the Permissions tab with the Calendar folder's default permissions.

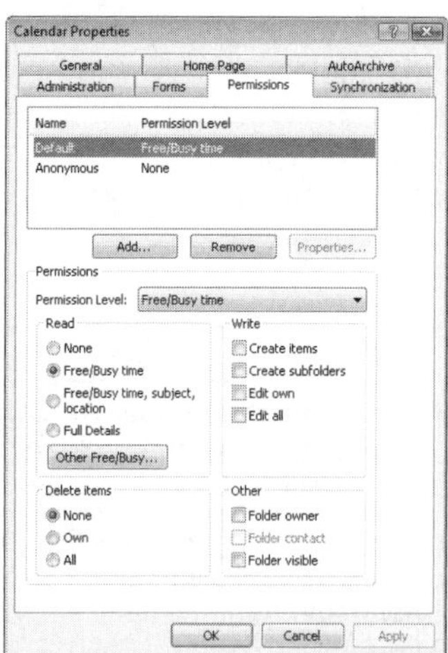

Figure 36-1. The default permissions for a calendar are set to Free/Busy Time.

To allow all users to view details of the calendar, you need to assign Reviewer permission to the default user. A *default user* is any user who is logged in. (An *anonymous user* is any user, whether or not he or she is logged in. Default users are a subgroup of anonymous users.) Select Default in the Name column, and then change the permission level by selecting Reviewer in the Permission Level drop-down list.

INSIDE OUT Quickly share your calendar for review

You can also right-click the calendar and then click Share "Calendar." An e-mail is generated that grants permission, and you can add people that you want to share the calendar with to the To line. Reviewer (read-only) status is granted using this method. This approach not only shares the calendar but also automatically generates the e-mail message to inform the recipients that you have made the calendar available to them.

You might assign a permission of Publishing Author to users if they are colleagues who need to be able to schedule items for you as well as view your calendar.

To give users Publishing Author access to the calendar, follow these steps:

1. On the Permissions tab in the Calendar Properties dialog box, click Add to open the Add Users dialog box, shown in Figure 36-2. Alternatively, you can right-click the calendar in the Navigation Pane and then choose Change Sharing Permissions.

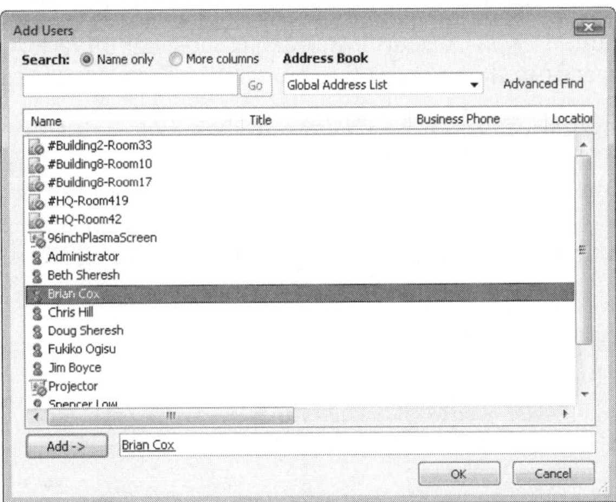

Figure 36-2. Add users to the Permissions tab so that you can specify their permissions for folder sharing.

2. Select a user or distribution list in the Add Users dialog box (hold down **Shift** and click to select a range of users, or hold down **Ctrl** and click to select multiple users), and then click Add. After you have selected all the users you want to add, click OK.

3. By default, Office Outlook 2007 adds users to the Permissions tab with Reviewer permission. To change the permission of a newly added user to Publishing Author, select the user's name, and then select the permission in the Permission Level drop-down list. Figure 36-3 shows the Permissions tab after these changes have been made.

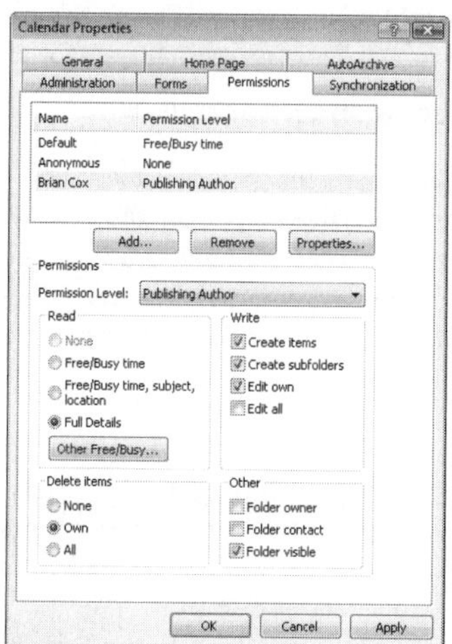

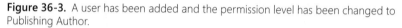

Figure 36-3. A user has been added and the permission level has been changed to Publishing Author.

As you can see in Figure 36-3, the permissions granted to a user can be configured manually using the check boxes in the bottom half of the Permissions tab. However, this is usually unnecessary because you can set most combinations of settings using the Permission Level drop-down list.

You can configure your Free/Busy settings by clicking the Other Free/Busy button. The Free/Busy Options dialog box is displayed, as shown in Figure 36-4, allowing you to set the amount of free/busy information you publish on the computer running Exchange Server and specify the frequency of updates. You can also configure your Internet free/busy publishing and search locations to set custom Internet addresses for your free/busy publishing and search locations.

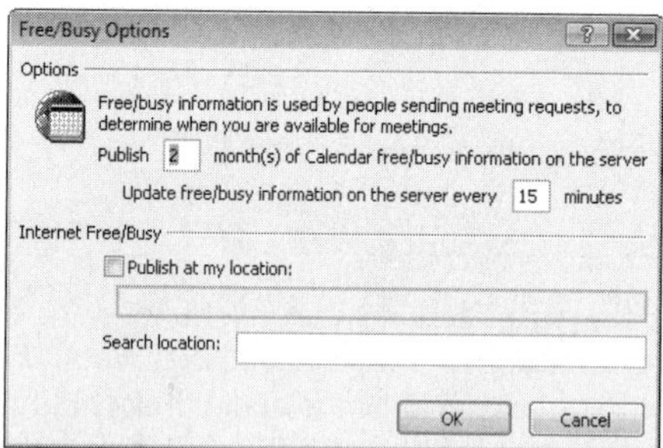

Figure 36-4. Configure your free/busy options for Exchange Server and Internet calendar publishing.

INSIDE OUT **Permissions and delegation are different**

Giving someone permission to view or modify your Calendar folder is not the same as assigning them as a delegate. Delegate permission gives the person the ability to send and receive meeting notices on your behalf. See Chapter 35, "Delegating Responsibilities to an Assistant," for details on assigning delegate permissions.

Managing Your Shared Calendar Information

By default, if you're using Exchange Server, your free/busy information is shared automatically with all other users on that server. If you want users who are not on your server to be able to view that information, or if you do not use Exchange Server at all, you can still share your free/busy information. You can also post your calendar information to other servers through File Transfer Protocol (FTP) or Hypertext Transfer Protocol (HTTP). For example, your company might set up its own server to enable users to share their calendar information with others, whether within the company (for example, if you don't use Exchange Server) or outside the company.

Note

This section focuses on how to publish your calendar information and configure Outlook 2007 to search for calendar information. See the section "Working with Group Schedules" later in this chapter to learn how to view others' calendar information.

TROUBLESHOOTING

Other users don't see your schedule changes

When you make changes to your schedule, those changes might not be visible right away to other users who need to see your free/busy times. By default, Outlook 2007 updates your free/busy information every 15 minutes. To change the frequency of these updates, click Tools, Options, and then click Calendar Options. Click Free/Busy Options, and then click Other Free/Busy to access the Update Free/Busy Information On The Server Every *n* Minutes option (shown earlier in Figure 36-4), which you can use to set the frequency of updates.

Publishing your calendar information makes it possible for others to see your free/busy times in Outlook 2007 when they need to schedule meetings with you or view or manage your calendar. Likewise, the free/busy times of people who publish their calendar information, and who give you access to that information, are visible to you in Outlook 2007. The ability to publish free/busy information to Web servers therefore brings group scheduling capabilities to Outlook 2007 users who do not have access to Exchange Server.

Understanding What Status Is Available

Exchange Server provides four free/busy states for a given time period: Free, Tentative, Busy, and Out Of Office. When you publish your calendar to Microsoft Office Online or a WebDAV server, you can specify which level of calendar detail is available to the viewing user. When you publish your free/busy information to a Web server or file server via FTP, HTTP, or a file, however, only Busy or No Information status is available. Consequently, if you view someone's free/busy information that is published to an FTP, an HTTP, or a file server, all time that the user has marked as Tentative or Out Of Office appears as Busy when you view his or her schedule in Outlook 2007. The only way to view Tentative and Out Of Office status is to pull that information directly from Exchange Server, from Microsoft Office Online, or from a WebDAV server (if the posting user has chosen to include detail in the calendar).

INSIDE OUT **Prevent free/busy publishing**

You can avoid publishing your free/busy information to any servers if you prefer. Choose Tools, Options, click Calendar Options, click Free/Busy Options, and then click Other Free/Busy. You can set the Publish *n* Months Of Calendar Free/Busy Information On The Server option to specify how much of your free/busy information is published. By setting this value to 0, no free/busy information is published, and your free/busy information will appear blank to other users.

Publishing Your Schedule

Microsoft Office Online is a central place on the Internet where you can publish your schedule. Publishing your schedule allows anyone (or only those you specify) to access your calendar information from anywhere on the Internet. This free Microsoft service is useful if you don't use Exchange Server but still want to share your calendar information with others, whether inside or outside your company. You can also use this Microsoft service in conjunction with Exchange Server, publishing your calendar information to the service to allow users outside your Exchange Server organization to view schedule status.

The following sections explain how to publish to the different types of calendar servers. Later in this chapter, you'll also learn how to set up your own free/busy server.

Publishing Your Calendar to Microsoft Office Online

Publishing your calendar to the Web using either Microsoft Office Online or another WebDAV server starts off the same way—you begin by right-clicking the calendar in the Navigation Pane and then choosing Publish To Internet, as shown in Figure 36-5. Alternatively, you could select the option to publish your calendar to a WebDAV server other than Microsoft Office Online by choosing the Publish To WebDAV Server option.

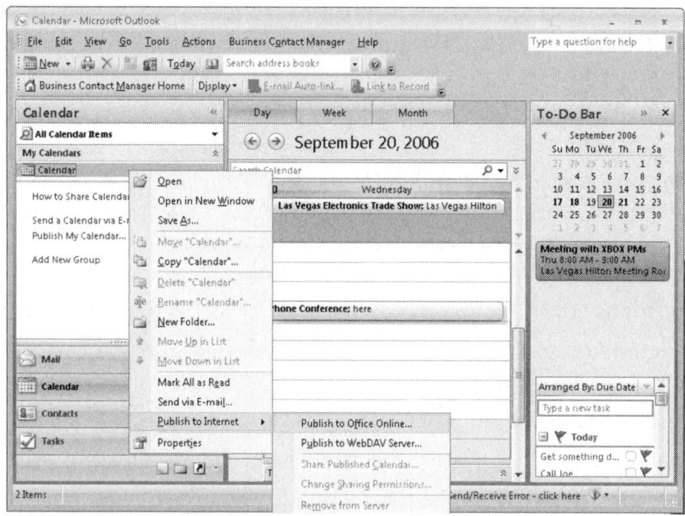

Figure 36-5. To publish your calendar to the Web, choose Publish To Internet, and then choose Publish To Office Online or Publish To WebDAV Server.

If you choose to publish your calendar to Microsoft Office Online, the Publish Calendar To Microsoft Office Online dialog box is displayed, as shown in Figure 36-6.

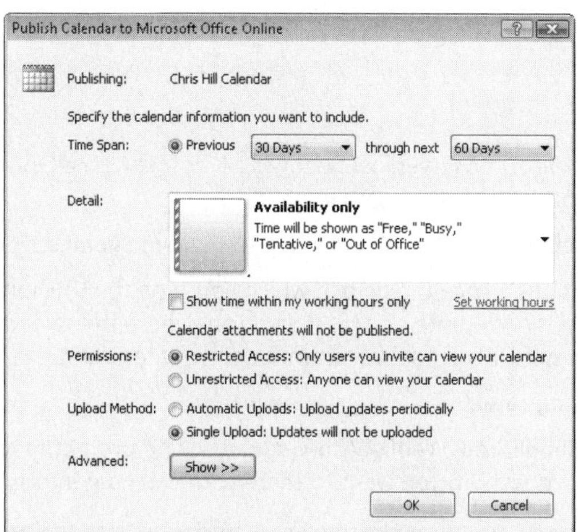

Figure 36-6. You can configure date range, details, access, and updates when publishing your calendar to Microsoft Office Online.

The Publish Calendar To Microsoft Online dialog box contains the following options:

- **Time Span** In this area, you can specify the range of calendar information by setting the Previous and Through Next options.
- **Detail** In this area, you can select the level of information detail that will be displayed to users viewing your calendar:

  Availability Only Only the availability status of the time will be displayed as Free, Busy, Tentative, or Out Of Office.

  Limited Details Displays the availability status as well as the Subject line of calendar items.

  Full Details Includes availability status and all information associated with the calendar items.

  Show Time Within My Working Hours Only You can limit the display of calendar information to only your working hours by selecting the Show Time Within My Working Hours Only check box. You can configure your working hours by clicking the Set Working Hours link.
- **Permissions** In this area, you can control the access to your published calendar:

  Restricted Access Limits access to your published calendar to people that you invite (via e-mail).

  Unrestricted Access Allows anyone to view your published calendar.
- **Upload Method** In this area, you can control the uploading of your calendar:

  Automatic Uploads Enables the automatic updating of your published calendar.

  Single Upload Enables the one-time publishing of your calendar with no further updates.
- **Advanced** By clicking the Show button in the Advanced area, you can elect to have private items also displayed and to have updates occur with the server's recommended frequency.

A Few Differences When Publishing to a WebDAV Server

If you are publishing to a WebDAV server instead of to Microsoft Office Online, the dialog box you'll see is slightly different from Figure 36-6:

- The dialog box title bar reads Publish Calendar To Custom Server.
- The dialog box contains a Location field in which you type the URL location of the WebDAV server and the Web site or virtual directory where the calendar files (*.ics) are stored—for example, **http://server.domain.com/calendars**.
- There is no Permissions area.

After you publish your calendar to a WebDAV server, you will be prompted to send e-mail invitations to others with whom you want to share your calendar information.

If this is your first connection to Microsoft Office Online, you will have to register for a Microsoft Windows Live™ ID (if you don't have one) and go through online registration for the Windows Live service before your calendar is published. You will be prompted to sign in to your Microsoft Office Online account, as shown in Figure 36-7.

Figure 36-7. Sign in to Microsoft Office Online to publish your calendar.

After your calendar has been published, you will be asked whether you want to send e-mail notifications to people whom you want to access your calendar.

> **Note**
>
> When sending e-mail invitations to others to access your calendar, Outlook 2007 will include this notice: "This calendar is shared with restricted permissions. To preview or subscribe to this calendar, you need to enroll the e-mail address to which this e-mail message was sent with a Windows Live ID account."

Your calendar information is now shared using Microsoft Office Online, and other users who have received your e-mail invitations can view that information.

Publishing to FTP, HTTP, and File Servers

You can also publish your free/busy schedule to another server using FTP, HTTP, or a share on a file server. For example, if you don't use Exchange Server in your company, you might set up a Web server on your network to enable users to publish and share their free/busy information. Using your own server eliminates the need to use the Microsoft Office Online service and the need for users to have a Microsoft Windows Live ID account (which is required to use the Microsoft Office Online service).

You can publish to local or remote FTP or HTTP servers, making it easy to publish free/busy information to servers outside your organization. For example, you might work at a division that doesn't have its own Web server, but the corporate office does have a server that you can use to publish your free/busy information. Publishing to a file requires a share on your computer or on a local file server. However, that doesn't mean that users who need to access that free/busy information must be located on the local network. You might publish your free/busy information to a share on your local Web server, for example, but remote users can then access that free/busy information through the Web server's HTTP-based URL.

You must know the correct URL for the server to configure the free/busy URL in Outlook 2007. Here are three examples:

- *http://www.tailspintoys.com/schedules/chill.vfb*
- *ftp://ftp.tailspintoys.com/schedules/chill.vfb*
- *f:\Schedules\Chill.vfb*

Note that schedule files use a .vfb file name extension. Also, the first two examples assume a virtual or physical folder named Schedules under the root of the specified server URL.

INSIDE OUT You can specify the URL with replaceable parameters

In addition to specifying the URL string explicitly, you can also use two replaceable parameters in the URL string:

- **%server%** This parameter represents the server portion of the e-mail address. For example, with the address chill@tailspintoys.com, %server% would resolve to tailspintoys.com. If you specified the URL http://%server%/schedules/chill.vfb, Outlook 2007 would resolve the server domain, and the resulting URL would be http://tailspintoys.com/schedules/chill.vfb.
- **%name%** This parameter represents the account portion of the e-mail address. Using the chill@tailspintoys.com example, %name% would resolve to chill. If you specified the URL http://%server%/schedules/%name%.vfb, for example, Outlook 2007 would resolve the URL to http://tailspintoys.com/schedules/chill.vfb.

If you need to include *www* in the URL, add it like this: **http://www.%server%/schedules/%name%.vfb**.

If your profile includes an Exchange Server account, specifying *%name%* in the URL string will result in Outlook 2007 trying to use the X.400 address from your Exchange Server account, causing the publishing of the free/busy information to fail. Instead of using the variable, specify an explicit name.

Why provide replaceable parameters if you can just type in the correct URL? You can use Group Policy to control the Outlook 2007 configuration, and one of the policies controls the free/busy publish and search URLs. You can define the publishing URL using replaceable parameters in the policy, and those parameters are then replaced when the user logs on, resulting in the correct URL for the user based on his or her e-mail address.

Configuring Outlook 2007 to publish to an FTP, an HTTP, or a file URL is easy. Follow these steps to configure Outlook 2007 to publish your free/busy information:

1. Choose Tools, Options.
2. Click Calendar Options, and then click Free/Busy Options.
3. Click Other Free/Busy.
4. In the Free/Busy Options dialog box, select Publish At My Location.
5. In the Publish At My Location text box, type the fully qualified path to the server on which your free/busy information is to be published.
6. In the Search location box, specify the server to search. This server will be used to view other users' free/busy information. (See the following section for additional details on configuring search locations.)
7. Click OK to close the Free/Busy Options dialog box.

Setting the Search Location for Free/Busy Information

The Free/Busy Options dialog box includes a Search Location box that specifies where Outlook 2007 will search for free/busy information when you create group schedules or meeting requests. Specify the URL or file share where the group's calendars are published, and Outlook 2007 will search the specified URL for free/busy information.

These global settings work in conjunction with Exchange Server, providing a search location for calendars not stored in Exchange Server. In addition to these global settings, you can also specify a search URL for individual contacts. You would specify the search URL in the contact if the contact's free/busy information is not stored on the Microsoft Office Online service or another server specified in the Search Location box.

Follow these steps to set the free/busy search URL for a contact:

1. Open the contact. In the Show group on the Contact tab, click Details.
2. Click in the Address field in the Internet Free-Busy area, and then type the URL as an HTTP, an FTP, or a file share. An FTP URL would look like this:

   ftp://ftp.domain.com/freebusy/JimBoyce.vfb
3. Click Save & Close.

Configuring FTP Authentication in Microsoft Windows XP for Free/Busy Searches

If you publish to an HTTP or a file URL that requires authentication, your Web browser or Microsoft Windows® itself will prompt you for a user name and password when Outlook 2007 attempts to connect. If you are publishing to an FTP site, however, you need to use a different method to specify the user name and password for the free/busy server. You cannot simply embed the user name and password in the publish/search string as you would when connecting to an FTP site from Microsoft Internet Explorer®. If you are using Windows XP, you can use the following steps to configure authentication information for connecting to FTP servers. Windows Vista™ does not support this operation.

Perform these steps to add authentication information for an FTP site in Outlook 2007:

1. In Outlook 2007, choose File, Open, Outlook Data File.
2. In the Open Outlook Data File dialog box, click the Look In drop-down list, and then select Add/Modify FTP Locations. Outlook 2007 displays the Add/Modify FTP Locations dialog box.
3. Type the FTP server name or IP address in the Name Of FTP Site box.
4. Select the User option, type a user name in the User box, and then type a password in the Password box.
5. Click Add, and then click OK. Click OK to close the Open Outlook Data File dialog box.

Refreshing Your Schedule

Free/busy information is refreshed automatically at the intervals set in the Free/Busy Options dialog box. (Choose Tools, Options, click Calendar Options, and then click Free/Busy Options to configure these settings.)

You can refresh free/busy information manually as well. First make sure that the Calendar folder is open, and then choose Tools, Send/Receive, Free/Busy Information. The free/busy information is updated from the server (Exchange Server or other selected free/busy server), and the free/busy information for the users is displayed in subsequent meeting requests.

Sharing Your Calendar Via E-Mail

Outlook 2007 enables you to send your calendar to other people via e-mail, either by clicking the Send A Calendar Via E-Mail link in the Navigation Pane or by right-clicking the calendar and then choosing Send Via E-Mail. A new mail message form will be opened, and the Send A Calendar Via E-Mail dialog box will be displayed, as shown in Figure 36-8. In this dialog box, you can select the calendar to send and configure the date range and amount of detail that the calendar contains. When you click Show in the Advanced area, you can enable the display of information marked as private, include attachments in the calendar, and specify the layout of the calendar as either Daily

Schedule or List Of Events. When you click OK, the calendar is written into the e-mail message as text and as an attachment.

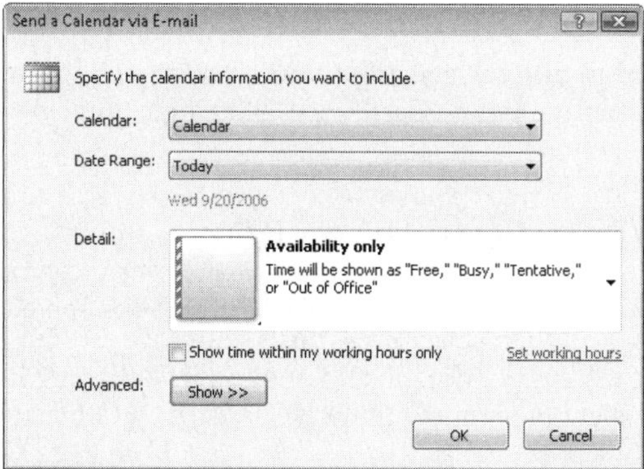

Figure 36-8. You can select a calendar and configure date range, details, and layout when e-mailing your calendar.

Sending a Link to Your Free/Busy Information Through E-Mail

To e-mail your free/busy information to others, you must first link that information to a vCard, as follows:

1. Open a contact item containing your own contact information.
2. In the Show area of the Contact tab, click Details. The Details page appears, as shown in Figure 36-9.

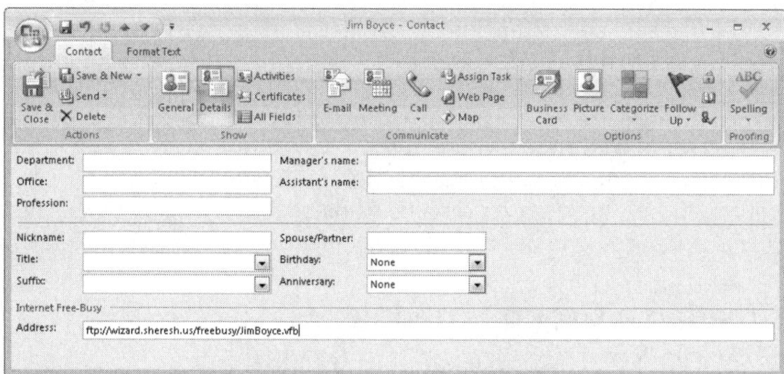

Figure 36-9. On the Details page of a contact form, you can specify the Internet free/busy server.

3. In the Address box in the Internet Free-Busy area, type the address of the server containing your free/busy information.
4. Click the Microsoft Office Button, click Save As, and then select Export To vCard File.

5. In the vCard File dialog box, type the name of the file, and then select the location where you want to save the file.

6. Click Save to create the vCard.

You can now send the vCard to other users, and they can reference your free/busy information. For more details about using vCards, see "Sharing Contacts with vCards" in Chapter 18.

Changing the Free/Busy Status of an Item

You can change the free/busy status of an item easily. One method is to right-click the item, choose Show Time As, and then select Free, Busy, Tentative, or Out Of Office. The second method is to open the item (by double-clicking or right-clicking it and then choosing Open), and then select Free, Busy, Tentative, or Out Of Office in the Show As drop-down list in the Options area.

Working with Group Schedules

Group scheduling is another very useful and important feature made possible by Outlook 2007. This section offers an overview of group scheduling to help you implement and manage it in your organization. Through the group scheduling features in Outlook 2007, managers and those who allocate resources in an organization can have easy access to schedule and contact information for all members of the organization. Managers can get an overview of what their teams are doing by viewing the team members' joint schedules. A receptionist who needs to locate employees can check the database for Outlook 2007 schedules, which can serve as an in/out board. Anyone who needs to plan a meeting can create and save a list of invitees to streamline the process. Scheduling is simplified because you can view free/busy information for all invitees in a single place.

As this section explains, you can use the Outlook 2007 group scheduling feature in three ways: by using your organization's internal Exchange Server database, by using your own free/busy server (or a third-party server), or by using the Microsoft Office Online service. You can use any of these in combination as needed.

Creating a Group Schedule

To see how the group scheduling feature can work in your organization, open the Outlook 2007 Calendar folder. Choose Actions, View Group Schedules to display the Group Schedules dialog box, shown in Figure 36-10.

> **Note**
>
> To open an existing group schedule, select it in the Group Schedules dialog box shown in Figure 36-10, and click Open.

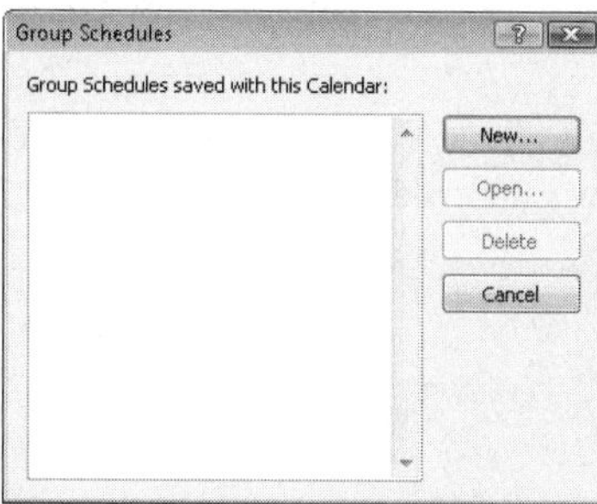

Figure 36-10. As you create custom group schedules, they're listed in the Group Schedules dialog box.

To create a new schedule, click New. In the Create New Group Schedule dialog box, shown in Figure 36-11, type a name for the new group schedule.

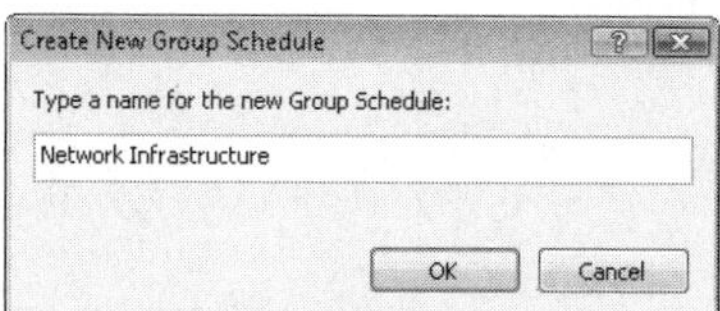

Figure 36-11. When naming schedules, use simple but descriptive names.

Use a name that is descriptive and easily identifiable (such as that shown in Figure 36-11). After you've entered a name, click OK. A window is displayed for the new group (and titled with the name of the new group), as shown in Figure 36-12.

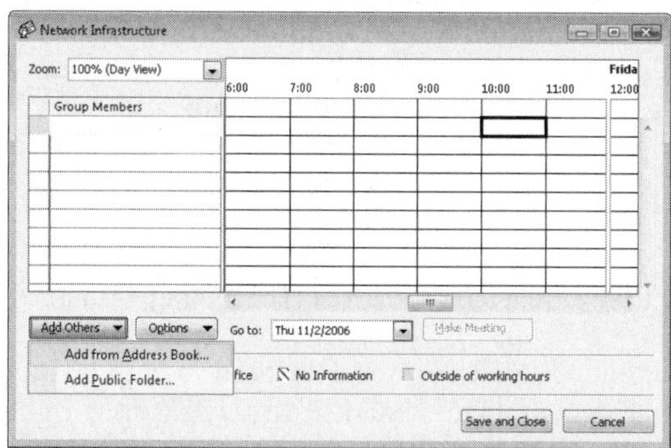

Figure 36-12. The group scheduling window is displayed for the Network Infrastructure group.

Next you must create a list of group members. In the group scheduling window, click Add Others. You can add members either from an address book or from a public folder. When you click Add From Address Book, Outlook 2007 opens the Select Members dialog box, shown in Figure 36-13.

Note

Alternatively, in the Group Members column (shown earlier in Figure 36-12), you can type the e-mail address of the person you want to add.

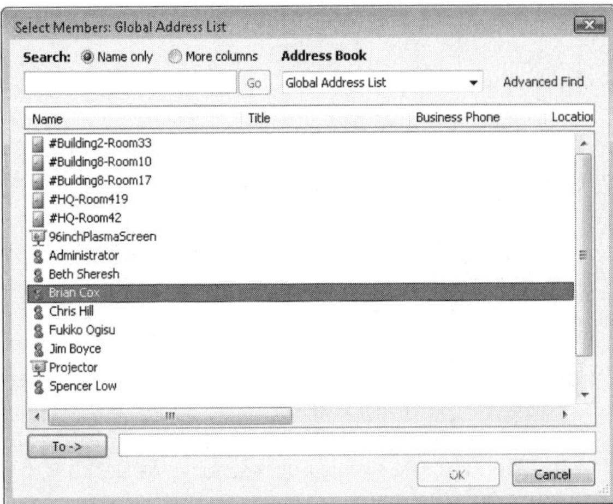

Figure 36-13. You can use the Select Members dialog box to add users to the group schedule.

The Select Members dialog box lists users who can be added to the group schedule list. You can use the Exchange Server Global Address List (GAL) or other address lists to which you have scheduling information access. (Additionally, any resources that need to be monitored, such as conference rooms or video equipment, can be added to this list.) Select each member you want to add to your new group, and then click To. You can also select a range of individuals or individual names by using the Shift and Ctrl keys. After you've added all the people who need to be included in this group, click OK to close the dialog box.

For information about how to schedule a resource, see "Scheduling Resources" in Chapter 21.

In the group scheduling window, you'll now see a list of the group members you selected, with each individual's schedule information displayed to the right, as shown in Figure 36-14. The legend at the bottom of the window indicates what the color coding represents.

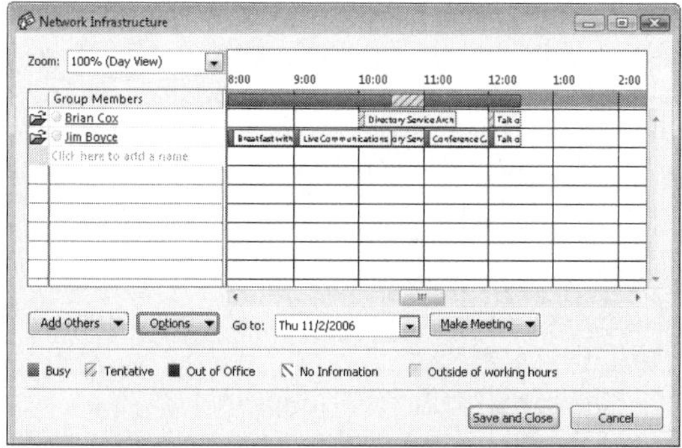

Figure 36-14. Scheduling information for each user in the group schedule is shown on a different line.

Each schedule shows blocks of time that are designated as follows:

- **Busy** The member is not available. You cannot schedule over this block of time. These appointments are shown in solid blue.
- **Tentative** The block of time is tentatively scheduled—perhaps an appointment for that time has not yet been confirmed or a meeting at that time is not a priority for the member. If you schedule over a tentative appointment, the member will need to decide which appointment to attend. Tentative appointments are colored with diagonal blue and white stripes.
- **Out Of Office** The member is on vacation, at a conference, or otherwise unavailable. These times are shown in purple.
- **Open** Open time for the group is indicated by gray areas. The member has no appointments or meetings on the calendar, and this block of time can be scheduled.
- **No Information** Exchange Server has no information about the member's schedule. Such blocks of time are shown as white areas with diagonal black lines (not included in Figure 36-14). This might indicate that the member does not use Outlook 2007, that the account is new, or that the account has problems.
- **Outside Of Working Hours** The times that are outside the set working hours of a member.

Note

If you have been given the appropriate permissions, you can view specific listings of meetings and appointments on a group member's schedule (as shown earlier in Figure 36-14), rather than seeing only color-coded blocks of time. Thus a manager or a receptionist could know not only that someone is out of the office but also where that person has gone. For privacy reasons, only users who are specifically given permission can view the details of other people's calendar entries. For information about giving other users permission to view your Calendar folder, see "Sharing Your Calendar" earlier in this chapter.

In Figure 36-14, the top bar of the group schedule is a composite of the individual schedules. This allows you to see at a glance which times are open for all group members. By scrolling left or right, you can check on previous or future times. You can also change views by using the Zoom drop-down list. In the example shown in Figure 36-15, a Week view of schedule information for the group is displayed.

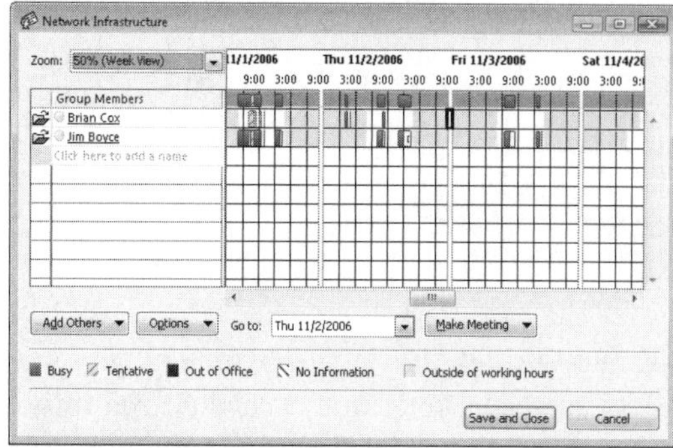

Figure 36-15. The Zoom drop-down list lets you select how much schedule information to display for the group.

Note that you can add members to the group even if they are not part of your organization. Just add them from your Contacts folder or whatever address book location in which their contact information is stored. As long as you have configured the appropriate free/busy search paths as explained earlier in this chapter, Outlook 2007 should be able to locate their free/busy information. However, keep in mind that only Exchange Server users' Tentative and Out Of Office times will appear as such in the group schedule. Members whose information is pulled from some other free/busy servers will have their Tentative and Out Of Office time shown simply as Busy.

Setting Up a Meeting or Sending Group E-Mail

You can use group schedules as a starting point for setting up a meeting or sending an e-mail message. Figure 36-16 shows some of the available options. When you choose one of these options, Outlook 2007 opens a new meeting request form or a message form, and you can create the meeting request or the message just as you normally would in Outlook 2007.

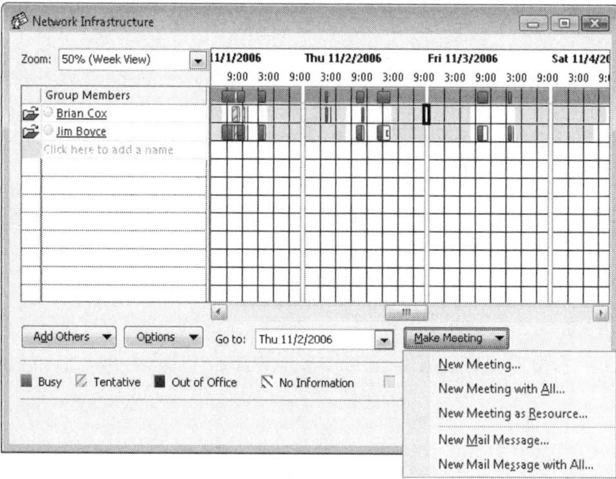

Figure 36-16. You can take a variety of actions based on the group schedule information.

Creating Your Own Free/Busy Server

If you don't have Exchange Server in your organization, you can still publish your free/busy information to enable others, whether inside or outside your organization, to view that information for scheduling purposes. As explained earlier in this chapter, Outlook 2007 can publish to FTP, HTTP, or file URLs. Which type you choose depends on the availability of such servers in your network, whether outside users need access to the free/busy information, and firewall and security issues for incoming access to the servers. For example, if your network does not allow FTP traffic through its firewalls but does allow HTTP, HTTP would be the choice for your free/busy server. However, keep in mind that publishing and searching are two different tasks that can use two different methods. You might have users internal to the network publish to a shared network folder, but outside users would access the information by HTTP. Naturally, this means that the target folder for publishing the free/busy information must also be a physical or virtual directory of the Web URL that outsiders use to view free/busy information. If your free/busy server must be located on the other side of a firewall from your users, FTP or HTTP would be a logical choice for publishing.

After you decide which access methods you need to provide for publishing and viewing free/busy information, it's a simple matter of setting up the appropriate type of server. There are no requirements specific to free/busy data for the server, so any FTP, HTTP, or file server will do the trick. Following are some points to keep in mind as you begin planning and deploying your free/busy server.

> **Note**
>
> You can use Microsoft Internet Information Services (IIS) running on Microsoft Windows 2000 Server or later to host free/busy FTP or HTTP virtual servers. If you need no more than a maximum of 10 concurrent connections, you can use Windows XP Professional or Windows Vista to host the site.

- **FTP** Set up the virtual server to allow both read and write permissions for the physical or virtual folder that will contain the free/busy data.

> **Note**
>
> For the best security, configure the server to require authentication and disallow anonymous access. Passing FTP authentication for free/busy information via Outlook 2007 isn't supported in Windows Vista, but you can do this in Windows XP. Keep in mind that you then need to provide authentication information to everyone who needs to access the server for free/busy information. Remember to configure NTFS file system permissions as needed to control access if the directory resides on an NTFS file system partition.

- **HTTP** The physical or virtual directory containing the free/busy data must be configured for both read and write permissions. If the directory resides on an NTFS file system partition, configure NTFS file system permissions as necessary to allow access to the directory as needed. You can disallow anonymous access if desired for greater security. Users who attempt to access the free/busy data are then required to provide a user name and password when publishing or searching.
- **File** Configure folder and file permissions as needed to allow users to access the shared directory. For better security, place the folder on an NTFS file system partition and use NTFS file system permissions to restrict access to the folder and its contents as needed.

Publishing Your Calendar as a Web Page

You can publish your calendar as an HTML file by clicking File and then choosing Save As Web Page. In the Save As Web Page dialog box, shown in Figure 36-17, you can specify the date range included, whether to include details, the background graphic, the calendar title, and the file name.

- **Duration** You can specify start and end dates to limit how much of your calendar is saved in the Web page.

- **Options** In this area, you can choose whether to include appointment details as well as select a background graphic for the Web page.
- **Save As** In this area, you can specify the title, path, and file name of the HTML file containing your Web page calendar. By default, the file name extension is set to .htm when saving your calendar.

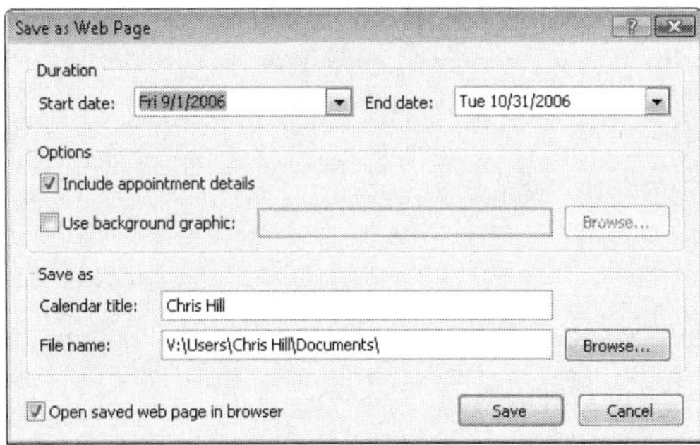

Figure 36-17. When saving your calendar as a Web page, you can specify calendar date range, details, background image, and file name.

CHAPTER 37
Integrating Outlook with Other Office Applications

Microsoft® Office Outlook® 2007 works well as a stand-alone application, but its real strength is realized when you integrate it with other 2007 Microsoft Office system applications. Most of us spend our days working in one or two main programs, such as a word processor or a database program, so most of our information is saved in files designed for those programs. For instance, you probably save letters and other correspondence in Microsoft Office Word 2007 files; save contact information in Office Outlook 2007; and save inventory, invoices, and other data in Microsoft Office Access 2007 or Microsoft Office Excel® 2007. With the Microsoft Office system, you can integrate it all, which enables you to choose the best tool for creating your information and the best tool for sharing or producing your data.

Some of the ways to integrate Outlook 2007 with other Microsoft Office system applications include the following:

- Using Outlook 2007 contacts for an Office Word 2007 mail merge
- Exporting Outlook 2007 contacts to Word 2007, Office Excel 2007, or Office Access 2007
- Importing contacts from Word 2007, Excel 2007, or Access 2007 into Outlook 2007
- Using Outlook 2007 notes in other Microsoft Office system applications

In this chapter, you'll learn about using Outlook 2007 and other Microsoft Office system applications to share information between applications. Instead of employing standard copy-and-paste or cut-and-paste techniques, you'll find out about ways to reuse your information in Outlook 2007 or another file format without retyping or re-creating the data.

Using Contacts for a Mail Merge in Word

The Outlook 2007 Contacts folder enables you to create contact entries to store information about a person, a group, or an organization. You can then use that contact data to create e-mail messages, set up meetings or appointments, or complete other tasks associated with a contact. Your contacts list can also be used as the data source to provide names, addresses, phone numbers, and other pertinent data to your mail merge documents.

You perform a *mail merge* in Word 2007 when you want to create multiple documents that are all based on the same letter or document but have different names, addresses, or other specific information (referred to as *merge data*). For instance, you might perform a mail merge operation when you want to do a mass mailing to your customers about a new product launch.

You begin by creating and saving a standard letter. Next, you place field codes where you want the recipient's address, the salutation, and other merge data to appear. *Field codes* are placeholders in documents where data will change. For instance, the name of the recipient should be a field code because it will change for each letter you send out.

You next create or assign a database to populate the field codes (that is, to insert the merge data). Word 2007 uses the database and contact information to create separate letters. You can then save these files or print each letter for your mass mailing.

> **Note**
>
> Before starting to set up a mail merge using your Outlook 2007 contact data, review your contact entries to make sure that the data is complete and current and that you don't have duplicate entries.

To perform a mail merge using Word 2007, follow these steps:

1. Start Word 2007.

> **Note**
>
> If you are using Outlook 2007 but are still using Office Word 2003, the initial steps of this procedure are different. To start a mail merge in Word 2003, click Tools, then Letters and Mailings, and then Mail Merge to open the task pane. From that point on (step 5), the wizard proceeds normally.

2. Click the Mailings tab on the Ribbon.

3. Click Start Mail Merge.

4. Click Step By Step Mail Merge Wizard (see Figure 37-1).

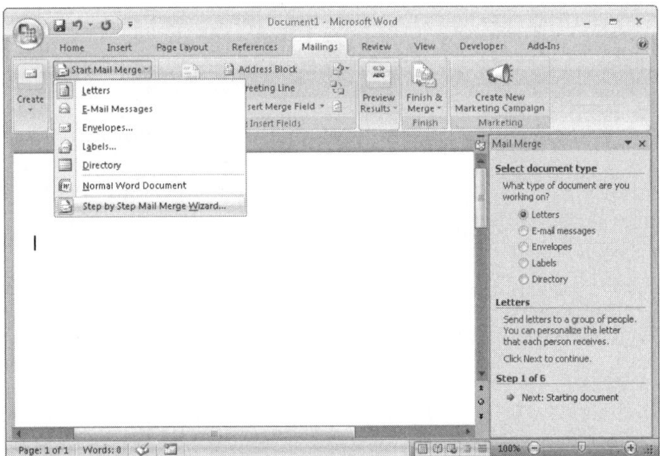

Figure 37-1. Start a mail merge by opening the Word 2007 Step By Step Mail Merge Wizard, which appears in the task pane on the right.

5. In the task pane, select the type of document to create, such as Letters, and then click Next: Starting Document at the bottom of the pane.

6. Select the document to use—for example, the current document. Click Next: Select Recipients.

7. Click Select from Outlook Contacts.

8. Select the Choose Contacts Folder option to open the Select Contacts dialog box (see Figure 37-2). (If you have configured Outlook 2007 to always prompt you for a profile, and Outlook 2007 is not open, you are asked to select a profile.)

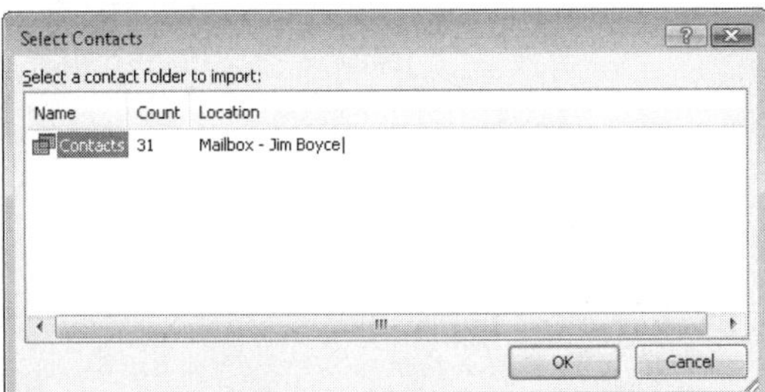

Figure 37-2. Select your Contacts folder here.

9. Select the folder that contains the contacts list you want to use, and then click OK to open the Mail Merge Recipients dialog box (see Figure 37-3).

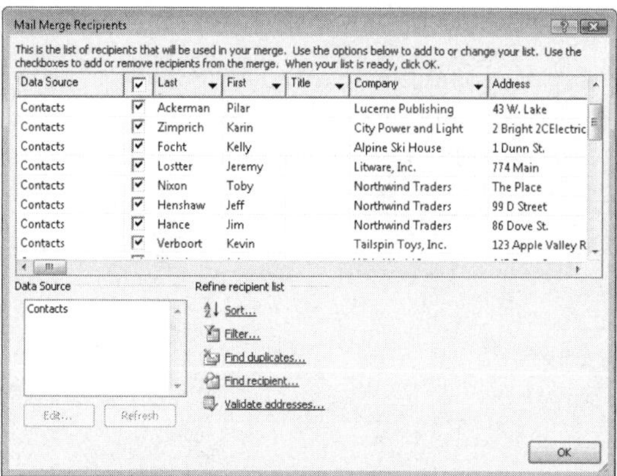

Figure 37-3. Select contacts to include in the mail merge from this dialog box.

10. Select the contacts you want to use to populate the mail merge document. All the contacts are selected by default. You can use the following methods to modify the selected list of contacts:
    - Select the check box in the Data Source column to choose all the contacts in the list (the default), or clear the check box to deselect all the contacts and then select individual contacts.
    - Click Sort to sort the contact list.
    - Click Filter to filter the list according to user-specified criteria.
    - Click Find Duplicates to locate duplicate names to clear them from the mail merge list.
    - Click Find Recipient to locate a specific name in your contact list.
    - Click Validate Addresses to use an add-in tool to verify that the addresses are valid.
    - Clear the check boxes next to the names of those you do not want to include in the mail merge.

Note

If you want to create a mailing list that is a subset of your Contacts folder, you can filter the contacts list with a custom view and then use the custom view to perform a mail merge from Outlook 2007.

See the "Performing a Mail Merge from Outlook" section later in this chapter.

11. Click OK.

12. Click Next: Write Your Letter.

13. Click Address Block to open the Insert Address Block dialog box (see Figure 37-4).

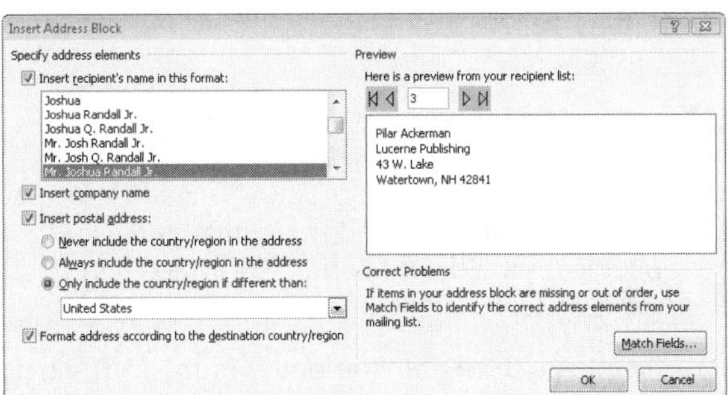

Figure 37-4. Set the address block field in this dialog box.

14. Using the options in this dialog box, specify the address fields and format you want to include in your letter. Click OK.

15. Click Greeting Line to insert and format a greeting line from your Contact information.

16. Click More Items to insert specific fields from your Contact information.

17. Write the body of your letter. When you finish, click Next: Preview Your Letters to see how the Outlook 2007 contact data looks in your letter. Figure 37-5 shows an example.

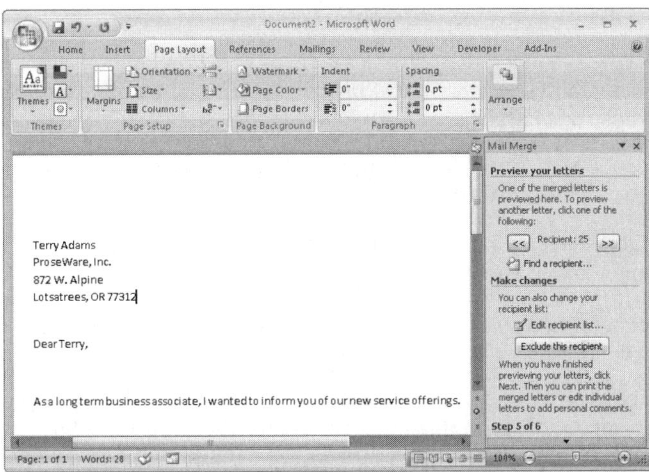

Figure 37-5. The address and salutation data in this letter came from an Outlook 2007 Contacts folder.

18. In the task pane, click Next: Complete The Merge to finish.

19. Finish editing your letter (or print it).

For detailed information about performing mail merges in Word 2007 and using other Word 2007 features, see *Microsoft Office Word 2007 Inside Out*, by Katherine Murray and Mary Millhollon (Microsoft Press, 2007).

Filtering Contacts in or out of the Merge

When you perform a mail merge from Word 2007, you can use selection criteria to determine which of the contacts are included in the mail merge set. For example, assume that you want to send a letter to all your contacts who have addresses in California and whose last names begin with the letter R.

In the Mail Merge Recipients dialog box (refer to Figure 37-3), each column includes a drop-down button next to the column heading. To specify selection criteria based on a particular column, click the drop-down button and choose one of the following commands:

- **All** Do not filter based on the selected column.
- **Blanks** Include only those contacts for which the selected field is blank. For example, choose this option under the E-Mail Address column to include all contacts who do not have an e-mail address in their contact record.
- **Nonblanks** Include only those contacts for which the selected field is not blank. For example, select this option under the Last field to include only those contacts whose Last Name field is not blank.
- **Advanced** Click this button to open the Filter And Sort dialog box, explained next.

If you click Advanced to open the Filter And Sort dialog box, shown in Figure 37-6, you can specify more-complex selection criteria. The following example includes those contacts whose last names start with R and whose State value equals California:

1. In the Mail Merge Recipients dialog box, click the drop-down button beside the Last field. Click Advanced.
2. From the first Field drop-down list, choose Last, choose Greater Than, and then enter **Q** in the Compare To field.
3. From the second Field drop-down list, choose Last, choose Less Than, and then enter **S** in the Compare To field.
4. Select State from the third Field drop-down list, choose Equal To from the Comparison drop-down list, and enter **CA** in the Compare To field. The dialog box should look similar to the one shown in Figure 37-6.

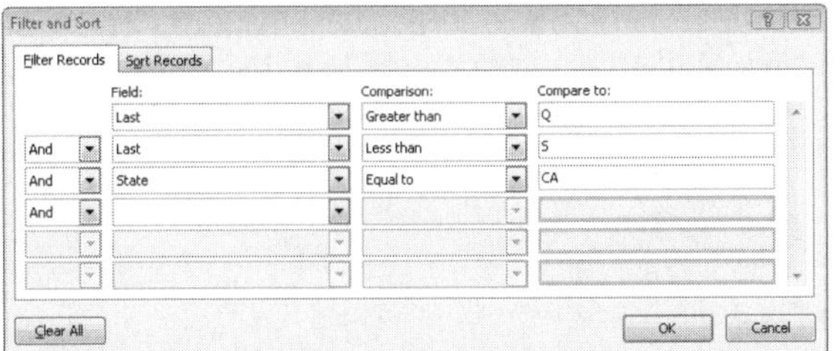

Figure 37-6. These settings select all contacts whose names start with R and whose addresses are in California.

5. Click OK to close the Filter And Sort dialog box. After a few moments, the Mail Merge Recipients list shows only those contacts whose last name begins with R and whose State value is listed as CA.

As you might have guessed from Figure 37-6, you can select OR instead of AND in the dialog box for a particular criterion. For example, you would use OR for the third criterion (step 4) to cause Outlook 2007 to include contacts in the mail merge if their names started with R or if they lived in California. A contact would also be included if both criteria were met.

Performing a Mail Merge from Outlook

As the previous sections illustrated, it's easy to perform a mail merge from Word 2007 and pull contact information from Outlook 2007. You can also filter the contacts to include only those that suit your needs.

You can also perform a mail merge from Outlook 2007. Starting from Outlook 2007 gives you a few advantages:

- **More control over contacts to be included** You can merge all the contacts in the current view of the Contacts folder or merge only those contacts you have selected in the folder.
- **Control over which fields to include** You can include all contact fields or only those fields that are visible in the current folder view.
- **Capability to save the contacts for later use** Outlook 2007 gives you the option of saving the contacts to a Word 2007 document to use for future reference or for future mail merges from Word 2007.

To begin a mail merge from Outlook 2007, select Contacts in the Navigation Pane, click Tools, and then click Mail Merge to open the Mail Merge Contacts dialog box. As Figure 37-7 illustrates, Outlook 2007 offers two options to control which contacts are included in the merge:

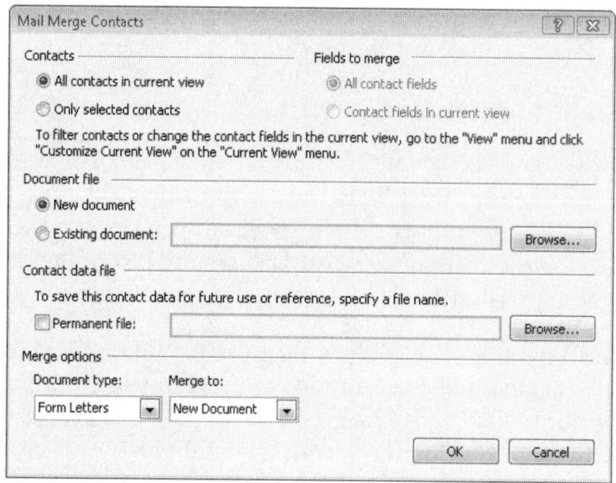

Figure 37-7. Use the Mail Merge Contacts dialog box to choose which contacts and fields to include in the merge.

- **All Contacts In Current View** Use this option to include all the contacts in the view, understanding that *all the contacts in the view* does not necessarily equate to *all contacts*. If you create a filtered view of the folder that excludes some of the contacts, those contacts will be excluded from the merge as well.
- **Only Selected Contacts** Choose this option to include only those contacts that you selected in the Contacts folder prior to choosing Tools, Mail Merge. To selectively include contacts, in the Contacts folder hold down the **Ctrl** key while clicking to select individual contacts, or press **Shift+Click** to select a range of contacts.

In addition to specifying which contacts are included, you can control which fields are included, excluding those you don't need. The following two options determine which fields are included:

- **All Contact Fields** Choose this option to include all the contact fields.
- **Contact Fields In Current View** Choose this option to include only the fields displayed in the current view. You can customize the view prior to choosing Tools, Mail Merge to filter in only specific fields.

Creating custom views to filter items in a folder is covered in detail in "Creating and Using Custom Views" in Chapter 27.

You can merge the contacts to a new document if you want or choose an existing document to use a Word 2007 document you have already created.

The merged contact information can be saved for later or repeated by checking Permanent File under Data Contact File and specifying a file name.

You can choose from a variety of document types for your merged information: form letters, mailing labels, envelopes, and catalogs. The output of the mail merge can be saved as a Word 2007 document, sent directly to a printer, or sent as e-mail to the contacts you have selected for the merge.

After you select your options in the Mail Merge Contacts dialog box and click OK, Outlook 2007 opens Word 2007, prepopulating the mail merge contact list and starting the document type you have specified. The rest of the process depends on the type of document you have selected.

- **Form letters or catalogs** To complete the mail merge for a form letter or catalog, choose the Mailings tab, click Start Mail Merge, and select the Step By Step Mail Merge Wizard. The wizard opens at step 3, in which you choose the contacts to include in the letter. Because you have already generated a contact list, the Use An Existing List option is already selected for you. You can then click Edit Recipient List to verify or fine-tune the list, or you can click Next: Write Your Letter to move to the next step.
- **Mailing labels or envelopes** Select options in the Mail Merge Helper dialog box to complete the mail merge and create mailing labels or envelopes. You can change the type of document you are creating or click Setup to choose a specific type of mailing label or envelope size. The data source is already selected, but you can change or edit the data source.

See the section "Using Contacts for a Mail Merge in Word" earlier in this chapter for detailed instructions on using the Mail Merge Wizard in Word 2007.

Exporting Contacts to Access

Another way to use Outlook 2007 contact information is to export the data to Access 2007, which is handy if you want to use contact data in database tables or reports. You could spend your time opening individual contact entries in Outlook 2007, copying information from the contact form, and then pasting the information into Access 2007 where you want it. However, Outlook 2007 makes the process much simpler. All you have to do is use the Import And Export Wizard and select Microsoft Access 2007 as the file to export to.

Here's how to export contact information to Access 2007:

1. In Outlook 2007, click File and then Import And Export to open the Import And Export Wizard.
2. Select Export To A File and then click Next.
3. On the wizard page shown in Figure 37-8, select Microsoft Access 97-2003 and then click Next.

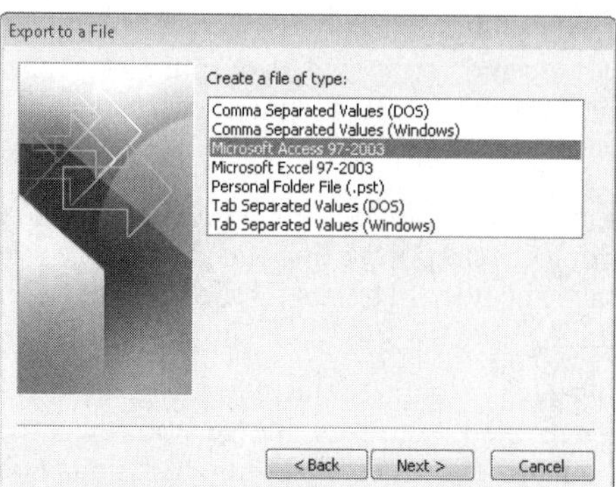

Figure 37-8. The Import And Export Wizard enables you to export to an Access 2007 file.

4. Select the folder from which to export data. In this case, select the Contacts folder (see Figure 37-9) or another folder that includes Outlook 2007 contact information. Click Next.

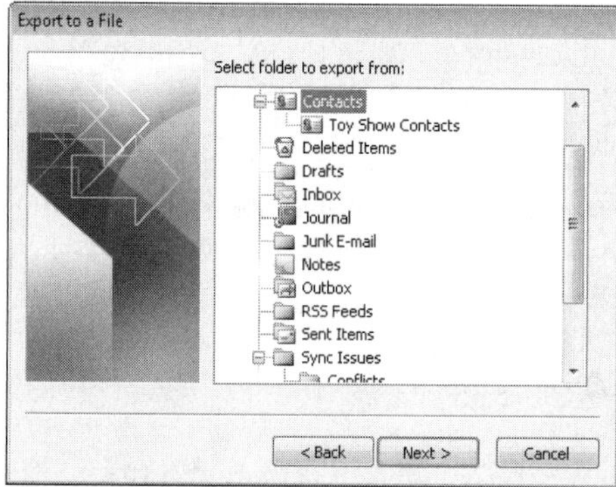

Figure 37-9. Select the folder from which you want to export.

5. Specify the folder and type a name for the export file. You can click Browse to browse to a folder and then click OK to select that folder. When you do this, the file is given an MDB extension to denote an Access 2007 database file. Click Next.

6. In the Export To A File dialog box, click Map Custom Fields. In this dialog box, you can verify that the Contacts fields are properly mapped to the Access database fields, add or remove field items, or modify the way the Outlook 2007 contacts list is saved in the new exported file (see Figure 37-10). When you finish working with field mapping, click OK.

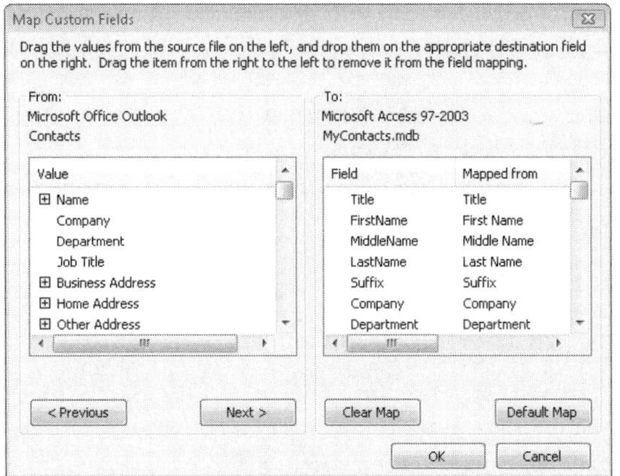

Figure 37-10. Modify field mappings in this dialog box.

7. Click Finish. Outlook 2007 exports the data from the Contacts folder and saves it in the specified file. You can now switch to Access 2007 and open the exported data as a table in that application.

For detailed information on working with Access 2007, see *Microsoft Office Access 2007 Inside Out*, by John L. Viescas and Jeff Conrad (Microsoft Press, 2007).

Importing Contacts from Access

Suppose that you've collected and stored contacts in an Access 2007 database, but you now want to use them in Outlook 2007. You can simply import the data to Outlook 2007 by using the Import And Export Wizard. During the import process, Outlook 2007 can see whether duplicate entries are being added to your contacts list and can then create, ignore, or replace them.

TROUBLESHOOTING

After replacing a duplicate entry in Outlook 2007, you see that you've lost data

Before you choose to allow Outlook 2007 to replace duplicate entries when importing a file, you should make sure that the items really are duplicates. Entries might erroneously appear to be duplicates if, for example, you have two contacts whose names are the same. For that reason, you might want to allow Outlook 2007 to create duplicate entries and then, after the import process is finished, go into the Outlook 2007 Contacts folder and manually remove any true duplicates.

Before you begin, make sure that the database you want to import is closed in Access 2007. If it isn't closed, you'll receive an error message when Outlook 2007 tries to find the data source.

Then follow these steps to import the data:

1. Switch to Outlook 2007 and choose File, Import And Export to open the Import And Export Wizard.
2. Select Import From Another Program Or File and then click Next.
3. Select Microsoft Access 97-2003 and click Next.
4. In the File To Import text box (see Figure 37-11), specify the Access 2007 file (MDB) that you want to import.

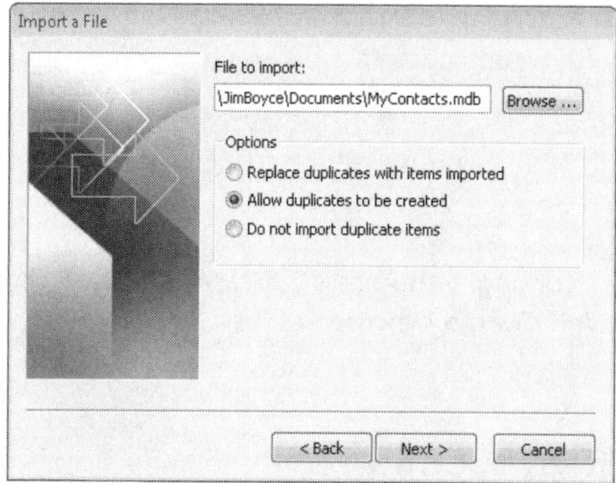

Figure 37-11. Specify the Access 2007 file to import and how Outlook 2007 should handle duplicates during the import process.

5. Specify how you want Outlook 2007 to handle duplicates, and then click Next.
6. Select the destination folder in which you want the imported data to be placed, such as the Contacts folder, and then click Next.
7. In the Import A File dialog box, click Map Custom Fields. In this dialog box, you can add or remove field items, modifying the way the Outlook 2007 contacts list is saved in the new imported file. When you finish reviewing or modifying the field mapping, click OK.
8. Click Finish to start the import process.

Exporting Contacts to Excel

You might also find it useful to export Outlook 2007 contact information to Excel 2007 worksheets. In Excel 2007, you can include the data in a spreadsheet of names and addresses for a contact management sheet, sort contact data in various ways, or perform other spreadsheet tasks with the data. Again, you simply use the Import And Export Wizard to create this Excel 2007 file.

Here's how to export contact information to Excel 2007:

1. In Outlook 2007, choose File, Import And Export to open the Import And Export Wizard.
2. Select Export To A File, and then click Next.
3. Select Microsoft Excel 97-2003, and then click Next.
4. Select the folder from which to export data. In this case, select the Contacts folder or another folder that includes Outlook 2007 contact information. Click Next.
5. Specify the folder and type a name for the export file. You can click Browse to browse to a folder, and then click OK to select that folder. When you do this, the file is given an XLS file extension to denote an Excel 2007 worksheet file. Click Next.
6. In the Export To A File dialog box, click Map Custom Fields. In this dialog box, you can add or remove field items, modifying the way the Outlook 2007 contacts list is saved in the new exported file. Click OK when you finish.
7. Click Finish. Outlook 2007 exports the data from the Contacts folder and saves it in the specified file.

> **Note**
>
> Another reason to export contact information is that you might need to share this data with others who do not use Outlook 2007 but do use Excel. Simply export the data to an Excel worksheet, open the worksheet, and modify or edit any column information. Then save the file and send it to the other users.

For detailed information on working with Excel 2007, see *Microsoft Office Excel 2007 Inside Out*, by Mark Dodge and Craig Stinson (Microsoft Press, 2007).

Importing Contacts from Excel

You import contact information from an Excel 2007 worksheet the same way you import from an Access 2007 database. Suppose that your coworker wants to send you contact information but is not running Outlook 2007. Ask the coworker to save the data in an Excel 2007 worksheet and send that file to you. You can then use the Import And Export Wizard to import the new contact information into Outlook 2007.

Before you begin the process, make sure that the worksheet you want to import is closed in Excel 2007. If it isn't closed, you'll receive an error message when Outlook 2007 tries to find the data source.

Then follow these steps to import the data:

1. Switch to Outlook 2007. Click File and then Import And Export to open the Import And Export Wizard.
2. Select Import From Another Program Or File, and then click Next.
3. Select Microsoft Excel 97-2003, and then click Next.
4. In the File To Import text box, type the name of the file or browse to the Excel 2007 file (XLS) that you want to import.
5. Specify how you want Outlook 2007 to handle duplicates, and then click Next.
6. Select the destination folder in which you want the imported data to be placed, such as the Contacts folder, and then click Next.
7. In the Import A File dialog box, click Map Custom Fields. In this dialog box, you can add or remove field items, modifying the way in which the imported items are saved in your Contacts list. When you finish verifying or modifying your field mappings, click OK.
8. Click Finish to start the import process. You might want to review your contacts to ensure that the data was imported the way you need it. If it wasn't, modify it as necessary in Outlook 2007.

Exporting Tasks to Office Applications

You can use the Import And Export Wizard to export other Outlook 2007 items. For example, you might want to export tasks to a Word 2007 or Excel 2007 file to view past or future assignments in a table format that can be easily edited or in a spreadsheet. You can then use this data in business correspondence, historical documents (such as a travel itinerary), event planning, work assignments, or presentations.

Follow these steps to export tasks to an Excel 2007 file:

1. In Outlook 2007, choose Click File, Import And Export to open the Import And Export Wizard.
2. Select Export To A File, and then click Next.
3. Select Microsoft Excel 97-2003, and then click Next.
4. Select the folder from which to export data. In this case, choose the Tasks folder or another folder that includes Outlook 2007 tasks. Click Next.
5. Specify the folder and type a name for the export file. You can click Browse to browse to a folder and then click OK to select that folder. When you do this, the file is given an XLS file extension to denote an Excel 2007 worksheet file. Click Next.

6. In the Export To A File dialog box, click Map Custom Fields. In this dialog box, you can add or remove field items, modifying the way Outlook 2007 task items are saved in the new imported file. Click OK when you finish.

7. Click Finish to start the export process and open the Set Date Range dialog box (see Figure 37-12).

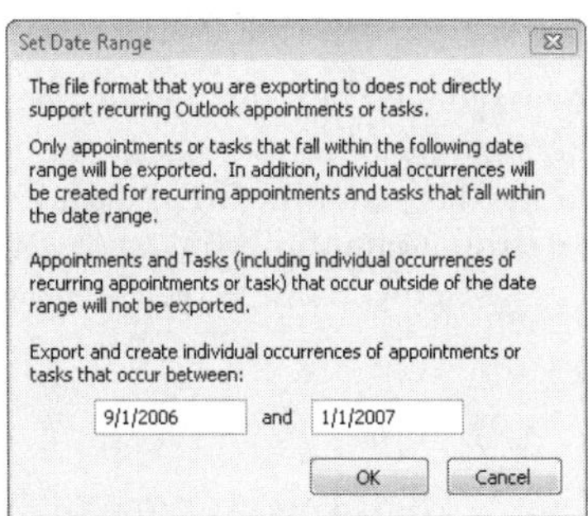

Figure 37-12. You might need to change the date range to include all the tasks you want to export.

8. Specify the date range for exported tasks. Some types of tasks are not directly exported or included, such as recurring tasks with recurrences that fall outside the date range you set. Modify the date range as necessary to include the tasks you want exported.

9. Click OK to start the export process. When it finishes, you can open the worksheet to review your tasks in Excel 2007.

Using Notes in Other Applications

Outlook 2007 notes are great when you need to create electronic "sticky" notes as a reminder of things to do in a document or project or of messages to send out. However, you are limited in how you can store information in notes and how you can use that information in other documents.

One way to reuse the information you placed in notes is to export the Notes folder and use that file in another application. Suppose that you have several notes that you want to archive and then remove from the Notes folder. Simply export the Notes folder to a tab-separated file and open the file in Word 2007, creating a document that contains the information.

Here's how to export the file:

1. In Outlook 2007, click File and then Import And Export to open the Import And Export Wizard.

2. Select Export To A File, and then click Next.

3. Select Tab-Separated Values (Windows), and then click Next.

4. Select the folder from which to export data. In this case, select the Notes folder or another folder that includes Outlook 2007 notes. Click Next.

5. Specify the folder and type a name for the export file. You can click Browse to browse to a folder and then click OK to select that folder. When you do this, the file is given a TXT extension to denote a text file (which you can open in Word 2007). Click Next.

6. In the Export To A File dialog box, click Map Custom Fields. In this dialog box, you can add or remove field items, modifying the way Outlook 2007 note items are saved in the new imported file. For example, you might want to remove the Note Color field (just drag and drop it out of the To: list of fields) because this field exports as a numeric value. When you finish verifying or modifying the field mappings, click OK.

7. Click Finish to begin the export process.

Open the file in Word 2007 to see how the Notes file is displayed. In the example shown in Figure 37-13, the tab-separated items are converted from text to a table using the Word 2007 table feature.

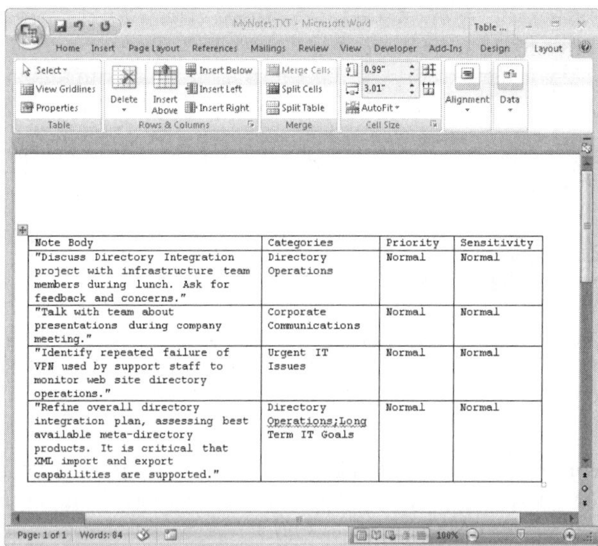

Figure 37-13. Your notes can be viewed in other Microsoft Office system applications, such as Word 2007.

CHAPTER 38

Integrating Microsoft Outlook and Microsoft Project

Software programs are designed to handle specific tasks or sets of tasks. For instance, Microsoft® Office Outlook® 2007 provides tools to perform several tasks, including creating and managing e-mail, setting up to-do lists, and organizing your contacts. You can even use Office Outlook 2007 to assign tasks, manage meetings, and keep track of events. When you need to manage a project, however, you might want to look into a project management program such as Microsoft Office Project 2007.

This chapter focuses on integrating Outlook 2007 and Office Project 2007. For instance, you'll learn how to set up a resource list in Project 2007 using Outlook 2007 contacts. In addition, you can use the Outlook 2007 reminder feature to send yourself alerts about tasks during a project's lifetime.

Before you learn how to integrate Outlook 2007 and Project 2007, you first need to look at what Project 2007 is and what you can do with it as a stand-alone program.

Overview of Microsoft Project

Project 2007 is an electronic project management tool. You can use Project 2007 to perform the following tasks:

- Create project plans
- Track projects from start to finish
- Capture important milestones during a project
- Use Budget Tracking to define a budget so project managers can allocate funds and track costs
- Send announcements to team contacts about the status of a project
- Use the Visual Report feature to create drill-down charts, graphs, and diagrams using Microsoft Office Excel® 2007 and Microsoft Office Visio® 2007

- Point out potential and actual problems during the course of a project
- Schedule meetings with important people

These are just a few examples of how Project 2007 makes it easy to view and manage your projects. Figure 38-1 shows one of the ways Project 2007 displays information related to your projects.

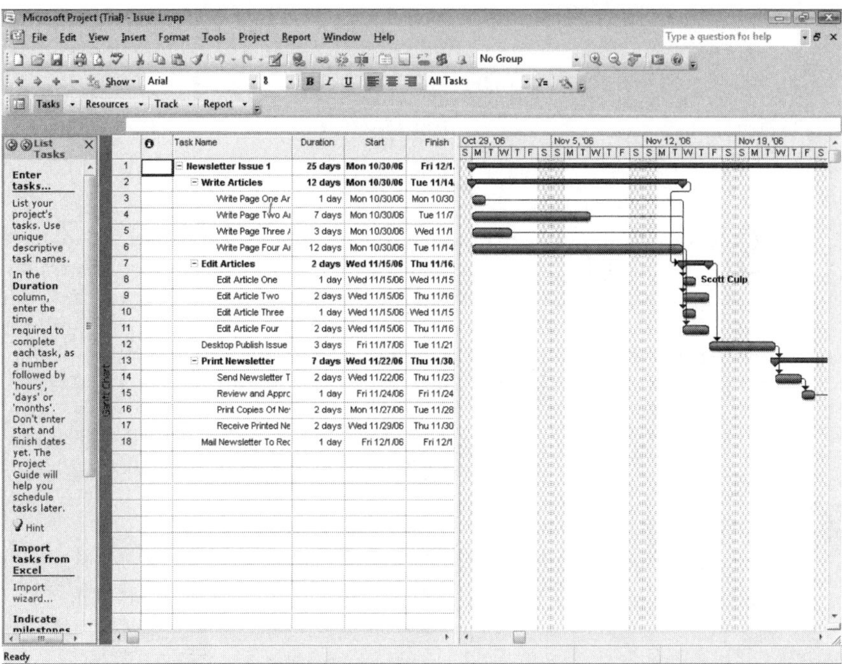

Figure 38-1. Use Project 2007 to organize, manage, and track projects for you, your team, or your entire organization.

Now let's look at some basic project management considerations as well as Project 2007 tasks and how to perform them.

Project Management Basics

Almost everyone–worker, homeowner, or organizational leader–works on some type of project. Some common projects include the following:

- Creating marketing material for an upcoming product launch
- Writing and publishing a book or newsletter
- Planning fundraising activities
- Renovating a room in your home
- Starting a new business

- Launching a Web site
- Managing employee training

Depending on the project you manage, you might need to keep track of a few or several hundred details. For example, some projects are small enough that you need to keep track of only two or three employees, a few material resources (such as a load of gravel or a small shipment of computers), and a start and finish date. For larger projects, you might need to monitor not only your own employees but also the schedules of related firms' employees and project budgets; you also might include milestones to ensure that your schedule stays on track.

Some projects don't require a robust software tool such as Project 2007. For instance, if you're put in charge of only one small project that can be finished in less than a day, you can probably track the project more efficiently with a scratch pad and pen. You shouldn't waste time starting Project 2007, entering new project criteria, mapping a Gantt chart, and then starting the project. Simply get the resources you need and finish the project as quickly as you can.

Suppose that you are assigned multiple small projects, a few medium-sized ones, and a large project that must all be completed over several months, however. A project management tool such as Project 2007 can help ensure that you remember the details and maintain the schedule.

Note

Business Contact Manager also functions as a program manager and might provide the basic tasks and reminders needed for your project management needs.

Keeping a Project in Balance

As a project gets under way (and while it's in progress), you must strive to keep three things in balance: scope, schedule, and resources.

A project's *scope* is the set of tasks required to finish the project. If you are remodeling a bathroom in your home or office, for example, you must finish specific tasks before your bathroom is considered complete. Some of these tasks might include designing a new floor plan, ordering bathtub and sink fixtures, setting up a plumbing contractor, and demolishing the existing bathroom. All these tasks make up the scope of the project.

Your project's *schedule* is the time required to complete the project's tasks and the order of those tasks. The schedule includes the obvious: projected start and finish dates. However, you must also consider scheduling other resource items, such as dates for the plumbing and heating personnel, the tile contractor, the electrician, and the inspector. Schedules should also include proposed receipt dates of any materials you need, such as custom faucet fixtures, lighting tracks, and a water filtration unit.

Finally, the *resources* for a project include the materials, equipment, and people necessary to complete the project. In many instances, you include not only contact information but also wage and benefit information for the people involved. (Benefits can include time off or holidays you must schedule around.) Likewise, materials and equipment connected with your project have related costs, operating expenses, and scheduling dynamics you must consider.

Another resource is where the project will take place. You must know the availability of the space throughout the project. In our example, the project's location is a bathroom, so you might not want to plan a renovation project to start when you are also hosting a large party. Similarly, if a project involves training employees, you don't want to schedule the training sessions to coincide with vacations or company-related events when an employee or group of employees will be out of town.

Microsoft Project's Four Project Management Steps

Project 2007 helps you with the four main project management steps:

- Defining the project
- Creating the project plan
- Tracking the project
- Finishing the project

When you define the project, you outline the goals, define the scope, determine the necessary resources, and estimate how much time is needed to complete the project. You should also add milestones and internal deadlines, such as the date you want a wall demolished.

The project plan is the blueprint for your project. In short, the plan specifies exactly what needs to be accomplished, who will complete each task, how much time is estimated for each task, which tasks are dependent on others to finish before they can start, and any constraints you want applied to a task or a schedule. An example of a task constraint, or dependency, is that you might need to hire an electrician to rough in electrical outlets before your drywall contractor puts up your walls. Completing the drywall is dependent on the completion of the electrical work. Constraints might also include starting a task on a specific date (such as not on a weekend or holiday because of higher contracting costs).

The strength of Project 2007 is that it can track your project's history from start to finish as long as you enter correct data and keep the information up to date. Project 2007 can compare the actual time to complete a task with the time you estimated (and budgeted for). It also can analyze resource requirements to determine whether a resource is overloaded or whether you have scheduled a resource to complete more than one task at the same time. (Your plumber can work on only one part of the bathroom at a time, for instance.) You can reformulate the plan to include additional resources, extend the project time, or redefine the scope of the project.

Even when a project is complete, your work isn't finished. For example, you might want to analyze the project so you can figure out how to manage a future project. Or you might have to gather project costs to review them with your manager or spouse. You might want to archive the project file for future reference.

Creating a Simple Project

To help you understand how Project 2007 works, this section shows you how to create a simple project plan for publishing a departmental newsletter.

Follow these steps to create the project:

1. Start Project 2007.
2. Choose File, Close to close the blank project.
3. Choose File, New.
4. In the New Project pane, click the Blank Project link (see Figure 38-2). A blank project window opens, and project tasks are shown in the Tasks pane. If the Tasks pane does not appear, choose View, Toolbars, Task Pane.

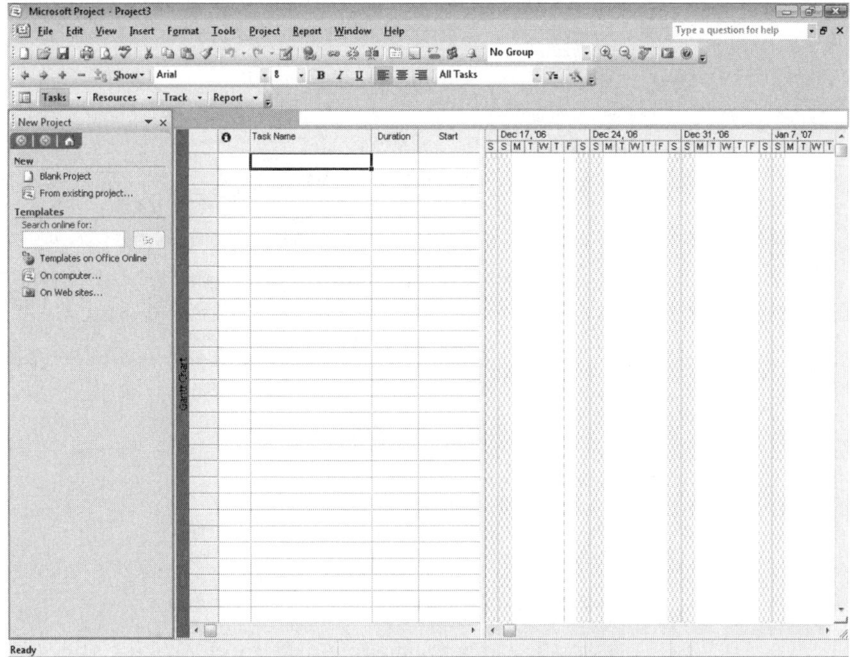

Figure 38-2. Start a new project by clicking the Blank Project link.

5. Click the Define The Project link; then enter a start or finish date. In this example, choose to start the project today.
6. Click Continue To Step 2.
7. Specify whether you want to use the new Microsoft Project Server 2007 to let you collaborate with others on your project. For now, click No.
8. Click Continue To Step 3.
9. Click Save And Finish to begin adding details about your project.

The Tasks pane shows several links to wizards that will walk you through adding details to your project. We'll walk you through two more to help get your project going.

To set up working times for your project, do the following:

1. Click the Define The Project's General Working Hours link in the Tasks pane (see Figure 38-3).

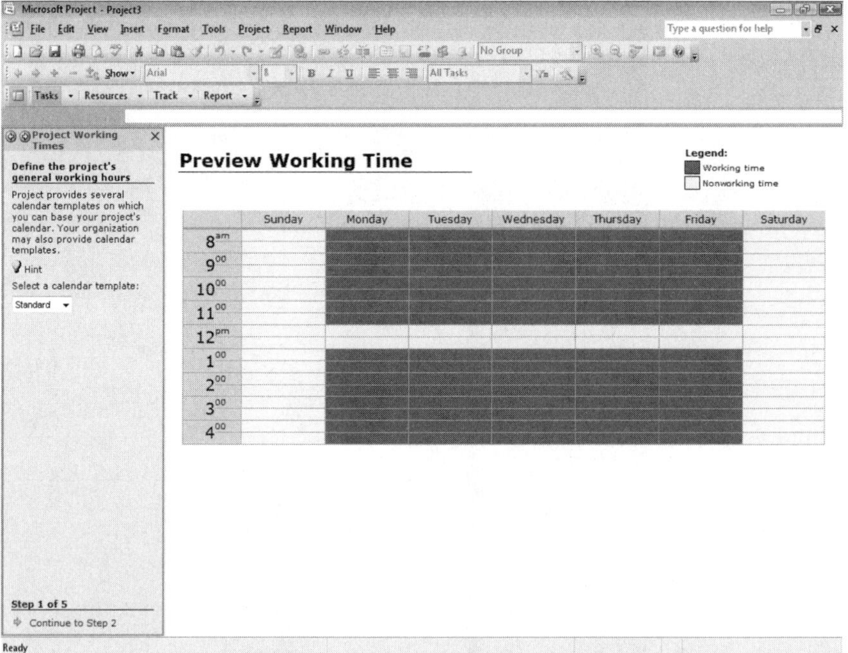

Figure 38-3. Set working times for your project here.

2. Select a calendar template from the Project Working Times drop-down list. Choose Standard, 24 Hours, or Night Shift to specify the type of hours your project will display. Select Standard for now.

3. Click Continue To Step 2.
4. In the Define The Work Week page, select the days of the week for your project.
5. Click I Want To Adjust The Working Hours Shown For One Or More Days Of The Week to change the times that are displayed as working and nonworking times. You can change one day at a time; you can also select new times and then click Apply To All Days to have your changes reflected on all days.
6. Click Continue To Step 3.
7. Click Change Working Time to set the holidays and days off you want to recognize during your project (see Figure 38-4).

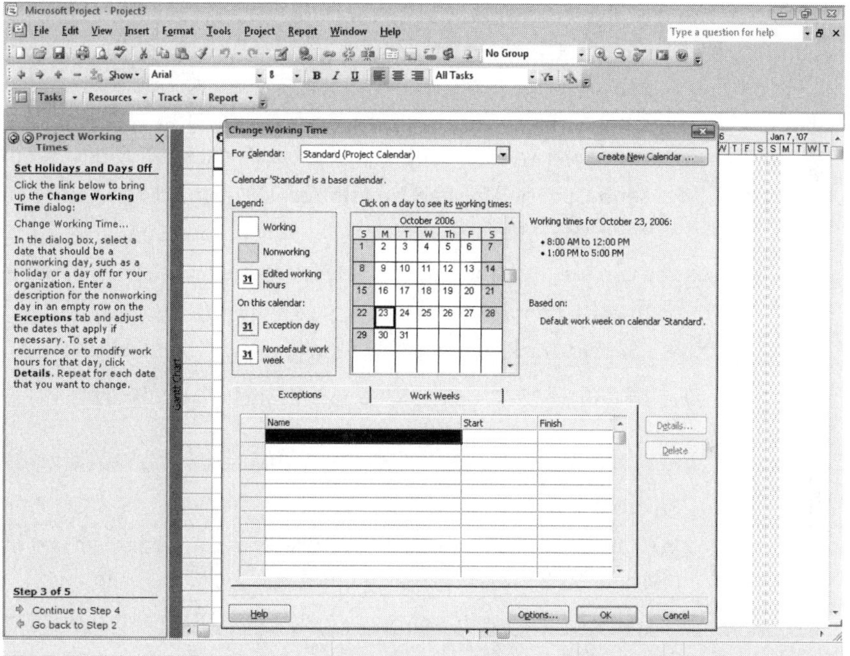

Figure 38-4. If you want to recognize holidays and days off during your project, use the Change Working Time dialog box.

8. Click OK when you finish setting up these special times.
9. Click Continue To Step 4.
10. Specify the default time units. Project 2007 starts you off by using the standard 8-hour days, 40-hour weeks, and 20-day months. Adjust these numbers as needed for your project.

11. Click Continue To Step 5.
12. Click Save And Finish to complete the Project Working Times task.
13. Choose File, Save to save the project. Enter the project name **Issue 1** and click Save.

Now you're ready to enter your task list. The task list for this example includes the following:

- **Write Each Article** In this four-page newsletter, each page will include one article named Page One Article, Page Two Article, and so on.
- **Create The Author List** Each article will have a separate author.
- **Define The Editor And Editor Dates** The newsletter will be edited by one editor.
- **Submit Articles To The Desktop Publisher** The newsletter will be desktop published by one person.
- **Submit The Newsletter To The Printer** The edited and desktop-published newsletter will be shipped to a printer on a specific date for printing.
- **Send Out The Finished Newsletter** The printed newsletter will be mailed to subscribers by a specific date.

As you can see from the list, a simple four-page newsletter can include many tasks, dates, and resources.

Now add these tasks to your new project using Gantt Chart view:

1. In Project 2007, on the View menu, click Gantt Chart.

> **Note**
>
> In Gantt Chart view, you can view your tasks as you enter them and see information that Project 2007 provides about the task.

2. In the Task Name box, type a task name, such as **Newsletter Issue 1**. Press Enter.
3. Continue adding tasks and durations. (If you're following along with the example, see Table 38-1 for the list of tasks and their durations.)
4. Order the tasks in the outline by indenting them, as shown in Table 38-1. (For instance, indent the Write Page One Article task two times.) To indent a task, click the Indent button on the Formatting toolbar.
5. Add predecessors, as indicated in Table 38-1. To do this, double-click a task and click the Predecessor tab. Click the Task Name column and select the predecessor in the drop-down list. Click OK to apply the change.

> **Note**
>
> In Project 2007, a *predecessor task* is a task that must start or finish before another task can begin. For example, before an article can be edited, it first must be written, so all editing tasks have a predecessor task of writing. You can specify predecessor tasks using the Predecessors tab of the Summary Task Information dialog box.

6. Check to be sure that your entries match those shown in Figure 38-5.
7. Choose File, Save to save the project.

Table 38-1 Tasks for Newsletter Issue 1

Task Name	Duration	Indents	Predecessor
Newsletter Issue 1	22 days	None	N/A
Write Articles	11 days	One	N/A
Write Page One Article	1 day	Two	N/A
Write Page Two Article	7 days	Two	N/A
Write Page Three Article	3 days	Two	N/A
Write Page Four Article	9 days	Two	N/A
Edit Articles	10 days	One	Write Articles
Edit Article One	1 day	Two	Write Page One Article
Edit Article Two	2 days	Two	Write Page Two Article
Edit Article Three	1 day	Two	Write Page Three Article
Edit Article Four	2 days	Two	Write Page Four Article
Desktop Publish Issue 1	3 days	One	Edit Articles
Print Newsletter	8 days	One	Desktop Publish Issue 1
Send Newsletter To Printer	2 days	Two	Desktop Publish Issue 1
Review And Approve Test Prints	1 day	Two	Send Newsletter To Printer
Print Copies Of Newsletter	2 days	Two	Review And Approve Test Prints
Receive Printed Newsletters	2 days	Two	Print Copies Of Newsletter
Mail Newsletter To Recipients	1 day	One	Receive Printed Newsletters

After you create your project plan, you can edit it for real data. For instance, suppose that the author of the article on page 4 needs an extra three days to complete it. Because everything that follows the authoring stage—editing, page layout, printing, and mailing—is dependent on the article being written, you must adjust your plan accordingly. To do this, change the duration date from 9 days to 12 days by clicking the Duration item in the Write Page Four Article row, and then use the spinner control to increase the duration. (You also can type the value and then press Enter.) Notice how this affects everything after the authoring stage.

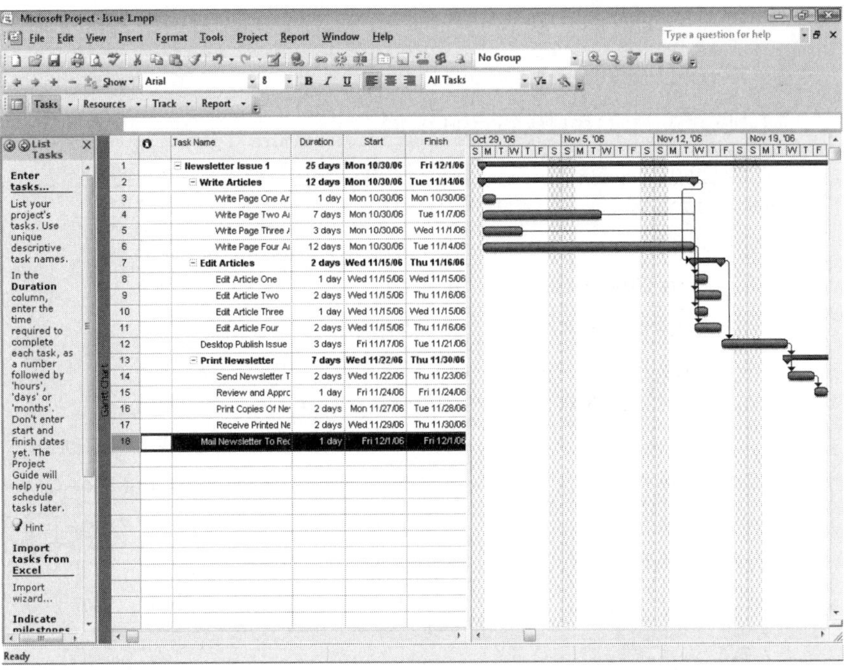

Figure 38-5. You can create a simple project plan, shown here in Project 2007.

This example, simple as it is, shows you how Project 2007 can manage and keep track of your projects. The next section looks at how you can integrate Project 2007 and Outlook 2007.

For more information on using Project 2007, visit the Microsoft Office Project Web site at *www.microsoft.com/office/project/.*

TROUBLESHOOTING

You're having trouble viewing and printing tasks and dependencies for projects

If you're having difficulties working with your projects, part of the problem might be that the project has grown too large, which can happen pretty easily. In this section, you learned how to create a simple project. This small project could easily grow into a large project if you expanded it to include marketing and advertisement tasks. In general, as you're creating your projects, you might want to consider breaking large tasks into smaller multiple tasks to make them more manageable. To do this, follow these steps:

1. On the View menu, choose Gantt Chart.
2. Hold down Ctrl and click the row heading of each task you want to break out as a new project.
3. Right-click and choose Cut Task.
4. Choose File, New.
5. Click Blank Project to display a blank project.
6. Choose Edit, Paste to paste the tasks into the new project.
7. Click File, Save and type a file name for the new project. Click Save.

Integrating Your Outlook Calendar

With the Outlook 2007 calendar, you can set up, manage, view, and set reminders for important meeting dates, events, and other activities. When you're working in Project 2007, you can set Outlook reminders to alert you when tasks need to start or finish.

To set an alert with an Outlook 2007 reminder, do the following:

1. In Project 2007, on the View menu, click Gantt Chart.
2. Select the task or tasks for which you want to set up reminders. Hold down the Ctrl key to select multiple tasks.
3. Choose View, Toolbars, Customize. Click the Commands tab, and then click Tools. Drag the Set Reminder button to a toolbar. Click Close. Click the Set Reminder button to display the Set Reminder dialog box.

4. Set the reminder options you want for the tasks. For example, to get a reminder two days before a task is scheduled to finish, type **2**, select Days in the drop-down list, and then select Finish in the Before The *n* Of The Selected Tasks drop-down list.
5. Click OK.

> **Note**
>
> Project 2007 warns you if you try to set a Start reminder after a task is scheduled to start or try to set a Finish reminder after a task is scheduled to finish.

Integrating Your Address Book

After you create an address book in Outlook 2007, you don't need to waste time typing resource names each time a project plan requires them. Instead, just use an Outlook 2007 address book from within Project 2007 to add resource names, addresses, and e-mail information. This saves time and eliminates errors you might introduce when retyping resource information.

Creating a Resource List

A resource list is a list of names, distribution lists, or other contact information you use when assigning a task. For instance, if you want to assign a particular editor to edit your newsletter articles, you can add that editor's name to a resource list compiled from your Outlook 2007 Contacts folder and then assign that editor to the Edit Articles task.

The following steps show how to create a resource list in Project 2007 using an Outlook 2007 address book:

1. In Project 2007, on the View menu, click Gantt Chart.
2. On the Standard toolbar, click Assign Resources to display the Assign Resources dialog box (see Figure 38-6).
3. Click the plus (+) sign to the left of Resource List Options.
4. Click Add Resources, and then click From Address Book to display your address book contacts. You can also select resources from Active Directory, such as conference rooms, video equipment, or other objects.
5. Select the resource you want to assign to project tasks.
6. In the Name list, select a resource name or distribution list and click Add to add this name to the resource list. You can use this name as a resource for any task in Project 2007.

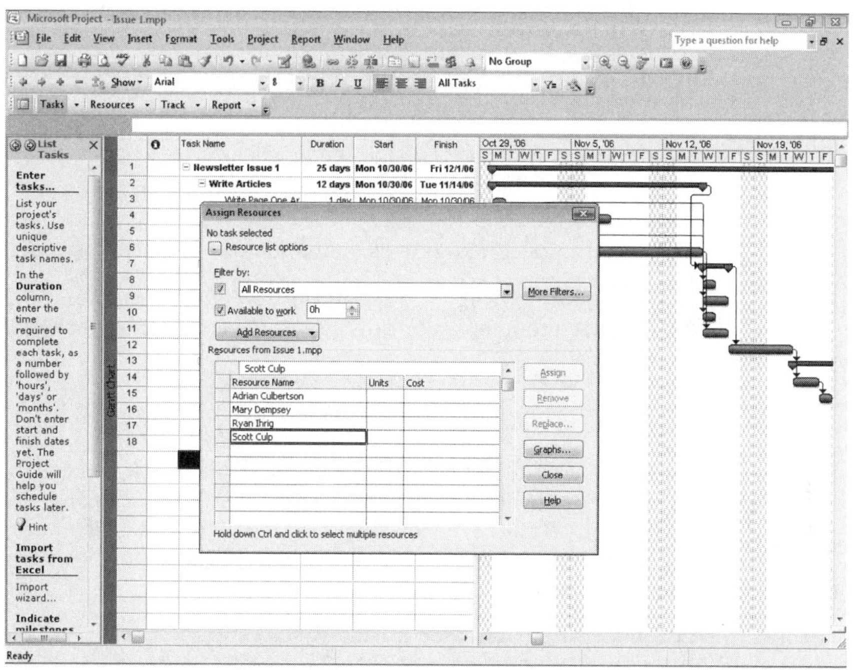

Figure 38-6. Use the Assign Resources dialog box from within Project 2007 to assign Outlook 2007 contacts as resources.

For a detailed discussion of distribution lists, see Chapter 6, "Managing Address Books and Distribution Lists." For more on assigning tasks to and working with contacts, see Chapter 14, "Creating and Managing Your Contacts."

7. Continue adding names as necessary.
8. After you finish adding names, click OK. The resources you selected are now part of the Assign Resources dialog box list.
9. Click Close to close the Assign Resources dialog box.

Note

In Project 2007, you can use a distribution list as you would in Outlook 2007 to make your work easier. To use a distribution list as a resource in Project 2007, create the distribution list in Outlook 2007, and then select the distribution list as shown in step 5 of the preceding procedure. A distribution list is handy if you must assign a task to multiple resources, such as a task in which multiple team members must attend a training class or multiple resources must be used to finish a construction job.

Assigning a Resource to a Task

After you create your resource list, you can assign resources to any tasks in Project 2007. The following steps show you how:

1. In Project 2007, on the View menu, click Gantt Chart.
2. In the Task Name column, select a task.
3. Click the Assign Resources toolbar button to display the Assign Resources dialog box.
4. Select a resource name or distribution list, and then click Assign.
5. Continue assigning resources as necessary.
6. After you finish, click Close.

To see a list of resources assigned to a task, double-click the task in the Task Name list, and then click the Resources tab (see Figure 38-7). You can also select resources here. To do so, click a row in the Resources list, click the down arrow, and then select a resource in the drop-down list. Click OK to close the dialog box and apply any changes you made to the list.

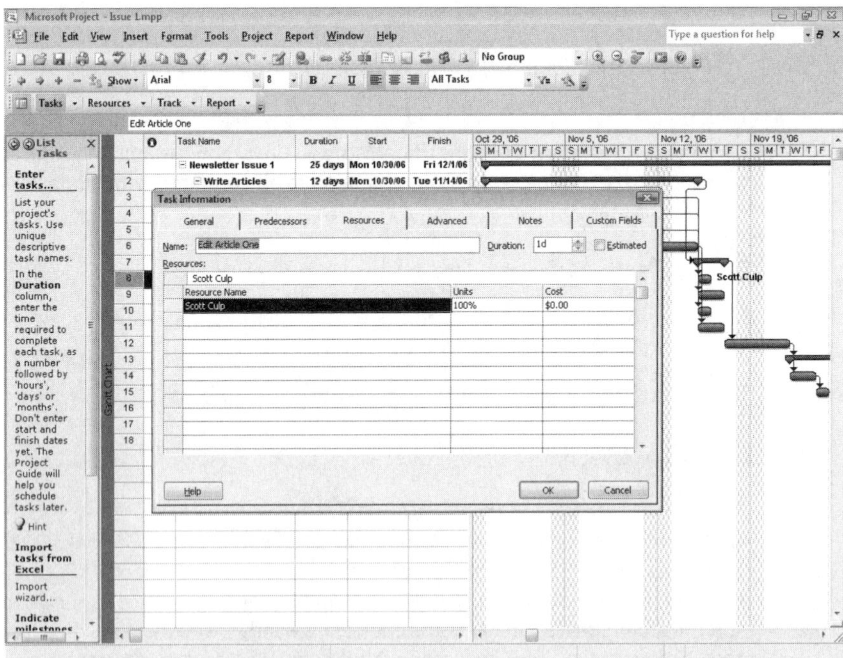

Figure 38-7. Click the Resources tab to review a list of resources assigned to a task.

Keeping Track of Your Progress

You can integrate the Outlook 2007 Journal feature with Project 2007 to keep a record of all the work you do on a project, including when you opened, saved, and printed the project file. This feature comes in handy, for example, when you want to find out which project file you worked on yesterday or last week, or which file you printed a few days ago.

To use the Outlook 2007 journal to track your project file work, do the following:

1. In Outlook 2007, choose Tools, Options.
2. Click the Preferences tab.
3. Click Journal Options.
4. In the Also Record Files From list, select Microsoft Project (see Figure 38-8).

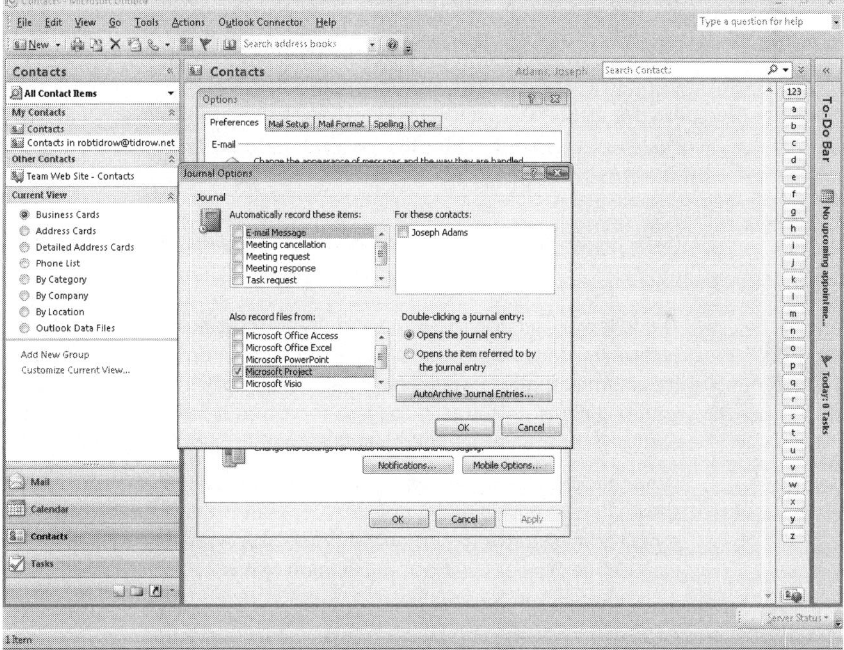

Figure 38-8. You can use the Outlook 2007 journal to keep journal information about your Project 2007 files.

5. Click OK to close the Journal Options dialog box, and then click OK again.

Now, as you use Project 2007, the journal will automatically keep track of the work you do on your Project 2007 files.

For more information about working with the Outlook 2007 journal, see Chapter 18, "Tracking Documents and Activities with the Journal."

Integrating Communication Features

One of the most difficult parts of managing a project is communicating with the people associated with a task or a set of tasks. If your company uses e-mail messages or the Internet, you can integrate the Outlook 2007 communication features with Project 2007 to help you effectively communicate with resources about task responsibilities.

With Office Project Server 2007, you can use Project 2007 to send messages to workgroup system members, also called teams. Workgroups can then use Project 2007 to assign tasks, send and receive task updates, accept or decline task assignments, and submit status reports. Team members can delegate tasks to other team members.

In addition to the collaborative features of Project Server 2007, members of a team can use e-mail messages, the Web, or both to exchange Project 2007 information. Project 2007 files can include hyperlinks to other supporting documents so that resources can quickly and easily access related documents. These documents might include a Microsoft Office Word 2007 document describing the project in detail, a cost-analysis worksheet in Office Excel 2007, or a related Web site you can view in Microsoft Internet Explorer®.

Note

The following section shows how to use the Outlook 2007 e-mail features to send and receive messages concerning task assignments, reporting status, and reporting updates. It's assumed that the workgroup functionality of Project 2007 is installed on your and your recipients' computers. To learn more about how to do this, consult the documentation that accompanies the Project 2007 and Project Server 2007 software.

Note that because e-mail systems and networks differ, the specific steps and features shown in this section might not work for your organization. Consult your network or e-mail administrator to find out whether your e-mail or local area network (LAN) system can use the Project 2007 communication features.

Allowing Tasks to Be Delegated to Other Team Members

Before you can assign tasks to other team members using the Project 2007 collaboration feature, you must configure Project 2007 to allow delegation of tasks. In addition, your Project Server 2007 must be configured to allow delegations. If you are not sure you can delegate tasks or if you have problems after following these steps, contact your system administrator for more information about your particular organization's server. In addition to setting up the server information, you must ensure that your tasks have resources assigned to them.

To allow team members (and yourself) to assign tasks to other team members, do the following:

1. Start Project 2007 if it is not already started.
2. Choose Tools, Options to open the Options dialog box.
3. Click the Collaborate tab.
4. From the Collaborate Using drop-down list, select Office Project Server 2007.
5. Type the path (Uniform Resource Locator [URL]) to the computer running Project Server 2007 (see Figure 38-9).

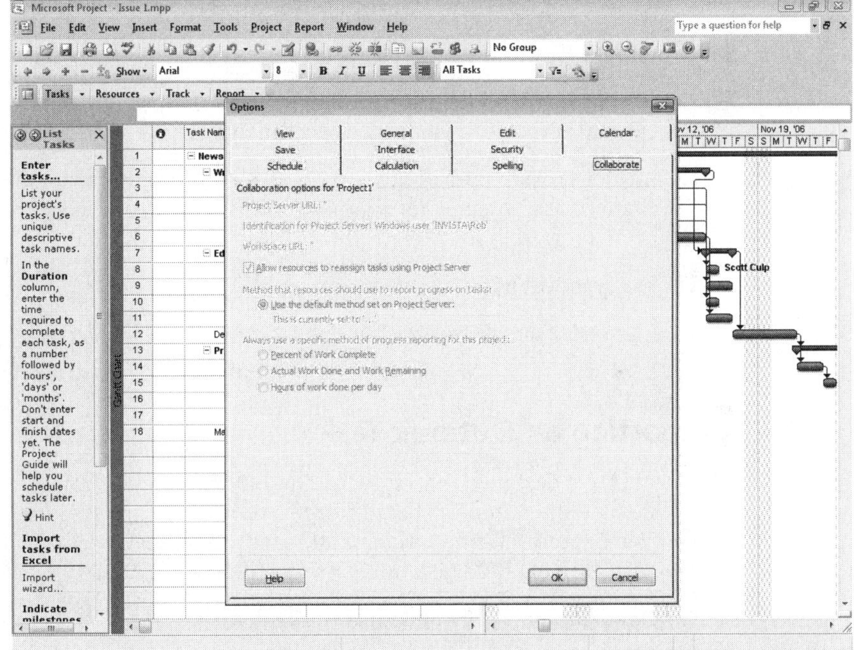

Figure 38-9. Before you can delegate tasks to other team members, configure Project 2007 to work with your company's Project Server 2007 computer.

6. Click Test Connection if you want to confirm that you typed the correct URL and that the server is working correctly.
7. Select the Allow Resources To Delegate Tasks Using Project Server check box.
8. Configure other settings on this tab as needed. For more information, see the Project 2007 documentation.
9. Click OK to save your settings.

Publishing Tasks

To delegate or publish tasks to other members, do the following:

1. Select the task you want to publish.
2. Right-click and choose Publish New And Changed Assignments.
3. Click OK when prompted to save the project.
4. Click Make Site Trusted if you need to specify that the server to which you are publishing is a trusted server. Note that if you are publishing to a Web site URL, you must make the Internet site trusted from within Internet Explorer before using Project 2007 to publish tasks.

Sending an Update

After your project gets under way, you will have slips in the schedule, updates to tasks, and other events that require you to modify your Project 2007 file. When these events occur, you need to update your team members appropriately, which you can do by using the Publish New And Changed Assignments feature, as follows:

1. In your project, update the task about which you want to publish a new or changed assignment. You cannot send an update unless the task has actually been updated first.
2. Save your project.
3. Right-click a task and choose Publish New And Changed Assignments, and then click OK.

Importing an Outlook Task

Project 2007 is designed to work with Outlook 2007 tasks. You can create a task in Outlook 2007 and then import that task into a project you are working on. This way, you do not have stray tasks in Outlook 2007 that should really be part of a project file. To import an Outlook 2007 task into a project, do the following:

1. Open Outlook 2007 and click the Task icon.
2. Create a new task and save it (see Figure 38-10).
3. Switch to Project 2007.
4. Choose Tools, Import Outlook Tasks.
5. Click Allow Access For 5 Minutes and click Yes if Outlook 2007 warns that another program is attempting to access e-mail addresses from your computer.
6. Select the check box next to the task you want to import in the Import Outlook Tasks dialog box, shown in Figure 38-11.
7. Click OK.

If necessary, you can move the task to another row and indent it under another task.

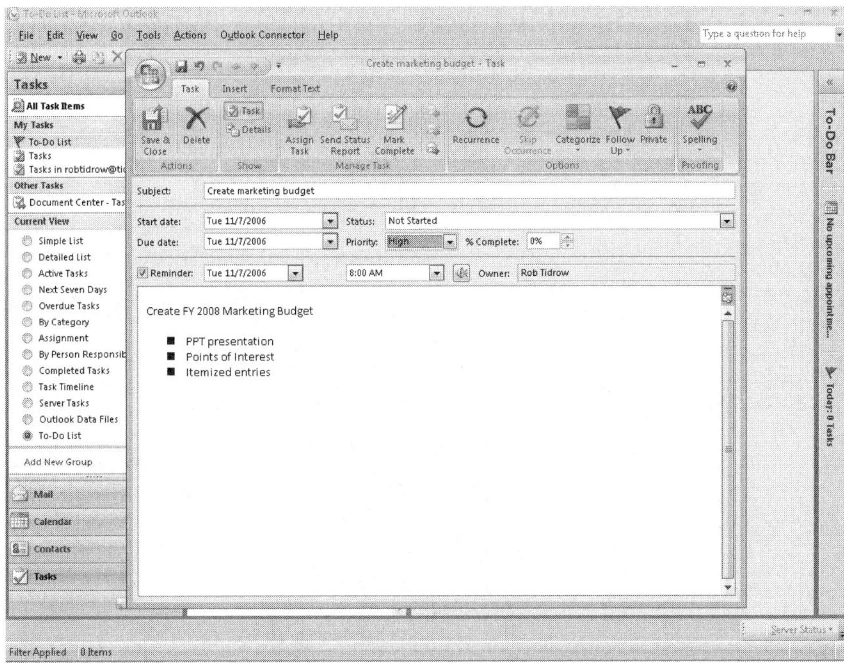

Figure 38-10. You can import an Outlook 2007 task into a project created in Project 2007.

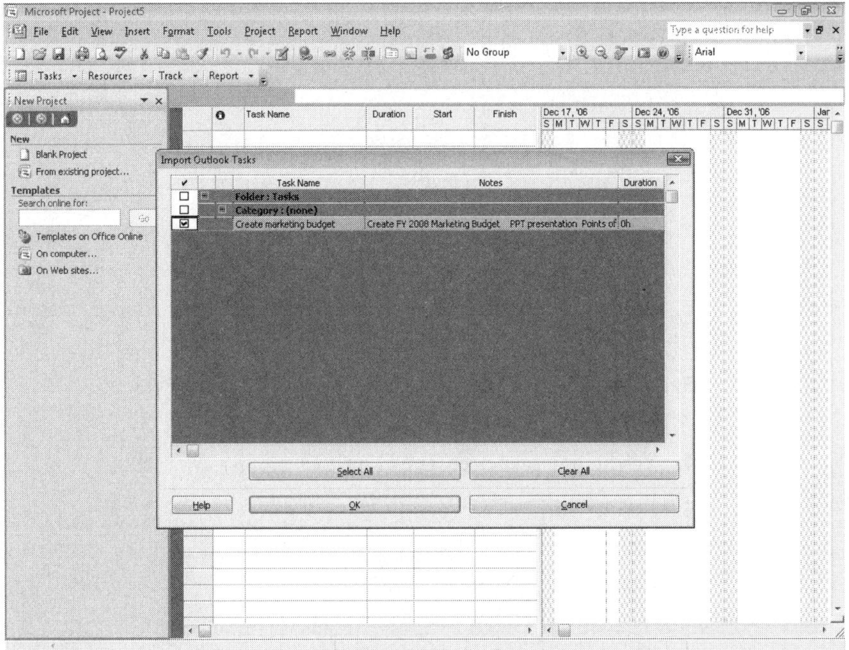

Figure 38-11. Select the task to import from this dialog box.

Sending a Microsoft Project File Using Outlook

One way you might want to share a Project 2007 file is to send it as a project file using Outlook 2007 e-mail. Recipients can then save the file to disk and open it in Project 2007, which enables them to view, modify, or print the Project 2007 file. Of course, everyone who receives the file must have Project 2007 installed on their computers.

To send a Project 2007 file this way, do the following:

1. In Project 2007, choose File, Send To, Mail Recipient (As Attachment) to display the message form (see Figure 38-12).

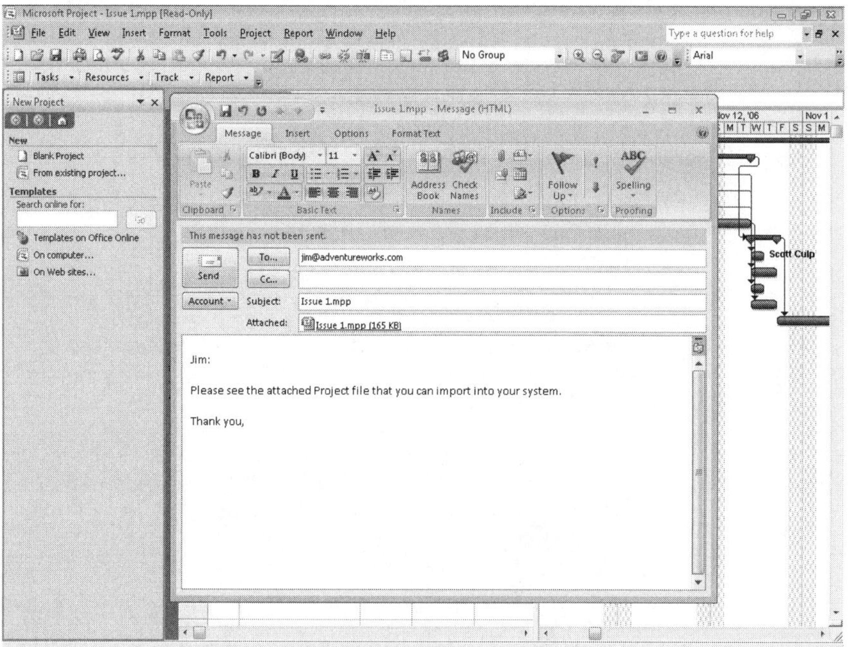

Figure 38-12. Send a Project 2007 file from Project 2007 using the Outlook 2007 e-mail features.

2. In the To box, type an e-mail address (or click To to access your address book). Add as many recipients as needed.
3. In the Subject box, type a subject. By default, Project 2007 uses the file name as the subject.
4. In the message area, type a message.
5. Click Send.

Routing a Microsoft Project File Using Outlook

You can also use Outlook 2007 to route a Project 2007 file. With routing, you send a file sequentially from one team member to the next or to all team members at one time. Use the former method if you want only one version of the file to be seen by all team members in the routing slip list. In this way, one member can review and modify the file before sending it to the next person on the routing slip. Use the latter method if you want all individuals to review and modify the file and return it directly to you.

> **Note**
>
> One downside of routing a file to a list of team members sequentially is that if someone in the routing list is out of the office for an extended time, your routed file could get stuck in that person's Inbox until they return, delaying any work you want to do on the file.

To route a Project 2007 file, follow these steps:

1. In Project 2007, choose File, Send To, Routing Recipient to display the Routing Slip dialog box.
2. Click Address to display the Address Book dialog box.
3. Select the recipients, and then click OK. The addresses are added to the To list, as shown in Figure 38-13.

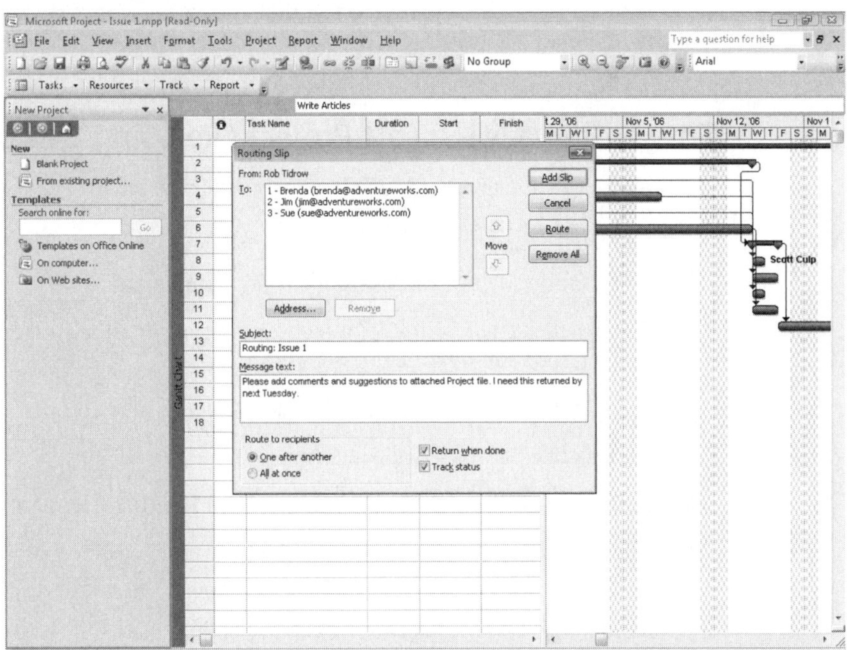

Figure 38-13. You can route a Project 2007 file using the Outlook 2007 routing features.

4. Click the up and down Move arrows to move recipients' locations in the list, specifying the order in which you want them to receive the routing slip. If you want everyone to receive a copy simultaneously, select the All At Once option at the bottom of the dialog box.
5. In the Subject box, type a subject.
6. In the Message text area, type a message.
7. If you want the Project 2007 file returned to you after all recipients have received it, select the Return When Done check box.
8. If you want Outlook 2007 to send you an e-mail notification each time the file is routed to the next recipient, select the Track Status check box. This process enables you to keep track of where the file is in the routing sequence.

> **Note**
>
> You can save the routing slip with the Project 2007 file if you are not ready to send it out yet. To do so, click Add Slip. To route the file, choose File, Send To, Next Routing Recipient, and then click OK.

9. When you're ready to start routing the file to specified recipients, click Route. If you receive a message telling you that another program is attempting to access your e-mail addresses, click Yes to continue. Outlook 2007 routes the file to the recipients.

Forwarding a Microsoft Project File Using Outlook

If a Project 2007 file is routed to you, you must forward it to the next person in the list.

To forward a Project 2007 file, follow these steps:

1. Open Outlook 2007 and view the routed message.
2. Double-click the Microsoft Project icon in the e-mail message to display the Project 2007 file.
3. In Project 2007, view and modify the project as needed.
4. Choose File, Save to save your changes.
5. In Project 2007, choose File, Send To, Next Routing Recipient.
6. Click OK when prompted to send the file to the specified person.

CHAPTER 39

Collaborating Online with Office

The term *collaboration* in the business world was once mainly a buzzword. Today, collaboration is not only a tangible process but also an extremely important one for most businesses and organizations. The capability to reach out through instant messaging to ask questions about a document or work behind the scenes of a conference call can be invaluable. The capability to see whether coworkers and business partners are online and available to answer questions about a document can be equally important. In today's competitive business market, these and other collaboration opportunities can have a significant impact on your personal productivity and your team's productivity.

There are new Microsoft® server and client components that support expanded collaboration capabilities, and while not all of them are part of the 2007 Microsoft Office system, they are all designed to integrate with the Microsoft Office system and extend the collaboration capabilities. In this chapter, we discuss new Microsoft server and client applications that support this enhanced ability to collaborate with others.

New Collaboration Features: Beyond Microsoft Office Outlook 2007

Microsoft Office Outlook® 2007 has features that support sharing information with others, such as sharing some or all of your calendar information or sharing access to your Office Outlook 2007 folders with coworkers. Microsoft has designed new client and server applications to leverage the functionality and common interface style of the Microsoft Office system and extend the ability to communicate with others and share information.

For more information about sharing your calendar, see Chapter 36, "Sharing Calendars."

Clearly one of the preeminent Microsoft server technologies that supports collaboration with the Microsoft Office system is Microsoft Office SharePoint® Server 2007. Interaction between Outlook 2007 and SharePoint Server is discussed in Chapter 40, "Collaboration with Outlook and Windows SharePoint Services."

In this chapter, we focus on the additional server and client programs that integrate with and extend the Outlook 2007 communication capabilities. Some of the new programs are common client or server applications designed to be installed on the company's network. Some of the other collaboration applications are rooted in Internet-based services designed to work with one or more client applications. The following list describes the Microsoft software tools that support collaboration in enterprise networks, as well as applications for Internet-based collaboration:

Microsoft network-based collaboration products:

- **Microsoft Office SharePoint Server 2007** Supports collaboration between people using Microsoft Office system applications.
- **Microsoft Office Live Communications Server** Supports collaboration between people using Microsoft Office Communicator.
- **Microsoft Office Communicator** This client software provides instant messaging, audio and video conferencing, and sending and receiving files, as well as sharing of whiteboards.

Microsoft Internet-based collaboration services for corporate/enterprise conferencing:

- **Microsoft Office Live Meeting** A Web-based service that provides dynamic collaboration capabilities suitable for corporate meetings and distributed conferences with vendors and partners as well as cross-enterprise development or project teams.
- **Live Meeting Console** The corresponding client application designed to work with Office Live Meeting.

Microsoft Internet-based collaboration services for individuals and small businesses:

- **Microsoft Office Live Collaboration** User-focused services designed to help individuals and small businesses establish a Web presence and connect with others, sharing documents, and calendars.

Microsoft Internet-based presence services for individuals and small businesses:

- **Microsoft Office Live Basics and Microsoft Office Live Essentials** Services designed to help individuals and small businesses establish a Web presence.

Using the Correct Collaboration Tools

With all of the new tools provided by Microsoft to support collaborative workflow, there might be some confusion about which technology to use. A range of interlocking communications technologies work with Outlook 2007 and the rest of the Microsoft

Office system applications to provide the means to dynamically collaborate with colleagues, customers, and the public.

Each of the server and client applications addresses particular communications needs and capabilities, so examining what each program is designed to do can give you some guidance as to which to choose. The following list briefly describes the core capabilities and uses of these new applications and service offerings:

- Use Office Communicator with Office Live Communications Server:
  - To establish instant messaging sessions with one or more members of your internal network.
  - To facilitate quick phone connections between project members.
  - To establish video conferencing between yourself and designated colleagues.
- Use Office Live Meeting:
  - To create dynamic collaborative multimedia conferences with distributed groups of people who are not sharing the same network.
  - To provide a simultaneous audio broadcast to a selected group of attendees for informational, marketing, or promotional purposes.
  - To support dynamic and interactive cooperative work on documents between project members working from different locations.
- Use Office SharePoint Server 2007:
  - To support the development of documents with distributed project teams.
  - To manage version control for content development.
- Use Office Live Collaboration:
  - To create a Web-accessible location for your small business information.
  - To provide an Internet-accessible point to share data with your customers, vendors, and partners.
- Use Office Live Basics or Office Live Essentials:
  - To create a Web presence for your small business.
  - To establish a domain name and related e-mail accounts.

Using Microsoft Office Live Communications Server

Live Communications Server provides services to support real-time communications between clients, supporting capabilities such as instant messaging and audio and video communications.

During installation, Live Communications Server must modify the Active Directory® directory service schema and must make additions to the forest and domain before the service installation can be completed. Once installed, Live Communications Server is managed via a Microsoft Management Console (MMC) snap-in. See the Live Communications Server documentation for details on installation and management.

Live Communications Server supports cross-organization federation (matching account names in different organizations to the people using them), enabling users in partner companies to find and communicate with people regardless of which company they are in. With additional licenses and provisioning (managing the configuration) of the connections, Live Communications Server can also perform federation with public instant messaging services such as MSN®, AOL, and Yahoo.

Office Communicator requires this server component to support its messaging and collaboration functionality. For corporate network environments, the Live Communications Server component must be installed and available to Communicator clients prior to operation.

Managing Your Live Communications Server

Live Communications Server is managed using the Live Communications Server MMC snap-in component. This snap-in component is not configured in the MMC console by default, however.

To add the Live Communications Server console to your Administrative Tools in Microsoft Windows Server® 2003, perform the following steps:

1. Click Start, Run, type **MMC**, and then press Enter.
2. Click File, Add/Remove Snap-In.
3. Click Add, and then select the Live Communications Server snap-in in the Add Standalone Snap-In dialog box.
4. Click Add, and then click Close.
5. Click OK to close the Add/Remove Snap-In dialog box.
6. Click File, Save, provide a name (such as Live Communications Server), and then click Save to save a link to the Live Communications Server console in Administrative Tools.

> **Note**
>
> The service that Live Communications Server uses might not start automatically the first time after it is installed. To start the service (or check its status), right-click My Computer, and then choose Manage. In the Computer Management console, browse to the Services node under Services And Applications. In Services, locate the Live Communications Server service, and verify that the Startup Type is set to Automatic and the Status is set to Started. If the service is not started, right-click on the service, and then choose Start.

Configuring User Accounts in the Live Communications Server Console

Once Live Communications Server is installed, you must configure user accounts in order to make use of the communication services. You will need to browse through the Forest and Domains nodes in the console to locate the Live Communications Servers And Pools node and then click to open it. Click the server name node beneath it, and then select the Users node, as shown in Figure 39-1.

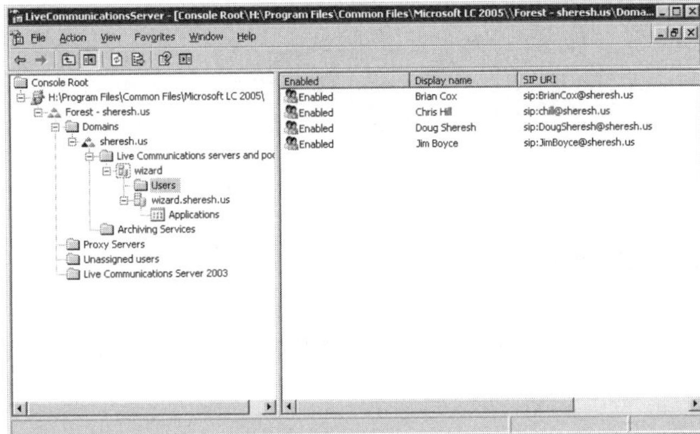

Figure 39-1. Configure user accounts in the Live Communications Server console.

To configure user accounts, follow these steps:

1. Right-click the Users node, and then choose Configure Users to start the Configure Users Wizard.
2. On the Configure User Settings page, select the user configuration settings appropriate to your environment, as shown in Figure 39-2.
   - Select Configure Federation to allow (or block) cross-service federation of user accounts.
   - Select Configure Remote Access to allow (or block) users remotely connecting to the Live Communications Server services.
   - Select Configure Archiving, and then select the desired archiving options.
   - Select Configure Public IM Connectivity to allow (or block) user connection to public instant messaging services (such as MSN).
3. Click Next, and then click Finish.

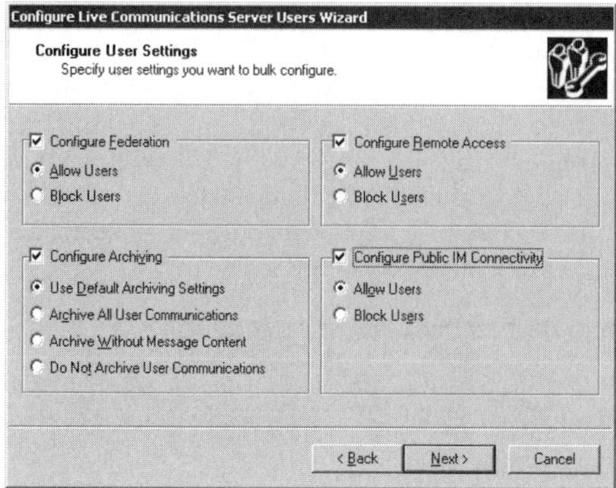

Figure 39-2. You can configure the settings for all user accounts.

Configuring User Accounts in Active Directory

If you want your users to use Live Communications Server to communicate with each other over your network, you must first enable the user accounts in Active Directory and then configure them to use Live Communications Server on your network. This is done by using the Active Directory Users And Computers console. The Live Communications Server installation process modifies the Active Directory schema, adding a Live Communications tab to the user account Properties dialog box.

To enable Live Communications Server for a specific user:

1. Open the Active Directory Users And Computers console.
2. Browse to the Users node, right-click the user's account name, and then choose Properties.
3. On the Live Communications tab, shown in Figure 39-3, select the Enable Live Communications For This User check box.

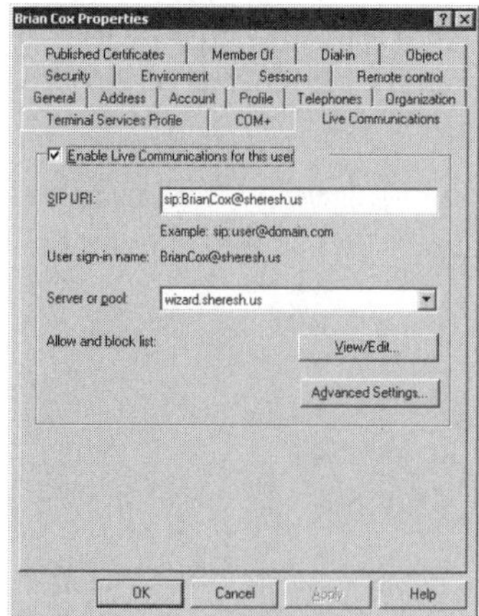

Figure 39-3. You can configure the Live Communications settings for a user account.

4. The Session Initiation Protocol (SIP) Uniform Resource Identifier (URI) field should contain the user's user logon name with an *SIP:* prefix. If not, enter the user's logon name in the form **SIP: <username>@<domain>.<tld>**.
5. In the Server Or Pool field, use the drop-down list to select the computer running Live Communications Server 2005.

To configure federation settings, to enable remote control, or to configure archiving settings, follow these steps:

1. On the Live Communications tab, click Advanced Settings.
2. In the User Advanced Settings dialog box, shown in Figure 39-4, select the federation settings appropriate for your connectivity requirements.

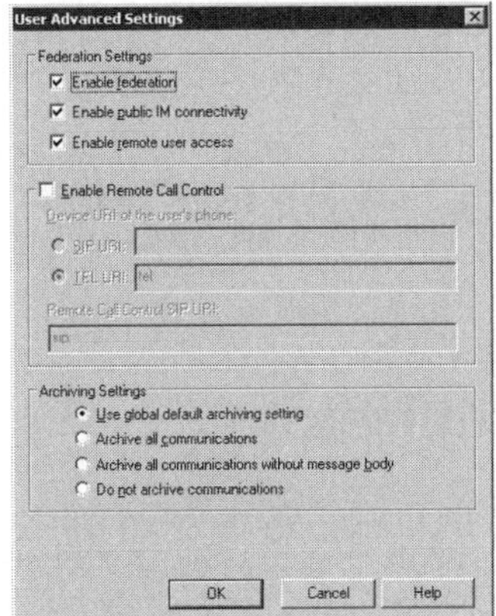

Figure 39-4. You can configure federation, remote access, and archiving settings.

3. If remote access is needed, select the Enable Remote Call Control check box, and then specify the related parameters.
4. In the Archive Settings area, select the desired archiving option.

In many cases, you will want to configure Live Communications Server settings for multiple users, and you can configure multiple users' settings simultaneously by selecting multiple accounts.

To enable Live Communications Server for a set of users:

1. Select all of the user accounts for which you want Live Communications Server available.
2. Right-click one of the user accounts, and then choose Enable Users For Live Communications to open the Enable Users Wizard. Click Next.
3. On the Select A Pool page, select the computer running Live Communications Server, and then click Next.

4. On the Enable Operation Status page, note the user accounts in the Succeeded Operations and the Failed Operations areas. The user accounts in the Succeeded Operations area have Live Communications Server enabled.
5. Click Finish.

To configure Live Communications Server for a selected set of users:

1. Select all of the user accounts for which you want to configure Live Communications Server.
2. Right-click one of the user accounts, and then choose Configure Live Communications Users to open the Configure Live Communications Server Users Wizard. Click Next.
3. On the Configure User Settings page (shown earlier in Figure 39-2), select the federation, remote access, and archiving options, and then click Next.
4. On the Configure Operations Status page, note the user accounts in the Succeeded Operations and Failed Operations areas. The user accounts in the Succeeded Operations area have the configuration changes set as you configured them in step 3. Click Finish.

Using Microsoft Office Communicator

Microsoft Office Communicator is not included in all versions of the Microsoft Office system–it is included, however, in Microsoft Office Professional Plus 2007 and in Microsoft Office Enterprise 2007. A demo version is available for free download from the Microsoft Web site:

office.microsoft.com/communicator

Communicator installation will normally be part of the Microsoft Office system installation (if obtained as part of a Microsoft Office system package), or you might need to individually install it from the download if you are using the demo version. In either case, you should install Communicator before proceeding with this section of the chapter.

Live Communications Server is a complementary and required component for Communicator providing essential server-side support for instant messaging and presence information, as well as audio and video communications. For scheduling information or free/busy information, Communicator requires Microsoft Exchange Server (versions 2000 through 2007).

Configuring Your Communicator Account

Communicator has a set of function-related menus containing groups of common operations, including the Connect, Contacts, View, and Action menus. To use Communicator, you must first configure it with the account information needed to connect to the server; therefore, we'll jump ahead to the Action menu to get your account set up. Once the account is established, we'll systematically explore how to use the capabilities available on all of the Communicator menus.

To set the account information, follow these steps:

1. Start Communicator.
2. Click Actions on the toolbar, and then select Options.
3. In the Options dialog box, select the Accounts tab, as shown in Figure 39-5.

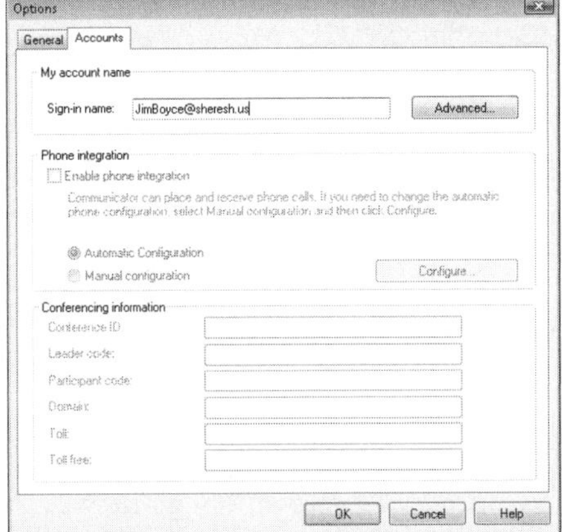

Figure 39-5. Configure your Communicator account by specifying your account name in the Sign-In Name box.

4. In the Sign-In Name box, type the account name that you sign in with. For internal networks using Active Directory, the sign-in name corresponds to your user principal name (UPN) that was configured in Active Directory, in the form <username>@<domain>.<tld>. Click OK.

To connect to the server, follow these steps:

1. Start Communicator.
2. Click the Sign In button, shown in Figure 39-6, or choose Connect, Sign In.

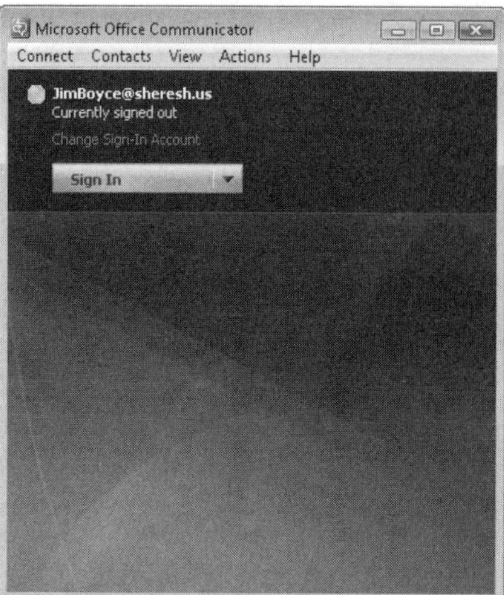

Figure 39-6. You can connect to the Live Communications Server by clicking the Sign In button or choosing Connect, Sign In.

Communicator then connects to the server and changes the display to reflect that you are now online. Any contacts that you have assigned are shown (by default, this list is initially blank until you add contacts), along with a Find field to search for contacts, as shown in Figure 39-7.

Figure 39-7. Once you are signed in, your contacts list is displayed (initially empty).

Using Your Account to Sign In

The Connect menu provides your sign-in and sign-out options, as well as the ability to sign in using another account via the Sign In As option. As shown in Figure 39-8, the sign-in options are disabled after you have signed in. You can change the default account that you use to connect to the server by choosing the Change Sign-In Account option and then changing the account information specified on the Accounts tab in the Options dialog box.

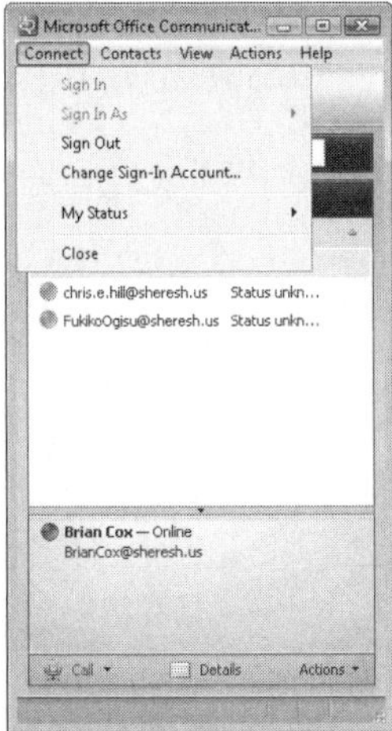

Figure 39-8. Set your sign-in account options using the Connect menu.

The My Status option lets you set the status of your Communicator account and indicates the current state of your account when displayed, as shown in Figure 39-9. Using this menu, you can set your online status to Online, Busy, Do Not Disturb, Be Right Back, Away, and Appear Offline, and you can opt to reset the status of your account with the Reset Status option.

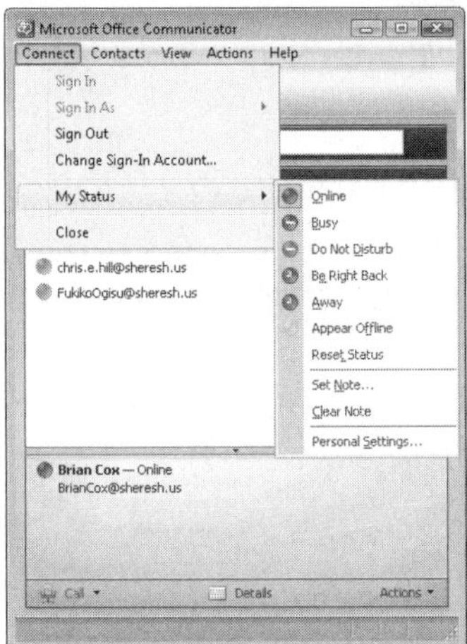

Figure 39-9. Set your sign-in account options using the Connect menu.

The Set Note option lets you attach a note to your account, displaying a note after your name in your own Communicator window and displaying a note icon for other users who have your account added to their list, as shown in Figure 39-10. Selecting the user name or note icon causes the note contents to be displayed as a ScreenTip, and if your user account is selected, the note is displayed at the bottom of the Communicator window. The note set with the Set Note option can be removed with the Clear Note option.

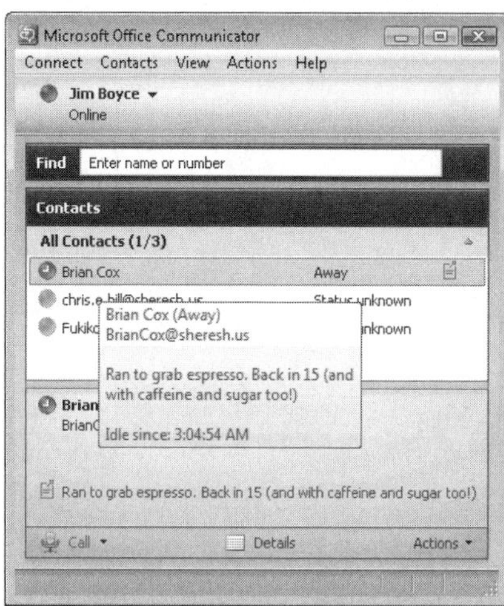

Figure 39-10. You can set a note on your account to be displayed for people who have you in their contacts list.

The Personal Settings option on the Connect menu takes you to the Rules tab in the Options dialog box, letting you specify rules for handling your status display. For more information about settings in the Options dialog box, see "Managing Communicator Configuration Settings" later in this chapter.

Managing Contacts in Communicator

To communicate with other people, you must add their accounts to your list of contacts. The Contacts menu in Communicator lets you add, delete, and review contact information and lets you establish groups of contacts for organizational purposes, as shown in Figure 39-11.

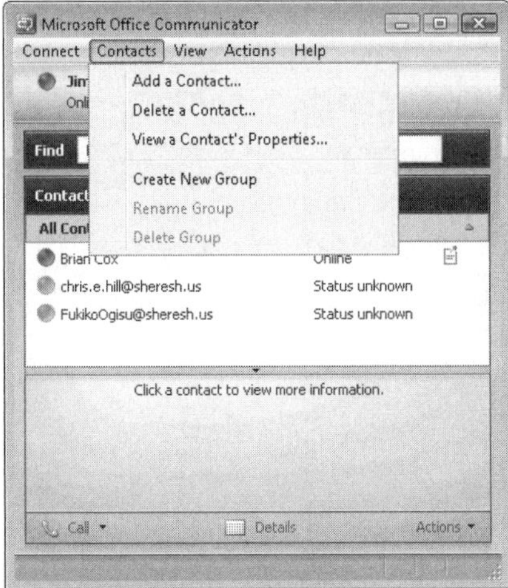

Figure 39-11. You can create a contacts list by adding new contacts or organize contacts into groups.

To add a new contact in Communicator, follow these steps:

1. Choose Contacts, Add A Contact.
2. The Add A Contact Wizard appears, as shown in Figure 39-12, prompting you to add a contact either by entering the e-mail address or sign-in name or by searching for the contact. If you know the account (sign-in) name or e-mail address of the contact that you want to add, select By E-Mail Address Or Sign-In Name; otherwise, select Search For A Contact. Click Next.

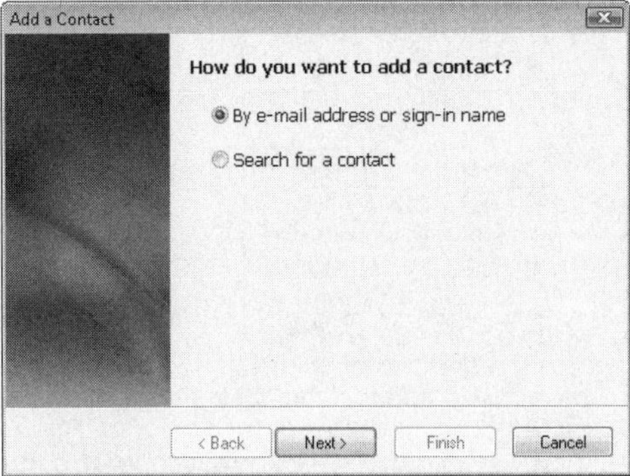

Figure 39-12. You can add a contact by specifying a name and an e-mail address or by searching for the contact.

3. Type the account (sign-in) name or e-mail address of the contact that you want to look for, as shown in Figure 39-13, and then click Next.

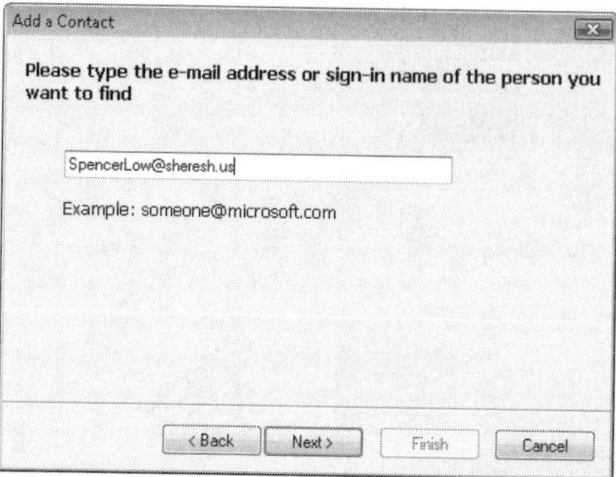

Figure 39-13. Enter the e-mail address or sign-in name for the contact.

4. Once the account is located and added to your contacts list, the account addition is confirmed, and you are provided an opportunity to assign the contact to a group, as shown in Figure 39-14. By default, the only group is the All Contacts group, and all new contacts are added to it. If you have created groups for your contacts (discussed shortly), select the group to add the new contact to, and then type the account (sign-in) name or e-mail address of the contact that you want to add to your list. Click Finish to finish adding contacts, or click Next if you want to add more contacts.

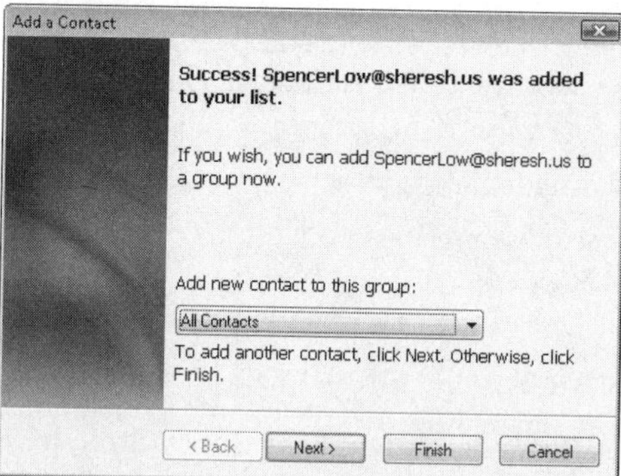

Figure 39-14. Select the group to add the contact to.

5. When you have finished, the contacts are shown in your contacts list, as shown in Figure 39-15, and you can start communicating with them using the Communicator instant messaging and audio and video connectivity features.

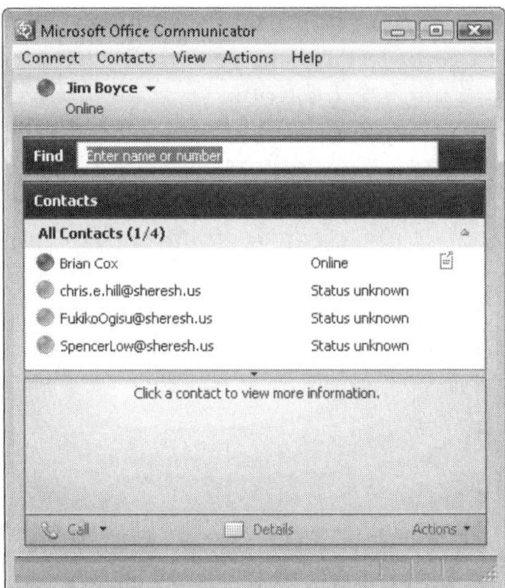

Figure 39-15. The contacts list displays the contacts you have added with their availability status.

Deleting a Contact in Communicator

You can delete a contact from your list easily by choosing Contacts, Delete A Contact. In the Delete A Contact dialog box, select the name of the contact that you want to delete, and then click OK. You will be asked to confirm the deletion–click Yes to delete the contact, or click No to retain the contact. You can also select the contact and then press Delete. Click Yes to remove the contact from your list or No to keep it.

Viewing a Contact's Properties

To review a contact's information, including Status, Idle Since, Calendar, Note, and Phone Numbers settings, click Contacts, View A Contact's Properties, select the contact that you want to view, and then click OK. You can also right-click a contact and then choose Properties.

Establishing Groups for Your Contacts List

You can establish groups to organize your contacts into. If you have many contacts in your list, for example, you might want to subdivide them into groups by department (Development, Sales, Support, and so on), by role (Managers, Technical Leads, and so on), or by any other grouping classification that is useful to you. One of the advantages of organizing your contacts by group is that you can start a conversation with the entire group–a feature that is particularly useful for groups of contacts that are all involved in the same project.

To create a group, simply choose Contacts, Create New Group. The new group will be automatically displayed in the Contacts list, and you will be prompted to assign a name for it. After you have created and named the group, you can move contacts into the group by dragging them into the new group or by right-clicking the contact, choosing Move Contact To, and then selecting the group to move the contact into. In the example shown in Figure 39-16, the Infrastructure Team group was created and two contacts were moved into it. Notice that once you create a group, the All Contacts group is renamed Other Contacts.

Figure 39-16. The groups and related contacts are displayed in the Contacts list.

Deleting a group is a straightforward process of right-clicking the group and then choosing Delete Group—however, deleting a group will also delete the contacts within the group. If you want to retain some or all of the contacts but want to remove the group, move the contacts to another group first, and then delete the group. Renaming a group is likewise simple—just right-click on the group, choose Rename Group, and then type in the new group name. In this case, all of the contacts are retained.

Controlling the Communicator Display

You can change the display of the contact information in Communicator by using the View menu, as shown in Figure 39-17. By default, the Show Friendly Name, Show Extended Status Icons (such as the Note icon), and Tabs options are selected. The Show Extended View option displays contact information such as notes with the contact name. You can keep the Communicator window always visible on the screen by selecting the Always On Top option. To view the entire list of files that have been sent to you via Communicator, you can select the Received Files option, and the list of files that you have received is displayed.

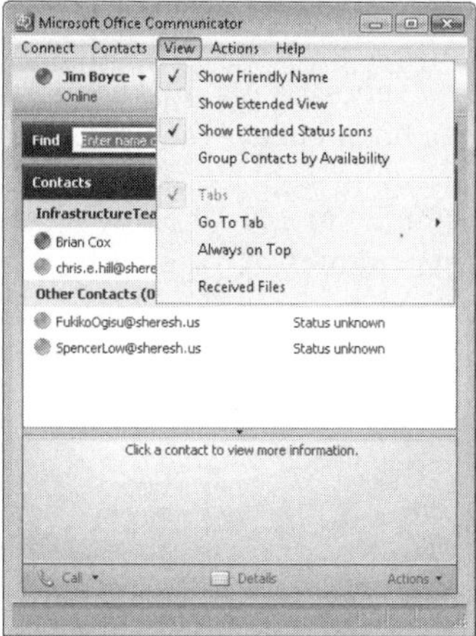

Figure 39-17. You can specify what information is displayed with the contacts.

Communicating with Others

To communicate with people in your Communicator contacts list, you can either use the Actions menu, shown in Figure 39-18, or right-click the contact and then select the desired action (such as Send An Instant Message). In addition to initiating instant messaging, audio, and video communications, you can also choose Send E-Mail or Send A File. The Audio And Video Tuning Wizard will assist you in configuring the audio and video settings. Choosing Options on the Actions menu displays the Options dialog box, in which you can configure Communicator settings.

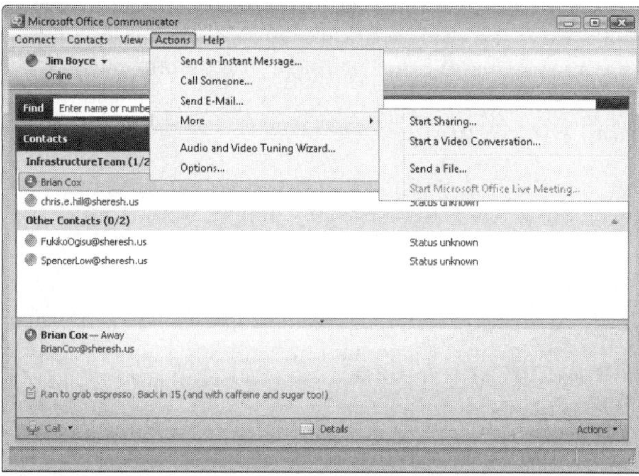

Figure 39-18. The Actions menu lets you instant message, call, send e-mail, send a file, or even start audio and video conversations with people in your contacts list.

Starting an Instant Message Session

You can initiate an instant message session by choosing Actions, Send An Instant Message. The Send An Instant Message dialog box displays the list of contacts—to start an instant message session with a contact, select the contact, and then click OK. The Conversation window is displayed, as shown in Figure 39-19, showing the participants in the meeting and displaying the ongoing instant messaging conversation.

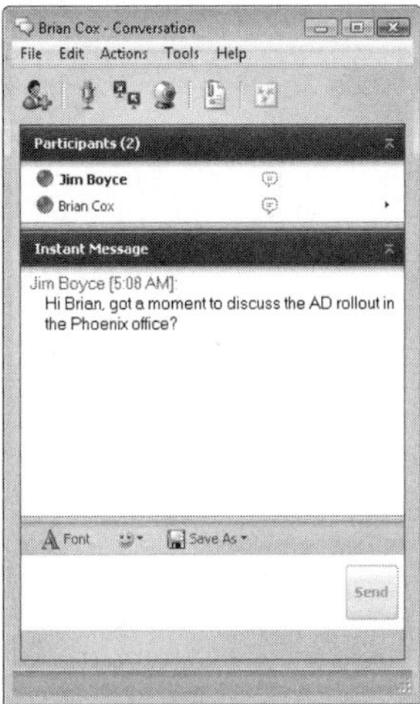

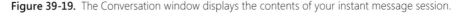

Figure 39-19. The Conversation window displays the contents of your instant message session.

The menus in the Conversation window let you control and save the instant message session, and otherwise include the same options as the Communicator window menus. The Actions menu, however, has the additional option Invite Someone To Join This Conversation, enabling you to add other people to the instant message session.

Sending an E-Mail Message

You can send e-mail to anyone on your contacts list by choosing Action, Send E-Mail, or by right-clicking a contact and then choosing Send E-Mail. Your default e-mail client opens an e-mail form, with the selected contact e-mail address in the To field. Just fill in the message body, select any attachments or other content, and send the message to the intended recipient.

Configuring Your Audio and Video

The Audio And Video Tuning Wizard analyzes your microphone, speakers, and video camera and checks to make sure that they are working correctly. To test your audio and video hardware, first verify that your hardware is connected properly—the microphone is plugged in, the speakers are plugged in and turned on, and your video camera is connected. Then choose Actions, Audio And Video Tuning Wizard. The wizard will walk you through testing your audio and video equipment—simply read each of the steps and then click Next when you are ready to proceed.

Communicating with Audio

You can call a contact by right-clicking the contact's name in the Conversation dialog box, choosing Call, and then selecting either a displayed phone number or Computer. If you are calling computer to computer, each party to the call must have a full-duplex sound card and a functioning microphone and speaker system (or USB equivalent). When you call using the phone number, Communicator initiates and manages the phone call, and also allows you to forward calls and put calls on hold.

Sharing an Application or a Whiteboard

In Communicator, to share an application or a whiteboard with a contact, select the contact, choose Action, More, and then select Start Sharing. In the Sharing Controls area of the Conversation window, select Start Application Sharing or Whiteboard.

Communicating with Video

For Communicator to establish a video conversation, both you and the recipient must have video-capable and audio-capable computers, and you have to perform audio and video tuning. Once you have completed the Audio And Video Tuning Wizard, you can begin a video session with a contact by choosing Action, More, and then selecting Start A Video Conversation. Once the recipient has accepted the conversation, the video session is established in the Conversation window, as shown in Figure 39-20. You can use the video controls to switch videos, stop a video conversation, or show the video full screen.

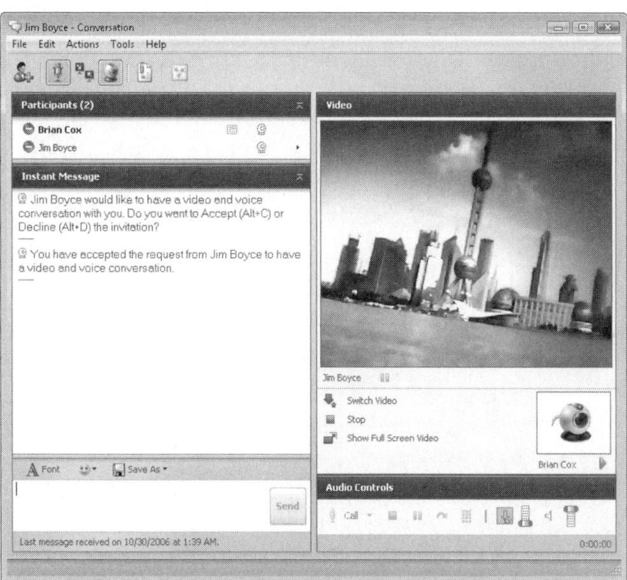

Figure 39-20. The Conversation window displays the video content from the remote user's video session.

Sending Files to Contacts

You can share files with your contacts by using the Send A File option in Communicator. To send files to someone on your contacts list, either choose Action, More, click Send A File, and then select the contact to receive the file, or right-click a contact and then choose Send A File. The Send A File dialog box opens—browse to the file that you want to send, select the file, and then click Open. Communicator is ready to send the file immediately, but it requires the contact to agree to receive the file before transmission occurs. The contact can press **Alt+C** to accept the file and have it saved to the default file transfer folder, **Alt+S** to save the file to a different folder, or **Alt+D** to decline the file transfer. If you want to cancel the file transfer that you initiated, press **Alt+Q**.

Using Office Live Meeting

If Office Live Meeting is installed, you can begin a Live Meeting session with a contact by choosing Action, More and then selecting Start Microsoft Office Live Meeting. For more information about using Live Meeting, see "Using Microsoft Office Live Meeting" later in this chapter.

Managing Communicator Configuration Settings

The configuration settings for Communicator 2005/2007 are available in the Options dialog box, accessible by choosing Actions and then choosing Options.

The Personal Tab

To include phone numbers with your contact information, you can use the Personal tab to enter phone numbers for work, mobile, home, and others, as shown in Figure 39-21. Next to each number you enter is a check box so you can specify whether the phone number is published with your contact information. You can also specify which personal information manager you use or select None. Communicator does not automatically complete these fields with information from either Active Directory or the Outlook Address Book, so if you want to make this information available to others, you must do so manually.

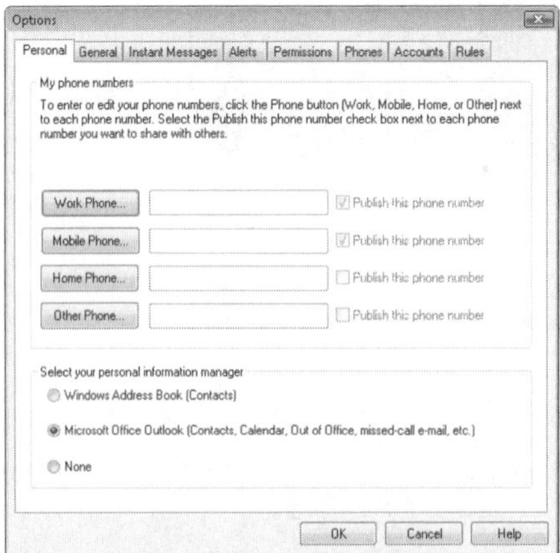

Figure 39-21. On the Personal tab you set your phone numbers and default information manager.

The General Tab

You can configure several options for Communicator on the General tab, shown in Figure 39-22, including specifying whether to Automatically Run Communicator When I Log On To Windows and whether to Automatically Open The Main Window When Communicator Starts. (Both of these options are selected by default.)

The File Transfer field lets you select the folder where you want files that are sent to you to be stored. (By default, the files will be stored in the My Received Files folder under the Documents folder in your user profile.) To have Communicator operate in a language different from the default, click the drop-down list in the Language area, and then select the preferred language.

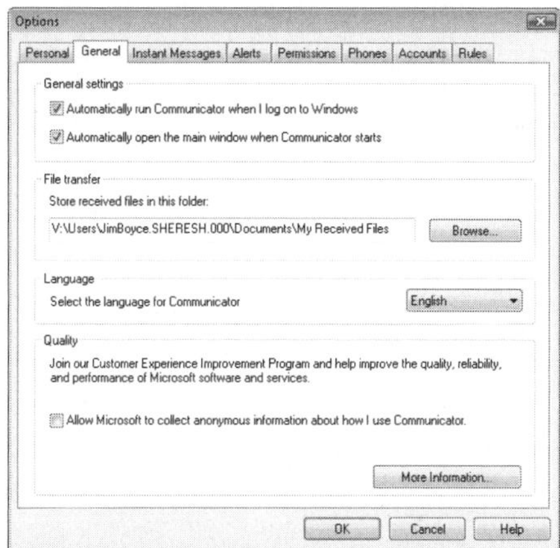

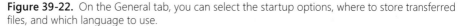

Figure 39-22. On the General tab, you can select the startup options, where to store transferred files, and which language to use.

The Instant Messages Tab

To control the font used in your instant messaging with other people on your contacts list, select the Instant Messages tab, shown in Figure 39-23, and then click Change Message Font. In the Change My Message Font dialog box, select the font, size, style, and color to use in your instant messaging, and then click OK. You can also enable or disable the availability of emoticons in your messages and turn on or off the time stamping of messages.

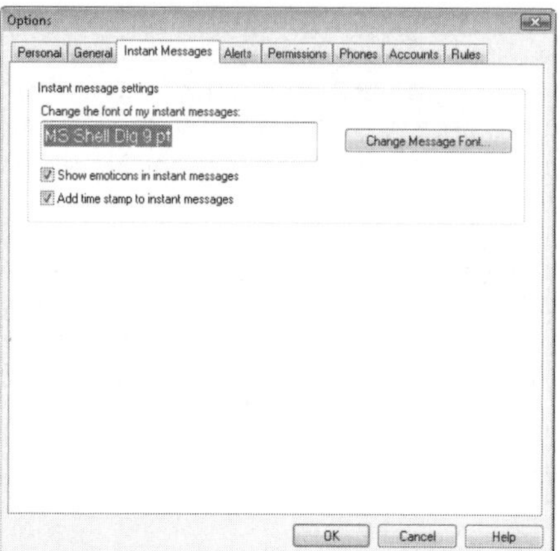

Figure 39-23. Set the font style and color to use to use in your messages, and control emoticons and time stamps.

The Alerts Tab

The Alerts tab, shown in Figure 39-24, enables you to control when Communicator displays status and incoming conversation alerts and whether to use sound in signaling the alert. You can set Communicator to show alerts for all contacts or only for tagged contacts and to determine when to do so dependent on status (either Busy or Do Not Disturb). By clicking Configure Sounds, you can specify what sounds are used in alerts by configuring the Communicator options (Background Message, Incoming Call, and others) in the Sounds dialog box.

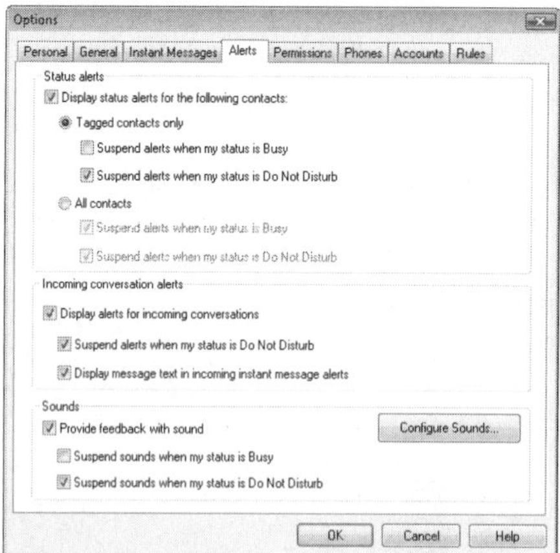

Figure 39-24. You can control when alerts are displayed and whether to use sound in the alert.

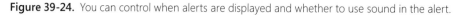

The Permissions Tab

On the Permissions tab, shown in Figure 39-25, you can specify how you are added to other people's lists of contacts, and you can select who can see your status, send instant messages or files, and add you to their contacts list. You can choose to allow or block any specific user account that you add to the Permissions List. The All Other Contacts account has the option to set permissions to Allow, Block, or Notify. There is also an option to control how contacts from outside your Active Directory domain are handled—the Block Instant Messages From Federated Contacts Who Are Not Allowed To See My Status check box limits which federated user accounts can send instant messages.

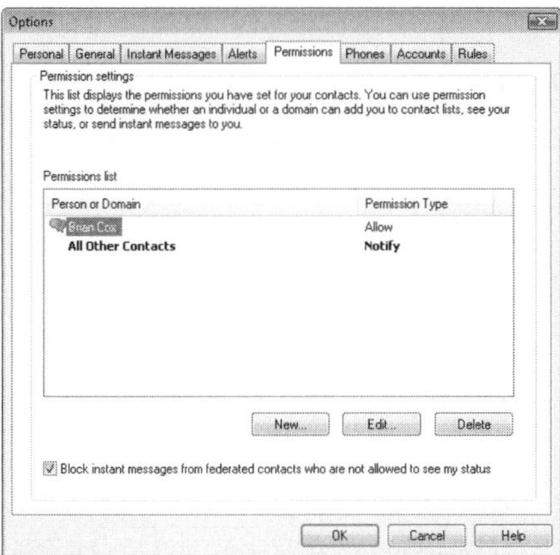

Figure 39-25. The Permissions tab lets you set Allow, Block, or Notify permissions for other contacts.

The Phones Tab

You can configure how Communicator handles calling of other contacts on the Phones tab, shown in Figure 39-26, where you can set the default device to use for phone dialing. The Call Forwarding area enables configuration of the Communicator call forwarding operations.

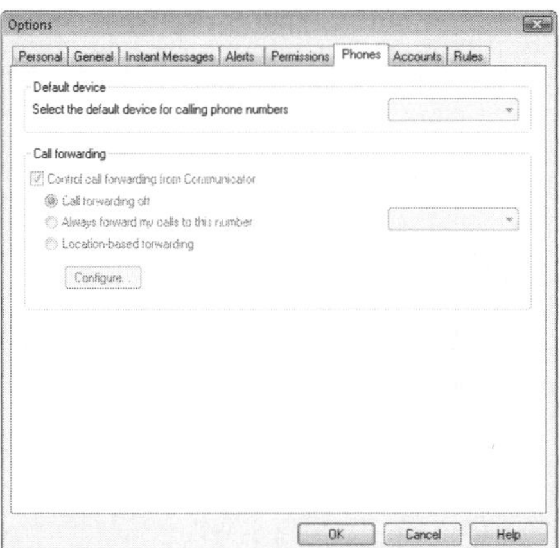

Figure 39-26. The Phones tab lets you set how Communicator performs dialing and call forwarding.

The Accounts Tab

You set the basic configuration for Communicator on the Accounts tab, shown in Figure 39-27, specifying the Sign-In Name and configuring the Phone Integration and Conferencing Information settings.

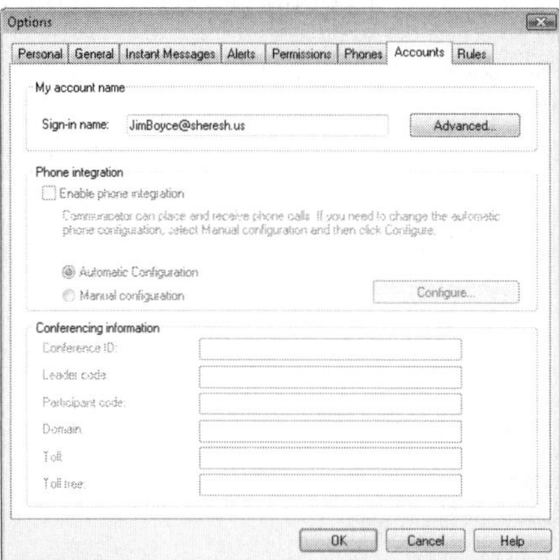

Figure 39-27. Use the Accounts tab to set the Sign-In Name as well as phone and conferencing information.

To configure the Live Communications Server address and protocol, click Advanced to display the Advanced Connection Settings dialog box, shown in Figure 39-28. Click Configure Settings, specify the Live Communications Server address in the Server Name Or IP Address field, and then specify the protocol by selecting either the TCP or the TLS protocol under Connect Using.

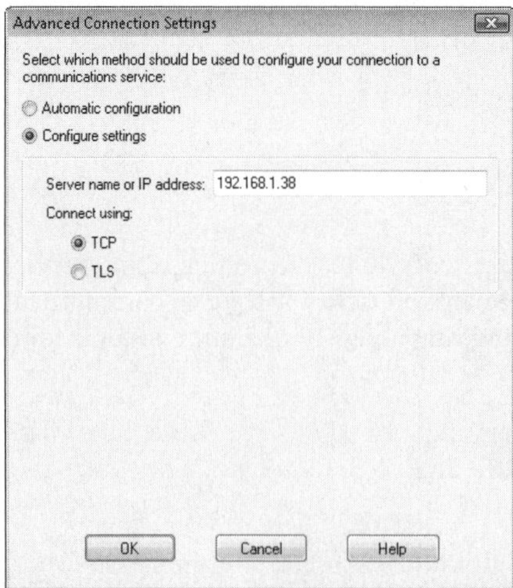

Figure 39-28. The Advanced Connection Settings dialog box enables you to specify the Live Communications Server address and protocol.

The Rules Tab

To establish the criteria for when Communicator changes your online status to Away or Do Not Disturb, configure the options on the Rules tab, shown in Figure 39-29. In the Status area, you can set the idle time limit when your status changes to Away by clicking the drop-down list and then selecting the time delay. You can also configure options to Enable Do Not Disturb on your phone and control Microsoft Office Outlook Integration. (These options are selected by default.) These Outlook 2007 options let Communicator Automatically Retrieve Out Of Office Settings From Outlook, and you can opt to have it Update My Status And Contact List Based On Calendar Data. You can also have Communicator send you e-mail when a call is missed or when a call is automatically forwarded from this computer. The Windows Media® Player check box enables you to have Microsoft Windows Media Player pause when you are using Communicator for phone, voice, and video conversations.

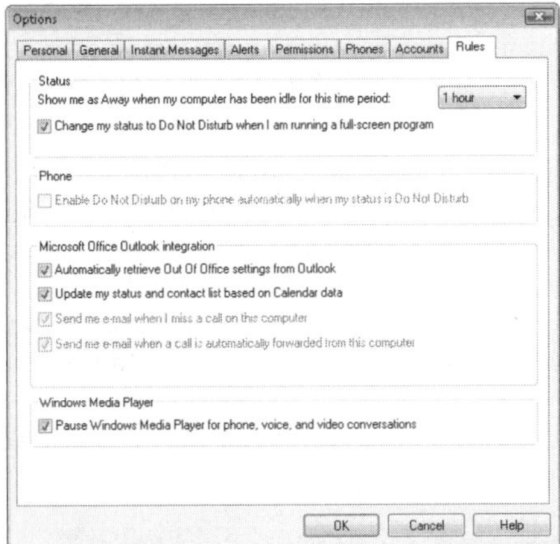

Figure 39-29. You can use the Rules tab to control when Communicator switches to Away or Do Not Disturb status, as well as to configure integration with Outlook 2007.

Using Microsoft Office Live Meeting

Microsoft Office Live Meeting is a hosted Web-based conferencing service that enables you to leverage the features of the Microsoft Office system to communicate in a media-rich format across the Internet, providing a new online suite of tools for collaboration with colleagues and customers.

From small-scale project-related meetings to larger-scale conferences with hundreds of customers, Live Meeting supports the interactive sharing of documents, graphics, and presentations.

Live Meeting features integration with Microsoft Office system applications, including Outlook 2007 and Microsoft Office Visio® 2007, and you can initiate Live Meeting sessions from any of them. Because Live Meeting leverages the common user interface of the Microsoft Office system, it's easy for participants to come up to speed and quickly use the capabilities of Live Meeting.

Live Meeting includes an audio streaming technology called Internet Audio Broadcast, which lets you provide a unidirectional audio stream to meeting participants.

To use Live Meeting, you must have a Microsoft Office Live Meeting account established, and you have to download and install the Live Meeting software.

Example of Using Live Meeting Services in Real Life

One of our colleagues reported on her company's extensive use of Live Meeting as a tool for providing formal training and as a means of conducting less formal "brown bag" sessions for staff at remote offices. Live Meeting is also increasingly used in her company to support client conferences, enabling internal staff and clients in geographically dispersed locations to communicate. The group editing capabilities provide an enormous benefit in document and contract development, as they let all stakeholders review, comment, and implement changes during the session.

Because Live Meeting sessions can be recorded, her company always records training sessions to provide an offline means of delivering training material to new staff or to staff who were unable to attend the live training session. Live Meeting is also being used to develop an internal library of technical and policy information collected from local and remote subject matter experts in irregularly scheduled Live Meeting sessions focused on topics of current concern or importance. By recording the Live Meeting sessions, the company is able to amass a growing library of the collective wisdom, perspective, and technical insight provided in the dynamic interchange of the top subject matter experts that the company has access to.

Setting Up Live Meeting

To use Live Meeting, you must set up a Live Meeting account and then download and install the Live Meeting application. Microsoft provides a 14-day free trial for you to test and review the capabilities provided by Live Meeting. See the information at the following URL for more information:

office.microsoft.com/livemeeting

After you sign up for the free trial, the confirmation information and access URL will be sent to the e-mail address that you provided during registration. Prior to using Live Meeting, you should download and install the Live Meeting Console application.

There are a few additional considerations when setting up a Live Meeting session:

- When setting up a Live Meeting connection (prior to the meeting), you have a link that you send to the presenter(s) and a different link that you send to the attendees.
- You also set up a conference call to support the audio portion of the Live Meeting session. You can either perform the call management or have Live Meeting operators assist you.
- If you are presenting developed content (such as content in the form of a Microsoft Office PowerPoint® 2007 presentation), you upload the material to the Live Meeting server prior to the meeting and share it so that all other attendees can view the material.

Using the Microsoft Live Meeting Add-In Pack

The Microsoft Live Meeting Add-In Pack lets you conduct conferencing from all of the Microsoft Office system applications, as well as from Microsoft's instant messaging clients (including Microsoft Windows Messenger, MSN Messenger, and Microsoft Office Communicator). The Microsoft Live Meeting Add-In Pack enables you to use Outlook 2007 to:

- Schedule a Live Meeting session, set default options for the meeting, and override defaults as needed.
- Specify which participants in the meeting will be presenters and specify others as attendees to the meeting, and send different meeting invitations to presenters and attendees.

Joining a Live Meeting Session

After registering a Live Meeting session, you receive a URL to connect to a tutorial on the features of Live Meeting. When you go to this URL, you will be prompted with pre-configured Name, Meeting ID, and Meeting Key fields, and you click Join Meeting to start the first Live Meeting session. The site will attempt to detect the Windows-based Live Meeting console, and if it fails to detect the console, it will offer to use a Web-based console, let you install the Windows-based Live Meeting console, or run the existing Windows-based Live Meeting console. (If you have already installed the console, select this option.)

Your first Live Meeting session is prearranged with a brief slide-based tutorial on how the Windows-based Live Meeting console works. The console, shown in Figure 39-30, contains a standard Windows menu bar, a set of default toolbars, and a Resources pane on the left showing the current presentation, the current presenter(s), and the audience and audio information. To the right of the Resources pane is a pane that displays the thumbnail images of the content that is being presented, and a questions and answers area appears at the bottom of the console.

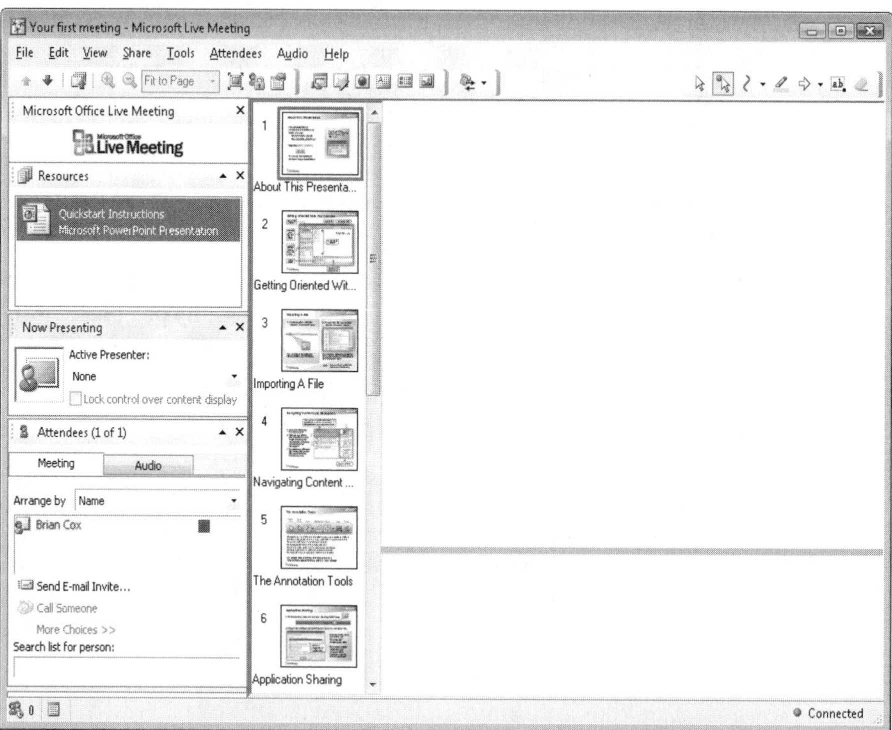

Figure 39-30. The Office Live Meeting console displays both presentation material and information about the meeting presenters and attendees.

You can use the Live Meeting menus to configure your connection to the meeting and how information is displayed:

- **File** The File menu provides options to Print To PDF, Exit, and End Session.
- **View** The View menu lets you change how the meeting materials are displayed (such as Full Screen) as well as control the display of thumbnails and meeting information.
- **Edit** The Edit menu provides the standard Windows Edit menu options–Undo, Cut, Copy, Paste, Delete, and Select All, as well as Move Up and Move Down, which enable you to change the order of presentation materials.
- **Share** The Share menu includes options to Share Document To View, Share Document To Edit, and Share Application. In addition, you can share your Whiteboard, Web, Text, Poll, and Snapshot, supporting substantial collaboration options in your Live Meeting session.
- **Tools** The Tools menu lets you configure the User Preferences, Manage Resources, Annotations, Polling, and Recording options, and even Start Remote Desktop Sharing for interactive demonstrations of real system operations.

- **Attendees** The Attendees menu manages attendee permissions; assigns the presenter for the meeting; sends e-mail invitations; starts, blocks, or unblocks chat sessions; and locks the meeting to prevent further attendees.
- **Audio** The Audio menu controls all audio aspects of your Live Meeting session, including muting your own or another's phone, identifying phones, and creating and managing conference calls. Additionally, you can start an Internet audio broadcast (as well as stop or listen to one) and manage the Internet audio broadcast settings.

When working in a Live Meeting session, you have a set of Annotations tools at your disposal that let you and all attendees collaborate on the presentation. These tools include:

- A Selector Arrow tool that lets you manipulate annotations.
- A Laser Pointer tool that enables you to point to items in the presentation.
- A Draw tool that is used to draw on the presentation.
- A Highlighter tool that uses color to highlight portions of the presentation.
- A Stamps tool that lets you place predefined shapes on the presentation.
- A Text tool that enables you to write comments on the presentation.
- An Eraser tool that lets you remove the annotations.

Purchasing Microsoft Live Meeting Services

To purchase the Microsoft Live Meeting services package that is most appropriate for your application, visit the following Web sites. The first Web site provides a detailed breakdown of the plans available for purchasing Live Meeting services. The second URL takes you directly to where you can purchase Live Meeting services. The second Web site is also accessible from the first site by clicking the Buy Now link at the end of the first paragraph in the Retail Pricing section.

- *www.microsoft.com/office/livemeeting/howtobuy/default.mspx*
- *https://main.placeware.com/ordering/lmbuy_it/but_it.cfm*

The Microsoft Office Live Services

In addition to its other collaboration features, downloadable collaboration applications (such as Communicator), and Web-based collaboration tools such as Live Meeting, Microsoft has also introduced a new set of Web-based collaboration services. The Microsoft Office Live services are focused around extending the Microsoft Office system functionality and user interface style to a set of Web-based tools that you can use to share your work with colleagues and customers.

The Microsoft Office Live services are available in three levels: Office Live Basics, Office Live Collaboration, and Office Live Essentials.

Office Live Basics

The Office Live Basics service lets you register a domain and associated e-mail addresses, featuring free initial domain registration and hosting of the associated Web site. Office Live Basics provides a Site Designer tool for designing and editing your Web site, as well as providing site statistics and tools to analyze site traffic and produce traffic reports. This offering includes e-mail accounts linked to the domain you register with your Office Live Basics account.

- **E-mail accounts** Up to 25 accounts, with 2 GB of e-mail storage per account
- **Space to store Web site content** Up to 500 MB
- **Data transfer per month** Up to 10 GB

To get more information about the Office Live Basics, go to the following Web site:

officelive.microsoft.com/OfficeLiveBasic.aspx

Office Live Essentials

The Office Live Essentials service also lets you register a domain name and set up a hosted Web site. The Office Live Essentials account includes up to 50 e-mail accounts linked to the domain you register at the time you set up your account. Like the other Office Live offerings, the Office Live Essentials service includes free initial domain registration and e-mail accounts linked to your domain. Office Live Essentials also includes Office Live Business Contact Manager for tracking your customers, projects, and related tasks. The features of Office Live Essentials include: .

- **E-mail accounts** Up to 50 accounts, with 2 GB of e-mail storage per account
- **Space to store Web site content** Up to 1 GB
- **Data transfer per month** Up to 15 GB
- **Storage for business applications and workspaces** Up to 500 MB
- **Number of users allowed in workspaces and business applications** Up to 10 users

To get more information about the Office Live Essentials service, go to the following Web site:

office.microsoft.com/en-us/officelive/FX101534271033.aspx

Office Live Premium

The Office Live Premium service includes the domain registration (with paid annual renewals), 50 e-mail accounts, and Web site hosting—all of the features of Office Live Essentials and Office Live Basics. Office Live Premium supports Shared Sites, a suite of business and human resources applications, and online workspaces that you can share with customers and partners.

Office Live Premium also includes Office Live Business Contact Manager for tracking your customers, projects, and related tasks, as well as 20 additional online applications. The features of Office Live Essentials include:

- **E-mail accounts** Up to 50 accounts, with 2 GB of e-mail storage per account
- **Space to store Web site content** Up to 2 GB
- **Data transfer per month** Up to 20 GB
- **Storage for business applications and workspaces** Up to 1 GB
- **Number of users allowed in workspaces and business applications** Up to 20 users

To get more information about the Office Live Premium service, go to the following Web site:

office.microsoft.com/en-us/officelive/FX101945591033.aspx

To compare the Office Live Basics, Essentials, and Premium service offerings, go to the following Web site:

office.microsoft.com/en-us/officelive/FX101925601033.aspx

Office Live Collaboration

The Office Live Collaboration service lets you set up an unlimited number of shared Web sites and includes a suite of business-oriented Web-based applications to assist you in running your business. These business applications are grouped into Customer Manager, Company Calendar, Employee Directory, Project Manager, and Inquiries Tracker. You can set up shared Web sites to share information with others—whether employees, vendors, or customers—and control access permissions to the documents you store there so that only authorized people can view or modify content. In addition, you can establish business and vendor workspaces to collaborate on projects with other firms. This service offering also supports the creation of a Human Resources Workspace to maintain critical and sensitive information that must remain confidential. Likewise, you can also establish a Small Business Accounting (SBA) Workspace in which you can share your Microsoft Office Small Business Accounting file with your accountant.

Note

Office Live Collaboration differs from the other Office Live offerings (Basics, Essentials, and Premium) in that it does not provide a Web presence nor does it provide e-mail accounts.

The Office Live Collaboration service is not free, however—this service will cost a low monthly fee.

To get more information about the Office Live Collaboration service, go to the following Web site:

officelive.microsoft.com/OfficeLiveCollaboration.aspx

PART 8

Working with Office Server and SharePoint Services

CHAPTER 40

Collaboration with Outlook and Windows SharePoint Services

Microsoft® Windows® SharePoint® Services 3.0 is a collaboration tool used to build Web sites for team members to share data such as contacts and documents. One of the biggest advantages of Windows SharePoint Services other than the fact that it allows team members to share information and collaborate easily is that it fully integrates with the 2007 Microsoft Office system. Windows SharePoint Services allows you to share documents created with Microsoft Office system applications and even lets you share contacts stored in Microsoft Office Outlook® 2007 with other team members.

Understanding Windows SharePoint Services Collaboration

Windows SharePoint Services 3.0 is a workgroup-class, Web-based portal product that can be used for collaboration, including document management for a team or workgroup within an organization. Each team requiring this collaboration functionality will typically have its own SharePoint site that team members can use to share documents, have threaded discussions, share lists of important information, and more.

Windows SharePoint Services is a Web-based tool, but it also provides integration with Microsoft Office system applications. Windows SharePoint Services provides a number of collaboration features, including the following:

- **Document sharing** Document sharing allows you to store documents on the SharePoint site, which can then be accessed by other team members. This is useful for sharing project-related documents, for example, or any other document that other team members might need access to. In addition to simple document storage, document sharing provides version control tools such as document check-in and checkout so that a document is not accidentally modified by more than one user at a time.

- **Picture libraries** Picture libraries are similar to document libraries in that they store pictures that can be shared among team members. This is basically a Web-based photo album.
- **Lists** Lists are formatted lists of information. The list format can vary based on the type of information being stored. A number of lists are predefined, such as Announcements, which are displayed on the main SharePoint Home page; Calendar, which can contain events relating to your team or project; Links, which stores Web links to pages that your team will find useful or interesting; and Tasks, which helps your team members keep track of work.
- **Discussion boards** Discussion boards allow team members to have threaded discussions on specific subjects. Discussion boards are useful to replace e-mail exchanges when more than two people are involved, as those involved can place comments and replies directly in the appropriate thread rather than exchanging a large number of e-mail messages.
- **Surveys** Surveys are simply a method of polling other team members for information.

As stated earlier, one of the key features of Windows SharePoint Services is its ability to integrate with Microsoft Office system applications. The features in Windows SharePoint Services that integrate with the Microsoft Office system include document sharing, which can be done from almost any Microsoft Office system application; lists, which can be synchronized with Microsoft Office Excel® 2007 or Microsoft Office Access 2007 files; and Calendar lists, contacts, and alerts, which can be linked into Office Outlook 2007. In addition, Microsoft SharePoint Designer can be used to edit and customize the Windows SharePoint Services pages. This chapter focuses mainly on the integration of SharePoint and Outlook 2007. SharePoint and Outlook 2007 have the tightest integration, as they are both collaboration tools, although each has a different focus.

Setting Up Alerts

Alerts (formerly called *subscriptions* in an earlier version of the software) are used when you want to be notified when content on the SharePoint site changes. Alerts are sent through e-mail. To set up an alert, follow these steps:

1. Locate the content for which you want to configure the alert. This can be virtually anything on the SharePoint site.
2. Click an item in a library. A menu appears, as shown in Figure 40-1. Select Alert Me to be alerted when that item is changed.
3. The New Alert page, shown in Figure 40-2, displays the e-mail address to which alerts will be sent. On this page, select the types of changes you want to be alerted about. Some of the options shown in the figure are not available if you are configuring an alert for a specific item. You can be alerted about all changes; item additions, changes, or deletions; or updates to discussions involving the selected item or library.

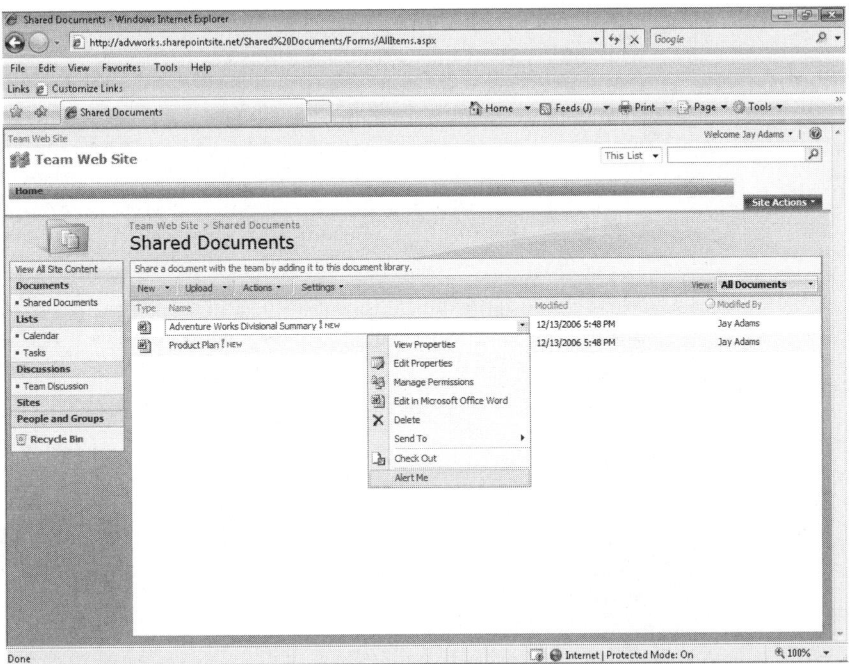

Figure 40-1. Select Alert Me to get an e-mail alert when a specific item has been changed.

4. Select the frequency for alerts from this item or library. The default setting sends an alert message every time the alert is triggered. You can also elect to receive only a daily or weekly summary of alerts. These options are useful if the item or library for which you are configuring the alert changes often.
5. Click OK, and the alert will be configured.

After you have created an alert, you will be notified each time the alert criteria set on the New Alert page are met. You can view a list of all of the alerts you have configured on the site by clicking View My Existing Alerts On This Site on the New Alert page. The My Alerts On This Site page, shown in Figure 40-3, shows all of the alerts you have configured on the site. You can delete an alert by selecting the check box next to the alert you want to delete and then clicking Delete Selected Alerts. It is also possible to add an alert for a list or document library (although not individual items) on the My Alerts On This Site page. Click Add Alert, select the library or list for the alert, and then click Next. Set the options on the New Alert page as described earlier in this section.

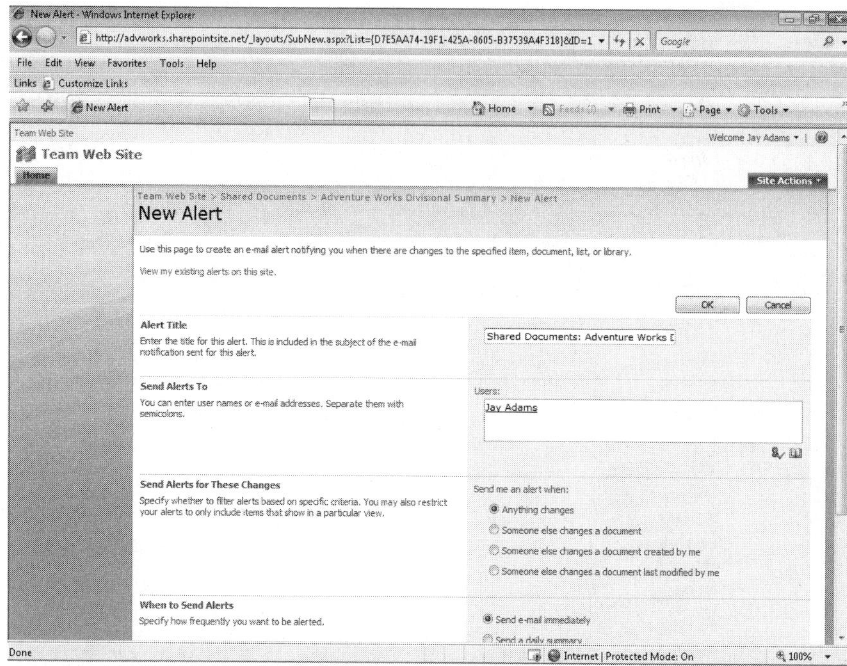

Figure 40-2. The New Alert page is used to configure the alert.

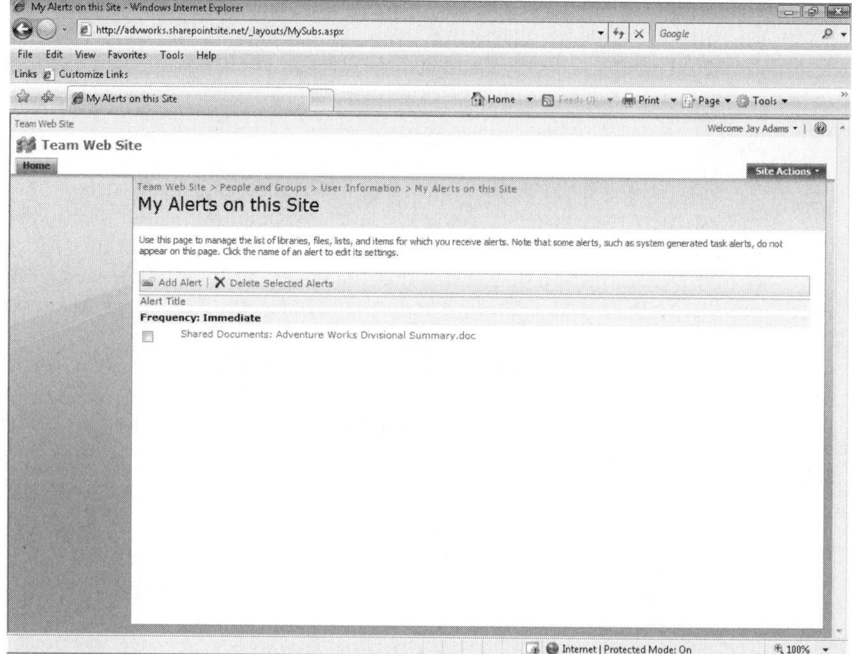

Figure 40-3. You can see all alerts you have configured on the site on the My Alerts On This Site page, which is accessible from the New Alert page.

Working with Shared Documents

Document sharing is simple with Windows SharePoint Services and can be done in one of two ways. If you have an existing Microsoft Office system document, it is an easy process to add the document to a document library in Windows SharePoint Services. If you don't already have a document created, you can create the document directly in the Windows SharePoint Services site. When you create a document in the Windows SharePoint Services site, the appropriate application opens automatically. When the document is saved, it is placed in the site automatically. In addition to creating and adding documents to the Windows SharePoint Services site, you can do a number of things with existing documents in Windows SharePoint Services: You can edit or remove existing documents, and you can use features such as document version history, check-out, and check-in to control versions.

Uploading a Document

To upload a document to a document library, follow these steps:

1. Locate and open the document library by clicking the library name (such as Shared Documents) on the Home page. Usually the library names appear under the Documents item on the Quick Launch bar.
2. In the document library, click the down arrow next to the Upload button. Click Upload Document to upload a single file, or click Upload Multiple Documents to upload several files at once.
3. On the Upload Document page, shown in Figure 40-4, click Browse, locate the file to upload, and then click Open. You can also click Upload Multiple Files to open a Microsoft Windows Explorer–style browser from which you can select multiple files to upload.
4. Existing files with the same name as the file or files being uploaded are not overwritten by default. If you want to overwrite any existing files, click the Overwrite Existing Files check box.
5. After you have specified or selected the files to upload, click OK. The documents are uploaded, and the Documents page appears.

You will now see the uploaded file listed in the document library.

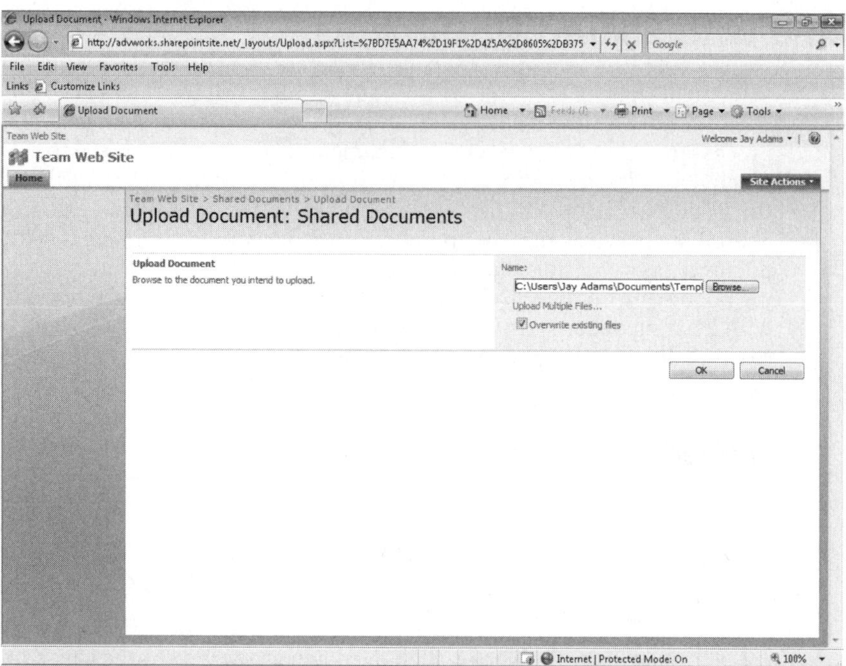

Figure 40-4. The Upload Document page is used to upload files to the document library.

Creating a Document from the Site

In addition to the preceding method of uploading an existing document to the document library, you can also create a new document directly from the document library site. The new document is created using the document template associated with the document library. By default, the Microsoft Office Word 2007 document template is associated with the Shared Documents library that is created when Windows SharePoint Services is installed. The Document Template setting is configured when a new document library is created, and you can set it for an existing library by clicking Settings on the document list and then clicking Document Library Settings. Click the Advanced Settings link, modify the Document Template setting, and then click OK.

To create a new document from your SharePoint site, follow these steps:

1. Open the document library in which you want to create the new document.
2. Click New, and then choose New Document, shown in Figure 40-5.

   The Microsoft Office system application associated with the document template specified for the selected document library is downloaded and opened in its native application, such as Microsoft Office Word 2007. Figure 40-5 shows how the SharePoint site communicates with Office Word 2007 to open up the default document template. Create and then save the new document to the document library.

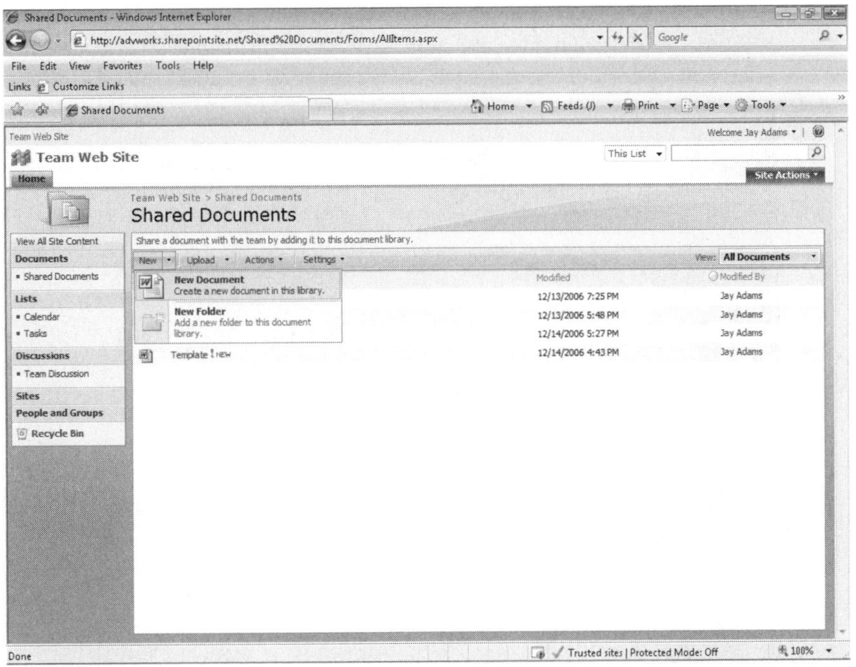

Figure 40-5. Click the New Document item on the New menu to create a new document from the SharePoint site.

Your newly created document will now be shown in the document library.

Working with Existing Documents and Version Control

Document options for each item in a document library are found in the item's drop-down menu. Position the mouse pointer over a document name, and a drop-down arrow appears. When you click the arrow, the Item drop-down menu appears. This menu was shown earlier in Figure 40-1. From this menu, you can edit the document (clicking the document name also has this effect); edit the document properties, which include the name and a descriptive title for the document; and delete the document from the library.

The key features in a shared document library are the version control features. In Windows SharePoint Services, these features include the ability to check a document in and out as well as view its version history. When you check out a document, other users can no longer edit the document until you return it to the document library by checking it in.

To check out a document, simply choose Check Out on the Item drop-down menu, as shown in Figure 40-6. Click OK when warned that you are about to check out the document. The icon in the Type column changes to display a green arrow to indicate that the document is checked out. After you specify that you want to check out the document, click the Item drop-down arrow again and click Edit In Microsoft Office

Word (or whichever application name appears). The document is downloaded to your computer and displayed in the application for editing. Perform your edits. Click the Microsoft Office Button and then Save to have Word 2007 save the document to the SharePoint site.

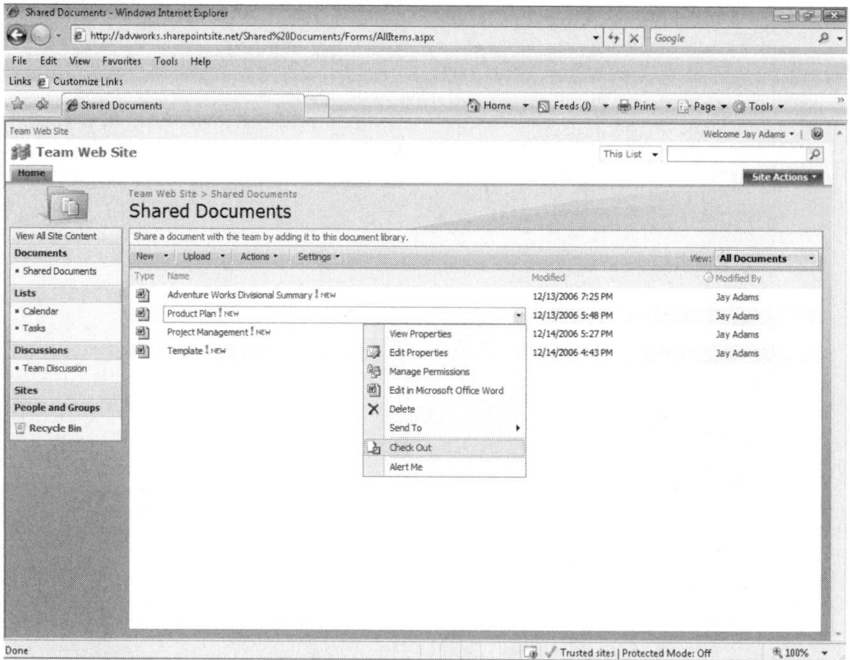

Figure 40-6. Use this drop-down list to check out documents from your SharePoint site.

When you have finished editing, you can close the document on your system and then return to the SharePoint site and check in the document. Checking a document back in to the document library is handled from the same drop-down menu as checking out. Click the Item drop-down arrow, and then click Check In. The Check In page shown in Figure 40-7 is displayed. Enter any comments for the version history, and then click OK. A message box appears, asking whether you want to continue. Click Yes. The document is then checked in.

INSIDE OUT

Force the check-in of a document

A user in the Administrator site group can force the checking in of a document even if another user has it checked out. This can be useful if a user checks out a document and forgets to check it back in and then leaves for the day, for example. An administrator can forcibly check the document back in so that other users can work with it. Changes made while the document was checked out might be lost in this case.

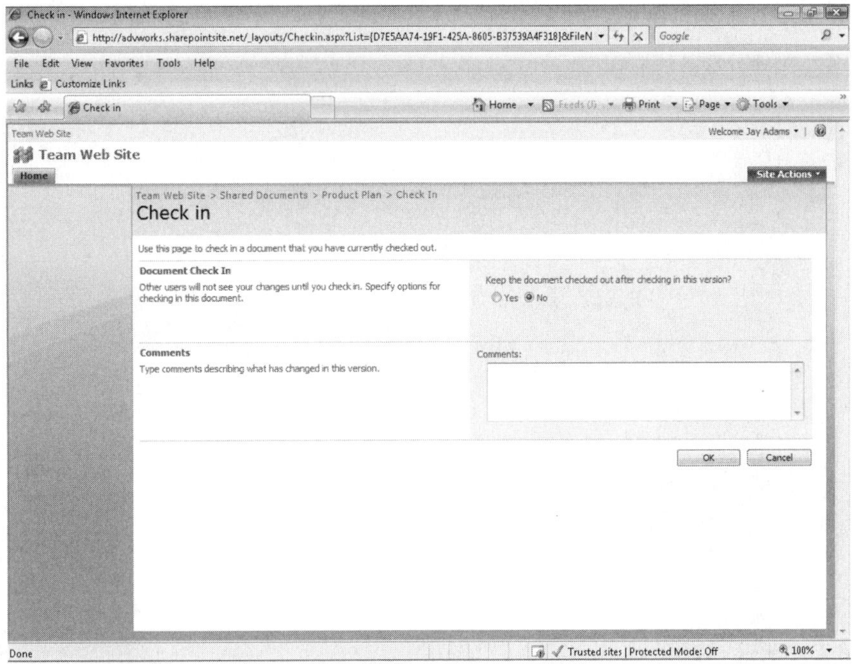

Figure 40-7. The Check In page is used to check in a document.

In the document library, choose Version History on the Item drop-down menu for a document. If version history is enabled for the document library, every time a document is checked in, it will appear in the version history, as shown in Figure 40-8. You can view each version of the document by hovering the mouse pointer over the date and time for a version and then clicking View. You also can restore a document by clicking the Restore option on this drop-down menu. You can delete old versions by clicking Delete Minor Versions.

INSIDE OUT Enable version history

Version history can be enabled from the Versions Saved page by clicking Site Actions and then clicking Site Settings on the right side of the screen. Under Site Administration, click Site Libraries And Lists, click Customize "Shared Documents," and then click Versioning Settings. Specify the level of version history to retain in the Document Version History area, and then click OK when you have finished.

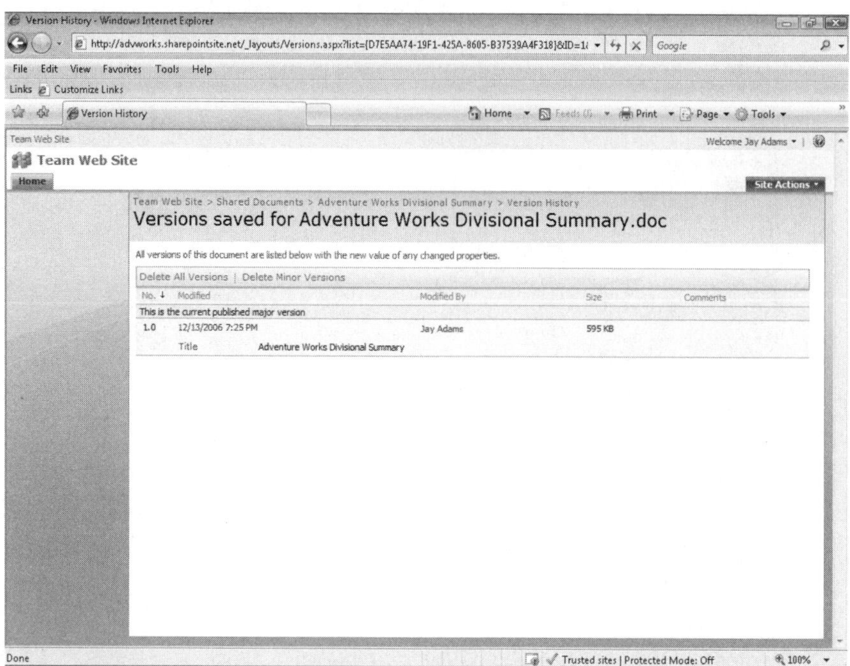

Figure 40-8. The Versions Saved page shows the document's version history and can be used to restore old versions of the document.

Working with Shared Contacts

Windows SharePoint Services 2.0 provides lists that can be used to share a variety of information. One of the defined list types is contacts, which is used to store contact information in a way similar to the Contacts folder in Outlook 2007. Shared contacts work only with SharePoint Services 2.0, not with the latest version of SharePoint (SharePoint Services 3.0).

Viewing Contacts on a Windows SharePoint Services Site

To view contacts on a Windows SharePoint Services 2.0 site, click Documents And Lists at the top of any Windows SharePoint Services 2.0 page. The contacts lists are in the Lists area of the page. By default, a list named Contacts is created when Windows SharePoint Services is installed; you might have more lists of contacts on your site. Click a contacts list name to view the list, as shown in Figure 40-9. From this list, you can add, edit, and delete contacts. An Item drop-down menu for contacts will be displayed if you hover the mouse pointer over the last name of a specific contact.

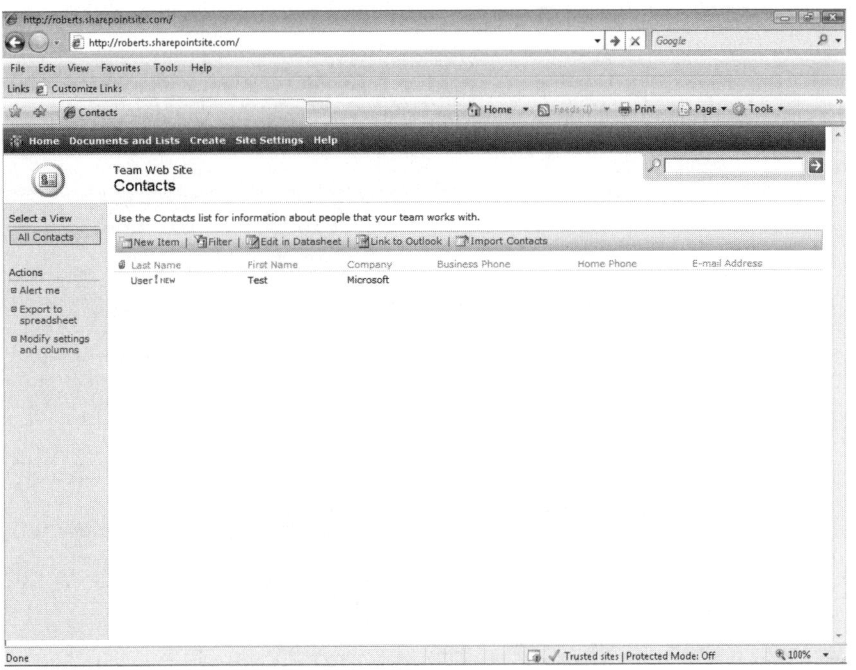

Figure 40-9. A contacts list shows the contact information in the familiar SharePoint 3.0 layout.

Linking Windows SharePoint Services 2.0 Contacts Lists to Outlook

If you frequently use contacts in your Windows SharePoint Services team site, it might be a lot of effort to open the team site every time you need a contact. Windows SharePoint Services and Outlook 2007 provide a method of linking a contacts list from Windows SharePoint Services directly into Outlook 2007 so that the contacts in the Windows SharePoint Services site show up as a contacts folder in Outlook 2007. However, contacts lists linked from Windows SharePoint Services into Outlook 2007 cannot be edited; they can only be read. You must add, edit, or delete contacts in a linked folder directly in the SharePoint Server 2.0 site.

To link a contacts list in Windows SharePoint Services into Outlook 2007, open the contacts list, click Actions, and then click Connect To Outlook. Outlook 2007 will start if needed. Microsoft Internet Explorer® displays a message asking whether it is OK to continue; click Yes. The message box shown in Figure 40-10 appears. This message box notifies you that a SharePoint site is attempting to link to Outlook 2007 and that the site is not trusted by default. Verify that the site URL in the message box is correct, and then click Yes.

> **Note**
>
> The message box notifying you that SharePoint is attempting to link to Outlook 2007 appears so that rogue SharePoint sites cannot link into Outlook 2007 without your knowledge or permission.

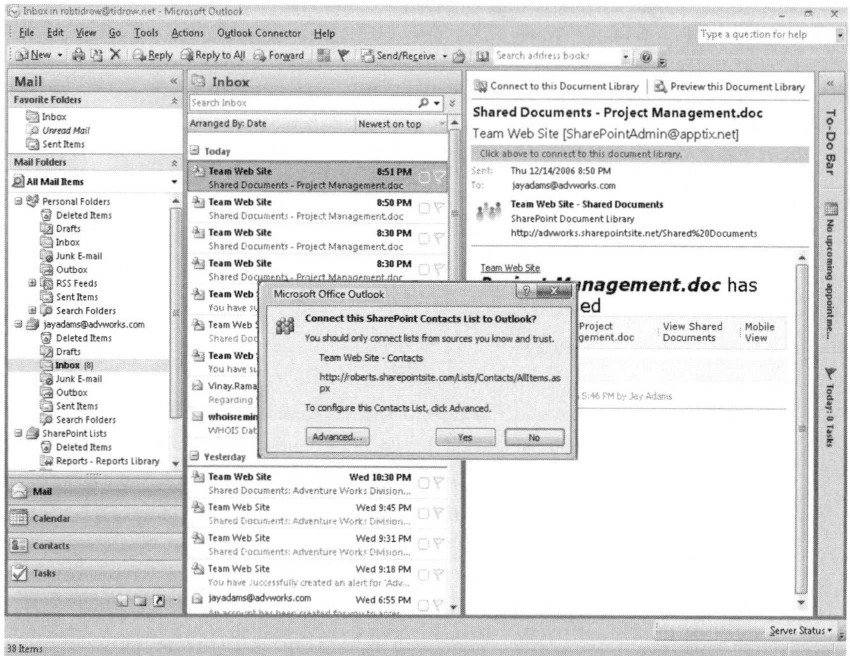

Figure 40-10. When you attempt to link a SharePoint contacts list to Outlook 2007, a message box appears, allowing you to verify that the SharePoint site is trusted before the link is created.

After you click Yes in this message box, the contacts list is linked into Outlook 2007, as shown in Figure 40-11. You now have two contacts folders in Outlook 2007, Contacts and Team Web Site–Contacts. You can open the new contacts folder linked from Windows SharePoint Services and view contacts, but you cannot add, edit, or delete contacts. (See the section "Copying Contacts from Outlook to Windows SharePoint Services 2.0" later in this chapter for more information.)

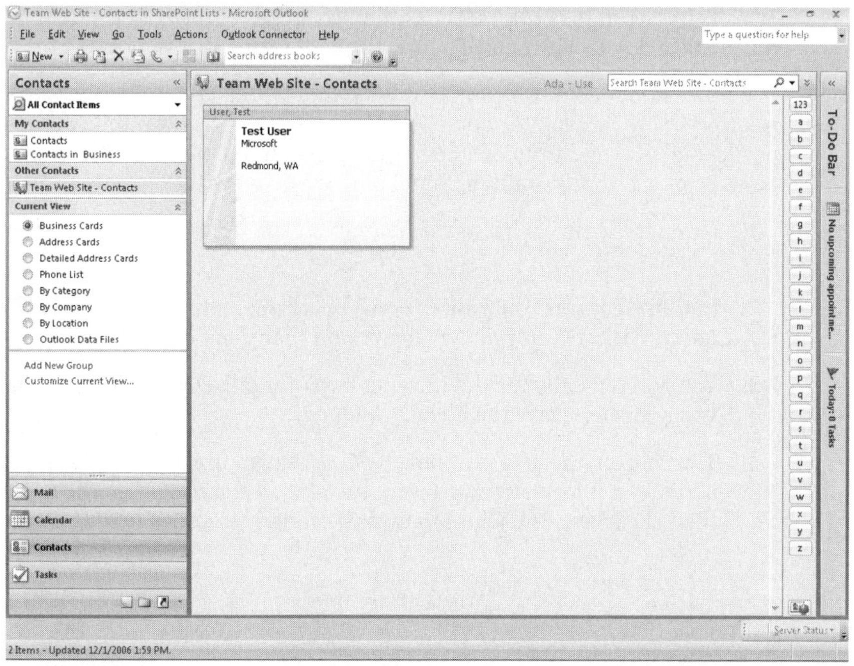

Figure 40-11. The new contacts folder linked from Windows SharePoint Services 2.0 is shown in Outlook 2007.

> **Note**
>
> The name in the Team Web Site—Contacts folder preceding the dash is the name of the SharePoint site, and the name following the dash is the name of the contacts list within the SharePoint site. If the name of the linked contacts list in Windows SharePoint Services were Project Contacts, for example, the linked folder in Outlook 2007 would be named Team Web Site—Project Contacts.

Copying Contacts from Windows SharePoint Services 2.0 to Outlook

Synchronizing contacts from Windows SharePoint Services 2.0 to Outlook 2007 is useful if you need access to an entire contacts list stored in a SharePoint site, but it is also possible to copy contacts from SharePoint to Outlook 2007. This is useful if you need only a few contacts from Windows SharePoint Services in Outlook 2007 for use on a regular basis, or if you need the contacts stored in a single contacts folder in Outlook 2007. Note that if you edit the contact, your changes are not reflected in the Windows

SharePoint Services contacts list, as the two copies of the contact are independent. See the next section to learn how to copy the contact back to Windows SharePoint Services.

The process for copying a contact from Windows SharePoint Services to Outlook 2007 is surprisingly simple. Windows SharePoint Services has the ability to export and import contacts to and from contacts lists on a SharePoint site in vCard (.vcf) format. To copy a contact from Windows SharePoint Services to Outlook 2007, follow these steps:

1. Open the contacts list in the SharePoint site from which you want to copy the contact.
2. Find the contact you want to copy, hover the mouse pointer over the contact's last name, click the drop-down arrow, and then click Export Contact.
3. You will typically see the Internet Explorer File Download dialog box, prompting you to open or save the file. Click Open.
4. The contact opens in Outlook 2007, as shown in Figure 40-12. Enter any additional information you want saved with the contact in the contact form, and then click Save And Close to save the contact in your Outlook 2007 Contacts folder.

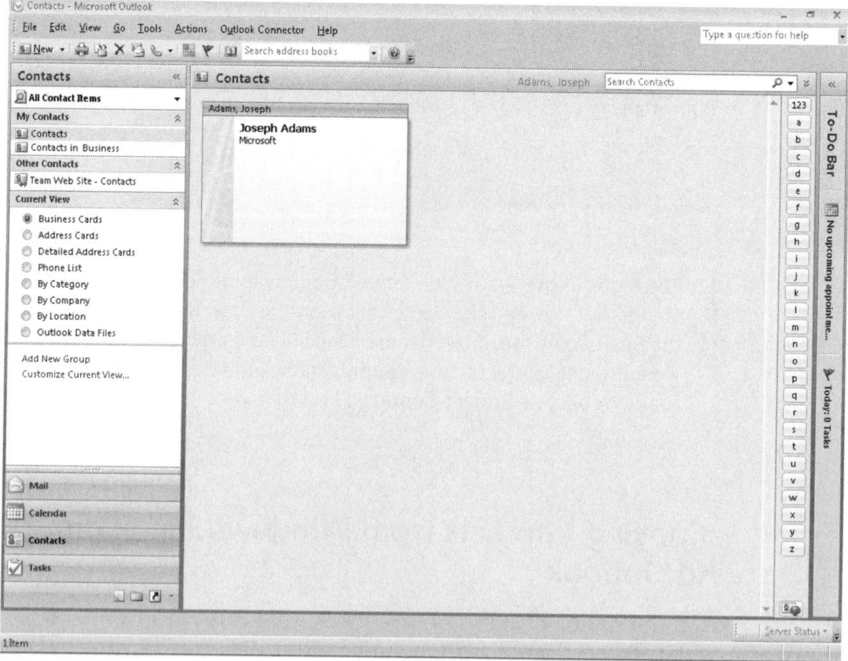

Figure 40-12. When you export a contact from the SharePoint site, the contact information opens in the Outlook 2007 contact form and you can save it to your Contacts folder.

Copying Contacts from Outlook to Windows SharePoint Services 2.0

The preceding two sections covered how to get your contacts from Windows SharePoint Services into Outlook 2007, but the ability to move Outlook 2007 contacts into Windows SharePoint Services is just as useful. If you are creating a Web site for your team, for example, and need to get a number of contacts from each team member's Contacts folder in Outlook 2007 into the Windows SharePoint Services contacts list, using the Import Contacts feature is much easier than adding each contact by hand. To copy contacts from Outlook 2007 to a SharePoint site, follow these steps:

1. In the SharePoint site, open the contacts list into which you want to import contacts.
2. Click Import Contacts.
3. In the Select Users To Import dialog box, shown in Figure 40-13, select the Outlook 2007 contacts folder containing the contact to import in the Show Names From The drop-down list. The Contacts folder is selected by default.

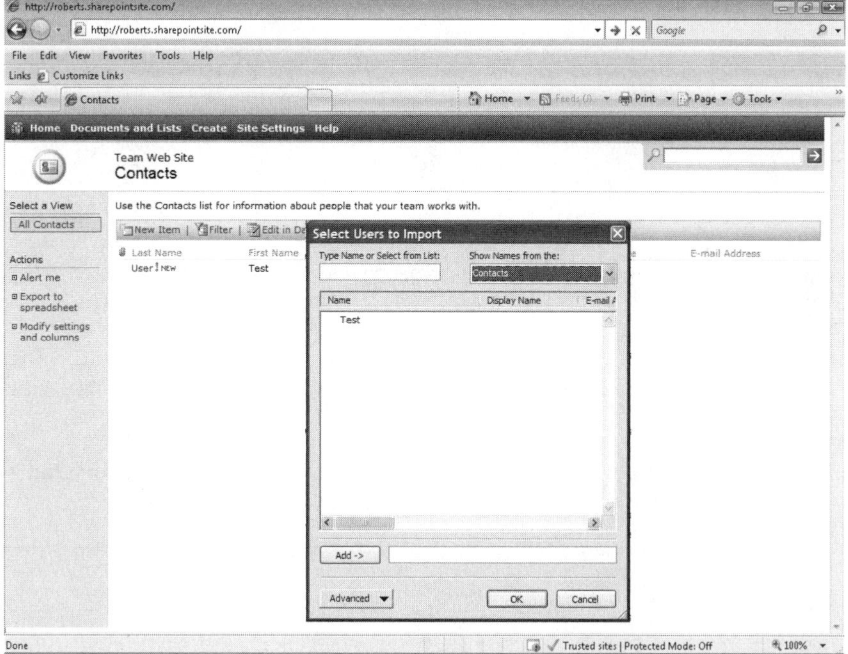

Figure 40-13. The Select Users To Import dialog box is used to select the contacts to import from Outlook 2007.

4. Select a contact in the list, click Add, and then click OK.
5. When the message box shown in Figure 40-14 is displayed, click Yes to allow access to the Outlook 2007 data. This message box warns you that someone is

trying to access your data. If you will be adding more contacts from Outlook 2007, selecting the Allow Access For check box and specifying a time interval in the Select Users To Import dialog box prevents this message box from being displayed again for the length of time selected.

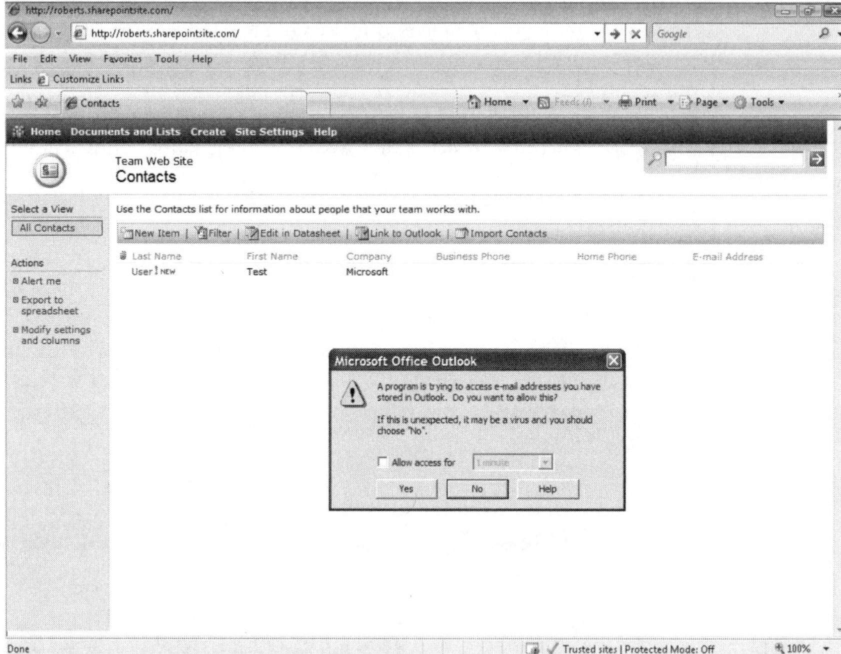

Figure 40-14. When someone tries to access your data stored in Outlook 2007, such as when importing contacts into Windows SharePoint Services, you are notified and can grant or deny access.

> **Note**
>
> Contacts stored in Outlook 2007 must have an associated e-mail address, or they will not appear in the Select Users To Import dialog box.

The contact will now be shown in the contacts list in the SharePoint site.

Linking a Team Calendar to Outlook

A SharePoint Calendar list in SharePoint 3.0 can be linked to Outlook 2007. A Calendar list is used to maintain important events and is shared by the team members using the site. The Calendar list is created by default when Windows SharePoint Services is installed. Click Home and then click Calendar in the Lists area on the Quick Launch bar.

There are three ways to view events: Calendar view, All Events view, and Current Events view. These views are selected in the Calendar drop-down list. All Events view shows a listing of events, and Calendar view shows events in a traditional calendar format. The view you select has no effect on linking to Outlook 2007. When a Calendar list is linked to Outlook 2007, it is shown in the Outlook 2007 calendar format.

To link a Calendar list to Outlook 2007, follow these steps:

1. On the Quick Launch bar, click Calendar.
2. Click Actions, and then click Connect To Outlook.
3. A message box is displayed, warning you that a SharePoint folder is being added to Outlook 2007. (You might also get a message from Internet Explorer asking whether you want to continue. Click Yes, and then you'll see the message from Outlook 2007.) Click Yes to add the folder. This message box is similar to the one shown earlier in Figure 40-10, but instead of prompting you to connect a contacts list to Outlook 2007, you are prompted to connect a calendar to Outlook.

When the calendar is linked to Outlook 2007, it is displayed as shown in Figure 40-15. You can see the new calendar listed in the Navigation Pane on the left. Linked Calendar lists are read-only in Outlook 2007. To add, edit, or delete events, you must do so within the SharePoint site.

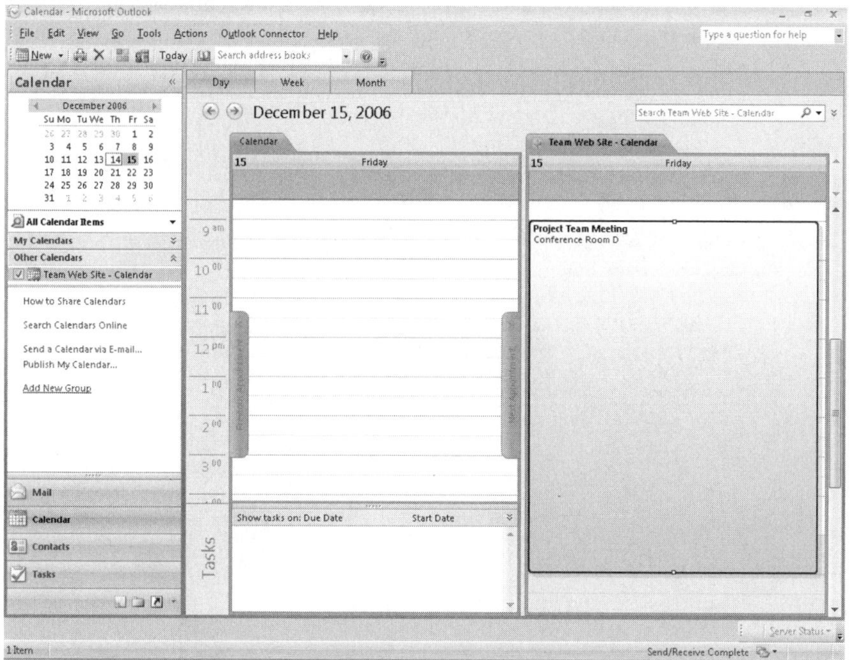

Figure 40-15. The calendar linked from the SharePoint site is shown in Outlook 2007.

Configuring Alerts in Outlook

We looked at alerts earlier in this chapter, in the section "Setting Up Alerts." Whereas alerts in Windows SharePoint Services are sent through e-mail messages, Outlook 2007 includes integration that allows for the simple management of alert messages from a SharePoint site. The Outlook 2007 Manage Alerts tab in the Rules And Alerts dialog box provides links directly into the correct SharePoint site pages for alert management.

To manage SharePoint alerts from Outlook 2007, follow these steps:

1. Configure an alert for a resource on the SharePoint site. The alert notification will be sent to you through e-mail and will appear in your Inbox.
2. Ensure that a mail folder is open.
3. Choose Tools, Rules And Alerts. The Rules And Alerts dialog box appears.
4. Click the Manage Alerts tab, shown in Figure 40-16. Wait for Outlook 2007 to retrieve alert information from the SharePoint site.

> **Note**
>
> You must configure the first alert manually from the SharePoint site because when an alert is processed by Outlook 2007, the site is *trusted*, and you can then manage alerts from the Rules And Alerts dialog box. It is possible to manage alerts without first configuring an alert through the SharePoint site if an administrator adds the site as a trusted domain for alerts.

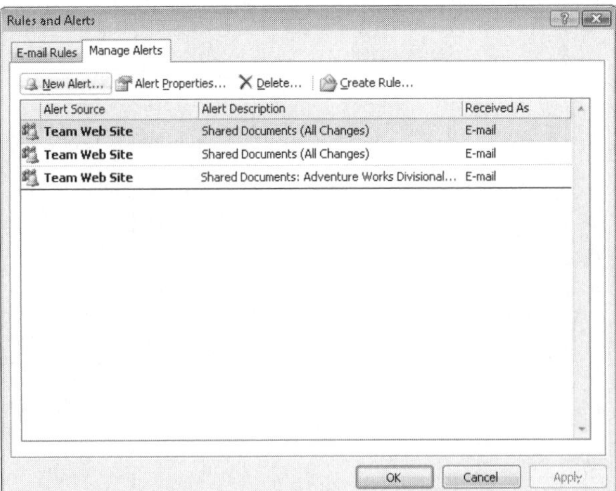

Figure 40-16. The Manage Alerts tab in the Rules And Alerts dialog box is used to manage SharePoint alerts directly from within Outlook 2007.

Adding Alerts from Outlook

You can now work with alerts directly within the client computer running Outlook 2007. To add a new alert, follow these steps:

1. Click New Alert on the Manage Alerts tab in the Rules And Alerts dialog box.
2. Expand Sources Currently Sending Me Alerts in the New Alert dialog box.
3. Select the SharePoint site in the list, as shown in Figure 40-17, and then click Open. You can also type the URL for the SharePoint site in the Web site Address box and then click Open.

Figure 40-17. Select the SharePoint site in which to create the new alert in the list in the New Alert dialog box.

4. The New Alert page in the SharePoint site opens automatically in a Web browser, as shown in Figure 40-18. Select the list or document library for which to set the alert, and then click Next.
5. Set the alert type and frequency as described in "Setting Up Alerts" earlier in this chapter.
6. Click OK to set the alert. You are then taken to the My Alerts On This Site page in the SharePoint site to review your alerts.
7. Switch to Outlook 2007.
8. Click the OK button to close the Rules And Alerts dialog box.
9. On the Tools menu, click Rules And Alerts.
10. Click the Manage Alerts tab in the Rules And Alerts dialog box. The new alert is shown on the Manage Alerts tab in the Rules And Alerts dialog box.

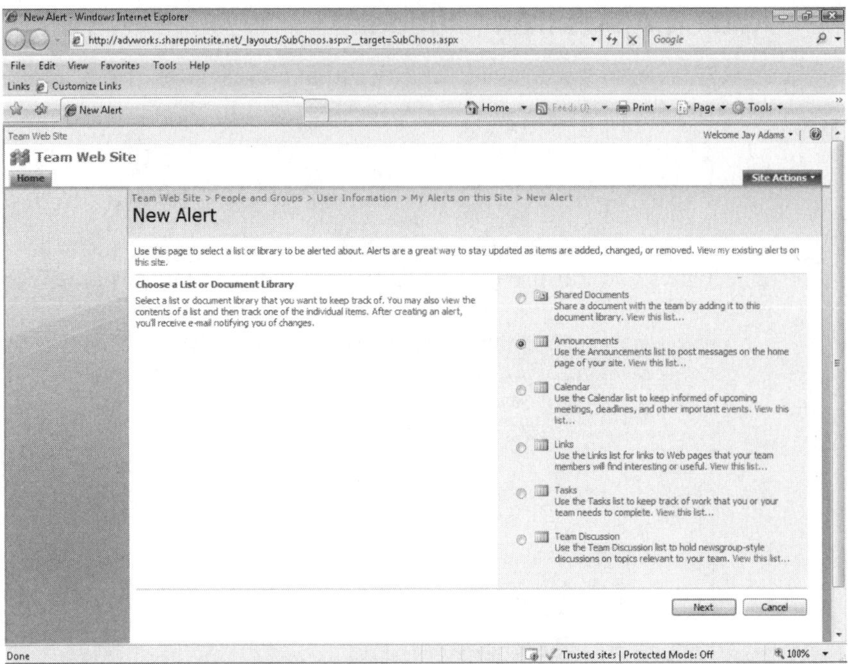

Figure 40-18. The New Alert page in the SharePoint site opens when you select the site from the list in the New Alert dialog box and click Open.

Editing and Deleting Alerts from Outlook

In addition to adding alerts directly from within Outlook 2007, you can edit existing alerts by following these steps:

1. Select the alert you want to edit on the Manage Alerts tab in the Rules And Alerts dialog box, and then click Alert Properties.
2. The Alert Properties dialog box opens, as shown in Figure 40-19. This dialog box shows the alert source as a clickable link to the home page of the SharePoint site and includes a link to the main alerts management page in SharePoint. Click Modify Alert to edit the alert.
3. The Edit Alert page in the SharePoint site opens in the Web browser. Make any changes you need on the Edit Alert page, and then click OK. You can also click Delete to remove the alert.

You can also remove alerts on the Manage Alerts tab by selecting the alert and then clicking Delete. You are prompted to verify the deletion, and the alert is removed when you click Yes.

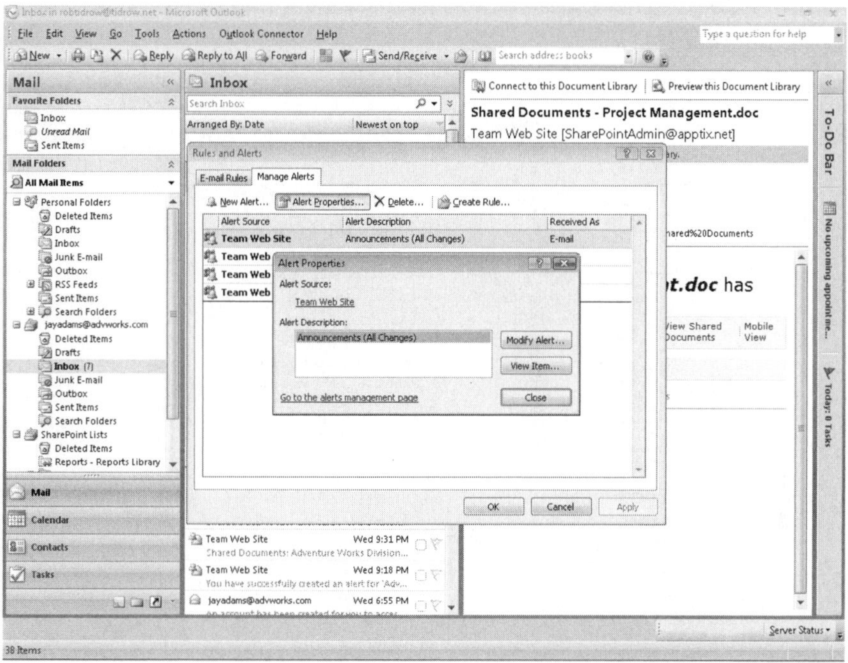

Figure 40-19. The Alert Properties dialog box is used to edit existing alerts from Outlook 2007.

Rules Based on Alerts

If you have a lot of alerts configured in a SharePoint site (or multiple sites), they can fill your mailbox quickly and distract from other messages. Outlook 2007 provides a simple way to create rules based on alerts. As you learned in Chapter 11, "Processing Messages Automatically," rules are used to process messages when they arrive in your mailbox. To configure a rule based on an alert, follow these steps:

1. Select the alert for which to configure a rule on the Manage Alerts tab in the Rules And Alerts dialog box.
2. Click Create Rule.
3. The Create Rule dialog opens, as shown in Figure 40-20. Specify what Outlook 2007 should do when it receives the selected alert. You can have Outlook 2007 display the alert in the New Item Alert window, play a sound, and move the message to a new folder.

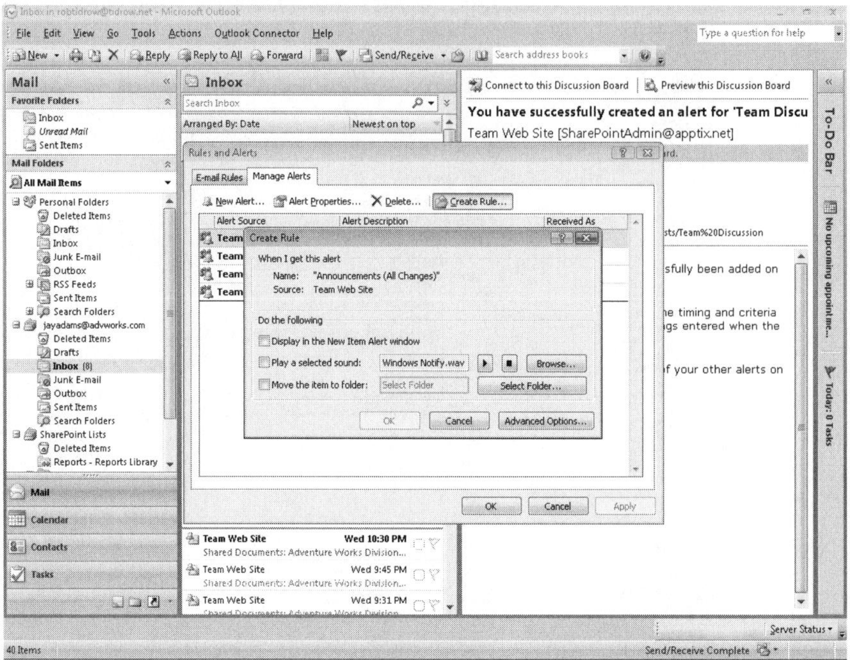

Figure 40-20. The Create Rule dialog box is used to create a rule based on an alert.

4. You can click Advanced Options to open the Rules Wizard and go into more detailed configuration for the rule. Use of the Rules Wizard is explained in Chapter 11, "Processing Messages Automatically." In most cases, this is not necessary for a basic alert.

5. Click OK to create the rule.

When the rule is created, the Success dialog box, shown in Figure 40-21, is displayed. You are notified that the rule is a client-side rule and given the option to run the rule against your mailbox immediately to find any messages that fit the rule criteria.

After you click OK in the Success dialog box, you can see the newly created rule by clicking the E-Mail Rules tab in the Rules And Alerts dialog box, which is already open.

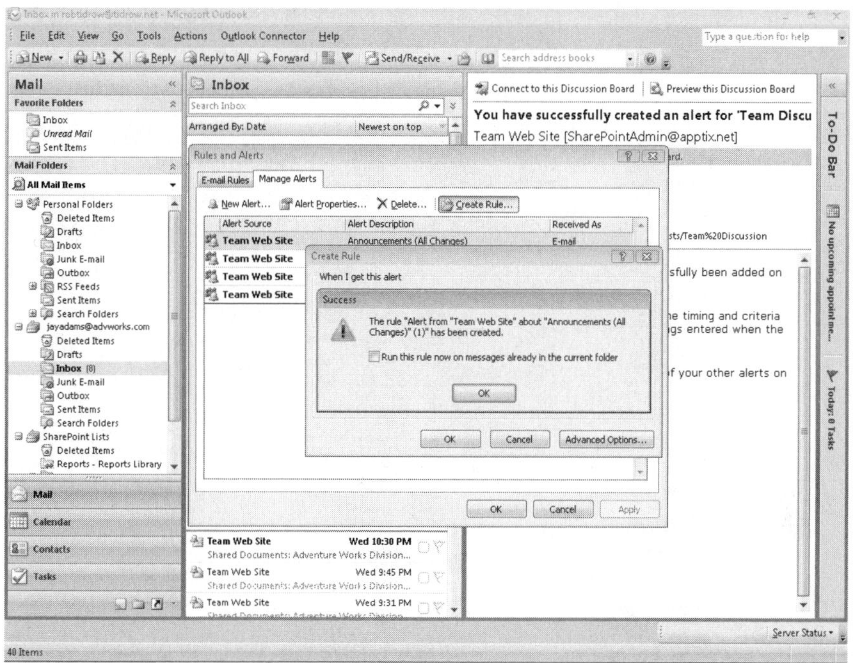

Figure 40-21. When the rule based on an alert is created, the Success dialog box is shown.

Using Outlook to Work with SharePoint Libraries and Files

In Outlook 2007, you can connect a SharePoint library to Outlook 2007. This makes the library and its items available within Outlook 2007 so that you don't have to use a Web browser to view and work with them—you can use Outlook 2007 instead. For example, you might want to have a list of current project documents that have been uploaded to your team's SharePoint site as you create e-mail messages to update your team members, support staff, and management.

By having the list of documents appear in Outlook 2007, you can quickly view the document name, its status, and other information without leaving Outlook 2007. Also, if you open a SharePoint document from within Outlook 2007, that file is stored locally on your hard drive while you view it. This makes the document open faster and reduces network traffic. If you make any edits to the document, you then check in the file to the SharePoint site. Files are stored on your hard drive in your personal folders (.pst) file.

Connecting a SharePoint Library to Outlook

To use Outlook 2007 to view and work with your SharePoint documents, you first connect a SharePoint library to Outlook 2007. This enables SharePoint and Outlook 2007 to synchronize your files so that you can have them available for offline use in Outlook 2007.

To connect a library to Outlook 2007, follow these steps:

1. In a library, click the Actions menu. This menu contains a list of actions that you can perform in this library, as shown in Figure 40-22.

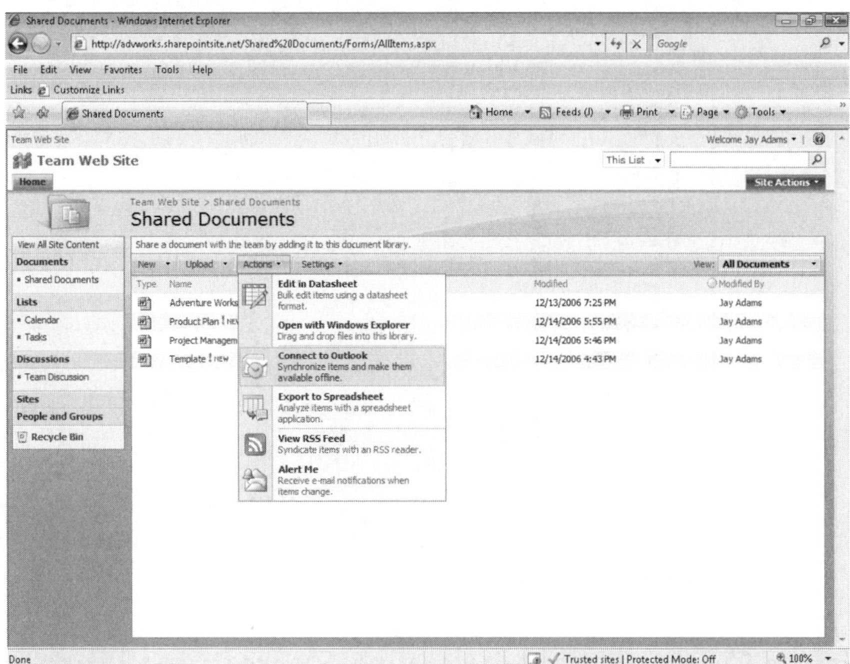

Figure 40-22. You can connect a SharePoint library to Outlook 2007 by using the Actions menu.

2. Click Connect To Outlook. A warning message might appear, telling you that you should connect lists only from sources you trust.

3. Click Yes. The Outlook Send/Receive Progress window appears as the library is connected. When finished, Outlook 2007 displays the library as a SharePoint list, as shown in Figure 40-23.

The libraries you connect to Outlook 2007 are in a folder named SharePoint Lists. The SharePoint Lists folder provides a view of file names, previews of documents, and links to download the files for viewing or editing.

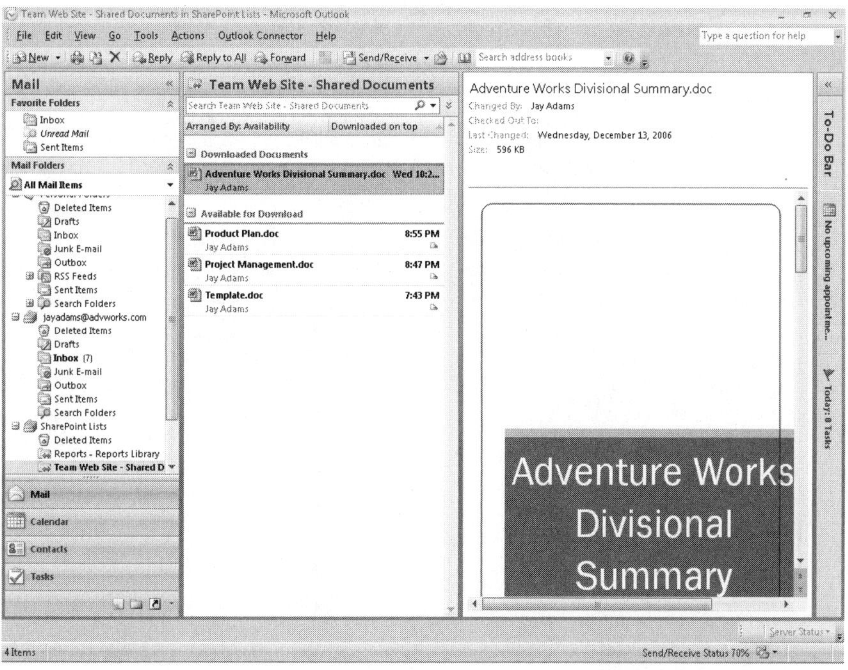

Figure 40-23. Outlook 2007 displays the connected library as a SharePoint Lists item.

Downloading Files from a SharePoint Library to Outlook

Sometimes when you connect a SharePoint library to Outlook 2007, the library is too large to download to your local hard drive. Instead, Outlook 2007 displays a group named Available For Download in the message list area, as shown in Figure 40-24. You can use this group to select individual files that you want to download to Outlook 2007. You can use the **Ctrl** key to select multiple files to download. Some files might include a button in the preview window labeled Download This Document. Click that button to download the file.

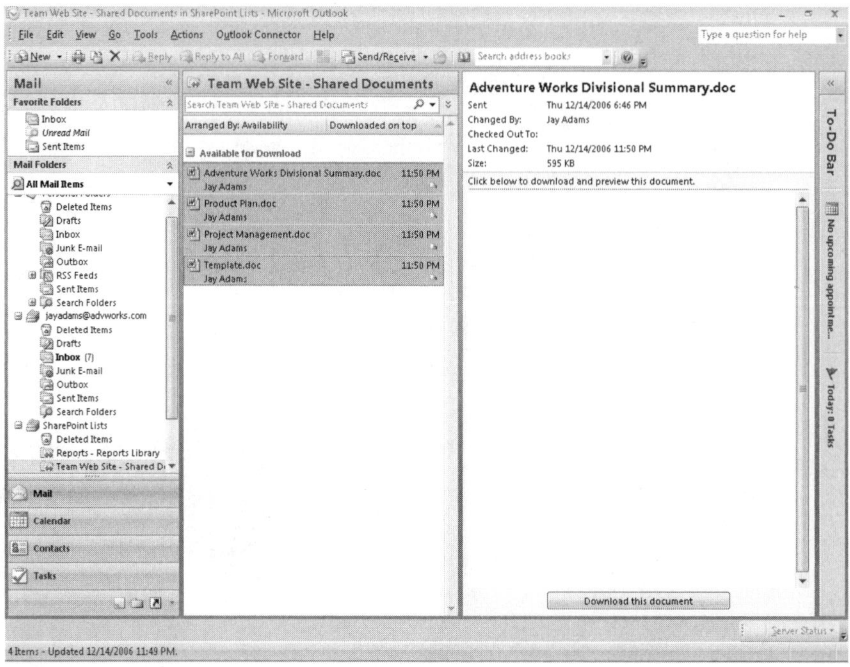

Figure 40-24. You can download files from SharePoint with Outlook 2007.

Opening Files from a SharePoint Site in Outlook

Once you have a SharePoint library connected to Outlook 2007, you can open files stored in that library from within Outlook 2007. Outlook 2007 enables you to view a number of different file formats, including the following:

- Microsoft Word documents
- Microsoft Excel worksheets
- Microsoft PowerPoint® presentations
- Pictures

To open a SharePoint library file in Outlook 2007, browse to a folder in the SharePoint Lists folder in the Outlook 2007 Navigation Pane. Click a folder to display that folder's list of files in the messages list. Files are displayed here just like e-mail messages. Each file, however, includes information about that file, such as name, file format, last user to edit the file, checkout information, modification date and time, and size. Figure 40-25 shows the messages list pane resized to display all the file details for files listed in the Team Web Site–Shared Documents SharePoint List.

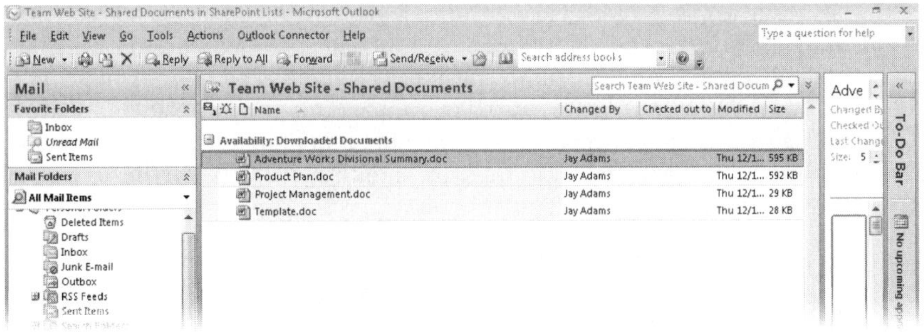

Figure 40-25. Outlook 2007 shows file details for files connected from SharePoint.

To open a file, you can click it to display the file in the Outlook 2007 Reading Pane. For example, Figure 40-26 shows a Microsoft Word file displayed in the Reading Pane.

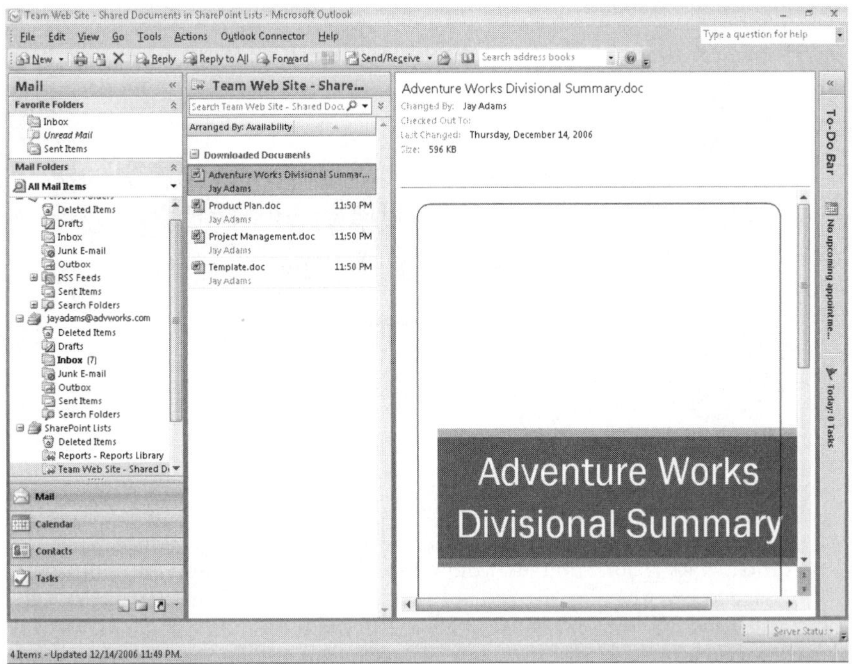

Figure 40-26. Outlook 2007 shows file details for files connected from SharePoint.

Editing Files from a SharePoint Site in Outlook

Not only can you open and view SharePoint files in Outlook 2007, you also can edit them. Before doing so, however, you should return to the SharePoint site and check out the document so that no one else can work on the document while you are working on it. (Outlook 2007 does not provide a way to check out the document locally.)

To edit the file, double-click it. Outlook 2007 displays a warning message about opening files from trustworthy sources only. Click Open to continue. The file opens in the default application for that file format (for example, an .xls file opens in Excel 2007, .ppt in PowerPoint 2007, and so on). For applications compatible with SharePoint Services 3.0, a banner appears across the top of document telling you that the document is an offline server document and that you should save the file to the server later, as shown in Figure 40-27.

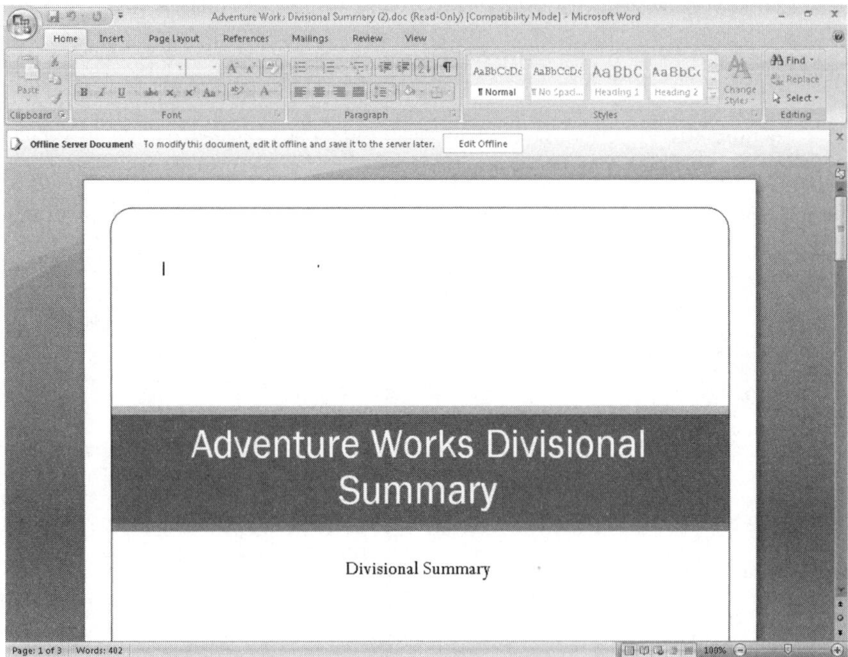

Figure 40-27. The Offline Server Document banner reminds you that the file you are editing needs to be updated to the server later.

Click the Edit Offline button. A message box appears, telling you that the document will be stored on your computer in the SharePoint Drafts folder. Click OK, and then edit the file. After you complete your edits, click the Microsoft Office Button and then click Save to save the file. Then click the Microsoft Office Button and click Close. If you are connected to your SharePoint site at this time, the Edit Offline dialog box appears. You can click the Update button to update the SharePoint site with your edited file. (You also can click Do Not Update Server to update the server later.)

When you click the Update button, the application (such as Word 2007) saves the changes to the SharePoint site.

If you chose not to update the files using the Update button, return to Outlook 2007, and then click the Send/Receive button when you are ready to update your files. Outlook 2007 synchronizes with the SharePoint Site to save your changes in the online library.

Removing SharePoint Files in Outlook

You can remove one or more files from a SharePoint library list in Outlook 2007 without actually removing the documents from the SharePoint library. The document remains on the server, but it is removed from your cached list in Outlook 2007. This feature simplifies browsing libraries that contain a large number of items.

To remove files from a SharePoint library list that have been connected to Outlook, follow these steps:

1. In the Outlook 2007 Navigation Pane, select the library that contains the files you want to remove.
2. Click the file that you want to remove. To remove multiple files, press **Ctrl** as you click the files.
3. Right-click the file, and then choose Remove Offline Copy, as shown in Figure 40-28.

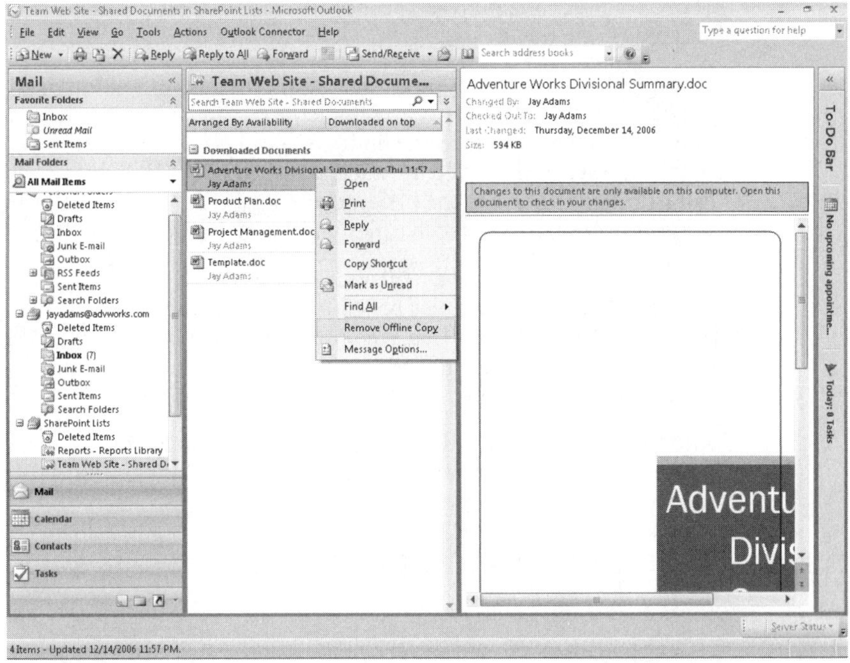

Figure 40-28. You can remove an offline file from Outlook 2007 but keep it in your SharePoint site.

When you remove a file from Outlook 2007, the Reading Pane removes the preview of the file and makes the file available for download. Outlook 2007 moves the file to the Available For Download group and adds a Download This Document button to the file.

Removing SharePoint Folders in Outlook

If you don't need a particular library anymore, you can easily remove it from Outlook 2007. Removing the library does not affect it on the SharePoint site but only removes it from the Navigation Pane in Outlook 2007. One thing to keep in mind, however, is that if you have not sent updates to the SharePoint site before you delete the folder, you will lose any edits you made to the offline files.

To remove a SharePoint folder, right-click it in the Navigation Pane. On the shortcut menu that appears, click Delete <NameOfLibrary>. The <NameOfLibrary> item is the name of the library you are removing. Click Yes.

Using E-Mail to Add a File to a SharePoint Library

If the SharePoint document library is configured to accept documents by e-mail, you can add a document to a library simply by sending an e-mail message, with the document attached, to the library. This is handy if you do not want to go through the process of opening your Web browser, connecting to your SharePoint site, locating a library, and uploading the file to it.

To use this feature, you need to know the e-mail address for the library you plan to send the file to. Some organizations include the e-mail address for libraries in their address book. If you have access to the library's settings, click the Settings button while viewing the library in your Web browser, and then click the library setting command (such as List Setting). Look in the List Information area for an E-Mail Address item. If your library is configured to receive files via e-mail, the address will appear here.

Others might include the e-mail address as part of the library's description—for example, placing the address beneath the title of the library so that users can see it while viewing the library in a Web browser. After you get the address, if your company does not already include the address in your Contacts folder or in the Outlook Address Book, add it your Contacts folder.

After you get the e-mail address, return to Outlook 2007, and then create your message. Attach the file that you want to send to the SharePoint site. Add the address of the library in the To box, and then click Send.

Note

Some organizations use SharePoint groups so that users can send an e-mail message and attachment to other members in a group. When you do this, the attached file is automatically added to the SharePoint site. If this is the case, type the address of the SharePoint group in the To box instead of the library address. The SharePoint group will already have the library address configured.

PART 9

Using Outlook with Exchange Server

CHAPTER 41

Configuring the Exchange Server Client

Although you can use Microsoft® Office Outlook® 2007 with other types of mail servers, you derive the greatest benefit when you use Office Outlook 2007 with Microsoft Exchange Server. Added benefits include the Out Of Office Assistant, the ability to recall messages, the ability to delegate functions to an assistant, the use of server-side message rules, and many other collaboration features.

You can connect to Exchange Server using any of several protocols, including Post Office Protocol 3 (POP3), Network News Transfer Protocol (NNTP), Internet Message Access Protocol (IMAP), and even Hypertext Transfer Protocol (HTTP). This means two things: you can connect to an Exchange Server using e-mail clients other than Outlook 2007 (Microsoft Outlook Express or Eudora, for example), and you can use a service provider other than the Exchange Server client within Outlook 2007 (such as POP3) to connect to the server, assuming that the server is appropriately configured. To get all the benefits afforded by the combination of Outlook 2007 and Exchange Server, however, you must use the Exchange Server service provided with Outlook 2007.

This chapter explains how to add the Exchange Server client to an Outlook 2007 profile and configure its settings.

For detailed information about adding other service providers to an Outlook 2007 profile, see Chapter 3, "Configuring Outlook Profiles and Accounts." You'll find additional information about setting up Internet e-mail accounts in Chapter 7, "Using Internet Mail Accounts."

Outlook as an Exchange Server Client

The Microsoft Exchange Server service in Outlook 2007 allows you to use Outlook 2007 as a client for Exchange Server. Of all the services supported by Outlook 2007, Exchange Server offers the broadest range of functionality, providing excellent support for collaboration, information sharing, group scheduling, and more.

The remaining chapters in Part 9, "Using Outlook with Exchange Server," cover a broad range of topics to help you use Outlook 2007 effectively as an Exchange Server client.

Setting up an Exchange Server account in Outlook 2007 isn't difficult, but it does require several steps, as follows:

1. If you are running Outlook 2007 for the first time, in the Outlook 2007 Startup Wizard, go to the Choose E-Mail Service page. To reach this page if you have run Outlook 2007 previously and your profile already includes a mail account, right-click the Outlook icon on the Start menu, select the profile, and then choose Properties. Click E-Mail Accounts, and then click New on the E-Mail tab in the Account Settings dialog box.
2. Select the Microsoft Exchange, POP3, IMAP, or HTTP option, and then click Next.
3. The Auto Account Setup page, shown in Figure 41-1, gives you a place to specify your name, e-mail address, and password. If AutoDiscover is properly configured on the computer running Exchange Server and in your network environment, you can enter your name, e-mail address, and password as it is set on the server, click Next, and have Outlook 2007 determine the settings necessary to connect to your server. However, the following steps assume that you are not able to use AutoDiscover and must configure the account manually.

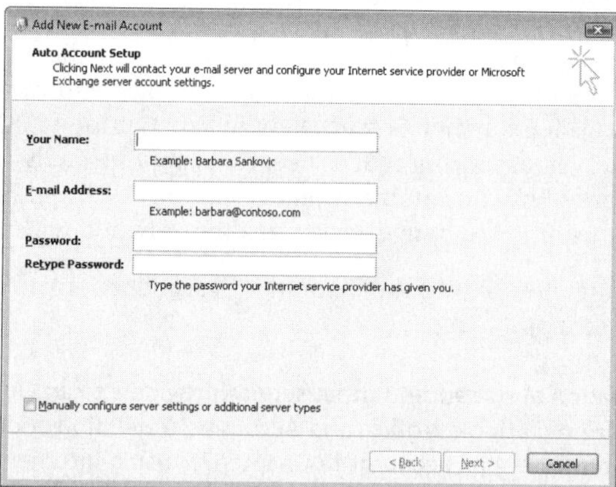

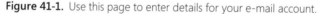

Figure 41-1. Use this page to enter details for your e-mail account.

> **Note**
>
> AutoDiscover requires that your computer be able to resolve the autodiscover host in your domain. For example, if your computer resides in the tailspintoys.com domain, your computer must be able to resolve autodiscover.tailspintoys.com to the servers on the tailspintoys.com network that are providing AutoDiscover services. For more details on AutoDiscover, see the Exchange Server 2007 documentation.

4. If you don't want to use AutoDiscover, choose Manually Configure Server Settings Or Additional Server Types, and then click Next.
5. Choose Microsoft Exchange, and then click Next.
6. On the Microsoft Exchange Settings page, shown in Figure 41-2, specify the following information:

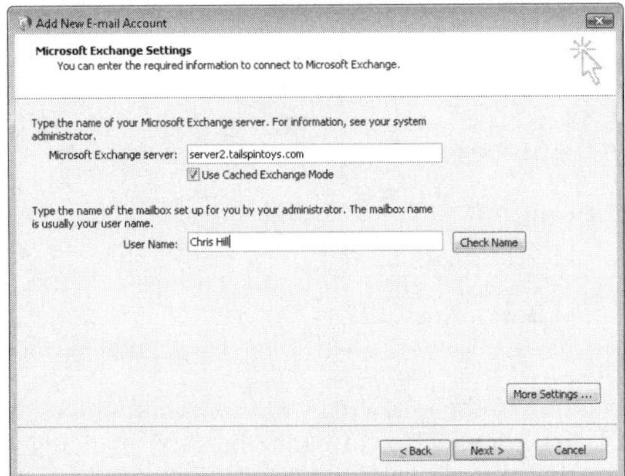

Figure 41-2. Configure basic Exchange Server settings on the Microsoft Exchange Settings page.

Microsoft Exchange Server Specify the NetBIOS or Domain Name Service (DNS) name of the computer running Exchange Server or its IP address. You don't have to include a double backslash (\\) before the server name.

Use Cached Exchange Mode Select this check box to have Outlook 2007 create a locally cached copy of your entire Exchange Server mailbox on your local computer. Outlook 2007 creates an offline folder store (.ost) file in which to store the mailbox and works from that cached copy, handling synchronization issues automatically.

User Name Specify the name of your mailbox on the server. You can specify your logon account name or mailbox name. For example, you might use **chill** or **Chris Hill**.

Check Name After you enter your logon or mailbox name, click Check Name to check the specified account information against the information on the server. If you specify your logon name, clicking Check Name automatically changes the user name to your mailbox name. Outlook 2007 indicates a successful check by underlining the user name. If you are connecting to the server using remote procedure call (RPC) over HTTP, do not click Check Name–you must configure the connection first because Outlook 2007 must be able to communicate with the server to check your name.

7. Click More Settings to open the Microsoft Exchange dialog box, shown in Figure 41-3.

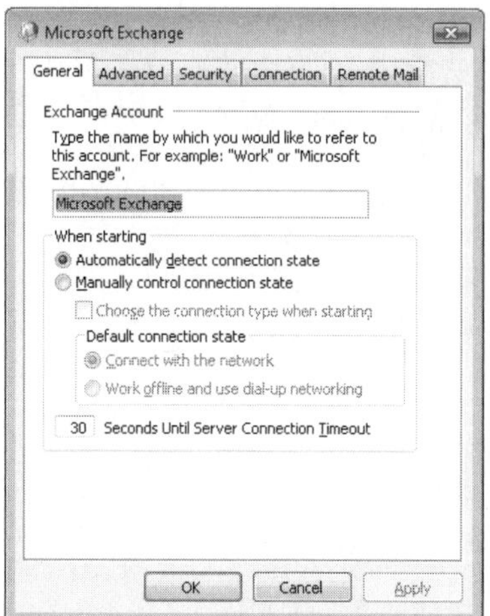

Figure 41-3. Use the Microsoft Exchange dialog box to configure additional options.

8. Use the information in the following sections to configure additional settings if needed, and then click OK to close the Microsoft Exchange dialog box. Click Next, and then click Finish.

Configuring General Properties

You use the General tab in the Microsoft Exchange dialog box (shown earlier in Figure 41-3) to configure the account name, the connection state, and other general settings, as follows:

- **Exchange Account** Specify the name under which the account appears in your Outlook 2007 configuration. This name has no bearing on the Exchange Server name or your account name. For example, you might name the account Office E-Mail, Work Account, or Microsoft Exchange Server.
- **Automatically Detect Connection State** Direct Outlook 2007 to detect the connection state (offline or online) at startup and choose the appropriate state. Use this option if your computer is connected to the network all the time. Use this option also if you're setting up an Exchange Server account on a notebook computer under a profile you use when the notebook is connected to the network.
- **Manually Control Connection State** Control the connection state at startup. Choose this option if you're setting up an Exchange Server account on a computer that is sometimes disconnected from the network (a notebook computer, for example) or that always accesses the computer running Exchange Server remotely.

Choose one of the following suboptions, depending on how you want Outlook 2007 to connect to the server:

Choose The Connection Type When Starting Specify which method Outlook 2007 uses to connect to the computer running Exchange Server at startup. If this check box is selected, Outlook 2007 prompts you each time it starts, asking whether you want to connect to the network or work offline. Clear this check box if you want Outlook 2007 to make that determination.

Connect With The Network Connect to the computer running Exchange Server through the network rather than initiating a dial-up connection. Use this option if your computer is hard-wired to the network or always online, such as with a Digital Subscriber Line (DSL), cable modem, or other persistent remote connection.

Work Offline And Use Dial-Up Networking Use dial-up networking to connect to the computer running Exchange Server. Specify the connection options on the Connection tab.

For information about setting connection options, see "Configuring Connection Properties" later in this chapter.

- **Seconds Until Server Connection Timeout** Specify the time-out for connection attempts to the computer running Exchange Server. If you are working remotely over a slow connection, increase this value to give Outlook 2007 more time to establish the connection to the server.

INSIDE OUT Increase TCP Time-Out for On-Demand Connections

If you use Internet Connection Sharing or demand-dial router connections, you've no doubt had your client computer time out while waiting for the Internet Connection Sharing or demand-dial router to establish a connection. This can cause a remote connection to the Exchange Server computer to fail.

TCP sets a retransmission timer when it attempts the first data transmission for a connection, with an initial retransmission time-out value of 3 seconds. TCP doubles the retransmission time-out value for each subsequent connection attempt and by default attempts retransmission two times. The first attempt is made at 3 seconds, the second at 3 + 6 seconds, and the third at 3 + 6 + 12 seconds, for a maximum time-out of 21 seconds. Increasing the initial retransmission timer to 5 seconds results in a total maximum time-out of 5 + 10 + 20, or 35 seconds.

The initial TCP retransmission time-out is defined by the registry value HKEY_LOCAL_MACHINE\System\CurrentControlSet\Services\Tcpip\Parameters\InitialRtt. The InitialRtt value is a REG_DWORD with a valid range from 0 to 65,535 and specifies the time-out in milliseconds.

The number of connection attempts is defined by the registry setting HKEY_LOCAL_MACHINE\System\CurrentControlSet\Services\Tcpip\Parameters\TcpMaxDataRetransmissions. The TcpMaxDataRetransmissions value is also a REG_DWORD with a valid range of 0 to 65,535.

Configuring Advanced Properties

You use the Advanced tab in the Microsoft Exchange dialog box, shown in Figure 41-4, to configure additional mailboxes to open as well as security and offline processing settings. Why use additional mailboxes? You might own two mailboxes on the server and need access to both of them. For example, if you are the system administrator, you probably need to manage your own account as well as the Administrator account. Or perhaps you've been delegated as an assistant for a set of mailboxes and need to access them to manage someone's schedule. The Advanced tab is where you add mailboxes that you own or for which you've been granted delegate access.

Figure 41-4. Use the Advanced tab to configure additional, Cached Exchange Mode, and offline file settings.

The options on the Advanced tab are:

- **Open These Additional Mailboxes** Define the set of mailboxes you want Outlook 2007 to open. These can be mailboxes that you own or for which you've been granted delegate access.
- **Use Cached Exchange Mode** Have Outlook 2007 create and work from a locally cached copy of your mailbox. This setting corresponds to the Use Cached Exchange Mode setting on the Exchange Server Settings page of the E-Mail Accounts Wizard.
- **Download Shared Folders** Select this option if you want Outlook 2007 to download the contents of shared folders, such as other users' Inbox or Calendar folders made available to you through delegate permissions or Microsoft Office SharePoint® folders.
- **Download Public Folder Favorites** Select this check box if you want Outlook 2007 to cache the public folders you have added to the Favorites folder in the Public Folders branch. Before selecting this check box, consider how much replication traffic you will experience if the folders in your Favorites folder contain a large number of posts and are very active.

- **Offline Folder File Settings** Set up an .ost file to use as your data cache while working offline. You need to use an .ost file only if the account is configured to store your data in your Exchange Server mailbox. If your primary data file is a personal folders (.pst) file, or if you don't work offline, you don't need an .ost file.

Configuring Security Properties

The settings on the Security tab, shown in Figure 41-5, control whether Outlook 2007 encrypts data between the client computer and the server and how authentication is handled.

Figure 41-5. Use the Security tab to configure security settings.

- **Encrypt Data Between Microsoft Office Outlook And Microsoft Exchange Server** Determine whether Outlook 2007 uses encryption to secure transmission between your system and the server. Select this check box to enable encryption for greater security.
- **Always Prompt For Logon Credentials** Select this check box if you want Outlook 2007 to prompt you for your logon credentials each time it needs to connect to the server. This is useful if you are concerned that others who have access to your computer might be accessing your mailbox.
- **Logon Network Security** Specify the type of authentication to use when connecting to Exchange Server. The Password Authentication option causes Exchange Server to use Microsoft Windows NT® LAN Manager (NTLM) challenge/response to authenticate on the server using your current logon account credentials. This is the standard authentication mechanism in Windows NT domains. Kerberos Password Authentication is the default authentication mechanism for Microsoft Windows® 2000 Server and later domains. You can choose either of these or choose the Negotiate Authentication option to have Outlook 2007 attempt both.

Configuring Connection Properties

The Connection tab in the Microsoft Exchange dialog box, shown in Figure 41-6, allows you to specify how your computer connects to Exchange Server. You can connect through the local area network (LAN), through dial-up networking, or through a third-party dialer such as the one included with Microsoft Internet Explorer®. The LAN connection option applies if you're connecting over a hard-wired connection–for example, when your computer is connected to the same network as the server. You should also use the LAN option if you connect to the server over a shared dial-up connection hosted by another computer.

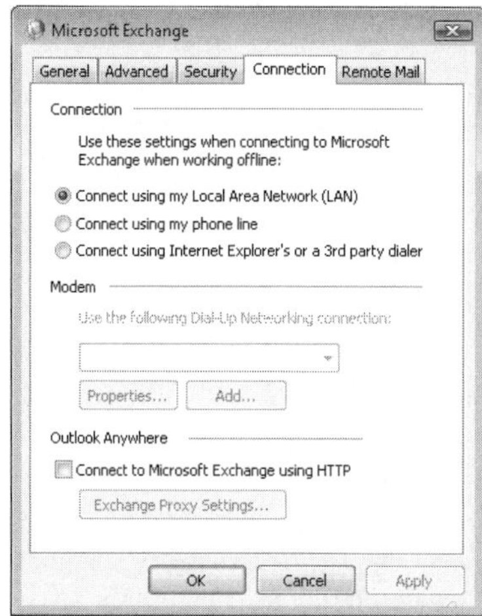

Figure 41-6. Use the Connection tab to specify how Outlook 2007 connects to Exchange Server.

Click Connect Using My Phone Line to use an existing dial-up networking connection or to create a new dial-up connection. Select the desired connection in the drop-down list, and then click Properties if you need to modify the dial-up connection. Click Add if you need to add a dial-up connection.

If you want to connect to the Internet or your remote network using the dialer included in Internet Explorer or a dialer included in a third-party dial-up client, click Connect Using Internet Explorer's Or A 3rd Party Dialer.

The Outlook Anywhere group of controls lets you configure Outlook 2007 to connect to Exchange Server using HTTP. The capability to use HTTP to connect to a remote computer running Exchange Server provides an additional connection option for Outlook 2007 users and can drastically reduce administrative overhead. Administrators no longer need to provide virtual private network (VPN) access to the network or configure VPN client software for users to access the computer running Exchange Server from remote locations. HTTP access also provides native access to the computer running Exchange Server as an alternative to Outlook Web Access (OWA) for users.

The Connect To Microsoft Exchange Using HTTP check box, if selected, causes Outlook 2007 to connect to the Exchange Server computer using the HTTP protocol. To configure additional settings, click Exchange Proxy Settings to open the Microsoft Exchange Proxy Settings dialog box, shown in Figure 41-7.

Figure 41-7. Specify settings for the HTTP connection in the Microsoft Exchange Proxy Settings dialog box.

Configure settings in this dialog box using the following list as a guide:

- **Use This URL To Connect To My Proxy Server For Exchange** Specify the URL that serves as the access point for the server. The default is <server>/RPC, where <server> is the Web address of the Exchange front-end server. An example is *httpmail.boyce.us/rpc*. Omit the *https://* prefix.
- **Connect Using SSL Only** Select this check box to connect to the server using Secure Sockets Layer (SSL). Note that Outlook 2007 changes the URL prefix to *https://* for the URL. (See the preceding option.)
- **Only Connect To Proxy Servers That Have This Principal Name In Their Certificate** Specify the principal name for the remote proxy server for SSL authentication.
- **On Fast Networks, Connect Using HTTP First, Then Connect Using TCP/IP** When Outlook 2007 senses a fast connection to the server, attempt HTTP first and then fall back to TCP/IP if HTTP fails.
- **On Slow Networks, Connect Using HTTP First, Then Connect Using TCP/IP** When Outlook 2007 senses a slow connection to the server, attempt HTTP first and then fall back to TCP/IP if HTTP fails.
- **Use This Authentication When Connecting To My Proxy Server For Exchange** Select the authentication method to use to authenticate on the remote computer running Exchange Server. Choose the type of authentication required by the front-end server.

Verifying Connection Status

After you have finished configuring Outlook 2007 to use RPC over HTTP to connect to your computer running Exchange Server, you can verify the type of connection it is using. Hold down the **Ctrl** key, right-click the Outlook 2007 icon in the system tray, and then choose Connection Status to open the Microsoft Exchange Connection Status dialog box, shown in Figure 41-8.

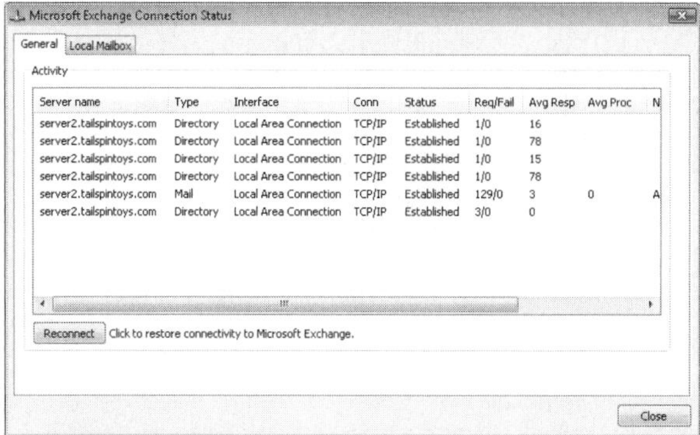

Figure 41-8. Determine the connection type in the Microsoft Exchange Connection Status dialog box.

Testing AutoConfiguration

Outlook 2007 supports automatic account configuration, which means that Outlook 2007 can attempt to determine your account settings automatically. With Exchange Server 2007, Outlook 2007 relies on being able to identify and communicate with the autodiscover host for your domain, such as autodiscover.tailspintoys.com. This host corresponds to a virtual server hosted on the computer running Exchange Server. With earlier versions of Exchange Server, you must specify your name, e-mail address, and account password, and then Outlook 2007 attempts to identify the appropriate server based on that information.

To be able to resolve the fully qualified autodiscover host name, your client computer must be pointed to a DNS server that hosts the records for the autodiscover host or that can forward a query to the appropriate DNS server(s).

After your client computer is appropriately configured to resolve the autodiscover host, you can use a feature in Outlook 2007 to test the capability to discover account information. If you are having difficulties viewing free/busy information or using the Out Of Office Assistant, the inability of the client to contact the autodiscover host could be the problem.

To test the connection, create an Outlook 2007 profile, with or without a valid e-mail account. Start Outlook 2007, hold down the **Ctrl** key, and right-click the Outlook 2007 icon in the system tray. Choose Test E-Mail AutoConfiguration to open the Test E-Mail AutoConfiguration dialog box, shown in Figure 41-9.

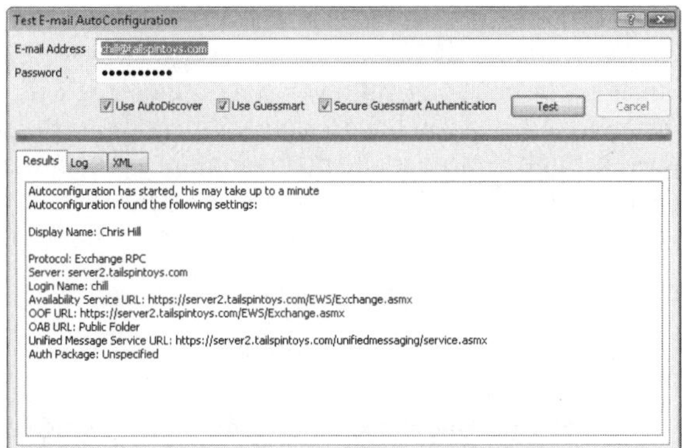

Figure 41-9. Use the Test E-Mail AutoConfiguration dialog box to test AutoDiscover functionality.

Type the e-mail address for your Exchange Server account in the E-Mail Address field, type your e-mail account password in the Password field, and then click Test. If Auto-Configure succeeds, the dialog box will display information similar to that shown in Figure 41-9. If AutoConfigure fails, the dialog box will display an error message indicating that it was unable to determine the correct settings. If you receive the error, verify that the client is configured for the appropriate DNS server(s) and retest.

Configuring Remote Mail Properties

You can use the Remote Mail tab in the Microsoft Exchange dialog box, shown in Figure 41-10, to configure how Outlook 2007 processes messages for your Exchange Server account through remote mail.

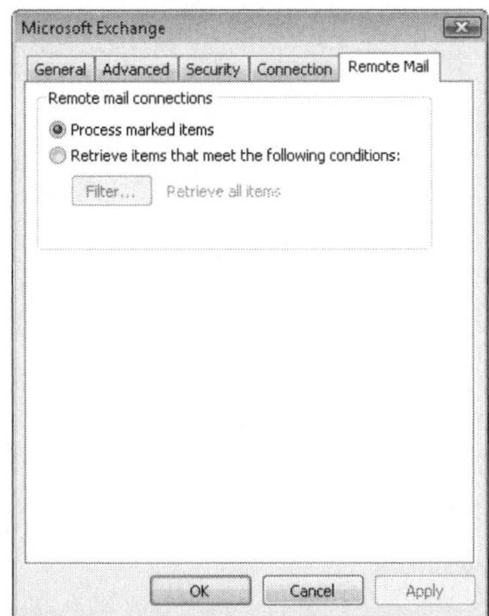

Figure 41-10. Use the Remote Mail tab to configure how Outlook 2007 processes messages through remote mail.

Chapter 41

With remote mail, you can download message headers without downloading the message body or attachments, which allows you to review messages without downloading them. This is particularly useful if you have a message with a very large attachment waiting for download and you have a slow connection to the server. Being able to preview messages through remote mail and optionally delete messages without downloading them is also useful when you have a corrupted message in your message store that is preventing you from downloading your messages normally.

The following list explains the options on the Remote Mail tab:

- **Process Marked Items** When using remote mail, retrieve all items you have marked for download.
- **Retrieve Items That Meet The Following Conditions** When using remote mail, retrieve only items that meet the conditions defined by the specified filter (see the following item).
- **Filter** Click to open the Filter dialog box, in which you specify conditions the message must meet for Outlook 2007 to download it from the server.

For detailed information about remote mail with non–Exchange Server accounts, see Chapter 15, "Receiving Messages Selectively." See Chapter 43, "Working Offline and Remotely," for details on using remote mail with Exchange Server accounts.

CHAPTER 42

Using Outlook with Exchange Server

This chapter focuses on some common messaging topics related specifically to Microsoft® Exchange Server, such as recalling sent messages, setting messages to expire, and working with the Global Address List (GAL). This chapter also covers voting, which is another feature that relies on Exchange Server. Other chapters cover many topics that are more specifically applicable to the Outlook 2007 messaging capabilities. For example, see Chapter 8, "Sending and Receiving Messages," to learn about message composition, replies, and using send/receive groups to synchronize your Exchange Server mailbox.

Sending Messages

When you send messages in Outlook 2007 while connected to Exchange Server, you have more options than you do when you use a regular Internet mail account–for example, you have the ability to recall messages, and you have access to a GAL.

To send a new message, you have three choices:

- In the Inbox or another message folder, click the New toolbar button.
- Choose File, New, Mail Message.
- Click the arrow next to the New toolbar button, and then choose Mail Message.

Whichever method you use, a new message form opens, as shown in Figure 42-1.

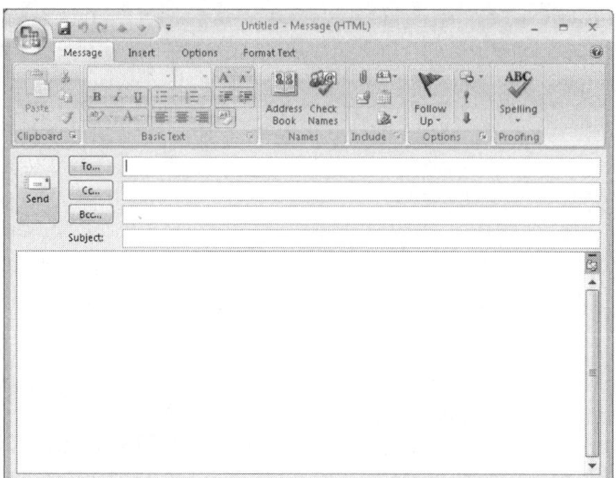

Figure 42-1. Write a message and choose the options for this message using the standard message form.

Addressing Messages

You can designate the recipients of your message in two ways. The first method is to click To or Cc (or Bcc) to open the Select Names dialog box, shown in Figure 42-2. By default, the GAL is displayed.

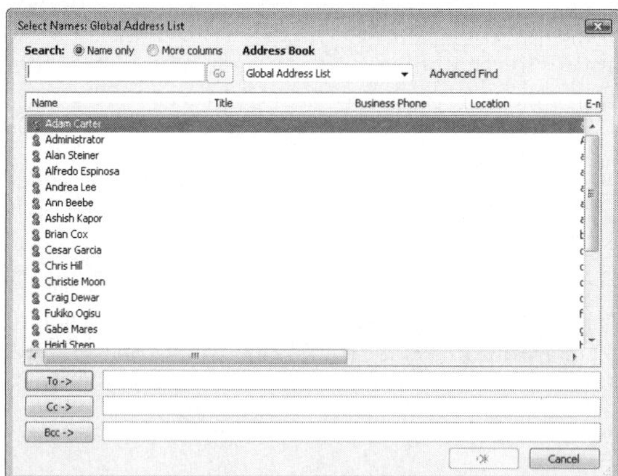

Figure 42-2. The Select Names dialog box displays the available address books.

The GAL contains all users in the entire organization, except those who are explicitly hidden. An Exchange administrator can define other address lists on the computer running Exchange Server to filter addresses by any criteria, such as location, name, or department.

To add a message recipient, select the recipient in the list, and then click To, Cc, or Bcc. Double-click a recipient in the To, Cc, or Bcc field to view the recipient's properties so that you can verify his or her contact information.

One of the most useful features of the Select Names dialog box is the Find feature. Click Advanced Find to open the Find dialog box, shown in Figure 42-3. You can search the address book by any of the criteria shown, such as Title, Company, or Department. The ability to search the address book is most useful when you have a large organization and no additional address lists are defined.

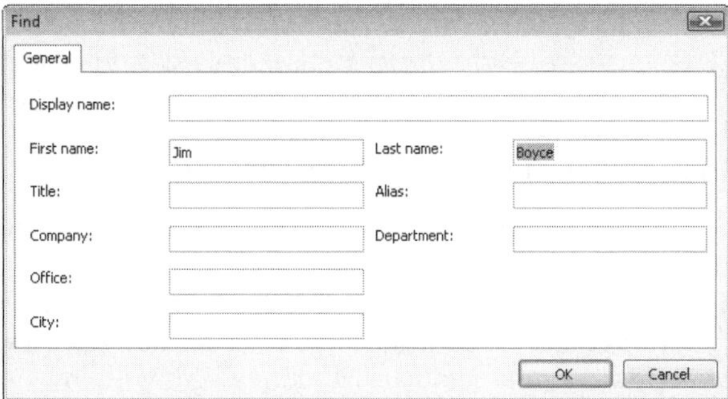

Figure 42-3. You can search the address list for recipients matching specific criteria.

The second way to add recipients to a message is the simplest: Type the recipient's name or alias in the To, Cc, or Bcc field on the message form. An Exchange *alias* is another way of referring to an account. In most cases, an alias is the same as a user's Microsoft Windows® user name.

INSIDE OUT Cut your typing time

You don't have to type the complete name or alias in an address field, as long as the part of the name you type is unique. For example, if only one name in the address book matches *Bob*, you can type **Bob** as the recipient, even if the recipient's name is Bob Smith and the alias is *bob.smith*. If the recipient's name is Robert Smith and the alias is *bob. smith*, you can type either **Rob** or **bob**—both will resolve to Robert Smith.

Checking Names

As soon as you finish typing a recipient's name and move the insertion point out of the text box, Outlook 2007 checks the name. If the name is not unique or can't be found, it is underlined in red. When this occurs, you'll need to manually check the name.

You can also check a recipient's name by clicking Check Names in the Names group on the Message tab on the Ribbon or by pressing **Ctrl+K**. When a problem arises, a

Check Names dialog box appears, indicating whether the name is not unique or not found. When the name is not unique, all matches are displayed so that you can make a selection.

> **Note**
>
> If the name you typed is causing a problem, check the spelling of the name. This sounds simple enough, but a small mistake can prevent the name from being resolved. You might need to use the GAL or another address list to find the correct name.

Setting Message Importance and Sensitivity

When you set the level of importance for a message, an icon indicating the level is displayed by default in the mailbox folders of the message recipients (although they can remove the Importance field from their message window). By default, messages are sent with normal importance and display no icon. Messages designated with a high importance level have a red exclamation mark, and messages with low importance are displayed with a blue down arrow.

You can set the importance level (or priority level) of a message in two ways. You can click either the red exclamation mark or the blue down arrow in the Options group on the Message tab on the Ribbon, shown in Figure 42-4. If you click either button again, the message returns to normal importance. You can also click the small Message Options button in the Options group on the Message tab to open the Message Options dialog box, shown in Figure 42-5, and then make your selection in the Importance drop-down list.

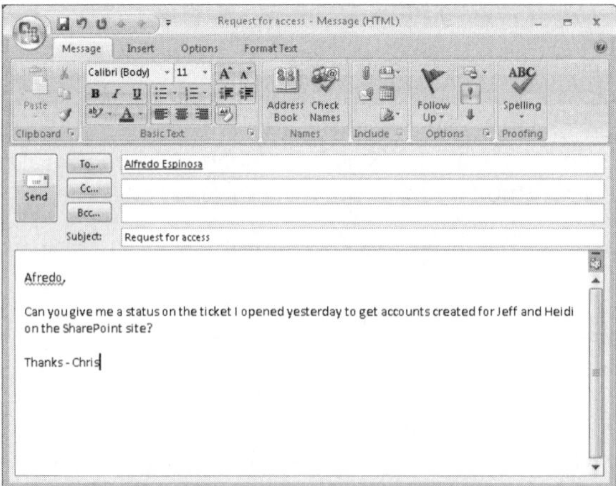

Figure 42-4. Click the High Importance button in the Options group on the Message tab to set the priority of a message.

Chapter 42

INSIDE OUT Use importance levels

Changing the importance level of a message does more than simply change the way the message is displayed to the recipient. Many types of mail transports, such as X.400, use the message importance level as a means for determining message routing. Messages with high importance are given a higher priority in the queue and are sent before low-importance messages. (Actually, the process is more complex than that, but the intricacies of mail routing are beyond the scope of this book.) It is poor etiquette to send all your messages with high priority set; if you overuse the setting, recipients will start to ignore the importance settings completely.

Message sensitivity, like message importance, appears as a flag on the message that the recipient sees. By default, message sensitivity is not shown in the Outlook 2007 message folder views. (You can add it to the view, of course, by choosing View, Current View, Customize Current View, clicking the Fields button, and then configuring options in the Show Fields dialog box.) However, if the message sensitivity is set to other than Normal (the default), Outlook 2007 displays the sensitivity level when the message is opened or viewed in the Reading Pane. You can set one of four levels of sensitivity–Normal, Personal, Private, or Confidential–in the Sensitivity drop-down list in the Message Options dialog box (shown in Figure 42-5).

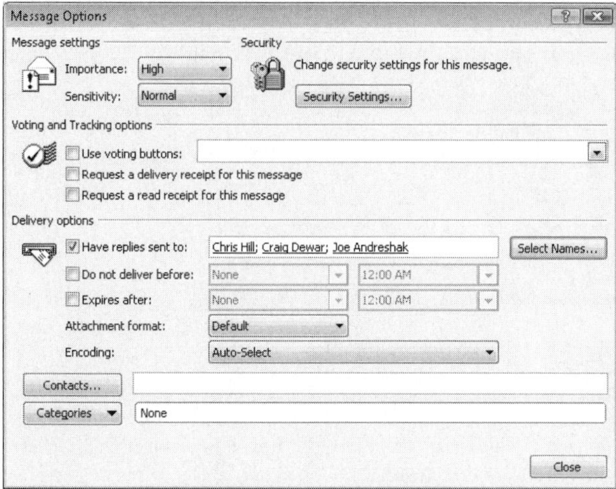

Figure 42-5. Replies to your message will now be sent not to you but to the listed recipients.

Redirecting Replies

If for some reason you don't want to receive the reply to your message, you can have the reply sent to someone else.

To redirect a reply, follow these steps:

1. With the message form open, click the Message Options button in the Options group on the Message tab to open the Message Options dialog box.
2. Select the Have Replies Sent To check box; your name (the sender) is added as a recipient in the text box.
3. Delete your name from the text box, and either type each recipient's name (separated by semicolons) or click Select Names to select the names from the address book. Select each name in the list, click Reply To, and then click OK to have Outlook 2007 add those names to the Have Replies Sent To box. Click Close to save these options.

Each recipient listed in the Have Replies Sent To box receives any replies to the selected message. Figure 42-5, shown earlier, shows the Message Options dialog box with redirected replies.

Using Delivery and Read Receipts

Delivery and read receipts are useful tracking features. The delivery receipt is sent to you when the message is delivered. The read receipt is sent when the message's status changes from unread to read. (This status can change automatically in the Reading Pane, when the recipient opens the message, or when the recipient right-clicks the message and chooses Mark As Read.) Delivery and read receipts are not supported on all mail clients. Most mail clients that do support them allow the recipient to choose not to send receipts, so you can't always rely on these receipts to confirm what you need to know. Figure 42-6 shows an example of a delivery receipt.

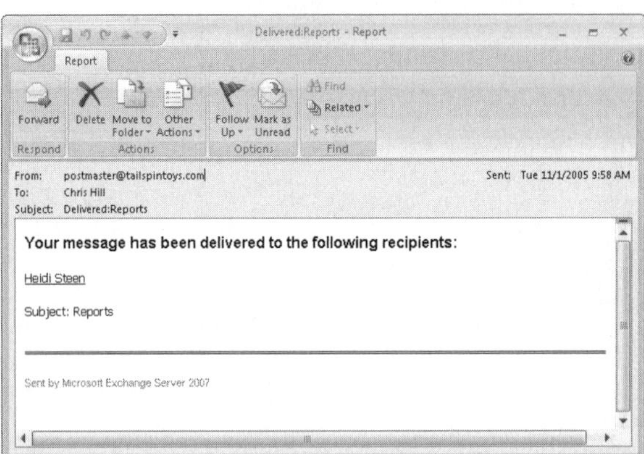

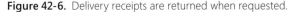

Figure 42-6. Delivery receipts are returned when requested.

To set a delivery receipt, a read receipt, or both for a message, follow these steps:

1. In the message form, click the Message Options button in the Options group on the Message tab to open the Message Options dialog box, shown in Figure 42-7.

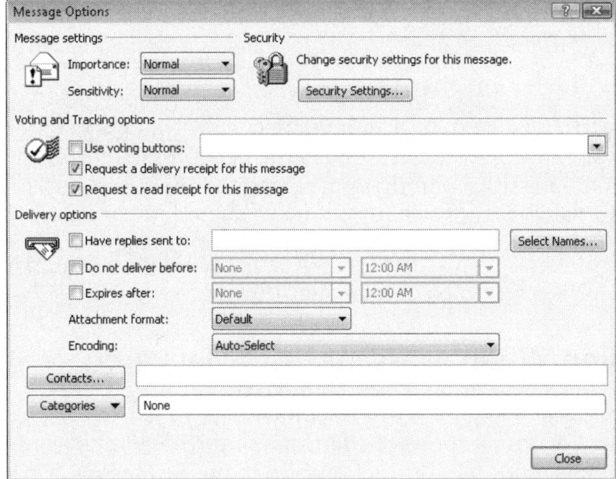

Figure 42-7. You can request receipts in the Message Options dialog box.

2. Select the Request A Delivery Receipt For This Message check box, the Request A Read Receipt For This Message check box, or both.

3. Click Close.

You can set up your mail to request delivery and read receipts by default for each message you send out. To do so, follow these steps:

1. In Outlook 2007, choose Tools, Options to open the Options dialog box.

2. On the Preferences tab, click E-Mail Options, and then click Tracking Options to open the Tracking Options dialog box.

3. In the For All Messages I Send, Request area, select Read Receipt, Delivery Receipt, or both.

4. Click OK three times to close the three dialog boxes.

Note

In the Tracking Options dialog box, you can prevent Outlook 2007 from sending read receipts to the senders of messages you receive (by selecting the Never Send A Response option). You can also direct Outlook 2007 to move any receipts to a specified folder (by selecting the After Processing, Move Receipts To option).

Saving Messages

By default, Outlook 2007 saves messages you send by placing copies of the messages in the Sent Items folder. New outgoing messages are also saved to the Drafts folder every three minutes. To specify how new, unsent messages should be automatically saved, follow these steps:

1. Choose Tools, Options.
2. On the Preferences tab, click E-Mail Options, and then click Advanced E-Mail Options.
3. Select the folder in which unsent items should be saved in the AutoSave Items In drop-down list, turn AutoSave on or off, and set the AutoSave interval.
4. Click OK to close each of the dialog boxes.

Controlling When Messages Are Delivered

When a message is sent, it is delivered immediately by default. You can, however, delay message delivery until a specified time for an individual message. To do so, click the Message Options button in the Options group on the Message tab to open the Message Options dialog box. Select the Do Not Deliver Before check box, and then set the date and time using the drop-down lists. Because delayed sending is a feature of Exchange Server, you can exit Outlook 2007 as soon as you click Send—the message will wait in your Outbox on the server until the delivery time arrives.

Setting Messages to Expire

Just as you can delay the delivery of a message, you can also set a message to expire. The message expires and is removed from the recipient's mailbox after a specified period of time whether or not it has been read. You might want to have a message expire if its contents become outdated after a certain amount of time, or if you want to ensure that the message is deleted. To set this option, open the Message Options dialog box, select the Expires After check box, and then set a date and time. The message will no longer be available to the recipient after that time.

> **Note**
>
> The capability to set a message to expire is not a security feature but simply causes the message to be deleted after the specified period. Use Information Rights Management (IRM), covered in Chapter 14, "Securing Your System, Messages, and Identity," to prevent messages from being forwarded, copied, or printed.

Assigning a Category to a Message

You assign a category to a message by clicking Categories in the Message Options dialog box and then choosing a color category. These categories can be used for sorting, grouping, and filtering messages.

For complete information about assigning and working with categories, see Chapter 5, "Creating and Using Categories."

Recalling a Sent Message Before It Is Read

There are many reasons why you might want to recall a message. For example, perhaps the message contains a mistake or is now obsolete. You can recall a message you have sent as long as the recipient has not read it and the message is still stored on a computer running Exchange Server. Messages sent to recipients using other mail servers cannot be recalled.

To recall a sent message, double-click the message in the Sent Items folder to open it. Click Other Actions in the Actions group on the Ribbon, and then click Recall This Message to open the dialog box shown in Figure 42-8. Select whether you want to simply delete all unread copies of the message or delete them and replace them with another message. You can also receive a response reporting the success or failure of each recall attempt.

CAUTION!

For a number of reasons, sometimes unread messages cannot be recalled. You should always take the time to verify the content of a message before sending it.

Figure 42-8. This dialog box is displayed when you attempt to recall a message.

Copying Global Addresses to Your Contacts Folder

On occasion, you might want to copy addresses from the GAL to your personal Contacts folder. For example, maybe you use a Personal Digital Assistant (PDA) or smartphone that synchronizes your Contacts folder to your mobile device. The device would not synchronize the GAL, but you might want a few entries available on your mobile device. You can copy those items to the Contacts folder, and from there, they can be synchronized to your mobile device.

You can easily copy addresses from the GAL to your Contacts folder by following these steps:

1. Choose Tools, Address Book, or click the Address Book button on the toolbar.
2. Click the address you want to add to your Contacts folder. You can also select multiple addresses using the **Shift** and **Ctrl** keys.
3. Choose File, Add To Contacts. The entry from the GAL opens in a contact form.
4. Make any necessary changes.
5. Click Save And Close. The contact information is now stored in your Contacts folder.

Voting in Outlook

Another feature in Outlook 2007 that takes advantage of Exchange Server is voting. The Outlook 2007 voting feature is useful when you want to solicit input from a group of message recipients. Perhaps you are looking for approval on a proposal, you are holding an informal election in your organization, or you just want to get the group's input on an issue.

With the voting feature, you solicit and tally votes from the group. Outlook 2007 provides predefined voting responses, but you can also create your own. In this section, you'll learn how to include voting buttons in messages, tally returned votes, and configure voting options.

Here's how voting works in general: You create a message containing the question or document on which the group will be voting. Next you add voting buttons to the message. Then you send the message. Recipients cast their vote by clicking the appropriate button. Outlook 2007 prompts them to confirm the vote and then sends the reply message back to you.

Sending a Message for a Vote

Sending a message for a vote is simple. In fact, as long as you want to use one of the Outlook 2007 default set of voting options, the process takes only a few clicks.

Using the Default Voting Responses

Use the following steps to create a message and add voting buttons to it:

1. Start Outlook 2007, and then open a new message or open an existing message from your Drafts folder.
2. On the Message tab, in the Options group, click the Message Options button to open the Message Options dialog box.
3. In the Voting And Tracking Options area, select the Use Voting Buttons check box. In the drop-down list, select the group of voting buttons you want to include, as shown in Figure 42-9.

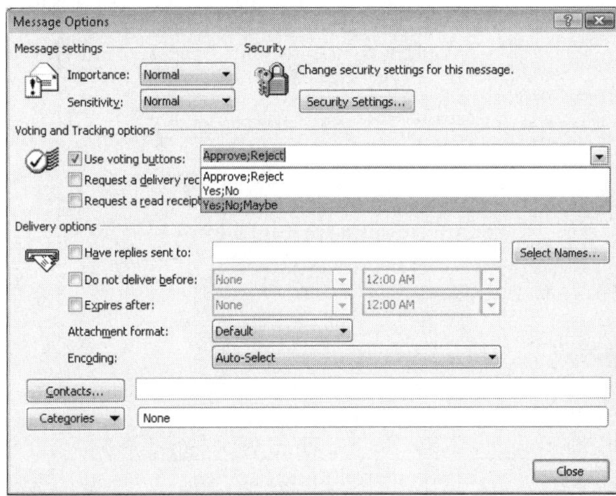

Figure 42-9. Select the voting buttons you want to include using the Message Options dialog box.

4. Click Close.
5. Edit your message. Include any message attachments and configure message options such as importance level if needed.
6. Click Send to send the message.

Using Custom Responses

Outlook 2007 doesn't limit you to the default sets of voting options (such as Accept/Reject). You can create your own set that includes the responses you need for any situation. For example, suppose that you're planning a company appreciation banquet and need to finalize the menu. You want to give everyone a choice of entree and collect those responses for the caterer. What better way to do that than electronically through Outlook 2007?

Here's how:

1. Compose your message.
2. On the Message tab, in the Options group, click Message Options to open the Message Options dialog box.
3. Select the Use Voting Buttons check box.
4. Click the text field in the Use Voting Buttons drop-down list. Delete the existing text. Type your custom vote options separated by semicolons, as shown in Figure 42-10.

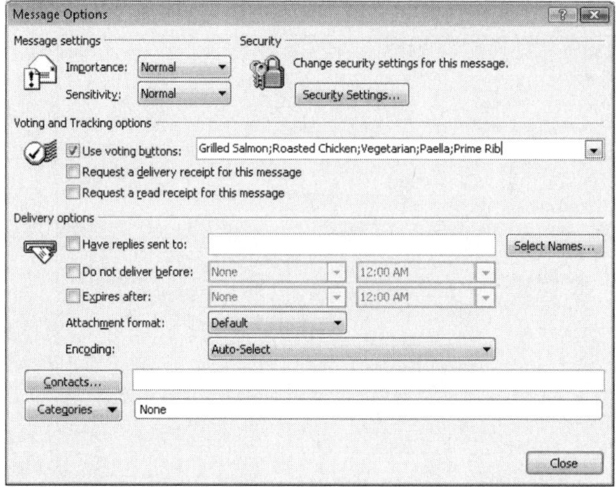

Figure 42-10. You can create custom vote responses in the Use Voting Buttons text field.

5. Click Close.
6. Make any final adjustments to the message as needed.
7. Click Send.

Casting Your Vote

When you receive a message that includes voting buttons, Outlook 2007 displays a message in the InfoBar to indicate that you can vote. Click the InfoBar, and then choose an item, as shown in Figure 42-11. In addition, Outlook 2007 displays a message in the Reading Pane, if it's open, to prompt you to vote, as shown in Figure 42-12.

Voting is easy: just select an option to cast your vote. Outlook 2007 displays a simple dialog box asking whether you want to send the vote now or edit your response. To send the message without modification, select Send The Response Now. To cast your vote and open the message as a reply so that you can include text in your response, select Edit The Response Before Sending.

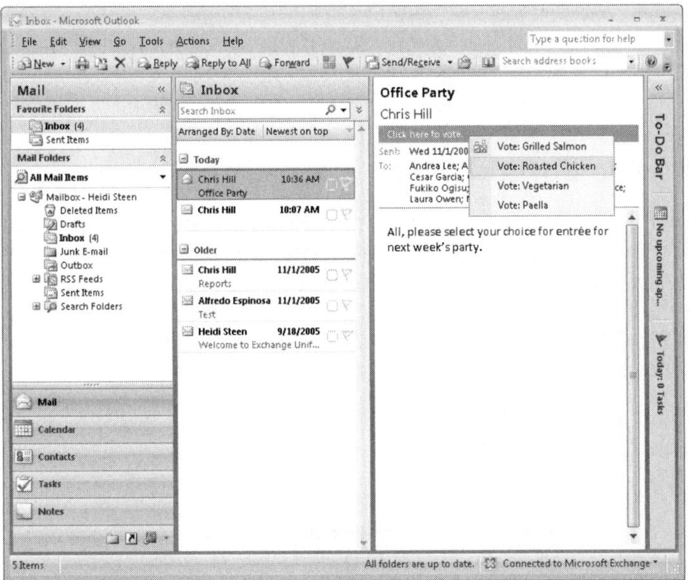

Figure 42-11. The Reading Pane shows a message prompting you to vote.

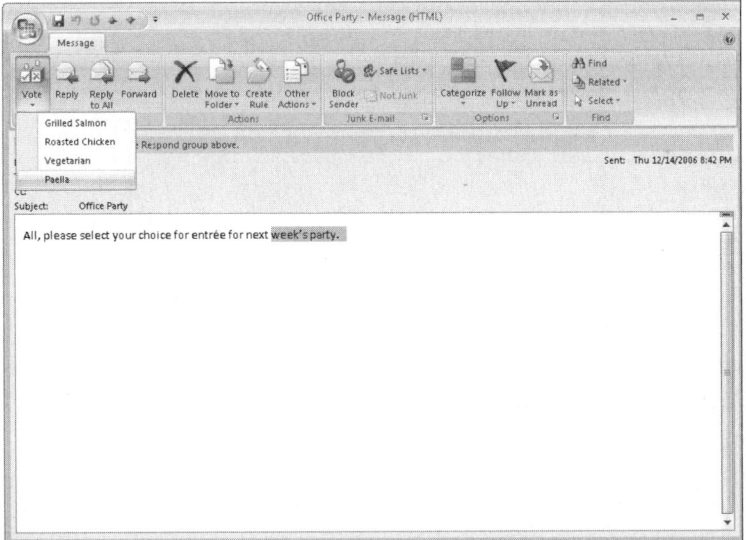

Figure 42-12. You can also vote by clicking the Vote button on the Ribbon.

> **Note**
>
> Outlook 2007 doesn't automatically close the message window when you cast a vote, which makes it easy to accidentally vote more than once. You must close the message window manually.

When you cast a vote, Outlook 2007 changes the subject of the message to include your vote. For example, if the original subject is Choose An Entree and you click the Grilled Salmon option, the subject of the reply returned to the sender is Grilled Salmon: Choose An Entree.

Viewing and Sorting Votes

Votes come back to you in the form of messages. You can view the vote summary in a few ways. If the Reading Pane is displayed, you can click the message header, click the summary message in the InfoBar, and then choose View Voting Responses, as shown in Figure 42-13. Or you can open the Sent Items folder, open the original message, and then click the Tracking button in the Show group on the Ribbon. Either method displays the Tracking results, shown in Figure 42-14.

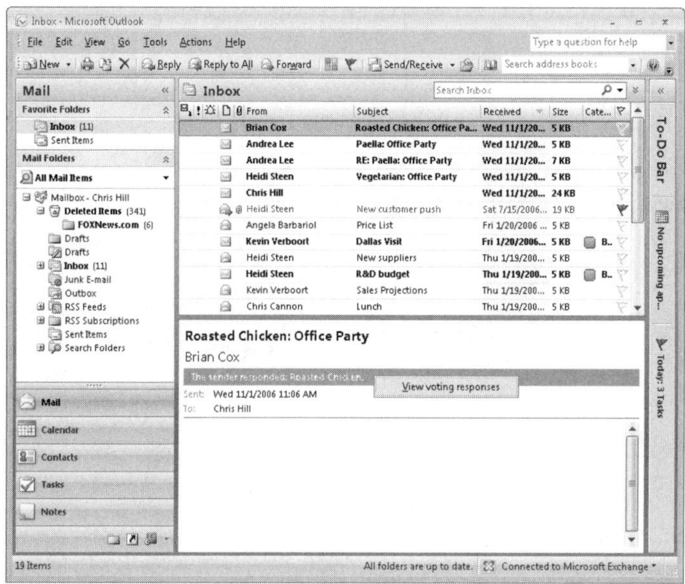

Figure 42-13. Click the summary message in the InfoBar to display the Tracking page.

> **INSIDE OUT** **Voting suggestions**
>
> Don't rely on Outlook 2007 as a voting tool for crucial questions. It is an acceptable tool, however, for such issues as choosing entrees and polling for parking problems. Keep in mind that although a person can vote more than once, only the first vote is recorded; this can be confusing if you aren't expecting that behavior. Note also that the voting buttons are not removed from the message after the recipient votes.

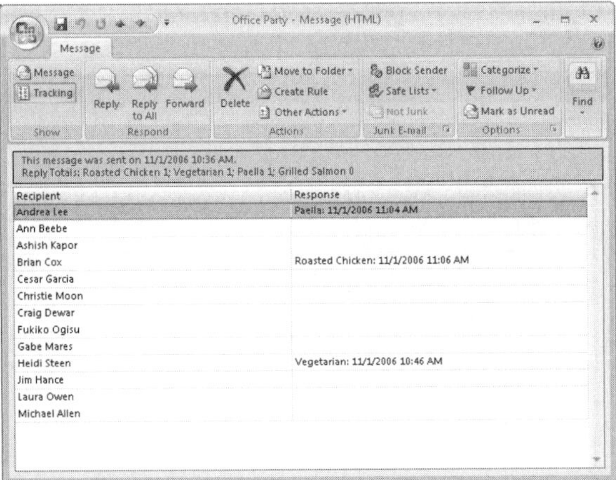

Figure 42-14. Open the message from the Sent Items folder as an alternative way to access the Tracking page.

The Tracking pane summarizes the votes, with individual responses displayed one per line. The responses are also totaled in the InfoBar. If you want a printout of the vote responses, print the messages with the Tracking page visible.

Unfortunately, Outlook 2007 doesn't give you a way to sort the vote tally. You can, however, copy the data to Microsoft Office Excel® 2007 to sort it.

To copy voting data to Office Excel 2007, follow these steps:

1. Select the rows that you want to copy. (Select a row, and then hold down the **Shift** key to select contiguous responses or hold down the **Ctrl** key to select noncontiguous ones.)
2. Press **Ctrl+C** to copy the data to the Clipboard.
3. Start Microsoft Excel.
4. Select a cell in the worksheet and then press **Ctrl+V** to paste the data.
5. Choose Data, Sort to open the Sort dialog box, and then click OK to accept the default settings and sort the spreadsheet.

Setting Options for Voting

You can configure options in Outlook 2007 to configure how Outlook 2007 handles voting. To configure these settings, follow these steps:

1. Start Outlook 2007, and then choose Tools, Options.
2. On the Preferences tab, click E-Mail Options.

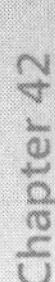

3. Click Tracking Options to open the Tracking Options dialog box, shown in Figure 42-15.

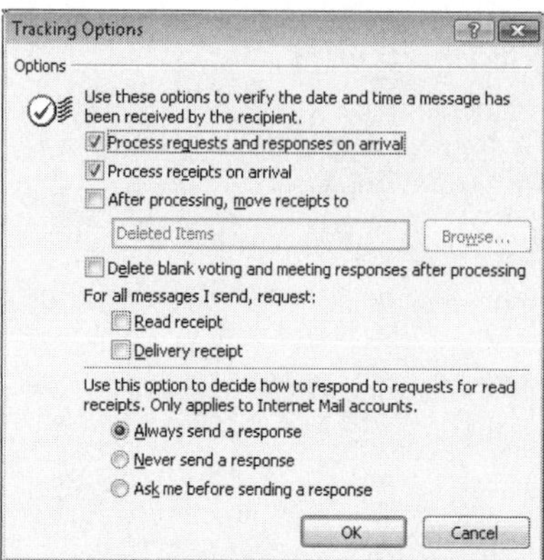

Figure 42-15. Use the Tracking Options dialog box to configure voting options.

The Tracking Options dialog box includes the following options that relate to voting:

Process Requests And Responses On Arrival Outlook 2007 processes and tallies responses when they arrive. If you clear this check box, you must open each response to have Outlook 2007 tally it.

Delete Blank Voting And Meeting Responses After Processing Outlook 2007 deletes voting responses that have no additional comments added to them.

4. Select the options you want to use, and then click OK to close the Tracking Options dialog box. Click OK twice more to close the E-Mail Options dialog box and the Options dialog box.

TROUBLESHOOTING

Votes aren't being automatically tallied

The Outlook 2007 capability to automatically tally votes without the user having to open each message might not be apparent at first. It can take several minutes even on a completely idle system for Outlook 2007 to process the messages. If you need to process the responses more quickly, select all the responses, right-click the selection, and then choose Open Selected Items to open them all at once. Keep in mind, however, that you'll end up with an open message form for each response, which you'll then have to close.

CHAPTER 43

Working Offline and Remotely

Microsoft® Office Outlook® 2007 provides several features that enable you to work offline (while you are not connected to your mail server) as well as from a remote location. Using the offline feature and Outlook 2007's offline storage, which contains copies of all the folders and items in your Microsoft Exchange Server mailbox, you can work with contacts, messages, and other items stored in your mailbox without being connected to the server (except to perform periodic synchronizations). You can create and delete items, add folders, and make other changes while offline; Outlook 2007 synchronizes those changes the next time you connect to the server and perform a send/receive operation.

A key feature in Outlook 2007 that supports remote use is remote mail, which enables you to process message headers without downloading the message bodies. You can preview message headers, delete messages from the server without downloading them, and perform other selective processing. Although you can perform similar tasks with POP3, Internet Message Access Protocol (IMAP), and HTTP accounts, only Exchange Server accounts can take advantage of the filters and other options provided through send/receive groups.

Note

This chapter focuses on the offline and remote features in Outlook 2007 used in conjunction with Exchange Server.

If you are looking for ways to work offline and remotely using other types of e-mail servers and accounts, see Chapter 15, "Receiving Messages Selectively."

Offline vs. Remote

Offline use and remote use are two separate aspects of using Outlook 2007. When you work offline, your computer is not connected to the computer running Exchange Server. This usually means you're working on a computer that uses a dial-up connection to the server or on a portable computer that you connect to the server through a docking station or a wireless access point on the local area network (LAN). You can be working offline even while your computer is connected to the LAN when the Exchange Server is down for maintenance, or you can deliberately set Outlook 2007 offline.

You can perform most of the same operations offline that you perform when you're connected to the server. You can create messages, contacts, and other Outlook 2007 items; schedule meetings; and carry out other common Outlook 2007 tasks. The items you create and the changes you make to your folders and their contents, however, are made to the offline store instead of to your Exchange Server mailbox store. When you reconnect to the server, Outlook 2007 synchronizes the offline store with the mailbox store. Any items that arrived in the mailbox while you were working offline are added to your offline store when Outlook 2007 performs the synchronization. This behavior is the same whether you use Cached Exchange Mode and work from a locally cached copy of your mailbox or simply add an offline store (OST) file to your profile–the main difference is in how Outlook 2007 synchronizes the online and offline mailboxes.

In contrast, working remotely generally means working with Outlook 2007 from a location other than the LAN on which the Exchange Server is located. For example, you might dial in to your LAN with a modem, connect to it through the Internet, or even connect through a demand-dial connection between two offices. Whatever your location, you can be working either offline or online when you work remotely. The only consideration is whether you are connected to the server. If you are not connected to the server, you are working offline and remotely. If you are connected to the server, you are simply working remotely.

With the Outlook 2007 remote mail features, you can read message headers without downloading the message itself. Remote mail is useful when you receive a very large message in your mailbox and don't want to download it, when your mailbox contains a corrupted message that is preventing you from downloading other messages, or when your mailbox contains a message infected by a worm or virus. You can connect with remote mail, delete the message without reading or downloading it, and continue processing the other messages normally. This capability is also generically useful in low-bandwidth situations to give you greater control over which messages you choose to download.

Establishing a Remote LAN Connection

To work remotely, you need to establish a remote connection to the server. How you accomplish this depends on the connection options available on your LAN and how the network administrator configured the LAN. The following are the most common methods for establishing a remote LAN connection:

- **Dial up access directly to the LAN** In this scenario, the LAN includes a Remote Access Services (RAS) server that enables clients to dial directly to the network using a modem or other device (such as an Integrated Services Digital Network [ISDN] connection). The RAS server can be the computer running Exchange Server or another server on the network, depending on the size of the organization and the load on the Exchange Server. Depending on the configuration of the RAS server, dial-up clients might have access to the network or only to the computer running Exchange Server.
- **Connect through a virtual private network connection over the Internet** If your LAN is connected to the Internet and includes a virtual private network (VPN) server, one of the options for retrieving e-mail messages is to create a VPN connection to the LAN and then connect to the computer running Exchange Server. A VPN server enables clients to establish secure connections to the network through a public network such as the Internet.
- **Use a demand-dial connection between two networks** If you have two or more offices, those offices might connect using a demand-dial connection. The connection might take place over a standard dial-up line, or use ISDN or another communication method. The demand-dial interface enables the two routers that connect the offices to establish the connection when a client requests it, such as when you connect to synchronize your Outlook 2007 data.
- **Use HTTP to connect to the server** Outlook 2007 includes support for HTTP as a communications protocol when used with Exchange Server 2003 or Exchange Server 2007, enabling you to connect to your Exchange Server remotely (such as from the Internet) without using a VPN connection.

> **Note**
>
> You can connect to an Exchange Server through the Internet without configuring Outlook 2007 to use RPC over HTTP. However, doing so requires that you open several ports on the firewall that, for security reasons, really should not be opened. For that reason, this method is neither recommended nor explained in this chapter.

Because this book focuses specifically on Outlook 2007 and its integration with Exchange Server, the details of how to set up a RAS or a VPN server aren't covered.

Using HTTP to Connect

Using HTTP as the communications protocol for your Exchange Server is a useful remote access method that eliminates the need for you to run VPN software on your client computer. It also eliminates the need for the network administrator to support those VPN connections. Most networks already have port 80 open for HTTP and port 443 open for secure HTTP (HTTPS) through Secure Sockets Layer (SSL), so providing HTTP-based access to Exchange Server requires only some setup on the computer running Exchange Server and configuring Outlook 2003 to use HTTP.

> **Note**
>
> HTTP-based access to Exchange Server requires Exchange Server 2003 or later and Outlook 2003 or later.

Chapter 41, "Configuring the Exchange Server Client," explains how to configure the Exchange Server client for Outlook 2007, including setting up the account to use HTTP and configuring the server, so that information isn't repeated here. Beyond those steps, there is really nothing else to do to start using HTTP to access your mailbox. However, here is some advice:

- **Use Cached Exchange Mode and synchronize from the LAN at least once** To reduce the load on the server and the amount of bandwidth you will use connecting to the server, consider using Cached Exchange Mode, which creates a locally cached copy of your mailbox on your computer. Before connecting remotely, connect to the server on your LAN and allow Outlook 2007 to synchronize the cache with your mailbox. By synchronizing from the LAN rather than a remote connection, you will likely decrease the amount of time required to complete the synchronization, particularly if your mailbox contains a large amount of data.
- **Use RPC and TCP/IP when connected locally to the network** The default settings for using HTTP in Outlook 2007 to connect to your Exchange Server cause Outlook 2007 to attempt a connection with RPC over TCP/IP for a fast connection before it attempts to use HTTP. Leave this setting at its default to provide better performance when you connect to the server from your LAN. Change this setting only if your Exchange Server requires an HTTP connection to the server.

Working Offline with Outlook 2007 and Exchange Server

There are a few specific issues and settings you need to consider when working with Outlook 2007 offline. This section explains how to configure the Outlook 2007 startup mode and offline folders and how to use an offline address book.

Configuring Startup Options

When you start Outlook 2007, it attempts by default to determine the online or offline status of the server. If the server is unavailable and Outlook 2007 is configured with an OST file, Outlook 2007 starts in offline mode and uses the offline folder specified in your profile for displaying existing items and storing new items (such as e-mail messages) before synchronizing with Exchange Server. With Cached Exchange Mode enabled, Outlook 2007 automatically uses the local cache (stored in an OST file) and attempts to synchronize the cached copy with your Exchange Server mailbox if a server connection is available. If you configured autodial in your operating system, Outlook 2007 dials the connection to the Internet service provider (ISP) or RAS server. However, you might want to exercise more control over the Outlook 2007 startup mode and when it connects. For example, you might prefer to have Outlook 2007 start in offline mode so that you can compose messages or perform other tasks before you connect and synchronize with the server.

You configure startup options by setting the properties for the Exchange Server account in your profile, as outlined in the following steps:

1. Right-click the Office Outlook icon on the Start menu and then click Properties or double-click the Mail icon in Control Panel (Classic View).
2. If you don't use multiple profiles, skip to step 3. If you use multiple profiles, click Show Profiles. Select the profile you want to change and then click Properties.
3. Click E-Mail Accounts.
4. Select the Exchange Server account and then click Change.
5. If you decide to use Cached Exchange Mode, you can click the Use Cached Exchange Mode option; otherwise, click More Settings and then click the General tab (see Figure 43-1.)

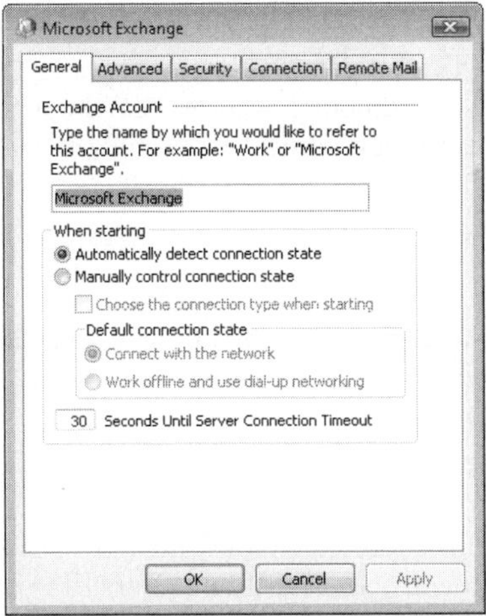

Figure 43-1. Use the General tab to configure startup options for Outlook 2007.

6. Configure the following settings:

Automatically Detect Connection State Outlook 2007 detects the connection state at startup and enters online or offline mode accordingly (selected by default).

Manually Control Connection State You control the connection state when Outlook 2007 starts. The following three options work in combination with this option.

Choose The Connection Type When Starting Outlook 2007 prompts you to select the connection state when it starts. This enables you to select between online and offline states.

Connect With The Network Connect through your local LAN to Exchange Server. You can use this option if you connect to the Internet through a dedicated connection such as a cable modem or a Digital Subscriber Line (DSL) connection (selected by default).

Work Offline And Use Dial-Up Networking Start in an offline state and use Dial-Up Networking to connect to Exchange Server. On the Connection tab, specify the dial-up connection you want to use.

Seconds Until Server Connection Timeout Specify the timeout, in seconds, for the server (30 seconds by default). Outlook 2007 attempts a connection for the specified amount of time; if Outlook 2007 is unable to establish a connection in the specified period, it times out. You might want to increase this setting if you connect to the Internet through a shared dial-up connection hosted by another computer on your LAN.

Increase TCP/IP timeout

You might want to change your TCP/IP timeout values if you change the Seconds Until Server Connection Timeout option in Outlook 2007. Increasing the TCP/IP timeout increases the length of time that your computer waits for TCP/IP connections to succeed before timing out, a feature that is particularly useful with dial-up or unreliable connections.

See the sidebar "Increase TCP Time-Out for On-Demand Connections" in Chapter 41 for details on configuring the TCP/IP timeout.

Using Offline Folders

Although you don't have to use offline folders when you work with Exchange Server over a remote connection, you do need a set of offline folders to work offline. If you haven't set up offline folders and can't connect to the remote server, Outlook 2007 won't start. One of your first tasks after you create your dial-up connection and configure your Exchange Server account should be to configure a set of offline folders. Note, however, that you don't have to perform this step if you configure Outlook 2007 to use Cached Exchange Mode for your Exchange Server account. When you enable Cached Exchange Mode, Outlook 2007 automatically creates an offline store for you.

See Chapter 41 for more information on enabling Cached Exchange Mode.

You can associate one set of offline folders with the Exchange Server account in your profile. The offline file has an OST file extension and stores a copy of all the folders and items in your Exchange Server mailbox. Outlook 2007 synchronizes the data between the two. For example, suppose that you create an e-mail message and a new contact item while working offline. The message goes in the Outbox folder of the offline store, and the new contact item goes in the Contacts folder of the offline store. When you next connect to the server and perform synchronization, Outlook 2007 moves the message in the local Outbox to the Outbox folder on your Exchange Server, and the message then gets delivered. Outlook 2007 also copies the new contact item in your local Contacts folder to the Contacts folder stored on the Exchange Server. Any additional changes, including those at the server (such as new e-mail messages waiting to be delivered), are copied to your local offline folders.

> **Note**
>
> The OST file does not appear as a separate set of folders in Outlook 2007. In effect, Outlook 2007 uses it transparently when your computer is offline.

An OST file, like a personal folders (PST) file, contains Outlook 2007 folders and items. One difference, however, is that you can have only one OST file, but you can have multiple PST files. Also, Outlook 2007 synchronizes the offline store with your Exchange Server automatically but does not provide automatic synchronization for PST files.

For more information on adding PST files to a profile, see "Adding Other Data Stores," in Chapter 3, "Configuring Outlook Profiles and Accounts."

Follow these steps to configure offline storage with an OST file:

1. If Outlook 2007 is running, click Tools, Account Settings. Otherwise, right-click the Office Outlook icon on the Start menu, click Properties, and then click E-Mail Accounts.
2. Select the Exchange Server account and click Change.
3. To use offline folders without Cached Exchange Mode, clear the Use Cached Exchange Mode check box in the Change E-Mail Account dialog box.
4. Click More Settings and then click the Advanced tab.
5. Click Offline Folder File Settings to open the dialog box shown in Figure 43-2.

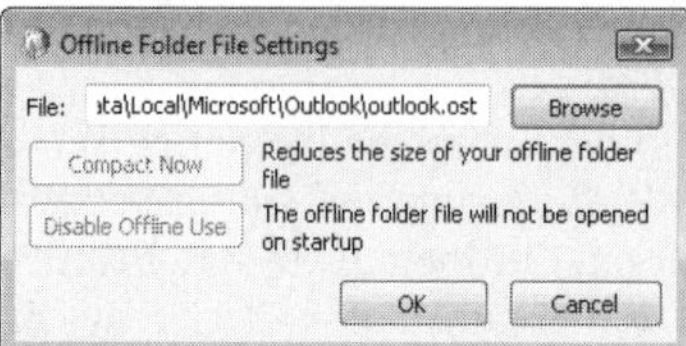

Figure 43-2. Specify the file name and other settings for the OST file.

6. In the File box, specify a path and name for the OST file and click OK.
7. On the Advanced tab, click OK.
8. Click Next and then click Finish.

> **Note**
>
> This option to configure the offline folder store might be dimmed (disabled) if you have only an Exchange e-mail account configured, yet it can be enabled if you have multiple types of e-mail accounts. If you have a POP3 account configured, for example, and you add an Exchange account, the capability to configure the offline storage location is enabled.

Synchronizing with the Exchange Server Mailbox

After you add an OST file to your profile, you need to synchronize the file with your Exchange Server mailbox at least once before you can work offline.

Follow these steps to synchronize your offline folders:

1. Connect to the remote network where the computer running Exchange Server is located using the Internet, a dial-up connection to a remote access server on the remote LAN, or other means (such as ISDN, cable modem, or DSL). A LAN connection will give you the best performance for the initial synchronization.
2. Open Outlook 2007.
3. Click Tools, Send/Receive, This Folder (Microsoft Exchange); or select Tools, Send/Receive, Microsoft Exchange Only, Inbox. Outlook 2007 then synchronizes with the Exchange Server.

> **Note**
>
> If you specified a name for the account other than the default computer running Exchange Server, select that account name on the Send/Receive menu. You'll find the account name on the General tab of the account's Properties dialog box.

Synchronizing with Send/Receive Groups

The preceding section explained how to synchronize your offline folders and your Exchange Server mailbox. Sometimes, though, you might not want to synchronize all folders each time you perform a send/receive operation. You can use send/receive groups to define the actions that Outlook 2007 takes when sending and receiving. For example, you might want to create a send/receive group that sends only mail waiting in your local Outbox and doesn't retrieve waiting messages from the server.

For a detailed discussion of send/receive groups, see "Controlling Synchronization and Send/Receive Times" in Chapter 8, "Sending and Receiving Messages."

Using an Offline Address Book

Whether you're composing messages offline or creating tasks to assign to others, chances are good that you want access to your Exchange Server address book so that you can address messages to other users in your organization. If the Global Address List (GAL) doesn't change very often on the server (if, for example, employee turnover at your company is low), you can get by with downloading the offline address book infrequently. Otherwise, you'll need to update the offline address book more often.

> **Note**
>
> You can download additional address lists from the server if the Exchange Server administrator has created additional address books and given you the necessary permissions to access them. Additional address books give you quick access to addresses that are sorted using different criteria than the GAL uses or access to other addresses not shown in the GAL (such as external contacts).

To download the address book manually whenever you want an update, follow these steps:

1. Click Tools, Send/Receive, Download Address Book to open the Offline Address Book dialog box (see Figure 43-3).
2. Select options as needed from the following:

   Download Changes Since Last Send/Receive Download only changes made since the last time you performed a send/receive operation. Clear this check box to download the entire address list.

   Full Details Download all address information, including phone, fax, and office location. You must select this option if you want to send encrypted messages because you need the users' digital signatures.

   No Details Download only e-mail addresses and no additional address book details.

Figure 43-3. Use the Offline Address Book dialog box to specify options for downloading the offline address book.

3. Click OK to download the address book.

In addition to performing manual offline address book updates, you also can configure a send/receive group to download the address book.

Follow these steps to do so:

1. In Outlook 2007, click Tools, Send/Receive, Send/Receive Settings, Define Send/Receive Groups.
2. Select the send/receive group in which you want to configure the address book download and then click Edit.
3. On the Accounts bar, select your Exchange Server account (see Figure 43-4).

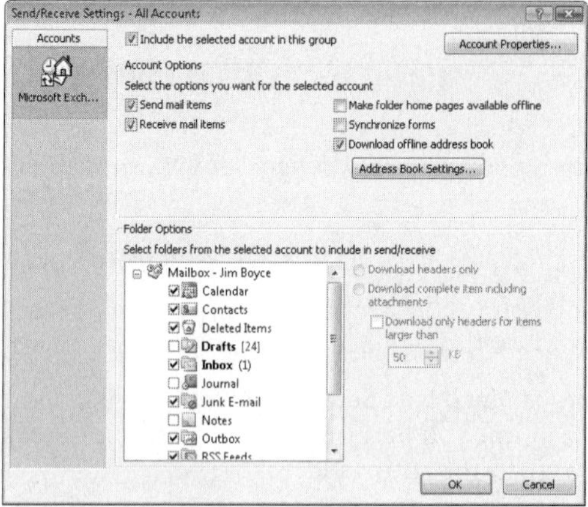

Figure 43-4. You can configure automatic offline address book synchronization.

4. Select the Download Offline Address Book check box and then click Address Book Settings to open the Offline Address Book dialog box.

5. Configure settings as necessary in the Offline Address Book dialog box (discussed in the preceding set of steps) and then click OK.

6. Click OK to close the Send/Receive Settings dialog box.

Each time you synchronize folders using the send/receive group, Outlook 2007 downloads the offline address book according to the settings you specified. You probably don't want to configure this option for the default All Accounts send/receive group unless you have a fast connection to the server and your offline address book changes frequently. One option is to create a send/receive group that downloads only the offline address book and does not process any other folders. However, this is essentially the same as choosing Tools, Send/Receive, Download Address Book. Consider how often you need to download the address book and work that task into your send/receive groups as you see fit.

Using Remote Mail

The Outlook 2007 remote mail feature enables you to manage your messages without downloading them from the server. With remote mail, you connect to the e-mail server, download the headers for new messages, and disconnect. You can take your time reviewing the message headers to decide which ones you want to download, which ones you want to delete without reading, and which ones can remain on the server for later. Then you can connect again and download the messages you've marked to retrieve, leaving the others on the server or deleting them, depending on how you marked the message headers.

To learn how to work with headers using remote mail, see "Working with Message Headers" in Chapter 15.

Remote mail is useful when you have a message with a very large attachment waiting on the server, and you want to retrieve only your most critical messages without spending the time or connect charges to download the attachment. You can connect with remote mail and select the messages for downloading, leaving the one with the large attachment on the server for when you have more time or are back in the office and can download it across the network or through a broadband Internet connection.

If you want to configure how Outlook 2007 handles synchronization with Cached Exchange Mode and Exchange Server 2003—and are not specifically interested in using remote mail—see the section "Configuring Cached Exchange Mode Synchronization" later in this chapter.

Remote mail is also useful when a corrupt message in your mailbox might prevent Outlook 2007 from downloading your messages. You can connect with remote mail, delete the problem message without attempting to download it, and then continue working normally.

Note

The remote mail feature, strictly defined, works only with Exchange Server accounts; but Outlook 2007 also provides features similar to remote mail for POP3, IMAP, and HTTP accounts.

For details on performing selective processing for other types of accounts, see "Understanding Remote Mail Options" in Chapter 15.

Unless you are using Outlook 2007 (or 2003) in combination with Exchange Server 2007 (or Exchange Server 2003), remote mail is available with Exchange Server only when you are working offline. The commands that would otherwise enable you to download headers and work with other remote mail features are unavailable when Outlook 2007 is working in online mode. You can use remote mail with any version of Exchange Server–it does not require Exchange Server 2003. However, Outlook 2007 behaves differently with remote mail if you are connecting to Exchange Server 2007 (or Exchange Server 2003), as the next section explains.

Using Remote Mail Preview with Exchange Server

When you are working with Outlook 2007 with an Exchange 2000 Server, the icon in the selected message header is different from those of the other messages that have already been downloaded. The icon indicates that the header has been downloaded but the message body has not. Clicking the header shows a message in the Reading Pane that the message has not yet been downloaded. Outlook 2007 does not offer a preview of the message.

When you connect to an Exchange Server 2007 (or Exchange Server 2003) mailbox, however, Outlook 2007 does provide a message preview, as shown in Figure 43-5. Outlook 2007 displays the first few lines of the message in the Reading Pane and adds a Mark This Message For Download button in the Reading Pane. You can click the button to mark the message for download. The button changes to Unmark This Message For Download when you mark the message. The marking options available when right-clicking on the message in the Inbox toggle between Mark To Download Message(s) and Unmark Select Headers.

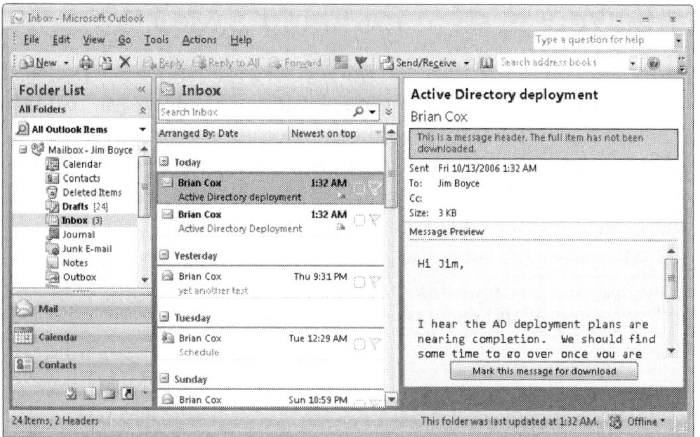

Figure 43-5. Outlook 2007 provides a preview of a message with remote mail when connected to an Exchange Server 2007 (or Exchange Server 2003) mailbox.

Remote Mail vs. Offline Folders

Remote mail and offline folders fulfill two different functions. Offline folders enable you to synchronize your local offline folders with your Exchange Server mailbox, enabling you to work offline. Remote mail enables you to manage headers remotely without downloading their associated messages. You'll probably use both at one time or another. In fact, to use remote mail, you must either use an offline folder (OST with or without Cached Exchange Mode) or configure your mail for delivery to a set of personal folders.

Note

You can achieve much the same effect with send/receive groups as you can with remote mail. For example, you can configure a send/receive group to download only message headers and not message bodies and then perform a send/receive operation on that group to retrieve the message headers. To accomplish this selective downloading for an Exchange Server account with send/receive groups, however, you must be connecting to an Exchange Server 2007 or Exchange Server 2003 account. Outlook 2007 by default downloads full items for Exchange Server 5.5 and Exchange 2000 Server accounts.

Configuring Your System for Remote Mail

You must configure your Exchange Server account for offline use and add an offline folder file to your configuration, or you must add a PST file to the configuration and configure it as the delivery store for mail. In most cases, you probably don't want to use a PST file to store your Exchange Server messages (which is a local e-mail store), preferring to leave the messages on the Exchange Server. For Exchange Server accounts, therefore, an offline file, either with or without Cached Exchange Mode, is the way to go.

To learn how to enable Cached Exchange Mode, see "Outlook as an Exchange Server Client" in Chapter 41.

Before you can work offline, you must first synchronize the OST file with your Exchange Server mailbox. Generally, you can do so by simply connecting to the Exchange Server computer and performing a full send/receive operation.

For information on configuring your Exchange Server account for offline use without Cached Exchange Mode, see the "Using Offline Folders" section earlier in this chapter.

Downloading Message Headers

When processing messages selectively, you first download the message headers and then decide what actions you want to perform with each message, based on its header.

Downloading message headers for an account is easy: In Outlook 2007, open the Inbox (or other mail folder) and click Tools, Send/Receive, Download Headers In This Folder. Or, if you have more than one account, you can choose Tools, Send/Receive, Microsoft Exchange Only, Download Inbox Headers.

Outlook 2007 then performs a send/receive operation but downloads only headers from the specified folder.

For more information, see "Processing Headers with Send/Receive Groups" later in this chapter.

If you are working from a dial-up connection and want to save on connect charges or identify spam, you can disconnect the dial-up connection and review your messages offline to decide what action to take on each.

The icon for a message header with an associated message that has not been downloaded is the standard envelope icon, just as it is for downloaded but unread messages. However, Outlook 2007 also includes an icon in the Header Status column of the Inbox to indicate that the message has not yet been downloaded. Figure 43-5 shows examples of the icons that Outlook 2007 uses to indicate downloaded headers and messages marked for download.

You'll find the commands for marking and unmarking messages in the Send/Receive menu (click Tools, Send/Receive). When you have finished marking messages as needed, click Tools, Send/Receive, Process Marked Headers In This Folder to process the headers only in the current folder, or choose Process All Marked Headers to process marked headers in all folders.

If you need more details on working with message headers, see "Working with Message Headers" in Chapter 15.

Forcing Remote Mail Functionality with a LAN Connection

As indicated earlier in this chapter, remote mail is available only when Outlook 2007 is working offline unless you are using Outlook 2007 in combination with Exchange Server 2007 or Exchange Server 2003. In most situations, you won't need to use remote mail when working with a LAN connection, but remote mail can still be useful with a LAN. For example, you might have a corrupted message in your Inbox that you would like to delete.

To force remote mail for a LAN connection when you are using Cached Exchange Mode and Exchange 2000 Server or earlier, simply place Outlook 2007 in an offline state. Click the Online indicator in the status bar and choose Work Offline to place Outlook 2007 in offline mode (or click File, Work Offline). When you finish using remote mail and want to place Outlook 2007 in online mode again, click the Disconnected indicator in the status bar and choose Work Offline again to return to online status.

Follow these steps if you want Outlook 2007 to start up in an offline state:

1. Open the properties for the Exchange Server account in your profile and click More Settings.
2. On the General tab, select Manually Control Connection State; then select the Work Offline And Use Dial-Up Networking option.
3. Click OK, Next, Finish, OK, and then restart Outlook 2007, which will start in offline mode with remote mail features available.

> **Note**
>
> Alternatively, if you put Outlook into offline mode (via File, Work Offline or by selecting the option on the status bar menu), it will stay in offline mode until you deselect the Work Offline option. Even if you close Outlook 2007 and reopen it, the offline mode, once selected, persists until online mode is selected.

Processing Headers with Send/Receive Groups

Instead of working with message headers manually, as explained in this chapter, you might prefer to process them automatically by configuring remote mail options in a send/receive group. This section explains how to do that.

Remote mail provides options that you can use to control how it handles the downloading of mail items. Although you can add remote mail to any send/receive group, it is good practice to set up a separate send/receive group just for remote mail. That way, you can process messages through remote mail by simply synchronizing folders with that particular send/receive group.

Configuring Header Processing for Exchange Server

When you configure a send/receive group for Exchange Server 2003 or Exchange Server 2007, the process on the Outlook side is the same. To configure header processing, use the following steps:

1. Click Tools, Send/Receive, Send/Receive Settings, Define Send/Receive Groups.
2. Click New to create a new Send/Receive group or click Edit to modify an existing one.
3. In the Send/Receive Settings dialog box for the group, select the Exchange Server account in the Accounts list.
4. Click a folder in the folder list, then configure the options for the folder, choosing between the following options:

   Download Headers Only Download only the headers of the e-mail message.

   Download Complete Item Including Attachment Download the headers, the body of the e-mail message, and any attachments. This is the standard receive operation.

   Download Only Headers For Items Larger Than Download only the headers for e-mail messages that exceed the size that you specify in the drop-down list.

Configuring Cached Exchange Mode Synchronization

In most respects, most of the remote mail features are the same regardless of the remote Exchange Server type. When you are using Outlook 2007 with Exchange Server 2007 or Exchange Server 2003 and Cached Exchange Mode, however, you can control the way Outlook 2007 downloads messages or headers without placing Outlook 2007 in offline mode. Outlook 2007 makes additional commands available from the status bar when you are working with an Exchange Server 2007 or Exchange Server 2003 account in Cached Exchange Mode. Click the Outlook 2007 icon in the status bar to access the commands shown in Figure 43-6.

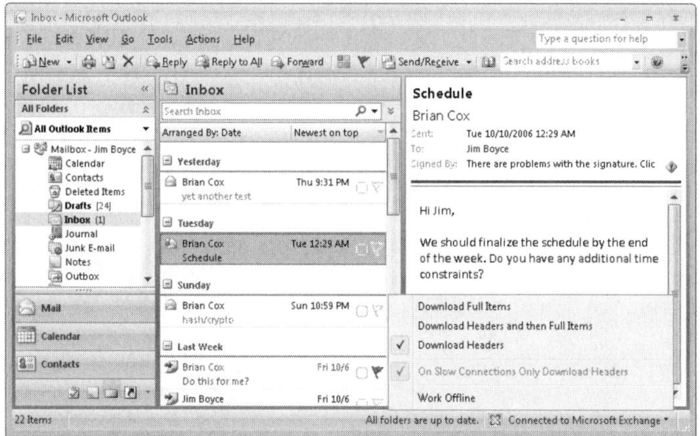

Figure 43-6. Control synchronization settings for Cached Exchange Mode from the status bar.

The commands available by clicking the status bar include the following:

- **Download Full Items** Download headers, bodies, and attachments when synchronizing the local cache with the remote mailbox.
- **Download Headers And Then Full Items** Download headers first; after all headers are downloaded, begin downloading message bodies and attachments.
- **Download Headers** Download only headers without message bodies or attachments.
- **On Slow Connections Only Download Headers** If Outlook 2007 detects a slow connection, download headers only. If this option is not selected, Outlook 2007 uses the setting you specified (see the preceding three options) regardless of the connection speed.
- **Work Offline** Place Outlook 2007 in offline mode. Also choose this command when offline to place Outlook 2007 in online mode.

PART 10
Mobility

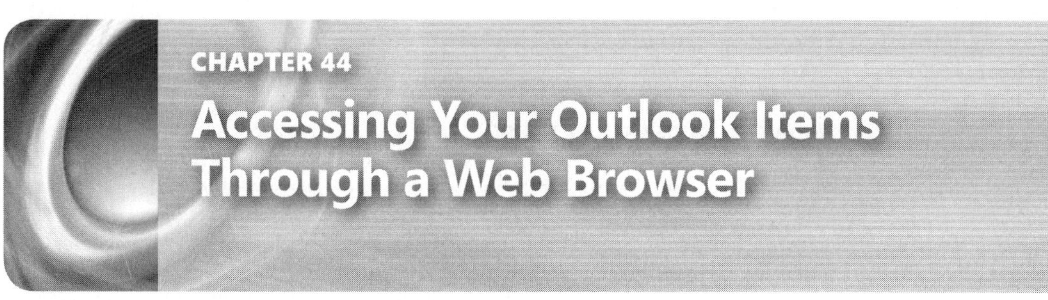

CHAPTER 44
Accessing Your Outlook Items Through a Web Browser

Microsoft first introduced Microsoft® Office Outlook® Web Access in Microsoft Exchange Server 5.0 so that clients could access their Exchange Server mailboxes through a Web browser. Microsoft has made significant improvements in Office Outlook Web Access in each new version of Exchange Server to provide support for a larger number of users, better performance, and improved functionality for clients. The latest version of Outlook Web Access in Microsoft Exchange Server 2007 provides most of the functionality of the Microsoft Office Outlook 2007 client.

This chapter explores Outlook Web Access to help you learn why it can be an important feature to implement and how to best put it to work for you, and also to help you put it to work as an alternative or complement to Microsoft Office Outlook 2007.

Overview of Outlook Web Access

With Outlook Web Access and a Web browser, users can send and receive messages, view and modify their calendars, and perform most of the other tasks available through Office Outlook 2007. The features and appearance of Outlook Web Access depend on the version of Exchange Server that is hosting Outlook Web Access. Each successive version of Exchange Server adds a new look and new capabilities.

Outlook 2007 provides full access to an Exchange Server mailbox. Although Outlook Web Access isn't intended as a replacement for Outlook 2007, it is useful for roaming users who want to access the most common mailbox features when they don't have access to their personal Outlook 2007 installation. Linux, Unix, and Macintosh users can also benefit from Outlook Web Access by accessing Exchange Server mailboxes and participating in workgroup messaging and scheduling. In addition, Outlook Web Access can save the administrative overhead and support associated with deploying Outlook 2007 to users who don't need everything that Outlook 2007 has to offer. These users can use a free Web browser to access many functions provided by Exchange Server. However, you must still purchase a client access license for each user or device that accesses the Exchange Server computer, even if the users do not use Outlook 2007 to connect to the server.

Outlook Web Access Features

Because e-mail is the primary function of Exchange Server and Outlook 2007, Outlook Web Access supports e-mail access. Users can view message headers and read messages (see Figure 44-1) as well as send, reply to, forward, and delete messages. This last capability—deleting messages—might seem commonplace, but it is a useful feature. If your mailbox contains a very large attachment or a corrupted message that is preventing you from viewing your messages in Outlook 2007, you can use Outlook Web Access to delete the message without downloading or reading it. Just open your mailbox in your Web browser, select the message header, and delete the message.

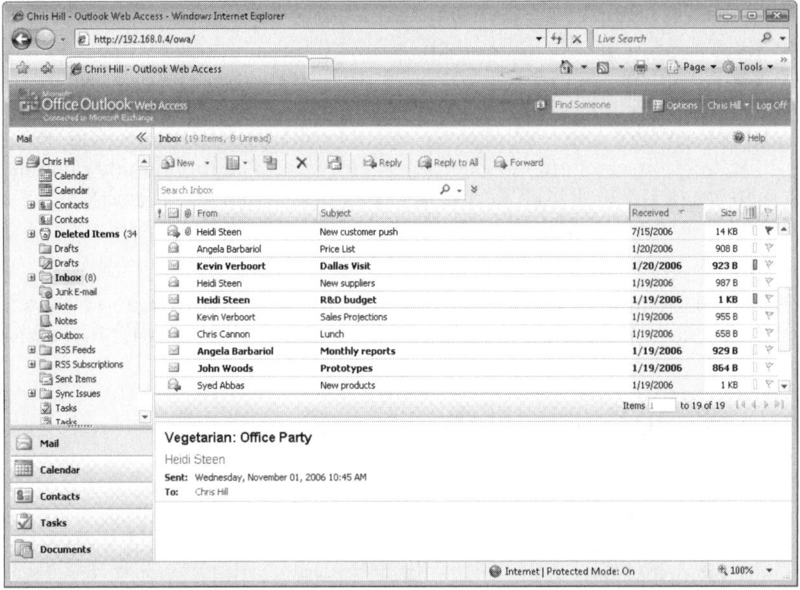

Figure 44-1. Using Outlook Web Access, you can access your Inbox through a Web browser.

> **Note**
>
> You can also use the Outlook 2007 remote mail feature to download only message headers, not message bodies. This capability is useful when you need to get your mail without downloading a message with a large attachment.

For details on using remote mail with Exchange Server, see the section "Using Remote Mail" in Chapter 43, "Working Offline and Remotely." For details on using remote mail with other types of e-mail servers, see the section "Understanding Remote Mail Options" in Chapter 15, "Receiving Messages Selectively."

Exchange 2000 Server and Exchange Server 2003 and 2007 offer additional features for messaging with Outlook Web Access. For example, Outlook Web Access in these versions of Exchange Server supports Hypertext Markup Language (HTML)-based messages as well as rich text messages. You also can access embedded objects in messages (another feature not supported by Exchange Server 5.*x*).

As mentioned earlier, you're not limited to just messaging–you can also access your Calendar folder through Outlook Web Access. You can view and modify existing items and create appointments (see Figure 44-2). You can't perform all the same scheduling tasks through Outlook Web Access that you can with Outlook 2007, but the ability to view your schedule and add appointments is useful, particularly when you're working from a remote location or on a system without Outlook 2007 installed.

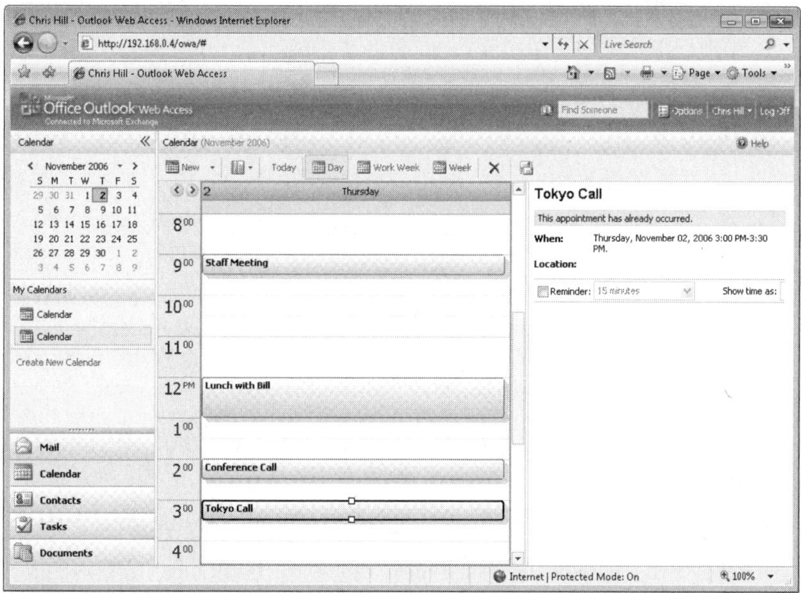

Figure 44-2. Use Outlook Web Access to manage your schedule as well as your e-mail messages.

Contacts are another type of item you can manage through Outlook Web Access. You can view and modify existing contact items and add new ones (see Figure 44-3). Other features in Outlook Web Access in Exchange 2000 Server and later include support for ActiveX® objects, multimedia messages, and public folders containing contact and calendar items.

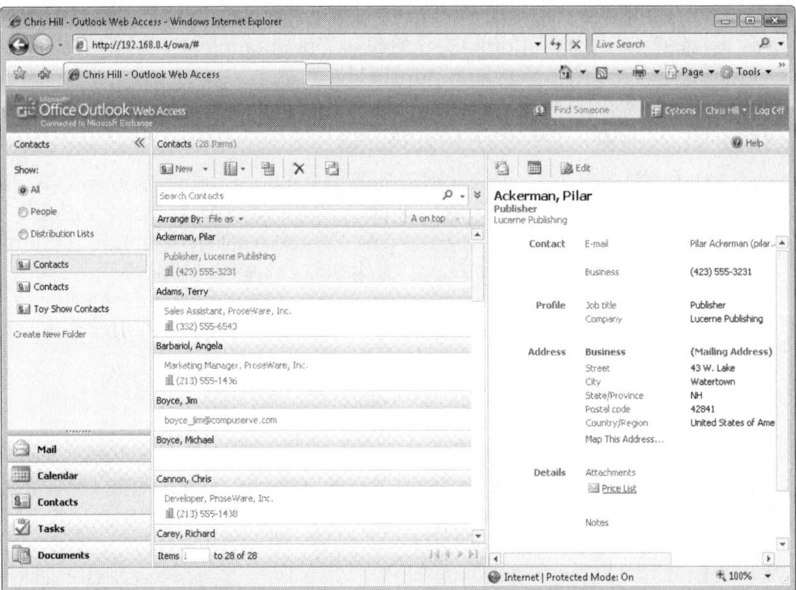

Figure 44-3. You can also work with your Contacts folder through Outlook Web Access.

Exchange Server 2003 adds new features for Outlook Web Access that are not included in Exchange 2000 Server. For example, the Outlook Web Access interface more closely matches the Office Outlook 2003 interface, and Outlook Web Access also adds spell checking, access to task lists, Secure Multipurpose Internet Mail Extensions (S/MIME) support, and HTML content blocking. These features carry forward into Exchange Server 2007. Outlook Web Access in Exchange Server 2007 also offers some new features:

- Schedule Out of Office messages and send to internal and/or external recipients
- Use the Scheduling Assistant to efficiently book meetings
- Access SharePoint® documents without a VPN or tunnel using LinkAccess
- Use WebReady Document Viewing to read attachments in HTML even if the application that created the document is not installed locally
- Access RSS subscriptions
- View content in Managed E-Mail Folders
- Retrieve voice mail or fax messages through Unified Messaging integration
- Search the Global Address List (GAL)
- Improved security and the capability for administrators to force HTML-only document viewing to prevent data from being left on public computers

- Self-service support to enable users to request a Unified Messaging PIN reset, issue a remote wipe request to wipe a lost or stolen mobile device, and manage the safe and blocked senders lists
- A light Outlook Web Access interface for use on slow connections
- Support for quick searches
- Capability to retrieve documents from a SharePoint link without requiring a VPN connection to the SharePoint site
- Use HTML to translate and view a variety of document types, including Office documents and PDF documents, without having the native application installed on the client computer
- Prelicensing of Information Rights Management (IRM)–protected content for faster client retrieval

For all its usefulness, Outlook Web Access has some limitations, but these limitations depend on the version of Exchange Server you use. For example, you can access your Tasks folder with Outlook Web Access in Exchange 2000 Server, but you can't create tasks. With Outlook Web Access in Exchange Server 2003 and 2007, however, you can create tasks. Likewise, you can view the Journal folder with Outlook Web Access 2000, but you can't add journal entries. With Outlook Web Access in Exchange Server 2003, you can view journal entries and post messages to the Journal folder, but you cannot create new journal items. Outlook Web Access with Exchange Server 2007 provides no access to the Journal.

You can't use your mailbox offline through Outlook Web Access as you can through Outlook 2007 and an offline folder (OST) file. Unlike Outlook 2007, Outlook Web Access doesn't support timed delivery and expiration for messages. However, Outlook Web Access provides a spell checker and includes the capability to define message rules for Outlook Web Access.

Web Browser Options

To access your mailbox through Outlook Web Access, you can use any Web browser that supports JavaScript and HTML version 3.2 or later, including Microsoft Internet Explorer® 4.0 or later and Netscape 4.0 or later. Some features, however, rely on Internet Explorer 5 or later, including drag-and-drop editing, shortcut menus, and native Kerberos authentication. In addition, browsers that support Dynamic HTML (DHTML) and Extensible Markup Language (XML) offer a richer set of features than those that do not. For example, Internet Explorer 5.*x* and later offer an interface for Outlook Web Access that is much closer to the native Outlook 2007 client, including a folder tree for navigating and managing folders as well as a Reading Pane.

> **Note**
>
> Kerberos authentication enables users to access multiple resources across the enterprise with a single set of user credentials, which is a capability Microsoft refers to as *single sign-on*.

Authentication Options

Outlook Web Access in Exchange 2000 Server provides three options for authentication:

- **Basic Use clear text and simple challenge/response to authenticate access.** This option offers the broadest client support but also offers the least security because passwords are transmitted as clear text.
- **Integrated Windows** Use the native Microsoft Windows authentication method for the client's operating system. On systems running Microsoft Windows 2000, for example, Internet Explorer uses Kerberos to authenticate on the server. Other Windows platforms–including Microsoft Windows 9*x*, Microsoft Windows NT®, and Microsoft Windows Me–use NTLM challenge/response rather than Kerberos. Integrated Windows authentication provides better security than basic authentication because passwords are encrypted. The client doesn't need to enter authentication credentials because the browser uses the client's Windows logon credentials to authenticate on the Outlook Web Access server.

> **Note**
>
> Microsoft Windows NT LAN Manager (NTLM) challenge/response authentication is the default authentication mechanism in Windows platforms earlier than Windows 2000.

- **Anonymous** Use anonymous access for public folders in the Exchange Server store. This option can simplify administration.

Exchange Server 2003 and Exchange Server 2007 support some additional options because of additions in IIS 6.0:

- **Digest Authentication** This authentication method works only with Active Directory® accounts. It offers the benefit of sending passwords as a hash rather than in plain text. However, to use digest authentication, you must configure Active Directory to allow reversible encryption, which reduces security. See the Active Directory online documentation for Microsoft Windows 2000 Server and Microsoft Windows Server® 2003 for more detailed information on reversible encryption.
- **.NET Passport Authentication** This method enables users to authenticate with their Microsoft Passports.

In addition to these authentication methods, Outlook Web Access supports the use of Secure Sockets Layer (SSL) to provide additional security for remote connections.

Using Outlook Web Access

After your Exchange Server administrators install and configure Outlook Web Access on the server, users can begin accessing their mailboxes through their Web browsers rather than (or in conjunction with) Outlook 2007. This section explains how to connect to the computer running Exchange Server and use Outlook Web Access to access your mailbox.

> **Note**
>
> This section assumes that you are connecting to Exchange Server 2007 with Outlook Web Access. If you have an earlier version of Exchange Server, the features available to you are slightly different.

Connecting to the Server

Typically, you connect to the Exchange Server computer through the URL *http://*<server>*/exchange*, where <server> is the DNS name, IP address, or NetBIOS name of the server. This URL isn't set in stone. The system administrator might have changed the virtual directory name for security purposes. Check with the system administrator if you're not sure what URL to use to connect to the Exchange Server computer.

> **Note**
>
> Windows Internet Naming Service (WINS) maps NetBIOS names (computer names) to IP addresses, performing a service similar to that provided by DNS (although DNS maps host names, not NetBIOS names). You can use an Lmhosts file to perform NetBIOS name-to-address mapping without a WINS server, just as you can use a Hosts file to perform host name-to-address mapping without a DNS server.

Depending on the server's authentication settings, you might be prompted to log on. Enter your user name and password for the Exchange Server account. If the account resides in a different domain from the one in which the server resides, enter the account name in the form *<domain>**<account>*, where *<domain>* is the logon domain and *<account>* is the user account.

When you connect to your mailbox, you should see a page similar to the one shown in Figure 44-4 for Exchange Server 2007. Earlier versions of Exchange Server show a somewhat different interface (Outlook Web Access 5.5, not shown, is considerably different). Outlook Web Access opens your Inbox by default, but you can switch to other folders as needed.

The left pane functions much as the Navigation Pane does in Outlook 2007 (or, in the case of Exchange 2000 Server or Exchange Server 5.5, as the Outlook Bar in Outlook 2002 or earlier), and you can select folders from it. (Throughout this chapter, I'll refer to the left pane as the Navigation Pane for simplicity.) The right pane changes to show the folder's contents.

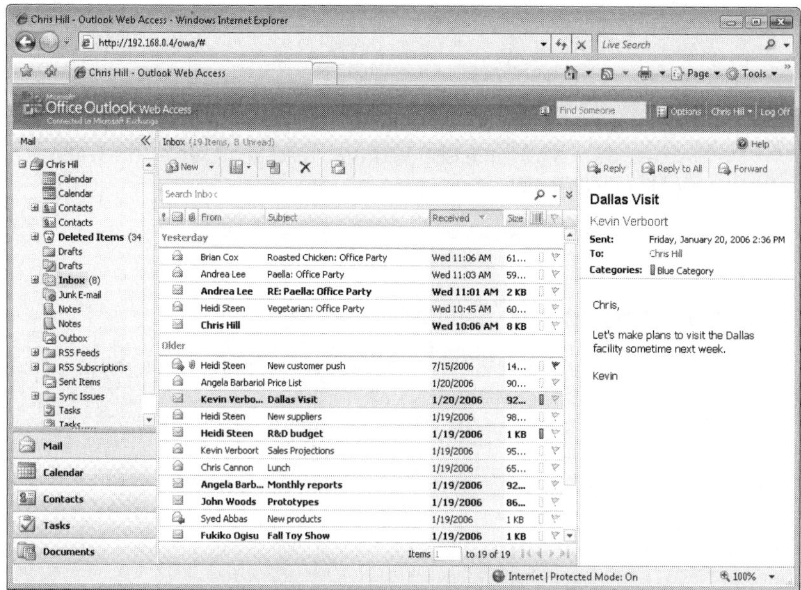

Figure 44-4. This is a typical look at a mailbox in Outlook Web Access.

> **Note**
>
> The interface for Outlook Web Access changed slightly between Exchange Server 5.5 and Exchange 2000 Server, and even more so from Exchange 2000 Server to Exchange Server 2003. The following sections assume that you're using Outlook Web Access to access Exchange Server 2007, but the procedures are similar for Outlook Web Access with earlier versions of Exchange Server. Also note that some features are not available with Outlook Web Access and Exchange Server 5.5 or with versions of Internet Explorer earlier than 5.0. Certain other features, such as rules, are only available with Exchange Server 2003 or Exchange Server 2007.

Sending and Receiving Messages

Outlook Web Access automatically shows your current messages when you connect. To read a message, double-click its header to display a window similar to the one shown in Figure 44-5.

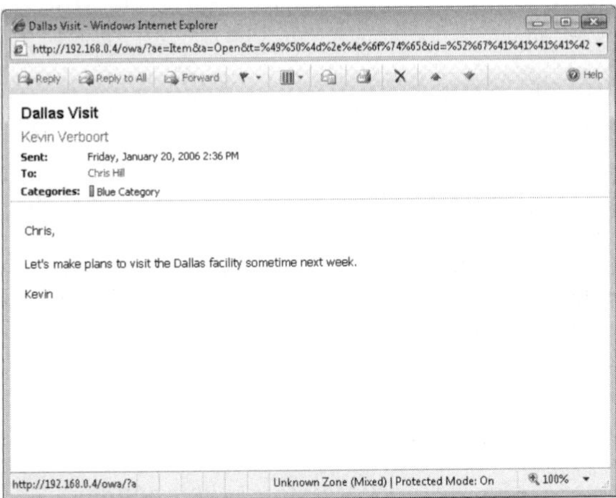

Figure 44-5. Outlook Web Access displays messages in a separate window.

As in Outlook 2007, you can reply to or forward e-mail messages. Simply click Reply or Reply To All to reply to a message or click Forward to forward a message. Outlook Web Access opens a form similar to the one shown in Figure 44-6. Add addresses as needed and type your text. If you want to add an attachment, click the Attach File toolbar button. Outlook Web Access opens the window shown in Figure 44-7 so that you can add one or more attachments to the message.

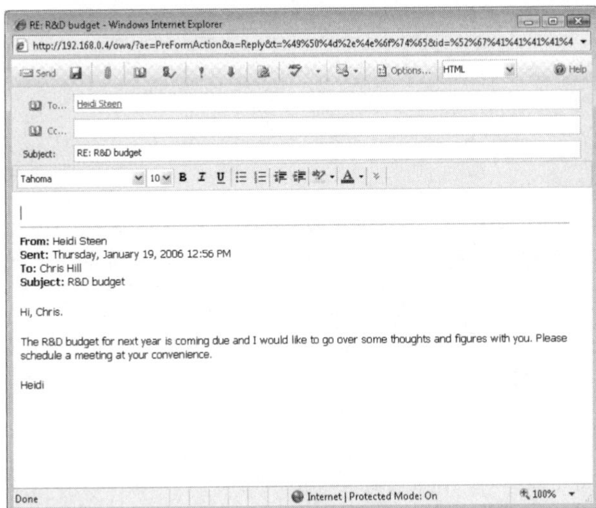

Figure 44-6. This is the Outlook Web Access form generated for a reply.

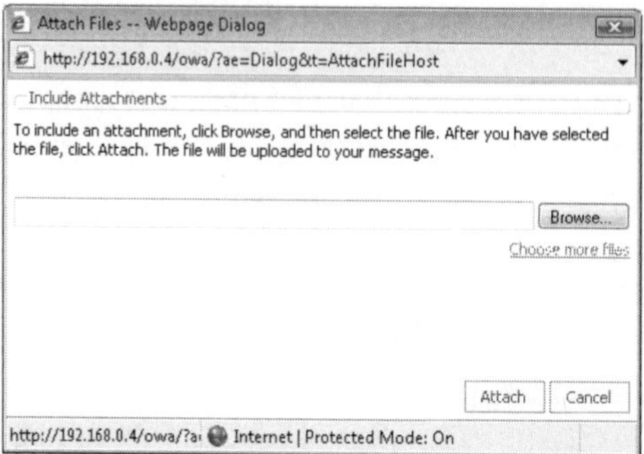

Figure 44-7. Outlook Web Access enables you to add attachments to e-mail messages.

When you want to create a message, click the New toolbar button (refer to Figure 44-4). Outlook Web Access opens a form similar to the one shown previously in Figure 44-5. You can specify addresses, attachments, body text, and other message properties.

> **Note**
>
> To check for new messages, click the Check Messages toolbar button.

You can set a handful of options for a new message by clicking the Options toolbar button with the new message form open. These options correspond to some of the options available in Outlook 2007 (see Figure 44-8).

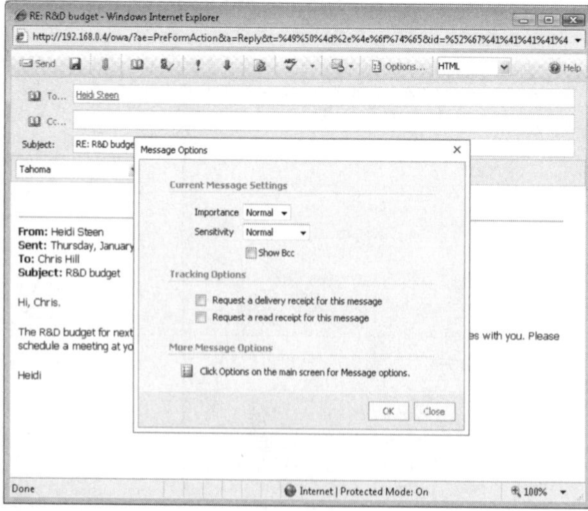

Figure 44-8. Configure message options such as Importance.

> **Note**
>
> If you maintain a lot of messages in your Inbox, they probably don't all fit on one page. Outlook Web Access displays the number of pages in your Inbox at the top of the window to the right of the toolbar. You can type a page number or use the arrow buttons to page through the Inbox.

Sorting Messages

By default, Outlook Web Access displays messages sorted by date and time received in multiline view. You can sort the messages by other properties as well. To do so, select the drop-down menu beside Arrange By and choose the field by which you want to sort messages (see Figure 44-9). Outlook Web Access also provides a Single-Line View option. You can click the Single Line button on the toolbar to turn off multiline display. To sort messages in Single-Line view, simply click the column header for the column by which you want to sort messages.

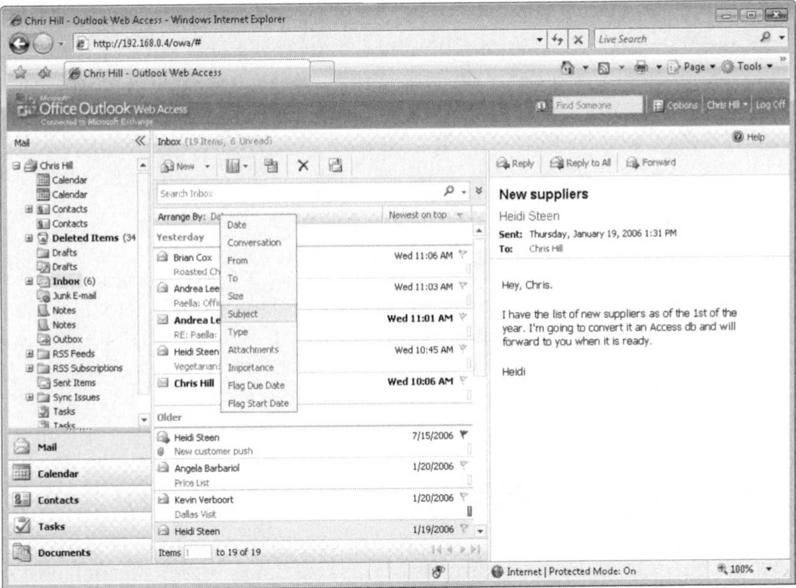

Figure 44-9. You can sort messages by one of several fields.

Copying and Moving Messages

You can copy and move messages by dragging in Outlook Web Access. Open the folder containing the messages you want to copy or move. If the target folder is hidden, scroll and expand folders as needed in the Navigation Pane to display the folder in the folder list. To move messages, drag them from the right pane to the destination folder in the folder list. If you want to copy the messages instead of moving them, hold down the Ctrl key while dragging.

Deleting Messages

Deleting messages in Outlook Web Access is a good way to clean out your mailbox when you don't have Outlook 2007 handy. It's also particularly useful for deleting large or corrupted messages that would otherwise prevent Outlook 2007 from downloading your messages normally.

To delete messages in Outlook Web Access, just select the messages and click the Delete toolbar button. Outlook Web Access moves the messages to the Deleted Items folder.

Working with Other Folders

Outlook Web Access does not limit you to working only with your Inbox. You can work with your Mail, Calendar, Contacts, and Tasks folders. With Outlook Web Access 2007, you can also work with SharePoint libraries and file servers configured on the Exchange Server computer by the Exchange Server administrator(s). When you select a different folder in the Navigation Pane, Outlook Web Access 2007 displays the contents of the selected folder in the right pane.

Renaming and Deleting Folders

While in Outlook Web Access 2007, you can rename and delete folders in your Exchange Server mailbox that you have created–but note that you cannot rename or delete the default Outlook 2007 folders. To perform either of the first two actions, display the folder in the Navigation Pane, right-click that folder, and then choose either Rename or Delete.

Working with Calendar, Contacts, and Other Items

In addition to working with the Inbox or other message folders, you can also manage your schedule, tasks, and contacts list on Exchange Server through Outlook Web Access.

Calendar Folder

To manage your schedule, click the Calendar icon in the Navigation Pane. Outlook Web Access updates the right pane to display your Calendar folder. Click the toolbar buttons to choose between Today, Day, Week, and Work Week views. The page also includes a Date Navigator similar to the one in Outlook 2007, which you can use to select dates (see Figure 44-10).

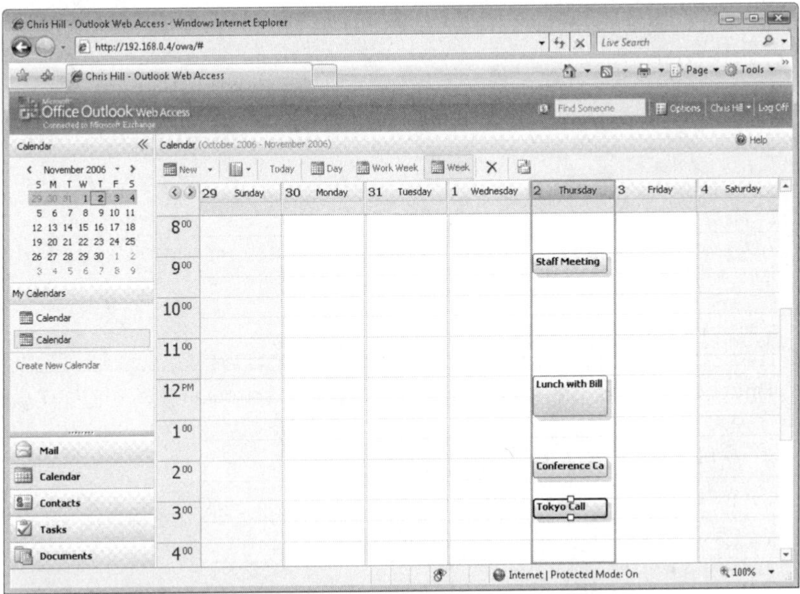

Figure 44-10. You can view and modify your schedule in Outlook Web Access.

Click the New toolbar button or click the arrow beside New and choose Appointment to display an appointment form similar to the one in Outlook 2007. Use the appointment form to specify the title, the time, and other properties for an appointment, just as you would in Outlook 2007.

Contacts Folder

You can also view and manage contacts in Outlook Web Access. Click the Contacts icon in the Navigation Pane to display the Contacts folder (see Figure 44-11).

Simply double-click a contact entry in the list to open a form that contains detailed information for that contact. Click New on the toolbar to open the form shown in Figure 44-12, which you can use to create new contact entries. Click Save And Close to save a new contact entry or to save changes to an existing contact entry.

As when you are working with your mail folders, you can click the drop-down button beside Arrange By to choose a different field for sorting contacts. To locate a contact, click in the Search Contacts text field and click the magnifying glass icon (which turns to a red X icon during the search). Click the red X to clear the search results.

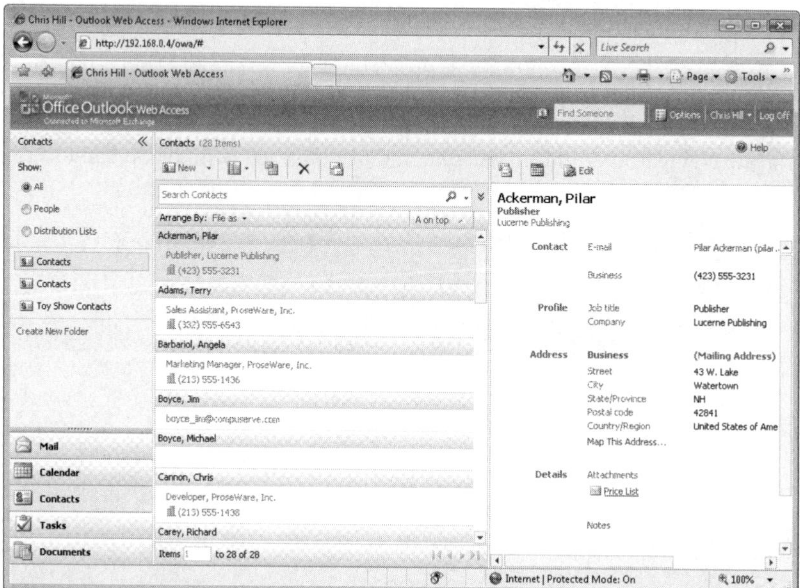

Figure 44-11. You can view and manage the Contacts folder in Outlook Web Access.

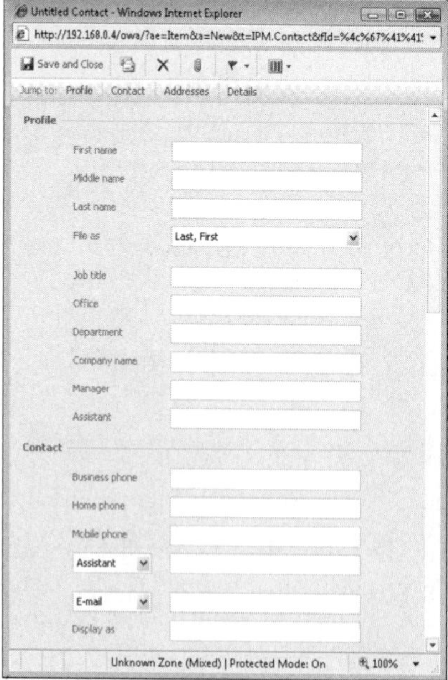

Figure 44-12. The form for creating contact entries in Outlook Web Access is similar to the contact form in Outlook 2007.

Other Folders

In Outlook Web Access 2007, you can also work with the Tasks folder. With Outlook Web Access 2003, you can also work with the Journal and Notes folders. Outlook Web Access 2003 enables you to create messages, contact items, distribution lists, appointments, tasks, and folders. You can view but not create items in the Journal folder. Earlier versions of Outlook Web Access restrict you to creating messages, contact items, and appointments.

Configuring the Out Of Office Assistant in Outlook Web Access

The Out Of Office Assistant automatically responds to messages when you are out of the office. The Out Of Office Assistant functions essentially as a server-side rule, replying to messages as they arrive in your Inbox. Although you usually configure the Out Of Office Assistant in Outlook 2007, you can also configure it in Outlook Web Access.

For details on using the Out Of Office Assistant, see the section "Creating Automatic Responses with the Out Of Office Assistant" in Chapter 13, "Automatically Responding to Messages."

To configure the Out Of Office Assistant in Outlook Web Access, connect to the server using your Web browser and click Options to view the Options page (see Figure 44-13), and then click Out Of Office Assistant to view the Out Of Office Assistant properties. To turn on the Out Of Office Assistant, select Send Out Of Office Auto-Replies. Outlook Web Access 2007 enables you to specify two different replies: one for people inside your organization and one for people outside the organization. When you are satisfied with the autoreply text, click Save to save the changes. When you want to turn off the Out Of Office Assistant, open the Options page again and select Do Not Send Out Of Office Auto-Replies.

> **Note**
>
> In Outlook Web Access 2000, click the Shortcuts group on the Outlook Bar and then click Options to open the Options page.

Configuring Other Options for Outlook Web Access

You can also use the Outlook Web Access Options page (see Figure 44-14) to set many other options for Outlook Web Access (in addition to the Out Of Office Assistant, as just discussed). You can configure date and time options, calendar options, and contact options; and you can also change your password. You can configure reminders, set up a signature for outgoing messages, set spelling options, and configure many additional options, all of which are essentially the same as those available in Outlook 2007 and covered elsewhere in this book.

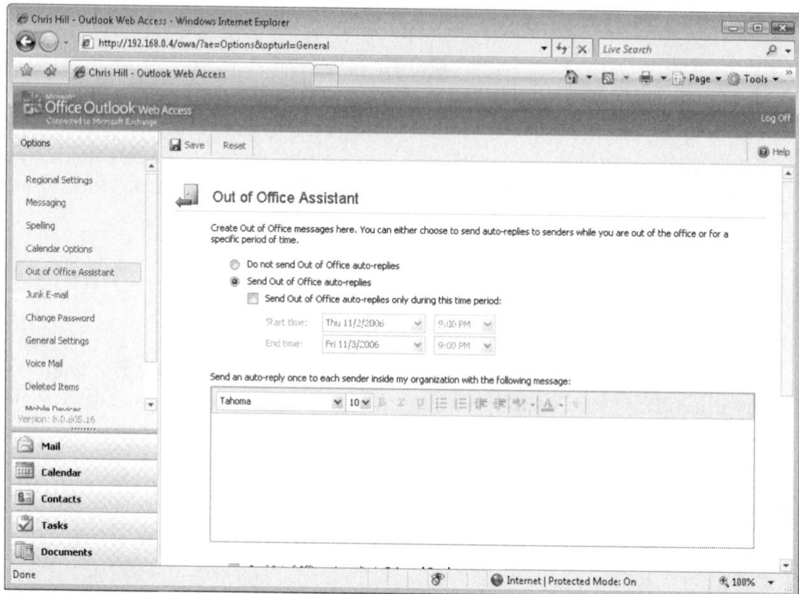

Figure 44-13. Configure the Out Of Office Assistant in Outlook Web Access.

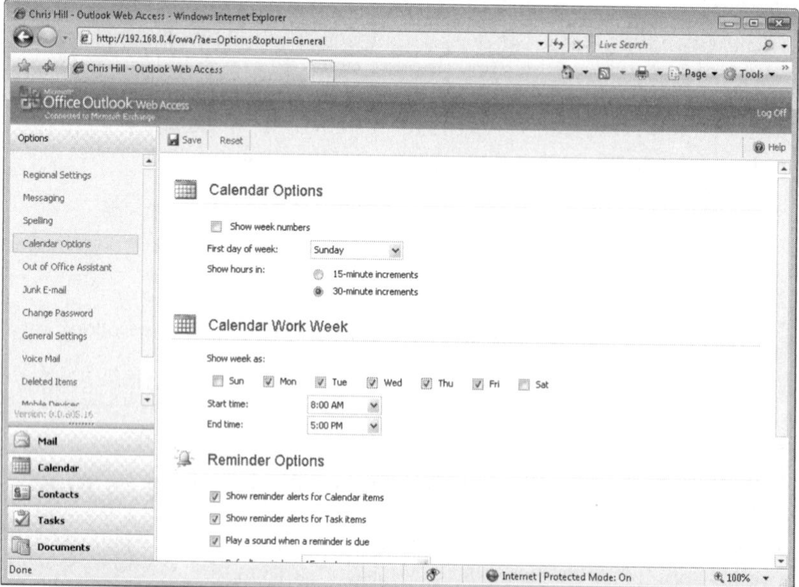

Figure 44-14. Use additional Options pages to configure additional Outlook Web Access options.

CHAPTER 45

Making Outlook Mobile

In the past, mobile users were much the exception rather than the rule. Today, users often work from home, from the road, and from remote offices. Personal Digital Assistants (PDAs) and smartphones are more and more common. All of these things make the mobility features built into Microsoft® Exchange Server and Microsoft Office Outlook® 2007 extremely important.

This chapter covers Office Outlook 2007 mobility features. For example, new in Outlook 2007 is the Mobile Service Account provider, which integrates Outlook 2007 with your mobile phone service. You'll learn in this chapter to configure the Mobile Service Account, send text messages, and use other mobile service features.

This chapter also explores Outlook Anywhere, also known as RPC over HTTP (remote procedure call over Hypertext Transfer Protocol), to enable users to connect to Exchange Server across the Internet. Outlook Anywhere enables administrators to provide remote access to Exchange Server without resorting to virtual private network (VPN) connections or exposing their networks to attack by opening the otherwise-required ports in the firewall.

Before we look at the mobility features offered by Exchange Server and Outlook 2007, let's take a look at mobility in general.

Why Mobility Is Important

In modern offices, the requirement for mobility has increased dramatically with the introduction of technologies such as high-speed broadband Internet connections to the home, the proliferation of wireless Internet connections, and sending data over cellular connections. Employee expectations have changed with these technologies, especially among those workers who are frequently out of the office on business, such as sales teams and executives. These users expect that they will be able to access their e-mail and other collaboration information whether they are in a hotel, at the airport, at a customer site, or at a remote office.

Along with the expectation that they can access their mail, mobile users are looking for more functionality while on the road than simple mail access. With Outlook 2007 and Exchange Server 2007 providing full collaboration functionality as outlined elsewhere in this book, simple Web mail is not enough to satisfy these users' requirements. Most mobile users now want full access to all of these features from outside the office too.

Mobility features are important for a number of reasons. However, the driving force behind the implementation of all mobility features and products is that they increase the speed of doing business and improve productivity. Mobility solutions, especially those integrated with collaboration products such as Outlook 2007 and Exchange Server, provide this speed and allow employees to conduct business from disparate locations. In a nutshell, e-mail has become the primary mechanism for conducting business in many companies. Anytime/anywhere access to that e-mail, as well as chat and other collaboration capabilities, is crucial.

Overview of Mobility Features in Exchange Server

Microsoft made many changes to Exchange Server to vastly improve mobility features over earlier versions of Microsoft Exchange. Features that were included in a separate product, Mobile Information Server, in Exchange 2000 Server are now included in Exchange Server 2003. A number of new features have been added to Exchange Server 2003, and features existing in earlier versions have been improved.

Mobility features introduced in Exchange 2003 fit into four main categories:

- **Cached Exchange Mode** Enables users to cache their mailboxes to their local computers, making it possible to work offline. Changes are synchronized with the computer running Exchange Server the next time Outlook 2007 connects to the server.
- **RPC over HTTP** A method of providing access to a computer running Exchange Server to remote clients without requiring any kind of VPN connection. RPC over HTTP allows clients to connect using Outlook 2007 directly over the Internet using a publicly accessible port.
- **Outlook Web Access (OWA)** Microsoft has provided OWA with several versions of Microsoft Exchange, but the main complaints have traditionally been that the OWA interface does not match that of Microsoft Outlook and that a number of Microsoft Outlook features do not exist in OWA. The version of OWA included in Exchange Server 2003 addressed both of those concerns by more closely resembling the Outlook 2003 interface and including a number of important Outlook 2003 features.
- **Mobile device support** Mobile devices such as PDAs with wireless network access and mobile phones with PDA-type interfaces have become ubiquitous in many organizations, especially among mobile staff. These devices provide portability because they are much smaller than laptop computers, and they provide much of the functionality of larger systems. Exchange Server 2003

provides a number of tools to integrate with Pocket PC and smartphone devices. Traditionally, hand-held devices have had the capacity to synchronize only with an existing application, such as synchronizing mail from Microsoft Outlook on a laptop or desktop with a PDA. Exchange Server 2003 has the capability to work with hand-held devices in real time rather than relying on synchronization, using these features:

Exchange ActiveSync Enabled by default, Microsoft Exchange ActiveSync® is used to synchronize data from an Exchange Server mailbox to a hand-held Pocket PC or smartphone device running Microsoft Pocket Outlook.

Outlook Mobile Access Outlook Mobile Access, not enabled by default, is used to provide Exchange Server mailbox access to devices that are Internet capable but are not Pocket PC or smartphone devices with Microsoft Pocket Outlook. Although a separate product from OWA, Outlook Mobile Access is similar to OWA in that it provides browser-based access to an Exchange Server mailbox. Whereas OWA runs on Web browsers on full-size computers, Outlook Mobile Access runs on Wireless Application Protocol (WAP) browsers on mobile devices.

Microsoft has also improved and added to these features in Exchange Server 2007. These improvements include:

- **Search improvements** ActiveSync enables users to query both the local device store and the entire Exchange Server mailbox when searching from a mobile device in an over-the-air search. This capability enables users to retrieve data from the server quickly and efficiently when needed.
- **Direct push** Mobile devices that support ActiveSync receive updates from the server as soon as the items (such as new e-mail messages) arrive at the server. This capability keeps users' mobile data up to date in an efficient way.
- **Consistent user experience for a variety of devices** The Exchange Server 2007 ActiveSync protocol is licensed for use by Microsoft Windows Mobile®, Nokia, Symbian, Motorola, Sony Ericsson, Palm, and DataViz, providing a broad range of mobile device options for organizations.
- **Mobile device security and management** Administrators can enforce mobile device policies, such as strong personal identification numbers (PINs), and can force a data and application wipe of the mobile device over the air in the event the device is lost or stolen. Exchange Server 2007 supports per-user policies for these operations.
- **Remote access to data hosted by Microsoft Windows SharePoint® Services sites and file server resources through LinkAccess** LinkAccess enables administrators to make SharePoint content and documents from file servers available to mobile device users without requiring a VPN connection to these resources.
- **Calendar and Out Of Office improvements** Exchange Server 2007 adds new features that improve a user's capability to access the calendar from a mobile device, manage meeting requests, and send Out Of Office replies from the device.

- **OWA improvements** As discussed in Chapter 44, "Accessing Your Outlook Items Through a Web Browser," OWA is enhanced in Exchange Server 2007 to give you access to the new Out Of Office features, self-service features, and more. See Chapter 44 for details.
- **Unified messaging** Exchange Server 2007 implements several voice-mail capabilities, enabling users to retrieve voice messages and faxes through Outlook 2007, OWA, and their mobile devices. Users can request a reset of their voice-mail PIN and set other voice-mail options from OWA, access their mailboxes by phone, and redirect voice messages to a cell phone or desk phone.

Using Outlook Anywhere for Remote Access to Exchange Server

Outlook Anywhere, called RPC over HTTP in Exchange Server 2003 and Outlook 2003, enables administrators to make Exchange Server connections available to remote users without requiring a VPN connection to the server's network. Outlook Anywhere uses HTTP and/or HTTP Secure (HTTPS) over ports 80 and 443 to enable Outlook 2007 to communicate with Exchange Server.

Outlook Anywhere offers a handful of benefits:

- **Simplified remote access** Users do not need to establish a VPN connection to the server's network to connect to Exchange Server. This simplifies the user experience and drastically reduces administrative overhead that would otherwise be required to support those VPN connections.
- **Better security** Without Outlook Anywhere, an Exchange administrator would have to open several ports in the organization's firewalls to enable the Outlook 2007 traffic to pass in and out, presenting a large security risk. Because Outlook Anywhere works through ports 80 and 443, which are very likely already enabled for Web browsing, the administrator need not open any additional ports.

Outlook 2003 and Outlook 2007 both support Outlook Anywhere/RPC over HTTP. Chapter 41, "Configuring the Exchange Server Client," explains how to configure an Exchange Server account to use Outlook Anywhere to connect to the server. The combination of Outlook Anywhere and Cached Exchange Mode, also discussed in Chapter 41, gives Outlook 2007 users the combined benefits of easy remote access across the Internet and the capability to work offline.

Using Outlook Mobile Service Accounts

Outlook Mobile Service, a new feature in Outlook 2007, lets you integrate Outlook 2007 with mobile phones. With Outlook Mobile Service, you can:

- **Send text and multimedia messages from Outlook 2007 to mobile phones.** Outgoing messages are placed in your Sent Items folder, just as for e-mail messages.

- **Have e-mail messages, reminders, and calendar summaries forwarded to your mobile phone.** This feature is a great productivity tool for people who are on the move often and need continual access to their Outlook 2007 items.
- **Send messages to e-mail and mobile phone recipients at the same time.** You do not need to send messages separately to e-mail and phone recipients. Instead, you can choose a selection of recipient addresses, and Outlook 2007 sends the message as needed based on the selected address types.
- **Easily retrieve cell phone numbers of your existing contacts.** Use the Mobile Address Book to quickly locate the cell phone numbers of your contacts. You don't need to store this information separately. Instead, the Mobile Address Book ties into your existing Contacts folder.

Adding the Outlook Mobile Service Account

Before you can take advantage of Outlook Mobile Service in Outlook 2007, you need to add the service to your profile. Follow these steps to do so:

1. Right-click the Outlook 2007 icon on the Start menu and then choose Properties, or open the Mail applet from Control Panel.
2. In the Mail Setup dialog box, click Show Profiles to open the Mail dialog box, select the profile in which you want to add Outlook Mobile Service, and then click Properties.
3. Click E-Mail Accounts to display the E-Mail tab in the Account Settings dialog box, shown in Figure 45-1.

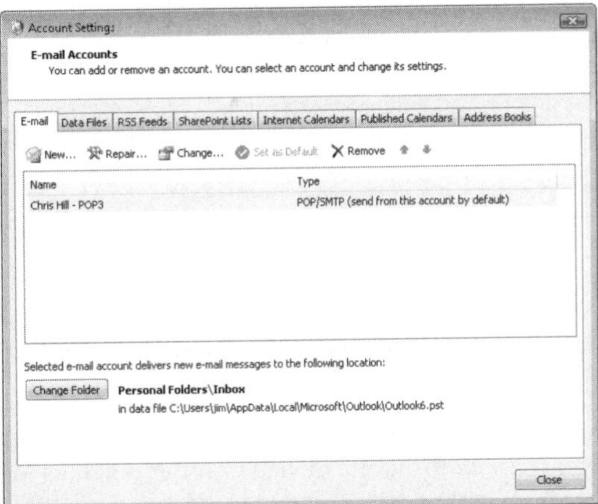

Figure 45-1. Use the Account Settings dialog box to add the Outlook Mobile Service account.

4. Click New to start the Add New E-Mail Account Wizard, select Other, select Outlook Mobile Service (Text Messaging), and then click Next.

5. On the Account Settings page of the Add New Outlook Mobile Service Account dialog box, shown in Figure 45-2, enter your service provider information. If you don't have a provider set up yet or don't know the appropriate settings, click the link to Microsoft Office Online to browse to a Web page where you can select and configure a provider. The resulting Web pages will guide you through the setup process.

> **Note**
>
> Microsoft offers a service called SMS Link for Microsoft Office Outlook 2007 that supports (at the time of the initial Outlook 2007 release) Alltel, Nextel, Sprint PCS, and Verizon Wireless. If you use a different service, browse to the Microsoft Office Online site from the link on the Account Settings page to determine current support status for your provider.

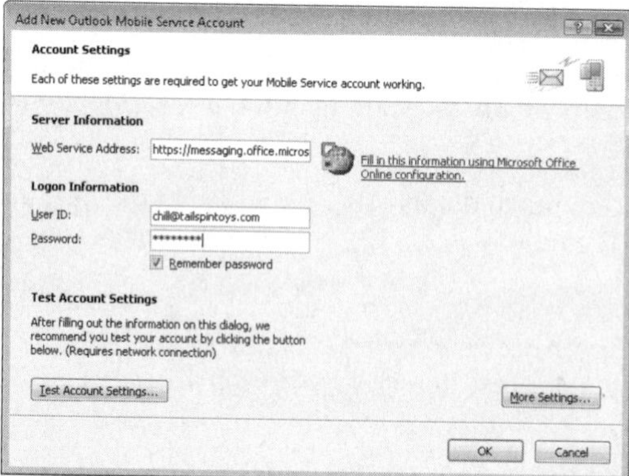

Figure 45-2. Use the Account Settings page to configure your Outlook Mobile Service account.

6. If you want to test the service, click Test Account Settings. Outlook 2007 tests the settings and gives you the option of sending a test message to your mobile phone.

7. Click More Settings to open the Outlook Mobile Service Information and Settings dialog box, shown in Figure 45-3. Here you can change the account name to something other than your mobile device number (such as My Mobile Account) and also change your phone number. Click OK when you've finished.

8. Click OK, click Close, and then click Finish to apply the change. Restart Outlook 2007 to access the new mobile features.

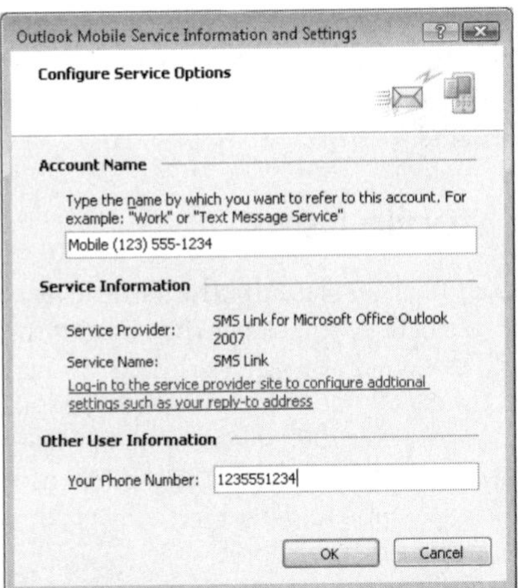

Figure 45-3. Use the Configure Service Options page to configure additional options for your Outlook Mobile Service account.

Using the Mobile Address Book

Outlook 2007 automatically adds the Mobile Address Book to your profile when you add Outlook Mobile Service to the profile. The Mobile Address Book is not a separate physical address book where contacts are stored. Instead, the Mobile Address Book hooks into your existing Contacts folder to retrieve contacts that have mobile device numbers.

To use the Mobile Address Book, click the Address Book icon on the Outlook 2007 toolbar, or click To, Cc, or Bcc in a message form. Either action displays the Address Book dialog box. In the Address Book drop-down list, select Contacts (Mobile) under the Mobile Address Book group. Outlook 2007 then displays all contacts from your Contacts folder that have a mobile number assigned, as shown in Figure 45-4.

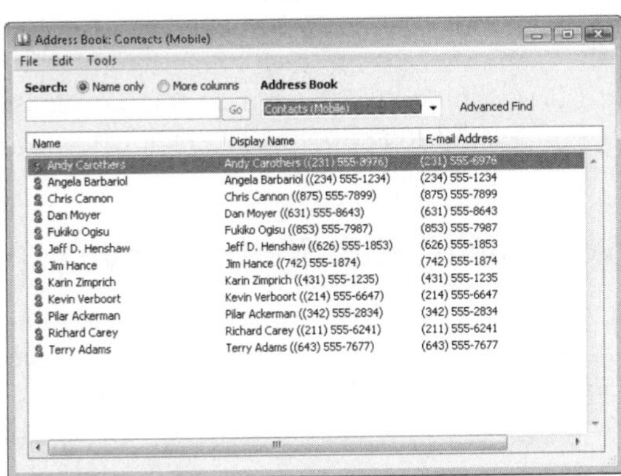

Figure 45-4. Use the Mobile Address Book to quickly access contacts' mobile device numbers.

Because the Mobile Address Book looks up contacts in your Contacts folder, it isn't necessary to add contacts specifically to the Mobile Address Book. Instead, simply make sure that you specify a device number in the Mobile field of each contact as needed when you create the contacts.

Sending Messages to Mobile Users

Sending a message to a mobile device is essentially the same as sending a message to an e-mail address. The only difference is that you select the contact in the Mobile Address Book rather than the Contacts folder, GAL, or other address book.

To do so, follow these steps:

1. Start a new e-mail message.
2. Click To, Cc, or Bcc to open the Address Book.
3. Select Contacts (Mobile) in the Address Book drop-down list.
4. Select one or more mobile recipients, and then click To, Cc, or Bcc as needed to add the addresses to the appropriate field.
5. If you need to send the message to e-mail recipients as well, select the appropriate address book in the Address Book drop-down list, and then add addresses to the To, Cc, and Bcc fields as needed.
6. Click OK to close the Address Book.
7. Add subject, message body, and other information as needed, and then click Send.

Forwarding Messages to Mobile Devices

Depending on your mobile account type, you can forward messages as either text messages or multimedia messages. To forward a message as a text message to a mobile recipient, select the message in Outlook 2007, and then choose Actions, Forward As Text Message. To forward as a multimedia message, choose Actions, Forward As Multimedia Message. In both cases, Outlook 2007 opens a standard message form. Click To, Cc, or Bcc; open the Mobile Address Book; select recipients; and then send the message.

Forwarding Outlook Items to Your Mobile Devices

You can configure Outlook 2007 to send alerts to your mobile device. For example, perhaps you want reminders and a calendar summary sent to your mobile device. Or maybe you'll be out of the office for several hours and want your new messages redirected to your mobile device. You can accomplish both of these tasks with the Outlook Mobile Service account.

Forward Alerts and Summaries

Outlook Mobile Service can forward reminders to your mobile device, as well as a summary of your next day's calendar items. Follow these steps to configure forwarding of these items:

1. In Outlook 2007, choose Tools, Options to open the Options dialog box.
2. On the Preferences tab, click Notifications to open the Outlook Mobile Notification dialog box, shown in Figure 45-5.

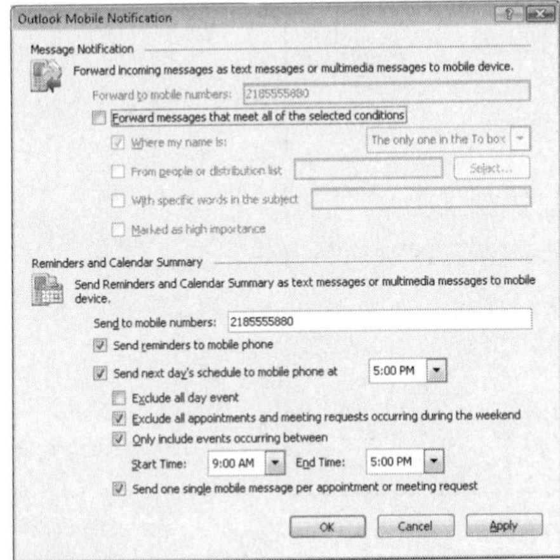

Figure 45-5. Use the Outlook Mobile Notification dialog box to configure forwarding of reminders and calendar summaries.

3. In the Reminders And Calendar Summary area, select Send Reminders To Mobile Phone.
4. Type your mobile device number in the Send To Mobile Numbers box.
5. To have calendar summaries sent, select Send Next Day's Schedule To Mobile Phone At, and then specify the time of day you want the summary sent.
6. Configure the remaining options as desired. You can exclude all-day events, exclude weekend items, specify a time frame for items to be included, and specify that Outlook 2007 send one message for each appointment or meeting request.
7. Click OK, and then click OK again to close the Options dialog box.

Forward Messages

You can configure Outlook Mobile Service to forward messages to your mobile phone based on conditions that you specify, including how your name appears in the message, the sender, words in the subject, and message importance. Follow these steps to configure message forwarding to your mobile device:

1. In Outlook 2007, choose Tools, Options, and then click Notifications on the Preferences tab.
2. Select Forward Messages That Meet All Of The Selected Conditions, as shown in Figure 45-6.

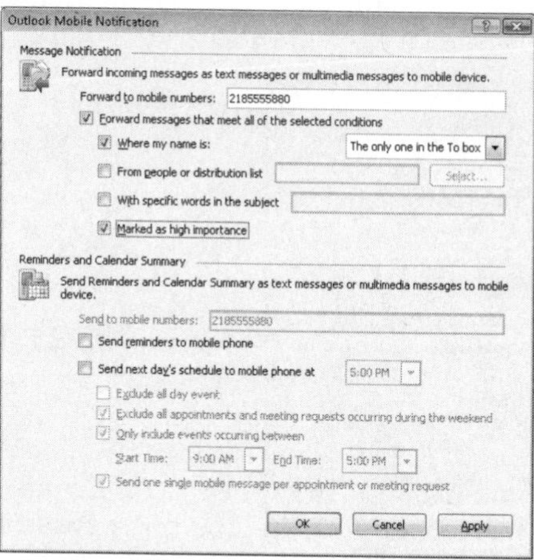

Figure 45-6. Use the Outlook Mobile Notification dialog box to configure forwarding of reminders and calendar summaries.

3. Type your mobile device number in the Forward To Mobile Numbers text box.
4. Select the conditions that you want to apply for messages to be forwarded.
5. Click OK, and then click OK again to close the Options dialog box.

Setting Outlook Mobile Service Options

Outlook Mobile Service offers a selection of options that you can use to control how text and multimedia messages are sent. To set these options, choose Tools, Options, and then click Mobile Options to open the Mobile Options dialog box, shown in Figure 45-7. Set options as desired, click OK, and then click OK again to close the Options dialog box.

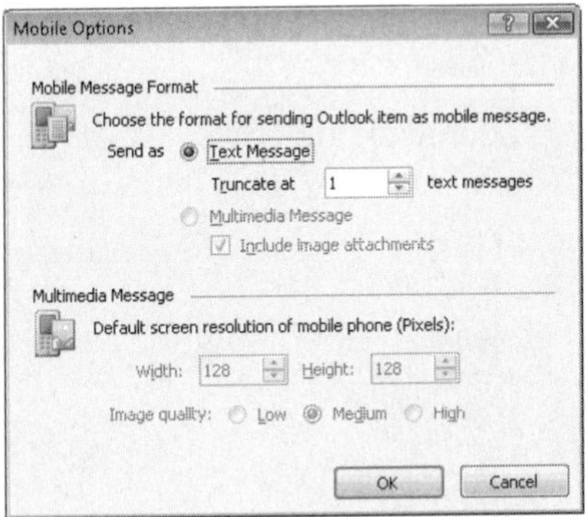

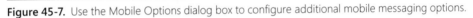

Figure 45-7. Use the Mobile Options dialog box to configure additional mobile messaging options.

Using a Mobile Signature

The section "Using Signatures" in Chapter 9 explains how to add a signature for each e-mail account. For example, perhaps you use one signature for a business account and a different signature for a personal account. Outlook 2007 treats Outlook Mobile Service like any other e-mail account, which means that you can add a signature specifically for your mobile messages. To specify the signature, choose Tools, Options, and then click the Mail Format tab. Click Signatures, and if the signature you want to use for mobile messages doesn't exist yet, click New to create the signature, type the name for the signature, and then click OK. On the E-Mail Signature tab, select Outlook Mobile Service in the E-Mail Account drop-down list, and then select the signature that you want to use for the account. Create or edit the signature, and then click OK twice to return to Outlook 2007.

See "Using Signatures" in Chapter 9 to learn more about creating and using signatures.

Index to Troubleshooting Topics

Index

B

C

D

E

F

M

N

O

P

Q

R

U

V

W

About the Authors

Jim Boyce has been a freelance author and consultant for almost 20 years, and has authored and co-authored over 50 books on computer operating systems, hardware, and applications. Jim has written about a wide range of technology topics such as Windows and UNIX operating systems, Microsoft Office applications, PC upgrade and maintenance, and Visual Basic programming. Jim is a former Contributing Editor for WINDOWS Magazine and a frequent contributor to Microsoft.com, techrepublic.com, The Office Letter (www.officeletter.com), and other print and online publications. In past lives, Jim has been a draftsman, college instructor, ISP owner/operator, and consultant. Jim is now a Sr. Practice and Process Manager for Affiliated Computer Services (ACS) and operations manager for one of ACS' IT support facilities.

Beth Sheresh (CNE) is a seasoned technical writer with more than 15 years of computer industry experience including writing and editing technical books, network administration and consulting, and technical training design, development, and delivery. Her writing projects have covered directory services and other networking technologies including IT provisioning, security, and Windows. Beth's books include *Understanding Directory Services* (two editions) and the *Microsoft Windows NT Server Administrators Bible–Option Pack Edition* as well as chapters of *Microsoft Windows Server 2003 Inside Out*. She recently directed the design and development of operations manuals and administrative training materials for the initial Active Directory implementation of a Fortune 500 company.

Doug Sheresh (MCSE) is an IT professional with over two decades of experience that encompasses network administration, consulting, technical support management, and managing technical writing projects. His expertise includes all aspects of technical training course development, from design and content creation to training delivery. Earlier, while at Microsoft, he was instrumental in the design and development of Microsoft's technical training for Windows 95, Windows 3.1, and MS-DOS, and was the lead technical writer of the *Microsoft Windows 95 Resource Kit*. He was also the project manager and coauthor of *Understanding Directory Services, 2nd Edition* and *Microsoft Windows NT Server Administrators Bible–Option Pack Edition*. His technical training projects for Fortune 500 companies include the design and development of the MOF Operations Assessment training, as well as Active Directory and SMS administration training. Recent writing includes technical materials on IT regulatory compliance, automated IT provisioning, contributing to a Windows Server 2003 book, and developing Windows Server 2003 administration operations manuals.

What do you think of this book?

We want to hear from you!

Do you have a few minutes to participate in a brief online survey?

Microsoft is interested in hearing your feedback so we can continually improve our books and learning resources for you.

To participate in our survey, please visit:

www.microsoft.com/learning/booksurvey/

...and enter this book's ISBN-10 number (appears above barcode on back cover*). As a thank-you to survey participants in the United States and Canada, each month we'll randomly select five respondents to win one of five $100 gift certificates from a leading online merchant. At the conclusion of the survey, you can enter the drawing by providing your e-mail address, which will be used for prize notification only.

Thanks in advance for your input. Your opinion counts!

* Where to find the ISBN-10 on back cover

Example only. Each book has unique ISBN.

Microsoft Press

No purchase necessary. Void where prohibited. Open only to residents of the 50 United States (includes District of Columbia) and Canada (void in Quebec). For official rules and entry dates see:

www.microsoft.com/learning/booksurvey/